CONTENTS

BOOK ONE

Introduction to Literature

PART ONE
The Essay

LANGUAGE

LEARNING

THE IMPACT OF SCIENCE

THE HUMAN EQUATION

THE MASS MEDIA

ALTON C. MORRIS
BIRON WALKER
PHILIP BRADSHAW
University of Florida

JOHN C. HODGES
Late of the University of Tennessee

MARY E. WHITTEN
North Texas State University

FIFTH EDITION

COLLEGE ENGLISH
the first year

HARCOURT, BRACE & WORLD, INC.

New York / Chicago / San Francisco / Atlanta

THE POET AS SINGER

THE POET AS WIT AND HUMORIST

THE POET AS PORTRAYER OF CHARACTER

THE POET AS ELEGIST

THE POET AS CRITIC AND PHILOSOPHER

BOOK TWO

Fundamentals of Speaking, Listening, and Writing 711

x

 *FOREWORD*

The welcome accorded the four earlier editions of *College English: The First Year* by teachers of freshman English has prompted the editors and the publishers to offer yet a fifth. This new edition has fresh selections in every section but preserves unchanged the fundamental objectives of its predecessors—to improve the student's reading skill, to develop his appreciation of the various types of literature, and to assist him to become a better writer, speaker, and listener.

College English has two main divisions: Book One contains a number of carefully selected essays, short biographies, short stories, plays, and poems; Book Two gives a concise treatment of the fundamentals of speaking and listening, a section on Rhetorical Guidelines, and a complete handbook.

Book One contains forty-six essays with a host of new names—Bigelow, Cousins, Fiedler, Frankel, Gibson, Heathorn, Kael, Lamb, Lazarus, Miller, Pachter, Perry, Rovere, Sarnoff, Trilling, Wheeler, and Wilson. The essays were chosen to improve reading skill and to stimulate the student's interest in and discussion of contemporary thought. They are timely but not narrowly dated, mature but within the understanding of the first-year student. If read thoughtfully, they should provide valuable standards of writing and speaking. The biographical section contains a representation of new names added to many old favorites—selections by Agee, Bryant, Kempton, and Ridgeway. There are new short stories by Cheever, Dürrenmatt, McCullers, and Warner; plays by Anouilh, Miller, and Synge; and poems by Childers, Crane, Dugan, Eberhart, Gunn, Lowell, Lucian, Miles, Morris, Nemerov, Nims, Picasso, Prévert, Reed, Schwartz, Simpson, Stephens, and Witt. The selections in Book One, representing six major literary types, have been included not so much because they represent an author, a period, a movement, or a nationality but because they are arresting and meaningful for the student reader and because they have genuine literary merit.

Book Two first emphasizes the need—personal, social, and professional—for proficiency in speaking and listening and presents the basic principles which will aid the student to speak and listen with greater effectiveness. It then illustrates the basic principles of effective writing through an examination of the major forms of discourse—exposition, argument, description, and narration. The rhetoric section has been modified, and the number of writing lessons related to the rhetorical principles has been increased to twenty-four. These lessons provide assignments and give the student step-by-step instructions for working them out.

The sixth edition of the *Harbrace College Handbook,* included here, is concerned both with the mechanics of written English and with the art of composition. It not only contains rules and illustrations drawn from the best modern usage but presents certain rhetorical principles which supplement the Rhetorical Guidelines.

The *Study Guide,* accompanying the text, shares the inclusiveness of the text itself. The questions raised there are designed (1) to make the preparation of assignments more thorough and informative for the student and (2) to give the instructor a convenient teaching guide and a motivation for class discussion. Growing out of the essays are exercises that test for the central idea, analyze the organization and the rhetorical principles utilized, improve vocabulary, acquaint the student with some indispensable library reference works, provide systematic dictionary study, and suggest subjects for talks and themes. The questions for biography, short story, drama, and poetry analyze ideas and content and focus upon the work as literature, frequently giving special attention to its theme, feeling, and tone. The *Study Guide* also contains assignment problems for speaking designed to help the student to work out the ideas contained in Book Two. And, last, it contains drills to accompany the *Handbook;* these exercises emphasize the fundamentals of writing with which students have the greatest difficulty.

Seven essays in Book One constitute a special reading project in the *Study Guide* with directions for carrying out the project, tests on reading comprehension and rate, and a chart on which the student may record his progress. (There are two sets of exercise materials for these seven essays—one set for class discussion and the other for the special reading project.)

Thus, *College English* presents in one volume the materials for a complete first-year English course. If the book contains more than can be used in many such courses, its abundance will allow each instructor considerable choice in the selection of his materials and the added chance to vary them from term to term, as is indicated in the "Note to the Instructor."

We reaffirm our continued indebtedness to all former editors of *College English: The First Year,* especially to J. Hooper Wise, who first conceived the need for this text to enrich the study of English for the first-year student and who helped to shape the character of the text.

In the preparation of this edition, especially the *Study Guide,* our thanks are due Denver Baughan, Kenneth Byron, Motley Deakin, Winifred Dusenbury, James R. Hodges, John A. Penrod, Joseph Vogel, and Butler H. Waugh, all of the University of Florida. To all of these and to our many associates here and in other colleges who have offered helpful suggestions for this edition we express our sincere appreciation.

A. C. M.
B. H. W.
P. B.

✤ NOTE TO THE INSTRUCTOR

The editors of *College English: The First Year* look upon Book One as an anthology, perhaps more precisely a *treasury*, of literary pieces of quality and variety. We believe that these thoughtfully chosen selections will go far to meet the needs of any first-year course devoted to the nature and use of language and to the critical reading of literature and intended thereby to improve the essential skills of reading, writing, speaking, and listening. The results to be gained are greater awareness of the verbal arts and skills and sharper critical standards for understanding, applying, and evaluating them.

Book One by design contains more reading than can be discussed in the usual time allotted for the freshman course. By omitting some of the selections, the instructor can adjust with considerable nicety the overall reading difficulty to the level of reading achievement his class has attained. By intention the selections do vary widely in difficulty. For success in college today, the student must be prepared to read well many kinds of demanding material. Therefore, each essay section presents at least one comparatively easy essay accompanied by more difficult ones. For example, in the section entitled The Mass Media Cary's simplicity in "The Mass Mind: Our Favorite Folly" presents a marked contrast in difficulty to McLuhan's "Sight, Sound, and the Fury." This same principle of varying the difficulty of materials has been followed in the selections representing the other types of literature. In the short story section the straightforwardness of Hardy and Crane is countered with the subtlety of Cheever and Dürrenmatt. In the poetry we have consciously included many variations of difficulty from the directness of Morris' "The Haystack in the Floods" to the indirection of Wilbur's "Lamarck Elaborated."

The essays are concerned with ideas that a first-year college student needs as an immediate intellectual environment for his collegiate study, especially for his study of language and literature. Within each essay section, we have attempted to provide as broad coverage of the subject as feasible while following a somewhat logical progression from the more elementary to the more involved ideas. In earlier editions much the same arrangements proved quite satisfactory in actual classroom practice.

Teachers who have been using the earlier editions have found that several sound and satisfactory arrangements of the literary selections are possible. We suggest that an instructor acquaint himself with the contents and devise an arrangement that will best serve his special situation and purposes. In order merely to indicate a few of the possible plans, we list five: (1) emphasizing literary types, (2) centering on language and observing its applications in the literary selections, (3) focusing initially on reading comprehension and writing improvement through the use of the literary pieces, (4) grouping literary materials around specific ideas or themes, or (5) using only the essays in the first term of the first-year course and then turning to the other literary genres in the second term.

No suggestions from the editors of *College English*, however, can be as valuable as the creative use of these materials by a staff sensitive to student needs.

THOMAS HARDY

When I Set Out for Lyonnesse

When I set out for Lyonnesse,
  A hundred miles away,
  The rime was on the spray,
And starlight lit my lonesomeness
When I set out for Lyonnesse
  A hundred miles away.

What could bechance at Lyonnesse
  While I should sojourn there
  No prophet durst declare,
Nor did the wisest wizard guess
What would bechance at Lyonnesse
  While I should sojourn there.

When I came back from Lyonnesse
  With magic in my eyes,
  All marked with mute surmise
My radiance rare and fathomless,
When I came back from Lyonnesse
  With magic in my eyes.

WHEN I SET OUT FOR LYONNESSE Reprinted with permission of the publisher from *Collected Poems* by Thomas Hardy. Copyright 1925 by The Macmillan Company.

BOOK ONE

Introduction
to Literature

The chief purpose of the study of literature is to intensify one's awareness of the quality and variety of human experience. A literary work therefore possesses greatness by virtue of the power it is able to exert, through means peculiar to it as a form of art, over the imaginative life of attentive readers. Literary works have a wide range of complexity. At one end of the scale we find the brief expression of personal emotion such as Edna St. Vincent Millay's "I Know I Am But Summer." The middle reaches are represented by the contained fervency of E. M. Forster's familiar essay "What I Believe" and by the buoyancy of Eudora Welty's "A Worn Path." At the other end stands such accumulated force and complexity as in the Greek tragedy *Antigonê*. But however modest or grand in scope a poem, a play, a novel, or an essay may be, the reader must participate actively and eagerly for full realization of its experience. The person who has read many books with understanding has shared in many lives, vividly different from one another, and has added richness and perspective to his sum total of experience—to the outer and inner events of his own life.

Experience, it is said, is a costly teacher. Direct experience is often desirable, despite its cost, but not all our experience can or need be acquired directly. It is possible to avoid disaster, for instance, and yet lay hold of the quality of character that disaster sometimes creates, or at least reveals. The imaginative projection of ourselves into the consciousness of others, through literature, yields experiences that would be too strenuous to endure without hazard in actual life, and yet can chasten and humanize us, bringing us to a better understanding of ourselves and others. The range of such vicarious experiences is surprisingly large and varied—from the outrageous to the sublime—but they are most meaningful to the reader when they complement his actual experiences. Steinbeck's "The Chrysanthemums" holds much meaning for any woman who has even vaguely felt herself beckoned by something beyond her daily life, and Yeats' "Down by the Salley Gardens" cuts deep into the man who already regrets that he has restrained himself from tasting more freely life's pleasures.

But literature, however closely allied to actual experience, is not an exact reproduction or transcript of happenings, feelings, and scenes. That is, literature is not so much like a photograph of life as it is like a series of portraits or interpretations. Life is so crowded with details as to seem nearly chaotic to most of us at times, but each work of literature is a selection of details combined to suggest a coherent impression of life. The artist does not give us masses of unassimilated knowledge. He imposes form upon the materials he uses and through this form suggests meaning. Organization is what gives us this sense of meaning. Test the truth of this statement by analyzing any one of the stories in the group of short stories in this text; see how little in the way of details— of description or character or action—the author actually gives us, how much he suggests or implies.

The central importance of this selection and organization of materials is especially well illustrated by the short story, because within its brief limits the author must select and organize his material with unusual care and skill. For example, when Hemingway wishes to show that even a ruffian can be touched by the mystery and tragedy of life, he chooses to put his material into a monologue, centers the action upon a single shipwreck, and places the story offshore from Key West. But selectivity goes beyond the simple limitation of character and incident; it involves also the choice of those personalities and events that will most economically and richly convey the theme of the story.

The meaning that emerges from organization and selection in any work of literature cannot be adequately conveyed in a summary. To perceive the full quality of the experience interpreted, we have to become sensitively aware of every part and relationship; and the comprehension we finally achieve will depend in part on the scope of our own consciousness. As one contemporary critic has suggested, the effect of a work of art on the consciousness of various readers is like the effect of pebbles falling into pools of water: the ripples always move out to the far edge of each pool, but some pools are larger than others.

Literature appeals to both mind and heart. Therefore our whole being is involved in the response to it. Sometimes full comprehension of a poem or of an experience comes in a flash of illumination which enlarges our consciousness and lifts us to a different plane of being. Robert Frost records such an incident in the following lines:

> The way a crow
> Shook down on me
> The dust of snow
> From a hemlock tree
>
> Has given my heart
> A change of mood
> And saved some part
> Of a day I had rued.[1]

[1] DUST OF SNOW From *Complete Poems of Robert Frost.* Copyright 1923 by Holt, Rinehart and Winston, Inc. Copyright renewed 1951 by Robert Frost. Reprinted by permission of Holt, Rinehart and Winston, Inc.

The sudden illumination here spoken of yields a deep understanding, an unusual insight, a discovery. No doubt all of us have such moments of poetic insight when past knowledge and present awareness come to focus upon a single point of understanding: these are among our most memorable experiences. Readers of imaginative literature may share these moments with artists. This is reading at its best—creative reading, building and enriching the mind.

The Essay

Probably no form of written composition records the varied interests of man and the temper of his times more completely and accurately than the essay. Bacon and Montaigne, originators of the form, reflect the taste of the Renaissance for proverbial and utilitarian lore. Eighteenth-century essayists represent the wit, gossip, and learned talk that was heard in the coffee houses and drawing rooms of Addison's and Steele's London. The essays of Hazlitt, Lamb, Ruskin, Carlyle, Darwin, Huxley, Thoreau, and Emerson reveal the social, literary, and scientific ferment of the nineteenth century in England and America. Today the genre has an even broader range of subject matter, a wider variety of types, and a greater audience. It not only reflects the interests of contemporary man and the complexity of his century, but provides a sounding board for his ideas, aspirations, and fears. Thus the essay continues to increase in popularity and usefulness as a means by which the reader can obtain ideas, knowledge, opinion, and counsel.

The essay received its name from the title of Montaigne's first collection of short prose writings—*Essais* (attempts)—and from its beginning was considered an "attempt" to communicate. The term still retains this meaning but today especially signifies a more polished prose selection that has a worthwhile idea and an artistic presentation. The term *article* suggests a timely treatment that lacks some of the literary quality of the essay. The article, though important and interesting for a time, may soon lose its importance and interest, while the essay is more likely to achieve a permanent place as a document of both intellectual significance and literary merit.

Essays traditionally have been classified by type, but in view of their present variety and range, no classification scheme seems very accurate today. Though numerous terms have been used to denote categories, perhaps two are sufficient— informal (or personal) and formal. The informal essay has a natural, instinctive, free flow of ideas rather than the tight, logical structure of the formal essay. It is conversational in tone, often frankly reminiscent, and tends to be unstudied in effect, whereas the formal essay uses language and style that maintain more esthetic distance from both the subject and the reader. Formal and informal essays are in evidence in many kinds of current publications. Most of the formal essays appear in scholarly, professional, and technical journals and in books and magazines of fairly limited circulation.

Informal essays are published most often in popular magazines and newspapers. It is apparent that most of the essays one reads today are informal.

Whether formal or informal, essays are a repository of ideas from various areas of knowledge. Though reading essays may require greater background, concentration, and skill than other literary forms demand, the reader is rewarded with increased knowledge and understanding of vital ideas, opinions, and judgments representative of the best thinking of the ablest writers of the time—the *summum bonum* of good literature.

ROBERT GRAVES

The Cool Web

Children are dumb to say how hot the day is,
How hot the scent is of the summer rose,
How dreadful the black wastes of evening sky,
How dreadful the tall soldiers drumming by.

But we have speech, to chill the angry day,
And speech, to dull the rose's cruel scent.
We spell away the overhanging night,
We spell away the soldiers and the fright.

There's a cool web of language winds us in,
Retreat from too much joy or too much fear:
We grow sea-green at last and coldly die
In brininess and volubility.

But if we let our tongues lose self-possession,
Throwing off language and its watery clasp
Before our death, instead of when death comes,
Facing the wide glare of the children's day,
Facing the rose, the dark sky and the drums,
We shall go mad no doubt and die that way.

THE COOL WEB From *Collected Poems 1955* by Robert Graves, published by Doubleday & Company, Inc., and Cassell & Company, Ltd. © 1955 International Authors N.V. Reprinted by permission of International Authors N.V. and A. P. Watt & Son.

EDWARD SAPIR

Language Defined

Edward Sapir (1884–1939) came to America from Germany at the age of five. His studies of the languages of the American Indian established his reputation as an authority on the relationships between language and anthropology. The author of many seminal articles on linguistics, Sapir summarized his conclusions concerning principles of language in his book *Language,* 1921.

In this essay Sapir discusses some of the different theories about the origins of language. He offers his own theory of language and discusses the problem of whether thinking without language is possible.

1. Speech is so familiar a feature of daily life that we rarely pause to define it. It seems as natural to man as walking, and only less so than breathing. Yet it needs but a moment's reflection to convince us that this naturalness of speech is but an illusory feeling. The process of acquiring speech is, in sober fact, an utterly different sort of thing from the process of learning to walk. In the case of the latter function, culture, in other words, the traditional body of social usage, is not seriously brought into play. The child is individually equipped, by the complex set of factors that we term biological heredity, to make all the needed muscular and nervous adjustments that result in walking. Indeed, the very conformation of these muscles and of the appropriate parts of the nervous system may be said to be primarily adapted to the movements made in walking and in similar activities. In a very real sense the normal human being is predestined to walk, not because his elders will assist him to learn the art, but because his organism is prepared from birth, or even from the moment of conception, to take on all those expenditures of nervous energy and all those muscular adaptations that result in walking. To put it concisely, walking is an inherent, biological function of man.

2. Not so language. It is of course true that in a certain sense the individual is predestined to talk, but that is due entirely to the circumstance that he is born not merely in nature, but in the lap of a society that is certain, reasonably certain, to lead him to its traditions. Eliminate society and there is every reason to believe that he will learn to walk, if, indeed, he survives at all. But it is

just as certain that he will never learn to talk, that is, to communicate ideas according to the traditional system of a particular society. Or, again, remove the new-born individual from the social environment into which he has come and transplant him to an utterly alien one. He will develop the art of walking in his new environment very much as he would have developed it in the old. But his speech will be completely at variance with the speech of his native environment. Walking, then, is a general human activity that varies only within circumscribed limits as we pass from individual to individual. Its variability is involuntary and purposeless. Speech is a human activity that varies without assignable limit as we pass from social group to social group, because it is a purely historical heritage of the group, the product of long-continued social usage. It varies as all creative effort varies— not as consciously, perhaps, but none the less as truly as do the religions, the beliefs, the customs, and the arts of different peoples. Walking is an organic, an instinctive, function (not, of course, itself an instinct); speech is a non-instinctive, acquired, "cultural" function.

3. There is one fact that has frequently tended to prevent the recognition of language as a merely conventional system of sound symbols, that has seduced the popular mind into attributing to it an instinctive basis that it does not really possess. This is the well-known observation that under the stress of emotion, say of a sudden twinge of pain or of unbridled joy, we do involuntarily give utterance to sounds that the hearer interprets as indicative of the emotion itself. But there is all the difference in the world between such involuntary expression of feeling and the normal type of communication of ideas that is speech. The former kind of utterance is indeed instinctive, but it is non-symbolic; in other words, the sound of pain or the sound of joy does not, as such, indicate the emotion, it does not stand aloof, as it were, and announce that such and such an emotion is being felt. What it does is to serve as a more or less automatic overflow of the emotional energy; in a sense, it is part and parcel of the emotion itself. Moreover, such instinctive

cries hardly constitute communication in any strict sense. They are not addressed to any one, they are merely overheard, if heard at all, as the bark of a dog, the sound of approaching footsteps, or the rustling of the wind is heard. If they convey certain ideas to the hearer, it is only in the very general sense in which any and every sound or even any phenomenon in our environment may be said to convey an idea to the perceiving mind. If the involuntary cry of pain which is conventionally represented by "Oh!" be looked upon as a true speech symbol equivalent to some such idea as "I am in great pain," it is just as allowable to interpret the appearance of clouds as an equivalent symbol that carries the definite message "It is likely to rain." A definition of language, however, that is so extended as to cover every type of inference becomes utterly meaningless.

4. The mistake must not be made of identifying our conventional interjections (our oh! and ah! and sh!) with the instinctive cries themselves. These interjections are merely conventional fixations of the natural sounds. They therefore differ widely in various languages in accordance with the specific phonetic genius of each of these. As such they may be considered an integral portion of speech, in the properly cultural sense of the term, being no more identical with the instinctive cries themselves than such words as "cuckoo" and "killdeer" are identical with the cries of the birds they denote or than Rossini's treatment of a storm in the overture to "William Tell" is in fact a storm. In other words, the interjections and sound-imitative words of normal speech are related to their natural prototypes as is art, a purely social or cultural thing, to nature. It may be objected that, though the interjections differ somewhat as we pass from language to language, they do nevertheless offer striking family resemblances and may therefore be looked upon as having grown up out of a common instinctive base. But their case is nowise different from that, say, of the varying national modes of pictorial representation. A Japanese picture of a hill both differs from and resembles a typical modern European painting of the same

kind of hill. Both are suggested by and both "imitate" the same natural feature. Neither the one nor the other is the same thing as, or, in any intelligible sense, a direct outgrowth of, this natural feature. The two modes of representation are not identical because they proceed from differing historical traditions, are executed with differing pictorial techniques. The interjections of Japanese and English are, just so, suggested by a common natural prototype, the instinctive cries, and are thus unavoidably suggestive of each other. They differ, now greatly, now but little, because they are builded out of historically diverse materials or techniques, the respective linguistic traditions, phonetic systems, speech habits of the two peoples. Yet the instinctive cries as such are practically identical for all humanity, just as the human skeleton or nervous system is to all intents and purposes a "fixed," that is, an only slightly and "accidentally" variable, feature of man's organism.

5. Interjections are among the least important of speech elements. Their discussion is valuable mainly because it can be shown that even they, avowedly the nearest of all language sounds to instinctive utterance, are only superficially of an instinctive nature. Were it therefore possible to demonstrate that the whole of language is traceable, in its ultimate historical and psychological foundations, to the interjections, it would still not follow that language is an instinctive activity. But, as a matter of fact, all attempts so to explain the origin of speech have been fruitless. There is no tangible evidence, historical or otherwise, tending to show that the mass of speech elements and speech processes has evolved out of the interjections. These are a very small and functionally insignificant proportion of the vocabulary of language; at no time and in no linguistic province that we have record of do we see a noticeable tendency towards their elaboration into the primary warp and woof of language. They are never more, at best, than a decorative edging to the ample, complex fabric.

6. What applies to the interjections applies with even greater force to the sound-imitative words. Such words as "whippoorwill," "to

mew," "to caw" are in no sense natural sounds that man has instinctively or automatically reproduced. They are just as truly creations of the human mind, flights of the human fancy, as anything else in language. They do not directly grow out of nature, they are suggested by it and play with it. Hence the onomatopoetic theory of the origin of speech, the theory that would explain all speech as a gradual evolution from sounds of an imitative character, really brings us no nearer to the instinctive level than is language as we know it today. As to the theory itself, it is scarcely more credible than its interjectional counterpart. It is true that a number of words which we do not now feel to have a sound-imitative value can be shown to have once had a phonetic form that strongly suggests their origin as imitations of natural sounds. Such is the English word "to laugh." For all that, it is quite impossible to show, nor does it seem intrinsically reasonable to suppose, that more than a negligible proportion of the elements of speech or anything at all of its formal apparatus is derivable from an onomatopoetic source. However much we may be disposed on general principles to assign a fundamental importance in the languages of primitive peoples to the imitation of natural sounds, the actual fact of the matter is that these languages show no particular preference for imitative words. Among the most primitive peoples of aboriginal America, the Athabaskan tribes of the Mackenzie River speak languages in which such words seem to be nearly or entirely absent, while they are used freely enough in languages as sophisticated as English and German. Such an instance shows how little the essential nature of speech is concerned with the mere imitation of things.

7. The way is now cleared for a serviceable definition of language. Language is a purely human and non-instinctive method of communicating ideas, emotions, and desires by means of a system of voluntarily produced symbols. These symbols are, in the first instance, auditory and they are produced by the so-called "organs of speech." There is no discernible instinctive basis in human speech

as such, however much instinctive expressions and the natural environment may serve as a stimulus for the development of certain elements of speech, however much instinctive tendencies, motor and other, may give a predetermined range or mold to linguistic expression. Such human or animal communication, if "communication" it may be called, as is brought about by involuntary, instinctive cries is not, in our sense, language at all.

8. I have just referred to the "organs of speech," and it would seem at first blush that this is tantamount to an admission that speech itself is an instinctive, biologically predetermined activity. We must not be misled by the mere term. There are, properly speaking, no organs of speech; there are only organs that are incidentally useful in the production of speech sounds. The lungs, the larynx, the palate, the nose, the tongue, the teeth, and the lips, are all so utilized, but they are no more to be thought of as primary organs of speech than are the fingers to be considered as essentially organs of piano-playing or the knees as organs of prayer. Speech is not a simple activity that is carried on by one or more organs biologically adapted to the purpose. It is an extremely complex and ever-shifting network of adjustments—in the brain, in the nervous system, and in the articulating and auditory organs—tending towards the desired end of communication. The lungs developed, roughly speaking, in connection with the necessary biological function known as breathing; the nose, as an organ of smell; the teeth, as organs useful in breaking up food before it was ready for digestion. If, then, these and other organs are being constantly utilized in speech, it is only because any organ, once existent and in so far as it is subject to voluntary control, can be utilized by man for secondary purposes. Physiologically, speech is an overlaid function, or, to be more precise, a group of overlaid functions. It gets what service it can out of organs and functions, nervous and muscular, that have come into being and are maintained for very different ends than its own.

9. It is true that physiological psychologists speak of the localization of speech in the brain. This can only mean that the sounds of speech are localized in the auditory tract of the brain, or in some circumscribed portion of it, precisely as other classes of sounds are localized; and that the motor processes involved in speech (such as the movements of the glottal cords in the larynx, the movements of the tongue required to pronounce the vowels, lip movements required to articulate certain consonants, and numerous others) are localized in the motor tract precisely as are all other impulses to special motor activities. In the same way control is lodged in the visual tract of the brain over all those processes of visual recognition involved in reading. Naturally the particular points or clusters of points of localization in the several tracts that refer to any element of language are connected in the brain by paths of association, so that the outward, or psycho-physical, aspect of language is of a vast network of associated localizations in the brain and lower nervous tracts, the auditory localizations being without doubt the most fundamental of all for speech. However, a speech-sound localized in the brain, even when associated with the particular movements of the "speech organs" that are required to produce it, is very far from being an element of language. It must be further associated with some element or group of elements of experience, say a visual image or a class of visual images or a feeling of relation, before it has even rudimentary linguistic significance. This "element" of experience is the content or "meaning" of the linguistic unit; the associated auditory, motor, and other cerebral processes that lie immediately back of the act of speaking and the act of hearing speech are merely a complicated symbol of or signal for these "meanings," of which more anon. We see therefore at once that language as such is not and cannot be definitely localized, for it consists of a peculiar symbolic relation—physiologically an arbitrary one—between all possible elements of consciousness on the one hand and certain selected elements localized in the auditory, motor, and other cerebral and nervous tracts on the other. If language can be said to be definitely "localized" in the brain, it is only in that gen-

eral and rather useless sense in which all aspects of consciousness, all human interest and activity, may be said to be "in the brain." Hence, we have no recourse but to accept language as a fully formed functional system within man's psychic or "spiritual" constitution. We cannot define it as an entity in psycho-physical terms alone, however much the psycho-physical basis is essential to its functioning in the individual.

10. From the physiologist's or psychologist's point of view we may seem to be making an unwarrantable abstraction in desiring to handle the subject of speech without constant and explicit reference to that basis. However, such an abstraction is justifiable. We can profitably discuss the intention, the form, and the history of speech, precisely as we discuss the nature of any other phase of human culture—say art or religion—as an institutional or cultural entity, leaving the organic and psychological mechanisms back of it as something to be taken for granted. Accordingly, it must be clearly understood that this introduction to the study of speech is not concerned with those aspects of physiology and of physiological psychology that underlie speech. Our study of language is not to be one of the genesis and operation of a concrete mechanism; it is, rather, to be an inquiry into the function and form of the arbitrary systems of symbolism that we term languages.

11. I have already pointed out that the essence of language consists in the assigning of conventional, voluntarily articulated, sounds, or of their equivalents, to the diverse elements of experience. The word "house" is not a linguistic fact if by it is meant merely the acoustic effect produced on the ear by its constituent consonants and vowels, pronounced in a certain order; nor the motor processes and tactile feelings which make up the articulation of the word; nor the visual perception on the part of the hearer of this articulation; nor the visual perception of the word "house" on the written or printed page; nor the motor processes and tactile feelings which enter into the writing of the word; nor the memory of any or all of these experiences. It is only when these, and possibly still other, associated experiences are automatically associated with the image of a house that they begin to take on the nature of a symbol, a word, an element of language. But the mere fact of such an association is not enough. One might have heard a particular word spoken in an individual house under such impressive circumstances that neither the word nor the image of the house ever recur in consciousness without the other becoming present at the same time. This type of association does not constitute speech. The association must be a purely symbolic one; in other words, the word must denote, tag off, the image, must have no other significance than to serve as a counter to refer to it whenever it is necessary or convenient to do so. Such an association, voluntary and, in a sense, arbitrary as it is, demands a considerable exercise of self-conscious attention. At least to begin with, for habit soon makes the association nearly as automatic as any and more rapid than most.

12. But we have traveled a little too fast. Were the symbol "house"—whether an auditory, motor, or visual experience or image—attached but to the single image of a particular house once seen, it might perhaps, by an indulgent criticism, be termed an element of speech, yet it is obvious at the outset that speech so constituted would have little or no value for purposes of communication. The world of our experiences must be enormously simplified and generalized before it is possible to make a symbolic inventory of all our experiences of things and relations and this inventory is imperative before we can convey ideas. The elements of language, the symbols that ticket off experience, must therefore be associated with whole groups, delimited classes, of experience rather than with the single experiences themselves. Only so is communication possible, for the single experience lodges in an individual consciousness and is, strictly speaking, incommunicable. To be communicated it needs to be referred to a class which is tacitly accepted by the community as an identity. Thus, the single impression which I have had of a particular house must be identified with all my other impressions of it. Further, my generalized

memory or my "notion" of this house must be merged with the notions that all other individuals who have seen the house have formed of it. The particular experience that we started with has now been widened so as to embrace all possible impressions or images that sentient beings have formed or may form of the house in question. This first simplification of experience is at the bottom of a large number of elements of speech, the so-called proper nouns or names of single individuals or objects. It is, essentially, the type of simplification which underlies, or forms the crude subject of, history and art. But we cannot be content with this measure of reduction of the infinity of experience. We must cut to the bone of things, we must more or less arbitrarily throw whole masses of experience together as similar enough to warrant their being looked upon—mistakenly, but conveniently—as identical. This house and that house and thousands of other phenomena of like character are thought of as having enough in common, in spite of great and obvious differences of detail, to be classed under the same heading. In other words, the speech element "house" is the symbol, first and foremost, not of a single perception, nor even of the notion of a particular object, but of a "concept," in other words, of a convenient capsule of thought that embraces thousands of distinct experiences and that is ready to take in thousands more. If the single significant elements of speech are the symbols of concepts, the actual flow of speech may be interpreted as a record of the setting of these concepts into mutual relations.

13. The question has often been raised whether thought is possible without speech; further, if speech and thought be not but two facets of the same psychic process. The question is all the more difficult because it has been hedged about by misunderstandings. In the first place, it is well to observe that whether or not thought necessitates symbolism, that is speech, the flow of language itself is not always indicative of thought. We have seen that the typical linguistic element labels a concept. It does not follow from this that the use to which language is put is always or even mainly conceptual. We are not in ordinary life so much concerned with concepts as such as with concrete particularities and specific relations. When I say, for instance, "I had a good breakfast this morning," it is clear that I am not in the throes of laborious thought, that what I have to transmit is hardly more than a pleasurable memory symbolically rendered in the grooves of habitual expression. Each element in the sentence defines a separate concept or conceptual relation or both combined, but the sentence as a whole has no conceptual significance whatever. It is somewhat as though a dynamo capable of generating enough power to run an elevator were operated almost exclusively to feed an electric doorbell. The parallel is more suggestive than at first sight appears. Language may be looked upon as an instrument capable of running a gamut of psychic uses. Its flow not only parallels that of the inner content of consciousness, but parallels it on different levels, ranging from the state of mind that is dominated by particular images to that in which abstract concepts and their relations are alone at the focus of attention and which is ordinarily termed reasoning. Thus the outward form only of language is constant; its inner meaning, its psychic value or intensity, varies freely with attention or the selective interest of the mind, also, needless to say, with the mind's general development. From the point of view of language, thought may be defined as the highest latent or potential content of speech, the content that is obtained by interpreting each of the elements in the flow of language as possessed of its very fullest conceptual value. From this it follows at once that language and thought are not strictly coterminous. At best language can but be the outward facet of thought on the highest, most generalized, level of symbolic expression. To put our viewpoint somewhat differently, language is primarily a prerational function. It humbly works up to the thought that is latent in, that may eventually be read into, its classifications and its forms; it is not, as is generally but naïvely assumed, the final label put upon the finished thought.

14. Most people, asked if they can think

without speech, would probably answer, "Yes, but it is not easy for me to do so. Still I know it can be done." Language is but a garment! But what if language is not so much a garment as a prepared road or groove? It is, indeed, in the highest degree likely that language is an instrument originally put to uses lower than the conceptual plane and that thought arises as a refined interpretation of its content. The product grows, in other words, with the instrument, and thought may be no more conceivable, in its genesis and daily practice, without speech than is mathematical reasoning practicable without the lever of an appropriate mathematical symbolism. No one believes that even the most difficult mathematical proposition is inherently dependent on an arbitrary set of symbols, but it is impossible to suppose that the human mind is capable of arriving at or holding such a proposition without the symbolism. The writer, for one, is strongly of the opinion that the feeling entertained by so many that they can think, or even reason, without language is an illusion. The illusion seems to be due to a number of factors. The simplest of these is the failure to distinguish between imagery and thought. As a matter of fact, no sooner do we try to put an image into conscious relation with another than we find ourselves slipping into a silent flow of words. Thought may be a natural domain apart from the artificial one of speech, but speech would seem to be the only road we know of that leads to it. A still more fruitful source of the illusive feeling that language may be dispensed with in thought is the common failure to realize that language is not identical with its auditory symbolism. The auditory symbolism may be replaced, point for point, by a motor or by a visual symbolism (many people can read, for instance, in a purely visual sense, that is, without the intermediating link of an inner flow of the auditory images that correspond to the printed or written words) or by still other, more subtle and elusive, types of transfer that are not so easy to define. Hence the contention that one thinks without language merely because he is not aware of a coexisting auditory imagery is very far indeed

from being a valid one. One may go so far as to suspect that the symbolic expression of thought may in some cases run along outside the fringe of the conscious mind, so that the feeling of a free, non-linguistic stream of thought is for minds of a certain type a relatively, but only a relatively, justified one. Psycho-physically, this would mean that the auditory or equivalent visual or motor centers in the brain, together with the appropriate paths of association, that are the cerebral equivalent of speech, are touched off so lightly during the process of thought as not to rise into consciousness at all. This would be a limiting case—thought riding lightly on the submerged crests of speech, instead of jogging along with it, hand in hand. The modern psychology has shown us how powerfully symbolism is at work in the unconscious mind. It is therefore easier to understand at the present time than it would have been twenty years ago that the most rarefied thought may be but the conscious counterpart of an unconscious linguistic symbolism.

15. One word more as to the relation between language and thought. The point of view that we have developed does not by any means preclude the possibility of the growth of speech being in a high degree dependent on the development of thought. We may assume that language arose pre-rationally—just how and on what precise level of mental activity we do not know—but we must not imagine that a highly developed system of speech symbols worked itself out before the genesis of distinct concepts and of thinking, the handling of concepts. We must rather imagine that thought processes set in, as a kind of psychic overflow, almost at the beginning of linguistic expression; further, that the concept, once defined, necessarily reacted on the life of its linguistic symbol, encouraging further linguistic growth. We see this complex process of the interaction of language and thought actually taking place under our eyes. The instrument makes possible the product, the product refines the instrument. The birth of a new concept is invariably foreshadowed by a more or less strained or extended use of old linguistic material; the concept does not

tions being visible to the eye. However, it is well known what excellent use deaf-mutes can make of "reading from the lips" as a subsidiary method of apprehending speech. The most important of all visual speech symbolisms is, of course, that of the written or printed word, to which, on the motor side, corresponds the system of delicately adjusted movements which result in the writing or typewriting or other graphic method of recording speech. The significant feature for our recognition in these new types of symbolism, apart from the fact that they are no longer a by-product of normal speech itself, is that each element (letter or written word) in the system corresponds to a specific element (sound or sound-group or spoken word) in the primary system. Written language is thus a point-to-point equivalence, to borrow a mathematical phrase, to its spoken counterpart. The written forms are secondary symbols of the spoken ones—symbols of symbols so close is the correspondence that they not only in theory but in the actual ice of certain eye-readers and, possibly, tain types of thinking, be entirely substi- for the spoken ones. Yet the auditory- associations are probably always latent least, that is, they are unconsciously into play. Even those who read and ithout the slightest use of sound im- e, at last analysis, dependent on it. merely handling the circulating me- money, of visual symbols as a con- stitute for the economic goods and the fundamental auditory symbols. possibilities of linguistic transfer lly unlimited. A familiar example e telegraph code, in which the tten speech are represented by lly fixed sequence of longer or Here the transfer takes place en word rather than directly s of spoken speech. The letter code is thus a symbol of a bol. It does not, of course, in that the skilled operator, in an understanding of a tele- eeds to transpose the indi- f ticks into a visual image

of the word before he experiences its normal auditory image. The precise method of reading off speech from the telegraphic communication undoubtedly varies widely with the individual. It is even conceivable, if not exactly likely, that certain operators may have learned to think directly, so far as the purely conscious part of the process of thought is concerned, in terms of the tick-auditory symbolism or, if they happen to have a strong natural bent toward motor symbolism, in terms of the correlated tactile-motor symbolism developed in the sending of telegraphic messages.

20. Still another interesting group of transfers are the different gesture languages, developed for the use of deaf-mutes, of Trappist monks vowed to perpetual silence, or of communicating parties that are within seeing distance of each other but are out of earshot. Some of these systems are one-to-one equivalences of the normal system of speech; others, like military gesture-symbolism or the gesture language of the Plains Indians of North America (understood by tribes of mutually unintelligible forms of speech) are imperfect transfers, limiting themselves to the rendering of such grosser speech elements as are an imperative minimum under difficult circumstances. In these latter systems, as in such still more imperfect symbolisms as those used at sea or in the woods, it may be contended that language no longer properly plays a part but that the ideas are directly conveyed by an utterly unrelated symbolic process or by a quasi-instinctive imitativeness. Such an interpretation would be erroneous. The intelligibility of these vaguer symbolisms can hardly be due to anything but their automatic and silent translation into the terms of a fuller flow of speech.

21. We shall no doubt conclude that all voluntary communication of ideas, aside from normal speech, is either a transfer, direct or indirect, from the typical symbolism of language as spoken and heard or, at the least, involves the intermediary of truly linguistic symbolism. This is a fact of the highest importance. Auditory imagery and the correlated motor imagery leading to articulation

attain to individual and independent life until it has found a distinctive linguistic embodiment. In most cases the new symbol is but a thing wrought from linguistic material already in existence in ways mapped out by crushingly despotic precedents. As soon as the word is at hand, we instinctively feel, with something of a sigh of relief, that the concept is ours for the handling. Not until we own the symbol do we feel that we hold a key to the immediate knowledge or understanding of the concept. Would we be so ready to die for "liberty," to struggle for "ideals," if the words themselves were not ringing within us? And the word, as we know, is not only a key; it may also be a fetter.

16. Language is primarily an auditory system of symbols. In so far as it is articulated it is also a motor system, but the motor aspect of speech is clearly secondary to the auditory. In normal individuals the impulse to speech first takes effect in the sphere of auditory imagery and is then transmitted to the motor nerves that control the organs of speech. The motor processes and the accompanying motor feelings are not, however, the end, the final resting point. They are merely a means and a control leading to auditory perception in both speaker and hearer. Communication, which is the very object of speech, is successfully effected only when the hearer's auditory perceptions are translated into the appropriate and intended flow of imagery or thought or both combined. Hence the cycle of speech, in so far as we may look upon it as a purely external instrument, begins and ends in the realm of sounds. The concordance between the initial auditory imagery and the final auditory perceptions is the social seal or warrant of the successful issue of the process. As we have already seen, the typical course of this process may undergo endless modifications or transfers into equivalent systems without thereby losing its essential formal characteristics.

17. The most important of these modifications is the abbreviation of the speech process involved in thinking. This has doubtless many forms, according to the structural or functional peculiarities of the individual mind.

The least modified form is that known a "talking to one's self" or "thinking aloud. Here the speaker and the hearer are identified in a single person, who may be said to communicate with himself. More significan is the still further abbreviated form in which the sounds of speech are not articulated at all. To this belong all the varieties of silent speech and of normal thinking. The auditory centers alone may be excited; or the impulse to linguistic expression may be communicated as well to the motor nerves that communicate with the organs of speech but be inhibited either in the muscles of these organs or at some point in the motor nerves themselves; or, possibly, the auditory centers may be only slightly, if at all, affected, the speech process manifesting itself directly in the motor sphere. There must be still other types of abbreviation. How common is the excitation of the motor nerves in silent speech, in which audible or visible articulations result, is by the frequent experience of fatigue speech organs, particularly in the lary unusually stimulating reading or thinking.

18. All the modifications so far are directly patterned on the typ of normal speech. Of very great importance is the possibility of the whole system of speech other terms than those that the typical process. This pr seen, is a matter of sounds intended to produce thes of vision is not brought suppose that one not lated sounds but see selves as they are speaker. Clearly, if ciently high degr ing these move the way is ope symbolism—th placed by th that corres system h cause w tory-m an in

are, by whatever devious ways we follow the process, the historic fountain-head of all speech and of all thinking. One other point is of still greater importance. The ease with which speech symbolism can be transferred from one sense to another, from technique to technique, itself indicates that the mere sounds of speech are not the essential fact of language, which lies rather in the classification, in the formal patterning, and in the relating of concepts. Once more, language, as a structure, is on its inner face the mold of thought. It is this abstracted language, rather more than the physical facts of speech, that is to concern us in our inquiry.

22. There is no more striking general fact about language than its universality. One may argue as to whether a particular tribe engages in activities that are worthy of the name of religion or of art, but we know of no people that is not possessed of a fully developed language. The lowliest South African Bushman speaks in the forms of a rich symbolic system that is in essence perfectly comparable to the speech of the cultivated Frenchman. It goes without saying that the more abstract concepts are not nearly so plentifully represented in the language of the savage, nor is there the rich terminology and the finer definition of nuances that reflect the higher culture. Yet the sort of linguistic development that parallels the historic growth of culture and which, in its later stages, we associate with literature is, at best, but a superficial thing. The fundamental groundwork of language—the development of a clear-cut phonetic system, the specific association of speech elements with concepts, and the delicate provision for the formal expression of all manner of relations—all this meets us rigidly perfected and systematized in every language known to us. Many primitive languages have a formal richness, a latent luxuriance of expression, that eclipses anything known to the languages of modern civilization. Even in the mere matter of the inventory of speech the layman must be prepared for strange surprises. Popular statements as to the extreme poverty of expression to which primitive languages are doomed are simply myths. Scarcely less impressive than the universality of speech is its almost incredible diversity. Those of us that have studied French or German, or, better yet, Latin or Greek, know in what varied forms a thought may run. The formal divergences between the English plan and the Latin plan, however, are comparatively slight in the perspective of what we know of more exotic linguistic patterns. The universality and the diversity of speech lead to a significant inference. We are forced to believe that language is an immensely ancient heritage of the human race, whether or not all forms of speech are the historical outgrowth of a single pristine form. It is doubtful if any other cultural asset of man, be it the art of drilling for fire or of chipping stone, may lay claim to a greater age. I am inclined to believe that it antedated even the lowliest developments of material culture, that these developments, in fact, were not strictly possible until language, the tool of significant expression, had itself taken shape.

SUSANNE K. LANGER

The Language Line

Susanne K. Langer (1895–   ) has long been recognized as an authority on symbolic logic, philosophy, and esthetics. In 1962 she retired as head of the Department of Philosophy at Connecticut College, where she is now professor emeritus and research scholar. Her books, *Philosophy in a New Key*, 1942, and *Feeling and Form*, 1953, established that man is unique as a symbol-maker, that symbolic transformation is a basic function of his brain and one of his essential needs. *Philosophical Sketches*, 1962, contains the preliminary material for a larger work, now in progress, on the human mind and emotions.

In "The Language Line" Mrs. Langer discusses the nature of discursive language, its origin, and its purposes. Specifically, she states that man's use of symbols is the characteristic that creates the line of demarcation between him and the beast.

1. The trait that sets human mentality apart from every other is its preoccupation with symbols, with images and names that *mean* things, rather than with things themselves. This trait may have been a mere sport of nature once upon a time. Certain creatures do develop tricks and interests that seem biologically unimportant. Pack rats, for instance, and some birds of the crow family take a capricious pleasure in bright objects and carry away such things for which they have, presumably, no earthly use. Perhaps man's tendency to see certain forms as *images,* to hear certain sounds not only as signals but as expressive tones, and to be excited by sunset colors or starlight, was originally just a peculiar sensitivity in a rather highly developed brain. But whatever its cause, the ultimate destiny of this trait was momentous; for all human activity is based on the appreciation and use of symbols. Language, religion, mathematics, all learning, all science and superstition, even right and wrong, are products of symbolic expression rather than direct experience. Our commonest words, such as "house" and "red" and "walking," are symbols; the pyramids of Egypt and the mysterious circles of Stonehenge are symbols; so are dominions and empires and astronomical universes. We live in a mind-made world, where the things of prime importance are images or words that embody ideas and feelings and attitudes.

2. The animal mind is like a telephone exchange; it receives stimuli from outside through the sense organs and sends out appropriate responses through the nerves that govern muscles, glands, and other parts of the body. The organism is constantly interacting with its surroundings, receiving messages and acting on the new state of affairs that the messages signify.

3. But the human mind is not a simple transmitter like a telephone exchange. It is more like a great projector; for instead of

THE LANGUAGE LINE   From *The Lord of Creation* by Susanne K. Langer. Reprinted from the January 1944 issue of *Fortune* magazine by Special Permission; © 1944 Time Inc.

merely mediating between an event in the outer world and a creature's responsive action, it transforms or, if you will, distorts the event into an image to be looked at, retained, and contemplated. For the images of things that we remember are not exact and faithful transcriptions even of our actual sense impressions. They are made as much by what we think as by what we see. It is a well-known fact that if you ask several people the size of the moon's disk as they look at it, their estimates will vary from the area of a dime to that of a barrel top. Like a magic lantern, the mind projects its ideas of things on the screen of what we call "memory"; but like all projections, these ideas are transformations of actual things. They are, in fact, *symbols* of reality, not pieces of it.

4. A symbol is not the same thing as a sign; that is a fact that psychologists and philosophers often overlook. All intelligent animals use signs; so do we. To them as well as to us sounds and smells and motions are signs of food, danger, the presence of other beings, or of rain or storm. Furthermore, some animals not only attend to signs but produce them for the benefit of others. Dogs bark at the door to be let in; rabbits thump to call each other; the cooing of doves and the growl of a wolf defending his kill are unequivocal signs of feelings and intentions to be reckoned with by other creatures.

5. We use signs just as animals do, though with considerably more elaboration. We stop at red lights and go on green; we answer calls and bells, watch the sky for coming storms, read trouble or promise or anger in each other's eyes. That is animal intelligence raised to the human level. Those of us who are dog lovers can probably all tell wonderful stories of how high our dogs have sometimes risen in the scale of clever sign interpretation and sign using.

6. A sign is anything that announces the existence or the imminence of some event, the presence of a thing or a person, or a change in a state of affairs. There are signs of the weather, signs of danger, signs of future good or evil, signs of what the past has been. In every case a sign is closely bound up with something to be noted or expected in experience. It is always a part of the situation to which it refers, though the reference may be remote in space and time. Insofar as we are led to note or expect the signified event we are making correct use of a sign. This is the essence of rational behavior, which animals show in varying degrees. It is entirely realistic, being closely bound up with the actual objective course of history—learned by experience, and cashed in or voided by further experience.

7. If man had kept to the straight and narrow path of sign using, he would be like the other animals, though perhaps a little brighter. He would not talk, but grunt and gesticulate and point. He would make his wishes known, give warnings, perhaps develop a social system like that of bees and ants, with such a wonderful efficiency of communal enterprise that all men would have plenty to eat, warm apartments—all exactly alike and perfectly convenient—to live in, and everybody could and would sit in the sun or by the fire, as the climate demanded, not talking but just basking, with every want satisfied, most of his life. The young would romp and make love, the old would sleep, the middle-aged would do the routine work almost unconsciously and eat a great deal. But that would be the life of a social, superintelligent, purely sign-using animal.

8. To us who are human, it does not sound very glorious. We want to go places and do things, own all sorts of gadgets that we do not absolutely need, and when we sit down to take it easy we want to talk. Rights and property, social position, special talents and virtues, and above all our ideas, are what we live for. We have gone off on a tangent that takes us far away from the mere biological cycle that animal generations accomplish; and that is because we can use not only signs but symbols.

9. A symbol differs from a sign in that it does not announce the presence of the object, the being, condition, or whatnot, which is its meaning, but merely *brings this thing to mind*. It is not a mere "substitute sign" to which we react as though it were the object

itself. The fact is that our reaction to hearing a person's name is quite different from our reaction to the person himself. There are certain rare cases where a symbol stands directly for its meaning: in religious experience, for instance, the Host is not only a symbol but a Presence. But symbols in the ordinary sense are not mystic. They are the same sort of thing that ordinary signs are; only they do not call our attention to something necessarily present or to be physically dealt with—they call up merely a conception of the thing they "mean."

10. The difference between a sign and a symbol is, in brief, that a sign causes us to think or act *in face of* the thing signified, whereas a symbol causes us to think *about* the thing symbolized. Therein lies the great importance of symbolism for human life, its power to make this life so different from any other animal biography that generations of men have found it incredible to suppose that they were of purely zoological origin. A sign is always embedded in reality, in a present that emerges from the actual past and stretches to the future; but a symbol may be divorced from reality altogether. It may refer to what is *not* the case, to a mere idea, a figment, a dream. It serves, therefore, to liberate thought from the immediate stimuli of a physically present world; and that liberation marks the essential difference between human and non-human mentality. Animals think, but they think *of* and *at* things; men think primarily *about* things. Words, pictures, and memory images are symbols that may be combined and varied in a thousand ways. The result is a symbolic structure whose meaning is a complex of all their respective meanings, and this kaleidoscope of *ideas* is the typical product of the human brain that we call the "stream of thought."

11. The process of transforming all direct experience into imagery or into that supreme mode of symbolic expression, language, has so completely taken possession of the human mind that it is not only a special talent but a dominant, organic need. All our sense impressions leave their traces in our memory not only as signs disposing our practical reactions in the future but also as symbols, images representing our *ideas* of things; and the tendency to manipulate ideas, to combine and abstract, mix and extend them by playing with symbols, is man's outstanding characteristic. It seems to be what his brain most naturally and spontaneously does. Therefore his primitive mental function is not judging reality, but *dreaming his desires*.

12. Dreaming is apparently a basic function of human brains, for it is free and unexhausting like our metabolism, heartbeat, and breath. It is easier to dream than not to dream, as it is easier to breathe than to refrain from breathing. The symbolic character of dreams is fairly well established. Symbol mongering, on this ineffectual, uncritical level, seems to be instinctive, the fulfillment of an elementary need rather than the purposeful exercise of a high and difficult talent.

13. The special power of man's mind rests on the evolution of this special activity, not on any transcendently high development of animal intelligence. We are not immeasurably higher than other animals; we are different. We have a biological need and with it a biological gift that they do not share.

14. Because man has not only the ability but the constant need of *conceiving* what has happened to him, what surrounds him, what is demanded of him—in short, of symbolizing nature, himself, and his hopes and fears—he has a constant and crying need of *expression*. What he cannot express, he cannot conceive; what he cannot conceive is chaos, and fills him with terror.

15. If we bear in mind this all-important craving for expression we get a new picture of man's behavior; for from this trait spring his powers and his weaknesses. The process of symbolic transformation that all our experiences undergo is nothing more nor less than the process of *conception*, which underlies the human faculties of abstraction and imagination.

16. When we are faced with a strange or difficult situation, we cannot react directly, as other creatures do, with flight, aggression, or any such simple instinctive pattern. Our whole reaction depends on how we manage to conceive the situation—whether we cast it in a definite dramatic form, whether we see

it as a disaster, a challenge, a fulfillment of doom, or a fiat of the Divine Will. In words or dreamlike images, in artistic or religious or even in cynical form, we must *construe* the events of life. There is great virtue in the figure of speech, "I can *make* nothing of it," to express a failure to understand something. Thought and memory are processes of *making* the thought content and the memory image; the pattern of our ideas is given by the symbols through which we express them. And in the course of manipulating those symbols we inevitably distort the original experience, as we abstract certain features of it, embroider and reinforce those features with other ideas, until the conception we project on the screen of memory is quite different from anything in our real history.

17. Conception is a necessary and elementary process; what we do with our conceptions is another story. That is the entire history of human culture—of intelligence and morality, folly and superstition, ritual, language, and the arts—all the phenomena that set man apart from, and above, the rest of the animal kingdom. As the religious mind has to make all human history a drama of sin and salvation in order to define its own moral attitudes, so a scientist wrestles with the mere presentation of "the facts" before he can reason about them. The process of *envisaging* facts, values, hopes, and fears underlies our whole behavior pattern; and this process is reflected in the evolution of an extraordinary phenomenon found always, and only, in human societies—the phenomenon of language.

18. Language is the highest and most amazing achievement of the symbolistic human mind. The power it bestows is almost inestimable, for without it anything properly called "thought" is impossible. The birth of language is the dawn of humanity. The line between man and beast—between the highest ape and the lowest savage—is the language line. Whether the primitive Neanderthal man was anthropoid or human depends less on his cranial capacity, his upright posture, or even his use of tools and fire, than on one issue we shall probably never be able to settle —whether or not he spoke.

19. In all physical traits and practical responses, such as skills and visual judgments, we can find a certain continuity between animal and human mentality. Sign using is an ever evolving, ever improving function throughout the whole animal kingdom, from the lowly worm that shrinks into his hole at the sound of an approaching foot, to the dog obeying his master's command, and even to the learned scientist who watches the movements of an index needle.

20. This continuity of the sign-using talent has led psychologists to the belief that language is evolved from the vocal expressions, grunts and coos and cries, whereby animals vent their feelings or signal their fellows; that man has elaborated this sort of communion to the point where it makes a perfect exchange of ideas possible.

21. I do not believe that this doctrine of the origin of language is correct. The essence of language is symbolic, not signific; we use it first and most vitally to formulate and hold ideas in our own minds. Conception, not social control, is its first and foremost benefit.

22. Watch a young child that is just learning to speak play with a toy; he says the name of the object, e.g.: "Horsey! horsey! horsey!" over and over again, looks at the object, moves it, always saying the name to himself or to the world at large. It is quite a time before he talks to anyone in particular; he talks first of all to himself. This is his way of forming and fixing the *conception* of the object in his mind, and around this conception all his knowledge of it grows. *Names* are the essence of language; for the *name* is what abstracts the conception of the horse from the horse itself, and lets the mere idea recur at the speaking of the name. This permits the conception gathered from one horse experience to be exemplified again by another instance of a horse, so that the notion embodied in the name is a general notion.

23. To this end, the baby uses a word long before he *asks for* the object; when he wants his horsey he is likely to cry and fret, because he is reacting to an actual environment, not forming ideas. He uses the animal language of *signs* for his wants; talking is still a

purely symbolic process—its practical value has not really impressed him yet.

24. Language need not be vocal; it may be purely visual, like written language, or even tactual, like the deaf-mute system of speech; but it *must be denotative*. The sounds, intended or unintended, whereby animals communicate do not constitute a language, because they are signs, not names. They never fall into an organic pattern, a meaningful syntax of even the most rudimentary sort, as all language seems to do with a sort of driving necessity. That is because signs refer to actual situations, in which things have obvious relations to each other that require only to be noted; but symbols refer to ideas, which are not physically there for inspection, so their connections and features have to be represented. This gives all true language a natural tendency toward growth and development, which seems almost like a life of its own. Languages are not invented; they grow with our need for expression.

25. In contrast, animal "speech" never has a structure. It is merely an emotional response. Apes may greet their ration of yams with a shout of "Nga!" But they do not say "Nga" between meals. If they could *talk about* their yams instead of just saluting them, they would be the most primitive men instead of the most anthropoid of beasts. They would have ideas, and tell each other things true or false, rational or irrational; they would make plans and invent laws and sing their own praises, as men do.

STUART CHASE

Words and the World View

Stuart Chase (1888–   ), a well-known writer on social and economic subjects, abandoned an accountant's life to pursue a writing career. His popular books on such topics as labor relations, conservation, consumer education, and semantics have given thousands of readers an insight into the influence of these subjects on their lives. Among his books are *The Tyranny of Words*, 1938; *The Proper Study of Mankind*, 1948; *Power of Words*, 1954; *Some Things Worth Knowing: A Generalizer's Guide to Useful Knowledge*, 1958; *Live and Let Live*, 1960; *American Credos*, 1962; and *Money to Grow On*, 1964.

In this essay, from *Power of Words*, Mr. Chase discusses the broad implications of language systems—how these actually control our thoughts and our cultural outlook.

1. Linguistics as a study of patterned sounds has been called the most exact of all the social sciences. One can predict with it, and

WORDS AND THE WORLD VIEW   From *Power of Words*, copyright, 1953, 1954, by Stuart Chase. Reprinted by permission of Harcourt, Brace & World, Inc.

prediction is the ultimate test of any science. From this rigorous base, some linguists, especially the late Benjamin Lee Whorf, graduated into a larger inquiry: How does a given language mold the thought of the man whose mother tongue it is, and his view of nature and the world? In this inquiry the vistas are even more exciting, though prediction is probably lower.

2. Whorf, had he lived, might have become another Franz Boas or William James, so brilliant were his powers of projecting scientific data into fruitful generalizations. He died in 1941 at the age of forty-four. A graduate of M.I.T., he became an executive of the Hartford Fire Insurance Company, and took up linguistics as a hobby. Presently it became his consuming interest. His skill in deciphering Mexican inscriptions brought him to the attention of the scientific world and the close friendship of Edward Sapir. In 1930 the Social Science Research Council gave him a grant to go to Yucatan. Maya and Aztec languages led him to the live speech of American Indians, and he spent two years on Hopi alone.

3. Whorf's only book is a Hopi dictionary, an unpublished manuscript, now in the possession of Clyde Kluckhohn. He published some thirty articles in the learned journals, and might well have gone on to give the world one of the great classics of social science.

4. The forms of a man's thoughts, he said, are controlled by patterns learned early, of which the man is mostly unconscious. Thinking is a language process, whether in English, Russian, or Hopi. Every language is a complex system, with three main functions.

1. To communicate with other persons.
2. To communicate with oneself, or, as we say, think.
3. To mold one's whole outlook on life.

5. As he uses words, "a person notices or neglects types of relationships and phenomena, he channels his reasoning, and builds the house of his consciousness." This conclusion, says Whorf, has been largely neglected by the philosophers, but stands on unimpeachable evidence.

6. Thinking follows the tracks laid down in one's own language; these tracks will converge on certain phases of "reality," and completely bypass phases which may be explored in other languages. In English, for instance,

we say, "look at that wave." But a wave in nature never occurs as a single phenomenon. In the Hopi language they say, "look at that slosh." The Hopi word, whose nearest equivalent in English is "slosh," gives a closer fit to the actual physics of wave motion, connoting movement in a mass. (This is only one of several tough matters in physics where Hopi does better than English.)

7. Perhaps the majority of linguists today, though they are not prepared to follow Whorf all the way, do recognize the vital part which language plays in thought and culture. The study of *metalinguistics*, as they call it, is thus described by Trager and Smith:

> Not only does it deal with *what* people talk about and *why*, but also considers *how* they use the linguistic system, and how they react to its use. This leads further to the consideration of how the linguistic system affects the behavior, both conscious and unconscious, and the world-view, of the speaker. . . .

Contrasted with microlinguistics, which takes a long time to reach a unit as large as the sentence, the meta- or super-linguistics considers the "organization of sentences into discourse, and the relation of the discourse to the rest of the culture."

UNCONSCIOUS ASSUMPTIONS

8. Most of us were brought up to believe that talking is merely a tool which something deeper called "thinking" puts to work. Thinking, we have assumed, depends on laws of reason and logic common to all mankind. These laws are said to be implicit in the mental machinery of humans, whether they speak English or Choctaw. Languages, it follows, are simply parallel methods for expressing this universal logic. On this assumption it also follows that any logical idea can be translated unbroken, or even unbent, into any language. A few minutes in the glass palace of the United Nations in New York will quickly disabuse one of this quaint notion. Even such a common concept as "democracy" may not survive translation.

9. Another set of assumptions underlying Western culture, says Whorf, imposes upon

the universe two grand cosmic forms: *space* and *time*. *Space* in our thinking is static, three-dimensional, and infinite; beyond the last area is always another area. *Time* is kinetic and one-dimensional, flowing perpetually and smoothly from the past to the present and into the future. It took the genius of Einstein to correct these cosmic assumptions, and most of us are still firmly wedded to them.

10. The assumptions underlying the culture of the Hopi also impose two grand cosmic forms upon the universe: the *objective* and the *subjective;* the manifest and the unmanifest. The first is everything accessible to the human senses, without distinction between past and present. The second is "the realm of expectancy, of desire and purpose, of vitalizing life, of efficient causes, of thought thinking itself out . . . into manifestation." It exists in the hearts and minds of animals, plants, mountains, as well as men. This subjective realm is intensely real to a Hopi, "quivering with life, power and potency."

11. All languages contain terms of cosmic grandeur. English includes "reality," "matter," "substance," "cause," "energy," as well as "space" and "time." Hopi includes the cosmic term *tunátya,* meaning a special and exalted kind of "hope." It is a verb, not a noun—the action of hoping, the stirring toward hope—and is bound up with communal ceremonies, like prayers for the harvest, and for the forming of rain clouds.

12. The ancient Greeks believed, among other things, in a universal rule of reason. This came easily because their language structure, like all Indo-European tongues, followed what is called the "subject-predicate" form. If there is a verb there must be a noun to make it work; it could not exist in its own right as pure action. The ancient Greeks, as well as all Western peoples today, say "the light flashed." Something has to be there to make the flash; "light" is the subject; "flash" is the predicate. The whole trend of modern physics, however, with its emphasis on the *field,* is away from subject-predicate propositions. A Hopi Indian, accordingly, is the bet-

ter physicist when he says *"Reh-pi"*—"flash!"—one word for the whole performance, no subject, no predicate, and no time element. (Children tend to do this too.) In Western languages we are constantly reading into nature ghostly entities which flash and perform other miracles. Do we supply them because our verbs require substantives in front of them?

13. Again, the Hopi language does not raise the question whether things in a distant village exist at the same present moment as things in one's own village. Thus it avoids the idea of *simultaneity,* which has plagued Western scientists for generations, and was only banished by relativity. The thoughts of a Hopi about events always include *both* space and time, for neither is found alone in his world view. Thus his language gets along adequately without tenses for its verbs, and permits him to think habitually in terms of space-time. For a Westerner really to understand relativity, he must abandon his spoken tongue altogether and take to the special language of calculus. But a Hopi, Whorf implies, has a sort of calculus built into him.

LINGUISTIC RELATIVITY

14. Whorf emphasizes that Hopi is only one language of one small tribe, and that there are thousands of other tongues, each imposing a unique view of nature and the cosmos upon those who speak it. Here is still another kind of relativity, a very important kind. No human is free to describe nature with strict objectivity; for he is a prisoner of his language. A trained linguist can do better because he, at least, is aware of the bondage, and can look at nature through a variety of frames. A physicist can do better by using the language of mathematics. Semanticists are now painfully learning how to do better. It is not easy for anybody. Says Whorf:

> We are thus introduced to a new principle of relativity, which holds that all observers are not led by the same physical evidence to the same picture of the universe, unless their linguistic backgrounds are similar, or can in some way be calibrated.

15. Indo-European languages can be calibrated with each other: English, Italian, Spanish, French, Russian, German, Latin, Greek, and the rest, back to Indo-Hittite, all use the subject-predicate form. All speakers of these languages are capable of observing the world in a roughly similar way, at least on the high levels of "time," "space," and "matter." Hopi cannot be calibrated with them; neither can Chinese, nor thousands of other languages, living and dead.

CHINESE AND WESTERN LANGUAGES

16. Speakers of Chinese dissect nature and the universe very differently from Western speakers, with a profound effect upon their systems of belief. A Chinese writer, Chang Tung-sun, vigorously supports the relativity thesis in a monograph comparing his culture with that of the West.[1]

17. Kant imagined that he was dealing in universal categories in *The Critique of Pure Reason,* but actually, says Chang, he was only discussing standard forms of Western thought, a very limited approach. Kant's logic was of the subject-predicate variety, which is not normal in Chinese. An intelligent Chinese gentleman does not know what Kant is talking about—unless he learns some Western tongue in which to read Kant's words. (To some readers this will raise another interesting question: Did Kant himself know what he was talking about?)

18. Our Western verb "to be," observes Chang, used with an adjective predicate, implies the existence of the adjective as an independent quality. When we say "this is yellow and hard," we tend to assume the existence of two qualities, "yellowness" and "hardness," which suggests to a Chinese something Chang calls a "cosmic substance." "The substance is characterized by its attributes, and the attributes are attributed to the substance," says Chang, in considerable astonishment at such a circular performance. The verb "to be" creates great congeries of identities, and blossoms in Aristotle's laws of logic,

[1] *ETC,* Spring 1952.

of which the first is the law of identity, "A is A." . . .

19. No such law is possible in the Chinese language, where logic follows a quite different path. In Chinese, one does not attribute existence to "yellowness" and "hardness," or to polar words like "longness" and "shortness." Rather one says: "the long and the short are mutually related"; "the difficult and easy are mutually complementary"; "the front and the rear are mutually accompanying."

20. In the West we say, "This is the front of the car, and that is the rear, and let's have no more nonsense about it!" But in the Chinese view, Westerners are guilty of considerable nonsense in creating "frontness" and "rearness" as entities. Even a Westerner can see that if a car is torn in two in a crash, the part with the radiator grille becomes the "front," and the part toward the now severed windshield becomes the "rear"—*of that segment.* We can see, if we work hard enough, that there are no such entities as "frontness" or "rearness," "difficulty" or "easiness," "length" or "shortness," by themselves out there. The Chinese language has this useful correction built in; we Westerners, have to sweat it out with the help of linguistics, semantics, and mathematics.

21. Linguists have also emphasized that Chinese is a "multi-valued" language, not primarily two-valued like English and Western languages generally. We say that things must be "good" or "bad," "right" or "wrong," "clean" or "dirty," "capitalistic" or "socialistic," "black" or "white"—ignoring shades of gray. When an economist talks about a middle road between "Socialism" and "Capitalism," both camps vie in their ferocity to tear him apart. (I have been that unhappy economist.)

22. Speakers of Chinese set up no such grim dichotomies; they see most situations in shades of gray, and have no difficulty in grasping the significance of a variety of middle roads. As a result, Chinese thought has been traditionally tolerant, not given to the fanatical ideologies of the West. Racial, religious, and doctrinal conflicts have been hard to maintain in China, because a Chinese speaker does not

possess an unshakable confidence that he is totally right and that you are totally wrong. Observe that this is not a moral judgment, but structural in the language.

MARXISM IN CHINA?

23. This happy lack of bi-polar thinking raises a most interesting question. Communism, as formulated by Marx and developed by Lenin, is rigidly bi-polar. The heroic worker stands against the wicked capitalist and one or the other must go down. There is no place for shades of gray or for innocent bystanders in this two-valued struggle. Those who are not with us are against us! Look at almost any bulletin of the National Association of Manufacturers, or at any issue of the *Daily Worker*. Which side are you on?

24. Russian is an Indo-European language, and the two-sided choice is readily accepted by its speakers. The choice was accepted, too, by top leaders of the Chinese Communists today, for they went to Moscow to be indoctrinated, and to learn the Russian language. But 400 million Chinese have not been to Moscow or learned Russian, or any other Indo-European language, and there is small prospect of their doing so.

25. How, then, can the Chinese people become good ideological Communists, if it is impossible for them to take seriously the central idea of Marxism? Professor Nathaniel Peffer, of Columbia University, a specialist on the Far East, observes that the Chinese culture has endured many conquerors but has always managed to absorb them. Then he asks a related question: Will not the little group of "Reds" in control of the Chinese state be absorbed too? At first these leaders were accepted, he says, as part of the process of the great Chinese revolution which began in 1911. After its completion, the world may find that it was a *Chinese* revolution, not a communist one. In any event the language barrier to Marxism is formidable.

MORE SIDELIGHTS ON ENGLISH

26. The Wintu Indians of North America are even more shy of the law of identity (A is A) than the Chinese, says D. D. Lee, writing in the *International Journal of American Linguistics.*[2] We say, "this *is* bread," but in Wintu they say, "we call this bread." They avoid the "is of identity," and so are less likely to confuse words with things. When a Wintu speaks of an event not within his own experience, he never affirms it but only suggests, "perhaps it is so." When Lee asked her informant the word for "body," she was given a term signifying "the whole person." Thus the Wintus seem to have antedated the psychosomatic school.

27. The Coeur d'Alene Indians of Idaho have long antedated other modern scientists. They do not speak in terms of simple cause-and-effect relations as we do, but rather in terms of *process,* as Western scientists are now painfully learning to do. Their language requires speakers to discriminate between three causal processes, denoted by three verb forms: growth, addition, secondary addition. "If, given a more sophisticated culture," says Whorf, "their thinkers erected these now unconscious discriminations into a theory of triadic causality, fitted to scientific observations, they might thereby produce a valuable intellectual tool for science." Our specialists can do this by taking thought, fortified with mathematics, but the Coeur d'Alenes seem to do it automatically.

28. In Nootka, a language of Vancouver Island Indians, a number of English nouns turn into verbs. A speaker does not say "a house," but "a house occurs." The suffixes indicate the duration of the house-event: "a long-lasting house," "a temporary house," "a future house," "a house that used to be," "what started out to be a house."

29. Eskimo, as we have noted, breaks down our single term "snow" into many words for different kinds of snow. Aztec, however, goes in the opposite direction; here we find one word, though with different terminations, for "snow," "ice," and "cold"! In Hopi, "wave," "flame," "meteor," and "lightning" are all verbs, suiting their dynamic quality. Looking into the August sky, a Hopi says: *"Reh-pi."* "It meteors!"

---

[2] 1944. Quoted by L. Doob.

30. It is easier to recite the story of William Tell in the Algonquin language than in English, because it has enough possessive pronouns to make a distinction between "his," as applied to Tell, and as applied to his son. As a writer I must continually watch my step with English pronouns, lest they trip me up.

31. Linguistic relativity makes it clear that Newton took his concepts of Absolute Space and Absolute Time, not so much out of profound cogitation, as out of the language he spoke. They had been lying there for thousands of years. Both "time" and "space" affect the behavior of everyone in Western culture.

32. "Time," especially, causes us to be oriented toward calendars, dates, "the course of history," timetables, clocks, time wages, races against time, accounting, compound interest, actuarial statistics, annals, diaries, the age of the rocks, of the earth, of the solar system, of the universe. The concept of time impels us to look ahead in planning programs, schedules, appropriations, balanced budgets. Our love affair with time causes other cultures, whose languages permit a less hurried outlook, to regard us as somewhat mad.

SUMMARY OF LINGUISTICS

33. The linguists are making us realize that language is not a tool with which to uncover a deeper vein of reason, universal to all thinkers, but a shaper of thought itself. Shaping the thought, it helps to shape the culture, as in the Western cult of time. They are making us realize that we get our view of the world outside our heads probably as much from the words inside as from independent observation. When we try to become independent observers, furthermore, these words, unless we take special precautions, may distort the vision. There is no reason to suppose that English, French, Spanish, or any other Western language, with its two-valued logic, its subject-predicate form, and its law of identity, is the ultimate in a communication system.

34. A study of other cultures and their languages brings humility, together with a deeper understanding of human behavior. It brings a new concept of human brotherhood. Though the language systems differ widely, yet in their order, harmony, and subtle power of apprehending reality, they show that all men are equal. This equality, Whorf observes, is invariant and independent of race, civilization, ethical development, degree of sophistication, science, art. Such a conclusion may shock those who hold that progress is linear, with Western man on its topmost rung; but it is the conclusion to which the study of linguistics strongly points.

35. Scientists have continually collided with the unconscious assumptions imbedded in language. If their work was to continue in an orderly way, they had to improve communication. So they have invented new languages, such as tensor calculus and multivalued logic; they have erected new concepts such as the operational definition; they have sharpened ordinary language to the most exact and economical statement possible. The results of this housecleaning have been spectacular.

KENNETH G. WILSON

English Grammars and the Grammar of English

Kenneth G. Wilson (1923–   ), professor of English at the University of Connecticut since 1951, is a specialist in medieval language and literature and applied linguistics. He is co-editor of *Essays on Language and Usage*, 1963, and *Harbrace Guide to Dictionaries*, 1963. As a contributing specialist in the preparation of the *Standard College Dictionary*, 1963, he wrote this essay which appears as part of the introductory material. Professor Wilson lectures frequently on pertinent present-day linguistic topics and often serves as consultant to English departments during periods of curriculum revision.

In this compendious essay the author provides a clarification of the current ways of describing the grammatical system of English.

1. The word "grammar," used loosely, can refer to nearly everything about a language from its sounds and spelling to syntax and semantics. We often use it to mean usage in speech or writing compared with current standards of correctness: "Her grammar was awful." Or a grammar can be a book, usually a textbook, on any of these aspects of a language. Modern students of the language, however, also understand two narrower meanings, which are our particular concern in this essay:

1. *The* grammar of a language is the system of devices which carry the structural "meanings" of that language in speech and writing. This system specifies the way words in a given language are related to each other, so that we may extract meaning beyond the relatively simple lexical or dictionary meanings of the words themselves.

2. A grammar is a description of *the* grammar of a language. That is, any full description of the patterned system of signals employed by a language is *a* grammar of that language. Although the system itself (*the* grammar) may remain relatively constant, our grammars—our descriptions of the system—may improve. We may come to write more accurate, more efficient descriptions.

2. This distinction between *the* grammar as the system itself and *a* grammar as any description of the system is the source of much confusion when linguists address laymen, and often when grammarians address each other. A few statements about the grammar of English will help to clarify the problem.

3. The grammar of a language changes in time, but the rate of change is relatively slow when compared with that of words and meanings. Since the grammatical system is not fixed while the language is in use, we can expect to have to re-describe it periodically in order to keep abreast of the changes. For example, the

grammar of English during the Renaissance included a question pattern which reversed the subject and verb: *Feels the king sick?* We still retain that pattern with *be* and *have* (*Is the king sick?*), but we rarely use it with other verbs. Instead, we have a relatively new pattern with the word *do*: *Does the king feel sick?* Since changes like this come very slowly, however, *a* grammar of *the* grammar will, if accurate, be useful on most counts for many years, though not for centuries.

4. The English grammatical system is peculiar to English. No other language has a grammar quite like it, though closely related languages such as Norwegian and Dutch show many points of grammatical similarity, and other Indo-European languages such as Latin and French display at least a few. But descriptions of none of these languages will fit the English grammatical system, any more than descriptions of English will fit theirs. There may be some grammatical devices which every known language shares with every other, but so far we do not know what they are. For example, German and Finnish have case, and so does English, but there are languages which lack case entirely. Comparing the grammars of various languages is instructive, but each grammar is unique; each belongs only to its own language.

5. The system of English grammar, then, is the object for study—the same system that little children usually master with no formal instruction by the age of four or five. By imitating the speech they hear, and by trial and error, they learn to use the language; they come to "know" English grammar. They cannot talk *about* it, perhaps, but they know it at least to the extent of being able to use it unconsciously and with great precision.

6. That the system exists and that every native user responds to it are perhaps most quickly illustrated by a nonsense sentence: *These foser glipses have volbicly merfed the wheeple their preebs.* Although we do not know what most of the words mean (except for the "empty" words, *These, have, the,* and *their*), we "know" the grammar of the sentence. We can identify every part of speech; we can assert that *glipses* is a plural noun

and a subject, that *volbicly* is an adverb modifying the verb phrase *have merfed,* and that *wheeple* is probably an indirect object. We know this, even though we do not know the "full," lexically meaningful words. The words we do recognize contain very little lexical meaning (try to define *the*), but give us considerable grammatical "meaning."

7. We have learned objectively a great deal about this grammatical system, about the features which signal the grammatical meanings to which we respond. In what follows, we shall examine three different grammars of English, three different methods of describing the grammar of contemporary English: *traditional grammars, descriptive grammars, and generative grammars.* We can learn a good deal about our language from each, because each has certain advantages over the others, just as each has certain flaws. But examination of all three should lead us closer to the ultimate goal, a clear view of the system itself.

8. Underlying each of these three kinds of grammar is the single purpose of describing in rules and generalizations the contemporary system of signaling grammatical meaning in English. The best of these grammars, obviously, will be the one that is most accurate and most efficient. It will need to be accurate because of course we want our description to be right, no matter how complicated this may make it. Ideally, we would like the description to be efficient, too, because we want our grammar to be teachable. We want to be able to teach English to foreigners, and we want to be able to help the native user of the language make better choices among the possible alternative grammatical structures English affords. To do this, we will need to be able to give him rigorously accurate information about where these choices lie, and we will also need a description efficient enough to permit him to learn quickly what he needs to know.

9. Finally, however, there is an even more important reason for seeking the best description of the English grammatical system. Language is perhaps the most distinctive and most basic of all human activities; it sets us

apart from all other animals. As a humane study, as an end in itself, therefore, language merits our every effort to understand what it is and how it works. The liberally educated man will find all his attempts at following the socratic injunction, "Know thyself," leading him sooner or later to the study of the language he uses. This means, among other things, studying its grammar.

TRADITIONAL GRAMMARS OF ENGLISH

10. It is not our purpose here to write a history of English grammars, but we will nevertheless begin with the oldest and most respected of grammatical descriptions, the traditional grammars of English. The word *traditional* suggests that these grammars are old, and that they have had that kind of approval which stems from custom and long use. In fact, traditional grammars were first devised during the Renaissance, and they were based primarily on the grammars of classical Latin then current, since Latin seemed to the English grammarians of that era the most nearly perfect language the world afforded. At the outset, these English grammars were neither very accurate nor very efficient; they were usually attempts to find in English the equivalents of forms and constructions which could be found in Latin, or, failing that, to insist that such forms be developed and that English grammar be corrected and improved to meet that standard. This side of traditional grammars—their reforming zeal in the effort to make English grammar conform to the system of Latin grammar—we usually call prescriptive, because these grammarians attempted to prescribe what English should be, rather than to describe what it currently was.

11. In recent years the quarrel between prescriptive and descriptive grammarians has been confused and unfortunate, since in the process some excellent traditional grammars, which were in many ways descriptive, have been wrongly accused of the same prescriptivism which had at so many points been typical of earlier traditional grammars. The real quarrel is not between description and prescription, but between describing and failing to describe.

12. In the beginning, many of the traditional grammars were poor things, inaccurate and inefficient. But by the nineteenth century there existed some really excellent traditional grammars, highly detailed and impressively accurate, which, given the limitations of their assumptions, were as descriptive as many modern grammars of English. It is that sort of traditional grammar which sheds real light on the grammar of English, and that is the sort we will examine here.

13. The distinguishing fact about traditional grammars is that they are notional: they are based on meaning rather than form or syntax. The chief weaknesses of the traditional grammars stem from that notional point of departure. These grammars are circular in their reasoning: they can describe the English sentence only by first understanding the total meaning of that sentence. Knowing that a sentence is a question or a statement, they can begin to describe the way it is put together. They can then name and describe the parts of the sentence and discuss their relationships in great detail. But the primary assumptions all depend on the total meaning of the sentence. This practice results in both strengths and weaknesses.

14. No brief discussion of traditional grammars will fully demonstrate the strengths of those grammars, primarily because the main strength of traditional grammars lies in their meticulously recorded details. Indeed, they *require* an almost endless listing of details because they are obliged to work from outside the language, from specific sentences; they cannot penetrate to the principles which will organize sentences yet unuttered or unwritten. Therefore their bulk is enormous and they are inefficient. (Because of that inefficiency they have been terribly watered down in textbook versions so as to be almost worthless.) Their main characteristics, then, are great inefficiency, great accuracy, and great length—there are no really good short ones. Here, therefore, we will merely illustrate methods.

15. Traditional grammars usually begin

with the definition of a *sentence:* Curme's [1] is a good one: "A sentence is an expression of a thought or feeling by means of a word or words used in such form and manner as to convey the meaning intended." [2] Kinds of sentences then follow, with distinctions based on the meaning we see in them: exclamatory, declarative, and interrogative, or command, statement, and question. This kind of grammar classifies the sentences it encounters by grasping their intention, their meaning. Then it turns to a discussion of the parts and their internal arrangements.

16. The chief point of interest here is that from meaning-based points of departure our traditional grammar has now begun to define and classify according to function in the sentence. That it begins in meaning and ends in function is an illustration of its circular reasoning. Consider the sentence *John gave Mary the book.* It is a sentence because it expresses a complete thought, a meaning. It is a statement because it asserts. This is notional reasoning. But next we shift the ground. *John* is the subject of the sentence because it expresses the actor, the doer of the action expressed by the verb; *gave* is the simple predicate because it expresses the action the actor did; *Mary* is the indirect object because it is the receiver of the action specified in subject and predicate; and *book* is the direct object because it is the thing acted upon. This is a bald statement of the traditional grammatical reasoning, but it illustrates fairly well: we identify the parts functionally only by knowing first what the sentence means. In effect, the chief weakness is this circularity. For this reason syntax is not a strong point of traditional grammars.

17. Overlapping categories also cause awkwardness. When we classify a group of objects we must use the same criteria for all of them: if we class some birds according to color and some according to size, we will not have a coherent set of observations. Our categories must be discrete, and we must apply

them uniformly to all the materials under study.

18. Once past the primary assumptions, however, traditional grammars go on to describe a wealth of syntactic detail. They make a distinction between phrases and clauses, the latter containing subjects and predicates, the former not, and they observe how these fit into the simple sentence or connect to it as modifiers, compounds, or dependencies of various sorts. All these parts and their functions are named, and we end with a very detailed account of the kinds of constructions in English sentences and how they function, usually elaborately illustrated with real examples.

19. A second line of development in traditional grammars is the examination of the smaller units, the *parts of speech.* Some traditional grammars begin here; all of them eventually define the parts of speech. Again, these classifications are based on either meaning or function or both. And some classifications, like the pronoun, may also be based partly on form, although this is usually only a peripheral consideration.

20. The main fact is this: meaning is the basis for defining the two most important of the traditional parts of speech, the noun and the verb. A noun, for example, is defined in traditional grammars as "the name of a person, place, or thing," or as "a word used as the name of a thing, quality, or action." We can identify and classify nouns, then, only by knowing their referents, the concepts or things for which they stand. In these traditional, notional grammars the noun as a part of speech is defined notionally.

21. Traditional grammars usually identify eight parts of speech: noun, verb, adjective, adverb, preposition, conjunction, pronoun, and interjection. The *nouns*—sometimes called substantives—are name-words. They can be further subdivided into proper and common nouns, proper nouns being the names of particular people, places, events, organizations, etc., which English usually distinguishes formally only by capitalization in writing. All other nouns, usually not capitalized, are com-

[1] George O. Curme, *Syntax* (New York, 1931) and *Parts of Speech and Accidence* (New York, 1935).
[2] Curme, *Syntax,* p. 1.

mon nouns. (Other groupings of nouns are also notional: categories such as collective nouns and abstract nouns are defined in traditional grammars on the basis of their meaning or on the basis of logic: *committee,* a collective noun, is described as being either singular or plural, depending on the unanimity of the membership, on whether it is thought of as a unit or a collection of individuals. This is a notional distinction.) Traditional grammars lean rather heavily on the written language, as the distinction between common and proper nouns shows. (A further circularity is often added to the layman's view of language as he decides that proper nouns are proper nouns *because* we capitalize them!) The notions behind the distinction are usually clear in speech too, although if context is missing we can think of isolated examples—*the city* and *the City,* for example—which are distinctive only in writing.

22. Once the traditional grammar has identified nouns by their meanings, it turns almost at once to examine the function of nouns; it becomes clear that words we have classed as nouns serve regularly as subjects, objects of various kinds, and predicate complements. And then we discover some of these same nouns used apparently as adjectives, as in "The *chocolate* cake was made of dark *chocolate.*" The functions become extremely complex and require elaborate illustration and classification. Again, accuracy leads away from efficiency.

23. *Adjective* definitions in traditional grammars are partly notional too, but mainly they are functional; they are notional only in that they depend on our ability to identify nouns notionally so that we can then identify adjectives and pronouns by means of their functional relationships to nouns.

24. In traditional grammars, an adjective is a word "that modifies a noun or a pronoun." Curme's definition[3] continues, "i.e., a word that is used with a noun or pronoun to describe or point out the living being or lifeless thing designated by the noun or pronoun: a *little* boy, *that* boy, *this* boy, a *little* house."

[3] *Parts of Speech and Accidence,* p. 42.

This is a functional definition. Further classes are both notional and functional. Adjectives are either descriptive or limiting: *"little* boy" is descriptive, *"this* boy" is limiting. This is a notional distinction. Adjectives are also either attributive (placed before or in immediate contact with the noun) or predicative (following a verb like *be*). This is a functional distinction. And the whole class depends on the prior, notional identification of the noun.

25. The *pronoun* is even more complex and is also classed by form—formally. The base definition in a traditional grammar usually goes something like the one from this dictionary: a pronoun is "a word that may be used instead of a noun or noun phrase (personal, relative, demonstrative, indefinite, and reflexive pronouns), or as an adjective (adjective pronoun), or to introduce a question (interrogative pronoun)." In each of these categories our identification depends ultimately on our identification of nouns. It is notional first, and then functional.

26. But this then raises an interesting point: how do we tell nouns from pronouns if functionally they do the same work? The answer is "partly from meaning, partly from form." Pronouns take most of their meaning (except for the grammatical matter of case) from the nouns they replace. They have no other referents, as can be seen from the definitions of the various pronouns in this dictionary. But their forms are distinctive, since they are a small, finite list of words. The personal pronouns, for example, show many distinctive formal characteristics: case (*I, my, mine,* and *me*), number (*I* and *we*), person (*I, you,* and *he*), and gender (*he, she,* and *it*). But the personal pronouns are a finite list, and we are not likely to add new ones as readily—or at least as speedily—as we add other words to the vocabulary. Pronominal changes occur of course, but only very slowly. (Note how long it is taking to lose completely the *thou, thy, thine, thee,* and *ye* forms, which have been disappearing for hundreds of years.) Thus the pronoun illustrates an even greater circularity of reasoning in traditional grammars, since form, function, and meaning all are used as

bases for identifying and classifying pronouns.

27. The definition of the *verb* in traditional grammars is also notional, perhaps with an overtone of functionalism. Curme says, "The verb is that part of speech that predicates, assists in predications, asks a question, or expresses a command: 'The wind *blows.*' 'He *is* blind.' '*Did* he *do* it?' '*Hurry!*'" [4] This is a notional definition. Verbs are further classed as transitive or intransitive (verbs that require or do not require an object), linking or auxiliary. These are functional classifications.

28. The other parts of speech—adverb, preposition, conjunction, and interjection—are similar mixtures of notional and functional distinctions. The chief flaw is the circularity of reasoning which stems from the notional point of departure. The chief virtue of these traditional grammars when they are well done is that they are so fully detailed. The terminology developed for classrooms has been a hindrance to later grammars in some ways, but ultimately it has served as a useful standard: no modern grammar can be said to be accurate, however high its apparent efficiency, if it cannot account for all the varieties of construction so fully delineated in the best traditional grammars. The traditional terminology is still useful.

29. Two other problems of traditional grammars are worth noting here. The first is the question of functionalism and the special variety of traditional grammar which grew up during the thirties and forties of this century under the name *functional grammars.*

30. At their best, functional grammars were written by traditional grammarians who were trying to avoid some of the circular reasoning and overlapping categories of meaning-based descriptions. By describing subjects, objects, and other functional categories and then classing words and constructions solely on the basis of their use in these functions or positions in the sentence, these grammarians felt they could write a more rational grammatical description of English. They did succeed in increasing efficiency somewhat, but ultimately

[4] *Ibid.*, p. 63.

at the cost of losing much detail which was the strength of the traditional grammars.

31. At their worst, functional grammars became a worthless watering-down of the detail of the good traditional grammars. *Functional* became a synonym for practical or useful; the teaching of English in the schools had come around to an almost exclusive interest in the most common mistakes in usage made by students, and since functional grammar seemed to be simpler to teach than the more elaborate traditional descriptions, it was the work of only a decade to destroy almost completely the effectiveness of full traditional grammars and replace them with truncated, diluted imitations which were called "functional."

32. A second problem with traditional grammar was its orientation almost exclusively to the written language. Spelling, punctuation, and the written versions of grammatical constructions were the material for analysis, and as a result many people came to feel that the written language was the standard from which the spoken language was a sloppy falling-away. This had awkward consequences for the writing of grammars: it meant that many constructions regularly heard in the language were simply not described because they were not encountered in the written language. It meant too that the system of grammar—*the* grammar of English—began to be viewed as a consciously learned thing, a subject composed of the terminology—the names of parts and functions—which the grammarians had invented originally to describe the grammar. The means became—and in many minds has remained—confused with the end.

33. We have much to thank traditional grammars for; they have managed to examine the details of written English and to describe and classify them with splendid accuracy and thoroughness. They have supplied us with useful terminology for the discussion of many aspects of grammar. And many of their particular observations remain, circular reasoning or no, the clearest and best accounts we have of some of the small but vexing problems we encounter when we try to describe the grammar of English. No student of the language

can sensibly ignore traditional grammars of English.

34. But in the end, traditional grammars have not solved the problem. Mainly because they work from outside the language, because they can only classify and describe the endless numbers of existing sentences, they lead us to parsing and naming of parts. But they do not help us very much in our effort to describe the system of patterns the child "knows," and they do not give us the kinds of generalizations we need for efficiency. Above all, they do not give us knowledge of the rules of the English grammar so that we can see precisely how sentences yet unuttered and unwritten will inevitably be formed. They do not tell us how or why.

DESCRIPTIVE GRAMMARS OF ENGLISH

35. The term *descriptive grammars* is arbitrary, used here to designate those attempts at describing the grammar of English which are based on the methods of modern descriptive linguistics. These grammars have several marked advantages over most traditional grammars.

1. They begin with the spoken language.
2. They begin with forms and work back to meaning, irrespective of whether the form is an inflectional suffix, an intonation marker, or a slot in a set pattern.
3. They try to work exclusively with grammatical meaning rather than with total meaning.
4. Since they consciously attempt to generalize, they are often very efficient.

36. The writing of descriptive grammars goes back more than thirty years. The descriptive linguistic work of men like Leonard Bloomfield and Edward Sapir marks the beginning in this country of·the kind of careful analysis of all aspects of language which led to the writing of descriptive grammars.

37. Descriptive English grammars are extremely accurate on phonology and morphology; they are perhaps less successful in describing syntax, especially the larger units. Good structural grammars tend to be more candid about their weaknesses, however, than those traditional grammars which with their pedagogical aims often sought to present a logically coherent grammar of English sometimes even at the expense of accuracy.

38. Descriptive grammars of English describe four major kinds of grammatical signal. These are the patterned devices which give us, usually with considerable redundancy, the grammatical meanings of our utterances:

1. Signals from the *forms* of words.
2. Signals from the *function words*.
3. Signals from the *order* of words and word groups.
4. Signals from the *intonation* of words or word groups.

These signals can be investigated in several reasonable orders, but the distinguishing characteristic of descriptive grammars is their interest in describing the spoken language; this interest makes sound the most helpful starting point.

39. Descriptive grammars, therefore, generally begin with the phonemes, which while not grammatical signals in themselves, since they have no meaning, are nonetheless the important basic concept. A *phoneme* is one of the distinctive classes of sounds in a language. Of all the hundreds of speech noises the human voice can make, only a relative few are distinctive or significant in any given language. In English there are twenty-four consonant phonemes, three of which are often called semivowels (/h/, /w/, and /y/). These consonant sounds are distinctive in English; one can neither speak nor understand English unless he can make and identify these sounds. In fact, any native English-speaking listener will constantly try to class all speech sounds he hears into one of the phonemes of English. He cannot help himself.

40. But the phoneme is only a category, not a finite sound. The difference between *phonetics* (the study of speech sounds) and *phonemics* (the study of the significant speech sound classes in a given language) illustrates this distinction: a *phonetic* description of an utterance reports exactly the nature and qualities of the sounds, whether they are significant in the language or not. It gets every

detail. A *phonemic* transcription is much more gross. Because /t/ and /d/ are phonemic (i.e., significantly distinctive) in English, this kind of transcription will note when each one occurs, but it will not be interested in the many variations of these two sounds (as in a more or less sharply exploded [t] which a phonetic transcription would record). Phonemics needs only to tell the /t/ from the /d/ and from all other phonemes of English, so that it can distinguish *matter* /mǽtər/ from *madder* /mǽdər/. Note that *phonemic* transcriptions are enclosed between virgules; *phonetic* transcriptions, between brackets. The following list shows the special phonemic symbols used in this essay and their equivalents in the pronunciation key of the *Standard College Dictionary: Text Edition;* all other phonemic characters are identical with the key: /æ/ = a; /ey/ = ā; /iy/ = ē; /č/ = ch; /ay/ = ī; /j/ = j; /ŋ/ = ng; /ow/ = ō; /ɔ/ = ô; /aw/ = ou; /uw/ = o͞o; /ə/ = u; /š/ = sh; /ð/ = th; /ž/ = zh.

41. In addition to the twenty-four consonant phonemes in English there are nine vowel phonemes. There are also at least seven diphthongs (vowel plus semi-vowel) common to most dialects, and other diphthongs peculiar to one or two dialects.

42. These vowel and consonant phonemes —the segmental phonemes—are not the only significant sounds in English. Stress too is phonemic, and so are pitch and clause terminals. The four stresses, four pitches, and three clause terminals comprise the suprasegmental phonemes, the phonemes which make the intonation contour of English. Another phoneme, open juncture, is considered segmental by some, suprasegmental by others. The intonation curve or contour (sometimes called *prosody*) contains important grammatical signals in the spoken language.

43. English has four levels of *stress,* labeled (from heaviest to lightest) primary / ´ /, secondary / ^ /, tertiary / ` /, and weak or unstressed / ˘ /. A one-syllable word spoken alone has a primary stress: /yés/. Two-syllable words have a primary and one other stress when they are spoken in isolation:

/névər/ /spíydbòwt/. Most of the time, in utterances of three or more syllables, we make our distinctions among three of these levels: primary, either secondary or tertiary, and weak, or primary, secondary, and either tertiary or weak. Occasionally, however, English grammatical meanings depend on our distinguishing all four levels. We can hear all four in the phrase *the red greenhouse* /ðə̆ rêd gríynhàws/. *Green house* and *greenhouse* /grîyn háws/ and /gríynhàws/ are distinguished from each other mainly by difference in stress pattern; the stresses help us tell an adjective plus noun from a compound. These four levels of stress are phonemic in English.

44. *Pitch* is also phonemic in English. There are four levels, usually numbered from lowest to highest, all relative rather than absolute. Every speaker and every listener distinguishes the four. /gôw | hów \ m/ illustrates levels 2, 3, and 1. /gôw | hówm/, a question, is distinguished from the command partly by the fact that pitch remains on third level instead of falling to first. *"Go home!" he screamed* illustrates the fourth level of pitch: /gôw | hów \ m hîy skríymd/. These four levels of pitch are phonemic in English.

45. Finally, open juncture and clause terminals are phonemic in English. Close juncture is the relationship which exists between segmental phonemes in sequence, as within most words. *Open juncture* /+/ helps us distinguish *sly twitch* from *slight witch* /slây + | twí \ č/ from /slâyt + | wí \ č/. Open juncture is sometimes described as a slight pause, sometimes as a modification of the phonemes on either side of the juncture, but in any case it is clearly a thing we listen for: *I scream* /ây + | skríy \ m/ and *ice cream* /âys + | kríy \ m/ can be distinguished from each other only because of the difference in placement of the open juncture, which so often separates our words for us.

46. *Clause terminals* require a definition of *clause* different from that used in traditional grammars. In descriptive grammars a clause is a string of segmental phonemes under a single pitch contour containing one primary stress and marked at both ends either by silence or a terminal. There are three clause terminals, described in descriptive grammars as level, rising, or falling, since they appear to be modifications of pitch within one of the numbered levels of pitch.

47. Falling clause terminals occur at the ends of many utterances (we use either /↘/ or /#/ to transcribe this phoneme, and we sometimes call it a double cross juncture):

I'm going home. /âym + gòwĭŋ + ⌐hów ↘ m ↘ /. When the utterance ends, the voice trails off and down from the first level of pitch.

48. Rising clause terminals occur most frequently between larger syntactic units in the utterance and at the ends of some questions: *Fred, who came late, missed his dinner.*

/fré ↘ d ↗ hūw + kêym + ⌐ léy ↘ t ↗ mîstĭz + ⌐ dín ↘ ɔ̆r ↘ /. Rising clause terminals are transcribed either /↗/ or /‖/, and are sometimes called double bar junctures.

49. Level clause terminals /→/, or single bar junctures /|/, are the least noticeable of the terminal breaks in a sequence of phonemes, just slightly stronger than an open juncture: *Their best outfielder hit a home run.*

/ðèr + bêst + ⌐ áwt ↘ fîyldɔ̆r → hît + ɔ̆ + hôwm + ⌐ rɔ̆ ↘ n ↘ /.

50. These four stresses, four pitches, open juncture, and three clause terminals are phonemic in English. This means that like the segmental phonemes, these suprasegmental phonemes are significant English sounds. Individually they have no meaning. A third level pitch at the end of a segment or clause does not mean *question* by itself, any more than a rising clause terminal in that position does. The two together, however, at the end of a full intonation contour, e.g., /$_2$³′³↗/, do mean question, provided, of course, that no stronger signal interferes. Usually intonation, the grammatical meaning attached to an intonation curve, is strong enough to counteract or modify the effects of other grammatical signals—for example: *He's a sailor.* /hîyz + ɔ̆ + ⌐ séyl ↘ ɔ̆r ↘ /. In this utterance we have a /$_2$³′$_1$↘/ curve, which, in conjunction with other signals, can signify a statement. A /$_2$³′³↗/ pattern for the same segment will mean question, despite other signals signifying a statement: /hîyz + ɔ̆ + ⌐ séylɔ̆r ↗ / (incredulous). A /$_2$³′$_2$↗/ contour will signify an included or incomplete utterance: /hîyz + ɔ̆ + ⌐ séyl ↘ ɔ̆r ↗ / *He's a sailor, but* . . .

51. A *morpheme* is hard to define, since it too is merely a category; perhaps it will suffice in a general discussion such as this to say that a morpheme—which is composed of one or more phonemes—is the smallest meaningful unit in a language. Sometimes the meaning is lexical, as in {kæt} and many affixes; sometimes it is grammatical. In the paragraph above we have examples of intonation contours which are morphemic; that is, they can carry meaning—in this instance, grammatical meaning. These morphemes are grammatical signals in the spoken language. In the written language, we replace them with punctuation, capitalization, and italics as far as is possible and necessary. The relationship between intonation and punctuation is not exact, just as that between the segmental phonemes and the conventional spelling of English is not exact, but in both instances the system is roughly efficient. When we read, we normally throw primary stresses toward the end of each segment: *Give me the ball.* This sentence has its primary stress on *ball*. If we want to stress *me*, as opposed to someone else, we have to write the sentence "Give *me* the ball" or "Give ME the ball" /gîv + ⌐ míy + ↘ ðɔ̆ + bɔ̂l ↘ /.

52. The suprasegmental phonemes of stress, pitch, and clause terminals, then, are necessary to descriptive grammars of English because in contours these phonemes become morphemic; they contain grammatical meaning. The segmental phonemes are necessary because in clusters they too contain meaning, both lexical and grammatical. We can describe these segmental forms more accurately by seeing them in their phonemic transcriptions than by seeing them conventionally spelled.

53. Let us turn next to the segmental morphemes of English which contain grammatical meaning. First are those morphemes which are the grammatical "endings" or *inflections* as follows:

1. *Plurals of nouns.* The main morphemic pattern is usually called the -*s* plural inflection. It turns out to have three forms when we examine it phonemically: The plural of *ship* is *ships* /šips/; we add /s/. The plural of *dog* is *dogs* /dogz/; we add /z/. The plural of *dish* is *dishes* /dišɨz/; we add /ɨz/. If we make new words we form their plurals on this major pattern, accommodating the form of the inflection to the final sounds of the singular.

There are several minor patterns too. They fall mainly into two groups, those from older English patterns such as *man:men, woman:women, foot:feet,* and *ox:oxen* (which make their plurals either by changing a vowel or adding an -*en* inflection), plus *sheep* and *deer* (which add no inflection for the plural); and those patterns which came from other languages along with words we borrowed: *alumnus: alumni, genus:genera, criterion:criteria,* etc. There are a good many of these minor patterns, some exhibited in only a word or two, and others, especially those from Latin, in a good many. But the list of patterns is finite.

The dominant pattern is the so-called *s*-plural pattern, the {-Z$_1$} morpheme. We can see the force of that pattern by watching two factors—the word's history and the frequency of its use—work to make borrowed words conform to the dominant pattern. *Stadium,* for example, while it retains the Latin form *stadia* in some uses, has even more commonly developed the standard {-Z$_1$} form *stadiums* for its plural. The older English forms, such as *man:men,* apparently are retained primarily because of frequency of use; we are used to hearing them with the older forms. Children, however, always learn the dominant pattern first, and will often be heard experimenting with *man:mans* until they observe the difference in practice around them.

2. *Genitives of nouns.* A second morphemic pattern which signals grammatical meaning is the genitive inflection for nouns, often called the {-Z$_2$} inflection. It has exactly the same form as the {-Z$_1$} inflection's major pattern—/s/ after voiceless consonants except for /s/, /š/, and /č/; /z/ after voiced consonants and vowels, except for /z/, /ž/, and /ǰ/; and /ɨz/ after the six exceptions.

Genitives are formally recognizable, then, in the spoken form. When a word already carrying the plural inflection turns genitive, we usually do not add the genitive inflection, so the distinction is lost in speech. In writing we move the apostrophe: *boss: boss's* (singular), *bosses:bosses'* (plural). If the singular already ends in /s/, /z/, or /ɨz/, we have two possible courses for making a genitive: add nothing, as in *Keats* /kiyts/:*Keats'* /kiyts/, or add the relevant genitive inflection anyway: *Keats* /kiyts/: *Keats's* /kiytsɨz/.

3. *Past tense (preterit) and past participles of verbs.* The major pattern, often called the dental suffix, is the so-called weak verb pattern used in the majority of English verbs. To form the past tense and past participle, this pattern adds /t/, /d/, or /ɨd/, according to the sound at the end of the infinitive. *Fish* adds /t/ to become /fišt/; *rig* adds /d/ to become /rigd/; *bat* adds /ɨd/ to become /bætɨd/.

The strong verb patterns, such as that of *swim, swam, swum,* are a second morphemic series for signaling tense. The Old

English Class III pattern of *swim* has the largest number of verbs left in it, but there are examples of all seven classes still in use: *drive-drove-driven* (I), *freeze-froze-frozen* (II), *spring-sprang-sprung* (III), *steal-stole-stolen* (IV), *speak-spoke-spoken* (V), *shake-shook-shaken* (VI), and *grow-grew-grown* (VII). Charles C. Fries counted sixty-six of these strong verbs still displaying these older patterns, twenty-four of them reduced, however, to two forms, such as *shine, shone, shone* and *swing, swung, swung*.[5] If we add new verbs to the vocabulary, we make them conform to the weak or dental suffix pattern: the past tense of *garf* is /garft/. We can find a few verbs, like *dive* and *prove*, which maintain two sets of forms for preterit and past participles, apparently because they have begun but not completed the switch to the weak pattern. There are also a few other patterns for a handful of verbs like *be, have, go,* and *do*, but the entire list of patterns for verbs is not very long.

4. *Third person singular present-tense verb inflection.* This inflection is also morphemically distinctive. It is usually called the {-Z₃} inflection, because it is formed exactly like the major pattern for plurals of nouns and genitives of nouns: *I go* /gow/: *he goes* /gowz/; *I please* /pliyz/: *he pleases* /pliyzɨz/; *I sleep* /sliyp/: *he sleeps* /sliyps/.

5. *Present participles of verbs.* The -*ing* /-iŋ/ form for present participles in English is also a morpheme.

6. *Verb subjunctives.* There are still some morphemic signals for the subjunctive mood in English, although we have dropped a good many of the older forms and, where we do retain the concept, often signal it by means of function words such as *should*. The inflections show up chiefly in the verbs *be, have,* and *do,* in object clauses after verbs such as *ask, command,* and *request,* and in conditional clauses, especially those with the function word *if*. Other verbs also show a subjunctive occasionally, but since it is much reduced in

use, and since it shows up only in the third person singular of the present tense of most verbs ("If he *arrive* in time, we'll be safe"), examples are not often encountered except in the most formal discourse or after verbs like *ask* or *request*. Mainly the subjunctive appears with *be* and *have*, both as full verbs and as auxiliaries (function words): "If I *be* in time," "if you *be* given a chance," "if he *have* a place for me." Since *be* also has the distinctive *was* form in the past indicative first and third person singular, the subjunctive *were* is distinctive there too: "if I *were* you," "if he *were* here."

7. *Adjectives.* In adjectives there are morphemic patterns of inflection for the comparative and superlative degrees. /ər/ and /ɨst/ are added to nearly all one-syllable adjectives (*big* /bigər/ /bigɨst/) and to two-syllable adjectives of relatively high frequency (*happy* /hæpiyər/ /hæpiyɨst/), but to almost no three-or-more-syllable adjectives. The comparative and superlative functions are accomplished by the function words *more, most, less,* and *least* where the inflections do not occur (*beautiful, more beautiful, most beautiful*).

8. *Pronouns.* The pronouns have distinctive forms. In addition to the personal pronouns, which have distinctive forms for case, number, person, and—in third person singular—gender, *who* and *whom* are distinguished for case, *this* and *these* and *that* and *those* for number, and *who* and *which* for one aspect of gender.

9. *Other morphemic indicators.* Finally, grammatical information is given us morphemically by a long series of word-forming affixes (both prefixes and suffixes), by vowel changes which occur medially, and by shifts in stress, all of which make functional change in English possible. Here are a few sample pairs:

arrive, v.	*arrival,* n.
defend, v.	*defense,* n.
true, a.	*truth,* n.
way, n.	*away,* adv.
súbject, n.	*subjéct,* v.
big, a.	*bigness,* n.

[5] *American English Grammar* (New York, 1940), p. 61.

friend, n.   *befriend,* v.
broad, a.   *abroad,* adv.[6]

54. These nine categories of morphemic signals comprise the main grammatical information given in English by morphology. To them we must add the description of the intonation morphemes described earlier. Modern grammars of English find these descriptions, based on the spoken language, to be accurate and efficient generalizations of part of the English grammatical system. Further generalizations, such as those we have mentioned in connection with spelling and punctuation above, are needed to adapt them to the written language.

55. We turn next to the grammatical information that comes from function words, but here it is useful to pause first to consider what descriptive grammars do with *parts of speech.* Two distinct approaches, plus an adaptation of these, are apparent:

1. Some descriptive linguists use morphology alone to define the parts of speech, and simply exclude from the parts of speech those words which do not fit strict morphological categories. Nouns are words which can be inflected for the plural and for the genitive, verbs are words which can be inflected for the past tense, past participle, etc., and adjectives are words which can be inflected for the comparative and superlative. These parts of speech can also be identified by the contrastive morphemic affixes mentioned above.

2. Other descriptive linguists use function or position in the sentence as the exclusive criterion for classing parts of speech. Nouns or Class I words (mainly but not exclusively nouns formally defined) are words which can fit in the positions of subject and objects in a sentence such as *"John* gave *Mary* the *book,"* or in positions after prepositions in patterns such as "in the *night"* and "on the *table."*

Verbs in this system are words which fit in the position of *goes, given,* and *was* in the following sentences: "John *goes* to school." "John has *given* the book to Mary." "John *was* sick."

Adjectives are then words which fit either after verbs in patterns such as "John was *sick"* (or exclusively there) or before nouns in patterns such as "the *sick* boy."

Adverbs have more positions: before or after verbs, as in "John went *willingly"* and "John *willingly* went," at the beginnings or ends of sentences, as in *"Willingly,* John went home" and "John went home *willingly,"* or before adjectives, as in *"pleasingly* plump" (although this last position is not accepted by a good many grammarians, who prefer to classify words which appear in this position as function words).

This positional classification of parts of speech turns up two kinds of lists of words: huge, open-ended lists of nouns, verbs, adjectives, and adverbs, and finite lists, often very short, of auxiliaries, prepositions, pronouns, articles, and the like. In other words, most of these positional classifications describe four parts of speech plus several finite lists of function words.

3. Finally, there are reconciliations of formal and positional bases of classification in modern grammars. For example, we can, as James Sledd does,[7] describe adjectives as words which inflect for the comparative and superlative, and then, after noting the positions in which these adjectives will function, we can classify as adjectivals all other words and word groups which, while they will not inflect for comparison, will function in the same structural positions as do these formally distinctive adjectives. Similarly, we can distinguish between nouns (a formal category) and nominals (a positional category which includes and is typical of nouns, but which contains other words and word groups), verbs and verbals, etc.

56. In any event, a rigorously formal or rigorously positional description of parts of speech—or a combined method—leads us to

---

[6] A nearly complete list appears in Charles C. Fries, *The Structure of English* (New York, 1952), pp. 110–41.

[7] *A Short Introduction to English Grammar* (New York, 1959), pp. 79 ff.

the third of the main kinds of grammatical signals distinguished by descriptive English grammars: *function words.*

57. We may designate function words either by labeling them with arbitrary symbols (type A, type B, etc.) or with descriptive labels, often ones borrowed for convenience from traditional grammars. The number of categories varies with the assumptions of the grammarian, but generally we will find at least these groups, all of which are finite lists of words which, while they may contain full lexical meanings, are usually "empty" or partly "empty" words, whose main meaning is grammatical.

1. *Auxiliaries* are words such as *may, shall, be,* and *have* that combine in various ways with verbs. *Do,* for example, lives a separate life both as verb and as auxiliary; some list it also as a special question-asking function word: "*Did* he *do* it?" In speech *have* and *has* distinguish the full verb from the function word in the present tense: *I have two books* /hæv/, and *I have to go home* /hæf/. These function words signal *verb* or *predication,* and when we use them, they rather than the verb itself take the inflections for number and tense which make for agreement of subject and verb and for logical sequence of tenses.

2. *Prepositions* are a finite list of function words which signal a special structure of modification: "the man *in* the street." These structures always have noun (or nominal) objects, and they can fit as units anywhere that nominals, adjectivals, or adverbials can fit.

3. *Determiners* are a longer but still finite list of words which mark constructions headed by nouns or nominals. *The, a, an, this, that,* etc., are determiners: "*these* boys," "*the* big house."

4. *Conjunctions* are a short finite list of function words which relate words or larger structures to each other. There are two parts to the list: one, fairly small, is composed of words such as *and* and *but,* which are used to join words or constructions in parallel: "John *and* I came *and* sat here

and there early *and* often, *and* we liked the atmosphere." The other, larger part contains conjunctions which relate subordinate or dependent structures, mainly those with verbs in them, to the main part of the sentence. "*Since* he came, we've been busy." "I like her *because* she's gay."

5. *Pronouns* are often not classed in descriptive grammars as function words but as a special group of nominals. Since they have limited and mainly grammatical meanings, however, and since they comprise short, finite lists of forms, they can fit the broad definition of function words. They can also be broken up into lists which classify largely under other function-word and part-of-speech classes.

6. *Interrogatives* are a finite list of function words used as the first element in questions, especially with *be* and the function word *do.* "*When* is he coming?" "*Who* does he think he is?" Obviously some of these overlap with pronouns.

7. *Intensives* are a group of function words which fit before adjectives or adjectivals in modification patterns. *Very* in "It's a *very* large order," and "He felt *very* sick," is the most common word of the class.

8. Finally, various modern grammars add function word classes for a handful of words almost empty of other than grammatical meaning. *Not,* for example, and its contracted form *n't,* mean *negative. There,* as in "There *there* is a place" (the first *there* is an adverb, the second the function word), means a transposed sentence pattern wherein the subject follows the verb.

58. After function words we come finally to the description of *syntax* as descriptive grammars treat it. Syntax deals with the kinds of grammatical meaning signaled by the order of words in an utterance and with the order of smaller units within various contained structures.

59. In the first place, most descriptive grammars use a different sort of definition of the sentence, a definition based on the spoken language, although of course it is adaptable

to the written language as well. These definitions vary according to the grammarian's assumptions, but at any rate they are never notional. Here are two typical definitions:

1. A sentence is an utterance, either from silence to silence, or from $/_2{}^{3/3}\nearrow/$ or any falling clause terminal to silence, to $/_2{}^{3/3}\nearrow/$, or to any falling clause terminal.
2. A sentence is an utterance which elicits certain responses. In this definition, statements elicit nods or other tacit or verbal signs of agreement or comprehension, questions elicit answers, and commands elicit action responses.

60. Classification of sentences on this second ground leads us to generalizations about what Charles C. Fries calls "situation utterances" and "response utterances," [8] two classes which differ or can differ grammatically mainly in that response utterances can be fragmentary, without predication. "On Tuesday" is a response utterance, an answer to a question.

61. Most descriptive grammars treat syntactic relationships by means of description of *immediate constituents;* hence descriptive grammars are often called immediate-constituent grammars. Briefly, immediate-constituent analysis consists in discovering how sentences are put together by taking them apart according to hierarchies of grammatical relationships. Unlike the parsing of traditional grammars, however, IC analysis uses an order dictated by the several structures themselves, which W. Nelson Francis calls modification, predication, complementation, and coordination. "All larger structures," says Francis, "are simply combinations of these. . . ." [9]

1. *Modification.* There are various forms of this, depending on what part of speech or positional substitute functions as the head of the structure. If a noun or nominal is head, we get a structure such as: *a sunny day,* with *day* as head. *A day with sun, a day having sun,* and *a day which is sunny*

[8] *The Structure of English,* pp. 37 ff.
[9] *The Structure of American English* (New York, 1958), pp. 292 ff.

are all structures of modification. IC analysis takes the syntactic relationships apart in hierarchical layers which we can describe graphically in various ways:

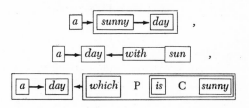

etc. (P means *predication;* C means *complementation.*) This process can be continued as each structure is broken up, until we have reached the ultimate constituents, the individual words and their morphemic components.

2. *Predication.* This is the relationship keyed to subject and verb, but of course it can be much more complex:

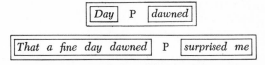

are the immediate constituents of two sentences. The parts of the second sentence can then be analyzed into their immediate constituents.

3. *Complementation.* These are the structures that include the developments of full predicates. To complete the IC analysis of the last example above, we break down the IC's,

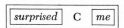

These structures account for all sorts of object complements and subject complements and their modifiers.

4. *Coordination.* These structures are usually parallel constructions joined by a coordinator—usually a function word, a conjunction:

(Some modern grammarians prefer to do without this structural class, arguing that there are more consistent explanations. For example, most instances of subordinate class structure would be classified under "modification" in this scheme.)

62. IC analysis may look a bit like the diagraming traditional grammar often uses in teaching, in order to make parsing and naming of parts more graphic, but there is a vital difference in purpose and assumptions. In IC analysis we are concerned with identifying and discovering the function of layers of grammatical structures. We seek grammatical meaning only. We want to show how English sentences work—the main goal of all descriptive English grammars.

GENERATIVE GRAMMARS OF ENGLISH

63. The newest of grammatical theories are embodied in attempts, so far not fully worked out in all details, but clearly very promising, to write what are called generative grammars of English. In many ways generative grammars are merely a special development of descriptive grammars, rather than a completely new departure: the phrase analysis, the structured strings of morphemes, and the materials which make possible the statement of morphophonemic rules in generative grammars all stem directly from modern descriptive linguistic investigation. All owe a good deal to descriptive grammars. But generative grammars differ from descriptive grammars in certain primary assumptions: Generative grammars are predicated on a slightly different definition of the grammar of English than that used by most descriptive grammars. For one thing, it is a definition which tries to predict the possible grammatical forms sentences may take, rather than simply to describe after the fact the forms that sentences already written or uttered have taken. This definition says that the grammar of English is a set of laws or rules which we "know," which enables us to utter English sentences and only English sentences. Generative grammars try to state those rules which "generate" all possible English sentences and only English sentences. These grammars rest on several important observations from mathematics and communication

theory. Paul Roberts' computer analogy is probably as descriptive as any general statement.[10] It assumes that we, like computers, have certain built-in laws and the information to use with those laws. We unconsciously abstract the laws from our trial and error imitation as children, and we soon reach the point where we do not have to imitate sentences we have heard. We come to "know" rules which let us form completely new sentences that meet the criteria of English grammar.

64. An objective knowledge of English grammar is of course the generative grammarians' goal. And, building in large part upon the details—such as those of morphology and phrase structure—worked out by linguists whose descriptions of English provided us with our descriptive grammars, such men as Noam Chomsky, Robert B. Lees, and others have begun to state the rules of that grammar.

65. The main lines of their investigations are these: we begin with the description of kernel sentences—a list of simple, declarative, active sentences with no complex elements, no complex developments of verb or noun phrases. From these we can derive all other sentences by means of rules for *transformations*—rules which change or develop a kernel sentence by developing one or more of its phrase structures into different but still grammatical parts of a different but still grammatical English sentence.

66. We work with structured strings of morphemes—those same morphemes the modern grammarians uncovered for us. Then finally we can arrive at any particular sentence by applying the morphophonemic rules—the third part of a generative grammar—which will enable us to convert any properly structured string of morphemes, transformed or not, into either a written or spoken English sentence.

67. This newest grammatical description promises to tell us still more about how the language works, and it promises especially to help us grasp syntax as descriptive grammars have not always been completely successful in doing. For example, it describes the kernel sentences "lions growl" and "John raises flow-

[10] *English Sentences* (New York, 1962), p. 1.

ers." Regular transformations give us "the growling of lions" and "the raising of flowers," but as transformations from two different kernel sentences. We can then see a reasonable explanation for the ambiguity of "the shooting of the hunters": the relation of *shoot* to *hunters* is different in the two kernels from which the ambiguous structure can be derived ("hunters shoot" and "John shoots hunters"), since ". . . neither 'they growl lions' nor 'flowers raise' are grammatical kernel sentences." [11]

68. Above all, generative grammars promise to be able to help us toward the solution of one of the hardest problems grammars have had to deal with: how to state the rules that make the grammar of our sentences predictable, instead of our being obliged by our grammatical descriptions only to analyze sentences we have already written or spoken. Full generative or transformational grammars remain to be written, but in their present state they already have told us a great deal, and their future looks very bright.

CONCLUSION

69. The grammar of modern American English has been described by many grammars —traditional, descriptive, and now generative. We now know that grammar is best studied

[11] These examples and the quotation are from Noam Chomsky, *Syntactic Structures* (The Hague, 1957), p. 89.

apart from semantics, that the system itself can be better delineated if we avoid the notional naming of parts.

70. We know too that the signals of English grammar can be described, that we can get grammatical information from morphemes (intonational, inflectional, and word-forming morphemes), from function words (which are morphemes too), and from syntactic patterns of strings of morphemes. We know also that much of the terminology of the traditional grammars, under different definition, is useful to us in our descriptions, as is the full notional system of traditional grammars in reminding us of what we need to know about the relation of grammar to total meaning. We know further that close attention to the spoken language and its sounds has enabled us to see more precisely what it is that is being patterned in English grammar; descriptive grammars have taught us that, as they have also shown us something about the hierarchies of constituent analysis. We know too that the grammar of English is peculiar to English, an analytic language which is precisely like no other language on earth.

71. In short, we know a great deal—although by no means all—about the grammar of English, and it is clear that at present the study of all three grammars of English is necessary for the man who wishes fully and consciously to understand his language, how he uses it, and how it uses him.

BERGEN EVANS

Grammar for Today

Bergen Evans (1904–   ) is professor of English at Northwestern University and a frequent participant on radio and television programs, having begun several years ago as a lively moderator of a popular television show "Down You Go." The appearance in 1957 of a volume he and his sister Cornelia edited, *A Dictionary of Contemporary American Usage,* created much criticism, both favorable and unfavorable.

In this essay he gives his reasons for believing that contemporary descriptive grammar is more valid than the traditional prescriptive grammar.

1. In 1747 Samuel Johnson issued a plan for a new dictionary of the English language. It was supported by the most distinguished printers of the day and was dedicated to the model of all correctness, Philip Dormer Stanhope, Fourth Earl of Chesterfield. Such a book, it was felt, was urgently needed to "fix" the language, to arrest its "corruption" and "decay," a degenerative process which, then as now, was attributed to the influence of "the vulgar" and which, then as now, it was a mark of superiority and elegance to decry. And Mr. Johnson seemed the man to write it. He had an enormous knowledge of Latin, deep piety, and dogmatic convictions. He was also honest and intelligent, but the effect of these lesser qualifications was not to show until later.

2. Oblig'd by hunger and request of friends, Mr. Johnson was willing to assume the role of linguistic dictator. He was prepared to "fix" the pronunciation of the language, "preserve the purity" of its idiom, brand "impure" words with a "note of infamy," and secure the whole "from being overrun by . . . low terms."

GRAMMAR FOR TODAY   From *The Atlantic Monthly,* March, 1960. Copyright © 1960, by The Atlantic Monthly Company, Boston, Mass. 02116. Reprinted with permission.

3. There were, however, a few reservations. Mr. Johnson felt it necessary to warn the oversanguine that "Language is the work of man, a being from whom permanence and stability cannot be derived." English "was not formed from heaven . . . but was produced by necessity and enlarged by accident." It had, indeed, been merely "thrown together by negligence" and was in such a state of confusion that its very syntax could no longer "be taught by general rules, but [only] by special precedents."

4. In 1755 the *Dictionary* appeared. The noble patron had been given a great deal more immortality than he had bargained for by the vigor of the kick Johnson had applied to his backside as he booted him overboard. And the *Plan* had been replaced by the *Preface,* a sadder but very much wiser document.

5. Eight years of "sluggishly treading the track of the alphabet" had taught Johnson that the hopes of "fixing" the language and preserving its "purity" were but "the dreams of a poet doomed at last to wake a lexicographer." In "the boundless chaos of living speech," so copious and energetic in its disorder, he had found no guides except "experience and analogy." Irregularities were "inherent in the

tongue" and could not be "dismissed or re-formed" but must be permitted "to remain untouched." "Uniformity must be sacrificed to custom . . . in compliance with a numberless majority" and "general agreement." One of the pet projects of the age had been the establishment of an academy to regulate and improve style. "I hope," Johnson wrote in the *Preface*, that if "it should be established . . . the spirit of English liberty will hinder or destroy [it]."

6. At the outset of the work he had flattered himself, he confessed, that he would reform abuses and put a stop to alterations. But he had soon discovered that "sounds are too volatile and subtle for legal restraints" and that "to enchain syllables and to lash the wind are equally undertakings of pride unwilling to measure its desires by its strength." For "the causes of change in language are as much superior to human resistance as the revolutions of the sky or the intumescence of the tide."

7. There had been an even more profound discovery: that grammarians and lexicographers "do not form, but register the language; do not teach men how they should think, but relate how they have hitherto expressed their thoughts." And with this statement Johnson ushered in the rational study of linguistics. He had entered on his task a medieval pedant. He emerged from it a modern scientist.

8. Of course his discoveries were not strikingly original. Horace had observed that use was the sole arbiter and norm of speech and Montaigne had said that he who would fight custom with grammar was a fool. Doubtless thousands of other people had at one time or another perceived and said the same thing. But Johnson introduced a new principle. Finding that he could not lay down rules, he gave actual examples to show meaning and form. He offered as authority illustrative quotations, and in so doing established that language is what usage makes it and that custom, in the long run, is the ultimate and only court of appeal in linguistic matters.

9. This principle, axiomatic today in grammar and lexicography, seems to exasperate a great many laymen who, apparently, find two

hundred and five years too short a period in which to grasp a basic idea. They insist that there are absolute standards of correctness in speech and that these standards may be set forth in a few simple rules. To a man, they believe, of course, that they speak and write "correctly" and they are loud in their insistence that others imitate them.

10. It is useless to argue with such people because they are not, really, interested in language at all. They are interested solely in demonstrating their own superiority. Point out to them—as has been done hundreds of times—that forms which they regard as "corrupt," "incorrect," and "vulgar" have been used by Shakespeare, Milton, and the Bible and are used daily by 180 million Americans and accepted by the best linguists and lexicographers, and they will coolly say, "Well, if they differ from me, they're wrong."

11. But if usage is not the final determinant of speech, what is? Do the inhabitants of Italy, for example, speak corrupt Latin or good Italian? Is Spanish superior to French? Would the Breton fisherman speak better if he spoke Parisian French? Can one be more fluent in Outer Mongolian than in Inner Mongolian? One has only to ask such questions in relation to languages other than one's own, language within which our particular snobberies and struggles for prestige have no stake, to see the absurdity of them.

12. The language that we do speak, if we are to accept the idea of "corruption" and "decay" in language, is a horribly decayed Anglo-Saxon, grotesquely corrupted by Norman French. Furthermore, since Standard English is a development of the London dialect of the fourteenth century, our speech, by true aristocratic standards, is woefully middle-class, commercial, and vulgar. And American speech is lower middle-class, reeking of counter and till. Where else on earth, for instance, would one find crime condemned because it didn't *pay!*

13. In more innocent days a great deal of time was spent in wondering what was the "original" language of mankind, the one spoken in Eden, the language of which all

modern tongues were merely degenerate remnants. Hector Boethius tells us that James I of Scotland was so interested in this problem that he had two children reared with a deaf and dumb nurse on an island in order to see what language they would "naturally" speak. James thought it would be Hebrew, and in time, to his great satisfaction, it was reported that the children were speaking Hebrew!

14. Despite this experiment, however, few people today regard English as a corruption of Hebrew. But many seem to think it is a corruption of Latin and labor mightily to make it conform to this illusion. It is they and their confused followers who tell us that we can't say "I am mistaken" because translated into Latin this would mean "I am misunderstood," and we can't say "I have enjoyed myself" unless we are egotistical or worse.

15. It is largely to this group—most of whom couldn't read a line of Latin at sight if their lives depended on it—that we owe our widespread bewilderment concerning *who* and *whom*. In Latin the accusative or dative form would always be used, regardless of the word's position in the sentence, when the pronoun was the object of a verb or a preposition. But in English, for at least four hundred years, this simply hasn't been so. When the pronoun occurs at the beginning of a question, people who speak natural, fluent, literary English use the nominative, regardless. They say "Who did you give it to?" not "Whom did you give it to?" But the semiliterate, intimidated and bewildered, are mouthing such ghastly utterances as a recent headline in a Chicago newspaper: WHOM'S HE KIDDING?

16. Another group seems to think that in its pure state English was a Laputan tongue, with logic as its guiding principle. Early members of this sect insisted that *unloose* could only mean "to tie up," and present members have compelled the gasoline industry to label its trucks *Flammable* under the disastrous insistence, apparently, that the old *Inflammable* could only mean "not burnable."

17. It is to them, in league with the Latinists, that we owe the bogy of the double negative. In all Teutonic languages a doubling of the negative merely emphasizes the nega-

tion. But we have been told for a century now that two negatives make a positive, though if they do and it's merely a matter of logic, then three negatives should make a negative again. So that if "It doesn't make no difference" is wrong merely because it includes two negatives, then "It doesn't never make no difference" ought to be right again.

18. Both of these groups, in their theories at least, ignore our idiom. Yet idiom—those expressions which defy all logic but are the very essence of a tongue—plays a large part in English. We go to school and college, but we go to *the* university. We buy two dozen eggs but a couple *of* dozen. *Good and* can mean *very* ("I am good and mad!") and "a hot cup of coffee" means that the coffee, not the cup, is to be hot. It makes a world of difference to a condemned man whether his reprieve is *upheld* or *held up*.

19. There are thousands of such expressions in English. They are the "irregularities" which Johnson found "inherent in the tongue" and which his wisdom perceived could not and should not be removed. Indeed, it is in the recognition and use of these idioms that skillful use of English lies.

20. Many words in the form that is now mandatory were originally just mistakes, and many of these mistakes were forced into the language by eager ignoramuses determined to make it conform to some notion of their own. The *s* was put in *island*, for instance, in sheer pedantic ignorance. The second *r* doesn't belong in *trousers*, nor the *g* in *arraign*, nor the *t* in *deviltry*, nor the *n* in *passenger* and *messenger*. Nor, so far as English is concerned, does that first *c* in *arctic* which so many people twist their mouths so strenuously to pronounce.

21. And grammar is as "corrupted" as spelling or pronunciation. "You are" is as gross a solecism as "me am." It's recent, too; you won't find it in the Authorized Version of the Bible. *Lesser, nearer*, and *more* are grammatically on a par with *gooder*. *Crowed* is the equivalent of *knowed* or *growed*, and *caught* and *dug* (for *catched* and *digged*) are as "corrupt" as *squoze* for *squeezed* or *snoze* for *sneezed*.

22. Fortunately for our peace of mind most people are quite content to let English conform to English, and they are supported in their sanity by modern grammarians and linguists.

23. Scholars agree with Puttenham (1589) that a language is simply speech "fashioned to the common understanding and accepted by consent." They believe that the only "rules" that can be stated for a language are codified observations. They hold, that is, that language is the basis of grammar, not the other way round. They do not believe that any language can become "corrupted" by the linguistic habits of those who speak it. They do not believe that anyone who is a native speaker of a standard language will get into any linguistic trouble unless he is misled by snobbishness or timidity or vanity.

24. He may, of course, if his native language is English, speak a form of English that marks him as coming from a rural or an unread group. But if he doesn't mind being so marked, there's no reason why he should change. Johnson retained a Staffordshire burr in his speech all his life. And surely no one will deny that Robert Burns' rustic dialect was just as good a form of speech as, and in his mouth infinitely better as a means of expression than, the "correct" English spoken by ten million of his southern contemporaries.

25. The trouble is that people are no longer willing to be rustic or provincial. They all want to speak like educated people, though they don't want to go to the trouble of becoming truly educated. They want to believe that a special form of socially acceptable and financially valuable speech can be mastered by following a few simple rules. And there is no lack of little books that offer to supply the rules and promise "correctness" if the rules are adhered to. But, of course, these offers are specious because you don't speak like an educated person unless you are an educated person, and the little books, if taken seriously, will not only leave the lack of education showing but will expose the pitiful yearning and the basic vulgarity as well, in such sentences as "Whom are you talking about?"

26. As a matter of fact, the educated man uses at least three languages. With his family and his close friends, on the ordinary, unimportant occasions of daily life, he speaks, much of the time, a monosyllabic sort of shorthand. On more important occasions and when dealing with strangers in his official or business relations, he has a more formal speech, more complete, less allusive, politely qualified, wisely reserved. In addition he has some acquaintance with the literary speech of his language. He understands this when he reads it, and often enjoys it, but he hesitates to use it. In times of emotional stress hot fragments of it may come out of him like lava, and in times of feigned emotion, as when giving a commencement address, cold, greasy gobbets of it will ooze forth.

27. The linguist differs from the amateur grammarian in recognizing all of these variations and gradations in the language. And he differs from the snob in doubting that the speech of any one small group among the language's more than 300 million daily users constitutes a model for all the rest to imitate.

28. The methods of the modern linguist can be illustrated by the question of the grammatical number of *none*. Is it singular or plural? Should one say "None of them is ready" or "None of them are ready"?

29. The prescriptive grammarians are emphatic that it should be singular. The Latinists point out that *nemo*, the Latin equivalent, is singular. The logicians triumphantly point out that *none* can't be more than one and hence can't be plural.

30. The linguist knows that he hears "None of them are ready" every day, from people of all social positions, geographical areas, and degrees of education. He also hears "None is." Furthermore, literature informs him that both forms were used in the past. From Malory (1450) to Milton (1650) he finds that *none* was treated as a singular three times for every once that it was treated as a plural. That is, up to three hundred years ago men usually said *None is*. From Milton to 1917, *none* was used as a plural seven times for every four times it was used as a singular. That is, in the past three hundred years men often said

None is, but they said *None are* almost twice as often. Since 1917, however, there has been a noticeable increase in the use of the plural, so much so that today *None are* is the preferred form.

31. The descriptive grammarian, therefore, says that while *None is* may still be used, it is becoming increasingly peculiar. This, of course, will not be as useful to one who wants to be cultured in a hurry as a short, emphatic permission or prohibition. But it has the advantage of describing English as it is spoken and written here and now and not as it ought to be spoken in some Cloud-Cuckoo-Land.

32. The descriptive grammarian believes that a child should be taught English, but he would like to see the child taught the English actually used by his educated contemporaries, not some pedantic, theoretical English designed chiefly to mark the imagined superiority of the designer.

33. He believes that a child should be taught the parts of speech, for example. But the child should be told the truth—that these are functions of use, not some quality immutably inherent in this or that word. Anyone, for instance, who tells a child—or anyone else —that *like* is used in English only as a preposition has grossly misinformed him. And anyone who complains that its use as a conjunction is a corruption introduced by Winston cigarettes ought, in all fairness, to explain how Shakespeare, Keats, and the translators of the Authorized Version of the Bible came to be in the employ of the R. J. Reynolds Tobacco Company.

34. Whether formal grammar can be taught to advantage before the senior year of high school is doubtful; most studies—and many have been made—indicate that it can't. But when it is taught, it should be the grammar of today's English, not the obsolete grammar of yesterday's prescriptive grammarians. By that grammar, for instance, *please* in the sentence "Please reply" is the verb and *reply* its object. But by modern meaning *reply* is the verb, in the imperative, and *please* is merely a qualifying word meaning "no discourtesy intended," a mollifying or de-imperatival adverb, or whatever you will, but not the verb.

35. This is a long way from saying "Anything goes," which is the charge that, with all the idiot repetition of a needle stuck in a groove, the uninformed ceaselessly chant against modern grammarians. But to assert that usage is the sole determinant in grammar, pronunciation, and meaning is *not* to say that anything goes. Custom is illogical and unreasonable, but it is also tyrannical. The latest deviation from its dictates is usually punished with severity. And because this is so, children should be taught what the current and local customs in English are. They should not be taught that we speak a bastard Latin or a vocalized logic. And they should certainly be disabused of the stultifying illusion that after God had given Moses the Commandments He called him back and pressed on him a copy of Woolley's *Handbook of English Grammar.*

36. The grammarian does not see it as his function to "raise the standards" set by Franklin, Lincoln, Melville, Mark Twain, and hundreds of millions of other Americans. He is content to record what they said and say.

37. Insofar as he serves as a teacher, it is his business to point out the limits of the permissible, to indicate the confines within which the writer may exercise his choice, to report that which custom and practice have made acceptable. It is certainly not the business of the grammarian to impose his personal taste as the only norm of good English, to set forth his prejudices as the ideal standard which everyone should copy. That would be fatal. No one person's standards are broad enough for that.

SIMEON POTTER

The Sentence

Simeon Potter (1898–   ), Baines Professor of English Language and Philology at Liverpool University from 1945 to 1965 (now professor emeritus) is internationally known as a scholar, teacher, writer, and lecturer. Among his many books on the English language and linguistics are *Our Language,* 1950; *Cheshire Place-Names,* 1954; *Language in the Modern World,* 1960; and *English Life and Speech,* 1964.

In this essay Mr. Potter discusses the basic kinds of English sentence patterns, showing that although the word order of the sentence tends to follow standard forms, sentence patterns still offer a great deal of flexibility to a skillful user.

1. We do not learn to frame sentences instinctively, as we learn to breathe or to walk. We repeat sentences from memory and we vary them by analogy. Imagine for a moment that all the sentences you have uttered during the course of the last two weeks are somewhere accurately recorded and that you can now scrutinize them at leisure. You will probably find them to be surprisingly varied: long and short; simple, double, multiple, and complex; statements, commands, wishes, questions, and exclamations; balanced, periodic, and loose. The words have been largely of your own choosing, but the sentences have seldom been of your own making. You have inherited them from the immediate, the distant, and the long-distant past. You have carried with you in your mind a certain number of sentence-patterns, few or many according to your individual linguistic capacity, and into these patterns you have fitted and varied the words expressing your thoughts and desires.

THE SENTENCE From *Our Language,* 1950, by Simeon Potter. Reprinted by permission of the publishers, Penguin Books Inc.

2. A child may echo the sounds it hears without being conscious of the meanings of separate words. Because English is, in the main, an analytic language (in spite of reviving synthetic tendencies . . .), the sentence is the most important unit of English speech. The sentence is more important even than the word. Revelling in the exercise of its imitative faculty, a child will attempt, however imperfectly, to babble whole sentences. A schoolboy may be word-perfect in his recitation of a long and difficult poem while remaining blissfully ignorant of the poet's intention and meaning. "If hopes were dupes, fears may be liars," I say to console a friend. He may like the words and repeat them, and yet neither of us may pause to reflect upon the astounding personifications implied by Clough in this oft-repeated line. "Genuine poetry," Mr. T. S. Eliot has reminded us, "can communicate before it is understood." A lovely sentence may haunt my memory—

And I shall have some peace there, for peace
　comes dropping slow,
Dropping from the veils of the morning to where
　the cricket sings

—and I may often murmur it to myself without being at all conscious of linguistic form, or function, or even of meaning. Nevertheless, the effective speaker and writer of prose is he who does not merely *catch* his sentence-patterns but who *grips* them and wields them with well-controlled purpose. In addition to possessing a ready command of vocabulary, the good speaker must be endowed with an unerring sense of rhythm. Even the most gifted orator, however, cannot depart too far from the speech patterns accepted by the community in which he lives without running the grave risk of being misapprehended or of being only partially understood. In ordinary affirmations the subject is followed by the predicate, consisting of verb and object or complement. In all the Indo-European languages the sentence is normally bipartite. Basically it is a two-in-one. It is a binary unit. The subject is that to which the speaker wishes to draw the hearer's attention and the predicate is that which the speaker has to say about that subject. If I utter a defective sentence it is probably because, for some reason or other, I have failed to keep these two things clear in my mind. In order to put it right, I have only to ask myself the simple questions: What am I talking about? What have I to say about it? Or, in other words: What is my subject? What do I predicate of that subject? As Edward Sapir has so well said (*Language*, p. 36),

> The major functional unit of speech, the sentence . . . is the linguistic expression of a proposition. It combines a subject of discourse with a statement in regard to this subject. Subject and predicate may be combined in a single word, as in Latin *dico;* each may be expressed independently, as in the English equivalent, *I say;* each or either may be so qualified as to lead to complex propositions of many sorts. No matter how many of these qualifying elements (words or functional parts of words) are introduced, the sentence does not lose its feeling of unity so long as each and every one of them falls in place as contributory to the definition of either the subject of discourse or the core of the predicate.

3. The predicate may indeed have preceded the subject in Proto-Indo-European, as in Modern Welsh, as in parenthetical "said he," or as in H. G. Wells's stylistic mannerism "Came a pause." The sentence-type *Down came the rain,* which is as old as Chaucer, finds its normal place in Modern German. Emphatic *down* comes first, the verb retains second place, and so the subject falls into the final position. It has been computed that the subject precedes the predicate in less than half of King Alfred's sentences, and if we study the shapes assumed by certain concrete locutions during the last thousand years or so, we detect a gradual shifting towards the modern order: subject, verb and object. Old English *mē gelīciaþ bēc* "To me are pleasing books" becomes modern English *I like books.* The vocables are identical, but the case of the pronoun has been altered from dative to nominative and the grammatical subject has been shifted from the things to the person. Since loving and liking are primarily active feelings, Modern English, it might be claimed, is here more rational than Old English. The modern grammatical subject becomes identical with the logical and the psychological one. Similarly, both *If you like* and *If you please* have derived historically from *If to you it may be pleasing* (*you* being dative of the pronoun and *like* and *please* third person singular of the present subjunctive) very much as in French *s'il vous plaît,* or Dutch *als 't u blieft* or old-fashioned German *wenn es Ihenen gefällt,* where, however, in all three languages, the verb is in the indicative. A still more striking example of the shifting of the grammatical subject to the first place in the sentence, without any resulting change in the position of the pronoun, is seen in *He was given the book* in which *the book* is "retained object." In the corresponding sentence in Old English, however, *the book* is the grammatical subject, *Him wæs gegiefen sēo bōc,* "(To) him was given the book." Similarly Chaucer's *It am I*, in which the grammatical subject is *I* (Old English *Hit eom ic*, Latin *Ego sum*), becomes Modern English *It is I.* In Chaucer's day the subjective character of *I* was still so strong that, in spite of word order, *It am I* sounded just as natural as Old French *Ce suis je.* French has certainly gone further than

English in normalizing *C'est moi.* "L'état, c'est moi," said Louis XIV as long ago as in the seventeenth century, not "L'état, c'est je." *It is me* is regarded by many to be too colloquial for literary use. At the same time, the feeling predominates that, apart from grammatical structure, a verb should be followed by the accusative. No one, as Otto Jespersen pointed out, would venture to suggest changing Shelley's emphatic *me* in *Ode to the West Wind—*

> Be thou, Spirit fierce,
> My spirit! Be thou *me,* impetuous one!

No one is shocked by the ungrammatical *Fare thee well* instead of *Fare (go) thou well.*

4. In the sentence *It's me* the neuter pronoun *it* has no separate meaning. It is a meaningless substitute which brings this simple statement into the usual pattern of subject, and complement. In the casual observations *It is blowing hard, It is cold,* and *It is raining,* you might too readily assume that the neuter pronoun stands for *the wind, the weather,* and *the rain* respectively. "For the rain it raineth every day" sang the clown at the end of *Twelfth Night,* and Robert Louis Stevenson wrote playfully in his verses for children—

> The rain is raining all around
> It falls on field and tree.

After a little reflection you will probably conclude that *it* in *It is raining* is merely a substitute for the subject of the impersonal verb and that it expresses an action or a condition of things without reference to any agent.

5. Swift defined a good style as the use of proper words in proper places. The proper places will vary considerably according to degrees of emphasis. Usage has left many parts of the sentence relatively free and these we can vary to suit our purpose. Coleridge laid much stress on the importance of word order. He defined poetry, you may remember, as "the best words in the best order." In the words of the greatest poets "there is," Coleridge asserted, "a reason assignable not only for every word, but for the position of every word." In the well-ordered sentence the hearer or the reader will receive no jolt or check. As Herbert Spencer observed, "things which are to be thought of together must be mentioned as closely as possible together." Naturally we place together such words as are more closely associated in meaning. We say "a big brown dog" rather than "a brown big dog," "a handsome young man" and not "a young handsome man," and "a kind old gardener" and not "an old kind gardener." So, too, we place together those phrases which are most closely associated in our minds. "Delighted to make your acquaintance" we say upon being introduced and not, as in German, "Delighted your acquaintance to make."

6. The classification of sentences is not a difficult matter. Sentences are of three kinds according to *form:* simple ("I know it"), compound ("I know it and I am proud of it"), and complex ("I know that he will come"). They are of four kinds according to *function:* statement ("I know it"), command-wish ("Long live the King!"), question ("Are you coming?"), and exclamation ("How good you are!"). The verb generally comes before the subject in wishes and questions. As we pass from a simple to a complex sentence we do not, as in some other languages, change the order of the words: "I hope (that) he will come. He will, I hope, come. Presumably he will come." But in German we are bound to say: "Ich hoffe, er wird kommen. Ich hoffe, dass er kommen wird. Hoffentlich (vermutlich) wird er kommen."

7. Sentences may be further categorized according to *style* as loose, balanced, and periodic, although this division is of its very nature somewhat vague and ill defined. All three types of sentence are good and a master of English will weave them skilfully into the varied fabric of style. In the so-called *loose* sentence the writer or speaker states fact after fact just as these occur to him, freely and artlessly. Daniel Defoe opens *The Life and Adventures of Robinson Crusoe* with a long, loose, rambling sentence which nevertheless grips our attention at once:

> I was born in the year 1632, in the city of York, of a good family, though not of that country, my father being a foreigner of Bremen, who settled first at Hull: he got a

good estate by merchandise, and leaving off his trade, lived afterward at York, from whence he had married my mother, whose relations were named Robinson, a very good family in that country, and from whom I was called Robinson Kreutznoer; but, by the usual corruption of words in England, we are now called, nay, we call ourselves, and write our name Crusoe, and so my companions always called me.

The style is conversational. We seem to hear the author talking quietly to us in the first person and telling us the story of his life. This imaginary autobiography seems at once factual and real. As the writer tells us about the time and the place of his birth, about his parentage and his name, he adds clause to clause pleasantly. The sentence might well have ended after the first clause, "I was born in the year 1632"; or it might have ended in at least thirteen other places after that. On the other hand, it might have gone on and on for many pages. There is no ambiguity, no obscurity, and no tautology. The reader receives no mental check. All is easy and natural. But behind this apparent artlessness there is art concealed, and behind this easy and natural prose—Defoe was writing in the year 1719—lay more than ten centuries of linguistic change and development. There is probably no surer way of appreciating the maturity and concreteness of Defoe's prose than by translating it into some foreign tongue.

8. In the *periodic* sentence the climax comes at the close. The reader is held in suspense until at last he hears what he has long been waiting for, and only then is he able to comprehend the meaning of the sentence as a whole. It is a style cultivated to good effect by the orators of classical antiquity, Demosthenes and Cicero, as well as those of modern times, Burke and Gladstone. When, in *The Laws of Ecclesiasticall Politie*, Richard Hooker reflected upon what might be the subsequent fate of man if the ordinances of nature should fail, he expressed himself in a stately and sonorous prose far different from Defoe's:

Now if nature should intermit her course, and leave altogether though it were but for a while the observation of her own laws; if those principal and mother elements of the world, whereof all things in this lower world are made, should lose the qualities which now they have; if the frame of that heavenly arch erected over our heads should loosen and dissolve itself; if celestial spheres should forget their wonted motions, and by irregular volubility turn themselves any way as it might happen; if the prince of the lights of heaven, which now as a giant doth run his unwearied course, should as it were through a languishing faintness begin to stand and to rest himself; if the moon should wander from her beaten way, the times and seasons of the year blend themselves by disordered and confused mixture, the winds breathe out their last gasp, the clouds yield no rain, the earth be defeated of heavenly influence, the fruits of the earth pine away as children at the withered breasts of their mother no longer able to yield them relief: what would become of man himself, whom these things now do all serve?

The language is highly rhythmical and the imagery is Biblical, reminiscent of Isaiah, the Psalms, and the Book of Job. The word-picture is painted with consummate art. After a long and steady climb upward over successive terraces of conditional clauses, the reader descends swiftly with the final rhetorical question.

9. As an example of a shorter but no less effective period we might consider the sentence in his *Autobiography* in which Edward Gibbon describes the birth of the idea of his great *History:*

It was at Rome, on the 15th of October 1764, as I sat musing amidst the ruins of the Capitol, while the barefooted friars were singing vespers in the temple of Jupiter, that the idea of writing the decline and fall of the city first started to my mind.

In Rome, ruinous and Christian, late in the afternoon in the fall of the year, the inspiration came to the historian. The word-picture is brief, but it is artistically perfect. The rhythm is stately and entirely satisfying. The reader is held in suspense to the end.

10. Had he wished, and had he been less of an artist, Gibbon might have said exactly the same things in a different way, arranging them in their logical and grammatical order:

The idea of writing the decline and fall of the city first started to my mind as I sat musing amidst the ruins of the Capitol at Rome on the 15th of October 1764, while the barefooted friars were singing vespers in the temple of Jupiter.

What has happened? It is not merely that a periodic sentence has been re-expressed as a loose one. The emphasis is now all wrong and the magnificent cadence of the original is quite marred. All is still grammatically correct, but "proper words" are no longer in "proper places." The passage has quite lost its harmonious rhythm.

11. The *balanced* sentence satisfies a profound human desire for equipoise and symmetry and it has long been at home in English as in Hebrew, Greek, and Latin, and many other languages both ancient and modern. It may express two similar thoughts in *parallelism* or two opposing ones in *antithesis*. Such proverbial sayings as *Like master like man, More haste less speed, First come first served,* and *Least said soonest mended* probably represent a primitive Indo-European sentence-type which survives in many lands.

12. "Children sweeten labours," wrote Francis Bacon, "but they make misfortunes more bitter: they increase the cares of life, but they mitigate the remembrance of death." Speaking at the Guildhall, London, on October 9, 1805, just one fortnight after the Battle of Trafalgar, William Pitt declared: "England has saved herself by her exertions and will, I trust, save Europe by her example." No less memorable was the balanced sentence uttered in the House of Lords by Edward Viscount Grey of Fallodon on August 3, 1914, on the eve of Britain's entry into the First World War: "The lamps are going out all over Europe: we shall not see them lit again in our lifetime."

13. English sentence-patterns show infinite variety and *loose, periodic,* and *balanced* are only relative terms. The best writers shape their sentences in such a way as to give just the right degree of emphasis, and this they must achieve, in written language, by word order alone. Now it is certainly not surprising that in a language like ours, with such a long history behind it, some patterns have become blended, mixed, or, to use the technical term, "contaminated," and that some of these "contaminations" have been sanctioned by usage. "I am friendly with him" and "We are friends" ("He and I are friends") have become contaminated and so have produced "I am friends with him." It is an idiom or manner of expression peculiar to English. "I am friends with him" cannot be translated literally into French, German, or Italian, though it is as old as Shakespeare. "I am good friends with my father," says Prince Hal (1 *Henry the Fourth,* III. iii. 202), "and may do any thing." "But whom say ye that I am?" (*St. Matthew,* xvi, 15) is frequently quoted from the King James Bible as an example of an ungrammatical accusative *whom* used as the complement of the verb *to be.* Is it, then, an error? Perhaps no direct yes or no can be given in answer to this question. The sentence is a good example of a blending of "Who say ye that I am?" and "Whom say ye me to be?" That is all. The English poets, even the very greatest of them, have occasionally indulged in such contaminations of sentence-structures, refusing to be bound by strict rules. "I should have liked to have been there," someone will say. Clearly this is a blending of "I should like (I wish now as I look back) to have been there" and "I should have liked (but unfortunately I was unable) to be there." "They each did their best" is likewise a mixture of "They all (all of them) did their best" and "Each of them did his best."

14. If it is true that we repeat sentences from memory and vary them by analogy, and that we do not really frame sentences in any other way, then we should perhaps look upon all analogous creations with a kind and indulgent eye. "Do like I do" is no worse than Elizabethan "Do like as I do." "Do like me" and "Do as I do" mark a desirable distinction, but it would be well to recognize that the distinction is more stylistic than grammatical. "What are you doing of?" is the Cockney's analogous creation, based upon "What are you doing?" and "What are you thinking of?" "I would say" and "I should like to say" are blended and so we hear "I would like to say," an undesirable form which is helped on its way to acceptance by the gen-

eral tendency, especially in North America and in Ireland, to ignore the (relatively recent) traditional distinctions between *shall* (*should*) in the first person and *will* (*would*) in the second and third. "It looks as though" is now on everyone's lips—"It looks as though there will be a general election (or anything else for that matter) soon." "It looks to me," said Burke in 1790 (*Reflections on the Revolution in France*) "as if I were in a great crisis." The verb to-day would be in the past subjective (or subjunctive equivalent) if people were conscious of the precise implication: "It appears as would or might be the case if." But "It looks as though" has come to be a mere substitute for "apparently, probably, by all appearances," and it is now invariably followed by the future tense. "You and I will decide between us" has influenced "Let you and me decide" which becomes "Let you and I decide" on the lips of the heedless, who no longer think of "Let us decide" as "Allow us to decide" supplanting "Decide we," the old ~~jussive~~. Whatever the grammarians may say, there is abundant evidence in many languages for the use of the superlative degree in a comparison of only two persons or things. Nevertheless, "Which (selective) is the stronger of the two?" is more satisfactory than "Who is the strongest of the two?" If we say "He was one of the kindest men that has ever lived" we break that favourite rule of the prescriptive grammarians which states that the verb in a relative clause should agree with its nearer antecedent. Doubtless we are thereby confusing "He was the kindest man that ever lived" and "He was one of the kindest men that have ever lived." We may confuse "The reason why printing is slow is that paper is scarce" and "Printing is slow because paper is scarce" and, as a result, we say "The reason why printing is slow is because paper is scarce." If we are observant and alert, we shall probably hear many interesting "contaminations," such as these, both tolerable and intolerable, every day of our lives.

15. Another interesting thing we shall observe is the way in which natural emphasis overrides strict logic in word order. "He only died last week" may be denounced by modern precisians on the ground that it flouts one of those rules of proximity whereby the modifying adverb should be placed as near as possible to the word, phrase or clause it modifies. "He died only last week" or "It was only last week that he died" should stand. Stress, intonation, and pause, however, make everything clear, or even clearer, when *only* is detached. "He only died last week" implies no ambiguity and no misplaced emphasis. Shakespeare himself wrote in Sonnet xciv—

The summer's flower is to the summer sweet
Though to itself it only live and die

—and not "Though only to itself" or "Though to itself alone," the latter cadence seeming certainly preferable to my modern ear. Mr. Vernon Bartlett once opened a wireless talk on world affairs with the words: "I am not an expert on China. I have only been there twice in my life." Natural emphasis and intonation were just right: the hearer's attention was arrested at once. "I have been there only twice in my life" would have sounded unnatural and pedantic in comparison. Language, after all, is more psychological than logical. So, too, in regard to the placing of the preposition, we should do well to divest ourselves of the notion that it is "an inelegant word to end a sentence with" and that, just because it is called a *pre-position*, it must therefore "be placed before." In Old English (*ūs betwēonan* "between us") as in Latin (*pāx vōbiscum* "peace be with you"), there were *postpositions* and the tradition has been kept alive through centuries of English poetry: "the table round" (Shakespeare); "stoutly struts his dames before" (Milton); "my heart within" (Scott); "the willowy hills and fields among" (Tennyson); "I will go to France again, and tramp the valley through" (Flecker). The final preposition became a butt for the nineteenth-century grammarians, who averred that the most careful writers avoided it and that the Authorized Version of the Bible contained not one instance of it. As a matter of fact, the curious reader will not go far in the Book of Genesis before encountering an example in Chapter xxviii: "I will not leave thee, until I have done that which I have spoken to thee of." It is a remarkable fact that even Dryden, that acknowledged master of English prose, criticized Ben Jonson's conversational style adversely on the ground that it showed the "common fault" of putting the preposition at the end, a fault which, Dryden added, "I have but lately observed in my own writings." Indeed, when revising his *Essay of Dramatic Poesy*, Dryden went so far as to rewrite the sentences in which an end preposition occurred and his illustrious example was followed by others. To-day we accept the final preposition as permissible and desirable in such natural and spontaneous expressions as "What are you thinking of?" and "I sometimes wonder what the world is coming to." Phrasal verbs, consisting of verbs joined with adverbs and prepositions, are now in such frequent use that, in order to avoid the prepositional ending entirely, a speaker would sometimes be driven to perpetrate an intolerably artificial sentence. Against such a clumsy sentence, according to Sir Ernest Gowers (*Plain Words*, p. 74), Mr. Winston Churchill is said to have added the marginal comment: "This is the sort of English up with which I will not put." Sir Ernest goes on to tell the story of a nurse who contrived to get no fewer than four prepositions together at the end of a sentence when she asked a child: "What did you choose that book to be read to out of for?" And did the child understand? If stress, rhythm, intonation, and pause were right, yes. The nurse "said what she wanted to say perfectly clearly, in words of one syllable, and what more can one ask?" You may have observed, by the way, that *out* in "read to out of for" is really an adverb or, if you will, that *out-of* is a prepositional compound consisting of adverb and preposition. At any rate, the dividing line between prepositions and adverbs is often shadowy and vague.

16. The English sentence, then, is something of a paradox. Word order has become more significant than hitherto, far more important than in Old, Middle, or Tudor English, and yet it has retained enough of its elasticity to give to the skilful speaker all the scope and power he needs. We English have inherited our sentence-patterns, but we have abundant freedom to vary words, phrases, and clauses within those inherited patterns. We shall be effective as speakers and as writers if we can say clearly, simply, and attractively just what we want to say and nothing more. If we really have something worth saying, then we are bound by the nature and necessities of our language to say it as simply as ever we can. If we have something very abstruse and complex to say, then, of course, we cannot say it simply, but we shall endeavour to say it as clearly as the theme permits. We shall vary our style, our vocabulary and our speech-level to suit the occasion and, at the same time, we shall never lose sight of the needs and capacities of our hearers. If, following the wise counsel of Aristotle, we keep these three things constantly in mind—our subject-matter, our purpose, and our audience—all will be well.

F. L. LUCAS

On the Fascination of Style

Frank Laurence Lucas (1894–   ), Yorkshire-born and Cambridge-educated, is presently fellow and lecturer of King's College, Cambridge. He is a distinguished poet, scholar, translator, anthologist, and literary critic. In 1964–65 he was Charles Eliot Norton Professor of Poetry at Harvard University. The variety and scope of his knowledge are reflected in the titles of some of his books, among which are *Greek Poetry for Everyman*, 1951; *From Many Times and Lands: A Volume of Poems*, 1953; *Greek Drama for Everyman*, 1954; *Style*, 1955; *Tennyson*, 1957; *Literature and Psychology*, 1957; *The Art of Living: Four Eighteenth-Century Minds—Hume, Horace Walpole, Burke, Benjamin Franklin*, 1959; *The Greatest Problem, and Other Essays*, 1960; and *The Drama of Ibsen and Strindberg*, 1962.

While we tend to seek style in the way we dress, the way we play golf, and all our other modes of living, we are indifferent, says Mr. Lucas, to our style in writing. Drawing on more than forty years of experience, he passes along some hints that may help others improve their writing style.

1. When it was suggested to Walt Whitman that one of his works should be bound in vellum, he was outraged—"Pshaw!" he snorted, "—hangings, curtains, finger bowls, chinaware, Matthew Arnold!" And he might have been equally irritated by talk of style; for he boasted of "my barbaric yawp"—he would *not* be literary; his readers should touch not a book but a man. Yet Whitman took the pains to rewrite *Leaves of Grass* four times, and his style is unmistakable. Samuel Butler maintained that writers who bothered about their style became unreadable but he bothered about his own. "Style" has got a bad name by growing associated with precious and superior persons who, like Oscar Wilde, spend a morning putting in a comma, and the afternoon (so he said) taking it out again. But such

abuse of "style" is misuse of English. For the word means merely "a way of expressing oneself, in language, manner, or appearance"; or, secondly, "a *good* way of so expressing oneself"—as when one says, "Her behavior never lacked style."

2. Now there is no crime in expressing oneself (though to try to *im*press oneself on others easily grows revolting or ridiculous). Indeed one cannot help expressing oneself, unless one passes one's life in a cupboard. Even the most rigid Communist, or Organization-man, is compelled by Nature to have a unique voice, unique fingerprints, unique handwriting. Even the signatures of the letters on your breakfast table may reveal more than their writers guess. There are blustering signatures that swish across the page like cornstalks bowed before a tempest. There are cryptic signatures, like a scrabble of lightning across a cloud, suggesting that behind is a lofty divinity

whom all must know, or an aloof divinity whom none is worthy to know (though, as this might be highly inconvenient, a docile typist sometimes interprets the mystery in a bracket underneath). There are impetuous squiggles implying that the author is a sort of strenuous Sputnik streaking round the globe every eighty minutes. There are florid signatures, all curlicues and danglements and flamboyance, like the youthful Disraeli (though these seem rather out of fashion). There are humble, humdrum signatures. And there are also, sometimes, signatures that are courteously clear, yet mindful of a certain simple grace and artistic economy—in short, of style.

3. Since, then, not one of us can put pen to paper, or even open his mouth, without giving something of himself away to shrewd observers, it seems mere common sense to give the matter a little thought. Yet it does not seem very common. Ladies may take infinite pains about having style in their clothes, but many of us remain curiously indifferent about having it in our words. How many women would dream of polishing not only their nails but also their tongues? They may play freely on that perilous little organ, but they cannot often be bothered to tune it. And how many men think of improving their talk as well as their golf handicap?

4. No doubt strong silent men, speaking only in gruff monosyllables, may despise "mere words." No doubt the world does suffer from an endemic plague of verbal dysentery. But that, precisely, is bad style. And consider the amazing power of mere words. Adolf Hitler was a bad artist, bad statesman, bad general, and bad man. But largely because he could tune his rant, with psychological nicety, to the exact wavelength of his audiences and make millions quarrelsome-drunk all at the same time by his command of windy nonsense, skilled statesmen, soldiers, scientists were blown away like chaff, and he came near to rule the world. If Sir Winston Churchill had been a mere speechifier, we might well have lost the war; yet his speeches did quite a lot to win it.

5. No man was less of a literary aesthete than Benjamin Franklin; yet this tallow-chandler's son, who changed world history, regarded as "a principal means of my advancement" that pungent style which he acquired partly by working in youth over old *Spectators;* but mainly by being Benjamin Franklin. The squinting demagogue, John Wilkes, as ugly as his many sins, had yet a tongue so winning that he asked only half an hour's start (to counteract his face) against any rival for a woman's favor. "Vote for you!" growled a surly elector in his constituency. "I'd sooner vote for the devil!" "But in case your friend should not stand . . . ?" Cleopatra, that ensnarer of world conquerors, owed less to the shape of her nose than to the charm of her tongue. Shakespeare himself has often poor plots and thin ideas; even his mastery of character has been questioned; what does remain unchallenged is his verbal magic. Men are often taken, like rabbits, by the ears. And though the tongue has no bones, it can sometimes break millions of them.

6. "But," the reader may grumble, "I am neither Hitler, Cleopatra, nor Shakespeare. What is all this to me?" Yet we all talk—often too much; we all have to write letters—often too many. We live not by bread alone but also by words. And not always with remarkable efficiency. Strikes, lawsuits, divorces, all sorts of public nuisance and private misery, often come just from the gaggling incompetence with which we express ourselves. Americans and British get at cross-purposes because they use the same words with different meanings. Men have been hanged on a comma in a statute. And in the valley of Balaclava a mere verbal ambiguity, about *which* guns were to be captured, sent the whole Light Brigade to futile annihilation.

7. Words can be more powerful, and more treacherous, than we sometimes suspect; communication more difficult than we may think. We are all serving life sentences of solitary confinement within our own bodies; like prisoners, we have, as it were, to tap in awkward code to our fellow men in their neighboring cells. Further, when A and B converse, there take part in their dialogue not two characters, as they suppose, but six. For there is A's real self—call it A_1; there is also A's picture

of himself—A_2; there is also B's picture of A—A_3. And there are three corresponding personalities of B. With six characters involved even in a simple tête-à-tête, no wonder we fall into muddles and misunderstandings.

8. Perhaps, then, there are five main reasons for trying to gain some mastery of language:

We have no other way of understanding, informing, misinforming, or persuading one another.

Even alone, we think mainly in words; if our language is muddy, so will our thinking be.

By our handling of words we are often revealed and judged. "Has he written anything?" said Napoleon of a candidate for an appointment. "Let me see his *style*."

Without a feeling for language one remains half-blind and deaf to literature.

Our mother tongue is bettered or worsened by the way each generation uses it. Languages evolve like species. They can degenerate; just as oysters and barnacles have lost their heads. Compare ancient Greek with modern. A heavy responsibility, though often forgotten.

9. Why and how did I become interested in style? The main answer, I suppose, is that I was born that way. Then I was, till ten, an only child running loose in a house packed with books, and in a world (thank goodness) still undistracted by radio and television. So at three I groaned to my mother, "Oh, I *wish* I could read," and at four I read. Now travel among books is the best travel of all, and the easiest, and the cheapest. (Not that I belittle ordinary travel—which I regard as one of the three main pleasures in life.) One learns to write by reading good books, as one learns to talk by hearing good talkers. And if I have learned anything of writing, it is largely from writers like Montaigne, Dorothy Osborne, Horace Walpole, Johnson, Goldsmith, Montesquieu, Voltaire, Flaubert and Anatole France. Again, I was reared on Greek and Latin, and one can learn much from translating Homer or the Greek Anthology, Horace or Tacitus, if one is thrilled by the originals

and tries, however vainly, to recapture some of that thrill in English.

10. But at Rugby I could *not* write English essays. I believe it stupid to torment boys to write on topics that they know and care nothing about. I used to rush to the school library and cram the subject, like a python swallowing rabbits; then, still replete as a postprandial python, I would tie myself in clumsy knots to embrace those accursed themes. Bacon was wise in saying that reading makes a full man; talking, a ready one; writing, an exact one. But writing from an empty head is futile anguish.

11. At Cambridge, my head having grown a little fuller, I suddenly found I *could* write —not with enjoyment (it is always tearing oneself in pieces)—but fairly fluently. Then came the War of 1914–18; and though soldiers have other things than pens to handle, they learn painfully to be clear and brief. Then the late Sir Desmond MacCarthy invited me to review for the *New Statesman;* it was a useful apprenticeship, and he was delightful to work for. But I think it was well after a few years to stop; reviewers remain essential, but there are too many books one *cannot* praise, and only the pugnacious enjoy amassing enemies. By then I was an ink-addict—not because writing is much pleasure, but because not to write is pain; just as some smokers do not so much enjoy tobacco as suffer without it. The positive happiness of writing comes, I think, from work when done—decently, one hopes, and not without use—and from the letters of readers which help to reassure, or delude, one that so it is.

12. But one of my most vivid lessons came, I think, from service in a war department during the Second War. Then, if the matter one sent out was too wordy, the communication channels might choke; yet if it was not absolutely clear, the results might be serious. So I emerged, after six years of it, with more passion than ever for clarity and brevity, more loathing than ever for the obscure and the verbose.

13. For forty years at Cambridge I have tried to teach young men to write well, and have come to think it impossible. To write

really well is a gift inborn; those who have it teach themselves; one can only try to help and hasten the process. After all, the uneducated sometimes express themselves far better than their "betters." In language, as in life, it is possible to be perfectly correct—and yet perfectly tedious, or odious. The illiterate last letter of the doomed Vanzetti was more moving than most professional orators; 18th Century ladies, who should have been spanked for their spelling, could yet write far better letters than most professors of English; and the talk of Synge's Irish peasants seems to me vastly more vivid than the later styles of Henry James. Yet Synge averred that his characters owed far less of their eloquence to what he invented for them than to what he had overheard in the cottages of Wicklow and Kerry:

> CHRISTY: It's little you'll think if my love's a poacher's, or an earl's itself, when you'll feel my two hands stretched around you, and I squeezing kisses on your puckered lips, till I'd feel a kind of pity for the Lord God is all ages sitting lonesome in His golden chair.
>
> PEGEEN: That'll be right fun, Christy Mahon, and any girl would walk her heart out before she'd meet a young man was your like for eloquence, or talk at all.

14. Well she might! It's not like that they talk in universities—more's the pity.

15. But though one cannot teach people to write well, one can sometimes teach them to write rather better. One can give a certain number of hints, which often seem boringly obvious—only experience shows they are not.

16. One can say: Beware of pronouns—they are devils. Look at even Addison, describing the type of pedant who chatters of style without having any:

> Upon enquiry I found my learned friend had dined that day with Mr. Swan, the famous punster; and desiring *him* to give me some account of Mr. Swan's conversation, *he* told me that *he* generally talked in the Paronomasia, that *he* sometimes gave in to the Plocé, but that in *his* humble opinion *he* shone most in the Antanaclasis.

What a sluttish muddle of *he* and *him* and *his!* It all needs rewording. Far better repeat a noun, or a name, than puzzle the reader, even for a moment, with ambiguous pronouns. Thou shalt not puzzle thy reader.

17. Or one can say: Avoid jingles. The B.B.C. news bulletins seem compiled by earless persons, capable of crying round the globe: "The enemy is re*port*ed to have seized this im*port*ant *port,* and reinforcements are hurrying up in sup*port.*" Any fool, once told, can hear such things to be insupportable.

18. Or one can say: Be sparing with relative clauses. Don't string them together like sausages, or jam them inside one another like Chinese boxes or the receptacles of Buddha's tooth. Or one can say: Don't flaunt jargon, like Addison's Mr. Swan, or the type of modern critic who gurgles more technical terms in a page than Johnson used in all his *Lives* or Sainte-Beuve in thirty volumes. But dozens of such snippety precepts, though they may sometimes save people from writing badly, will help them little toward writing well. Are there no general rules of a more positive kind, and of more positive use?

19. Perhaps. There *are* certain basic principles which seem to me observed by many authors I admire, which I think have served me and which may serve others. I am not talking of geniuses, who are a law to themselves (and do not always write a very good style, either); nor of poetry, which has different laws from prose; nor of poetic prose, like Sir Thomas Browne's or De Quincey's, which is often more akin to poetry; but of the plain prose of ordinary books and documents, letters and talk.

20. The writer should respect truth and himself; therefore honesty. He should respect his readers; therefore courtesy. These are two of the cornerstones of style. Confucius saw it, twenty-five centuries ago: "The Master said, The gentleman is courteous, but not pliable: common men are pliable, but not courteous."

21. First, honesty. In literature, as in life, one of the fundamentals is to find, and be, one's true self. One's true self may indeed be unpleasant (though one can try to better it); but a false self, sooner or later, becomes disgusting—just as a nice plain woman, painted to the eyebrows, can become horrid. In writ-

ing, in the long run, pretense does not work. As the police put it, anything you say may be used as evidence against you. If handwriting reveals character, writing reveals it still more. You cannot fool *all* your judges *all* the time.

22. Most style is not hone̲st enough. Easy to say, but hard to practice. A writer may take to long words, as young men to beards—to impress. But long words, like long beards, are often the badge of charlatans. Or a writer may cultivate the obscure, to seem profound. But even carefully muddied puddles are soon fathomed. Or he may cultivate eccentricity, to seem original. But really original people do not have to think about being original—they can no more help it than they can help breathing. They do not need to dye their hair green. The fame of Meredith, Wilde or Bernard Shaw might now shine brighter, had they struggled less to be brilliant; whereas Johnson remains great, not merely because his gifts were formidable but also because, with all this prejudice and passion, he fought no less passionately to "clear his mind of cant."

23. Secondly, courtesy̲—respect fo̲r̲ t̲h̲e̲ reader̲. From this follow several other basic principles of style. Clarity is one. For it is boorish to make your reader rack his brains to understand. One should aim at being impossible to misunderstand—though men's capacity for misunderstanding approaches infinity. Hence Molière and Po Chu-i tried their work on their cooks; and Swift his on his menservants—"which, if they did not comprehend, he would alter and amend, until they understood it perfectly." Our bureaucrats and pundits, unfortunately, are less considerate.

24. Brevit̲y̲ is another basic principle. For it is boorish, also, to waste your reader's time. People who would not dream of stealing a penny of one's money turn not a hair at stealing hours of one's life. But that does not make them less exasperating. Therefore there is no excuse for the sort of writer who takes as long as a marching army corps to pass a given point. Besides, brevity is often more effective; the half can say more than the whole, and to imply things may strike far deeper than to state them at length. And because one is particularly apt to waste words on preambles

before coming to the substance, there was sense in the Scots professor who always asked his pupils—"Did ye remember to tear up that fir-r-st page?"

25. Here are some instances that would only lose by lengthening:

It is useless to go to bed to save the light, if the result is twins. (Chinese proverb.)

My barn is burnt down—
Nothing hides the moon. (Complete Japanese poem.)

Je me regrette. (Dying words of the gay Vicomtesse d'Houdetot.)

I have seen their backs before. (Wellington, when French marshals turned their backs on him at a reception.)

Continue until the tanks stop, then get out and walk. (Patton to the Twelfth Corps, halted for fuel supplies at St. Dizier, 8/30/44.)

26. Or there is the most la̲co̲nic̲ diplomatic note on record: when Philip of Macedon wrote to the Spartans that, if he came within their borders, he would leave not one stone of their city, they wrote back the one word—"If."

27. Clarity comes before even brevity. But it is a fallacy that wordiness is necessarily clearer. Metternich when he thought something he had written was obscure would simply go through it crossing out everything irrelevant. What remained, he found, often became clear. Wellington, asked to recommend three names for the post of Commander-in-Chief, India, took a piece of paper and wrote three times—"Napier." Pages could not have been clearer—or as forcible. On the other hand the lectures, and the sentences, of Coleridge became at times bewildering because his mind was often "wiggle-waggle"; just as he could not even walk straight on a path.

28. But clarity and brevity, though a good beginning, are only a beginning. By themselves, they may remain bare and bleak. When Calvin Coolidge, asked by his wife what the preacher had preached on, replied "Sin," and, asked what the preacher had said, replied, "He

was against it," he was brief enough. But one hardly envies Mrs. Coolidge.

29. An attractive style requires, of course, all kinds of further gifts—such as variety, good humor, good sense, vitality, imagination. Variety means avoiding monotony of rhythm, of language, of mood. One needs to vary one's sentence length (this present article has too many short sentences; but so vast a subject grows here as cramped as a djin in a bottle); to amplify one's vocabulary; to diversify one's tone. There are books that petrify one throughout, with the rigidly pompous solemnity of an owl perched on a leafless tree. But ceaseless facetiousness can be as bad; or perpetual irony. Even the smile of Voltaire can seem at times a fixed grin, a disagreeable wrinkle. Constant peevishness is far worse, as often in Swift; even on the stage too much irritable dialogue may irritate an audience, without its knowing why.

30. Still more are vitality, energy, imagination gifts that must be inborn before they can be cultivated. But under the head of imagination two common devices may be mentioned that have been the making of many a style—metaphor and simile. Why such magic power should reside in simply saying, or implying, that A is like B remains a little mysterious. But even our unconscious seems to love symbols; again, language often tends to lose itself in clouds of vaporous abstraction, and simile or metaphor can bring it back to concrete solidity; and, again, such imagery can gild the gray flats of prose with sudden sunglints of poetry.

31. If a foreigner may for a moment be impertinent, I admire the native gift of Americans for imagery as much as I wince at their fondness for slang. (Slang seems to me a kind of linguistic fungus; as poisonous, and as short-lived, as toadstools.) When Matthew Arnold lectured in the United States, he was likened by one newspaper to "an elderly macaw pecking at a trellis of grapes"; he observed, very justly, "How lively journalistic fancy is among the Americans!" General Grant, again, unable to hear him, remarked: "Well, wife, we've paid to see the British lion, but as we can't hear him roar, we'd better go home." By simile and

metaphor, these two quotations bring before us the slightly pompous, fastidious, inaudible Arnold as no direct description could have done.

32. Or consider how language comes alive in the Chinese saying that lending to the feckless is "like pelting a stray dog with dumplings," or in the Arab proverb: "They came to shoe the pasha's horse, and the beetle stretched forth his leg"; in the Greek phrase for a perilous cape—"stepmother of ships"; or the Hebrew adage that "as the climbing up a sandy way is to the feet of the aged, so is a wife full of words to a quiet man"; in Shakespeare's phrase for a little England lost in the world's vastness—"in a great Poole, a Swan's nest"; or Fuller's libel on tall men—"Ofttimes such who are built four stories high are observed to have little in their cockloft"; in Chateaubriand's "I go yawning my life"; or in Jules Renard's portrait of a cat, "well buttoned in her fur." Or, to take a modern instance, there is Churchill on dealings with Russia:

> Trying to maintain good relations with a Communist is like wooing a crocodile. You do not know whether to tickle it under the chin or beat it over the head. When it opens its mouth, you cannot tell whether it is trying to smile or preparing to eat you up.

What a miracle human speech can be, and how dull is most that one hears! Would one hold one's hearers, it is far less help, I suspect, to read manuals on style than to cultivate one's own imagination and imagery.

33. I will end with two remarks by two wise old women of the civilized 18th Century.

34. The first is from the blind Mme. du Deffand (the friend of Horace Walpole) to that Mlle. de Lespinasse with whom, alas, she was to quarrel so unwisely: "You must make up your mind, my queen, to live with me in the greatest truth and sincerity. You will be charming so long as you let yourself be natural, and remain without pretension and without artifice." The second is from Mme. de Charrière, the Zélide whom Boswell had once loved at Utrecht in vain, to a Swiss girl friend: "Lucinde, my clever Lucinde, while you wait for the Romeos to arrive, you have nothing

better to do than become perfect. Have ideas that are clear, and expressions that are simple." (*"Ayez des idées nettes et des expressions simples."*) More than half the bad writing in the world, I believe, comes from neglecting those two very simple pieces of advice.

35. In many ways, no doubt, our world grows more and more complex; sputniks cannot be simple; yet how many of our complexities remain futile, how many of our artificialities false. Simplicity too can be subtle—as the straight lines of a Greek temple, like the Parthenon at Athens, are delicately curved, in order to look straighter still.

ARNOLD LAZARUS

Language-learning Objectives: A Checklist

Arnold Lazarus (1914–   ) received his doctorate from the University of California, Los Angeles, in 1957 and has taught at Santa Monica City College, Los Angeles State College, and the University of Texas. Since 1962, he has directed English education for teachers at the English Curriculum Center at Purdue University. He contributes frequently to professional journals in linguistics and English education.

This list of twenty specific language-learning objectives can serve as a guide for teacher and student in their study of language and literature.

Pupil performance in "English" consists of listening, speaking, reading, writing, and reasoning, though not necessarily in that audio-lingual sequence. Spelled out, these "-ings" can also be identified as "skills" (or "arts") and as "understandings." Thus a skills objective might be "writing clear exposition," for example, while an understandings objective might be "getting differential meanings from differential simple-sentence patterns." The present checklist is concerned primarily with understandings or concept objectives rather than with arts or skills objectives, though it

cannot avoid a certain amount of overlap. This checklist also reflects a trend toward bridging what one linguist has called the "innocent gap," in pedagogy, between the language of communication and the language of literature.

Here, then, is the checklist:

1. To understand that language is one but only one kind of human behavior, one but only one of various devices for signaling communication.

2. To understand that various cultures categorize their contexts (their experiences and realities) variously; that notions about the other fellow's spoken language as "primitive" or "less sophisticated" than ours are nonsense.

3. To understand that even within our

Western cultures—even within the United States—subcultures use different, not necessarily better or worse, language patterns.

4. To understand that there is no such real split in usage as absolutely "correct" vs. "incorrect"; that various "standard" and "nonstandard" classifications ("general" or "nongeneral USA") are based on regional and occasional levels of acceptability or prestige; that "formal," "informal" (or "colloquial") and "slang" are not levels but rather functional varieties of usage subsumed under the levels; that further refining Kenyon's and Gove's distinctions there remain what Martin Joos and others have called the continua and clocks of usage.

5. To understand that whenever a speaker in literature or life makes an utterance, he always reveals one or more of the following: his historical era, his geographical stance (country, region, locality), his age (infancy, childhood, adolescence, adulthood, senility), his sex (male, female, effeminate, tomboyish), the age and sex of his audience, the size of his audience (from intimate to public), his formal education (lack of education, half-education, "prestige dialects"), his socioeconomic status (a continuum from slave through various kinds of follower to various kinds of leader and power elites), his cultural milieu's values, sports, and pastimes.

6. To understand that "grammar" is not a set of rules for usage but rather a set (or sets) of descriptions of meanings characteristically signaled by an utterance's (a) structure, (b) lexical context, and (c) context.

7. To understand that structural and contextual meanings are signaled largely by intonational clues, by such suprasegmentals as pitch, stress, and juncture—structural elements just as indispensable to one's silent reading as to one's oral interpretation of poetry, fiction, drama, and the like.

8. To understand that meanings are signaled partly by utterance *patterns*—simple-sentence patterns, compound-sentence patterns, complex-sentence patterns, etc.; that ellipses and reduced forms of these patterns occur about as frequently as do simple-sentence patterns but that the most frequent

simple-sentence patterns include (a) the S-V, (b) the S-V-O, (c) the S-V-iO-O, (d) the S-LV-C, (LV = linking verb and C = complement), and (e) the expletive-V-S ("It is morning").

9. To understand that word groups filling noun slots and verb slots comprise the chief building blocks of utterances regardless of how one dissects these clusters into more immediate constituents.

10. To understand and recognize such words (often called "form words") as those that change their forms by means of "-s," "-ly," "-ed," "-en," and by means of other morphemes under whatever labels; and such words (often called "function words") as determiners, connectors, and subordinators, under whatever labels; to distinguish such coordinating signals as *and, but, or* from such subordinating signals as *who, which, that, since, when, although, because,* and *if.*

11. To understand and distinguish among verbals and verbal phrases; to recognize, e.g., which participles go with which nouns or noun substitutes as a prerequisite to understanding what is being said, especially in poetry and difficult prose; to sort out, chiefly by context, the participles, transitive gerunds, and intransitive gerunds; to relish the ambivalence, intended or not, in an utterance like "She enjoys swimming, boating, and exciting dates."

12. To understand and differentiate between phrases and clauses, between independent or coordinate clauses on the one hand and dependent or subordinate clauses on the other; to observe that certain structurally subordinate clauses do not necessarily signal logical subordination ("I had only gone one block when I realized my blunder," for example, is a perfectly idiomatic utterance).

13. To understand that devices for signaling subordination are not just subordinate clauses but also such syntactic structures as appositives, verbal phrases, and absolute phrases.

14. To understand that—except for certain ellipses understandable in context—it takes at least one independent clause to make a simple sentence; two or more independent clauses to

make a compound sentence; one independent joined to one or more dependents—any number of dependents and in any position—to make a complex sentence, etc.

15. To understand that—aside from Noam Chomsky's concept of "the kernel of the language" as *the set* of sentences produced when we apply obligatory transformations to the terminal strings of the grammar"—many a basic simple sentence frequently "transforms" (a loose but operational description) to a question, a negation, a passive, etc., and often, in poetry, to an inversion; that apprehending such *systems* (the more scholarly notion of what "transformations" really are) increases the probabilities that one will apprehend what he reads.

16. To understand that even though meaning is signaled only partly by lexical content lexical content cannot be dismissed—neglect hardly intended by the structuralists, who only wanted more recognition for the great amount of meaning signaled by structure as well; that a knowledge of etymology and language history informs one's understanding of literary pieces; that recognizing the various meanings which affixes (prefixes, infixes, suffixes) signal in various situations is rewarding, as is an understanding of the inflection level-

ing which has occurred since Anglo-Saxon times; that language is constantly changing; that guardians self-appointed to keep our language "pure" are deluding themselves.

17. To understand that language as lexicon is an imperfect representation of whatever words stand for; that there are simply not enough words to go around for things; that words are not things but rather abstractions—symbols pulled out of things—which may or may not be arranged in a hierarchy as more or less abstract, more or less general and specific.

18. To understand that the language of context *suggests* meaning—that it often suggests more than it denotes, that it is connotative of what Hayakawa calls "snarls" and "purrs" as well as of intended "neutrals."

19. To understand that written language is not only an art ("selective representation") but also an imperfect representation of spoken language, and yet a representation with its own structures and conventions often differing markedly from those of spoken language.

20. To understand that the meaning of a literary work is signaled somewhat mutually by its *genre, mode* (i.e., romance, or tragedy, or comedy, or satire, etc.), *tone,* and *context.*

 *LEARNING*

JAMES THURBER

Many Moons

Once upon a time, in a kingdom by the sea, there lived a little Princess named Lenore. She was ten years old, going on eleven. One day Lenore fell ill of a surfeit of raspberry tarts and took to her bed.

The Royal Physician came to see her and took her temperature and felt her pulse and made her stick out her tongue. The Royal Physician was worried. He sent for the King, Lenore's father, and the King came to see her.

"I will get you anything your heart desires," the King said. "Is there anything your heart desires?"

"Yes," said the Princess. "I want the moon. If I can have the moon, I will be well again."

Now the King had a great many wise men who always got for him anything he wanted, so he told his daughter that she could have the moon. Then he went to the throne room and pulled a bell cord, three long pulls and a short pull, and presently the Lord High Chamberlain came into the room.

The Lord High Chamberlain was a large, fat man who wore thick glasses which made his eyes seem twice as big as they really were. This made the Lord High Chamberlain seem twice as wise as he really was.

"I want you to get the moon," said the King. "The Princess Lenore wants the moon. If she can have the moon, she will get well again."

"The moon?" exclaimed the Lord High Chamberlain, his eyes widening. This made him look four times as wise as he really was.

"Yes, the moon," said the King. "M-o-o-n, moon. Get it tonight, tomorrow at the latest."

The Lord High Chamberlain wiped his forehead with a handkerchief and then blew his nose loudly. "I have got a great many things for you in my time, your Majesty," he said. "It just happens that I have with me a list of the things I have got for you in my time." He pulled a long scroll of parchment out of his

MANY MOONS © 1943 James Thurber. Published by Harcourt, Brace & World, Inc. Reprinted by permission of Mrs. James Thurber.

pocket. "Let me see, now." He glanced at the list, frowning. "I have got ivory, apes, and peacocks, rubies, opals, and emeralds, black orchids, pink elephants, and blue poodles, gold bugs, scarabs, and flies in amber, hummingbirds' tongues, angels' feathers, and unicorns' horns, giants, midgets, and mermaids, frankincense, ambergris, and myrrh, troubadors, minstrels, and dancing women, a pound of butter, two dozen eggs, and a sack of sugar—sorry, my wife wrote that in there."

"I don't remember any blue poodles," said the King.

"It says blue poodles right here on the list, and they are checked off with a little check mark," said the Lord High Chamberlain. "So there must have been blue poodles. You just forget."

"Never mind the blue poodles," said the King. "What I want now is the moon."

"I have sent as far as Samarkand and Araby and Zanzibar to get things for you, your Majesty," said the Lord High Chamberlain. "But the moon is out of the question. It is 35,000 miles away and it is bigger than the room the Princess lies in. Furthermore, it is made of molten copper. I cannot get the moon for you. Blue poodles, yes; the moon, no."

The King flew into a rage and told the Lord High Chamberlain to leave the room and to send the Royal Wizard to the throne room.

The Royal Wizard was a little, thin man with a long face. He wore a high red peaked hat covered with silver stars, and a long blue robe covered with golden owls. His face grew very pale when the King told him that he wanted the moon for his little daughter, and that he expected the Royal Wizard to get it.

"I have worked a great deal of magic for you in my time, your Majesty," said the Royal Wizard. "As a matter of fact, I just happen to have in my pocket a list of the wizardries I have performed for you." He drew a paper from a deep pocket of his robe. "It begins: 'Dear Royal Wizard: I am returning herewith the so-called philosopher's stone which you claimed—' no, that isn't it." The Royal Wizard brought a long scroll of parchment from another pocket of his robe. "Here it is," he said. "Now, let's see. I have squeezed blood out of turnips for you, and turnips out of blood. I have produced rabbits out of silk hats, and silk hats out of rabbits. I have conjured up flowers, tambourines, and doves out of nowhere, and nowhere out of flowers, tambourines and doves. I have brought you divining rods, magic wands, and crystal spheres in which to behold the future. I have compounded philters, unguents, and potions, to cure heartbreak, surfeit, and ringing in the ears. I have made you my own special mixture of wolfbane, nightshade, and eagles' tears, to ward off witches, demons, and things that go bump in the night. I have given you seven league boots, the golden touch, and a cloak of invisibility—"

"It didn't work," said the King. "The cloak of invisibility didn't work."

"Yes, it did," said the Royal Wizard.

"No, it didn't," said the King. "I kept bumping into things, the same as ever."

"The cloak is supposed to make you invisible," said the Royal Wizard. "It is not supposed to keep you from bumping into things."

"All I know is, I kept bumping into things," said the King.

The Royal Wizard looked at his list again. "I got you," he said, "horns from Elfland, sand from the Sandman, and gold from the rainbow. Also a spool of thread, a paper of needles, and a lump of beeswax—sorry, those are things my wife wrote down for me to get her."

"What I want you to do now," said the King, "is to get me the moon. The Princess Lenore wants the moon, and when she gets it, she will be well again."

"Nobody can get the moon," said the Royal Wizard. "It is 150,000 miles away, and it is made of green cheese, and it is twice as big as this palace."

The King flew into another rage and sent the Royal Wizard back to his cave. Then he rang a gong and summoned the Royal Mathematician.

The Royal Mathematician was a bald-headed, nearsighted man, with a skullcap on his head and a pencil behind each ear. He wore a black suit with white numbers on it.

"I don't want to hear a long list of all the things you have figured out for me since 1907," the King said to him. "I want you to figure out right now how to get the moon for the Princess Lenore. When she gets the moon, she will be well again."

"I am glad you mentioned all the things I have figured out for you since 1907," said the Royal Mathematician. "It so happens that I have a list of them with me."

He pulled a long scroll of parchment out of a pocket and looked at it. "Now let me see. I have figured out for you the distance between the horns of a dilemma, night and day, and A and Z. I have computed how far is Up, how long it takes to get to Away, and what becomes of Gone. I have discovered the length of the sea serpent, the price of the priceless, and the square of the hippopotamus. I know where you are when you are at Sixes and Sevens, how much Is you have to have to make an Are, and how many birds you can catch with the salt in the ocean—187,796,132, if it would interest you to know."

"There aren't that many birds," said the King.

"I didn't say there were," said the Royal Mathematician. "I said if there were."

"I don't want to hear about seven hundred million imaginary birds," said the King. "I want you to get the moon for the Princess Lenore."

"The moon is 300,000 miles away," said the Royal Mathematician. "It is round and flat like a coin, only it is made of asbestos, and it is half the size of this kingdom. Furthermore, it is pasted on the sky. Nobody can get the moon."

The King flew into still another rage and sent the Royal Mathematician away. Then he rang for the Court Jester. The Jester came bounding into the throne room in his motley and his cap and bells, and sat at the foot of the throne.

"What can I do for you, your Majesty?" asked the Court Jester.

"Nobody can do anything for me," said the King mournfully. "The Princess Lenore wants the moon, and she cannot be well till she gets it, but nobody can get it for her. Every time I ask anybody for the moon, it gets larger and farther away. There is nothing you can do for me except play on your lute. Something sad."

"How big do they say the moon is," asked the Court Jester, "and how far away?"

"The Lord High Chamberlain says it is 35,000 miles away, and bigger than the Princess Lenore's room," said the King. "The Royal Wizard says it is 150,000 miles away, and twice as big as this palace. The Royal Mathematician says it is 300,000 miles away, and half the size of this kingdom."

The Court Jester strummed on his lute for a little while. "They are all wise men," he said, "and so they must all be right. If they are all right, then the moon must be just as large and as far away as each person thinks it is. The thing to do is find out how big the Princess Lenore thinks it is, and how far away."

"I never thought of that," said the King.

"I will go and ask her, your Majesty," said the Court Jester. And he crept softly into the little girl's room.

The Princess Lenore was awake, and she was glad to see the Court Jester, but her face was very pale and her voice very weak.

"Have you brought the moon to me?" she asked.

"Not yet," said the Court Jester, "but I will get it for you right away. How big do you think it is?"

"It is just a little smaller than my thumbnail," she said, "for when I hold my thumbnail up at the moon, it just covers it."

"And how far away is it?" asked the Court Jester.

"It is not as high as the big tree outside my window," said the Princess, "for sometimes it gets caught in the top branches."

"It will be very easy to get the moon for you," said the Court Jester. "I will climb the tree tonight when it gets caught in the top branches and bring it to you."

Then he thought of something else. "What is the moon made of, Princess?" he asked.

"Oh," she said, "it's made of gold, of course, silly."

The Court Jester left the Princess Lenore's room and went to see the Royal Goldsmith. He had the Royal Goldsmith make a tiny round golden moon just a little smaller than the thumbnail of the Princess Lenore. Then he had him string it on a golden chain so the Princess could wear it around her neck.

"What is this thing I have made?" asked the Royal Goldsmith when he had finished it.

"You have made the moon," said the Court Jester. "That is the moon."

"But the moon," said the Royal Goldsmith, "is 500,000 miles away and is made of bronze and is round like a marble."

"That's what you think," said the Court Jester as he went away with the moon.

The Court Jester took the moon to the Princess Lenore, and she was overjoyed. The next day she was well again and could get up and go out in the gardens to play.

But the King's worries were not yet over. He knew that the moon would shine in the sky again that night, and he did not want the Princess Lenore to see it. If she did, she would know that the moon she wore on a chain around her neck was not the real moon.

So the King sent for the Lord High Chamberlain and said, "We must keep the Princess Lenore from seeing the moon when it shines in the sky tonight. Think of something."

The Lord High Chamberlain tapped his forehead with his fingers thoughtfully and said, "I know just the thing. We can make some dark glasses for the Princess Lenore. We can make them so dark that she will not be able to see anything at all through them. Then she will not be able to see the moon when it shines in the sky."

This made the King very angry, and he shook his head from side to side. "If she wore dark glasses, she would bump into things," he said, "and then she would be ill again." So he sent the Lord High Chamberlain away and called the Royal Wizard.

"We must hide the moon," said the King, "so that the Princess Lenore will not see it when it shines in the sky tonight. How are we going to do that?"

The Royal Wizard stood on his hands and then he stood on his head and then he stood on his feet again. "I know what we can do," he said. "We can stretch some black velvet curtains on poles. The curtains will cover all the palace gardens like a circus tent, and the Princess Lenore will not be able to see through them, so she will not see the moon in the sky."

The King was so angry at this that he waved his arms around. "Black velvet curtains would keep out the air," he said. "The Princess Lenore would not be able to breathe, and she would be ill again." So he sent the Royal Wizard away and summoned the Royal Mathematician.

"We must do something," said the King, "so that the Princess Lenore will not see the moon when it shines in the sky tonight. If you know so much, figure out a way to do that."

The Royal Mathematician walked around in a circle, and then he walked around in a square, and then he stood still. "I have it!" he said. "We can set off fireworks in the gardens every night. We will make a lot of silver fountains and golden cascades, and when they go off, they will fill the sky with so many sparks that it will be as light as day and the Princess Lenore will not be able to see the moon."

The King flew into such a rage that he began jumping up and down. "Fireworks would keep the Princess Lenore awake," he said. "She would not get any sleep at all and she would be ill again." So the King sent the Royal Mathematician away.

When he looked up again, it was dark outside and he saw the bright rim of the moon just peeping over the horizon. He jumped up in a great fright and rang for the Court Jester. The Court Jester came bounding into the room and sat down at the foot of the throne.

"What can I do for you, your Majesty?" he asked.

"Nobody can do anything for me," said the King, mournfully. "The moon is coming up again. It will shine into the Princess Lenore's bedroom, and she will know it is still in the sky and that she does not wear it on a golden chain around her neck. Play me something on your lute, something very sad, for when the Princess sees the moon, she will be ill again."

The Court Jester strummed on his lute. "What do your wise men say?" he asked.

"They can think of no way to hide the moon that will not make the Princess Lenore ill," said the King.

The Court Jester played another song, very softly. "Your wise men know everything," he said, "and if they cannot hide the moon, then it cannot be hidden."

The King put his head in his hands again and sighed. Suddenly he jumped up from his throne and pointed to the windows. "Look!" he cried. "The moon is already shining into the Princess Lenore's bedroom. Who can explain how the moon can be shining in the sky when it is hanging on a golden chain around her neck?"

The Court Jester stopped playing his lute. "Who could explain how to get the moon when your wise men said it was too large and too far away? It was the Princess Lenore. Therefore the Princess Lenore is wiser than your wise men and knows more about the moon than they do. So I will ask *her.*" And before the King could stop him, the Court Jester slipped quietly out of the throne room and up the wide marble staircase to the Princess Lenore's bedroom.

The Princess was lying in bed, but she was wide awake and she was looking out the window at the moon shining in the sky. Shining in her hand was the moon the Court Jester had got for her. He looked very sad, and there seemed to be tears in his eyes.

"Tell me, Princess Lenore," he said mournfully, "how can the moon be shining in the sky when it is hanging on a golden chain around your neck?"

The Princess looked at him and laughed. "That is easy, silly," she said. "When I lose a tooth, a new one grows in its place, doesn't it?"

"Of course," said the Court Jester. "And when the unicorn loses his horn in the forest, a new one grows in the middle of his forehead."

"That is right," said the Princess. "And when the Royal Gardener cuts the flowers in the garden, other flowers come to take their place."

"I should have thought of that," said the Court Jester, "for it is the same way with the daylight."

"And it is the same way with the moon," said the Princess Lenore. "I guess it is the same way with everything." Her voice became very low and faded away, and the Court Jester saw that she was asleep. Gently he tucked the covers in around the sleeping Princess.

But before he left the room, he went over to the window and winked at the moon, for it seemed to the Court Jester that the moon had winked at him.

JAMES HARVEY ROBINSON

On Various Kinds of Thinking

James Harvey Robinson (1863–1936), one of the most influential historians of his day, insisted that history must be viewed in relation to the political, social, and cultural forces underlying historical events. Among his notable writings are *The Mind in the Making*, 1921; *The Humanizing of Knowledge*, 1923; *The Ordeal of Civilization*, 1926; and *The Human Comedy*, 1937.

"On Various Kinds of Thinking," from *The Mind in the Making*, is a penetrating analysis of the ways of thinking, which aids the reader to view critically his own thought processes.

Good sense is, of all things among men, the most equally distributed; for everyone thinks himself so abundantly provided with it that those even who are the most difficult to satisfy in everything else do not usually desire a larger measure of this quality than they already possess. —DESCARTES

We see man to-day, instead of the frank and courageous recognition of his status, the docile attention to his biological history, the determination to let nothing stand in the way of the security and permanence of his future, which alone can establish the safety and happiness of the race, substituting blind con-

fidence in his destiny, unclouded faith in the essentially respectful attitude of the universe toward his moral code, and a belief no less firm that his traditions and laws and institutions necessarily contain permanent qualities of reality.   —WILLIAM TROTTER

ON VARIOUS KINDS OF THINKING

1. The truest and most profound observations on Intelligence have in the past been made by the poets and, in recent times, by story-writers. They have been keen observers and recorders and reckoned freely with the emotions and sentiments. Most philosophers, on the other hand, have exhibited a grotesque ignorance of man's life and have built up systems that are elaborate and imposing, but quite unrelated to actual human affairs. They have almost consistently neglected the actual process of thought and have set the mind off as something apart to be studied by itself. *But no such mind, exempt from bodily processes, animal impulses, savage traditions, infantile impressions, conventional reactions, and traditional knowledge, ever existed,* even in the case of the most abstract of metaphysicians. Kant entitled his great work *A Critique of Pure Reason.* But to the modern student of mind pure reason seems as mythical as the pure gold, transparent as glass, with which the celestial city is paved.

2. Formerly philosophers thought of mind as having to do exclusively with conscious thought. It was that within man which perceived, remembered, judged, reasoned, understood, believed, willed. But of late it has been shown that we are unaware of a great part of what we perceive, remember, will, and infer; and that a great part of the thinking of which we are aware is determined by that of which we are not conscious. It has indeed been demonstrated that our unconscious psychic life far outruns our conscious. This seems perfectly natural to anyone who considers the following facts:

3. The sharp distinction between the mind and the body is, as we shall find, a very ancient and spontaneous uncritical savage prepossession. What we think of as "mind" is so intimately associated with what we call "body" that we are coming to realize that the one cannot be understood without the other. Every thought reverberates through the body, and, on the other hand, alterations in our physical condition affect our whole attitude of mind. The insufficient elimination of the foul and decaying products of digestion may plunge us into deep melancholy, whereas a few whiffs of nitrous monoxide may exalt us to the seventh heaven of supernal knowledge and godlike complacency. And *vice versa,* a sudden word or thought may cause our heart to jump, check our breathing, or make our knees as water. There is a whole new literature growing up which studies the effects of our bodily secretions and our muscular tensions and their relation to our emotions and our thinking.

4. Then there are hidden impulses and desires and secret longings of which we can only with the greatest difficulty take account. They influence our conscious thought in the most bewildering fashion. Many of these unconscious influences appear to originate in our very early years. The older philosophers seem to have forgotten that even they were infants and children at their most impressionable age and never could by any possibility get over it.

5. The term "unconscious," now so familiar to all readers of modern works on psychology, gives offense to some adherents of the past. There should, however, be no special mystery about it. It is not a new animistic abstraction, but simply a collective word to include all the physiological changes which escape our notice, all the forgotten experiences and impressions of the past which continue to influence our desires and reflections and conduct, even if we cannot remember them. What we can remember at any time is indeed an infinitesimal part of what has happened to us. We could not remember anything unless we forgot almost everything. As Bergson says, the brain is the organ of forgetfulness as well as of memory. Moreover, we tend, of course, to become oblivious to things to which we are thoroughly accustomed, for habit blinds us

to their existence. So the forgotten and the habitual make up a great part of the so-called "unconscious."

6. If we are ever to understand man, his conduct and reasoning, and if we aspire to learn to guide his life and his relations with his fellows more happily than heretofore, we cannot neglect the great discoveries briefly noted above. We must reconcile ourselves to novel and revolutionary conceptions of the mind, for it is clear that the older philosophers, whose works still determine our current views, had a very superficial notion of the subject with which they dealt. But for our purposes, with due regard to what has just been said and to much that has necessarily been left unsaid (and with the indulgence of those who will at first be inclined to dissent), *we shall consider mind chiefly as conscious knowledge and intelligence, as what we know and our attitude toward it—our disposition to increase our information, classify it, criticize it, and apply it.*

7. We do not think enough about thinking, and much of our confusion is the result of current illusions in regard to it. Let us forget for the moment any impressions we may have derived from the philosophers, and see what seems to happen in ourselves. The first thing that we notice is that our thought moves with such incredible rapidity that it is almost impossible to arrest any specimen of it long enough to have a look at it. When we are offered a penny for our thoughts we always find that we have recently had so many things in mind that we can easily make a selection which will not compromise us too nakedly. On inspection we shall find that even if we are not downright ashamed of a great part of our spontaneous thinking it is far too intimate, personal, ignoble or trivial to permit us to reveal more than a small part of it. I believe this must be true of everyone. We do not, of course, know what goes on in other people's heads. They tell us very little and we tell them very little. The spigot of speech, rarely fully opened, could never emit more than driblets of the ever renewed hogshead of thought— *noch grösser wie's Heidelberger Fass.* We find it hard to believe that other people's thoughts are as silly as our own, but they probably are.

8. We all appear to ourselves to be thinking all the time during our waking hours, and most of us are aware that we go on thinking while we are asleep, even more foolishly than when awake. When uninterrupted by some practical issue we are engaged in what is now known as a *reverie.* This is our spontaneous and favorite kind of thinking. We allow our ideas to take their own course and this course is determined by our hopes and fears, our spontaneous desires, their fulfillment or frustration; by our likes and dislikes, our loves and hates and resentments. There is nothing else anything like so interesting to ourselves as ourselves. All thought that is not more or less laboriously controlled and directed will inevitably circle about the beloved Ego. It is amusing and pathetic to observe this tendency in ourselves and in others. We learn politely and generously to overlook this truth, but if we dare to think of it, it blazes forth like the noontide sun.

9. The reverie or "free association of ideas" has of late become the subject of scientific research. While investigators are not yet agreed on the results, or at least on the proper interpretation to be given to them, there can be no doubt that our reveries form the chief index to our fundamental character. They are a reflection of our nature as modified by often hidden and forgotten experiences. We need not go into the matter further here, for it is only necessary to observe that the reverie is at all times a potent and in many cases an omnipotent rival to every other kind of thinking. It doubtless influences all our speculations in its persistent tendency to self-magnification and self-justification, which are its chief preoccupations, but it is the last thing to make directly or indirectly for honest increase of knowledge.[1] Philosophers usu-

---

[1] The poet-clergyman, John Donne, who lived in the time of James I, has given a beautifully honest picture of the doings of a saint's mind: "I throw myself down in my chamber and call in and invite God and His angels thither, and when they are there I neglect

ally talk as if such thinking did not exist or were in some way negligible. This is what makes their speculations so unreal and often worthless.

10. The reverie, as any of us can see for himself, is frequently broken and interrupted by the necessity of a second kind of thinking. We have to make practical decisions. Shall we write a letter or no? Shall we take the subway or a bus? Shall we have dinner at seven or half past? Shall we buy U. S. Rubber or a Liberty bond? Decisions are easily distinguishable from the free flow of the reverie. Sometimes they demand a good deal of careful pondering and the recollection of pertinent facts; often, however, they are made impulsively. They are a more difficult and laborious thing than the reverie, and we resent having to "make up our mind" when we are tired, or absorbed in a congenial reverie. Weighing a decision, it should be noted, does not necessarily add anything to our knowledge, although we may, of course, seek further information before making it.

RATIONALIZING

11. A third kind of thinking is stimulated when anyone questions our belief and opinions. We sometimes find ourselves changing our minds without any resistance or heavy emotion, but if we are told that we are wrong we resent the imputation and harden our hearts. We are incredibly heedless in the formation of our beliefs, but find ourselves filled with an illicit passion for them when anyone proposes to rob us of their companionship. It is obviously not the ideas themselves that are dear to us, but our self-esteem,

God and His angels for the noise of a fly, for the rattling of a coach, for the whining of a door. I talk on in the same posture of praying, eyes lifted up, knees bowed down, as though I prayed to God, and if God or His angels should ask me when I thought last of God in that prayer I cannot tell. Sometimes I find that I had forgot what I was about, but when I began to forget it I cannot tell. A memory of yesterday's pleasures, a fear of to-morrow's dangers, a straw under my knee, a noise in mine ear, a light in mine eye, an anything, a nothing, a fancy, a chimera in my brain troubles me in my prayer."—Quoted by ROBERT LYND, *The Art of Letters*, pp. 46–47.

which is threatened. We are by nature stubbornly pledged to defend our own from attack, whether it be our person, our family, our property, or our opinion. A United States Senator once remarked to a friend of mine that God Almighty could not make him change his mind on our Latin-America policy. We may surrender, but rarely confess ourselves vanquished. In the intellectual world at least peace is without victory.

12. Few of us take the pains to study the origin of our cherished convictions; indeed, we have a natural repugnance to so doing. We like to continue to believe what we have been accustomed to accept as true, and the resentment aroused when doubt is cast upon any of our assumptions leads us to seek every manner of excuse for clinging to them. *The result is that most of our so-called reasoning consists in finding arguments for going on believing as we already do.*

13. I remember years ago attending a public dinner to which the Governor of the state was bidden. The chairman explained that His Excellency could not be present for certain "good" reasons; what the "real" reasons were the presiding officer said he would leave us to conjecture. This distinction between "good" and "real" reasons is one of the most clarifying and essential in the whole realm of thought. We can readily give what seem to us "good" reasons for being a Catholic or a Mason, a Republican or a Democrat, an adherent or opponent of the League of Nations. But the "real" reasons are usually on quite a different plane. Of course the importance of this distinction is popularly, if somewhat obscurely, recognized. The Baptist missionary is ready enough to see that the Buddhist is not such because his doctrines would bear careful inspection, but because he happened to be born in a Buddhist family in Tokio. But it would be treason to his faith to acknowledge that his own partiality for certain doctrines is due to the fact that his mother was a member of the First Baptist church of Oak Ridge. A savage can give all sorts of reasons for his belief that it is dangerous to step on a man's shadow, and a newspaper editor can advance plenty of arguments against the Bolsheviki. But neither

of them may realize why he happens to be defending his particular opinion.

14. The "real" reasons for our beliefs are concealed from ourselves as well as from others. As we grow up we simply adopt the ideas presented to us in regard to such matters as religion, family relations, property, business, our country, and the state. We unconsciously absorb them from our environment. They are persistently whispered in our ear by the group in which we happen to live. Moreover, as Mr. Trotter has pointed out, these judgments, being the product of suggestion and not of reasoning, have the quality of perfect obviousness, so that to question them

> . . . is to the believer to carry skepticism to an insane degree, and will be met by contempt, disapproval, or condemnation, according to the nature of the belief in question. When, therefore, we find ourselves entertaining an opinion about the basis of which there is a quality of feeling which tells us that to inquire into it would be absurd, obviously unnecessary, unprofitable, undesirable, bad form, or wicked, we may know that that opinion is a nonrational one, and probably, therefore, founded upon inadequate evidence.[2]

15. Opinions, on the other hand, which are the result of experience or of honest reasoning do not have this quality of "primary certitude." I remember when as a youth I heard a group of business men discussing the question of the immortality of the soul, I was outraged by the sentiment of doubt expressed by one of the party. As I look back now I see that I had at the time no interest in the matter, and certainly no least argument to urge in favor of the belief in which I had been reared. But neither my personal indifference to the issue, nor the fact that I had previously given it no attention, served to prevent an angry resentment when I heard *my* ideas questioned.

16. This spontaneous and loyal support of our preconceptions—this process of finding "good" reasons to justify our routine beliefs—is known to modern psychologists as "rationalizing"—clearly only a new name for a very ancient thing. Our "good" reasons ordinarily have no value in promoting honest enlightenment, because, no matter how solemnly they may be marshaled, they are at bottom the result of personal preference or prejudice, and not of an honest desire to seek or accept new knowledge.

17. In our reveries we are frequently engaged in self-justification, for we cannot bear to think ourselves wrong, and yet have constant illustrations of our weaknesses and mistakes. So we spend much time finding fault with circumstances and the conduct of others, and shifting on to them with great ingenuity the onus of our own failures and disappointments. *Rationalizing is the self-exculpation which occurs when we feel ourselves, or our group, accused of misapprehension or error.*

18. The little word *my* is the most important one in all human affairs, and properly to reckon with it is the beginning of wisdom. It has the same force whether it is *my* dinner, *my* dog, and *my* house, or *my* faith, *my* country, and *my* God. We not only resent the imputation that our watch is wrong, or our car shabby, but that our conception of the canals of Mars, of the pronunciation of "Epictetus," of the medicinal value of salicine, or the date of Sargon I, are subject to revision.

19. Philosophers, scholars, and men of science exhibit a common sensitiveness in all decisions in which their *amour propre* is involved. Thousands of argumentative works have been written to vent a grudge. However stately their reasoning, it may be nothing but rationalizing, stimulated by the most commonplace of all motives. A history of philosophy and theology could be written in terms of grouches, wounded pride, and aversions, and it would be far more instructive than the usual treatments of these themes. Sometimes, under Providence, the lowly impulse of resentment leads to great achievements. Milton wrote his treatise on divorce as a result of his troubles with his seventeen-year-old wife, and when he was accused of being the leading spirit in a new sect, the Divorcers, he wrote his noble *Areopagitica* to prove his right to say what he thought fit, and incidentally to

[2] *Instincts of the Herd*, p. 44.

establish the advantage of a free press in the promotion of Truth.

20. All mankind, high and low, thinks in all the ways which have been described. The reverie goes on all the time not only in the mind of the mill hand and the Broadway flapper, but equally in weighty judges and godly bishops. It has gone on in all the philosophers, scientists, poets, and theologians that have ever lived. Aristotle's most abstruse speculations were doubtless tempered by highly irrelevant reflections. He is reported to have had very thin legs and small eyes, for which he doubtless had to find excuses, and he was wont to indulge in very conspicuous dress and rings and was accustomed to arrange his hair carefully.[3] Diogenes the Cynic exhibited the impudence of a touchy soul. His tub was his distinction. Tennyson in beginning his "Maud" could not forget his chagrin over losing his patrimony years before as the result of an unhappy investment in the Patent Decorative Carving Company. These facts are not recalled here as a gratuitous disparagement of the truly great, but to insure a full realization of the tremendous competition which all really exacting thought has to face, even in the minds of the most highly endowed mortals.

21. And now the astonishing and perturbing suspicion emerges that perhaps almost all that had passed for social science, political economy, politics, and ethics in the past may be brushed aside by future generations as mainly rationalizing. John Dewey has already reached this conclusion in regard to philosophy.[4] Veblen [5] and other writers have revealed the various unperceived presuppositions of the traditional political economy, and now comes an Italian sociologist, Vilfredo Pareto, who, in his huge treatise on general sociology, devotes hundreds of pages to substantiating a similar thesis affecting all the social sciences.[6] This

conclusion may be ranked by students of a hundred years hence as one of the several great discoveries of our age. It is by no means fully worked out, and it is so opposed to nature that it will be very slowly accepted by the great mass of those who consider themselves thoughtful. As a historical student I am personally fully reconciled to this newer view. Indeed, it seems to me inevitable that just as the various sciences of nature were, before the opening of the seventeenth century, largely masses of rationalizations to suit the religious sentiments of the period, so the social sciences have continued even to our own day to be rationalizations of uncritically accepted beliefs and customs.

22. *It will become apparent as we proceed that the fact that an idea is ancient and that it has been widely received is no argument in its favor, but should immediately suggest the necessity of carefully testing it as a probable instance of rationalization.*

HOW CREATIVE THOUGHT TRANSFORMS THE WORLD

23. This brings us to another kind of thought which can fairly easily be distinguished from the three kinds described above. It has not the usual qualities of the reverie, for it does not hover about our personal complacencies and humiliations. It is not made up of the homely decisions forced upon us by everyday needs, when we review our little stock of existing information, consult our conventional preferences and obligations, and make a choice of action. It is not the defense of our own cherished beliefs and prejudices just because they are our own—mere plausible excuses for remaining of the same mind. On the contrary, it is that peculiar species of thought which leads us to *change* our mind.

24. It is this kind of thought that has raised man from his pristine, subsavage ignorance and squalor to the degree of knowledge and comfort which he now possesses. On his capacity to continue and greatly extend this

[3] Diogenes Laërtius, book v.
[4] *Reconstruction in Philosophy.*
[5] *The Place of Science in Modern Civilization.*
[6] *Traité de Sociologie Générale, passim.* The author's term *"derivations"* seems to be his precise way of expressing what we have called the "good" reasons, and his *"residus"* correspond to the "real" reasons. He well says, *"L'homme éprouve le besoin de raison-*

ner, et en outre d'étendre un voile sur ses instincts et sur ses sentiments"—hence, rationalization. (P. 788.) His aim is to reduce sociology to the "real" reasons. (P. 791.)

kind of thinking depends his chance of groping his way out of the plight in which the
most highly civilized peoples of the world now
find themselves. In the past this type of thinking has been called Reason. But so many misapprehensions have grown up around the
word that some of us have become very suspicious of it. I suggest, therefore, that we
substitute a recent name and speak of "creative
thought" rather than of Reason. *For this kind
of meditation begets knowledge, and knowledge is really creative inasmuch as it makes
things look different from what they seemed
before and may indeed work for their reconstruction.*

25. In certain moods some of us realize that
we are observing things or making reflections
with a seeming disregard of our personal preoccupations. We are not preening or defending ourselves; we are not faced by the necessity of any practical decision, nor are we
apologizing for believing this or that. We are
just wondering and looking and mayhap seeing
what we never perceived before.

26. Curiosity is as clear and definite as any
of our urges. We wonder what is in a sealed
telegram or in a letter in which some one else
is absorbed, or what is being said in the
telephone booth or in low conversation. This
inquisitiveness is vastly stimulated by jealousy, suspicion, or any hint that we ourselves
are directly or indirectly involved. But there
appears to be a fair amount of personal interest in other people's affairs even when they
do not concern us except as a mystery to be
unraveled or a tale to be told. The reports of
a divorce suit will have "news value" for many
weeks. They constitute a story, like a novel
or play or moving picture. This is not an example of pure curiosity, however, since we
readily identify ourselves with others, and
their joys and despair then become our own.

27. We also take note of, or "observe," as
Sherlock Holmes says, things which have
nothing to do with our personal interests and
make no personal appeal either direct or by
way of sympathy. This is what Veblen so well
calls "idle curiosity." And it is usually idle
enough. Some of us when we face the line of
people opposite us in a subway train im-

pulsively consider them in detail and engage
in rapid inferences and form theories in regard to them. On entering a room there are
those who will perceive at a glance the degree of preciousness of the rugs, the character
of the pictures, and the personality revealed
by the books. But there are many, it would
seem, who are so absorbed in their personal
reverie or in some definite purpose that they
have no bright-eyed energy for idle curiosity.
The tendency to miscellaneous observation we
come by honestly enough, for we note it in
many of our animal relatives.

28. Veblen, however, uses the term "idle
curiosity" somewhat ironically, as is his wont.
It is idle only to those who fail to realize that
it may be a very rare and indispensable thing
from which almost all distinguished human
achievement proceeds. For it may lead to
systematic examination and seeking for things
hitherto undiscovered. For research is but
diligent search which enjoys the high flavor
of primitive hunting. Occasionally and fitfully
idle curiosity thus leads to creative thought,
which alters and broadens our own views and
aspirations and may in turn, under highly
favorable circumstances, affect the views and
lives of others, even for generations to follow.
An example or two will make this unique
human process clear.

29. Galileo was a thoughtful youth and
doubtless carried on a rich and varied reverie.
He had artistic ability and might have turned
out to be a musician or painter. When he had
dwelt among the monks at Valambrosa he had
been tempted to lead the life of a religious.
As a boy he busied himself with toy machines
and he inherited a fondness for mathematics.
All these facts are of record. We may safely
assume also that, along with many other subjects of contemplation, the Pisan maidens
found a vivid place in his thoughts.

30. One day when seventeen years old he
wandered into the cathedral of his native
town. In the midst of his reverie he looked up
at the lamps hanging by long chains from
the high ceiling of the church. Then something very difficult to explain occurred. He
found himself no longer thinking of the building, worshipers, or the services; of his artistic

or religious interests; of his reluctance to become a physician as his father wished. He forgot the question of a career and even the *graziosissime donne*. As he watched the swinging lamps he was suddenly wondering if mayhap their oscillations, whether long or short, did not occupy the same time. Then he tested this hypothesis by counting his pulse, for that was the only timepiece he had with him.

31. This observation, however remarkable in itself, was not enough to produce a really creative thought. Others may have noticed the same thing and yet nothing came of it. Most of our observations have no assignable results. Galileo may have seen that the warts on a peasant's face formed a perfect isosceles triangle, or he may have noticed with boyish glee that just as the officiating priest was uttering the solemn words, *ecce agnus Dei*, a fly lit on the end of his nose. To be really creative, ideas have to be worked up and then "put over," so that they become a part of man's social heritage. The highly accurate pendulum clock was one of the later results of Galileo's discovery. He himself was led to reconsider and successfully to refute the old notions of falling bodies. It remained for Newton to prove that the moon was falling, and presumably all the heavenly bodies. This quite upset all the consecrated views of the heavens as managed by angelic engineers. The universality of the laws of gravitation stimulated the attempt to seek other and equally important natural laws and cast grave doubts on the miracles in which mankind had hitherto believed. In short, those who dared to include in their thought the discoveries of Galileo and his successors found themselves in a new earth surrounded by new heavens.

32. On the 28th of October, 1831, two hundred and fifty years after Galileo had noticed the isochronous vibrations of the lamps, creative thought and its currency had so far increased that Faraday was wondering what would happen if he mounted a disk of copper between the poles of a horseshoe magnet. As the disk revolved an electric current was produced. This would doubtless have seemed the idlest kind of an experiment to the stanch business men of the time, who, it happened, were just then denouncing the child-labor bills in their anxiety to avail themselves to the full of the results of earlier idle curiosity. But should the dynamos and motors which have come into being as the outcome of Faraday's experiment be stopped this evening, the business man of to-day, agitated over labor troubles, might, as he trudged home past lines of "dead" cars, through dark streets to an unlighted house, engage in a little creative thought of his own and perceive that he and his laborers would have no modern factories and mines to quarrel about had it not been for the strange practical effects of the idle curiosity of scientists, inventors, and engineers.

33. The examples of creative intelligence given above belong to the realm of modern scientific achievement, which furnishes the most striking instances of the effects of scrupulous, objective thinking. But there are, of course, other great realms in which the recording and embodiment of acute observation and insight have wrought themselves into the higher life of man. The great poets and dramatists and our modern story-tellers have found themselves engaged in productive reveries, noting and artistically presenting their discoveries for the delight and instruction of those who have the ability to appreciate them.

34. The process by which a fresh and original poem or drama comes into being is doubtless analogous to that which originates and elaborates so-called scientific discoveries; but there is clearly a temperamental difference. The genesis and advance of painting, sculpture, and music offer still other problems. We really as yet know shockingly little about these matters, and indeed very few people have the least curiosity about them.[7] Nevertheless, creative intelligence in its various forms and ac-

---

[7] Recently a re-examination of creative thought has begun as a result of new knowledge which discredits many of the notions formerly held about "reason." See, for example, *Creative Intelligence*, by a group of American philosophic thinkers; John Dewey, *Essays in Experimental Logic* (both pretty hard books); and Veblen, *The Place of Science in Modern Civilization*. Easier than these and very stimulating are Dewey, *Reconstruction in Philosophy*, and Woodworth, *Dynamic Psychology*.

tivities is what makes man. Were it not for its slow, painful, and constantly discouraged operations through the ages man would be no more than a species of primate living on seeds, fruit, roots, and uncooked flesh, and wandering naked through the woods and over the plains like a chimpanzee.

35. The origin and progress and future promotion of civilization are ill understood and misconceived. These should be made the chief theme of education, but much hard work is necessary before we can reconstruct our ideas of man and his capacities and free ourselves from innumerable persistent misapprehensions. There have been obstructionists in all times, not merely the lethargic masses, but the moralists, the rationalizing theologians, and most of the philosophers, all busily if unconsciously engaged in ratifying existing ignorance and mistakes and discouraging creative thought. Naturally, those who reassure us seem worthy of honor and respect. Equally naturally those who puzzle us with disturbing criticisms and invite us to change our ways are objects of suspicion and readily discredited. Our personal discontent does not ordinarily extend to any critical questioning of the general situation in which we find ourselves. In every age the prevailing conditions of civilization have appeared quite natural and inevitable to those who grew up in them. The cow asks no questions as to how it happens to have a dry stall and a supply of hay. The kitten laps its warm milk from a china saucer, without knowing anything about porcelain; the dog nestles in the corner of a divan with no sense of obligation to the inventors of upholstery and the manufacturers of down pillows. So we humans accept our breakfasts, our trains and telephones and orchestras and movies, our national Constitution, our moral code and standards of manners, with the simplicity and innocence of a pet rabbit. We have absolutely inexhaustible capacities for appropriating what others do for us with no thought of a "thank you." We do not feel called upon to make any least contribution to the merry game ourselves. Indeed, we are usually quite unaware that a game is being played at all.

36. We have now examined the various classes of thinking which we can readily observe in ourselves and which we have plenty of reasons to believe go on, and always have been going on, in our fellow-men. We can sometimes get quite pure and sparkling examples of all four kinds, but commonly they are so confused and intermingled in our reverie as not to be readily distinguishable. The reverie is a reflection of our longings, exultations, and complacencies, our fears, suspicions, and disappointments. We are chiefly engaged in struggling to maintain our self-respect and in asserting that supremacy which we all crave and which seems to us our natural prerogative. It is not strange, but rather quite inevitable, that our beliefs about what is true and false, good and bad, right and wrong, should be mixed up with the reverie and be influenced by the same considerations which determine its character and course. We resent criticisms of our views exactly as we do of anything else connected with ourselves. Our notions of life and its ideals seem to us to be *our own* and as such necessarily true and right, to be defended at all costs.

37. *We very rarely consider, however, the process by which we gained our convictions.* If we did so, we could hardly fail to see that there was usually little ground for our confidence in them. Here and there, in this department of knowledge or that, some one of us might make a fair claim to have taken some trouble to get correct ideas of, let us say, the situation in Russia, the sources of our food supply, the origin of the Constitution, the revision of the tariff, the policy of the Holy Roman Apostolic Church, modern business organization, trade unions, birth control, socialism, the League of Nations, the excess-profits tax, preparedness, advertising in its social bearings; but only a very exceptional person would be entitled to opinions on all of even these few matters. And yet most of us have opinions on all these, and on many other questions of equal importance, of which we may know even less. We feel compelled, as self-respecting persons, to take sides when they come up for discussion. We even sur-

prise ourselves by our omniscience. Without taking thought we see in a flash that it is most righteous and expedient to discourage birth control by legislative enactment, or that one who decries intervention in Mexico is clearly wrong, or that big advertising is essential to big business and that big business is the pride of the land. As godlike beings why should we not rejoice in our omniscience?

38. It is clear, in any case, that our convictions on important matters are not the result of knowledge or critical thought, nor, it may be added, are they often dictated by supposed self-interest. Most of them are *pure prejudices* in the proper sense of that word. We do not form them ourselves. They are the whisperings of "the voice of the herd." We have in the last analysis no responsibility for them and need assume none. They are not really our own ideas, but those of others no more well informed or inspired than ourselves, who have got them in the same careless and humiliating manner as we. It should be our pride to revise our ideas and not to adhere to what passes for respectable opinion, for such opinion can frequently be shown to be not respectable at all. We should, in view of the considerations that have been mentioned, resent our supine credulity. As an English writer has remarked:

"If we feared the entertaining of an un-verifiable opinion with the warmth with which we fear using the wrong implement at the dinner table, if the thought of holding a prejudice disgusted us as does a foul disease, then the dangers of man's suggestibility would be turned into advantages." [8]

39. The purpose of this essay is to set forth briefly the way in which the notions of the herd have been accumulated. This seems to me the best, easiest, and least invidious educational device for cultivating a proper distrust for the older notions on which we still continue to rely.

40. The "real" reasons, which explain how it is we happen to hold a particular belief, are chiefly historical. Our most important opin-

[8] Trotter, *op. cit.*, p. 45. The first part of this little volume is excellent.

ions—those, for example, having to do with traditional, religious, and moral convictions, property rights, patriotism, national honor, the state, and indeed all the assumed foundations of society—are, as I have already suggested, rarely the result of reasoned consideration, but of unthinking absorption from the social environment in which we live. Consequently, they have about them a quality of "elemental certitude," and we especially resent doubt or criticism cast upon them. So long, however, as we revere the whisperings of the herd, we are obviously unable to examine them dispassionately and to consider to what extent they are suited to the novel conditions and social exigencies in which we find ourselves to-day.

41. The "real" reasons for our beliefs, by making clear their origins and history, can do much to dissipate this emotional blockade and rid us of our prejudices and preconceptions. Once this is done and we come critically to examine our traditional beliefs, we may well find some of them sustained by experience and honest reasoning, while others must be revised to meet new conditions and our more extended knowledge. But only after we have undertaken such a critical examination in the light of experience and modern knowledge, freed from any feeling of "primary certitude," can we claim that the "good" are also the "real" reasons for our opinions.

42. I do not flatter myself that this general show-up of man's thought through the ages will cure myself or others of carelessness in adopting ideas, or of unseemly heat in defending them just because we have adopted them. But if the considerations which I propose to recall are really incorporated into our thinking and are permitted to establish our general outlook on human affairs, they will do much to relieve the imaginary obligation we feel in regard to traditional sentiments and ideals. Few of us are capable of engaging in creative thought, but some of us can at least come to distinguish it from other and inferior kinds of thought and accord to it the esteem that it merits as the greatest treasure of the past and the only hope of the future.

HAROLD TAYLOR

The Private World of the Man with a Book

Harold Taylor (1914–   ), writer, teacher, and college president, began his career in 1939 at the University of Wisconsin. In 1945 he accepted the presidency of Sarah Lawrence College and became the nation's youngest college president. Mr. Taylor's ideas about college presidents, the education of women, communism, and the role of education in a democracy are set forth in his collection of essays *On Education and Freedom*, 1954.

Mr. Taylor's essay, a plea for the restoration of a personal involvement in both reading and education, becomes more meaningful when one is aware that Mr. Taylor practices what he preaches—he resigned the presidency of Sarah Lawrence College in 1959 to return to teaching and writing.

1. The temptation of the educator is to explain and describe, to organize a body of knowledge for the student, leaving the student with nothing to do. I have never been able to understand why educators do this so often, especially where books are concerned. Much of the time they force their students to read the wrong books at the wrong time, and insist that they read them in the wrong way. That is, they lecture to the students about what is in the books, reduce the content to a series of points that can be remembered, and, if there are discussions, arrange them to deal with the points.

2. Schools and colleges thus empty books of their true meaning, and addict their students to habits of thought that often last for the rest of their lives. Everything must be reduced to a summary, ideas are topic sentences, to read is to prepare for a distant test. This is why so many people do not know how

THE PRIVATE WORLD OF THE MAN WITH A BOOK From the *Saturday Review*, January 7, 1961. Reprinted by permission of the *Saturday Review* and the author.

to read. They have been taught to turn books into abstractions.

3. This goes against everything we know about what it means to read a book in real life, life, that is to say, which is uncorrupted by educational purpose. There is only one way to read a book, to give yourself up to it, alone, without instruction as to what you should be finding in it, without the necessity of making it into a series of points, but enjoying it, coming to know in personal terms what is in the mind of the writer. Only after that should there be discussion, criticism, comment by the educators. Otherwise education becomes too much like another kind of real life, the kind in which nobody reads the book, everyone reads the reviews, and everyone talks as if he knew the book.

4. The difficulty is that something happens to educators, and to other people, when they think or talk about education. They draw themselves to their full height and make large statements. They seem not to think that what applies to human experience in general may also apply to experience in schools and col-

leges. They assume that there is something peculiar about education which demands that unless a book is read out of a sense of duty, as a piece of "material" to be "covered," in order for the reader to become "educated," it is not serving the cause of education.

5. Yet most of the most important experiences that truly educate cannot be arranged ahead of time with any precision. All the educator can do is to surround the student with a rich variety of intellectual and personal experience chosen with a view to quickening his mind and emotions into action. The ends are achieved by indirect means—something said in private conversation one day in the street, a remark by a teacher in the middle of a discussion, a book picked up in someone's room. When George Saintsbury was once asked how to interest the young in good literature, he replied, "Leave books around."

6. I grew up in a city that was culturally sterile, in a college whose curriculum lacked intellectual vitality. There were no little magazines, no experimental theatres, no dance groups, no philosophical movements, no strong views held, no centers of new effort. Those of us who were happy to know about Auden, Spender, MacNeice, Isherwood, Malraux, Faulkner, Hemingway, Melville, James, Dostoevsky, Tolstoy, Dewey, or Marx were quite rare, and we pursued our illicit reading without benefit of curriculum or librarians.

7. We read and talked in our rooms, in the newspaper office, in drugstores, and found the writers who meant most to us in little bookstores and reading rooms, where one person speaks of a book to another, where the books have been left around. In this way we learned what it was like to become so involved with an idea that sleep was impossible, or, to put it more broadly, to possess an intellectual life of our own. We did the educational things required of us, because that was what the educators wanted. We did them well, won prizes for them. But our real lives were elsewhere.

8. From that day to this I have never been able to understand why educators do not seize upon this truth and make it the center of their educational plans, make one life of the double

lives which students lead. The heart of education, where books are concerned, is to get the student alone with a book, in a right state of mind.

9. Students are made to read more than they can ever enjoy, too little of too many things, in a way calculated to destroy personal involvement with the writer. The brighter the student, the more he is asked to read, until he develops prodigious skill in reading quickly and cleverly, for purposes of taking examinations and talking in discussions. Students are always reading to deadlines, in order to return books to the library, in order to answer questions and prove only that they have covered the ground. The educational system thus becomes a barrier to the creation by the student of a body of knowledge of his own.

10. True learning is not a matter of the formal organization of knowledge of books. It is a series of personal experiences. The written word makes public a state of mind; it transfers from private to public expression a set of ideas and facts that might otherwise remain unknown. For the writer, it is more than communication. It is the revelation, to oneself as writer, of things that have been hidden, now forced into expression.

11. On the other side, the side of the reader, it is the revelation of one person to another, a personal communication in an impersonal world. The reader in his true role is a private person, learning what another private person has to tell him. He may be seated in a library with a thousand others, but his way of knowing is by taking to himself the writer whose book he is reading. The teacher exists to get his students ready to read for and by themselves.

12. I would mark down as one of the physical barriers to the free flow of knowledge in the university and the American community, the absence of a sufficient number of intimate little bookshops and reading rooms where the librarian or the owner who loves books and knows what is in them has assembled a spread of inviting titles to capture the affection and involvement of the reader who comes as a welcome guest.

13. We will not have the atmosphere for

learning or the true content of learning until we have teachers who themselves haunt the bookshops and who think of librarians as friends and companions in the pursuit of ideas rather than as clerks and custodians of book collections. Nor will we have the atmosphere for learning in our colleges and in our libraries unless we have librarians who work directly with teachers and students because they want to, and because they too are involved in the intellectual life of their own time.

14. My plea is for the restoration of the personal element in modern life and in modern education at a time when everything is pushing us into collective states of mind, when intellectuals huddle together in committees that issue reports in anonymous prose, when so many people are willing to strip themselves of their personal qualities in order to become clusters of approved characteristics.

15. It is a time when everybody talks and nobody listens. Instead, people exchange statements which each thinks will raise himself in the estimate of the other. Had we in the United States in recent months been listening to intelligent private persons in Cuba, Japan, Korea, Turkey, and elsewhere in Asian countries, we would have known that their best thinking and their deepest motivations were not of a kind that could respond to the policies which our government had designed for them and so innocently applied.

16. Most communications to the world by governments are calculated efforts at raising the level of impersonality and at concealment of the reality with which they are concerned. This habit of concealment in public speech has crept into private discourse and is seen, for example, in the loss of the old-fashioned habit of writing personal letters which are so honestly personal that they are not intended for eventual publication.

17. At another level, it has meant no longer asking our students for private essays each week which can give their teachers an understanding of who the student is and what are his honest thoughts, what are his weaknesses and inadequacies, what are his strengths, his needs, his hopes. Instead we seek for ways in which he can provide answers to questions he would never dream of asking, answers that merely reflect the demands we make upon him for information on topics of our choosing.

18. In the United States we justify our impersonality and lack of sensitivity to students by referring to the growing size of the student body, the excess of numbers of students who thus cannot be dealt with in personal ways, and we turn to technology for more devices to do the teaching for us. This is surely sensible where mechanical tasks, like keeping records, can be done mechanically, where films and television can bring the immediacy of the outside world into the school and college, or in cases where information is to be conveyed quickly and effectively.

19. But as far as the deeper aims of education are concerned, the problem is not how to distribute more information to larger numbers of students. That, as we have seen, is fairly easy to solve. You put more students into the same classes and pump the material in.

20. The question is: What intellectual, personal, and moral qualities are we developing in our students? What are they learning to care about? What are they doing with their lives?

21. It is as if we were deliberately turning back from the real problems, and keeping ourselves busy while we hope they will go away. We are asking not to know our students by what they say in writing or in speech, but to know whether or not they possess correct information as revealed in mechanical tests that can be graded like eggs, by nonhuman means.

22. What has happened is that many of the concepts of an American public-relations culture and the mass media have been transferred from the realm of business and industry into education, and the university has been organized not as a place where student talent is nurtured but as a bureaucracy for the dissemination of information. It has its own organization man, its own managerial class, its own habits of the market place by which the man with the largest amount of published academic prose commands the highest salary and receives the ultimate reward of the university

—not to have to teach. With the combination of speeded-up sabbaticals, foundation grants, and continuous leaves of absence, the criterion of highest prestige for the university scholar will soon be that he is excused even from residence at the university and will be paid simply for the privilege of listing his name in the faculty roster. In the meantime, there are students.

23. We must teach these students and citizens the necessity of withdrawal into their own thoughts as a preparation for independent thinking and independent action. They must learn to feel their own emotions, not those that are considered culturally appropriate by the educational authorities or politically correct by their government. This is why the question of what books should be in the curriculum is one that should be decided, not by committees, but by teachers who themselves can enter into the experience of the young and feel with them the impulses of their own time, by teachers who know the responses the young are making to their own society.

24. Each generation has its own truth, its own private world, its own way of knowing, and we who are educators would be wise to listen to them for the knowledge they can bring. The young have the supreme advantage of not having been here before; they are not yet settled, they have almost no history and they can consider the world freshly (that is, they can and do when they talk to each other), and they test and retest the ideas that are old and known and reputable. They reject some, they revive and re-create others.

25. The comradeship of the young both sustains them in their own image of themselves and gives them the emotional sustenance they need for the independence of their lives. They live apart from us, they hold themselves back, and from the untouchable center of their personal lives they look distantly at our existence and our knowledge as items possessed by beings on a different planet. They are not what they seem to the professor who merely looks at the faces before him. He cannot be certain even of their attention, since they have learned how to occupy a classroom and look attentive while they take their minds elsewhere. He cannot be sure of their respect, since they have learned how to be quiet and how to act respectfully. The silence of the present generation has been in many ways deceptive, and it is false to assume that the silence has meant either consent or lack of creative and critical thought. They have played the system but have not been convinced of its claim to be believed in.

26. They are not to be presented with the familiar lists of the Great Books with an air of authority vested in the educators and the curriculum-makers. The students must be asked to determine for themselves which books are great, which ideas are viable, which values are compelling. To do otherwise is to use the familiar brand-name approach as a form of intellectual propaganda, like saluting the flag or bowing to royalty. It is to take the young through an educational tour of the museums of literature, to inspire a dutiful and pious attitude to authors rather than an attitude of expectancy and involvement.

27. If our aim is to create a vivid sense of awareness of the joy in learning and the satisfaction of intellectual mastery, we must trust the student to come away from his experience with the authors we ask him to read with ideas and convictions of his own. From the point of view of the student, every idea is inert until it comes alive in his consciousness. But first he must learn to read in personal terms, to invest himself in the reading, to bring something of his own to the book. If the books in his education are ill-chosen, or chosen chiefly on the basis of scholarly correctness, the student can bring almost nothing of himself to the enterprise, because what the author is saying corresponds to nothing in his lived experience. In order to learn how to expand that experience in imagination, to make links to the past and to cultures alien to his own, he must first learn how to come close to books and ideas themselves, he must have an experience with the immediacy of ideas. This involves a different way of choosing books for his education, and usually a sequence different from conventional chronology or historical periods.

28. If he reads, for example, in order to be able to tell an eighteenth-century rationalist from a nineteenth-century romantic, he may very well not be able to tell more than this, nor be able to enter into the experience of the writer whose work he is studying. Or he may simply be able to say to himself that he has read the best representatives of all the great periods in cultural history.

29. Whenever we take a writer out of his natural element, that is, treat him as other than a human being who is writing what he knows, we run the risk of destroying his value to the reader by making him represent a category of thought to which he has been assigned after the fact, usually after his death. In graduate schools, this unnatural treatment of writers leads to the continual preoccupation with tracing influences, classifying authors into categories, and otherwise drawing attention away from the writer himself. The writer must be allowed to stand on his own feet. Indeed, his greatness is established by the fact that he continues to stand on his own feet from generation to generation, and that

he is perpetually rediscovered for himself and for what he has to say.

30. The student who is being educated is in fact discovering his own self and learning how to relate it to other selves. At its best, education is a series of private conversations in which all sham, pretense, and intellectual hypocrisy or name-dropping is stripped away and the student is free to respond with honesty to the intellectual and personal situation in which he finds himself. This is why it is so important to keep the student's situation as free of educational formalities as possible, to insist upon some version of the tutorial system, to resist all efforts to build an impersonal administrative machine in place of a fascinating intellectual community, to assure that the student and the teacher are known to each other and that the student may thus benefit by the fact that his individuality is known, recognized, and respected.

31. For it is finally in the individual response of one person to another—whether through books or in person—that the heart of the matter rests.

LANCELOT LAW WHYTE

Where Do Those Bright Ideas Come From?

Lancelot Law Whyte (1896–   ), a British physicist and jet-propulsion engineer who is also a social scientist and philosopher, is deeply concerned with the need for a continuing flow of new ideas. He has published in his professional field and on other subjects of special interest—*Archimedes, or the Future of Physics,* 1927; *Everyman Looks Forward,* 1948; *The Next Development in Man,* 1948; *The Unitary Principle in Physics and Biology,* 1949; *Aspects of Form,* 1951; *Accent on Form,* 1954; *The Atomic Problem: A Challenge to Physicists and Mathematicians,* 1961; and other books.

In answering the question about the origin of creative thought, Mr. Whyte makes suggestions about the conditions which may stimulate the unconscious process. To some degree the ideas in this essay extend the discussion of the element of "reverie" in James Harvey Robinson's essay "On Various Kinds of Thinking."

> . . . as imagination bodies forth
> The forms of things unknown, . . .
> —*A Midsummer Night's Dream*

1. There are few experiences quite so satisfactory as getting a good idea. You've had a problem, you've thought about it till you were tired, forgotten it and perhaps slept on it, and then flash! when you weren't thinking about it suddenly the answer has come to you, as a gift from the gods. You're pleased with it, and feel good. It may not be right, but at least you can try it out.

2. Of course all ideas don't come like that, but the interesting thing is that so many do, particularly the most important ones. They burst into the mind, glowing with the heat of creation. How they do it is a mystery. Psychology does not yet understand even the ordinary processes of conscious thought, but the emergence of new ideas by a "leap in thought," as Dewey put it, is particularly intriguing, because they must have come from somewhere. For the moment let us assume that they come from the "unconscious." This is reasonable, for the psychologists use this term to describe mental processes which are unknown to the subject, and creative thought consists precisely in what was unknown becoming known.

3. We have all experienced this sudden arrival of a happy idea, but it is easiest to examine it in the great creative figures, many of whom experienced it in an intensified form and have put it on record in their memoirs and letters. One can draw examples from genius in any realm, from religious mysticism, philosophy, and literature to art and music, and even in mathematics, science, and technical invention, though these are often thought to rest solely on logic and experiment. It seems that all truly creative activity depends in some degree on these signals from the unconscious, and the more highly intuitive the person, the sharper and more dramatic the signals become.

4. Here, for example, is Richard Wagner conceiving the prelude to "Rhinegold," as told

WHERE DO THOSE BRIGHT IDEAS COME FROM? By Lancelot Law Whyte, from *Harper's Magazine*, July 1951. © 1951 Harper & Brothers, Inc. Reprinted by permission of A. Watkins, Inc.

by Wagner himself and recounted by Newman in his biography. Wagner had been occupied with the general idea of the "Ring" for several years, and for many weary months had been struggling to make a start with the actual composition. On September 4, 1863, he reached Spezia sick with dysentery, crawled to a hotel, could not sleep for noise without and fever within, took a long walk the next day, and in the afternoon flung himself on a couch intending to sleep. And then at last the miracle happened for which his subconscious mind had been crying out for so many months. Falling into a trance-like state, he suddenly felt, he says, as though he were sinking in a mighty flood of water:

> The rush and roar soon took musical shape within my brain as the chord of E-flat major, surging incessantly in broken chords. . . . Yet the pure triad of E-flat major never changed, but seemed by its steady persistence to impart infinite significance to the element in which I was sinking. I awoke from my half-sleep in terror, feeling as though the waves were rushing high above my head. I at once recognized that the orchestral prelude to the "Rhinegold," which for a long time I must have carried about within me, yet had never been able to fix definitely, had at last come to being within me; and I quickly understood the very essence of my own nature: the stream of life was not to flow to me from without, but from within.

5. In this example, which is exceptional only in the violence of the emotions, the conscious mind at the moment of creation knew nothing of the actual processes by which the solution was found. As a contrast we may take a famous story: the discovery by Henri Poincaré, the great French mathematician, of a new mathematical method called the Fuchsian functions. For here we see the conscious mind, in a person of the highest ability, actually watching the unconscious at work, if that paradox may be allowed. Poincaré describes how he came to write his first treatise on these functions.

> For a fortnight I had been attempting to prove that there could not be any function analogous to what I have since called the Fuchsian functions. I was at that time very ignorant. Every

understanding

day I sat down at my table and spent an hour or two trying a great number of combinations, and I arrived at no result. One night I took some black coffee, contrary to my custom, and was unable to sleep. A host of ideas kept surging in my head; I could almost feel them jostling one another, until two of them coalesced, so to speak, to form a stable combination. When morning came, I had established the existence of one class of Fuchsian functions. . . . I had only to verify the results, which took only a few hours.

6. While the Wagner story illustrates the sudden explosion of a new conception into consciousness, in this one we see the conscious mind observing the new combinations being formed in that part of the mind whose operations are normally beyond the range of conscious attention. A third type of creative experience is exemplified by the dreams which came to Descartes at the age of twenty-three and determined the path he was to follow for the rest of his life. Descartes tells how he had vainly searched for certainty, first in the world of books, and then in the world of men, and how in a triple dream on November 10, 1619, he made the crucial discovery that he could only find certainty in his own thoughts, *cogito ergo sum*. This dream filled him with intense religious enthusiasm, because it had brought to him the "simple and fertile idea, all sparkling with angelic luster" (Maritain), which provided the foundation of the "admirable science" which it was his mission to create. Freud classified this dream as one of those whose content is very close to conscious thought.

7. Wagner's, Poincaré's, and Descartes' experiences are representative of countless others in every realm of culture. The unconscious is certainly the source of instinctive activity and therefore sometimes of conflict with the demands of reason, as Freud emphasized. But in creative thought the unconscious is responsible, not for conflict, but for the production of new organized forms from relatively disorganized elements.

8. The processes of creative activity display several striking features. One of the most frequent is the occurrence of flashes of insight outside the hours of regular work, during periods of physical activity or at odd moments of reverie or relaxation when the mind is daydreaming. Poincaré tells how the further steps of his discovery of the Fuchsian functions came to him, with a sense of absolute certainty, "just as I put my foot on the step" (of a wagonette), and again, "as I was crossing the street." Similar examples are endless, and give comforting glimpses of the ordinary daily life of genius. Mozart got the idea for the melody of the "Magic Flute" quintet while playing billiards, Berlioz found himself humming a musical phrase he had long sought in vain as he rose from a dive while bathing in the Tiber, Sir William Hamilton, a great mathematical physicist, thought of quaternions (a new mathematical method) while strolling with his wife in the streets of Dublin, and the chemist Kekulé saw the atoms dancing in mid-air and so conceived his theory of atomic groupings while riding on the top of a London bus.

9. So familiar is this phenomenon that many have taken advantage of it and have developed techniques to woo their shy genius. The prolific Haydn, with 125 symphonies and hundreds of other compositions to his credit, says, "When my work does not advance I retire into the oratory with my rosary, and say an Ave; immediately ideas come to me." Many, like Hamilton, have found that walking encourages the appearance of ideas. Thus Mozart tells how "taking a drive or walking after a good meal, or in the night when I cannot sleep, thoughts crowd into my mind as easily as you could wish"; James Watt saw how the waste of heat in a steam engine could be avoided by condensing steam, in a flash of inspiration on a walk to the golf house; Helmholtz, the German scientist and philosopher, records how "happy ideas . . . come particularly readily during the slow ascent of hills on a sunny day"; and many persons devoted to creative work have carried scraps of paper with them everywhere so that nothing of the precious flashes of revelation shall be lost.

10. "Sleeping on it" also produces good results. Sir Walter Scott used to say to himself,

"Never mind, I shall have it at seven o'clock tomorrow morning." Gauss, one of the greatest mathematicians, put as heading to his paper on the "Law of Induction" the note: "Found 23rd January 1835—7.0 A.M. before rising." And Helmholtz says, "Often they come as soon as one wakes up in the morning."

11. The suddenness with which ideas come is often stressed. "You feel a little electric shock striking you in the head . . . that is the moment of genius"; so Buffon, the French biologist. In the "Hymn to Intellectual Beauty" Shelley writes:

Sudden, thy shadow fell on me:
I shrieked, and clasped my hands in ecstasy.

In Chopin, according to George Sand, who knew him intimately, "creation was spontaneous, miraculous . . . it would come sudden, sublime."

12. Thinkers, artists, and scientists have all described the sense of precision and inevitability, the loss of freedom of choice, or feeling of possession by an impersonal force which accompanies the creative moment. Blake declares, "I have written the poem . . . without premeditation, and even against my will," and Jacob Boehme, the German mystic of the early seventeenth century, says: "Before God I do not know how the thing arises in me, without the participation of my will. I do not even know that which I must write." Van Gogh describes how he had "a terrible lucidity at moments, when nature is so glorious. In those days, I am hardly conscious of myself and the picture comes to me like a dream." Walt Whitman says that the "fruition of beauty is no chance of hit or miss—it is as inevitable as life—it is as exact and plumb as gravitation." Russel Wallace, who published the theory of natural selection simultaneously with Darwin, expresses the views of many thinkers in saying, "Ideas and beliefs are not voluntary acts."

13. Moreover the new ideas come before they can be justified or applied. Thus Bernard Shaw's Joan of Arc says, "The voices come first, and I find the reasons after." This feature is most remarkable in the realm of science and of mathematics. Sir Isaac Newton wrote of a geometrical theorem: "It is plain to me by the fountain I draw it from, though I will not undertake to prove it to others." Like most intuitive mathematicians, he usually got the result before he could prove it; indeed one discovery of his (on the roots of equations) was only proved two hundred years later. Gauss says of one of his mathematical discoveries:

At last I succeeded, not by painful effort, but so to speak by the grace of God. As a sudden flash of truth the enigma was solved. For my part I am not in a position to point to the thread which joins what I knew previously to what I have succeeded in doing.

14. In the field of applied mathematics intuitive guessing sometimes proves superior to ordinary calculation. Edison says:

In all the work connected with the building of the first Central Station, the greatest bugbears I had to contend with were the mathematicians. I found after a while that I could guess a good deal closer than they could figure, so I went on guessing.

A similar example is to be found in the design of complex electric valves, where practical, intuitive knowledge has played a major role, and one of the best living valve engineers is said to use only the multiplication table! The genius of many great experimenters, such as Faraday and Rutherford, lay in an exceptionally powerful intuition resulting from a passionate and sustained interest in a definite field of inquiry.

15. Owing to the heightened interest in psychology many studies of creative thought have been made recently, and the majority of these trace the creative element to the unconscious in the individual mind. This interpretation is supported by the recorded views of many creative personalities. Schiller held that "poetry sets out from the unconscious," and since the middle of the nineteenth century countless others have ascribed their inspiration to the working of the unconscious. But

this must not be interpreted in a one-sided manner, for all thought depends on the co-operation of conscious and unconscious. The supreme type of creative thought, in certain realms at least, appears to depend on an intimate blending of unconscious and conscious processes, when both work in harmony.

16. A few writers, disliking the conception of the unconscious, have held that all true mental work is conscious, that new ideas arise by the chance association of previously formed ideas, and that "inspiration" is a romantic fiction. But this view is scarcely tenable, for an important part of all mental activity takes place behind the scenes. The working of memory and association normally lies outside the field of conscious attention, and it is only their results which flash into our awareness.

17. Graham Wallas, an English sociologist, divided the process of creative thought into four stages: conscious *Preparation,* unconscious *Incubation,* the flash of *Illumination,* and the conscious *Verification* (or application). There is as yet no accepted psychological or physiological theory of the operations of the unconscious which lead to the creation of new patterns during the period of incubation, perhaps because the sharp separation of "physical" and "mental" processes in our dualistic language has delayed the advance of a science of thought. But it seems clear that no mere rearrangement of unchanged elements can account for what happens in the unconscious creative processes. The conscious mind performs such mechanical rearrangements all the time. But the creative imagination does more: it actually changes the character of the separate elements given to it, in course of molding them into a new unity.

18. Hadamard, a French mathematician now in the United States, suggests that mathematical invention is choice guided by the aesthetic sense. That is not wide enough to cover all creation, which sometimes involves not merely choice, but in addition the molding of the elements so that they can combine to form a new whole. The coalescence, or growing together, of elements into a new unit may *change* them. This creative reshaping is evident in all branches of culture. The new unity grows out of the old and is as different from the elements that were used to make it, as the living organism is from the foodstuffs which it absorbs and assimilates. Indeed the creative processes of the mind share many features with the synthetic processes which occur throughout all living organisms.

19. It is therefore natural that the analogy of growth has often been used for creative thought. Keats liked the symbol of plant growth: "Let us open our leaves like a flower and be passive and receptive—budding patiently under the eve of Apollo." Tchaikovsky speaks of the

germ of a future composition [coming] suddenly. . . . If the soil is ready . . . it takes root with extraordinary force and rapidity, shoots up through the earth, puts forth branches, leaves, and finally blossoms. I cannot describe the creative process in any other way than by this simile.

20. But growth requires a seed, and the heart of the creative process lies in the production of the original fertile nucleus from which growth can proceed. This initial step in all creation consists in the establishment of a new unity from disparate elements, of order out of disorder, of shape from what was formless. The mind achieves this by the plastic reshaping, so as to form a new unit, of a selection of the separate elements derived from experience and stored in memory. Intuitions arise from richly unified experience. Henry James spoke of the "deep well of unconscious cerebration," and Coleridge of the "inward creatrix" which "establishes a center, as it were, a sort of nucleus in this reservoir of the soul."

21. Professor Lowes, in *The Road to Xanadu,* a superb study of the ways of the poetic imagination, speaks of the "incredible facility with which in the wonder-working depths of the unconscious the fragments which sink incessantly below the surface fuse and assimilate and coalesce."

22. This process of the establishment of new forms must occur in patterns of nervous

activity in the brain, lying below the threshold of consciousness, which interact and combine to form more comprehensive patterns. Experimental physiology has not yet identified this process, for its methods are as yet insufficiently refined, but it may be significant that a quarter of the total bodily consumption of energy during sleep goes to the brain, even when the sense organs are at rest, to maintain the activity of ten thousand million brain cells. These cells, acting together as a single organ, achieve the miracle of the production of new patterns of thought. No calculating machine can do that, for such machines can "only do what we know how to design them to do," and these formative brain processes obey laws which are still unknown.

23. Can any practical conclusions be drawn from the experience of genius? Is there an art of thought for the ordinary person? Certainly there is no single road to success; in the world of the imagination each has to find his own way to use his own gifts. Yet a study of those who have been successful suggests some elementary hints towards a hygiene of the unconscious mind.

24. A wide range of interests is an advantage, since valuable clues may be drawn from unexpected fields. High specialism may lead to sterility.

25. When a particular task makes no progress, one can go on with something else and return to the first later on. It may pay to keep several jobs running in parallel.

26. Periods of relaxation are important, such as an hour or two alone, when no definite task is undertaken and the time is kept free for pondering over anything that comes into one's mind.

27. Finally, the less haste the better. New ideas come less easily when the mind is strained by anxiety or tense with impatience to achieve a definite result. The new grows at its own pace—"as inevitable as life."

JAMES J. GIBSON

Constancy and Invariance in Perception

James J. Gibson (1904–   ), professor of psychology and chairman of the Department of Psychology at Cornell University since 1949, is a major researcher into the mysteries of perception. He studied problems of depth perception for the Air Force in World War II, and after the war published *The Perception of the Visual World*, 1950. He was a Fulbright Scholar at Oxford University in 1955–56 and a fellow at the Institute for Advanced Study in 1958–59. Recently he was invited as a fellow to the Center for Advanced Study in the Social Sciences at Stanford University.

In this essay, included in *The Nature and Art of Motion*, a volume edited by the noted artist Gyorgy Kepes, Mr. Gibson considers the mysteries of our perceiving and comes to the tentative conclusion that the stimuli that produce changing sensations are not the same as those that produce constant perceptions, out of which one discovers "the finer properties of the world."

1. Why do things look as they do? Why do they appear, on the whole, pretty much as they are? The makers of things-to-be-seen need to understand how we see. So also, for that matter, do the *consumers* of things-to-be-seen—those of us who enjoy looking at artifacts of any sort, particularly at pictures. Perceiving for its own sake—contemplating, registering, detecting, discriminating, and comprehending—is not only a pleasure, it is useful. It can even be thought of as a sort of discipline. Artists have long believed that in making "art" they learn to perceive "nature," and that they can thereby show the rest of us how to see it better. Artists are bound to be psychologists insofar as they are concerned with the psychological question of how a perceiver does what he does. By the same token the perception-psychologist ought to be concerned with art.

2. The psychology of perception, however, is a large field with a long history, a bewildering series of controversies, and a vast amount of evidence on both sides of the issues. It includes the study of the physiology of sensations at one extreme, and the philosophy of knowledge at the other. A bare introduction to the subject is given in a long and difficult book by E. G. Boring entitled *Sensation and Perception in the History of Experimental Psychology.*[1] Any artist who even attempts to read everything important that has been written about it is a bold man. Gombrich has recently done so in his study of the psychology of pictorial representation.[2] Although he found the literature illuminating, he also found it full of contradictions.

3. The central puzzle of perception, I believe, is the problem of what is called constancy. This term is not very familiar outside

of psychology, and I shall try to explain what the term means and why it is considered so important.

4. Constancy is the tendency to perceive an object as the same despite changing sense-impressions. One sees the size of an object fairly well at quite different distances from the eye. One sees the shape of the face of an object correctly even when it is slanted or inclined to the line of sight, i.e., foreshortened. The impression of "extent" changes with distance and the impression of "form" changes with inclination, but the perception, on the whole, does not. Likewise both the perception of surface-color and of white-black do not seem to vary much with the color and intensity of the light entering the eye (which change with varying illumination, or shadows) but depend on a property of the surface —the differential absorbing and reflecting of incident light. These three facts are called size constancy, shape constancy, and color constancy, and a great number of experiments have been carried out in psychological laboratories to discover the conditions under which they occur, to measure the tendencies, and to test the theories which purport to explain them. It is fair to say that these facts are as much a puzzle now as they were half a century ago when they began to be studied.

5. The constancies of size, shape, and color are not the whole of the matter. It is becoming clear that there is a much larger set of constancies in perception, not so easily labelled. All of them involve a discrepancy between the sense impression and the experience of the ordinary naïve observer. Some of these are worth describing, in order to show the scope of the problem.

6. *Constancy of perceived space.* Not only is the size of a single rigid body seen to be the same at different distances and the shape the same from different viewpoints, but also the size and shape of two bodies in different places can be compared. Their dimensions and proportions are visible. Moreover, the apparent distances between bodies, as well as the objects themselves, remain constant. One can match the separation of two things which are far off with two things nearby. Similarly,

[1] E. G. Boring, *Sensation and Perception in the History of Experimental Psychology,* New York, Appleton-Century-Crofts (1942).
[2] E. H. Gombrich, *Art and Illusion: A Study in the Psychology of Pictorial Representation,* New York, Pantheon (1960).

CONSTANCY AND INVARIANCE IN PERCEPTION George Braziller, Inc.—from *The Nature and Art of Motion* edited by Gyorgy Kepes, reprinted with permission of the publisher. © 1965 George Braziller, Inc.

one can say whether the edges of a road running off into the distance (or two stretched strings controlled by an experimenter) are parallel or not. What remains constant in such situations is the scale of things and the intervals between things. It is the ground, not just the bodies resting on the ground, that keeps the same size and shape in experience.

7. One can put these facts in another way by saying that what men are conscious of are the surfaces of their environment, and the *layout* of these surfaces. So far as the evidence goes, this also holds true for children and, on behavioral evidence, for animals. Observers are not ordinarily conscious of the patchwork of colors in the field of view as this is determined by the laws of perspective. Instead they perceive the environing surfaces with their edges, corners, slants, convexities, concavities, and interspaces. These are, of course, the pathways and obstacles, the places and things, the goals and the dangers of the terrestrial world. They are identified by their surface properties, including texture and differential reflectance of light. They have to be seen as constant, where they are, in order to be identified for what they are.

8. Historically, the central problem of perception has been taken to be how we see depth and distance, the so-called third dimension of space. The psychologist and the painter have been led to ask what the clues or cues may be for tridimensional perception as distinguished from bidimensional sensation. It begins to be evident, however, that the heart of the problem is not so much how we see objects in depth as how we see the constant layout of the world around us. Space as such, empty space, is not visible but surfaces are.

9. *The apparent rigidity of the phenomenal world.* Whenever an observer moves from place to place, the pattern of his field of view —that is, the optic array that determines his retinal image [3]—undergoes a perspective transformation. This follows, of course, from the facts of perspective at a stationary point.

[3] J. J. Gibson, "Ecological optics," in *Vision Research* (1:1961), pp. 253–262.

There is a deformation of this array as a whole and in every part. The visual sense-impression, therefore, changes with every change of position. Unless an observer holds his head unnaturally still and fixes his eye, his visual field is alive with transformation. A sensation of "form," then, is an extreme rarity in life; what normally stimulates the eye is a continuous transformation in time. Nevertheless perception is of rigid things, of a rigid ground, and of constant separations between fixed things. The phenomenal world is not distorted during locomotion, although it ought to be if perception is based on sensation.

10. The same perspective transformation of the field that occurs when the head is moved from right to left appears simultaneously in one eye relative to the other when both eyes are open. This disparity of the two fields, the mismatch of pattern, yields a sensation called double imagery. But perception is not doubled and the mismatch can only be noticed if a man attends to his subjective sense-impressions instead of to the world.

11. *Other discrepancies between sensation and perception.* The set of color-patches which make up the visual field continually change in a jerky fashion as the eyes scan the array of ambient light. We move our eyes from one fixation point to another several times a second during waking life. We also blink frequently. The sense impressions, therefore, are highly unstable and interrupted. But an obvious characteristic of perception is its stability and continuity. The world does not seem to move as the retinal image moves over the retina. Here is another sort of constancy.

12. Human visual sensation is clear only in the center of the field corresponding to the central fovea of the eye at each momentary fixation. It is a fleeting impression. But visual perception, being extended over time and depending on the whole array of ambient light, may be clear in all directions. The momentary sensation is bounded by the margins of the cone of light rays that can enter the eye. But visual perception is unbounded. We are aware of a world that surrounds us like a panorama, not a cone of rays. I have described

these contrasts more fully in Chapter 3 of *The Perception of the Visual World.*[4]

13. *Constancy in perception other than visual.* The stability of perception with unstable sensations holds true for all the receptive systems, not only the visual system. Just as the visible world does not seem to rotate 90° when one lies down on his side, although the retinal image does, so the tangible ground and the direction of gravity do not seem to swing upward, although the tactual impression has shifted from one's feet to one's flank and the weights in the sacs of the inner ear now pull sideways to the head. Instead of the ground changing, one feels that *he* has changed and the earth has not.

14. Sensations of touch are often radically different from perceptions of touch. One gets a tactual impression whenever the skin is pushed in, usually by contact with a solid body. But when one touches an object with the fingers he feels the object, not the contacts. When you move your groping fingers over an unfamiliar object with eyes closed you will experience its shape, size, proportions, and rigidity but you will be almost wholly unaware of the sequence of cutaneous impressions. The same single object, a pencil for example, is felt whether you hold it with two, three, four, or five fingers, and this means with two, three, four, or five different sensations at different places on the skin. In short the perception is unitary despite diversity of the impressions. When you press on a surface lightly or heavily you do not feel the changing intensity of the impression; you feel only the unchanging solidity of the object. When you move your hand over the edges and corners of a rigid body, you do not feel the cutaneous motion over the skin; you feel a motionless object with a moving hand. The perception is constant and stable although the sensations are changing and mobile.

15. The channels for stimulus information that we have arbitrarily separated and called "senses" are normally active and exploratory,

not passive and receptive. It begins to be clear, I think, that the passive arousal of sensations, as these have been studied by sensory physiologists, is not typical of the way perception works in life.

16. One more example may be offered, from hearing. The sensory qualities of auditory experience are said to be loudness, pitch, and tonal complexity. A great deal is known about the corresponding variables of physical sound. But the perceptions arising in auditory experience are of outer happenings, inanimate events, cries, and the speech of our fellow men. The perceiving of speech sounds is largely independent of loudness, pitch, and tonal complexity. The proof is that we hear the same speech whether it is whispered or shouted, voiced or sung, produced by male or female vocal organs. The critical speech sounds, the phonemes, depend on properties of sound that are invariant, that is, properties which do not change when the level of intensity or the level of pitch is altered.

17. *Theories of the invariance of perception with varying sensations.* How can the experience of a constant world arise from the ever changing flux of sensory impressions? This is the central puzzle. If the data of sense vary, how can the perception of unvarying places and things be explained? The constancies of size, shape, and color of objects together with all the other sorts of constancy are the principal reason for theories of perception.

18. Theories of perception go back for hundreds of years and have occupied the best efforts of some of the greatest thinkers in history. They cannot be here summarized, but they can be classified roughly. They seem to fall into three types: first, those that appeal to innate ideas or the rational faculties of the mind for making the sensory data intelligible; second, those that appeal to past experience, memory, or learning for supplementing and interpreting the sensory data; and a third, a recent theory which asserts that the sensory chaos is organized by a spontaneous process of self-distribution in the brain.

19. It should be noted that all these theories assume without question that sense im-

[4] J. J. Gibson, *The Perception of the Visual World,* Boston, Houghton Mifflin (1950).

pressions are somehow the cause of perception but not a sufficient cause. They are taken to be the occasion for perception, the basis for it, or the raw material from which perception is constructed. These theories all take for granted the poverty of the senses and seek for a special process in the mind or the brain to supplement them. They assume that the organs of sense are passive, or merely receptive, accepting whatever physical stimulation enters as if they were merely windows. The activity of perception is supposed to be an internal or subjective process. Meaning is supposed to come from inside, not from outside. These assumptions, as will appear later, can be challenged. It might be that no special process is necessary to explain perception, and that in fact perception is not based on sensation. But this is getting ahead of the story.

20. *The theory of innate ideas and faculties.* It is possible to suppose that perceiving, although occasioned by having sensations, is chiefly a matter of intuition. The idea of a constant and fixed Euclidean space, for example, may be simply a part of the inborn capacity of the human mind. The continually changing perspectives of visual sensation are interpreted in terms of this abstract concept as rigid objects. But the mind is informed by its own preconceptions, not by the sense impressions.

21. *The theory of the accumulation of past experience.* By far the most popular theory of perception is that of empiricism, as contrasted with nativism. Concepts and general ideas are taken to be learned, not inborn. They are the residue of all the fleeting perspectives of the past. We have learned that objects are constant in shape and size and color and therefore we unwittingly interpret our sensations in accordance with what we have learned about objects. According to Helmholtz, the process is one of "unconscious inference," the sense data serving only as clues to the real nature of the objects.

22. This explanation, or one of its many variants, is so widely accepted that many people have never heard of any other. It has the virtue of emphasizing training or learning

instead of the mysterious faculties of the mind. It allows for the possibility of the improvement of our perceptual abilities with the accumulation of memories. But as an explanation it is weak and it was destructively criticized a generation ago by the proponents of another theory, especially by Koffka.[5]

23. *The theory of sensory organization. Gestalt theory.* Koffka asked how a perceiver could be supposed to learn about objects if all he had to go on were the flux of meaningless sensations. How could a child learn to see an object without ever seeing one? A theory of association, or of the learning of clues, cannot explain it unless the objectivity of an object is given at some time. There was evidence to suggest, moreover, that inexperienced animals and children did not behave as if they confused a large far object with a near small object—in short that they did not see their retinal images in the first place.

24. The *Gestalt* theorists proposed that a process of sensory organization instead of association was the explanation of perception. The nature of the nervous system is such that organization takes place spontaneously. Experience is structured; it comes in a field and, at the very least, there is always a "figure" on a "ground." It is never wholly meaningless, even at the start.

25. Koffka also made the acute observation that, in perceiving an object, we do not separately see a retinal size and then a distance, or a retinal shape and then a slant; instead we see all at once a size-at-a-distance, or a shape-at-a-slant. The relationship between the members of these pairs is invariant in experience, he noted, the visual angle for a given object being reciprocal to distance and the perspective flattening being concomitant with slant. Form and space are linked together, as it were, not separable. It is only a step from this idea to the hypothesis that a shape-at-a-slant may actually be given as an invariant within two variables of optical stimulation, although this is a step that Koffka did not take.

26. The *Principles of Gestalt Psychology*

[5] K. Koffka, *Principles of Gestalt Psychology*, New York, Harcourt Brace (1935).

was certainly the most knowledgeable book on visual perception ever written, and it is still a good foundation for new knowledge. *Gestalt* theory has been called a modern form of nativism and there is a grain of truth in this observation, for the hypothetical "laws of visual organization" bear some analogy to innate forms of apprehension. But the trend or direction of the theory was novel and its emphasis on structure, order, articulation, pattern, and the "total field" of perception is still to be followed up. The proposed laws of organization have not been verified experimentally. But some kind of organization in perception is a fact. The question is where it comes from. Perhaps it comes from outside, not inside.

27. *The relation between stimuli and their sources in the environment.* It was only in the era of *Gestalt* theory that the paradox of perceptual constancy became clear, although it has been the root of the difficulty all along. In my terminology, it is the invariance of perception with varying sensations. The other side of the problem is, the invariance of physical objects with what seem to be varying physical stimuli.

28. One must not confuse the stimuli for the eyes, the ears, and the skin with the sources of these stimuli in the environment. The light, the sound, and the mechanical energy respectively must be distinguished from the objects that reflect light, emit sound, or come in contact with the skin. The impinging physical energy is called the *proximal* stimulus, the stimulus proper, and the external object or event is called the *distal* or *distant* stimulus. The sense organs are excited only by proximal stimuli but what the perceiver is aware of are distal stimuli. This is the other side of the paradox of perceptual constancy. The environment is constant, the stimuli are changing, the sensations are changing, and the perception is constant. The distance, depth, solidity, and permanence of the environment seem to be lost in the proximal stimuli and in the sensory impressions but they turn up again, almost miraculously, in perception. The third dimension of space is said to be lost in the two-dimensional visual image but restored by

some activity of the mind (or the memory, or the brain) in visual experience.

29. The study of the senses has always involved the study of proximal stimuli, and experimenters have been applying energies to the sense organs of their subjects to see what happens for more than a century. A great deal more is now known about stimuli than when the theories were first formulated. It used to be thought that they were bits of energy, points and movements. But the evidence accumulates that the field of stimulation and the flow of stimulation are what is important in arousing sense organs. Both the field and the flow must have a pattern or structure. What excites the eye, for example, is not an even distribution of light but at least one contrast or margin; and not a fixed level of intensity but a change. The effective stimuli are gradients and transients, and this is as true for the ear and the skin as it is for the eye.

30. It used to be thought that stimuli could not possibly represent their sources in the world. Objects do not get into the eye; only light can enter. It is true that an object cannot be *replicated* in light rays, but the properties of its surface can be *specified* by them. Perspective carries some information about the object, and change of perspective carries still more.[6] An observer who has "looked at all sides of a thing" is one who has sensed it in all possible perspectives. As he moves around it his eyes are stimulated by a whole family of serial transformations. The perspective forms change from moment to moment, but note that they change in perfectly orderly and in completely reversible ways. It has been taken for granted that the ever changing form of the stimulus is a chaos which cannot possibly contain the solid form of the object. But perhaps it can. The true shape of the object may be implicit in the serial transformations. In that case, order does not have to be imposed on the momentary stimuli; it is already there in the sequential stimulus.

31. The relation between orderly stimuli and their sources, then, may not be as tenuous as we have thought in the past. The varying

[6] J. J. Gibson, *The Perception of the Visual World*, Ch. 7.

stimuli which go with unvarying objects in the world may have an unvarying component. And this leads us back to the theory of perception.

32. *A new approach to the invariance of perception.* I have a suspicion that the theories of perception have been on the wrong track. It has often been true in the history of thought that a puzzling problem cannot be solved but has to be reformulated, and perhaps this is true of the problem of constancy.

33. The invariance of perception with varying sensations ought to lead to the conclusion that sensations do not cause perceptions. But that seems to go against common sense, for we perceive only when the sense organs are stimulated—otherwise we only imagine or remember or guess the facts of the world. The way out may be this: that sensory experience is a special self-conscious kind of awareness while perceptual experience is unself-conscious and direct. The latter does not depend on the former. Perception is not mediated by sensations, nor based on sensations.

34. This requires that the stimuli causing sensations be different from those causing perceptions. This is a new idea, not at all evident but very promising when it is considered. The individual is bathed in a sea of energy at all times, and the stimulus energies that his receptors can pick up are a flowing array. Light, sound, and physical touchings are patterned, both simultaneously and successively. The hypothesis is that the flowing array has two components, one of change and one of non-change.

35. This hypothesis can be sharpened by borrowing from mathematics two notions. One is that of *transformations* and the other is that of *invariants under transformation.* These terms, although not taught us in beginning geometry, are fundamental. They are much more useful than the notion of "form" as the Greeks conceived it.[7] Stimuli are not static forms but serial transformations which are nevertheless lawful. A static form is simply a

special case of continued non-transformation. Transformation, in mathematics, is not simply change but permanence in change. The specific hypothesis is that the invariant component in a transformation carries information about an object and that the variant component carries other information entirely, for example, about the relation of the perceiver to the object. When an observer attends to certain invariants he perceives objects; when he attends to certain variants he has sensations.

36. This hypothesis is incomplete (and probably the same thing can be said in another way) but it explains the constancy of objective perception without recourse to theories of a subjective process. It also explains how perception can be, in effect, focused on the sources of stimulation, although it is in fact wholly dependent on the stimulation itself. For the permanent properties of the outer world—its texture, edges, layout, solidity, stability, and the fact of gravity—are undoubtedly specified by invariant properties in the visual and tactual stimulus flux. We can thus understand why perceiving is so often correct without recourse to difficult philosophical theories.

37. Extra hypotheses are needed about what I have called the variant component of stimulus transformation. They are speculative, and need investigation. For one thing, we must suppose that there is a difference between perspective transformations and other transformations. In vision, a perspective transformation results from a movement of the object relative to the observer or of the observer relative to the object. But if the thing observed is fluid or viscous or ephemeral or changeable in itself, not simply moveable, a quite different sort of transformation occurs in the light to the eye. The difference is quite noticeable.[8] If the thing observed is broken or disrupted still another transformation occurs, a permutation of order in the stimulus, and the event is visible as such.

38. Another extra hypothesis is needed about

[7] J. J. Gibson, "What is a form?," in *Psychological Review* (58:1951), pp. 403–412; idem., "Optical motions and transformations as stimuli for visual perception," in *Psychological Review* (64:1957), pp. 288–295.

[8] K. von Fieandt and J. J. Gibson, "The sensitivity of the eye to two kinds of continuous transformation of a shadow-pattern," in *Journal of Experimental Psychology.* (57:1959), pp. 344–347.

self-produced transformations of the stimulus-array as contrasted with those not dependent on action of one's own. In moving one's eyes, or head, or body, or in manipulating external objects, one changes the optical stimulus array in whole or part. Each action has its own family of transformations, and each is accompanied by a family of other feelings. We can thus control our responses and explore the possibilities of new stimulation. Locomotion, for example, is guided in this way. We even hear our own footsteps. But some changes in the pattern of light or touch or sound are not self-produced in this circular fashion. They are object-produced. The absence of circularity may well be the feature of these stimuli that gives the corresponding perceptions their external reference. A clue to the whole muddle of explaining how experi-ence can be both external and internal, both objective and subjective, may lie here.

39. Still another hypothesis is needed about the way in which perception develops in the child, and how discrimination improves in the adult. Presumably it is a matter of the growth and the education of attention. The theory that the infant has only meaningless sensations based on raw stimuli and later enriches these impressions with memories is not good enough. The child learns, but what he probably learns is to fix on the subtle variables of stimulation instead of only the crude ones. He does not have to construct a constant world out of ever changing perspectives but he does have to discover the finer properties of the world that lie hidden in these transformations.

L. A. G. STRONG

The Poetic Approach to Reality

Leonard Alfred George Strong (1896–1958) was a British teacher, writer, and critic who published novels, poems, short stories, detective stories, children's stories, biographies, and critical studies. Among his critical works are *Common Sense About Poetry*, 1931; *Common Sense About Drama*, 1937; *The Sacred River: An Approach to James Joyce*, 1949; and *The Writer's Trade*, 1953. His autobiography, *Green Memory*, was published in 1961.

In "The Poetic Approach to Reality" Strong explains why one person's interpretation of reality may be quite different from another's, why the poet's view of the world is not unreal, but only another way of seeing.

1. A lorry, laden with loose sheets of corrugated iron, passes along a suburban road at two in the morning. The hideous clatter rouses

THE POETIC APPROACH TO REALITY Reprinted from *Common Sense About Poetry* by L. A. G. Strong, by permission of Alfred A. Knopf, Inc. Copyright 1931 by L. A. G. Strong. Renewed, 1959 by Sylvia Strong.

some sleepers altogether. On a few fortunate others it produces no impression. The remainder hear the noise, but it does not wake them. They are aware of it under the disguise of a dream. A retired naval officer dreams of a prolonged sea-fight. His daughter, who keeps house for him, dreams that the new maid has dropped the laden breakfast tray at the top of the kitchen stairs: crockery and all bump their way down in a series of resounding crashes. A young man dreams that he is watching a football match. He has a police rattle in his hand, and whirls it to encourage his team. But it gets out of control. It whirls on and on, making a noise so loud and terrifying that the whole game stops, and everyone looks at him accusingly. An old man dreams that his naughty grandson is persistently banging the door to anger him. And so on, *ad infinitum,* as the lorry crashes on its nefarious way between the rows of silent houses.

2. Each of these dreams is an *interpretation* of the disturbance in the road. It is a personal interpretation, appropriate to each dreamer, of the external reality which caused them all to dream.

3. This, with one or two important qualifications, is a parable of the poet's attitude towards reality. It does *not* mean that he is in a bemused or sleeping condition with regard to the realities of life. It does *not* mean that his view of them is a chimaera. Before we establish what it *does* mean, we must first decide what we mean by reality. More bother and misunderstanding are caused by people reading the same term in different ways than by any fundamental lack of contact with the truth. Most of our big abstractions are question-begging terms, unless we limit them, and decide from what point of view we are to look at them. Pilate's famous "What is truth?" is a historic reminder that this star to which we aspire can shine with many colours. "Reality" is as difficult.

4. There will always be a practical, *useful* element in our ideas of everyday reality. A chair is something made of wood (or something very like it), upholstered (apparently) with leather (or so we believe), upon which we can SIT (the most important point, for us, and the most easily verified). Yet this practical account of it would not satisfy an expert in furniture, nor a scientist. Each would wish to go beyond the evidence given by our unaided senses. The different accounts they will arrive at, with magnifying glass and expert technical knowledge, with all the lore of energy and electrons, may be exceedingly inter-

esting: but they are of less immediate interest to us than our own primary concern with the chair's comfort and desirability as a thing to sit on. In the same way, the medicine we have been ordered after meals is expressed for our doctor and chemist by a formula of chemical symbols: for us, by a dark red liquid with a thick sediment and a disagreeable flavour. The Forth Bridge is, for us, difficult to disentangle from the various sense-impressions and associations which we experience in crossing it, or in our memory of crossing it: impressions of sight and sound, associations of holiday time, or of any time or occasion with which it is connected in our minds: anything but a series of metallurgical formulae and equations of stress and strain. Our ideas of the Forth Bridge and of the medicine are local and personal interpretations of reality: and our unaided senses will not do more than provide us with data for these interpretations. My *unaided* senses (unless I have had special training) will not tell me the proportionate ingredients in the medicine, any more than they will deduce from the prescription what the medicine will look like, taste like, and what effect it will have upon my system. In fact, the prescription, the pharmaceutical and scientific account of the medicine, is far less real to me than the medicine as I experience it, since I do not understand the prescription, and would not know if it represented a tonic, a sedative, or a deadly poison. In this practical sense, the prescription is not real to me.

5. Many statements of astronomical fact are incomprehensible to us, because we cannot picture the aeons and distances involved. We can talk quite glibly of "a billion light years," but the expression conveys no picture of reality to our minds. Mathematical statements of these vast relationships would be incomprehensible to us; as incomprehensible as an astronomical and evolutionary account of the universe would have been to the first readers of the Book of Genesis. *I suggest that what is incomprehensible to a man is not real to him.*

6. To come back a moment to the Forth Bridge. You will probably have noticed that I dishonestly slipped the idea of associations

into our notions of its reality: and probably you objected to yourself that these were easily separable, and that it was at the best a sentimental error to include them. I slipped them in on purpose: for the question is not as simple as it looks. The reality apparent to our senses *must always be an interpretation* of the objects perceived through the senses. We may supplement it in various ways, with microscopes, etc.; we may learn, by the exercise of reason, to amend and correct it, to build up a great structure from it: but what our unaided senses give us remains an interpretation only. Often it will include something which is not a property of the object. If our only acquaintance with the Forth Bridge is by crossing it in the train, we may associate noise with the Forth Bridge. Noise, though clearly not a property of the Forth Bridge, recurs to our mind the moment we think of the Bridge. A man born deaf would not include noise in his idea of the Bridge. But for a man born blind the noise would be his only way of recognising it. The noise would come to his mind as instinctively as the picture of the Bridge comes to ours. He would have a mental sound, instead of a mental picture. For him, the noise would not be a property separable from the Bridge: or, at any rate, it would be no more separable than the look of the Bridge is for us. We think the look of the Bridge a criterion of its reality, because it is an aspect of it which we share with the great majority of other people. For blind men, the noise would be the criterion. We have no right to say that noise is not a part of the Bridge's reality, unless we are prepared to admit that visual appearance is not a part of its reality either: for both are the sense data which tell human brains that the train in which they are travelling has reached the Bridge. A deaf man and a blind man, sitting in the same train, both know when they are crossing the Bridge. In other words, each receives data which interpret to his brain the reality "Bridge."

7. Ants, we are told, by means of their antennae, can perceive the size and shape of a smell. The very idea of this is barely intelligible to us, for these properties do not figure in the interpretation of a smell given by our imperfectly associated senses. Yet, to an ant, the shape of a smell is part of its reality.

8. In the same way, to certain animals objects appear magnified twice their "real" size. Thus they hesitate to attack human beings, who seem to them less relatively insignificant than they "really" are.

9. In plain fact, we depend upon evidence which is not nearly as conclusive as we should like to think. We depend upon our five senses, and only get authority for their account from the fact that the great majority of our fellow creatures roughly agree with us. The blind, the colour blind, the deaf, etc., we can exclude, because they suffer from a defect in these five senses, and receive only a partial account of external reality. But the account we receive is also partial, and frequently misleading.

10. In the middle of a circular amphitheatre stands a grand piano. From one side of the circle a green spotlight is turned upon the piano: from the other, a red spotlight. Let us imagine the seats of the amphitheatre filled with savages who have not previously seen a grand piano: people, that is, who depend upon their unaided senses for an idea of its nature. It stands to reason that their judgment of its appearance, texture, colour, etc., will depend upon where each of them is sitting. We can almost contemptuously allow for the differences of view due to perspective (which we understand), and can eliminate the coloured lights, because, however they may delude the savages, they are not "real" properties of the grand piano. But—neither is the ordinary light of day, by which we are accustomed to measure *our* ideas of the piano!

11. Little by little, however we dislike it, we are forced to the conclusion that what our senses tell us is only an interpretation. External reality produces upon them an effect which they interpret after their own nature, as the dreamers interpreted the noise of the lorry. Our senses are not *wrong*. The prescription, when duly made up, does look red, and does taste beastly. On that, the majority of normal human tastes are agreed. The Forth Bridge does look as you and I think it looks, and does, when suitably stimulated by the passing train, give forth the sounds we are agreed on hearing. Each of the savages (we can see)

is right, *from his own point of view,* in the account he gives of the piano—though they will fight bitterly among themselves over the truth of their differing accounts: as bitterly as we fight over politics, taste, religion, and other matters. To *deny* the evidence of the senses leads us to sheer scepticism and negation. One must start with something.

12. The more practical view is that there are different aspects of reality, as of the grand piano: the abstract (prescription, equation, formula) aspect, and the personal, or local (taste, appearance, interpretation) aspect.

13. "The stars are pretty twinkling rogues, that light us home," says a character in one of Sedley's plays: and though his statement would be useless to an astronomer, it was perfectly relevant to his circumstances and his frame of mind. It was an idea: an interpretation: a local reality. "That's not my idea of a hot cross bun," complained a girl in the hotel where I was staying last Easter: by which she meant it was not what she called a *real* hot cross bun.

14. The same difference will be found in our regard for time and space. A dreary, dusty, hot walk, when we are returning angrily from a fruitless errand, will affect us quite differently from the same distance, even the same walk under the same physical conditions, when we are hurrying to a delightful rend'vous. Fifteen minutes of pain in the dentist's chair, or of anxiety in awaiting some result, feel infinitely longer than fifteen minutes when our mind is happily occupied. Yet each aspect of time and distance is *real*.

15. We thus arrive at a table which we can set down roughly thus:

Price	Value
Chemical prescription	Nasty red medicine
Formulae, equation of stress, etc.	Forth Bridge
Three quarters of a mile	Endless dreary walk
Fifteen minutes	Hours and hours
Fact	Idea

16. The left-hand column denotes the world of facts: the right-hand column the world of values. (I do not mean that values are not facts: but they are not objective. The human contribution to them includes emotion; it is not perception only. The value you attach to a keepsake worth nothing in the market is a private and local reality. It does not obtain objectively, outside, independently of your personal regard for the keepsake.) In their professional capacity, mathematicians, chemists, and scientists prefer the left-hand column; philosophers and artists prefer the right. There is no contradiction between the two columns. They are different aspects of reality; different views of the grand piano; different ways of looking at the world.

17. *The poetic approach to reality is via the right-hand column.*

18. Once we accept this, the objection that poetry is unreal will be narrowed down to a new meaning. It will not mean, "Is poetry out of touch with fact?" but, "Is a particular poem true to the world of values?" It will, that is to say, be concerned with the difference between good poetry and bad.

JOHN HENRY NEWMAN

Knowledge Viewed in Relation to Learning

John Henry Newman (1801–1890), churchman and writer, was born in London and educated at Oxford University, where he later became vicar of St. Mary's Church. In 1845 he renounced his Anglican Church affiliation for Roman Catholicism, and in 1879 he became cardinal of St. George in Velabro. Among his writings are sermons and tracts on a variety of subjects; a spiritual autobiography, *Apologia pro Vita Sua,* 1864; poems—*Lyra Apostolica,* 1836, *The Dream of Gerontius,* 1866, and others; two novels—*Loss and Gain,* 1848, and *Callista,* 1856; and a series of lectures given in Dublin entitled *The Idea of a University,* 1852.

In "Knowledge Viewed in Relation to Learning" Cardinal Newman describes the interaction between knowledge, learning, and philosophy, and with a profound insight appraises a liberal education.

1. It were well if the English, like the Greek language, possessed some definite word to express, simply and generally, intellectual proficiency or perfection, such as "health," as used with reference to the animal frame, and "virtue," with reference to our moral nature. I am not able to find such a term;—talent, ability, genius, belong distinctly to the raw material, which is the subject-matter, not to that excellence which is the result of exercise and training. When we turn, indeed, to the particular kinds of intellectual perfection, words are forthcoming for our purpose, as, for instance, judgment, taste, and skill; yet even these belong, for the most part, to powers or habits bearing upon practice or upon art, and not to any perfect condition of the intellect, considered in itself. Wisdom, again, is certainly a more comprehensive word than any other, but it has a direct relation to conduct, and to human life. Knowledge, indeed, and

From KNOWLEDGE VIEWED IN RELATION TO LEARNING, Discourse VI in *The Idea of a University,* 1852, by John Henry Newman.

Science express purely intellectual ideas, but still not a state or quality of the intellect; for knowledge, in its ordinary sense, is but one of its circumstances, denoting a possession or a habit; and science has been appropriated to the subject-matter of the intellect, instead of belonging in English, as it ought to do, to the intellect itself. The consequence is that, on an occasion like this, many words are necessary, in order, first, to bring out and convey what surely is no difficult idea in itself,—that of the cultivation of the intellect as an end; next, in order to recommend what surely is no unreasonable object; and lastly, to describe and make the mind realize the particular perfection in which that object consists. Everyone knows practically what are the constituents of health or of virtue; and everyone recognizes health and virtue as ends to be pursued; it is otherwise with intellectual excellence, and this must be my excuse, if I seem to anyone to be bestowing a good deal of labor on a preliminary matter.

2. In default of a recognized term, I have

called the perfection or virtue of the intellect by the name of philosophy, philosophical knowledge, enlargement of mind, or illumination; terms which are not uncommonly given to it by writers of this day: but, whatever name we bestow on it, it is, I believe, as a matter of history, the business of a University to make this intellectual culture its direct scope, or to employ itself in the education of the intellect,—just as the work of a Hospital lies in healing the sick or wounded, of a Riding or Fencing School, or of a Gymnasium, in exercising the limbs, of an Almshouse, in aiding and solacing the old, of an Orphanage, in protecting innocence, of a Penitentiary, in restoring the guilty. I say, a University taken in its bare idea, and before we view it as an instrument of the Church, has this object and this mission; it contemplates neither moral impression nor mechanical production; it professes to exercise the mind neither in art nor in duty; its function is intellectual culture; here it may leave its scholars, and it has done its work when it has done as much as this. It educates the intellect to reason well in all matters, to reach out towards truth, and to grasp it.

II

3. This, I said in my foregoing Discourse, was the object of a University, viewed in itself, and apart from the Catholic Church, or from the State, or from any other power which may use it; and I illustrated this in various ways. I said that the intellect must have an excellence of its own, for there was nothing which had not its specific good; that the word "educate" would not be used of intellectual culture, as it is used, had not the intellect had an end of its own; that had it not such an end, there would be no meaning in calling certain intellectual exercises "liberal," in contrast with "useful," as is commonly done; that the very notion of a philosophical temper implied it, for it threw us back upon research and system as ends in themselves, distinct from effects and works of any kind; that a philosophical scheme of knowledge, or system of sciences, could not, from the nature of the case, issue in any one definite art or pursuit,

as its end; and that, on the other hand, the discovery and contemplation of truth, to which research and systematizing led, were surely sufficient ends, though nothing beyond them were added, and that they had ever been accounted sufficient by mankind.

4. Here then I take up the subject; and, having determined that the cultivation of the intellect is an end distinct and sufficient in itself, and that, so far as words go it is an enlargement or illumination, I proceed to inquire what this mental breadth, or power, or light, or philosophy consists in. A Hospital heals a broken limb or cures a fever: what does an Institution effect, which professes the health, not of the body, not of the soul, but of the intellect? What is this good, which in former times, as well as our own, has been found worth the notice, the appropriation, of the Catholic Church?

5. I have then to investigate, in the Discourses which follow, those qualities and characteristics of the intellect in which its cultivation issues or rather consists; and, with a view of assisting myself in this undertaking, I shall recur to certain questions which have already been touched upon. These questions are three: viz., the relation of intellectual culture, first, to *mere* knowledge; secondly, to *professional* knowledge; and thirdly, to *religious* knowledge. In other words, are *acquirements* and *attainments* the scope of a University Education? or *expertness in particular arts and pursuits?* or *moral and religious proficiency?* or something besides these three? These questions I shall examine in succession, with the purpose I have mentioned; and I hope to be excused, if, in this anxious undertaking, I am led to repeat what, either in these Discourses or elsewhere, I have already put upon paper. And first, of *Mere Knowledge*, or Learning, and its connection with intellectual illumination or Philosophy.

III

6. I suppose, the *primâ-facie* view which the public at large would take of a University, considering it as a place of Education, is nothing more or less than a place for acquiring a great deal of knowledge on a great

many subjects. Memory is one of the first developed of the mental faculties; a boy's business when he goes to school is to learn, that is, to store up things in his memory. For some years his intellect is little more than an instrument for taking in facts, or a receptacle for storing them; he welcomes them as fast as they come to him; he lives on what is without; he has his eyes ever about him; he has a lively susceptibility of impressions; he imbibes information of every kind; and little does he make his own in a true sense of the word, living rather upon his neighbors all around him. He has opinions, religious, political, and literary, and for a boy, is very positive in them and sure about them; but he gets them from his schoolfellows, or his masters, or his parents, as the case may be. Such as he is in his other relations, such also is he in his school exercises; his mind is observant, sharp, ready, retentive; he is almost passive in the acquisition of knowledge. I say this in no disparagement of the idea of a clever boy. Geography, chronology, history, language, natural history, he heaps up the matter of these studies as treasures for a future day. It is the seven years of plenty with him: he gathers in by handfuls, like the Egyptians, without counting; and though, as time goes on, there is exercise for his argumentative powers in the Elements of Mathematics, and for his taste in the Poets and Orators, still, while at school, or at least, till quite the last years of his time, he acquires, and little more; and when he is leaving for the University, he is mainly the creature of foreign influences and circumstances, and made up of accidents, homogeneous or not, as the case may be. Moreover, the moral habits, which are a boy's praise, encourage and assist this result; that is, diligence, assiduity, regularity, dispatch, persevering application; for these are the direct conditions of acquisition, and naturally lead to it. Acquirements, again, are emphatically producible, and at a moment; they are a something to show, both for master and scholar; an audience, even though ignorant themselves of the subjects of an examination, can comprehend when questions are answered and when they are not. Here again is a reason why mental culture is in the minds of men identified with the acquisition of knowledge.

7. The same notion possesses the public mind, when it passes on from the thought of a school to that of a University: and with the best of reasons so far as this, that there is no true culture without acquirements, and that philosophy presupposes knowledge. It requires a great deal of reading, or a wide range of information, to warrant us in putting forth our opinions on any serious subject; and without such learning the most original mind may be able indeed to dazzle, to amuse, to refute, to perplex, but not to come to any useful result or any trustworthy conclusion. There are indeed persons who profess a different view of the matter, and even act upon it. Every now and then you will find a person of vigorous or fertile mind, who relies upon his own resources, despises all former authors, and gives the world, with the utmost fearlessness, his views upon religion, or history, or any other popular subject. And his works may sell for a while; he may get a name in his day; but this will be all. His readers are sure to find in the long run that his doctrines are mere theories, and not the expression of facts, that they are chaff instead of bread, and then his popularity drops as suddenly as it rose.

8. Knowledge then is the indispensable condition of expansion of mind, and the instrument of attaining to it; this cannot be denied, it is ever to be insisted on; I begin with it as a first principle; however, the very truth of it carries men too far, and confirms to them the notion that it is the whole of the matter. A narrow mind is thought to be that which contains little knowledge; and an enlarged mind, that which holds a great deal; and what seems to put the matter beyond dispute is, the fact of the great number of studies which are pursued in a University, by its very profession. Lectures are given on every kind of subject; examinations are held; prizes awarded. There are moral, metaphysical, physical Professors; Professors of language, of history, of mathematics, of experimental science. Lists of questions are published, wonderful for their range and depth, variety and difficulty; treatises are written,

which carry upon their very face the evidence of extensive reading or multifarious information; what then is wanting for mental culture to a person of large reading and scientific attainments? what is grasp of mind but acquirement? where shall philosophical repose be found, but in the consciousness and enjoyment of large intellectual possessions?

9. And yet this notion is, I conceive, a mistake, and my present business is to show that it is one, and that the end of a Liberal Education is not mere knowledge, or knowledge considered in its *matter;* and I shall best attain my object, by actually setting down some cases, which will be generally granted to be instances of the process of enlightenment or enlargement of mind, and others which are not, and thus, by the comparison, you will be able to judge for yourselves, Gentlemen, whether Knowledge, that is, acquirement, is after all the real principle of the enlargement, or whether that principle is not rather something beyond it.

IV

10. For instance, let a person, whose experience has hitherto been confined to the more calm and unpretending scenery of these islands, whether here or in England, go for the first time into parts where physical nature puts on her wilder and more awful forms, whether at home or abroad, as into mountainous districts; or let one, who has ever lived in a quiet village, go for the first time to a great metropolis,—then I suppose he will have a sensation which perhaps he never had before. He has a feeling not in addition or increase of former feelings, but of something different in its nature. He will perhaps be borne forward, and find for a time that he has lost his bearings. He has made a certain progress, and he has a consciousness of mental enlargement; he does not stand where he did, he has a new center, and a range of thoughts to which he was before a stranger.

11. Again, the view of the heavens which the telescope opens upon us, if allowed to fill and possess the mind, may almost whirl it round and make it dizzy. It brings in a flood of ideas, and is rightly called an intellectual

enlargement, whatever is meant by the term.

12. And so again, the sight of beasts of prey and other foreign animals, their strangeness, the originality (if I may use the term) of their forms and gestures and habits and their variety and independence of each other, throw us out of ourselves into another creation, and as if under another Creator, if I may so express the temptation which may come on the mind. We seem to have new faculties, or a new exercise for our faculties, by this addition to our knowledge; like a prisoner, who, having been accustomed to wear manacles or fetters, suddenly finds his arms and legs free.

13. Hence Physical Science generally, in all its departments, as bringing before us the exuberant riches and resources, yet the orderly course, of the Universe, elevates and excites the student, and at first, I may say, almost takes away his breath, while in time it exercises a tranquilizing influence upon him.

14. Again, the study of history is said to enlarge and enlighten the mind, and why? because, as I conceive, it gives it a power of judging of passing events, and of all events, and a conscious superiority over them, which before it did not possess.

15. And in like manner, what is called seeing the world, entering into active life, going into society, traveling, gaining acquaintance with the various classes of the community, coming into contact with the principles and modes of thought of various parties, interests, and races, their views, aims, habits and manners, their religious creeds and forms of worship,—gaining experience how various yet how alike men are, how low-minded, how bad, how opposed, yet how confident in their opinions; all this exerts a perceptible influence upon the mind, which it is impossible to mistake, be it good or be it bad, and is popularly called its enlargement.

16. And then again, the first time the mind comes across the arguments and speculations of unbelievers, and feels what a novel light they cast upon what he has hitherto accounted sacred; and still more, if it gives in to them and embraces them, and throws off as so much prejudice what it has hitherto held,

and, as if waking from a dream, begins to realize to its imagination that there is now no such thing as law and the transgression of law, that sin is a phantom, and punishment a bugbear, that it is free to sin, free to enjoy the world and the flesh; and still further, when it does enjoy them, and reflects that it may think and hold just what it will, that "the world is all before it where to choose," and what system to build up as its own private persuasion; when this torrent of willful thoughts rushes over and inundates it, who will deny that the fruit of the tree of knowledge, or what the mind takes for knowledge, has made it one of the gods, with a sense of expansion and elevation,—an intoxication in reality, still, so far as the subjective state of the mind goes, an illumination? Hence the fanaticism of individuals or nations, who suddenly cast off their Maker. Their eyes are opened; and, like the judgment-stricken king in the Tragedy, they see two suns, and a magic universe, out of which they look back upon their former state of faith and innocence with a sort of contempt and indignation, as if they were then but fools, and the dupes of imposture.

17. On the other hand, Religion has its own enlargement, and an enlargement, not of tumult, but of peace. It is often remarked of uneducated persons, who have hitherto thought little of the unseen world, that, on their turning to God, looking into themselves, regulating their hearts, reforming their conduct, and meditating on death and judgment, heaven and hell, they seem to become, in point of intellect, different beings from what they were. Before, they took things as they came, and thought no more of one thing than another. But now every event has a meaning; they are mindful of times and seasons, and compare the present with the past; and the world, no longer dull, monotonous, unprofitable, and hopeless, is a various and complicated drama, with parts and an object, and an awful moral.

v

18. Now from these instances, to which many more might be added, it is plain, first,

that the communication of knowledge certainly is either a condition or the means of that sense of enlargement or enlightenment, of which at this day we hear so much in certain quarters: this cannot be denied; but next, it is equally plain, that such communication is not the whole of the process. The enlargement consists, not merely in the passive reception into the mind of a number of ideas hitherto unknown to it, but in the mind's energetic and simultaneous action upon and towards and among those new ideas, which are rushing in upon it. It is the action of a formative power, reducing to order and meaning the matter of our acquirements; it is a making the objects of our knowledge subjectively our own, or, to use a familiar word, it is a digestion of what we receive, into the substance of our previous state of thought; and without this no enlargement is said to follow. There is no enlargement, unless there be a comparison of ideas one with another, as they come before the mind, and a systematizing of them. We feel our minds to be growing and expanding *then,* when we not only learn, but refer what we learn to what we know already. It is not the mere addition to our knowledge that is the illumination; but the locomotion, the movement onwards, of that mental center, to which both what we know, and what we are learning, the accumulating mass of our acquirements, gravitates. And therefore a truly great intellect, and recognized to be such by the common opinion of mankind, such as the intellect of Aristotle, or of St. Thomas, or of Newton, or of Goethe (I purposely take instances within and without the Catholic pale, when I would speak of the intellect as such), is one which takes a connected view of old and new, past and present, far and near, and which has an insight into the influence of all these one on another; without which there is no whole, and no center. It possesses the knowledge, not only of things, but also of their mutual and true relations; knowledge, not merely considered as acquirement, but as philosophy.

19. Accordingly, when this analytical, distributive, harmonizing process is away, the mind experiences no enlargement, and is not

reckoned as enlightened or comprehensive, whatever it may add to its knowledge. For instance, a great memory, as I have already said, does not make a philosopher, any more than a dictionary can be called a grammar. There are men who embrace in their minds a vast multitude of ideas, but with little sensibility about their real relations towards each other. These may be antiquarians, annalists, naturalists; they may be learned in the law; they may be versed in statistics; they are most useful in their own place; I should shrink from speaking disrespectfully of them; still, there is nothing in such attainments to guarantee the absence of narrowness of mind. If they are nothing more than well-read men, or men of information, they have not what specially deserves the name of culture of mind, or fulfills the type of Liberal Education.

20. In like manner, we sometimes fall in with persons who have seen much of the world, and of the men who, in their day, have played a conspicuous part in it, but who generalize nothing, and have no observation, in the true sense of the word. They abound in information in detail, curious and entertaining, about men and things; and, having lived under the influence of no very clear or settled principles, religious or political, they speak of every one and every thing, only as so many phenomena, which are complete in themselves, and lead to nothing, not discussing them, or teaching any truth, or instructing the hearer, but simply talking. No one would say that these persons, well informed as they are, had attained to any great culture of intellect or to philosophy.

21. The case is the same still more strikingly where the persons in question are beyond dispute men of inferior powers and deficient education. Perhaps they have been much in foreign countries, and for any they receive, in a passive, otiose, unfruitful way, the various facts which are forced upon them there. Seafaring men, for example, range from one end of the earth to the other; but the multiplicity of external objects, which they have encountered, forms no symmetrical and consistent picture upon their imagination; they see the tapestry of human life, as it were on the wrong side, and it tells no story. They sleep, and they rise up, and they find themselves, now in Europe, now in Asia; they see visions of great cities and wild regions; they are in the marts of commerce, or amid the islands of the South; they gaze on Pompey's Pillar, or on the Andes; and nothing which meets them carries them forward or backward, to any idea beyond itself. Nothing has a drift or relation; nothing has a history or a promise. Everything stands by itself, and comes and goes in its turn, like the shifting scenes of a show, which leave the spectator where he was. Perhaps you are near such a man on a particular occasion, and expect him to be shocked or perplexed at something which occurs; but one thing is much the same to him as another, or, if he is perplexed, it is as not knowing what to say, whether it is right to admire, or to ridicule, or to disapprove, while conscious that some expression of opinion is expected from him; for in fact he has no standard of judgment at all, and no landmarks to guide him to a conclusion. Such is mere acquisition, and I repeat, no one would dream of calling it philosophy.

VI

22. Instances, such as these, confirm, by the contrast, the conclusion I have already drawn from those which preceded them. That only is true enlargement of mind which is the power of viewing many things at once as one whole, of referring them severally to their place in the universal system, of understanding their respective values, and determining their mutual dependence. Thus is that form of Universal Knowledge, of which I have on a former occasion spoken, set up in the individual intellect, and constitutes its perfection. Possessed of this real illumination, the mind never views any part of the extended subject-matter of Knowledge without recollecting that it is but a part, or without the associations which spring from this recollection. It makes everything in some sort lead to everything else; it would communicate the image of the whole to every separate portion, till that whole becomes in imagination like a spirit,

everywhere pervading and penetrating its component parts, and giving them one definite meaning. Just as our bodily organs, when mentioned, recall their function in the body, as the word "creation" suggests the Creator, and "subjects" a sovereign, so, in the mind of the Philosopher, as we are abstractedly conceiving of him, the elements of the physical and moral world, sciences, arts, pursuits, ranks, offices, events, opinions, individualities, are all viewed as one, with correlative functions, and as gradually by successive combinations converging, one and all, to the true center.

23. To have even a portion of this illuminative reason and true philosophy is the highest state to which nature can aspire, in the way of intellect; it puts the mind above the influences of chance and necessity, above anxiety, suspense, unsettlement, and superstition, which is the lot of the many. Men, whose minds are possessed with some one object, take exaggerated views of its importance, are feverish in the pursuit of it, make it the measure of things which are utterly foreign to it, and are startled and despond if it happens to fail them. They are ever in alarm or in transport. Those on the other hand who have no object or principle whatever to hold by, lose their way, every step they take. They are thrown out, and do not know what to think or say, at every fresh juncture; they have no view of persons, or occurrences, or facts, which come suddenly upon them, and they hang upon the opinion of others, for want of internal resources. But the intellect, which has been disciplined to the perfection of its powers, which knows, and thinks while it knows, which has learned to leaven the dense mass of facts and events with the elastic force of reason, such an intellect cannot be partial, cannot be exclusive, cannot be impetuous, cannot be at a loss, cannot but be patient, collected, and majestically calm, because it discerns the end in every beginning, the origin in every end, the law in every interruption, the limit in each delay; because it ever knows

where it stands, and how its path lies from one point to another. It is the τετράγωνος [1] of the Peripatetic, and has the "nil admirari" [2] of the Stoic,—

Felix qui potuit rerum cognoscere causas,
Atque metus omnes, et inexorabile fatum
Subjecit pedibus, strepitumque Acherontis
    avari. [3]

There are men who, when in difficulties, originate at the moment vast ideas or dazzling projects; who, under the influence of excitement, are able to cast a light, almost as if from inspiration, on a subject or course of action which comes before them; who have a sudden presence of mind equal to any emergency, rising with the occasion, and an undaunted magnanimous bearing, and an energy and keenness which is but made intense by opposition. This is genius, this is heroism; it is the exhibition of a natural gift, which no culture can teach, at which no Institution can aim; here, on the contrary, we are concerned, not with mere nature, but with training and teaching. That perfection of the Intellect, which is the result of Education, and its *beau idéal*, to be imparted to individuals in their respective measures, is the clear, calm, accurate vision and comprehension of all things, as far as the finite mind can embrace them, each in its place, and with its own characteristics upon it. It is almost prophetic from its knowledge of history; it is almost heartsearching from its knowledge of human nature; it has almost supernatural charity from its freedom from littleness and prejudice; it has almost the repose of faith, because nothing can startle it; it has almost the beauty and harmony of heavenly contemplation, so intimate is it with the eternal order of things and the music of the spheres. . . .

[1] [Foursquare.]
[2] [To be excited by nothing. Horace, *Epistles*.]
[3] [Fortunate the man who can understand the causes of things and who casts under foot all fears and inexorable fate and the roar of greedy Acheron. Virgil, *Georgics*.]

WILLIAM G. PERRY, JR.

Examsmanship and the Liberal Arts: A Study in Educational Epistemology

William G. Perry, Jr. (1913–   ) is a member of the faculty and director of the Bureau of Study Counsel at Harvard University. He and Charles Preston Whitlock co-produced a set of sixteen reading films in 1949 and twice since have revised them, the most recent revision in 1959. Mr. Perry has contributed to many professional journals, including *Harvard Educational Review* and *Journal of General Education*. This essay was his contribution to *Examining in Harvard College: A Collection of Essays by Members of the Harvard Faculty*.

Mr. Perry examines here two diametrically opposed definitions of knowledge: one, represented by the term "cow," is the application of facts without understanding; the other, "bull," is the application of understanding with few or no facts.

1. "But sir, I don't think I really deserve it, it was mostly bull, really." This disclaimer from a student whose examination we have awarded a straight "A" is wondrously depressing. Alfred North Whitehead invented its only possible rejoinder: "Yes sir, what you wrote is nonsense, utter nonsense. But ah! Sir! It's the right *kind* of nonsense!"

2. Bull, in this university, is customarily a source of laughter, or a problem in ethics. I shall step a little out of fashion to use the subject as a take-off point for a study in comparative epistemology. The phenomenon of bull, in all the honor and opprobrium with which it is regarded by students and faculty, says something, I think, about our theories of knowledge. So too, the grades which we

EXAMSMANSHIP AND THE LIBERAL ARTS: A STUDY IN EDUCATIONAL EPISTEMOLOGY Reprinted by permission of the publishers from William G. Perry, Jr. in *Examining at Harvard College;* Cambridge, Mass.: Harvard University. Distributed by Harvard University Press.

assign on examinations communicate to students what these theories may be.

3. We do not have to be out-and-out logical-positivists to suppose that we have something to learn about "what we think knowledge is" by having a good look at "what we do when we go about measuring it." We know the straight "A" examination when we see it, of course, and we have reason to hope that the student will understand why his work receives our recognition. He doesn't always. And those who receive lesser honor? Perhaps an understanding of certain anomalies in our customs of grading good bull will explain the students' confusion.

4. I must beg patience, then, both of the reader's humor and of his morals. Not that I ask him to suspend his sense of humor but that I shall ask him to go beyond it. In a great university the picture of a bright student attempting to outwit his professor while his professor takes pride in not being outwitted is certainly ridiculous. I shall report just such

a scene, for its implications bear upon my point. Its comedy need not present a serious obstacle to thought.

5. As for the ethics of bull, I must ask for a suspension of judgment. I wish that students could suspend theirs. Unlike humor, moral commitment is hard to think beyond. Too early a moral judgment is precisely what stands between many able students and a liberal education. The stunning realization that the Harvard Faculty will often accept, as evidence of knowledge, the cerebrations of a student who has little data at his disposal, confronts every student with an ethical dilemma. For some it forms an academic focus for what used to be thought of as "adolescent disillusion." It is irrelevant that rumor inflates the phenomenon to mythical proportions. The students know that beneath the myth there remains a solid and haunting reality. The moral "bind" consequent on this awareness appears most poignantly in serious students who are reluctant to concede the competitive advantage to the bullster and who yet feel a deep personal shame when, having succumbed to "temptation," they themselves receive a high grade for work they consider "dishonest."

6. I have spent many hours with students caught in this unwelcome bitterness. These hours lend an urgency to my theme. I have found that students have been able to come to terms with the ethical problem, to the extent that it is real, only after a refined study of the true nature of bull and its relation to "knowledge." I shall submit grounds for my suspicion that we can be found guilty of sharing the students' confusion of moral and epistemological issues.

I

7. I present as my "premise," then, an amoral *fabliau*. Its hero-villain is the Abominable Mr. Metzger '47. Since I celebrate his virtuosity, I regret giving him a pseudonym, but the peculiar style of his bravado requires me to honor also his modesty. Bull in pure form is rare; there is usually some contamination by data. The community has reason to be grateful to Mr. Metzger for having created an instance of laboratory purity, free from any

adulteration by matter. The more credit is due him, I think, because his act was free from premeditation, deliberation, or hope of personal gain.

8. Mr. Metzger stood one rainy November day in the lobby of Memorial Hall. A junior, concentrating in mathematics, he was fond of diverting himself by taking part in the drama, a penchant which may have had some influence on the events of the next hour. He was waiting to take part in a rehearsal in Sanders Theatre, but, as sometimes happens, no other players appeared. Perhaps the rehearsal had been canceled without his knowledge? He decided to wait another five minutes.

9. Students, meanwhile, were filing into the Great Hall opposite and taking seats at the testing tables. Spying a friend crossing the lobby toward the Great Hall's door, Metzger greeted him and extended appropriate condolences. He inquired, too, what course his friend was being tested in. "Oh, Soc. Sci. something-or-other." "What's it all about?" asked Metzger, and this, as Homer remarked of Patroclus, was the beginning of evil for him.

10. "It's about Modern Perspectives on Man and Society and All That," said his friend. "Pretty interesting, really."

11. "Always wanted to take a course like that," said Metzger. "Any good reading?"

12. "Yeah, great. There's this book"—his friend did not have time to finish.

13. "Take your seats please" said a stern voice beside them. The idle conversation had somehow taken the two friends to one of the tables in the Great Hall. Both students automatically obeyed; the proctor put blue books before them; another proctor presented them with copies of the printed hour-test.

14. Mr. Metzger remembered afterwards a brief misgiving that was suddenly overwhelmed by a surge of curiosity and puckish glee. He wrote "George Smith" on the blue book, opened it, and addressed the first question.

15. I must pause to exonerate the Management. The Faculty has a rule that no student may attend an examination in a course in which he is not enrolled. To the wisdom of

this rule the outcome of this deplorable story stands witness. The Registrar, charged with the enforcement of the rule, has developed an organization with procedures which are certainly the finest to be devised. In November, however, class rosters are still shaky, and on this particular day another student, named Smith, was absent. As for the culprit, we can reduce his guilt no further than to suppose that he was ignorant of the rule, or, in the face of the momentous challenge before him, forgetful.

16. We need not be distracted by Metzger's performance on the "objective" or "spot" questions on the test. His D on these sections can be explained by those versed in the theory of probability. Our interest focuses on the quality of his essay. It appears that when Metzger's friend picked up his own blue book a few days later, he found himself in company with a large proportion of his section in having received on the essay a C+. When he quietly picked up "George Smith's" blue book to return it to Metzger, he observed that the grade for the essay was A—. In the margin was a note in the section man's hand. It read "Excellent work. Could you have pinned these observations down a bit more closely? Compare . . . in . . . pp. . . ."

17. Such news could hardly be kept quiet. There was a leak, and the whole scandal broke on the front page of Tuesday's *Crimson*. With the press Metzger was modest, as becomes a hero. He said that there had been nothing to it at all, really. The essay question had offered a choice of two books, Margaret Mead's *And Keep Your Powder Dry* or Geoffrey Gorer's *The American People*. Metzger reported that having read neither of them, he had chosen the second "because the title gave me some notion as to what the book might be about." On the test, two critical comments were offered on each book, one favorable, one unfavorable. The students were asked to "discuss." Metzger conceded that he had played safe in throwing his lot with the more laudatory of the two comments, "but I did not forget to be balanced."

18. I do not have Mr. Metzger's essay before me except in vivid memory. As I recall, he

took his first cue from the name Geoffrey, and committed his strategy to the premise that Gorer was born into an "Anglo-Saxon" culture, probably English, but certainly "English speaking." Having heard that Margaret Mead was a social anthropologist, he inferred that Gorer was the same. He then entered upon his essay, centering his inquiry upon what he supposed might be the problems inherent in an anthropologist's observation of a culture which was his own, or nearly his own. Drawing in part from memories of table-talk on cultural relativity and in part from creative logic, he rang changes on the relation of observer to observed, and assessed the kind and degree of objectivity which might accrue to an observer through training as an anthropologist. He concluded that the book in question did in fact contribute a considerable range of " 'objective,' and even 'fresh,' " insights into the nature of our culture. "At the same time," he warned, "these observations must be understood within the context of their generation by a person only partly freed from his embeddedness in the culture he is observing, and limited in his capacity to transcend those particular tendencies and biases which he has himself developed as a personality in his interaction with this culture since his birth. In this sense the book portrays as much the character of Geoffrey Gorer as it analyzes that of the American people." It is my regrettable duty to report that at this moment of triumph Mr. Metzger was carried away by the temptations of parody and added, "We are thus much the richer."

19. In any case, this was the essay for which Metzger received his honor grade and his public acclaim. He was now, of course, in serious trouble with the authorities.

20. I shall leave him for the moment to the mercy of the Administrative Board of Harvard College and turn the reader's attention to the section man who ascribed the grade. He was in much worse trouble. All the consternation in his immediate area of the Faculty and all the glee in other areas fell upon his unprotected head. I shall now undertake his defense.

21. I do so not simply because I was ac-

quainted with him and feel a respect for his intelligence; I believe in the justice of his grade! Well, perhaps "justice" is the wrong word in a situation so manifestly absurd. This is more a case in "equity." That is, the grade is equitable if we accept other aspects of the situation which are equally absurd. My proposition is this: if we accept as valid those C grades which were accorded students who, like Metzger's friend, demonstrated a thorough familiarity with the details of the book without relating their critique to the methodological problems of social anthropology, then "George Smith" deserved not only the same, but better.

22. The reader may protest that the C's given to students who showed evidence only of diligence were indeed not valid and that both these students and "George Smith" should have received E's. To give the diligent E is of course not in accord with custom. I shall take up this matter later. For now, were I to allow the protest, I could only restate my thesis: that "George Smith's" E would, in a college of liberal arts, be properly a "better" E.

23. At this point I need a short-hand. It is a curious fact that there is no academic slang for the presentation of evidence of diligence alone. "Parroting" won't do; it is possible to "parrot" bull. I must beg the reader's pardon, and, for reasons almost too obvious to bear, suggest "cow."

24. Stated as nouns, the concepts look simple enough:

cow (pure): data, however relevant, without relevancies.
bull (pure): relevancies, however relevant, without data.

25. The reader can see all too clearly where this simplicity would lead. I can assure him that I would not have imposed on him this way were I aiming to say that knowledge in this university is definable as some neuter compromise between cow and bull, some infertile hermaphrodite. This is precisely what many diligent students seem to believe: that what they must learn to do is to "find the right mean" between "amounts" of detail and "amounts" of generalities. Of course this is not the point at all. The problem is not quantita-

tive, nor does its solution lie on a continuum between the particular and the general. Cow and bull are not poles of a single dimension. A clear notion of what they really are is essential to my inquiry, and for heuristic purposes I wish to observe them further in the celibate state.

26. When the pure concepts are translated into verbs, their complexities become apparent in the assumptions and purposes of the students as they write:

To cow (v. intrans.) or the act of cowing:
    To list data (or perform operations) without awareness of, or comment upon, the contexts, frames of reference, or points of observation which determine the origin, nature, and meaning of the data (or procedures). To write on the assumption that "a fact is a fact." To present evidence of hard work as a substitute for understanding, without any intent to deceive.

To bull (v. intrans.) or the act of bulling:
    To discourse upon the contexts, frames of reference and points of observation which would determine the origin, nature, and meaning of data if one had any. To present evidence of an understanding of form in the hope that the reader may be deceived into supposing a familiarity with content.

27. At the level of conscious intent, it is evident that cowing is more moral, or less immoral, than bulling. To speculate about unconscious intent would be either an injustice or a needless elaboration of my theme. It is enough that the impression left by cow is one of earnestness, diligence, and painful naiveté. The grader may feel disappointment or even irritation, but these feelings are usually balanced by pity, compassion, and a reluctance to hit a man when he's both down and moral. He may feel some challenge to his teaching, but none whatever to his one-ups-manship. He writes in the margin: "See me."

28. We are now in a position to understand the anomaly of custom: As instructors, we always assign bull an E, *when we detect it;* whereas we usually give cow a C, *even though it is always obvious.*

29. After all, we did not ask to be confronted with a choice between morals and understand-

ing (or did we?). We evince a charming humanity, I think, in our decision to grade in favor of morals and pathos. "I simply *can't* give this student an E after he has *worked* so hard." At the same time we tacitly express our respect for the bullster's strength. We recognize a colleague. If he knows so well how to dish it out, we can be sure that he can also take it.

30. Of course it is just possible that we carry with us, perhaps from our own school-days, an assumption that if a student is willing to work hard and collect "good hard facts" he can always be taught to understand their relevance, whereas a student who has caught onto the forms of relevance without working at all is a lost scholar.

31. But this is not in accord with our experience.

32. It is not in accord either, as far as I can see, with the stated values of a liberal education. If a liberal education should teach students "how to think," not only in their own fields but in fields outside their own—that is, to understand "how the other fellow orders knowledge," then bulling, even in its purest form, expresses an important part of what a pluralist university holds dear, surely a more important part than the collecting of "facts that are facts" which schoolboys learn to do. Here then, good bull appears not as ignorance at all but as an aspect of knowledge. It is both relevant and "true." In a university setting good bull is therefore of more value than "facts," which, without a frame of reference, are not even "true" at all.

33. Perhaps this value accounts for the final anomaly: as instructors, we are inclined to reward bull highly, *where we do not detect its intent,* to the consternation of the bullster's acquaintances. And often we do not examine the matter too closely. After a long evening of reading blue books full of cow, the sudden meeting with a student who at least understands the problems of one's field provides a lift like a draught of refreshing wine, and a strong disposition toward trust.

34. This was, then, the sense of confidence that came to our unfortunate section man as

he read "George Smith's" sympathetic considerations.

II

35. In my own years of watching over students' shoulders as they work, I have come to believe that this feeling of trust has a firmer basis than the confidence generated by evidence of diligence alone. I believe that the theory of a liberal education holds. Students who have dared to understand man's real relation to his knowledge have shown themselves to be in a strong position to learn content rapidly and meaningfully, and to retain it. I have learned to be less concerned about the education of a student who has come to understand the nature of man's knowledge, even though he has not yet committed himself to hard work, than I am about the education of the student who, after one or two terms at Harvard is working desperately hard and still believes that collected "facts" constitute knowledge. The latter, when I try to explain to him, too often understands me to be saying that he "doesn't *put in enough generalities.*" Surely he has "put in *enough* facts."

36. I have come to see such quantitative statements as expressions of an entire, coherent epistemology. In grammar school the student is taught that Columbus discovered America in 1492. The *more* such items he gets "right" on a given test the more he is credited with "knowing." From years of this sort of thing it is not unnatural to develop the conviction that knowledge consists of the accretion of hard facts by hard work.

37. The student learns that the more facts and procedures he can get "right" in a given course, the better will be his grade. The more courses he takes, the more subjects he has "had," the more credits he accumulates, the more diplomas he will get, until, after graduate school, he will emerge with his doctorate, a member of the community of scholars.

38. The foundation of this entire life is the proposition that a fact is a fact. The necessary correlate of this proposition is that a fact is either right or wrong. This implies that the

standard against which the rightness or wrongness of a fact may be judged exists *someplace* —perhaps graven upon a tablet in a Platonic world outside and above *this* cave of tears. In grammar school it is evident that the tablets which enshrine the spelling of a word or the answer to an arithmetic problem are visible to my teacher who need only compare my offerings to it. In high school I observe that my English teachers disagree. This can only mean that the tablets in such matters as the goodness of a poem are distant and obscured by clouds. They surely exist. The pleasing of befuddled English teachers degenerates into assessing their prejudices, a game in which I have no protection against my competitors more glib of tongue. I respect only my science teachers, authorities who *really know*. Later I learn from them that "this is only what we think *now*." But eventually, surely. . . . Into this epistemology of education, apparently shared by teachers in such terms as "credits," "semester hours" and "years of French" the student may invest his ideals, his drive, his competitiveness, his safety, his self-esteem, and even his love.

39. College raises other questions: by whose calendar is it proper to say that Columbus discovered America in 1492? How, when and by whom was the year 1 established in this calendar? What of other calendars? In view of the evidence for Leif Ericson's previous visit (and the American Indians), what historical ethnocentrism is suggested by the use of the word "discover" in this sentence? As for Leif Ericson, in accord with what assumptions do you order the evidence?

40. These questions and their answers are not "more" knowledge. They are devastation. I do not need to elaborate upon the epistemology, or rather epistemologies, they imply. A fact has become at last "an observation or an operation performed in a frame of reference." A liberal education is founded in an awareness of frame of reference even in the most immediate and empirical examination of data. Its acquirement involves relinquishing hope of absolutes and of the protection they afford against doubt and the glib-tongued

competitor. It demands an ever widening sophistication about systems of thought and observation. It leads, not away from, but *through* the arts of gamesmanship to a new trust.

41. This trust is in the value and integrity of systems, their varied character, and the way their apparently incompatible metaphors enlighten, from complementary facets, the particulars of human experience. As one student said to me: "I used to be cynical about intellectual games. Now I want to know them thoroughly. You see I came to realize that it was only when I knew the rules of the game cold that I could tell whether what I was saying was tripe."

42. We too often think of the bullster as cynical. He can be, and not always in a light-hearted way. We have failed to observe that there can lie behind cow the potential of a deeper and more dangerous despair. The moralism of sheer work and obedience can be an ethic that, unwilling to face a despair of its ends, glorifies its means. The implicit refusal to consider the relativity of both ends and means leaves the operator in an unconsidered proprietary absolutism. History bears witness that in the pinches this moral superiority has no recourse to negotiation, only to force.

43. A liberal education proposes that man's hope lies elsewhere: in the negotiability that can arise from an understanding of the integrity of systems and of their origins in man's address to his universe. The prerequisite is the courage to accept such a definition of knowledge. From then on, of course, there is nothing incompatible between such an epistemology and hard work. Rather the contrary.

44. I can now at last let bull and cow get together. The reader knows best how a productive wedding is arranged in his own field. This is the nuptial he celebrates with a straight A on examinations. The masculine context must embrace the feminine particular, though itself "born of woman." Such a union is knowledge itself, and it alone can generate new contexts and new data which can unite in their turn to form new knowledge.

45. In this happy setting we can congratulate in particular the Natural Sciences, long thought to be barren ground to the bullster. I have indeed drawn my examples of bull from the Social Sciences, and by analogy from the Humanities. Essay-writing in these fields has long been thought to nurture the art of bull to its prime. I feel, however, that the Natural Sciences have no reason to feel slighted. It is perhaps no accident that Metzger was a mathematician. As part of my researches for this paper, furthermore, a student of considerable talent has recently honored me with an impressive analysis of the art of amassing "partial credits" on examinations in advanced physics. Though beyond me in some respects, his presentation confirmed my impression that instructors of Physics frequently honor on examinations operations structurally similar to those requisite in a good essay.

46. The very qualities that make the Natural Sciences fields of delight for the eager gamesman have been essential to their marvelous fertility.

III

47. As priests of these mysteries, how can we make our rites more precisely expressive? The student who merely cows robs himself, without knowing it, of his education and his soul. The student who only bulls robs himself, as he knows full well, of the joys of inductive discovery—that is, of engagement. The introduction of frames of reference in the new curricula of Mathematics and Physics in the schools is a hopeful experiment. We do not know yet how much of these potent revelations the very young can stand, but I suspect they may rejoice in them more than we have supposed. I can't believe they have never wondered about Leif Ericson and that word "discovered," or even about 1492. They have simply been too wise to inquire.

48. Increasingly in recent years better students in the better high schools and preparatory schools *are* being allowed to inquire. In fact they appear to be receiving both encouragement and training in their inquiry. I have the evidence before me.

49. Each year for the past five years all freshmen entering Harvard and Radcliffe have been asked in freshman week to "grade" two essays answering an examination question in History. They are then asked to give their reasons for their grades. One essay, filled with dates, is 99% cow. The other, with hardly a date in it, is a good essay, easily mistaken for bull. The "official" grades of these essays are, for the first (alas!) C+ "because he has worked so hard," and for the second (soundly, I think) B+. Each year a larger majority of freshmen evaluate these essays as would the majority of the faculty, and for the faculty's reasons, and each year a smaller minority give the higher honor to the essay offering data alone. Most interesting, a larger number of students each year, while not overrating the second essay, award the first the straight E appropriate to it in a college of liberal arts.

50. For us who must grade such students in a university, these developments imply a new urgency, did we not feel it already. Through our grades we describe for the students, in the showdown, what we believe about the nature of knowledge. The subtleties of bull are not peripheral to our academic concerns. That they penetrate to the center of our care is evident in our feelings when a student whose good work we have awarded a high grade reveals to us that he does not feel he deserves it. Whether he disqualifies himself because "there's too much bull in it," or worse because "I really don't think I've worked that hard," he presents a serious educational problem. Many students feel this sleaziness; only a few reveal it to us.

51. We can hardly allow a mistaken sense of fraudulence to undermine our students' achievements. We must lead students beyond their concept of bull so that they may honor relevancies that are really relevant. We can willingly acknowledge that, in lieu of the date 1492, a consideration of calendars and of the word "discovered," may well be offered with intent to deceive. We must insist that this does not make such considerations intrinsically immoral, and that, contrariwise, the date 1492 may be no substitute for them. Most of all,

we must convey the impression that we grade understanding qua understanding. To be convincing, I suppose we must concede to ourselves in advance that a bright student's understanding is understanding even if he achieved it by osmosis rather than by hard work in our course.

52. These are delicate matters. As for cow, its complexities are not what need concern us. Unlike good bull, it does not represent partial knowledge at all. It belongs to a different theory of knowledge entirely. In our theories of knowledge it represents total ignorance, or worse yet, a knowledge downright inimical to understanding. I even go so far as to propose that we award no more C's for cow. To do so is rarely, I feel, the act of mercy it seems. Mercy lies in clarity.

53. The reader may be afflicted by a lingering curiosity about the fate of Mr. Metzger. I hasten to reassure him. The Administrative Board of Harvard College, whatever its satanic reputations, is a benign body. Its members, to be sure, were on the spot. They delighted in Metzger's exploit, but they were responsible to the Faculty's rule. The hero stood in danger of probation. The debate was painful. Suddenly one member, of a refined legalistic sensibility, observed that the rule applied specifically to "examinations" and that the occasion had been simply an hour-test. Mr. Metzger was merely "admonished."

 THE IMPACT OF SCIENCE

E. B. WHITE

The Door

Everything (he kept saying) is something it isn't. And everybody is always somewhere else. Maybe it was the city, being in the city, that made him feel how queer everything was and that it was something else. Maybe (he kept thinking) it was the names of the things. The names were tex and frequently koid. Or they were flex and oid or they were duroid (sani) or flexsan (duro), but everything was glass (but not quite glass) and the thing that you touched (the surface, washable, crease-resistant) was rubber, only it wasn't quite rubber and you didn't quite touch it but almost. The wall, which was glass but thrutex, turned out on being approached not to be a wall, it was something else, it was an opening or doorway—and the doorway (through which he saw himself approaching) turned out to be something else, it was a wall. And what he had eaten not having agreed with him.

He was in a washable house, but he wasn't sure. Now about those rats, he kept saying to himself. He meant the rats that the Professor had driven crazy by forcing them to deal with problems which were beyond the scope of rats, the insoluble problems. He meant the rats that had been trained to jump at the square card with the circle in the middle, and the card (because it was something it wasn't) would give way and let the rat into a place where the food was, but then one day it would be a trick played on the rat, and the card would be changed, and the rat would jump but the card wouldn't give way, and it was an impossible situation (for a rat) and the rat would go insane and into its eyes would come the unspeakably bright imploring look of the frustrated, and after the convulsions were over and the frantic racing around, then the passive stage would set in and the willingness to let anything be done to it, even if it was something else.

He didn't know which door (or wall) or opening in the house to jump at, to get through, because one was an opening that wasn't a door (it was a void, or koid) and the other was a wall that wasn't an opening, it was a sanitary cupboard of the same color. He caught a glimpse of his eyes staring into his eyes, in the thrutex, and in them was the expression he had seen in the picture of the rats— weary after convulsions and the frantic racing around, when they were willing and did not mind having anything done to them. More and more (he kept saying) I am confronted by a problem which is incapable of solution (for this time even if he chose the right door, there would be no food behind it) and that is what madness is, and things seeming different from what they are. He heard, in the house where he was, in the city to which he had gone (as toward a door which might, or might not, give way), a noise—not a loud noise but more of a low prefabricated humming. It came from a place in the base of the wall (or stat) where the flue carrying the filterable air was, and not far from the Minipiano, which was made of the same material nailbrushes are made of, and which was under the stairs. "This, too, has been tested," she said, pointing, but not at it, "and found viable." It wasn't a loud noise, he kept thinking, sorry that he had seen his eyes, even though it was through his own eyes that he had seen them.

First will come the convulsions (he said), then the exhaustion, then the willingness to let anything be done. "And you better believe it *will* be."

All his life he had been confronted by situations which were incapable of being solved, and there was a deliberateness behind all this, behind this chang- ing of the card (or door), because they would always wait till you had learned to jump at the certain card (or door)—the one with the circle—and then they would change it on you. There have been so many doors changed on me, he said, in the last twenty years, but it is now becoming clear that it is an impossible situation, and the question is whether to jump again, even though they ruffle you in the rump with a blast of air—to make you jump. He wished he wasn't standing by the Minipiano. First they would teach you the prayers and the Psalms, and that would be the right door (the one with the circle) and the long sweet words with the holy sound, and that would be the one to jump at to get where the food was. Then one day you jumped and it didn't give way, so that all you got was the bump on the nose, and the first bewilderment, the first young bewilderment.

I don't know whether to tell her about the door they substituted or not, he said, the one with the equation on it and the picture of the amoeba reproducing itself by division. Or the one with the photostatic copy of the check for thirty-two dollars and fifty cents. But the jumping was so long ago, although the bump is . . . how those old wounds hurt! Being crazy this way wouldn't be so bad if only, if only. If only when you put your foot forward to take a step, the ground wouldn't come up to meet your foot the way it does. And the same way in the street (only I may never get back to the street unless I jump at the right door), the curb coming up to meet your foot, anticipating ever so delicately the weight of the body, which is somewhere else. "We could take your name," she said, "and send it to you." And it wouldn't be so bad if only you could read a sentence all the way through without jumping (your eye) to something else on the same page; and then (he kept thinking) here was that man out in Jersey, the one who started to chop his trees down, one by one, the man who began talking about how he would take his house to pieces, brick by brick, because he faced a problem incapable of solution, probably, so he began to hack at the trees in the yard, began to pluck with trembling fingers at the bricks in the house. Even if a house is not washable, it is worth taking down. It is not till later that the exhaustion sets in.

But it is inevitable that they will keep changing the doors on you, he said, because that is what they are for; and the thing is to get used to it and not let it unsettle the mind. But that would mean not jumping, and you can't. Nobody can not jump. There will be no not-jumping. Among rats, perhaps, but among people never. Everybody has to keep jumping at a door (the one with the circle on it) because that is the way everybody is, specially some people. You wouldn't want me, standing here, to tell you, would you, about my friend the poet (deceased) who said, "My heart has followed all my days something I cannot name"? (It had the circle on it.) And like many poets, although few so beloved, he is gone. It killed him, the jumping. First, of course, there were the preliminary bouts, the convulsions, and the calm and the willingness.

I remember the door with the picture of the girl on it (only it was spring), her arms outstretched in loveliness, her dress (it was the one with the circle on it) uncaught, beginning the slow, clear, blinding cascade—and I guess we would all like to try that door again, for it seemed like the way and for a while it was the way, the door would open and you would go through winged and exalted (like any rat) and the food would be there, the way the Professor had it arranged, everything O.K., and you had chosen the right door for the world was young. The time they changed that door on me, my nose bled for a hundred hours—how do you like that, Madam? Or would you prefer to show me further through this so strange house, or you could take my name and send it to me, for although my heart has followed all my days something I cannot name, I am tired of the jumping and I do not know which way to go, Madam, and I am not even sure that I am not tired beyond the endurance of man (rat, if you will) and have taken leave of sanity. What are you following these days, old friend, after your recovery from the last bump? What is the name, or is it something you cannot name? The rats have a name for it by this time, perhaps, but I don't know what they call it. I call it plexikoid and it comes in sheets, something like insulating board, unattainable and ugli-proof.

And there was the man out in Jersey, because I keep thinking about his terrible necessity and the passion and trouble he had gone to all those years in the indescribable abundance of a householder's detail, building the estate and the planting of the trees and in spring the lawn-dressing and in fall the bulbs for the spring burgeoning, and the watering of the grass on the long light evenings in summer and the gravel for the driveway (all had to be thought out, planned) and the decorative borders, probably, the perennials and the bug spray, and the building of the house from plans of the architect, first the sills, then the studs, then the full corn in the ear, the floors laid on the floor timbers, smoothed, and then the carpets upon the smooth floors and the curtains and the rods therefor. And then, almost without warning, he would be jumping at the same old door and it wouldn't give: they had changed it on him, making life no longer supportable under the elms in the elm shade, under the maples in the maple shade.

"Here you have the maximum of openness in a small room."

It was impossible to say (maybe it was the city) what made him feel the way he did, and I am not the only one either, he kept thinking—ask any doctor if I am. The doctors, they know how many there are, they even know where the trouble is only they don't like to tell you about the prefrontal lobe because that means making a hole in your skull and removing the work of centuries. It took so long coming, this lobe, so many, many years. (Is it something you read in the paper, perhaps?) And now, the strain being so great, the door having been changed by the Professor once too often . . . but it only means a whiff of ether, a few deft strokes, and the higher animal becomes a little easier in his mind and more like the lower one. From now on, you see, that's the way it will be, the ones with the small prefrontal lobes will win because the other ones are hurt too much by this incessant bumping. They can stand just so much, eh, Doctor? (And what is that, pray, that you have in your hand?) Still, you never can tell, eh, Madam?

He crossed (carefully) the room, the thick carpet under him softly, and went toward the door carefully, which was glass and he could see himself in it, and which, at his approach, opened to allow him to pass through; and beyond he half expected to find one of the old doors that he had known, perhaps the one with the circle, the one with the girl her arms outstretched in loveliness and beauty before him. But he saw instead a moving stairway, and descended in light (he kept thinking) to the street below and to the other people. As he stepped off, the ground came up slightly, to meet his foot.

JUDITH WHEELER

The Electronic Age

Judith Wheeler (1934–   ) is a senior research associate with The Carnegie Study of the Education of Educators. Her article "The Electronic Age" grew out of her collaboration with Charles E. Silberman on a series of articles on automation first published in *Fortune* and now available as a book entitled *The Myths of Automation*, 1966. She and Mr. Silberman have also collaborated in a critique of the writings of Marshall McLuhan.

"The Electronic Age" asserts that writers are increasingly needed as interpreters because the world presents more and more experience that "lies beyond the limits of our personal lives."

1. Donald Barthelme's story, "The Balloon," in a recent issue of *The New Yorker*, conjured a gigantic balloon that expanded during a night and a morning over a large part of Manhattan. There had been "a flood of original ideas in all media, works of singular beauty as well as significant milestones in the history of inflation, but at that moment there was only *this balloon*, concrete particular, hanging there." It transformed the lives of the people. They talked of little else; they tested it for toxic effect, analyzed it for philosophical significance, and found in it the explanation of their psychic disturbances. Discussion of the *meaning* of the balloon, however, was quickly abandoned because meanings "are rarely even looked for now, except in cases involving the simplest, safest phenomena." It was easier to adapt to the balloon, to be submerged by it.

THE ELECTRONIC AGE By Judith Wheeler, from the *Saturday Review*, June 4, 1966. Reprinted by permission of the author and the publisher.

2. In a way, "the electronic age" is our gigantic, overblown balloon, hanging there. Its manifestations intrude during more and more of the hours of our days, and there are few sanctuaries left. We have approached it from all angles, yet its meaning eludes us.

3. It is not as though it came upon us in a night and a morning, however: in 1942 General David Sarnoff gave notice that television would "bring to the home a complete means of instantaneous participation in the sights and sounds of the outer world." It was, he said, the "ultimate form of communication." Whether television has quite lived up to this promise is not settled, but it is clear that it can offer the illusion of "real life" better than any other medium. And its "truthfulness" transforms the impact of other media. A New York taxi-driver says he doesn't care if *all* the newspapers go out of business: "I like the news on TV. There you can see for yourself what's happening." Television's "sights and sounds of the outer world" have proved they

can mystify, excite, instruct, horrify, even ennoble their audience. We seem to have all the values of art along with the comforting/awesome awareness that *those* people are *real*.

4. Perhaps this is why critic John Aldridge, in his new book *Time to Murder and Create*, finds that the novel is no longer "the primary source of our information about the varieties of experience that lie beyond the limits of our personal lives. . . ." Mr. Aldridge is right. But it is also true that we don't need more information; we are in the midst of a data explosion. The possibilities for conveying information have proliferated to such an extent, and they feed so voraciously on "reality," that as Marshall McLuhan, director of the Center for Culture and Technology at the University of Toronto, says, the world itself has become "a sort of museum of objects that have been encountered before in some other medium."

5. Yet, paradoxically, the more we encounter these "objects," the more inscrutable they seem to be. Each rendition of the object in a different medium, or in the same medium at different times, or in several media at the same time, seems to give it luster. Familiarity breeds unfamiliarity just as a word repeated over and over suddenly sounds mysterious. We have more and more information, and suddenly no understanding. We experience a great deal that lies "beyond the limits of our personal lives," and things are more unreasonable than ever. A tourist promotion film on South Africa shows a stately parade of well-dressed citizens (white) at garden parties, in skyscraper offices, at splendid resorts. Toward the end the narrator describes South Africa's abundant crop yields, and on the screen are the only Negroes in the film—women with baskets of fruit on their heads waiting in line to have their loads checked. This film was shown in New York theaters during the weeks when television offered the 1964 Harlem and Rochester race riots.

6. The incongruousness of this film would have gone unremarked twenty years ago, and not because there was less sensitivity about race relations. As the taxi-driver said, you can see for yourself—and the whole world is watching. One American first heard that there was rioting in Watts last summer from a priest in the cathedral at Palma, Majorca, who had seen the "difficulties," as he politely called them, on television. How do you think about a world where the news of an ongoing riot 6,000 miles distant is dropped into the immense dark silence of a fourteenth-century Spanish cathedral?

7. The point is, can we still talk about something that lies beyond the limits of our personal lives? The old limits of time and space have been drastically altered, and the new limits are not obvious. Nor is it clear any longer what "authentic" experience is. Mr. Aldridge writes, "We are vicariously informed about experience to the point where we do not need to *have* experience, and if we do have it, we very often feel it to be less compelling than the secondhand version of it that we already possess." This is an odd statement to make in a decade of activism. But perhaps mere activity is not experience. To a large extent we think of "an experience" as something personal, raised out of the flux of daily life by virtue of having a beginning, a middle, and an end, very like a book or a play. But more and more, with the bombardment of information, experience becomes process without end. And direct personal experience becomes indistinguishable from the vicarious, the compelling secondhand version, when the doings of the outer world are brought to us on television, as they happen. We know at the same moment as the astronaut whether his shot is successful. It is not only real life; it is real time.

8. A writer can make this museum of objects, this collection of random sights and sounds, relevant to each of us. He separates us from the "mass audience," and makes us feel important. He even makes us feel wise. Television shows us what we do; writers try to tell us why. Television turns reality into news; writers make news into reality. As we probe farther into physical space, deeper into human awareness; as we devour our world, the only one left may be the one the writers make.

THE NEW COMPUTER AGE:
A SYMPOSIUM

Many well-qualified observers in both the sciences and the humanities see the next two or three decades as probably the most crucial in the history of man. Two modern technical innovations support this opinion: the harnessing of nuclear power and the development of the computer. The implications of nuclear energy for good and evil are now comparatively well known, but the potential effects of the computer are less known and understood. The four brief essays that follow represent a cross section of comment upon the possible benefits and dangers of a computerized society.

DAVID SARNOFF

No Life Untouched

General David Sarnoff (1891–   ), probably best known as the Chairman of the Board of the Radio Corporation of America, was born in Russia and came to the United States at the age of eight. He is the recipient of a most impressive array of honors and awards in such diverse areas as education, communications, science, and government. Typical of his achievements was his promotion in 1944 to Brigadier General of the Army.

In "No Life Untouched" General Sarnoff discusses the versatility of the computer, records the rapid growth of its use, and foresees that society will direct its future use toward the betterment of life.

1. In our increasingly complex world, information is becoming the basic building block of society. However, at a time when the acquisition of new scientific information alone is approaching a rate of 250 million pages annually, the tide of knowledge is overwhelming the human capability for dealing with it. So man must turn to a machine if he hopes to contain the tide and channel it to beneficial ends.

2. The electronic computer, handling millions of facts with the swiftness of light, has given contemporary meaning to Aristotle's vision of the liberating possibilities of machines: "When looms weave by themselves, man's slavery will end." By transforming the way in which he gathers, stores, retrieves, and uses information, this versatile instrument is helping man to overcome his mental and physical limitations. It is vastly widening his intellectual horizon, enabling him better to comprehend his universe, and providing the means to master that portion of it lying within his reach.

3. Although we are barely in the second decade of electronic data processing, the outlines of its influence on our culture are beginning to emerge. Far from depersonalizing the individual and dehumanizing his society, the computer promises a degree of personalized service never before available to mankind.

4. By the end of the century, for the equivalent of a few dollars a month, the individual will have a vast complex of computer services at his command. Information utilities will make computing power available, like electricity, to thousands of users simultaneously. The computer in the home will be joined to a national and global computer system that provides services ranging from banking and travel facilities to library research and medical care. High-speed communications devices, linked to satellites in space, will transmit data to and from virtually any point on earth with the ease of a dial system. Students, businessmen, scientists, government officials, and

NO LIFE UNTOUCHED By General David Sarnoff, from the *Saturday Review*, July 23, 1966. Reprinted by permission of the author and the publisher.

housewives will converse with computers as readily as they now talk by telephone.

5. In the health field, computers will be employed to maintain a complete medical profile on every person in the country from the hour of birth. The record will be constantly updated by a regional computer for immediate access by doctors or hospital personnel. The computer also will maintain files on every known ailment, its symptoms, diagnosis, and treatment. A doctor will communicate a patient's symptoms to the computer center and within seconds receive suggestions for treatment based both on the symptoms and the patient's history.

6. Computers will handle the nation's fiscal transactions from a central credit information exchange, to which all banks, business enterprises, and individuals will be connected. Purchases will be made, funds invested, and loans issued by transfers of credit within the computer without a dollar or penny physically exchanging hands. Even the soil will be computerized. The long-range outlook for agriculture includes new sensing devices that will be placed on larger farms, feeding information to the computer on soil moisture, temperature, weather outlook, and other details. The computer will calculate the best crops to plant, the best seeding times, the amount of fertilizer, and even the correct harvesting time for maximum yield.

7. Some of the most profound changes wrought by the computer will be in education. Here, the machine will do more than assist students to solve problems and to locate up-to-date information: It will fundamentally improve and enrich the entire learning process. The student's educational experience will be analyzed by the computer from the primary grades through university. Computer-based teaching machines, programed and operated by teachers thoroughly trained in electronic data processing techniques, will instruct students at the rate best suited to each individual. The concept of mass education will give way to the concept of personal tutoring, with the teacher and the computer working as a

team. Computers will bring many new learning dimensions to the classroom. For example, they will simulate nuclear reactors and other complex, dangerous, or remote systems, enabling students to learn through a form of experience what could formerly be taught only in theory.

8. The computer's participation in the field of learning will continue long after the end of formal education. The government estimates that 50 per cent of the jobs to be held ten years from now do not even exist today. With this tremendous rate of occupational obsolescence, future generations of Americans may pursue two or three careers during their lifetimes. The home computer will aid in developing career mobility by providing continuing self-instruction.

9. Just as it is recasting the educational process, the computer is also fundamentally changing the production and distribution of the printed word. Five centuries ago, Gutenberg broke words into individual letters. Electronic composition now breaks the letters into tiny patterns of dots that are stored in the computer's memory. Any character can be called up by the computer, written on the face of a cathode ray tube, and reproduced on film or paper in thousandths of a second. Nothing moves except the electrons.

10. When the electronic computer first appeared in composition rooms and printing shops several years ago, its job was to hyphenate words and justify text. But the computer, working at speeds of thousands of words a minute, was driving mechanical typesetting devices capable of setting only a few words per minute. Now, the development of computerized composition makes it possible to set text at hundreds of lines per minute. Photographs and drawings will be set the same way. Since the printed picture is itself a dot structure, the computer can electronically scan any photograph or drawing, reduce it to dots and store it, then retrieve it and beam it on a cathode ray tube for immediate reproduction.

11. In the future, electronics will develop processes that will make it possible to go from final copy and illustrations to printing in one integrated electronic process. One result will be that newspapers, in the foreseeable future, will no longer be printed in a single location. Instead, they will be transmitted through computers in complete page form to regional electronic printing centers that will turn out special editions for the areas they govern. Local news and advertising will be inserted on the spot. Eventually, the newspaper can be reproduced in the home through a small copying device functioning as part of a home communications center.

12. Basic changes also will come to other areas of the printed word. For example, of the more than one billion books published every year, almost half are textbooks. The growth of knowledge and the factor of obsolescence mean that these texts must be supplemented by a professor's mimeographed notes. Today, these notes have a small distribution of only a few hundred copies. Computers will make it possible to catalogue this information and thus broaden its availability.

13. At the turn of the century, most large universities will not only have electronic composition systems that allow them to reprint original research, theses, or course notes upon demand; they will also have a computerized information retrieval library. This process of information retrieval can be duplicated in almost any other field. The scientist will have the latest technical papers culled by the computer and reproduced in the laboratory or home. The computer will bring to the attorney all the pertinent laws, decisions, and precedents on any case that concerns him. The business executive need not rush to the office every morning; most of the information he will need to conduct his business will be run off for him at home, and he will have two-way national and global closed-circuit television, via satellites, for meetings and conferences.

14. Some of these developments are probabilities, some of them are certainties, and all of them are or soon will be within the capabilities of the computer art. But one fact is absolute: the incredible growth of the computer in numbers, power and availability.

15. In just ten years, the typical electronic data processor has become ten times smaller,

100 times faster and 1,000 times less expensive to operate. These trends will continue, and our national computing power, which is doubling every year, will soon be sufficient to make the computer a genuinely universal tool.

16. In 1956, there were fewer than 1,000 computers in the United States. Today, there are 30,000, or more than $11 billion worth; and by 1976 the machine population may reach 100,000. And these figures will, of course, be greatly increased through the growth of data processing in other nations.

17. A decade ago, our machines were capable of 12 billion computations per hour; today, they can do more than 20 trillion, and by 1976 —a decade from now—they will attain 400 trillion—or about two billion computations per hour for every man, woman and child. Quite evidently, the threshold of the computer age has barely been crossed.

18. Nevertheless, for all its potential to stretch the mind a thousandfold, it is perhaps necessary to point out that the computer is still a thing—that it cannot see, feel, or act unless first acted upon. Its value depends upon man's ability to use it with purpose and intelligence. If his postulates are wrong, the computerized future can only be a massive enlargement of human error.

19. Ramsay MacDonald once warned against "an attempt to clothe unreality in the garb of mathematical reality." Computers echo this warning. For they cannot usurp man's unique ability to blend intuition with fact, to feel as well as to think. In the end, this remains the basis of human progress.

20. The task ahead will be to assign to the machine those things which it can best do, and reserve for man those things which he must provide and control. It is my conviction that society will adjust itself to the computer and work in harmony with it for the genuine betterment of life.

VERNON F. MILLER

The Town Meeting Reborn

Vernon F. Miller (1919–   ) is at present pastor of the City Church of the Brethren in Goshen, Indiana. Since 1941 he has had wide experience, here and abroad, in such areas as mass media, psychiatry and guidance, social work, and religion.

This essay suggests a way by which the computerized mass media can be used to promote both individuality and a sense of community for modern society.

1. Contemporary mass media have been accused of creating a mass culture in which

THE TOWN MEETING REBORN By Rev. Vernon F. Miller, from the *Saturday Review*, July 23, 1966. Reprinted by permission of the author and the publisher.

the individual is lost in a depersonalized society of unrelated persons. But reversal of this prospect is possible. Mass media can be the vehicle for individual involvement in modern life. If we combine contemporary mass media with modern computer systems, we will have the means to help restore responsibility to the individual and a new sense of community in our society.

2. Our representative democracy began in an era when all members of a given community could get together to discuss an issue from all sides. With the expansion of population, we lost much of the personal involvement and evaluation by "the people." But the combination of mass media with the potential of computerized response can bring every citizen into as vital a relationship with his government as was possible in town-meeting days. Moreover, modern man will have more time for involvement in government. How can computerized public opinion involve each citizen?

3. The basic concept can be suggested by this sample format of a television program. An issue of national policy is chosen. Panel members experienced in the field under discussion present varying or opposing points of view. Debate patterns are followed with opportunity for rebuttal and pursuing of specific points in question. A view-screen is available for film clips and statistics. Each person in the studio audience of several hundred has three response buttons on the arm of his seat: "yes," "no," and "?." These feed to the computer.

4. The audience has been chosen from the area on a random selection basis conforming to procedures of opinion polls. Each person is assigned a specific seat. The computer correlates data by the usual classifications, age, sex, etc. The audience hears the information from the panel. Then questions are asked of the audience. Each person responds to each question by pressing a button. Answers are tabulated in the computer. Immediately the results are shown. The moderator, a person skilled in opinion-poll science, interprets trends. The panel discusses these trends. Finally, the audience asks questions.

5. This type of opinion poll is significantly improved over current procedures, for all respondents are asked the questions simultaneously, and there are no accidental variations in inflections or surrounding conversations. More important, the answer is given on the basis of thoughtful consideration of the issues.

6. Opinion polls influence decisions that set the directions of national life. We should be concerned when these important decisions are influenced by inherited, off-the-cuff, uninformed, unexamined answers. We can use mass media and electronic responses to sharpen our judgments.

7. There is even greater potential to restore individual responsibility toward government when another step is added: the response of the home audience. Current opinion-poll samplings are so small that most people have never been asked an opinion on any subject. They think they will never be polled. They see informing programs, but do not push themselves to make a decision about how they believe the issue should be solved. They have information, but have not practiced the art of responsible reaction.

8. Viewers across the nation can be motivated to come to decisions and register opinions. Each viewer would have a porta-punch card. On it would be printed several basic questions. With a toothpick, he could punch out the "yes" or "no" holes. In the morning he could drop this card in the mail. Very shortly this mass response would be tabulated and reported, and every citizen would see the tabulation that included his expression of opinion.

9. In the near future, it will be possible to tabulate the viewer's decision response immediately by use of his telephone. When push-button phones are in general use, the different number digits can be used to send responses to questions. Present engineering would not accommodate thousands of simultaneous calls in a metropolitan area. However, if a large business with multiple-phone lines would allow usage of its facilities at night, a large number could be recorded over a two- or three-hour period. The computer could even ask each question by the phone, indicating which digit to push for a "yes," "no," or "?." For more complex surveys, it could ask different questions depending on the previous answers.

10. Beyond cultivation of decision response by the individual viewer by means of punch-cards or telephones, still another step is pos-

sible: the neighborhood group-response. A person is really never sure how fully he believes an idea until he has expressed it in his own words to another person. In the give and take of conversation he can correct errors, and be open to new insights. A group can come out with a creative new concept that no one person had at the beginning.

11. We could organize our neighborhoods into groups of eight to twelve persons. We did this with block captains and air-raid wardens in World War II, and, to the extent that it helps recapture government of the people, it might be our best security against World War III. An issue might be selected for each month of the year. Newspaper feature articles, public-think letters, radio-talk programs, and local television panel discussions would draw out people's ideas at the local level. National magazines might document background material, and each television network could present a documentary or debate as outlined earlier. On the fourth week of the month, neighborhood groups would meet. They would have a printed discussion guide and porta-punch cards. After a thorough discussion of the alternatives, they would record their opinions on the punch-cards and send them in.

12. Most people tend to gather with groups who think as they do. These groups would tend to mix people of different political, religious, and fraternal groupings. The concept of deliberative assembly where speakers are listened to for truth is largely absent even in Congress. There used to be more than 500 cities with more than one newspaper; now there are only seventy-five; and television news for the entire nation comes primarily from three networks. Thus the proposed techniques would help rediscover the values of debate of both sides of an issue.

13. They also could be valuable training for the role of the citizen at election time. They could help him focus on issues rather than the personality of a candidate, and they could be the framework for a forum open to all candidates regardless of their financial ability to purchase advertising.

14. Moreover, these techniques and practices for a people's government in mass society could become our most valuable item of foreign aid. The capacity for informed individual participation in law and order is a basic need in both old and new nations, as well as a requisite for world peace. But we must practice this capacity ourselves before we presume to share it with others.

NORMAN COUSINS

The Computer and the Poet

Norman Cousins (1912–   ), long a distinguished editor of the *Saturday Review*, is also president of Saturday Review, Inc. Although he is a versatile man who has received honors and awards in many fields, he is chiefly a writer. Among his books are *Modern Man Is Obsolete*, 1945; *Dr. Schweitzer of Lambarene*, 1960; and *In Praise of Folly*, 1961.

In "The Computer and the Poet" Mr. Cousins argues that the poet's cast of mind is needed to help determine the meaning of facts—to convert knowledge to wisdom.

1. The essential problem of man in a computerized age remains the same as it has always been. That problem is not solely how to be more productive, more comfortable, more content, but how to be more sensitive, more sensible, more proportionate, more alive. The computer makes possible a phenomenal leap in human proficiency; it demolishes the fences around the practical and even the theoretical intelligence. But the question persists and indeed grows whether the computer will make it easier or harder for human beings to know who they really are, to identify their real problems, to respond more fully to beauty, to place adequate value on life, and to make their world safer than it now is.

2. Electronic brains can reduce the profusion of dead ends involved in vital research. But they can't eliminate the foolishness and decay that come from the unexamined life. Nor do they connect a man to the things he has to be connected to—the reality of pain in others; the possibilities of creative growth in himself; the memory of the race; and the rights of the next generation.

3. The reason these matters are important in a computerized age is that there may be a tendency to mistake data for wisdom, just as there has always been a tendency to confuse logic with values, and intelligence with insight. Unobstructed access to facts can produce unlimited good only if it is matched by the desire and ability to find out what they mean and where they would lead.

4. Facts are terrible things if left sprawling and unattended. They are too easily regarded as evaluated certainties rather than as the rawest of raw materials crying to be processed into the texture of logic. It requires a very unusual mind, Whitehead said, to undertake the analysis of a fact. The computer can provide a correct number, but it may be an irrelevant number until judgment is pronounced.

5. To the extent, then, that man fails to make the distinction between the intermediate operations of electronic intelligence and

THE COMPUTER AND THE POET By Norman Cousins, from the *Saturday Review*, July 23, 1966. Reprinted by permission of the author and the publisher.

the ultimate responsibilities of human decision and conscience, the computer could prove a digression. It could obscure man's awareness of the need to come to terms with himself. It may foster the illusion that he is asking fundamental questions when actually he is asking only functional ones. It may be regarded as a substitute for intelligence instead of an extension of it. It may promote undue confidence in concrete answers. "If we begin with certainties," Bacon said, "we shall end in doubts; but if we begin with doubts, and we are patient with them, we shall end in certainties."

6. The computer knows how to vanquish error, but before we lose ourselves in celebration of the victory, we might reflect on the great advances in the human situation that have come about because men were challenged by error and would not stop thinking and probing until they found better approaches for dealing with it. "Give me a good fruitful error, full of seeds, bursting with its own corrections," Ferris Greenslet wrote. "You can keep your sterile truth for yourself."

7. The biggest single need in computer technology is not for improved circuitry, or enlarged capacity, or prolonged memory, or miniaturized containers, but for better questions and better use of the answers. Without taking anything away from the technicians, we think it might be fruitful to effect some sort of junction between the computer technologist and the poet. A genuine purpose may be served by turning loose the wonders of the creative imagination on the kinds of problems being put to electronic tubes and transistors. The company of poets may enable the men who tend the machines to see a larger panorama of possibilities than technology alone may inspire.

8. A poet, said Aristotle, has the advantage of expressing the universal; the specialist expresses only the particular. The poet, moreover, can remind us that man's greatest energy comes not from his dynamos but from his dreams. The notion of where a man ought to be instead of where he is; the liberation from cramped prospects; the intimations of im-

mortality through art—all these proceed naturally out of dreams. But the quality of a man's dreams can only be a reflection of his subconscious. What he puts into his subconscious, therefore, is quite literally the most important nourishment in the world.

9. Nothing really happens to a man except as it is registered in the subconscious. This is where event and feeling become memory and where the proof of life is stored. The poet—and we use the term to include all those who have respect for and speak to the human spirit—can help to supply the subconscious with material to enhance its sensitivity, thus safeguarding it. The poet, too, can help to keep man from making himself over in the image of his electronic marvels. For the danger is not so much that man will be controlled by the computer as that he may imitate it.

10. The poet reminds men of their uniqueness. It is not necessary to possess the ultimate definition of this uniqueness. Even to speculate on it is a gain.

R. J. HEATHORN

Learn with BOOK

R. J. Heathorn (1914–   ), a native of England now living in Surrey, contributes essays to both British and American periodicals.

This ironic parable provokes a thoughtful reappraisal of the contribution the print medium has made, and can continue to make, to human culture.

1. A new aid to rapid—almost magical—learning has made its appearance. Indications are that if it catches on, all the electronic gadgets will be so much junk. The new device is known as Built-in Orderly Organized Knowledge. The makers generally call it by its initials, BOOK.

2. Many advantages are claimed over the old-style learning and teaching aids on which most people are brought up nowadays. It has no wires, no electric circuits to break down. No connection is needed to an electricity power point. It is made entirely without mechanical parts to go wrong or need replacement.

3. Anyone can use BOOK, even children, and it fits comfortably into the hands. It can be conveniently used sitting in an armchair by the fire.

4. How does this revolutionary, unbelievably easy invention work? Basically BOOK consists only of a large number of paper sheets. These may run to hundreds where BOOK covers a lengthy program of information. Each sheet bears a number in sequence, so that the sheets cannot be used in the wrong order. To make it even easier for the user to

keep the sheets in the proper order they are held firmly in place by a special locking device called a "binding."

5. Each sheet of paper presents the user with an information sequence in the form of symbols, which he absorbs optically for automatic registration on the brain. When one sheet has been assimilated a flick of the finger turns it over and further information is found on the other side. By using both sides of each sheet in this way a great economy is effected, thus reducing both the size and cost of BOOK. No buttons need to be pressed to move from one sheet to another, to open or close BOOK, or to start it working.

6. BOOK may be taken up at any time and used by merely opening it. Instantly it is ready for use. Nothing has to be connected up or switched on. The user may turn at will to any sheet, going backwards or forwards as he pleases. A sheet is provided near the beginning as a location finder for any required information sequence.

7. A small accessory, available at trifling extra cost, is the BOOKmark. This enables the user to pick up his program where he left off on the previous learning session. BOOKmark is versatile and may be used in any BOOK.

8. The initial cost varies with the size and subject matter. Already a vast range of BOOKs is available, covering every conceivable subject and adjusted to different levels of aptitude. One BOOK, small enough to be held in the hands, may contain an entire learning schedule. Once purchased, BOOK requires no further cost; no batteries or wires are needed, since the motive power, thanks to the ingenious device patented by the makers, is supplied by the brain of the user.

9. BOOKs may be stored on handy shelves and for ease of reference the program schedule is normally indicated on the back of the binding.

10. Altogether the Built-in Orderly Organized Knowledge seems to have great advantages with no drawbacks. We predict a big future for it.

ERICH FROMM

The Marketing Orientation

Erich Fromm (1900–   ) was born in Frankfurt, Germany, and received his Ph.D. from the University of Heidelberg. Since 1940 he has lectured in several American universities. He has also written many significant books and articles, most of which are concerned with some aspect of psychology. Among the books are *Escape from Freedom,* 1941; *Man for Himself,* 1947, from which this essay was taken; *The Sane Society,* 1955; *The Art of Loving,* 1956; *Sigmund Freud's Mission,* 1958; *May Man Prevail?* 1961; *Life Without Illusions,* 1962; *The Heart of Man,* 1964; and *You Shall Be as Gods,* 1966.

In "The Marketing Orientation" Mr. Fromm explores the influence of the marketplace on the development of the individual personality, and draws some interesting conclusions about the means by which success is achieved in our society.

1. The marketing orientation developed as a dominant one only in the modern era. In order to understand its nature one must consider the economic function of the market in modern society as being not only analogous to this character orientation but as the basis and the main condition for its development in modern man.

2. Barter is one of the oldest economic mechanisms. The traditional local market, however, is essentially different from the market as it has developed in modern capitalism. Bartering on a local market offered an opportunity to meet for the purpose of exchanging commodities. Producers and customers became acquainted; they were relatively small groups; the demand was more or less known, so that the producer could produce for this specific demand.

3. The modern market [1] is no longer a meeting place but a mechanism characterized by abstract and impersonal demand. One produces for this market, not for a known circle of customers; its verdict is based on laws of supply and demand; and it determines whether the commodity can be sold and at what price. No matter what the *use value* of a pair of shoes may be, for instance, if the supply is greater than the demand, some shoes will be sentenced to economic death; they might as well not have been produced at all. The market day is the "day of judgment" as far as the *exchange value* of commodities is concerned.

4. The reader may object that this description of the market is oversimplified. The producer does try to judge the demand in advance, and under monopoly conditions even obtains a certain degree of control over it. Nevertheless, the regulatory function of the market has been, and still is, predominant enough to have a profound influence on the character formation of the urban middle class

[1] Cf., for the study of history and function of the modern market, K. Polanyi's *The Great Transformation* (New York: Rinehart & Company, 1944).

THE MARKETING ORIENTATION From *Man for Himself* by Erich Fromm. Copyright 1947 by Erich Fromm. Reprinted by permission of Holt, Rinehart and Winston, Inc.

and, through the latter's social and cultural influence, on the whole population. The market concept of value, the emphasis on exchange value rather than on use value, has led to a similar concept of value with regard to people and particularly to oneself. The character orientation which is rooted in the experience of oneself as a commodity and of one's value as exchange value I call the marketing orientation.

5. In our time the marketing orientation has been growing rapidly, together with the development of a new market that is a phenomenon of the last decades—the "personality market." Clerks and salesmen, business executives and doctors, lawyers and artists all appear on this market. It is true that their legal status and economic positions are different: some are independent, charging for their services; others are employed, receiving salaries. But all are dependent for their material success on a personal acceptance by those who need their services or who employ them.

6. The principle of evaluation is the same on both the personality and the commodity market: on the one, personalities are offered for sale; on the other, commodities. Value in both cases is their exchange value, for which use value is a necessary but not a sufficient condition. It is true, our economic system could not function if people were not skilled in the particular work they have to perform and were gifted only with a pleasant personality. Even the best bedside manner and the most beautifully equipped office on Park Avenue would not make a New York doctor successful if he did not have a minimum of medical knowledge and skill. Even the most winning personality would not prevent a secretary from losing her job unless she could type reasonably fast. However, if we ask what the respective weight of skill and personality as a condition for success is, we find that only in exceptional cases is success predominantly the result of skill and of certain other human qualities like honesty, decency, and integrity. Although the proportion between skill and human qualities on the one hand and "personality" on the other hand as prerequisites for success varies, the "personality factor" al-

important

ways plays a decisive role. Success depends largely on how well a person sells himself on the market, how well he gets his personality across, how nice a "package" he is; whether he is "cheerful," "sound," "aggressive," "reliable," "ambitious"; furthermore what his family background is, what clubs he belongs to, and whether he knows the right people. The type of personality required depends to some degree on the special field in which a person works. A stockbroker, a salesman, a secretary, a railroad executive, a college professor, or a hotel manager must each offer different kinds of personality that, regardless of their differences, must fulfill one condition: to be in demand.

7. The fact that in order to have success it is not sufficient to have the skill and equipment for performing a given task but that one must be able to "put across" one's personality in competition with many others shapes the attitude toward oneself. If it were enough for the purpose of making a living to rely on what one knows and what one can do, one's self-esteem would be in proportion to one's capacities, that is, to one's use value; but since success depends largely on how one sells one's personality, one experiences oneself as a commodity or rather simultaneously as the seller *and* the commodity to be sold. A person is not concerned with his life and happiness, but with becoming salable. This feeling might be compared to that of a commodity, of handbags on a counter, for instance, could they feel and think. Each handbag would try to make itself as "attractive" as possible in order to attract customers and to look as expensive as possible in order to obtain a higher price than its rivals. The handbag sold for the highest price would feel elated, since that would mean it was the most "valuable" one; the one which was not sold would feel sad and convinced of its own worthlessness. This fate might befall a bag which, though excellent in appearance and usefulness, had the bad luck to be out of date because of a change in fashion.

8. Like the handbag, one has to be in fashion on the personality market, and in order to be in fashion one has to know what kind of personality is most in demand. This knowledge is transmitted in a general way throughout the whole process of education, from kindergarten to college, and implemented by the family. The knowledge acquired at this early stage is not sufficient, however; it emphasizes only certain general qualities like adaptability, ambition, and sensitivity to the changing expectations of other people. The more specific picture of the models for success one gets elsewhere. The pictorial magazines, newspapers, and newsreels show the pictures and life stories of the successful in many variations. Pictorial advertising has a similar function. The successful executive who is pictured in a tailor's advertisement is the image of how one should look and be, if one is to draw down the "big money" on the contemporary personality market.

9. The most important means of transmitting the desired personality pattern to the average man is the motion picture. The young girl tries to emulate the facial expression, coiffure, gestures of a high-priced star as the most promising way to success. The young man tries to look and be like the model he sees on the screen. While the average citizen has little contact with the life of the most successful people, his relationship with the motion-picture stars is different. It is true that he has no real contact with them either, but he can see them on the screen again and again, can write them and receive their autographed pictures. In contrast to the time when the actor was socially despised but was nevertheless the transmitter of the works of great poets to his audience, our motion-picture stars have no great works or ideas to transmit, but their function is to serve as the link an average person has with the world of the "great." Even if he cannot hope to become as successful as they are, he can try to emulate them; they are his saints and because of their success they embody the norms for living.

10. Since modern man experiences himself both as the seller and as the commodity to be sold on the market, his self-esteem depends on conditions beyond his control. If he is "successful," he is valuable; if he is not, he is worthless. The degree of insecurity which re-

sults from this orientation can hardly be over-estimated. If one feels that one's own value is not constituted primarily by the human qualities one possesses, but by one's success on a competitive market with ever-changing conditions, one's self-esteem is bound to be shaky and in constant need of confirmation by others. Hence one is driven to strive relentlessly for success, and any setback is a severe threat to one's self-esteem; helplessness, insecurity, and inferiority feelings are the result. If the vicissitudes of the market are the judges of one's value, the sense of dignity and pride is destroyed.

11. But the problem is not only that of self-evaluation and self-esteem but of one's experience of oneself as an independent entity, of one's *identity* with *oneself*. . . . The mature and productive individual derives his feeling of identity from the experience of himself as the agent who is one with his powers; this feeling of self can be briefly expressed as meaning "*I am what I do.*" In the marketing orientation man encounters his own powers as commodities alienated from him. He is not one with them but they are masked from him because what matters is not his self-realization in the process of using them but his success in the process of selling them. Both his powers and what they create become estranged, something different from himself, something for others to judge and to use; thus his feeling of identity becomes as shaky as his self-esteem; it is constituted by the sum total of roles one can play: "*I am as you desire me.*"

12. Ibsen has expressed this state of selfhood in Peer Gynt: Peer Gynt tries to discover his self and he finds that he is like an onion—one layer after the other can be peeled off and there is no core to be found. Since man cannot live doubting his identity, he must, in the marketing orientation, find the conviction of identity not in reference to himself and his powers but in the opinion of others about him. His prestige, status, success, the fact that he is known to others as being a certain person are a substitute for the genuine feeling of identity. This situation makes him utterly dependent on the way others look at him and forces him to keep up the role in which he once had become

successful. If I and my powers are separated from each other then, indeed, is my self constituted by the price I fetch.

13. The way one experiences others is not different from the way one experiences oneself. Others are experienced as commodities like oneself; they too do not present *themselves* but their salable part. The difference between people is reduced to a merely quantitative difference of being *more or less* successful, attractive, hence valuable. This process is not different from what happens to commodities on the market. A painting and a pair of shoes can both be expressed in, and reduced to, their exchange value, their price; so many pairs of shoes are "equal" to one painting. In the same way the difference between people is reduced to a common element, their price on the market. Their individuality, that which is peculiar and unique in them, is valueless and, in fact, a ballast. The meaning which the word *peculiar* has assumed is quite expressive of this attitude. Instead of denoting the greatest achievement of man—that of having developed his individuality—it has become almost synonymous with *queer*. The word *equality* has also changed its meaning. The idea that all men are created equal implied that all men have the same fundamental right to be considered as ends in themselves and not as means. Today, equality has become equivalent to *interchangeability*, and is the very negation of individuality. Equality, instead of being the condition for the development of each man's peculiarity, means the extinction of individuality, the "selfishness" characteristic of the marketing orientation. Equality was conjunctive with difference, but it has become synonymous with "in-difference" and, indeed, indifference is what characterizes modern man's relationship to himself and to others.

14. These conditions necessarily color all human relationships. When the individual self is neglected, the relationships between people must of necessity become superficial, because not they themselves but interchangeable commodities are related. People are not able and cannot afford to be concerned with that which is unique and "peculiar" in each other. How-

ever, the market creates a kind of comradeship of its own. Everybody is involved in the same battle of competition, shares the same striving for success; all meet under the same conditions of the market (or at least believe they do). Everyone knows how the others feel because each is in the same boat: alone, afraid to fail, eager to please; no quarter is given or expected in this battle.

15. The superficial character of human relationships leads many to hope that they can find depth and intensity of feeling in individual love. But love for one person and love for one's neighbor are indivisible; in any given culture, love relationships are only a more intense expression of the relatedness to man prevalent in that culture. Hence it is an illusion to expect that the loneliness of man rooted in the marketing orientation can be cured by individual love.

16. Thinking as well as feeling is determined by the marketing orientation. Thinking assumes the function of grasping things quickly so as to be able to manipulate them successfully. Furthered by widespread and efficient education, this leads to a high degree of intelligence, but not of reason. For manipulative purposes, all that is necessary to know is the surface features of things, the superficial. The truth, to be uncovered by penetrating to the essence of phenomena, becomes an obsolete concept—truth not only in the prescientific sense of "absolute" truth, dogmatically maintained without reference to empirical data, but also in the sense of truth attained by man's reason applied to his observations and open to revisions. Most intelligence tests are attuned to this kind of thinking; they measure not so much the capacity for reason and understanding as the capacity for quick mental adaptation to a given situation; "mental adjustment tests" would be the adequate name for them. For this kind of thinking the application of the categories of comparison and of quantitative measurement—rather than a thorough analysis of a given phenomenon and its quality—is essential. All problems are equally "interesting" and there is little sense of the respective differences in their importance. Knowledge itself becomes a com-

modity. Here, too, man is alienated from his own power; thinking and knowing are experienced as a tool to produce results. Knowledge of man himself, psychology, which in the great tradition of Western thought was held to be the condition for virtue, for right living, for happiness, has degenerated into an instrument to be used for better manipulation of others and oneself, in market research, in political propaganda, in advertising, and so on.

17. Evidently this type of thinking has a profound effect on our educational system. From grade school to graduate school, the aim of learning is to gather as much information as possible that is mainly useful for the purposes of the market. Students are supposed to learn so many things that they have hardly time and energy left to *think*. Not the interest in the subjects taught or in knowledge and insight as such, but the enhanced exchange value knowledge gives is the main incentive for wanting more and better education. We find today a tremendous enthusiasm for knowledge and education, but at the same time a skeptical or contemptuous attitude toward the allegedly impractical and useless thinking which is concerned "only" with the truth and which has no exchange value on the market.

18. Although I have presented the marketing orientation as one of the non-productive orientations, it is in many ways so different that it belongs in a category of its own. The receptive, exploitative, and hoarding orientations have one thing in common: each is one form of human relatedness which, if dominant in a person, is specific of him and characterizes him. The marketing orientation, however, does not develop something which is potentially in the person (unless we make the absurd assertion that "nothing" is also part of the human equipment); its very nature is that no specific and permanent kind of relatedness is developed, but that the very changeability of attitudes is the only permanent quality of such orientation. In this orientation, those qualities are developed which can best be sold. Not one particular attitude is predominant, but the emptiness which can be filled most quickly with the desired quality. This quality, how-

ever, ceases to be one in the proper sense of the word; it is only a role, the pretense of a quality, to be readily exchanged if another one is more desirable. Thus, for instance, respectability is sometimes desirable. The salesmen in certain branches of business ought to impress the public with those qualities of reliability, soberness, and respectability which were genuine in many a businessman of the nineteenth century. Now one looks for a man who instills confidence because he *looks* as if he had these qualities; what this man sells on the personality market is his ability to look the part; what kind of person is behind that role does not matter and is nobody's concern. He himself is not interested in his honesty, but in what it gets for him on the market. The premise of the marketing orientation is emptiness, the lack of any specific quality which could not be subject to change, since any persistent trait of character might conflict some day with the requirements of the market. Some roles would not fit in with the peculiarities of the person; therefore we must do away with them—not with the roles but with the peculiarities. The marketing personality must be free, free of all individuality.

RICHARD H. ROVERE

Technology and the Claims of Community

Richard H. Rovere (1915–   ) has held editorial positions with such periodicals as *Harper's, The American Scholar,* and *The New Yorker,* to which he regularly contributes a "Letter from Washington." He has published and edited many books, among them *The Eisenhower Years,* 1956; *The Orwell Reader,* 1956; *The American Establishment and Other Reports, Opinions, and Speculations,* 1962; and *Goldwater Caper,* 1965.

Mr. Rovere finds the chief cause of our diminished privacy to be the growing size and complexity of our technological society, and he foresees that it will become increasingly difficult to preserve individual privacy and still protect the public welfare.

1. It is repeatedly asserted by solicitous groups and individuals that the right of privacy—described once by Mr. Justice Brandeis as the "right to be let alone . . . the most comprehensive of rights and the right most

TECHNOLOGY AND THE CLAIMS OF COMMUNITY From *The American Scholar,* Autumn 1958. Reprinted by permission of the author and the publisher.

valued by civilized men"—is in sorry shape in this Republic today. The evidence is impressive. Wire tapping is epidemic; even where it is illegal, it flourishes, and some authorities believe that the number of telephones being monitored on any given day runs into the hundreds of thousands. "Bugging," the use of concealed electronic devices by absentee eavesdroppers, is an almost universal practice among policemen, private detectives, and both public and private investigators. People describing themselves as "investigators" are as numerous and as pestiferous, it often seems, as flies in late September. Each day, more and more of us are required to tell agencies of government more and more about ourselves; and each melancholy day, government agencies are telling more and more about us. Someone in the F.B.I.—not Mr. Hoover, certainly, but someone—slips a "raw" file to a favored congressman; the President instructs the Bureau of Internal Revenue to turn over income tax returns to an investigating committee; the Defense Department gives medical records to an insurance adjuster. The existence of the files, apart from their disclosure, may itself be regarded as a violation of privacy; we are compelled to leave bits and pieces of ourselves in many places where we would just as soon not be.

2. Broadly speaking, invasions of privacy are of two sorts, both on the increase. There are those, like wire tapping and bugging and disclosure of supposedly confidential documents, that could conceivably be dealt with by changes in law or public policy. Then there are those that appear to be exercises of other rights—for example, freedom of speech, of the press, of inquiry. A newspaper reporter asks an impertinent personal question; the prospective employer of a friend wishes to know whether the friend has a happy sex life; a motivational researcher wishes to know what we have against Brand X deodorant; a magazine wishing to lure more advertisers asks us to fill out a questionnaire on our social, financial and intellectual status. Brandeis' "right to be let alone" is unique in that it can be denied us by the powerless as well as by the powerful —by a teen-ager with a portable radio as well as by a servant of the law armed with a subpoena.

3. Most of those who publicly lament the decline of privacy talk as if they believe that the causes are essentially political; they seem to feel that enemies of individual rights are conspiring to destroy privacy just as certain of them have sought, in recent years, to destroy the right to avoid self-incrimination. Some also see privacy eroding as a consequence of a diminishing respect for it. I think there may be something in both points, although a good deal less in the first than in the second; but it seems to me that the really important causes lie elsewhere—in our advancing technology and in the growing size and complexity of our society. Until the early part of this century, the right of privacy was seldom invoked. Though its broadest and most binding guarantee is in the Fourth Amendment to the Constitution, which affirms "the right of the people to be secure in their persons, houses, papers, and effects" and prohibits unreasonable searches and seizures, it was not until 1905 that a court squarely upheld the right of privacy. The jurisdiction was Georgia, and the court laid it down as a common-law proposition that "the right of privacy has its foundations in the instincts of nature." In a thinly populated land, with government touching only lightly on the everyday lives of citizens and with a technology so primitive that people had to depend on their own eyes and ears to know what others were up to, men armed with the Fourth Amendment and with the squirrel gun permitted them under the Second Amendment could pretty well attend to their own privacy. Mostly, one supposes, it was not thought of as a "right" to be protected but as a condition of life cherished by some and merely accepted by others.

4. But then came the camera, the telephone, the graduated income tax, and later the tape recorder, the behavioral scientist, television (now being used to follow us as we move about supermarkets and department stores as a kind of radar for the light-fingered), the professional social worker, "togetherness" and a host of other developments that are destructive of privacy as a right and as a condition. Soundproofing is the only technological contribution I can think of that has been an aid to the right to be let alone. The rest have lent themselves to invasions of privacy, and the end is not yet in sight. Wire tapping, for example, is now in the process of being fully automated; where formerly the number of wires that could be tapped was limited by the

number of personnel that could be assigned to sitting around all day waiting for a conversation to intercept, today innumerable phones can be monitored entirely by machines. Someday, no doubt, we shall be spied upon from space platforms equipped with television cameras. And all this time the welfare state has been developing—in the main, of course, as a response to technology. It may be that a disrespect for privacy has been on the increase, too, but what is certain is that those of a trespassing inclination are infinitely better equipped today and have infinitely more excuses for their incursions. I rather think this is the essential thing, for I believe that if the Georgia court was correct in saying that the "instincts of nature" provided foundations for the right of privacy, the same thing may also be cited as a source of motive power for those who assume the right to violate privacy. Was it not Senator McCarthy who screamed bloody murder when the Post Office Department ran a "mail cover" on his correspondence? (In a mail cover, postal officials do not open mail but examine envelopes and wrappings with a view to learning the identity of a victim's correspondents.) No doubt his outrage was as genuine as it was noisy. There is a hermit spirit in each of us, and also a snooper, a census taker, a gossipmonger and a brother's keeper.

5. Technology has forced the surrender of a measure of privacy in many different ways. It may be a man's business whether he drinks or not, but if he wishes to drive a car or fly an airplane or perform brain operations, society's need to inquire into his drinking habits must surely override his right to privacy in this serious matter. Government is society's instrument in such affairs, and the more responsibilities we saddle it with, the more we require it to take a hand in our lives. If we wish it to protect us against quacks, frauds, swindlers, maniacs and criminals, we must give it powers of prosecution, punishment and licensing. We can be reasonably certain that its tendency will be to go too far (the American Civil Liberties Union reports with distress that in some places tile layers must now be licensed by public authority), but we may—

indeed, it seems to me that most of us do —judge its excesses to be less dangerous than complete laissez faire or laissez passer. Technology has made us all a great deal more dependent upon one another than we ever were in the past and necessarily, therefore, less able to protect our own privacy. Once we could labor alone—now there is a division of labor which relates my work to yours. Once we traveled alone—now our mobility is collectivized, and while we have a legitimate concern over the habits of the man at the controls, whose private life we find it necessary to investigate, we also constitute ourselves a captive audience and a group of hostages to those in whom the instincts of nature that lead to compulsive trespassing are more powerful than those that make sometime recluses of us all.

6. In my view, which may be eccentric, it gains us nothing to denounce J. Edgar Hoover or those who descend to what Mr. Justice Holmes called the "dirty business" of wire tapping—or even to expend rhetoric on the death of solitude in our kind of civilization, as William Faulkner now and then does when he feels himself affronted by the attentions of the press. If there is any way at all out of the fish bowl, it will be found only by facing some hard facts of life today. For one thing, there is no stopping the technology that extends our senses by wires and waves and electrical impulses. For another, it is difficult —if, indeed, it is possible—to distinguish, morally and practically, between the use of these devices and the use of the senses unaided. I think that wire tapping is a dirty business, but I am not sure that I can find much logic to support my belief so long as I am willing to countenance the older, unmechanized ways by which society apprehends criminals. What is the moral difference between tapping a telephone wire and straining one's ears to overhear a conversation believed by the participants to be private? What is the moral difference between putting an ear to a keyhole and bugging a room? Or between using any and all bugging devices and planting spies and informers in the underworld? Or between carrying a concealed tape re-

corder to an interview and carrying a concealed plan to commit to memory as much
of the talk as the memory can retain? Society
needs detectives, or so at least I believe, and
the means they employ have never been
lovely and have almost always involved the
violation of privacy.

7. So far as morality is concerned, I doubt
if a valid distinction can be made between
primitive and advanced techniques. But a
practical distinction can be made, and in fact
has been made (wire tapping *is* either outlawed or restricted by law in every American
jurisdiction), and the rationale is not very
different from that which proscribes mechanical devices in most sports. Whether or not
wire tapping is dirty business in the Holmes-
ian sense, it is dirty pool, and this applies,
or soon will, one suspects, to most other gadgets. It may be no more immoral than other
means used for the same end—any more than
killing with thermonuclear weapons is more
immoral than killing with a club—but somehow the advantage it gives to the police side
is offensive to sportsmanship, and the numbers that can be bagged by automated spying,
like the numbers that can be killed by a hydrogen bomb, make it seem more offensive to
our humanity. Against this, it can be argued
that crime and subversion have also benefited
by science and that their adversaries should
not have to fight a horse cavalry war against
them. But the fact of the matter is that it is
not narcotics peddlers whose privacy has been
more efficiently violated by the use of the
new techniques; the net has not been drawn
tighter against society's enemies—it has simply been spread for a larger catch. And here
another practical distinction can be made,
even though a moral one comes hard. It is
one thing to deceive and trap a dope pusher
by almost any means available, and quite
another to tap the phone of, let us say, a
philanthropic foundation on the chance of
turning up a relationship between it and some
citizen of a heretical turn of mind. To be
sure, the underworld members of the Apa-
lachin rally have every bit as much right
to privacy as Robert M. Hutchins. But the
law in its wisdom has found a way to draw
a line between the two without denying their
equality; this is the doctrine of "probable
cause," embodied as the condition for sei-
zure and arrest in the same Fourth Amendment that keeps most of us out of the broad
net of policemen merely fishing for evidence
in our homes and among our papers and
effects.

8. It seems to me that it is by no means
too late for law and public policy to deal
with violations of privacy that are undertaken
by zealous guardians of the peace and the
public order. In all probability, wire tapping
and the many forms of bugging can never
be wholly eliminated, even where they are
outlawed and the penalties for their use are
severe; they suit the police mentality too well,
and they may be easily employed without
fear of detection. Moreover, there are circumstances in which even the most ardent civil
libertarians would be forced to approve their
use. But the third degree and the rubber
truncheon also suit the police mentality, and
free societies have managed to reduce their
use to a point where they are not regarded
as essential characteristics of the machinery of
law enforcement. Probable cause, with high
standards for the determination of probability,
would seem a basic safeguard against present
excesses. Another would be an extension of
the rule of the inadmissibility of wire-tap
evidence; this, of course, is the rule in the
federal courts today, and it has not stopped
the F.B.I. and God knows how many other
government agencies from tapping wires in
the hope of learning where admissible evidence may be turned up. But there is no reason why the rule of inadmissibility might
not be strengthened in such a way as to give
ordinary criminal defendants a chance at ac-
quittals and reversals whenever the prosecution's case has been made by playing dirty
pool. The police, like merchants, do not care
for profitless ventures, and somewhere, no
doubt, there is a point at which most of the
profit can be taken out of the indiscriminate
wire tapping and bugging that is being employed today. Mr. Justice Murphy used to

say that there was no means of preserving the liberties of citizens so efficacious as making the denial of those liberties disadvantageous to the police power.

9. Nothing will be done, however, along this line unless a certain amount of public pressure builds up against a catch-as-catch-can view of law enforcement and in defense of the right of privacy. And even if abuses of the police power were checked, we would be left with all those invasions that are the work not of the police power, but of other public authorities and of a multitude of private ones. Here, as I see it, we encounter problems far knottier than those posed by technology in the service of law and order. We were willed a social order dedicated to the sovereignty of the individual but, again thanks mainly to technology, dependent for its functioning largely on the interdependence of lives. My behavior affects my neighbor in a hundred ways undreamed of a century ago. My home is joined to his by pipes and cables, by tax and insurance rates. If my labor is not immediately dependent on his, it is on that of other men down the street and across the continent. When I move about, my life is at my neighbor's mercy—and his, of course, at mine. I may build a high fence, bolt the doors, draw the blinds and insist that my time to myself is mine alone, but his devices for intrusion are limitless. My privacy can be invaded by a ringing telephone as well as by a tapped one. It can be invaded by an insistent community that seeks to shame me into getting up off my haunches to do something for the P.T.A. or town improvement or the American Civil Liberties Union—possibly, for this worthy organization, making a survey of invasions of privacy. My "right to be let alone" is a right I may cherish and from time to time invoke, but it is not a right favored by the conditions of the life I lead and am, by and large, pleased to be leading. If I were to think of it as any sort of absolute right, I would be as blind to the world about me as those who used to believe that the United States could assert and by itself defend its right to be let alone. No kind of sovereignty has ever been

absolute, but in the last century or so the decline has been staggering.

10. The meaningful invasions that are a consequence of the condition of our lives are, to be sure, those undertaken more or less in the name of the whole community: by organs of government other than the police, by the press, by education, by business. Against them, the law can offer few defenses without denying other freedoms and committing new invasions of privacy. The press has a right to describe Nathan Leopold's release from prison; whether it will exercise that right in the face of eloquent pleas not to do so is a matter of conscience and taste. In general, our rule is that those who lead part of their lives in public—politicians, entertainers, writers and others, including celebrated criminal defendants, who court the public favor in one way or another—have forfeited the right to invoke the common-law doctrine that "a person who unreasonably and seriously interferes with another's interest in not having his affairs known to others . . . is liable to the other." In England, Randolph Churchill may raise the roof because the press is, in his view, too nosey about the private life of Princess Margaret, but here there would be no one to defend the proposition that the press and public should be kept in the dark about the President's health, as the British public was once kept in the dark about the health of Randolph Churchill's father. And the same tests of public interest and relevance that apply in the community of the nation apply in every subcommunity. To a degree, we can control our privacy by controlling our mode of existence, and if we can never retain anything like complete mastery, we can at least attempt an approach to it. But the costs are heavy and to many, probably most, Americans excessive.

11. It is common for Europeans to say that privacy will die in America because we care nothing about it. "An American has no sense of privacy," Bernard Shaw wrote. "He does not know what it means. There is no such thing in the country." Foreigners frequently profess to be scandalized by American institutions that seem to them destructive of the

very idea of privacy—the standard sleeping car, for instance, and the now ubiquitous portable radio. Alistair Cooke has said that while in England good manners consist in not intruding oneself upon others, here they consist in being tolerant of those who lead their private life in public and remain a good sport about all noisy intrusions. I think the differences are real but insignificant. The British may piously talk of the royal family's right to privacy, but their gutter press makes more lives miserable than ours does. The French set great store by privacy, but they allow their police a license that Americans would never tolerate. (The French police operate on the theory that their work would be quite impossible if they were not allowed to run mail covers, ransack telegraph files and tap wires.) We are perhaps the most gregarious and community-minded of people and have developed social and technological interdependence further than any other, but it is still, I think, universally acknowledged that the man who tells another to "mind your own business" has justice on his side and speaks the common law. We are all in the same fix, and we all have to strike the same balance between our need for others and our need for ourselves alone.

ROBERT FROST

Desert Places

Snow falling and night falling fast, oh, fast
In a field I looked into going past,
And the ground almost covered smooth in snow,
But a few weeds and stubble showing last.

The woods around it have it—it is theirs.
All animals are smothered in their lairs.
I am too absent-spirited to count;
The loneliness includes me unawares.

And lonely as it is that loneliness
Will be more lonely ere it will be less—
A blanker whiteness of benighted snow
With no expression, nothing to express.

They cannot scare me with their empty spaces
Between stars—on stars where no human race is.
I have it in me so much nearer home
To scare myself with my own desert places.

CLARENCE HENRY FAUST

The Search for Answers

Clarence Henry Faust (1901–   ) has had a versatile career. He began in 1924 as an ordained minister and in 1928 entered academic life, becoming later the dean of the University of Chicago and subsequently the director of libraries at Stanford University. In 1950 he became president of the Fund for the Advancement of Education, established by the Ford Foundation, and in 1957 he was named vice president of the Ford Foundation, the position he now holds. Throughout his career he has maintained an interest in the religious problems of modern man. His publications include *Representative Selections* from the writings of Jonathan Edwards, 1935, which he coedited with Thomas H. Johnson; *The Decline of Puritanism*, 1954; and *Ideological Conflicts in Early American Books*, 1958.

In this essay Mr. Faust examines man's search for meaning in the modern world.

1. Man ought to feel more at home in the modern world. At least he should feel surer about himself and surer about the world around him than his ancestors did. For . . . we understand ourselves and the processes of the universe today much better than ever before, and we have vastly extended our ability to adapt the forces of the universe to our own purposes. It may well be that we sometimes overstate the facts when we talk about our increasing control of nature. But certainly it is true that in dozens of areas we can now de-

THE SEARCH FOR ANSWERS From *An Outline of Man's Knowledge of the Modern World* by Lyman Bryson. Copyright © 1960 by Catherine McGrattan Bryson, Executrix of the estate of Lyman Bryson. Reprinted by permission of Doubleday & Company, Inc., and published by McGraw-Hill Book Company, Inc.

feat, direct, control, or harness natural forces that our ancestors could only view in helpless awe or terror.

2. Yet we are not at ease in this Zion of our own making, not at all confident about ourselves and our place in the world. If anything, we are more troubled about these matters than were our ancestors. Day by day we seem to become less certain of our ability to make firm distinctions between what is right and what is wrong, less sure of the meaning and purpose of human life and of society, less assured about the place of humanity in the scheme of things; we are more hesitant about defining our role as individuals or as members of society, about assigning praise and blame to human actions, and about what our responsibilities to ourselves and others may be.

3. We do understand the processes of na-

ture better, but we are less sure that we understand the sum total of their significance. We know infinitely more about how to manipulate the forces around us, but are inclined to regard these forces as morally neutral. Although we find ourselves capable of unlocking the sources of atomic energy, we are fearfully aware that this incredible new power may become the instrument of race suicide, and none of us is deeply certain that the brave talk about harnessing these new powers for productive purposes in the satisfaction of human needs is more than unrealistic idealism or desperate wishful thinking.

4. This uncertainty afflicts most of us today, including many who adhere to a religious faith. We are often reminded that a larger proportion of our population belongs to some church body now than ever before in American history. And yet, it is certainly true that though millions of people today rely as happily on a church-centered faith as did anyone in the Middle Ages, church members are not exempt from the peculiar uncertainties and anxieties of our time. It is typical of our age that magazines (including religious publications), books, and broadcasting programs regularly present "individual approaches" and "philosophies" that are no more than modifications or interpretations of orthodox creeds. The point of view taken here grows out of the concerns common to those who are religiously inclined. It is implicit in this discussion that the solution of the problems which have their roots in these concerns must come, in part at least, from religious leaders who are prepared to fulfill the function they have fulfilled in the past; that is, who will develop a synthesis of our new knowledge, especially of our new scientific knowledge, in relation to the persistent problems and troubles of mankind. But such a solution is by no means inevitable, for it cannot be taken for granted that the necessary relationships and cross interpretations of science, philosophy, and theology will actually take place.

MAN'S SEARCH FOR VALUES

5. We seem now more than ever before to be trying to discover the source of all principles of what ought to be and all forces that promote the good in human affairs, simply in individual human desires or ideals, or in social decisions.

6. This attempt to individualize our values is evident in what seems to be a key word, perhaps *the* key word, of modern ethics, namely, responsibility. The highest praise we can give a good citizen is to describe him as a highly responsible person. And one of the most effective ways of attacking an aspirant for high public office is to suggest that he is irresponsible. Yet the word responsibility has for us an almost purely social or individual reference. The terms in which we define responsibility reflect what is either socially desirable or in accordance with individual conscience.

7. And yet it is obvious that we are troubled about the validity of these terms of reference. We praise and reward a social sense of responsibility, but at the same time we are concerned about the pressures to conformism which this interpretation of responsibility would seem to justify and increase. We admire the independent man, the man of firm perpendicularity, but are worried that what passes for individual conscience and conscientiousness may after all be merely the product of social conditioning.

8. This same uncertainty is further illustrated in the difficulty our educational institutions have in dealing with what we have come to call "values." The term values is at best ambiguous, for it can mean either that which is in itself truly valuable or that which has merely come to be valued. All of our terms of ultimate reference—"the public good" with respect to society, for example, and "maturity" or "adjustment to society" with respect to the individual—have the same unsatisfactory ultimate point of reference.

9. Our means of dealing with the problems of ethics, with values, with responsibility—in short, with what *ought* to be—seem all to have the same unhappy lack of reach, to fall short of anything beyond individual or social preference. Applying the most admirable modern refinements of the scientific method to these problems, we achieve descriptive but not normative conclusions. We know more and more about what makes people think and act as

they do and about how society operates, but we are less and less sure about the way we ought to behave and what makes a good society. If we assume that these matters are not amenable to scientific investigation but must depend upon some right posture of the emotions, upon some undefined "maturity" which cannot be rationally analyzed or justified but only appropriately appreciated or felt, then we have no way of discriminating ultimately between what is better and worse in human propensities. The feelings of the individual may be shaped by characteristics peculiar to him alone or may be merely culturally conditioned. It is well and good to be able to describe social aims, ideals, and commitments as products of historical processes; but that does not make it any the less difficult to justify them as in any sense right in themselves.

10. It is for these reasons that modern man, though he knows much more about the universe in which he lives and can mold it much more fully to his purposes, still does not feel at home in it and restlessly alternates between dependence upon individual conscience, which he fears may be merely personal and irresponsible, and conformity to society, which he fears may be no more than the product of historical accidents. Distressed and troubled by all these uncertainties, he at last has to seek some security in force—the force which within society is exerted through the pressures of self-interested advertising and propaganda, and which in the international area depends upon the creation of more and more potent weapons. Security comes to mean power, the power to maintain our status and to pursue our individual and social ends.

THE NEED FOR GUIDING PRINCIPLES

11. There can be no satisfactory or fundamental solution to the problem of ethics, no assurance about the real nature of good and evil, no confidence of ultimate success in the search for answers concerning the significance of man's career on this planet and the nature of his responsibilities to himself or to his society without a sense of the direction of the universe apart from man's desires and choices.

12. What our age then needs to establish is a sense of direction, not dogmatically but with sufficient confidence to make firm commitments and even sacrifices, some sense that the path laid out is in accord with the constitution and processes of the universe. It is easier to specify the conditions which must be met in a search for answers than to state the answers or even to point out the line of inquiry to be pursued. The conditions themselves are simple. What we need are some conceptions of the universe which hold out hope of a relationship between the human and the nonhuman, some conception which makes man feel at home in his world—not necessarily at ease in it or with himself but clearly and confidently aware of his successes and failures, or, to use older words, of his virtues and vices.

13. The kind of answer required in the search we are describing must contain the word "ought." The question is, what direction or directions *ought* the individual and society take? To satisfy this need, the answer must be more than a description of individual desires or wants or of social purposes and commitments. It is this requirement which makes the contemporary term "values" unsatisfactory, for it does not necessarily transcend human wishes and often merely denotes qualities which for some reason—conditioning, social pressure, or historical accident—have come to be valued.

14. It is for this reason that the search for ethical direction involves the idea of sacrifice. That which is in itself valuable (over and above being merely valued) has the characteristic that it demands in cases of conflict that we override what merely happens to be valued. The course of right action involves the willingness to give up desires in favor of the good, that is, in favor of what is valuable in itself; and right action requires the will to do so when the two are in conflict. In such circumstances sacrifice, or the readiness to sacrifice, becomes a mark of virtue. This is not to say that suffering or pain is itself a good thing or is in itself virtuous. It is a recognition of the fact that it may be painful to give up a desire because of a compelling sense of a purpose rooted in the nature of things, beyond man's wishes and wants.

15. It is here that modern man finds himself so much at a loss. The admirably effective

and productive methods by which he is able to lay hold of some aspects of the nature of things, the methods of the natural sciences, fail him; not because they are inadequate for their primary purpose, but because they do not reveal the basis of ethical choice. They do enable him to predict the sequences in the processes of things. They do provide him with the means of injecting himself into these processes so that he can direct them to satisfy his own desires and wants. But they do *not* tell him what direction he or a society ought to take. In nothing is this more evident than in the triumph of science in releasing atomic energy. The methods which unlocked those secrets provided a knowledge of natural processes and immense capacity for production or destruction. But they have given us no guide to the basic problems of war or peace.

16. We are at last driven to look inward for guides, to search our own feelings for direction. But here our difficulty is that human beings are patently moved by conflicting forces, that they exhibit aggressive as well as affectionate tendencies. And, as we have said, we find reasons to suppose or to fear that our feelings are either the result of peculiarly individual characteristics or are socially conditioned. Since we are conscious of many uncertainties, the distinctions we do make between right and wrong are set apart from purely factual or descriptive propositions by being called "preference statements" or "emotive language." The term "preference" reveals with even less ambiguity than the term "values" the limitations of our search for answers which would make it possible to discriminate clearly between what we prefer and what is really valuable—which would, in other words, put a moral demand upon us.

RELIGION, NATURAL LAW, AND THE UNIVERSE

17. In times past religion provided a conception of man's relation to the universe which gave his life meaning or taught him how to order his life in order to make it meaningful. In one way or another, religion has always attempted to establish a relationship between human purposes and aspirations and the scheme of the universe. By devices which in their primitive forms seem naïve, religion has

asserted the possibility of establishing a harmonious connection between human intentions and behavior and the universal course of things. If all that exists is under the firm and universal direction of a being who can be called "Father" or "King," there is hope that man's enterprises may be related to, judged, and given at least long-range assurance of success so long as they are compatible with the nonhuman nature and processes of the world. But the growing emphasis on the authority and reliability of the physical and social sciences has made it increasingly difficult for many modern people to accept or to use these terms with any conviction.

18. In the eighteenth century the concept of natural law, "the law of nature and of nature's god," served the same purpose as religion once did. The conception grew out of or implied the idea that the constitution and course of all things could appropriately be regarded as under laws which were not of man's devising but were written in the nature of things. Such a conception consequently provided a reference point for the appraisal of human organizations, laws, and courses of action. But despite our vastly increased knowledge of the regularity of natural processes, even this concept is no longer convincing to many modern men. The eighteenth-century farm boy and the city dwellers alike were constantly reminded of the forces of nature—the succession of the seasons, the processes of generation and growth, the frightful effects of disease. Since it was obvious that all of this was beyond human contrivance, the conception that it was the result of the operation of natural law was persuasive. But we now know that much that was once believed to be immutable in nature can be altered or controlled or directed by man. Modern technology daily performs more astonishing miracles and daily makes us less dependent upon and more distant from the processes of nature. Today's children know milk only as a nourishing liquid that is delivered in cartons, and the hurried modern businessman spans the continent in a few hours, in an elaborately contrived machine, and is conveyed from plane to city in another shiny piece of artifice and deposited in an air-conditioned hotel room. It is hardly

surprising that natural law is for many people today an archaic concept.

19. Today we live not by nature but by technology. But there are tremendous, if not insurmountable, difficulties in establishing a new sense of man's relatedness to the universe, as it is pictured by modern science. One difficulty is simply the overwhelming sense of its immensity. The astronomer's universe with its galaxies millions of light years away, each larger than our own but still an infinitesimal part of an expanding system, is hardly calculated to make the inhabitant of a small planet in a minor solar system feel at home in his world. Such a universe is almost beyond our comprehension. Yet the fundamental difficulty does not, I believe, depend on size alone. The man of the eighteenth-century living in America on the eastern edge of an as yet unexplored continent also had ample, if less spectacular, reason to feel relatively insignificant in the world he inhabited.

20. The real difficulty in feeling at home in the universe, in developing a sense of relationship to it and deriving therefrom convictions concerning what is in itself valuable and demanding beyond our immediate wants and wishes, is conceptual. The world of the modern physicist is conceptually utterly foreign to most of his contemporaries. Most of us, certainly, cannot conceive of a fourth dimension, or of particles with negative spin, and to all but a few the mathematical formulas of modern physics are as unintelligible as the markings on clay tablets made thousands of years ago by a people whose language has been utterly lost. So alien are these modern concepts that there are not even workable analogies to convey to us at least an inkling of what the universe is like and what it intends or at least where it is tending. We are benumbed by size and defeated by complexity.

THE RELATIONSHIP OF RELIGION AND PSYCHOLOGY

21. Human nature being what it is and its needs being what they are, it would be astonishing if there were not some groping beginnings and tentative conceptions of a possible new relation between modern man and his universe. Surely we are not quite as much at a loss as a contemplation of the empty niches in which man's older conceptions once stood would indicate. It is reasonable to suppose that somewhere in the burgeoning new sciences of our time and in the new techniques based upon them there are emerging fruitful new conceptions of man's relationship to the world around him and to processes not of his own making or willing.

22. Though we cannot yet discern their outlines, we can properly assume that the new conceptions must have some of the characteristics of the older ones. The concepts by which we once lived clearly established values and standards that existed quite apart from man's desires and choices. They pointed the direction for man's thoughts, feelings, and conduct and indicated the path which he could hope would bring him into harmony with the nature of things. In short, they provided a basis for ethics which was beyond individual and social interests, a foundation deeper than individual and social desires for discriminating between virtue and vice. They put demands upon men. They specified the nature and ground of sacrifice, that is, they established both the reason and the compulsion to forego immediate emotional pressures. As a result they created for man an important kind of relatedness, and while they did not necessarily provide ease and comfort for him, they did make a man feel at home in his world as he might feel at home in a family which he sometimes found demanding and even irksome but in which his relationships and responsibilities were clear.

23. If we ask where in modern man's thinking about himself and his world such criteria may in a measure be satisfied, we are driven to the conclusion, I think, that it is most likely to be found in the area explored by psychology and psychiatry. Of this, there are many signs. Modern parents read Dr. Spock as Puritan parents conned the Scriptures or the Calvinistic interpretations of them. Not a few individuals in our society relate themselves to a psychiatrist as our forefathers related themselves to a priest or parson. There seems

everywhere to be an increasing tendency to believe that many of the physical difficulties with which our medical men deal are ultimately best understood in terms of the psychological stresses of modern life, and that they can be treated most effectively by techniques which see mind and body as interrelated parts of the whole person.

24. The comparison between the religious and psychological approaches can be carried further. The demonic in human life, which used to be associated with the presence of evil, supernatural beings such as devils and witches, is now located in the realm in which psychology and psychiatry operate. We seem increasingly to suppose that there is an area beyond our immediate perception in the depths of the subconscious which in its functions has supplanted demonic hosts. Freud, Dr. Erik Erikson observes, has "unearthed mankind's daimonic inner world."

25. Psychology and psychiatry are also being called upon to establish a new foundation and new conceptions of virtue and vice. Moreover, there appears to be an increasing tendency to look for salvation in this area. Thomas Mann wrote prophetically when in *The Magic Mountain* he described the lecture of Dr. Krokowski at the sanitarium at Davos:

It seemed that at the end of his lecture Dr. Krokowski was making propaganda for psychoanalysis: with open arms he summoned all and sundry to come unto him. "Come unto me," he was saying, though not in those words. "Come unto me, all ye who are weary and heavy laden." And he left no doubt of his conviction that all those present *were* weary and heavy laden. He spoke of secret suffering, of shame and sorrow, of the redeeming power of the analytic. He advocated the bringing of light into the unconscious mind and explained how the abnormality was metamorphosed into the conscious emotion; he urged them to have confidence; he promised relief.

26. The close relationship between this new approach to the fundamental questions of life and the answers once supplied by religion is evidenced by the increasing interest which it arouses in churches and churchmen. In this connection the reports of a conference sponsored by the Group for the Advancement of Psychiatry on "Some Considerations of Early Attempts in Cooperation Between Religion and Psychiatry" is most illuminating. The participants at the meeting, which was held in 1957, included Protestant, Catholic, and Jewish theologians, as well as psychiatrists. Much was made on both sides of the fundamental differences between religion and psychiatry and between the problems of pastoral service and psychiatric practice. One of the participants took the position that "Religion gives a way of life; psychiatry is a branch of medicine which, it would appear from observation and reading, has been accepted by some as a way of life, or at least as a *Weltanschauung,* and this in spite of the disavowal by Freud of the possibility." Another, however, outlined a religious role for psychiatry:

The education and spiritual development of man was entirely in the hands of the Church in the early part of European civilization, and the clergy was, therefore, in a central position. In the centuries following the Reformation, personality development became increasingly a matter of education. Humanistic ideas of development superseded the older religious ideas. With the decline of religion and humanism at the turn of the century, the psychiatrist has moved into a unique position. He is now the recognized, scientifically trained expert on personality development and is expected to fulfill all functions previously divided among clergymen, educators, parents, and other agencies. If we now attempt to reestablish a relationship between psychiatry and religion, it must be recognized that long-range planning is necessary. At this moment of history, many patients cannot accept what religion has to offer. These individuals consider the psychiatrist to be the only firm reliance in the ocean of emotional currents. Therefore, the present role of the psychiatrist seems to be to make it possible for the patient to interact with his social and cultural environment.

27. What psychiatry presents to modern man is in effect something quite apart from man's conscious desires and choices. It proposes an insight into the direction of things which exist outside of conscious impulses and

wishes—an insight which seems to hold out the prospect of becoming a guide to good and evil in human feelings, thoughts, and conduct. In this sense, the processes of psychiatry do resemble the processes of religion. They promise to reveal to distressed and confused people what their feelings or their conduct mean in the light of the nature of things, or rather the substratum of things, in the human mind and in human association. And like religion, psychiatry frequently insists upon the critical importance of helping the individual himself to uncover and understand the hidden sources of behavior and feeling.

28. There are indeed many similarities between religion and psychiatry. But there are also differences and difficulties, for despite the bridges which are being thrown across the chasm between psychiatry and religion, there are still serious obstacles to communication between the two. Some psychiatrists say that men cannot get on without religion, but such statements seem to many religious leaders to make the unacceptable assumption that any religion will serve the purpose as well as another. Furthermore, the Freudian theory that religion is based largely on the Oedipus complex seems to be a destructive misconception of religion as it is conceived by most religious people. There are many such areas of difference. As Victor von Weizsacker has pointed out in reporting his discussions with Freud about the conflicts of psychoanalysis and religion, "One can no longer evade the question whether psychoanalysis has substituted for religion." Such substitution shocks many thoughtful religious people. Jacques Maritain, in his essay on *Freudianism and Psychoanalysis—A Thomist View*, takes care to distinguish between the method of psychoanalysis, Freudian psychology, and Freudian philosophy, and he sharply states his opinion:

. . . on the first plane [psychoanalytic method], Freud shows himself to be an investigator of genius. On the third plane [Freudian philosophy], he seems almost like a man obsessed. On the second plane [Freudian psychology], he appears to be an admirably penetrating psychologist, whose ideas, inspired by his astonishing instinct for discovery, are spoiled by a radical empiricism and an erroneous metaphysics that is unaware of itself.

29. In short, though he acknowledges certain therapeutic values in psychiatry, Maritain rejects its religious and moral implications: "The phenomena that psychotherapy attempts to modify are pathological phenomena and not moral faults. Its end is not to render people virtuous, but to restore them to health."

30. It would be bold to the point of foolhardiness to predict the course which the relationships of psychiatry and religion will take: whether differences will be sharpened and battle lines fixed; whether different territories will, as suggested by Maritain, be assigned to each; or whether reformulations on both sides will establish a productive peace. Much depends—everything, perhaps—on whether there will emerge a creative intellectual leadership which is capable of opening generally acceptable ways of dealing with the problem. There are reasons to expect that under such leadership fundamental concepts on both sides might be brought into a productive working relationship. For one thing, the growth of religious tolerance, which in America, at least, has been essential to peaceful coexistence of various religions in a united but pluralistic society, has tended to establish and make acceptable the view that there is some truth in every religious position and an element of universality in each. Furthermore, the resolution of the conflicts between science and religion which troubled the nineteenth century, especially after the rise of Darwinism, has left as a legacy the opinion that science does not necessarily threaten religious beliefs. There are, indeed, in our own earlier religious history some encouraging examples of the reconciliation of religion and psychology. The great task of our most original theologian and metaphysician, Jonathan Edwards, was the reinterpretation during the eighteenth century of Calvinistic theology in terms of the powerful new psychological concepts of John Locke, a reinterpretation which proceeded to the point where the process of salvation and

even the idea of the Trinity were reformulated in psychological terms.

31. In the final analysis, the success of efforts to find the terms in which man may have some sense of being at home in his universe depends upon the intellectual and spiritual power of any new religious leadership which may arise. Its intellectual power will be revealed by the depth of its insight into the implications of modern science, including psychology and psychiatry. Its spiritual power must rest upon the development of a view which is not merely contrived to meet the human need and desire for man's understanding of himself in relation to the world, but which also reflects the force of inescapable demands made by the universe on man. The faith, the hope, the ethical criteria of religion require the recognition that inescapable demands are imposed upon man and society, rather than being merely generated by men's problems and desires. In this sense the search for answers in this time of burgeoning scientific knowledge must be a religious search, and its products must have something of the force of revelation.

32. The search for such answers will, of course, inevitably go on. No matter how impressive our scientific knowledge may become, men will be restless until they can form a satisfactory picture of themselves in the kind of universe which science has revealed. The search will be a long, hard task, as long and hard as were those in the days when religion and philosophy provided a rationale for the evaluation of individual and social behavior. No task could be more vital to the welfare of mankind. The most urgent problem of the twentieth century is whether man today can discover and accept the demands which his conception of the universe puts upon him—the necessity to find his own place and society's place in the scheme of things before he destroys himself by the abuse of the powers which science has given him.

HARRY and BONARO OVERSTREET

Making Psychic Space for One Another

Harry Allen Overstreet (1875–   ), served for a decade as a member of the philosophy staff at the University of California. In 1911 he became head of the Department of Philosophy at the College of the City of New York, retiring in 1939. He has continued his intellectual activities in retirement—especially his writing. Among his many books are *A Guide to Civilized Leisure*, 1934; *Let Me Think*, 1939; and *The Great Enterprise*, 1952. Best known of his earlier works is *The Mature Mind*, 1949, a book that continues to draw both wide popular reading and critical acclaim.

Bonaro Wilkinson Overstreet (1902–   ) is also an educator and writer. Her first book was *Poetic Way of Release*, 1931; she has since published many other volumes, including *Footsteps on the Earth*, 1934; *Brave Enough for Life*, 1941; *Understanding Fear in Ourselves and Others*, 1951; and *Hands Laid Upon the Wind*, 1956.

In addition to writing individually, the Overstreets have collaborated on such well-known titles as *The Mind Alive,* 1954; *The Mind Goes Forth,* 1956; *What We Must Know About Communism,* 1958; *Iron Curtain,* 1963; and *Strange Tactics of Extremism,* 1963.

"Making Psychic Space for One Another," from *The Mind Goes Forth,* advances and illustrates the idea that creating one's own psychic space, or room for self-realization, requires first of all the concession of psychic space to others.

1. Where it is known in advance that crowds will compete for standing room, signs are often posted: PLEASE DON'T PUSH. These are to remind each individual that he is not the only one present and that his own share of the space will remain comfortably his only so long as pushing and shoving, elbowing and stepping on toes are kept to a minimum.

2. As soon as pushing and shoving begin, tempers are frayed, irritation takes over, and attention is diverted from the purpose that has brought people together. The man whose toe has been trampled, whose ribs have been jabbed, or who finds himself pinned against a wall, becomes quite simply a man on the defensive: angry or scared or both; not a man whose powers are focused for consideration or appreciation.

3. We know this in physical terms. . . . Also, we know it in psychological terms. If physical elbow-jabbing makes us want to jab back, so does psychological. If we can feel physically cornered, so we can feel mentally and emotionally cornered. We testify to this fact when we say, "I felt trapped," or, "He backed me up against a wall."

4. What this points to is clear: namely, that if we wish other people to think broadly and feel deeply in our presence, we must give them room to do so. We must provide space enough to hold the sort of thoughts and feelings we ask them to have. If, for example, we want them to consider all sides of

a subject, we must give them the mental chance to walk around it and look at it from all sides. It makes no sense for us to argue them into a corner where they can think only of how to hold their own against us or how to escape. If we want them to be people of vision, it makes no sense for us to suspend over them, like the sword of Damocles, our own particular viewpoint—letting them know that they had better see things as we see them, or else.

5. Energies marshaled for self-defense, attack, or escape are not simultaneously marshaled for quiet thought, warm affection, deep appreciation, long-range planning, or compassion. Before we yield, then, to the impulse to put another person on the spot, bludgeon him into compliance, or trap him into making a fool of himself, we must decide what kind of person we want him to become: what marshaling of his energies we hope to encourage.

6. In *The Little World of Don Camillo,* Giovanni Guareschi shows what happens when a normal town becomes a frightened one. No one planned the coming of the fear to that little town in the Po Valley. But the situation was ripe for it. Political partisanship between Communists and anti-Communists had been running high. Then an unplanned incident occurred. Smilzo, a leading Communist, was accidentally injured. His fellow Communists, finding him unconscious, jumped to the conclusion for which they had been emotionally set: a bomb had been thrown by the opposition. Who could have done it? They were ready with their answer: a certain man was said to have voiced a threat. As a mob

they surged off to this man's house, primed for violence.

7. The supposed murderer was at home with his wife and child: had been there all evening. But the mob was in no mood to see him as innocent. He was accused; threatened. Then, even while the argument continued in the farmhouse kitchen, someone in the mob outside shot at him through the window. He died next morning.

8. From that moment, fear stalked the town. Every man looked at every other with suspicion in his eyes. Before, people had been friends, neighbors, or openly acknowledged opponents; they were strangers now. Walled about by mutual fear, they were unable any longer to think the frank thoughts or make the frank movements of free men. Although physically the town lay unaltered—as large as ever—psychologically it had become too small for people to live in.

9. One evening shortly before Christmas, Don Camillo was at work in the rectory, touching up the figures of the crèche. There, Peppone, Mayor and leader of the Communist Party, found him. Peppone was his political enemy. Yet because they had been comrades in the resistance movement against the Fascists, they were united by bonds that came closer to being those of affection than either wanted to acknowledge.

10. Peppone was in a black mood. In the miasma of fear, he trusted no one, not even himself. He had relied, always, on his big fists. Now these were of no use to him. The enemy was a faceless emotion, not localized in a specific body that could be knocked down. Worst of all, he had, in his depression, begun to doubt the cause to which he had devoted his prowess.

"I'd like to give it all up," said Peppone, "but it can't be done."
"What stops you?"
"Stops me? With an iron bar in my hand I could stand up against a regiment!"
"Are you afraid?"
"I've never been afraid in my life!"
"I have, Peppone. Sometimes I am frightened."

Peppone's next remark was one that he could not possibly have given a few moments earlier:
"Well; so am I, sometimes," he said, and his voice was almost inaudible.[1]

11. What made possible this final admission of Peppone's, so out of character with his burly strength and Communistic belligerence? To answer this question, we might take the liberty of revising the conversation. Suppose it had gone this way:

"Are you afraid?"
"I've never been afraid in my life!"
"That's what *you* say! I'll bet you're scared stiff right now!"

12. Would Peppone then have acknowledged his fear? Obviously, he would not and could not have done so. There was nothing in his way of life to make him meek in the face of such a challenge. He could answer as he did only because Don Camillo *made room for that answer by admitting his own fear.* When Don Camillo said, "I have, Peppone. Sometimes I am frightened," the rectory became, in psychological terms, a roomier place than all the rest of the town put together. It was the only place in town large enough to let fear in, let it be recognized and named, and yet not crowd out self-respect and mutual respect.

13. What Don Camillo did for Peppone—and thereby for himself and for the whole town—was a sort of thing we are repeatedly called upon to do for one another, and that we all too repeatedly fail to do. Instead, more often than it is pleasant to realize, we say something that guarantees the other person's remaining on the defensive: something equivalent to, "That's what *you* say! I'll bet you're scared stiff right now!" It takes a generously structured self to make for another person the kind of psychic space in which he can find room for both his self-respect and the acknowledgement of his emotional problems and limitations.

14. Making psychic space for one another,

[1] Giovanni Guareschi, *The Little World of Don Camillo*, pp. 202–203. New York: Pellegrini and Cudahy, 1950.

in short, means, among other things, making room for thoughts and feelings that may not be pretty or brave or noble, but that are human—and that are harmful chiefly when "bottling up" and self-deception have made them explosive, surreptitious, or perverted.

15. One more question is here in order. Suppose Don Camillo had, by skepticism or contempt, forced Peppone into a corner where he had to keep up his boast that he had never been afraid. Would this have made him safer to have around? Would it have made him less likely to do the destructive things that scared men do? Obviously not. Only when Peppone admitted his fear did he stage a return from the world of fiction to the world of reality—where he could take his fears in hand. He was far less likely thereafter to indulge in the extravagant fictions of self-proving. When he said—though almost inaudibly—"Well; so am I, sometimes," he was speaking truth to himself no less than to Don Camillo; and he became more able, not less able, to help restore himself and his frightened community to sane and normal life.

16. People need room to recognize and acknowledge their less praiseworthy thoughts and emotions so that they can manage them while they are still manageable; but even more, perhaps, people need room to turn around when they find themselves going in the wrong direction. They need psychic space in which to correct errors—and move beyond them.

17. *Man is a mistake-maker.* This fact is at once his embarrassment and his glory. It is his embarrassment because his mistakes so often make him look stupid, in his own eyes and those of the people around him, and because they repeatedly get him into situations from which he does not know how to extricate himself. But it is his glory, also; for his power to make more mistakes, and more varied mistakes, than can be made by any lower animal is the badge of his having escaped from the tight prison of instinct and become an explorer of life's wider possibilities.

18. Likewise, however, *man is an ego-defending creature.* If his ego is put under threat every time he makes a mistake; if he is taunted, punished, or cast in the role of fool, he will almost certainly develop tactics of self-defense that are also tactics of self-deception and self-distortion. He will learn to disown his errors, or excuse them. Or, by way of compensation, he will become hypercritical of others. Or he will avoid situations that put him to the test. He may even convert his way of error into his "style of life"—as do those delinquents and criminals who take perverse pride in their antisocial skills. As a matter of self-defense, in brief, he will refuse to see himself as a mistake-maker—and so will both stunt his own growth and become a problem to other people.

19. This fact points up our obligation to let one another make a normal quota of mistakes, acknowledge them, learn from them, and move beyond them—keeping intact, all the while, a reasonable self-respect and self-confidence.

20. Most of us do not admire either people who never admit a mistake or those who never let anyone else forget a mistake: who time and time again drag up old errors as a basis for new reproaches. Furthermore, most of us hold to a religious philosophy that recognizes our human fallibility and our consequent need to forgive and be forgiven. Yet for all this, it seems, we try every dodge where our own mistakes are concerned, except the simple one of admitting them; and we often make it as hard as possible for other people to admit theirs. Instead of giving them room to turn around, and supportive companionship while they make the turn, we edge them into a corner—where they, after the manner of all trapped creatures, defend themselves as best they can.

21. This, we believe, is the tragic story back of many of the personality disorders, stubbornly maintained injustices, and rampant hostilities that so beset our private lives and public practices. It is the story of errors defended or disowned because those who have made them have seen no way, and have not been helped to find any way, in which to harmonize self-defense with the admission and correction of error.

22. We might consider, for example, one

sort of case that has become familiar in our time. Here, we will say, is a man who, during the thirties and the years of the Second World War, gave support of one kind or another to various groups that have since been classified as Communist "fronts." He made a donation here; signed a petition there; let his name be listed among the sponsors of a meeting; was briefly a member, though never a policy-making member, in one or more such organizations.

23. His "affiliations" expressed no commitment to Communism and certainly no intention of undermining our government. He donated, signed, sponsored, or joined because the groups, as portrayed in the materials made available to him, seemed wholly legitimate and humanitarian in purpose. He gave his support, in brief, in exactly the same spirit and for exactly the same reasons that he gave it, and has continued to give it, to other groups that have never been viewed with suspicion.

24. Because of a handful of such past "affiliations," however, he may now find himself officially or unofficially "listed," with his reputation and even his livelihood put under threat. It is a matter of vital importance not only to himself but also to his family, friends, and employer that his equivocal position be clarified. More than this, however, it is a matter of vital importance to our democracy itself, in a time when real dangers need to be distinguished from pseudo dangers, and when those who have deliberately infiltrated an organization must be distinguished from those who joined in good faith, that confusions of this sort be cleared up.

25. It is important, in this kind of a case, that no needless ambiguities remain; for each such ambiguity gives aid and comfort to destructive forces in our midst and provides a "cause" for those disturbed personalities that make their own importance out of pointing condemnatory fingers at their neighbors. It can be readily exploited by demagogues and by those new profiteers among us who have found that fear and suspicion are marketable commodities. It can, likewise, be turned to good account by the Communists themselves,

who most of all benefit by our mutual recriminations.

26. What is needed in such a case, in brief, is a quietly resolute determination to replace confusion with clarity. This determination, moreover, should characterize both the individual himself and those whose minds frame questions about his past. All too often, we know, it characterizes neither—and after enough condemnatory things have been said, on the one hand, and enough self-defensive things, on the other, and after enough people have rallied in support of each side, and enough publicity has been given to the denunciations and denials, there seems little room left for any movement toward understanding. The victory, then, belongs to those who thrive on confusion.

27. What commonly happens in such a case? And how does it comport with either the broad realities of the situation or the common integrities and decencies of our living together?

28. The challenged individual feels himself to be innocent—and feels that the open record of his life, taken in its entirety, testifies to that innocence. Also, he suspects that the chief reason why some of his most vociferous accusers never got caught themselves by any similarly ambiguous groups is that they have never supported *any* movement on the risky pioneering edge of society. Their "virtue," as he sees it, is not the keen discrimination they now charge him with having lacked, but simply a habit of social unconcern. This habit, now, by a turn of the wheel of history, is paying them peculiar dividends: enabling them to set themselves up as "experts in patriotism." The more he ponders this, the more deeply he feels the unfairness of his situation; and the more he feels, also, that to take any steps to set the record straight would be humiliating and unprincipled. Thus, *not* acknowledging past ignorances and errors becomes in itself a "cause."

29. If the individual in question does try to approach his most determined accusers with clarifying evidence, he may have the shocking experience, moreover, of discovering that even though they loudly demand that he clear

up his record, they do not want it cleared up. Moved by a sort of psychological "blood lust," they want him to be guilty. They want him to be guilty because they have called him so. Or they want him to be guilty because he is the sort of "liberal intellectual" or "scientist" whom they have long feared and distrusted, but whom they have never before had such a good chance to put on the spot. Therefore, they may—and frequently do—refuse even to talk with him. Or with a wholly complacent sense of their own virtue, they settle for calling him, not a Communist indeed, but a gullible "dupe" of the Communists.

30. Focusing with more and more anxiety and anger upon those who thus seem determined to misjudge or deliberately to injure him, the challenged individual is likely to lose sight of the fact that, in spite of the noise they make and the claims they make for themselves as experts, his accusers are not typical. They are not a majority—either among his neighbors or within his local or national government. Staring at them, however, until he sees their after-image everywhere, he makes them a majority in his own consciousness. He assumes that as they act, so people in general would act if he ventured toward them with his problem.

31. From that point on, he is in grim reality trapped by those who will not grant him psychic space. Feeling himself hemmed in, he cannot do quietly and simply what is called for: he cannot walk around the self-deluded few, and beyond them, toward those who may be variously confused by what they have heard about him, and confused also about what does and does not promote national security, but who still prefer facts to unfounded charges: who do not want to hate or to be unjust. He does not approach those, in or out of government, who want sanity to prevail—and who will give him all the room he needs for stretching his mind and clarifying his position—because he has persuaded himself that, outside his own particular group of supporters, such people are almost nonexistent.

32. If by good luck, however, or on good advice, he finds himself in the presence of someone who simply relaxes and says, "Tell me about it," he may abruptly discover what psychic space means. It is the kind of space in which broad realities can be looked at; in which thoughts can range widely; in which truths can be sorted out from among half-truths and falsehoods; and in which a human being can stand tall in self-respect even while he acknowledges that he has not always acted wisely and does not know all the answers.

33. When an individual is called a gullible dupe of the Communists, he has room only for the emotions and gestures of self-defense. But it is different where the person to whom he is talking says, "That was a different period of history, back there. It's hard to see how you could have detected Communist influence at that time in some of those groups. You probably didn't even have reason to look for it." Within the spacious generosity and realism of such a judgment, the individual can afford to wonder about his own attitudes and decisions—and to think aloud, perhaps, about the fact that more than once, in earlier years, he dismissed evidence of Communist infiltration as the trumped-up stock in trade of reactionaries and Fascists. Not being called blind, in short, he does not have to prove that he has always seen clearly. Not being called wrong, he does not have to prove himself right. Not being called guilty, he does not have to protest his innocence.

34. Given room, he can explore his own judgments, as well as those of his opponents and supporters. He can see fanaticism, demagoguery, and stereotyped thinking for what they are, without seeing himself as above reproach, or seeing as a fanatic or demagogue everyone who takes seriously the problem of Communist infiltration. Having received psychic space, he can move around in it; and far more than when he was rigidly on the defensive, he can grant such space to others—thereby helping to restore the sanity of our common life.

35. We need to give one another room, however, for far more than the correction of error. We need to give room for what is individually unique and constructively human in one another: curiosity about the make-up of

things, zest in experimentation, pride in accomplishment, creative imagination, appreciation of the beautiful, admiration, gratitude,
and love. For all of these we must provide
psychic space; for they make up the spaciousness of life.

36. Yet often, for reasons that lie deep within our own personalities, we do not make
room for them. We drive them into hiding
with our flippancies and pseudosophistica-
tions. We cut across them with our impatience.
We hedge them about with our dogmatisms,
our narrow definitions of the "practical,"
and our nervous definitions of the "proper."

37. More than thirty years ago, in her novel
So Big, Edna Ferber gave us a sentence that
summed up the contempt of the "practical"
man for the "impractical" lover of beauty:
"Cabbages is beautiful!"

38. Many readers will remember the story
of Selina who, left alone while still almost a
child, fed her hungry spirit on poetry and on
every beautiful thing that met her eyes. Out
of these she made her courage; and this courage took her out of Chicago, as a teen-age
girl, to teach in the Dutch school of High
Prairie. She was driven there seated beside
Klaas Pool, farmer and school director, in the
wagon in which he brought his garden produce to the Chicago market.

> So they jolted up the long Halstead road
> through the late October sunset. . . . Mile
> after mile of cabbage fields, jade-green against
> the earth. Mile after mile of red cabbage, a rich
> plummy Burgundy veined with black. Between
> these, heaps of corn were piled-up sunshine.
> Against the horizon an occasional patch of
> woods showed the late russet and bronze of
> oak and maple. These things Selina saw with
> her beauty-loving eyes. . . .

39. She saw them, and she responded as a
human being is equipped to respond: with the
joy of appreciation.

> "Oh, Mr. Pool!" she cried. "Mr. Pool! How
> beautiful it is here!"

40. Klaas Pool had been driving with his
eyes straight ahead. It took time for his mind
to receive her words even enough to be surprised by them. When they did work in, he
turned toward Selina a slow head and pale,
uncomprehending eyes:

> "Beautiful," he echoed, in puzzled interroga-
> tion. "What is beautiful?"

41. Then Selina made the mistake—if we
count it a mistake—that was to establish her,
at the very start of her teaching career in High
Prairie, as a proper object of heavy, obtuse
humor. She answered his question: "This! The
—the cabbages."

42. Klaas Pool "knew cabbages from seed to
sauerkraut; he knew and grew varieties from
the sturdy Flat Dutch to the early Wakefield."
But for Selina to see them as she did was incomprehensible absurdity.

> "Cabbages is beautiful!" his round pop eyes
> staring at her in a fixity of glee. "Cabbages is
> beautiful!" [2]

43. The humor of Klaas Pool was not malicious. He had no wish to make the young
girl at his side retreat from spontaneity into
a prim correctness: to retreat, as it were, from
being freely herself to being stiltedly the new
teacher. But because his own experience had
given him no room in which to hold together the two concepts of *beauty* and *cash
crop*, he could not grant to Selina her right to
see cabbages as beautiful.

44. We may not have the physical or mental heaviness of a Klaas Pool. Yet all too many
of us have definitions of the practical, the important, the efficient, the smart, the respectable, and the interesting that we impose like
strait jackets upon other people's thoughts
and feelings. We have our own ways of declaring that "everyone knows this"; or "anyone
in his right mind can see"; or "no one but
a sentimental fool would believe"—when what
we actually mean is that some people of our
own kind (who confirm us in our particular
pattern of life, as we confirm them in theirs)
thus "know," "see," and "refuse to believe."

45. There is one further type of space we
must grant to one another if we are to do what
is called for not only in behalf of individual

[2] Edna Ferber, *So Big*, pp. 23–25. New York: Grosset
and Dunlap, 1924.

growth but for the sake of democracy's fulfillment: we must make room for the *outsider*
to move in and become an *insider*.

46. The word *outsider* is one of the lonely
words of our language. It calls up the image
of the human being isolated from his kind:
not able to move into their fellowship; not
able to interpret what is going on, and therefor anxious and awkward in any approach
he tries to make; not able to contribute his
knowledge and skill, and to be valued accordingly.

47. We think of the displaced person, for
example, doomed to physical life in a cultural
vacuum. Around him, people put in their days
after the common manner of human beings.
They talk to one another—in a language
not his. They have work to do that is their
work. They have accustomed ways: ways that
are not intrinsically right or wrong, but which
constitute the easy "second nature" of their
communal life. They are free to express opinions about how things should be done; free,
when they feel like it, to judge and criticize.
It is *their* society. It is not his.

48. Or we think of the child of migrant
parents, dragged from school to school, from
one area of ripening crops to another: a child
who never stays long enough in any one classroom to feel easy with what is expected of
him, nor long enough on any playground to
make friends—so that he can feel confident
that where two or three of these are gathered
together, they will spontaneously widen their
circle to include him if he runs to join them.
He is the outsider against whom, intentionally or thoughtlessly, the other children keep
their circle closed.

49. Not in such drastic cases only, however,
can we recognize the outsider. We think of
the teen-ager who never knows why his words
and actions are not right by the standards
of the group: why he is marked as "different"
and "queer." Or we think of the individual
who is an outsider in his own family: quiet
among the boisterous; frail among those who
are proud of muscle; slow among the quick
of mind—and therefore one to be taunted
or handled with a too obvious patience or
looked at with eyes that are puzzled even when

they mean to be kind. Or we think of the
old person—an outsider under the roof of the
vigorous young—who knows that those who
help him, with brisk conscience, to find small
ways to occupy his hours, hold the unacknowledged belief that his proper occupation is to
die.

50. However we may have come by the experience of "outsideness"—however any person comes by it—the important thing is for
us to know what it does to a human being.
It excludes him. With reference to some part
of his world—some group, activity, field of
knowledge, scheme of values, even topic of
conversation—it leaves him in the dark: unsure of both his footing and his direction. He
cannot see—and therefore cannot do—what
would make him an insider.

51. If the situation from which he feels excluded is emotionally important to him; if,
try as he will, he cannot get on to the hang
of it; and if, further, the experience ties in
with many previous experiences of exclusion,
it may exert a deeply disruptive influence
on his personality. The individual's awareness,
in such a case, may become an in-turning
awareness—so that he cannot give to the objective world the sort of interest and attention that would make him, gradually, an
insider. His estimate of that world, moreover, may become progressively based on one
fact: that it has, or seems to have, shut him
out.

52. Here, for example, is a man who long
ago got off to a bad start in school. His home
gave him no friendliness with books. Neither
was it hospitable to "impractical" questions
nor to the sort of "idle" staring by which a
small boy becomes an insider to the world
of bugs, plants, clouds, and stars. From almost
his first day in school, being ignorant of much
that the other children knew, and inhibited
where they seemed emotionally free, he was
rated as "backward" by his teacher. His classmates, catching him time and again in some
ignorance that seemed to them incredible,
decided he didn't know anything.

53. He was an outsider—among the students, among books, among the gadgets and
natural objects the teacher brought in for illus-

tration. Whether in the classroom or on the playground, he experienced chiefly the sense that the human circle was closed against him. No one, not even the teacher, widened that circle to welcome him. He hated school. Or, in more precise psychological terms, *he hated being what school made him be; hated feeling about himself what school made him feel.*

54. This individual, now, is a man in his late forties. He has no use for "intellectuals." "If anyone blows up the world, it will be those guys." In his community, he is first to suspect the educated person—almost any educated person—of being disloyal. In his home, he is first to make sure that no kid of his will sit around with his nose in a book. The type of psychic space that was denied to him during his formative years, he now denies to others.

55. The concept of such space, however, does not need for its illumination merely one example after another. It is the core concept of our maturing psychological sciences. Wherever these sciences begin to have a genuine impact upon us, their primary effect is that of persuading people to give other people room to breathe, to move freely with their minds, to turn around if need be—and therefore to grow.

56. This development has had conspicuous triumphs in the field of parent-child relationships. Here, the essential insight is that growth will take place only where there is mental and emotional room for growth. Neither child nor adult will manifest an increasing good will and creativeness if he is kept so on the defensive that his energies are chiefly focused for fight and flight. The infant who screams in fear and rage when it is held so tightly that it cannot move when it wants to is, we might say, our whole humanity writ small.

57. The principle of space-making is oper-ating, also, in the emerging programs of human relations in industry. What these programs chiefly provide is more psychic space in situations of daily work than was there before.

58. In a certain New England mill town, factory buildings that have stood for generations were recently taken over by a new enterprise. The cubic footage of the buildings has not materially changed since the 1880's. The psychic "footage," however, has increased almost unbelievably. This particular mill was once a place where workers—men, women, and children—were treated as expendable; and where, if they wished to stay on the job, they kept their mouths shut and their minds empty of questions. Today, workers who go in through the same old doors to their allocated desks or machines move in an atmosphere of astonishing new spaciousness. If they see ways to improve production or human relationships, they can talk these out; and if they can make them seem even fairly practical, try them out. The enterprise still has, to be sure, its points of friction. Yet the contrast with what the same walls once contained dramatically illustrates the fact that where the psychological sciences move into industry, they become makers of a highly valuable product: breathing space for the minds of men.

59. When the priest, Don Camillo, said to Peppone, the Communist mayor, "Sometimes I am afraid," he gave Peppone room in which to say, in effect, "Me too." Wherever human beings are permitted to move from a strictly defensive position to one of free and honest association with their kind—and with their own thoughts—they begin to discover the common bases of their living together, and, no less, the unique and stimulating diversity of their many minds.

LOREN EISELEY

An Evolutionist Looks at Modern Man

Loren Eiseley (1907–   ) is a professor of anthropology, writer on science, and curator of the Early Man section of the University of Pennsylvania Museum. He is the author of many popular articles, books, short stories, and poems, as well as a contributor to scientific journals, and he has received a number of literary awards and medals. In 1957 he published the speculative book on evolution, *The Immense Journey*. Among his latest works are *Darwin's Century: Evolution and the Men Who Discovered It*, 1958; *The Firmament of Time*, 1960; *Francis Bacon and the Modern Dilemma*, 1961; and *The Mind as Nature*, 1962.

Mr. Eiseley reminds us here that man's future "will be achieved, if it is achieved at all, only in our individual hearts."

1. In the age of technology which now surrounds us, and which boasts of its triumphs over nature, one thing is ever more apparent to the anthropologist—the student of man. We have not really conquered nature because we have not conquered ourselves. It is modern man, *Homo sapiens,* "the wise" as he styles himself, who is now the secret nightmare of man. It is his own long shadow that falls across his restless nights and that follows soundlessly after the pacing feet of statesmen.

2. Not long ago I chanced to walk through the Hall of Man in one of the country's large museums. Persons of great learning had been instrumental in erecting those exhibits, and I hoped to find there some clue as to human destiny, some key that might unlock in a few succinct sentences the nature of man. The exhibit ended in a question mark before an atomic machine and a graph showing the almost incredible energy that now lay open to

AN EVOLUTIONIST LOOKS AT MODERN MAN   From the *Saturday Evening Post,* April 26, 1958. Reprinted by special permission of The Saturday Evening Post and the author. © 1958 The Curtis Publishing Company.

the hand of man. Needless to say, I agreed with the question mark which ended the history of humanity within that hall.

3. But as I turned and went in the other direction, step by step, eon by eon, back into the past, I came to a scarcely human thing crouched over a little fire of sticks and peering up at me under shaggy brows. The caption read: "Man begins his technological climb up the energy ladder. He discovers fire." I walked a short way backward and forward. I read the captions. I looked again at the creatures huddled over a fire of sticks—at the woman clutching a child to her breast. Again I searched the hall. This was the sum total of all that science had here seen fit to emphasize graphically as important to the human story. The hunters' tools were there, the economic revolution effected by agriculture was ably presented. Summarized before my eyes, populations grew, cities and empires rose and fell, and still man's energy accumulated.

4. One saw another thing. One saw the armored legions grow and grow until at last continent confronted continent and the powers

of death to a world lay in the hands of the descendants of that maned woman and her consort by the fire of sticks.

5. I hesitated again before those forgotten engines of the past, for it seemed to me that there was lacking here some clue, some vital essence of the creature man, and that I was looking upon stone and polished sword and catapult from some place just a little remote and distorted. "This is the history of man," the caption ran through my head, and at that moment, finally, I knew I was looking at the past through the eyes of a modern twentieth-century American, or for that matter, a Russian. There was no basic difference.

6. In that whole exhibit were ranged the energies of wheat and fire and oil, but of what man had dreamed in his relations with other men, there was little trace. Yet it is only on paper, or, in human heads, we might say in paraphrase of Shaw, that man has sought successfully to transcend himself, his appetites and his desires. In that great room was scarcely a hint of the most remarkable story of all, the rise of a value-creating animal and the way in which his intangible dreams had been modified and transformed to bring him to the world he faces today.

7. The educated public has come to accept the verdict of science that man, along with the plant and animal world about us, is the product of endless evolutionary divergence and change. In accepting this verdict of science, however, men have frequently failed to inquire in what way human evolution may differ from that of other animals, or by what extra dangers and responsibilities the human brain may be haunted. In the revolt from the fanatical religiosity of past centuries we have too often welcomed with open arms a dogmatic scientific naturalism which, like the devil with Faust, seemed to offer unlimited material power over nature while, at the same time, assuring us that our moral responsibilities were limited and excusable since we were, after all, only the natural evolutionary culmination of a line of apes that chanced to descend upon the ground.

8. Darwin and his compatriots, struggling to establish for their day a new and quite amazing interpretation of human history, placed great emphasis upon man's relationship to the animal world about him. Indeed, at times they overemphasized man's kinship with the existing apes, partly because of their anxiety to prove the reality of man's descent from lower forms of life, partly because in their lifetime the course of human evolution was very imperfectly known from fossils. The result was that Darwin's own interpretation of the early stages of human evolution wavered between a theory involving an early and Edenlike seclusion on some oceanic island, to a later more ferocious and competitive existence on one of the major continents.

9. These extremes of interpretation need not concern us now except to illustrate the hesitancy with which Darwin attempted to account for some of the peculiar qualities of man. Today we are well convinced of the general course of man's rise from some ancient anthropoid line. Each year new fossil evidence of this fact is brought to our attention. Each year the public grows more accustomed to this history, feels more at home in the natural world which it casually assumes to be dominated by struggle, by a dog-eat-dog interpretation of existence which descends to us from the Darwinian period.

10. Some time ago I had a letter from a professional friend of mine commenting upon the education his daughter was receiving at a polite finishing school. "She has been taught," he wrote to me a little sadly, "that there are two kinds of people, the tough- and the tender-minded. Her professor, whose science I will not name, informed her that the tough-minded would survive."

11. This archaic remark shook me. I knew it was not the product of the great selfless masters of the field, but it betrayed an attitude which demanded an answer. In that answer is contained the whole uniqueness of man. Man has not really survived by toughness in a major sense—even the great evolutionists Darwin and Wallace had had trouble with that aspect of man—instead, he has survived through tenderness. Man in his arrogance may boast that the battle is to the strong, that pity and affection are signs of weakness. Nevertheless, in

spite of the widespread popularity of such ideas, the truth is that if man at heart were not a tender creature toward his kind, a loving creature in a peculiarly special way, he would long since have left his bones to the wild dogs that roved the African grasslands where he first essayed the great adventure of becoming human.

12. The professor who growled to his class of future mothers about being tough-minded spent a childhood which is among the most helpless and prolonged of any living creature. If our parents had actually practiced certain of the philosophies that now flourish among us, or if our remote ancestors had achieved that degree of sophistication which would have enabled them to discount their social responsibilities for the day's pleasure, we—you and I and all of us—would never have enjoyed the experience of living.

13. Man, in the achievement of a unique gift—a thinking brain capable of weighing stars or atoms—cannot grow that brain in the nine months before birth. It is, moreover, a peculiarly plastic brain, intended to receive impressions from the social world around it. Instinct, unlike the case in the world of animals, is here reduced to a minimum. This brain must grow and learn, be able to profit by experience. In man much of that growth and learning comes after birth. The result is that the human infant enters the world in a peculiarly helpless and undeveloped condition. His childhood is lengthy because his developing brain must receive a large store of information and ways of behavior from the social group into which it is born. It must acquire the complicated tool of speech.

14. The demands of learning thus placed upon the human offspring are greater than in any other animal. They have made necessary the existence of a continued family, rather than the casual sex life of many of the lower animals. Although the family differs in many of its minor features in distinct societies, it is always and everywhere marked by its tender and continuing care of the human offspring through the lengthened period of childhood.

15. The social regulations of all human groups promote the welfare of the young.

Man's first normal experience of life involves maternal and paternal care and affection. It continues over the years of childhood. Thus the creature who strives at times to deny the love within himself, to reject the responsibilities to which he owes his own existence, who grows vocal about "tough-mindedness" and "the struggle for existence," is striving to reject his own human heritage. For without the mysteriously increased growth rate of the brain and the correlated willingness of fallible, loving adults to spend years in nursing the helpless offspring they have produced, man would long since have vanished from the earth.

16. We take the simple facts of human life too much for granted. To the student of human evolution this remarkable and unique adjustment of our peculiar infancy to a lengthened family relationship between adults is one of the more mysterious episodes in the history of life. It is so strange, in fact, that only in one group of creatures—that giving rise to man— has it been successfully developed in the three billion years or so that life has existed on the planet. Family life is a fact that underlies everything else about man—his capacity for absorbing culture, his ability to learn—everything, in short, that enables us to call him human. He is born of love and he exists by reason of a love more continuous than in any other form of life. Yet this, in all irony, is the creature who professes to pierce the shams of life and to live by tough-mindedness!

17. Let us see how this nascent and once-aspiring creature now lives in great danger of reentering the specialized trap that his ancestors escaped from ages ago when they evolved a brain capable of abstract thought. "Man is the dwarf of himself," Emerson once wrote, and never, perhaps, has he been more than dwarf than in this age where he appears to wield so much power. The only sign of health remaining to him is the fact that he is still capable of creeping out of the interior of his thickening crust of technological accomplishment to gaze around him with a sense of dissatisfaction and unease.

18. He has every reason to feel this way. For man has never lived before in so great an age of exterior accomplishment, so tre-

mendous a projection of himself into his machines, nor yet so disheartening a period in all that stands for the nobler aspects of the human dream. His spiritual yearnings to transcend his own evil qualities are dimming as he is constantly reminded of his animal past. His desire to fly away to Mars, still warring, still haunted by his own black shadow, is the adolescent escape mechanism of a creature who would prefer to infect the outer planets with his problems than to master them at home.

19. Even now in the enthusiasm for new discoveries, reported public interviews with scientists tend to run increasingly toward a future replete with more inventions, stores of energy, babies in bottles, deadlier weapons. Relatively few have spoken of values, ethics, art, religion—all those intangible aspects of life which set the tone of a civilization and determine, in the end, whether it will be cruel or humane; whether, in other words, the modern world, so far as its interior spiritual life is concerned, will be stainless steel like its exterior, or display the rich fabric of genuine human experience. The very indifference of many scientists to such matters reveals how far man has already gone toward the world of the "outside," of no memory, of contempt toward all that makes up the human tradition.

20. "Wars will be fought in space," prophesied a high military authority recently. "Teach children the hard things first." "Ah, but what hard things?" the teacher asks, because youth is shaped in the teaching and becomes what he is taught. Without spiritual insight and generosity, without the ability to rise beyond power and mechanical extensions, man will encounter in place of the nature which gave him birth only that vast, expanding genie rising from his own brain—himself. Nothing more terrible threatens to confront him in his final hour.

21. It is increasingly plain that if we read the past as a justification for a kind of moral complacency, an animal limit which justifies military remarks such as "man will always fight," we have not read it well. Until man came, it is true, the evolution of life had been

an evolution of parts. It had been hook and clutching bur and fang, struggling upward in an agelong effort. Life had been shaped by the blind forces of the inanimate world. All it had that was different was the will to crawl, the will to find the crevice, the niche, the foothold on this mountain of inanimate matter, and to hold its place against the forces which ever seek to disperse and destroy the substance of life. In all that prehuman world there had been no animal capable of looking back or forward. No living creature had wept above another's grave. There had been nothing to comprehend the whole.

22. For three billion years that rule remained unbroken. At the end of that time there occurred a small soundless concussion. In a sense it was the most terrible explosion in the world, because it forecast and contained all the rest. The coruscating heat of atomic fission, the red depths of the hydrogen bomb— all were potentially contained in a little packet of gray matter that, somewhere between about a million and 600,000 years ago, quite suddenly appears to have begun to multiply itself in the thick-walled cranium of a ground-dwelling ape.

23. The event itself took place in silence, the silence of cells multiplying at an enormous pace under a small bone roof, the silence of some great fungus coming up at night in a forest glade. The eruption had about it the utter unpredictability of nature when she chooses to bypass her accepted laws and to hurtle headlong into some new and unguessed experiment. Even the solar system has now felt the impact of that tiny, soundless explosion. The fact that it was the product of evolutionary forces does not lessen its remarkable quality.

24. For three billion years, until an ageless watcher might have turned away in weariness, nothing had moved but the slime and its creations. Toward the end of that time a small, unprepossessing animal sat on his haunches by a rock pile on a waste of open ground. He clutched a stick and chewed the end of it meditatively. He was setting the fuse of the great explosion. In his head was the first twinkle of that tenuous rainbow

a something that can be reshaped

bridge which stretches between earth and the city of the gods.

25. At that moment the ancestor of man had become the molder of things, rather than their victim, but he had, at the same time, suffered a major loss of instinctive adjustments to life. As the psychologist Jung very aptly remarks: "The forlornness of consciousness in our world is due primarily to the loss of instinct, and the reason for this lies in the development of the human mind over the past eon."

alone—unhappy

26. In a recent paper given before the Research Conference on Growth and Aging, my colleague, Dr. W. M. Krogman, remarked that "The mind of man, the learning potential of an evolved cerebral cortex, enabled him to focus upon the *quality* of things rather than mere quantity." Man has become, in other words, a value-creating animal. He sets his own goals and more and more exerts his own will upon recalcitrant matter and the natural forces of the universe. In this activity he has passed from the specialized evolution of the parts of the body to a projection of such "part" evolution upon his machines and implements. In this respect man is a unique being. Having achieved high intellectual ability, he may remain comparatively unchanged in structure while all around him other animals are still subjected to the old laws of specialized selection. His brain evolves parts and replaces them, but only upon man's mechanical inventions: his tools. This fact gives man a kind of freedom which none of the crawlers-up-the-mountain ever had. He is, as the philosopher Henri Bergson once remarked, a reservoir of indetermination; his power of choice for good or evil is enormous.

outer layer

rebellious

27. It is here that we come upon what I choose to call the "unnatural" aspect of man; unnatural, that is, in the sense that there is nothing else like it on the planet. Even Darwin confessed that his principle of limited perfection—that is, the conception that life would evolve only sufficiently to maintain itself in competition with other life or to adjust to changes in its environment—had been upset in the case of man. A part, such as a tooth or an eye, could reach perfection only for a given purpose in a particular environment. With man, however, Darwin professed to observe no foreseeable limit to the development of the mental faculties.

28. Psychology had once regarded human nature as something consisting of separate abilities given to man at the time of creation. Mind was a fixed, unchanging thing that molded history. Now it was to be seen as malleable and moving, subject like the body, though in a different and more mysterious way, to change. Perhaps, indeed, there was no such thing as human nature in the old fixed sense, except the human ability to become what it most desired in terms of the social world in which it existed. As we have seen, the mind's power of choice has opened to man a tremendous freedom, but it is a freedom whose moral implications only a few great spiritual leaders have fully grasped.

29. Increasingly, at the very height of the human achievement, there loom two obstacles which threaten to cast man back into the world of parts, tools and processes, in a way he has scarcely imagined. In fact there are times when it appears man is so occupied with the world he is now creating that he has already lost a sense for what may be missing in his society. He is deeply influenced by his knowledge of the past and the animal limitations which it seems to place upon his earlier spiritual aspirations. Equally, he confuses "progress" with his mechanical extensions which represent his triumph over the caprices of biological selection. Man, in a new way, shows formidable signs of taking the road of the dinosaurs, though by quite another track.

great + fearful

30. On a night during the period of the Korean War I sat with an old hunter at a campfire in the wilds of Wyoming. Around us in the mountain dark were geological strata that contained the remains of dinosaurs. My companion threw a log upon the fire. As the flames rose upward, I could see the bronzed old American face looking at me across the fire. It could have been a face from any period out of the frontier past. And it was the frontier that spoke to me from the man who had two sons in Korea.

31. "America," he said, "needs a strong enemy. It will keep her from getting fat and make her strong."

32. I nodded dubiously. It was a philosophy of the frontier, of the woods. But I saw in my mind's eye the fate of the colossi that lay about us in the stone. They had warred and thundered, shaken the earth with their tread, grown larger, armored themselves with great shields of bone, and teeth like bear traps. Spikes had glistened on their tails and foreheads. In the end they had vanished with their monstrous tumult, and some small, rat-like mammals and a few birds had come hesitantly into the arena they had vacated. It had been a war of parts, won, not by the participants, but by some small, relatively intelligent creatures that had hidden in the trees.

33. "We need a strong enemy," my friend repeated. I did not doubt it was being said also in the Siberian forests and on the Manchurian plains. Faster and faster labor the technicians, the scientists of parts. They labor so today. The pace grows ever swifter. Already, and I quote from one recent industrial report, "scientists and engineers can be utilized more effectively by confining their work almost entirely to the field of their specialization." This remark indicates the re-emergence of the war of parts, and if continued, it forecasts the death of all we claim as human. Such statements convey a failure to grasp that it is the creative thinker capable of using his brain out of the immediate context of his surroundings who is the *CHANGER* innovator, the religious leader, the artist, the man who in all ages has been, in the words of Lancelot Whyte, "the very creator of humanity."

34. "Man," John Burroughs once remarked, "is like the trainer of wild beasts who, at his peril, for one instant relaxes his mastery over them. Gravity, electricity, fire, flood, hurricane, will crush or consume him if his hands are unsteady or his wits tardy." It is true that man has been badly knocked about by raw nature, but that nature has never organized her powers for the deliberate purpose of destroying man. He has even benefited and had his wits sharpened by her vagaries. Man has survived

↓
UNUSUAL idEA on
HAPPENiNg

the long inexorable marchings of the glacial ice that pressed him back upon the Mediterranean and threatened his annihilation in Europe. He has left his bones under the boiling mud of volcanic upheavals. He has known drought and famine—the careless buffets of the storm that blows unceasingly through nature. He has seen cities go down, cities full of adept artisans and clever technicians, cities fallen to the sands when an old enemy cut off the water supply.

35. Who was that enemy? It was man. He is the other face of that nature man has feared. Now, in an age when man lays his hands upon the lightning, and heat in millions of degrees shudders in his confining mechanisms, an old shadow, a monstrous growing shadow, falls across the doorway of all the world's laboratories. It is merely man, merely the creature by the fire of sticks, merely the museum wielder of the sling and spear, but now grown large enough to shadow the sun. This creature thinks with all the malignant concentration that man has so far escaped in nature, and it thinks toward just one purpose—the creation of the ultimate weapon. Ultimate, ultimate, and still more ultimate, as if there were a growing secret zero in its mind.

36. So terrible is the fascination of that zero, so much does it appeal to some ancient power-loving streak in our still primitive natures, that whether men plan aggression or defense from it, they are, in degree, corrupted. At heart they know the word "neutral" has lost its meaning; that the blow, if it falls, will mean what the ultimate weapon means—death to green grass and singing bird, death to a world.

37. Nevertheless, as I have said, no creature in the world demands more love than man; no creature is less adapted to survive without it. Man is a paradox. Individually most men hate and fear war in spite of much of the talk of professional militarists about instinct. Men have to be drummed to war, propagandized to war, assured their cause is righteous. Even dictators have to render lip service to humanitarian principles. None of this sounds particularly as though an "instinct" for war ex-

isted. There are, instead, things from the old dark midnight of the past that suffice as well for evil purposes. Fear of the stranger, when the stranger was two eyes in the dark beyond the fire at a cave mouth; aggressive hungers that were stoked to a high pitch by nature in the million years of man's wandering across the wastes of an open world. Man is not completed—that is the secret of his paradoxical behavior. He is not made. He is, perhaps, about to be. Once long ago in the Middle Ages he was called *Homo duplex*—a thing half of dust and half of spirit. The term well expresses his predicament.

38. Today we know a great deal about human evolution, but as scientists we have failed, I sometimes think, to convey successfully to the public the marvel of the human transformation. We have shown man the anthropoidal skulls of his ancestors. We have convinced him that the human brain is an instrument of ancient origin which has not sprung full blown into being, but rather partakes of both the old and the new; that it includes the imperfections which are written into the substance of all moving and growing life. The vestigial organs that are concealed here and there in our bodies and which tell tales of the long past—of trees and waters in our lost ancestral world—have their corollary in the mind of man. His flashes of unreasoning temper, his frustrations, his occasional irrationalities are, some of them, echoes out of an older, more primitive machine. Yet signs of affection and mutual co-operation, love of beauty, dreams of a future life, can be traced into forms of man physically more primitive than ourselves.

39. Now, however, it is the present which concerns us—the present that creates tomorrow. Who contends for it—the rocket century with its vast zero looming over the future? The now is *our* responsibility, not that of the hoarse-voiced animal that came from the wood in a dream and made our today. Nor can we call to those pleasant, wide-browed people whom we strive to conjure up as inhabiting the comfortable future of our novels and dreams. They are lost in the unfathom-

able, formless future which we are engaged in shaping. Do we want them deeply? Do we want them enough, in the heavy-handed violence of this day, to live toward them at all cost, to struggle once more against the destructive forces of nature? To stand up and face, as every man must face, that ancient lurking shadow of himself? Is the price of acquiring brains, brains to look before and after in the universe, only to mean subservience to man after escaping subservience to nature that has lasted for a million years? Is it to mean acquiescence in the plans of those clever intellects who talk glibly of psychological "break-throughs" and the subliminal control of nations? Is it for this that men have labored up the dark pathway behind us and died often and blindly for some vision they could scarcely see?

40. A society has an image of itself, its way of life. This image is a wavering, composite picture reflected from millions of minds. If the image is largely compounded of the events of the present; if tradition is weak, the past forgotten, that image can alter by subtle degrees. A "cold war" such as we are fighting demands great tenacity in democratic institutions. Secrecy grows, technicians multiply, two great societies shoulder each other down a road that may look increasingly alike to both. The humane tradition—arts, letters, philosophy, the social sciences—threatens to be ignored as unrealistic in what has become a technological race for survival.

41. Man was a social animal long before he was man. But when he created huge societies and elaborated the world of culture that surrounds him today, he was acting, in some degree, consciously. Man, unlike the animal, is aware of the nature of his society. His conscious image of it is tremendously important in shaping what it will become. It is this that helps to build the human future, and why the future must be fought for day by day in the lives of innumerable and humble men.

42. Man, whether he engages in war or not, is in a pyramiding technological society whose values are largely directed outward upon things. The important fact in such a material

age is that we do not abandon or forget that man has always sought to transcend himself spiritually, and that this is part of his strange heritage. It is a heritage which must be preserved in our schools and churches, for in a society without deep historical memory, the future ceases to exist and the present becomes a meaningless cacophony. A future worth contemplating will not be achieved solely by flights to the far side of the moon. It will not be found in space. It will be achieved, if it is achieved at all, only in our individual hearts. This is the choice that has been presented man,

as a free agent, as one who can look before and after in the cosmos.

43. And if indeed men do achieve that victory, they will know, with the greater insight they will then possess, that it is not a human victory, but nature's new and final triumph in the human heart—perhaps that nature which is also God. "The rationality of man," a great theologian once wrote, "is the little telltale rift in Nature which shows there is something beyond or behind her." It remains for man, in his moral freedom, to prove that statement true.

GEORGE ORWELL

Shooting an Elephant

George Orwell (1903–50), whose real name was Eric Blair, was a British novelist, essayist, and satirist. He was born in Bengal, India, and after attending Eton from 1917 to 1921, he served for five years with the Indian Imperial Police in Burma. During the 1930's, Orwell spent several years writing fiction in Paris and one year fighting in the Spanish Civil War, in which he was badly wounded. Among his many books are *Animal Farm*, 1945; *Nineteen Eighty-Four*, 1949; *Shooting an Elephant*, 1950; *Homage to Catalonia*, 1952; and *Such, Such Were the Joys*, 1953.

In his reactions to human experience and behavior Orwell was primarily satirical. "Shooting an Elephant" is a stirring account of an experience that gave him an insight into the real nature of imperialism.

1. In Moulmein, in Lower Burma, I was hated by large numbers of people—the only time in my life that I have been important enough for this to happen to me. I was sub-

divisional police officer of the town, and in an aimless, petty kind of way anti-European feeling was very bitter. No one had the guts to raise a riot, but if a European woman went through the bazaars alone somebody would probably spit betel juice over her dress. As a police officer I was an obvious target and was baited whenever it seemed safe to do so. When a nimble Burman tripped me up on the football field and the referee (another Burman) looked the other way, the crowd yelled with hideous laughter. This happened more than once. In the end the sneering yellow faces of young men that met me everywhere, the insults hooted after me when I was at a safe distance, got badly on my nerves. The young Buddhist priests were the worst of all. There were several thousands of them in the town and none of them seemed to have anything to do except stand on street corners and jeer at Europeans.

2. All this was perplexing and upsetting. For at that time I had already made up my mind that imperialism was an evil thing and the sooner I chucked up my job and got out of it the better. Theoretically—and secretly, of course—I was all for the Burmese and all against their oppressors, the British. As for the job I was doing, I hated it more bitterly than I can perhaps make clear. In a job like that you see the dirty work of Empire at close quarters. The wretched prisoners huddling in the stinking cages of the lock-ups, the grey, cowed faces of the long-term convicts, the scarred buttocks of the men who had been flogged with bamboos—all these oppressed me with an intolerable sense of guilt. But I could get nothing into perspective. I was young and ill-educated and I had had to think out my problems in the utter silence that is imposed on every Englishman in the East. I did not even know that the British Empire is dying, still less did I know that it is a great deal better than the younger empires that are going to supplant it. All I knew was that I was stuck between my hatred of the empire I served and my rage against the evil-spirited little beasts who tried to make my job impossible. With one part of my mind I thought of the British Raj as an unbreakable tyranny, as something clamped down, in *saecula saeculorum,* upon the will of prostrate peoples; with another part I thought that the greatest joy in the world would be to drive a bayonet into a Buddhist priest's guts. Feelings like these are the normal by-products of imperialism; ask any Anglo-Indian official, if you can catch him off duty.

3. One day something happened which in a roundabout way was enlightening. It was a tiny incident in itself, but it gave me a better glimpse than I had had before of the real nature of imperialism—the real motives for which despotic governments act. Early one morning the sub-inspector at a police station the other end of the town rang me up on the 'phone and said that an elephant was ravaging the bazaar. Would I please come and do something about it? I did not know what I could do, but I wanted to see what was happening and I got on to a pony and started out. I took my rifle, an old .44 Winchester and much too small to kill an elephant, but I thought the noise might be useful *in terrorem.* Various Burmans stopped me on the way and told me about the elephant's doings. It was not, of course, a wild elephant, but a tame one which had gone "must." It had been chained up, as tame elephants always are when their attack of "must" is due, but on the previous night it had broken its chain and escaped. Its mahout, the only person who could manage it when it was in that state, had set out in pursuit, but had taken the wrong direction and was now twelve hours' journey away, and in the morning the elephant had suddenly reappeared in the town. The Burmese population had no weapons and were quite helpless against it. It had already destroyed somebody's bamboo hut, killed a cow and raided some fruit-stalls and devoured the stock; also it had met the municipal rubbish van and, when the driver jumped out and took to his heels, had turned the van over and inflicted violences upon it.

4. The Burmese sub-inspector and some Indian constables were waiting for me in the quarter where the elephant had been seen. It was a very poor quarter, a labyrinth of squalid bamboo huts, thatched with palm-leaf, winding all over a steep hillside. I remember that it was a cloudy, stuffy morning at the beginning of the rains. We began questioning the people as to where the elephant had gone and, as usual, failed to get any definite information. That is invariably the case in the East; a story always sounds clear enough at a distance, but the nearer you get to the scene of events the vaguer it becomes. Some of the people said

that the elephant had gone in one direction, some said that he had gone in another, some professed not even to have heard of any elephant. I had almost made up my mind that the whole story was a pack of lies, when we heard yells a little distance away. There was a loud, scandalized cry of "Go away, child! Go away this instant!" and an old woman with a switch in her hand came round the corner of a hut, violently shooing away a crowd of naked children. Some more women followed, clicking their tongues and exclaiming; evidently there was something that the children ought not to have seen. I rounded the hut and saw a man's dead body sprawling in the mud. He was an Indian, a black Dravidian coolie, almost naked, and he could not have been dead many minutes. The people said that the elephant had come suddenly upon him round the corner of the hut, caught him with its trunk, put its foot on his back and ground him into the earth. This was the rainy season and the ground was soft, and his face had scored a trench a foot deep and a couple of yards long. He was lying on his belly with arms crucified and head sharply twisted to one side. His face was coated with mud, the eyes wide open, the teeth bared and grinning with an expression of unendurable agony. (Never tell me, by the way, that the dead look peaceful. Most of the corpses I have seen looked devilish.) The friction of the great beast's foot had stripped the skin from his back as neatly as one skins a rabbit. As soon as I saw the dead man I sent an orderly to a friend's house nearby to borrow an elephant rifle. I had already sent back the pony, not wanting it to go mad with fright and throw me if it smelt the elephant.

5. The orderly came back in a few minutes with a rifle and five cartridges, and meanwhile some Burmans had arrived and told us that the elephant was in the paddy fields below, only a few hundred yards away. As I started forward practically the whole population of the quarter flocked out of the houses and followed me. They had seen the rifle and were all shouting excitedly that I was going to shoot the elephant. They had not shown much interest in the elephant when he was merely ravaging their homes, but it was different now

that he was going to be shot. It was a bit of fun to them, as it would be to an English crowd; besides they wanted the meat. It made me vaguely uneasy. I had no intention of shooting the elephant—I had merely sent for the rifle to defend myself if necessary—and it is always unnerving to have a crowd following you. I marched down the hill, looking and feeling a fool, with the rifle over my shoulder and an ever-growing army of people jostling at my heels. At the bottom, when you got away from the huts, there was a metalled road and beyond that a miry waste of paddy fields a thousand yards across, not yet ploughed but soggy from the first rains and dotted with coarse grass. The elephant was standing eight yards from the road, his left side towards us. He took not the slightest notice of the crowd's approach. He was tearing up bunches of grass, beating them against his knees to clean them and stuffing them into his mouth.

6. I had halted on the road. As soon as I saw the elephant I knew with perfect certainty that I ought not to shoot him. It is a serious matter to shoot a working elephant—it is comparable to destroying a huge and costly piece of machinery—and obviously one ought not to do it if it can possibly be avoided. And at that distance, peacefully eating, the elephant looked no more dangerous than a cow. I thought then and I think now that his attack of "must" was already passing off; in which case he would merely wander harmlessly about until the mahout came back and caught him. Moreover, I did not in the least want to shoot him. I decided that I would watch him for a little while to make sure that he did not turn savage again, and then go home.

7. But at that moment I glanced round at the crowd that had followed me. It was an immense crowd, two thousand at the least and growing every minute. It blocked the road for a long distance on either side. I looked at the sea of yellow faces above the garish clothes—faces all happy and excited over this bit of fun, all certain that the elephant was going to be shot. They were watching me as they would watch a conjurer about to perform a trick. They did not like me, but with the

magical rifle in my hands I was momentarily worth watching. And suddenly I realized that I should have to shoot the elephant after all. The people expected it of me and I had got to do it; I could feel their two thousand wills pressing me forward, irresistibly. And it was at this moment, as I stood there with the rifle in my hands, that I first grasped the hollowness, the futility of the white man's dominion in the East. Here was I, the white man with his gun, standing in front of the unarmed native crowd—seemingly the leading actor of the piece; but in reality I was only an absurd puppet pushed to and fro by the will of those yellow faces behind. I perceived in this moment that when the white man turns tyrant it is his own freedom that he destroys. He becomes a sort of hollow, posing dummy, the conventionalized figure of a sahib. For it is the condition of his rule that he shall spend his life in trying to impress the "natives," and so in every crisis he has got to do what the "natives" expect of him. He wears a mask, and his face grows to fit it. I had got to shoot the elephant. I had committed myself to doing it when I sent for the rifle. A sahib has got to act like a sahib; he has got to appear resolute, to know his own mind and do definite things. To come all that way, rifle in hand, with two thousand people marching at my heels, and then to trail feebly away, having done nothing—no, that was impossible. The crowd would laugh at me. And my whole life, every white man's life in the East, was one long struggle not to be laughed at.

8. But I did not want to shoot the elephant. I watched him beating his bunch of grass against his knees, with that preoccupied grandmotherly air that elephants have. It seemed to me that it would be murder to shoot him. At that age I was not squeamish about killing animals, but I had never shot an elephant and never wanted to. (Somehow it always seems worse to kill a *large* animal.) Besides, there was the beast's owner to be considered. Alive, the elephant was worth at least a hundred pounds; dead, he would only be worth the value of his tusks, five pounds, possibly. But I had got to act quickly. I turned to some experienced-looking Burmans who

had been there when we arrived, and asked them how the elephant had been behaving. They all said the same thing: he took no notice of you if you left him alone, but he might charge if you went too close to him.

9. It was perfectly clear to me what I ought to do. I ought to walk up to within, say, twenty-five yards of the elephant and test his behavior. If he charged, I could shoot; if he took no notice of me, it would be safe to leave him until the mahout came back. But also I knew that I was going to do no such thing. I was a poor shot with a rifle and the ground was soft mud into which one would sink at every step. If the elephant charged and I missed him, I should have about as much chance as a toad under a steam-roller. But even then I was not thinking particularly of my own skin, only of the watchful yellow faces behind. For at that moment, with the crowd watching me, I was not afraid in the ordinary sense, as I would have been if I had been alone. A white man musn't be frightened in front of "natives"; and so, in general, he isn't frightened. The sole thought in my mind was that if anything went wrong those two thousand Burmans would see me pursued, caught, trampled on and reduced to a grinning corpse like that Indian up the hill. And if that happened it was quite probable that some of them would laugh. That would never do. There was only one alternative. I shoved the cartridges into the magazine and lay down on the road to get a better aim.

10. The crowd grew very still, and a deep, low, happy sigh, as of people who see the theatre curtain go up at last, breathed from innumerable throats. They were going to have their bit of fun after all. The rifle was a beautiful German thing with cross-hair sights. I did not then know that in shooting an elephant one would shoot to cut an imaginary bar running from ear-hole to ear-hole. I ought, therefore, as the elephant was sideways on, to have aimed straight at his ear-hole; actually I aimed several inches in front of this, thinking the brain would be further forward.

11. When I pulled the trigger I did not hear the bang or feel the kick—one never does when a shot goes home—but I heard the devil-

ish roar of glee that went up from the crowd. In that instant, in too short a time, one would have thought, even for the bullet to get there, a mysterious, terrible change had come over the elephant. He neither stirred nor fell, but every line of his body had altered. He looked suddenly stricken, shrunken, immensely old, as though the frightful impact of the bullet had paralysed him without knocking him down. At last, after what seemed a long time —it might have been five seconds, I dare say— he sagged flabbily to his knees. His mouth slobbered. An enormous senility seemed to have settled upon him. One could have imagined him thousands of years old. I fired again into the same spot. At the second shot he did not collapse but climbed with desperate slowness to his feet and stood weakly upright, with legs sagging and head drooping. I fired a third time. That was the shot that did for him. You could see the agony of it jolt his whole body and knock the last remnant of strength from his legs. But in falling he seemed for a moment to rise, for as his hind legs collapsed beneath him he seemed to tower upward like a huge rock toppling, his trunk reaching skyward like a tree. He trumpeted, for the first and only time. And then down he came, his belly towards me, with a crash that seemed to shake the ground even where I lay.

12. I got up. The Burmans were already racing past me across the mud. It was obvious that the elephant would never rise again, but he was not dead. He was breathing very rhythmically with long rattling gasps, his great mound of a side painfully rising and falling. His mouth was wide open—I could see far down into caverns of pale pink throat. I waited a long time for him to die, but his breathing did not weaken. Finally I fired my two remaining shots into the spot where I thought his heart must be. The thick blood welled out of him like red velvet, but still he did not die. His body did not even jerk when the shots hit him, the tortured breathing continued without a pause. He was dying, very slowly and in great agony, but in some world remote from me where not even a bullet could damage him further. I felt that I had got to put an end to that dreadful noise. It seemed dreadful to see the great beast lying there, powerless to move and yet powerless to die, and not even to be able to finish him. I sent back for my small rifle and poured shot after shot into his heart and down his throat. They seemed to make no impression. The tortured gasps continued as steadily as the ticking of a clock.

13. In the end I could not stand it any longer and went away. I heard later that it took him half an hour to die. Burmans were bringing dahs and baskets even before I left, and I was told they had stripped his body almost to the bones by the afternoon.

14. Afterwards, of course, there were endless discussions about the shooting of the elephant. The owner was furious, but he was only an Indian and could do nothing. Besides, legally I had done the right thing, for a mad elephant has to be killed, like a mad dog, if its owner fails to control it. Among the Europeans opinion was divided. The older men said I was right, the younger men said it was a damn shame to shoot an elephant for killing a coolie, because an elephant was worth more than any damn Coringhee coolie. And afterwards I was very glad that the coolie had been killed; it put me legally in the right and it gave me a sufficient pretext for shooting the elephant. I often wondered whether any of the others grasped that I had done it solely to avoid looking a fool.

E. M. FORSTER

What I Believe

Edward Morgan Forster (1879–   ), one of England's most distinguished writers, is a lecturer and an honorary member of the American Academy of Arts and Letters. The holder of many awards, among which is membership in the Order of Companions of Honour to the Queen, he is best known as a novelist and literary critic. His books include *A Room with a View,* 1908; *Howard's End,* 1910; *A Passage to India,* 1924; *Abinger Harvest,* 1926; *Aspects of the Novel,* 1927; and two volumes of short stories, *The Celestial Omnibus,* 1911, and *The Eternal Moment,* 1928. A collection of his essays, *Two Cheers for Democracy,* appeared in 1951. In 1962 he wrote the libretto for the opera *Billy Budd.*

In "What I Believe," here reprinted from *Two Cheers for Democracy,* Mr. Forster presents his liberal beliefs on a wide range of subjects—faith, democracy, use of force, hero-worship, aristocracy, and Christianity.

1. I do not believe in Belief. But this is an age of faith, and there are so many militant creeds that, in self-defence, one has to formulate a creed of one's own. Tolerance, good temper and sympathy are no longer enough in a world which is rent by religious and racial persecution, in a world where ignorance rules, and science, who ought to have ruled, plays the subservient pimp. Tolerance, good temper and sympathy—they are what matter really, and if the human race is not to collapse they must come to the front before long. But for the moment they are not enough, their action is no stronger than a flower, battered beneath a military jack-boot. They want stiffening, even if the process coarsens them. Faith, to my mind, is a stiffening process, a sort of mental starch, which ought to be applied as sparingly as possible. I dislike the stuff. I do

not believe in it, for its own sake, at all. Herein I probably differ from most people, who believe in Belief, and are only sorry they cannot swallow even more than they do. My law-givers are Erasmus and Montaigne, not Moses and St. Paul. My temple stands not upon Mount Moriah but in that Elysian Field where even the immoral are admitted. My motto is: "Lord, I disbelieve—help thou my unbelief."

2. I have, however, to live in an Age of Faith—the sort of epoch I used to hear praised when I was a boy. It is extremely unpleasant really. It is bloody in every sense of the word. And I have to keep my end up in it. Where do I start?

3. With personal relationships. Here is something comparatively solid in a world full of violence and cruelty. Not absolutely solid, for Psychology has split and shattered the idea of a "Person," and has shown that there is something incalculable in each of us, which may at any moment rise to the surface and

destroy our normal balance. We don't know what we are like. We can't know what other people are like. How, then, can we put any trust in personal relationships, or cling to them in the gathering political storm? In theory we cannot. But in practice we can and do. Though A is not unchangeably A or B unchangeably B, there can still be love and loyalty between the two. For the purpose of living one has to assume that the personality is solid, and the "self" is an entity, and to ignore all contrary evidence. And since to ignore evidence is one of the characteristics of faith, I certainly can proclaim that I believe in personal relationships.

4. Starting from them, I get a little order into the contemporary chaos. One must be fond of people and trust them if one is not to make a mess of life, and it is therefore essential that they should not let one down. They often do. The moral of which is that I must, myself, be as reliable as possible, and this I try to be. But reliability is not a matter of contract—that is the main difference between the world of personal relationships and the world of business relationships. It is a matter for the heart, which signs no documents. In other words, reliability is impossible unless there is a natural warmth. Most men possess this warmth, though they often have bad luck and get chilled. Most of them, even when they are politicians, *want* to keep faith. And one can, at all events, show one's own little light here, one's own poor little trembling flame, with the knowledge that it is not the only light that is shining in the darkness, and not the only one which the darkness does not comprehend. Personal relations are despised today. They are regarded as bourgeois luxuries, as products of a time of fair weather which is now past, and we are urged to get rid of them, and to dedicate ourselves to some movement or cause instead. I hate the idea of causes, and if I had to choose between betraying my country and betraying my friend, I hope I should have the guts to betray my country. Such a choice may scandalise the modern reader, and he may stretch out his patriotic hand to the telephone at once and ring up the police. It would not have shocked

Dante, though. Dante places Brutus and Cassius in the lowest circle of Hell because they had chosen to betray their friend Julius Caesar rather than their country Rome. Probably one will not be asked to make such an agonizing choice. Still, there lies at the back of every creed something terrible and hard for which the worshipper may one day be required to suffer, and there is even a terror and a hardness in this creed of personal relationships, urbane and mild though it sounds. Love and loyalty to an individual can run counter to the claims of the State. When they do—down with the State, say I, which means that the State would down me.

5. This brings me along to Democracy, "even Love, the Beloved Republic, which feeds upon Freedom and lives." Democracy is not a Beloved Republic really, and never will be. But it is less hateful than other contemporary forms of government, and to that extent it deserves our support. It does start from the assumption that the individual is important, and that all types are needed to make a civilisation. It does not divide its citizens into the bossers and the bossed—as an efficiency-regime tends to do. The people I admire most are those who are sensitive and want to create something or discover something, and do not see life in terms of power, and such people get more of a chance under a democracy than elsewhere. They found religions, great or small, or they produce literature and art, or they do disinterested scientific research, or they may be what is called "ordinary people," who are creative in their private lives, bring up their children decently, for instance, or help their neighbours. All these people need to express themselves; they cannot do so unless society allows them liberty to do so, and the society which allows them most liberty is a democracy.

6. Democracy has another merit. It allows criticism, and if there is not public criticism there are bound to be hushed-up scandals. That is why I believe in the Press, despite all its lies and vulgarity, and why I believe in Parliament. Parliament is often sneered at because it is a Talking Shop. I believe in it *because* it is a talking shop. I believe in the

Private Member who makes himself a nuisance. He gets snubbed and is told that he is cranky or ill-informed, but he does expose abuses which would otherwise never have been mentioned, and very often an abuse gets put right just by being mentioned. Occasionally, too, a well-meaning public official starts losing his head in the cause of efficiency, and thinks himself God Almighty. Such officials are particularly frequent in the Home Office. Well, there will be questions about them in Parliament sooner or later, and then they will have to mind their steps. Whether Parliament is either a representative body or an efficient one is questionable, but I value it because it criticises and talks, and because its chatter gets widely reported.

7. So Two Cheers for Democracy: one because it admits variety and two because it permits criticism. Two cheers are quite enough: there is no occasion to give three. Only Love the Beloved Republic deserves that.

8. What about Force, though? While we are trying to be sensitive and advanced and affectionate and tolerant, an unpleasant question pops up: does not all society rest upon force? If a government cannot count upon the police and the army, how can it hope to rule? And if an individual gets knocked on the head or sent to a labour camp, of what significance are his opinions?

9. This dilemma does not worry me as much as it does some. I realise that all society rests upon force. But all the great creative actions, all the decent human relations, occur during the intervals when force has not managed to come to the front. These intervals are what matter. I want them to be as frequent and as lengthy as possible, and I call them "civilisation." Some people idealise force and pull it into the foreground and worship it, instead of keeping it in the background as long as possible. I think they make a mistake, and I think that their opposites, the mystics, err even more when they declare that force does not exist. I believe that it exists, and that one of our jobs is to prevent it from getting out of its box. It gets out sooner or later, and then it destroys us and all the lovely things which we have made. But it is not out all the time, for the

fortunate reason that the strong are so stupid. Consider their conduct for a moment in the Niebelung's Ring. The giants there have the guns, or in other words the gold; but they do nothing with it, they do not realise that they are all-powerful, with the result that the catastrophe is delayed and the castle of Walhalla, insecure but glorious, fronts the storms. Fafnir, coiled round his hoard, grumbles and grunts; we can hear him under Europe today; the leaves of the wood already tremble, and the Bird calls its warnings uselessly. Fafnir will destroy us, but by a blessed dispensation he is stupid and slow, and creation goes on just outside the poisonous blast of his breath. The Nietzschean would hurry the monster up, the mystic would say he did not exist, but Wotan, wiser than either, hastens to create warriors before doom declares itself. The Valkyries are symbols not only of courage but of intelligence; they represent the human spirit snatching its opportunity while the going is good, and one of them even finds time to love. Brünnhilde's last song hymns the recurrence of love, and since it is the privilege of art to exaggerate, she goes even further, and proclaims the love which is eternally triumphant and feeds upon freedom, and lives.

10. So that is what I feel about force and violence. It is, alas! the ultimate reality on this earth, but it does not always get to the front. Some people call its absences "decadence"; I call them "civilisation" and find in such interludes the chief justification for the human experiment. I look the other way until fate strikes me. Whether this is due to courage or to cowardice in my own case I cannot be sure. But I know that if men had not looked the other way in the past, nothing of any value would survive. The people I respect most behave as if they were immortal and as if society was eternal. Both assumptions are false: both of them must be accepted as true if we are to go on eating and working and loving, and are to keep open a few breathing holes for the human spirit. No millennium seems likely to descend upon humanity; no better and stronger League of Nations will be instituted; no form of Christianity and no alternative to Christianity will bring peace to the world or

integrity to the individual; no "change of heart" will occur. And yet we need not despair, indeed, we cannot despair; the evidence of history shows us that men have always insisted on behaving creatively under the shadow of the sword; that they have done their artistic and scientific and domestic stuff for the sake of doing it, and that we had better follow their example under the shadow of the aeroplanes. Others, with more vision or courage than myself, see the salvation of humanity ahead, and will dismiss my conception of civilisation as paltry, a sort of tip-and-run game. Certainly it is presumptuous to say that we *cannot* improve, and that Man, who has only been in power for a few thousand years, will never learn to make use of his power. All I mean is that, if people continue to kill one another as they do, the world cannot get better than it is, and that since there are more people than formerly, and their means for destroying one another superior, the world may well get worse. What is good in people—and consequently in the world—is their insistence on creation, their belief in friendship and loyalty for their own sakes; and though Violence remains and is, indeed, the major partner in this muddled establishment, I believe that creativeness remains too, and will always assume direction when violence sleeps. So, though I am not an optimist, I cannot agree with Sophocles that it were better never to have been born. And although, like Horace, I see no evidence that each batch of births is superior to the last, I leave the field open for the more complacent view. This is such a difficult moment to live in, one cannot help getting gloomy and also a bit rattled, and perhaps short-sighted.

11. In search of a refuge, we may perhaps turn to hero-worship. But here we shall get no help, in my opinion. Hero-worship is a dangerous vice, and one of the minor merits of a democracy is that it does not encourage it, or produce that unmanageable type of citizen known as the Great Man. It produces instead different kinds of small men—a much finer achievement. But people who cannot get interested in the variety of life, and cannot make up their own minds, get discontented over this, and they long for a hero to bow down before and to follow blindly. It is significant that a hero is an integral part of the authoritarian stock-in-trade today. An efficiency-regime cannot be run without a few heroes stuck about it to carry off the dullness —much as plums have to be put into a bad pudding to make it palatable. One hero at the top and a smaller one each side of him is a favourite arrangement, and the timid and the bored are comforted by the trinity, and, bowing down, feel exalted and strengthened.

12. No, I distrust Great Men. They produce a desert of uniformity around them and often a pool of blood too, and I always feel a little man's pleasure when they come a cropper. Every now and then one reads in the newspapers some such statement as: "The coup d'état appears to have failed, and Admiral Toma's whereabouts is at present unknown." Admiral Toma had probably every qualification for being a Great Man—an iron will, personal magnetism, dash, flair, sexlessness—but fate was against him, so he retires to unknown whereabouts instead of parading history with his peers. He fails with a completeness which no artist and no lover can experience, because with them the process of creation is itself an achievement, whereas with him the only possible achievement is success.

13. I believe in aristocracy, though—if that is the right word, and if a democrat may use it. Not an aristocracy of power, based upon rank and influence, but an aristocracy of the sensitive, the considerate and the plucky. Its members are to be found in all nations and classes, and all through the ages, and there is a secret understanding between them when they meet. They represent the true human tradition, the one permanent victory of our queer race over cruelty and chaos. Thousands of them perish in obscurity, a few are great names. They are sensitive for others as well as for themselves, they are considerate without being fussy, their pluck is not swankiness but the power to endure, and they can take a joke. I give no examples—it is risky to do that—but the reader may as well consider whether this is the type of person he would like to meet and to be, and whether (going farther with

me) he would prefer that this type should *not* be an ascetic one. I am against asceticism myself. I am with the old Scotsman who wanted less chastity and more delicacy. I do not feel that my aristocrats are a real aristocracy if they thwart their bodies, since bodies are the instruments through which we register and enjoy the world. Still, I do not insist. This is not a major point. It is clearly possible to be sensitive, considerate and plucky and yet be an ascetic too; if anyone possesses the first three qualities, I will let him in! On they go —an invincible army, yet not a victorious one. The aristocrats, the elect, the chosen, the Best People—all the words that describe them are false, and all attempts to organise them fail. Again and again Authority, seeing their value, has tried to net them and to utilise them as the Egyptian Priesthood or the Christian Church or the Chinese Civil Service or the Group Movement, or some other worthy stunt. But they slip through the net and are gone; when the door is shut, they are no longer in the room; their temple, as one of them remarked, is the Holiness of the Heart's Affection, and their kingdom, though they never possess it, is the wide-open world.

14. With this type of person knocking about, and constantly crossing one's path if one has eyes to see or hands to feel, the experiment of earthly life cannot be dismissed as a failure. But it may well be hailed as a tragedy, the tragedy being that no device has been found by which these private decencies can be transmitted to public affairs. As soon as people have power they go crooked and sometimes dotty as well, because the possession of power lifts them into a region where normal honesty never pays. For instance, the man who is selling newspapers outside the Houses of Parliament can safely leave his papers to go for a drink and his cap beside them: anyone who takes a paper is sure to drop a copper into the cap. But the men who are inside the Houses of Parliament—they cannot trust one another like that; still less can the Government they compose trust other governments. No caps upon the pavement here, but suspicion, treachery and armaments. The more highly public

life is organised the lower does its morality sink; the nations of today behave to each other worse than they ever did in the past, they cheat, rob, bully and bluff, make war without notice, and kill as many women and children as possible; whereas primitive tribes were at all events restrained by taboos. It is a humiliating outlook—though the greater the darkness, the brighter shine the little lights, reassuring one another, signalling: "Well, at all events, I'm still here. I don't like it very much, but how are you?" Unquenchable lights of my aristocracy! Signals of the invincible army! "Come along—anyway, let's have a good time while we can." I think they signal that too.

15. The Saviour of the future—if ever he comes—will not preach a new Gospel. He will merely utilise my aristocracy, he will make effective the good will and the good temper which are already existing. In other words, he will introduce a new technique. In economics, we are told that if there was a new technique of distribution, there need be no poverty, and people would not starve in one place while crops were being ploughed under in another. A similar change is needed in the sphere of morals and politics. The desire for it is by no means new; it was expressed, for example, in theological terms by Jacopone da Todi over six hundred years ago. "Ordina questo amore, O tu che m'ami," he said; "O thou who lovest me—set this love in order." His prayer was not granted, and I do not myself believe that it ever will be, but here, and not through a change of heart, is our probable route. Not by becoming better, but by ordering and distributing his native goodness, will Man shut up Force into its box, and so gain time to explore the universe and to set his mark upon it worthily. At present he only explores it at odd moments, when Force is looking the other way, and his divine creativeness appears as a trivial by-product, to be scrapped as soon as the drums beat and the bombers hum.

16. Such a change, claim the orthodox, can only be made by Christianity, and will be made by it in God's good time: man always has failed and always will fail to organise his own goodness, and it is presumptuous of him

to try. This claim—solemn as it is—leaves me cold. I cannot believe that Christianity will ever cope with the present world-wide mess, and I think that such influence as it retains in modern society is due to the money behind it, rather than to its spiritual appeal. It was a spiritual force once, but the indwelling spirit will have to be restated if it is to calm the waters again, and probably restated in a non-Christian form. Naturally a lot of people, and people who are not only good but able and intelligent, will disagree here; they will vehemently deny that Christianity has failed, or they will argue that its failure proceeds from the wickedness of men, and really proves its ultimate success. They have Faith, with a large F. My faith has a very small one, and I only intrude it because these are strenuous and serious days, and one likes to say what one thinks while speech is comparatively free: it may not be free much longer.

17. The above are the reflections of an individualist and a liberal who has found liberalism crumbling beneath him and at first felt ashamed. Then, looking around, he decided there was no special reason for shame, since other people, whatever they felt, were equally insecure. And as for individualism—there seems no way of getting off this, even if one wanted to. The dictator-hero can grind down his citizens till they are all alike, but he cannot melt them into a single man. That is beyond his power. He can order them to merge, he can incite them to mass-antics, but they are obliged to be born separately, and to die separately, and, owing to these unavoidable termini, will always be running off the totalitarian rails. The memory of birth and the expectation of death always lurk within the human being, making him separate from his fellows and consequently capable of intercourse with them. Naked I came into the world, naked I shall go out of it! And a very good thing too, for it reminds me that I am naked under my shirt, whatever its colour.

CHARLES FRANKEL

The Morality of Civil Disobedience

Charles Frankel (1917–   ) is a versatile editor and a provocative writer on many aspects of modern culture. Representative of his editorial works are *Rousseau's Social Contract,* 1947; *Issues in University Education,* 1959; and *The Golden Age of American Philosophy,* 1960. His books include *The Faith of Reason,* 1948; *The Case for Modern Man,* 1956; *The Democratic Prospect,* 1962; *The Love of Anxiety and Other Essays,* 1965, from which this essay was taken, and, most recently, *The Neglected Aspect of Foreign Affairs: American Educational and Cultural Policy Abroad,* 1966.

"The Morality of Civil Disobedience" examines both sides of the philosophical and practical question: Does the individual have the right to disobey the law when he believes it to be unjust?

1. For some time past an old and troublesome philosophical issue has been at the center of public events, and it is likely to remain there for some time to come. This is the question of the morality of civil disobedience. A teachers' union threatens a strike even though a state law prohibits strikes by public employees; advocates of civil rights employ mass demonstrations of disobedience to the law to advance their cause; the governor of a Southern state deliberately obstructs the enforcement of federal laws, and declares himself thoroughly within his rights in doing so. An observer can approve the motives that lead to some of these actions and disapprove others. All, nevertheless, raise the same fundamental question: Does the individual have the right—or perhaps the duty—to disobey the law when his mind, his conscience, or his religious faith tells him that the law is unjust?

2. The question is as old as Socrates. It has regularly propelled men into radical examination of the premises of personal morality and civic obligation and, indeed, of government itself. And it is an interesting question not only for its philosophical implications but because it has always been a painfully practical question as well, and never more so than today.

3. Our period in history is frequently described as "materialistic" and "conformist," an age in which governments have enormous powers to crush the bodies and anesthetize the minds of their subjects, and in which the great masses of men and women—presumably in contrast with men and women of other times—prefer to play it safe rather than raise questions of basic moral principle. It is to the point to note, however, that massive resistance to law, justified in the name of higher moral principles like "freedom," "equality," and "national independence," has been a conspicuous feature of our period, and one of its most effective techniques of social action. Millions of ordinary people with no preten-

THE MORALITY OF CIVIL DISOBEDIENCE   From *The Love of Anxiety,* Harper & Row, 1965. Published January 12, 1964, in *The New York Times* under the title "Is It Ever Right to Break the Law." © 1964 by The New York Times Company. Reprinted by permission.

sions to being either heroes or saints have employed it in India, in South Africa, in the resistance movements against the Nazis, and in the struggle for equality for Negroes in the United States.

4. Moreover, such massive resistance to law is by no means confined only to supremely glorious or dangerous causes; nor is it used only by revolutionaries, underdogs, or outsiders. During Prohibition, a large number of respectable, conservative Americans dutifully broke the law in defense of what they regarded as an inalienable human right. In this case, doing one's duty happened also to be agreeable and even fashionable, but this does not change the fact that many right-thinking citizens, who today condemn pacifists or integrationists for using illegal methods to advance their cause, have themselves used such methods happily and unashamedly.

5. When is it justified, then, for the citizen to act as his own legislator and to decide that he will or will not obey a given law?

6. An answer that covers all the issues this question raises cannot be given here, nor can a set of principles be proposed that will allow anyone to make automatic and infallible judgments concerning the legitimacy or illegitimacy of specific acts of civil disobedience. Such judgments require detailed knowledge of the facts of specific cases, and such knowledge is often unavailable to the outsider. Nevertheless, it is possible to indicate some of the principal issues that are raised by civil disobedience, some of the more common mistakes that are made in thinking about these issues, and, at least in outline, the approach that one man would take toward such issues.

7. We can begin, it seems to me, by rejecting one extreme position. This is the view that disobedience to the law can never be justified in any circumstances. To take this position is to say one of two things: either every law that exists is a just law, or a greater wrong is always done by breaking the law. The first statement is plainly false. The second is highly doubtful. If it is true, then the signers of the Declaration of Independence, and those Germans who refused to carry out Hitler's orders, committed acts of injustice.

8. It is possible, however, to take a much more moderate and plausible version of this position, and many quite reasonable people do. Such people concede that disobedience to the law can sometimes be legitimate and necessary under a despotic regime. They argue, however, that civil disobedience can never be justified in a democratic society, because such a society provides its members with legal instruments for the redress of their grievances.

9. This is one of the standard arguments that is made, often quite sincerely, against the activities of people like supporters of the Congress of Racial Equality, who set about changing laws they find objectionable by dramatically breaking them. Such groups are often condemned for risking disorder and for spreading disrespect for the law when, so it is maintained, they could accomplish their goals a great deal more fairly and patriotically by staying within the law, and confining themselves to the courts and to methods of peaceful persuasion.

10. Now it is perfectly true, I believe, that there is a stronger case for obedience to the law, including bad law, in a democracy than in a dictatorship. The people who must abide by the law have presumably been consulted, and they have legal channels through which to express their protests and to work for reform. One way to define democracy is to say that it is a system whose aim is to provide alternatives to civil disobedience. Nevertheless, when applied to the kind of situation faced, say, by CORE, these generalizations, it seems to me, become cruelly abstract.

11. The basic fallacy in the proposition that, in a democracy, civil disobedience can never be justified, is that it confuses the *ideals* or *aims* of democracy with the inevitably less than perfect accomplishments of democracy at any given moment. In accordance with democratic ideals, the laws of a democracy may give rights and powers to individuals which, in theory, enable them to work legally for the elimination of injustices. In actual fact, however, these rights and powers may be empty. The police may be hostile, the courts biased, the elections rigged—and the legal

remedies available to the individual may be unavailing against these evils.

12. Worse still, the majority may have demonstrated, in a series of free and honest elections, that it is unwavering in its support of what the minority regards as an unspeakable evil. This is obviously the case today in many parts of the South, where the white majority is either opposed to desegregation or not so impatient to get on with it as is the Negro minority. Are we prepared to say that majorities never err? If not, there is no absolutely conclusive reason why we must invariably give the results of an election greater weight than considerations of elementary justice.

13. It is true, of course, that one swallow does not make a summer, and that the test of legal democratic processes is not this or that particular success or failure, but rather the general direction in which these processes move over the long run. Still, the position that violation of the law is never justifiable so long as there are legal alternatives overstates this important truth. It fails to face at least three important exceptions to it.

14. In the first place, dramatic disobedience to the law by a minority may be the only effective way of catching the attention or winning the support of the majority. Most classic cases of civil disobedience, from the early Christians to Gandhi and his supporters, exemplify this truth. Civil disobedience, like almost no other technique, can shame a majority and make it ask itself just how far it is willing to go, just how seriously it really is committed to defending the status quo.

15. Second, there is the simple but painful factor of time. If a man is holding you down on a bed of nails, it is all very well for a bystander to say that you live in a great country in which there are legal remedies for your condition, and that you ought, therefore, to be patient and wait for these remedies to take effect. But your willingness to listen to this counsel will depend, quite properly, on the nature of the injury you are suffering.

16. Third, it is baseless prejudice to assume that observance of the law is *always* conducive

to strengthening a democratic system while disobedience to the law can never have a salutary effect. A majority's complacent acquiescence in bad laws can undermine the faith of a minority in the power of democratic methods to rectify manifest evils; yet a vigorous democracy depends on the existence of minorities holding just such a faith. Disobedience to bad laws can sometimes jolt democratic processes into motion. Which strengthens one's hope for democracy more— the behavior of the Negroes in Birmingham who broke municipal ordinances when they staged their protest marches, or the behavior of the police, using dogs and fire hoses to assert their legal authority?

17. Another factor should also be taken into account. In our federal system, there are often legitimate doubts concerning the legal validity, under our Constitution, of various state or local ordinances. Disobedience to these laws is in many cases simply a practical, though painful, way of testing their legality. But even where no thought of such a test is involved, there is often present a moral issue which no one can easily dodge—least of all the man whose personal dignity and self-respect are caught up in the issue. A citizen caught in a conflict between local laws and what he thinks will be upheld as the superior federal law can sometimes afford to wait until the courts have determined the issue for him. But often he cannot afford to wait, or must take a stand in order to force a decision. This is the situation of many Negro citizens in Southern states as they confront the conflict between local and federal laws.

18. Yet there is another side to the story. It would be a mistake to conclude from what has been said that civil disobedience is justified, provided only that it is disobedience in the name of higher principles. Strong moral conviction is not all that is required to turn breaking the law into service to society.

19. Civil disobedience is not simply like other acts in which men stand up courageously for their principles. It involves violation of the law. And the law can make no provision for its violation except to hold the offender liable to punishment. This is why President Kennedy was in such a delicate position at the time of the Negro demonstrations in Birmingham. He gave many signs that, as an individual, he was in sympathy with the goals of the demonstrators. As a political leader, he probably realized that these goals could not be attained without dramatic actions that crossed the line into illegality. But as Chief Executive he could not give permission or approval to such actions.

20. We may admire a man like Martin Luther King, who is prepared to defy the authorities in the name of a principle, and we may think that he is entirely in the right; just the same, his right to break the law cannot be officially recognized. No society, whether free or tyrannical, can give its citizens the right to break its laws: to ask it to do so is to ask it to proclaim, as a matter of law, that its laws are not laws. If anybody ever has a right to break the law, this cannot be a legal right under the law. It has to be a moral right against the law. And this moral right is not an unlimited right to disobey any law which one regards as unjust. It is a right that is hedged about, it seems to me, with important restrictions.

21. First of all, the exercise of this right is subject to standards of just and fair behavior. I may be correct, for example, in thinking that an ordinance against jaywalking is an unnecessary infringement of my rights. This does not make it reasonable, however, for me to organize a giant sit-down strike in the streets which holds up traffic for a week. Conformity to the concept of justice requires that there be some proportion between the importance of the end one desires to attain and the power of the means one employs to attain it.

22. When applied to civil disobedience, this principle constitutes a very large restriction. Civil disobedience is an effort to change the law by making it impossible to enforce the law, or by making the price of such enforcement extremely high. It is a case, as it were, of holding the legal system to ransom. It can arouse extreme passions on one side or the other, excite and provoke the unbalanced, and

make disrespect for the law a commonplace and popular attitude.

23. Moreover, although violence may be no part of the intention of those who practice civil disobedience, the risks of violence are present, and are part of what must be taken into account when a program of civil disobedience is being contemplated. In short, civil disobedience is a grave enterprise. It may sometimes be justified, but the provocation for it has to be equally grave. Basic principles have to be at issue. The evils being combated have to be serious evils that are liable to endure unless they are fought. And there should be reasonable grounds to believe that legal methods of fighting them are likely to be insufficient by themselves.

24. Nor is this the only limitation on the individual's moral right to disobey the law. The most important limitation is that his cause must be a just one. It was right for General de Gaulle to disobey Marshal Pétain; it was wrong for the commanders of the French Army in Algeria, twenty years later, to disobey General de Gaulle. Similarly, if it is absolutely necessary, and if the consequences have been properly weighed, then it is right to break the law in order to eliminate inequalities based on race. But it can never be necessary, and no weighing of consequences can ever make it right, to break the law in the name of Nazi principles. In sum, the goals of those who disobey the law have to lie at the very heart of what we regard as morality before we can say that they have a moral right to do what they are doing.

25. But who is to make these difficult decisions? Who is to say that one man's moral principles are right and another man's wrong? We come here to the special function that civil disobedience serves in a society. The man who breaks the law on the ground that the law is immoral asks the rest of us, in effect, to trust him, or to trust those he trusts, in preference to the established conventions and authorities of our society. He has taken a large and visible chance, and implicitly asked us to join him in taking that chance, on the probity of his personal moral judgment. In doing so, he has put it to us whether we are willing to take a similar chance on the probity of our own judgment.

26. Thomas Hobbes, who knew the trouble that rebels and dissenters convinced of their rectitude could cause, once remarked that a man may be convinced that God has commanded him to act as he has, but that God, after all, does not command other men to believe that this is so. The man who chooses to disobey the law on grounds of principle may be a saint, but he may also be a madman. He may be a courageous and lonely individualist, but he may also merely be taking orders and following his own crowd. Whatever he may be, however, his existence tends to make us painfully aware that we too are implicitly making choices, and must bear responsibility for the ones we make.

27. This, indeed, may be the most important function of those who practice civil disobedience. They remind us that the man who obeys the law has as much of an obligation to look into the morality of his acts and the rationality of his society as does the man who breaks the law. The occurrence of civil disobedience can never be a happy phenomenon; when it is justified, something is seriously wrong with the society in which it takes place. But the man who puts his conscience above the law, though he may be right or he may be wrong, does take personal moral responsibility for the social arrangements under which he lives. And so he dramatizes the fascinating and fearful possibility that those who obey the law might do the same. They might obey the law and support what exists, not out of habit or fear, but because they have freely chosen to do so, and are prepared to live with their consciences after having made that choice.

FREYA STARK

On Smuggling

Freya Madeline Stark (1893–   ), born in Paris, studied in Italy and at the University of London. She has been honored for her special diplomatic services to the British government in the Middle East and in the United States, and for her books about her travels and diplomatic experiences. In 1951 she received an honorary degree from the University of Glasgow, and in 1953 the Order of the British Empire. She has said that her life has been devoted to travel, mountaineering, and embroidery. But since 1933 she has also published many books; the most recent are *Alexander's Path*, 1958; *Riding to the Tigris*, 1959; *Dust in the Lion's Paw*, 1961 (a report of her mission to the United States to explain British policy in World War II); *The Journey's Echo*, 1963; and *Rome on the Euphrates*, 1967.

"On Smuggling," which appeared in *Holiday*, October 1966, reveals the author's deep insight into human nature and her ability to deal wisely with its manifestations.

1. On the French-Italian frontier, where I spent some years of my life, the husband of our cook happened to be a smuggler, and would go off on Tuesdays and Fridays with a band of colleagues, each carrying a note of 1,000 lire and 1,100 francs for the Italian and French gendarmes respectively at the pass of the Maritime Alps.

2. At this time—it was in the late 1940's—little boats would put out openly in the sunset from Menton or Ventimiglia and wait for a thin shred of darkness to land their goods on one side or the other of the border, while the posts on the main road waylaid the more legitimate travelers with infinite delays. Even there, evasions could be engineered.

3. The most ingenious one I heard of was that of a woman with her sick boy whose leg, wrapped in plaster, was to be X-rayed on the other side of the frontier at San Remo. The

police had been informed that this was a ruse at a time when gold was being largely smuggled across. They insisted on cutting open the plaster to see, and found nothing but the injured limb.

4. "What shall I do?" wailed the tearful mother as they plastered the leg up again. "The boy has to go to the hospital every week, and will you open it every time?"

5. "Never again, Madame: you need have no fears."

6. She was sent off in a cloud of apology, and able to return for a number of weeks after with her boy's leg lapped in gold, to the amusement of both sides of the border.

7. French Menton was nearer to my home than Italian Ventimiglia, and I would carry on a modest little household smuggling of my own in coffee—which was difficult to get in Italy at that time. In my father's day, I would slip an unnoticed parcel into his overcoat pocket and rely on the transparent integrity of his innocence to walk us through;

ON SMUGGLING From *Holiday*, October, 1966. Reprinted by permission of John Murray, Ltd.

but when I came to be alone, I would hold up my shopping bag and say, "Coffee," relying on the diplomatic cliché that the best disguise is the truth, and would usually walk on unchallenged. The sleepy old guard once came out from his little box and felt the beans through the bag and asked what they were; but it was a hot afternoon, and the siesta hour, and I said, "You had better not inquire"; and he kindly desisted. They came to know their usual clients, and on one occasion apologized to me for a new official whose zeal over a miserable jar of treacle had made me walk from a subsidiary post in the hills to the highroad. "He is young," they said. "He is still attached to the regulations."

8. One may notice in the course of a variegated life, that illegality need not always be disapproved of. The tolerance with which it is accepted is possibly due to a remote feeling that law is not infallible and human nature has its rights. No one has thought the worse of Shakespeare for poaching. Highwaymen and pirates have enjoyed a measure of sympathy, undeserved I should say, increasing, no doubt as their threat diminished and seas and roads became safer. And in the present state of our society, which does its best to think of security as normal, smuggling continues to hold a sort of extramural respectability. Men usually dislike it—from cowardice, I think, and not from virtue—but one may say that almost the whole female sex is addicted to it by nature, and here a psychologist might perhaps find one of the permanent differences between us.

9. Strangely enough, since I usually belong to the other party, I am personally inclined to side with the police. Perhaps this comes from my having lived so much on borderlands in Asia, where the odds are weighted heavily against them. I have never been able to evade them for long while riding near a frontier, and when caught by the police, have felt a sympathy for their hard and poorly rewarded and solitary lives. They eke them out, one must admit, with a scanty amount of plunder from the very poor; but their chief support is moral, and comes from man's simple loyalty, which he produces merely by banding himself with other men and devoting himself to something or someone out of sight. Watching the cheerful endurance and constant hardship of their lives, I came to have a great liking and respect for these tough people, many of them already grizzled in their service, who had to pay out of their own pockets for the horses they rode up and down the solitary lands they kept free from intruders and marauders, and whose best hope was to end up respectably in some remote village, with little but their memories and perhaps the rank of sergeant to keep them warm.

10. Even in more sophisticated places, one should never forget that a customs officer is human.

11. The Mediterranean world south of the Alps, having to steer the ship of civilization through such difficult waters and through so many centuries, has long ago come to terms both with its conscience and with the ups and downs of the customs officer's character. It is a world that still continues, in spite of every sort of injustice and oppression, to make life livable and pleasant through one millennium after another. Its basic characteristic is, I think, that it has an infinite optimism about human nature. It does not assume that one is wicked because one does wicked things. It goes on being polite through activities that would spell exclusion from clubs in Washington or London; for it recognizes morality, but treats it as a private possession, not to be too much mixed up with the art of living as such. It has seen too many landmarks removed, too many formulas exploded, to believe that there is an intrinsic difference between smoking a cigarette on one side of a border or the other. It limits its disapproval to those who are found out.

12. With any luck, one may be sure that the customs officer shares these views in his heart of hearts. His life, one must remember, is very boring. We come to him exhilarated by the intriguing variety of our little stratagems, and he has the weary task of frustrating them: he is grateful for any flash of interest or amusement. I once spent a long day in the *dogana* of Venice seeing some trunks of

household goods through labyrinths of paper. The trunks contained mostly old worn books, which I had thought of as perfectly easy, but it appeared that all literature required a permit from the Ministry of Interior before being allowed into Italy. The hours passed while this hurdle was being negotiated, and as I sat there on a hard chair thinking things about bureaucracy, a minor official passing by said pityingly: "We make you suffer, signora. We are all scoundrels, we people of the *dogana*."

13. "Well, not all of you," said I, "because you may remember that Saint Matthew was a customs officer."

14. This happily inspired remark was handed on; I could hear it passing in an enlivening way down the bleak and empty corridors; and it must have reached the august and private desk of the chief of customs, for my permit came in a matter of minutes, with no intervention from the Ministry of Interior.

15. Books are anyway a headache for the customs. Many countries still think that corruption comes from outside, and one cannot expect every customs officer to be erudite. One sympathizes with those in the United States who years ago excluded the poems of Ovid as pornographic. A more recent instance happened to a friend of mine landing in Egypt. He had been reading Aldous Huxley's *Grey Eminence* in the plane, and had it taken from him because the customs official, skipping at random, saw the name of Father Joseph and concluded that it must be some communist reference to Stalin.

16. The customs officer himself, however, if he likes their looks, will sometimes do his best to help his culprits through.

17. I have not done any serious smuggling myself, apart from taking a large, gold-backed, primitive Madonna across a border for a friend: but I have occasionally in the East had maps I did not wish to be deprived of, and kept them in a small, double-bottomed suitcase which I carried. When the War was over, a friend in Greece asked me to bring three lengths of expensive silk for her evening wear, and I foolishly packed them in the bottom of this case, and was instantly dis-

covered by the Greek who came on board at Corfu. It should be a smuggler's basic rule never to try to deceive a Greek. On this occasion my defeat was watched by the three Mediterranean ladies who shared my cabin; by several stewards and stewardesses lounging there; and by the customs officer and his two aides. All, with one accord, recognized a fellow human being in distress and came to my assistance.

18. "What is the silk worth?" said the officer, turning to the nearest woman beside him.

19. "Artificial," said she. "A few drachmas to the yard"—a lie that everyone took in the kindly way it was intended.

20. My friend's evening gowns were whittled down till they were not worth paying for; I was cautioned against the double-based suitcase; complimented the Greek officer on his quickness; and was allowed my three dress lengths free of charge.

21. This would probably not have happened north of the Alps. Tancred's mother, in Lord Beaconsfield's novel, anxious for her son's health and distressed at his predilection for the Orient, laments that he will not travel in "Protestant countries free from vermin": there is a line of demarcation not merely geographic between the Protestant north and pagan south. But the difference is, I think, not one of virtue—a matter anyway hard to assess in a relative world. It is rather due to the increase in the number of things the individual considers to be only his own proper business as he travels to the south.

22. If we like individuality—as indeed we do—we must not forget that variety is one of its ingredients, and it is no use to go on criticizing the Mediterranean for the patchwork system of its corporate life. (It remains to be seen, of course, when we have really got bureaucracy going, how long we can remain corporate ourselves.) However this may be, the Greco-Roman world, which still is the modern Mediterranean, discovered centuries ago that a body of regulations in the middle of one's path can be dealt with only by the most prompt and skillful circumvention. "*Fatta la legge, trovato l'inganno,*" the

Italians say: "Make a law and find the way around it."

23. In this age-long struggle of the individual against the Regulation, the government official, in whatever department it may be, is the adversary. But he is not therefore either black to your white or white to your black, as he would be in our ethical north. He is a human being like ourselves, who has chosen to make his career in the camp opposed to Human Nature, but retains the freedom as well as the power to be either easy or disagreeable to his friends. There are any number of hidden little bridges between the two Mediterranean camps. Nor is their intercourse quite as unknown as we in the north like to imagine it. During World War II, I twice had to cross into and out of England without time to have all my papers censored. The censor's rules were very strict, and I had a great many papers, collected for a tour on which I was being sent to the United States. I handed these in at the ports of arrival and departure, explaining why they were not sealed and stamped as they should have been, and on both occasions happened by great good fortune on an officer who knew my books and took it upon himself to think it safe to let me have my packet back unread. He, too, was using his individual judgment against the regulations; and the fact that one sort of official will use it for the general good, and another for his own, is just one of those exhilarating human problems that hamper the regulations all the time.

24. I must digress to another pleasant breach, one that happened in 1938, when the democratic nations imposed the blockade called "sanctions" on Mussolini at the beginning of the Abyssinian war. My mother, living at that time in Italy, sent a small strip of embroidery linen to me in England. The little sample lingered on its way, but a large sheet of paper reached me with a full description of the policy of sanctions and the consequent detention of my parcel by His Majesty's Customs: and I was so annoyed that I wrote back, explaining that I detested dictatorships in general, and Mussolini's in particular, but could not see how my embroidery linen could help while the tankers carrying oil were all allowed freely through. Some unknown official evidently felt the same, for the next post brought my parcel.

25. On looking back along the vista of my long and varied warfare with the customs, I am surprised to notice how many stimulating memories these meetings contain. Even the French, who tend to enjoy being disagreeable as soon as they put on a uniform, have given me pleasurable moments. There was a man on the *wagon-lit* who solved the problem of a new Paris suit: one could get 14 percent, as far as I remember, off its not inconsiderable price if one presented the parcel sealed and intact at the exit from France on the Simplon route, and one could avoid the Italian duty on it if it lay, innocent and unwrapped from its tissue papers, among one's ordinary clothes, after one emerged from the tunnel— a transformation performed by the attendant, who kept all the parcels in his cubbyhole on the train, and who told me he was in the habit of doing the same *"pour toutes les dames."* In the middle of the night, not long after the French customs had been pacified, he handed in my parcel from the corridor, and a hasty unpacking and repacking spread the cartons and name of Madame Grès into the darkness.

26. Another friendly helper appeared at the beginning of the War, when I was being sent to Aden and was trying to get into the Orient Express in Paris with far more luggage than was allowed.

27. "I have eight frontiers to cross," I explained, "and my luggage is full of things I don't want them to see."

28. "Let it go in," said the guard, looking fiercely at the shrinking passengers inside. "I, too, have worked for the intelligence service." (I may say that my suitcases mostly contained innocuous and indeed futile propaganda films such as *Sheep-Shearing in Yorkshire* and *Arts and Crafts in England Today*.)

29. Recollections of unkind customs officers are almost as agreeable as the others; they gave the pleasure of warfare without its serious pain.

30. There was a Frenchman on the Menton frontier whom I begged to let me and my car through quickly since my battery had given out and I was afraid, being a bad driver, to twist about in darkness on the Corniche road. He replied by going through every detail of my luggage with sadistic slowness, while I searched in a frenzy of hatred for the most wounding thing I could find to say. The War was just over, and patriotic feeling among the French ran high. "He is surely a *collaborateur*," I thought, and drawing a bow at a venture, said: "One can see, monsieur, that you never fought at Bir Hakim." Bir Hakim was the desert site where the Free French covered themselves with glory, and the mention of it must have touched some delicate and unsuspected chord. The wicked man leaped into the air as if I had run a needle into him.

31. "What makes you say that, mademoiselle?"

32. "That, monsieur," said I, noticing my advantage, "is a matter I mean to keep to myself."

33. I was luckily as innocent of contraband as could be, and when at last the darkness was falling, and my luggage had to be closed, my Frenchman's still furious comment was: "One says that the English are phlegmatic. I have never found them so."

34. "I presume no one has told you that women are phlegmatic?" was my retort. After which, as we were south of the Alps, he came around the barrier of the customs and shook hands.

35. Some years ago I was discussing the question of the Persian nomads with one of the Bakhtiari Khans in Isfahan. These tribes move twice a year, up to their summer or down to their winter pastures, and are a menace to the quiet farmers on their way. "We leave our villages and close our gates," my Persian mirza had told me long before, "when the tribes are passing by."

36. "In a few years," said the Bakhtiari (dressed in the best Scotch tweed and sipping his whisky), "we shall have no more nomads: they will be settled peacefully on their lands."

37. I took up what is a lost cause, since the process has already gone too far to stop; but I asked him whether the way of life that produces a maximum of independence, intelligence, toughness and self-reliance is not worth trying to preserve at almost any cost in the empty and barren stretches of earth.

38. The same argument, I think, holds in favor of smuggling.

39. Our chief enemy today is not Russia or Africa or China but mere boredom in a world in which the means of living may be ceasing to be totally absorbing. Even animals suffer from this monster as soon as they enjoy security, as anyone can see who has not taken his dog out for a walk. It threatens, unless carefully neutralized, to play havoc in a world under control.

40. Crime already begins to appear as the alternative to war.

41. Efforts are already being made to supply other and less damaging equivalents. Adventure—organized to be innocuous, or dangerous so as to be advertised; philanthropy—an almost boundless interference of efficient and inefficient people in other people's lives; even the pleasures of the imagination—as a last resort—are now being enlisted.

42. They all lack one or both of two indispensable ingredients: their appeal is either too narrow to be general or the stimulus of danger is wanting.

43. The art of smuggling has these requisites in a manageable form. It should not be despised. It is less expensive than war, and unlike crime, does no real harm to innocent people; it merely robs a government already usually engaged in robbing, and in any case produces no such sensible loss as to outbalance its individual enjoyment. It encourages initiative, and like mountaineering or sailing (which often enter into its curriculum), has a spice of danger of its own: and adds, moreover, the animating sensation of stepping temporarily outside the bureaucratic bonds. In this it may perhaps in its small way be compared to what the astronauts feel when they slide outside their satellites in space.

44. I have never, as far as I remember,

heard of anything either very cruel or vicious in the annals of smuggling, at any rate as practiced today. The worst I can remember is two carabinieri tied back to back by the outlaws in the mountains and left for their comrades of the next patrol to find; and the frontier guards of Mussolini shooting at embarrassed climbers when some caprice of an Alpine ridge forced them up the wrong side of the border.

45. Usually it is clear fun, not too expensive to either side. In the Persian summer, when the embassies go camping up the valley of the Lar, the military secretary had been looking forward to the use of his new fishing rod from London. The weeks went by, and it lay in the customs, marooned as if forever; and when the last day before his holiday came around, his servant volunteered to steal it out. With the help of some useful Oriental friend it was extracted from its package in the customs store, was used—no doubt with additional pleasure—by the military secretary, and replaced in unobserved safety when the holiday was over, to emerge and pay its duty in its official time.

46. On the borders of Egypt the camel caravans were used for the transport of hashish: the camels were fed with it, in pellets wrapped in some substance too hard to digest, at a carefully timed point that would cause them to be evacuated intact on the right (or wrong) side of the frontier.

47. I have never myself carried a narcotic of any kind, and when I found a few packets of opium hidden in my saddlebags by a Persian guide, I risked the mutiny of my small caravan by throwing them into a stream in sight of all.

48. The drug traffic is not amusing; it brings a dark spot into the map of this otherwise cheerful game and justifies the official contention that human nature is not to be trusted. If this were not so, if the individual used his judgment only to smuggle happiness and enjoyment across the borders of the world, and to leave such things as hashish and gelignite alone, the official position would indeed be untenable and frontiers even more idiotic than they are.

49. Even as it is, there is a fallacy inherent in the effort to substitute law for human nature, which—as I have been trying to show—will inevitably appear, however much you dress it up in uniform. "Dress them as you like; they will always run away," the King of Naples is reported to have said of his poor soldiers, and the only remedy is not to be found in the regulations as such, but lurks in whatever reality may exist behind a legal façade.

50. The persuasive strength of truth is in the long run the only substitute for crime, from the illegal smoking of a cigarette to the lighting of an atomic bomb: it is only through the conscience of mankind that these questions can be touched. I am not suggesting that this can be achieved, since Christianity and other religions also have tried for about 2,000 years and failed: but the difficulty of a path in the right direction does not make the easier and wrong one any more likely to lead one to one's goal: and the probability is that humanity in general will continue to think that a woman in Italy has as much claim to a whiff of French perfume as a woman in Paris. While this conviction persists in spite of economic laws, smuggling is most likely to continue; and as it offers one of the few harmless sports that can in any way be comparable to war, it is quite a good idea to make use of our silly frontiers while we have them, and let our youth be trained, as the Spartans trained theirs, by stealing. We are in a poor way, perhaps, and if we are reduced to seeing our good wheat stifled (largely by bureaucratic regulations), we may as well do whatever we can to extract some living virtue from among the tares.

 *THE MASS MEDIA*

GEORGE STARBUCK

Extravaganza

Radio Keith Orpheum R K
O Radio Pictures presents Sestina:
The Story of Six Strange Loves A Bill Scott-
Jay Ward Production starring Siobhan
McKenna Lionel Barrymore
Francis X. Bushman Carroll

Baker and Leo G. Carroll
and also featuring Kay
Kendall Diana Barrymore
and Cantinflas in the role of Señor Sestina
Musical Score by Ralph Vaughan
Williams played by John Scott

Trotter and the Orchestra with Hazel Scott
at the Hammond Organ and Diahann Carroll
Patachou Sarah and Vaughn
Monroe Danny and Sammy and Kay
Kyser and Starr and the Sestina
Chorus and Orchestra John Barrymore

played by himself John Barrymore
Jr. played by himself as a child From the F. Scott
Fitzgerald novella "The Sestina
Caper" Adapted by Karel
Čapek Screenplay by R. K.
Narayan and William Vaughn

EXTRAVAGANZA From *The New Yorker*, July 30, 1966. © 1966 The New Yorker Magazine, Inc.

Moody Gowns for the Misses Vaughn
Lombard Negri and Barrymore
by Irene Special material for the Danny Kaye
number the George C. Scott-Scott
Joplin number and the Carol
Burnett number and the songs "Sestina

Sestina" and "Beach Blanket Sestina"
by Adolph Green Directed by Erich von
Stroheim D. W. Griffith and Carol
Reed *M Squad* and *The Garry Moore
Show* will not be seen tonight so that Scott-
Tissue Kelloggs makers of Special K

The P. K. Wrigley Company and your Avon
Lady can bring you Ethel Barrymore J. Carrol
Naish and Randolph Scott in SESTINA.

HENRY M. PACHTER

In Defense of Television

Henry M. Pachter (1907–   ), born and educated in Germany, emigrated to France in 1933 and to America in 1941. Since 1949, he has been United Nations correspondent for Swiss and German newspapers, and since 1952, he has taught history at the New School for Social Research in New York City. His books include *Espagne: creuset politique,* which was published in 1939 and issued in a Spanish edition as *España: crisol político* in 1966; *Nazi-Deutsch,* 1944; *Paracelsus—Magic into Science,* 1951; and *Collision Course: The Cuban Missile Crisis,* 1963.

In this balanced consideration of television, Mr. Pachter defends it against a number of charges and suggests that its admitted weaknesses could be alleviated if its critics would invest some of their energy in directing its course.

1. Casting an indulgent eye on the merry-making of Flemish peasants, Breughel found it brutish, vulgar, lusty, gluttonous, bibulous and, possibly, dulling. Yet, nothing in his canvases suggests the suspicion that the feudal lords might have devised the popular culture of their time the better to keep the peasantry in submission. Pious monks might have believed that the Devil was to blame, but no serious historian would credit such views today. We condone superstition with reference only to our own culture. According to Gunther Anders (in *Dissent,* Winter 1956), e.g., a dark conspiracy has foisted television on us for the purposes of profit, deception and subjection:

1. "The mass producer . . . needs a mass broken up into the largest possible number of customers; he does not want all of his customers to consume one and the same product (as in looking at a movie together); he wants all to buy identical products" (as in watching television separately).

2. "The method allegedly intended to bring the object close to us, actually serves to veil the object, to alienate it or slowly to do away with it"; the implication is that capitalism needs unrealistic subjects who live in a "phantom world," as the title of the essay says.

3. "Mass production of the mass man himself was speeded up," meaning that by watching TV we acquire, without being aware of what is being done to us, the character of the crowd.

2. Assertion No. 1 obviously means to inform us of a more shattering discovery than the fact that the electronics industry is inter-

IN DEFENSE OF TELEVISION From *Dissent III.* Reprinted by permission of the publisher.

ested in the sale of television sets; after all, automobiles and refrigerators are sold without any "phantom" assisting. The real phantom which bothers our author is the little man behind the grey screen; isn't it difficult to realize how he got there, economically speaking? Someone paid to put him there, so he must be a "commodity"; and, reasoning further, one such commodity seen by a thousand people in a movie theatre must bring less profit, hence be less capitalistic than the same picture appearing a thousand times on a thousand little screens.

3. This is poor economics based on misunderstood technology, and primitive sociology too. A TV program supplies one identical product to a large mass, just as the movies; in both cases the admission price is calculated on the basis of cost and profit. Like any other enterprise, the entertainment industry does not count its customers, but the sales value of its product no matter whether it is divided into many or few lumps. But worse: How did "the mass producer" convert his "need" into a desire of his customers? It is one thing to say that some modern inventions came as a boon to industry; Mr. Anders implies quite another thing—that these inventions were so conceived, and we consumers were so conditioned, that the greatest number of goods can be sold at the highest profit. He still believes in the omnipotence of the overlords; his new version of the Iron Heel even gives them credit for a far more ambitious scheme: mass production, Mr. Anders says, has been so devised that "mass consumption produces mass man." As a witticism the *aperçu* might be superb; as a theory, expounded at nauseating leisure, it is misleading.

4. Consider this sentence: "The classical homeworker manufactures his wares in order to secure a minimum of consumer goods and leisure; the modern homeworker consumes a maximum of leisure products in order to help produce the mass man." The first "in order to" refers to the worker's intentions; the second "in order to," however, expresses the mystical power of the Iron Heel. An honest parallel to the latter statement would have been: "The classical homeworker manufactured goods in order to reproduce the social conditions which force him to manufacture more goods." Thus stated, we still have the primitive sociology, but at least the evil cycle of the producer society would be compared with the evil cycle of the consumer society.

5. Moreover, throughout his essay, as in the last quotation, Mr. Anders consistently idealizes and even idyllicizes the past. That noble worker in the Lord's vineyard seems never to have been conditioned by the ideologies of his terrestrial and spiritual overlords! That touching picture of the happy family, gathered around the big oaken table, seems never to have been marred by the tragedies which constitute up to 90 per cent of the thematic material in nineteenth century literature. Those lovers, before radio, must all have been highly articulate Cyranos, and no Christian ever needed the voice of a poet or the song of a musician to conquer first his shyness and thereafter the bride. Those heroes of yesterday never saw politics as a spectacle but went in there to fight it out for themselves; they never went to a circus, never read novels, penny dreadfuls and Radcliffe, never relied on newspapers for their knowledge of the world, never believed a Napoleon or a Mussolini before radio. Finally, these intellectual giants had no occasion to look at the world in an "idealistic" way, but were always aware of the reality behind the pictures that supplied their limited opportunities of information. What nonsense! All the indictments against "mass culture" are at least as old as Gutenberg—not to speak of Ovid. Ortega y Gasset added elegance and Anders adds brilliant confusion, punning happily along Heidegger alley where all lights are fueled by free association.

6. Granted that the new inventions may create opportunities for manipulation or tend to cripple our sensorial experience of the world; it still does not follow that mass communication methods doom our intelligence to misorientation. The truth is that at all times most public events are experienced vicariously and that each society has its special means of communicating to its citizens the preferred picture of reality; at all times did people rely on teachers, travelers, pictures and other second-hand information to form their view of the world. Today's mass media and extreme

mobility potentially increase our sources of information to the point of universality, where cross-checking has become easy and wilful distortion has become difficult. The walls of the city and the walls of the home have been laid down; the idols of the market and the idols of the cave have been blown to pieces— Mr. Anders claims that these old and whole-some walls, the protectors of the *penates,* have been replaced by a wide screen where the idols of the theatre simulate an unreal world.

7. I do not wish to belittle the difference between reading and viewing. Certainly the latter opens more opportunity to suggestion. Yet, not so long ago, the printed word was held almost sacred by the masses; from es-capist literature to tabloids, peoples at all times preferred to read and believe what reassured them, rather than what might shake their complacency. Of their own volition they gave the manipulators a monopoly of information. Today nobody thinks that the picture on the little screen represents the real world; every-body knows that the President uses makeup and tele-prompter; even the children who used to believe in Santa Claus know that Hopalong Cassidy is an actor. The television camera constantly prompts the experienced viewer to cheer the editor who switches to promising angles and selects the most interesting view-points. Mr. Anders is blind to the immense widening of our perceptive capacities through the camera.

8. While the possibility of deception is ever-present, the danger of deliberate manipula-tion and of "conditioning" through unconscious suggestion might even be declining. The ideals of our society may be less admirable than the virtues of ancient Rome; but if we live by them, not TV is to blame but the erosion of virtue that preceded popular culture. The loss of substance and certainty which characterizes the age began to be noticed eighty years ago by a generation of artists which did not call itself avant-garde but in relation to which our critics of TV are a sorry rear-guard. They first revealed the surface character of our ex-perience, but now we have run full circle: in popular experience, manipulation is visible

or suspected everywhere. We know that our environment is being manufactured for us, and after some more years, TV-experienced people may tend to believe nothing, just as they have become fairly immune to propa-ganda of other sorts. The illusions which we buy—a perfume, a movie, a popular song, a comedian on TV—do not fool us; they are consciously presented and accepted as illu-sions, not as truth. Far from living in a world of phantoms, we are facing the danger of com-plete disillusionment.

9. Another facet of this development is our loss of values. I deplore it as much as Mr. Anders does. But again—is the display of profligacy on big and small screens a cause or a symptom of the decline in the stature of our heroes? What had Hitler or Stalin that Cromwell or Cortez did not have? Is Gary Cooper less real than Robin Hood?

10. In this connection, Mr. Anders makes the shrewd remark that Socrates is being made over into a pal on TV and in popular science literature. The great men, he says, no longer are revered for their greatness but inserted into a world of appearances; they are known not for their unique substance but for that which the community of pals can understand. He might have addressed his reproach to Aristophanes, and he might have quoted in support of his own views any number of antique writers, beginning with Plato. They all complained that the *profanum vulgus* was taking over; they all hated themselves and others, begrudging the people their daily pleasures. I should have liked to meet Socra-tes; I understand he used to dine and wine with friends. He might not be less great for that. Plato's Socrates, whom Mr. Anders wishes to raise on a pedestal, is a completely phoney picture—a phantom, to use Mr. Anders's words. The mere fact that so many millions now can become familiar with him, makes Socrates a base commodity: "When the event can be . . . reproduced virtually any number of times, it acquires the characteristics of an assembly-line product; and when we pay for having it delivered to our homes, it is a com-modity." Only professional philosophers turned theologians make such elementary mistakes

in elementary logic. If I buy the print of a Rembrandt etching, not the meeting of Christ with the disciples at Emmaus is reproduced but its likeness; and neither the event nor Rembrandt's conception of it has become a commodity. What Mr. Anders means to say is much less mystical than the transubstantiation of an event into a commodity. Certain experiences—enjoying a work of art, meeting a great personality, reading a profound book—cannot be duplicated. The reproduction which pretends to be the original merely reminds us of it; the exciting moment of a live concert is not recorded along with the sound track; an "art appreciation course" substitutes learning for spontaneous perception. Manufacturers of such ersatz satisfaction surely would have us accept their wares for the real thing; clever producers even may exploit the real love affairs of a movie star or create suitable stories from the whole cloth to provide vicarious experiences for an audience that increasingly likes to have the proper feelings preassembled and delivered along with the "event." Not multiplication of the event, but vulgarization of its stand-in, not communication of an experience but pre-digestion of experience results in the stunted sensibility of mass culture.

11. In similar ways, totalitarian governments may create events for political exploitation; their policies often are designed to confirm the dream world where they keep their subjects. Occasionally they fall for their own phantasmagoria and walk into an abyss where they had seen a road to glory. Strangely enough, the totalitarian implications are not discussed by Mr. Anders, though everywhere else he insists on the modern-age nature of his phantom world. In the German version of his essay, which is more complete, however, he speaks of important mimesis phenomena which belong here. "In the beginning, there was broadcasting," he says ironically, "and the world was made to suit it." He concludes: "Were one of us to try and go forth in quest of the real world . . . he soon would be disappointed. For out there he would find nothing but models modeled after the pictures of which they are supposed to be the originals."

It may be unfair to polemicize against something that was not published; yet I feel that the published fragment does not do justice to Mr. Anders. He has developed an interesting theory of cognition which may apply to human nature. His may be a great discovery, occasioned by certain outstanding traits of perception which now are more visible than before. He is wrong, I submit, in trying to make a double discovery—namely, that these features are characteristic of the present society. A sociological analysis of knowledge must start out from sound sociology and careful use of history. Certainly, Orson Welles's famous radio invasion from Mars says something about the United States in the thirties—but have there not been panicky flights to the hills before, when a comet seemed to announce a new Flood? Certainly we pity the old ladies who start knitting baby clothes when their favorite soap opera heroine is pregnant; but did not Goethe get hundreds of letters from imaginary Lottes and did not would-be Werthers actually commit suicide?

12. Neither the economics nor the technical facilities of mass communication are to blame for the use which their owners make of them. We, on the other hand, are not helpless, powerless and hopeless in front of inexorable forces unleashed by industry's ingenuity or the Iron Heel's clever scheming. These phantoms were built up by the pseudo-radicalism of the snobs to justify their flight into the cultural preserve, a Messianic religion, political or other nihilisms. Not popular culture but their own craving for "alienation" keeps their eyes away from the realistic, "materialistic," Mr. Anders might say, conditions which must be changed. Mass entertainment can be debased by commercial or by political interests, but only if and while these interests retain their monopoly of communication. The ultra-left culture snobs from the start concede this monopoly to the interests. They have no real quarrel with the world as it is, except that they pretend not to like it that way. The hypocrites! They like it exactly in such a desperate state that they can lament about their impotence in facing it.

13. For the newest fashion in mass culture

is to scorn mass culture. Everybody does, nowadays; those who don't either are writing a book on mass culture or collect early jazz records. Conformism has come around full circle; one dares no longer be "conformist," enjoy any product of the entertainment industry, see differences between the two major parties, admit opinions which might be shared by the multitude. Those who cannot possibly be radicals on the left develop at least a radical or "new" conservatism; these nonconformists in reverse usually get along with the older variety of nonconformists in forward gear. In friendly competition, the two élites are trying to outdo each other at deriding the "mass." Members of their bi-partisan club display in their home a copy of *Partisan Review* together with a painting conceived in an advanced style (as to records, progressives favor Bach while new-conservatives may boast a Shostakovitch concerto played by Oistrakh), and are conversant with words such as alienation, popular culture, pseudo-whatever-fashion-is, anxiety, crowd, absurd and a few others, judicious use of which will silence the un-initiated and bring recognition from those who belong; many will grant you such recognition to be recognized themselves.

14. Nonconformist tolerance leaves a choice of many peculiar ways to exquisiteness. One may be an existentialist, a Marxist, a surrealist, a fascist—the crowd of frightened snobs will be so discriminating as not to discriminate against him. They may differentiate, though; through marginal differentiation between various crowds, each of them very distinctive, the crowd of the anti-crowds constitutes itself as an effective instrument of terror. No one ever dares to defy its edicts. To be amused by Groucho, to be excited by Armstrong, to be moved to tears by Molly Goldberg (or Werther, for that matter), amounts to backwardness, lack of sensitivity, vulgarity and cultural treason. One has to be alienated to be counted. For here is art, there is entertainment.

15. In their dread of being caught in a profane mood, would-be intellectuals alienate themselves from the sources of national experience and risk forfeiting their share in forming it. They refuse to see any transmission belt between popular and higher culture, or between popular ideologies and true ideals. Yet, popular culture may be a watered-down, vulgarized version of yesterday's class culture; it also may contain groping, unconscious adumbrations of tomorrow's means of expression. Contemporary indictments of jazz often are literal repetitions of similar pronouncements on the waltz 130 years ago. "Baroque" once had a meaning similar to our "kitsch," and already the suggestion has been made that the first half of this century may be known to, and admired by, posterity as the "Age of Kitsch." Kitsch, by the way, is most children's avenue to artistic expression—some never get beyond that stage, and much of the so-called folk culture, which often is favorably compared with our "mass culture," really is or was the mass culture of civilizations which knew few fashion changes. Though this difference may be decisive, it is precisely one where our mass culture and our nonconformists stand on the same side. Both fear nothing so much as yesterday's conformity. The mad chase for newness in "original creations" is fittingly aped on the assembly line of popular fashion. Mass production processes in the entertainment industries make its content repetitious, self-perpetuating, inflexible. It produces no original material but, on the contrary, transforms its consumer into a passive recipient of sense stimuli. There is no cross-fertilization, no participation in a creative process, but only the surrender to the narcotic effects of a merchandise. Popular culture no longer is entertainment which we provide for ourselves, but has become the supply of entertainment which we buy. All this is true, and serious, too. Our spectator sports, the Roman *circenses*, are opium for the crowds. Unable to escape the insanity of their existence, they purchase escape by the hour; incapable of facing their own feelings, they have sentimentality expressed for them; too sluggish to rebel against their impotence, they watch Superman conquer space and time.

16. Yet, these vicarious gratifications also express a yearning for a different world and reflect a search for a different humanity. The

material content of some escape literature even points to pre-conscious states of rebellion. Sometimes in curiously inverted forms Al Capp, through his "Li'l Abner" cartoon, projects the immolated image of humanity into crudely ironical utopias. It is a gross overstatement that the alienation process in popular culture has gone too far for remedy and return. There is no conformistic material that cannot be turned into nonconformist outcries. Kung Fu changed a few words in a simple calendar to express his political criticism and everybody can think of many superb works of art issued from the new media. The technical characteristics of printing, photographing, filming, broadcasting, television, recording do not restrict, but enlarge the range of our experience and the possibilities of expression.

LESLIE FIEDLER

The Middle Against Both Ends

Leslie Aaron Fiedler (1917–   ) is professor of English at State University of New York at Buffalo. He has published many volumes of essays, short stories, novels, and poetry, among them *The Image of the Jew in American Fiction,* 1959; the highly controversial *Love and Death in the American Novel,* 1960; *Pull Down, Vanity* (stories), 1962; *The Second Stone: A Love Story,* 1963; and *Back to China,* 1965. His latest publication is *Last Jew in America,* 1966.

In this essay the "subbooks" and "subarts" of mass culture are interpreted as unavoidable effects of industrialization and mass education, and their detractors are identified as pseudoliterate middlebrows who would denounce great literature just as strongly if they had any acquaintance with it.

1. I am surely one of the few people pretending to intellectual respectability who can boast that he has read more comic books than attacks on comic books. I do not mean that I have consulted or studied the comics —I have read them, often with some pleasure. Nephews and nieces, my own children, and the children of neighbors have brought them to me to share their enjoyment. An old lady on a ferry boat in Puget Sound once

THE MIDDLE AGAINST BOTH ENDS   From *Encounter V,* 1955. Reprinted by permission of the author and the publisher.

dropped two in my lap in wordless sympathy; I was wearing, at the time, a sailor's uniform.

2. I have somewhat more difficulty in getting through the books that attack them. I am put off, to begin with, by inaccuracies of fact. When Mr. Geoffrey Wagner in his *Parade of Pleasure* calls Superboy "Superman's brother" (he is, of course, Superman himself as a child), I am made suspicious. Actually, Mr. Wagner's book is one of the least painful on the subject; confused, to be sure, but quite lively and not in the least smug; though it

propounds the preposterous theory that the whole of "popular literature" is a conspiracy on the part of the "plutos" to corrupt an innocent American people. Such easy melodrama can only satisfy someone prepared to believe, as Mr. Wagner apparently does, that the young girls of Harlem are being led astray by the *double-entendres* of blues records!

3. Mr. Wagner's notions are at least more varied and subtle than Mr. Gershon Legman's, who cries out in his *Love and Death* that it is simply our sexual frustrations which breed a popular literature dedicated to violence. But Mr. Legman's theory explains too much: not only comic books but Hemingway, war, Luce, Faulkner, the status of women—and, I should suppose, Mr. Legman's own shrill hyperboles. At that, Mr. Legman seems more to the point in his search for some deeply underlying cause than Frederic Wertham, in *Seduction of the Innocent,* with his contention that the pulps and comics in themselves are schools for murder. That the undefined aggressiveness of disturbed children can be given a shape by comic books, I do not doubt; and one could make a good case for the contention that such literature standardizes crime woefully or inhibits imagination in violence, but I find it hard to consider so obvious a symptom a prime cause of anything. Perhaps I am a little sensitive on this score, having heard the charge this week that the recent suicide of one of our college freshmen was caused by his having read (in a course of which I am in charge) Goethe, Dostoevsky, and *Death of a Salesman.* Damn it, he *had* read them, and he *did* kill himself!

4. In none of the books on comics I have looked into, and in none of the reports of ladies' clubs, protests of legislators, or statements of moral indignation by pastors, have I come on any real attempt to understand comic books: to define the form, midway between icon and story; to distinguish the subtypes—animal, adolescent, crime, western, etc.; or even to separate out, from the deadpan varieties, tongue-in-cheek sports like *Pogo,* frank satire like *Mad,* or semisurrealist variations like *Plastic Man.* It would not take someone with the talents of an Aristotle, but merely with his method, to ask the rewarding questions about this kind of literature that he asked once about an equally popular and bloody genre: what are its causes and its natural form?

5. A cursory examination would show that the super-hero comic (*Superman, Captain Marvel, Wonder Woman,* etc.) is the final form; it is statistically the most popular with the most avid readers, as well as providing the only new legendary material invented along with the form rather than adapted to it.

6. Next, one would have to abstract the most general pattern of the myth of the super-hero and deduce its significance: the urban setting, the threatened universal catastrophe, the hero who never uses arms, who returns to weakness and obscurity, who must keep his identity secret, who is impotent, etc. Not until then could one ask with any hope of an answer: what end do the comics serve? Why have they gained an immense body of readers precisely in the past fifteen or twenty years? Why must they be disguised as children's literature though read by men and women of all ages? And having answered these, one could pose the most dangerous question of all: why the constant virulent attacks on the comics, and, indeed, on the whole of popular culture of which they are especially flagrant examples?

7. Strategically, if not logically, the last question should be asked first. Why the attacks? Such assaults by scientists and laymen are as characteristic of our age as puritanic diatribes against the stage of the Elizabethan Era, and pious protests against novel reading in the later eighteenth century. I suspect that a study of such conventional reactions reveals at least as much about the nature of a period as an examination of the forms to which they respond. The most fascinating and suspicious aspect of the opposition to popular narrative is its unanimity; everyone from the members of the Montana State Legislature to the ladies of the Parent Teachers Association of Boston, Massachusetts, from British M.P.'s to the wilder post-Freudians of two continents agree on this, though they may agree on nothing else. What they have in common is, I am afraid, the sense that they are all, according

to their lights, righteous. And their protests represent only one more example (though an unlikely one) of the notorious failure of righteousness in matters involving art.

8. Just what is it with which vulgar literature is charged by various guardians of morality or sanity? With everything: encouraging crime, destroying literacy, expressing sexual frustration, unleashing sadism, spreading anti-democratic ideas, and, of course, corrupting youth. To understand the grounds of such charges, their justification and their bias, we must understand something of the nature of the subart with which we are dealing.

9. Perhaps it is most illuminating to begin by saying that it is a peculiarly American phenomenon, an unexpected by-product of an attempt, not only to extend literacy universally, but to delegate taste to majority suffrage. I do not mean, of course, that it is found only in the United States, but that wherever it is found, it comes first from us, and is still to be discovered in fully developed form only among us. Our experience along these lines is, in this sense, a preview for the rest of the world of what must follow the inevitable dissolution of the older aristocratic cultures.

10. One has only to examine certain Continental imitations of picture magazines like *Look* or *Life* or Disney-inspired cartoon books to be aware at once of their debt to American examples and of the failure of the imitations. For a true "popular literature" demands a more than ordinary slickness, the sort of high finish possible only to a machine-produced commodity in an economy of maximum prosperity. Contemporary popular culture, which is a function of an industrialized society, is distinguished from older folk art by its refusal to be shabby or second-rate in appearance, by a refusal to know its place. It is a product of the same impulse which has made available the sort of ready-made clothing which aims at destroying the possibility of knowing a lady by her dress.

11. Yet the articles of popular culture are made, not to be treasured, but to be thrown away; a paperback book is like a disposable diaper or a paper milk-container. For all its competent finish, it cannot be preserved on dusty shelves like the calf-bound volumes of another day; indeed, its very mode of existence challenges the concept of a library, private or public. The sort of conspicuous waste once reserved for an élite is now available to anyone; and this is inconceivable without an absurdly high standard of living, just as it is unimaginable without a degree of mechanical efficiency that permits industry to replace nature, and invents—among other disposable synthetics—one for literature.

12. Just as the production of popular narrative demands industrial conditions most favorably developed in the United States, its distribution requires the peculiar conditions of our market places: the mass of democratized market. Subbooks and subarts are not distributed primarily through the traditional institutions: museums, libraries, and schools, which remain firmly in the hands of those who deplore mass culture. It is in drugstores and supermarkets and airline terminals that this kind of literature mingles without condescension with chocolate bars and soapflakes. We have reached the end of a long process, begun, let us say, with Samuel Richardson, in which the work of art has approached closer and closer to the status of a commodity. Even the comic book is a last descendant of *Pamela,* the final consequence of letting the tastes (or more precisely, the buying power) of a class unpledged to maintaining the traditional genres determine literary success or failure.

13. Those who cry out now that the work of a Mickey Spillane or *The Adventures of Superman* travesty the novel, forget that the novel was long accused of travestying literature. What seems to offend us most is not the further downgrading of literary standards so much as the fact that the medium, the very notion and shape of a book, is being parodied by the comics. Jazz or the movies, which are also popular urban arts, depending for their distribution and acceptance on developments in technology (for jazz, the phonograph), really upset us much less.

14. It is the final, though camouflaged, rejection of literacy implicit in these new forms which is the most legitimate source of distress; but all arts so universally consumed

have been for illiterates, even stained glass windows and the plays of Shakespeare. What is new in our present situation, and hence especially upsetting, is that this is the first art for *post*literates, i.e., for those who have refused the benefit for which they were presumed to have sighed in their long exclusion. Besides, modern popular narrative is disconcertingly not oral; it will not surrender the benefits of the printing press as a machine, however indifferent it may be to that press as the perpetuator of techniques devised first for pen or quill. Everything that the press can provide—except matter to be really read—is demanded: picture, typography, even in many cases the illusion of reading along with the relaxed pleasure of illiteracy. Yet the new popular forms remain somehow prose narrative or pictographic substitutes for the novel; even the cognate form of the movies is notoriously more like a novel than a play in its handling of time, space and narrative progression.

15. From the folk literature of the past, which ever since the triumph of the machine we have been trying sentimentally to recapture, popular literature differs in its rejection of the picturesque. Rooted in prose rather than verse, secular rather than religious in origin, defining itself against the city rather than the world of outdoor nature, a by-product of the factory rather than agriculture, present-day popular literature defeats romantic expectations of peasants in their embroidered blouses chanting or plucking balalaikas for the approval of their betters. The haters of our own popular art love to condescend to the folk; and on records or in fashionable night clubs in recent years, we have had entertainers who have earned enviable livings producing commercial imitations of folk songs. But contemporary vulgar culture is brutal and disturbing: the quasi-spontaneous expression of the uprooted and culturally dispossessed inhabitants of anonymous cities, contriving mythologies which reduce to manageable form the threat of science, the horror of unlimited war, the general spread of corruption in a world where the social bases of old loyalties

and heroisms have long been destroyed. That such an art is exploited for profit in a commercial society, mass produced by nameless collaborators, standardized and debased, is of secondary importance. It is the patented nightmare of us all, a packaged way of coming to terms with one's environment sold for a dime to all those who have rejected the unasked-for gift of literacy.

16. Thought of in this light, the comic books with their legends of the eternally threatened metropolis eternally protected by immaculate and modest heroes (who shrink back after each exploit into the image of the crippled newsboy, the impotent and cowardly reporter) are seen as inheritors, for all their superficial differences, of the *inner* impulses of traditional folk art. Their gross drawing, their poverty of language cannot disguise their heritage of aboriginal violence, their exploitation of the ancient conflict of black magic and white. Beneath their journalistic commentary on A-bomb and Communism, they touch archetypal material: those shared figures of our lower minds more like the patterns of dream than fact. In a world where men threaten to dissolve into their most superficial and mechanical techniques, to become their borrowed newspaper platitudes, they remain close to the impulsive, subliminal life. They are our not quite machine-subdued Grimm, though the Black Forest has become, as it must, the City; the Wizard, the Scientist; and Simple Hans, Captain Marvel. In a society which thinks of itself as "scientific"—and of the Marvelous as childish—such a literature must seem primarily children's literature, though, of course, it is read by people of all ages.

17. We are now in a position to begin to answer the question: what do the righteous really have against comic books? In some parts of the world, simply the fact that they are American is sufficient, and certain homegrown self-condemners follow this line even in the United States. But it is really a minor argument, lent a certain temporary importance by passing political exigencies. To declare oneself against "the Americanization of culture" is meaningless unless one is set

resolutely against industrialization and mass education.

18. More to the point is the attack on mass culture for its betrayal of literacy itself. In a very few cases, this charge is made seriously and with full realization of its import; but most often it amounts to nothing but an accusation of "bad grammar" or "slang" on the part of some school marm to whom the spread of "different than" seems to threaten the future of civilized discourse. What should set us on guard in this case is that it is not the fully literate, the intellectuals and serious writers, who lead the attack, but the insecure semi-literate. In America, there is something a little absurd about the indignant delegation from the Parent Teachers Association (themselves clutching the latest issue of *Life*) crying out in defense of literature. Asked for suggestions, such critics are likely to propose the *Reader's Digest* as required reading in high school—or to urge more comic-book versions of the "classics": emasculated Melville, expurgated Hawthorne, or a child's version of something "uplifting" like "The Fall of the House of Usher." In other countries, corresponding counterparts are not hard to find.

19. As a matter of fact, this charge is scarcely ever urged with much conviction. It is really the portrayal of crime and horror (and less usually sex) that the enlightened censors deplore. It has been charged against vulgar art that it is sadistic, fetishistic, brutal, full of terror; that it pictures women with exaggeratedly full breasts and rumps, portrays death on the printed page, is often covertly homosexual, etc., etc. About these charges, there are two obvious things to say. First, by and large, they are true. Secondly, they are also true about much of the most serious art of our time, especially that produced in America.

20. There is no count of sadism and brutality which would not be equally proved against Hemingway or Faulkner or Paul Bowles—or, for that matter, Edgar Allan Poe. There are certain more literate critics who are victims of their own confusion in this regard, and who will condemn a Class B movie for its images of flagellation or bloodshed only to praise in the next breath such an orgy of highminded sadism as *Le Salaire de la Peur*. The politics of the French picture may be preferable, or its photography; but this cannot redeem the scene in which a mud- and oil-soaked truckdriver crawls from a pit of sludge to reveal the protruding white bones of a multiple fracture of the thigh. This is as much horror-pornography as *Scarface* or *Little Caesar*. You cannot condemn *Superman* for the exploitation of violence, and praise the existentialist-homosexual-sadist shockers of Paul Bowles. It is possible to murmur by way of explanation something vague about art or catharsis; but no one is ready to advocate the suppression of anything merely because it is aesthetically bad. In this age of conflicting standards, we would all soon suppress each other.

21. An occasional Savonarola is, of course, ready to make the total rejection; and secretly or openly, the run-of-the-mill condemner of mass culture does condemn, on precisely the same grounds, most contemporary literature of distinction. Historically, one can make quite a convincing case to prove that our highest and lowest arts come from a common antibourgeois source. Edgar Allan Poe, who lived the image of the dandy that has been haunting high art ever since, also, one remembers, invented the popular detective story; and there is a direct line from Hemingway to O'Hara to Dashiell Hammett to Raymond Chandler to Mickey Spillane.

22. Of both lines of descent from Poe, one can say that they tell a black and distressing truth (we are creatures of dark impulse in a threatened and guilty world), and that they challenge the more genteel versions of "good taste." Behind the opposition to vulgar literature, there is at work the same fear of the archetypal and the unconscious itself that motivated similar attacks on Elizabethan drama and on the eighteenth-century novel. We always judge Gosson a fool in terms of Shakespeare; but this is not the point—he was just as wrong in his attack on the worst-written, the most outrageously bloody and bawdy plays of his time. I should hate my argument to be understood as a defense of

what is banal and mechanical and dull (there is, of course, a great deal!) in mass culture; it is merely a counterattack against those who are aiming through that banality and dullness at what moves all literature of worth. Anyone at all sensitive to the life of the imagination would surely prefer his kids to read the coarsest fables of Black and White contending for the City of Man, rather than have them spell out, "Oh, see, Jane. Funny, funny Jane," or read to themselves hygienic accounts of the operation of supermarkets or manureless farms. Yet most schoolboard members are on the side of mental hygiene; and it is they who lead the charge against mass culture.

23. Anyone old enough to have seen, say, *Rain* is on guard against those who in the guise of wanting to destroy savagery and ignorance wage war on spontaneity and richness. But we are likely to think of such possibilities purely in sexual terms; the new righteous themselves have been touched lightly by Freud and are firm believers in frankness and "sex education." But in the very midst of their self-congratulation at their emancipation, they have become victims of a new and ferocious prudery. One who would be ashamed to lecture his masturbating son on the dangers of insanity, is quite prepared (especially if he has been reading Wertham) to predict the electric chair for the young scoundrel caught with a bootlegged comic. Superman is our Sadie Thompson. We live in an age when the child who is exposed to the "facts of life" is protected from "the facts of death." In the United States, for instance, a certain Doctor Spock has produced an enlightened guide to childcare for modern mothers—a paperback book which sold, I would guess, millions of copies. Tell the child all about sex, the good doctor advises, but on the subject of death—hush!

24. By more "advanced" consultants, the taboo is advanced further toward absurdity: no bloodsoaked Grimm, no terrifying Andersen, no childhood verses about cradles that fall—for fear breeds insecurity; insecurity, aggression; aggression, war. There is even a "happy," that is to say, expurgated, Mother Goose in which the three blind mice have become "kind mice"—and the farmer's wife no longer hacks off their tails, but "cuts them some cheese with a carving knife." Everywhere the fear is endemic, the fear of the very names of fear; those who have most ardently desired to end warfare and personal cruelty in the world around them, and are therefore most frustrated by their persistence, conspire to stamp out violence on the nursery bookshelf. This much they can do anyhow. If they can't hold up the weather, at least they can break the bloody glass.

25. This same fear of the instinctual and the dark, this denial of death and guilt by the enlightened genteel, motivates their distrust of serious literature, too. Faulkner is snubbed and the comic books are banned, not in the interests of the classics or even of Robert Louis Stevenson, as the attackers claim, but in the name of a literature of the middle ground which finds its fictitious vision of a kindly and congenial world attacked from above and below. I speak now not of the few intellectual converts to the cause of censorship, but of the main body of genteel book-banners, whose idol is Lloyd Douglas or even A. J. Cronin. When a critic such as Mr. Wagner is led to applaud what he sees as a "trend" toward making doctors, lawyers, etc., the heroes of certain magazine stories, he has fallen into the trap of regarding middling fiction as a transmission belt from the vulgar to the high. There is no question, however, of a slow climb from the level of literature which celebrates newspaper reporters, newsboys, radio commentators (who are also superheroes in tight-fitting uniforms with insignia), through one which centers around prosperous professionals, to the heights of serious literature, whose protagonists are suicides full of incestuous longings, lady lushes with clipped hair, bootleggers, gangsters, and broken-down pugs. To try to state the progression is to reveal its absurdity.

26. The conception of such a "trend" is nothing more than the standard attitude of a standard kind of literature, the literature of slick-paper ladies' magazines, which prefers the stereotype to the archetype, loves poetic justice, sentimentality, and gentility,

and is peopled by characters who bathe frequently, live in the suburbs, and are professionals. Such literature circles mindlessly inside the trap of its two themes: unconsummated adultery and the consummated pure romance. There can be little doubt about which kind of persons and which sort of fables best typify our plight, which tell the truth—or better, a truth—in language of those to whom they speak.

27. In the last phrase, there is a rub. The notion that there is more than one language of art, or rather, that there is something not quite art, which performs art's function for most men in our society, is disquieting enough for anyone, and completely unacceptable to the sentimental egalitarian, who had dreamed of universal literacy leading directly to a universal culture. It is here that we begin to see that there is a politics as well as a pathology involved in the bourgeois hostility to popular culture. I do not refer only to the explicit political ideas embodied in the comics or in the literature of the cultural élite; but certainly each of these arts has a characteristic attitude: populist-authoritarian on the one hand and aristocratic-authoritarian on the other.

28. It is notorious how few of the eminent novelists or poets of our time have shared the political ideals we would agree are the most noble available to us. The flirtations of Yeats and Lawrence with fascism, Pound's weird amalgam of Confucianism, Jeffersonianism, and social credit, the modified Dixiecrat principles of Faulkner—all make the point with terrible reiteration. Between the best art and poetry of our age and the critical liberal reader there can be no bond of shared belief; at best we have the ironic confrontation of the skeptical mind and the believing imagination. It is this division which has, I suppose, led us to define more and more narrowly the "aesthetic experience," to attempt to isolate a quality of seeing and saying that has a moral value quite independent of *what* is seen or heard.

> Time that with this strange excuse
> Pardoned Kipling and his views,
> And will pardon Paul Claudel,
> Pardons him for writing well.

29. But the genteel middling mind which turns to art for entertainment and uplift, finds this point of view reprehensible; and cries out in rage against those who give Ezra Pound a prize and who claim that "to permit other considerations than that of poetic achievement to sway the decision would . . . deny the validity of that objective perception of value on which any civilized society must rest." We live in the midst of a strange two-front class war: the readers of the slicks battling the subscribers to the "little reviews" and the consumers of pulps; the sentimental-egalitarian conscience against the ironical-aristocratic sensibility on the one hand and the brutal-populist mentality on the other. The joke, of course, is that it is the "democratic" center which calls here and now for suppression of its rivals; while the élite advocate a condescending tolerance, and the vulgar ask only to be let alone.

30. It is disconcerting to find cultural repression flourishing at the point where middling culture meets a kindly, if not vigorously thought-out, liberalism. The sort of right-thinking citizen who subsidizes trips to America for Japanese girls scarred by the Hiroshima bombing, and deplores McCarthy in the public press, also deplores, and would censor, the comics. In one sense, this is fair enough; for beneath the veneer of slogans that "crime doesn't pay" and the superficial praise of law and order, the comics do reflect that dark populist faith which Senator McCarthy has exploited. There is a kind of "black socialism" of the American masses which underlies formal allegiances to one party or another: the sense that there is always a conspiracy at the centers of political and financial power; the notion that the official defenders of the commonwealth are "bought" more often than not; an impatience with moral scruples and a distrust of intelligence, especially in the expert and scientist; a willingness to identify the enemy, the dark projection of everything most feared in the self, on to some journalistically defined political opponent of the moment.

31. This is not quite the "fascism" it is sometimes called. There is, for instance, no European anti-Semitism involved, despite the con-

ventional hooked nose of the scientist-villain. (The inventors and chief producers of comic books have been, as it happens, Jews.) There is also no adulation of a dictator-figure on the model of Hitler or Stalin; though one of the archetypes of the Deliverer in the comics is called Superman, he is quite unlike the Nietzschean figure—it is the image of Cincinnatus which persists in him, an archetype that has possessed the American imagination since the time of Washington: the leader who enlists for the duration and retires unrewarded to obscurity.

32. It would be absurd to ask the consumer of such art to admire in the place of images that project his own impotence and longing for civil peace some hero of middling culture— say, the good boy of Arthur Miller's *Death of a Salesman*, who, because he has studied hard in school, has become a lawyer who argues cases before the Supreme Court and has friends who own their own tennis courts. As absurd as to ask the general populace to worship Stephen Daedalus or Captain Ahab! But the high-minded petty-bourgeois cannot understand or forgive the rejection of his own dream, which he considers as nothing less than the final dream of humanity. The very existence of a kind of art depending on allegiances and values other than his challenges an article of his political faith; and when such an art is "popular," that is, more read, more liked, more bought than his own, he feels his *raison d'être*, his basic life-defense, imperilled. The failure of the petty-bourgeoisie to achieve cultural hegemony threatens their dream of a truly classless society; for they believe, with some justification, that such a society can afford only a single culture. And they see, in the persistence of a high art and a low art on either side of their average own, symptoms of the re-emergence of classes in a quarter where no one had troubled to stand guard.

33. The problem posed by popular culture is finally, then, a problem of class distinction in a democratic society. What is at stake is the refusal of cultural equality by a large part of the population. It is misleading to think of popular culture as the product of a conspiracy of profiteers against the rest of us. This vener-

able notion of an eternally oppressed and deprived but innocent people is precisely what the rise of mass culture challenges. Much of what upper-class egalitarians dreamed for him, the ordinary man does not want—especially literacy. The situation is bewildering and complex, for the people have not rejected completely the notion of cultural equity; rather, they desire its symbol but not its fact. At the very moment when half of the population of the United States reads no *hard-covered* book in a year, more than half of all high-school graduates are entering universities and colleges; in twenty-five years almost all Americans will at least begin a higher education. It is clear that what is demanded is a B.A. for everyone, with the stipulation that no one be forced to read to get it. And this the colleges, with "objective tests" and "audio-visual aids," are doing their reluctant best to satisfy.

34. One of the more exasperating aspects of the cultural defeat of the egalitarians is that it followed a seeming victory. For a while (in the Anglo-Saxon world at least) it appeared as if the spread of literacy, the rise of the bourgeoisie, and the emergence of the novel as a reigning form would succeed in destroying both traditional folk art and an aristocratic literature still pledged to epic, ode, and verse tragedy. But the novel itself (in the hands of Lawrence, Proust, Kafka, etc.) soon passed beyond the comprehension of those for whom it was originally contrived; and the retrograde derivations from it—various steps in a retreat toward wordless narrative: digests, pulp fiction, movies, picture magazines—revealed that middling literature was not in fact the legitimate heir of either folk art or high art, much less the successor of both, but a *tertium quid* of uncertain status and value.

35. The middlebrow reacts with equal fury to an art that baffles his understanding and to one which refuses to aspire to his level. The first reminds him that he has not yet, after all, *arrived* (and, indeed, may never make it); the second suggests to him a condition to which he might easily relapse, one perhaps that might have made him happier with less effort (and here exacerbated puritanism is joined to baffled egalitarianism), even suggests

what his state may appear like to those a notch above. Since he cannot, on his own terms, explain to himself why anyone should choose any level but the highest (that is, his own), the failure of the vulgar seems to him the product of mere ignorance and laziness—a crime! And the rejection by the advanced artist of his canons strikes him as a finicking excess, a pointless and unforgivable snobbism.

Both, that is, suggest the intolerable notion of a hierarchy of values, the possibility of cultural classes in a democratic state; and before this, puzzled and enraged, he can only call a cop. The fear of the vulgar is the obverse of the fear of excellence, and both are aspects of the fear of difference: symptoms of a drive for conformity on the level of the timid, sentimental, mindless-bodiless genteel.

JOYCE CARY

The Mass Mind: Our Favorite Folly

Joyce Cary (1888–1957) was born in Ireland and educated at Oxford University. Appointed a colonial officer in Africa in 1913, he served there until ill health resulting from a wound received in the Cameroons Campaign of 1915–16 caused him to resign in 1920 and to return to England, where he settled down to be a writer. Among his twenty books are many novels—*Aissa Saved,* 1932; a trilogy—*Herself Surprised,* 1941, *To Be a Pilgrim,* 1942, and *The Horse's Mouth,* 1944; *A Fearful Joy,* 1949; and *Prisoner of Grace,* 1952. It was *The Horse's Mouth* that brought him recognition as a novelist of stature in both England and America. A critical work, *Art and Reality,* 1958, was published posthumously.

In "The Mass Mind: Our Favorite Folly" Cary utilizes his African experiences to dispute the current dogma that standardized production, education, and amusements have produced a standardized individual.

1. Every age, they say, has its special bit of nonsense. The eighteenth century had its noble savage, and the nineteenth, its automatic progress. Now we have this modern nonsense about the "mass man." We are all told constantly that people are becoming more and more standardized. That mass education, mass amusements, mass production, ready-

THE MASS MIND: OUR FAVORITE FOLLY Reprinted by permission of Curtis Brown Ltd. Copyright 1952 by Joyce Cary.

made clothes, and a popular dress are destroying all individuality—turning civilization into a nice, warmed, sterilized orphan asylum where all the little lost souls wear the same uniforms, eat the same meals, think the same thoughts, and play the same games.

2. This belief is now so completely accepted that it underlies half the writing and thinking of the time, like chalk under the downs. You don't see it but it gives shape to what you do see. If you deny it you will get exactly the

same response as Galileo when he said that the earth moved through the sky. You will be told, "Use your eyes. And don't talk nonsense. Look at the crowds in the street or at any football match. Go to the films, read the newspapers. Consider the disappearance of national dress all over the world—the immense development of laws restricting individual liberty, standardizing our lives. Go on a tour to famous sights—year by year there will be bigger crowds of morons gaping at them and listening to the spiel of some bored guide—a piece nicely designed to satisfy the mass mind."

3. And you will be referred to history and old travel accounts to learn how various and delightful the world was, in dress and thought and individuality, one hundred or even fifty years ago.

4. I was convinced of all this myself till I went to administer the affairs of a primitive tribe in Africa. There I found that the tribal mind was much more truly a mass mind than anything I had known in Europe. The nearest approximation to it was among illiterate peasantry in remote country districts. Tribesmen and primitive peasants are intensely narrow and conservative. Their very simple ideas and reactions guide them in a mysterious and dangerous world.

5. I found that young chiefs with enterprise and ambition were keen to learn about the world outside the tribe. If they got away with it, they tended to put on European dress. To them, European dress was not a mark of the mass mind, but of the free and independent mind.

6. Likewise, when a European peasantry becomes educated and enterprising, it breaks away from the national dress which seems a badge of servitude and backwardness. To tourists, no doubt, this is a misfortune. As a keen tourist and sight-seer, I wish all Scotsmen would wear the kilt and all Turks the tarboosh. I'm delighted that some are beginning to do so again. But these are individualists, eccentrics, nationalists—national dress is not a tribal uniform to them, but a proclamation of difference, an assertion of self.

7. Education, contact with other peoples, breaks up tribal uniformity of thought and custom, brings in new ideas. That is, it makes for difference. The celebrated eccentrics of former centuries were either lunatics—or educated men.

8. New ideas also make for conflict. Old African chiefs hated roads and railways: they said they brought in strangers who corrupted the young people with new ideas and made them rebellious. They were quite right. It is far easier to rule a primitive tribe than a modern democracy where every individual is ready to criticize the government, where everyone has his own ideas about politics and religion, and where dozens of societies, unions, religious sects claim independence and support ambitious leaders who are ready to fight at any time for their "rights."

9. The more education a man has the more likely he is to be independent in his views and obstinate in sticking to them. A committee of professors, I can assure you, is much harder to manage than a council of African chiefs.

10. And this throws light on another argument brought forward to prove that individuality is vanishing from the world—the enormous increase of law and regulation, the growing power of the police. In any primitive African tribe, law enforcement was in the hands of village chiefs. There was very little theft. I could leave my bungalow wide open and unguarded for three weeks at a time and nothing was ever taken. We had crimes of passion and crimes of witchcraft, but no criminal class, no crooks as you know them in the big city, no cranks, no anarchists—so we did not require an elaborate structure of law.

11. You do not need traffic police where there is no wheeled traffic. You do not need postal bylaws where no one knows how to write. But the modern state, simply because of the independence of its citizens, the complication of their demands, needs a huge machine of law and police. This is not a proof of the mass mind but the exact opposite—of a growing number of people who think and act for themselves, and, rightly or wrongly, are ready to defy the old simple rules founded on custom.

12. Thus, the modern state has lost its mass mind in getting education. But, you will say,

this education destroys the primitive mass mind only to replace it with a number of mob minds: in the crowds which queue for the films or a match, read the same newspapers, and shout for the same spellbinders. Mass education is driving out the sound, traditional culture to bring in a lot of half-baked slogans. It produces the shallow brain seeking only to be distracted from serious reflection.

13. But these "mobs" have no resemblance to those of the tribal world where every individual does the same thing at the same time—hunts, dances, drinks in the mass. Even if he had the will to do anything else, it would not be there to do. The modern individual has an immense choice of occupation and amusement. So that the "mass" of sight-seers at any show place today is actually composed of individuals who have freely chosen to join the crowd and will join a different one tomorrow. What looks like a proof of the mob mind is really evidence of spreading interests among the people and a variety of occupations. And if some of these interests are "popular," aimed at a crowd which is not very critical or reflective, they are a good deal more so than interests which were the only recourse of their ancestors—dog-fighting, bear-baiting, the fit-up melodrama or one-night stand, once a year, and booze.

14. In the best educated countries, you find the biggest demand for something new in amusement as well as for instruction. Education enlarges all the interests of a man. Apart from what he learns, he acquires a general curiosity and a wider taste.

15. Compare the press of today with that of a hundred or even fifty years ago. You will find a far greater variety of subjects appealing to a greater variety of tastes. You will find instructive articles on matters formerly dealt with only in the special magazines. Perhaps they don't aim at a learned audience, but they help the general reader to get some idea of what the experts are doing in atomic research or medicine or even astronomy. If you want to write a best seller, your best subject nowadays is probably cosmology.

16. But if a hundred thousand people are ready to buy a book on the nature of the universe, you have a mass demand at bookshops. The mass demand is not a proof of falling standards: it means that millions are being educated who would formerly have been left in the illiterate mass. There are "masses" reading learned works just as there are other "masses" going to popular films. The number of people with a good university education is many hundred times what it was fifty years ago, and that explains the immense development of arts and literature in experimental forms that would have had no chance of appreciation before. And in the millions in the next category who have just become literate in the last generation, whose reactions to education have given rise to this illusion of an increasing "mass mind," what we are seeing is not a collapse of standards, but a very rapid improvement. The crowds at the cinemas and the bus loads on the sight-seeing tours are on the way up. They have already left the mass; they are individuals seeking ideas for themselves.

17. The mass mind idea is not only a bit of nonsense, it is a dangerous nonsense. It leads to a profound defeatism, to the secret and unacknowledged belief that the dictators hold all the trumps.

18. The reasoning, when you bring it to light, is something like this. There are two kinds of education in the world: the free, which develops the individual according to his nature, and the specialized, which turns out doctors, scientists, mechanics—useful servants of the state or of industry. In a democracy each individual has both types. In the Soviet he gets only the specialized—the whole plan is to make him a state slave.

19. But it seems that free education merely debases the standards of thought and life by producing mob minds without spiritual strength. Meanwhile the Soviet acquires millions of workers, docile as serfs, yet skillful as our own craftsmen. Aiming deliberately at the creation of a mass mind it will easily defeat the free world, where opinions are shallow and divided.

20. But this is based on bad psychology. The West is not producing a mass mind, but a variety of strong minds with the richest sense of adventure and will for discovery. The East

is not succeeding in obtaining a mass mind either—it is going in the opposite direction. Merely by process of education, it is producing every year people who can at least think a little more freely than illiterate peasants, who are very likely therefore to think critical thoughts, however much they may hide them. That is why the task of dictatorship becomes constantly more difficult, why it is obliged to stiffen its grip, to hire more police, to bribe more spies, and to purge its own party, every year or so, of "deviators."

21. What I suggest is that no kind of education, however narrow, can produce the mass mind. The reason is that minds are creative,

that thoughts wander by themselves and cannot be controlled by the cleverest police. All education is free in this sense; it cannot be shut up within walls. To teach people to think, if only to make them more useful as soldiers and mechanics, is to open all thoughts to them —a whole world of new ideas. And though the dictator may wish to think of them as a proletariat they have already begun to leave the proletariat.

22. The "mass mind" is a delusion. How many dictators have been amazed when their rule, which seemed so strong, has collapsed in a few hours, without a friend?

MARSHALL MC LUHAN

Sight, Sound, and the Fury

Herbert Marshall McLuhan (1911–   ), Director of the Centre for Culture and Technology at the University of Toronto, has aroused a great deal of controversy with his theories of the ways in which communications systems alter man's cultural patterns. His book *The Mechanical Bride: Folklore of Industrial Man* was published in 1951; his recent books are *The Gutenberg Galaxy: The Making of Typographical Man*, 1962; *Understanding Media: The Extensions of Man*, 1964; *Culture Is Our Business*, 1967. He is also co-author of *The Medium Is the Massage*, 1967. In September 1967, Dr. McLuhan began a year's appointment to the Albert Schweitzer chair of Fordham University.

In "Sight, Sound, and the Fury" Dr. McLuhan reviews the historical and technical development of the mass media and explains the resemblance between the devices of the "verbivocovisual" media and human cognition. He warns of the need for critical awareness of the effects of the "fury" which the new sound and sight media produce.

1. On his recent visit to America, Roy Campbell mentioned that when Dylan Thomas had discovered he could read poetry

SIGHT, SOUND, AND THE FURY From the *Commonweal*, April 9, 1954. Reprinted by permission of the publishers.

on the radio, this discovery transformed his later poetry for the better. Thomas discovered a new dimension in his language when he established a new relation with the public.

2. Until Gutenberg, poetic publication meant the reading or singing of one's poems

to a small audience. When poetry began to exist primarily on the printed page, in the seventeenth century, there occurred that strange mixture of sight and sound later known as "metaphysical poetry" which has so much in common with modern poetry.

3. American colonization began when the only culture available to most men was that of the printed book. European culture was then, as now, as much an affair of music, painting, sculpture, and communication as it was of literature. So that to this day North Americans associate culture mainly with books. But, paradoxically, it is in North America that the new media of sight and sound have had the greatest popular sway. Is it precisely because we make the widest separation between culture and our new media that we are unable to see the new media as serious culture? Have four centuries of book-culture hypnotized us into such concentration on the content of books and the new media that we cannot see that the very form of any medium of communication is as important as anything that it conveys?

4. Ireland is perhaps the only part of the English-speaking world where the oral tradition of culture has strongly persisted in spite of the printed page. And Ireland has given us Wilde, Shaw, Yeats, Synge, and Joyce in recent years—all of them masters of the magic of the spoken word. A Ballynooley farmer who returned to Ireland from America said to his neighbor: "In three years I didn't meet a man who could sing a ballad, let alone compose one on his feet."

5. The printed page was itself a highly specialized (and spatialized) form of communication. In 1500 A.D. it was revolutionary. And Erasmus was perhaps the first to grasp the fact that the revolution was going to occur above all in the classroom. He devoted himself to the production of textbooks and to the setting up of grammar schools. The printed book soon liquidated two thousand years of manuscript culture. It created the solitary student. It set up the rule of private interpretation against public disputation. It established the divorce between "literature and life." It created a new and highly abstract culture be-cause it was itself a mechanized form of culture. Today, when the textbook has yielded to the classroom project and the classroom as social workshop and discussion group, it is easier for us to notice what was going on in 1500. Today we know that the turn to the visual on one hand, that is, to photography, and to the auditory media of radio and public address systems on the other hand, has created a totally new environment for the educational process.

6. André Malraux has recently popularized the notion of the art revolution of our time in his *Museum Without Walls.* His theme is that the picture book today can embrace a greater range of art than any museum. By bringing such a range of art within portable compass, however, it has changed even the painter's approach to painting. Again, it is not just a question of message, image, or content. The picture book as a museum without walls has for the artist a new technical meaning, just as for the spectator pictorial communication means a large but unconscious shift in his ways of thought and feeling.

7. We have long been accustomed to the notion that a person's beliefs shape and color his existence. They provide the windows which frame, and through which he views, all events. We are less accustomed to the notion that the shapes of a technological environment are also idea-windows. Every shape (gimmick or metropolis), every situation planned and realized by man's factive intelligence, is a window which reveals or distorts reality. Today when power technology has taken over the entire global environment to be manipulated as the material of art, nature has disappeared with nature-poetry. And the effectiveness of the classroom has diminished with the decline of the monopoly of book-culture. If Erasmus saw the classroom as the new stage for the drama of the printing press, we can see today that the new situation for young and old alike is classrooms without walls. The entire urban environment has become aggressively pedagogic. Everybody and everything has a message to declare, a line to plug.

8. This is the time of transition from the

commercial age, when it was the production and distribution of commodities which occupied the ingenuity of men. Today we have moved from the production of packaged goods to the packaging of information. Formerly we invaded foreign markets with goods. Today we invade whole cultures with packaged information, entertainment, and ideas. In view of the instantaneous global scope of the new media of sight and sound, even the newspaper is slow. But the press ousted the book in the nineteenth century because the book arrived too late. The newspaper page was not a mere enlargement of the book page. It was, like the movie, a new collective art form.

9. To retrace some of this ground, it will help to recall that in the *Phaedrus,* Plato argued that the new arrival of writing would revolutionize culture for the worse. He suggested that it would substitute reminiscence for thought and mechanical learning for the true dialectic of the living quest for truth by discourse and conversation. It was as if he foresaw the library of Alexandria and the unending exegeses upon previous exegeses of the scholiasts and grammarians.

10. It would seem that the great virtue of writing is its power to arrest the swift process of thought for steady contemplation and analysis. Writing is the translation of the audible into the visual. In large measure it is the spatialization of thought. Yet writing on papyrus and parchment fostered a very different set of mental habits from those we associate with print and books. In the first place silent reading was unknown until the macadamized, streamlined surfaces of the printed page arrived to permit swift traverse of the eye alone. In the second place, difficulty of access to manuscripts impelled students to memorize so far as possible everything they read. This led to encyclopedism, but also to having on tap in oral discourse one's entire erudition.

11. The child at school in the Middle Ages had first to make his own copies of texts from dictation. He had next to compile his own grammar and lexicon and commonplace book. The arrival of plenty of cheap, uniform, printed texts changed all this. The mechanization of writing by means of the assembly line of movable type speedily expanded the range of available reading and just as quickly reduced the habit of oral discourse as a way of learning. During the sixteenth century, however, a degree of equilibrium persisted between oral and written learning which we associate with the special excellence of Elizabethan drama, sermon, and poetry.

12. In the reverse direction, much of the vivid energy of American speech and writing in the twentieth century is the result of the movement away from book-culture toward oral communication. This nonliterary direction of speech has been felt to a much smaller degree in England and in Europe during the same period. Radio in particular has encouraged the return to the panel discussion and the round table. But the spontaneous move toward the seminar and class discussion as learning process has been helped by press and photography too, in so far as these have challenged the monopoly of the book.

13. Above all, the habits of the business community in demanding conference and discussion as the swift way of establishing insight into method and procedure in various specialized branches of business—these have prompted the new reliance on speech as a means of discovery. It is significant, for example, that the atomic physicists found that only by daily, face-to-face association could they get on with their tasks during the past war.

14. It has long been a truism that changes in material culture cause shifts in the patterns of the entire culture. The ancient road made possible armies and empires and destroyed the isolated city states of Greece. But the road depended in the first place on writing. Behind the imperial command of great land areas stood the written word in easily transportable form. In the nineteenth century the newspapers, especially after the telegraph, paid for new roads and faster transport by land and sea. The press altered the forms of government, and the telegraph brought secret diplomacy to an end. When events in Egypt or Russia, London, Paris, or New York were

known everywhere at once, the time for secret negotiation was reduced to hours and minutes. And the great national populations of the world, alerted and emotionalized by the press, could confront one another immediately for a showdown.

15. Printing had from the first fostered nationalism because the vernaculars with their large reading publics were more profitable to commercial publishers than Latin. The press has pushed this nationalism to its ultimate point. There it remains. But photography and movies, like music and painting, are international in their power of appeal. The power of pictures to leap over national frontiers and prejudices is well-known, for good and ill.

16. One aspect of the press deserves special comment in this same respect. The contents of newspapers, their messages and information, have steadily promoted nationalism. But the form of the newspaper page is powerfully inter-cultural and international. The unformulated message of an assembly of news items from every quarter of the globe is that the world today is one city. All war is civil war. All suffering is our own. So that regardless of the political line, or the time or the place, the mere format of the press exerts a single pressure. Basic acceptance of this fact is recorded in the steady weakening of interest in political parties everywhere.

17. From the point of view of its format, the press as a daily cross section of the globe is a mirror of the technological instruments of communication. It is the popular daily book, the great collective poem, the universal entertainment of our age. As such it has modified poetic techniques and in turn has already been modified by the newer media of movie, radio, and television. These represent revolutions in communication as radical as printing itself. In fact, they are "magic casements opening on the foam of perilous seas," on which few of us have yet ventured in thought, art or living. If Erasmus was the first to size up and exploit the printing press as a new force in art and education, James Joyce was the first to seize upon newspaper, radio, movie, and televsion to set up his "verbivocovisual" drama in *Finnegans Wake*. Pound and Eliot

are, in comparison with Joyce, timid devotees of the book as art form. But most of the difficulties which the ordinary person encounters with the poetry of Pound and Eliot disappear if it is viewed as a historical newsreel of persons, myths, ideas, and events with thematic musical score built in. Joyce had a much greater trust of language and reality than Pound or Eliot. By contrast they give their language and reality the Hollywood glamour treatment. Joyce is closer to a De Sica film with its awareness of the intimate riches of the most ordinary scenes and situations.

18. But the reader who approaches Pound, Eliot, and Joyce alike as exploiters of the cinematic aspects of language will arrive at appreciation more quickly than the one who unconsciously tries to make sense of them by reducing their use of the new media of communication to the abstract linear forms of the book page.

19. The basic fact to keep in mind about the movie camera and projector is their resemblance to the process of human cognition. That is the real source of their magical, transforming power. The camera rolls up the external world on a spool. It does this by rapid still shots. The projector unwinds this spool as a kind of magic carpet which conveys the enchanted spectator anywhere in the world in an instant. The camera records and analyzes the daylight world with more than human intensity because of the forty-five degree angle of the camera eye. The projector reveals this daylight world on a dark screen where it becomes a dream world.

20. The wonderful resemblance in all this to human cognition extends at least this far: in cognition we have to interiorize the exterior world. We have to recreate in the medium of our senses and inner faculties the drama of existence. This is the work of the *logos poietikos*, the agent intellect. In speech we utter that drama which we have analogously recreated within us. In speech we make or *poet* the world even as we may say that the movie parrots the world. Languages themselves are thus the greatest of all works of art. They are the collective hymns to existence. For in cognition itself is the whole of the poetic process.

But the artist differs from most men in his power to arrest and then reverse the stages of human apprehension. He learns how to embody the stages of cognition (Aristotle's "plot") in an exterior work which can be held up for contemplation.

21. Even in this respect the movie resembles the cognitive process since the daylight world which the camera rolls up on the spool is reversed and projected to become the magical dream world of the audience. But all media of communication share something of this cognitive character which only a Thomist vision of existence and cognition dare do justice to.

22. Television, for example, differs from the movie in the immediacy with which it picks up and renders back the visible. The TV camera is like the microphone in relation to the voice. The movie has no such immediacy of pick-up and feedback. As we begin to look into the inevitably cognitive character of the various media we soon get over the jitters that come from exclusive concern with any one form of communication.

23. In his *Theory of the Film*, Bela Balazs notes how

> the discovery of printing gradually rendered illegible the faces of men. So much could be read from paper that the method of conveying meaning by facial expression fell into desuetude. Victor Hugo wrote once that the printed book took over the part played by the cathedral in the Middle Ages and became the carrier of the spirit of the people. But the thousands of books tore the one spirit . . . into thousands of opinions . . . tore the church into a thousand books. The visible spirit was thus turned into a legible spirit and visual culture into a culture of concepts.

24. Before printing, a reader was one who discerned and probed riddles. After printing, it meant one who scanned, who skipped along the macadamized surfaces of print. Today at the end of that process we have come to equate reading skill with speed and distraction rather than wisdom. But print, the mechanization of writing, was succeeded in the nineteenth century by photography and then by the mechanization of human gesture in the movie. This was followed by the mechanization of speech in telephone, phonograph and radio. In the talkies, and finally with TV, came the mechanization of the totality of human expression, of voice, gesture, and human figure in action.

25. Each of these steps in the mechanization of human expression was comparable in its scope to the revolution brought about by the mechanization of writing itself. The changes in the ways of human association, social and political, were telescoped in time and so hidden from casual observers.

26. If there is a truism in the history of human communication it is that any innovation in the external means of communication brings in its train shock on shock of social change. One effect of writing was to make possible cities, roads, armies, and empires. The letters of the alphabet were indeed the dragon's teeth. The printed book not only fostered nationalism but made it possible to bring the world of the past into every study. The newspaper is a daily book which brings a slice of all the cultures of the world under our eyes every day. To this extent it reverses the tendency of the printing press to accentuate merely national culture. Pictorial journalism and reportage tend strongly in the same international direction. But is this true of radio? Radio has strengthened the oral habit of communication and extended it, via the panel and round table, to serious learning. Yet radio seems to be a form which also strengthens the national culture. Merely oral societies, for example, are the ultimate in national exclusiveness.

27. A group of us recently performed an experiment with a large group of students. We divided them into four sections and assigned each section to a separate communication channel. Each section got the identical lecture simultaneously, but one read it, one heard it as a regular lecture in a studio, one heard it on radio and one heard and saw it as a TV broadcast. Immediately afterwards we administered a quiz to determine apprehension and understanding of this new and difficult material. The TV section came out on top, then the radio section, then the studio, and the

reading section at the bottom. This was a totally unexpected result and it is too soon to
generalize; but it is quite certain that the so-
called mass media are not necessarily ordained to be channels of popular entertainment only.

28. It is "desirable" in thinking about the
new media that we should recall that buildings are mass communications and that the
first mechanical medium was print from movable type. In fact, the discovery of movable
type was the ancestor of all assembly lines, and
it would be foolish to overlook the impact of
the technological form involved in print on
the psychological life of readers. To overlook
this would be as unrealistic as to ignore
rhythm and tempo in music. Likewise it is
only common sense to recognize that the general situation created by a communicative
channel and its audience is a large part of that
in which and by which the individuals commune. The encoded message cannot be regarded as a mere capsule or pellet produced
at one point and consumed at another. Communication is communication all along the
line.

29. One might illustrate from sports. The
best brand of football played before fifty people would lack something of the power to
communicate. The large enthusiastic crowd is
necessary to represent the community at large,
just as the players enact a drama which ex-
ternalizes certain motivations and tensions in
the communal life which would not otherwise
be visible or available for audience participation. In India huge crowds assemble to experience "darshan," which they consider to occur
when they are massed in the presence of a
visible manifestation of their collective life.

30. The new media do something similar for
us in the West. Movies, radio, and TV establish certain personalities on a new plane of
existence. They exist not so much in themselves but as types of collective life felt and
perceived through a mass medium. Li'l Abner,
Bob Hope, Donald Duck, and Marilyn Mon-

roe become points of collective awareness and
communication for an entire society. And as
technology increasingly undertakes to submit the entire planet as well as the contents
of consciousness to the purposes of man's
factive intelligence, it behooves us to consider
the whole process of magical transformation
involved in the media acutely and extensively.

31. From this point of view it should be obvious, for example, that the framers of the
Hollywood morality code were operating with
a very inadequate set of perceptions and concepts about the nature of the movie medium.
Modern discussions of censorship, in the same
way, are helplessly tied to conceptions borrowed from book culture alone. And the defenders of book culture have seldom given
any thought to any of the media as art forms,
the book least of all. The result is that their
"defense" might as well be staged on an
abandoned movie lot for all the effect it has
on the actual situation.

32. When I wrote *The Mechanical Bride*
some years ago I did not realize that I was
attempting a defense of book culture against
the new media. I can now see that I was trying to bring some of the critical awareness
fostered by literary training to bear on the
new media of sight and sound. My strategy
was wrong, because my obsession with literary values blinded me to much that was actually happening for good and ill. What we
have to defend today is not the values developed in any particular culture or by any
one mode of communication. Modern technology presumes to attempt a total transformation of man and his environment. This calls
in turn for an inspection and defense of all
human values. And so far as merely human
aid goes, the citadel of this defense must be
located in analytical awareness of the nature
of the creative process involved in human
cognition. For it is in this citadel that science
and technology have already established
themselves in their manipulation of the new
media.

PAULINE KAEL

Zeitgeist or Poltergeist;
Or, Are Movies Going to Pieces?

Pauline Kael (1914–   ), author, lecturer, and film critic, has published articles in many American periodicals, and has worked on experimental films. She is now a contributing editor for *The New Republic*. Her book *I Lost It at the Movies*, 1965, a collection of criticism that questions modern movie trends, has occasioned considerable interest and controversy.

In this vigorous discussion Miss Kael maintains that true art makes complex experience intelligible, and charges that, in their emphasis on "cinematic" effects, movies are becoming dangerously arcane and academic.

1. The week before, at home, some academic friends had been over and as we talked and drank we looked at a television showing of Tod Browning's 1931 version of *Dracula*. Dwight Frye's appearance on the screen had us suddenly squealing and shrieking, and it was obvious that old vampire movies were part of our common experience. We talked about the famous ones, Murnau's *Nosferatu* and Dreyer's *Vampyr*, and we began to get fairly involved in the lore of the genre—the strategy of the bite, the special earth for the coffins, the stake through the heart versus the rays of the sun as disposal methods, the cross as vampire repellent, et al. We had begun to surprise each other by the affectionate, nostalgic tone of our mock erudition when the youngest person present, an instructor in English, said, in a clear, firm tone, "*The Beast with Five Fingers* is the greatest horror picture I've ever seen." Stunned that so bright a young man could display such shocking taste, preferring a Warner

Brothers forties mediocrity to the classics, I gasped, "But why?" And he answered, "Because it's completely irrational. It doesn't make any sense, and that's the true terror."

2. Upset by his neat little declaration—existentialism in a nutshell—by the calm matter-of-factness of it, and by the way the others seemed to take it for granted, I wanted to pursue the subject. But O. Henry's remark "Conversation in Texas is seldom continuous" applies to California, too. *Dracula* had ended, and the conversation shifted to other, more "serious" subjects.

3. But his attitude, which had never occurred to me, helped to explain some of my recent moviegoing experiences. I don't mean that I agree that *The Beast with Five Fingers* is a great horror film, but that his enthusiasm for the horror that cannot be rationalized by the mythology and rules of the horror game related to audience reactions that had been puzzling me.

4. Last year I had gone to see a famous French film, Georges Franju's *Eyes Without a Face*, which had arrived in San Francisco in a dubbed version called *The Horror Chamber*

of Dr. Faustus and was playing on a double-horror bill in a huge Market Street theater. It was Saturday night and the theater, which holds 2646, was so crowded I had trouble finding a seat.

5. Even dubbed, *Eyes Without a Face,* which Franju called a "poetic fantasy," is austere and elegant: the exquisite photography is by the great Shuftan, the music by Maurice Jarre, the superb gowns by Givenchy. It's a symbolist attack on science and the ethics of medicine, and though I thought this attack as simpleminded in its way as the usual young poet's denunciation of war or commerce, it is in some peculiar way a classic of horror.

6. Pierre Brasseur, as a doctor, experiments systematically, removing the faces of beautiful young kidnaped women, trying to graft them onto the ruined head of his daughter. He keeps failing, the girls are destroyed and yet he persists—in some terrible parody of the scientific method. In the end, the daughter—still only eyes without a face—liberates the dogs on which he also experiments and they tear off *his* head.

7. It's both bizarrely sophisticated (with Alida Valli as his mistress doing the kidnaping in a black leather coat, recalling the death images from Cocteau's *Orpheus*) and absurdly naive. Franju's style is almost as purified as Robert Bresson's, and although I dislike the mixture of austerity and mysticism with blood and gore, it produced its effect—a vague, floating, almost lyric sense of horror, an almost abstract atmosphere, impersonal and humorless. It has nothing like the fun of a good old horror satire like *The Bride of Frankenstein* with Elsa Lanchester's hair curling electrically instead of just frizzing as usual, and Ernest Thesiger toying with mandrake roots and tiny ladies and gentlemen in glass jars. It's a horror film that takes itself very seriously, and even though I thought its intellectual pretensions silly, I couldn't shake off the exquisite, dread images.

8. But the audience seemed to be reacting to a different movie. They were so noisy the dialogue was inaudible; they talked until the screen gave promise of bloody ghastliness.

Then the chatter subsided to rise again in noisy approval of the gory scenes. When a girl in the film seemed about to be mutilated, a young man behind me jumped up and down and shouted encouragement. "Somebody's going to *get* it," he sang out gleefully. The audience, which was, I'd judge, predominantly between fifteen and twenty-five, and at least a third feminine, was as pleased and excited by the most revolting, obsessive images as that older, mostly male audience is when the nudes appear in *The Immoral Mr. Teas* or *Not Tonight, Henry.* They'd gotten what they came for: they hadn't been cheated. But nobody seemed to care what the movie was about or be interested in the logic of the plot—the reasons for the gore.

9. And audiences have seemed indifferent to incomprehensible sections in big expensive pictures. For example, how is it that the immense audience for *The Bridge on the River Kwai,* after all those hours of watching a story unfold, didn't express discomfort or outrage or even plain curiosity about what exactly happened at the end—which through bad direction or perhaps sloppy editing went by too fast to be sorted out and understood. Was it possible that audiences no longer cared if a film was so untidily put together that information crucial to the plot or characterizations was obscure or omitted altogether? *What Ever Happened to Baby Jane?* was such a mess that *Time,* after calling it "the year's scariest, funniest and most sophisticated thriller," got the plot garbled.

10. In recent years, largely because of the uncertainty of producers about what will draw, films in production may shift from one script to another, or may be finally cut so that key sequences are omitted. And the oddity is that it doesn't seem to matter to the audience. I couldn't tell what was going on in parts of *55 Days at Peking.* I was flabbergasted when *Cleopatra,* with no hint or preparation, suddenly demonstrated clairvoyant powers, only to dispense with them as quickly as she had acquired them. The audience for *The Cardinal* can have little way of knowing whose baby the priest's sister is having, or of understanding how she can be in labor for days,

screaming in a rooming house, without anybody hearing her. They might also be puzzled about how the priest's argument against
her marriage, which they have been told is
the only Catholic position, can, after it leads
to her downfall and death, be casually dismissed as an error.

11. It would be easy to conclude that people go to see a "show" and just don't worry if
it all hangs together so long as they've got
something to look at. But I think it's more
complicated than that: audiences used to have
an almost rational passion for getting the story
straight. They might prefer bad movies to
good ones, and the *Variety* list of "all-time top
grossers" (such as *The Greatest Show on Earth*
and *Going My Way*) indicates that they did,
but although the movies might be banal or
vulgar, they were rarely incoherent. A movie
had to tell some kind of story that held together: a plot had to parse. Some of the appreciation   for   the   cleverness   of,   say,
Hitchcock's early thrillers was that they distracted you from the loopholes, so that, afterwards, you could enjoy thinking over how
you'd been tricked and teased. Perhaps now
"stories" have become too sane, too explicable,
too commonplace for the large audiences who
want sensations and regard the explanatory
connections as mere "filler"—the kind of stuff
you sit through or talk through between jolts.

12. It's possible that television viewing,
with all its breaks and cuts, and the inatten-
tion, except for action, and spinning the dial
to find some action, is partly responsible for
destruction of the narrative sense—that delight
in following a story through its complications
to its conclusion, which is perhaps a child's
first conscious artistic pleasure. The old staples
of entertainment—inoffensive genres like the
adventure story or the musical or the ghost
story or the detective story—are no longer
commercially safe for moviemakers, and it
may be that audiences don't have much more
than a TV span of attention left: they want to
be turned on and they spend most of their
time turning off. Something similar and related
may be happening in reading tastes and habits: teen-agers that I meet have often read

Salinger and some Orwell and *Lord of the
Flies* and some Joyce Cary and sometimes
even Dostoyevsky, but they are not interested
in the "classic" English novels of Scott or
Dickens, and what is more to the point, they
don't read the Sherlock Holmes stories or even
the modern detective fiction that in the thirties and forties was an accepted part of the
shared experience of adolescents. Whatever
the reasons—and they must be more than TV,
they must have to do with modern life and
the sense of urgency it produces—audiences
can no longer be depended on to respond to
conventional forms.

13. Perhaps they want much more from entertainment than the civilized, but limited rational pleasures of genre pieces. More likely,
and the box-office returns support this, they
want something different. Audiences that enjoy the shocks and falsifications, the brutal
series of titillations of a *Mondo Cane*, one
thrill after another, don't care any longer
about the conventions of the past, and are too
restless and apathetic to pay attention to motivations and complications, cause and effect.
They want less effort, more sensations, more
knobs to turn.

14. A decade ago, *The Haunting*, an efficient, professional and to all appearances
"commercial" genre piece, might have made
money. By the end of 1963, its grosses in the
United States and Canada, according to *Variety*, were $700,000. This may be compared
with $9,250,000 for *Irma La Douce*, $4,600,000
for *The Birds*, $3,900,000 for *55 Days at Pe-
king*—all three, I think, much less enjoyable
movies, or to be more exact, terrible movies,
and in varying degrees pointless and incomprehensible. A detective genre piece, *The List
of Adrian Messenger*, also incomparably better than the three films cited, and with a tricky
"star" selling campaign, grossed only $1,500,-
000. It's easy to imagine that Robert Wise,
after the energetic excesses of *West Side
Story*, turned to *The Haunting* for a safe, sane
respite, and that John Huston, after wrestling
with *Freud*, turned to an intriguing detective
story like *Adrian Messenger* for a lucrative,
old-fashioned holiday. But what used to be
safe seems now to be folly. How can audiences

preoccupied with identity problems of their own worry about a case of whodunit and why and how? Following clues may be too much of an effort for those who, in the current teen-age phrase, "couldn't care less." They want shock treatment, not diversion, and it takes more than ghosts to frighten them.

15. *The Haunting* is set in that pleasantly familiar "old dark house" that is itself an evil presence, and is usually inhabited by ghosts or evil people. In our childhood imaginings, the unknowable things that have happened in old houses, and the whispers that someone may have died in them, make them mysteri-ous, "dirty"; only the new house that has known no life or death is safe and clean. But so many stories have used the sinister dark house from-which-no-one-can-escape and its murky gardens for our ritual entertainment that we learn to experience the terrors as pleasurable excitations and reassuring remind-ers of how frightened we used to be before we learned our way around. In film, as in story, the ambiance is fear; the film specialty is gathering a group who are trapped and helpless. (Although the women are more eas-ily frightened, the men are also powerless. Their superior strength doesn't count for much against unseen menaces: this may explain why the genre was often used for a male comedian —like Bob Hope in *The Ghost Breakers*. Russ Tamblyn serves a similar but feeble cowardly-comic function in *The Haunting*.) The action is confined to the house and grounds (the maze); the town is usually far away, just far enough away so that "nobody will hear you if you scream."

16. In recent years film festivals and art houses have featured a peculiar variant of the trapped-in-the-old-dark-house genre (Buñuel's *The Exterminating Angel* is the classic new ex-ample), but the characters, or rather figures, are the undead or zombies of the vampire movies. "We live as in coffins frozen side by side in a garden"—*Last Year at Marienbad*. "I'm dead"—the heroine of *Il Mare*. "They're all dead in there"—the hostess describing the party of *La Notte*. Their vital juices have been sucked away, but they don't have the reveal-ing marks on the throat. We get the message:

alienation drains the soul without leaving any marks. Or, as Bergman says of his trilogy, "Most of the people in these three films are dead, completely dead. They don't know how to love or to feel any emotions. They are lost because they can't reach anyone outside of themselves." This "art" variant is a message movie about failure of communication and lack of love and spiritual emptiness and all the rest of that. It's the closest thing we've got to a new genre but it has some peculiarities. The old dark house was simply *there*, but these symbolic decadent or sterile surroundings are supposed to reflect the walking death of those within the maze. The characters in the old dark house tried to solve the riddle of their imprisonment and tried to escape; even in *No Exit* the drama was in *why* the characters were there, but in the new hotel-in-hell mov-ies the characters don't even want to get out of the maze—nor one surmises do the direc-tors, despite their moralizing. And audiences apparently respond to these films as modern and relevant just because of this paralysis and inaction and minimal story line. If in the group at the older dark house, someone was not who we thought he was, in the new dull party gatherings, it doesn't matter who any-body is (which is a new horror).

17. Although *The Haunting* is moderately elegant and literate and expensive, and the di-rector gussies things up with a Marienbadish piece of statuary that may or may not be the key to something or other, it's basically a tra-ditional ghost story. There is the dedicated scientist who wants to contribute to science in some socially unacceptable or scientifically reproachable area—in this case to prove the supernatural powers of the house. (The sci-entist is, somewhat inexplicably, an anthro-pologist; perhaps Margaret Mead has set the precedent for anthropologists to dabble in and babble on anything—so that the modern con-cept of the anthropologist is like the old con-cept of the philosopher or, for that matter, the scientist.) And, in the expository style tra-ditional for the genre, he explains the lore and jargon of psychic research, meticulously separating out ghost from poltergeist and so on. And of course the scientist, in the great

tradition of *Frankenstein*, must have the abnormal or mad assistant: the role that would
once have belonged to Dwight Frye is here
modernized and becomes the Greenwich Village lesbian, Claire Bloom. And there is the
scientist's distraught wife who fears that her
husband's brilliant career will be ruined, and
so on. The chaste heroine, Julie Harris (like
an updated Helen Chandler, Dracula's anemic
victim), is the movies' post-Freudian concept
of the virgin: repressed, hysterical, insane—
the source of evil.

18. It wasn't a great movie but I certainly
wouldn't have thought that it could offend
anyone. Yet part of the audience at *The
Haunting* wasn't merely bored, it was hostile—
as if the movie, by assuming interests they
didn't have, made them feel resentful or inferior. I've never felt this kind of audience
hostility toward crude, bad movies. People
are relaxed and tolerant about ghoulish
quickies, grotesque shockers dubbed from
Japan, and chopped-up Italian spectacles that
scramble mythologies and pile on actions, one
stupidity after another. Perhaps they prefer
incoherent, meaningless movies because they
are not required to remember or connect.
They can feel superior, contemptuous—as they
do toward television advertising. Even when
it's a virtuoso triumph, the audience is contemptuous toward advertising, because, after
all, they see through it—they know somebody
is trying to sell something. And because, like a
cheap movie obviously made to pry money out
of them, that is all advertising means, it's OK.
But the few, scattered people at *The Haunting* were restless and talkative, the couple
sitting near me arguing—the man threatening
to leave, the woman assuring him that something would happen. In their terms, they were
cheated: nothing happened. And, of course,
they missed what was happening all along,
perhaps because of nervous impatience or a
primitive notion that the real things are physical, perhaps because people take from art
and from popular entertainment only what
they want; and if they are indifferent to story
and motive and blank out on the connections,
then a movie without physical action or crass
jokes or built-in sentimental responses has

nothing for them. I am afraid that the young
instructor in English spoke for his times, that
there is no terror for modern audiences if a
story is carefully worked out and follows a tradition, even though the tradition was developed and perfected precisely to frighten en-
tertainingly.

19. No wonder that studios and producers
are unsure what to do next, scan best-seller
lists for trends, consult audience-testing polls,
anxiously chop out what a preview audience
doesn't like. The New York *Times* chides the
representatives of some seven companies who
didn't want to invest in *What Ever Happened
to Baby Jane?* but how could businessmen,
brought up to respect logic and a good commercial script, possibly guess that this confused mixture of low camp and Grand Gui-
gnol would delight the public?

•   •   •

20. It is not just general audiences out for
an evening's entertainment who seem to have
lost the narrative sense, or become indifferent
to narrative. What I think are processes of
structural disintegration are at work in all
types of movies, and though it's obvious that
many of the old forms were dead and had to
be broken through, it's rather scary to see
what's happening—and not just at the big pic-
ture-palaces. Art-house films are even more
confusing. Why, at the end of Godard's *My
Life to Live*, is the heroine shot, rather than
the pimp that the rival gang is presumably
gunning for? Is she just a victim of bad marks-
manship? If we express perplexity, we are
likely to be told that we are missing the
existentialist point: it's simply fate, she had
to die. But a cross-eyed fate? And why is
there so little questioning of the organization
of *My Name Is Ivan* with its lyric interludes
and patriotic sections so ill assembled that
one might think the projectionist had scrambled the reels? (They often do at art houses,
and it would seem that the more sophisticated
the audience, the less likely that the error
will be discovered. When I pointed out to a
theater manager that the women in *Brink of
Life* were waiting for their babies after they
had miscarried, he told me that he had been

playing the film for two weeks and I was his first patron who wasn't familiar with Bergman's methods.)

21. The art-house audience accepts lack of clarity as complexity, accepts clumsiness and confusion as "ambiguity" and as style. Perhaps even without the support of critics, they would accept incoherence just as the larger audience does: they may feel that movies as incomprehensible as *Viridiana* are more relevant to their experience, more true to their own feelings about life, and more satisfying and complex than works they can understand.

22. I trust I won't be mistaken for the sort of boob who attacks ambiguity or complexity. I am interested in the change from the period when the meaning of art and form in art was in making complex experience simple and lucid, as is still the case in *Knife in the Water* or *Bandits of Orgosolo,* to the current acceptance of art as technique, the technique which in a movie like *This Sporting Life* makes a simple, though psychologically confused, story look complex, and modern because inexplicable.

23. It has become easy—especially for those who consider "time" a problem and a great theme—to believe that fast editing, out of normal sequence, which makes it difficult, or impossible, for the audience to know if any action is taking place, is somehow more "cinematic" than a consecutively told story. For a half century movies have, when necessary, shifted action in time and place and the directors generally didn't think it necessary to slap us in the face with each cut or to call out, "Look what I can do!" Yet people who should know better will tell you how "cinematic" *The Loneliness of the Long Distance Runner* or *This Sporting Life* is—as if fiddling with the time sequence was good in itself, proof that the "medium" is really being used. Perhaps, after a few decades of indoctrination in high art, they are convinced that a movie is cinematic when they don't understand what's going on. *This Sporting Life,* which Derek Hill, among others, has called the best feature ever made in England, isn't gracefully fragmented, it's smashed. The chunks are so heavy and humorless and, in an odd way,

disturbing, that we can tell the film is meant to be bold, powerful, tragic.

24. There's a woman writer I'd be tempted to call a three-time loser: she's Catholic, Communist, and lesbian; but she comes on more like a triple threat. She's in with so many groups that her books are rarely panned. I thought of her when I read the reviews of *This Sporting Life:* this film has it made in so many ways, it carries an identity card with all the outsiders. The hero is "bewildered," the heroine "bruised" and "afraid of life," the brutal rugby games are possibly a "microcosm of a corrupt society," and the film murkily suggests all sorts of passion and protest, like a group of demonstrators singing "We Shall Overcome" and leaving it to you to fill in your own set of injustices. For *Show* magazine, "The football scenes bear the aspect of a savage rite, with the spectators as participants hungry for sacrifice. The love story . . . is simply another kind of scrimmage, a battle between two people who cannot communicate . . ." For the New York *Times,* the film "translates the confusions and unrequited longings of the angry young men and women of our time into memorable universal truths." (I wish the review would spell out one or two of them for us.) The *Times* has an unusual interpretation of the love story: "The woman . . . only succumbs to him physically and the real roots he seeks are unattainable." This reminds me of my confusion as a schoolgirl when a jazz musician who had been introduced to me during the break called out "Dig you later" as he went back to the stand.

25. In the *Observer,* Penelope Gilliatt offers extraordinary praise: "*This Sporting Life* is a stupendous film. It has a blow like a fist. I've never seen an English picture that gave such expression to the violence and the capacity for pain that there is in the English character. It is there in Shakespeare, in Marlowe, in Lawrence and Orwell and Hogarth, but not in our cinema like this before. *This Sporting Life* is hard to write about because everything important about it is really subverbal." But then so are trees and animals and cities. Isn't it precisely the artist's task to give form to his experience and the critic's task to verbalize

on how this has been accomplished? She goes on to write of the hero, "The events almost seem to be happening to him in the dark. Half of them are told while he is under dentist's gas, in flashback, which is a clumsy device if one is telling a story but the natural method if one is searching around a character." English dental hygiene is notorious; still, isn't telling a story, with or without gas and flashbacks, a pretty good "natural" method of searching around a character? But something *more* seems to be involved: "The black subjective spirit of the film is overpowering. It floods the sound track, which often has a peculiar resonance as though it were happening inside one's own head." Sort of a sunken cathedral effect? The bells are clanging in the reviewers' heads, but what's happening on the screen?

26. In one way or another, almost all the enthusiasts for a film like this one will tell you that it doesn't matter, that however you interpret the film, you will be right (though this does not prevent some of them from working out elaborate interpretations of *Marienbad* or *The Eclipse* or *Viridiana*). Walter Lassally says that "Antonioni's oblique atmospheric statements and Buñuel's symbolism, for example, cannot be analyzed in terms of good or bad . . . for they contain, in addition to any obvious meanings, everything that the viewer may read into them." Surely he can read the most onto a blank screen?

27. There's not much to be said for this theory except that it's mighty democratic. Rather pathetically, those who accept this Rorschach-blot approach to movies are hesitant and uneasy about offering reactions. They should be reassured by the belief that whatever they say is right, but as it refers not to the film but to them (turning criticism into autobiography) they are afraid of self-exposure. I don't think they really believe the theory—it's a sort of temporary public convenience station. More and more people come out of a movie and can't tell you what they've seen, or even whether they liked it.

28. An author like David Storey may stun them with information like "[*This Sporting Life*] works purely in terms of feeling. Only frivolous judgments can be made about it in conventional terms of style." Has he discovered a new method of conveying feeling without style? Or has he simply found the arrogance to frustrate normal responses? No one wants to have his capacity for feeling questioned, and if a viewer tries to play it cool, and discuss *This Sporting Life* in terms of corrupt professional football, he still won't score on that muddy field: there are no goalposts. Lindsay Anderson, who directed, says, "*This Sporting Life* is not a film about sport. In fact, I wouldn't really call it a story picture at all. . . . We have tried to make a tragedy . . . we were making a film about something unique." A tragedy without a story is unique all right: a disaster.

29. In movies, as in other art forms, if you are interested only in technique or if you reject technique, the result is just about the same: if you have nothing to express it is very much like thinking you have so much to express that you don't know how to say it. Something related to absorption in technique is involved in the enthusiasm of young people for what is called "the New American Cinema," though these films are often made by those who reject craftsmanship as well as meaning. They tend to equate technique with science and those who produced the Bomb. This approach, which is a little like the attack on scientific method in *Eyes Without a Face*, is used to explain why they must make movies without taking time to learn how. They're in a hurry, and anyway, technique might corrupt them.

30. The spokesmen for this cinema attack rationality as if it were the enemy of art ("as/the heavy Boots of Soldiers and Intellect/march across the/flowerfields of subconscious" and so forth by Jonas Mekas). They have composed a rather strange amalgam in which reason = lack of feeling and imagination = hostility to art = science = the enemy = Nazis and police = the Bomb. Somewhere along the line, criticism is also turned into an enemy of art. The group produces a kind of euphoric publicity which is published in place of criticism, but soon it may have semi-intellectually respectable critics. In the *Nation* of April 13, 1964, Susan Sontag published an

extraordinary essay on Jack Smith's *Flaming Creatures* called "A Feast for Open Eyes" in which she enunciates a new critical principle: "Thus Smith's crude technique serves, beautifully, the sensibility embodied in *Flaming Creatures*—a sensibility based on indiscriminateness, without ideas, beyond negation." I think in treating indiscriminateness as a *value*, she has become a real swinger. Of course we can reply that if anything goes, nothing happens, nothing works. But this is becoming irrelevant. In Los Angeles, among the independent film makers at their midnight screenings I was told that I belonged to the older generation, that Agee-alcohol generation they called it, who could not respond to the new films because I didn't take pot or LSD and so couldn't learn just to *accept* everything. This narcotic approach of torpid acceptance, which is much like the lethargy of the undead in those failure-of-communication movies, may explain why those films have seemed so "true" to some people (and why the directors' moralistic messages sound so false). This attitude of rejecting critical standards has the dubious advantage of accepting everyone who says he is an artist as an artist and conferring on all his "noncommercial" productions the status of art. Miss Sontag is on to something and if she stays on and rides it like Slim Pickens, it's the end of criticism—at the very least.

31. It's ten years since Dylan Thomas answered Maya Deren's call for a new poetry of film with "I'm not at all sure that I want such a thing, myself, as a poetic film. I think films fine as they are, if only they were better! . . . I like stories, you know—I like to see something going on." Movies have changed in these ten years, disastrously in the last few years; they have become "cinema."

32. At the art-house level, critics and audiences haven't yet discovered the beauty of indiscriminateness, but there's a lot of talk about "purely visual content"—which might be called the principle of ineffability. *Time* calls Resnais's *Muriel* "another absorbing exercise in style." Dwight Macdonald calls *Marienbad* " 'pure' cinema, a succession of images enjoyable in themselves." And Richard Roud, who was responsible (and thus guilty) for the film selection at the New York Film Festivals, goes all the way: films like *La Notte*, he says, provide an "experience in pure form."

33. Once matters reach this plane, it begins to seem almost unclean to raise issues about meaning and content and character, or to question the relevance of a sequence, the quality of a performance. Someone is sure to sneer, "Are you looking for a paraphrasable content? A film, like a poem, *is*." Or smile pityingly and remind you that Patroni Griffi had originally intended to call *Il Mare* "Landscape with Figures"; doesn't that tell you how you should look at it? It does indeed, and it's not my idea of a good time. After a few dismal experiences we discover that when we are told to admire a film for its pure form or its structure, it is going to exhibit irritating, confusing, and ostentatious technique, which will, infuriatingly, be all we can discover in it. And if we should mention that we *enjoy* the dramatic and narrative elements in movies, we are almost certain to be subjected to the contemptuous remark, "Why does cinema have to *mean* something? Do you expect a work by Bach to *mean* something?"

34. The only way to answer this is by some embarrassingly basic analysis, pointing out that words, unlike tones, refer to something and that movie images are rarely abstract or geometric designs, and that when they include people and places and actions, they have implications, associations. Robbe-Grillet, the scenarist of *Marienbad*, may say that the film is a pure construction, an object without reference to anything outside itself, and that the existence of the two characters begins when the film begins and ends ninety-three minutes later, but, of course, we are not born when we go in to see a movie—though we may want to die by the time we leave. And we can't even leave *Marienbad* behind because, although it isn't particularly memorable (it isn't even particularly offensive), a kind of creeping Marienbadism is the new aesthetics of "poetic" cinema. This can only sound like pedantry to those interested in "pure" art who tend to consider analysis as an enemy,

anyway (though many of them are in it). The very same people who say that a movie shouldn't mean anything, that art is beyond meaning, also say that it must be seen over and over again because it reveals more meaning with subsequent viewings. And although the structure of many of the new films is somehow supposed to be the art, we are frowned upon if we question the organization of the material. There is nothing, finally, that we are allowed to question or criticize. We are supposed only to interpret—and that as we wish.

35. The leaders of this new left-wing formalism are Resnais, who gives us his vision of a bomb-shattered, fragmented universe, and Antonioni, the master practitioner of the fallacy of expressive form, who sets out to demonstrate that boredom (and its accompanying eroticism) is the sickness of our time (but doesn't explain how it helps to add to it). If their characters have a curious way of using their sophisticated vacuity as a come-on, are they not in their creators' image? They make assignations (as in *The Eclipse*), but nobody comes.

36. The movie houses may soon look as desolate as *Il Mare*—set in Capri in winter. I've never seen so many people sleeping through movies as at Lincoln Center: no wonder there is talk of "cinema" achieving the social status of opera. A few more seasons of such art and it will be evidence of your interest in culture and your sense of civic responsibility if you go to the movies.

37. The "techniques" of such films are so apparent, so obtrusive, that they may easily be assumed to be "advanced," "modern," "new." It's perfectly true you don't come out of an older movie like Renoir's *La Grande Illusion*, or Flaherty's *Man of Aran*, or Bergman's *Smiles of a Summer Night* saying, "What technique!" Nor do you come out of a concert by Serkin exclaiming about his technique—you're thinking of the music. But those who adore José Iturbi always say, "What technique!"; what *else* is there to respond to? And the comment—which means how fast he can play or how ostentatiously—is not so very far from the admiration for Antonioni or Torre

Nilsson or Bresson's *Trial of Joan of Arc* (though they are generally admired for how slow they can play).

38. My attitude to what is happening to movies is more than a little ambivalent. I don't think that my own preferences or the preferences of others for coherence and wit and feeling are going to make much difference. Movies are going to pieces; they're disintegrating, and the something called cinema is not movies raised to an art but rather movies diminished, movies that look "artistic." Movies are being stripped of all the "nonessentials" —that is to say, faces, actions, details, stories, places—everything that makes them entertaining and joyful. They are even being stripped of the essentials—light (*The Eclipse*), sound (*The Silence*), and movement in some of the New American Cinema films (there is sure to be one called *Stasis*). It's obvious that the most talented film artists and the ones most responsive to our time and the attitudes of Camus and Sartre are the ones moving in this direction. The others, those trying to observe the older conventions, are usually (though not always) banal, trivial, ludicrously commercial, and out of touch, somehow. It is the highest talents, the most dedicated, who are driven to the dead end of "pure" cinema— just as our painters are driven to obliterate the image, and a dramatist like Beckett to reduce words to sounds.

39. Cinema, I suspect, is going to become so rarefied, so private in meaning, and so lacking in audience appeal that in a few years the foundations will be desperately and hopelessly trying to bring it back to life, as they are now doing with theater. The parallel course is, already, depressingly apparent. Clancy Sigal's (admiring) account of Beckett's *Endgame* might have been written of Bergman's *The Silence*:

> *Endgame's* two main characters . . . occupy a claustrophobic space and a deeply ambiguous relationship. . . . Outside, the world is dead of some great catastrophe. . . . The action of the play mainly comprises anxious bickering between the two principal characters. Eventually, Clov dresses for the road to leave Hamm, and Hamm prepares for death, though

we do not see the moment of parting . . . none of the actors is quite sure what the play is about, Beckett affects complete ignorance of the larger implications. "I only know what's on the page," he says with a friendly gesture.

40. Is Beckett leading the way or is it all in the air? His direction that the words of *Play* should be spoken so fast that they can't be understood is paralleled by Resnais's editing of *Muriel* so fast that you can't keep track of what's going on. Penelope Gilliatt writes, "You may have to go to the film at least twice, as I did, before the warmth of it seeps through . . ."; Beckett has already anticipated the problem and provided the answer with the stage direction, "Repeat play exactly."

41. When movies, the only art which everyone felt free to enjoy and have opinions about, lose their connection with song and dance, drama, and the novel, when they become cinema, which people fear to criticize just as they fear to say what they think of a new piece of music or a new poem or painting, they will become another object of academic study and "appreciation," and will soon be an object of excitement only to practitioners of the "art." Although *L'Avventura* is a great film, had I been present at Cannes in 1960, where Antonioni distributed his explanatory statement, beginning, "There exists in the world today a very serious break between science on the one hand . . . ," I might easily have joined in the hisses, which he didn't really deserve until the following year, when *La Notte* revealed that he'd begun to believe his own explanations—thus making liars of us all.

42. When we see Dwight Macdonald's cultural solution applied to film, when we see the prospect that movies will become a product for "Masscult" consumption, while the "few who care" will have their High Culture cinema, who wants to take the high road? There is more energy, more originality, more excitement, more *art* in American kitsch like *Gunga Din, Easy Living,* the Rogers and Astaire pictures like *Swingtime* and *Top Hat,* in *Strangers on a Train, His Girl Friday, The Crimson Pirate, Citizen Kane, The Lady Eve,*

To Have and Have Not, The African Queen, Singin' in the Rain, Sweet Smell of Success, or more recently, *The Hustler, Lolita, The Manchurian Candidate, Hud, Charade,* than in the presumed "High Culture" of *Hiroshima Mon Amour, Marienbad, La Notte, The Eclipse,* and the Torre Nilsson pictures. As Nabokov remarked, "Nothing is more exhilarating than Philistine vulgarity."

43. Regrettably, one of the surest signs of the Philistine is his reverence for the superior tastes of those who put him down. Macdonald believes that "a work of High Culture, however inept, is an expression of feelings, ideas, tastes, visions that are idiosyncratic and the audience similarly responds to them as individuals." No. The "pure" cinema enthusiast who doesn't react to a film but feels he should, and so goes back to it over and over, is not responding as an individual but as a compulsive good pupil determined to appreciate what his cultural superiors say is "art." Movies are on their way into academia when they're turned into a matter of duty: a mistake in judgment isn't fatal, but too much anxiety about judgment is. In this country, respect for High Culture is becoming a ritual.

44. If debased art is kitsch, perhaps kitsch may be redeemed by honest vulgarity, may become art. Our best work transforms kitsch, makes art out of it; that is the peculiar greatness and strength of American movies, as Godard in *Breathless* and Truffaut in *Shoot the Piano Player* recognize. Huston's *The Maltese Falcon* is a classic example. Our first and greatest film artist D. W. Griffith was a master of kitsch: the sentiment and melodrama in his films are much more integral to their greatness than the critics who lament Griffith's lack of mind (!) perceive.

45. The movies are still where it happens, not for much longer perhaps, but the movies are still the art form that uses the material of our lives and the art form that we use. I am not suggesting that we want to see new and bigger remakes of the tired old standbys of the film repertory: who wants to see the new *Cimarron,* another *Quo Vadis?* And meanings don't have to be spread out for us like a free-lunch counter. There are movies that

are great experiences like *Long Day's Journey into Night,* and just a few years back there were movies which told good stories—movies like *The Treasure of Sierra Madre, From Here to Eternity, The Nun's Story.*

46. People go to the movies for the various ways they express the experiences of our lives, and as a means of avoiding and postponing the pressures we feel. This latter function of art—generally referred to disparagingly as escapism—may also be considered as refreshment, and in terms of modern big city life and small town boredom, it may be a major factor in keeping us sane.

47. In the last few years there has appeared a new kind of filmgoer: he isn't interested in movies but in cinema. A great many of the film makers are in this group: they've never gone to movies much and they don't care about them. They're interested in what they can do in the medium, not in what *has* been done. This is, of course, their privilege, though I would suggest that it may explain why they have such limited approaches to film. I'm more puzzled by the large numbers of those who are looking for *importance* in cinema. For example, a doctor friend called me after he'd seen *The Pink Panther* to tell me I needn't "bother" with that one, it was just slapstick. When I told him I'd already seen it and had a good time at it, he was irritated; he informed me that a movie should be more than a waste of time, it should be an exercise of taste that will enrich your life. Those looking for importance are too often contemptuous of the crude vitality of American films, though this crudity is not always offensive, and may represent the only way that energy and talent and inventiveness can find an outlet, can break through the planned standardization of mass entertainment. It has become a mark of culture to revere the old slapstick (the Mack Sennett two-reelers and early Chaplins that aren't really as great as all that) and put down the

new. But in a movie as shopworn as *Who's Been Sleeping in My Bed?* there is, near the end, an almost inspired satirical striptease by Carol Burnett. *The Nutty Professor* is too long and repetitive, but Jerry Lewis has some scenes that hold their own with the silent classics. I enjoyed *The Prize,* which opens badly but then becomes a lively, blatant entertainment; but there's no point in recommending it to someone who wants his life enriched. I couldn't persuade friends to go see *Charade,* which although no more than a charming confectionery trifle was, I think, probably the best American film of last year— as artificial and enjoyable in its way as *The Big Sleep.* The word had got around that it isn't *important,* that it isn't *serious,* that it doesn't do anything for you.

48. Our academic bureaucracy needs something alive to nourish it and movies still have a little blood which the academics can drain away. In the West several of the academic people I know who have least understanding of movies were suddenly interested by Laurence Alloway's piece called "Critics in the Dark" in *Encounter.* By suggesting that movie criticism had never gotten into the right hands —i.e., theirs, and by indicating *projects,* and by publishing in the prestigious *Encounter,* Alloway indicated large vistas of respectability for future film critics. Perhaps also they were drawn to his condescending approach to movies as a pop art. Many academics have always been puzzled that Agee could *care* so much about movies. Alloway, by taking the position that Agee's caring was a maladjustment, re-established their safe, serene worlds in which if a man gets excited about an idea or an issue, they know there's something the matter with him. It's not much consolation, but I think the cinema the academics will be working over will be the cinema they deserve.

 *THE ARTS*

DYLAN THOMAS

A Visit to America

Across the United States of America, from New York to California and back, glazed, again, for many months of the year, there streams and sings for its heady supper a dazed and prejudiced procession of European lecturers, scholars, sociologists, economists, writers, authorities on this and that and even, in theory, on the United States of America. And, breathlessly, between addresses and receptions, in planes and trains and boiling hotel bedroom ovens, many of these attempt to keep journals and diaries.

At first, confused and shocked by shameless profusion and almost shamed by generosity, unaccustomed to such importance as they are assumed, by their hosts, to possess, and up against the barrier of a common language, they write in their notebooks like demons, generalising away, on character and culture and the American political scene. But, towards the middle of their middle-aged whisk through middle-western clubs and universities, the fury of the writing flags; their spirits are lowered by the spirit with which they are everywhere strongly greeted and which, in ever increasing doses, they themselves lower; and they begin to mistrust themselves, and their reputations—for they have found, too often, that an audience will receive a lantern-lecture on, say, Ceramics, with the same uninhibited enthusiasm that it accorded the very week before to a paper on the Modern Turkish Novel. And, in their diaries, more and more do such entries appear as, "No way of escape!" or "Buffalo!" or "I am beaten," until at last they cannot write a word. And, twittering all over, old before their time, with eyes like rissoles in the sand, they are helped up the gangway of the home-bound liner by kind bosom friends (of all kinds and bosoms) who boister them on the back, pick them up again, thrust bottles, sonnets, cigars, addresses, into their pockets, have a farewell party in their cabin, pick them up again, and, snickering and yelping, are gone: to wait at the dockside for another boat from Europe and another batch of fresh, green lecturers.

There they go, every spring, from New York to Los Angeles: exhibitionists, polemicists, histrionic publicists, theological rhetoricians, historical hoddy-doddies, balletomanes, ulterior decorators, windbags and bigwigs and humbugs, men in love with stamps, men in love with steaks, men after millionaires' widows, men with elephantiasis of the reputation (huge trunks and teeny minds), authorities on gas, bishops, best-sellers, editors looking for writers, writers looking for publishers, publishers looking for dollars, existentialists, serious physicists with nuclear missions, men from the B.B.C. who speak as though they had the Elgin marbles in their mouths, pot-boiling philosophers, professional Irishmen (very lepri-corny), and, I am afraid, fat poets with slim volumes.

And see, too, in that linguacious stream, the tall monocled men, smelling of saddle soap and club armchairs, their breath a nice blending of whisky and fox's blood, with big protruding upper-class tusks and county mustaches, presumably invented in England and sent abroad to advertise *Punch*, who lecture to women's clubs on such unlikely subjects as "The History of Etching in the Shetland Islands"; and the brassy-bossy men-women, with corrugated-iron perms, and hippo hides, who come, self-announced, as "ordinary British housewives," to talk to rich minked chunks of American matronhood about the iniquity of the Health Services, the criminal sloth of the miners, the *visible* tail and horns of Mr. Aneurin Bevan, and the fear of everyone in England to go out alone at night because of the organised legions of coshboys against whom the police are powerless owing to the refusal of those in power to equip them with revolvers and to flog to ribbons every adolescent offender on any charge at all.

And there shiver and teeter also, meek and driven, those British authors unfortunate enough to have written, after years of unadventurous forgotten work, one bad novel which became enormously popular on both sides of the Atlantic. At home, when success first hit them, they were mildly delighted; a couple of literary luncheons went sugar-tipsy to their heads, like the washing sherry served before those luncheons; and perhaps, as the lovely money rolled lushly in, they began to dream, in their moony writers' way, of being able to retire to the country, keep wasps (or was it bees?) and never write another lousy word. But in come the literary agent's triggermen and the publisher's armed narks: "You must go to the States and make a Personal Appearance. Your novel is *killing* them over there, and we're not surprised either. You must go round the States lecturing to women." And the inoffensive writers, who have never dared lecture anyone, let alone women—they are frightened of women, they do not understand women, they write about women as creatures that never existed, and the women lap it up—these sensitive plants cry out, "But what shall we lecture about?"

"The English Novel."

"I don't read novels."

"Great Women in Fiction."

"I don't like fiction *or* women."

But off they are wafted, first class, in the plush bowels of the *Queen Victoria*, with a list of engagements long as a New York menu or a half-hour with a book by Charles Morgan, and soon they are losing their little cold-as-goldfish paw in the great general glutinous handshake of a clutch of enveloping hostesses.

I think, by the way, that it was Ernest Raymond, the author of *Tell England*, who once made a journey round the American women's clubs, being housed and entertained at each small town he stopped at, by the richest and largest and furriest lady available. On one occasion he stopped at some little station and was met, as usual, by an enormous motor-car full of a large horn-rimmed businessman—looking exactly like a large horn-rimmed businessman on the films—and his roly-poly pearly wife. Mr. Raymond sat with her in the back of the car, and off they went, the husband driving. At once, she began to say how utterly delighted she and her husband and the committee were to have him at their Women's Literary and Social Guild, and to compliment him on his books.

"I don't think I've ever, in all my life, enjoyed a book so much as *Sorrel and Son*," she said. "What you don't know about human nature! I think Sorrel is one of the most beautiful characters ever portrayed."

Ernest Raymond let her talk on, while he stared, embarrassed, in front of him. All he could see were the double chins that her husband wore at the back of his neck. On and on she gushed in praise of *Sorrel and Son* until he could stand it no longer.

"I quite agree with you," he said. "A beautiful book indeed. But I'm afraid I didn't write *Sorrel and Son*. It was written by an old friend of mine, Mr. Warwick Deeping."

And the large horn-rimmed double-chinned husband at the wheel said, without turning: "Caught again, Emily."

See the garrulous others, also, gabbing and garlanded from one nest of culture-vultures to another: people selling the English way of life and condemning the American way as they swig and guzzle through it; people resurrecting the theories of surrealism for the benefit of remote parochial female audiences who did not know it was dead, not having ever known it had been alive; people talking about Etruscan pots and pans to a bunch of dead pans and wealthy pots in Boston. And there, too, in the sticky thick of lecturers moving across the continent black with clubs, go the foreign poets, catarrhal troubadours, lyrical one-night-standers, dollar-mad nightingales, remittance-bards from at home, myself among them booming with the worst.

Did we pass one another, en route, all unknowing, I wonder; one of us spry-eyed, with clean, white lectures and a soul he could call his own, going buoyantly west to his remunerative doom in the great state university factories; another returning dog-eared as his clutch of poems and his carefully typed impromptu asides? I ache for us both. There one goes, unsullied as yet, in his Pullman pride, toying—oh boy!—with a blunderbuss bourbon, being smoked by a large cigar, riding out to the wide-open spaces of the faces of his waiting audience. He carries, besides his literary baggage, a new, dynamic razor, just on the market, bought in New York, which operates at the flick of a thumb, but cuts the thumb to the bone; a tin of new shaving-lather which is worked with the other, unbleeding, thumb, and covers not only the face but the whole bathroom and, instantly freezing, makes an arctic, icicled cave from which it takes two sneering bellboys to extract him; and, of course a nylon shirt. This, he dearly believes, from the advertisements, he can himself wash in his hotel, hang to dry overnight, and put on, without ironing, in the morning. (In my case, no ironing was needed, for, as someone cruelly pointed out in print, I looked, anyway, like an unmade bed.)

He is vigorously welcomed at the station by an earnest crew-cut platoon of giant collegiates, all chasing the butterfly culture with net, notebook, poison bottle, pin and label, each with at least thirty-six terribly white teeth, and nursed away, as heavily gently as though he were an imbecile rich aunt with a short prospect of life, into a motor-car in which, for a mere fifty miles or so travelled at poet-breaking speed, he assures them of the correctness of their assumption that he is half-witted by stammering inconsequential answers in an over-British accent to their genial questions about what international conference Stephen Spender might be attending at the moment, or the reactions of British poets to the work of a famous American whose name he did not know or catch. He is then taken to a small party of only a few hundred people all of whom hold the belief that what a visiting lecturer needs before he trips on to the platform is just enough martinis so that he can trip off the platform as well. And, clutching his explosive glass, he is soon contemptuously dismissing, in a flush of ignorance and fluency, the poetry of those androgynous literary ladies with three names who produce a kind of verbal ectoplasm to order as a waiter dishes up spaghetti—only to find that the fiercest of these, a wealthy huntress of small, seedy lions (such as himself), who stalks the middle-western bush with ears and rifle cocked, is his hostess for the evening. Of the lecture, he remembers little but the applause and maybe two questions: "Is it true that the young English intellectuals are *really* psychological?" or, "I always carry Kierkegaard in my pocket. What do you carry?"

Late at night, in his room, he fills a page of his journal with a confused, but scathing, account of his first engagement; summarises American advanced education in a paragraph that will be meaningless tomorrow; and falls to sleep where he is immediately chased through long, dark thickets by a Mrs. Mabel Frankincense Mehaffey, with a tray of martinis and lyrics.

And there goes the other happy poet bedraggledly back to New York which struck him all of a sheepish never-sleeping heap at first, but which seems to him now, after the ulcerous rigours of a lecturer's spring, a haven cosy as toast, cool as an icebox, and safe as skyscrapers.

KENNETH CLARK

Art and Society

Sir Kenneth Mackenzie Clark (1903–   ), an English writer, has had an illustrious career in the history and criticism of art. He has held such posts as the directorship of the National Gallery, London; the Slade Professorship of Fine Art at Oxford University; and the chairmanship of the Arts Council of Great Britain. Books of his include *The Gothic Revival*, 1929; *Leonardo da Vinci*, 1939; *Moments of Vision*, 1954; *The Nude*, 1956; *Looking at Pictures*, 1960; *Provincialism*, 1962; and *Ruskin Today*, 1963.

Drawing upon his encyclopedic knowledge of the history of the visual arts, Mr. Clark discusses three "laws" which deal with the relationship of art to society. He predicts, with measured optimism, the future of art in a materialistic society.

1. Art is an extensive word. In this essay I limit it to the branch of art that I know best, the visual arts: and I take this term to cover everything made in response to the feeling that certain events or objects of contemplation, seen or imagined, are so important that they must be recorded; and that certain objects of use are so important that they must be enriched. These two aspects of visual art I refer to as image and ornament. They used to be called "fine art" and "applied art," and in the nineteenth century were severely distinguished from one another. Today we tend to minimize this distinction. We believe that the form-creating instinct can express itself in both ornament and image; all ornament, however

ART AND SOCIETY From *Harper's Magazine*, August 1961. Reprinted by permission of the author.

abstract, suggests some visual experience; all images, however factual, reveal some sense of design. Both are forms of order. And both are sacramental. "What is this sacrament?" as the catechism says. "The outward and visible sign of an inward and spiritual grace." Both image and ornament are revelations of a state of mind and social temper.

2. Having accepted this basic unity, however, these two branches of visual art show very great differences, especially in their relationship to society, and I shall consider them separately. I think it true to say that all image art of any value has been made by, or on behalf of, a small minority: not necessarily a governing class in a political sense, but a governing class in an intellectual and spiritual sense. Since I shall often refer to this minority, I must decide what to call it. Plato's "gover-

nors" is too narrow a term, Rousseau's *volonté générale* is too wide and too mysterious. For the sake of brevity I have referred to it as an *élite;* although in fact it is not elected, and may be drawn from any class of society.

3. Images are not made for fun. In fact it is almost true to say that all image art of value illustrates or confirms a system of belief held by an elite, and very often is employed consciously as a means of maintaining that system. Obvious examples are the theocratic art of Egypt, the Parthenon with its Olympian embodiment of Greek philosophy, the stained glass of Chartres and Bourges illustrating not only Christian legend but the whole superstructure of patristic theology, the temples of Angkor and Borobudur, the Basilica of Assisi and its Buddhist equivalent Ajanta, the Stanze of Raphael, and so forth, down to David's picture of the Oath of the Horatii. The list could be expanded till in the end it would include most of the greatest visible feats of human imagination and all of those which are in any way related to society and do not depend solely on the genius of an individual artist. It seems that an image achieves the concentration, clarity, and rhythmic energy which make it memorable only when it illustrates or confirms what a minority believes to be an important truth.

4. The images provided for the majority by the elite may be more, or less, popular. Franciscan art in the thirteenth century and Baroque art in the seventeenth century were two attempts to create a new repertoire of images which should be more popular than that which preceded it. Both consciously exploited emotionalism. But the artists who gave the finest expression of those styles—let us say Cimabue and Bernini—were working for a small group of patrons, and were deeply receptive of their ideas. Bernini's Saint Theresa became a popular image; it revealed to the majority a hidden need. But it was Bernini's own invention and in its origin it owed nothing to popular demands. Even the images which we first believe to have a popular origin—for example those charming woodcuts known as *images d' Epinal*—are for the most part naïve and imperfect memories of images already invented for the elite by such an artist as Philippe de Champagne. The only exceptions I can think of are those anecdotal strips which simply tell a story, often with the help of balloons of text. Such were the illustrations of late antique manuscripts, the painting of popular artists like Pacino di Bonaguida, the *Biblia Pauperum* and its derivatives, and a number of Japanese scrolls, like the comic animals attributed to Toba Sojo. These, I believe, are the only forms of autochthonous popular image art before the nineteenth century, and I mention them now because they reveal a fundamental characteristic of all popular art: that it is concerned with narration.

5. At first sight ornament would seem to be a more popular form of expression than image. Ornament has the character of a language—nineteenth-century writers used, quite properly, to speak of the grammar of ornament—and in so far as it is a living language it is accepted almost unconsciously by the majority. However there is this difference, that whereas language seems to have evolved unconsciously from mass needs, a system of ornament has seldom been invented by "the people." In fact I can think of only one exception: the pottery of the Mexican Indians, which is outstandingly beautiful and does seem to be a genuine popular creation. In Europe good folk ornament turns out almost always to be a cruder rendering of a minority style; and I think the same is true of China, India, Persia, and the whole Moslem culture. I would even extend this to the most vital and expressive of all ornament styles—that produced by the so-called folk-wandering peoples. I believe that the finest Scythian ornaments were by a great artist working for a chief, and that most of what has been discovered in Scandinavia or Scotland is a half-understood imitation of these aristocratic adornments.

6. In ornament the ulterior motive is less strong than in the image. It does not openly recommend a system. But no one maintains that it exists solely to please the eye, and lacks ulterior motive altogether. It is an assertion of status—whether in a cope or crown or crosier or *portail royal* or precious reliquary. This fact,

which has been worked out in detail by Marxist historians, is taken by them as a condemnation of art; and, as everyone knows, Veblen coined for it the expression "conspicuous waste." This expression is apt, but I do not find it at all damaging. All art is waste in a material sense; and the idea that things should be made more precious-looking in accordance with the status of the user seems to me entirely fitting. I think that a bishop should have finer vestments than a deacon and that the portal of a cathedral should be more richly ornamented than the door of a warehouse. I would go further, and say that ornament is inseparable from hierarchy. It is not only the result, but the cause of status. The carving on the corner capitals of the Doge's Palace and the central window of the Palazzo Farnese confer a kind of kingship on those points of the buildings. In a democratic building, where all windows are equal, no ornament is permissible; although I understand that the higher executives may have more windows.

7. So I would deduce from history this first law (in the Ruskinian sense) of the relationship of art and society: that visual art, whether it takes the form of images or ornament, is made by a minority for a minority, and would add this rider, that the image-making part is usually controlled in the interests of a system, and that the ornamental part is usually the index of status.

8. Created by a minority: yes, but accepted by the majority unquestionably, eagerly, and with a sense of participation. The degree of physical participation in the great popular works of art is hard to assess. We know that in the building of the Gothic cathedrals—Chartres is the most familiar example—whole villages moved to be nearer the work, and men were prepared to learn subsidiary crafts in order to help the professional masons. We can assume that the same was true of Borobudur or Ellora, although the economic status of the workers may have been different. A parallel in modern life would be the building of a great liner in Clydebank, where the whole life of the town depends on the work. But apart from this active participation, one has only to read the accounts of how in the great ages of artistic creation works of art were brought into existence—the long and serious thought which preceded the commission, the public anxiety about its progress, the joy when it was at last accomplished, and the procession in which it was carried to its destination, to the sound of bells and singing of a Te Deum—one has only to come upon such documents, common enough in the Middle Ages and Renaissance, and applicable, surely, to Olympia and the Acropolis of Athens, to recognize that the society of those times needed art, believed without question in the value of art, and participated imaginatively in its making. So this would be my second law: that a healthy and vital relationship between art and society exists when the majority feel that art is absolutely necessary to them, to confirm their beliefs, to inform them about matters of lasting importance, and to make the invisible visible.

9. Now in saying that this is the *healthiest* relationship between art and society, I must not be understood as saying that these are the *only* circumstances under which good works of art can be produced. Even before 1870 great pictures were painted by individuals who had no relationship with society at all and whose work was distasteful or incomprehensible to the majority. Rembrandt and Turner, in their later phases, are obvious examples. In the history of art, as in all history, nothing poses a more delicate problem of interpretation than the relationship between individual genius and the general will. But even if we believe, as I am inclined to do, that inspiration is more likely to illuminate an individual than a mass and that all the memorable forms of art were originally invented by individuals of genius, we must agree that at certain periods these individuals are isolated, at others they enlist behind them a whole army of assent and participation.

10. Nor is this direct relationship of need and unquestioning belief certain to produce good art. Artistic faculties are somewhat unequally—we may think unfairly—distributed among the peoples of the globe; and although the relationship may be sound, not all needs

have the same validity. However, I am sufficiently a Ruskinian to believe that when a society, over a long period, produces an art
which is lacking in vitality and imaginative
power, but which nevertheless seems to be
accepted by the majority, there is something
wrong with that society.

11. This brings me back to the part of my
opening definition, where I said that art was
a sacrament; and I must now consider how an
inward and spiritual grace can be given outward and visible form. The answer is, through
symbols. A symbol is a sort of analogy in the
physical sphere for some spiritual or intellectual experience. Usually it is the concentration
of several related experiences so complex that
they cannot be expressed in any rational form,
and so intense that a physical symbol suggests
itself unconsciously. We know from the saints
of every religion that the most poignant spiritual experiences demand expression by physical analogies, and, in spite of Pascal and
Spinoza, we may infer that spiritual experiences which remain abstract are not usually
very intense. Symbols may start as a result of
private revelations, but their value in art depends on the degree to which they can be
felt and accepted by others. In fact nearly all
intensely felt symbols have some universal
quality, which makes them comprehensible
even when their maker believes them to be
peculiar to himself. But it is also true that the
sacramental character of art is far more easily achieved when the principal objects of
belief have already been given a symbolic
form which is generally recognized and accepted: in other words, when there is an
established mythology and iconography.

12. In this question of art and society the
importance of an accepted iconography cannot be overstated. Without it the network of
beliefs and customs which holds a society together may never take shape as art. If an
iconography contains a number of sufficiently
powerful symbols, it can positively alter a
philosophic system. The points of dogma for
which no satisfactory image can be created
tend to be dropped from popular religious exposition, and episodes which have scarcely
occupied the attention of theologians tend to

grow in importance if they produce a compelling image. I would go so far as to say that
the failure to discover a satisfactory symbol
for the Holy Ghost has seriously impaired our
concept of the Trinity.

13. Let me give an example of iconographic
triumph and disaster from one painter in one
place: Titian in Venice. In the Frari his sublime image of the Assumption of the Virgin is
so corporeally convincing that it provided a
point of departure for Baroque painting, and
this image was to float in the background of
Catholic imagination down to our own day.
In the "Salute" is Titian's painting of Pente-
cost, a work over which he took great pains,
but without success. It was the final blow to
a subject which had never found an impressive iconographical form, and which in spite
of its theological importance, gradually faded
from the consciousness of popular Catholicism. Let me take another example from
Buddhism. It had been categorically laid down
that the Buddha must not be portrayed, and
in the earliest scenes of his life, such as those
on the stupa at Sanchi, the central point of
each episode is left a blank—an empty chair
or a deserted boat. This insult to the image-
making faculty was not to be borne, and a
representation of the Buddha was finally accepted. But where did it come from? From
the imitation, in the fringes of the Buddhist
world, of some Praxitelian Apollo. Thus the
most extreme example of spirituality was embodied by the most concrete expression of
physical beauty. Conversely, dogma may triumph over the popular love of imagery in a
theocratic society, and produce an iconography, like that of later Buddhism, with its
10,000 Buddhas, which deprives images of all
artistic quality.

14. Lest it should be thought that this question of iconography does not apply to modern
life, let me add that it is not confined to dogmatic religion. For example, the iconography
of the Romantic Movement from 1790 to 1830
was almost as compulsive as if it had been laid
down by the Council of Trent. The tiger—in
Blake, Stubbs, Géricault, Delacroix, Barye,
and a dozen lesser artists; the cloud—in
Wordsworth and Byron, Shelley, Turner, and
Constable; the shipwreck—in Byron, Turner,

Goya, Géricault, Delacroix, and Victor Hugo: these are symbols of Romanticism, used and accepted unconsciously because they expressed the new worship of nature and power, and a new sense of destiny. I think it would be a mistake to call this state of mind a religion. That word should be reserved for beliefs which are based on a book of holy writ and involve certain formal observances. But at least we can say that the belief in nature, which expressed itself in the landscape painting of the nineteenth century and has remained the most productive source of popular art to this day, is a non-material belief. It is something which cannot be justified by reason alone and seems to lift the life of the senses onto a higher plane.

15. This suggests another "law" in the relationship of art and society: that it is valuable only when the spiritual life is strong enough to insist on some sort of expression through symbols. No great social arts can be based on material values or physical sensations alone.

16. This "law" leads me to consider the problem of luxury art. Now, it would be dishonest for me to take a puritanical or Veblenist view of luxury art. Moreover there is a point—Watteau's "Enseigne de Gersaint" is an example—at which the sensuous quality of luxury art is so fine that it offers a spiritual experience. We are playing with words and concepts which, as we breathe on them, become alive and flutter from our hands. Still, the fact remains that, in the long run, luxury art implies the reverse of what I have called a healthy relationship between art and society and so has a deadening effect. The most obvious example is the art of eighteenth-century France, where, however, the arrogant elaboration demanded by powerful patrons is sometimes sweetened, and given lasting value, by a reasonable belief in the *douceur de vivre*. But the predominance of luxury art in the eighteenth century is a short and harmless episode compared to that long slumber of the creative imagination which lasted from the end of the second century B.C. to the third century A.D. For almost five hundred years not a single new form of any value was invented except, perhaps, in architecture. Works from the preceding centuries were reproduced in-

terminably—made smoother and sweeter for private collectors, bigger and coarser for the public.

17. What can we say of the relations of this art to the society which produced and accepted it? That no one believed in its symbols; that no one looked to it for confirmation or enlightenment. In short that no one wanted it, except as a conventional form of display. The Romans did not want art and they did not make it; but they collected it.

18. The problem of luxury art is complicated by the fact that the periods in which it predominates are usually periods when the art of the past is collected and esteemed. This was obviously the case in Hellenized Rome and in eighteenth-century England; conversely the idea of collecting and displaying works of an earlier period was hardly known in those cultures where the need for art was strong and widely diffused. One must distinguish, of course, between the fruitful use by artists of earlier works, which took place in thirteenth-century Rheims no less than in fifteenth-century Florence, and the competitive accumulation of collectors. The feeling for the art of the past in Donatello or Ghiberti is entirely different from that of the eighteenth-century connoisseurs—at once more passionate and more practical. "How can I use these admirable inventions to give my own message?" "How can I surpass them in truth or expressive power?" These are the questions aroused by the work of the past in the great ages of art. In periods of luxury art, on the other hand, works of the past are collected at worst for reasons of prestige and at best in order to establish a standard of taste. The concept of good taste is the virtuous profession of luxury art. But one cannot imagine it existing in the twelfth century, or even in the Renaissance; and without going into the complex question of what the words can mean, I am inclined to doubt if a completely healthy relationship between art and society is possible while the concept of good taste exists.

19. Such, then, are the deductions that I would make from studying the history of art; and I have ventured, in the nineteenth-century manner, to call them laws. It is arguable

that this word should never be applied to the historical process: we see too little. But at least we can say that these are strong probabilities which should be our first criteria when we come to examine the relations of art to society at the present day. In doing so I may be allowed one assumption: that fundamentally human beings have not changed. The picture of human nature which we derive from the Book of Kings or the Fourth Dynasty Egyptian portrait heads in Cairo and Boston is much the same as what we know today, and I think we may safely assume that it will take more than television and the internal combustion engine to change us. In fact, I would suppose that we have more in common with the Middle Ages than our fathers had, because to us universal destruction is an actual possibility, whereas to our fathers it was only a pious fiction. However, if human nature has not changed, human society has; and changed as the result of a basic shift of mental outlook.

20. This change can be described in one word: materialism. The word has taken on a pejorative sense, but materialism has been the source of achievements which have added immeasurably to the well-being and happiness of mankind. Whether as the dialectical materialism of the East or the liberal materialism of the West, it has given to masses of men a new standard of living, a new sense of status, and a new hope. These benefits have been achieved because materialism has been the philosophical basis of two outstanding human activities, one in the moral and one in the intellectual sphere: humanitarianism and science. These are the integrating forces of our culture, and they are as powerful, and as all-pervasive, as was Christianity in the Middle Ages.

21. Now, how does this underlying philosophy of materialism relate to art? One cannot help being aware of one very serious obstacle. Materialism and all its children are dedicated to measurement. Bentham's philosophy was based on the greatest good for the greatest *number*. Democracy depends on counting the *number* of votes. All social studies are based on statistics. Science, although it claims to have outgrown that phase, reached its present position by an unprecedented accuracy of measurement.

22. In its century of triumph, measurement has even become an article of faith. The potential of faith in the human mind is probably fairly constant, but it attaches itself to different ideas or manifestations at different periods. The bones of the Saints, the Rights of Man, psychoanalysis—all these have been the means of precipitating a quantity of faith which is always in solution. People probably believe as much nonsense today as they did in the Middle Ages; but we demand of our precipitant that it *look* as if it could be proved—that it appear to be measurable. People might have believed in art during the last fifty years if its effects could have been stated in an immense table of figures or a very complicated graph; of course they would not have checked the figures or understood the graph, but the existence of these symbols of measurement would have sustained their faith.

23. But we cannot measure the amount of satisfaction which we derive from a song. We cannot even measure the relative greatness of artists, and attempts to do so by giving marks, popular in the eighteenth century, produced ridiculous results; Giulio Romano always came out top of the poll, which as we all know, by some unanalyzable form of knowledge, is incorrect. The more honest philosophers of materialism have recognized that art cannot be measured in material terms. Bentham invented the unforgettable comparison between pushpin and poetry, coming down on the side of pushpin because more people wanted it. Poetry he defined as "misrepresentation," which is the liberal counterpart to Veblen's "conspicuous waste." The philosophers of dialectical materialism have accepted art only in so far as its magical properties have conceded the right to enjoy and even to produce art among the rights of minorities. Art is the opiate of the few.

24. How are the philosophic assumptions of materialism reflected in the actual status of art in modern society? It is incontrovertible that fine art, as the word is usually understood, is the preserve of a very small minority. We must not be bamboozled by the claim that

more people listen to "good" music or visit picture galleries; nor even by the fact that a few of us have tricked the unsuspecting viewer into looking at old pictures on television. Similar claims could be made for the nineteenth century—for example, during the Manchester Art Treasures Exhibition in 1857, special trains ran from all over England, and whole factories closed down in order that the workers could enjoy the experience of art; and yet the next fifty years saw the consolidation of a Philistinism unequaled since the Roman Republic.

25. Anyone who has been concerned with those "arts" which really depend on the support of a majority—the cinema, television, or wholesale furnishing—knows that the minority which is interested in art is so small as to be irrelevant in any serious calculation. In England, the majority is not merely apathetic, but hostile to art. A recent example was the film of *The Horse's Mouth,* which the exhibitors would not show (in spite of brilliant acting and hilarious comedy) simply because the leading character was an artist. If only, they said, he had been a schoolmaster or a doctor! This is perfectly understandable. The existence of these freakish members of society whose usefulness cannot be demonstrated, but who often seem to be enjoying themselves and sometimes even to be making money, is an affront to the ordinary hard-working man. It is fair to say that in spite of this feeling, artists are treated tolerantly in democratic countries.

26. We should be grateful for this tolerance, but does it not fall far short of my second condition for a healthy relationship between art and society: that the majority feel art to be absolutely necessary to them; that they are not merely consumers, but participants; and that they receive works of art as the expression of their own deepest feelings?

27. Before answering this question, I must look back at my original definition of the word "art." Do the majority still feel that material things must be made more precious? Do they still feel that certain images are so important that they must be preserved? In a sense the answer is "yes." The majority still want ornament on their clothes, their furnishing fabrics, their wallpapers, and many objects of daily use. More than this, they still mind very much how things look, independent of their utility. Whether it be dress or automobile design, they are still in the grip of style. They and the designers are swept along by a blind destiny, a mysterious force which they cannot analyze, but of which they are acutely conscious when they look back at the fashions of twenty years ago.

28. But no one pretends that, in the last fifty years, the use of ornament has revealed a satisfactory relationship between art and society. Ruskin and William Morris supposed that this was due to the intervention of the machine. But this theory turns out to be applicable only to the Gothic style. In almost every other style the machine is an extended tool that can be used with confidence; and for that matter a great deal of the ornament of the past, from the Viking goldsmith work of Sutton Hoo to the inlaid panels of the Taj Mahal, is entirely devoid of manual sensibility and might just as well have been made by a machine.

29. From a technical point of view, the premises on which ornamental art is produced have not greatly changed. When we examine it in the light of my other laws, however, the change is considerable. With a single exception, the ornament favored by the majority is no longer made for an elite; and it no longer has any underlying sense of symbolic meaning. In one branch of art—in architecture—it has almost ceased to exist; and although we have now grown used to buildings without ornament, the historian must record that this is a unique event in the history of art, and one which would certainly have shocked those famous architects of the past who gave so much thought to the character of their ornament, and counted upon it at all points of focus and transition. The great refusal of modern architecture was perhaps a necessary purge and had certain health-giving consequences. But often it is simply an impoverishment, an excuse for meanness and a triumph for the spirit that denies. That it is not the expression of a popular will we learn when we look down the blank face of a modern building into the shop windows at its base; and this leads me to

the exception I mentioned just now: it is women's dress. There, it seems to me, the compulsion is so strong that a healthy relationship between art and society is never lost. I am not suggesting that all fashions are equally good—of course there are moments of failing invention and false direction. But they always right themselves because there is an indestructible *volonté générale*—an interaction between the elite and the masses, a sense of status and an unconscious feeling for symbolism.

30. If the position of ornament in modern society is uneasy and incomplete, the position of image art has suffered a far more drastic change, owing to the invention of the camera. The public hunger for memorable and credible images has in no way declined, but it is satisfied every day by illustrated papers; and the love of landscape which, as I said, was one of the chief spiritual conquests of the nineteenth century, is fed by colored postcards. I am not denying that there is an element of art in press photography; I will also admit that I derive a pleasure from colored postcards which must, I suppose, be called aesthetic. I prefer a good colored postcard to a bad landscape painting. But in both these projections of the image, much of what we believe gives art its value is necessarily omitted. There is selection, but no order, and no extension of the imaginative faculty.

31. To realize how destructive has been the effect of the camera on image art, consider the art of portraiture. The desire to hand down one's likeness to posterity produced one of the chief social arts of the postmedieval world. It did so because the portrait painters of the time had behind them an immense weight of *volonté générale*. The sitters participated because they knew that their desire to perpetuate their likenesses could not be achieved in any other way. Now, no one supposes that a photograph, however skillful, is comparable with a Goya as a work of art, or even as a likeness. But the fact that photography exists, and can tell us far more accurately than a mediocre painting what people looked like, has knocked away the foundation upon which portraiture rested. There is no longer a feeling of participation in the sitters. The portrait painter no longer feels

that he is really needed, any more than ornament is need on a building; and so he, too, has become an anachronism.

32. The portrait is typical of the decline of confidence in art which is felt unconsciously by the mass of people as a result of the camera. There is however one form of popular imagery which is not entirely dependent on photography, and that is the poster. Here, a number of my conditions for a healthy relationship between art and society obtain. Posters are made on behalf of a minority and aim at supporting some belief; they appeal to a majority, and millions of people derive from them what they take to be information about matters which they believe to be important. Moreover, posters achieve their effects through the use of symbols, and it is a curious fact that the ordinary man will accept in posters a symbolic treatment, a freedom from realism, which he would not accept in a picture framed in a gallery, simply because a poster does not exist for its own sake, but is concerned with something he needs. All this is true, and yet we know that in spite of many effective and memorable posters, advertising has not produced an art comparable to the windows of Chartres Cathedral; and never can. The reason is, of course, that it lacks what I have called the sacramental element in art. I said earlier that the nearest equivalent in modern life to the building of a medieval cathedral was the construction of a giant liner. But the liner is built for the convenience of passengers and the benefit of shareholders. The cathedral was built to the glory of God. One might add that advertising art is concerned with lies, of a relatively harmless and acceptable kind; but one must remember that the great art of the past was also concerned with lies, often of a much more dangerous kind. The difference is not one of truth, but of the different realms to which these two forms of art belong—the realm of matter and the realm of spirit.

33. I need not press any further the point that the philosophy of materialism is hostile to art. But what about its two noble kinsmen, humanitarianism and science? Although they are to a great extent committed to measure-

ment, they are not wholly materialistic. They recognize values which we may call moral, intellectual, and even aesthetic. They are the integrating beliefs of the last 150 years. How are they connected with art?

34. The more enlightened supporters of humanitarianism have often bewailed the fact that art seems to have flourished in societies which were quite the reverse of humane. Yet we feel instinctively that this is natural; that kindness, mildness, decency, are not as likely to produce art as violence, passion, and ruthlessness. One of the most ancient and persistent images in art is the lion devouring a horse or deer; and it must puzzle the humanitarian mind that this bloodthirsty episode came to be accepted as a suitable decoration for pagan sarcophagi; then entered Christian iconography as a symbol of the spiritual life; and finally became the dominating motif of the only great religious painter of the nineteenth century, Delacroix. The answer is given in Blake's *Marriage of Heaven and Hell,* and I will not be so foolish as to elaborate it. But I may quote the words of a great living painter: "It isn't enough to have the eyes of a gazelle; you also need the claws of a cat in order to capture your bird alive and play with it before you eat it and so join its life to yours." To put it less picturesquely, art depends on a condition of spiritual energy, which must devour and transform all that is passive and phlegmatic in life, and no amount of good will can take the place of this creative hunger.

35. I am not saying that violence and brutality *beget* art, or that there is not still far too much violence and brutality left in the world. The bright new towns in our welfare state are an achievement of which humanity may be proud. But do not let us suppose that this peaceful, humdrum, hell-free, de-Christianized life has been achieved without loss. And apart from the unlikeliness of art being forged at such a low temperature, the doctrine of equality and the drift toward equality, on which such a society depends, run counter to one of my first laws. We have many reliable indications of what Mr. and Mrs. Honest Everyman really want. We don't need surveys and questionnaires—only a glance at suburban or provincial furniture stores and television advertisements. There we see the art of a prosperous democracy—the art that is easily unwrapped—the art of least resistance. This would not matter much, were it not that Gresham's law—that bad money drives out good—is equally true of spiritual currency; and we are all surrounded by far more bad art than we are aware of. I observed during the war, when the amount of conspicuous waste was cut down in the interest of economy, and objects of daily use, like teacups, were made without even a curve, let alone a pattern, that the appetite for real works of art was much keener and more discriminating than it was before.

36. With science the position is rather different. It is not so much a soil in which art will not grow as it is a rival crop. The development of physical science in the last hundred years has been one of the most colossal efforts the human intellect has ever made. Now, I think it is arguable that human beings can produce, in a given epoch, only a certain amount of creative power, and that this is directed to different ends at different times; and I believe that the dazzling achievements of science during the last seventy years have deflected many of those skills and endowments which go to the making of a work of art. To begin with, there is the sheer energy. In every molding of a Florentine palace we are conscious of an immense intellectual energy, and it is the absence of this energy in the nineteenth-century copies of Renaissance buildings which makes them seem so dead. To find a form with the same vitality as the window moldings of the Palazzo Strozzi, I must wait till I get back into an airplane, and look at the relation of the engine to the wing. That form is alive, not (as used to be said) because it is functional—many functional shapes are entirely uninteresting—but because it is animated by the breath of modern science.

37. The deflections from art to science are the more serious because these are not, as used to be supposed, two contrary activities, but draw on many of the same capacities of the human mind. In the last resort each depends on the imagination. Artist and scientist alike

are trying to give concrete form to dimly apprehended ideas. Both, in the words of Aristotle's famous definition of poetry, are hoping "to see similars in dissimilars." "All science," says Dr. Bronowski, "is the search for unity in hidden likenesses, and the starting point is an image, because then the unity is before our mind's eye." He gives the example of how Copernicus' notion of the solar system was inspired by the old astrological image of man with the signs of the Zodiac distributed about his body, and notices how Copernicus uses warm-blooded expressions to describe the chilly operations of outer space. "The earth conceives from the sun" or "The sun rules a family of stars." Our scientists are no longer as anthropomorphic as that; but they still depend on humanly comprehensible images, and the valid symbols of our time, invented to embody some scientific truth, have taken root in the popular imagination. Do those red and blue balls connected by rods really resemble a type of atomic structure? I am too ignorant to say, but I accept the symbol just as an early Christian accepted the Fish or the Lamb, and I find it echoed or even (it would seem) anticipated in the work of modern artists like Kandinsky and Miró.

38. Finally there is the question of popular interest and approval. The position of science in the modern world illustrates clearly what I meant by a vital relationship with society. Science is front-page news; every child has a scientific toy; small boys dream of space ships; big boys know how to make a radio set. What does a compulsory visit to an art museum mean compared to this? An opportunity to fool about and hide behind the showcases? And, at the other end of the scale, the research scientist has universities competing for his favors with millions of dollars' worth of plant and equipment, while principalities and powers wait breathless for his conclusions. So he goes to work, as Titian once did, confident that he will succed, because he knows that everybody needs him.

39. Such are the conclusions which force themselves upon me when I examine, in the light of history, the present relations of art and society. Those who care for art and feel a sense of loyalty to their own times may feel it their duty to refute these conclusions, but I think they will find it difficult to do so without straining the evidence. Does this mean that a broadly based social art is unlikely to appear for a long time? I am inclined to think so. This is not as catastrophic as it sounds. At least 90 per cent of our fellow countrymen get on very well without art, and I don't quite know why we should bother about them or try to persuade them to take an interest. No one tries to persuade me to take an interest in racing. And yet some instinct I can neither define nor defend makes me believe that people without art are incomplete and that posterity will have a poor opinion of them; and so I peer anxiously into the dark scene I have described. This is what I find.

40. The fact that art is not only tolerated, but actually supported by government and municipal funds, although it is hardly worth a single vote and practically no politician has the faintest belief or interest in it, shows that it has retained some of its magic power. The unbelieving majority still recognize that the believing minority, in picture galleries and concert halls, achieve a state of mind of peculiar value. There are very few people who have never had an aesthetic experience, either from the sound of a band or the sight of a sunset or the action of a horse. The words "beauty" and "beautiful" often pass the lips of those who have never looked at a work of art—oftener, perhaps, than they pass the lips of museum curators—and some meaning must be attached to them.

41. I believe that the majority of people really long to experience that moment of pure, disinterested, nonmaterial satisfaction which causes them to ejaculate the word "beautiful"; and since this experience can be obtained more reliably through works of art than through any other means, I believe that those of us who try to make works of art more accessible are not wasting our time. But how little we know of what we are doing. I am not even sure that museum art and its modern derivatives, however extended and skillfully contrived, will ever bring about a healthy re-

lationship between art and society. It is too deeply rooted in cultural values which only a small minority can acquire.

42. Here we reach the crux of the problem: the nature of the elite. It was my first conclusion that art cannot exist without one, my second that the elite must inspire confidence in the majority. During the last hundred years values in art have been established by a minority so small and so cut off from the sources of life, that it cannot be called an elite in my sense of the word. Let us call it a priesthood, and add that in preserving its mysteries from the profanation of all-conquering materialism, it has made them rather too mysterious. There is something admirable in all forms of bigotry, but I do not believe that we can return to a healthy relationship between art and society over so narrow a bridge. On the contrary, I believe that our hope lies in an expanding elite, an elite drawn from every class, and with varying degrees of education, but united in a belief that nonmaterial values can be discovered in visible things.

43. Is it fatuous to interpret the large sale of books on art and the relative success of certain television programs as a sign that such an elite is forming? But even if these are genuine snowdrops, and not paper flowers stuck in the woods by hopeful highbrows, many obstacles will remain. There is a lack of an iconography. There is the glut of false art which blunts our appetites. There is even the danger that true art may be degraded through the media of mass communications. But I believe that all these obstacles can be overcome if only the *need* for art, which lies dormant and unperceived in the spirit of every man, yet is manifested by him unconsciously every day, can be united with the *will* to art which must remain the endowment, and the responsibility, of the happy few.

E. M. FORSTER

Art for Art's Sake[1]

Edward Morgan Forster (1879–   ), one of England's most distinguished writers, is a lecturer and an honorary member of the American Academy of Arts and Letters. (Other biographical details are given in the headnote for his "What I Believe," page 172.)

In this essay Mr. Forster emphasizes the chaotic, unstable nature of the material universe and discusses the function of art in it.

[1] An address delivered before the American Academy of Arts and Letters in New York, 1949.

ART FOR ART'S SAKE From *Two Cheers for Democracy*, copyright, 1938, 1939, 1947, 1949, 1951, by E. M. Forster. Reprinted by permission of Harcourt, Brace & World, Inc.

1. I believe in art for art's sake. It is an unfashionable belief, and some of my statements must be of the nature of an apology. Fifty years ago I should have faced you with more confidence. A writer or a speaker who chose "Art for Art's Sake" for his theme fifty years

ago could be sure of being in the swim, and could feel so confident of success that he sometimes dressed himself in esthetic costumes suitable to the occasion—in an embroidered dressing gown, perhaps, or a blue velvet suit with a Lord Fauntleroy collar; or a toga, or a kimono, and carried a poppy or a lily or a long peacock's feather in his medieval hand. Times have changed. Not thus can I present either myself or my theme today. My aim rather is to ask you quietly to reconsider for a few minutes a phrase which has been much misused and much abused, but which has, I believe, great importance for us—has, indeed, eternal importance.

2. Now we can easily dismiss those peacock's feathers and other affectations—they are but trifles—but I want also to dismiss a more dangerous heresy, namely the silly idea that only art matters, an idea which has somehow got mixed up with the idea of art for art's sake, and has helped to discredit it. Many things, besides art, matter. It is merely one of the things that matter, and high though the claims are that I make for it, I want to keep them in proportion. No one can spend his or her life entirely in the creation or the appreciation of masterpieces. Man lives, and ought to live, in a complex world, full of conflicting claims, and if we simplified them down into the esthetic he would be sterilised. Art for art's sake does not mean that only art matters, and I would also like to rule out such phrases as "The Life of Art," "Living for Art," and "Art's High Mission." They confuse and mislead.

3. What does the phrase mean? Instead of generalising, let us take a specific instance—Shakespeare's *Macbeth,* for example, and pronounce the words, "*Macbeth* for *Macbeth's* sake." What does that mean? Well, the play has several aspects—it is educational, it teaches us something about legendary Scotland, something about Jacobean England, and a good deal about human nature and its perils. We can study its origins, and study and enjoy its dramatic technique and the music of its diction. All that is true. But *Macbeth* is furthermore a world of its own, created by

Shakespeare and existing in virtue of its own poetry. It is in this aspect *Macbeth* for *Macbeth's* sake, and that is what I intend by the phrase "art for art's sake." A work of art—whatever else it may be—is a self-contained entity, with a life of its own imposed on it by its creator. It has internal order. It may have external form. That is how we recognise it.

4. Take for another example that picture of Seurat's which I saw two years ago in Chicago—"*La Grande Jatte.*" Here again there is much to study and to enjoy: the pointillism, the charming face of the seated girl, the nineteenth-century Parisian Sunday sunlight, the sense of motion in immobility. But here again there is something more; "*La Grande Jatte*" forms a world of its own, created by Seurat and existing by virtue of its own poetry: "*La Grande Jatte*" pour "*La Grande Jatte*": *l'art pour l'art.* Like *Macbeth* it has internal order and internal life.

5. It is to the conception of order that I would now turn. This is important to my argument, and I want to make a digression, and glance at order in daily life, before I come to order in art.

6. In the world of daily life, the world which we perforce inhabit, there is much talk about order, particularly from statesmen and politicians. They tend, however, to confuse order with orders, just as they confuse creation with regulations. Order, I suggest, is something evolved from within, not something imposed from without; it is an internal stability, a vital harmony, and in the social and political category, it has never existed except for the convenience of historians. Viewed realistically, the past is really a series of *dis*orders, succeeding one another by discoverable laws, no doubt, and certainly marked by an increasing growth of human interference, but disorders all the same. So that, speaking as a writer, what I hope for today is a disorder which will be more favourable to artists than is the present one, and which will provide them with fuller inspirations and better material conditions. It will not last—nothing lasts—but there have been some advantageous disorders in the

past—for instance, in ancient Athens, in Renaissance Italy, eighteenth-century France, periods in China and Persia—and we may do something to accelerate the next one. But let us not again fix our hearts where true joys are not to be found. We were promised a new order after the first world war through the League of Nations. It did not come, nor have I faith in present promises, by whomsoever endorsed. The implacable offensive of Science forbids. We cannot reach social and political stability for the reason that we continue to make scientific discoveries and to apply them, and thus to destroy the arrangements which were based on more elementary discoveries. If Science would discover rather than apply—if, in other words, men were more interested in knowledge than in power—mankind would be in a far safer position, the stability statesmen talk about would be a possibility, there could be a new order based on vital harmony, and the earthly millennium might approach. But Science shows no signs of doing this: she gave us the internal combustion engine, and before we had digested and assimilated it with terrible pains into our social system, she harnessed the atom, and destroyed any new order that seemed to be evolving. How can man get into harmony with his surroundings when he is constantly altering them? The future of our race is, in this direction, more unpleasant than we care to admit, and it has sometimes seemed to me that its best chance lies through apathy, uninventiveness, and inertia. Universal exhaustion might promote that Change of Heart which is at present so briskly recommended from a thousand pulpits. Universal exhaustion would certainly be a new experience. The human race has never undergone it, and is still too perky to admit that it may be coming and might result in a sprouting of new growth through the decay.

7. I must not pursue these speculations any further—they lead me too far from my terms of reference and maybe from yours. But I do want to emphasize that order in daily life and in history, order in the social and political category, is unattainable under our present psychology.

8. Where is it attainable? Not in the astronomical category, where it was for many years enthroned. The heavens and the earth have become terribly alike since Einstein. No longer can we find a reassuring contrast to chaos in the night sky and look up with George Meredith to the stars, the army of unalterable law, or listen for the music of the spheres. Order is not there. In the entire universe there seem to be only two possibilities for it. The first of them—which again lies outside my terms of reference—is the divine order, the mystic harmony, which according to all religions is available for those who can contemplate it. We must admit its possibility, on the evidence of the adepts, and we must believe them when they say that it is attained, if attainable, by prayer. "O thou who changest not, abide with me," said one of its poets. *"Ordina questo amor, o tu che m'ami,"* said another: "Set love in order, thou who lovest me." The existence of a divine order, though it cannot be tested, has never been disproved.

9. The second possibility for order lies in the esthetic category, which is my subject here: the order which an artist can create in his own work, and to that we must now return. A work of art, we are all agreed, is a unique product. But why? It is unique not because it is clever or noble or beautiful or enlightened or original or sincere or idealistic or useful or educational—it may embody any of those qualities—but because it is the only material object in the universe which may possess internal harmony. All the others have been pressed into shape from outside, and when their mold is removed they collapse. The work of art stands up by itself, and nothing else does. It achieves something which has often been promised by society, but always delusively. Ancient Athens made a mess—but the *Antigone* stands up. Renaissance Rome made a mess—but the ceiling of the Sistine got painted. James I made a mess—but there was *Macbeth.* Louis XIV—but there was *Phèdre.* Art for art's sake? I should just think so, and more so than ever at the present time. It is the one orderly product which our muddling race has produced. It is the cry of a

thousand sentinels, the echo from a thousand labyrinths; it is the lighthouse which cannot be hidden: *c'est le meilleur témoignage que nous puissions donner de notre dignité.*[2] *Antigone* for *Antigone's* sake, *Macbeth* for *Macbeth's*, "La Grande Jatte" pour "La Grande Jatte."

10. If this line of argument is correct, it follows that the artist will tend to be an outsider in the society to which he has been born, and that the nineteenth-century conception of him as a Bohemian was not inaccurate. The conception erred in three particulars: it postulated an economic system where art could be a full-time job, it introduced the fallacy that only art matters, and it overstressed idiosyncrasy and waywardness—the peacock-feather aspect—rather than order. But it is a truer conception than the one which prevails in official circles on my side of the Atlantic—I don't know about yours: the conception which treats the artist as if he were a particularly bright government advertiser and encourages him to be friendly and matey with his fellow citizens, and not to give himself airs.

11. Estimable is mateyness, and the man who achieves it gives many a pleasant little drink to himself and to others. But it has no traceable connection with the creative impulse, and probably acts as an inhibition on it. The artist who is seduced by mateyness may stop himself from doing the one thing which he, and he alone, can do—the making of something out of words or sounds or paint or clay or marble or steel or film which has internal harmony and presents order to a permanently disarranged planet. This seems worth doing, even at the risk of being called uppish by journalists. I have in mind an article which was published some years ago in the London *Times*, an article called "The Eclipse of the Highbrow," in which the "Average Man" was exalted, and all contemporary literature was censured if it did not toe the line, the precise position of the line being naturally known to the writer of the article. Sir Kenneth Clark, who was at that time director of our

[2] [It is the best testimony that we can give of our dignity.]

National Gallery, commented on this pernicious doctrine in a letter which cannot be too often quoted. "The poet and the artist," wrote Clark, "are important precisely because they are not average men; because in sensibility, intelligence, and power of invention they far exceed the average." These memorable words, and particularly the words "power of invention," are the Bohemian's passport. Furnished with it, he slinks about society, saluted now by a brickbat and now by a penny, and accepting either of them with equanimity. He does not consider too anxiously what his relations with society may be, for he is aware of something more important than that—namely the invitation to invent, to create order, and he believes he will be better placed for doing this if he attempts detachment. So round and round he slouches, with his hat pulled over his eyes, and maybe with a louse in his beard, and—if he really wants one—with a peacock's feather in his hand.

12. If our present society should disintegrate—and who dare prophesy that it won't? —this old-fashioned and démodé figure will become clearer: the Bohemian, the outsider, the parasite, the rat—one of those figures which have at present no function either in a warring or a peaceful world. It may not be dignified to be a rat, but many of the ships are sinking, which is not dignified either—the officials did not build them properly. Myself, I would sooner be a swimming rat than a sinking ship—at all events I can look around me for a little longer—and I remember how one of us, a rat with particularly bright eyes called Shelley, squeaked out, "Poets are the unacknowledged legislators of the world," before he vanished into the waters of the Mediterranean.

13. What laws did Shelley propose to pass? None. The legislation of the artist is never formulated at the time, though it is sometimes discerned by future generations. He legislates through creating. And he creates through his sensitiveness and his power to impose form. Without form the sensitiveness vanishes. And form is as important today, when the human race is trying to ride the whirlwind, as it ever was in those less agitat-

ing days of the past, when the earth seemed solid and the stars fixed, and the discoveries of science were made slowly, slowly. Form is not tradition. It alters from generation to generation. Artists always seek a new technique, and will continue to do so as long as their work excites them. But form of some kind is imperative. It is the surface crust of the internal harmony, it is the outward evidence of order.

14. My remarks about society may have seemed too pessimistic, but I believe that society can only represent a fragment of the human spirit, and that another fragment can only get expressed through art. And I wanted to take this opportunity, this vantage ground, to assert not only the existence of art but its pertinacity. Looking back into the past, it seems to me that that is all there has ever been: vantage grounds for discussion and creation, little vantage grounds in the changing chaos, where bubbles have been blown and webs spun, and the desire to create order has found temporary gratification, and the sentinels have managed to utter their challenges, and the huntsmen, though lost individually, have heard each other's calls through the impenetrable wood, and the lighthouses have never ceased sweeping the thankless seas. In this pertinacity there seems to me, as I

grow older, something more and more profound, something which does in fact concern people who do not care about art at all.

15. In conclusion, let me summarize the various categories that have laid claim to the possession of Order.

1. The social and political category. Claim disallowed on the evidence of history and of our own experience. If man altered psychologically, order here might be attainable; not otherwise.

2. The astronomical category. Claim allowed up to the present century, but now disallowed on the evidence of the physicists.

3. The religious category. Claim allowed on the evidence of the mystics.

4. The esthetic category—the subject of this article. Claim allowed on the evidence of various works of art; and on the evidence of our own creative impulses, however weak these may be, or however imperfectly they may function. Works of art, in my opinion, are the only objects in the material universe to possess internal order, and that is why, though I don't believe that only art matters, I do believe in Art for Art's Sake.

T. K. WHIPPLE

Machinery, Magic, and Art

Thomas King Whipple (1890–1939), who was a professor of English at the University of California for several years, published magazine articles such as this one in the *Saturday Review*. In 1928 his *Spokesmen*, a book appraising the chief American authors of the 1920's, made its appearance.

In contrast to Forster's statements in "Art for Art's Sake," Whipple maintains that art must serve a useful purpose. Only when it does so, he holds, will art and the artist regain their proper importance in society.

1. Some people seem to feel, vaguely and perhaps uncomfortably, that the arts somehow ought to be thought of as important. We permit our children in school to give their time to music and drawing. Our self-made men often devote part of their hard-won earnings to paintings or old books. As soon as our cities accumulate a little spare capital, they start public libraries and orchestras and art galleries. Nevertheless, the lot of the arts is not an altogether happy one. The practitioner of any art is apt to feel that the homage paid the arts is largely sham, and that he is in reality surrounded by a vast ocean of indifference and incomprehension. He and his cohorts are inclined to take to scolding the public or the nation. And the public, on the other hand, when at intervals it is seized with compunction and decides to investigate what is happening in the arts, is likely to find itself puzzled and vexed, and forced to the conclusion that the modern painter or musician or poet "only does it to annoy." It gladly returns to its old favorites, or to its old unconcern.

2. Meanwhile, becalmed upon this windless sea of neglect, the artists and their hangers-on degenerate into connoisseurs and virtuosos and technicians, and quarrel over the functions and purposes of their several arts, and lament the crassness of the modern age. Yet the responsibility for the present unsatisfactory state of affairs must be charged chiefly to the artists. The modern age—for all the disparagement of it which we hear from those who do not belong to it in spirit—is as good as another, if not better. And the public is on the whole right—right in its sense both that the arts ought to be important, and that they somehow aren't. Surely, everyone has a drastic, vital need of art—for reasons which I shall try to set forth later on. And for a long time now the arts have done little to fill this need. In other words, they neglect their most important function.

3. Both artists and critics are apparently unaware of the function I have in mind. In the

MACHINERY, MAGIC, AND ART From the *Saturday Review*, July 11, 1931. Reprinted by permission of the publishers.

theoretical discussions which rage among the specialists, many purposes are propounded—and these, it is true, the arts fulfil: they give much pleasure, they afford self-expression to many, they supply a representation, an interpretation, a criticism, of life. At their best, they do what Robert Frost says art should do —"strip life to form." Yet the fact remains that nowadays painting and music and literature are luxury products, epiphenomena—and this condition, I insist, is both wrong and needless. It is due to the arts having forsaken their essential office.

4. To turn to the one art that really flourishes in our time is instructive—engineering, and especially mechanical engineering. The fact that this is not a fine art, but a utilitarian one, long prevented it from being recognized as an art at all. However, the presupposition that nothing useful can be art, a notion general among both the esthetic clans and the laity, is directly opposite to truth, and has wrought great harm. On the contrary, there ought to be no fine arts, but only useful ones. And mechanical engineering has prospered because there is no doubt as to what it accomplishes, and because that is something everybody wants done: it transmits and regulates power, and everyone wants command of power, ever more power. Thus, this one art that thrives has two lessons to teach the fine arts: that any art can flourish if it will satisfy a strong universal desire; and that what men crave is power. In other words, I suggest that artists set themselves the same end as mechanicians, the communication and control of power. This is the all-important function which modern art has abandoned.

5. Of late there has been some talk, and very interesting talk, too, about machines as works of art. Why not reverse the process, and look at works of art as machines? Such an identification of art and machinery is not unwarranted. In the beginning, they were one and the same thing, they served the same single object, the gaining and ruling of power. This was in the days when they were both indistinguishable parts of primitive magic. As they have developed and differentiated, however, machinery has remained true to its origi-

nal purpose, but has specialized in handling only physical power. Art, on the other hand, which should specialize in conveying psychological power, has relinquished its office. Consequently, it finds itself in the doldrums, although it has vital work to do that can be done by no other agency. The world has urgent need of it; both the world and art would benefit if the arts could be persuaded to resume their original and proper business, to play once again the rôle they played in early magic.

6. The mention of magic ought not to be too surprising. It has long been recognized that in primitive magic lies a chief source of both science and art. Magic is the savage's engineering, his technology. It is his effort to get command of power and direct it to his own purpose. By mimicry, incantation, and the other methods of magic, he undertakes to control the wind and the rains, to induce fecundity in his tribe, to make his crops grow. Always he has in view, according to his lights, what Bacon foretold as the chief service of natural science, "the relief of man's estate." And it must be remembered that to him magic is in a sense not magic, and certainly not to be divided from science and art. To divert the waters of a stream to his cornfield, to sprinkle it with holy meal, and to make a song or a statue for the benefit of his grain, are for him not only equally valid, but essentially similar means of attaining his end.

7. Furthermore, it must be remembered also that, not discriminating as we do between objective and subjective, he sees physical and psychological energy as all one. He conceives of a universal potency in which all things share to a greater or lesser degree; the terms of the Maori and of the Sioux for this potency, *mana* and *wakanda* respectively. have come into wide use among anthropologists. The common American word is "medicine." Just as we wish above everything to get at what we call energy and use it for ourselves, so the savage wishes to avail himself of what he calls *mana*—the two words mean much the same thing. From the individual's private relations with the Powers Above and Below to the communal rites of the whole tribe, runs the same motive, the winning and directing of power.

8. After all, the ways of the savage are not so utterly different from our own. In time of war, for instance, as we invent new explosives and machine guns, he makes himself the best bow and arrows that he can. His fighters do their war dances; our soldiers march and sing. He paints the Thunderbird and other mighty spirits on his equipment to get their assistance; we try to reassure ourselves in our churches that Omnipotence is with us. It is curious to reflect how many of our devices for keeping up our morale, or for sustaining our tribal *wakanda*, are like those of the savage—that is, are magical. And very effective these devices are, too, as everybody knows.

9. For unquestionably there is truth in magic, as well as delusion—but it is psychological, not scientific truth. The love song or the war song, the amulet in which he has faith, beyond doubt render a man more irresistible in love or war, if only by heartening him. By similar means, it is probable, medicine men have succeeded in curing many illnesses. In the fertility rites of spring, we may question the efficacy of the ceremony with reference to the crops, but we have no reason to question its efficacy with reference to the tribe itself. In relation to external objects, we know that magic fails; but we ought to know also that with reference to the practitioners themselves it is likely to succeed: by means of it, they gain an access of energy—they gain the power they desire.

10. No one, I am sure, who has ever witnessed a genuine magical ceremony will question its effectiveness. Even the ignorant and infidel bystander gains from it a tremendous lift, a renewal, and an enhancement of strength. After all, we have our bodies, we are part animal, and to get a proper relation to our bodily animal energies, instincts, powers —the groundwork of our lives—is of enormous benefit.

11. Magic, then, insofar as it is efficacious and true, might be described as a kind of psychological machinery—that is, a set of devices by which the human being is enabled to avail himself of augmented psychological power, to

raise his vitality. "Psychic energy," to be sure, may be only a metaphor, a figure of speech which we use to cover our ignorance, because we know too little to speak literally and exactly. Indeed, we might as well use the primitive terms, and call it *mana, wakanda,* "medicine," mysterious potency. But the phenomenon itself, in some form or other, I am sure, is familiar to everyone; everyone, that is, must be conscious at times of possessing a peculiar abundance of vigor, and at other times of its dearth. We have various methods of securing this vigor; the primitive secures it by the practice of magic.

12. Among the means by which magic works, the two most important, I suspect, are images and rhythm. The savage sings, he dances, he beats his drum—magical practices are replete with rhythmical activities. And rhythmical activity, as we all know from our own experience, sets free our latent energies. Probably it affects our breathing, the beating of our hearts, and the other bodily processes which are themselves rhythmical, speeding them up or toning them down, heightening them and making them more regular. At any rate, whatever the cause, the effect of rhythm is familiar enough, from the savage's war dance to the congregational singing in church and to modern dancing.

13. As for images, their potency is perhaps less generally recognized. But consider the part played by images in magical procedure —in the typical case, for instance, of the warrior's magic, whether individual or communal. First of all, he holds before his mind an image of success, of victory; he pictures himself irresistibly slaying huge numbers of the enemy. Thus he gains confidence, and therefore power. Furthermore, he imagines himself receiving aid from nature; he keeps in his mind an image of Wind or Sun, thus associating and identifying himself with forces mightier than his own. So his own little "medicine" is enlarged by drawing upon the great "medicines" of the world, and he is bucked up, he feels that "virtue" has entered into him. A war song of the Blackfeet, rendered by Miss Eda Lou Walton, illustrates the process:

The earth is my home,
It is powerful.
Water speaks in foam,
It is powerful.
There sits a hill,
It is powerful.
I go now to kill,
I am powerful!

14. Strong as the image in the mind may be, however, its strength is immensely increased if it is embodied in something, and so objectified and externalized. The mere association of it with some external object seems to be of much help: the possession of a wolf's tooth or an eagle's feather, for example, aids in addressing prayer for ferocity or speed to the Wolf or Eagle Spirit—aids, presumably, by making more vivid and real the images involved. Still more effective is a drawing, a picture, a carving of wood or stone—any such representation of the Power to be won. This is the "image" in the sense of effigy or likeness, as in the Biblical phrase, "graven image." It is noteworthy that no religion has been able to get along without such images for long—a testimonial to the inability of most people to hold a mental image without help, and to the superior efficacy of the objective image. To the methods of achieving this result should be added the embodying of an image in the mimicry and movements of a dance, and the snaring of it in the words and music of a song. These last methods are of special consequence, because they unite strikingly the two most effectual of the instruments of magic, rhythm, and image.

15. According to the civilized view, the savage, in the act of creating his charm, whether fetish or song or dance, frees and utilizes latent energy in himself; and thereafter the charm has the capacity at proper moments again to make latent energy available, through working upon him with imagery and rhythm. But this, of course, is not at all the savage's view. He believes that the charm itself possesses the *mana;* and he further believes that once the charm is made, its *mana* becomes transferable. The original owner and maker, by giving his talisman to someone else, or by teaching his song or his dance to

another, can pass on with it its "medicine." Thus, a man, for instance, who makes a good hunting dance or song may be thought a great benefactor of his tribe. And quite properly, too, for these charms do no doubt produce much the same psychological effect upon others as upon the creators of them. So the man who devises a good war dance may make better fighters of all his clansmen, by enhancing their belligerent ardor.

16. It must be clear by this time what a large part magic has played in the origin of the arts. Other sources also may have contributed: probably wood was carved and pictures drawn for the mere fun of it; probably from the beginning some songs were sheer outbursts of spontaneous feeling. But serious art, art that mattered, was pretty well tied up with magic; a work of art was a magical machine, a contrivance for capturing *mana*, potency. Songs and dances were spells, charms; rituals and pantomimes developed into drama and opera and choral singing; modern fiction is related to the ceremonial rehearsing of sacred myths; and painting and sculpture began mainly in primitive fetishes and idols. Bach and Beethoven are lineal descendants of early shamans and medicine men. Art as well as science has grown out of the basic impulse which underlies magic. But whereas science, at least applied science, has remained true to its first aim, the arts, in our world, have drifted far away.

17. That is my complaint of them. In surrendering their practical usefulness, they have relinquished their chief excuse for being. And only, I am sure, when they return to their first function, when they become again channels of power, will they regain the robust vitality and the wide acceptance and understanding which they have forfeited. For everyone craves more vital energy, more medicine or *wakanda,* and when artists supply it, they will no longer have cause to complain of public indifference. The triumphs and services of science and engineering are no more momentous, I venture to say, in utilizing natural resources, than might be the triumphs and services of art in utilizing human resources.

18. All art that amounts to much has been true to its original function, and has attained its end by magical means—by rhythm and images, embodied, externalized images. The Greek tragedies were not performed, nor the Gothic cathedrals built, we may be sure, merely to gratify the esthetic sense, but to do something, to perform work on the beholders. Later artists, too, have been conscious of this aspect of their work. When Browning describes the effect on a band of pirates of listening to poetry, he says:

And then, because Greeks are Greeks,
And hearts are hearts, and *poetry is power*,
They all outbrake in a great joyous laughter
With much love.

The effect of, say, imagist verse on bands of Americans is very different from that. And before deciding that Americans are insensitive, let us ask "Is this poetry power?" Of all qualities demanded of poetry nowadays, we hear least of this, that it communicate power. And most of the poets, too, seem to have forgotten this purpose. But Browning was well aware of it, as witness his "Saul," in which David by singing wins Saul back from death to life, and in which Browning himself exemplifies the fact that poetry can be power, can be charged and surcharged with tremendous "medicine."

19. From the artist's point of view, Byron has said the last word: as the artist gives shape and body to his imaginings, he gets back from them the vitality he imparts, and thus increases the life that is in him:

'Tis to create, and in creating live
A being more intense, that we endow
With form our fancy, gaining as we give
The life we image.

20. The artist expends much energy, but somehow he gets back more. This is the magical and mysterious effect of artistic creation. It is as if the images, hidden in his mind, contained great stores of energy, but locked up, latent, inert, which are set free and made available. To take a conspicuous example of figures which have the kind of power in question, think of Michael Angelo's Night or his Adam: these figures, we may suppose, lay

secretly in Michael Angelo's mind, unknown to himself, rich in inactive power; then, as they rose before his mind at the moment of conception, and still more, vastly more, as he projected them in marble and in paint, this power was liberated and flooded his consciousness, so that, in Byron's words, he gained, as he gave it, the life he imaged, and lived "a being more intense." In other words, we may be sure that Night or Adam had for Michael Angelo the value that his fetish or his charm has for a savage—an embodiment and a source of supernal energy, of *wakanda*, of mysterious potency. Just as the primitive carves or paints or sings to get at this potency, so does the artist.

21. And just as the charm, together with its power, is transferable, so also—luckily for most of us—is the work of art. It is as if a great musical composition or building or play were an inexhaustible reservoir or store of energy. It transmits to us the power which its creator poured into it. Upon it we can draw for a heightening of vitality, for more abundant life. Nor should it be assumed that only the stately and sublime works of art possess this quality; on the contrary, much popular art has it, and indeed I question whether any art or artist that altogether lacks it can be widely popular. For example, I should say that "The Big Parade" and Charlie Chaplin and Fannie Brice and "Old Man River" and Zane Grey all have more or less of it. Perhaps, indeed, at present the lowbrow arts have more of it than the highbrow. But at any time people will flock to the artist who will move them, do something to them—who will give them that enhancement of life which we all crave. We care so much for it that we will even suffer to get it—and this, I am sure, is why we enjoy tragic art. In spite of the pain involved, the tragic spectacle exalts our own sense of life; it transmits to us the artist's passion and energy, and so gives us a lift, an augmented vitality. Freudians, and others before them, have maintained that all art, and tragedy in particular, is of service chiefly in cleansing bosoms of perilous stuff. But surely art's function is less important as a purgative or a safety-valve than as an unbounded source of energy.

22. I have suggested that art works upon us as magic works upon the savage—by rhythm, and by embodied images. But I think the effect of art is more understandable if for *rhythm* the larger term, *order* or *harmony*, is substituted. If a poem, a statue, or a building is patterned or ordered in form as it should be, if it is a harmonious embodiment of power, it conveys that power to us in order and harmony, and so induces a corresponding harmony in ourselves. Now most of us are seldom in a wholly harmonious state; most of the time much of our energy is absorbed and wasted in strains and conflicts, outer and inner; we do not often, so to speak, hit on all cylinders. Therefore, to be harmonized is for us to be energized—to be "put in order," literally, is to experience an increase of power. This is why form is all-important in art; it corresponds to efficiency in a machine; the power involved, instead of being lost, is communicated so as to do the work it ought to do.

23. If the form enables the power to be transmitted, the carrier of that power is the image. The importance of imagination is grossly underestimated today, probably because for various reasons modern life is marked by an exaggerated objectivity. But for all our externality, our running away from ourselves into outer circumstances and hectic activity, our lives are still largely ruled by images. We imagine ourselves wealthy, or powerful, or learned, or famous, or irresistible in love, or having exciting adventures, and we set ourselves to acquire what we have imagined. Many men and women, possessed by imagination, have cast themselves for rôles beyond their capacities, and striven to be superhuman heroes or saints or sages. For weal or woe, images have dominion over us, and it is of the utmost consequence that we be aware of them, conscious of what is happening, that we be not obsessed by them but judge their fitness for ourselves and our situation. And art, by embodying them in some external medium, helps us to this awareness, enables us to avoid obsession, to distinguish between ourselves and these images. It does not shear them of their power, but it changes that power from obsessive to beneficial.

24. Miss Rebecca West's phrase, "the potent image," is a good one. I have not meant to imply that any or every image is potent; most of them are not. One may imagine oneself walking downstairs or washing one's face, but the image has no special value for oneself or anyone else. And only potent images have value for art. The most valuable are those which are racial or national, or still better universal. The figure of Don Quixote has been of enormous worth to Spain; the figure of Robin Hood has had a particular attraction for Englishmen. Perhaps the nearest that America has come to such "potent images" is in Lincoln or Jesse James—the mythical, not the historical figures—or in the Indian. The Viking appeals to all northern races. Such figures as Prometheus, the Fire-bringer, or Faust, the man who sold himself to the devil, have a world-wide significance. The potent image, however, need not be human or even naturalistic. Oddly enough, it may even be mathematical. The embodiments in architecture and in music of abstract imagination, of pure form, can be as moving as any. There is no way, so far as I know, of telling which images will have potency, and which will not—but the quality itself is unmistakable.

25. Sometimes it looks as if modern artists by preference busied themselves with impotent images. They seem to avoid images which profoundly move themselves or anyone else, to be distrustful of imagination and above all of emotion. And they have their reward, in comparative neglect and misunderstanding. The public cannot be expected to comprehend, much less to care violently about, subtle problems of technique. But meanwhile, unfortunately, the public suffers even more than the artists from this state of affairs. To be sure, there is all the art of the past to draw upon, but somehow with the lapse of time works of art suffer a gradual loss of power. By no means a total loss, of course, or we should be hard put to it—but it would be absurd to suppose that the "Bacchae" of Euripides or "Le Misanthrope" of Molière can mean as much to us as to their original audiences. The images which were potent in ancient Greece or under the Ancien Régime are naturally much less potent in the twentieth century United States.

26. For these reasons, if we are to get the power which only art can give us, we must have artists of our own to convey it. And we are not without them. There is little ground to complain of our architects. Some of our writers perform their functions. Musicians seem less satisfactory; and only a few sculptors or painters in the United States aim at transmitting power. Just now, this function has been largely relegated to the cheapest practitioners—in literature, for instance, to Zane Grey and Edgar Rice Burroughs. However, there is no reason to suppose that the public prefers inadequate and incompetent art. O'Neill has not lacked his audiences, and even a poem—witness "John Brown's Body" —if it will do its job, can attract hordes of readers. But the public in its demands has been faithful to the original purpose of art; it asks magic and power, and if good artists deny it, it turns to bad ones.

27. The result is deplorable all round. While the artists take for their motto "No compromise with the public taste" and wither away in minute elaboration of their individual, private, and insignificant moods and sensations and skills, the public feeds on husks and straw. Yet I cannot believe that our artists are incapable of conceiving powerful forms and images of more than personal significance, which would profoundly stir them, and therefore us too. I believe rather that, misapprehending their function, they do not solicit such forms and images. For too long they have thought of themselves as playing no social rôle. It is as if a savage, instead of using his magic for the major purpose of living, were to use it only for private entertainment; as if a mechanical engineer, instead of helping get the world's work done, were to design only toys to amuse himself. We need the artists, as we need imperatively the kind of life and power which only they can supply. Let us beg them not to desert us utterly.

CLEMENT GREENBERG

The Case for Abstract Art

Clement Greenberg (1909–   ), a painter and art critic, has published many articles on art and has edited for *The Nation, Commentary,* and the *Partisan Review.* He has published full-length works on Miró and Matisse and is now completing a book on Jackson Pollock, the American painter. His *Art and Culture,* a collection of critical essays, appeared in 1961.

In this essay Mr. Greenberg defends "modernist art in general, or abstract art in particular" against the charge that it is pathological. Though Greenberg, Forster, and Whipple have varied points of view on the value and function of art, their views to some degree supplement and illuminate each other.

1. Many people say that the kind of art our age produces is one of the major symptoms of what's wrong with the age. The disintegration and, finally, the disappearance of recognizable images in painting and sculpture, like the obscurity in advanced literature, are supposed to reflect a disintegration of values in society itself. Some people go further and say that abstract, nonrepresentational art is pathological art, crazy art, and that those who practice it and those who admire and buy it are either sick or silly. The kindest critics are those who say it's all a joke, a hoax, and a fad, and that modernist art in general, or abstract art in particular, will soon pass. This sort of thing is heard or read pretty constantly, but in some years more often than others.

2. There seems to be a certain rhythm in the advance in popularity of modernist art, and a certain rhythm in the counterattacks which try to stem it. More or less the same works or arguments are used in all the po-

THE CASE FOR ABSTRACT ART From the *Saturday Evening Post,* August 1, 1959. Reprinted by special permission of The Saturday Evening Post and the author. © 1959 The Curtis Publishing Company.

lemics, but the targets usually change. Once it was the impressionists who were a scandal, next it was Van Gogh and Cézanne, then it was Matisse, then it was cubism and Picasso, after that Mondrian, and now it is Jackson Pollock. The fact that Pollock was an American shows, in a backhanded way, how important American art has lately become.

3. Some of the same people who attack modernist art in general, or abstract art in particular, happen also to complain that our age has lost those habits of disinterested contemplation, and that capacity for enjoying things as ends in themselves and for their own sake, which former ages are supposed to have cultivated. This idea has been advanced often enough to convert it into a cliché. I hate to give assent to a cliché, for it is almost always an oversimplification, but I have to make an exception in this case. While I strongly doubt that disinterested contemplation was as unalloyed or as popular in ages past as is supposed, I do tend to agree that we could do with more of it in this time, and especially in this country.

4. I think a poor life is lived by any one

who doesn't regularly take time out to stand and gaze, or sit and listen, or touch, or smell, or brood, without any further end in mind, simply for the satisfaction gotten from that which is gazed at, listened to, touched, smelled or brooded upon. We all know, however, that the climate of Western life, and particularly of American life, is not conducive to this kind of thing; we are all too busy making a living. This is another cliché, of course. And still a third cliché says that we should learn from Oriental society how to give more of ourselves to the life of the spirit, to contemplation and meditation, and to the appreciation of what is satisfying or beautiful in its own sole right. This last is not only a cliché, but a fallacy, since most Orientals are even more preoccupied than we are with making a living. I hope that I myself am not making a gross and reductive simplification when I say that so much of Oriental contemplative and aesthetic discipline strikes me as a technique for keeping one's eyes averted from ugliness and misery.

5. Every civilization and every tradition of culture seem to possess capacities for self-cure and self-correction that go into operation automatically, unbidden. If the given tradition goes too far in one direction it will usually try to right itself by going equally far in the opposite one. There is no question but that our Western civilization, especially in its American variant, devotes more mental energy than any other to the production of material things and services; and that, more than any other, it puts stress on interested, purposeful activity in general. This is reflected in our art, which, as has been frequently observed, puts such great emphasis on movement and development and resolution, on beginnings, middles, and endings—that is, on dynamics. Compare Western music with any other kind, or look at Western literature, for that matter, with its relatively great concern with plot and over-all structure and its relatively small concern with tropes and figures and ornamental elaborations; think of how slow-moving Chinese and Japanese poetry is by comparison with ours, and how much it delights in static situations; and how uncertain the narrational logic of non-Western fiction tends to be. Think of how encrusted

and convoluted Arabic poetry is by contrast even with our most euphuistic lyrical verse. And as for non-Western music, does it not almost always, and literally, strike us as more monotonous than ours?

6. Well, how does Western art compensate for, correct, or at least qualify its emphasis on the dynamic—an emphasis that may or may not be excessive? And how does Western life itself compensate for, correct, or at least qualify its obsession with material production and purposeful activity? I shall not here attempt to answer the latter question. But in the realm of art an answer is beginning to emerge of its own accord, and the shape of part of that answer is abstract art.

7. Abstract decoration is almost universal, and Chinese and Japanese calligraphy is quasi-abstract—abstract to the extent that few occidentals can read the characters of Chinese or Japanese writing. But only in the West, and only in the last fifty years, have such things as abstract pictures and free-standing pieces of abstract sculpture appeared. What makes the big difference between these and abstract decoration is that they are, exactly, pictures and free-standing sculpture—solo works of art meant to be looked at for their own sake and with full attention, and not as the adjuncts, incidental aspects, or settings of things other than themselves. These abstract pictures and pieces of sculpture challenge our capacity for disinterested contemplation in a way that is more concentrated and, I daresay, more conscious than anything else I know of in art. Music is an essentially abstract art, but even at its most rarefied and abstract, and whether it's Bach's or the middle-period Schoenberg's music, it does not offer this challenge in quite the same way or degree. Music tends from a beginning through a middle toward an ending. We wait to see how it "comes out"—which is what we also do with literature. Of course, the *total* experience of literature and music is completely disinterested, but it becomes that only at a further remove. While undergoing the experience we are caught up and expectant as well as detached—disinterested and at the same time interested in a way resembling that in which we are interested in how things turn

out in real life. I exaggerate to make my point—aesthetic experience *has* to be disinterested, and when it is genuine it always is, even when bad works of art are involved—but the distinctions I've made and those I've still to make are valid nevertheless.

8. With representational painting it is something like what it is with literature. This has been said before, many times before, but usually is order to criticize representational painting in what I think is a wrong-headed when not downright silly way. What I mean when I say, in this context, that representational painting is like literature, is that it tends to involve us in the interested as well as the disinterested by presenting us with the images of things that are inconceivable outside time and action. This goes even for landscapes and flower pieces and still lifes. It is not simply that we sometimes tend to confuse the attractiveness of the things represented in a picture with the quality of the picture itself. And it is not only that attractiveness as such has nothing to do with the abiding success of a work of art. What is more fundamental is that the meaning—as distinct from the attractiveness—of what is represented becomes truly inseparable from the representation itself. That Rembrandt confined impasto—thick paint, that is—to his highlights, and that in his later portraits especially these coincide with the ridges of the noses of his subjects is important to the artistic effect of these portraits. And that the effectiveness of the impasto, as impasto—as an abstract element of technique—coincides with its effectiveness as a means of showing just how a nose looks under a certain kind of light is also genuinely important. And that the lifelike delineation of the nose contributes to the evocation of the personality of the individual to whom the nose belongs is likewise important. And the manner and degree of insight into that individual's personality which Rembrandt exhibits in his portrait is important too. None of these factors can be, or ought to be, separated from the legitimate effect of the portrait as a picture pure and simple.

9. But once we have to do with personalities and lifelikeness we have to do with things from which we cannot keep as secure a distance for the sake of disinterestedness as we can, say, from abstract decoration. As it happens, the whole tendency of our Western painting, up until the later stages of impressionism, was to make distance and detachment on the part of the spectator as insecure as possible. It laid more of a stress than any other tradition on creating a sculpture-like, or photographic, illusion of the third dimension, on thrusting images at the eye with a lifelikeness that brought them as close as possible to their originals. Because of their sculptural vividness, Western paintings tend to be far less quiet, far more agitated and active—in short, far more explicitly dynamic—than most non-Western paintings do. And they involve the spectator to a much greater extent in the practical and actual aspects of the things they depict and represent.

10. We begin to wonder what we think of the people shown in Rembrandt's portraits, *as* people; whether or not we would like to walk through the terrain shown in a Corot landscape; about the life stories of the burghers we see in a Steen painting; we react in a less than disinterested way to the attractiveness of the models, real or ideal, of the personages in a Renaissance painting. And once we begin to do this we begin to participate in the work of art in a so-to-speak practical way. In itself this participation may not be improper, but it does become so when it begins to shut out all other factors. This it has done and does, all too often. Even though the connoisseurs have usually been able in the long run to prefer the picture of a dwarf by Velasquez to that of a pretty girl by Howard Chandler Christy, the enjoyment of pictorial and sculptural art in our society has tended, on every other level than that of professional connoisseurship, to be excessively "literary," and to center too much on merely technical feats of copying.

11. But, as I've said, every tradition of culture tends to try to correct one extreme by going to its opposite. And when our Western tradition of painting came up at last with reservations about its forthright naturalism, these quickly took the form of an equally forthright antinaturalism. These reservations started with late impressionism, and have now cul-

minated in abstract art. I don't at all wish to be understood as saying that it all happened because some artist or artists decided it was time to curb the excesses of realistic painting, and that the main historical significance of abstract art lies in its function as an antidote to these. Nor do I wish to be understood as assuming that realistic or naturalistic art inherently needs, or ever needed, such a thing as an antidote. The motivations, conscious and unconscious, of the first modernist artists, and of present modernists as well, were and are quite different. Impressionism itself started as an effort to push naturalism further than ever before. And all through the history of art—not only in recent times—consequences have escaped intentions.

12. It is on a different, and more impersonal, and far more general level of meaning and history that our culture has generated abstract art as an antidote. On that level this seemingly new kind of art has emerged as an epitome of almost everything that disinterested contemplation requires, and as both a challenge and a reproof to a society that exaggerates, not the necessity, but the intrinsic value of purposeful and interested activity. Abstract art comes, on this level, as a relief, an archexample of something that does not have to mean, or be useful for, anything other than itself. And it seems fitting, too, that abstract art should at present flourish most in this country. If American society is indeed given over as no other society has been to purposeful activity and material production, then it is right that it should be reminded, in extreme terms, of the essential nature of disinterested activity.

13. Abstract art does this in very literal and also in very imaginative ways. First, it does not exhibit the illusion or semblance of things we are already familiar with in real life; it gives us no imaginary space through which to walk with the mind's eye; no imaginary objects to desire or not desire; no imaginary people to like or dislike. We are left alone with shapes and colors. These may or may not remind us of real things; but if they do, they usually do so incidentally or accidentally—on our own responsibility as it were; and the genuine enjoyment of an abstract picture does

not ordinarily depend on such resemblances.

14. Second, pictorial art in its highest definition is static; it tries to overcome movement in space or time. This is not to say that the eye does not wander over a painted surface, and thus travel in both space and time. When a picture presents us with an illusion of real space, there is all the more inducement for the eye to do such wandering. But ideally the whole of a picture should be taken in at a glance; its unity should be immediately evident, and the supreme quality of a picture, the highest measure of its power to move and control the visual imagination, should reside in its unity. And this is something to be grasped only in an indivisible instant of time. No expectancy is involved in the true and pertinent experience of a painting; a picture, I repeat, does not "come out" the way a story, or a poem, or a piece of music does. It's all there at once, like a sudden revelation. This "at-onceness" an abstract picture usually drives home to us with greater singleness and clarity than a representational painting does. And to apprehend this "at-onceness" demands a freedom of mind and untrammeledness of eye that constitute "at-onceness" in their own right. Those who have grown capable of experiencing this know what I mean. You are summoned and gathered into one point in the continuum of duration. The picture does this to you, willy-nilly, regardless of whatever else is on your mind; a mere glance at it creates the attitude required for its appreciation, like a stimulus that elicits an automatic response. You become all attention, which means that you become, for the moment, selfless and in a sense entirely identified with the object of your attention.

15. The "at-onceness" which a picture or a piece of sculpture enforces on you is not, however, single or isolated. It can be repeated in a succession of instants, in each one remaining an "at-onceness," an instant all by itself. For the cultivated eye, the picture repeats its instantaneous unity like a mouth repeating a single word.

16. This pinpointing of the attention, this complete liberation and concentration of it, offers what is largely a new experience to most

people in our sort of society. And it is, I think, a hunger for this particular kind of experience that helps account for the growing popularity of abstract art in this country: for the way it is taking over in the art schools, the galleries, and the museums. The fact that fad and fashion are also involved does not invalidate what I say. I know that abstract art of the latest variety—that originating with painters like Pollock and Georges Mathieu—has gotten associated with progressive jazz and its cultists; but what of it? That Wagner's music became associated with German ultranationalism, and that Wagner was Hitler's favorite composer, still doesn't detract from its sheer quality as music. That the present vogue for folk music started, back in the 1930's, among the Communists doesn't make our liking for it any the less genuine, or take anything away from folk music itself. Nor does the fact that so much gibberish gets talked and written about abstract art compromise it, just as the gibberish in which art criticism in general abounds, and abounds increasingly, doesn't compromise art in general.

17. One point, however, I want to make glaringly clear. Abstract art is not a special kind of art; no hard-and-fast line separates it from representational art; it is only the latest phase in the development of Western art as a whole, and almost every "technical" device of abstract painting is already to be found in the realistic painting that preceded it. Nor is it a superior kind of art. I still know of nothing in abstract painting, aside perhaps from some of the near-abstract cubist works that Picasso, Braque and Léger executed between 1910 and 1914, which matches the highest achievements of the old masters. Abstract painting may be a purer, more quintessential form of pictorial art than the representational kind, but this does not of itself confer quality upon an abstract picture. The ratio of bad abstract painting to good is actually much greater than the ratio of bad to good representational painting. Nonetheless, the very best painting, the major painting, of our age is almost exclusively abstract. Only on the middle and lower levels of quality, on the levels below the first-rate—which is, of course, where most of the art that gets pro-

duced places itself—only there is the better painting preponderantly representational.

18. On the plane of culture in general, the special, unique value of abstract art, I repeat, lies in the high degree of detached contemplativeness that its appreciation requires. Contemplativeness is demanded in greater or lesser degree for the appreciation of every kind of art, but abstract art tends to present this requirement in quintessential form, at its purest, least diluted, most immediate. If abstract art—as does happen nowadays—should chance to be the first kind of pictorial art we learn to appreciate, the chances are that when we go to other kinds of pictorial art—to the old masters, say, and I hope we all do go to the old masters eventually—we shall find ourselves all the better able to enjoy them. That is, we shall be able to experience them with less intrusion of irrelevancies, therefore more fully and more intensely.

19. The old masters stand or fall, their pictures succeed or fail, on the same ultimate basis as do those of Mondrian or any other abstract artist. The abstract formal unity of a picture by Titian is more important to its quality than what that picture images. To return to what I said about Rembrandt's portraits, the whatness of what is imaged is not unimportant—far from it—and cannot be separated, really, from the formal qualities that result from the way it is imaged. But it is a fact, in my experience, that representational paintings are essentially and most fully appreciated when the identities of what they represent are only secondarily present to our consciousness. Baudelaire said he could grasp the quality of a painting by Delacroix when he was still too far away from it to make out the images it contained, when it was still only a blur of colors. I think it was really on this kind of evidence that critics and connoisseurs, though they were almost always unaware of it, discriminated between the good and the bad in the past. Put to it, they more or less unconsciously dismissed from their minds the connotations of Rubens' nudes when assessing and experiencing the final worth of his art. They may have remained aware of the pinkness as a *nude* pinkness, but it was a pinkness

and a nudity devoid of most of their usual associations.

20. Abstract paintings do not confront us with such problems. Or at least the frequenting of abstract art can train us to relegate them automatically to their proper place; and in doing this we refine our eyes for the appreciation of non-abstract art. That has been my own experience. That it is still relatively rare can be explained perhaps by the fact that most people continue to come to painting through academic art—the kind of art they see in ads and in magazines—and when and if they discover abstract art it comes as such an overwhelming experience that they tend to forget everything produced before. This is to be deplored, but it does not negate the value, actual or potential, of abstract art as an introduction to the fine arts in general, and as an introduction, too, to habits of disinterested contemplation. In this respect, the value of abstract art will, I hope, prove far greater in the future than it has yet. Not only can it confirm instead of subverting tradition; it can teach us, by example, how valuable so much in life can be made without being invested with ulterior meanings. How many people I know who have hung abstract pictures on their walls and found themselves gazing at them endlessly, and then exclaiming, "I don't know what there is in that painting, but I can't take my eyes off it." This kind of bewilderment is salutary. It does us good not to be able to explain, either to ourselves or to others, what we enjoy or love; it expands our capacity for experience.

HUBERT LAMB

Music in the Age of Zak

Hubert Weldon Lamb (1909–   ), music critic and composer, is chairman of the Music Department at Wellesley College. After graduating from Harvard University, Mr. Lamb studied composition in Paris, and subsequently was awarded a Guggenheim Fellowship. Characteristic of his musical acumen is an engaging article entitled "High Fidelity—To What?" which appeared in the January 1960 issue of *Harper's Magazine*.

"Music in the Age of Zak," given as an Honors Day address at Wellesley, challenges the so-called aleatory music as nonmusic in which abstruse manipulation has produced a spurious and trivial musical novelty.

1. Non-music, like the sister non-arts, lends itself to parody. The Philistine who playfully concocts a non-painting or a non-poem and

MUSIC IN THE AGE OF ZAK   From *Harper's Magazine*, May 1963. Copyright © 1963 by Harper's Magazine Inc. Reprinted from the May 1963 issue of *Harper's Magazine* by permission of the author.

succeeds in attracting serious public attention, to the subsequent embarrassment of connoisseurs and critics, can properly take satisfaction. He has not only fooled the professionals; he has exposed sham. It's best, certainly, not to keep it a secret if the idol has clay feet.

2. Piotr Zak's *Mobile for Tape and Percussion*—performed not long ago over the BBC and identified as an example of the newest in "aleatory music"—was accepted without objection by the audience and received with polite and serious attention by critics. When later it was revealed that Zak didn't exist and that the concoction was a hoax, perpetrated by two pranksters who "went around the studio" banging instruments, a few critics commented briefly on the implications of its reception. If the professional evaluators and the listening public were unable to distinguish a flippant parody from a genuine work of art, how was one to be sure any basic distinction existed? And if none existed, what reason was there to believe that "aleatory music" itself might not be a hoax? And if the shadow of suspicion was to fall on this kind of avant-garde music, what about other kinds?

3. Answers to these questions are worth looking into if we wish to distinguish between music and non-music. And it isn't aestheticians alone who are concerned. Music has become, in our society, a larger enterprise than ever before. Customers at record stores, patrons at box offices, fellowship committees of colleges and universities, foundations, and, through the Fulbright Act, the government itself—not to mention composers and performers—are all investors of time, thought, or money, in the present and future of music. Some of the investments are enlightened and productive. But support is too often given, in the name of Progress, to alluring enterprises which have little or nothing to do with music. *Caveat emptor.* It's up to the investor to distinguish between musical fraud and honesty. He clearly needs, in the Age of Zak, to know more both about the products he helps to produce and about their usefulness to society. And perhaps he should also know more about what the word "music" means.

4. Milton Babbitt, our leading apologist for "electronic music," recently produced a short article for the laity. He took as his point of departure the statement, "Music is, of course, sound." This is fine, as far as it goes. It suits Mr. Babbitt's particular purposes, and everyone, of course, would agree with it. But it doesn't go far enough to be generally useful.

It doesn't stipulate that the sounds of music are sounds of a certain kind; nor does it suggest that we can have music only when such sounds occur in coherent succession.

5. We lead our lives surrounded by sounds, and most of them are meaningful to us. The buzzer tells the office girls to take a coffee break. The ambulance siren says somebody has to get to the hospital in a hurry. And the town fire horn, of course, says there's a fire. But to someone standing directly across the street from the fire station, what the horn *says* is less important than the shattering physical impact of its sound. This is true also of the close thunderclap. Such sounds are not important to us because they state facts or raise or answer questions. They impose themselves on us primarily as *events to be experienced*, not as *signals to be interpreted*.

6. It's not necessary for a sound of this sort to be loud. The quiet lapping of waves is not important to us because of what it says about the weather or about fluid dynamics. We respond to it simply as a delightful sound. And we respond similarly to the thrush's song at sunset, not for what it tells us, but for what it is.

7. For purely musical purposes the composer can make use only of sounds that are events to be experienced. The musical sound is therefore necessarily free of significant factual, extramusical connotation. The search for explanations is as out of place at a concert as it is at a fireworks display, where speculation as to chemical content and packaging is clearly irrelevant. We *experience* fireworks. And we *experience* music. We're missing the point altogether if, in the bassoon's chromatic descent in the coda of the *Eroica's* first movement, we look for illustrations of the laws of acoustics or for insight into Beethoven's home life in 1804.

8. The experience of music has to do with metamorphosis. Eliot comments penetratingly on the nature of that experience, in *The Dry Salvages:*

> . . . music heard so deeply
> That it is not heard at all, but you are the music
> While the music lasts. . . .

9. We have all watched parades. As the band approaches, the sounds of the music stimulate us, setting off reactions in our bodily chemistry and affecting the way we feel. Until the band has moved away into the distance, our dispositions are not our own but are dispositions imposed upon us by the music. In the presence of marches and of dance music, whether or not we march or dance, we become marchers and dancers through an induced realignment of our feelings in keeping with what we hear.

10. Such metamorphosis may be thought of as a branch of magic. The composer and the performer are magicians, whose sole function is to enchant those who listen. The magic may be either black or white, that of the *Ça ira* of the French Revolution or of *Throw Out the Lifeline*. It may serve the purposes of the honky-tonk, the cathedral, the concert hall, or the living room. Music may be interesting. It may be enlightening. It may be entertaining. But its single indispensable attribute is its effectiveness as an agent of metamorphosis.

11. The production and dissemination of music in our society is big business. Distributors of canned music—from the self-effacing Muzak air-freshener and the beguiling radio commercial to the pornophony of the disk jockey's turntable and the jukebox—thrive because their products, for better or worse, bewitch those who listen to them. There's a market for magic; and that market is by no means limited to the magic of the tawdry and the tasteless. In concert halls, in performing groups, professional and amateur, in school and college classes, Americans show themselves aware of good music and deeply sensitive to it. Nor are we provincial in our tastes. The American audience is prepared to find enchantment in a Balinese dance, a medieval organum, a Viennese symphony of the 1880s, or a Bach cantata. And it's prepared to find enchantment, too, in what belongs particularly to us. The esteem in which our leading composers are held bears witness both to the American listener's readiness to accept our own new music and to the validity of that music itself.

12. Ives, Piston, Hanson, Thomson, Copland, and many others less well known, have given American music in our century a stature it never possessed before. This has been an era of solid and enlightened accomplishment. But, unhappily, it has seen the rise, here as in Europe, of a variety of non-musical aberrations sponsored, in music's name, by disenchanted experimenters, to whom the uses of the mathematician and the physicist are more congenial than those of the musician, and the enchantment of audiences is of little or no concern. And these aberrations, thanks partly to their shock value and partly to the persuasive casuistry of the proponents and their followers, have survived and flourished despite the apathy of a musically literate and discriminating public.

13. The search for progress by the avant-garde has reflected, in part, the restless and uncareful pursuit of novelty characteristic of our society. It has also reflected an unhappy inability to come to terms with a past which one is unwilling to accept and unable to reject.

14. Discovery, of course, is essential to art. The composer is an explorer, a Cortez or a Champlain, prepared to suffer hardship and frustration in the uncertain hope of returning, later on, with something negotiable. It's necessary for the composer to produce something of a sort not previously produced, and to the extent that he is aware of yesterday, he must take it into account. But yesterday in music now begins not thirty or forty years ago, as it used to, but somewhere around 1200 A.D. And if a knowledgeable composer, embarrassed by the old masters looking over his shoulder, becomes convinced that his music must stand in its flaming novelty as a rejection *in toto* of yesterday's, it's small wonder, in this age of rockets, that the temptation to go into orbit should prove irresistible.

15. The major musical explorations of our century, to date, were well launched by the mid-'twenties. In music, as in the other arts, it was a time of unrest and self-conscious searching for new identities. Stravinsky, Prokofiev, Bartók, and others had already presided over the musical liquidation of the nineteenth century. Their early music, in its barbaric

vigor and primitivism, had earned them the reputation of revolutionaries. But as they matured in music, what they wrote began to sound disconcertingly traditional: the Prokofiev of the *Third Piano Concerto* (1921), the Stravinsky of *Apollon Musagète* (1928), and the Ravel of the *Piano Concerto in G* (1931), of which, to Ravel's evident satisfaction, an admirer used the phrase *"tout à fait Bach"* in congratulating him after the premiere.

16. There had, after all, been no revolution. The word "revolution," as Bartók pointed out, seems, in fact, to have little application in music. Western music has progressed continuously, by a process of stylistic evolution, since the invention of polyphony in the twelfth century. Time after time, dedication to a set of prevailing fashions has led to excess and satiety, and music has reverted to a middle ground. It turned away in the Renaissance from the overinvolved complexity of the fifteenth century. It turned away in the time of Beethoven from the excessive formalities of Classicism. And early in our century the main current, predictably, turned away from the confusion and extravagance of the late Romantic style. The majority of the supposed iconoclasts, having freed themselves of their ungainly inheritance, set out, in the 'twenties and 'thirties, on a course wholly in keeping with traditional methods and purposes.

17. Schoenberg and his fellow explorers did not take part in this movement. Anyone familiar with Schoenberg's youthful work—*Transfigured Night* (1899) and the early songs—will be aware that he was a prodigiously gifted musician. He was also, by nature, an experimenter, a formulator of theories, and an articulate spokesman. But as a progressive in a time of change, Schoenberg differed from his non-Viennese counterparts. He was, in temperament and attitude, the child of post-Wagnerian Romanticism. The others were not. And when the others, for the most part, had turned their backs on the heritage of the late nineteenth century, Schoenberg and his followers were continuing to build on an ex-

tension of that heritage itself. And their building—since its foundations lay in a style already well past its vital maturity—quite naturally took peculiar forms.

18. They were composing a forbidding, obscure, implacably dissonant music in which theories, musical and supra-musical, played an important part. In making no concessions to the listener, this new music appealed strongly to the avant-garde disciple who was still in search of revolution and was disappointed at not finding it elsewhere. Here was something, whether he *liked* it or not, that really seemed to speak for a new era. It was incisive, unbending, and often unpalatable. It had about it a quality of audacity and uninhibited experiment that made it seem at home in the disillusionment and confusion of the postwar society.

19. But there's a fallacy here. Composers aren't spokesmen for their societies. They write music, not commentaries. Except in such practical matters as performance resources and varying consumer demands, the connection between a music and its place and time of origin has always been tenuous at best. We look in vain in the Mozart *Clarinet Concerto* (1791) for evidence either of the poverty in which the composer was forced to live or of concern over the disquieting news of the Terror in France. Nor do we find in *Les Noces* of Stravinsky (completed in Switzerland in 1917) any reflections of the holocaust in Western Europe, though Stravinsky was profoundly aware of its horrors.

20. Music is not a language. It's simply music. The violin is incapable of sounding truth as opposed to falsehood, nor can it take part in arguments. It is useful exclusively for the production of events in sound; and those events, whether they originate in a time of trouble or not, will be without significance if they fail to enchant. The phenomenon of music exists only because people are *changed* by music and under its influence they enjoy *themselves*.

21. During the Blitz, a musician friend of mine in London carried in his wallet a little poem of Robert Herrick which he had clipped from a newspaper. It reads:

Give me a man that is not dull,
When all the world with rifts is full:
But unamaz'd dares clearly sing,
Whenas the roof's a-tottering:
And, though it falls, continues still
Tickling the Citterne with his quill.

22. Here is someone who, confronted with calamity, prefers, by means of music, to remain aloof from his surroundings. He's not concerned with commentaries. He doesn't sing to bear witness to unhappy circumstances, but simply for the joy, in the face of that circumstance, of singing. In despair or not, he's interested only in enchantment. And the more appealing the music is, the better his purposes are served.

23. If music were representational—if it could transmit ideas instead of merely specifying sensations—we might well have in music an emphasis on the shocking and the calamitous comparable to that in the literary arts, in painting, and in sculpture. But music, like architecture, cannot present commentaries through which the distasteful can be made palatable and illuminating.

24. In combination with pantomime or with words, music, of course, can dispose us to an acute awareness of meanings. It's this faculty of music that lies behind our rich heritage of opera. But we must distinguish between the composer and the librettist. In scenes of confusion and horror, it's not the music that's confused and horrible. The composer's job is solely to project an appropriate enchantment, and to do this he must observe the *Rules of Order.*

25. The very first rule of music is that it shall be orderly. The enchantment of an audience is necessarily a cumulative process, and it depends upon the setting up of expectations, whether those expectations are fulfilled or not. Expectations cannot take shape in disorder. An incoherent music, however arresting its sonorities, will project at best a very shallow magic. Chaotic music is not a music eloquent of chaos—it's simply chaos itself.

26. The validity of a piece of music can be judged only in terms of a listener's response to it. The listener will be affected partly by the sounds themselves and partly by the musical implications of the sounds. Order in music has to do, then, not merely with what the listener hears but with what he makes of it. And what he makes will depend on his grasp of implications. He will be led continually to expect consequences implicit in what he hears. The Strauss waltz may conform too much to his expectations, and he'll find it dull. The *Grosse Fuge* of Beethoven may conform too little, and he'll find it confusing and unapproachable. But so long as he's in the presence of music, the listener is obliged, consciously or not, to react to the expected and the unexpected. The more acute his hearing and the wider his experience in music, the more deeply he will be affected by the extreme subtleties of implication upon which the accomplished magician depends.

27. The experiments of Schoenberg in the years before and immediately following the first world war resulted in music ingeniously ordered in theory and meticulously disordered in effect. In the compositions of the late Romantics—Mahler, Richard Strauss, and the young Schoenberg—tonality, through excessive chordal alteration, had become sufficiently confused to cause the listener often to lose track of destinations and to fail to distinguish the excursion from the road home. In Schoenberg's "atonality" there is no home. The twelve tones of the chromatic scale are equal in function and in importance; and tonal order —both in melody and harmony—and the implications resting on such an order, are therefore excluded.

28. It's not surprising, in view of Schoenberg's musical orientation and his readiness to experiment, that he should have developed a music to which the *Rules of Order,* in any normal sense, would not apply. Nor is it surprising, in view of his natural predisposition to theory, that he should have devised a methodical approach to the composition of such music. In 1923 he first used the so-called "serial" method of composition in which the composer confines himself exclusively to manipulation, in various melodic and chordal forms, of a basic sequence of tones.

29. The invention of this ingenious pro-

cedure did not lead, either in Schoenberg's music or in that of his associates, to a stylistic revolution. It was a method suited to purposes they had been sharing before. It was not dangerous for them. But in the decades to follow, it was to prove dangerous for music.

30. The danger has lain partly in the disorderly nature of the product the serial method is designed to produce, and partly in the fact that the method is a *system*. It's in the nature of systems to grow on their own. And the more a system proliferates, the more the application of it tends to become an end in itself. And, as everyone knows, systems in art provide a ready refuge for incompetence.

31. The systematic serial procedure, during the second quarter of the century, attracted increasing attention among the followers of Schoenberg-the-theorist who shared neither the background, the genius, nor the objectives of Schoenberg-the-musician. At their hands, System came to control every aspect of music; and submission to an evolving micro-orthodoxy of systematic perfection took on a quality of dedication it never possessed for Schoenberg.

32. The thoroughly up-to-date serialist of the 1960s—a follower of Stockhausen or of Boulez—will produce a composition made up, in melody, harmony, rhythm, dynamic scheme, and even in the specification of color, entirely of derivations systematically related to its basic formulae. His composition is, thus, an integral and exclusive realization of possibilities inherent in its point of departure. And some who speak for the serialists point out that this rigorous technical integrity is in line with the master works of the past, which are so often characterized by extreme economy of material and by concentration upon abstruse manipulation.

33. Procedural subtlety, of course, has played a part in music since the beginning, and often a very important part. Many of our richest experiences as listeners stem from the composer's eloquent application of principle. But in traditional music such application is functional. The elaborate isorhythm of the fifteenth-century Burgundians and the canonic writing of Bach are not abstract. They serve directly to enrich the listener's experience.

34. The proper serialist, in contrast, does not intend his audience to be aware of his ingenuity in manipulating materials. His composition contains order to the highest degree. But that order, a reflection only of involved, abstract calculation, is not to be heard. It is, in fact, an integral part of the finished product only because it dictated what that product might and might not contain. The analyst who painstakingly numbers notes in a serial score, seeking to unravel its technical complexities, will uncover no secrets of musical importance. His study, at best, can serve only to demonstrate the composer's patience and ingenuity. He need not look for the kinds of order that give rise to expectations. The avoidance of such order is one of the focal proprieties of serialism.

35. A composer, of course, can conform to parts of the serialist dogma while rejecting other parts. He can make use of certain of the procedures for purposes alien to the total serialist orthodoxy. Stravinsky, in the course of his gradual conversion to serialism, with half-a-century of traditional composition behind him, has again demonstrated, as Berg and many others had demonstrated before, that partial adherence to serialist disciplines is not incompatible with a traditional result. But, Stravinsky, from the beginning, has been a practitioner of functional order; and he has brought to his practice of serialism a cast of mind and a respect for traditional objectives distinctly out of keeping with rigorous serialist practice. It's worthwhile to note, however, that since Stravinsky first used serial procedures, the old magic has been most in evidence where, as in the *Septet* and in parts of *Agon*, the techniques of serialism are modified and restricted and are clearly not at odds with traditional purposes.

36. In its intellectuality and its rejection of traditional objectives and responsibilities, serialism is at home in 1963. And under Webern's influence, at the hands of a small company of gifted latterday Impressionists with a

very special flair for subtle and affecting sonority, serial procedure has recently played a part in provocative enterprises. But its widespread vogue among composers-at-large and their students has resulted in quantities of incoherent, kaleidoscopic pseudo-music—"washboard twelve-tone," to use Thomas Schippers' happy phrase—eloquent only sporadically and often by accident, constructed by craftsmen whose primary allegiance is not to the production of affecting musical experience but to the manipulation of hidden, secret orders.

37. If disordered music is hard on the audience, it's harder still on the performer. Everyone knows that complicated music is more difficult to play than simple music, and that in very complicated music even the masters make mistakes. But it's not generally known that disordered music poses performance problems that defy solution by traditional methods.

38. The experienced performer has learned that there is, even in a specified meter and tempo, no such thing as an absolute quarter-note. Quarter-notes are longer or shorter, depending on their context. And players of instruments that are not pre-tuned, as the piano and organ are, know that pitch, too, is relative. Recent research [1] has demonstrated that even when an overall pitch basis is specified, one E-flat differs markedly from another, depending both on other notes sounding with it and on the melodic design. How the performer sounds a particular E-flat quarter-note depends therefore, both in pitch and duration, on how he interprets its function in context. And to make that interpretation, he must be able to perceive an underlying order.

39. It's small wonder that so many performers, including the majority of our reigning virtuosi, have failed—in the face not of difficulty but of impossibility—to embrace the cause of disordered music with enthusiasm. Nor is it strange that some proponents of the avant-grade should have welcomed the opportunity of dispensing with performers alto-

gether. The opportunity came with the invention of the electronic recording machine.

40. To anyone who knows what fun it is to fool around with tape recorders, it's unnecessary to explain part of the impetus behind the rapid development of "electronic music." The tape recorder is not merely versatile, it invites experiment. It has enabled us to carry patterns of sound around like pieces of string and to assemble them into composite constructions by cutting them, splicing them, and superposing one on another. Patterns may be readily modified in pitch and speed, and they may be reversed. Oscillating tubes, as sources of pure sound, combined with filtering devices provide a limitless variety of sound structures. And it's possible, by means of electronic circuitry, to extend or to compress patterns of sound without altering their pitch. (The "composer," if he wished, could in fact construct an exactly accurate "performance" of *The Star-spangled Banner* which would last precisely forty-eight hours and another, perhaps preferable, lasting half a second.)

41. "Electronic music" is obviously an ingenious and altogether fascinating novelty. And here is something which, both in quality of sound and in design, can be wholly free of evocations of an unwelcome musical past. It really belongs to us, and no one can say it doesn't. It can contribute notably to our understanding both of sound itself and of the perception of sound. But the apologists are mistaken in thinking that they see in their *assemblages* the foundations of a new music.

42. These heterogeneous sounds that materialize, convolute, and vanish, often against the background of an anonymous, vacant silence, are not primarily events to be experienced. To the uninitiated they are reminders of the familiar: the distant foghorn, the pressure hammer in the hotel plumbing, the scream of diving aircraft. And to the initiated they give rise to speculations about sound structure and modification. Initiates or not, then, when we attend a session of "electronic music" we're all preoccupied with explanations—with the interpretation of signals. By our definition these are therefore not sounds

[1] See Charles R. Shackford, "Some Aspects of Perception," *Journal of Music Theory* (November 1961, April 1962, November 1962).

of music, and no matter how astutely they may be arranged, they cannot serve as bases for the development of musical implications.

43. And have the apologists forgotten that music is a performing art in which performers act upon audiences and audiences upon performers, and that fortune, good or ill, and the hazards of temperament are essential ingredients? In dispensing with the performer, they have overcome difficulties and eliminated risks. But ease and safety are to be had only at a price. These constructions may intrigue, fascinate, amuse, or terrify; but they are powerless to enchant.

44. It's dangerous, in our time, particularly in the field of electronics, to suggest that anything is impossible. "Electronic music" is new, and it's identified with a rapidly developing technology. Present experiments, which belong essentially in the "sound effect" category, may lead to experiments in *music*. They may not. A body of traditions, which one could take for granted, might be developed. The technicians, by electronic means, might be freed from their burdensome involvement in minute procedural detail to devote themselves more to the responsibilities of artists. Some sort of performance control might be introduced to lend the quality of uniqueness to each listening experience. But whether our children, or our grandchildren, even with these advances, will experience the joys of music through the agency of this impersonal facsimile equipment will remain, still, to be seen.

45. It's inevitable, perhaps, in a society shaped by technology, in which know-how takes precedence over know-what, that the musician should seek identity with his age through procedural elegance and abstruse experiment. And he sees around him, reflected in the work of his brother artists, a tide of revolution against which it would seem both reactionary and futile to attempt to stand.

46. Composers may well envy architects. Architecture has new materials and a new technology. But before the composer places his trust in the invention of new instruments—or the maltreatment of old ones—he should take a backward glance. Western music has

got along, for more than twenty-five hundred years, for the most part with direct descendants of Nebuchadnezzar's "cornet, flute, harp, sackbut, psaltery, dulcimer, and all kinds of music." It has got along well, and not for lack of ingenuity and enterprise. It's the composer's job to produce magic, not intriguing auditory curiosities. And magic flourishes far more readily in familiar surroundings, which one can take for granted, than in an environment of distracting oddity.

47. And before he seeks to align himself with the new painters, sculptors, poets, and dramatists, the composer should note an interesting fact. If these arts have gained a new vitality by rejecting tradition, it's because the practitioners of the avant-garde have sacrificed meaningful representation in favor of direct experience in which intellectual interpretation is largely superfluous. The avant-garde artist deals not in stories but in shapes, lines, and colors; the dramatist not in plot but in situation. And neither is concerned with "meaning" in the traditional sense. What has happened, in other words, is that the painters, the sculptors, the poets, and the dramatists have deserted their traditional areas and set up shop where the musician has always been in business.

48. "Aleatory music"—in which organization, in large part, is left to chance—is calculated, of course, to interest both the mathematician and the student of aesthetics. It takes its place naturally as a product of the search for progress through abstruse manipulation. And anyone who has kept up with the experiments of John Cage and others is aware that its performance can make for intriguing theatre. But taken as music, this branch of the avant-garde stands as the ultimate absurdity in the evolving aesthetic of disorder.

49. In presenting Mr. Zak's aleatory *Mobile*, then, the perpetrators of the English hoax chose a telling target. Zak is the integral embodiment of the fallacies which have spread confusion in music, fostering the spurious and diverting attention from the authentic for more than a quarter of a century.

50. It's the investor's business, whether he's a promoter, a purchaser, or a producer of mu-

sic, to distinguish between the Zaks and the musicians. Fraud in art, like creeping dishonesty in public office, flourishes in an atmosphere of resignation and apathy. It's the investor's business not to be taken in by the fake ovation and the articulate apology.

51. And the investor shouldn't forget that the magic of music possesses a unique power to align enchanted listeners in singleness and sympathy. In a world in which fear of imminent, total destruction by warfare has become commonplace, the opportunity provided by music to reach across barriers of race and ideology clearly justifies investment on a large scale. But that investment must be made in works of genuine originality, not in trivial, spurious novelties, whether those novelties purport to represent today's world or not.

52. In music, thanks to the primitive nature of the perceptive mechanism which initiates our response, we are traditionalists by necessity. We'd have a choice in this only if we could redesign the human physique. Whether we might wish to see it otherwise or not, man listens and reacts essentially as he always has. And music, therefore, though perpetually new, must in essence remain what it has always been.

53. The experience the investor has gained in dealing with Machaut, Monteverdi, Mozart, and Mahler, will apply as well in dealing with the contemporaries. He will know authenticity by what happens to him when he's in the presence of it. And the discriminating investor, who's not taken in by fads, will find in offerings of authentic new music an abundance of preferred risks.

 *LITERATURE*

JOHN KEATS

On First Looking into Chapman's Homer

Much have I traveled in the realms of gold,
   And many goodly states and kingdoms seen;
   Round many western islands have I been
Which bards in fealty to Apollo hold.
Oft of one wide expanse had I been told
   That deep-browed Homer ruled as his demesne;
   Yet did I never breathe its pure serene
Till I heard Chapman speak out loud and bold:
Then felt I like some watcher of the skies
   When a new planet swims into his ken;
Or like stout Cortez when with eagle eyes
   He stared at the Pacific—and all his men
Looked at each other with a wild surmise—
   Silent, upon a peak in Darien.

BONARO OVERSTREET

Little Story, What Now?

Bonaro Wilkinson Overstreet (1902–   ), writer and lecturer, has chiefly concerned herself with the problems of contemporary life. Among her books are *Poetic Way of Release,* 1931; *A Search for a Self,* 1938; *How to Think About Ourselves,* 1948; and *Understanding Fear in Ourselves and Others,* 1951. She has collaborated with her husband, Harry Allen Overstreet, on such widely known books as *The Mind Alive,* 1954; *What We Must Know About Communism,* 1958; *The War Called Peace: Khrushchev's Communism,* 1961; *The Iron Curtain: Where Freedom's Offensive Begins,* 1963; and *Strange Tactics of Extremism,* 1963. She has also written three volumes of poetry.

In "Little Story, What Now?" Mrs. Overstreet presents a study of the nineteenth-century short story and its twentieth-century modifications. While many critics despair that the true short story has been altered unmercifully by modern writers, she sees the changes more as variations and adaptations of the traditional forms.

1. Is it really time to weave funeral wreaths for the short story? We gather that impression from various critics who tell us, dolefully, that this well-beloved form is not what it once was. But must all things die that are not what they once were?

2. The short story has had a peculiar history—and in this history lies a clue to why critics pronounce elegies over it whenever it shows an unfamiliar face. Most literary types belong to the ages. The short story belongs to the nineteenth century.

3. The short story that bears that trademark

LITTLE STORY, WHAT NOW? From the *Saturday Review,* November 22, 1941. Reprinted by permission of the *Saturday Review* and the author.

is, first of all, a story with a plot—a close-knit structure that can be seen steadily and whole. In the well-constructed story of plot, of incident and coincident, things happen—and nothing happens that does not push the story along toward its climax. The skillful writer of the nineteenth-century story had his materials as well in hand, as obedient to his organizing will, as had the strong man who spanned a continent with a railroad. He, too, in his own way, was a competent executive.

4. A respect for action and the fruits of action, however, is not an isolated phenomenon. Psychologically, it cannot be. It has to be underwritten by two basic faiths. Joined with these, action becomes an efficient means to an

end. Without them, it becomes—as it became during the twenties of our own century—a frenetic means of escape from having to think about ends. These two faiths necessary to an eager respect for action permeated nineteenth-century thinking—and the nineteenth-century short story.

5. The first of these faiths was simply that it is possible—indeed, natural—for people to know the difference between right and wrong. The short story might have its villain—drunk-ard, thief, exploiter, snob, traitor, foreclosers of a mortgage, or what not—but there was a clear assumption, accepted alike by author and public, that the behavior of such a villain went counter to something so fundamental in the scheme of things that he must repent or perish. The life of action, in fiction or out, can command respect when, and only when, the basic code of values is taken for granted—and rare indeed in the nineteenth century were stories of ethical *laissez faire*.

6. The second faith was that people are, for the most part, what they seem to be. They may be torn by temptations, but their struggles are aboveboard—part of their conscious, active ex-perience. They may be afraid, but their fears attach to known causes in the objective world and can be overcome by fitting activity. They may be guilty of deceit, but scarcely of self-deceit: they know well enough what they are up to, and sooner or later they give them-selves away by their conduct. Here, again, is a faith that must accompany an eager belief in action: for since men of action cannot be forever hunting out obscure motives and hidden clues, they have to assume a reliable correspondence between inner character and outward behavior. In the nineteenth century people commonly assumed such a correspon-dence. Story writers did likewise, and based their plots upon it.

7. What of the twentieth century? It is not, in the same sense as the nineteenth, marked by *eventfulness*. To say this may seem para-doxical—even absurd. For more things happen every day, every minute, than ever before. But *eventfulness* is a psychological as well as a physical matter—and the twentieth century is dog-tired of action: action that goes on be-cause it cannot seem to stop; that is always having to go on to counterbalance other action that is likewise going on because it cannot stop.

8. What event, now—what physical discov-ery, or new mechanism—can stir the satiated, event-ridden imagination of man to visions of a brave new world? Our age-old Icarian dream took shape in the first clumsy aeroplane that lifted its wings from the earth; and within two decades the bombing plane was dumping its loads of death upon cities. If we take this as symbolic of what has happened to one after another of the machines and enterprises to which we attached our faith, we can say that the dropped bombs have ripped raw caverns not only in the streets of cities but in the hearts of men; they have reduced to rubble not only our houses but our hopes. It was a splendid thing for man to invent a plane that could conquer space. But what value is there in his inventing a plane that can merely hold its own against another death-dealing plane: hold its own, that is, until the enemy model is im-proved so that he will have to improve his own model to hold his own? Not by such a vicious circle as this can an eager faith in action be kept alive.

9. In the twentieth century, because we have lost the faiths that must underpin a con-fident life of action, we are being thrown back upon a study of human nature—human mo-tives, fears, wants, prejudices. The drama of our century is the drama of what goes on in the mind. The outward action—whether it be the slightest gesture of a hand or the ruthless invasion of one nation by another—is signifi-cant only as it throws light upon the obscure mental and emotional states that have bred it.

10. The characteristic science of our cen-tury is psychology. It has naturalized in our speech such words and phrases as *inferiority complex, stream of consciousness, inhibition, the subconscious, frustration, rationalization.* These are not action-words. They reflect our growing need to understand what goes on in the hidden corners of our human nature.

11. What of the short story in our century? Its future is as unpredictable as that of all our

other institutions. But this we can say: during the past several decades it has become a more and more expert medium for the expression of our deep concern about human moods and motives—moods and motives that have shown themselves to be far less transparent than we once thought they were.

12. Two protests commonly made against the current short story are, first, that it specializes in the unpleasant and abnormal and, second, that it is formless—has no plot. (Thus Irvin S. Cobb, in a recent interview in the *New York Times*, spoke the mind of disgruntled critics and public alike when he said, "I couldn't do these things they publish now, with no beginning and no end and a little incest in the middle.") Both of these charges against the short story can be maintained with a show of reason. But the sober critic who cares more about understanding the new than expressing his nostalgia for the old may choose to suspend judgment—may suspect that these faults are transition-faults. The nineteenth-century story-teller was a master of plot. His twentieth-century fellow, seeing that life was not made up of neatly parcelled collections of incidents, took his rebel stand: let his stream-of-consciousness dictate his words. The nineteenth-century writer—for reasons of common faith—wrought happy endings even out of situations that seemed logically to promise little happiness. The twentieth-century writer—for reasons of common cynicism—first turned to the unhappy and abnormal. Anyone, however, who makes an unbiased approach to the short stories being written today will realize, I think, that these are no longer either formless or swaggeringly dedicated to the sordid.

13. The twentieth-century story-teller is becoming, in his own way, a master of rigorous form. But to understand this form, we must recognize that it is dictated by psychological materials and processes, not primarily by events in the objective world. Its logic is not, and cannot be, that of dovetailed incidents that total up to a precise plot—a plot that any teacher of English can outline on a blackboard. Its logic is the complex logic of mental and emotional experience. Associate linkages, personal memories and fears and faiths, ra-

tionalized reasons for behavior, subsurface thinking that goes on in contradiction to surface talk—all these, and a multitude of other factors, must be recognized by the writer, today, as part of the deeper logic of any given situation. In determining its outcome, they may be far more important than are objective events.

14. Some readers complain that nothing happens in modern stories. But we all know from our own experience that a great deal can be happening—that volcanic changes in mind and mood can take place—when there is scarcely a surface ripple for the casual observer to detect. Objective events are necessary for drama in inverse proportion to the psychological charge that a situation carries. If little is thought or felt, much must happen; if much is thought and felt, no elaborate stacking-up of incidents is necessary for dramatic catharsis through pity and fear. The pity and fear of human thinking and feeling is what dictates the strict form which the twentieth-century story is learning to impose upon itself.

15. As for the complaint that stories are deliberately unpleasant, I think the answer must be that they are as unpleasant as sincerity makes them—neither more nor less. When first-rate nineteenth-century writers made a clear distinction between right and wrong, and provided in their plot for the triumph of the former, they were not insincere. They were not trying to be a good influence, nor to furnish their readers with an easy avenue of escape from ugliness. The confidence they expressed in the basic rationality of life was their own sincere confidence. The happy ending became a trivial formula only when genuine faith no longer gave it solid meaning. The twentieth-century rebellion has been against formulated insincerity, against stories that went on using the spent trappings of faith after the faith had gone. Moralists who now urge that writers should be purveyors of good cheer had best recognize the dubiousness of their own position: they are asking that writers practise a profound insincerity—and that is an odd thing for moralists to ask. The average man, today, does not go at life with confident faith. He does not believe all is well with

the world, nor that providence insures a happy ending to all our human tangles. Is it probable that the writer, more sensitive than the average, can go through today's world clothed in a sense of glory?

16. The happy-ending story still exists as an avenue of escape for millions. But what kind of escape do we really want our writers to provide? Do we ask only that they provide us with a few moments of forgetfulness? Or do we ask that they, with their peculiar power to go beyond the obvious, so add to our own understanding of the life we live that we can become, because of our companionship with them, better equipped to see with our eyes and hear with our ears?

17. It seems to me that the short story, today, far from being in a state of decline, is approaching a state where it can rightly mean more than it has ever meant. As it becomes increasingly deft in its power to portray our individual and social complexity, it will offer a veritable treasure house of insight-materials not only to lay readers whose main preoccu-

pation is living with their human fellows but to sociologists and psychologists. At a time when an understanding of human behavior seems the only alternative to racial suicide, we can thank our lucky stars that our short-story writers, with full sincerity, are at the job of trying to understand. If they ask us to face unpleasant realities, that is certainly not more than life itself is asking. And if they work to mature a form that is true to the intricate logic of their psychological materials, we would do ill to complain that their stories do not have a traditional array of incidents woven into a close-knit plot.

18. The short story has enjoyed one rich period of development. It is entering upon another period which, I believe, promises even greater richness, more subtle wisdom and beauty. In a changing world, this new development may be cut short by altered conditions. But if the twentieth-century story has a chance to mature along the lines of its present growth, it will make its own unique place in literary history.

EDITH HAMILTON

The Idea of Tragedy

Edith Hamilton (1867–1963), one of the great authorities on classical culture, served as headmistress at Bryn Mawr College from 1896 to 1922. In 1950 she received the National Achievement Award. Her many books are primarily studies of Greek, Roman, and Hebrew cultures, among them being *Witness to the Truth: Christ and His Interpreters,* 1948, and *Age of Heroes,* 1959. Perhaps the best known of her works is *The Greek Way,* 1930, from which this selection is taken.

As Miss Hamilton says, "tragedy is a strange matter"; scholars disagree as to its essence. In this essay she not only describes what tragedy makes us feel, but attempts to identify its essential elements.

1. The great tragic artists of the world are four, and three of them are Greek. It is in tragedy that the pre-eminence of the Greeks can be seen most clearly. Except for Shakespeare, the great three, Aeschylus, Sophocles, Euripides, stand alone. Tragedy is an achievement peculiarly Greek. They were the first to perceive it and they lifted it to its supreme height. Nor is it a matter that directly touches only the great artists who wrote tragedies; it concerns the entire people as well, who felt the appeal of the tragic to such a degree that they would gather thirty thousand strong to see a performance. In tragedy the Greek genius penetrated farthest and it is the revelation of what was most profound in them.

2. The special characteristic of the Greeks was their power to see the world clearly and at the same time as beautiful. Because they were able to do this, they produced art distinguished from all other art by an absence of struggle, marked by a calm and serenity which is theirs alone. There is, it seems to assure us, a region where beauty is truth, truth beauty. To it their artists would lead us, illumining life's dark confusions by gleams fitful indeed and wavering compared with the fixed light of religious faith, but by some magic of their own, satisfying, affording a vision of something inconclusive and yet of incalculable significance. Of all the great poets this is true, but truest of the tragic poets, for the reason that in them the power of poetry confronts the inexplicable.

3. Tragedy was a Greek creation because in Greece thought was free. Men were thinking more and more deeply about human life, and beginning to perceive more and more clearly that it was bound up with evil and that injustice was of the nature of things. And then, one day, this knowledge of something irremediably wrong in the world, came to a poet with his poet's power to see beauty in the truth of human life, and the first tragedy was written. As the author of a most distinguished book on the

THE IDEA OF TRAGEDY Reprinted from *The Greek Way* by Edith Hamilton. By permission of W. W. Norton & Company, Inc. Copyright 1930, 1942 by W. W. Norton & Company, Inc.

subject says: "The spirit of inquiry meets the spirit of poetry and tragedy is born." Make it concrete: early Greece with her godlike heroes and hero-gods fighting far on the ringing plains of windy Troy; with her lyric world, where every common thing is touched with beauty—her twofold world of poetic creation. Then a new age dawns, not satisfied with beauty of song and story, an age that must try to know and to explain. And for the first time tragedy appears. A poet of surpassing magnitude, not content with the old sacred conventions, and of a soul great enough to bear new and intolerable truth—that is Aeschylus, the first writer of tragedy.

4. Tragedy belongs to the poets. Only they have "trod the sunlit heights and from life's dissonance struck one clear chord." None but a poet can write a tragedy. For tragedy is nothing less than pain transmuted into exaltation by the alchemy of poetry, and if poetry is true knowledge and the great poets guides safe to follow, this transmutation has arresting implications.

5. Pain changed into, or, let us say, charged with, exaltation. It would seem that tragedy is a strange matter. There is indeed none stranger. A tragedy shows us pain and gives us pleasure thereby. The greater the suffering depicted, the more terrible the events, the more intense our pleasure. The most monstrous and appalling deeds life can show are those the tragedian chooses, and by the spectacle he thus offers us, we are moved to a very passion of enjoyment. There is food for wonder here, not to be passed over, as the superficial have done, by pointing out that the Romans made a holiday of a gladiator's slaughter, and that even today fierce instincts, savage survivals, stir in the most civilized. Grant all that, and we are not a step advanced on the way to explaining the mystery of tragic pleasure. It has no kinship with cruelty or the lust for blood.

6. On this point it is illuminating to consider our everyday use of the words *tragedy* and *tragic*. Pain, sorrow, disaster, are always spoken of as depressing, as dragging down—the dark abyss of pain, a crushing sorrow, an

overwhelming disaster. But speak of tragedy and extraordinarily the metaphor changes. Lift us to tragic heights, we say, and never anything else. The depths of pathos but never of tragedy. Always the height of tragedy. A word is no light matter. Words have with truth been called fossil poetry, each, that is, a symbol of a creative thought. The whole philosophy of human nature is implicit in human speech. It is a matter to pause over, that the instinct of mankind has perceived a difference, not of degree but of kind, between tragic pain and all other pain. There is something in tragedy which marks it off from other disaster so sharply that in our common speech we bear witness to the difference.

7. All those whose attention has been caught by the strange contradiction of pleasure through pain agree with this instinctive witness, and some of the most brilliant minds the world has known have concerned themselves with it. Tragic pleasure, they tell us, is in a class by itself. "Pity and awe," Aristotle called it, "and a sense of emotion purged and purified thereby." "Reconciliation," said Hegel, which we may understand in the sense of life's temporary dissonance resolved into eternal harmony. "Acceptance," said Schopenhauer, the temper of mind that says, "Thy will be done." "The reaffirmation of the will to live in the face of death," said Nietzsche, "and the joy of its inexhaustibility when so reaffirmed."

8. Pity, awe, reconciliation, exaltation—these are the elements that make up tragic pleasure. No play is a tragedy that does not call them forth. So the philosophers say, all in agreement with the common judgment of mankind, that tragedy is something above and beyond the dissonance of pain. But what it is that causes a play to call forth these feelings, what is the essential element in a tragedy, Hegel alone seeks to define. In a notable passage he says that the only tragic subject is a spiritual struggle in which each side has a claim upon our sympathy. But, as his critics have pointed out, he would thus exclude the tragedy of the suffering of the innocent, and a definition which does not include the death of Cordelia or of Deianira cannot be taken as final.

9. The suffering of the innocent, indeed, can itself be so differently treated as to necessitate completely different categories. In one of the greatest tragedies, the *Prometheus* of Aeschylus, the main actor is an innocent sufferer, but, beyond this purely formal connection, that passionate rebel, defying God and all the powers of the universe, has no relationship whatever to the lovely, loving Cordelia. An inclusive definition of tragedy must cover cases as diverse in circumstance and in the character of the protagonist as the whole range of life and letters can afford it. It must include such opposites as Antigone, the high-souled maiden who goes with open eyes to her death rather than leave her brother's body unburied, and Macbeth, the ambition-mad, the murderer of his king and guest. These two plays, seemingly so totally unlike, call forth the same response. Tragic pleasure of the greatest intensity is caused by them both. They have something in common, but the philosophers do not tell us what it is. Their concern is with what a tragedy makes us feel, not with what makes a tragedy.

10. Only twice in literary history has there been a great period of tragedy, in the Athens of Pericles and in Elizabethan England. What these two periods had in common, two thousand years and more apart in time, that they expressed themselves in the same fashion, may give us some hint of the nature of tragedy, for far from being periods of darkness and defeat, each was a time when life was seen exalted, a time of thrilling and unfathomable possibilities. They held their heads high, those men who conquered at Marathon and Salamis, and those who fought Spain and saw the Great Armada sink. The world was a place of wonder; mankind was beauteous; life was lived on the crest of the wave. More than all, the poignant joy of heroism had stirred men's hearts. Not stuff for tragedy, would you say? But on the crest of the wave one must feel either tragically or joyously; one cannot feel tamely. The temper of mind that sees tragedy in life has not for its opposite the temper that sees joy. The opposite pole to the tragic view of life is the sordid view. When humanity is seen as devoid of dignity and significance, trivial, mean, and sunk in dreary hopelessness, then

the spirit of tragedy departs. "Sometime let gorgeous tragedy in sceptred pall come sweeping by." At the opposite pole stands Gorki with *The Lower Depths.*

11. Other poets may, the tragedian must, seek for the significance of life. An error strangely common is that this significance for tragic purposes depends, in some sort, upon outward circumstance, on

> pomp and feast and revelry,
> With mask, and antique pageantry—

Nothing of all that touches tragedy. The surface of life is comedy's concern; tragedy is indifferent to it. We do not, to be sure, go to Main Street or to Zenith for tragedy, but the reason has nothing to do with their dull familiarity. There is no reason inherent in the house itself why Babbitt's home in Zenith should not be the scene of a tragedy quite as well as the Castle of Elsinore. The only reason it is not is Babbitt himself. "That singular swing toward elevation" which Schopenhauer discerned in tragedy, does not take any of its impetus from outside things.

12. The dignity and the significance of human life—of these, and of these alone, tragedy will never let go. Without them there is no tragedy. To answer the question, what makes a tragedy, is to answer the question wherein lies the essential significance of life, what the dignity of humanity depends upon in the last analysis. Here the tragedians speak to us with no uncertain voice. The great tragedies themselves offer the solution to the problem they propound. It is by our power to suffer, above all, that we are of more value than the sparrows. Endow them with a greater or as great a potentiality of pain and our foremost place in the world would no longer be undisputed. Deep down, when we search out the reason for our conviction of the transcendent worth of each human being, we know that it is because of the possibility that each can suffer so terribly. What do outside trappings matter, Zenith or Elsinore? Tragedy's preoccupation is with suffering.

13. But, it is to be well noted, not with all suffering. There are degrees in our high estate of pain. It is not given to all to suffer alike.

We differ in nothing more than in our power to feel. There are souls of little and of great degree, and upon that degree the dignity and significance of each life depend. There is no dignity like the dignity of a soul in agony.

> Here I and sorrows sit;
> Here is my throne, bid kings come bow to it.

14. Tragedy is enthroned, and to her realm those alone are admitted who belong to the only true aristocracy, that of all passionate souls. Tragedy's one essential is a soul that can feel greatly. Given such a one and any catastrophe may be tragic. But the earth may be removed and the mountains be carried into the midst of the sea, and if only the small and shallow are confounded, tragedy is absent.

15. One dark page of Roman history tells of a little seven-year-old girl, daughter of a man judged guilty of death and so herself condemned to die, and how she passed through the staring crowds sobbing and asking, "What had she done wrong? If they would tell her, she would never do it again"—and so on to the black prison and the executioner. That breaks the heart, but is not tragedy, it is pathos. No heights are there for the soul to mount to, but only the dark depths where there are tears for things. Undeserved suffering is not in itself tragic. Death is not tragic in itself, not the death of the beautiful and the young, the lovely and beloved. Death felt and suffered as Macbeth feels and suffers is tragic. Death felt as Lear feels Cordelia's death is tragic. Ophelia's death is not a tragedy. She being what she is, it could be so only if Hamlet's and Laertes' grief were tragic grief. The conflicting claims of the law of God and the law of man are not what make the tragedy of the *Antigonê.* It is Antigonê herself, so great, so tortured. Hamlet's hesitation to kill his uncle is not tragic. The tragedy is his power to feel. Change all the circumstances of the drama and Hamlet in the grip of any calamity would be tragic, just as Polonius would never be, however awful the catastrophe. The suffering of a soul that can suffer greatly—that and only that, is tragedy.

16. It follows, then, that tragedy has nothing to do with the distinction between Real-

ism and Romanticism. The contrary has always been maintained. The Greeks went to the myths for their subjects, we are told, to insure remoteness from real life which does not admit of high tragedy. "Realism is the ruin of tragedy," says the latest writer on the subject. It is not true. If indeed Realism were conceived of as dealing only with the usual, tragedy would be ruled out, for the soul capable of a great passion is not usual. But if nothing human is alien to Realism, then tragedy is of her domain, for the unusual is as real as the usual. When the Moscow Art Players presented the *Brothers Karamazoff* there was seen on the stage an absurd little man in dirty clothes who waved his arms about and shuffled and sobbed, the farthest possible remove from the traditional figures of tragedy, and yet tragedy was there in his person, stripped of her gorgeous pall, but sceptred truly, speaking the authentic voice of human agony in a struggle past the power of the human heart to bear. A drearier setting, a more typically realistic setting, it would be hard to find, but to see the play was to feel pity and awe before a man dignified by one thing only, made great by what he could suffer. Ibsen's plays are not tragedies. Whether Ibsen is a realist or not—the Realism of one generation is apt to be the Romanticism of the next—small souls are his dramatis personae and his plays are dramas with an unhappy ending. The end of *Ghosts* leaves us with a sense of shuddering horror and cold anger against a society where such things can be, and these are not tragic feelings.

17. The greatest realistic works of fiction have been written by the French and the Russians. To read one of the great Frenchmen's books is to feel mingled despair and loathing for mankind, so base, so trivial and so wretched. But to read a great Russian novel is to have an altogether different experience. The baseness, the beast in us, the misery of life, are there as plain to see as in the French book, but what we are left with is not despair and not loathing, but a sense of pity and wonder before mankind that can so suffer. The Russian sees life in that way because the Russian genius is primarily poetical; the French genius is not. *Anna Karénina* is a tragedy; *Madame Bovary* is not. Realism and Romanticism, or comparative degrees of Realism, have nothing to do with the matter. It is a case of the small soul against the great soul and the power of a writer whose special endowment is *"voir clair dans ce qui est"* against the intuition of a poet.

18. If the Greeks had left no tragedies behind for us, the highest reach of their power would be unknown. The three poets who were able to sound the depths of human agony were able also to recognize and reveal it as tragedy. The mystery of evil, they said, curtains that of which "every man whose soul is not a clod hath visions." Pain could exalt and in tragedy for a moment men could have sight of a meaning beyond their grasp. "Yet had God not turned us in his hand and cast to earth our greatness," Euripides makes the old Trojan queen say in her extremity, "we would have passed away giving nothing to men. They would have found no theme for song in us nor made great poems from our sorrows."

19. Why is the death of the ordinary man a wretched, chilling thing which we turn from, while the death of the hero, always tragic, warms us with a sense of quickened life? Answer this question and the enigma of tragic pleasure is solved. "Never let me hear that brave blood has been shed in vain," said Sir Walter Scott, "it sends an imperious challenge down through all the generations." So the end of a tragedy challenges us. The great soul in pain and in death transforms pain and death. Through it we catch a glimpse of the Stoic Emperor's Dear City of God, of a deeper and more ultimate reality than that in which our lives are lived.

JOHN CIARDI

. . . an ulcer, gentlemen, is an unwritten poem

John Ciardi (1916–   ) is poetry editor of the *Saturday Review* and director of the Bread Loaf Writers' Conference. From 1953 to 1961 he was on the English staff of Rutgers University. His first volume of poetry—*Homeward to America, 1940*—won him the Hopwood Award for Poetry, and he has received numerous other honors for his excellence as a poet. Among his other volumes of poetry are *Other Skies, 1947; From Time to Time, 1951; As If, 1955; I Marry You, 1958; How Does a Poem Mean?* 1959; *In the Stoneworks, 1961; You Read to Me, I'll Read to You, 1962; Dialogue with an Audience, 1963; Person to Person, 1964;* and a long poem, *The King Who Saved Himself from Being Saved, 1965.* He has also translated Dante's *Inferno* and *Purgatorio.*

". . . an ulcer, gentlemen, is an unwritten poem" analyzes the kind of human behavior poetry represents and describes the peculiar ability of poetry to enlarge man's "sense of possibility."

1. The poet in our times is a figure of estrangement and he knows it. He not only knows it, he has grown used to the fact and does not much mind it. The truth seems to be, for that matter, that the poet—outside those Golden Ages of folk-poetry now long gone—never did reach more than a few special people in any culture.

2. In the past, however, poets have managed to persuade themselves that they were some sort of social force. Elizabethan poets liked to claim that their sonnets conferred immortality on the ladies they wrote about. The seventeenth-century satirists were especially fond of the idea that by "holding folly up to ridicule" they purified the intellect of their age. More recently Shelley found it possible to assert that "Poets are the unacknowledged legislators of the world." And even within the last twenty-five years, the social poets of the thirties may be cited as having seriously believed that their poems of social protest had a measurable effect on the government of nations.

3. Stephen Spender, looking back on the mood of poetry in the thirties from the vantage point of 1950, summarized the poet's then-sense of himself as very much a warrior of the practical world:

> It was still possible then to think of a poem as a palpable, overt, and effective anti-fascist action. Every poetic assertion of the dignity of the individual seemed to be a bullet fired in the war against human repression.

4. I know of no sane poet today who persuades himself that the action of his art and imagination has any significant consequence in the practical reality of Dow-Jones averages, election returns, and state-of-the-nation.

Wherever the practical world may be, Auden has defined the position of poetry in our time:

For poetry makes nothing happen: it survives
In the valley of its saying where executives
Would never want to tamper; it flows south
From ranches of isolation and the busy griefs,
Raw towns that we believe and die in; it survives,
A way of happening, a mouth.

5. But now—perhaps to prove that poets are no prophets—the executives have wanted to tamper. Under the auspices of the College English Association a group of leading business executives have been meeting regularly with writers and teachers of the liberal arts; and from their problems in the practical world of business management, they seem to be asking seriously what meeting there can be between the arts and the practicalities of industry.

6. The answer to these questions may well be that the poets and the practical men would be mutually happier in leaving one another strictly alone, the poets on their ranches of isolation practising a way of happening, and the practical men in their cities of numbered and lettered glass doors busily pushing the buttons of the world.

7. For the gap that divides the poet from the practical man is real. Nor will it be measurably closed by pointing out that some men have functioned with distinction in both the poetical and the practical imagination. There was a director of public works named Chaucer, there was a bricklayer named Ben Jonson, there was a good soldier named Richard Lovelace—one could compile endlessly. But all that such a list would prove is that some men are ambidextrous: it would not eliminate the distinction between the right hand and the left.

8. A poem is a kind of human behavior. Plowing a field, running a chemical experiment, and analyzing the character of a job-applicant are also kinds of human behavior. The poem may, of course, be about any one of these human actions; but when the poem deals with them, it does so in nonpractical ways. The poet who writes about plowing a field may find significance in the *idea* of plowing, or he may describe plowing so richly that the riches of the description become a self-pleasing idea in themselves. He does not, however, turn physical soil, plant an actual crop, and take it to the literal human diet by way of a negotiable cash market. In the same way, the poet may create a powerfully penetrating picture of the character of the man the business executive is interviewing for a job. But when the poet has finished his analysis, he has no need to make a payroll decision and to assign the man to a specific job in a specific department.

9. Poetry and practicality are in fact two different worlds with two different orders of experience and of imagination. The poet enters his world as an *as if:* he writes *as if* he were plowing a field, *as if* he were conducting a chemical experiment, *as if* he were analyzing a real man seated before him. He is free with a stroke of the pen to change the lineaments of the world he has imagined. The work-sheets of a poem by Karl Shapiro contain a monumental example of this freedom to *as if* at will.

10. Setting out to describe the (*as if*) dome of darkness that settles over a city at night, he writes in his first draft: "Under the fatherly dome of the universe and the town." Now "fatherly dome" cannot fail to imply a theological universe in the mind of God the Father. For reasons that need not be examined here, Shapiro, in his second draft, rephrased the idea "Under the dome of zero." Simply by changing one central word, Shapiro swung the universe itself from the theological concept of "father" to the scientific concept of "zero." And the poem continued to follow itself as if the process of reversing thirty centuries of human attitudes in a single word amounted to nothing whatever.

11. The practical man has no such large freedom. He enters a world called *is*. When he is at work, he *is* plowing a field, he *is* assembling chemical appartus, he *is* interviewing an actual man whose name appears on the census listings and who *is* offering his services in return for real and taxable wages.

12. It is only natural, moreover, that men who give their attention to either of these two worlds should not be especially well disposed to the other. Poets tend to think very little of stockbrokers, and stockbrokers tend to think even less—if at all—of poets. And the fact is that some of the best poetry of our times has been written on what may be called an inverted sense of reality, an order of imagination that asserts openly or by implication that what the practical men do is meaningless and that only the *as if* of the vicarious imagination has a place in the final mind of man. So Wallace Stevens, in a poem significantly titled "Holiday in Reality," lists a series of things seen and says of them: "These are real only if I make them so," and concludes:

Intangible arrows quiver and stick in the skin
And I taste at the root of the tongue the unreal
Of what is real.

13. It may be very much to the point that Wallace Stevens, in another part of his imagination, is a vice-president of the Hartford Accident and Indemnity Company and a specialist in claims on surety bonds. Obviously, however, Wallace Stevens cannot look into his surety bond claims and send in a report that "These are real only if I make them so." That difference between the world of practical solutions and the world of the vicarious imagination must not be blinked away.

14. What must be borne in mind, rather, is the fact that no sane human being is exclusively a practical man. The plant manager may be the most mechanically efficient of calculators during his waking hours; and still his dreams or his nightmares will be human and impractical. What is his order of reality and of business efficiency when he first holds his newborn child? Or when, as some men must in time, he stands by his child's grave? What is his order of reality when he steps out of a late conference and finds a hurricane shaking the earth? Or his wife is ill and the telephone rings: In one ear he hears his assistant howling that the sub-contractor sent the wrong parts and that a rush order is delayed, while with the other he hears the doctor close the bedroom door and start down the stairs to tell him his wife will or will not recover. Which of these realities is more real than the other to live to?

15. The poem does not care and cannot care what happens to that rush order. The poem is of the humanity of the man. And despite the tendency . . . [to admire] only those men who "do things" and to scorn "dreamers," the fact is that no man can be wholly practical or wholly impractical, and that the humanity of any man's life requires some, at least, of both orders of the imagination.

16. There is no poetry for the practical man. There is poetry only for the mankind of the man who spends a certain amount of his life turning the mechanical wheel. But let him spend too much of his life at the mechanics of practicality and either he must become something less than a man, or his very mechanical efficiency will become impaired by the frustrations stored up in his irrational human personality. An ulcer, gentlemen, is an unkissed imagination taking its revenge for having been jilted. It is an unwritten poem, a neglected music, an unpainted watercolor, an undanced dance. It is a declaration from the mankind of the man that a clear spring of joy has not been tapped, and that it must break through, muddily, on its own.

17. Poetry is one of the forms of joy, the most articulate, the most expanding, and, therefore, the most fulfilling form. It is no separation from the world; it is the mankind of the world, the most human language of man's uncertain romance with the universe.

18. Despite the slanders of high-minded schoolmarms and even of some of the poets themselves, poetry is not a moral thing. It is a life thing. It is like hunger, or sex-drive, or the pleasure of stretching one's muscles. It exists. It is of the liveness of the man. Because the man is various, it may be mixed in him with the moral or the amoral, with the lofty or the coarse, with the sententious or the foppish, with the brilliant or the trivial. But where the living gift of poetry is real, it

survives all added characteristics. Whatever the situation of the poet's learning, morals, or psychic base, the stomach wrinkles, the glands secrete, the consciousness evolves, and the gift, if there is gift in the man, answers to the rhythm of its own living. As natively as a child sways to music, as blindly as a mouth sucks, as darkly as the hand of the sleeping man reaches to touch the woman and rests resolved and assured when it has found her—just so the human being needs the motion and repose that a good poem is. And just so, the man who has not been estranged from himself by busy motions, not only needs, but knows he needs, these fulfillments.

19. The moralist to the contrary, the impulse to poetry is a play impulse. It will not do to call it anything more high-sounding than that. It is necessary, rather, to see that poetic play is of the very fiber of life and that it runs equally through child's prattle, the designer's pleasure in finding and following the shape of his idea, and the substance of all religious ritual.

20. Form, whether in rhythm (time) or in mass (space), is inseparable from our perception of the world. To respond to form and to take the inevitable next step, which is to re-imagine it, is inseparable from the act of sentience a human life is.

21. That act of imagination and of re-imagination is not easy. It is better than easy: it is joyous. It is what Robert Frost called "the pleasure of taking pains." Taking pains is inseparable from human satisfaction. Every game ever developed by mankind is a way of inventing a difficulty for the sake of overcoming it. The lines a child draws for hopscotch, the rules chess players agree upon, the hurdles a track man puts in his way, are deliberately selected ways of making things hard for oneself. It would be easier to play hopscotch without the lines, but it would be no fun.

22. Poets throughout history have been men who played their life's game against form. However painful the overt subject of the good poem, the dance of the form has been the same life-dance for joy. Keats' sonnet, "On First Looking into Chapman's Homer," is a poem on a happy subject. His sonnet, "When I have fears that I may cease to be," is overtly addressed to his unhappy certainty of his impending death. Keats even concludes his brooding with a statement that nothing in the world matters:

> —then on the shore
> Of the wide world I stand alone, and think
> Till love and fame to nothingness do sink.

But though love and fame and world and time might sink to nothing, the rhymes still fall carefully into place, the meter is kept, the images follow, and the form completes itself in an open performance of the joy and the significance of making the poem well. Even in writing of his death the poet dances his life. Whatever the subject of the poem may seem to be, its true subject is the play of form which asserts, shapes, and fulfills the need of the man. Keats thinking about his death was a tragic man. Keats finding the form of his imagination that could best express and hold his feelings about his death was a joyous man.

23. Now, if we ask what sort of human behavior a poem is, we may answer, "it is this dance." The practical-minded man may still object that the dance accomplishes nothing: Keats was not spared his death, and nothing in the act of giving shape to his dark thoughts had any effect on the reality of his tubercular lung. True, the poem moved nothing in the physical world. But equally true—even more true—in the act of writing Keats became more alive to himself. And whatever may or may not be measured in foot-pounds, that which gives life to life is a human good.

24. But there is more than the basic dance of joy in the human action of Keats' poem. In essence, Keats has found an act of joy wherewith to express the fact of loss. "Grief brought to numbers cannot be so fierce." All life is attended by losses: an action that can convert those very losses to joys must certainly seem an indispensable human resource.

25. And the more sensitively alive a man is, the more certainly his life must scar him. But it is only the *is*-reality that scars. In the act of re-imagining that reality and of capturing it into the *as-if* of poetic form, the poem releases

the mind from the bonds of body and situation. Because the poet is free to *as-if* as many realities as he likes, he can, by that much, see his life as part of all other realities. He can imagine himself from outside himself. And he can imagine himself into the mind and feeling of other men. He is ready to acquire both sympathy and understanding.

26. In shorter terms than these there is no good poetry. And no man who lives his life in shorter terms than these is sufficiently alive. The poet is a man at play, but in Robert Frost's phrase, "the work is play for mortal stakes." However sternly the moralist may frown at this emphasis on the play function of poetry, the supreme statements of man's passion on the planet have been made by those men who were most alive to this play.

27. For in the pursuit of form, one not only finds but enlarges himself. "Endure a change of imagination," says the good poem. It is a long thing to be a man. And it is nothing a man may accomplish unaided. Poetry, by storing the world's best imagination, not only transmits experiences from the past of the race, but teaches the man an enlargement of his own sense of possibility.

28. Imagine, for example, a Greek musician of the Golden Age stumbling out of a time machine into the presence of one of our great symphony orchestras just as Toscanini led it into a Beethoven symphony. However passionately that Greek had devoted himself to his lyre and his harp, he never could have imagined the possibility of such music even as he responds to it and is filled by it. It is unlikely in fact that he could begin to understand the music. When we listen to a symphony, we listen with part of the heritage of the race, with the history that has evolved the tradition of that music, and the imaginary Greek would be missing that memory. As in time, however, he acquired that memory, he would certainly be filled with new possibilities, possibilities he could never have imagined unaided.

29. In a very real sense, all of us are that Greek. Left to ourselves we could not hope to have accomplished enough of the imagination of the race to sense our own possibilities and our own humanity. The presence of a true work of art is always an expansion of the human sense.

30. None of these extensions of the human being, to be sure, are useful in tightening a bolt or in adding a column of figures. A man especially sensitive to this life-play may in fact be too variable in his imagination for mechanical and mathematical accuracy. But to define the practical man in terms as mechanical as bolts and adding machines is to define practically no man at all. What is more practical in world and time than a good human being? Let there be good men and the machine will not want.

JOHN GALSWORTHY

A Novelist's Allegory

John Galsworthy (1867–1933), English novelist and playwright, won the Nobel Prize for Literature in 1932. His *Forsyte Saga*, 1922—a trilogy of novels (*The Man of Property*, 1906; *In Chancery*, 1920; and *To Let*, 1921)—depicts the frustrations and subsequent deterioration that result from an overweening possessive instinct in a middle-class family of Victorian England. Though his fame rests largely upon his work as a novelist,

he also wrote plays—among them *The Silver Box,* 1906; *Strife,* 1909; and *Justice,* 1910
—in which he portrays social problems in a realistic but unbiased manner.

In this allegory, from *The Inn of Tranquillity,* 1912, Galsworthy deftly states the fiction
writer's purpose in writing and the writer's function in society.

1. Once upon a time the Prince of Felicitas had occasion to set forth on a journey. It was a late autumn evening with few pale stars and a moon no larger than the paring of a finger nail. And as he rode through the purlieus of his city, the white mane of his amber-coloured steed was all that he could clearly see in the dusk of the high streets. His way led through a quarter but little known to him, and he was surprised to find that his horse, instead of ambling forward with his customary gentle vigour, stepped carefully from side to side, stopping now and then to curve his neck and prick his ears—as though at some thing of fear unseen in the darkness; while on either hand creatures could be heard rustling and scuttling, and little cold draughts as of wings fanned the rider's cheeks.

2. The Prince at last turned in his saddle, but so great was the darkness that he could not even see his escort.

3. "What is the name of this street?" he said.

4. "Sire, it is called the Vita Publica."

5. "It is very dark." Even as he spoke his horse staggered, but, recovering its foothold with an effort, stood trembling violently. Nor could all the incitements of its master induce the beast again to move forward.

6. "Is there no one with a lanthorn in this street?" asked the Prince.

7. His attendants began forthwith to call out loudly for anyone who had a lanthorn. Now, it chanced that an old man sleeping in a hovel on a pallet of straw was awakened by these cries. When he heard that it was the Prince of Felicitas himself, he came hastily,

A NOVELIST'S ALLEGORY is reprinted with the permission of Charles Scribner's Sons from *The Inn of Tranquillity* by John Galsworthy. Copyright 1912 Charles Scribner's Sons; renewal copyright 1940 Ada Galsworthy.

carrying his lanthorn, and stood trembling beside the Prince's horse. It was so dark that the Prince could not see him.

8. "Light your lanthorn, old man," he said.

9. The old man laboriously lit his lanthorn. Its pale rays fled out on either hand; beautiful but grim was the vision they disclosed. Tall houses, fair court-yards, and a palm-grown garden; in front of the Prince's horse a deep cesspool, on whose jagged edges the good beast's hoofs were planted; and, as far as the glimmer of the lanthorn stretched, both ways down the rutted street, paving stones displaced, and smooth tessellated marbles; pools of mud, the hanging fruit of an orange-tree, and dark, scurrying shapes of monstrous rats bolting across from house to house. The old man held the lanthorn higher; and instantly bats flying against it would have beaten out the light but for the thin protection of its horn sides.

10. The Prince sat still upon his horse, looking first at the rutted space that he had traversed and then at the rutted space before him.

11. "Without a light," he said, "this thoroughfare is dangerous. What is your name, old man?"

12. "My name is Cethru," replied the aged churl.

13. "Cethru!" said the Prince. "Let it be your duty henceforth to walk with your lanthorn up and down this street all night and every night,"—and he looked at Cethru: "Do you understand, old man, what it is you have to do?"

14. The old man answered in a voice that trembled like a rusty flute:

15. "Aye, aye!—to walk up and down and hold my lanthorn so that folk can see where they be goin'."

16. The Prince gathered up his reins; but

the old man, lurching forward, touched his stirrup.

17. "How long be I to go on wi' thiccy job?"

18. "Until you die!"

19. Cethru held up his lanthorn, and they could see his long, thin face, like a sandwich of dried leather, jerk and quiver, and his thin gray hairs flutter in the draughts of the bats' wings circling round the light.

20. " 'Twill be main hard!" he groaned; "an' my lanthorn's nowt but a poor thing."

21. With a high look, the Prince of Felicitas bent and touched the old man's forehead.

22. "Until you die, old man," he repeated; and bidding his followers to light torches from Cethru's lanthorn, he rode on down the twisting street. The clatter of the horses' hoofs died out in the night, and the scuttling and the rustling of the rats and the whispers of the bats' wings were heard again.

23. Cethru, left alone in the dark thoroughfare, sighed heavily; then, spitting on his hands, he tightened the old girdle round his loins, and slinging the lanthorn on his staff, held it up to the level of his waist, and began to make his way along the street. His progress was but slow, for he had many times to stop and rekindle the flame within his lanthorn, which the bats' wings, his own stumbles, and the jostlings of footpads or of revelers returning home, were for ever extinguishing. In traversing that long street he spent half the night, and half the night in traversing it back again. The saffron swan of dawn, slow swimming up the sky-river between the high roof-banks, bent her neck down through the dark air-water to look at him staggering below her, with his still smoking wick. No sooner did Cethru see that sunlit bird, than with a great sigh of joy he sat him down, and at once fell asleep.

24. Now when the dwellers in the houses of the Vita Publica first gained knowledge that this old man passed every night with his lanthorn up and down their street, and when they marked those pallid gleams gliding over the motley prospect of cesspools and garden gates, over the sightless hovels and the rich-carved frontages of their palaces; or saw them stay

their journey and remain suspended like a handful of daffodils held up against the black stuffs of secrecy—they said:

25. "It is good that the old man should pass like this—we shall see better where we're going; and if the Watch have any job on hand, or want to put the pavements in order, his lanthorn will serve their purpose well enough." And they would call out of their doors and windows to him passing:

26. "Hola! old man Cethru! All's well with our house, and with the street before it?"

27. But, for answer, the old man only held his lanthorn up, so that in the ring of its pale light they saw some sight or other in the street. And his silence troubled them, one by one, for each had expected that he would reply:

28. "Aye, aye! All's well with *your* house, Sirs, and with the street before it!"

29. Thus they grew irritated with this old man who did not seem able to do anything but just hold his lanthorn up. And gradually they began to dislike his passing by their doors with his pale light, by which they could not fail to see, not only the rich-carved frontages and scrolled gates of court-yards and fair gardens, but things that were not pleasing to the eye. And they murmured amongst themselves: "What is the good of this old man and his silly lanthorn? We can see all we want to see without him; in fact, we got on very well before he came."

30. So, as he passed, rich folk who were supping would pelt him with orange-peel and empty the dregs of their wine over his head; and poor folk, sleeping in their hutches, turned over, as the rays of the lanthorn fell on them, and cursed him for that disturbance. Nor did the revelers or footpads treat the old man civilly, but tied him to the wall, where he was constrained to stay till a kind passer-by released him. And ever the bats darkened his lanthorn with their wings and tried to beat the flame out. And the old man thought: "This be a terrible hard job; I don't seem to please nobody." But because the Prince of Felicitas had so commanded him, he continued nightly to pass with his lanthorn up and down the street; and every morning as the saffron swan came

swimming overhead, to fall asleep. But his sleep did not last long, for he was compelled to pass many hours each day in gathering rushes and melting down tallow for his lanthorn; so that his lean face grew more than ever like a sandwich of dried leather.

31. Now it came to pass that the Town Watch having had certain complaints made to them that persons had been bitten in the Vita Publica by rats, doubted of their duty to destroy these ferocious creatures; and they held investigation, summoning the persons bitten and inquiring of them how it was that in so dark a street they could tell that the animals which had bitten them were indeed rats. Howbeit for some time no one could be found who could say more than what he had been told, and since this was not evidence, the Town Watch had good hopes that they would not after all be forced to undertake this tedious enterprise. But presently there came before them one who said that he had himself seen the rat which had bitten him, by the light of an old man's lanthorn. When the Town Watch heard this they were vexed, for they knew that if this were true they would now be forced to prosecute the arduous undertaking, and they said:

32. "Bring in this old man!"

33. Cethru was brought before them trembling.

34. "What is this we hear, old man, about your lanthorn and the rat? And in the first place, what were you doing in the Vita Publica at that time of night?"

35. Cethru answered: "I was just passin' with my lanthorn!"

36. "Tell us—did *you* see the rat?"

37. Cethru shook his head: "My lanthorn seed the rat, maybe!" he muttered.

38. "Old owl!" said the Captain of the Watch: "Be careful what you say! If you saw the rat, why did you then not aid this unhappy citizen who was bitten by it—first, to avoid that rodent, and subsequently to slay it, thereby relieving the public of a pestilential danger?"

39. Cethru looked at him, and for some seconds did not reply; then he said slowly: "I were just passin' with my lanthorn."

40. "That you have already told us," said the Captain of the Watch; "it is no answer."

41. Cethru's leathern cheeks became wine-coloured, so desirous was he to speak, and so unable. And the Watch sneered and laughed, saying: "This is a fine witness."

42. But of a sudden Cethru spoke:

43. "What would I be duin'—killin' rats; tidden my business to kill rats."

44. The Captain of the Watch caressed his beard, and looking at the old man with contempt, said:

45. "It seems to me, brothers, that this is an idle old vagabond, who does no good to anyone. We should be well advised, I think, to prosecute him for vagrancy. But that is not at this moment the matter in hand. Owing to the accident—scarcely fortunate—of this old man's passing with his lanthorn, it would certainly appear that citizens have been bitten by rodents. It is then, I fear, our duty to institute proceedings against those poisonous and violent animals."

46. And amidst the sighing of the Watch, it was so resolved.

47. Cethru was glad to shuffle away, unnoticed, from the Court, and sitting down under a camel-date tree outside the City Wall, he thus reflected:

48. "They were rough with me! I done nothin', so far's I can see!"

49. And a long time he sat there with the bunches of the camel-dates above him, golden as the sunlight. Then, as the scent of the lyrio flowers, released by evening, warned him of the night dropping like a flight of dark birds on the plain, he rose stiffly, and made his way as usual toward the Vita Publica.

50. He had traversed but little of that black thoroughfare, holding his lanthorn at the level of his breast, when the sound of a splash and cries for help smote his long, thin ears. Remembering how the Captain of the Watch had admonished him, he stopped and peered about, but owing to his proximity to the light of his own lanthorn he saw nothing. Presently he heard another splash and the sound of blowings and of puffings, but still unable to see clearly whence they came, he was forced in bewilderment to resume his march. But he

had no sooner entered the next bend of that obscure and winding avenue than the most lamentable, lusty cries assailed him. Again he stood still, blinded by his own light. Somewhere at hand a citizen was being beaten, for vague, quick-moving forms emerged into the radiance of his lanthorn out of the deep violet of the night air. The cries swelled, and died away, and swelled; and the mazed Cethru moved forward on his way. But very near the end of his first traversage, the sound of a long, deep sighing, as of a fat man in spiritual pain, once more arrested him.

51. "Drat me!" he thought, "this time I *will* see what 'tis," and he spun round and round, holding his lanthorn now high, now low, and to both sides. "The devil an' all's in it tonight," he murmured to himself; "there's some 'at here fetchin' of its breath awful loud." But for his life he could see nothing, only that the higher he held his lanthorn the more painful grew the sound of the fat but spiritual sighing. And desperately, he at last resumed his progress.

52. On the morrow, while he still slept stretched on his straw pallet, there came to him a member of the Watch.

53. "Old man, you are wanted at the Court House; rouse up, and bring your lanthorn."

54. Stiffly Cethru rose.

55. "What be they wantin' me fur now, mester?"

56. "Ah!" replied the Watchman, "they are about to see if they can't put an end to your goings-on."

57. Cethru shivered, and was silent.

58. Now when they reached the Court House it was patent that a great affair was forward; for the Judges were in their robes, and a crowd of advocates, burgesses, and common folk thronged the carven, lofty hall of justice.

59. When Cethru saw that all eyes were turned on him, he shivered still more violently, fixing his fascinated gaze on the three Judges in their emerald robes.

60. "This then is the prisoner," said the oldest of the Judges; "proceed with the indictment!"

61. A little advocate in snuff-coloured clothes rose on little legs, and commenced to read:

62. "Forasmuch as on the seventeenth night of August fifteen hundred years since the Messiah's death, one Celestine, a maiden of this city, fell into a cesspool in the Vita Publica, and while being quietly drowned, was espied of the burgess Pardonix by the light of a lanthorn held by the old man Cethru; and, forasmuch as, plunging in, the said Pardonix rescued her, not without grave risk of life and the ruin of his clothes, and today lies ill of fever; and forasmuch as the old man Cethru was the cause of these misfortunes to the burgess Pardonix, by reason of his wandering lanthorn's showing the drowning maiden, the Watch do hereby indict, accuse, and otherwise place charge upon this Cethru of 'Vagabondage without serious occupation.'

63. "And, forasmuch as on this same night the Watchman Filepo, made aware, by the light of this said Cethru's lanthorn, of three sturdy footpads, went to arrest them, and was set on by the rogues and wellnigh slain, the Watch do hereby indict, accuse, and otherwise charge upon Cethru complicity in this assault, by reasons, namely, first, that he discovered the footpads to the Watchman and the Watchman to the footpads by the light of his lanthorn; and, second, that, having thus discovered them, he stood idly by and gave no assistance to the law.

64. "And, forasmuch as on this same night the wealthy burgess Pranzo, who, having prepared a banquet, was standing in his doorway awaiting the arrival of his guests, did see, by the light of the said Cethru's lanthorn, a beggar woman and her children groveling in the gutter for garbage, whereby his appetite was lost completely; and, forasmuch as he, Pranzo, has lodged a complaint against the Constitution for permitting women and children to go starved, the Watch do hereby indict, accuse, and otherwise make charge on Cethru of rebellion and of anarchy, in that willfully he doth disturb good citizens by showing to them without provocation disagreeable sights, and doth moreover endanger the laws by causing persons to desire to change them.

65. "These be the charges, reverend Judges, so please you!"

66. And having thus spoken, the little advocate resumed his seat.

67. Then said the oldest of the Judges:

68. "Cethru, you have heard; what answer do you make?"

69. But no word, only the chattering of teeth, came from Cethru.

70. "Have you no defense?" said the Judge: "these are grave accusations!"

71. Then Cethru spoke.

72. "So please your Highnesses," he said, "can I help what my lanthorn sees?"

73. And having spoken these words, to all further questions he remained more silent than a headless man.

74. The Judges took counsel of each other, and the oldest of them thus addressed himself to Cethru:

75. "If you have no defense, old man, and there is no one will say a word for you, we can but proceed to judgment."

76. Then in the main aisle of the Court there rose a youthful advocate.

77. "Most reverend Judges," he said in a mellifluous voice, clearer than the fluting of a bell-bird, "it is useless to look for words from this old man, for it is manifest that he himself is nothing, and that his lanthorn is alone concerned in this affair. But, reverend Judges, bethink you well: Would you have a lanthorn ply a trade or be concerned with a profession, or do aught indeed but pervade the streets at night, shedding its light, which, if you will, is vagabondage? And, Sirs, upon the second count of this indictment: Would you have a lanthorn dive into cesspools to rescue maidens? Would you have a lanthorn to beat footpads? Or, indeed, to be any sort of partisan either of the Law or of them that break the Law? Sure, Sirs, I think not. And as to this third charge of fostering anarchy—let me but describe the trick of this lanthorn's flame. It is distilled, most reverend Judges, of oil and wick, together with that sweet secret heat of whose birth no words of mine can tell. And when, Sirs, this pale flame has sprung into the air swaying to every wind, it brings vision to the human eye. And, if it be charged on this old man Cethru that he and his lanthorn by reason of their showing not only the good but the evil bring no pleasure into the world, I ask, Sirs, what in the world is so dear as this power to see—whether it be the beautiful or the foul that is disclosed? Need I, indeed, tell you of the way this flame spreads its feelers, and delicately darts and hovers in the darkness, conjuring things from nothing? This mechanical summoning, Sirs, of visions out of blackness is benign, by no means of malevolent intent; no more than if a man, passing two donkeys in the road, one lean and the other fat, could justly be arraigned for malignancy because they were not both fat. This, reverend Judges, is the essence of the matter concerning the rich burgess, Pranzo, who, on account of the sight he saw by Cethru's lanthorn, has lost the equilibrium of his stomach. For, Sirs, the lanthorn did but show that which was there, both fair and foul, no more, and no less: and though it is indeed true that Pranzo is upset, it was not because the lanthorn maliciously produced distorted images, but merely caused to be seen, in due proportions, things which Pranzo had not seen before. And surely, reverend Judges, being just men, you would not have this lanthorn turn its light away from what is ragged and ugly because there are also fair things on which its light may fall; how, indeed, being a lanthorn, could it, if it would? And I would have you note this, Sirs, that by this impartial discovery of the proportions of one thing to another, this lanthorn must indeed perpetually seem to cloud and sadden those things which are fair, because of the deep instincts of harmony and justice planted in the human breast. However unfair and cruel, then, this lanthorn may seem to those who, deficient in these instincts, desire all their lives to see naught but what is pleasant, lest they, like Pranzo, should lose their appetites—it is not consonant with equity that this lanthorn should, even if it could, be prevented from thus mechanically buffeting the holiday cheek of life. I would think, Sirs, that you should rather blame the queazy state of Pranzo's stomach. The old man has said that

he cannot help what his lanthorn sees. This is a just saying. But if, reverend Judges, you deem this equiposed, indifferent lanthorn to be indeed blameworthy for having shown in the same moment, side by side, the skull and the fair face, the burdock and the tiger-lily, the butterfly and toad, then, most reverend Judges, punish it, but do not punish this old man, for he himself is but a flume of smoke, thistledown dispersed—nothing!"

78. So saying, the young advocate ceased.

79. Again the three Judges took counsel of each other, and after much talk had passed between them, the oldest spoke:

80. "What this young advocate has said seems to us to be the truth. We cannot punish a lanthorn. Let the old man go!"

81. And Cethru went out into the sunshine. . . .

82. Now it came to pass that the Prince of Felicitas, returning from his journey, rode once more on his amber-coloured steed down the Vita Publica.

83. The night was dark as a rook's wing, but far away down the street burned a little light, like a red star truant from heaven. The Prince riding by descried it for a lanthorn, with an old man sleeping beside it.

84. "How is this, Friend?" said the Prince. "You are not walking as I bade you, carrying your lanthorn."

85. But Cethru neither moved nor answered.

86. "Lift him up!" said the Prince.

87. They lifted up his head and held the lanthorn to his closed eyes. So lean was that brown face that the beams from the lanthorn would not rest on it, but slipped past on either side into the night. His eyes did not open. He was dead.

88. And the Prince touched him, saying: "Farewell, old man! The lanthorn is still alight. Go, fetch me another one, and let him carry it!" . . .

LIONEL TRILLING

Sherwood Anderson

Lionel Trilling (1905–   ), writer and the George Woodberry Professor of Literature and Criticism at Columbia University, began his versatile literary career with a critical study, *Matthew Arnold*, 1939. This was followed by *E. M. Forster* and *The Liberal Imagination*, 1943; a novel, *The Middle of the Journey*, 1947; *Letters of John Keats*, 1950; and a series of essays, *The Opposing Self*, 1955. His most recent work is a series of essays on learning and literature, *Beyond Culture*, 1965.

"Sherwood Anderson" is a literary critic's evaluation of that writer's strengths and weaknesses. Trilling believes that although Anderson's writing does not adequately represent reality or depict true sensory or social experience, it reflects truthfully the cultural situation of its time.

1. I find it hard, and I think it would be false, to write about Sherwood Anderson without speaking of him personally and even emotionally. I did not know him; I was in his company only twice and on neither occasion did I talk with him. The first time I saw him was when he was at the height of his fame; I had, I recall, just been reading *A Story-Teller's Story* and *Tar*, and these autobiographical works had made me fully aware of the change that had taken place in my feelings since a few years before when almost anything that Anderson wrote had seemed a sort of revelation. The second time was about two years before his death; he had by then not figured in my own thought about literature for many years, and I believe that most people were no longer aware of him as an immediate force in their lives. His last two novels (*Beyond Desire* in 1932 and *Kit Brandon* in 1936) had not been good; they were all too clearly an attempt to catch up with the world, but the world had moved too fast; it was not that Anderson was not aware of the state of things but rather that he had suffered the fate of the writer who at one short past moment has had a success with a simple idea which he allowed to remain simple and to become fixed. On both occasions —the first being a gathering, after one of Anderson's lectures, of eager Wisconsin graduate students and of young instructors who were a little worried that they would be thought stuffy and academic by this Odysseus, the first famous man of letters most of us had ever seen; the second being a crowded New York party—I was much taken by Anderson's human quality, by a certain serious interest he would have in the person he was shaking hands with or talking to for a brief, formal moment, by a certain graciousness or gracefulness which seemed to arise from an innocence of heart.

2. I mention this very tenuous personal impression because it must really have arisen

SHERWOOD ANDERSON   From *The Liberal Imagination* by Lionel Trilling. Copyright 1941, 1947, by Lionel Trilling. Reprinted by permission of The Viking Press, Inc.

not at all from my observation of the moment but rather have been projected from some unconscious residue of admiration I had for Anderson's books even after I had made all my adverse judgments upon them. It existed when I undertook this notice of Anderson on the occasion of his death, or else I should not have undertaken it. And now that I have gone back to his books again and have found that I like them even less than I remembered, I find too that the residue of admiration still remains; it is quite vague, yet it requires to be articulated with the clearer feelings of dissatisfaction; and it needs to be spoken of, as it has been, first.

3. There is a special poignancy in the failure of Anderson's later career. According to the artistic morality to which he and his friends subscribed—Robert Browning seems to have played a large if anonymous part in shaping it—Anderson should have been forever protected against artistic failure by the facts of his biography. At the age of forty-five, as everyone knows, he found himself the manager of a small paint factory in Elyria, Ohio; one day, in the very middle of a sentence he was dictating, he walked out of the factory and gave himself to literature and truth. From the wonder of that escape he seems never to have recovered, and his continued pleasure in it did him harm, for it seems to have made him feel that the problem of the artist was defined wholly by the struggle between sincerity on the one hand and commercialism and gentility on the other. He did indeed say that the artist needed not only courage but craft, yet it was surely the courage by which he set the most store. And we must sometimes feel that he had dared too much for his art and therefore expected too much merely from his boldness, believing that right opinion must necessarily result from it. Anderson was deeply concerned with the idea of justification; there was an odd, quirky, undisciplined religious strain in him that took this form; and he expected that although Philistia might condemn him, he would have an eventual justification in the way of art and truth. He was justified in some personal way, as I have tried

to say, and no doubt his great escape had something to do with this, but it also had the effect of fatally fixing the character of his artistic life.

4. Anderson's greatest influence was probably upon those who read him in adolescence, the age when we find the books we give up but do not get over. And it now needs a little fortitude to pick up again, as many must have done upon the news of his death, the one book of his we are all sure to have read, for *Winesburg, Ohio* is not just a book, it is a personal souvenir. It is commonly owned in the Modern Library edition, very likely in the most primitive format of that series, even before it was tricked out with its vulgar little ballet-Prometheus; and the brown oilcloth binding, the coarse paper, the bold type crooked on the page, are dreadfully evocative. Even the introduction by Ernest Boyd is rank with the odor of the past, of the day when criticism existed in heroic practical simplicity, when it was all truth against hypocrisy, idealism against philistinism, and the opposite of "romanticism" was not "classicism" but "realism," which—it now seems odd—negated both. As for the Winesburg stories themselves, they are as dangerous to read again, as paining and as puzzling, as if they were old letters we had written or received.

5. It is not surprising that Anderson should have made his strongest appeal, although by no means his only one, to adolescents. For one thing, he wrote of young people with a special tenderness; one of his best-known stories is called "I Want To Know Why": it is the great adolescent question, and the world Anderson saw is essentially, and even when it is inhabited by adults, the world of the sensitive young person. It is a world that does not "understand," a world of solitude, of running away from home, of present dullness and far-off joy and eventual fulfillment; it is a world seen as suffused by one's own personality and yet—and therefore—felt as indifferent to one's own personality. And Anderson used what seems to a young person the very language to penetrate to the heart of the world's mystery, what with its rural or primeval willingness to say things thrice over, its reiterated "Well . . ." which suggests the groping of boyhood, its "Eh?" which implies the inward-turning wisdom of old age.

6. Most of us will feel now that this world of Anderson's is a pretty inadequate representation of reality and probably always was. But we cannot be sure that it was not a necessary event in our history, like adolescence itself; and no one has the adolescence he would have liked to have had. But an adolescence must not continue beyond its natural term, and as we read through Anderson's canon what exasperates us is his stubborn, satisfied continuance in his earliest attitudes. There is something undeniably impressive about the period of Anderson's work in which he was formulating his characteristic notions. We can take, especially if we have a modifying consciousness of its historical moment, *Windy MacPherson's Son*, despite its last part which is so curiously like a commercial magazine story of the time; *Marching Men* has power even though its political mysticism is repellent; *Winesburg, Ohio* has its touch of greatness; *Poor White* is heavy-handed but not without its force; and some of the stories in *The Triumph of the Egg* have the kind of grim quaintness which is, I think, Anderson's most successful mood, the mood that he occasionally achieves now and then in his later short pieces, such as "Death in the Woods." But after 1921, in *Dark Laughter* and *Many Marriages*, the books that made the greatest critical stir, there emerges in Anderson's work the compulsive, obsessive, repetitive quality which finally impresses itself on us as his characteristic quality.

7. Anderson is connected with the tradition of the men who maintain a standing quarrel with respectable society and have a perpetual bone to pick with the rational intellect. It is a very old tradition, for the Essenes, the early Franciscans, as well as the early Hasidim, may be said to belong to it. In modern times it has been continued by Blake and Whitman and D. H. Lawrence. Those who belong to the tradition usually do something more about the wrong way the world goes than merely

to denounce it—they *act out* their denunciations and assume a role and a way of life. Typically they take up their packs and leave the doomed respectable city, just as Anderson did. But Anderson lacked what his spiritual colleagues have always notably had. We may call it *mind,* but *energy* and *spiritedness,* in their relation to mind, will serve just as well. Anderson never understood that the moment of enlightenment and conversion—the walking out—cannot be merely celebrated but must be developed, so that what begins as an act of will grows to be an act of intelligence. The men of the anti-rationalist tradition mock the mind's pretensions and denounce its restrictiveness; but they are themselves the agents of the most powerful thought. They do not of course really reject mind at all, but only mind as it is conceived by respectable society, "I learned the Torah from all the limbs of my teacher," said one of the Hasidim. They think with their sensations, their emotions, and, some of them, with their sex. While denouncing intellect, they shine forth in a mental blaze of energy which manifests itself in syntax, epigram, and true discovery.

8. Anderson is not like them in this regard. He did not become a "wise" man. He did not have the gift of being able to throw out a sentence or a metaphor which suddenly illuminates some dark corner of life—his role implied that he should be full of "sayings" and specific insights, yet he never was. But in the preface to *Winesburg, Ohio* he utters one of the few really "wise" things in his work, and, by a kind of irony, it explains something of his own inadequacy. The preface consists of a little story about an old man who is writing what he calls "The Book of the Grotesque." This is the old man's ruling idea:

> That in the beginning when the world was young there were a great many thoughts but no such thing as a truth. Man made the truths himself and each truth was a composite of a great many vague thoughts. All about in the world were truths and they were all beautiful.
> The old man listed hundreds of the truths in his book. I will not try to tell you all of them. There was the truth of virginity and the

truth of passion, the truth of wealth and of poverty, of thrift and of profligacy, of carelessness and abandon. Hundreds and hundreds were the truths and they were all beautiful.

> And then the people came along. Each as he appeared snatched up one of the truths and some who were quite strong snatched up a dozen of them.
> It was the truths that made the people grotesques. The old man had quite an elaborate theory concerning the matter. It was his notion that the moment one of the people took one of the truths to himself, called it his truth, and tried to live his life by it, he became a grotesque and the truth he embraced became a falsehood.

9. Anderson snatched but a single one of the truths and it made him, in his own gentle and affectionate meaning of the word, a "grotesque"; eventually the truth itself became a kind of falsehood. It was the truth—or perhaps we must call it a simple complex of truths—of love-passion-freedom, and it was made up of these "vague thoughts": that each individual is a precious secret essence, often discordant with all other essences; that society, and more particularly the industrial society, threatens these essences; that the old good values of life have been destroyed by the industrial dispensation; that people have been cut off from each other and even from themselves. That these thoughts make a truth is certain; and its importance is equally certain. In what way could it have become a falsehood and its possessor a "grotesque"?

10. The nature of the falsehood seems to lie in this—that Anderson's affirmation of life by love, passion, and freedom had, paradoxically enough, the effect of quite negating life, making it gray, empty, and devoid of meaning. We are quite used to hearing that this is what excessive intellection can do; we are not so often warned that emotion, if it is of a certain kind, can be similarly destructive. Yet when feeling is understood as an answer, a therapeutic, when it becomes a sort of critical tool and is conceived of as excluding other activities of life, it can indeed make the world abstract and empty. Love and passion, when considered as they are by Anderson as a means of attack upon the order of the

respectable world, can contrive a world which is actually without love and passion and not worth being "free" in.[1]

11. In Anderson's world there are many emotions, or rather many instances of a few emotions, but there are very few sights, sounds, and smells, very little of the stuff of actuality. The very things to which he gives moral value because they are living and real and opposed in their organic nature to the insensate abstractness of an industrial culture become, as he writes about them, themselves abstract and without life. His praise of the race horses he said he loved gives us no sense of a horse; his Mississippi does not flow; his tall corn grows out of the soil of his dominating subjectivity. The beautiful organic things of the world are made to be admirable not for themselves but only for their moral superiority to men and machines. There are many similarities of theme between Anderson and D. H. Lawrence, but Lawrence's far stronger and more sensitive mind kept his faculty of vision fresh and true; Lawrence had eyes for the substantial and even at his most doctrinaire he knew the world of appearance.

12. And just as there is no real sensory experience in Anderson's writing, there is also no real social experience. His people do not really go to church or vote or work for money, although it is often said of them that they do

[1] In the preface of *The Sherwood Anderson Reader*, Paul Rosenfeld, Anderson's friend and admirer, has summarized in a remarkable way the vision of life which Anderson's work suggests: "Almost, it seems, we touch an absolute existence, a curious semi-animal, semi-divine life. Its chronic state is banality, prostration, dismemberment, unconsciousness; tensity with indefinite yearning and infinitely stretching desire. Its manifestation: the non-community of cranky or otherwise asocial solitaries, dispersed, impotent and imprisoned. . . . Its wonders—the wonders of its chaos—are fugitive heroes and heroines, mutilated like the dismembered Osiris, the dismembered Dionysius. . . . Painfully the absolute comes to itself in consciousness of universal feeling and helplessness. . . . It realizes itself as feeling, sincerity, understanding, as connection and unity; sometimes at the cost of the death of its creatures. It triumphs in anyone aware of its existence even in its sullen state. The moment of realization is tragically brief. Feeling, understanding, unity pass. The divine life sinks back again, dismembered and unconscious."

these things. In his desire for better social relationships Anderson could never quite see the social relationships that do in fact exist, however inadequate they may be. He often spoke, for example, of unhappy, desperate marriages and seemed to suggest that they ought to be quickly dissolved, but he never understood that marriages are often unsatisfactory for the very reasons that make it impossible to dissolve them.

13. His people have passion without body, and sexuality without gaiety and joy, although it is often through sex that they are supposed to find their salvation. John Jay Chapman said of Emerson that, great as he was, a visitor from Mars would learn less about life on earth from him than from Italian opera, for the opera at least suggested that there were two sexes. When Anderson was at the height of his reputation, it seemed that his report on the existence of two sexes was the great thing about him, the thing that made his work an advance over the literature of New England. But although the visitor from Mars might be instructed by Anderson in the mere fact of bisexuality, he would still be advised to go to the Italian opera if he seeks fuller information. For from the opera, as never from Anderson, he will acquire some of the knowledge which is normally in the possession of natives of the planet, such as that sex has certain manifestations which are socially quite complex, that it is involved with religion, politics, and the fate of nations, above all that it is frequently marked by the liveliest sort of energy.

14. In their speech his people have not only no wit, but no idiom. To say that they are not "real" would be to introduce all sorts of useless quibbles about the art of character creation; they are simply not *there*. This is not a failure of art; rather, it would seem to have been part of Anderson's intention that they should be not there. His narrative prose is contrived to that end; it is not really a colloquial idiom, although it has certain colloquial tricks; it approaches in effect the inadequate use of a foreign language; old slang persists in it and elegant archaisms are consciously used, so that people are constantly

having the "fantods," girls are frequently referred to as "maidens," and things are "like unto" other things. These mannerisms, although they remind us of some of Dreiser's, are not the result, as Dreiser's are, of an effort to be literary and impressive. Anderson's prose has a purpose to which these mannerisms are essential—it has the intention of making us doubt our familiarity with our own world, and not, we must note, in order to make things fresher for us but only in order to make them seem puzzling to us and remote from us. When a man whose name we know is frequently referred to as "the plowmaker," when we hear again and again of "a kind of candy called Milky Way" long after we have learned, if we did not already know, that Milky Way is a candy, when we are told of someone that "He became a radical. He had radical thoughts," it becomes clear that we are being asked by this false naïveté to give up our usual and on the whole useful conceptual grasp of the world we get around in.

15. Anderson liked to catch people with their single human secret, their essence, but the more he looks for their essence the more his characters vanish into the vast limbo of meaningless life, the less they are human beings. His great American heroes were Mark Twain and Lincoln, but when he writes of these two shrewd, enduring men, he robs them of all their savor and masculinity, of all their bitter resisting mind; they become little more than a pair of sensitive, suffering happy-go-luckies. The more Anderson says about people, the less alive they become—and the less lovable. Is it strange that, with all Anderson's expressed affection for them, we ourselves can never love the people he writes about? But of course we do not love people for their essence or their souls, but for their having a certain body, or wit, or idiom, certain specific relationships with things and· other people, and for a dependable continuity of existence: we love them for being there.

16. We can even for a moment entertain the thought that Anderson himself did not love his characters, else he would not have so thoroughly robbed them of substance and hustled them so quickly off the stage after their small essential moments of crisis. Anderson's love, however, was real enough; it is only that he loves under the aspect of his "truth"; it is love indeed but love become wholly abstract. Another way of putting it is that Anderson sees with the eyes of a religiosity of a very limited sort. No one, I think, has commented on the amount and quality of the mysticism that entered the thought of the writers of the twenties. We may leave Willa Cather aside, for her notion of Catholic order differentiates her; but in addition to Anderson himself, Dreiser, Waldo Frank, and Eugene O'Neill come to mind as men who had recourse to a strong but undeveloped sense of supernal powers.

17. It is easy enough to understand this crude mysticism as a protest against philosophical and moral materialism; easy enough, too, to forgive it, even when, as in Anderson, the second births and the large revelations seem often to point only to the bosom of a solemn bohemia, and almost always to a lowering rather than a heightening of energy. We forgive it because some part of the blame for its crudity must be borne by the culture of the time. In Europe a century before, Stendhal could execrate a bourgeois materialism and yet remain untempted by the dim religiosity which in America in the twenties seemed one of the likeliest of the few ways by which one might affirm the value of spirit, but then Stendhal could utter his denunciation of philistinism in the name of Mozart's music, the pictures of Cimabue, Masaccio, Giotto, Leonardo, and Michelangelo, the plays of Corneille, Racine, and Shakespeare. Of what is implied by these things Anderson seems never to have had a real intimation. His awareness of the past was limited, perhaps by his fighting faith in the "modern," and this, in a modern, is always a danger. His heroes in art and morality were few: Joyce, Lawrence, Dreiser, and Gertrude Stein, as fellow moderns; Cellini, Turgenev; there is a long piece in praise of George Borrow; he spoke of Hawthorne with contempt, for he could not understand Hawthorne except as genteel, and he said of Henry James

that he was "the novelist of those who hate," for mind seemed to him always a sort of malice. And he saw but faintly even those colleagues in art whom he did admire. His real heroes were the simple and unassuming, a few anonymous Negroes, a few craftsmen, for he gave to the idea of craftsmanship a value beyond the value which it actually does have —it is this as much as anything else that reminds us of Hemingway's relation to Anderson—and a few racing drivers of whom Pop Geers was chief. It is a charming hero worship, but it does not make an adequate antagonism to the culture which Anderson opposed, and in order to make it compelling and effective Anderson reinforced it with what is in effect the high language of religion, speaking of salvation, of the voice that will not be denied, of dropping the heavy burden of this world.

18. The salvation that Anderson was talking about was no doubt a real salvation, but it was small, and he used for it the language of the most strenuous religious experience. He spoke in visions and mysteries and raptures, but what he was speaking about after all was only the salvation of a small legitimate existence, of a quiet place in the sun and moments of leisurely peace, of not being nagged and shrew-ridden, nor deprived of one's due share of affection. What he wanted for himself and others was perhaps no more than what he got in his last years: a home, neighbors, a small daily work to do, and the right to say his say carelessly and loosely and without the sense of being strictly judged. But between this small, good life and the language which he used about it there is a discrepancy which may be thought of as a willful failure of taste,

an intended lapse of the sense of how things fit. Wyndham Lewis, in his attack in *Paleface* on the early triumphant Anderson, speaks of Anderson's work as an assault on responsibility and thoughtful maturity, on the pleasures and uses of the mind, on decent human pride, on Socratic clarity and precision; and certainly when we think of the "marching men" of Anderson's second novel, their minds lost in their marching and singing, leaving to their leader the definitions of their aims, we have what might indeed be the political consequences of Anderson's attitudes if these were carried out to their ultimate implications. Certainly the precious essence of personality to which Anderson was so much committed could not be preserved by any of the people or any of the deeds his own books delight in.

19. But what hostile critics forget about Anderson is that the cultural situation from which his writing sprang was actually much as he described it. Anderson's truth may have become a falsehood in his hands by reason of limitations in himself or in the tradition of easy populism he chose as his own, but one has only to take it out of his hands to see again that it is indeed a truth. The small legitimate existence, so necessary for the majority of men to achieve, is in our age so very hard, so nearly impossible, for them to achieve. The language Anderson used was certainly not commensurate with the traditional value which literature gives to the things he wanted, but it is not incommensurate with the modern difficulty of attaining these things. And it is his unending consciousness of this difficulty that constitutes for me the residue of admiration for him that I find I still have.

GORDON E. BIGELOW

A Primer of Existentialism

Gordon E. Bigelow (1919–   ), professor of English at the University of Florida, was born in Springfield, Massachusetts. He received his Ph.D. degree from The Johns Hopkins University in 1950. In 1961 he was a Fulbright Lecturer in American Literature at the University of Vienna. In addition to writing numerous articles on a variety of topics, he has recently focused his interest on the works of Marjorie Kinnan Rawlings. His book-length appraisal of her literary accomplishment, *Frontier Eden: The Literary Career of Marjorie Kinnan Rawlings,* was published in 1966.

"A Primer of Existentialism" is a succinct statement of the major tenets of the existentialist credo of man as expressed in literature.

1. For some years I fought the word by irritably looking the other way whenever I stumbled across it, hoping that like dadaism and some of the other "isms" of the French *avant garde* it would go away if I ignored it. But existentialism was apparently more than the picture it evoked of uncombed beards, smoky basement cafes, and French beatniks regaling one another between sips of absinthe with brilliant variations on the theme of despair. It turned out to be of major importance to literature and the arts, to philosophy and theology, and of increasing importance to the social sciences. To learn more about it, I read several of the self-styled introductions to the subject, with the baffled sensation of a man who reads a critical introduction to a novel only to find that he must read the novel before he can understand the introduction. Therefore, I should like to provide here something most discussions of existentialism take for granted, a simple state-

A PRIMER OF EXISTENTIALISM   From *College English,* December 1961. Reprinted with the permission of the National Council of Teachers of English and Gordon Bigelow.

ment of its basic characteristics. This is a reckless thing to do because there are several kinds of existentialism and what one says of one kind may not be true of another, but there is an area of agreement, and it is this common ground that I should like to set forth here. We should not run into trouble so long as we understand from the outset that the six major themes outlined below will apply in varying degrees to particular existentialists. A reader should be able to go from here to the existentialists themselves, to the more specialized critiques of them, or be able to recognize an existentialist theme or coloration in literature when he sees it.

2. A word first about the kinds of existentialism. Like transcendentalism of the last century, there are almost as many varieties of this *ism* as there are individual writers to whom the word is applied (not all of them claim it). But without being facetious we might group them into two main kinds, the *ungodly* and the *godly*. To take the ungodly or atheistic first, we would list as the chief spokesmen among many others Jean-Paul Sartre, Albert Camus, and Simone de Beau-

voir. Several of this important group of French writers had rigorous and significant experience in the Resistance during the Nazi occupation of France in World War II. Out of the despair which came with the collapse of their nation during those terrible years they found unexpected strength in the single indomitable human spirit, which even under severe torture could maintain the spirit of resistance, the unextinguishable ability to say "No." From this irreducible core in the human spirit, they erected after the war a philosophy which was a twentieth-century variation of the philosophy of Descartes. But instead of saying "I think, therefore I am," they said "I can say No, therefore I exist." As we shall presently see, the use of the word "exist" is of prime significance. This group is chiefly responsible for giving existentialism its status in the popular mind as a literary-philosophical cult.

3. Of the godly or theistic existentialists we should mention first a mid-nineteenth-century Danish writer, Søren Kierkegaard; two contemporary French Roman Catholics, Gabriel Marcel and Jacques Maritain; two Protestant theologians, Paul Tillich and Nicholas Berdyaev; and Martin Buber, an important contemporary Jewish theologian. Taken together, their writings constitute one of the most significant developments in modern theology. Behind both groups of existentialists stand other important figures, chiefly philosophers, who exert powerful influence upon the movement—Blaise Pascal, Friedrich Nietzsche, Henri Bergson, Martin Heidegger, Karl Jaspers, among others. Several literary figures, notably Tolstoy and Dostoievsky, are frequently cited because existentialist attitudes and themes are prominent in their writings. The eclectic nature of this movement should already be sufficiently clear and the danger of applying too rigidly to any particular figure the general characteristics of the movement which I now make bold to describe:

4. *Existence before essence.* Existentialism gets its name from an insistence that human life is understandable only in terms of an individual man's existence, his particular experience of life. It says that a man *lives* (has existence) rather than *is* (has being or essence), and that every man's experience of life is unique, radically different from everyone else's and can be understood truly only in terms of his involvement in life or commitment to it. It strenuously shuns that view which assumes an ideal of Man or Mankind, a universal of human nature of which each man is only one example. It eschews the question of Greek philosophy, "*What is mankind?*" which suggests that man can be defined if he is ranged in his proper place in the order of nature; it asks instead the question of Job and St. Augustine, "*Who am I?*" with its suggestion of the uniqueness and mystery of each human life and its emphasis upon the subjective or personal rather than the objective or impersonal. From the outside a man appears to be just another natural creature; from the inside he is an entire universe, the center of infinity. The existentialist insists upon this latter radically subjective view, and from this grows much of the rest of existentialism.

5. *Reason is impotent to deal with the depths of human life.* There are two parts to this proposition—first, that human reason is relatively weak and imperfect, and second, that there are dark places in human life which are "nonreason" and to which reason scarcely penetrates. Since Plato, Western civilization has usually assumed a separation of reason from the rest of the human psyche, and has glorified reason as suited to command the nonrational part. The classic statement of this separation appears in the *Phaedrus*, where Plato describes the psyche in the myth of the chariot which is drawn by the white steeds of the emotions and the black unruly steeds of the appetites. The driver of the chariot is Reason who holds the reins which control the horses and the whip to subdue the surging black steeds of passion. Only the driver, the rational nature, is given human form; the rest of the psyche, the nonrational part, is given a lower, animal form. This separation and exaltation of reason is carried further in the allegory of the cave in the *Republic*. You recall the sombre picture of human life with which the story begins: men are chained in the dark in a cave, with their backs to a

flickering firelight, able to see only uncertain shadows moving on the wall before them, able to hear only confused echoes of sounds. One of the men, breaking free from his chains, is able to turn and look upon the objects themselves and the light which casts the shadows; even, at last, he is able to work his way entirely out of the cave into the sunlight beyond. All this he is able to do through his reason; he escapes from the bondage of error, from time and change, from death itself, into the realm of changeless eternal ideas or Truth, and the lower nature which had chained him in darkness is left behind.

6. Existentialism in our time, and this is one of its most important characteristics, insists upon reuniting the "lower" or irrational parts of the psyche with the "higher." It insists that man must be taken in his wholeness and not in some divided state, that whole man contains not only intellect but also anxiety, guilt, and the will to power—which modify and sometimes overwhelm the reason. A man seen in this light is fundamentally ambiguous, if not mysterious, full of contradictions and tensions which cannot be dissolved simply by taking thought. "Human life," said Berdyaev, "is permeated by underground streams." One is reminded of D. H. Lawrence's outburst against Franklin and his rational attempt to achieve moral perfection: "The Perfectability of Man! . . . The perfectability of which man? I am many men. Which of them are you going to perfect? I am not a mechanical contrivance. . . . It's a queer thing is a man's soul. It is the whole of him. Which means it is the unknown as well as the known. . . . The soul of man is a dark vast forest, with wild life in it." The emphasis in existentialism is not on idea but upon the thinker who has the idea. It accepts not only his power of thought, but his contingency and fallibility, his frailty, his body, blood, and bones, and above all his death. Kierkegaard emphasized the distinction between *subjective* truth (what a person *is*) and *objective* truth (what the person *knows*), and said that we encounter the true self not in the detachment of thought but in the involvement and agony of choice and in the pathos of commitment to our choice. This distrust of rational systems helps to explain why many existential writers in their own expression are paradoxical or prophetic or gnomic, why their works often belong more to literature than to philosophy.

7. *Alienation or estrangement.* One major result of the dissociation of reason from the rest of the psyche has been the growth of science, which has become one of the hallmarks of Western civilization, and an ever-increasing rational ordering of men in society. As the existentialists view them, the main forces of history since the Renaissance have progressively separated man from concrete earthy existence, have forced him to live at ever higher levels of abstraction, have collectivized individual man out of existence, have driven God from the heavens, or what is the same thing, from the hearts of men. They are convinced that modern man lives in a fourfold condition of alienation: from God, from nature, from other men, from his own true self.

8. The estrangement from God is most shockingly expressed by Nietzsche's anguished cry, "God is dead," a cry which has continuously echoed through the writings of the existentialists, particularly the French. This theme of spiritual barrenness is a commonplace in literature of this century, from Eliot's "Hollow Man" to the novels of Dos Passos, Hemingway, and Faulkner. It often appears in writers not commonly associated with the existentialists as in this remarkable passage from A Story-Teller's Story, where Sherwood Anderson describes his own awakening to his spiritual emptiness. He tells of walking alone late at night along a moonlit road when,

I had suddenly an odd, and to my own seeming, a ridiculous desire to abase myself before something not human and so stepping into the moonlit road, I knelt in the dust. Having no God, the gods having been taken from me by the life about me, as a personal God has been taken from all modern men by a force within that man himself does not understand but that is called the intellect, I kept smiling at the figure I cut in my own eyes as I knelt in the road. . . .

There was no God in the sky, no God in myself, no conviction in myself that I had the power to believe in a God, and so I merely knelt in the dust in silence and no words came to my lips.

In another passage Anderson wondered if the giving of itself by an entire generation to mechanical things was not really making all men impotent, if the desire for a greater navy, a greater army, taller public buildings, was not a sign of growing impotence. He felt that Puritanism and the industrialism which was its offspring has sterilized modern life, and proposed that men return to a healthful animal vigor by renewed contact with simple things of the earth, among them untrammeled sexual expression. One is reminded of the unkempt and delectable raffishness of Steinbeck's *Cannery Row* or of D. H. Lawrence's quasi-religious doctrine of sex, "blood-consciousness" and the "divine otherness" of animal existence.

9. Man's estrangement from nature has been a major theme in literature at least since Rousseau and the Romantic movement, and can hardly be said to be the property of existentialists. But this group nevertheless adds its own insistence that one of modern man's most urgent dangers is that he builds ever higher the brick and steel walls of technology which shut him away from a health-giving life according to "nature." Their treatment of this theme is most commonly expressed as part of a broader insistence that modern man needs to shun abstraction and return to "concreteness" or "wholeness."

10. A third estrangement has occurred at the social level and its sign is a growing dismay at man's helplessness before the great machine-like colossus of industrialized society. This is another major theme of Western literature, and here again, though they hardly discovered the danger or began the protest, the existentialists in our time renew the protest against any pattern or force which would stifle the unique and spontaneous in individual life. The crowding of men into cities, the subdivision of labor which submerges the man in his economic function, the burgeoning of centralized government, the growth of advertising, propaganda, and mass media of entertainment and communication—all the things which force men into Riesman's "Lonely Crowd"— these same things drive men asunder by destroying their individuality and making them live on the surface of life, content to deal with things rather than people. "Exteriorization," says Berdyaev, "is the source of slavery, whereas freedom is interiorization. Slavery always indicates alienation, the ejection of human nature into the external." This kind of alienation is exemplified by Zero, in Elmer Rice's play "The Adding Machine." Zero's twenty-five years as a bookkeeper in a department store have dried up his humanity, making him incapable of love, of friendship, of any deeply felt, freely expressed emotion. Such estrangement is often given as the reason for man's inhumanity to man, the explanation for injustice in modern society. In Camus' short novel, aptly called *The Stranger,* a young man is convicted by a court of murder. This is a homicide which he has actually committed under extenuating circumstances. But the court never listens to any of the relevant evidence, seems never to hear anything that pertains to the crime itself; it convicts the young man on wholly irrelevant grounds—because he had behaved in an unconventional way at his mother's funeral the day before the homicide. In this book one feels the same dreamlike distortion of reality as in the trial scene in *Alice in Wonderland,* a suffocating sense of being enclosed by events which are irrational or absurd but also inexorable. Most disturbing of all is the young man's aloneness, the impermeable membrane of estrangement which surrounds him and prevents anyone else from penetrating to his experience of life or sympathizing with it.

11. The fourth kind of alienation, man's estrangement from his own true self, especially as his nature is distorted by an exaltation of reason, is another theme having an extensive history as a major part of the Romantic revolt. Of the many writers who treat the theme, Hawthorne comes particularly close to the emphasis of contemporary existentialists. His Ethan Brand, Dr. Rappaccini, and Roger Chillingworth are a recurrent figure who represents the dislocation in human nature which

results when an overdeveloped or misapplied intellect severs "the magnetic chain of human sympathy." Hawthorne is thoroughly existential in his concern for the sanctity of the individual human soul, as well as in his preoccupation with sin and the dark side of human nature, which must be seen in part as his attempt to build back some fullness to the flattened image of man bequeathed to him by the Enlightenment. Whitman was trying to do this when he added flesh and bone and a sexual nature to the spiritualized image of man he inherited from Emerson, though his image remains diffused and attenuated by the same cosmic optimism. Many of the nineteenth-century depictions of man represent him as a figure of power or of potential power, sometimes as daimonic, like Melville's Ahab, but after World War I the power is gone; man is not merely distorted or truncated, he is hollow, powerless, faceless. At the time when his command over natural forces seems to be unlimited, man is pictured as weak, ridden with nameless dread. And this brings us to another of the major themes of existentialism.

12. *"Fear and trembling," Anxiety.* At Stockholm when he accepted the Nobel Prize, William Faulkner said that "Our tragedy today is a general and universal physical fear so long sustained by now that we can even bear it. There are no longer problems of the spirit. There is only one question: When will I be blown up?" The optimistic vision of the Enlightenment which saw man, through reason and its extensions in science, conquering all nature and solving all social and political problems in a continuous upward spiral of Progress, cracked open like a melon on the rock of World War I. The theories which held such high hopes died in that sickening and unimaginable butchery. Here was a concrete fact of human nature and society which the theories could not contain. The Great Depression and World War II deepened the sense of dismay which the loss of these ideals brought, but only with the atomic bomb did this become an unbearable terror, a threat of instant annihilation which confronted all men, even those most insulated by the thick crust of material goods and services. Now the most un-thinking person could sense that each advance in mechanical technique carried not only a chromium and plush promise of comfort but a threat as well.

13. Sartre, following Kierkegaard, speaks of another kind of anxiety which oppresses modern man—"the anguish of Abraham"—the necessity which is laid upon him to make moral choices on his own responsibility. A military officer in wartime knows the agony of choice which forces him to sacrifice part of his army to preserve the rest, as does a man in high political office, who must make decisions affecting the lives of millions. The existentialists claim that each of us must make moral decisions in our own lives which involve the same anguish. Kierkegaard finds that this necessity is one thing which makes each life unique, which makes it impossible to speculate or generalize about human life, because each man's case is irretrievably his own, something in which he is personally and passionately involved. His book *Fear and Trembling* is an elaborate and fascinating commentary on the Old Testament story of Abraham, who was commanded by God to sacrifice his beloved son Isaac. Abraham thus becomes the emblem of man who must make a harrowing choice, in this case between love for his son and love for God, between the universal moral law which says categorically, "thou shalt not kill," and the unique inner demand of his religious faith. Abraham's decision, which is to violate the abstract and collective moral law, has to be made not in arrogance but in fear and trembling, one of the inferences being that sometimes one must make an exception to the general law because he is (existentially) an exception, a concrete being whose existence can never be completely subsumed under any universal.

14. *The encounter with Nothingness.* For the man alienated from God, from nature, from his fellow man and from himself, what is left at last but Nothingness? The testimony of the existentialists is that this is where modern man now finds himself, not on the highway of upward Progress toward a radiant Utopia but on the brink of a catastrophic precipice, below which yawns the absolute void,

an uncompromised black Nothingness. In one sense this is Eliot's Wasteland inhabited by his Hollow Man, who is

> Shape without form, shade without color
> Paralyzed force, gesture without motion.

This is what moves E. A. Robinson's Richard Cory, the man who is everything that might make us wish that we were in his place, to go home one calm summer night and put a bullet through his head.

15. One of the most convincing statements of the encounter with Nothingness is made by Leo Tolstoy in "My Confession." He tells how in good health, in the prime of life, when he had everything that a man could desire—wealth, fame, aristocratic social position, a beautiful wife and children, a brilliant mind and great artistic talent in the height of their powers, he nevertheless was seized with a growing uneasiness, a nameless discontent which he could not shake or alleviate. His experience was like that of a man who falls sick, with symptoms which he disregards as insignificant; but the symptoms return again and again until they merge into a continuous suffering. And the patient suddenly is confronted with the overwhelming fact that what he took for mere indisposition is more important to him than anything else on earth, that it is death! "I felt the ground on which I stood was crumbling, that there was nothing for me to stand on, that what I had been living for was nothing, that I had no reason for living. . . . To stop was impossible, to go back was impossible; and it was impossible to shut my eyes so as to see that there was nothing before me but suffering and actual death, absolute annihilation." This is the "Sickness Unto Death" of Kierkegaard, the despair in which one wishes to die but cannot. Hemingway's short story, "A Clean, Well-Lighted Place," gives an unforgettable expression of this theme. At the end of the story, the old waiter climbs into bed late at night saying to himself, "What did he fear? It was not fear or dread. It was a nothing which he knew too well. It was all a nothing and a man was nothing too. . . . Nada y pues nada, y nada y pues nada." And then because he has experienced the death of God he goes on to recite the Lord's Prayer in blasphemous despair: "Our Nothing who are in Nothing, nothing be thy nothing. . . ." And then the Ave Maria, "Hail nothing, full of nothing. . . ." This is stark, even for Hemingway, but the old waiter does no more than name the void felt by most people in the early Hemingway novels, a hunger they seek to assuage with alcohol, sex, and violence in an aimless progress from bar to bed to bull-ring. It goes without saying that much of the despair and pessimism in other contemporary authors springs from a similar sense of the void in modern life.

16. *Freedom.* Sooner or later, as a theme that includes all the others, the existentialist writings bear upon freedom. The themes we have outlined above describe either some loss of man's freedom or some threat to it, and all existentialists of whatever sort are concerned to enlarge the range of human freedom.

17. For the avowed atheists like Sartre freedom means human autonomy. In a purposeless universe man is *condemned* to freedom because he is the only creature who is "self-surpassing," who can become something other than he is. Precisely because there is no God to give purpose to the universe, each man must accept individual responsibility for his own becoming, a burden made heavier by the fact that in choosing for himself he chooses for all men "the image of man as he ought to be." A man *is* the sum total of the acts that make up his life—no more, no less—and though the coward has made himself cowardly, it is always possible for him to change and make himself heroic. In Sartre's novel, *The Age of Reason*, one of the least likable of the characters, almost overwhelmed by despair and self-disgust at his homosexual tendencies, is on the point of solving his problem by mutilating himself with a razor, when in an effort of will he throws the instrument down, and we are given to understand that from this moment he will have mastery over his aberrant drive. Thus in the daily course of ordinary life must men shape their becoming in Sartre's world.

18. The religious existentialists interpret man's freedom differently. They use much the same language as Sartre, develop the same

themes concerning the predicament of man, but always include God as a radical factor. They stress the man of faith rather than the man of will. They interpret man's existential condition as a state of alienation from his essential nature which is God-like, the problem of his life being to heal the chasm between the two, that is, to find salvation. The mystery and ambiguity of man's existence they attribute to his being the intersection of two realms. "Man bears within himself," writes Berdyaev, "the image which is both the image of man and the image of God, and is the image of man as far as the image of God is actualized." Tillich describes salvation as "the act in which the cleavage between the essential being and the existential situation is overcome." Freedom here, as for Sartre, involves an acceptance of responsibility for choice and a *commitment* to one's choice. This is the meaning of faith, a faith like Abraham's, the commitment which is an agonizing sacrifice of one's own desire and will and dearest treasure to God's will.

19. A final word. Just as one should not expect to find in a particular writer all of the characteristics of existentialism as we have described them, he should also be aware that some of the most striking expressions of existentialism in literature and the arts come to us by indirection, often through symbols or through innovations in conventional form. Take the preoccupation of contemporary writers with time. In *The Sound and the Fury,* Faulkner both collapses and expands normal clock time, or by juxtapositions of past and present blurs time into a single amorphous pool. He does this by using various forms of "stream of consciousness" or other techniques which see life in terms of unique, subjective experience—that is, existentially. The conventional view of externalized life, a rational orderly progression cut into uniform segments by the hands of a clock, he rejects in favor of a view which sees life as opaque, ambiguous, and irrational—that is, as the existentialist sees it. Graham Greene does something like this in *The Power and the Glory.* He creates a scene isolated in time and cut off from the rest of the world, steamy and suffocating as if a bell jar had been placed over it. Through this atmosphere fetid with impending death and human suffering, stumbles the whiskey priest, lonely and confused, pursued by a police lieutenant who has experienced the void and the death of God.

20. Such expressions in literature do not mean necessarily that the authors are conscious existentialist theorizers, or even that they know the writings of such theorizers. Faulkner may never have read Heidegger—or St. Augustine—both of whom attempt to demonstrate that time is more within a man and subject to his unique experience of it than it is outside him. But it is legitimate to call Faulkner's views of time and life "existential" in this novel because in recent years existentialist theorizers have given such views a local habitation and a name. One of the attractions, and one of the dangers, of existential themes is that they become like Sir Thomas Browne's quincunx: once one begins to look for them, he sees them everywhere. But if one applies restraint and discrimination, he will find that they illuminate much of contemporary literature and sometimes the literature of the past as well.

SEAN O'CASEY

The Harp in the Air Still Sings

Sean O'Casey (1880–1964), an Irish playwright, is known for his highly individual and beautiful prose style and as an outspoken critic in matters of literary, social, and religious significance. Of his several plays written between 1923 and 1946, the best known are *Juno and the Paycock*, 1924 (for which he received the Hawthornden Prize in 1926); *The Plough and the Stars*, 1926; and *Red Roses for Me*, 1942. Although he continued to write plays, in his later years he gave his attention to writing several volumes of reminiscences including *I Knock at the Door*, 1939; *Pictures in the Hallway*, 1942; *Inishfallen, Fare Thee Well*, 1949; *Rose and Crown*, 1952; *Mirror in My House*, 1958; and *Autobiographies*, a two-volume work, 1963. Among his last works was a collection of essays, *Under a Colored Cap: Articles Merry and Mournful with Comments and a Song*, 1964.

"The Harp in the Air Still Sings," written in Mr. O'Casey's characteristic "harpstrung prose," reveals his unquenchable optimism and love of life. Speaking of this essay, Mr. O'Casey wrote to the editors, "If you think it worthwhile that it may do something to encourage the young to fight for life, till sense and sensibility bring about a way wherein the young can live a full time, doing many things, not great, but useful and bright, lasting till the sleep of old age forces them to go apart and rest from their labors, you're welcome to the article."

1. Many have tried, more are still trying, to frighten hope from the human heart, but all find it hard to coax away, or root it out, though, God help them, they do their best. To them hope springs infernal in the human breast, and they mock at any writer who guards and cherishes it still. Present-day writers of poem, play or novel seem to set words down as they stand before a wailing wall; each writes with "his hand on his bosom, his head on his knee chanting oh, willow, oh, willow, oh, willow!"

2. The brightest and best of their sons of the morning totter through the time like those who had just finished a marathon dance of a

THE HARP IN THE AIR STILL SINGS Reprinted from the *New York Times Magazine*, January 19, 1959. Reprinted by permission of the author.

week's duration, and had drunken too much liquor during the passing of the dance tunes, and now feel too damn weary for words to tell. Their characters or ideas drag their feet, like the spirits of the hypocrites shod in lead, shuffling about in Dante's Inferno; they keep eyes closed to show man was born blind; they hold arm and hand limp as if power of movement never reigned in either of them. But their mouths are never shut; they keep up the warning wail sent out by Sean O'Dwyer of the Glen that man has been worsted in the fight, and that life has taken a false name. To them life is a drunken sailor, a roaring, sly, staggering misery, with nothing living knowing what to do with him; and more, a bloodier villain than terms can give him out to be.

Hope not, love not, ye hopeless sons of clay;
  Hope's brightest wreaths are made of earthly
    flowers,
Things that are made to fade and fall away
  Ere they have blossom'd for a few short hours.

Oh, Lord! But it isn't true, for earthly flowers
are lovely; and when one dies another takes
its place to bloom as fair; and so sweet flowers
shall last till time has ceased to be.

3. Caroline Sheridan Norton wrote this
verse, and died three years before I was born
to sing a different song, facing those who have
followed this lady singing her song in a variety of keys—Kafka, Orwell, Eliot, Mauriac,
Beckett, Genet, Ionesco, Greene, Camus, leading a host of following intelligentsia—a great
galaxy of darkened stars dulling the human
sky.

4. Most of them are very fine writers indeed
but, to me, it seems they are setting down the
history of life as a Doomsday Book; though
Beckett wears his rue with a difference. He is
a poet, of course, but there is humor as well
as music in his prose. One has but to listen to
good artists speaking it within a monologue
or in the little group of "Waiting for Godot"
or "All Who Fall" to hear the music and feel
a touch from humor in the twisting, sad re-
countal.

5. Gloomy and full of expanding doubt in
humankind as these may be, they are fine artists, and so are stimulating in their darkened
vision as Joyce is, too, and a few others. In
Beckett, perhaps also in Mauriac, there is a
deep compassionate feeling for the many woes
of man. It is the minor spirits, who follow and
crib their ideas from the masters, that spread
despair and the woe of life the world over,
without the exaltation of the fine style of their
betters; these who persuade, or labor to persuade, life that the good earth is but a mad-
house, a jail, and a morgue. A bright place to
live in surely! Trying even to teach light to
counterfeit a gloom. Every sentence they write
abandons life, yet they themselves cling to it
as the ivy clings to the wall, grip it with all
their might, and seek a doctor when they feel
a cold coming.

6. It's not a new thing, this angry rejection
of the facts and stresses of life; the hasty shout

and the shaking of a fist in thought and in
word at God and the world. Time and again
the lusty, ever active Elizabethans rail at nature, at God's way, and at the frequent disappointments of life. Thus Chapman's Mont-
surry:

Since all earth's pleasures are so short and small,
Th'way t'enjoy it is t'abjure it all.

And another exclaims crossly:

  What is the pleasure of life
  But the good hours of an ague?

7. Life, too, often puts on the Black Cap for
Shakespeare; in many a part of his plays and
sonnets he wails at fortune, mocks at life, at
the dangers life must meet, at its terrible uncertainty, its rare joys as uncertain as the uncertain glory of an April day; rails blasphe-
mously even against the God he is said to have
believed in:

As flies to wanton boys are we to the gods,
They kill us for their sport.

But Shakespeare doesn't stay very long with
his sorrows; he sings and dances even in the
midst of them, come into these yellow sands
and then take hands, foot it featly here and
there—and already he has forgotten his dejection.

8. He can weep following Hamlet's or Lear's
bier, but he can soon hurry away to the Boar's
Head to drink a flagon of sack with Falstaff.
Despondency met him in the theater, in the
street at times, halting to say a few words in
his ear; but the poet was always in a crowd of
thoughts and things so that he soon lost sight
of his dismal adviser in the animated hurly-
burly of his activities.

9. Milton, too, had his dark moments. Pen-
sive souls accosted him, lost spirits troubled
him; he saw Samson in deep and angry misery.
But among them he saw Laughter holding
both his sides. Young Keats, assailed by many,
a bed his home for most of the time, dying, yet
sang like a linnet, and we hear his song still.
The romantic Byron, who cloaked himself at
times in stately gloom, yet wrote the gay satire
Childe Harold, yet in it all, joy was not always
absent from the pilgrim's face; sang many a

lovely song, and crammed an immense amount of work into a gallant and gadding life.

10. It is recorded somewhere that the solemn and stately poet Yeats complaining dejectedly of the Theatre Company's failure to speak parts in a play the way he wanted them spoken, gestured toward a goat, used in another play, and moaned that this animal was the one living thing there knowing what to do and how to act truly, never making a mistake. The poet was interrupted by an outcry from a stagehand, "Ay looka Mister Yeats, looka, the blasted goat's atin' the stage ivy!" The stately and solemn poet looked, saw, and turned aside to give time and space to a merry laugh. Laughter is always pulling us aside from dejection; and we hurt ourselves and hurt others when we refuse to feel laughter tugging at our sleeve.

11. In most plays written yesterday or today, there never seems to be room for a laugh, or for any rough or gentle belief in the greatness of life or the goodness of man; no admiration for, no enjoyment in, the wonder of his ways. They think only of their own personal importance. A book has just been put out packed with the plays of yesterday; they are faced by a preface from Kenneth Tynan, who thinks them to be plays of rebellion. No interest in politics, rebels only against uniformity, ignoring capitalism, communism, using cult-language, wearing eccentric dress, exulting in private philosophies, separating themselves (as they think) from the communal society in which they live. A very safe form of rebellion; a rebellion of personal bawling.

12. No one can escape from the society in which he lives. Anyone who thinks himself a rebel because he's dressed differently isn't armed against society even with a blunt pin. Anyone in America or Great Britain can, if so desiring, wear the gayest of colors, and no one will wish to hike him off to jail. Myself when young wore a gay kilt, a gayer shawl, pinned with a big brooch, and a bonnet sporting an eagle's feather, and I felt no more concern walking Dublin streets than a MacKenzie or a McCloud would feel in Edinburgh town dressed in the kilts of their clans. An old man now, I like bright jerseys and gaily colored

caps, but I never feel separate from the doctor, the scientist, or the business man who dress in conformity with the manner of their professions.

13. One play tells us that "everybody's wedged in; nobody can move; nobody counts"; and another shouts, "Rules, Laws, Guides, Promises, Terms, Guarantees, Traditions: into the pot with the whole bloody lot of them!" A third says, "Have you got your permit and your promise? They'll prove to you either that you live in the best possible world or that you *will* do, and they'll prove it either by dialectic or by the Bible. But can you wait that long? Have you ever given your instinct a chance to say whether you are happy or not, or whether you want to kill or not?"

14. A grand gospel! A nice lot we'd be, and a fine condition of life we'd live, if there were neither rule nor law! We might exist, but we couldn't live without them. They are necessary for our civil and social salvation. Our problem is not to do away with them, but to make them better, more sensible for all: national rules and international rules.

15. We take our cue from nature that has her own. Nice thing if the earth suddenly got stubborn, saying, "I'm fed up with moving, I'll stay where I am," and halted in the winter solstice, so that we should never again see the darling buds of May! We are under rule when we go to work, when we go to church, when we go to hospital, when we go to play, and we'll be under rule when we get to heaven or go to hell.

16. Rebels! These aren't rebels against any stupidity, any injustice, but merely runners-away from life. The fault in life lies not in the stars above them, not in the earth beneath, not in the people with whom they live, but in themselves. They seem to think the rhythm of the universe starts from them, and the tick of time's clock goes with their heart's deadbeat.

17. Frustration, disappointment, grief is the portion of all; these are personal, and life takes little or no notice of them, but goes on living. Like pain, these things must be borne, must be conquered as they come, so that we can leave their loneliness, and enter into the grand

fight again. Man is the only life on earth which can see its form and love its grandeur; he has enriched the earth, for without him it would have no meaning, and look dead, be dead. He has ennobled the star we stand on; exceptional souls give things exceptional beauty.

18. When Jesus looked and saw the lilies of the field and said to those around Him, "I say unto you that even Solomon in all his glory was not arrayed like one of these," He gave the blossoms an eternal beauty; and when Shakespeare, looking at another flower in an English field, said,

Daffodils
That come before the swallow dares, and take
The winds of March with beauty

he gave the flowers a beauty and a courage unrecognized before.

19. Mankind teems with brave men and women and good Samaritans. However rough the sea, the lifeboat goes out to deliver perishing men from stormy waters and a battered ship. When cholera appears in Egypt, planes from every nation come sailing in to banish the curse. In a bombing raid a young nurse stays in a ward from which patients cannot be removed, and dies there with them.

20. There is a threatened epidemic of smallpox in Glasgow, and surgeons and nurses isolate themselves with the afflicted; a patient, doctor, and nurse die, but the threatened danger is over. A lad of thirteen sees two girls sinking in the sea; he goes out, brings in one, goes again and, after a fine fight, brings the other girl safe, too. Life will never want for heroes, mostly unhonored and unsung, but always there, and ready to act.

21. Our world has grandeur and life has hope. In spite of the despair of the beats and the wailers, the harp in the air still sings the melody of hope, and hope in action will sing on everlastingly till, maybe, a thousand million years from now time gives its last sigh, and all things go.

PART TWO

Biography

The earliest biographers were probably those minstrels who praised the deeds of heroes in extemporaneous song. As a hero's exploits increased—in fact or in imagination—the songs grew in length and number, until at last the total reached epic proportions. Such, for instance, was the genesis of our most ancient epics, the *Iliad* and the *Odyssey*. Almost as ancient, and strictly speaking more biographical, are the accounts of the lives of the prophets in the Old Testament.

The earliest example of the carefully wrought, formal type of biography was Plutarch's *Parallel Lives*, written in the first century A.D., which presented in a series of contrasting pairs the lives of a number of famous Greeks and Romans. Plutarch's chief concern was with men as types of moral excellence or moral weakness, rather than as individuals endowed with complex personal characteristics.

During the centuries of development between Plutarch's *Lives* and the biography as we know it today, biographical writing took many forms, including miraculous lives of the saints and a multitude of chronicle accounts of kings and conquerors. The compelling motives in these biographical endeavors were largely didactic or commemorative. In the sixteenth and seventeenth centuries, however, a greater degree of curiosity about how other people thought and lived was reflected in such experiments in biographical writing as prefatory biographical essays, character sketches, printed funeral sermons, letters, and diaries. In short, emphasis was placed on the historical rather than the ethical motive, and more attention was given to the individual as a secular being.

The next stage in the development of biography centers around two prominent eighteenth-century writers—Samuel Johnson and James Boswell. Johnson insisted that the whole truth be given about a man: "If a man is to write *A Panegyrick*, he may keep vices out of sight; but if he professes to write *A Life*, he must write it as it was." James Boswell followed this dictum of his master and in consequence established for biography a permanent place as a type of literature. In *The Life of Samuel Johnson,* one of the most fascinating books in all of English literature, Boswell captured Johnson's individuality, wit, wisdom, and arrogance. As a work of art, Boswell's masterpiece possesses charm, realism, psychological analysis, and force far surpassing that of any of its predecessors.

The spirit of scientific accuracy and the respect for exhaustive scholarly research that characterized the late nineteenth century resulted in long, detailed biographies of the "life and times" type. These not only recounted the events of a man's life but used that life as a center around which to organize a history of the times in which the character lived. As a consequence, nineteenth-century biographies are of great scope: Lockhart's life of his father-in-law, Sir Walter Scott, was first published in ten volumes; Froude's *Life of Carlyle*, in four volumes; Forster's *Life of Dickens*, in three volumes.

In recent years biographical writing has undergone the same extension of technique and purpose noticeable in other literary genres. Murray Kempton and James Ridgeway's "Romans" illustrates how a befitting objectivity can enhance the enjoyment of biography and give the reader confidence in the biographer's integrity. Sir Arthur Bryant's "Becket" demonstrates how a recording of the events in which a man participated can be used to tell the story of his life.

Similarly, good autobiography today does much more than detail an account of a person's own life. George Orwell, in "Shooting an Elephant" (in Part One), uses a personal experience to support an expository theme. Marjorie Kinnan Rawlings' autobiographical account of "The Pound Party," with her careful handling of character, scene, and incident, makes an impact upon the reader comparable to that of the short story. Archie Carr's "The Black Beach" demonstrates how a relationship established by chance while Carr was on a scientific expedition is made interesting through the medium of a well-written personal narrative.

Among modern readers biographical writing competes keenly in popularity with other types of literature. Perhaps for this reason many recent biographers have drawn heavily on modern psychology for method in character analysis and on drama and the short story for techniques of presenting their subjects. Emphasis in this kind of writing is on character and personality. A person's shortcomings and follies, his merits and his virtues—all are displayed with equal exactitude. Modern biography, notable for its clever, crisp, and highly readable style, at its best combines Plutarch's effective use of anecdotes, Boswell's skill in character analysis and ability to reproduce vivid conversation, and the scientific demand for truth and factual accuracy which marked the nineteenth-century taste.

Every scantling of information or clue to character found in letters, journals, diaries, conversations of friends or enemies, published works, and magazine articles becomes the substance of biography. It has been said that Lytton Strachey, the eminent English biographer, read and studied a roomful of books and other printed matter in order to write his two-hundred-page life of Queen Victoria.

Autobiographical writing has followed a course paralleling that of biography, with even closer attention to the selection of significant detail and a refreshing liveliness of style. Experimentation in autobiographical writing started when man first began keeping a record of his life in memoirs, diaries, letters, and chronicles. However, the early eighteenth century marks the first use of the word *autobiography* to describe a narrative with the writer's life constituting the central framework. Autobiography as a literary form is perhaps as popular today as biography, though not as extensively written.

The enjoyment of reading biography will be heightened if the reader observes closely the choice of illustrative detail—detail that not only gives literary or historical perspective but presents the subjects as human beings endowed with traits of genius of differing kinds. So it is with all good biography: in reading it one broadens one's store of factual knowledge and gains an understanding of human behavior. In addition one can come intimately to know important people and find history personalized.

ESTHER R. B. WAGNER

The Stern and Rock-Bound Coast of Chicago

Esther R. B. Wagner (1917–   ), a teacher and writer, is a Chicagoan by birth and a Westerner by adoption, who went East to Bryn Mawr College for her education. Her first novel, *The Gift of Rome,* 1961, a story about a murder trial in ancient Rome, was written in collaboration with her husband, John Wagner. In addition, she has written stories for the *Atlantic Monthly, Harper's,* and *The New Yorker.* At present she is a professor of English at the University of Puget Sound in Tacoma, Washington.

"The Stern and Rock-Bound Coast of Chicago," a charming personal narrative, relates Mrs. Wagner's observations of the French and their system of education, with its age-old conservative tradition in educational techniques and examination procedures. Her story brings into bold relief the difference between the American and French systems of university training.

In Paris in the late thirties, the French seemed a bit sad and sour about France. We American students had not expected this. A group of us—girls from Wellesley, Vassar, Bryn Mawr; boys from Brown, Amherst, Dartmouth—were spending our junior year there under a special arrangement between our colleges and the University of Paris. An American organization had been formed to preside over this arrangement, and over us. We studied French literature, philosophy, art, and history, and we lived with French families that the organization found for us. For all our American bounce, we had come in intellectual humility—second-generation Gauls in the Roman

forum, full of a frontier energy but with our minds hungry for the essences of civilization. We wanted to hear the French talk about France, and to receive light through their speech. But the French kept saying *"Pauvre France!"* and talking about America. Young Frenchmen took us—the American girls—to night clubs to hear Negro orchestras, and there lectured us about American jazz. We muttered feebly the names of Hal Kemp and Eddy Duchin, and were given shocked glances. Other young men asked us about Faulkner. We shook our heads and mumbled, wanting to hear about Mauriac. They rolled up their eyes and shrugged.

Ellen, who was in my dormitory at college, shared quarters with me in Paris too. We lived with a dignified French family, all of whose members were rather elderly. They were kind to us, and always courteous, but we found at once that the conversation of French people older than our young men put our simple minds into a state of complete confusion. And I believe the rest of our group had the same experience. Soon, in my letters to my home, in Chicago, I stopped writing about the French people, and took to describing only landscapes and furniture. But for Ellen and me, during two hours a week, there was at least one place where we got what we had come to find.

Every Monday and Wednesday, we rose early, stuffed ourselves with bread and marmalade and chocolate, and ran to catch the bus that took us to the Sorbonne for the early lecture of Professor Gelin (as I will call him) on the Literature of the Middle Ages and the Renaissance. This was one of the Courses in French Civilization that were given exclusively for foreign students. It was not required, and Ellen and I were almost the only Americans who had signed up for it. We sat in a huge amphitheatre, surrounded by scribbling Swedes, Danes, and Norwegians, a number of Swiss, a few Germans, and many English. Note-taking and concentration filled the air around us, but we did not take notes. For one thing, we had discovered, to our total mystification, that you could buy the Professor's lectures, complete, in any little bookstore near the Sorbonne, and that his book on the subject—containing many of the lectures almost verbatim and elaborated with considerable bibliography—was also available there for a few francs. So we felt that the pressure was off. But the real reason we dispensed with notes was that Professor Gelin was, for us, an object of such beauty and grace that we felt we could not afford to take our eyes from his glorious white-bearded, deep-eyed face for a single instant.

He would lean across his dark lectern and speak to us of Villon's mother, and, raising one long, yellow hand, would recite verses in his deep, unshaken old voice—"*Qui pour moy ot douleur amère, Dieu le sçait, et mainte tristesse . . .*" —with infinite deliberation, touching the mute "e"s with infinite delicacy, and our breath would stop in our throats. Then,

with the curious effect of slow motion that distinguished all his gestures, he would lower his hand to the lectern and pause for a moment, looking at us from under his heavy lids. He would talk of the tavern signs in Villon, and of the students' Paris they evoked, and his voice, his beard, his eyelids were, for a long, beautiful hour each week, our Paris. Villon's Paris was the instrument he played, for our delight.

The American student group was well taken care of in Paris. At a charming old building in the Rue de Chevreuse, we were intellectually massaged and ministered to by a corps of special tutors, who assigned us essays to write and readings to report on, and who watched over our French and briefed us for the examinations. They taught us to write *dissertations* in the French style, and once we had grasped the fact that no one was interested in our personal thoughts—that in a *dissertation* we were simply expected to repeat in a ritually organized, methodically graceful fashion what we had read and heard about the subject, confining our originality to the selection of phrases and figures of speech—we found ourselves able to perform the task with considerable ease. We simply had to forget, for the moment, our American professors' obsession with "independent thought" and the individual ordering of materials. As the term went on, we learned to quote, with *élan* and *finesse*, and to forget about documentation. Ellen and I, our French and our mental processes having been hammered into shape relentlessly at our American college, which had a faculty notorious for its unwillingness to fool, did rather well at this. Our French friends laughed at our early *dissertations*, full of our private notions concerning the beauties of Racine, but they nodded in approval at our later ones, full of recapitulations of the best authorities and ornamented with familiar examples.

So, at the term's end, we sailed confidently into the examination hall for our *écrit*—the long written examination—for Professor Gelin's course. We plumped ourselves down, at a reasonable distance from each other, among our Swiss and Swedish colleagues, their faces gray after white nights of study, and waited for the neatly printed examination questions to be passed out.

They came, and in spite of my confidence, my heart, out of habit, beat faster at the first sight of them, and my breath shortened. And then, in the midst of this, came a thudding instant of recognition. The examination consisted of a *dissertation* to be written on any one of three subjects, and the first subject was one that our tutors had dredged up out of the files of past examinations and had given us two weeks before as the theme for a practice essay, "The Clerical Element in French Medieval Literature." On this topic, Ellen and I had already disported ourselves with imagery and curlicues. My essay had begun with an elaborate simile comparing the clerical element in medieval literature to the cathedral of Chartres. My tutor, the widow of a celebrated medievalist, had clucked with pleasure over it and had ironed out my awkward subordinate clauses, showing me how to brandish the French participle. The paper had continued with a discussion of the religious drama and the saints' lives, and had repeated, in a souped-up form, Professor Gelin's remarks on Villon's "Ballad for His Mother" as a prayer to the Virgin. It had ended with a whimsical little coda, throwing up for discussion the question of whether the vast *anti*clerical literature of the Middle Ages was not really a part of this immense subject—a sort of subhead, to be entitled "The Anticlerical Element in French Medieval Literature."

Gleefully, I plunged into the opening paragraph. The phrases and epithets of my essay came back to me like the notes of some familiar tune. I grinned as I wrote. An hour and a half flicked by, and I could already see the peroration coming. I leaned back in my chair for a breath, and looked around me.

Earnest Teutonic faces, heavy Swiss ones, beautiful Danish ones—all twisted with effort, lips telling over obscure beads of thought—hovered above stained papers full of outlines and sketch notes. There was Annelies Vischer, of Basel, eyes rolling in her head in a fury of concentration; there was gray-eyed Ragnar Nillson, of Uppsala, with his dark frown. I was acquainted with many of the students I saw around me, and knew how they lived. Most of them had little rooms in the quarter or in the Le Corbusier barracks of the Cité Universitaire; they ate sparsely and sensibly, drinking bocks at the students' café, saving for a bottle of wine. They worked in the chill library of the Sorbonne or in the enormous, frowsty reading room of the Bibliothèque Sainte-Geneviève; we Americans read our own texts in our own comfortable rooms or in the warm, charmingly furnished little reading room of our group headquarters in the Rue de Chevreuse.

And now, all of a sudden, the thought of that ease, the thought of our skilled and patient tutors working with us, guiding us, preparing for our consumption all the hard material these others had to wrench out for themselves, closed over me like warm, smothering feathers. I felt as if I were in a huge nest. I thought of the terrible prosperity of our country—the unmentioned great barrier that all along had stood between us and our European friends. And then I remembered—with horror —that all French examinations are graded on a competitive basis. Anyone's doing well—my doing well—automatically meant the downgrading of all those doing less well. A wave of revulsion against my smooth, trained-poodle *dissertation* surged in my throat and gagged me.

In anguish, I turned to catch Ellen's eye. She was five seats back in the next row, and was twiddling her pen in blue fingers, wondering idly, I knew, why her fountain pens always leaked, since nobody ever could find what was wrong with them. Ellen was a girl whose attitude toward the world combined, to an odd degree, deep sensitivity and relaxed detachment. She felt things, but she failed to get excited. She had spent her girlhood in English schools, in summer houses in France and Saxony, in a sedate boarding school in Boston, in a don's house in Cambridge, according to the vagaries of her widely travelled, widely connected parents, and she had lost, somewhere along the way, all capacity for surprise, for feeling that things were out of order, out of hand, or even peculiar. Yet she seldom was bored, largely because she took extreme care to avoid situations where ennui might take hold of her.

I caught her wide violet gaze and raised my eyebrows at her, signalling, "Which did you choose?"

She held up two fingers. The question I had answered was No. 1 on the sheet. So even Ellen had felt the revulsion I had felt, but earlier—in time! Shame filled my heart. Ellen slumped in her seat, laid down her pen, and yawned.

I cast aside my paper and began all over again, writing feverishly on the second question. About an hour remained. The new subject was a rather fancy one—something about the philosophy of late medieval poetry as a prelude to that of the Renaissance. With time, I could have done it easily, out of Professor Gelin's lectures and the elaborations of our tutor. As it was, writing rapidly, I made orthographic mistakes, and left out words, while my panicked mind more and more let go its hold of the relevant quotations. It was a sad little scribble that I handed in at the end of the hour.

As we stumbled out of the airless, sweat-smelling room, I told Ellen what I had done, and why. She turned her great eyes on me, with something as near to surprise as she ever came. She said, "You're crazy! If they give those old questions, they have to expect that some of us will have seen them. It's just a chance they take. The files are open to everybody, after all."

"Well, why didn't you—"

"What, write on that old thing again?" she said. "Remember, I had to do mine twice. I'm so sick of that Clerical Element! *Anything* but three more hours of *that!*"

Within three days, I received a summons to the office of Mr. Harcourt, the academic dean in charge of our American students' organization. He was a man of great mental agility—an American who spoke a rapid, crackling French with a pure accent. He could be charming, but not for Ellen and me. His large face and small, rather chubby build aroused the dark female impatience always induced in us by American males whom we considered unattractive—though, God knows, we were will-

ing and happy to put up with some very peculiar specimens indeed, if they were French, or even English.

"Mademoiselle!" snapped Harcourt, waving me to a seat with his ivory cigarette holder—a gesture that immediately caused me to summon up all my talent for being annoying. Mr. Harcourt made a fetish of addressing all students exclusively in French. Ordinarily, I made a strenuous effort with my dipthongs, "a"s, and nasals, trying to sound well trained. Now I honked and flatted, and tried to sound, and even look, as Midwestern as possible. "I know I didn't do very well on Professor Gelin's exam," I said.

"Didn't do very well!" said Harcourt. "You failed. Flatly."

Clearly, he expected this to be disastrous news, but he did not know how bad it was. I had failed miserably in geology at college, and it was only because of the strenuous efforts of the French Department and the willingness of the college authorities to postpone my repetition of the course that I had been allowed to come to Paris at all. Now to fail a course at the Sorbonne—

"Is there any explanation you can offer?" Harcourt asked.

I told him exactly why I had done what I had. I knew the story would fill him with impatience, and it did. He said what Ellen had said—that such coincidences were certain to happen, and that the University was responsible for avoiding them.

"In a week's time," Harcourt continued, his little eyes crinkling, "the Dean of your college's Graduate School, who is also head of its French Department, will arrive in Paris for her half-year sabbatical leave. She will, of course, inquire about the progress of the college's students here. I fear I can promise you a disagreeable scene with her."

I was silent for a minute, and then asked "Is that all, Monsieur?" in a tone as near to rude as I dared make it. Harcourt treated me to one of his cold, silent stares, and said, "That is all, Mademoiselle."

During the next week, I ate small dinners and no breakfasts, and my landlady began to mutter about my liver, an organ that the entire

French nation is pathologically conscious of. Then it came—the beastly little *pneu* from the Dean, praying me, in neat French, to be willing to lunch with her at her hotel the next day. My fear was not only a fear of justice, of punitive measures; I feared the unknown as well. The Dean of the Graduate School was not a familiar figure to undergraduates—not even to those in her own department. I had seen her but once, and then shrouded in the mysteries of full academic dress, in a procession during some college festivity in my freshman year.

Her hotel was an old and distinguished one in a famous ancient quarter, far from the plebeian grandeurs of the Georges V and the Crillon. The next noon, in my best black wool dress and a good hat, I went there; and the worn, unfashionable distinction of the place made me feel even more a suppliant than I had when I set out.

I had myself announced, and for a few minutes sat waiting in the lobby. Then the gold gate of the little automatic elevator creaked open, and there emerged the most enormous woman I had ever seen. There was a kind of Triassic quality about her, an aura of a creature remaining from some lost age. Her shape was not the shape of an ordinary fat woman, but, in truth, she was not fat; she was just enormous, and without recognizable female shape—no pendulous bosom, no protruding stomach. Her hair was sparse and gray, and stood out in little puffs from under the tight black turban she wore. As I rose, she paused in her massive progress and fixed me with her eyes—small in her great face—making up her mind that I must be the student she was looking for. Struggling to dominate the fear that her aspect and my situation combined to unleash on me, I moved hesitantly toward her. She raised a mighty arm and held out a hand.

Calling me by name, she greeted me in English, in the most beautiful, warm voice imaginable, and a charming vivacious smile lit up that landscape of a face like a sun. As I took her hand, warm and dry and firm-fingered, in my damp one, I became confusedly aware of the youthfulness of her complexion, its lively pink-and-white, and the frivolous wrinkles around her eyes. Above all, I was conscious

that the great Dean was trying hard not to laugh out loud.

"Auguste has our luncheon ready," she said, in the suavest of tones. "I think you may appreciate the mussels. I thought perhaps a Rhine wine, though of course Auguste considers this a bit graceless of me, coming, as he does, from the Côte de Beaune."

She swept ahead of me with her inimitable gait, which had no hint of waddle or lumber; it was a kind of wheeled locomotion. Auguste, the headwaiter, seated her swiftly and with tenderness. She waved me to a seat imperially, but with another of her Sun Queen smiles. She gave me a small Russian cigarette from a silver case, and then took one herself and inserted it in an improbable black silver-mounted holder. As we lit up and settled back, I saw her watching me, through a cloud of lilac smoke, with what seemed an expression of direct and simple pleasure. She began to converse, introducing subjects of interest, telling me about the new French House to be installed at the college, inquiring about the extent of my sightseeing in the Touraine and in Paris, pressing for news of the other students. She gave me a deft and highly valuable little lesson in how to manage the mussels. She called me by my first name. Academic subjects were not exactly avoided; they simply failed to make an appearance.

After the delicate and lovely little soufflé that ended our meal, Auguste helped the Dean to her feet, with the air of one performing a rather complicated operation skillfully and lovingly, and ushered us from the room, the Dean making mysterious jokes with him about his native province, and trying to put me in touch with them by speaking French to me, for the first time. Before I knew what was happening, the two of us were in the fragile, dangerous elevator, creaking up to her room. Here, I decided, would come the Inquisition.

Still talking in her clear, effortless voice, in her beautiful sentences, which always came out in a form so controlled you could feel their balance and elegance, or their ease and informality, like a texture, she moved ahead of me down a long corridor and let me into a room that perfectly exemplified the classic atmosphere of the entire hotel. She motioned me to a chair, seated herself, and went through the cigarette-lighting ritual again.

"Now," she said, "let's talk about *you*." Then she burst into a laugh, as gay and charming as the laugh of a young girl in some Musset comedy or Verlaine poem—unsmirched by the elements of snort, snicker, and giggle that are, alas, components of the laughter of most actual young girls.

Harcourt had told her the whole story, but first she had heard it from old Professor Gelin himself, who had heard it from Harcourt over the phone. A sudden image flashed into my mind of those two faces bent over rickety French telephones—Harcourt's heavy gray-and-pink one, his little eyes and his excellent French snapping and crackling, and the grave, deep-eyed countenance of Professor Gelin, with its princely beard, attentive, considering, trying to take it all in.

"Well, my dear," said the Dean, an incredible set of dimples sparkling in her cheeks, "it seems you've made an old man very, very happy. Professor Gelin is telling your story all over Paris as a sort of fable, with the moral 'Americans are at bottom Puritans, though they may try to appear to be hedonists.' Frenchmen like Professor Gelin, you know, have read and heard a great deal about American Puritanism and the New England conscience. They appreciate Hawthorne, and they have read Henry James on the subject of the American conscience in Europe. But"—she looked long at the glowing end of her cigarette, raised her fine, arched brows, and made a bit of a *moue*—"*hélas*, they don't really *see* much of it. They don't see much of what they're always looking for when they look at Americans. And now Professor Gelin is utterly delighted with his New Englander—his *Nouvelle-Anglaise*, as he calls you—whose stern and rock-bound forebears suddenly interfered with her normal mental processes and produced that odd bit of conduct."

"I'm *not* from New England!" I said, full of an obscure protest, feeling that I was being rearranged, pushed around.

"I know. Chicago!" said the Dean, laughing again.

"And it wasn't really *that* so much. I mean, not *ethics* so much. I just thought—well, *you* know—we have all the tutors and everything . . ."

"I know," she said softly.

"I really just did something dumb, that's all," I said. "Stupid. Nobody should parlay it into a thing about New England. *New England!*" Indignation began to enter my voice.

"Well," said the Dean, "not much harm's been done. You'll make up your credit in summer school at Chicago or Madison. You could do something with my friend Vareuil, at Chicago, an excellent Proust man. We'll see. In the meantime, try not to behave in such an exotic manner."

"I think I'd better tell Professor Gelin," I said. "I wouldn't like him to go on thinking—After all, I *like* him." I waited, and then added impulsively, "He sort of *is* Paris, for me."

The Dean smiled. "He's from the Savoie," she said. "A really extravagant landscape."

"Well, I'd better tell him I'm *not* from New England," I said stubbornly. "That had nothing to do with it!"

The Dean's face changed. Humor and sadness were in her half smile; a deep worldliness and a faint melancholy, a blend of lucidity and gentleness, transformed that vast expanse of countenance. She kept silent a full minute.

"Professor Gelin is old and poor." She communicated a very black period at the end of this short sentence. "As we get older, our little provincialisms give us more and more pleasure. Sometimes a rather simplified view is a source of pure delight. Do whatever you like, my dear." She extinguished her cigarette.

I rose to go. She did not rise, but turned toward me in her chair. The soft afternoon sunlight fell across her face. I stood before her for a moment, then said, "Mr. Harcourt said he could promise me a disagreeable scene with you."

We smiled at each other. "Poor Mr. Harcourt," said the Dean.

The next week, in one of the corridors of the Sorbonne library, Professor Gelin saw me coming toward him and stopped me by putting up his hand, palm out. In his deep, measured voice, he spoke to me, in French, with musical pauses and a mogul courtesy, inquiring about the Dean and my new program of study. Then he said, "Dear Mademoiselle, soon—not too soon, of course, I hope with all my heart—you will return to your own country." Was he using the word *"pays"* in the French sense, meaning one's native region? "Have you missed it, your country, in our France? Is it very beautiful there?"

His old eyes rested full on me; I could feel the weight of an attention profound yet delicate. Now was the time for honesty—Chicago, Lake Michigan. Or was it, really? An inspiration vibrated through me like a shock. In a gentle voice that Mr. Harcourt would never have recognized, I answered, "In my country, Monsieur, the rocks are very black and the gulls are very white."

The heavy lids lifted suddenly, and a great,

blazing look came from his eyes. "Ah!" said Professor Gelin, and smiled. Gravely he held out his hand for me to shake.

What could I have given the old man that would have been of any value to him? I knew almost nothing of America anyhow. His huge intelligence had no use for any claptrap about the Wrigley Building or the stockyards. As the magnificent old Savoyard had been golden hours of Paris to me, I could be a sharp moment of Puritan New England to him. I had told him nothing, but I had made something for him—a little picture, an object. I turned from the graceless building and walked down the steep hill to the gravelled Luxembourg Gardens, feeling small, feeling foreign and not quite myself—and yet not quite so young as before, and slightly, just slightly, more at home in the world.

LILLIAN SMITH

Memory of a Large Christmas

Lillian Smith (1897–1966), a teacher, editor, and writer, has traveled extensively in England, Italy, France, India, China, and Brazil but has spent most of her life in the rural South, out of which much of her writing stems. From 1936 to 1946 she was coeditor and publisher of *South Today,* a magazine devoted to Southern problems. She gained prominence as a writer with the publication of her highly controversial novel *Strange Fruit,* 1944, which was followed by three nonfiction works—*Killers of the Dream,* 1949; *The Journey,* 1954; and *Now Is the Time,* 1955—and a novel, *One Hour,* 1959. In 1950 she was awarded a Special Citation for Distinguished Contribution to American Letters by the National Book Award Committee.

"Memory of a Large Christmas," from her book of the same title, is a portrait of Christmas as she knew it in her childhood. But in a larger perspective, "Memory of a Large Christmas" is a biography of a way of American life that flourished in the nineteenth century and lingered on in the South until the first decades of the twentieth century.

Everything about our family was big: there were nine of us and our mother and father and a cousin or two, and Little Grandma when it was her turn to stay with us, and Big Grandma when it was hers, and there were three bird dogs and four cats and their kittens and once a small alligator and a pet coon. And the house took them all in. And still there were empty corners and stairways and pantries, and maybe the winter parlor would have nobody in it, but if it did you could go to the summer parlor, or if you felt too crowded you could slip in the closet under the stairs and crawl on and on until it grew small and low, then you could get down on your stomach and crawl way back where things were quiet and dim, and sometimes you liked that.

But not often. Most of the time you wanted to be with the others racing round the veranda, or huddled up somewhere playing games. It was only when Big Grandma came that we began to scramble for hide-outs, for Big Grandma filled up the whole place. She could scrouge even Christmas.

We dreaded her coming. We'd moan, Oh Mama why! And our mother would look at us, her dark eyes growing darker, darker, then she'd say softly, "Your grandmother is very good with the hog killing."

My big brothers, two, three, four of them would launch a collective protest: old Japers and Desto from the farm could handle the hogs. And Papa was there. Why Big Grandma! She gets in the way, showing the men how hogs should be stuck, calling them to do this and that, and all the time hogs squealing and Grandma getting too close to the knives and the wind blowing smoke every which away from fires under pots where water is heating for the scraping, oh Mama!

Mother soothed her rebellious sons, "Remember the sausage. Nobody can make sausage as good as your grandmother's; she knows just how to dry the sage and rub and crumble it just right and how much red pepper to put in and she never puts in too much fat." Mother was expert in the fine usages of reiteration, "And she stuffs the skins just right," turning to the Twelve Year Old—"last year you helped her and you loved it."

"I didn't have no sense last year. I was just a kid."

Mother's voice begged. "You love her sausage and hot biscuits, everyone of you—"

"But Mama—"

"You love her sausage, remember."

Yes, we did. But we didn't love Big Grandma. Especially at Christmas.

Christmas began when pecans started falling. The early November rains loosened the nuts from their outer shells and sent them plopping like machine gun bullets on the roof of the veranda. In the night, you'd listen and you'd know IT would soon be here.

IT was *not* Thanksgiving. We skipped that day. At school, there were exercises, yes, and we dressed up like New England Pilgrims and play-acted Priscilla and Miles Standish and made like we had just landed on Plymouth Rock. But the truth is, the only Plymouth Rocks we saw in our minds were the black and white hens scratching round at the hen house. In those days, the Pilgrims and Thanksgiving did not dent the imaginations of little Southerners, some of whose parents wouldn't concede they had a thing to be thankful for, anyway. It was football that elevated the day into a festival—but that was later than these memories.

We eased over the national holiday without one tummy ache. Turkey? that was Christmas. Pumpkin pie? not for us. Sweet potato pie was Deep South dessert in the fall. We had it once or twice a week. Now and then, Mother varied it with sweet potato pone—rather nice if you don't try it often: raw sweet potato was grated, mixed with cane syrup, milk, eggs and spices and slowly baked, then served with thick unbeaten cream; plain, earthy, caloric and good. But not Christmasy.

Pecans were. Everybody in town had at least one tree. Some had a dozen. No matter. Pecans were prestige. They fitted Christmas.

And so you lay there, listening to the drip

MEMORY OF A LARGE CHRISTMAS From *Memory of a Large Christmas* by Lillian Smith. By permission of W. W. Norton & Company, Inc. Decorations by Constance McMillan. Copyright © 1961, 1962 by Lillian Smith. First Edition.

drip of rain and plop plop of nuts, feeling something good is going to happen, something good and it won't be long now. And you'd better sneak out early in the morning before your five brothers and three sisters and get you a few pecans and hide them. Strange how those nuts made squirrels out of us. Nothing was more plentiful and yet we hid piles of them all over the place. Of course, when there are nine of you and the cousins, you get in the habit of hiding things.

Our father chose the auspicious Monday to shake the trees. (Our weekly school holiday was Monday.) The shaking occurred after breakfast. He would stay long enough from the mill to get us well organized. You organized nine kids and the cousins when Big Grandma was around; if you didn't, she would take over—and there'd be a riot.

I cannot remember a nonconforming breakfast on tree-shaking day, but on ordinary days breakfast could be highly unpredictable. One never knew where rebellion would break out.

Our father customarily arose at five o'clock, drank a cup of coffee, walked to the mill, got things going there; got the logging train off to the woods, the mules off to the turpentine farm, got things going at the planing mill, the dry kiln, the shingle mill and the big mill, got things going at the commissary, going at the office, going at the ice plant, going at the Supply Store which he owned half interest in, and at the light plant and water works which he owned three-quarters interest in. Then, with everything going, he walked home to have breakfast with his children.

We were all in the dining room when he came back. A fire was sputtering in the fireplace if the day was cold, the bay window was fluttering with windy white curtains and sunshine and the nervous cage of the canary who was being stalked by one of the cats. The big long table was spread with a white Irish damask cloth—one of Mother's few self-indulgences. There were platters at each end of mullet roe (crisply fried), or perhaps, smothered steak; there were three bowls of grits, and four plates of thin light biscuits and two dishes of homemade butter and three pitchers of cane syrup scattered in between.

We each had our place. The two oldest sat on either side of our mother; the two youngest sat in high chairs on either side of our father; the others sat according to age in between. You took your turn sitting by Big Granny. You sat under duress, for not only was she wide, she had a habit of reaching over to your plate with her fork when both your hands were busy and spearing the morsel you had saved for last. On the walnut-paneled wall, behind the picture (lambs huddling in terrible snow storm) was a small shelf on which lay the Bible and a thin peach-sprout switch. The Bible was read every morning. The thin switch was used to quell whatever disorder was popping up among the younger ones.

We sat down. Our father read briefly from the Bible, closed it, rested his hand on it for a moment as though it gave him strength (and I think it did) then put it back on the shelf. He returned to the table, looked round at his nine, smiled, studied a face now and then as though it was new, beamed at mother, then encouragingly asked for our verses. Each of us then said what we had gleaned from the Bible. The youngest always said, *Jesus wept.* The next one always said, *God is love.* The others were on their own. Verses began with the oldest and came down like a babbling stream to the youngest.

It was usually routine. But there were sudden uprisings. One morning, the six-year-old when his turn came, calmly shouted "Jesus wept!" Silence. A scream from the youngest, "He tant have Thesus wept, he tant it's mine he tant he tant—" A scream from the four-year-old, "He tant have my Dod is love neider he tant he tant he tant—"

"Sssh . . . nobody's going to take your Jesus wept or your G—" He turned to the deviationist. "Why, son," he asked gravely, "did you say your little sister's verse?"

"I'm tired," said son. Father looked at Mother. Mother looked at the tired one who flashed his softest smile on her. When Father was not present it worked. No response now. He looked at Big Granny who could be fetched by it, too, but B. G. had seized the opportunity to spear a big piece of roe from an unguarded plate. Six-year-old swallowed hard, "I'm plumb wore out," he quavered.

Dissent more often came from the higher echelons. There was the summer when Age Fifteen decided it was time for subversion. He came close to bringing off·a successful *coup* by the simple and highly effective device of teaching the *Song of Solomon* to one and all, even the littlest. He trained with cruel disregard of all the things we wanted to dream about or run and do. His sense of timing was superb; his dominance over us was complete, for we adored Age Fifteen whose imagination never went to sleep, we would have loved to move into his mythic mind and live there forever with him. So we chanted our lines, as he ordered, and rechanted—quick, quick, he'd say, no wait, be ready, hook on now; and finally, we were zipping along like a chain reaction and he announced we were ready.

The morning came. He led off with "How beautiful are thy feet with shoes, O prince's daughter . . . thy navel is like a round goblet which wanteth not liquor . . . thy two breasts are like two young roes that are twins . . . thy neck . . ." Each picked up his split-second cue and carried on, and it was climaxed by the two-year-old who piped out gaily, "Tay me wif flagons, tomfort me wif apples for I am thick of love."

And there was the time when one of the sisters—eleven years old that year—craving economy of effort and a smidge of excitement, specialized in the Begats. Each morning this pigtailed plump daughter sang out to the dining room her story of begetting: "Enos lived ninety years and begat Cainan . . . And Cainan lived seventy years and begat Mahalaleel . . . and Mahalaleel lived sixty-five years and begat Jared"—etc.

The parents could play it cool when they wanted to. For three mornings, they quietly ignored the giggles of the eight and the cousins, as Eleven Year Old begatted. But Eleven was too proud of her memory and her acrobatic skill with Semitic names and she loved the spotlight. The next morning she hung on

to Genesis and begat and begat and begat. Her audience was hysterical. Then the two youngest, giggling wildly about what they could not comprehend, seized the chance to steal a biscuit before the Blessing and promptly choked on their dual pleasures, and our father, beating alternately on two little wheezy backs, yelled (a measure reserved for near-disaster) Stop it, you!

Age Eleven, a thinskinned if loquacious show-off, blushed and began to cry silently. And Big Granny who had been having a ball spearing food off the platters along with the littlest ones put a sausage on the conquered one's plate and told her to hush and eat, eating would make any thing all right and WHAT DID THE POOR CHILD DO THAT WAS SO WRONG she shouted from *her* soapbox, seizing this chance to heckle her son-in-law.

Our father looked at Mother. And Mother swiftly said, "Papa, please say the Blessing—the other verses can wait until tomorrow."

But on tree-shaking day we were meek. We said proper verses, we bowed our heads for the Blessing, we ate quickly, did not kick each other or yap at Big Grandma.

The moment we were excused from the table we ran to the linen closet for old sheets and spread them under the trees as our father directed. We got the baskets without being told. We were gloriously good. Even the little ones listened when Papa told them not to cry if the nuts hit their heads—anyway, they didn't need to get under the tree, did they? Of course, they needed to get under the tree but they said yessuh and waved him goodby as he walked down the tiled walk which led to the street which led to his office.

The one chosen to shake the tree first was usually the eldest. But now and then, an ambitious underling snatched the honor away by bringing in wood for all twelve fireplaces without being told to or washing and polishing Mother's brougham and offering to drive her out to Cousin Lizzie's; or maybe, he cleaned (with his sisters' help) all twenty-two lamp chimneys. (The town's young electric light plant was still pretty unstable; one never knew what to count on; but my father took care of that, too, by arranging a signal of two quick blinks and one delayed one, which was the communal code for *light your oil lamps quick!* Even on its placid evenings, the light plant turned "the juice" off at nine-thirty.)

Whoever won by fair or foul means the title of shaker of the tree did a pull-up to the first limb, hefted himself to the next, skittered into the branches and began to shake. Thousands of nuts fell until sheets were covered and thickening. Everybody was picking up and filling the baskets, except the little ones who ran round and round, holding their hands up to catch the raining nuts, yelping when hit, dashing to safety, rolling over the big boys' bird dogs, racing back. The inevitable moment came when the smallest girl whined "I gotta peepee I gotta—" But nobody was going to take her to what Mother called the Garden House, nobody was in that kind of sacrificial mood. When the piteous cries could no longer be ignored, one of the older boys sang out, My gosh, don't you know how? And shamed and desperate, she crept behind a bush as she had seen our retriever do. Soon she was back, holding up her damp hands to catch the falling nuts, begging the shaker to shake her some and everybody was begging for more nuts on his side of the tree, for his turn shaking, for another basket—

This was how Christmas began for us. Soon, the nuts had been stored in old pillow cases. Our neighbors used croker sacks, I don't know why we preferred old pillow cases. After a few days of what our mother called "seasoning" the picking out of the nut meats took place. This was Little Granny's job, if it was her turn to be with us. We'd gather in her room and sit close to the hearth listening to her soft easy stories of panthers in the Big Swamp when she was young, how she shot one between the eyes in 1824, and of the war with the Seminoles; and every now and then, she put a broken piece of nut in our mouths; and we loved her and her stories. But when Big Granny was there, she shooed us away, ensconced herself in a rocker in a sunny place on the circular veranda, and as she rocked and

sang *Bringing in the Sheaves,* she carefully cracked the nuts (she was good at it) and got them out whole; and she'd put three halves in the fruit jar and plop one in her mouth for the road, but finally quarts and quarts of pecan halves were ready for the fruit cake, and the date and pecan cake, and the Waldorf salad and the chicken salad and the chewy syrup candy you make from cane syrup with lots of homemade butter and lots of nuts—the kind you put on the back veranda for the cold air to harden while watchers take turns shooing the hen away and the bird dogs away and the cat—

Christmas was coming nearer. It was December. A cold frosty week was upon us and our father said it was fine for hog-killing. This, too, was on Monday. We were all present. The hogs were brought in from the farm, two black wash pots were brought from Aunt Chloe's backyard where she lived in our backyard; and an awful Thing which the Fifteen-Year-Old—specializing in the French Revolution at the moment—called the "guillotine." The word made the blood flow in imaginations where already enough was flowing to streak the day with horror. The guillotine was a two-by-six plank nailed to two strong posts which were firmly embedded in the ground. There was a pulley-and-chain attached. It served as a rack from which to hang the hogs while they were being cleaned. But first they were dipped in boiling water and scraped—a witchbrewed process which turned black hogs to white hogs, stunning the young spectators—then, after the scraping, the gambrel stick was fastened to the tendons of each leg and the hogs were hoisted up to the rack and split open and entails and heart and liver and lights tumbled into big tubs on the ground beneath them.

There are lacunae in my memory. I felt a profound ambivalence about this day. I longed for it and dreaded it like death. To us all it was orgy and holocaust, wild pleasure and terror that pounded the heart and dilated the pupils of eyes. But even so, on the perimeter somewhere beyond words but *there,* were visions of platters of sausage and crisp spareribs and backbone and rice and liver-'n'-lights stew and and . . .

So we awoke at dawn. We dressed and went out to watch the men build the fire and heat the water in the big black pots. We never took our eyes from them but crept closer, closer to the massive preparations for these primitive rites. And then, the moment came when Desto and Japers threw a squealing hog to the ground and stuck it in the throat and then lifted three or four hundred pounds of mortally wounded but still struggling flesh into the steaming barrel. By this time the youngest was running his legs off to get to Grandma's room—any grandma would do now. But the others, in a state either of paralysis or hypnosis, stayed on. And in the sudden hush came the moment when the blood began to spurt. And now, the Seven-Year-Old and her younger sister were scampering to the parlor where if you hid behind the piano you couldn't hear a sound. Two tense faces peered out now and then, but bodies were reluctant to follow; and it was only when the more curious crept to the back porch to see what was happening that she saw the big steel knife raised to slit the hog's belly. She shot through the door to the parlor and crouched behind the piano, whitefaced and tightlipped. The less daring whispered, What did you see? what did you see? But you could only shake your head.

Squatting there, behind the upright piano whose back was painted gold and stamped with the letters *Kranich & Bach,* smelling the musty dark carpet and looking at the carved walnut and damask furniture and the blue Victorian glass vases, you somehow pushed out the terror, the sense of unlimited violence. Your sister whispered, "Let's play dolls." But to play dolls on this day! No. You buried your face against the cold frame of the piano and waited waited waited until silence came from the outside where death and blood and squeals and glistening steel blades and smoke had driven tranquillity off the face of the earth.

Then you crept out. You had to know what was happening in the vast silence. So you eased through the wide hall, eased to the back porch, and down the steps—.

Nothing was happening. It was like a dream: it was over. Nothing was hanging there. Nothing was squealing. No anything was anywhere. The big wooden table was clean and bare of all but the white enameled dish pans and stew pots where Mama and the women seemed to be washing up things. And you saw that Mama's autumn rosebushes were blooming just as they had yesterday. The pump was dripping as it had done all your life. The big washpots were gone. Nothing left but smoldering ashes. You walked closer. Something strange and magic had occurred: death had been transmuted into Food For The Family. You saw that Desto and Japers were stacking ordinary hams and bacon meat, and shoulders and backbone, in neat piles and sprinkling a little salt over them. And there were your brothers, blowing the bladders into wonderful balloons and suddenly you were yelling, Let me let me let me its my turn. . . . Now, the youngest was creeping out, and Age Thirteen who had hidden upstairs in the library with a book sauntered out with cool nonchalance as though unaware anything extraordinary had been going on. . . . And now, in an instant, ALL THE WORLD turned into a Good Place with a Good Father and a Good Mother and a Good Granny who made good sausage, and a Good Japers who said, Little Sister, come here, Old Japers will show you how to cut a pork chop.

You went to him: and the big black hand covered the small white hand, and holding firmly to the long steel knife, the two together pressed down down on something, then Japers whispered, Hold tight! and you did, and he lifted your hand and his and the knife and came down hard—and lo, the two of you had cut a pork chop. And he was saying softly, I sho do like pork chops, don't you, Little Sister? and you whispered back, I sho do, Japers. And the two words had changed the whole world.

Tension eased from faces and pupils of eyes lost dilation and suddenly everybody went wild with confidence, wild with atavistic triumph, for once again, Man—black man and white man together—had won a victory over the animal world. And now, the kids were yelling, Let me grind its my turn, let me let me let me, and they'd grind a few times and then sneezing from the sage and pepper they'd abandon Big Granny and the sausage and run round the dim cavernous smokehouse, peering in the bins where salt meat from last year still lay, and looking at dark brown greenish moldish hams hanging from the rafters where they had cured in the smoke last winter, sniffing the salt-hickory-sugar-phosphorus of old ashes, traces of which were there from last year and the year before and the year before and the year—dashing out, now to the yard where a setting sun threw shafts of light across dark pecan trees, turning the women's faces a warm mahogany and yellowing the white pans. Racing now to the woodhouse for kindling, glad to help tote in wood for the twelve fireplaces tonight, glad to be a part of the big human family, glad to belong to the house where you were born.

Big and endless, that house. I am sure that were I to see it now, it would seem shrunken in size, for all these years it has been growing in my memory and, too, I had only a small world to measure it by when I was a child.

Our mother and father started their marriage in bleak disordered Reconstruction days with almost no money at all. They began in a two-room house set in the middle of a town block on College Street. As each child came along my father added a room, and the year in between—for we arrived regularly like steps—if he had lucked out with his business ventures he'd add something extra: a winter parlor one year; a summer parlor; and when waterworks came to our town he added four bathrooms; and one prosperous year he built a fifteen-foot veranda round the whole house, except the wing where the dining room and kitchen were. There were deep mysterious closets in almost every room and some of them had small doors at the rear through which you could crawl in the dark edging one shoulder through, then the other—and suddenly there you'd be: on the ground under the house among great squatting brick pillars which held the big house on their backs. In the dim eerie light you'd see, maybe, a toad-frog close to your hand blinking at you, and you'd feel it didn't think you belonged here,

and sometimes, just as you were sliding through the narrow hole you were sure the big squatting pillars were saying things but they never spoke while you were there. A winding halfdark stairway led to the second floor from the wide hall which in itself was a room with fireplace and mantel and pictures on the walls and a black tufted leather couch. And there was a stairway on the back veranda which was an answered prayer for the older boys who could sneak in late from their night-prowling without Mother calling out to them.

As the house grew, the block of land where it stood was extended in depth to two and a half blocks and in the back were barn and stables and carriage-room and gardens and a field; and upstairs in the barn along with the bales of hay were trapezes and training bars; and out in the back, beginning at the roof, was a shoot-the-chute which started off steeply but eased into a gradual decline that ended in the back field. We kept it greased with yellow "bar-soap" and lard, and I cannot remember whether our sturdy little behinds took the full brunt of it or whether we had a small wood carriage in which to sit. On the front lawn were a tennis court and croquet ground and a big rope swing hanging from a high limb of a live-oak.

As my father added to the house he added something to the church across the street— for he tithed—so we grew up together, church and home and family and town.

As you might suspect, he was not only a business man but a ritual maker and entrepreneur: turning routine family matters into rites that held style and significance and transforming ordinary events into Big Occasions. Being what he was, it would have seemed incredible to him not to have his children participate in the annual event of hog killing, so he ordered the hogs brought in from his farm and started things off by being there when the hogs were stuck and hung to be cleaned, although he might leave—after he had got things going—for his office at the mill.

After hog-killing, Christmas pushed us. Overnight the drab stores gushed forth like illuminated fountains with choice imported china dishes, sets of silver, fancy leather wallets and toilet kits, and elegant initialed white linen handkerchiefs for the men and boys, and manicure sets and perfumes and laces and silver toilet sets and sewing baskets for the women and girls, and in the jeweler's store were watches and gold pins and rings and necklaces and everywhere toys and red wagons and fire engines and tin soldiers and gold boxes of candy spangled with red velvet poinsettias, and even in the meat market there were stacks of Roman candles and sparklers and firecrackers. (We southerners were still too sullen to celebrate the Fourth, and saved our fireworks for Christmas.)

Dolls were everywhere: "penny dolls," twenty-dollar dolls, boy dolls and girl dolls, dressed dolls and naked dolls, and French bisque dolls and "china head" dolls were in drugstores, drygoods stores; the hardware store had them, too, tucked in front of the plows, perched on the yellow mule collars, decorating the ends of the snuff shelf.

You went round saying boldly, There's a beautiful doll in Mr. Pennington's store only it hasn't any clothes on, but it would look beautiful in a hemstitched white polka-dotted dress with little red ribbons. And you said it in time, for you hoped, although you dared not breathe it, that its dress would be made by Miss Ada. You had not quite given up your belief in Santa, you stubbornly held on, but you had begun to guess that Santa might have a difficult time without Miss Ada's help. So, playing it safe, you wrote a letter and kneeling on the hearth in your mother's bedroom you watched for the moment when, if you let go, the updraft from the flames would whoosh your message to the North Pole. But, having acquired a smidge of your mother's canniness, you also persuaded the Seventeen-year-old to take another letter out to Miss Ada's, in case Santa dropped by.

Poor Miss Ada, the town called her. After her old mother's death, she lived alone in the mosscovered house under tall cedars at the edge of the grave yard. The day before her wedding, Miss Ada's fiancé died of typhoid fever; and she was left on the edge of a wedding day she could not enter and could not leave. Sometimes, you'd see her in her white satin gown wandering among the tombstones, stooping to stroke a carved lamb or rubbing the moss on an urn, and she'd be smiling and talking to herself, or maybe, laughing loud at something very funny. At other times she'd be sobbing. And you'd hide behind a cedar and listen, then everything would swing round inside you—and you ran home quick. When you got there you called, "Mama!" And when her calm voice answered, you said, "Nothing—just wanted to know where you were."

After a time, people noticed how thin she was, and slowly, they realized Miss Ada needed money for food. But nobody knew what to do. Until a poet in our town—who made up wonderful poems after he'd polished off half a pint or so which he kept by the rattan chair where he sat most days in his back yard under a chinaberry tree—suggested Miss Ada dress Santa's dolls. Everybody knew instantly this was exactly as it should be. And ever afterward, she dressed Santa's dolls and some for birthdays, too. And it was not long before little girls began to feel Santa hadn't treated them right if their dolls were not dressed by Miss Ada—although they didn't *know* it was Miss Ada, they only half guessed it was; and the mystery, the doubt, rimming their faith gave ambience to the delicate garments.

The more the illuminated fountains gushed, the deeper the nine of us were plunged in financial complexities. For there were so many to buy presents for—not only each other but the grandmas and the cousins and the cook, and the cook's husband and her grandson and the nurse, and Desto and Japers and the washerwoman out at Mt. Pisgah, who came in once a week in her rickety wagon to bring the huge white bundles of washed and ironed clothes; and teacher at school and teacher at Sunday School.

To manage it all, we toted in wood, cleaned lamp chimneys, ran to the meat market for the steak for supper, swept Grandma's room, made our beds without being told, swept the tiled walks that led to the street, washed our mother's handkerchiefs, washed our father's socks, offered to wash his feet after he'd walked home from the office. And sometimes he'd let us, as he sat reading the *Savannah News* or the *Florida Times-Union*. We'd bring a basin and mother's lavender soap and wash his feet and powder them with the Spiro he liked to use, then slip a fresh pair of socks on the moist feet, and bring his carpet slippers. And sometimes, we'd hear him say to Mother, "The children are getting mighty thoughtful." And his blue eyes would twinkle and he'd chuckle and Mother's dark eyes would laugh and they seemed to have such nice secrets— though there were thunder and lightning times, too, and silences that raced your heart, but these you didn't think about at Christmas.

We evolved all kinds of money-making schemes, such as reselling our newspapers and magazines to the neighbors. But our mother stopped that one flat. One brother suggested we sell our summer clothes at a smash bargain in mill town, but Dad stopped that one. We settled for less speculative ventures, the older ones taking jobs in the stores after school hours. We kids earned what we spent. We were not rich people, not as wealth is thought of in the cities. We were just small-town people who lived in an ample and comfortable way. We were given little spending money: a nickel was nice, a dime was big, a quarter rich, a dollar was a dream.

The younger ones skittered along contenting themselves with whatever they could improvise for the grown folks. Once I gave my father a pincushion made of a piece of red velvet from an old hat of Mother's, which I scrunched up and filled with bird seed snitched from the shelf where the canary's food was kept, and centered with a gilt button found on the floor when my brother was home from military school. My father seemed to like it; he told me he'd never had a red velvet pincushion in all his life and had never used pins but he was not too old to learn, and he thought it was fine that I could do something besides rattle my tongue.

But the older ones didn't feel they could skin by like that. There was one historical year when the fifteen-year-old with his disciples, a thirteen-year-old brother, and the cook's grandson, named Town Marshal, decided we had neglected the parents. They should be given Nice Things—things that could be heirlooms, Age Fifteen announced. He had been reading to Town and his brother novels about English manors and French châteaux, and lately he'd been specializing in Carlyle's *French Revolution*. Looking round our rambling barn of a house he couldn't find much the fourth and fifth generation would cling to—certainly nothing they'd lay down their lives for. He said to Age Thirteen and Town, "Take these old brass beds: do you know what they are?" His empathetic audience shook their heads. "They're the status quo. Would you die for them?" No, the mob shouted. "O.K.," he said, "then we gotta do something." Age Thirteen and Town, like many disciples, increased in fervor more rapidly than did their mahatma and went round for days staring into space. Inclined to be absentminded, anyway, Age Thirteen became more so and left his violin—which as he said, was almost a Stradivarius—out on the back veranda in Big Granny's rocking chair. This was about as absentminded as you can get. The only reason there was not total disaster was that Mother got there first. But Big Grandma seized the opportunity to say, "The boy is just like his grandfather, all time thinking about music and books, talking about things nobody can understand; the only reason you have to be thankful," she announced to her daughter, "is he can't speak six languages like his poor grandfather; if he starts that, he'll starve to death down here."

Little Miss Curiosity, a natural to head up any government's espionage system, caught on that something was brewing. She slipped away from Desto's granddaughter who was babysitting the younger ones, and hid behind the Cape jasmine bush.

Town was talking as usual—which was every moment Age Fifteen wasn't holding forth. The others were listening. Town was saying:

"Why don't we ketch the freight train when it slows down on Sandy Hill at Tuten's, and ride to New York?"

"Then what?"

"Then we could ketch a boat and hide in a corner somewheres and ride to that little French town named Have."

"Lee Have," corrected Age Thirteen.

"O.K. Then we'd ketch another freight train to the castle—"

"What castle?"

"One we been studyin about—Verse All."

"Verse Alley," corrected Age Thirteen.

"Verse Illey," corrected Age Fifteen. "Then what," he pushed Town.

"Then we'd—we'd walk up those steps real slow and easy right into the Hall of Mirrors, like we had business there."

"What business?"

"Business with the king. I'm the ambassador from Africa and I have business with Louis the Fourteenth—and you two can be my retinue."

Silence.

Town glanced at Age Thirteen, "You can play your violin." Silence. "And you can play your guitar," glancing at Age Fifteen. Silence. Town, who was the soul of tact, studied the faces of his two friends. With a change of pace, he said, "I know what! I'll be the ambassador from Africa and you be the sheriff and deputy from Dixieland. How'd that be?"

"Fine," said his friends. Age Thirteen added slowly, "And we can wear a big silver star."

Town interrupted. "The ambassador can wear one, too. All of us can wear a star," he added tactfully.

"You wear a crown," said Age Thirteen. "We wear a silver star."

"Nope," said Town firmly. "My name is Town Marshal and that gives me a right to wear a star. All of us can wear one."

"That makes sense," said Age Fifteen, who knew when he'd met his match. "Then what?" he asked Town.

"Then," said Town, "we get washed up for supper and eat a little somep'n and then we have a talk with the king; then the king says he's had a hard day, and he'd better get to bed and we say we tired, too. So—everything gets quiet and the help goes to bed and then we slip back into the Hall of Mirrors and while you two roll up a rug I take down a big gold looking glass and we sneak out the back door and make it for the freight train which is blowing down at the crossing and we know we better hurry, so we hot foot it down the road and the whistle is blowing two shorts so we know it's going to stop at the water tank and we—"

"Lord help us," said Age Fifteen, suddenly coming to. "Town, you the biggest fool in this family!"

"He is not," shouted Age Thirteen, "you the biggest fool in this family, you just scared to try it, me and Town we'd cut the king's head off to bring our parents some heirlooms—you all time thinking up things then when Town tells you how to do it, you get scared, that's what—you leave Town alone—"

"Kids!" sneered Age Fifteen and walked away.

But the next day he was holding forth. "Down to brass tacks," he was saying—a phrase of our father's. "Town, you quit your big talk, and you do, too," he said turning to Town's chum. "The two of you got work to do. We got to find some heirlooms. It's only eight days to Christmas. Now you go to the Supply Store and look over the place, go down in the basement and everywhere—there might be something; I'll go to the jewelry store and the hardware store—and the cotton warehouse—"

"And we'll go to the Opera House and look through that stuff—"

"Trash," said Age Fifteen. "Stage sets are trash, waste of time—"

"We going anyway," said Town. "Somep'n might turn up."

"Somep'n might," Age Thirteen.

Age Fifteen studied Town's face. "How you goin get there?"

The lights turned on from Town's chin to his hair line. "Easy," he said. "We goin slip round to the back of the Supply Store, then we walk like nothin on our minds to behind the hardware store, then we cut through to the livery stable and look round at the horses and when nobody's noticing we sneak in the back of the feed store, real easy, and go round the front way to Sandlin's mule lot and we stay there a little, then we stop at the calaboose and talk to everybody there and—"

"When you goin get to the Opera House?"

"We'll get there," said Town, still lit up. "We gotta throw em off our tracks, see? We cut through the ball diamond and back round to Mr. Peeple's gin, then we head straight for the Opera House, but easy like we don't exactly know where we're going, then we stop by the grocery store and ask old Mr. Brown if there's somep'n we can do for him—"

"Better not," said Age Thirteen, "he'll find somep'n."

Town smiled in a superior way, "We don't *do* it, see? we say yessuh but we don't *do* it, see? we just make like we're goin to then we light out for the alley fast as we can and when we come to the back of the Opera House, we shake the windows and find one we can push up and we climb in and then we go without making a sound up the back stairs—"

"I'll meet you at three-thirty, in front of the drugstore," said Fifteen.

"Thought you had a Christmas job," said Thirteen.

"I'll start day after tomorrow."

The next two afternoons were spent casing all the joints. Afterward, the three gathered at the boys' "garden house" to talk it over. (There was a g. h. for the girls and one on the opposite side of Mother's flower garden for the boys.) Miss Curiosity, whose extrasensory equipment was working overtime, slid through the woodhouse, round the back of Aunt Chloe's, backtracked, then crept round a clump of Cape jasmine and hid behind the boys' g. h. so she could find out what they were up to.

"Nothing fit to be an heirloom," Age Thirteen was saying.

"This town's full of trash," said Town.

"There's one watch that'd do," said Age Fifteen, "at the jewelry store; it has five diamonds, but it's a wrist watch and that's too new. You got to be careful about heirlooms, next year it might be out of style and nobody would look at it—" He studied Town's face. "What you think, Town?"

"Well, I tell you," said Town in a slow, judicious voice, "nothing in this town fit to be an heirloom cept one thing—and it's a

beaut. It's a beaut and it won't go out of style—"

"Tell you, it won't do," urged Thirteen Year Old.

"Well now, I'm not so sure. It's a real beaut and it's not going to break up, it's built solid and the handles are made out of real silver—"

"You talking like Big Granma," said Fifteen, "get to the point. What is it?"

Town glanced at Age Thirteen's rapt face. Age Thirteen shrugged in futile attempt to break the spell.

"Well," said Town, "it's the prettiest coffin you ever saw. We slipped up to the second floor when Mr. Pennington wasn't looking—"

"Went to see the appendix and the liver and egg they got there in alcohol," said the thirteen-year-old. "Town didn't get to see 'em." The others had when the WCTU lady lectured at school on the evils of drinking.

"We looked at that," said Town, "and then we looked at the coffins. And right in the front there was a beaut. It has big silver handles and silver knobs and it's gray and I opened it—"

"You—" Fifteen Year Old succumbed to total awe.

"Sure," said Town, "I just opened it to see what it looked like inside. Things these days, they're likely to look better outside than inside. It's a beaut, I'm telling you, all satin. I reached in and pulled at it—"

"You—" Fifteen was humbled to the dust.

"Sure. To see if it was strong. You gotta be careful these days. Everything seemed first class. It'll last easy to the fourth or fifth generation and I bet it looks even better then than—"

Fifteen Year Old couldn't speak. Horror and ecstatic admiration were tearing him to pieces. Town went on, "Nothing but trash in this town except—"

Fifteen was coming to. "Lord help us—" he whispered, "it's great—it's absolutely great—it's absolu—" then he caught a mean glimpse of reality. "Town, you're the craziest fool in this family, I swear to—"

"He is not," said Age Thirteen. "It makes sense. It won't wear out and it's a beaut, all right; real silver handles—"

"But how you goin use it?" Age Fifteen pushed. "Which one you goin to give it to?"

Silence. But only for a second. Town solved it. "Both," he said judiciously. "Give it to both. Then the one who needs it first will use it."

Town's powers of hypnosis were superb. All he needed do was relax and stare hard. He stared hard at Age Fifteen who muttered, "Fair enough."

But reality had the edge even on Town. "We can't do it," said the fifteen-year-old, after a long moment of hypnotic assent. He stopped. Studied the ground. Looked at Town, and once more the spell worked. "It'd be absolutely—it'd be absolu—" he lit out for the wild blue yonder—"You see, we let the kids go through their stockings first and play a minute or so with their little old dolls and little old toy stoves and tea-sets and little old red fire engine and all that, while the three of us sneak out to the woodhouse where we got it hidden then we bring it right through the hall and into—" He crashed. "Nope. We can't do it, Town. We just can't."

Town sighed. "Did cost a lot of money."

"How much?"

"Four hundard and fifty—"

Fifteen's eyes bugged out—

"You better not steal that coffin," yelped Miss Curiosity, "it's for old Mr. Askew sure as the world, he's dying and sure as the world it's for him—"

Paralysis set in. Town slowly lifted one finger, made the sign of the circle: that meant hold still. He said easy-like, "Well boys, reckon I'd better be helping my grandma and you better be helping yours—" and with that he got up real slow and made a dash round the g. h. and when Miss Curiosity saw him coming, she took to her heels through the lane, circled round the barn and back through the woodhouse into the rose garden—saw the three were gaining on her and there was nowhere to go but the magnolia tree, so she ran through the passageway of the house and pulled up the tree like a monkey and was half way to the top when the boys reached it. "You leave me alone," she shrieked, "Papa said everybody in this family had to treat each other like human beings."

"You ain't no human being," Town called up the tree where Miss Curiosity had now swung out to a high thin limb, that would not have held the big boys, and clung there swaying in the wind.

"You sho ain't," yelled Thirteen.

They stood peering up at her, utterly thwarted.

"Let's cut her liver 'n' lights out," suggested Town.

"We goin cut your liver 'n' lights out," yelled Thirteen.

And Miss Curiosity, sure as the world they would if she came down, clung to that final sprout of the magnolia, until her father came home at supper time and promised her safe conduct to the dining room, under certain conditions.

Everybody went to work next day to earn Christmas money and even Miss Curiosity heard no more talk of heirlooms.

Christmas Eve came. All day, Mother and Grandma and the cook and the two oldest sisters worked in the kitchen. Fruit cakes had been made for a month, wrapped in clean white towels and stored in the dark pantry. But the lean pork had to be ground for pork salad, the twenty-eight-pound turkey had to have its head chopped off, and then it must be picked and cleaned and hung high in the passageway between house and dining room, and then, of course, you had to put a turkey feather in your hair and make like you were Indians; then coconuts had to be grated for ambrosia and for the six-layered coconut cake and the eight coconut custard pies, and you helped punch out the eyes of the coconuts; then of course you needed to drink some of the coconut milk, and as you watched the grownups grate the nut meats into vast snowy mounds you nibbled at the pieces too small to be grated—and by that time, you felt sort of dizzy but here came the dray from the depot bringing the barrel of oysters in the shell (they were shipped from Apalachicola), and you watched them cover the barrel with ice, for you can't count on north Florida's winter staying winter. It was time, then, to lick the pan where the filling for the Lord Baltimore cake had been beaten and somebody laid down the caramel pan—but you tried to lick it and couldn't, you felt too glazy-eyed and poked out. And finally, you lay down on the back porch in the warm sun and fell asleep.

When you woke up it was almost dark. The sun had dropped behind the woodhouse. Curls of smoke floated from the chimney of the cook's house in the back yard. Her husband was smoking his pipe on the porch and Town, his grandson, was lounging on the steps reading a book. Town read everything Thirteen and Fifteen read, although he went to school only three months each year, for that was all the school there was for Town to go to. But his two friends taught him what they learned each day and he kept right up with them— although, maybe, they didn't know they were teaching and he didn't know he was learning. They just liked to do everything together so they did it. Now Town's grandfather was speaking to him: you saw Town move inside to lie before the fire and continue his reading; you knew he had been told what your father told you, "It'll ruin your eyes in that light."

In the kitchen they were preparing supper. You didn't want it. You played round with your spoon. Your mother came to your chair, felt your cheek, leaned down and felt your head with her lips to see if you had fever. You liked this so much, sometimes you played sick to get her to do it. She decided you didn't need any Castoria (the family answer to everything wrong with children) but Big Granny called out to say she might as well give you Castor Oil, everybody ought to be given a jigger of Castor Oil on Christmas Eve to make way for Christmas.

Mother did not seem to hear but accelerated stocking-hanging. Twelve were hung. The foresighted had reserved Big Granny's weeks ahead, the laggards made do with Aunt Chloe's (first choice) or Mother's (second choice). The long black stockings hung from the mantel in Mother's bedroom each with a name on it.

Five o'clock, next morning, the little ones were scrambling round the fireplace, feeling in the dark for theirs. Mother, in her bed, did not stir. Father, in the adjoining room, turned over, muttered *my my my*. The rule was, you tiptoed and you whispered and you looked through your stocking but you couldn't touch the big presents lying right there before you until you had dressed.

So you took down your knobby stocking and in the light from the fire which someone had thrown kindling on, you dug in. And all the time, there—on a fine new doll rocker—sat the beautiful doll Miss Ada (well, maybe) had dressed but you dared not touch it until you had washed your face and put on your clothes. You stood and stared at it and then you saw a tea-set and you stared at it and the suspense was almost unendurable. But at that moment, a big sister appeared and offered to help you dress quick, and then, suddenly, Mother was in her wrapper and our father was tiptoeing in from his room, making like he didn't know what it was all about. This big act of Absolute Astonishment which he staged each year gave an extra polish to an already shining moment. Where did it all come from! what a fire engine! what a doll! what a tea-set! what soldiers! what a rocking horse—

Finally, we went to breakfast. No verses on this day. We sat down to a table which held the same breakfast every Christmas: before my father's place, in an enormous platter, was a cold gelatiny hog's head which had been boiled with bay leaves and spices, a few pickled pig's feet were with it, and up and down the long table were three big platters of sausage and bowls of grits and plates of biscuits, and butter and syrup.

We waited for Mother. She came in from the kitchen, flushed from last-minute doings, and sat down. Then Fifteen and Thirteen got up again, looking solemn, walked to the corner of the bay window. With a fine flick of the wrist, the fifteen-year-old uncovered the small children's table (the overflow table when company was present). Behold! the future heirlooms. You felt a letdown, having overheard the plans and knowing what might have been there. But the others gaped admiration. The boys had presented the parents with eighteen plates, each with a splendid fish painted on it, and eighteen side dishes for the bones. The oldest then made a presentation speech on the necessity for heirlooms. He said in times of revolutionary unrest heirlooms had a most stabilizing effect, they gave a thrust to one's patriotism (or something to that effect), and he and his brother were making the gift not so much to the parents as to the fourth and fifth generation. And then everybody applauded, for he was a natural—you felt like applauding whenever you saw him.

(Later, you heard your father ask where in the name of heaven did the boys get enough money to buy all those dishes. They must have cost plenty! Mother said they probably did. "But where . . ." and then he did a double-take. "Not . . ." "I'm afraid so," was the reply. In January, when the bills came in, he found the donors had done what he half guessed and Mother's intuition confirmed: they had charged them to his account at the Supply Store.)

After the excitement of the unexpected gift subsided, our father took down the Bible and opened it at the second chapter of St. Luke. Nine pairs of eyes turned toward him as we waited to hear what we had heard every Christmas of our lives:

> And it came to pass in those days that there went out a decree from Caesar Augustus, that all the world should be taxed. And Joseph also went . . . unto the city of David, which is called Bethlehem: . . . to be taxed with Mary his espoused wife, being great with child. And the days were accomplished that she should be delivered. And she brought forth her first-born son, and wrapped him in swaddling clothes, and laid him in a manger. . . . And there were in the same country shepherds abiding in the field, keeping watch over their flock by night. And, lo, the angel of the Lord . . .

As he read in his deep warm voice, we followed the words, knowing them by heart. We knew, too, that to him it was not only the story of the Christ Child but of Every Child, every new beginning, every new chance for peace on earth. When he was done, we bowed our heads: he thanked God for "all the good things which we do not merit" and asked His blessing on all who were suffering and in need in every country in the whole world, and then he asked

for courage, courage to have vision, for "without vision the people perish."

The bay window was bright. Fire and cat were purring. Canary was at peace. Mother sat between her two eldest home from college, and her eyes were big and dark and somehow sad and tender, and there was flour on her nose. A good silence was settling on us. Then the youngest one said, "I fink Thesus was a fine little fellow"—and a sausage perched on top of the pile shivered and rolled off the platter toward him. And everybody laughed and began to eat breakfast.

In the middle of the day we had dinner. But by the time the dinner bell rang and we assembled in the dining room, we had little space left for turkey and Mother's succulent dressing made of nuts and oysters and celery and eggs and bread and turkey "essence" for we had been nibbling all morning on raisins and candy and crystallized fruit and pecans (which were cracked and in bowls, everywhere). The next day, and the next, the results of the cooking and baking that had gone on for days would be more appreciated. After all, there is no better time to eat a piece of coconut pie than after you have been racing round for hours and someone says, Let's have a piece of coconut pie! You stop, everybody goes to the pantry, and you eat a piece of pie, then you get a spoon and scoop out a little cold turkey dressing, then you pick up an olive, then you take a piece of stuffed celery left over from Christmas, and then you dash out to the back yard and climb up on the roof of the woodhouse and call the others to come up there . . .

On Christmas afternoon, we went visiting and our friends came visiting us and sometimes we'd meet half way between our houses. We girls had, of course, to show off our dolls and books and sewing baskets and manicure sets and the big boys had to show off their bicycles and shotguns and the little boys showed off their red wagons and fire engines. But before dark we were home again and a stillness settled down on the house.

And then, after things had been quiet a long time, our father would call out, "Where are the boys? It's about time to get our fireworks organized." But he knew: the boys—and the girls—were on their own beds, each in his own room or corner of a room, looking things over more closely or reading (books by the piles came at Christmas time). And now, each face had become its own, settling in its own private curves, its own secret question marks, its own wisting or wondering lines. Each had crawled into his secret hide-out. Thirteen-year-old in his corner might be playing a new Mozart concerto he had wanted, or polishing his new gun; fifteen-year-old might be reading the new big dictionary which he had especially asked for, the nine-year-old philosopher might be squatting at the window, face like a buddha, looking deep into eternal matters as was his way. Suddenly one of them would stop, look around as though he had never met the others and turn a cartwheel or two, then they were all turning cartwheels or wrasslin with each other and you'd hear them thumping the floor and rolling off beds and maybe the slats would fall out and the whole bed come tumbling down.

Then our father would call up and say, "I'm waiting, boys!" And there'd be three or four *yessirs* and you'd hear them dashing down the backstairs or the hall stairs and soon you'd hear our father planning the fireworks which would be set off at eight o'clock.

After the Big Illumination, when Roman candles and rockets and cannon crackers were shot off on the front lawn at the proper and dramatic moment by the big boys and Town and our father, while the little ones raced round with sparklers and firewheels and small firecrackers, all the family and sometimes a few stray friends would dash into the dining room for oyster stew, and oysters on the shell, and fried oysters; and there'd be a waving of tomato catsup and horse-radish bottles and somebody would drop a raw oyster on a rug and a big sister would clean it up . . . .

And now everything fades out. And one knows only that there must have been a slow stumbling exhaustion which ended in bed. And finally, the old house was still. And whatever was said was said by the toadfrog underneath the house or by the great pillars which held the house and its children and the par-

ents and Big Grandma or Little Grandma secure on their giant shoulders.

Every Christmas it was like this until the First World War. Then things turned upside down: the new world began to squeeze the old too hard. The world market which the naval stores industry depended upon grew very dizzy indeed; we children of a small inland town heard daily talk of the seas and the ships, and the blockade, and the Germans and the Russians and the British and strange names and strange places entered our lives and have, of course, stayed there. I heard my father had "over-stretched" himself and I was sure he had; but I was as sure as could be that no matter how much "stretching" he had done he'd never fail to do what he set out to do, and the stretching would turn out to be his magic way of stepping across a wide chasm from where he was to a more exciting place.

But this time, it did not happen quite as I had expected. Our father lost his mills and his turpentine stills, the light plant and ice plant and store and the house that never quite ended—and we moved to our small summer cottage in the mountains.

There was nothing dismal about that moving, for my father departed like an explorer setting out for an unknown continent. He actually succeeded in convincing everybody but Mother that our new life was going to be more interesting than our old, that mountains were more beautiful than swamps and lily-covered ponds and oaks heavy with moss, that we'd never forget our first spring when we would see dogwood in bloom on the hills. (And of course, we have never forgot the beauty he spoke of—nor the deeper, mythic fascination of the swamps and cypress and sand and great oaks where we were born and where our memories still live.)

The move to the mountains, by the time Dad had planned it, had acquired all the drama and tension and highlights of a Great Hegira. He leased three big freight cars and stored the household furniture and the piano and the dishes and trunks full of Mother's linens and our things in two of them. (Certain large pieces of furniture they must have sold or given away, for I have never seen them since.) In the third freight car were the cow and the horses and the dogs and crates of pure-bred Leghorns from his farm plus feed for the long journey, plus farm implements plus tools and toys plus two of the brothers —and two of the young Negroes from the farm who were completely entranced by our father's stories of mountains and red earth and the great gorge at Tallulah Falls and asked to go along on this adventure.

It was a bit difficult to come down to the size of our small summer cottage after our father's big build-up but we managed it, somehow. He had a way of diverting us from nostalgic moods by arriving home from the little mountain town with two newly purchased feisty black mules, or a Duroc-Jersey sow, or maybe a hundred small apple trees. "What are we going to do with them?" Mother would ask quietly. "Mama, we are going to farm; this is going to be the finest little farm you ever saw. You will raise the prettiest pure-bred pigs in North Georgia and think what this hill will look like with a hundred apple trees in bloom in the spring!"

We were not alone in being poor. Times were hard in the South—much harder for most than for us, as our father often reminded us. Our region was deep in a depression long before the rest of the country felt it—indeed, it had never had real prosperity since the Civil War—only spotty surges of easy money. But even the bank did not know—and it knew plenty—how little money we managed on those years. It got worse instead of better as time passed. And there came a winter when my younger sister and I, who were in Baltimore preparing ourselves to be a great pianist (me) and a great actress (her) felt we were needed at home. We had been supporting ourselves in our schools but even so, we felt the parents needed us.

It was our barter year: Dad would take eggs to town, swap them for flour or cornmeal or coffee, and do it so casually that nobody suspected it was necessary. They thought he was so proud of his wife's Leghorns that he wanted to show their achievements to his friends at the stores. Eggs from the hens, three pigs which he had raised, milk and butter from the cow, beans he grew and dried, and apples from a few old trees already on the property—that was about it. It was enough. For Mother could take cornmeal, mix it with flour, add soda and buttermilk and melted butter, a dab of sugar and salt, and present us with the best hot cakes in the world. Her gravy made of drippings from fried side meat, with flour and milk added and crushed black pepper would have pleased Escoffier or any other great cook. And when things got too dull, my sister and I would hitch up the two feisty mules to the wagon and go for as wild a ride as one wanted over rough clay winter roads.

Nevertheless, the two of us had agreed to skip Christmas. You don't always have to have Christmas, we kept saying to each other. Of course not, the other would answer.

We had forgot our father.

In that year of austerity, he invited the chain gang to have Christmas dinner with us. The prisoners were working the state roads, staying in two shabby red railroad cars on a siding. Our father visited them as he visited "all his neighbors." That night, after he returned from a three-hour visit with the men, we heard him tell Mother about it. She knew what was coming. "Bad place to be living," he said. "Terrible! Not fit for animals much less—" He sighed. "Well, there's more misery in the world than even I know; and a lot of it is unnecessary. That's the wrong part of it, it's unnecessary." He looked in his wife's dark eyes. She waited. "Mama," he said softly, "how about having them out here for Christmas. Wouldn't that be good?" A long silence. Then Mother quietly agreed. Dad walked to town —we had no car—to tell the foreman he would like to have the prisoners and guards come to Christmas dinner.

"All of them?" asked the chain-gang foreman.

"We couldn't hardly leave any of the boys out, could we?"

Close to noon on Christmas Day we saw them coming down the road: forty-eight men in stripes, with their guards. They came up the hill and headed for the house, a few laughing, talking, others grim and suspicious. All had come, white and Negro. We had helped Mother make two caramel cakes and twelve sweet potato pies and a wonderful backbone-and-rice dish (which Mother, born on the coast, called pilau); and there were hot rolls and Brunswick stew, and a washtub full of apples which our father had polished in front of the fire on Christmas Eve. It would be a splendid dinner, he told Mother who looked a bit wan, probably wondering what we would eat in January.

While we pulled out Mother's best china —piecing out with the famous heirloom fish plates—our father went from man to man shaking hands, and soon they were talking freely with him, and everybody was laughing at his funny—and sometimes on the rare side —stories. And then, there was a hush, and we in the kitchen heard Dad's voice lifted up: "And it came to pass in those days—"

Mother stayed with the oven. The two of us eased to the porch. Dad was standing there, reading from St. Luke. The day was warm and sunny and the forty-eight men and their guards were sitting on the grass. Two guards with guns in their hands leaned against trees. Eight of the men were lifers; six of them, in pairs, had their inside legs locked together; ten were killers (one had bashed in his grandma's head), two had robbed banks, three had stolen cars, one had burned down his neighbor's house and barn after an argument, one had raped a girl—all were listening to the old old words.

When my father closed the Bible, he gravely said he hoped their families were having a good Christmas, he hoped all was well "back home." Then he smiled and grew hearty. "Now boys," he said, "eat plenty and have a good time. We're proud to have you today. We would have been a little lonely if you hadn't come. Now let's have a Merry Christmas."

The men laughed. It began with the Negroes, who quickly caught the wonderful absurdity, it spread to the whites and finally all were laughing and muttering Merry Christ-

mas, half deriding, half meaning it, and my father laughed with them for he was never unaware of the absurd which he seemed deliberately, sometimes, to whistle into his life.

They were our guests, and our father moved among them with grace and ease. He was soon asking them about their families, telling them a little about his. One young man talked earnestly in a low voice. I heard my father say, "Son, that's mighty bad. We'll see if we can't do something about it." (Later he did.)

When Mother said she was ready, our father asked "Son," who was one of the killers, to go help "my wife, won't you, with the heavy things." And the young man said he'd be mighty glad to. The one in for raping and another for robbing a bank said they'd be pleased to help, too, and they went in. My sister and I followed, not feeling as casual as we hoped we looked. But when two guards moved toward the door my father peremptorily stopped them with, "The boys will be all right." And "the boys" were. They came back in a few minutes bearing great pots and pans to a serving table we had set up on the porch. My sister and I served the plates. The murderer and his two friends passed them to the men. Afterward, the rapist and two bank robbers and the arsonist said they'd be real pleased to wash up the dishes. But we told them nobody should wash dishes on Christmas—just have a good time.

That evening, after our guests had gone back to their quarters on the railroad siding, we sat by the fire. The parents looked tired. Dad went out for another hickory log to "keep us through the night," laid it in the deep fireplace, scratched the coals, sat down in his chair by the lamp. Mother said she had a letter from the eldest daughter in China—would Papa read it? It was full of cheer as such letters are likely to be. We sat quietly talking of her family, of their work with a religious organization, of China's persisting troubles after the 1911 revolution.

We were quiet after that. Just rested together. Dad glanced through a book or two that his sons had sent him. Then the old look of having something to say to his children settled on his face. He began slowly:

"We've been through some pretty hard times, lately, and I've been proud of my family. Some folks can take prosperity and can't take poverty; some can take being poor and lose their heads when money comes. I want my children to accept it all: the good and the bad, for that is what life is. It can't be wholly good; it won't be wholly bad." He looked at our mother, sitting there, tired but gently involved. "Those men, today—they've made mistakes. Sure. But I have too. Bigger ones maybe than theirs. And you will. You are not likely to commit a crime but you may become blind and refuse to see what you should look at, and that can be worse than a crime. Don't forget that. Never look down on a man. Never. If you can't look him straight in the eyes, then what's wrong is with you." He glanced at the letter from the eldest sister. "The world is changing fast. Folks get hurt and make terrible mistakes at such times. But the one I hope you won't make is to cling to my generation's sins. You'll have plenty of your own, remember. Changing things is mighty risky, but not changing things is worse—that is, if you can think of something better to change

to. . . . Mama, believe I'll go to bed. You about ready?"

On the stairs, he stopped. "But I don't mean, Sister, you got to get radical." He laughed. His voice dropped to the soft tones he used with his younger children. "We had a good Christmas, didn't we?" He followed our mother up the stairs.

My younger sister and I looked in the fire. What our future would be, we did not know. The curve was too sharp, just here; and sometimes, the dreaming about a curve you can't see round is not a thing you want to talk about. After a long staring in the fire, we succumbed to a little do-you-remember. And soon we were laughing about the fifteen-year-old and Town and the thirteen-year-old and their heirloom year, and the hog killing and the Song of Solomon and the tree-shaking and Big Grandma's sausage, the best as our mother used to say that anybody could make, with just enough red pepper and sage . . . .

And now the fire in front of us was blurring. My sister said softly, "It was a large Christmas."

"Which one?"

"All of them," she whispered.

ARCHIE CARR

The Black Beach

Archie Carr (1909–   ), distinguished Graduate Research Professor of Biological Sciences at the University of Florida, has been a member of the faculty there since 1937. While on leave of absence from 1944 to 1949, he taught biology at the Escuela Agrícola Panamericana in Honduras. His *High Jungles and Low*, 1953, records his impressions of Honduras and Nicaragua. This volume was followed by *The Windward Road*, 1956 (from which "The Black Beach" was taken), an account of Mr. Carr's search for turtles along the shores of Costa Rica. "The Black Beach," which originally appeared in *Mademoiselle*, was chosen by the O. Henry Memorial Award editors for inclusion in *Prize Stories 1956*. Two recent books relate his experiences as a naturalist in Africa: *Ulando*, 1964, and *Land and Wild Life in Africa*, 1964.

Although "The Black Beach" is a report of a real experience, the carefully controlled unfolding of events and the development of character might justify calling it a short story.

It was on the black beach that I met Mrs. Ybarra. It was the long, lonesome, log-strewn stretch from Tortuguero to Parismina. You don't see many people on that beach. Perhaps the chances against our meeting reinforced the impression Mrs. Ybarra made on me and caused her to seem more noteworthy than she really was. That you must judge when you have learned the circumstances.

I was looking for nests of trunkback turtles. I had walked five miles and had found no sign—no fresh trail that was not clearly that of hawksbill or green turtle. Even the greens were scarce. There was just a sprinkling of early layers in the van of the big nesting migration—the "fleet," as the people on the beach call it—which was already long overdue. It was nearing noon of a flaming, cloudless day and the land breeze had killed the trade wind.

Two miles back I had met the Siquirres dogs—the seasonally feral packs of curs that Paco had pointed out from the plane two days before. Each May the dogs gather on the beach from Siquirres and the other towns along the railroad far inland, called by some unknown cue to cross as much as thirty miles of jungle, marsh and mangrove swamp and meet the fleet and batten on turtle eggs for the season. There were eight dogs in the pack I met, and they were hungry and irritable. They ran yapping before me for a while, as if they thought I was somehow to blame for the lateness of the fleet, and then they dashed off over the low dunes and disappeared among the coco plums. Besides the dogs and a scurrying sand crab now and then I had seen no living thing on land.

THE BLACK BEACH From *The Windward Road* by Archie Carr, by permission of Alfred A. Knopf, Inc. Copyright 1955 by Archie Carr.

Seaward there was little more—no boat to watch, no cruising fin, no whitecaps even, nor any bar or promontory to break the sweeping surf line. Once in a thousand steps there came the thin, lost cry of a tern hidden out among the heat waves.

Once, for a moment, a black patch showed on the burnished, blue-white swells just beyond the breakers where a shoal of anchovy had come up from wherever they had been to flip and play and circle at the surface. I stopped to see what hungry things would gather from the sea and the air, as they always gather about such schools. Almost at once the jacks came—big, flat, gleaming five-pounders that slashed and ripped at the edges of the anchovy cloud, knocking chunks of it into the air in showers of chrome splinters, and sometimes throwing themselves out too in short parabolas, head over tail, stiff and sheepish-looking. I thought what I could do among the jacks with a bass rod and a Johnson spoon.

I shuffled on through the fine, hot sand. It was light, powdery dust of pumice and black glass that let you sink ankle-deep. It was so hot it burned my shanks above my shoe tops. The beach was piled with stranded timber —immense silver trunks of cedar and laurel and *cedro macho* from the Costa Rican rivers and mahogany from Panama or Nicaragua, stolen from the loggers by decades of June floods and then thrown back again onto the black beach by the wild seas that batter this open coast. No tropical beach is fun to walk on at cloudless, windless midday. This one, with its endless, monstrous jetsam to send you weaving from the deep, hot dunes down into the brawling surf and back again, made following the narrow strip above high-water mark, where turtle trails are laid, a trying job. My ardor for trunkback nests was failing under the sun and I was on the point of crawling beneath a propped log to sleep out the midday calm when I saw what I had come after.

It was a short, broad-limbed V deeply engraved in the beach above the tide zone. The limbs of the V—the trails to and from the disturbed patch—were nearly as wide as the wheel trail of a tractor, and indeed the whole system of marks seemed to show that a heavy, wheeled vehicle had come up from the sea, had sunk deep in the sand drift and, after a great deal of backing and filling and churning, had returned to the water.

It was the nest of a trunkback. It was the first I had ever seen but there was no mistaking it. It was the first ever recorded for Central America, but its significance to me far transcended that statistic. To me it was the long-sought land sign of a sea creature I had looked for since childhood—a monster of the deep ocean guided ashore one time in each year by the primal reptile drive to dig a hole in earth and drop in it the seeds of trunkbacks for tomorrow, and cover the hole with toeless flat feet, and pound back down to the sea and never look behind—the last vestige of landcraft left to a bloodline sea-bound for a hundred million years, and left then but to one sex for one hour on one night in the year.

For a while I just stood and looked at the nest. After a bit the trance of lightheaded exultation ran out and I put down my camera bag and canteen and set about appraising the site where the turtle had worked. There was a great deal of it. A female trunkback often weighs a thousand pounds or more and is full of a fanatical kind of gland-given zeal that would almost pass for ingenuity. Everything she does is calculated to keep her eggs from being dug up again. She can't hide the fact that she was on the beach, so she confounds the egg-hunter with a plethora of clues. In this case the area of flung sand in which I had to prospect for the egg chamber was at least fifteen feet in diameter and roughly circular in outline. Since it offered no evidence, at least to my eye, by which the field for search might be narrowed down, I had to cover every square foot of it; and since the

clutch of eggs might lie waist-deep beneath the sand the job ahead was imposing.

I took up my egg stick. After making a few random test holes here and there I began moving systematically back and forth across the site, punching as deeply as I could drive the stick. When I had completed a regular and closely spaced gridwork of holes and had found nothing I began to realize that the slim section of cane I had found effective enough in prospecting for the nests of hawksbill and green turtles was too feeble for the work at hand. To get down through the hard sand that lay below the surface drift I needed a pole with backbone—something I could plant and swing my weight on.

I began looking about the beach for something suitable. I tested one silvery stick after another but all were either crooked as a snake or punky and spineless from salt water and sun. I found a section of timber bamboo that was sound, but you don't split stuff like that with a pocketknife, which was the only tool I carried. Halfheartedly I trimmed and sharpened a leaf stem of coco palm, and this collapsed at the first thrust.

I wanted the nest badly, and with the mounting realization that I probably would not get it my frustration grew apace. I cursed my lack of foresight in not bringing a machete. I grabbed up a sphere of drifted pumice stone and tried to put an edge on my knife blade with it, but the rounded face of the stone collapsed like sugar candy and only polished the metal. In a peevish fit I threw the stone at the face of a laurel log and it went to pieces there.

Suddenly a slight blue feist dog burst from behind the log and started shrieking at me, lifting its feet in indignation and looking backward at intervals as if for support from a source hidden from me by the rise of the log.

Then, for an instant, I saw a face above the six-foot loom of the trunk, and then the face was gone. I ran around the end of the log and saw a woman on horseback retreating at a dead run in the direction from which she had come. I could hear the splatting of the horse's feet in the wave wash and I could see in the slant of the rider's back that she was not party to the flight but was trying to stop and turn the horse. It was the horse who was alarmed at the sudden, unprecedented sight and stink of gringo behind a log on the black beach—not Mrs. Ybarra.

Mrs. Ybarra no doubt took an unenthusiastic view of me too. But she was a woman inured to the shocks of life on this beach. She was not the sort to turn back because of a stranger there, no matter how unaccounted for. She gradually dominated the horse and brought it to a grudging halt a hundred yards down the beach and turned it. I could see that it was an ash-colored *criollo* stallion—one of the tough, runty and cruelly selected remnants of the old Spanish horse that somehow survived the odds against horseflesh on this tropical shore and that now, salt-cured, *torsola*-proof and vampire-tolerant and economical with its tissue water as a camel, will single-foot all night in sand fetlock-deep.

The example under Mrs. Ybarra had the odd, ratlike face and ewe-necked silhouette they all have. He came back toward me under pressure, against his judgment, his eyes rolling. He came because the will of his rider was stronger than his will.

As she approached Mrs. Ybarra steered her mount down-beach to pass well seaward of me, gripping the reins firmly and drumming at the horse's tight belly with her heels. She gave me a quick look.

"*Adios*," she said.

Adios said that way means you are going on by. In a matrix of circumstance such as this it becomes a bivalent greeting, a salutation with connotation that a parting will follow immediately. It is a hello-good-by and a word that, so far as I know, has no counterpart in English or North American. Spanish can be shaded delicately. It is nowhere near as simple as my textbooks and teachers made out.

There was, of course, no reason at all why Mrs. Ybarra should not go on by. But at the moment she spoke I saw the pearly gleam of new turtle eggs in two arroba baskets swinging from her saddle; and this made it unthinkable that she should ride on and leave me with my dilemma.

So I said "*Buenas tardes*," and the shift in salutation changed our relationship at once and made it a point of courtesy for her to rein up, a bit warily, and see what my intentions were.

She was not the sort of woman you would expect to see on this beach, even supposing you were expecting women of any sort. She was a short, turnip-shaped woman with a thin-lipped Madonna's face and a mass of snuff-colored hair piled under a man's old felt hat tied on with a scarf. She had spindly Spanish legs and a big bosom bound in by a bodice of muslin. She wore a brown cotton smock, and a skirt of the same stuff was cleverly tucked under and around her legs because she rode astride and not sidesaddle like the women in Honduras. Her racial origin and place in life were not evident from her appearance. She looked like no Costa Rican I had ever seen. Except for her almost-black skin and reddish hair, and for the shameless way she straddled the high wooden pack saddle, she more closely approached the kind of women you see in the mountains of Matagalpa or of southern Honduras, where the century of hardship the old revolutions brought bred thin-faced women with more than their share of character. She had much in common with them and much in common with her horse. She was weather-beaten, but she had the quiet confidence that goes with a full stomach.

"*Buenas tardes*," she said, stopping her horse. "The widow of Ybarra from Panal, this side of Parismina."

"Do you know what kind of a turtle did that?" I asked.

"Why not? *Es de canal*—a trunkback."

"That's what I thought," I said. "How do you know?"

"Only a trunkback tears up the beach like that. All this beach is torn up by trunkbacks. It's hard to ride except near the water."

I looked up and down the beach and for the first time noticed that the sand in front of the dunes had an oddly uneven topography that was not part of the wind-piled dune system and not like any beach I had even seen before.

"Some of that is where the animals dig for eggs when the fleet of green turtles comes, but mostly it's trunkbacks that pile the sand like that. Like this nest here. . . . But why don't you go on a way? I saw several *carey* nests in the light sand yonder, and some of green turtles—various. I dug two." She patted the side of one of the egg baskets.

"I don't want hawksbill eggs," I said, "or green turtle either. I'm looking for trunkback eggs."

"They're not as good as *carey* eggs. They have a little taste."

"I don't want to eat them," I said. "I want to measure them."

She looked at me deprecatingly.

"They're this big. *Asi de grande.*" She cupped her hand to show me how big.

"I mean exactly. And I want to take pictures of them."

"They are very deep. A yard—yard and a half. The animals can't find them. Even the tigers. Even the Siquirres dogs that dig out all the rest don't try to dig trunkback eggs."

"I don't care how long it takes," I said. "I would dig all afternoon if I knew there was a nest there. Maybe this one scratched and went back. Loggerheads do that."

She studied the tumbled sand for a moment. Then she wagged her finger from side to side in front of her face in the gesture of negation that all Latins use.

"*Puso—*" she said. "*Ahí puso.*"

"But how do you find the nest?" I asked. "I've punched all around here and couldn't find a soft place anywhere."

Again she wagged her finger at me.

"You didn't punch deep enough. There is no soft place in a *canal* nest. You just have to find it. Please, what time is it? Midday?"

I brushed the sweat-soaked sand from the face of my watch.

"A quarter after. Are you in a hurry?"

"Today the Spaniard pays the Mosquitos. I am going to collect a debt and I want to get there before they are all drunk. I saw the airplane Thursday, and they will all be drunk by dark."

"How much is the debt?" I said.

"There are two of them. They add up to eight *colones.*"

"All right, look. I'll pay you ten if you will help me find the turtle nest."

She looked at the sand in front of her horse again and then up at the sun. She sighed and swung a leg over the tall saddle frame and stepped to the ground.

"We will try it." She said it with no great enthusiasm.

She led the horse into the sprinkled shade of a ragged old *mangineal,* the only real tree anywhere on the foreshore, and tied the reins to a branch.

"That is a poison tree," I said.

"It doesn't molest horses."

"But how about your hands? You have to hold the reins."

"Don't worry. It doesn't molest me either. Only the juice, or the smoke when it burns."

"I wouldn't tie a horse to that tree for anything," I said.

"It's all right. You are a stranger here and haven't found yourself."

She drew a wasted sliver of a machete from a rawhide scabbard tied to the saddle. She walked back to the turtle nest and called to the feist and it came bouncing down from the beach grass, eager to serve her with all its talents. She leaned and scratched suggestively at the sand to interest the dog in the place.

"*Huevos,*" she said.

I winced, because this word said by itself like that usually means something quite different; but the dog understood and began to dig in a crab hole six feet from the turtle nest.

"Don't be an imbecile," Mrs. Ybarra said. "Here—dig here!"

The dog dropped his ears, hurt by the tone of the words; then he moved over and started digging in the turtle nest.

"With green turtles and *careyes* Filin never deceives himself. With trunkbacks he doesn't serve. Let him dig here awhile. I have to cut a stick. You come too! You can climb better."

We pushed through the sea grapes and sea oats and coco plums, and behind the dunes we came to a coppice of tightly spaced saplings. We stopped and Mrs. Ybarra peered about in the dense thicket until she found what she wanted.

"*Aquel.*" She pointed into the dim interior of the thicket. "If you climb that *palito* and trim it we can get it out."

I shinnied up the slim, smooth stem and trimmed off all the branches I could reach. Then I slid down and cut the trunk through at the ground and dragged it out into the clear. Mrs. Ybarra cut a five-foot section from the stem, skinned the bark from it and tapered one end to a point.

"Ya," she said. "Maybe with this."

When we got back the feist had lost interest in the turtle nest and was digging out another sand crab hole.

"He doesn't serve," Mrs. Ybarra said.

She planted the tip of the stick in the center of the nest and pushed. The point grated to a stop in the dense sand two feet down. She tried again a foot away with the same result. She punched a dozen holes and from each the stick emerged only dusted with fine sand. She stopped and studied the site again on hands and knees, plucking at each twig or bit of debris that protruded above the ploughed surface. After a while she found a newly broken end of beach morning glory stem, and when she pulled on this a good three feet of green vine came out of the sand.

"Maybe here," she said. "The *canal* buried the vine."

She took up the stick and probed carefully all around where the vine had been. Still the rod broke through no nest roof and came out smeared with no yolk. Finally she stopped and shook her head.

"It is *fregada*, this question of the *canal* nests," she said.

She wiped her eyes with the backs of her forearms. Her hair was falling out from under her hat and the sweat-stuck sand had frosted the dark shine of her face. I thought I could see misgiving in her expression.

"I don't believe there's anything here," I said.

"Don't deceive yourself. *Aquí puso*—she laid here. It is sure. Always it is like this. The *canal* is—ooo—very big. Her leg is like this—" She measured against her own thigh. "She reaches to a great depth and she is heavy and she packs the sand back with her belly harder than it was before. And the worst is she

ploughs so much ground it is hard to locate the nest. If you do find the eggs they are too big to eat with comfort. It is not worth the trouble. But maybe if we both push on the stick. . . . The place should be exactly there."

I have seen a water witch point out the spot for a well with the judicious precision with which Mrs. Ybarra aimed the tip of her stick. She sighted as if she were aiming a rifle at the head of a snake.

"Exactly there," she repeated.

She stuck the point in the sand and we both leaned on the shaft and it broke with a snap and split back in our hands.

"It broke," Mrs. Ybarra said. "The wood was tender. . . . Look, do you want to try any more? I think it will be easier if you go out at night and find the *canal* when she is laying and before she has covered. Any time when the moon is over the sea, not over the land. In the black sand pieces they come out every night—one, two, three—to lay."

I said I thought she was right. I dug in my pocket and from under the sand there brought out some Costa Rican bills. I counted ten colons and held them out to her, saying I was grateful for her help and was sorry she had got so hot and sandy.

"Ah, no," she said. "I can't accept that. I said I would find the eggs. You owe me nothing. I'll reach the village in plenty of time."

"No, look—I stopped you. I'm going to put the money in your saddlebag."

I turned and walked toward the *mangineal* tree behind the screen of tall sea oats. My first sight of Mrs. Ybarra's horse was his feet waving and kicking in the air, all four of them. I ran toward him in sudden panic and burst through the grass and saw him on his back writhing and jerking and bending his short, stiff backbone in impossible, convulsive arcs.

"Come, quick, look at your horse!" I yelled.

She came running.

"Oh, my sainted mother, is he scratching? Yes, my God, he is scratching! He always scratches when he is hot, and I forgot to watch —and look at my *carga*! A la—! Get up! You! Flojo! Stand up!"

She seized a piece of driftwood and began pounding the horse on his unprotected underside. He stopped rolling and in awkward haste floundered to his feet and stood with flaring nostrils, ears back and eyes rolling at his mistress, stung and puzzled.

He was a frightful thing to see. The bridle was bunched at his chin. The saddle and the empty egg baskets and some bundles that had not broken their moorings hung beneath him, and a disheveled game rooster dangled from a cinch ring between his forelegs. His back and sides were heavily smeared with a thick, uneven mixture of egg yolks and whites and black sand, in which, here and there about his surface, leaves and rotting *mangineal* apples and bits of turtle egg shell were stuck. He looked as if a two-year-old child had made a frosting for him. He shook himself violently but looked no better for it.

A feeling of despondency spread over me. This poor woman; what misery I had brought her. How utterly my stubbornness had wrecked her hopes and her day. I turned to her, in my shame ready to crawl or to force on her every last colon I could claw out of my pockets.

She was laughing.

"What a barbarity!" she shrieked. "What a brutal animal! Oh, my sainted mother, what animal more brutal!"

She was so clearly delighted that I looked back at the horse with new eyes, and this time he looked funny to me too and I started to laugh. We both laughed for a long time.

After a while I said: "I am sorry. The blame is all mine. What can we do?"

"No," she said, "it doesn't matter. I only have to bathe the horse."

She began to untangle the bridle, stopping at intervals to bend over and shake and screech with laughter. I helped her unfasten the cinches and disengage the confusion of saddle and *carga*. She took the machete and cut some clumps of grass, which she doubled and bunched and bound to make a brush. She shed her shoes and smock and skirt and strode off to the surf clad only in sacklike nether garment, leading the horse by the bridle.

I hurriedly made a crude copy of her grass brush; then I rolled up my trousers and followed her into the water.

Within fifteen minutes the little horse was clean, or nearly so, his blue barb skin show-ing through matted wet hair and only a few patches of coagulated yolk clinging to him here and there. Mrs. Ybarra led him back to the tree and rubbed his back with handfuls of dry grass and spread on the burlap saddle blanket. She tidied up the saddle a bit and I heaved it on the horse and fastened the cinches while she rearranged the *carga*. The gamecock was dead but seemed remarkably intact for having been under a horse. Mrs. Ybarra chopped part way through his neck with the machete and hung the body low on the saddle to bleed on the ground. Then she slipped on her skirt and dropped her shoes into one of the baskets. She brushed at the sand on her arms and put on her smock, then swung herself into the saddle.

Once again I held out the thin sheaf of bills.

"*Vea*," I said cajolingly. "It was my fault that you lost the eggs and the cock died."

"*Qué va!* The cock was to kill and there will be eggs enough. There is no lack of *carey* eggs and the fleet will not be long coming. Will you be going back now?"

I told her I was going on. I must have seemed depressed at the prospect, because she said:

"All right—there's a *cocal* no more than there—just a little way. You can get a *pipa* there (a drinking coconut) and there is shade. Then if you go on six miles there is another *cocal*, and my house is there. If you go that far it is almost certain that I can show you a *canal* tonight, laying on the high tide."

I thanked her and said I couldn't go that far. Without her noticing I slipped the money into the basket where her shoes were.

"I'm going to dig another *canal* nest," I said. "I don't believe this one laid."

"Ay-eeee," she yelped. "You will kill yourself for nothing. She laid. This one laid. Right there. No *canal* nest will be easier to dig than this one."

"O.K.," I said. "But I'm not going to dig here any more. I'll be seeing you."

She gave me a look of what I think was pity, then set her mount in motion with her bare heels, guided him into the surf wash and squeezed him into the mincing single-foot he would hold all the way to Tortuguero. Then she turned and waved. "*Adios, pues*," she said.

The little feist saw her leaving and ran to take the lead. A first sudden breath of the afternoon breeze wiped the gleam from the water and turned it black. The horse's hoof splash faded in the distance and when it was gone the only sounds were the roll of the waves and the fitful piping of a tern as it slipped and tilted on the swelling trade wind.

MARJORIE KINNAN RAWLINGS

The Pound Party

Marjorie Kinnan Rawlings (1896–1953) was born in Washington, D.C., and began writing and selling stories at the age of eleven. In 1928 she bought a seventy-two-acre orange grove at Cross Creek, a small out-of-the-way village in central Florida. In the next few years she became well acquainted with Florida people and their customs. Her attachment to this part of the Florida scene was exhibited in her first novel, *South Moon Under*, 1933.

The Yearling, 1938, introduced one of the most appealing boy characters in fiction since Huckleberry Finn. It won for Marjorie Rawlings a Pulitzer Prize for fiction and was a Book-of-the-Month Club choice. In recognition of the understanding with which she had recorded the life of the "Florida cracker," Rollins College in 1939 awarded her an honorary Doctor of Laws degree and in 1941 the University of Florida bestowed upon her the Doctor of Humane Letters degree. Other books by Mrs. Rawlings include *When the Whippoorwill*, 1940, a collection of short stories, and *Cross Creek*, 1942, an autobiographical account of her experiences in her Florida home.

"The Pound Party," a personal narrative describing a folk custom of rural Florida, reveals the author's keen awareness of people and place and incident. Written in a simple style, this autobiographical sketch is marked by warmth, perceptiveness, and good humor.

We pay no attention to a newcomer at the Creek. There is no more formal getting-acquainted than among the rabbits in the woods and the birds in the trees. When anyone has been here long enough, sooner or later his path crosses that of the other inhabitants and friendship or enmity or mere tolerance sets in.

I was never welcomed to the Creek except by Martha, or my presence acknowledged. If I stayed, that was my own business, so long as I minded it. If I did not stay, no one would be surprised and there was no point in making overtures to me. But how was I to have known this and that the Townsends' invitation to a pound party was not a social gesture? I took it at face value.

I knew vaguely that a family lived half a mile away as tenants in Cow Hammock. A lean brown-eyed man who looked like John the Baptist often walked down the sand road in front of my house, scuffling up the dust with long bare feet. A pretty woman with a baby in her arms sometimes walked with him, or followed him an hour later, or sometimes appeared mysteriously with him only on his way back, as though she had gone off to the Creek in the night and he had come after her by daylight. Actually, I found, they fished both from Cow Hammock Landing and from Cross Creek, and one or the other might take the rowboat back and forth. Apparently countless children loitered along the road, like beads set far apart in a string, sometimes in little knots, sometimes singly. They resembled neither St. John nor the woman, but among themselves were as alike as peas in a pod and precisely the color of that vegetable when a little wilted. I began speaking to the children and they answered, not the conventional "Hey!" but "How-do," politely. Apparently none of them went to school, although I believe it was that winter that the school bus began collecting children from the Creek. Once a wagon went by, lurching in the ruts, filled to overflowing with these passers-by, integrated at last into one family. They were the Townsends, and a community to themselves, aloof by choice. There were enough of them to need no other contacts. One day two of the small girls appeared at my back door.

The oldest said rapidly, before she should forget the memorized words, "I'm Ella May, and Mama says we're having a pound party tomorrow evening and she'd be proud did you come."

It came to me that this was the first neighborly gesture I had encountered at the Creek. I was touched.

I said, "I'd be glad to. But what is a pound party?"

"Everybody brings a pound of something. Sugar, or butter, or candy, or a cake. A cake's fine. Such as that."

The evening of the party was clear as glass and I walked the half-mile to Cow Hammock. Remembering the swarm of little Townsends, and adding a houseful of guests in my mind's eye, I had doubled my largest cake recipe and

baked it in a roasting pan. I thought I must be early, for there was no one in the shabby house but the Townsends. The children were watching and at sight of me scattered within.

I heard a sibilant, "Here she comes."

The suspicion had not yet touched me not only that they knew I should be the sole arrival, but that the party had been built around the probability of my innocent acceptance. The Townsends were in their Sunday best, fresh-scrubbed and uncomfortable. The girls were starched, the boys in stiff clean blue overalls and shirts. I was given a seat on a bench along a wall. Behind me a ragged screen over the open window let in a steady stream of mosquitoes, attracted by the oil lamp on the table. Ella May was assigned with a newspaper to sit beside me and fan my legs to keep them from biting me. When Ella May lagged, Beatrice took up the paper. Their work was enthusiastic but inadequate to the ingenuity of mosquitoes. I slapped furtively. My cake had the place of honor on the bare deal table in the center of the room. A Townsend layer cake dripping sticky icing was pushed modestly to one side. The rest of the refreshments provided by the hostess consisted of a bucket of water, a ten-cent jar of peanut butter and a nickel box of soda crackers.

She said easily, "We'll wait a while to eat, just in case."

I made conversation as best I could. We talked of the heavy crop of blackberries, of the Hamon sow that could not be kept up, no matter how one tried, of the summer rains and of the fishing. Mr. Townsend spoke up brightly when we reached the fishing. Fishing was not only the family livelihood but its delight. The Townsends would have sat all day with poles if they had been millionaires.

"I'll bring you a mess of bream one day," he said.

The talk ebbed. The mosquitoes buzzed and the Townsends slapped automatically. The lamp flickered in a gust of wind.

Mrs. Townsend said, "Be nice, did you blow some, Floyd."

Mr. Townsend echoed, "Blow some, Floyd."

Floyd, the oldest, long, thin and pale, brought out a mouth organ from his pocket and drew up a straight wooden chair. He began to pat his foot before he started his tune. Into the patting came suddenly the whine of the mouth organ. The tune, formless, unrecognizable, was mournful. One sad phrase repeated itself over and over. Other Townsends took up the patting and the rickety floor shook to the thumping. Floyd stopped abruptly.

Mrs. Townsend said to the air, "Be nice, did Preston dance."

Preston was five, the youngest weaned Townsend. The older children seized him and dragged him from the doorway. He hung his head but made no resistance. They seemed to prop him up, then retreated and left him standing alone. Floyd took up his tune. Preston stood staring vacantly. The tune and the party seemed no concern of his. As though one note had set off a mechanical spring, he began to shuffle his feet. His body was still. His arms jerked a little, like a broken jack-in-the-box. His feet shuffled back and forth without rhythm. He might have been trying to keep his footing on a slippery treadmill. This was the dance. I expected him to stop in a moment but he kept it up. The tune, the dance, were endless.

Mrs. Townsend said complacently, "Preston holds out good, don't he?"

The compliment seemed a signal, for he stopped as suddenly as he had begun.

Mrs. Townsend said, "We just as good to eat."

She passed the crackers in one hand and the tiny jar of peanut butter, with a spoon in it, in the other. Eyes followed her hungrily. I refused, to the relief of the eyes. I had a dipper of water and as small a piece of cake as I dared take and yet be courteous. The two cakes disappeared as though a thundershower had melted them. The party was obviously over. Mrs. Townsend accompanied me outside the house and to the head of the path. She looked up into a cloudless and starlit sky.

"I reckon the threat of bad weather kept the others away," she said placidly.

I inquired about pound parties at the Creek, and my gullibility was verified. Yet the occasion had been truly a party, and the Townsends had done their best to make it festive.

I decided that I should go any time I was invited, and should see to it that a larger jar of peanut butter was provided. After the party, the Townsend children and I were great friends. Ella May and Beatrice came almost every day to visit me. Dorsey and Floyd and Glenwood came to do odd chores. They were thin, grave boys and very capable. They moved slowly, like old men, and had the look of age that hunger puts on children. The boys were the right size to climb into the pecan trees and shake down and gather the nuts. The crop was heavy that year, and the filled sacks and baskets amounted to many hundred pounds.

The boys were asked, "What would you do if you had a dollar for every one of those pecans?"

There was silence while the thought of wealth was contemplated.

Dorsey said slowly, "First off, I'd get me a whole plug of Brown Mule tobaccy, all for myself."

Floyd said, "I'd have all I want of rich folks' rations—light bread and jelly."

The questioner went on, "What, no cornbread?"

Glenwood said quickly, "Oh yes. We know you got to have cornbread to grow on."

One week in the next spring the whole family left off its fishing and picked, without enthusiasm, the heavy crop of beans. Their pay on Saturday totaled thirty-six dollars. I thought happily how far this would go. I pictured the big sack of groceries that night, with money laid by for future needs, seed and fertilizer perhaps for a garden of their own. On Monday morning Floyd came to the house.

"Could you let us have two dollars," he asked, "to get us some rations?"

Their money had surely been stolen from them, or the heavy hand of poor folks' luck had made them lose it in some fashion.

"But what happened to the thirty-six dollars you had on Saturday?"

Floyd's pale face was bright with pleasure.

"We bought us an ottymobile," he said.

They were somehow a challenge. I have never known a more exquisite courtesy than the whole family possessed. There were good blood and breeding back of them. I have known no one with more gracious manners. The children were intelligent. Their finances were a problem beyond me and would evidently have to take care of themselves, but it seemed to me that the children's futures held something better than a precarious living fishing on Orange Lake. The two great needs, where I could give tangible help, were their health and their education.

Their green color came from a lifetime of hookworm. I persuaded the mother and father to let the children be treated. The tetrachlorethylene capsules were dispensed free by the state. I obtained capsules and instructions, and set off for the Townsend house one Saturday night. One by one I handed out the preliminary doses of Epsom salts. I gave orders about no further food. On Sunday morning I trudged back again and saw the capsules safely down the Townsends. I departed with the sense of smugness common to all meddlers, leaving word that in ten days we would repeat the treatment. When the ten days were up, the mother refused point blank to let the children be treated again.

"It made them sick," she said.

"Of course it made them sick. They were eaten up with hookworm."

She shook her head.

" 'Twouldn't be safe to give that medicine to them again," she said firmly. "It must of been stale. You can't trust nothin' is free."

I was beaten there, and passed on slyly to the matter of education. Once safely in school, I was sure the visiting county nurse would have a chance for a fresh battle against the hookworms. I would give clothes, I said, to all the children who would go to school. St. John and his wife consulted and it was agreed that Dorsey and Glenwood, Ella May and Beatrice, might condescend to be clothed and to allow the school bus from the village to stop for them.

I am no seamstress, the holding of a threaded needle in my hand producing an acute stomach-ache. But a long line of Methodist preachers behind me has left the evil thought in the blood of my brain that the more difficult a job, the more certainly one must apply oneself to its mastering. I bought yards of good gingham and sat hour after hour, developing stomach ulcers, I was certain, at the sewing machine. The girls came for fittings and had light bread and jelly as reward. I turned out creditable dresses, nicely trimmed, and went at the job of underwear. I cut down my own two woolen coats for Ella May and Beatrice. I bought shirts and pants for the boys. I took my bundles with a missionary's pride to the Townsends and modest pleasure was shown in my products. I arranged for the school bus to stop at the entrance to Cow Hammock. I went home and took a large dose of bicarbonate of soda.

The next morning one of the smaller children brought me a dress length of very good silk.

"Mama says will you please make a dress for her."

I took the material to the Townsend house, puzzled, unwilling as yet to be outraged. Mama was on the lake, fishing. I was shown some of Mama's other garments. Mama was a much better seamstress than I—but if the Lord sends forth a strangely agreeable slave to the sewing machine, surely it is pleasanter and more profitable to spend one's time on the lovely lake, dangling a bamboo pole for bream. I left the material and word that my offer to sew for the Townsends applied only to those in need of education, not to those who had advanced in philosophy far beyond me.

The children went to school just long enough to make ownership of the clothes indisputable. Then they were all home again, playing in the sandy yard, or as a special treat, taken along on the fishing parties.

"They didn't like school," St. John informed me gently.

It would be satisfying, if sad, to tell of their tragic maturities. I can only report that they have grown up as healthy as any one else, and within the limits of their congenital leisureliness, are living as active and prosperous lives as their neighbors. I am sometimes haunted by the feeling that it is I who could have learned of the Townsends.

MURRAY KEMPTON and JAMES RIDGEWAY

Romans

James Murray Kempton (1918–   ), editor and reporter, was born in Baltimore, Maryland, and received his academic training at The Johns Hopkins University. His work as a journalist brought him the Sidney Hillman Foundation Award for Reporting in 1950. In addition to serving as publicity director for the American Labor Party and as reporter for the *New York Post* and the *Wilmington* (North Carolina) *Morning Star*, he held the editorship of *The New Republic* from 1963 to 1965. He is the author of *Part of Our Time*, 1955, a series of historical sketches of personages of the 1930's.

James Fowler Ridgeway (1936–   ), editor and reporter, was educated at Princeton University. He is associate editor of *The New Republic*, and has been writing articles and editorials on domestic politics for that magazine since 1962.

"Romans," a verbal candid-camera account of events and reactions attending the death of the late President Kennedy, is written in a restrained and objectively tempered style.

Robert Frost wrote 50 years ago, "nothing is true except as a man or men adhere to it—to live for it, to spend themselves on it, to die for it." We need this spirit even more than money or institutions or agreements.
—JOHN F. KENNEDY, November 18, 1963

By Saturday night, even the television seemed worn out by attempt and failure and ceased to comment and gave over to a succession of photographs of the columns and the windows and the corners of the White House and of the shadows of the great Lincoln head in Springfield and to a voice reciting "Oh, Captain, My Captain." It is to be, then, the grand style. But the ship has not weathered every storm; Mr. Kennedy is not Abraham Lincoln; not because he is more or less, but because he is a remembered physical

ROMANS From *The New Republic*, December 7, 1963. Reprinted by permission of *The New Republic*, copyright 1963, Harrison-Blaine of New Jersey, Inc.

presence and Mr. Lincoln an image of the plastic arts. One's own time is personal, not historical. Just how long will it be before many of us will want to read a book about the day Mr. Kennedy was shot?

The news of the President's assassination was given by a taxi driver to three gentlemen as they left a hotel on Arlington Street in Boston. They turned right around and hurried back inside to attend to their investments. Packed with students and businessmen a shuttle plane from Boston to Washington waited for permission to take off when the captain came on the intercom: "Folks, up here on the flight deck we've been listening to the news and the President is dead." There was only time to hear one woman say, "How dreadful" before three men went back to discussing plan specifications. A college student reading *Agamemnon* paid no visible attention. One of his notes read, "love-in-hate."

The plane took off, the stewardess collected the money and started to serve drinks. Then the captain was back again. They had been listening to more news, that is trying to listen to news because their real job was to hear flight control. There had been a gun battle in Dallas; a patrolman was killed; the police had taken a man in a movie theater. Vice President Johnson was now the President. The talk of business went on through this, and stopped only when the captain again interrupted to say that the new President had been sworn in aboard an aircraft. A few laughed.

They ask too much of us when they ask us to act up to the grand style. We are not an emotionally affluent people. And yet some of us always complained that Mr. Kennedy did not seem quite emotionally committed enough. But now someone remembered with special affection a moment late in the 1960 campaign. Mr. Kennedy was in a motorcade and the Democratic governor who was with him said how wonderful it was to feel the love with which these crowds pressed forward to feel the touch of their candidate. "Oh, dry up," Mr. Kennedy said. It seemed now somehow a special grace in him that he used only the real in emotion and abstained from fabricating the expected. He had too much respect for the grand style to counterfeit it; how much truer to him might we have been if we had come down in scale and if the many of us who must have remembered the lines from *Cymbeline* had thought them proper to speak

> Fear no more the heat of the sun,
>   Nor the furious winter's rages.
> Thou thy worldly task hast done,
>   Home art thou and ta'en thy wages.
> Golden lads and girls all must,
> As chimney sweepers, come to dust.

Cymbeline is a Roman play. The Kennedys are a Roman family; America seems only a Roman crowd. For us alone in it, there is only a terrible irritation with God and with self and with every other face that is left.

Friday night caught most of the President's Cabinet away from the city. All that could be collected from his official establishment came to Andrews Air Force base to meet the dead man come back from Dallas.

Everything mechanical intruded as it would intrude all weekend. The lights were vagrant, savage and aimless; the planes came and went on distracting irrelevant missions. The face of Undersecretary of Commerce Roosevelt seemed the ruin of his father's. Every uncared-for lank of Senator Dirksen's hair, every fold under every chin seemed for the moment our own fault.

For we had lost in the instant the hope of beginning again. Reason might argue that the sense of a new start was already gone. The main story in the morning's *Washington Post* had detailed the exculpations of a Congressman who had made a 1,000 percent profit from the stock of a company which had enjoyed his good offices with the Internal Revenue Service. The very Senate which dissipated in shock at the news from Texas had just before been waspishly disputing the privileges and emoluments of elective office. For weeks it had been hard to remember anyone in Washington talking about anything except who was getting what from whom. Mr. Kennedy seemed to be wasting in his city and to be nourished only by the great crowds in the countryside. The films from Dallas, painful as they were, reinforced the feeling that he was his old self only away from Washington. It could be argued then that we would see a time when we recognized that all that promise had been an illusion; but you need only look at hope lain dead to know how easy it is to look forward to regret. It had been less than three years since Mr. Kennedy had announced that a new generation was taking up the torch; now old General de Gaulle and old Mr. Mikoyan were coming to see the young man buried.

The great red and white plane of the President of the United States came to Andrews at last bearing all the transition in one horrid large economy-size package. There was a portable yellow elevator to bring Mrs. Kennedy and Attorney-General Kennedy down with a casket that looked like a ship's chest. Half of Lyndon Johnson could be seen waiting in the open door behind them. Mrs. Kennedy's weeds as a widow had to be what some said was a strawberry and some said was a raspberry-colored campaign suit. Everything mechanical that did not intrude functioned badly; the elevator seemed to stall; Mrs. Kennedy tried a door of the ambulance, which did not work, and the Attorney-General, with a deliberation unbroken as hers was, found one which did and she was gone at last, the high Roman figure that she would be all weekend.

So Mr. Johnson came on, tall as ever but wearing the glasses which his image of himself has always thought unsuitable to state occasions, emptied by his misfortune of all his vanity, small and large, and of almost everything else. His lips seemed wet, his chin uncertain; there was a fear that he might be a man who would cry in public and who there was enough his better to blame him? He said something into the microphones that was identifiable only as being hoarse, broken and undeservedly apologetic, and then his new household gathered around him. And the eye as cruel to everyone else as the heart was cruel to self, focused and saw only the hearing aid of an Undersecretary. The next morning, Mr. Johnson had repaired his interior and left off resenting himself, as all of us had better do if we are to get about our business.

As the people waited the passing of the cortege on Sunday some of them squabbled over who was to stand on the step ladder and shoot the first pictures and at what speed and at what lens opening. A mother trying to tune up a transistor radio said to a pouting child, "I want you to understand one thing. This is very important to me." Amidst the people came a teenager with a portable tape recorder. He stuck out a microphone and said, "Sir, on this day of national mourning how do you feel?" Coming away from the Capitol after viewing the bier, a man with a camera slung over his head, said to another man with a camera, "Did you get any good pictures?"

One sat in the Senate press room away from the rotunda on Sunday night and read a wire service report on the tributes paid to the patriotism of Jack Ruby by the master of ceremonies of Mr. Ruby's strip parlor. There was a story about the good fortune of the Dallas citizen who had been in at the death with his movie camera and had sold the films to *Life* for $40,000. The National Football League had played its full Sunday schedule; every seat in Yankee Stadium was filled with mourners. One thought with respect—it was not possible to be grateful to anyone—of Randall Jarrell for having known enough soon enough to have written a book and called it *A Sad Heart at the Supermarket.*

Then a man spoke up and said:

"She came in with the children this afternoon when the rotunda was first opened and she was standing and waiting and the kid looked up at the dome and began to walk around, and she bent over and touched him and he looked up and she straightened her shoulders to show him how to stand at attention, and he did it for about ten seconds. You know, I wish it was a dynasty and the kid was taking over and she was the regent."

Monday was sunny and for those to whom life is a picture, the Capitol was the best and largest color television screen anyone could hope for. A boy sat on his father's shoulders and his father told him to use the Number One setting. The band began "Hail to the Chief," the boy raised his camera and instructed his father not to move. Behind them a woman put a child on her shoulders; the child must have tickled her because she kept laughing, comfortably, and this pleasant distraction continued until the coffin could be detected from its flag to be coming out and she left off and pointed her finger and said with undiminished gaiety, "See, there he is." One left and walked past a girl clutching a paperback. Then suddenly there was one man kneeling with his hands over his eyes and his hat on the sidewalk, and it was impossible not to stop and put a hand upon his shoulder and not to begin to hope that a chain might be put together again.

In front of St. Matthew's the crowd was quieter. The bands and the soldiers went by, the pipers last; and then, like thunder, there was Mrs. Kennedy with the Senator on one side and the Attorney-General on the other and ramrods up their spines. And behind them, the powers and potentates of the earth; the Kennedys were marching with all of Madame Tussaud's in their train, as though Charles de Gaulle had been created a Marshal of France and Haile Selassie I the Lion of Judah only for this last concentrated moment. The powers and potentates waited; Mrs. Kennedy, for the moment made flesh again, gathered her children. Cardinal Cushing came down, under his mitre, looking, to his credit, a trifle irritated with God; we could be grateful for the Catholics and grateful to them for providing one Cardinal who looked like a Prince of the Church.

And the children in their sunny pale blue coats began walking with their mother up the stairs, the little boy stumbling only at the vestibule and then they were gone. We had lived awhile with old Romans; now the doors were closing and we must make do with ourselves.

JAMES AGEE

Undirectable Director

James Agee (1910–1955), biographer, screen writer, and poet, was born in Knoxville, Tennessee. He received his academic training at Exeter Academy and Harvard University, where he was editor of *The Advocate*. His best-known works are a volume of poetry, *Permit Me Voyage*, 1934; a collection of biographical portraits, *Let Us Now Praise Famous Men*, 1941; and a number of screen plays and film biographies—*The Quiet One*, 1949, *The African Queen*, 1950, and *Mr. Lincoln*, 1953, which was produced three times on NBC Television as a documentary on *Omnibus*. In 1958 he received, posthumously, the Pulitzer Prize in Letters Fiction for *A Death in the Family*, 1956. During the last years of his life he spent most of his time in Hollywood, working with Charles Laughton and John Huston.

"Undirectable Director," a poignant biography of John Huston, one of Hollywood's outstanding directors, is done in the poetic and lively style characteristic of all of Agee's writing.

The ant, as every sluggard knows, is a model citizen. His eye is fixed unwaveringly upon Security and Success, and he gets where he is going. The grasshopper, as every maiden

UNDIRECTABLE DIRECTOR   From *Agee on Film* by James Agee, Copyright 1950, © 1958 by James Agee Trust. Reprinted by permission of Grosset & Dunlap, Inc.

ant delights in pointing out, is his reprehensible opposite number: a hedonistic jazz-baby, tangoing along primrose paths to a disreputable end. The late Walter Huston's son John, one of the ranking grasshoppers of the Western Hemisphere, is living proof of what a lot of nonsense that can be. He has beaten the ants at their own game and then some, and he has managed that blindfolded, by accident, and largely just for the hell of it. John was well into his twenties before anyone could imagine he would ever amount to more than an awfully nice guy to get drunk with. He wandered into his vocation as a writer of movie scripts to prove to a girl he wanted to marry that he amounted to more than a likable bum. He stumbled into his still deeper vocation as a writer-director only when he got sick of seeing what the professional directors did to his scripts. But during the ten subsequent years he has won both Security aplenty (currently $3,000 a week with MGM and a partnership in Horizon Pictures with his friend Sam Spiegel) and Success aplenty (two Oscars, a One World Award and such lesser prizes as the Screen Directors' Guild quarterly award which he received last week for his *Asphalt Jungle*).

Yet these are merely incidental attainments. The first movie he directed, *The Maltese Falcon,* is the best private-eye melodrama ever made. *San Pietro,* his microcosm of the meaning of war in terms of the fight for one hill town, is generally conceded to be the finest of war documentaries. *Treasure of Sierra Madre,* which he developed from B. Traven's sardonic adventure-fable about the corrosive effect of gold on character, is the clearest proof in perhaps twenty years that first-rate work can come out of the big commercial studios.

Most of the really good popular art produced anywhere comes from Hollywood, and much of it bears Huston's name. To put it conservatively, there is nobody under fifty at work in movies, here or abroad, who can excel Huston in talent, inventiveness, intransigence, achievement or promise. Yet it is a fair bet that neither money, nor acclaim, nor a sense of dedication to the greatest art medium of his century have much to do with Huston's staying at his job: he stays at it because there is nothing else he enjoys so much. It is this tireless enjoyment that gives his work a unique vitality and makes every foot of film he works on unmistakably his.

Huston seems to have acquired this priceless quality many years ago at the time of

what, in his opinion, was probably the most crucial incident in his life. When he was about twelve years old he was so delicate he was hardly expected to live. It was interminably dinned into him that he could never possibly be quite careful enough, and for even closer protection he was put into a sanitarium where every bite he ate and breath he drew could be professionally policed. As a result he became virtually paralyzed by timidity; "I haven't the slightest doubt," he still says, "that if things had gone on like that I'd have died inside a few more months." His only weapon was a blind desperation of instinct, and by day not even that was any use. Nights, however, when everyone was asleep, he used to sneak out, strip, dive into a stream which sped across the grounds and ride it down quite a steep and stony waterfall, over and over and over. "The first few times," he recalls, "it scared the living hell out of me, but I realized—instinctively anyhow—it was exactly fear I had to get over." He kept at it until it was the one joy in his life. When they first caught him at this primordial autotherapy the goons were of course aghast; but on maturer thought they decided he might live after all.

The traits revealed in this incident are central and permanent in Huston's character. Risk, not to say recklessness, are virtual reflexes in him. Action, and the most vivid possible use of the immediate present, were his personal salvation; they have remained lifelong habits. Because action also is the natural language of the screen and the instant present is its tense, Huston is a born popular artist. In his life, his dealings and his work as an artist he operates largely by instinct, unencumbered by much reflectiveness or abstract thinking, or any serious self-doubt. Incapable of yesing, apple-polishing or bootlicking, he instantly catches fire in resistance to authority.

Nobody in movies can beat Huston's record for trying to get away with more than the traffic will bear. *San Pietro* was regarded with horror by some gentlemen of the upper brass as "an antiwar picture" and was cut from five reels to three. *Treasure,* which broke practically every box-office law in the game and won three Oscars, was made over the virtually dead bodies of the top men at Warners' and was advertised as a Western. *The Asphalt Jungle* suggests that in some respects big-town crime operates remarkably like free enterprise. Huston seldom tries to "lick" the problem imposed by censorship, commercial queasiness or tradition; he has learned that nothing is so likely to settle an argument as to turn up with the accomplished fact, accomplished well, plus a bland lack of alternative film shots. And yet after innumerable large and small fights and a fair share of defeats he can still say of his movie career, "I've never had any trouble." Probably the whitest magic that protects him is that he really means it.

Nonetheless his life began with trouble—decorated with the best that his Irish imagination, and his father's, could add to it. He was born John Marcellus Huston on August 5, 1906 in Nevada, Missouri, a hamlet which his grandfather, a professional gambler, had by the most ambitious version of the family legend acquired in a poker game. John's father, a retired actor, was in charge of power and light and was learning his job, while he earned, via a correspondence course. Before the postman had taught him how to handle such a delicate situation, a fire broke out in town, Walter overstrained the valves in his effort to satisfy the fire department, and the Hustons decided it would be prudent to leave what was left of Nevada before morning. They did not let their shirttails touch their rumps until they hit Weatherford, Texas, another of Grandfather's jackpots. After a breather they moved on to St. Louis (without, however, repeating the scorched-earth policy), and Walter settled down to engineering in dead earnest until a solid man clapped him on the shoulder and told him that with enough stick-to-itiveness he might well become a top-notch engineer, a regular crackerjack. Horrified, Walter instantly returned to the stage. A few years later he and his wife were divorced. From there on out the child's life lacked the stability of those early years.

John divided his time between his father and mother. With his father, who was still some years short of eminence or even solvency, he shared that bleakly glamorous continuum of three-a-days, scabrous fleabags and the cindery, ambling day coaches between, which used to be so much of the essence of the American theater. John's mother was a newspaperwoman with a mania for travel and horses (she was later to marry a vice-president of the Northern Pacific), and she and her son once pooled their last ten dollars on a 100-to-1 shot—which came in. Now and then she stuck the boy in one school or another, but mostly they traveled—well off the beaten paths.

After his defeat of death by sliding down the waterfall, there was no holding John. In his teens he became amateur lightweight boxing champion of California. A high-school marriage lasted only briefly. He won twenty-three out of twenty-five fights, many in the professional ring, but he abandoned this promise of a career to join another of his mother's eccentric grand tours. He spent two years in the Mexican cavalry, emerging at twenty-one as a lieutenant. In Mexico he wrote a book, a puppet play about Frankie and Johnny. Receiving, to his astonishment, a $500 advance from a publisher, he promptly entrained for the crap tables of Saratoga where, in one evening, he ran it up to $11,000, which he soon spent or gambled away.

After that Huston took quite a friendly interest in writing. He wrote a short story which his father showed to his friend Ring Lardner, who showed it to his friend H. L. Mencken, who ran it in the *Mercury*. He wrote several other stories about horses and boxers before the vein ran out. It was through these stories, with his father's help that he got his first job as a movie writer. He scripted *A House Divided*, starring his father, for William Wyler. But movies, at this extravagant stage of Huston's career, were just an incident. At other stages he worked for the New York *Graphic* ("I was the world's lousiest reporter"), broke ribs riding steeplechase, studied painting in Paris, knocked around with international Bohemians in London and went on the bum in that city when his money ran out and he was too proud to wire his father. At length he beat his way back to New York where, for a time, he tried editing the *Midweek Pictorial*. He was playing Abraham Lincoln in a Chicago WPA production when he met an Irish girl named Leslie Black and within fifteen minutes after their meeting asked her to marry him. When she hesitated he hotfooted it to Hollywood and settled down to earn a solid living as fast as possible. Marrying Leslie was probably the best thing that ever happened to him, in the opinion of Huston's wise friend and studio protector during the years at Warner Brothers, the producer Henry Blanke. Blanke remembers him vividly during the bachelor interlude: "Just a drunken boy; hopelessly immature. You'd see him at every party, wearing bangs, with a monkey on his shoulder. Charming. Very talented but without an ounce of discipline in his make-up." Leslie Huston, Blanke is convinced, set her husband the standards and incentives which brought his abilities into focus. They were divorced in 1945, but in relation to his work he has never lost the stability she helped him gain.

At forty-four Huston still has a monkey and a chimpanzee as well, but he doesn't escort them to parties. His gray-sleeted hair still treats his scalp like Liberty Hall and occasionally slithers into bangs, but they can no longer be mistaken for a Bohemian compensation. He roughly suggests a jerked-venison version of his father, or a highly intelligent cowboy. A little over six feet tall, quite lean, he carries himself in a perpetual gangling-graceful slouch. The forehead is monkeyishly puckered, the ears look as clipped as a show dog's; the eyes, too, are curiously animal, an opaque red-brown. The nose was broken in the prize ring. The mouth is large, mobile and gap-toothed. The voice which comes out of this leatheriness is surprisingly rich, gentle and cultivated. The vocabulary ranges with the careless ease of a mountain goat between words of eight syllables and of four letters.

Some friends believe he is essentially a deep introvert using every outside means available as a form of flight from self-recognition—in other words, he is forever sliding down the waterfall and instinctively fears to stop. The same friends suspect his work is all that keeps him from flying apart. He is wonderful company, almost anytime, for those who can stand the pace. Loving completely unrestrained and fantastic play, he is particularly happy with animals, roughhousers and children; a friend who owns three of the latter describes him as "a blend of Santa Claus and the Pied Piper." His friendships range from high in the Social Register to low in the animal kingdom, but pretty certainly the friend he liked best in the world was his father, and that was thoroughly reciprocated. It was a rare and heart-warming thing, in this Freud-ridden era, to see a father and son so irrepressibly pleased with each other's company and skill.

He has an indestructible kind of youthfulness, enjoys his enthusiasms with all his might and has the prompt appetite for new knowledge of a man whose intelligence has not been cloyed by much formal education. He regrets that nowadays he can read only two or three books a week. His favorite writers are Joyce, his friend Hemingway (perhaps his closest literary equivalent) and, above all, O'Neill; it was one of the deepest disappointments of his career when movie commitments prevented his staging the new O'Neill's *The Iceman Cometh*. His other enjoyments take many forms. He still paints occasionally. He is a very good shot and a superlative horseman; he has some very promising runners of his own. He likes money for the fun it can bring him, is extremely generous with it and particularly loves to gamble. He generally does well at the races and siphons it off at the crap tables. He is a hard drinker (Scotch) but no lush, and a heavy smoker. Often as not he forgets to eat. He has a reputation for being attractive to women, and rough on them. His fourth wife is the dancer, Ricky Soma; their son Walter was born last spring. He makes most of his important decisions on impulse; it was thus he adopted his son Pablo in Mexico. The way he and his third wife, Evelyn Keyes, got married is a good example of Huston in action. He suggested they marry one evening in Romanoff's a week after they met, borrowed a pocketful of money from the prince, tore out to his house to pick up a wedding ring a guest had mislaid in the swimming pool and chartered Paul Mantz to fly them to Las Vegas where they were married that night.

Huston's courage verges on the absolute, or on simple obliviousness to danger. In Italy during the shooting of *San Pietro,* his simian curiosity about literally everything made him the beau ideal of the contrivers of booby traps; time and again he was spared an arm, leg or skull only by the grace of God and the horrified vigilance of his friend Lieutenant Jules Buck. He sauntered through mine fields where plain man feared to tread. He is quick to get mad and as quick to get over it. Once in Italy he sprinted up five flights of headquarters stairs in order to sock a frustrating superior officer; arriving at the top he was so winded he could hardly stand. Time enough to catch his breath was time enough to cool off; he just wobbled downstairs again.

Huston is swiftly stirred by anything which appeals to his sense of justice, magnanimity or courage: he was among the first men to stand up for Lew Ayres as a conscientious objector, he flew to the Washington hearings on Hollywood (which he refers to as "an obscenity") and sponsored Henry Wallace (though he voted for Truman) in the 1948 campaign. Some people think of him, accordingly, as a fellow traveler. Actually he is a political man chiefly in an emotional sense: "I'm against *anybody,*" he says, "who tries to tell anybody else what to do." The mere sight or thought of a cop can get him sore. He is in short rather less of a Communist than the most ultramontane Republican, for like perhaps five out of seven good artists who ever lived he is—to lapse into technical jargon —a natural-born antiauthoritarian individualistic libertarian anarchist, without portfolio.

A very good screen writer, Huston is an even better director. He has a feeling about telling a story on a screen which sets him apart from most other movie artists and from all nonmovie writers and artists. "On paper," he says, "all you can do is say something happened, and if you say it well enough the reader believes you. In pictures, if you do it right, *the thing happens, right there on the screen.*"

This means more than it may seem to. Most movies are like predigested food because they are mere reenactments of something that happened (if ever) back in the scripting stage. At the time of shooting the sense of the present is not strong, and such creative energy as may be on hand is used to give the event finish, in every sense of the word, rather than beginning and life. Huston's work has a unique tension and vitality because the maximum of all contributing creative energies converge at the one moment that counts most in a movie—the continuing moment of committing the story to film. At his best he makes the story tell itself, makes it seem to happen for the first and last time at the moment of recording. It is almost magically hard to get this to happen. In the *Treasure* scene in which the bandits kill Bogart, Huston wanted it to be quiet and mock-casual up to its final burst of violence. He told two of his three killers— one a professional actor, the other two professional criminals—only to stay quiet and close to the ground, and always to move when Bogart moved, to keep him surrounded. Then he had everyone play it through, over and over, until they should get the feel of it. At length one of them did a quick scuttling slide down a bank, on his bottom and his busy little hands and feet. A motion as innocent as a child's and as frightening as a centipede's, it makes clear for the first time in the scene that death is absolutely inescapable, and very near. "When he did that slide," Huston says, "I knew they had the feel of it." He shot it accordingly.

Paradoxically in this hyperactive artist of action, the living, breathing texture of his best work is the result of a working method which relies on the utmost possible passiveness. Most serious-minded directors direct too much: "Now on this word," Huston has heard one tell an actor, "I want your voice to break." Actors accustomed to that kind of "help" are often uneasy when they start work with Huston. "Shall I sit down here?" one asked, interrupting a rehearsal. "*I* dunno," Huston replied. "You tired?" When Claire Trevor, starting work in *Key Largo,* asked for a few pointers, he told her, "You're the kind of drunken dame whose elbows are always a little too big, your voice is a little too loud, you're a little too polite. You're very sad, very resigned. Like this," he said, for short, and leaned against the bar with a peculiarly heavy, gentle disconsolateness. It was the leaning she caught onto (though she also used everything he said); without further instruction of any kind, she took an Oscar for her performance. His only advice to his father was a whispered, "Dad, that was a little too much like Walter Huston." Often he works with actors as if he were gentling animals; and although Bogart says without total injustice that "as an actor he stinks," he has more than enough mimetic ability to get his ideas across. Sometimes he discards instruction altogether: to get a desired expression from Lauren Bacall, he simply twisted her arm.

Even on disastrously thin ice Huston has the peculiar kind of well-earned luck which Heaven reserves exclusively for the intuitive and the intrepid. One of the most important roles in *Treasure* is that of the bandit leader, a primordial criminal psychopath about whom the most fascinating and terrifying thing is his unpredictability. It is impossible to know what he will do next because it is impossible to be sure what strange piece of glare-ice in his nature will cause a sudden skid. Too late for a change, it turned out that the man who played this role, though visually ideal for it, couldn't act for shucks. Worried as he was, Huston had a hunch it would turn out all right. It worked because this inadequate actor was trying so hard, was so unsure of what he was doing and was so painfully confused and angered by Huston's cryptic passivity. These several kinds of strain and uncertainty, sprung against the context of the story, made a living image of the almost unactable, real thing; and that had been Huston's hunch.

In placing and moving his characters within a shot Huston is nearly always concerned above all else to be simple and spontaneous rather than merely "dramatic" or visually

effective. Just as he feels that the story belongs to the characters, he feels that the actors should as fully as possible belong to themselves. It is only because the actors are so free that their several individualities, converging in a scene, can so often knock the kinds of sparks off each other which cannot be asked for or invented or foreseen. All that can be foreseen is that this can happen only under favorable circumstances; Huston is a master at creating such circumstances.

Each of Huston's pictures has a visual tone and style of its own, dictated to his camera by the story's essential content and spirit. In *Treasure* the camera is generally static and at a middle distance from the action (as Huston says, "It's impersonal, it just looks on and lets them stew in their own juice"); the composition is—superficially—informal, the light cruel and clean, like noon sun on quartz and bone. Most of the action in *Key Largo* takes place inside a small Florida hotel. The problems are to convey heat, suspense, enclosedness, the illusion of some eighteen hours of continuous action in two hours' playing time, with only one time lapse. The lighting is stickily fungoid. The camera is sneakily "personal"; working close and in almost continuous motion, it enlarges the ambiguous suspensefulness of almost every human move. In *Strangers* the main pressures are inside a home and beneath it, where conspirators dig a tunnel. Here Huston's chief keys are lighting contrasts. Underground the players move in and out of shadow like trout; upstairs the light is mainly the luminous pallor of marble without sunlight: a cemetery, a bank interior, a great outdoor staircase.

Much that is best in Huston's work comes of his sense of what is natural to the eye and his delicate, simple feeling for space relationships: his camera huddles close to those who huddle to talk, leans back a proportionate distance, relaxing, if they talk casually. He loathes camera rhetoric and the shot-for-shot's-sake; but because he takes each moment catch-as-catch-can and is so deeply absorbed in doing the best possible thing with it he has made any number of unforgettable shots. He can make an unexpected close-up reverberate like a gong. The first shot of Edward G. Robinson in *Key Largo,* mouthing a cigar and sweltering naked in a tub of cold water ("I wanted to get a look at the animal with its shell off") is one of the most powerful and efficient "first entrances" of a character on record. Other great shots come through the kind of candor which causes some people to stare when others look away: the stripped, raw-sound scenes of psychiatric interviews in *Let There Be Light.* Others come through simple discretion in relating word and image. In *San Pietro,* as the camera starts moving along a line of children and babies, the commentator (Huston) remarks that in a few years they'll have forgotten there ever was a war; then he shuts up. As the camera continues in silence along the terrible frieze of shock and starvation, one realizes the remark was not the inane optimism it seemed: they, forgetting, are fodder for the next war.

Sometimes the shot is just a spark—a brief glint of extra imagination and perception. During the robbery sequence in *Asphalt Jungle* there is a quick glimpse of the downtown midnight street at the moment when people have just begun to hear the burglar alarms. Unsure, still, where the trouble is, the people merely hesitate a trifle in their ways of walking, and it is like the first stirrings of metal filings before the magnet beneath the paper pulls them into pattern. Very often the fine shot comes because Huston, working to please himself without fear of his audience, sharply condenses his storytelling. Early in *Strangers* a student is machine-gunned on the steps of Havana's university. A scene follows which is breath-taking in its surprise and beauty, but storytelling, not beauty, brings it: what seems to be hundreds of young men and women, all in summery whites, throw themselves flat on the marble stairs in a wave-like motion as graceful as the sudden close swooping of so many doves. The shot is already off the screen before one can realize its full meaning. By their trained, quiet unison in falling, these students are used to this. They expect it any average morning. And that suffices, with great efficiency, to suggest the Cuban tyranny.

Within the prevailing style of a picture, Huston works many and extreme changes and conflicts between the "active" camera, which takes its moment of the story by the scruff of the neck and "tells" it, and the "passive" camera, whose business is transparency, to receive a moment of action purely and record it. But whether active or passive, each shot contains no more than is absolutely necessary to make its point and is cut off sharp at that instant. The shots are cantilevered, sprung together in electric arcs, rather than buttered together. A given scene is apt to be composed of highly unconventional alternations of rhythm and patterns of exchange between long and medium and close shots and the standing, swinging and dollying camera. The rhythm and contour are very powerful but very irregular, like the rhythm of good prose rather than of good verse; and it is this rangy, leaping, thrusting kind of nervous vitality which binds the whole picture together. Within this vitality he can bring about moments as thoroughly revealing as those in great writing. As an average sample of that, *Treasure's* intruder is killed by bandits; the three prospectors come to identify the man they themselves were on the verge of shooting. Bogart, the would-be tough guy, cocks one foot up on a rock and tries to look at the corpse as casually as if it were fresh-killed game. Tim Holt, the essentially decent young man, comes past behind him and, innocent and unaware of it, clasps his hands as he looks down, in the respectful manner of a boy who used to go to church. Walter Huston, the experienced old man, steps quietly behind both, leans to the dead man as professionally as a doctor to a patient and gently rifles him for papers. By such simplicity Huston can draw the eye so deep into the screen that time and again he can make important points in medium shots, by motions as small as the twitching of an eyelid, for which most directors would require a close-up or even a line of dialogue.

Most movies are made in the evident assumption that the audience is passive and wants to remain passive; every effort is made to do all the work—the seeing, the explaining, the understanding, even the feeling. Huston is one of the few movie artists who, without thinking twice about it, honors his audience. His pictures are not acts of seduction or of benign enslavement but of liberation, and they require, of anyone who enjoys them, the responsibilities of liberty. They continually open the eye and require it to work vigorously; and through the eye they awaken curiosity and intelligence. That, by any virile standard, is essential to good entertainment. It is unquestionably essential to good art.

The most inventive director of his generation, Huston has done more to extend, invigorate and purify the essential idiom of American movies, the truly visual telling of stories, than anyone since the prime of D. W. Griffith. To date, however, his work as a whole is not on the level with the finest and most deeply imaginative work that has been done in movies—the work of Chaplin, Dovzhenko, Eisenstein, Griffith, the late Jean Vigo. For an artist of such conscience and caliber, his range is surprisingly narrow, both in subject matter and technique. In general he is leery of emotion—of the "feminine" aspects of art— and if he explored it with more assurance, with his taste and equipment, he might show himself to be a much more sensitive artist. With only one early exception, his movies have centered on men under pressure, have usually involved violence and have occasionally verged on a kind of romanticism about danger. Though he uses sound and dialogue more intelligently than most directors, he has not shown much interest in exploring the tremendous possibilities of the former or in solving the crippling problems of the latter. While his cutting is astute, terse, thoroughly appropriate to his kind of work, yet compared with that of Eisenstein, who regarded cutting as the essence of the art of movies, it seems distinctly unadventurous. In his studio pictures, Huston is apt to be tired and bored by the time the stages of ultrarefinement in cutting are reached, so that some of his scenes have been given perfection, others somewhat impaired, by film editors other than Huston. This is consistent with much that is free and improvisatory in his work and in his nature,

but it is a startling irresponsibility in so good an artist.

During his past few pictures Huston does appear to have become more of a "camera" man, and not all of this has been to the good. The camera sometimes imposes on the story; the lighting sometimes becomes elaborately studioish or even verges on the arty; the screen at times becomes rigid, overstylized. This has been happening, moreover, at a time when another of Huston's liabilities has been growing: thanks to what Henry Blanke calls his "amazing capacity for belief," he can fall for, and lose himself in, relatively mediocre material. Sometimes—as in *Asphalt Jungle*—he makes a silk purse out of a sow's ear, but sometimes—as in parts of *Strangers* and *Key Largo* —the result is neither silk nor sow.

Conceivably Huston lacks that deepest kind of creative impulse and that intense self-critical skepticism without which the stature of a great artist is rarely achieved. A brilliant adapter, he has yet to do a Huston "original," barring the war documentaries. He is probably too much at the mercy of his immediate surroundings. When the surroundings are right for him there is no need to talk about mercy: during the war and just after he was as hard as a rock and made his three finest pictures in a row. Since then the pictures, for all their excellence, are, like the surroundings, relatively softened and blurred. Unfortunately no man in Hollywood can be sufficiently his own master or move in a direct line to personally selected goals. After *Treasure*, Huston was unable to proceed to *Moby Dick* as he wanted to; he still is awaiting the opportunity to make Dreiser's *Jennie Gerhardt* and Dostoevski's *The Idiot* although he is at last shooting Stephen Crane's *The Red Badge of Courage*, which he has wanted to make for years. "This has got to be a masterpiece," he recently told friends, "or it's nothing."

There is no reason to expect less of it than his finest picture yet, for the better his starting material, the better he functions as an artist: he is one of the very few men in the world of movies who has shown himself to be worthy of the best. He has, in abundance, many of the human qualities which most men of talent lack. He is magnanimous, disinterested and fearless. Whatever his job, he always makes a noble and rewarding fight of it. If it should occur to him to fight for his life—his life as the consistently great artist

he evidently might become—he would stand a much better chance of winning than most people. For besides having talent and fighting ability, he has nothing to lose but his hide, and he has never set a very high value on that.

SIR ARTHUR BRYANT

The Holy Blissful Martyr

Sir Arthur Bryant (1899–   ), English writer and teacher, has been called by G. M. Trevellyan "a learned scholar who knows how to use his learning and scholar's life for the general good." He was awarded the Chesney Gold Medal of the Royal United Services Institution for his historical trilogy on the Napoleonic Wars, and he has distinguished himself as a biographer with full-length biographies of Samuel Pepys (three volumes), Charles II, Macaulay, George I, and Stanley Baldwin.

He has held the Watson Chair in American History Lectures at London University and at present is a lecturer at Oxford University. Among his books are *Dunkirk,* 1943; *The Story of England,* 1954; *The Turn of the Tide,* 1957; *Triumph in the West,* 1959; and *The Age of Chivalry,* 1964. His *Fire and the Rose,* 1966, from which this biographical sketch is taken, treats eight significant moments in British history. In it Sir Arthur has painted a broad canvas of English history, ranging from the seventeenth century to modern times.

"The Holy Blissful Martyr," which describes one of the moments "where time stood still," recounts the feud between Henry II and Thomas à Becket over the control of ecclesiastical privilege and jurisdiction, and dramatizes the conflict of wills in which Becket stakes his whole being regardless of his own martyrdom.

From every shire's end
Of Engeland to Canterbury they wend
The holy blissful martyr for to seek. . . .
—CHAUCER

High among the founders of the world of ideas and institutions we inherit was the king who eight hundred years ago created a framework for the Common Law. To his contemporaries the first Plantagenet was, like Napolean, a terrifying phenomenon. At the core of his being lay a daemonic energy. This ruthless, formidable man, with his bullet head, sandy, close-cropped hair and hoarse cracked voice, who ascended the throne of England at twenty-one and died before he was forty-seven, was always on the move, always imposing his will, always ordaining. His restless vitality drove both his wife and children to rebellion; slaving far into the night over the business of an empire that stretched from the Cheviots to the Pyrenees, and constantly travelling from place to place, he never wasted a moment or tolerated the least delay. Beneath his urbane manner and hail-fellow good humour ran the diabolical temper of the Angevins; there were times when he tore off his clothes in rage and gnawed the straw from his mattresses. All who opposed him were met with unrelenting, unscrupulous resolution.

Yet those who worked with Henry II loved him. The praises of his judges and Exchequer officials were based on more than flattery. For his devotion to their common task—the creation of order in his kingdom's affairs—was the consuming passion of his life.

Above all, he sought to make his rule endure. It is this that constitutes his claim to greatness. The supreme object of his crowded, stormy life was to create institutions that could preserve his inheritance after his death from the disintegrating forces that threaten all emergent societies. He used the prerogative to bring the whole system of freehold tenure under national law. By making the smaller landowner's right to his property dependent on royal instead of feudal courts, he struck at the root of the great lord's power over his military tenants. And he dealt a death-blow to trial-by-battle and private war. Selfish, crafty, unscrupulous, the great lawyer-king wielded the sword of justice "for the punishment of evil-doers and the maintenance of peace and quiet for honest men." His judges made his remedies available in every corner of the realm. With the precedents they enshrined in their judgments they little by little created a common law for all England. They established the same system for north, south, east and west, for town and country,

for Norman, Englishman and Welshman. They nationalised, as it were, the Law.

Henry's achievement was far in advance of his age. By the end of his reign there was no major offence against the public peace which could not bring the offender within range of a royal writ. Henceforward whoever gave law to England was to have a machinery by which it could be enforced—against the strong as well as the weak. The professional judges Henry trained, the courts in which they sat, the writs they devised to meet popular needs, and the judgments they left behind to guide their successors, helped to ensure that justice should be done even in the royal absence or in the reign of a weak or unjust sovereign. By making the Common Law the permanent embodiment of a righteous king sitting in judgment, the great Angevin established the English habit of obedience to law which has been the strongest of all the forces making for the nation's peaceful continuity and progress.

Yet, in trying to subject every part of the nation's life to the Law, the great Plantagenet fell foul of the one Power which in that age no prince could safely challenge. Wherever in western Europe man turned his eyes, he was confronted by the majesty of the Church. He could not read a book that churchmen had not written and copied by hand; unless he was a churchman trained by churchmen, he almost certainly could not read at all. Everything he did was blessed or cursed, approved or disapproved, explained and solemnised by the Church. He was baptised by it, married by it, buried by it. He went into battle calling on its saints to aid his arms; he sought a cure for his ills at its martyrs' shrines or in its holy waters and wells; he made his oaths on its sacred relics. Its superstitions, often touchingly beautiful, were part of his daily life. He prayed before the painted images of its saints and angels for help, comfort and forgiveness. The bells rang, and the familiar gargoyles grinned from the village church tower to guard him from demon or storm; he brought his corn to be blessed at its altars, and, repeating its hallowed Latin incantations,

danced round his apple trees to make them
fruitful. The very oxen of the fields, he believed, knelt in the byres on Christmas night
in remembrance of the manger birth.

The Church not only dominated men's
minds and imaginations. It enjoyed immense
wealth. In an age when most people lived in
huts little bigger or cleaner than pigsties, the
Church's buildings towered above the landscape and blazed with colour and jewels. And
it commanded in every country a host, not
of warriors, but of men and women disciplined
to its service. They ranged from scarlet-robed
cardinals and mitred archbishops to humble
parish-clerks, bellringers and church-sweepers
—members of the Minor Orders, as they were
called; from judges, lawyers and physicians
to the poor ragged students who begged and
sang their way along the roads of Europe to
hear the Church's famous doctors lecture on
theology and canon law in its cathedral schools
and universities. In its heyday in the twelfth
and thirteenth centuries, it has been reckoned,
one out of every thirty adult males was a
cleric of some kind.

To the pope or bishop of Rome, as Christ's
vicar on earth, lay an appeal from every man
and woman in Orders. A system of ecclesiastical or canon law, derived from early Christian and Roman practice and constantly added
to, provided the machinery—meticulous, bureaucratic, authoritative—for enforcing papal
control over all clerics. For by the twelfth
century the Roman Church had won for its
members almost complete exemption from the
processes of secular criminal law. If a cleric—
even a poor ragamuffin student—committed a
murder, burglary or other breach of the peace,
it claimed the exclusive right to try and punish him. And as the canon law forbade the use
of mutilation and the death sentence, and as
the keeping of prisons was costly, it relied for
punishment mainly on penance and spiritual
penalties. Any malefactor who could read or
mumble over a Latin text from the Bible—
the test of clerical status—and so claim "benefit of clergy," could escape the king's judges.
The worst that could befall him was a fine
or brotherly scourging or, in the last resort,

defrocking, in which case he remained free
to repeat his offence.

Thus Henry II, seeking to establish a common law for all Englishmen, was confronted
by ecclesiastical privileges incompatible with
his object. The Church's punishments were
far too light to maintain order in a violent
and unpoliced age. To the king's orderly and
autocratic mind it was intolerable that episcopal tenants-in-chief should have the right to
appeal over his head to foreign courts and
leave the realm to advance their suits against
him. It seemed equally so that papal legates,
over whose appointment he had no control,
should exercise judicial powers inside his
dominions and constrain, by threats of excommunication and suspension, those who
were his vassals and ministers.

For the Church sheltered so many beneath
its ample cloak that it formed a complete subsection of humanity. Had a majority of clerics
been what they were supposed to be—and the
best were—its claim to immunity from national Law would have been reasonable
enough. But most of them were merely ordinary men in clerical dress leading clerical lives.
Their leaders—though a few were saints and
many men of ability and learning—were as
given to pomp and luxury as the lay lords
by whose side they presided over realm and
neighbourhood. They entertained in halls off
plate of gold and silver, wore jewels, rings and
costly garments, kept fine horses, hounds,
hawks and armies of retainers, and travelled
with magnificent cortèges. Monks, who in
theory had withdrawn from the world to
mortify the flesh and exalt the spirit, lived in
a manner at startling variance, not only with
their own professions, but with the poverty-
stricken life of the countryside around them.
Other churchmen not in regular orders did not
even trouble to wear the outward garb of
piety, but went about, like the fashionable
chaplains of the feudal magnates, with curled
hair, pointed beards and effeminate clothes
or, like secular canons in non-monastic cathedrals, in fine linen instead of sheepskin. And
some, though mostly in minor orders, were
knaves and malefactors, as dangerous to the

public peace as any other criminals. In Worcestershire, in the early part of Henry II's reign, one of them raped a girl and then murdered her father; another, a canon of Bedford, slew a knight at Dunstable and, after being acquitted in the teeth of the evidence by the bishop's court, insulted a royal judge who had been sent to investigate the matter. It was such men that Henry II wished to bring under the Common Law.

He proceeded with great caution. As in his attacks on the powers of feudal magnates and their franchises he relied on subtly disguised and harmless-looking legal devices to bring the ecclesiastical courts under his control before anyone could realise what was happening. In this he was aided by the man he made his chancellor and who showed almost as small respect as he for clerical claims which conflicted with the needs of royal revenue and justice. It was characteristic of Henry's freedom from the prejudices of his age that this favourite counsellor was the son of a London merchant. Thomas Becket at the time of Henry's accession was archdeacon of Canterbury and the primate's legal adviser. Dark, handsome, and immensely tall, with a great hooked beak and wonderful vitality, this brilliant ecclesiastical lawyer became the young king's inseparable companion. As chancellor and keeper of the great seal he was loaded with gifts and favours; the wood-chopper, the contemptuous nobles called him after his homely origin. His wealth, splendour and vast train of retainers became the talk of England and France. The very bits of his horses' harness were made of silver. When in 1158 he went on an embassy to Paris to negotiate a marriage between his master's son and the French king's daughter, he rode on a magnificent charger, preceded by hundreds of knights and liveried choristers and with richly-caparisoned pack-horses ridden by monkeys in silks and velvets. A year later he led the royal army in Aquitaine and captured the city of Cahors, unseating a French champion in open tournament.

In 1162, wishing to have a loyal and subservient ecclesiastical collaborator, the king raised this low-born clerk to the supreme office of archbishop of Canterbury. With his aid, he felt, he would be able to bring the practice of every court in the land into line with the principles of law and order he was seeking to enforce. Brushing aside opposition, he induced the monastery chapter of Christ Church, Canterbury, to elect Becket to the vacant see, though he was not even ordained a priest until the day before his consecration as head of the English Church.

In doing so, however, the king made a grave miscalculation. For Becket, who received his sacred office with reluctance, had no sooner accepted it than, at the age of forty-five, he completely changed his way of life. The most resplendently arrayed and attended man in England, who had taken the field at the head of seven hundred of his own knights, worn the long-embroidered sleeves of a baron and once told his sovereign that his royal cloak was unfit to give a beggar, he now donned the black robes of a Canterbury monk, attended midnight masses, and daily—with his habitual ostentation—entertained and washed the feet of the filthiest beggars in Canterbury. A shameless pluralist who had collected benefices and prebendal stalls to support his magnificent entertainments, he insisted on resigning the chancellorship regardless of the entreaties of his sovereign, who had seen in the union of the primacy and the royal chancery the solution of his problems. He gave up coursing and hunting and the hawks and hounds in which he delighted. Most surprising and, for the king, disconcerting, he embraced the extreme theories of the clerical reformers. He became an ardent, unbending champion of the papacy. When the pallium—the symbol of spiritual authority—arrived from Rome, he walked barefoot through the streets to receive it.

For, with the thoroughness with which he did everything, Becket refused to serve two masters. Having been the most loyal of royal lieutenants, he now transferred his allegiance to a more powerful master and, as it seemed to the king, most ungratefully sacrificed his interests. Instead of applying his vast legal and business experience to subject ecclesiastical encroachments to Exchequer scrutiny, he used them to extend the rights and revenues of his see. He revived long-dormant claims, demanded the restoration of estates alienated by his predecessors, and insisted on receiving homage in place of the Crown from knights holding church-lands. When a fellow tenant-in-chief usurped an advowson, he summarily excommunicated him, thus depriving the Crown of his services, for no-one could have dealings with an excommunicated man. Nor would he yield an inch to the king's demands about criminous clerks. A tax reform, to which as chancellor he would have given whole-hearted support, was fiercely resisted by him in the Council. "By the eyes of God," declared the furious king, "it is not seemly for you to gainsay me." "By the reverence of those eyes by which you have sworn, my lord king," Becket replied, "not a penny shall be given from all my land or from the jurisdiction of the Church." [1] Even when Henry sought a papal dispensation for his bastard brother to marry an heiress within the prohibited degrees, instead of facilitating matters as a normal archbishop would have done, the primate refused to consider it. He seemed to go out of his way deliberately to enrage his former friend and benefactor.

Thus the king's attempts to bring the Church under the law was frustrated by the very man who had been his chief assistant and who, as the repository of his secret plans, was ideally situated to defeat them. His love for his brilliant lieutenant turned to bitter hatred. With all his resolution and cunning he set himself to remedy his mistake. He had at all costs to get Becket out of the key position in which he had so injudiciously placed him.

The two men—the one with the strongest throne in Europe, the other representing the international Church—seemed well matched. They had been the complement of one another and now became the antithesis. Each had the same imperious, overbearing will, each was thorough, persistent, and electric with restless energy, each had behind him a career of un-

broken triumph. And each knew, or thought he knew, his opponent by heart, for they had worked together in close companionship for seven years, and, so far as either was capable of love, had been fascinated by one another.

Yet within a year the king had completely outmanœuvred the tall, gaunt, dark archbishop. For, with all his boldness and courage, Becket lacked the virtues in which Henry, the Achilles' heel of his temper apart, was so strong. He had none of his capacity for patient statesmanship and *finesse* in handling political opinion. He was a perfectionist rather than a man of the world. During his seven years as chancellor he had shown himself a tireless organiser and worker, with a wonderful quickness and versatility. He possessed dazzling address and charm; could be all things to all men and, so long as he was not personally concerned, show considerable tact, and, though revealing his heart to none, win from subordinates affection and even devotion. But while he appealed to the multitude by his dramatic genius and emotional power, his equals could not depend on him. He was far too much of an egotist to be a good colleague. He lacked constancy and stability: was a man of extremes who lived on his nerves. He seemed capable of every attitude except moderation. He constantly laid himself open to criticism and suspicion by sudden changes of mood which appeared to responsible men insincere and in bad taste. They saw him as an exhibitionist who could never stop playing a part. To Gilbert Foliot, the austere and learned bishop of London who had been the leader of the Church party before Becket's elevation to the primacy, he seemed as much an upstart ecclesiastically as to the feudal magnates socially: a careerist who had never been a monk or even a priest and whose pretences to devotion were utterly insincere.

The king, who had been so well served and delighted by his chancellor's genius, understood his weaknesses perfectly: his vanity and hypersensitiveness, his inability not to overstate and dramatise his case, his pathological desire—the result of a lonely childhood—to win applause and justify himself. And in their relations with the English bishops and the

[1] *Materials for the History of Thomas Becket*, II, 373, cit. *English Historical Documents* II, 714.

pope, both of whose support was essential to Becket's position, he played the brilliant, excitable archbishop like a fish. First he joined issue with him over what was by far the weakest point in the Church's position—the trial of criminous clerks, to which a notorious murder and an equally notorious acquittal had just drawn everyone's attention. It was an issue on which the Church was divided and about which doubts were felt even by the pope. In October 1163 at a Council at Westminster Henry outlined his proposals for dealing with this pressing scandal. He did not challenge the Church's right to try its members, but demanded only that clerics found guilty by ecclesiastical courts of major crimes should be degraded and handed over to his offices for punishment. Those who could not be restrained from such outrages by the thought of their sacred orders, he pointed out, could scarcely be much wronged by the loss of them.

To this Becket, incapable of moderation and taking up, as always, the extreme position in any cause with which he was identified, replied that it would be a monstrous injustice to punish a man twice for the same offence. In a long, passionate speech he urged the king not to introduce into the kingdom a new discipline contrary to the decrees of the ancient fathers—"a new law of Christ," he called it, "by a new and strange kind of lord." At this Henry asked angrily whether he and his fellow bishops were prepared to swear to abide by the ancient customs of the realm. This put them in a quandary, for in the time of Henry's grandfather the Church had been subjected to many restraints which it had since shaken off. Yet in England an appeal to ancient custom was always hard to refuse. After a consultation, therefore, the archbishop replied that they would swear as their liege-lord requested, but with the customary proviso, "saving the rights of their order." At this Henry became extremely angry and stamped out in a rage, leaving the bishops to digest the fact that they were in for an uncomfortable and dangerous struggle. Next day he demanded from the primate the return of the castles and honours of Berkhamsted and

Eye which he had granted him during his chancellorship.

Having set the issue before the world—one in which he appeared to be asking nothing of his bishops but what was fair and reasonable—the king proceeded to drive a wedge between them and their leader. His instrument was the pope, Alexander III, a sensible man and no extremist, who, being engaged in a life-or-death struggle with the Emperor of the Germans, Frederick Barbarossa, during which he had been forced to take refuge in France, was exceedingly anxious to stand well with the English king. He therefore responded willingly to Henry's suggestions that he should hint to his quarrelsome metropolitan that it was no service to the Church to insult the Crown by refusing to swear to the ancient customs of the realm, and that some reasonable compromise over the trial of criminous clerks would be in the Holy See's interest. Confronted by surrender in such a quarter Becket—still a parvenu in the Church—felt that he had no choice but to give way. He therefore privately, and it seems rather impulsively, informed the king that the next time he was asked to swear to the ancient customs of the realm in public, he would do as he wished. It was characteristic of him that in taking this step he consulted nobody and refrained from informing his fellow bishops who had stood behind him so firmly at Westminster.

Immediately, in the January of 1164, the king called a council at his hunting-lodge at Clarendon. In that simple, childlike age, when men's minds were swayed by outward forms and ceremonies, it seemed essential to obtain from the archbishop and his colleagues a solemn and public declaration of what had been promised. Once more the primate was asked, in the presence of the barons and bishops, whether he would agree to clerics, found guilty of felony by ecclesiastical courts, being degraded and handed over to the king's judges for punishment. And once more the archbishop, who seemed almost incapable of meeting his old master in public without falling into a furious altercation, contended that it was contrary to divine law to punish a man twice for the same offence, and that a priest was a sacred being who could no more be sentenced by laymen than a father by his own child. Thereupon the king reminded him of his promise to swear to the ancient customs and constitutions without insulting qualifications. Then he sprang a bombshell on everyone by producing these in written form and asking the prelates to acknowledge them.

These sixteen carefully-prepared clauses, known to history as the Constitutions of Clarendon, set out, not unfairly, the relationship that had existed between Church and State in the time of Henry's grandfather Henry I. Some of them, like the proviso that no peasant's son should be ordained without his lord's assent, were undisputed. Others traversed what in the past thirty years had become the accepted practice of the Church. They included provisions for trying in the king's courts disputes about advowsons as a species of landed property, and for regulating reckless and blackmailing accusations brought by archdeacons against laymen for moral offences. And they laid down a procedure for dealing with criminous clerks: preliminary investigation before a lay judge, trial in the ecclesiastical courts in the presence of a royal observer, and, where guilt was proved, degradation and delivery to the king's officers for sentence and punishment.

The most contentious provisions were that no tenants-in-chief should be excommunicated, no cleric leave the realm and no appeal be made to Rome without the king's leave. And appeals in ecclesiastical disputes were to go from the archdeacon's court to the bishop's, from the bishop's to the archbishop's, and, unless permission were given for an appeal to Rome, from the archbishop to the king, who was to direct the archbishop's court how to decide the issue. This was tantamount to making the king supreme ecclesiastical judge in the realm—a principle which, however much it might conform with ancient English practice, ran diametrically counter to existing canon law. It struck at the international sovereignty of the Church and made the crown, as in Saxon and early Norman times,

the constitutional link between the pope and the English clergy.

It was one thing for Henry to try to restore the ancient unwritten and peculiarly English relations between Church and State in a tacit agreement with his own bishops, some of whom at least were sympathetic to views which had been held only a century before by such a primate as Lanfranc. But it was another to reduce these to writing and demand from churchmen a public avowal of principles which violated the disciplinary canons of their Church. The episcopal bench was appalled. For three days, in a series of violent arguments, the bishops stood solidly behind the primate in defence of what they deemed the liberties of the Church. Even when "the princes and nobles of the realm, waxing hot in their wrath, burst into the chamber, muttering and clamouring," and, shaking fists in their faces, declared that those who resisted the king were in deadly peril, they remained firm.

At this point Becket—vehemently reproached by the king for promising his agreement in private and humiliating him by breaking it in public—suddenly gave way. Without consulting his colleagues he announced that, as his lord and sovereign would have him perjure himself, he must do so. By refusing to add his seal to this grudging agreement, he made his surrender seem as great an insult to Henry as it seemed a betrayal to his colleagues. Subsequently he made his position still more invidious by suspending himself from the service of the altar as a penance for perjury. He also sent an emissary to the pope to ask forgiveness for betraying the Church.

The archbishop could hardly have played his cards worse. His colleagues, hopelessly confused and divided, had lost all confidence in him. Even those who most strongly upheld the principles for which he had contended felt that, as he had abandoned them, it was a needless and dishonest continuance of a regrettable controversy to qualify and repudiate his undertaking. The view of responsible laymen was that he had made himself ridiculous and, by his vanity and ungrateful provocation of his royal master, compromised the Church's position.

Henry had put his adversary in a cleft stick; the latter's resignation now seemed inevitable. Yet, in his determination to crush him, he had blundered himself. By setting down his claims in black and white, he had put the Church's defenders on their guard. This became apparent when he sent the Constitutions to the pope for ratification. For though the Holy Father, confronted by an imperialist anti-pope in Rome, was in greater need than ever of the English king's support, he could not publicly repudiate the doctrines for which his predecessors had fought. The denial of the right of ecclesiastical appeal struck at the Church's independence and unity and at one of the papacy's principal sources of income. While agreeing to six of the clauses, Alexander, as tactfully as possible, withheld his assent from the remainder. And he released Becket from any oath he might have made to observe them. He did not approve of the archbishop's attitude, but he could not do otherwise.

The pope's refusal to underwrite his Constitutions only made Henry the more determined to get rid of the man to whom he attributed the refusal. Meanwhile the latter further prejudiced his position by trying to escape from the country in a fishing-smack. That October the king called a meeting of the Council at Northampton and summoned the archbishop to appear before it for a technical breach of feudal law—the lonely, passionate man's failure, in his alternating moods of defiance and despair, to respond to a sheriff's writ, which should never in any case have been addressed to him. Working himself into one of his famous rages, Henry browbeat the Council, whose members needed little encouragement to avenge themselves on the primate, into sentencing him for his contempt of the royal court to the loss of all his own and his see's moveable goods. Then, without notice, he called on him to account for the vast sums which had passed through his hands' as chancellor. When Becket, seeing that the king was resolved on his ruin, offered a compensation of 2,000 marks, it was contemptuously refused.

At that moment Henry seemed to hold all the cards. He was the most powerful ruler in Europe, and the head of a State in which respect for the Crown was more deeply rooted than in any other. He had behind him a baronage which he had taught to join with him in governing the realm, and a knighthood deeply attached to the throne. Becket, in the eyes of every king's man and of many of his fellow prelates, was a low-born clerk, a parvenu whom his royal master had raised from a merchant's counter. In opposing his benefactor he had laid himself open to charges of the basest ingratitude.

Yet, by making him desperate, Henry drove his adversary back on something greater than either himself or the Church. He forced him on to the rock of the inner spirit. Though ill and afraid, the archbishop resolved to compromise no more and to take his stand, not merely on the Church's tenets, but on the cross of suffering and sacrifice it represented. By doing so he became the champion of thousands to whom the rights and wrongs of the constitutional principles under dispute meant nothing. Becket was not by nature a religious man; he was self-centred, egotistical, an artist and an autocrat. Though pure in life, and generous to his servants and retainers, he did not instinctively love men or turn the other cheek. He was neither meek nor humble. Indeed he was more arrogant than the king, who, for all his blind rages and high-handed ways, had a vein of everyday simplicity which the primate lacked.

Yet for the lonely, spectacular role he now chose Becket was superbly equipped. His towering height, his pale, sensitive face, the aquiline nose and restless penetrating eyes, the white feminine hands and quick eager movements made him look what he aspired to be, a saint and martyr. And the very theatricality and emotionalism that so annoyed high-born men of the world appealed to the hearts of common folk who only saw him from afar and knew nothing of his weaknesses. Here was a man who even in that age of pageantry and outward symbols made his meaning ten times clearer than anyone else, speaking to them across the immense barriers of rank and wealth. Almost alone among the rulers of the time he laid himself out to please the masses— the peasants and craftsmen of England who were without the rights and privileges, laws and liberties of the feudal lords. When he rode on visitation and the children of the poor were brought to him to confirm, he did not, like other prelates, bless them from the saddle. He dismounted and went through the formalities of the sacrament like a humble priest.

Through the king's vindictiveness Becket had reached solid ground. From that moment, despite all the odds against him, he never quitted it. "If you desire success in this world," one of the monks at his side counselled him, "make peace with the king. But if you wish to serve God, act fearlessly." It was what the archbishop had resolved to do. His enemies on the episcopal bench and many of his friends, faced by Henry's unrelenting fury, urged him to resign his see rather than to bring ruin on the Church. He refused either to do so or to plead in an issue which, if lost, would place every churchman at a despot's mercy. Declaring that all temporal power derived from God and that a son could not judge his spiritual father or a sheep his shepherd, he traversed his adversary's whole position and announced, in defiance of the Constitutions, that he would appeal to Rome against any sentence passed on him.

On the 13th October 1164 Becket was summoned before the Council to receive judgment. Before setting out from the monastery where he lodged he deliberately said a votive mass of St. Stephen, the first Christian martyr. Then, ordering the assembled bishops to excommunicate any who dared to lay hands on him, he entered the royal castle at Northampton, wearing his archbishop's cope and pallium and bearing his own cross. When the bishop of London protested, saying, "If you brandish your cross, the king will brandish his sword," Thomas replied, "The cross is the emblem of peace; I carry it for the protection of the whole English Church." All day, while the king and his barons sat in one room and Becket in another, and pleading bishops and threatening envoys constantly passed between them, the archbishop sat alone, hugging his cross and gazing on the crucifix. To his adversaries he seemed merely an angry, unreasonable man clinging to an untenable position—one who, as the bishop of London said, had always been a fool and always would be. To himself he seemed to be wrestling with wild beasts at Ephesus. "This is a fearful day," murmured one of his followers as angry baron after baron came in with summons and threat. "Ay," replied the archbishop, "but the Day of Judgment will be more fearful!"

As the bishops—even those most opposed to Becket—dared not, in face of his prohibition, join in judgment against him, the king demanded it from his earls and barons alone. But when the magnates made their way to the archbishop's chamber to inform him of the sentence, he rose and refused to hear them. "You are come to judge me," he cried, "it is not your right. . . . It is no sentence; I have not been heard. You cannot judge me. I am your spiritual father; you are lords of the household, lay powers, secular personages. I will not hear your judgment! Under protection of the Apostolic See I depart hence." Then, rising to his full height and bearing his cross, he swept into the darkening hall and towards the door, while knights and royal servants, rising from the straw-strewn floor and benches where they had dined, shouted, "Traitor!" "Perjurer!" Outside in the wet streets the people thronged round him to beg his blessing so that he could hardly control his horse.

That night, while the triumphant king issued a proclamation that no-one was to do him physical hurt, Becket rode out of Northampton in driving wind and rain and made his way in disguise to the coast. Three weeks later he landed in France.

For six years the archbishop remained an exile. The revenues of his see were confiscated, his kinsfolk banished, and his office declared forfeit. From the position he had taken up— that ultimate appeals affecting the Church must lie to the pope and not the king, and that no lay court had the right to lay hands on an anointed priest—nothing would move him. Attempts were made to negotiate a compromise by the pious king of France, who gave him shelter out of dislike for his English rival, by the pope who, despite his disapproval of the constitutions of Clarendon, was still deeply anxious to retain Henry's goodwill, by the bishops who found themselves between the devil and the deep sea and could not obey their temporal master without disobeying their spiritual. All were in vain and broke down on the enmity of two resolute and legalistically-minded men of genius, who brought out all that was most stubborn and violent in one another. From time to time, whenever the temporising pope permitted, Becket emerged from the French monasteries into which he had retired to a life of the sternest austerity, to hurl anathemas and excommunications at his fellow prelates for compromising with the king. Only the papal prohibition stopped him from treating the latter likewise.

Henry was equally unappeasable. But in the end the logic of events was too much for him. He could not govern Christian England without the Church. And, in an international age, himself an international ruler, he could not cut the English Church off from the universal Church and make himself, instead of the pope, its ruler. To ensure the peaceful succession of the crown and secure his successor's inheritance from the uncertainties of civil war—the fate that had befallen his own on his grandfather's death—he wished to have his eldest son crowned during his lifetime: a constitutional practice familiar in France, though hitherto unknown in England. But the consecration, which in a Christian realm was the binding part of a coronation, could only be performed—according to the custom both of Church and realm—by the archbishop of Canterbury. After waiting five years and trying vainly to get a papal dispensation to allow the ceremony to be performed by deputy, Henry took the law into his own hands and in June 1170 had the young prince crowned by Becket's enemies, the archbishop of York and the assisting bishops of London, Durham, Rochester and Salisbury.

Yet the king was well aware of his danger. He knew that the pope, who was by now on firmer ground in his duel with the emperor and anti-pope, was unlikely to condone such an invasion of the Church's control of its own hierarchy, and that opinion, both in England and on the continent, was hardening against him; unless he could soon negotiate some kind of public settlement with the archbishop, his dominions would almost certainly be laid under interdict and himself under excommunication. He knew too that Becket's host and champion, the king of France, was arming against him, and that many of his own barons, galled by his firm rule and strong measures, were awaiting an opportunity to rise.

He therefore intimated to the papal legates and French king, who were still trying to negotiate a settlement, that he was ready to make his peace with the archbishop, restore his forfeited estates and receive him back into his realm. Nothing was said about the Constitutions, but the presumption was that, as neither archbishop nor pope had accepted them, their enforcement was to be tacitly dropped. The great thing was to achieve a public reconciliation and the restoration of peace and normal religious life in England. A meeting between the two disputants took place in the French king's presence and they were apparently reconciled. But, though the restoration of the archbishop's lands and dignities was agreed, the customary kiss of peace, which he had demanded at a previous abortive meeting and which had been refused by the king, was neither given nor requested. The quarrel—and at heart both men knew it—had been patched up but not appeased.

In agreeing to return to England the primate knew the risk he was running from a passionate and injured autocrat of unpredictable moods. But his own safety was by now the last thing with which he was concerned. His only thought was of spiritual victory. Nor did he return unarmed. Before setting out he secured from the pope letters of suspension and excommunication against his fellow metropolitan of York and two of his own suffragan bishops for their part in crowning the young prince. Just as he was about to embark, he learnt that they were on their way to join the king in Normandy to consecrate royal nominees to five vacant English bishoprics. Faced with the prospect of a packed and hostile episcopal bench, Becket at once used the discretionary powers with which Alexander had armed him and launched the sentences of excommunication and suspension, hastily dispatching them to England before him.

Then on December 1st, 1170, having shown that he was prepared to abate not one tittle of the Church's authority, and avoiding the royal officials who, infuriated by his latest act of war, were waiting at Dover to seize him, he landed at his own cathedral's port of Sandwich. All the way to Canterbury the roads were lined with praying and rejoicing multitudes; it was like a triumphal procession. In the city he was welcomed with trumpets, psalms and organs. As he took his throne in the cathedral his face was transfigured with happiness. "My lord," one of his monks whispered to him, "it matters not now when you depart from the world. Christ has conquered! Christ is now king!"

When Henry in Normandy learnt what had happened and that Becket had announced that, though ready to absolve his suffragans on their doing penance, he had no power to withdraw the papal sentence on his fellow metropolitan, he flew into an ungovernable rage. "What idle and coward knaves have I nourished as vassals," he shouted, "that, faithless to their oaths, they suffer their lord to be mocked by a low-born priest!" Four knights—Reginald FitzUrse of Williton in Somerset, William de Tracey, Richard le Breton, and Hugh de Morville of Knaresborough—took the king at his word, and, without informing anyone of their intention, set out for England. There they made their way to Saltwood castle in Kent, the home of Becket's bitterest enemy, Sir Ranulf de Broc, the man who during his absence had farmed his see's revenues and who, with his retainers, was already waging open war against him.

On December 29th the four knights, with a rabble of de Broc's followers, arrived at Canterbury where the archbishop was sitting after dinner in his chamber. Ostentatiously refusing his servants' offer of food, they strode up to his chamber and sat down on the rushes before him, watching him in grim silence.

When after a time he addressed them they broke into curses, telling him that they had something to say to him by the king's command and asking if he would have it said in public. Then they told him that, unless he absolved the excommunicated bishops, he must immediately leave the realm. To which the archbishop replied that they should cease from brawling and that, as his trust was in Heaven, no sea should ever again come between him and his church. "I have not come back to flee again," he said; "here shall he who wants find me."

At that the knights sprang to their feet and began shouting. But the archbishop answered them in kind: "I am not moved by threats, nor are your swords more ready to strike than my soul is for martyrdom. Go, seek him who would fly from you. Me you will find foot to foot in the battle of the Lord." And as, amid tumult and insults, they withdrew to their waiting men, there was a flash of the same fiery spirit that had caused the archbishop six years before in the castle hall at Northampton to round on the king's mocking brother and call him bastard. He followed the intruders to the door and cried out after them defiantly, "Here, here, will you find me!"

Becket was now expecting immediate death. Indeed, it had become clear during the past few days that he was deliberately seeking it. In his Nativity sermon on Christmas Day he had told his hearers in the packed cathedral that they had already one Canterbury martyr—St. Alphege who had been pelted to death by drunken Danes—and that they might soon have another. And on the day before the knights arrived he had secretly sent two of his monks to the pope and, in bidding them farewell, shown that he never expected to see them again. That night at supper he remarked to those about him that he who must lose much blood must drink much wine.

By now it was nearly dark, and the monks had repaired to the cathedral for vespers. A few minutes later the four knights, having donned their armour in the courtyard, returned to the hall. But they found the door barred. While they were seeking another and battering in a shutter with an axe seized from a carpenter, Becket's clerks repeatedly urged him to take refuge in the cathedral. Fearing that they would all be massacred together, they dragged and pushed him as far as the church door. But when the monks, leaving their vespers, ran to meet him and tried to bolt the door behind him, he sternly refused, saying, "It is not meet to make a fortress of the house of prayer." Then, "driving all before him as a good shepherd doth his sheep," he made his way into the dark, silent cathedral. Almost immediately its peace was broken by the knights and their retainers pouring through the open cloister door, led by FitzUrse, in hauberk and with drawn sword, shouting, "Hither to me, king's men!" Then they all began shouting together, "Where is Thomas Becket, traitor to the king and realm?" The knights were completely covered in armour save for their eyes, and their swords were naked. At the sight the monks fled into the shadows and the dark crypt below.

Only three of his household now remained with the archbishop—William FitzStephen, his future biographer, Robert of Merton, his confessor, and an English monk named Grim who was holding the cross. As the clamour behind increased, Becket suddenly stopped and, descending the steps from the choir, called out in a clear voice, "Lo! here am I, no traitor to the king but a priest. What do you seek from me? I am ready to suffer in His Name who redeemed me by His blood." Whereupon the armed men came shouting and clattering through the darkness to where he stood beside a pillar in the transept. As they closed in to seize him, apparently intending to carry him off, they again called on him to absolve the excommunicated bishops. Rising above them in his great height, he answered: "There has been no satisfaction made, and I will *not* absolve them!" "Then you shall die this instant," cried one of the knights, "and receive your deserts." "I am ready to die for my Lord; may the Church through my blood obtain peace and liberty!" As he resisted their efforts to drag him away, the knights, fearing a rescue, began to strike furiously at him with their swords. A blow cut off his scalp, while another severed his cross-bearer's arm. Two

more blows brought him to his knees, and a fourth scattered his brains on the pavement. Then the murderers burst out of the cathedral to plunder his lodgings and make their escape before the city could be roused.

When that night in the desecrated cathedral the monks bent over the body of the proud, fastidious archbishop and stripped off his bloodstained Cistercian's habit to replace it by his pontifical vestments, they found to their amazement a covering of filthy sackcloth and a horsehair shirt, long worn and alive with lice. Beneath it they saw the festering weals of repeated self-scourging. Then, through their grief and fears, they rejoiced exceedingly. For they knew that he had been a true monk and a saint of God.

By death the archbishop had triumphed. As the news became known a thrill of horror ran through Christendom. The king against whom Becket had contended, collapsed in an agony of lamentation. Exchanging his robes for sackcloth he shut himself in his chamber, where for three days he refused all food and consolation, groaning and crying exceedingly and from time to time falling into a stupor. When he at last calmed down, he threw himself and his realm on the pope's mercy. If it was not to disintegrate, it was the only thing he could do.

But it was not the great alone who were shaken. The common people left their rulers in no doubts as to their attitude. Within a few hours of the murder rumours of miracles began to spread outwards from Canterbury. Four times, it was said, the candles round the bloodstained pall had been lit by invisible hands. A monk in the abbey had seen the archbishop in a vision going towards the high altar in episcopal robes; his deep, beautiful voice had joined in the singing of the introit. A blind woman who touched her eyes with a handkerchief dipped in his blood had regained her sight; others similarly afflicted who had prayed to him had been restored. "The blind see, the deaf hear, the dumb speak" wrote John of Salisbury, "the lame walk, the devils are cast out!" Meanwhile the de Brocs, who had threatened to move the body, were besieged in their castle by a furious crowd. The murderers, who began by boasting of their deed, are said to have fled to Scotland, where the people tried to hang them.

It was easy for twelfth century kings and lords to ignore the rights of the individual poor. But they could not ignore popular beliefs. In matters of faith neither monarch nor prelate had the last word. The Church represented and embodied the beliefs of the people. Because they were convinced that Becket was a saint, the pope, who had so often tried to restrain him during his life, was forced within two years of his death to canonise him. His shrine at Canterbury, blazing with jewels and surrounded by the discarded crutches of those he had cured, became the most famous place of pilgrimage in England. For a time the cult of St. Thomas almost rivalled that of the Virgin Mary. Churches were dedicated to him and memorials erected in lands as remote as Scandinavia and Iceland.

In his own land, whose fame he had blazoned through Christendom, Becket's name became better known and more honoured than any other of his age. Before the Reformation there can have been few English churches that did not have a retable, wall painting, window or other treasure depicting some scene in his troubled life. Even today, despite the wholesale destruction by sixteenth and seventeenth century iconoclasts, many survive, like the boss in the roof of the Norwich cloisters with its demons standing over the Canterbury murderers or the panel at Elham in Kent in which the saint defies the royal anger at Northampton. By a strange paradox—for it had been to strengthen the realm that Henry had fought against him—Becket lived on, not merely as a martyr, but as a national hero to a submerged and conquered people. A Norman born in England who had stood up to her foreign rulers and died at their hands, he became, in a modern writer's words, "one of the people of England as well as one of the saints of God."

In a constitutional historian's sense the martyrdom achieved comparatively little. It saved for English clerics the right of appeal to Rome in purely clerical matters. It established the immunity of criminous clerks from

lay justice. And it brought the English Church, beyond doubt or cavil, into line with the universal practice of the Roman Catholic Church and the canon law, even though that practice conferred on churchmen a greater independence than had been customary in the Anglo-Saxon and early Anglo-Norman State. As a result power in England, as elsewhere in western Europe, continued to be regarded, not as force to be operated by a single untrammelled will, but as a balance in which rulers were subjected to the check of the organised Christian conscience expressed through the Church. When four centuries later the rulers of England repudiated the authority of Rome, the habit of thought remained—a potent check to tyranny.

In everyday administrative practice, after the first shock of the murder had passed, it was the commonsense views of Henry that prevailed rather than the extreme and unrealistic claims of the archbishop. Of the sixteen Constitutions of Clarendon only those governing the freedom of appeals to Rome and the trial of criminous clerks were abandoned. The royal courts extended their control over advowsons and kept their jurisdiction over pleas for debt, except when the latter arose from wills and marriages—matters which had always been dealt with by ecclesiastical courts. The Crown continued to control, subject to certain formalities, the election of bishops and abbots, and to deny to English prelates the right to excommunicate their fellow tenants-in-chief without permission.

Yet Becket's martyrdom created an emotional content which for centuries remained of immense significance in English life and helped to form the enduring values of England. The Canterbury martyr created *The Canterbury Tales* and all the generations of pilgrims riding or tramping through the Kentish countryside "the holy blissful martyr for to seek." It was not the wordly ends for which Becket had fought that mattered after his death. It was the spiritual means with which he had fought for them. The immunity of clerics from lay jurisdiction meant as often as not the protection from justice of rogues and scoundrels; the right of appeal to Rome meant the submission of disputes, which might have been more expeditiously and justly settled at home, to the costly processes of bureaucratic procrastination and corruption in a foreign land. But that a man in high place who had notoriously loved, and to excess, the wealth and fine things of the world and enjoyed them in dazzling splendour, should voluntarily renounce them and live in exile and poverty, should mortify his body and at the end return to his native land to brave and suffer a violent death for the sake of an ideal, was to reveal the power of Christ and enhance the spiritual dignity of man. It is not easy for one who has lived fine to subdue the flesh, to face unarmed the naked swords of brutal warriors, to place himself in the power of insulting foes. Whoever voluntarily chooses these things is, whatever his failings, a great man. In this sense Becket was great—"great," as one of his followers put it, "in truth always and in all places,

great in the palace, great at the altar; great both at court and in the church; great, when going forth on his pilgrimage, great when returning, and singularly great at his journey's end." [2] Historians, who condemn him for contending against administrative measures which were in themselves reasonable, sometimes forget this. But his contemporaries who witnessed his martyrdom or those who heard of it from their fathers and went on pilgrimage to kneel on the steps where he died or touch with trembling fingers the bloodstained hem of his garments, saw it very clearly. For all the world's coarse obsessions and stupidity and blindness, the saints and martyrs have the last word. It is their triumph over the frailty of the body that causes man to believe in God.

[2] Herbert of Bosham, *Materials for the History of Thomas Becket*, III, 471, cit. M. D. Knowles, *Archbishop Thomas Becket*. Proceedings of British Academy XXXV (1949), 23.

PART THREE

The Short Story

The art of story-telling is doubtless older than the records of civilization. Even the so-called modern short story, which was the latest of the major literary types to evolve, has an ancient lineage. Perhaps the oldest and most direct ancestor of the short story is the *anecdote*—an illustrative story, straight to the point. The ancient *parable* and *fable*, starkly brief narratives used to enforce some moral or spiritual truth, anticipate the severe brevity and unity of some short stories written today. With the Middle Ages came such types as the *exemplum*, a brief story used to support the text of a sermon, and the *ballad*, folk verse centered about a dramatic episode. During the sixteenth, seventeenth, and eighteenth centuries numerous forerunners of the short story appeared, such as the *sketch* and the *tale*—loosely constructed prose narratives, not so compact, intense, and comprehensive as the short story. Though these early narratives sometimes bear close resemblance to the modern short story, few, if any, of them exemplify its specialized artistry.

THE DEVELOPMENT OF THE SHORT STORY. The short story as it is known today began with Nathaniel Hawthorne and Edgar Allan Poe. The first typical story of each of these writers was published in 1835—Poe's "Berenice" and Hawthorne's "The Ambitious Guest." Though it now seems naïve, Poe's horror story demonstrated the author's mastery of a new type of narrative. His characters may be strange, the action of his plots far removed from ordinary experience, and his scenes fantastic, but everything in his stories is subordinate to narrative suspense and emotional effect.

Hawthorne's stories are as closely knit and unified as Poe's. But Hawthorne, unlike Poe, is primarily a moralist, and his constant focus on a moral problem—selfishness, pride, ambition—is usually the unifying factor of his story. It was this quality in his work that caused Poe, when reviewing the *Twice-Told Tales* in 1842, to observe:

> A skillful literary artist has constructed a tale. If wise, he has not fashioned his thoughts to accommodate his incidents; but having conceived, with deliberate care, a certain unique or single effect to be wrought out, he then invents such incidents— he then combines such events as may best aid him in establishing this preconceived effect. If his very initial sentence tend not to the outbringing of this effect, then

he has failed in his first step. In the whole composition there should be no word written, of which the tendency, direct or indirect, is not to the one pre-established design.

This celebrated passage is now generally considered the first significant definition of the type. And, along with an earlier stricture in the same essay—a story must not be so long that it "cannot be read at one sitting"—Poe's phrase "a certain unique or single effect" remains, with remarkable accuracy, the hallmark of the short story even today. By 1842, then, Hawthorne and Poe had isolated and defined the essential character- istics of the short story—brevity, unity, intensity. Forty years later an American critic, Brander Matthews, rephrased Poe's definition and supplied a label: the short story, called the "Short-story" (spelled with a hyphen) "to emphasize the distinction between the Short-story and the story which is merely short." In the meantime, two other American writers had made significant contributions to this literary form: Bret Harte, with his stories of early life in California, started a vogue of local-color stories, and Henry James produced the first of his long series of peculiarly modern psychological investigations of the human mind and heart.

Later developments of the short story remain for the most part within the limits set by these writers and critics. One must not, however, overlook the far-reaching effect on the American short story of two foreign writers, Guy de Maupassant and Anton Chekhov. Maupassant showed remarkable ingenuity in inventing means to gain dramatic compression and considerable boldness in relentlessly subordinating every- thing to a central effect. The structural neatness of countless "plotted" stories owes, ultimately, something to Maupassant's technique. Chekhov's practice of presenting a segment of life, objective and seemingly plotless yet highly suggestive and penetrating, has been another influence on the short story—perhaps second to none in recent years. Many writers agree with Chekhov that life poses questions but has no answers for them. The artist, they believe, is therefore obliged only to give a unified impression of some part of life. The major development in the short story in recent decades has, in fact, been the work of a group of writers who seek to create an "impression." The great masters who influenced this group are, in addition to Chekhov and James, Gus- tave Flaubert, Stephen Crane, James Joyce, and D. H. Lawrence. Some of the best known of the group are Seán O'Faoláin, Franz Kafka, Frank O'Connor, Albert Camus, Marcel Aymé, and Friedrich Dürrenmatt in Great Britain and Europe, and Ernest Hemingway, William Faulkner, John Steinbeck, and Eudora Welty in the United States.

The flowering of the short story was one of the principal literary events of the first half of the twentieth century, especially in the United States, where the rapid growth of periodicals and the tempo and pressure of American life have provided special inducements. Scores of writers have discovered dynamic materials in the iso- lated communities and forgotten backwoods, the humdrum towns, the congested cities; they have presented the lost generation, the gangster, the neglected artist, the immi- grant, the lingering pioneer; they have written about Harlem, Chicago, Winesburg, the Prairies, the Appalachian Mountains, the Deep South.

THE ART OF THE SHORT STORY. An awareness of the essential characteristics already pointed out—brevity, unity, intensity—increases the reader's understanding and enjoyment of a short story. In addition, some knowledge of the specialized techniques by which these qualities are produced makes communication between writer and reader more satisfying.

Scene. In all forms of fiction, from the longest novel to the shortest short story, the basic elements are the same: scene, character, and action. The least important is scene, which in most instances merely "sets the stage" and, because of the premium on space in the short story, is handled as quickly as possible. Yet in some stories the scene is of basic importance—in "The Open Boat," for example, where the sea becomes the central force in the men's existence. And many of the most eminent authors (including Conrad and Faulkner) make scene contribute to the intensity of the story. Notice, for instance, how thoroughly Conrad treats scene in "The Lagoon" and how central that element is to the whole story.

Character. The primary concern of most authors is character: "Take care of character," Galsworthy said; "action and dialogue will take care of themselves." Theme and meaning evolve from the interrelation between a character and the circumstances of his life. Yet there is in the short story neither time nor space to show development or disintegration; this is the province of the novel. Furthermore, the focus is usually on one character; other characters are portrayed only in complementary detail. In Faulkner's "Spotted Horses," for instance, the main character is Flem Snopes. The other characters serve only to emphasize his personality and predicament. In most stories the main character is easily discovered. If the reader identifies the main character early in the story, he will more accurately understand the intricate relationships among the characters and consequently gain a fuller appreciation of what they do and say.

Action. For many readers action is the most important element of fiction. In fact the success of some stories—those of Saki, for example—rests mainly on an ingenious plot. Yet many of the best short-story writers today often minimize action, lest it destroy that delicate balance of all the elements on which their total achievement depends. Still, everyone agrees that some plot is indispensable. But the action by which plot is developed must, in the short story, be limited to a critical moment in the life of the chief character. His whole life history cannot be told; that again is the province of the novel. The essential of plot is conflict; it alone causes tension and creates suspense. The conflict may be of various kinds: it may be an inner conflict (as in "The Chrysanthemums"), a conflict among people (as in "The Three Strangers"), a conflict between the characters and their surroundings (as in "The Open Boat"). Ordinarily the action follows a definite pattern. It begins with the *incentive moment* (first point of conflict), develops through a series of entanglements (*complication*), reaches a peak of intensity (*climax*), and becomes disentangled in the *resolution.* Though it would hardly be wise to graph the action of a story, fixing precisely the incentive moment, the climax, and the moment of last suspense, it is helpful, even in casual reading, to note the beginning of the conflict, to follow the increasing tension to the highest point of interest, and to watch the suspense subside and come to rest.

Scene, character, and plot are combined into a continuum of existence, an illusion of reality, so that the reader willingly suspends disbelief and enters into the experience of the story. In working the elements into a pattern of continuous experience, the writer makes use chiefly of two techniques—summary and drama (sometimes referred to as the "long view" and the "short view"). If he decides to hurry over a certain part of the story, he simply describes or summarizes what happens. But those parts which are crucial he presents in vivid detail. In such parts the characters usually break into dialogue. Thus by using the long view the author can economize, and by using the short view, he can gain the intensity that marks the short story.

The elements of scene, character, and plot may be discovered by analyzing a story, but they are in reality inseparable; and the art of the short story in no small degree depends on the skill of the writer in making all of them illuminate the theme of the story. Furthermore, the action of the story itself must be related to the life that existed before the story began and will continue to exist after the story ends. It is the relation between the specific action of the story and this enveloping action that affords the shock of discovery in the resolution and gives the story meaning.

Though the major devices which constitute the art of the short story concern the handling of the basic elements of scene, character, and action, there are a few special techniques that are of particular importance to the reader.

Enveloping Action. Since the short story presents only a fragment of experience, the writer employs special techniques in order to give the reader a feeling that the fragment is a part of a continuous experience. Sometimes he begins and ends his story with a sentence or phrase that refers to the larger experience. More often, however, he interweaves the momentary events of the story with the routine action of the characters' lives in order to create this impression. For instance, in "The Three Strangers" the curious conduct and dialogue of the first two strangers is interrupted time and again by details that keep the reader aware that this confrontation is only a brief episode in the long flow of the lives of the Fennels and their guests. Through cumulative references the author develops in the reader an impression of the continuous experience from which the specific experience was extracted.

Point of View. For both the writer and reader of the short story, an important consideration is point of view, that is, through whose eyes the story is seen and by whose consciousness the material is interpreted. All stories are told from one of two broad points of view or from some variation of the two. In one of these, the *first person,* the author tells the story as if he knew only what one character—the narrator, speaking as the "I" in the story—knows about the story's events and characters. This one character to whose knowledge and understanding the author intentionally limits himself may be a main or a minor character or even an outside observer. "After the Storm," "Guests of the Nation," and "An Old Manuscript" are told from the first-person main-character point of view, and "Spotted Horses" from the first-person outside-observer point of view.

The second of the two broad points of view—generally called the *(omniscient-)* is used in various special ways, and the accepted terminology for these is unrevealing. In the first place, the word "omniscient" signifies that the author knows everything—not merely the externalities some spectator might see but also the inner workings of the minds of the characters. Second, all omniscient stories are necessarily third-person stories. With these two matters clearly in mind, the reader can distinguish the three main specializations of the omniscient story. First, *third person* is the designation given to the omniscient story in which the author freely moves inside and outside the minds of any and all characters; he knows all and may do as he chooses. "The Lagoon" is a typical third-person story. The second prominent type of the omniscient story, known as the *central intelligence,* limits the author to moving inside and outside the consciousness of only one character, either a major or minor one. In "The Open Boat" the journalist is the central intelligence, the one character whose mind Crane enters or withdraws from at will. The third most prominent variety is the *scenic.* Although the scenic is in reality an omniscient and third-person point of view, these features are subtly obscured. They are present, however; to deny them is equivalent to saying that a story can be told without a teller. It is enough to say that the scenic story does not invade the consciousness of any character; by being presented almost entirely through dialogue, it calls no attention to the identity of the teller. In effect, the teller is effaced almost to the point of non-existence. This is the technique used in "After You, My Dear Alphonse," a technique very similar to that used in Strindberg's play "The Stronger."

These narrative methods vary chiefly in two respects—the amount of freedom they allow and the degree of directness they permit. For the writer, fixing on a point of view is of utmost importance, since, if he is to realize the full value of his material, he must choose a convenient position from which to tell the story. For the reader, an awareness of point of view is also highly important, for once he has discovered through whose eyes he is to see what happens, the story unfolds more logically and can be more readily interpreted.

Language. In the modern short story, language is a critical component—hardly less decisive than in poetry. Since a story is built around a particular isolated experience, the language in which it is set down must suggest the quality of that experience: the language must be incisive, suggestive, and alert. In a well-written story, one need not read beyond the first few sentences to find words that reveal its unique quality. Since so much of a short story is often presented dramatically, the language of dialogue is of particular importance. Perhaps no modern writer excels William Faulkner in writing dialogue full of meaningful cadence and rhythm. In "Spotted Horses," for example, when Mrs. Armstid sees that her husband is about to buy a worthless horse from the Texas stranger and the swindler Flem Snopes, she says, "He hain't no more despair than to buy one of them things. And us not five dollars ahead of the pore house, he hain't no more despair." In context, which includes some vivid descriptive detail, this remark reveals, with poetic accuracy, the character and role of Mrs. Armstid, which are a significant part of the story.

Ethical Insight. To many readers the highest test of fiction is ethical insight into the world of universal and ideal truth. Modern short stories may still depend on adventure, but not necessarily on the adventure of action in strange and dangerous places. They may be concerned with adventure in understanding human nature— complex and contradictory, amusing and surprising, comic and tragic. As we have said, theme is developed by showing how the limited action of the story is related to the enveloping action of its background in life. It is the struggle between these two forces that constitutes the main tension, the resolution of which makes the point of the story.

In order for a writer to attain the unity required of a successful short story, his feeling toward scene, character, action, and theme must be consistent. Since a short story is usually read at one sitting, and since the focus is so narrow, a writer must be extraordinarily skillful in utilizing all the potential of his materials. It was, indeed, this central point of the art of the short story with which Poe was concerned when he observed that a "skillful literary artist" conceives "with deliberate care, a certain unique or single effect to be wrought out."

W. SOMERSET MAUGHAM

Appointment in Samarra

William Somerset Maugham (1874–1966), British author, was born in Paris and attended Heidelberg University. He was educated to be a doctor, achieved financial success through his dramas and popular success as a novelist. His greatest novel, *Of Human Bondage*, 1915, like most of his writing, treats the unpredictability of human conduct and the thralldom of man by his passions. His first published novel was *Liza of Lambeth*, 1897. His publications include more than forty novels, several collections of short stories, books of literary criticism, and other nonfiction—*The Gentleman in the Parlour*, 1930; an autobiography, *The Summing Up*, 1938; and *A Writer's Notebook*, 1949, excerpts from his journals. *Points of View*, 1958, reflected his interest in appraising fiction and its practitioners. His twenty-odd plays are chiefly drawing-room comedies.

"Appointment in Samarra" fulfills the essential requirements of a short story: it has strict unity, intensity, and, of course, brevity. Mr. Maugham's restraint gives the story a gem-like quality. Perhaps no story has ever made better use of dramatic irony.

There was a merchant in Bagdad who sent his servant to market to buy provisions, and in a little while the servant came back, white and trembling, and said, "Master, just now when I was in the market-place I was jostled by a woman in the crowd and when I turned I saw it was Death that jostled me. She looked at me and made a threatening gesture; now, lend me your horse, and I will ride away from this city and avoid my fate. I will go to Samarra and there Death will not find me." The merchant lent him his horse, and the servant mounted it, and he dug his spurs in its flanks and as fast as the horse could gallop he went. Then the merchant went down to the market-place and he saw Death standing in the crowd and he came to Death and said, "Why did you make a threatening gesture to my servant when you saw him this morning?" "That was not a threatening gesture," Death said. "It was only a start of surprise. I was astonished to see him in Bagdad, for I had an appointment with him tonight in Samarra."

APPOINTMENT IN SAMARRA From *Sheppey* by W. Somerset Maugham. Copyright 1933 by W. Somerset Maugham. Reprinted by permission of Doubleday & Company, Inc.

JOHN CHEEVER

The Swimmer

John Cheever (1912–   ) is an outstanding figure in contemporary American fiction. He has published both novels and short stories: *The Way Some People Live,* 1942; *The Enormous Radio,* 1954; *The Wapshot Chronicle,* 1957; *The Housebreaker of Shady Hill,* 1959; *Some People, Places and Things That Will Not Appear in My Next Novel,* 1961; *The Wapshot Scandal,* 1964; and *The Brigadier and the Golf Widow,* 1964.

"The Swimmer," like many of Cheever's short stories, presents his concern with well-to-do suburbanites. Neddy Merrill, as *Time* put it, "turns an unsuspected corner and falls off the edge of things into outer darkness."

It was one of those midsummer Sundays when everyone sits around saying: "I *drank* too much last night." You might have heard it whispered by the parishioners leaving church, heard it from the lips of the priest himself, struggling with his cassock in the *vestiarium,* heard it from the golf links and the tennis courts, heard it from the wildlife preserve where the leader of the Audubon group was suffering from a terrible hangover. "I *drank* too much," said Donald Westerhazy. "We all *drank* too much," said Lucinda Merrill. "It must have been the wine," said Helen Westerhazy. "I *drank* too much of that claret." This was at the edge of the Westerhazys' pool. The pool, fed by an artesian well with a high iron content, was a pale shade of green. It was a fine day. In the west there was a massive stand of cumulus cloud so like a city seen from a distance—from the bow of an approaching ship—that it might have had a name. Lisbon. Hackensack. The sun was hot. Neddy Merrill sat by the green water,

THE SWIMMER From *The Brigadier and the Golf Widow* by John Cheever. Copyright © 1964 by John Cheever.

one hand in it, one around a glass of gin. He was a slender man—he seemed to have the especial slenderness of youth—and while he was far from young he had slid down his banister that morning and given the bronze backside of Aphrodite on the hall table a smack, as he jogged toward the smell of coffee in his dining room. He might have been compared to a summer's day, particularly the last hours of one, and while he lacked a tennis racket or a sail bag the impression was definitely one of youth, sport, and clement weather. He had been swimming and now he was breathing deeply, stertorously as if he could gulp into his lungs the components of that moment, the heat of the sun, the intenseness of his pleasure. It all seemed to flow into his chest. His own house stood in Bullet Park, eight miles to the south, where his four beautiful daughters would have had their lunch and might be playing tennis. Then it occurred to him that by taking a dogleg to the southwest he could reach his home by water.

His life was not confining and the delight he took in this observation could not be explained by its suggestion of escape. He seemed to see, with a cartographer's eye, that string of swimming pools, that quasi-subterranean stream that curved across the county. He had made a discovery, a contribution to modern geography; he would name the stream Lucinda after his wife. He was not a practical joker nor was he a fool but he was determinedly original and had a vague and modest idea of himself as a lengendary figure. The day was beautiful and it seemed to him that a long swim might enlarge and celebrate its beauty.

He took off a sweater that was hung over his shoulders and dove in. He had an inexplicable contempt for men who did not hurl themselves into pools. He swam a choppy crawl, breathing either with every stroke or every fourth stroke and counting somewhere well in the back of his mind the one-two one-two of a flutter kick. It was not a serviceable stroke for long distances but the domestication of swimming had saddled the sport with some customs and in his part of the world a crawl was customary. To be embraced and sustained by the light green water was less a pleasure, it seemed, than the resumption of a natural condition, and he would have liked to swim without trunks, but this was not possible, considering his project. He hoisted himself up on the far curb—he never used the ladder—and started across the lawn. When Lucinda asked where he was going he said he was going to swim home.

The only maps and charts he had to go by were remembered or imaginary but these were clear enough. First there were the Grahams, the Hammers, the Lears, the Howlands, and the Crosscups. He would cross Ditmar Street to the Bunkers and come, after a short portage, to the Levys, the Welchers, and the public pool in Lancaster. Then there were the Hallorans, the Sachses, the Biswangers, Shirley Adams, the Gilmartins, and the Clydes. The day was lovely, and that he lived in a world so generously supplied with water seemed like a clemency, a beneficence. His heart was high and he ran across the grass. Making his way home by an uncommon route gave him the feeling that he was a pilgrim, an explorer, a man with a destiny, and he knew that he would find friends all along the way; friends would line the banks of the Lucinda River.

He went through a hedge that separated the Westerhazys' land from the Grahams', walked under some flowering apple trees, passed the shed that housed their pump and filter, and came out at the Grahams' pool. "Why, Neddy," Mrs. Graham said, "what a marvelous surprise. I've been trying to get you on the phone all morning. Here, let me get you a drink." He saw then, like any explorer, that the hospitable customs and traditions of the natives would have to be handled with diplomacy if he was ever going to reach his destination. He did not want to mystify or seem rude to the Grahams nor did he have the time to linger there. He swam the length of their pool and joined them in the sun and was rescued, a few minutes later, by the arrival of two carloads of friends from Connecticut. During the uproarious reunions he was able to slip away. He went down by the front of the Grahams' house, stepped over a thorny hedge, and crossed a vacant lot to the Hammers'. Mrs. Hammer, looking up from her roses, saw him swim by although she wasn't quite sure who it was. The Lears heard him splashing past the open windows of their living room. The Howlands and the Crosscups were away. After leaving the Howlands' he crossed Ditmar Street and started for the Bunkers', where he could hear, even at that distance, the noise of a party.

The water refracted the sound of voices and laughter and seemed to suspend it in midair. The Bunkers' pool was on a rise and he climbed some stairs to a terrace where twenty-five or thirty men and women were drinking. The only person in the water was Rusty Towers, who floated there on a rubber raft. Oh how bonny and lush were the banks of the Lucinda River! Prosperous men and women gathered by the sapphire-colored waters while caterer's men in white coats passed them cold gin. Overhead a red de Haviland trainer was circling around and around and around in the sky with something like the glee of a child in a swing. Ned felt a passing affection for the scene, a tenderness for the gathering, as if it was something he might touch. In the distance he heard thunder. As soon as Enid Bunker saw him she began to scream: "Oh look who's here! What a marvelous surprise! When Lucinda said that you couldn't come I thought I'd *die*." She made her way to him through the crowd, and when they had finished kissing she led him to the bar, a progress that was slowed by the fact that he stopped to kiss eight or ten other women and shake the hands of as many men. A smiling bartender he had seen at a hundred parties gave him a gin and tonic and he stood by the bar for a moment, anxious not to get stuck in any conversation that would delay his voyage. When he seemed about to be surrounded he dove in and swam close to the side to avoid colliding with Rusty's raft. At the far end of the pool he bypassed the Tomlinsons with a broad smile and jogged up the garden path. The gravel cut his feet but this was the only unpleasantness. The party was confined to the pool, and as he went toward the house he heard the brilliant, watery sound of voices fade, heard the noise of a radio from the Bunkers' kitchen, where someone was listening to a ballgame. Sunday afternoon. He made his way through the parked cars and down the grassy border of their driveway to Alewives' Lane. He did not want to be seen on the road in his bathing trunks but there was no traffic and he made the short distance to the Levys' driveway, marked with a private property sign and a green tube for the *New York Times*. All the doors and windows of the big house were open but there were no signs of life; not even a dog barked. He went around the side of the house to the pool and saw that the Levys had only recently left. Glasses and bottles and dishes of nuts were on a table at the deep end, where there was a bathhouse or gazebo, hung with Japanese lanterns. After swimming the pool he got himself a glass and poured a drink. It was his fourth or fifth drink and he had swum nearly half the length of the Lucinda River. He felt tired, clean, and pleased at that moment to be alone; pleased with everything.

It would storm. The stand of cumulus cloud —that city—had risen and darkened, and while

he sat there he heard the percussiveness of thunder again. The de Haviland trainer was still circling overhead and it seemed to Ned that he could almost hear the pilot laugh with pleasure in the afternoon; but when there was another peal of thunder he took off for home. A train whistle blew and he wondered what time it had gotten to be. Four? Five? He thought of the provincial station at that hour, where a waiter, his tuxedo concealed by a raincoat, a dwarf with some flowers wrapped in newspaper, and a woman who had been crying would be waiting for the local. It was suddenly growing dark; it was that moment when the pin-headed birds seem to organize their song into some acute and knowledgeable recognition of the storm's approach. Then there was a fine noise of rushing water from the crown of an oak at his back, as if a spigot there had been turned. Then the noise of fountains came from the crowns of all the tall trees. Why did he love storms, what was the meaning of his excitement when the door sprang open and the rain wind fled rudely up the stairs, why had the simple task of shutting the windows of an old house seemed fitting and urgent, why did the first watery notes of a storm wind have for him the unmistakable sound of good news, cheer, glad tidings? Then there was an explosion, a smell of cordite, and rain lashed the Japanese lanterns that Mrs. Levy had bought in Kyoto the year before last, or was it the year before that?

He stayed in the Levys' gazebo until the storm had passed. The rain had cooled the air and he shivered. The force of the wind had stripped a maple of its red and yellow leaves and scattered them over the grass and the water. Since it was midsummer the tree must be blighted, and yet he felt a peculiar sadness at this sign of autumn. He braced his shoulders, emptied his glass, and started for the Welchers' pool. This meant crossing the Lindleys' riding ring and he was surprised to find it overgrown with grass and all the jumps dismantled. He wondered if the Lindleys had sold their horses or gone away for the summer and put them out to board. He seemed to remember having heard something about the Lindleys and their horses but the memory was unclear. On he went, barefoot through the wet grass, to the Welchers', where he found their pool was dry.

This breach in his chain of water disappointed him absurdly, and he felt like some explorer who seeks a torrential headwater and finds a dead stream. He was disappointed and mystified. It was common enough to go away for the summer but no one ever drained his pool. The Welchers had definitely gone away. The pool furniture was folded, stacked, and covered with a tarpaulin. The bathhouse was locked. All the windows of the house were shut, and when he went around to the driveway in front he saw a for-sale sign nailed to a tree. When had he last heard from the Welchers—when, that is, had he and Lucinda last regretted an invitation to dine with them. It seemed only a week or so ago. Was his memory failing or had he so disciplined it in the repression of unpleasant facts that he had damaged his sense of the truth? Then in the distance he heard the sound of a tennis game. This cheered him, cleared away all his apprehensions and let him regard the overcast sky and the cold air with indifference. This was the day that Neddy Merrill swam across the county. That was the day! He started off then for his most difficult portage.

Had you gone for a Sunday afternoon ride that day you might have seen him, close to naked, standing on the shoulders of route 424, waiting for a chance to cross. You might have wondered if he was the victim of foul play, had his car broken down, or was he merely a fool. Standing barefoot in the deposits of the highway—beer cans, rags, and blowout patches—exposed to all kinds of ridicule, he seemed pitiful. He had known when he started that this was a part of his journey—it had been on his maps—but confronted with the lines of traffic, worming through the summery light, he found himself unprepared. He was laughed at, jeered at, a beer can was thrown at him, and he had no dignity or humor to bring to the situation. He could have gone back, back to the Westerhazys', where Lucinda would still be sitting in the sun. He had signed nothing, vowed nothing, pledged nothing not even to himself. Why, believing as he did, that all human obduracy was susceptible to common sense, was he unable to turn back? Why was he determined to complete his journey even if it meant putting his life in danger? At what point had this prank, this joke, this piece of horseplay become serious? He could not go back, he could not even recall with any clearness the green water at the Westerhazys', the sense of inhaling the day's components, the friendly and relaxed voices saying that they had *drunk* too much. In the space of an hour, more or less, he had covered a distance that made his return impossible.

An old man, tooling down the highway at fifteen miles an hour, let him get to the middle of the road, where there was a grass divider. Here he was exposed to the ridicule of the northbound traffic, but after ten or fifteen minutes he was able to cross. From here he had only a short walk to the Recreation Center at the edge of the Village of Lancaster, where there were some handball courts and a public pool.

The effect of the water on voices, the illusion of brilliance and suspense, was the same here as it had been at the Bunkers' but the sounds here were louder, harsher, and more shrill, and as soon as he entered the crowded enclosure he was confronted with regimentation. "ALL SWIMMERS MUST TAKE A SHOWER BEFORE USING THE POOL. ALL SWIMMERS MUST USE THE FOOTBATH. ALL SWIMMERS MUST WEAR THEIR IDENTIFICATION DISKS." He took a shower, washed his feet in a cloudy and bitter solution and made his way to the edge of the water. It stank of chlorine and looked to him like a sink. A pair of lifeguards in a pair of towers blew police whistles at what seemed to be regular intervals and abused the swimmers through a public address system. Neddy remembered the sapphire water at the Bunkers' with longing and thought that he might contaminate himself—damage his own prosperousness and charm—by swimming in this murk, but he reminded himself that he was an explorer, a pilgrim, and that this was merely a stagnant bend in the Lucinda River.

He dove, scowling with distaste, into the chlorine and had to swim with his head above water to avoid collisions, but even so he was bumped into, splashed and jostled. When he got to the shallow end both lifeguards were shouting at him: "Hey, you, you without the identification disk, get outa the water." He did, but they had no way of pursuing him and he went through the reek of suntan oil and chlorine out through the hurricane fence and passed the handball courts. By crossing the road he entered the wooded part of the Halloran estate. The woods were not cleared and the footing was treacherous and difficult until he reached the lawn and the clipped beech hedge that encircled their pool.

The Hallorans were friends, an elderly couple of enormous wealth who seemed to bask in the suspicion that they might be Communists. They were zealous reformers but they were not Communists, and yet when they were accused, as they sometimes were, of subversion, it seemed to gratify and excite them. Their beech hedge was yellow and he guessed this had been blighted like the Levys' maple. He called hullo, hullo, to warn the Hallorans of his approach, to palliate his invasion of their privacy. The Hallorans, for reasons that had never been explained to him, did not wear bathing suits. No explanations were in order, really. Their nakedness was a detail in their uncompromising zeal for reform and he stepped politely out of his trunks before he went through the opening in the hedge.

Mrs. Halloran, a stout woman with white hair and a serene face, was reading the *Times*. Mr. Halloran was taking beech leaves out of the water with a scoop. They seemed not surprised or displeased to see him. Their pool was perhaps the oldest in the county, a field-stone rectangle, fed by a brook. It had no filter or pump and its waters were the opaque gold of the stream.

"I'm swimming across the county," Ned said.

"Why, I didn't know one could," exclaimed Mrs. Halloran.

"Well, I've made it from the Westerhazys'," Ned said. "That must be about four miles."

He left his trunks at the deep end, walked to the shallow end, and swam this stretch.

As he was pulling himself out of the water he heard Mrs. Halloran say: "We've been *terribly* sorry to hear about all your misfortunes, Neddy."

"My misfortunes?" Ned asked. "I don't know what you mean."

"Why, we heard that you'd sold the house and that your poor children . . ."

"I don't recall having sold the house," Ned said, "and the girls are at home."

"Yes," Mrs. Halloran sighed. "Yes . . ." Her voice filled the air with an unseasonable melancholy and Ned spoke briskly. "Thank you for the swim."

"Well, have a nice trip," said Mrs. Halloran.

Beyond the hedge he pulled on his trunks and fastened them. They were loose and he wondered if, during the space of an afternoon, he could have lost some weight. He was cold and he was tired and the naked Hallorans and their dark water had depressed him. The swim was too much for his strength but how could he have guessed this, sliding down the banister that morning and sitting in the Westerhazys' sun? His arms were lame. His legs felt rubbery and ached at the joints. The worst of it was the cold in his bones and the feeling that he might never be warm again. Leaves were falling down around him and he smelled woodsmoke on the wind. Who would be burning wood at this time of year?

He needed a drink. Whiskey would warm him, pick him up, carry him through the last of his journey, refresh his feeling that it was original and valorous to swim across the county. Channel swimmers took brandy. He needed a stimulant. He crossed the lawn in front of the Hallorans' house and went down a little path to where they had built a house for their only daughter Helen and her husband Eric Sachs. The Sachses' pool was small and he found Helen and her husband there.

"Oh, *Neddy*," Helen said. "Did you lunch at Mother's?"

"Not *really*," Ned said. "I *did* stop to see your parents." This seemed to be explanation enough. "I'm terribly sorry to break in on you like this but I've taken a chill and I wonder if you'd give me a drink."

"Why, I'd *love* to," Helen said, "but there

hasn't been anything in this house to drink since Eric's operation. That was three years ago."

Was he losing his memory, had his gift for concealing painful facts let him forget that he had sold his house, that his children were in trouble, and that his friend had been ill? His eyes slipped from Eric's face to his abdomen, where he saw three pale, sutured scars, two of them at least a foot long. Gone was his navel, and what, Neddy thought, would the roving hand, bed-checking one's gifts at 3 A.M. make of a belly with no navel, no link to birth, this breach in the succession?

"I'm sure you can get a drink at the Biswangers'," Helen said. "They're having an enormous do. You can hear it from here. Listen!"

She raised her head and from across the road, the lawns, the gardens, the woods, the fields, he heard again the brilliant noise of voices over water. "Well, I'll get wet," he said, still feeling that he had no freedom of choice about his means of travel. He dove into the Sachses' cold water and, gasping, close to drowning, made his way from one end of the pool to the other. "Lucinda and I want *terribly* to see you," he said over his shoulder, his face set toward the Biswangers'. "We're sorry it's been so long and we'll call you *very* soon."

He crossed some fields to the Biswangers' and the sounds of revelry there. They would be honored to give him a drink, they would be happy to give him a drink, they would in fact be lucky to give him a drink. The Biswangers invited him and Lucinda for dinner four times a year, six weeks in advance. They were always rebuffed and yet they continued to send out their invitations, unwilling to comprehend the rigid and undemocratic realities of their society. They were the sort of people who discussed the price of things at cocktails, exchanged market tips during dinner, and after dinner told dirty stories to mixed company. They did not belong to Neddy's set— they were not even on Lucinda's Christmas card list. He went toward their pool with feelings of indifference, charity, and some unease, since it seemed to be getting dark and these

were the longest days of the year. The party when he joined it was noisy and large. Grace Biswanger was the kind of hostess who asked the optometrist, the veterinarian, the real-estate dealer and the dentist. No one was swimming and the twilight, reflected on the water of the pool, had a wintry gleam. There was a bar and he started for this. When Grace Biswanger saw him she came toward him, not affectionately as he had every right to expect, but bellicosely.

"Why, this party has everything," she said loudly, "including a gate crasher."

She could not deal him a social blow—there was no question about this and he did not flinch. "As a gate crasher," he asked politely, "do I rate a drink?"

"Suit yourself," she said. "You don't seem to pay much attention to invitations."

She turned her back on him and joined some guests, and he went to the bar and ordered a whiskey. The bartender served him but he served him rudely. His was a world in which the caterer's men kept the social score, and to be rebuffed by a part-time barkeep meant that he had suffered some loss of social esteem. Or perhaps the man was new and uninformed. Then he heard Grace at his back say: "They went for broke overnight—nothing but income—and he showed up drunk one Sunday and asked us to loan him five thousand dollars. . . ." She was always talking about money. It was worse than eating your peas off a knife. He dove into the pool, swam its length and went away.

The next pool on his list, the last but two, belonged to his old mistress, Shirley Adams. If he had suffered any injuries at the Biswangers' they would be cured here. Love— sexual roughhouse in fact—was the supreme elixir, the painkiller, the brightly colored pill that would put the spring back into his step, the joy of life in his heart. They had had an affair last week, last month, last year. He couldn't remember. It was he who had broken it off, his was the upper hand, and he stepped through the gate of the wall that surrounded her pool with nothing so considered as self-confidence. It seemed in a way to be his pool as the lover, particularly the illicit lover, enjoys the possessions of his mistress with an authority unknown to holy matrimony. She was there, her hair the color of brass, but her figure, at the edge of the lighted, cerulean water, excited in him no profound memories. It had been, he thought, a lighthearted affair, although she had wept when he broke it off. She seemed confused to see him and he wondered if she was still wounded. Would she, God forbid, weep again?

"What do you want?" she asked.

"I'm swimming across the county."

"Good Christ. Will you ever grow up?"

"What's the matter?"

"If you've come here for money," she said, "I won't give you another cent."

"You could give me a drink."

"I could but I won't. I'm not alone."

"Well, I'm on my way."

He dove in and swam the pool, but when he tried to haul himself up onto the curb he found that the strength in his arms and his shoulders had gone, and he paddled to the ladder and climbed out. Looking over his shoulder he saw, in the lighted bathhouse, a young man. Going out onto the dark lawn he smelled chrysanthemums or marigolds—some stubborn autumnal fragrance—on the night air, strong as gas. Looking overhead he saw that the stars had come out, but why should he seem to see Andromeda, Cepheus, and Cassiopeia? What had become of the constellations of midsummer? He began to cry.

It was probably the first time in his adult life that he had ever cried, certainly the first time in his life that he had ever felt so miserable, cold, tired, and bewildered. He could not understand the rudeness of the caterer's barkeep or the rudeness of a mistress who had come to him on her knees and showered his trousers with tears. He had swum too long, he had been immersed too long, and his nose and his throat were sore from the water. What he needed then was a drink, some company, and some clean dry clothes, and while he could have cut directly across the road to his home he went on to the Gilmartins' pool. Here, for the first time in his life, he did not dive but went down the steps into the icy water and swam a hobbled side stroke that he might have learned as a youth. He staggered with fatigue on his way to the Clydes' and paddled the length of their pool, stopping again and again with his hand on the curb to rest. He climbed up the ladder and wondered if he had the strength to get home. He had done what he wanted, he had swum the county, but he was so stupefied with exhaustion that his triumph seemed vague. Stooped, holding onto the gateposts for support, he turned up the driveway of his own house.

The place was dark. Was it so late that they had all gone to bed? Had Lucinda stayed at the Westerhazys' for supper? Had the girls joined her there or gone someplace else? Hadn't they agreed, as they usually did on Sunday, to regret all their invitations and stay at home? He tried the garage doors to see what cars were in but the doors were locked and rust came off the handles onto his hands. Going toward the house, he saw that the force of the thunderstorm had knocked one of the rain gutters loose. It hung down over the front door like an umbrella rib, but it could be fixed in the morning. The house was locked, and he thought that the stupid cook or the stupid maid must have locked the place up until he remembered that it had been some time since they had employed a maid or a cook. He shouted, pounded on the door, tried to force it with his shoulder, and then, looking in at the windows, saw that the place was empty.

THOMAS HARDY

The Three Strangers

Thomas Hardy (1840–1928), born near Dorchester, England, began his working career as an architect. However, poetry was such a compelling interest that he began to write it. Because he was not able to attract an audience for his poetry, he turned to writing short stories and novels for a livelihood. His first success as a novelist came in 1874 with the publication of *Far from the Madding Crowd*. Then followed his masterpieces, *The Return of the Native*, 1878; *The Mayor of Casterbridge*, 1886; *Tess of the D'Urbervilles*, 1891; and *Jude the Obscure*, 1895. In 1896, discouraged by harsh criticism of *Jude the Obscure* and now financially secure because of his earlier successes, Hardy returned to the writing of poetry and became one of the great English poets.

Hardy's main concerns as a writer are clearly shown in "The Three Strangers"—the unpredictable character of man's fate, the irony of life, the warmth of natural human response, and the authentic detailing of scene.

Among the few features of agricultural England which retain an appearance but little modified by the lapse of centuries may be reckoned the high, grassy and furzy downs, coombs, or eweleases, as they are indifferently called, that fill a large area of certain counties in the south and south-west. If any mark of human occupation is met with heron, it usually takes the form of the solitary cottage of some shepherd.

Fifty years ago such a lonely cottage stood on such a down, and may possibly be standing there now. In spite of its loneliness, however, the spot, by actual measurement, was not more than five miles from a county-town. Yet that affected it little. Five miles of irregular upland, during the long inimical seasons, with their sleets, snows, rains, and mists, afford withdrawing space enough to isolate a Timon or a Nebuchadnezzar; much less, in fair weather, to please that less repellent tribe, the poets, philosophers, artists, and others who "conceive and meditate of pleasant things."

Some old earthen camp or barrow, some clump of trees, at least some starved fragment of ancient hedge is usually taken advantage of in the erection of these forlorn dwellings. But, in the present case, such a kind of shelter had been disregarded. Higher Crowstairs, as the house was called, stood quite detached and undefended. The only reason for its precise situation seemed to be the crossing of two footpaths at right angles hard by, which may have crossed there and thus for a good five hundred years. Hence the house was exposed to the elements on all sides. But, though the wind up here blew unmistakably when it did blow, and the rain hit hard whenever it fell, the various weathers of the winter season were not quite so formidable on the coomb as they were imagined to be by dwellers on low ground. The raw rimes were not so pernicious as in the hollows, and the frosts were scarcely so severe. When the shepherd and his family who tenanted the house were pitied for their sufferings from the exposure, they said that upon the whole they were less inconvenienced by "wuzzes and flames" (hoarses and phlegms) than when they had lived by the stream of a snug neighboring valley.

The night of March 28, 182– was precisely one of the nights that were wont to call forth these expressions of commiseration. The level rainstorm smote walls, slopes, and hedges like the clothyard shafts of Senlac and Crecy. Such sheep and outdoor animals as had no shelter stood with their buttocks to the winds; while the tails of little birds trying to roost on some scraggy thorn were blown inside-out like umbrellas. The gable-end of the cottage was stained with wet, and the eavesdroppings flapped against the wall. Yet never was commiseration for the shepherd more misplaced. For that cheerful rustic was entertaining a large party in glorification of the christening of his second girl.

The guests had arrived before the rain began to fall, and they were all now assembled in the chief or living room of the dwelling. A glance into the apartment at eight o'clock on this eventful evening would have resulted in the opinion that it was as cozy and comfortable a nook as could be wished for in boisterous weather. The calling of its inhabitant was proclaimed by a number of highly polished sheep-crooks without stems that were hung ornamentally over the fireplace, the curl of each shining crook varying from the antiquated type engraved in the patriarchal pictures of old family Bibles to the most approved fashion of the last local sheep-fair. The room was lighted by half-a-dozen candles, having wicks only a trifle smaller than the grease which enveloped them, in candlesticks that were never used but at high-days, holy-days, and family feasts. The lights were scattered about the room, two of them standing on the chimney-piece. This position of candles was in itself significant. Candles on the chimney-piece always meant a party.

On the hearth, in front of a back-brand to give substance, blazed a fire of thorns, that crackled "like the laughter of the fool."

Nineteen persons were gathered here. Of these, five women, wearing gowns of various bright hues, sat in chairs along the wall; girls shy and not shy filled the window-bench; four men, including Charley Jake the hedge-carpenter, Elijah New the parish-clerk, and John Pitcher, a neighboring dairyman, the shepherd's father-in-law, lolled in the settle; a young man and maid, who were blushing over tentative *pourparlers* on a life-companionship, sat beneath the corner-cupboard; and an elderly engaged man of fifty or upward moved restlessly about from spots where his betrothed was not to the spot where she was. Enjoyment was pretty general, and so much the more prevailed in being unhampered by conventional restrictions. Absolute confidence in each other's good opinion begat perfect ease, while the finishing stroke of manner, amounting to a truly princely serenity, was lent to the majority by the absence of any expression or trait denoting that they wished to get on in the world, enlarge their minds, or do any eclipsing thing whatever—which nowadays so generally nips the bloom and *bonhomie* of all except the two extremes of the social scale.

Shepherd Fennel had married well, his wife being a dairyman's daughter from a vale at a distance, who brought fifty guineas in her pocket—and kept them there, till they should be required for ministering to the needs of a coming family. This frugal woman had been somewhat exercised as to the character that should be given to the gathering. A sit-still party had its advantages; but an undisturbed position of ease in chairs and settles was apt to lead on the men to such an unconscionable deal of toping that they would sometimes fairly drink the house dry. A dancing-party was the alternative; but this, while avoiding the foregoing objection on the score of good drink, had a counterbalancing disadvantage in the matter of good victuals, the ravenous appetites engendered by the exercise causing immense havoc in the buttery. Shepherdess Fennel fell back upon the intermediate plan of mingling short dances with short periods of talk and singing, so as to hinder any ungovernable rage in either. But this scheme was entirely confined to her own gentle mind: the shepherd himself was in the mood to exhibit the most reckless phases of hospitality.

The fiddler was a boy of those parts, about

twelve years of age, who had a wonderful dexterity in jigs and reels, though his fingers were so small and short as to necessitate a constant shifting for the high notes, from which he scrambled back to the first position with sounds not of unmixed purity of tone. At seven the shrill tweedle-dee of this youngster had begun, accompanied by a booming ground-bass from Elijah New, the parish-clerk, who had thoughtfully brought with him his favorite musical instrument, the serpent. Dancing was instantaneous, Mrs. Fennel privately enjoining the players on no account to let the dance exceed the length of a quarter of an hour.

But Elijah and the boy, in the excitement of their position, quite forgot the injunction. Moreover, Oliver Giles, a man of seventeen, one of the dancers, who was enamored of his partner, a fair girl of thirty-three rolling years, had recklessly handed a new crown-piece to the musicians, as a bribe to keep going as long as they had muscle and wind. Mrs. Fennel, seeing the steam begin to generate on the countenances of her guests, crossed over and touched the fiddler's elbow and put her hand on the serpent's mouth. But they took no notice, and fearing she might lose her character of genial hostess if she were to interfere too markedly, she retired and sat down helpless. And so the dance whizzed on with cumulative fury, the performers moving in their planet-like courses, direct and retrograde, from apogee to perigee, till the hand of the well-kicked clock at the bottom of the room had traveled over the circumference of an hour.

While these cheerful events were in course of enactment within Fennel's pastoral dwelling, an incident having considerable bearing on the party had occurred in the gloomy night without. Mrs. Fennel's concern about the growing fierceness of the dance corresponded in point of time with the ascent of a human figure to the solitary hill of Higher Crowstairs from the direction of the distant town. This personage strode on through the rain without a pause, following the little-worn path which, further on in its course, skirted the shepherd's cottage.

It was nearly the time of full moon, and on this account, though the sky was lined with a uniform sheet of dripping cloud, ordinary objects out of doors were readily visible. The sad wan light revealed the lonely pedestrian to be a man of supple frame; his gait suggested that he had somewhat passed the period of perfect and instinctive agility, though not so far as to be otherwise than rapid of motion when occasion required. At a rough guess, he might have been about forty years of age. He appeared tall, but a recruiting sergeant, or other person accustomed to the judging of men's heights by the eye, would have discerned that this was chiefly owing to his gauntness, and that he was not more than five-feet-eight or nine.

Notwithstanding the regularity of his tread, there was caution in it, as in that of one who mentally feels his way; and despite the fact that it was not a black coat nor a dark garment of any sort that he wore, there was something about him which suggested that he naturally belonged to the black-coated tribes of men. His clothes were of fustian, and his boots hobnailed, yet in his progress he showed not the mud-accustomed bearing of hobnailed and fustianed peasantry.

By the time that he had arrived abreast of the shepherd's premises the rain came down, or rather came along, with yet more determined violence. The outskirts of the little settlement partially broke the force of wind and rain, and this induced him to stand still. The most salient of the shepherd's domestic erections was an empty sty at the forward corner of his hedgeless garden, for in these latitudes the principle of masking the homelier features of your establishment by a conventional frontage was unknown. The traveler's eye was attracted to this small building by the pallid shine of the wet slates that covered it. He turned aside, and, finding it empty, stood under the pent-roof for shelter.

While he stood, the boom of the serpent within the adjacent house, and the lesser strains of the fiddler, reached the spot as an accompaniment to the surging hiss of the flying rain on the sod, its louder beating on the cabbage-leaves of the garden, on the eight or ten beehives just discernible by the path, and its dripping from the eaves into a row of buckets and pans that been placed under the walls of the cottage. For at Higher Crowstairs, as at all such elevated domiciles, the grand difficulty of housekeeping was an insufficiency of water; and a casual rainfall was utilized by turning out, as catchers, every utensil that the house contained. Some queer stories might be told of the contrivances for economy in suds and dishwaters that are absolutely necessitated in upland habitations during the droughts of summer. But at this season there were no such exigencies; a mere acceptance of what the skies bestowed was sufficient for an abundant store.

At last the notes of the serpent ceased and the house was silent. This cessation of activity aroused the solitary pedestrian from the reverie into which he had lapsed, and, emerging from the shed, with an apparently new intention, he walked up the path to the house-door. Arrived here, his first act was to kneel down on a large stone beside the row of vessels, and to drink a copious draught from one of them. Having quenched his thirst he rose and lifted his hand to knock, but paused with his eye upon the panel. Since the dark surface of the wood revealed absolutely nothing, it was evident that he must be mentally looking through the door, as if he wished to measure thereby all the possibilities that a house of this sort might include, and how they might bear upon the question of his entry.

In his indecision he turned and surveyed the scene around. Not a soul was anywhere visible. The garden-path stretched downward from his feet, gleaming like the track of a snail; the roof of the little well (mostly dry), the well-cover, the top rail of the garden-gate, were varnished with the same dull liquid glaze; while, far away in the vale, a faint whiteness of more than usual extent showed that the rivers were high in the meads. Beyond all this winked a few bleared lamplights through the beating drops—lights that denoted the situation of the county-town from which he had appeared to come. The absence of all notes of life in that direction seemed to clinch his intentions, and he knocked at the door.

Within, a desultory chat had taken the place of movement and musical sound. The hedge-carpenter was suggesting a song to the company, which nobody just then was inclined to undertake, so that the knock afforded a not unwelcome diversion.

"Walk in!" said the shepherd promptly.

The latch clicked upward, and out of the night our pedestrian appeared upon the door-mat. The shepherd arose, snuffed two of the nearest candles, and turned to look at him.

Their light disclosed that the stranger was dark in complexion and not unprepossessing as to feature. His hat, which for a moment he did not remove, hung low over his eyes, without concealing that they were large, open, and determined, moving with a flash rather than a glance round the room. He seemed pleased with his survey, and, bearing his shaggy head, said, in a rich deep voice, "The rain is so heavy, friends, that I ask leave to come in and rest awhile."

"To be sure, stranger," said the shepherd. "And faith, you've been lucky in choosing your time, for we are having a bit of a fling for a glad cause—though, to be sure, a man could hardly wish that glad cause to happen more than once a year."

"Nor less," spoke up a woman. "For 'tis best to get your family over and done with, as soon as you can, so as to be all the earlier out of the fag o't."

And what may be this glad cause?" asked the stranger.

"A birth and christening," said the shepherd.

The stranger hoped his host might not be made unhappy, either by too many or too few of such episodes, and being invited by a gesture to a pull at the mug, he readily acquiesced. His manner, which, before entering, had been so dubious, was now altogether that of a careless and candid man.

"Late to be traipsing athwart this coomb—hey?" said the engaged man of fifty.

"Late it is, master, as you say.—I'll take a seat in the chimney-corner, if you have nothing to urge against it, ma'am; for I am a little moist on the side that was next the rain."

Mrs. Shepherd Fennel assented, and made room for the self-invited comer, who, having got completely inside the chimney-corner, stretched out his legs and his arms with the exspansiveness of a person quite at home.

"Yes, I am rather cracked in the vamp," he said freely, seeing that the eyes of the shepherd's wife fell upon his boots, "and I am not well fitted either. I have had some rough times lately, and have been forced to pick up what I can get in the way of wearing, but I must find a suit better fit for working-days when I reach home."

"One of hereabouts?" she inquired.

"Not quite that—further up the country."

"I thought so. And so be I; and by your tongue you come from my neighborhood."

"But you would hardly have heard of me," he said quickly. "My time would be long before yours, ma'am, you see."

This testimony to the youthfulness of his hostess had the effect of stopping her cross-examination.

"There is only one thing more wanted to make me happy," continued the new-comer. "And that is a little baccy, which I am sorry to say I am out of."

"I'll fill your pipe," said the shepherd.

"I must ask you to lend me a pipe likewise."

"A smoke, and no pipe about 'ee?"

"I have dropped it somewhere on the road."

The shepherd filled and handed him a new clay pipe, saying, as he did so, "Hand me your baccy-box—I'll fill that too, now I am about it."

The man went through the movement of searching his pockets.

"Lost that too?" said his entertainer, with some surprise.

"I am afraid so," said the man with some confusion. "Give it to me in a screw of paper." Lighting his pipe at the candle with a suction that drew the whole flame into the bowl, he resettled himself in the corner and bent his looks upon the faint steam from his damp legs, as if he wished to say no more.

Meanwhile the general body of guests had been taking little notice of this visitor by reason of an absorbing discussion in which they were engaged with the band about a tune for the next dance. The matter being settled, they were about to stand up when an inter-ruption came in the shape of another knock at the door.

At sound of the same the man in the chimney-corner took up the poker and began stirring the brands as if doing it thoroughly were the one aim of his existence; and a second time the shepherd said, "Walk in!" In a moment another man stood upon the straw-woven door-mat. He too was a stranger.

This individual was one of a type radically different from the first. There was more of the commonplace in his manner, and a certain jovial cosmopolitanism sat upon his features. He was several years older than the first arrival, his hair being slightly frosted, his eyebrows bristly, and his whiskers cut back from his cheeks. His face was rather full and flabby, and yet it was not altogether a face without power. A few grog-blossoms marked the neighborhood of his nose. He flung back his long drab greatcoat, revealing that beneath it he wore a suit of cinder-gray shade throughout, large heavy seals, of some metal or other that would take a polish, dangling from his fob as his only personal ornament. Shaking the water-drops from his low-crowned glazed hat, he said, "I must ask for a few minutes' shelter, comrades, or I shall be wetted to my skin before I get to Casterbridge."

"Make yourself at home, master," said the shepherd, perhaps a trifle less heartily than on the first occasion. Not that Fennel had the least tinge of niggardliness in his composition; but the room was far from large, spare chairs were not numerous, and damp companions were not altogether desirable at close quarters for the women and girls in their bright-colored gowns.

However, the second comer, after taking off his greatcoat, and hanging his hat on a nail in one of the ceiling-beams as if he had been specially invited to put it there, advanced and sat down at the table. This had been pushed so closely into the chimney-corner, to give all available room to the dancers, that its inner edge grazed the elbow of the man who had ensconced himself by the fire; and thus the two strangers were brought into close companionship. They nodded to each other by way of breaking the ice of unacquaintance, and the first stranger handed his neighbor the family mug—a huge vessel of brown ware, having its upper edge worn away like a threshold by the rub of whole generations of thirsty lips that had gone the way of all flesh, and bearing the following inscription burnt upon its rotund side in yellow letters:

THERE IS NO FUN
UNTILL I CUM

The other man, nothing loth, raised the mug to his lips, and drank on, and on, and on— till a curious blueness overspread the countenance of the shepherd's wife, who had regarded with no little surprise the first stranger's free offer to the second of what did not belong to him to dispense.

"I knew it!" said the toper to the shepherd with much satisfaction. "When I walked up your garden before coming in, and saw the hives all of a row, I said to myself, 'Where there's bees there's honey, and where there's honey there's mead.' But mead of such a truly comfortable sort as this I really didn't expect to meet in my older days." He took yet another pull at the mug, till it assumed an ominous elevation.

"Glad you enjoy it!" said the shepherd warmly.

"It is goodish mead," assented Mrs. Fennel, with an absence of enthusiasm which seemed to say that it was possible to buy praise for one's cellar at too heavy a price. "It is trouble enough to make—and really I hardly think we shall make any more. For honey sells well, and we ourselves can make shift with a drop o' small mead and metheglin for common use from the comb-washings."

"O, but you'll never have the heart!" reproachfully cried the stranger in cinder-gray, after taking up the mug a third time and setting it down empty. "I love mead, when 'tis old like this, as I love to go to church o' Sundays, or to relieve the needy any day of the week."

"Ha, ha, ha!" said the man in the chimney-corner, who, in spite of the taciturnity induced by the pipe of tobacco, could not or would not refrain from this slight testimony to his comrade's humor.

Now the old mead of those days, brewed of the purest first year or maiden honey, four pounds to the gallon—with its due complement of white of eggs, cinnamon, ginger, cloves, mace, rosemary, yeast, and processes of working, bottling and cellaring—tasted remarkably strong; but it did not taste so strong as it actually was. Hence, presently, the stranger in cinder-gray at the table, moved by its creeping influence, unbuttoned his waistcoat, threw himself back in his chair, spread his legs, and made his presence felt in various ways.

"Well, well, as I say," he resumed, "I am going to Casterbridge, and to Casterbridge I must go. I should have been almost there by this time; but the rain drove me into your dwelling, and I'm not sorry for it."

"You don't live in Casterbridge?" said the shepherd.

"Not as yet; though I shortly mean to move there."

"Going to set up in trade, perhaps?"

"No, no," said the shepherd's wife. "It is easy to see that the gentleman is rich, and don't want to work at anything."

The cinder-gray stranger paused, as if to consider whether he would accept that definition of himself. He presently rejected it by answering, "Rich is not quite the word for me, dame. I do work, and I must work. And even if I only get to Casterbridge by midnight I must begin work there at eight tomorrow morning. Yes, het or wet, blow or snow, famine or sword, my day's work tomorrow must be done."

"Poor man! Then, in spite o' seeming, you be worse off than we?" replied the shepherd's wife.

"'Tis the nature of my trade, men and maidens. 'Tis the nature of my trade more than my poverty. . . . But really and truly I must up and off, or I shan't get a lodging in the town." However, the speaker did not move, and directly added, "There's time for one more draught of friendship before I go; and I'd perform it at once if the mug were not dry."

"Here's a mug o' small," said Mrs. Fennel. "Small, we call it, though to be sure 'tis only the first wash o' the combs."

"No," said the stranger disdainfully. "I won't

spoil your first kindness by partaking o' your second."

"Certainly not," broke in Fennel. "We don't increase and multiply every day, and I'll fill the mug again." He went away to the dark place under the stairs where the barrel stood. The shepherdess followed him.

"Why should you do this?" she said reproachfully, as soon as they were alone. "He's emptied it once, though it held enough for ten people; and now he's not contented wi' the small, but must needs call for more o' the strong! And a stranger unbeknown to any of us. For my part, I don't like the look o' the man at all."

"But he's in the house, my honey; and 'tis a wet night, and a christening. Daze it, what's a cup of mead more or less? There'll be plenty more next bee-burning."

"Very well—this time, then," she answered, looking wistfully at the barrel. "But what is the man's calling, and where is he one of, that he should come in and join us like this?"

"I don't know. I'll ask him again."

The catastrophe of having the mug drained dry at one pull by the stranger in cinder-gray was effectually guarded against this time by Mrs. Fennel. She poured out his allowance in a small cup, keeping the large one at a discreet distance from him. When he had tossed off his portion the shepherd renewed his inquiry about the stranger's occupation.

The latter did not immediately reply, and the man in the chimney-corner, with sudden demonstrativeness, said, "Anybody may know my trade—I'm a wheelwright."

"A very good trade for these parts," said the shepherd.

"And anybody may know mine—if they've the sense to find it out," said the stranger in cinder-gray.

"You may generally tell what a man is by his claws," observed the hedge-carpenter, looking at his own hands. "My fingers be as full of thorns as an old pincushion is of pins."

The hands of the man in the chimney-corner instinctively sought the shade, and he gazed into the fire as he resumed his pipe. The man at the table took up the hedge-carpenter's remark, and added smartly, "True; but the odd-ity of my trade is that, instead of setting a mark upon me, it sets a mark upon my customers."

No observation being offered by anybody in elucidation of this enigma, the shepherd's wife once more called for a song. The same obstacles presented themselves as at the former time—one had no voice, another had and would have proceeded, but finding him wanting in alacrity for catching her she sat down trembling.

"O, he's the—!" whispered the people in the background, mentioning the name of an ominous public officer. "He's come to do it! 'Tis to be at Casterbridge jail tomorrow—the man for sheep-stealing—the poor clock-maker we heard of, who used to live away at Shottsford and had no work to do—Timothy Summers, whose family were a-starving, and so he went out of Shottsford by the high-road, and took a sheep in open daylight, defying the farmer and the farmer's wife and the farmer's lad, and every man jack among 'em. He" (and they nodded towards the stranger of the deadly trade) "is come from up the country to do it because there's not enough to do in his own county-town, and he's got the place here now our own county man's dead; he's going to live in the same cottage under the prison wall."

The stranger in cinder-gray took no notice of this whispered string of observations, but again wetted his lips. Seeing that his friend in the chimney-corner was the only one who reciprocated his joviality in any way, he held out his cup towards that appreciative comrade, who also held out his own. They clinked together, the eyes of the rest of the room hanging upon the singer's actions. He parted his lips for the third verse; but at that moment another knock was audible upon the door. This time the knock was faint and hesitating.

The company seemed scared; the shepherd looked with consternation towards the entrance, and it was with some effort that he resisted his alarmed wife's deprecatory glance, and uttered for the third time the welcoming words, "Walk in!"

The door was gently opened, and another man stood upon the mat. He, like those who had preceded him, was a stranger. This time it was a short, small personage, of fair complexion, and dressed in a decent suit of dark clothes.

"Can you tell me the way to——?" he began, when, gazing round the room to observe the nature of the company amongst whom he had fallen, his eyes lighted on the stranger in cinder-gray. It was just at the instant when the latter, who had thrown his mind into his song, had forgotten the first verse. The stranger at the table, whose soul had now risen to a good working temperature, relieved the difficulty by exclaiming that, to start the company, he would sing himself. Thrusting one thumb into the arm-hole of his waistcoat, he waved the other hand in the air, and, with an extemporizing gaze at the shining sheep-crooks above the mantelpiece, began:

> O my trade it is the rarest one,
> > Simple shepherds all—
> My trade is a sight to see;
> For my customers I tie, and take them up on high,
> > And waft 'em to a far countree!

The room was silent when he had finished the verse—with one exception, that of the man in the chimney-corner, who, at the singer's word, "Chorus!" joined him in a deep bass voice of musical relish:

> And waft 'em to a far countree!

Oliver Giles, John Pitcher the dairyman, the parish-clerk, the engaged man of fifty, the row of young women against the wall, seemed lost in thought not of the gayest kind. The shepherd looked meditatively on the ground, the shepherdess gazed keenly at the singer, and with some suspicion; she was doubting whether this stranger were merely singing an old song from recollection, or was composing one there and then for the occasion. All were as perplexed at the obscure revelation as the guests at Belshazzar's Feast, except the man in the chimney-corner, who quietly said, "Second verse, stranger," and smoked on.

The singer thoroughly moistened himself from his lips inwards, and went on with the next stanza as requested:

> My tools are but common ones,
> > Simple shepherds all—
> My tools are no sight to see:
> A little hempen string, and a post whereon to swing,
> > Are implements enough for me!

Shepherd Fennel glanced round. There was no longer any doubt that the stranger was answering his question rhythmically. The guests one and all started back with suppressed exclamations. The young woman engaged to the man of fifty fainted half-way, with such a will that he scarcely heeded the interruption, silenced all whispers and inquiries by bursting into his third verse.

> Tomorrow is my working day,
> > Simple shepherds all—
> Tomorrow is a working day for me:
> For the farmer's sheep is slain, and the lad who did it ta'en,
> And on his soul may God ha' merc-y!

The stranger in the chimney-corner, waving cups with the singer so heartily that his mead splashed over on the hearth, repeated in his bass voice as before:

> And on his soul may God ha' merc-y!

All this time the third stranger had been standing in the doorway. Finding now that he did not come forward or go on speaking, the guests particularly regarded him. They noticed to their surprise that he stood before them the picture of abject terror—his knees trembling, his hand shaking so violently that the door-latch by which he supported himself rattled audibly: his white lips were parted, and his eyes fixed on the merry officer of justice in the middle of the room. A moment more and he had turned, closed the door, and fled.

"What a man can it be?" said the shepherd.

The rest, between the awfulness of their late discovery and the odd conduct of this third visitor, looked as if they knew not what to think, and said nothing. Instinctively they withdrew further and further from the grim gentleman in their midst, whom some of them seemed to take for the Prince of Darkness himself, till they formed a remote circle, an empty space of floor being left between them and him:

. . . circulus, cujus centrum diabolus.

The room was so silent—though there were more than twenty people in it—that nothing could be heard but the patter of the rain against the window-shutters, accompanied by the occasional hiss of a stray drop that fell down the chimney into the fire, and the steady puffing of the man in the corner, who had now resumed his pipe of long clay.

The stillness was unexpectedly broken. The distant sound of a gun reverberated through the air—apparently from the direction of the county-town.

"Be jiggered!" cried the stranger who had sung the song, jumping up.

"What does that mean?" asked several.

"A prisoner escaped from the jail—that's what it means."

All listened. The sound was repeated, and none of them spoke but the man in the chimney-corner, who said quietly, "I've often been told that in this county they fire a gun at such times; but I never heard it till now."

"I wonder if it is *my* man?" murmured the personage in cinder-gray.

"Surely it is!" said the shepherd involuntarily. "And surely we've zeed him! That little man who looked in at the door by now, and quivered like a leaf when he zeed ye and heard your song!"

"His teeth chattered, and the breath went out of his body," said the dairyman.

"And his heart seemed to sink within him like a stone," said Oliver Giles.

"And he bolted as if he'd been shot at," said the hedge-carpenter.

"True—his teeth chattered, and his heart seemed to sink; and he bolted as if he'd been shot at," slowly summed up the man in the chimney-corner.

"I didn't notice it," remarked the hangman.

"We were all a-wondering what made him run off in such a fright," faltered one of the women against the wall, "and now 'tis explained!"

The firing of the alarm-gun went on at intervals, low and sullenly, and their suspicions became a certainty. The sinister gentleman in cinder-gray roused himself. "Is there a constable here?" he asked, in thick tones. "If so, let him step forward."

The engaged man of fifty stepped quavering out from the wall, his betrothed beginning to sob on the back of the chair.

"You are a sworn constable?"

"I be, sir."

"Then pursue the criminal at once, with assistance, and bring him back here. He can't have gone far."

"I will, sir, I will—when I've got my staff. I'll go home and get it, and come sharp here, and start in a body."

"Staff!—never mind your staff; the man'll be gone!"

"But I can't do nothing without my staff—can I, William, and John, and Charles Jake? No; for there's the king's royal crown a painted on en in yaller and gold, and the lion and the unicorn, so as when I raise en up and hit my prisoner, 'tis made a lawful blow thereby. I wouldn't 'tempt to take up a man without my staff—no, not I. If I hadn't the law to gie me courage, why, instead o' my taking up him he might take up me!"

"Now, I'm a king's man myself, and can give you authority enough for this," said the formidable officer in gray. "Now then, all of ye, be ready. Have ye any lanterns?"

"Yes—have ye any lanterns?—I demand it!" said the constable.

"And the rest of you able-bodied—"

"Able-bodied men—yes—the rest of ye!" said the constable.

"Have you some good stout staves and pitchforks—"

"Staves and pitchforks—in the name o' the law! And take 'em in yer hands and go in quest, and do as we in authority tell ye!"

Thus aroused, the men prepared to give chase. The evidence was, indeed, though circumstantial, so convincing, that but little argument was needed to show the shepherd's guests that after what they had seen it would look very much like connivance if they did not instantly pursue the unhappy third stranger who could not as yet have gone more than a few hundred yards over such uneven country.

A shepherd is always well provided with lanterns; and, lighting these hastily, and with hurdle-staves in their hands, they poured out of the door, taking a direction along the crest of the hill, away from the town, the rain having fortunately a little abated.

Disturbed by the noise, or possibly by unpleasant dreams of her baptism, the child who had been christened began to cry heart-brokenly in the room overhead. These notes of grief came down through the chinks of the floor to the ears of the women below, who jumped up one by one, and seemed glad of the excuse to ascend and comfort the baby, for the incidents of the last half-hour greatly oppressed them. Thus in the space of two or three minutes the room on the ground-floor was deserted quite.

But it was not for long. Hardly had the sound of footsteps died away when a man returned round the corner of the house from the direction the pursuers had taken. Peeping in at the door, and seeing nobody there, he entered leisurely. It was the stranger of the chimney-corner, who had gone out with the rest. The motive of his return was shown by his helping himself to a cut piece of skimmer-cake that lay on a ledge beside where he had sat, and which he had apparently forgotten to take with him. He also poured out half a cup more mead from the quantity that remained, ravenously eating and drinking these as he stood. He had not finished when another figure came in just as quietly—his friend in cinder-gray.

"O—you here?" said the latter, smiling. "I thought you had gone to help in the capture." And this speaker also revealed the object of his return by looking solicitously round for the fascinating mug of old mead.

"And I thought you had gone," said the other, continuing his skimmer-cake with some effort.

"Well, on second thoughts, I felt there were enough without me," said the first confiden-

tially, "and such a night as it is, too. Besides, 'tis the business o' the Government to take care of its criminals—not mine."

"True; so it is. And I felt as you did, that there were enough without me."

"I don't want to break my limbs running over the humps and hollows of this wild country."

"Nor I neither, between you and me."

"These shepherd-people are used to it—simple-minded souls, you know, stirred up to anything in a moment. They'll have him ready for me before morning, and no trouble to me at all."

"They'll have him, and we shall have saved ourselves all labor in the matter."

"True, true. Well, my way is to Caster-bridge; and 'tis as much as my legs will do to take me that far. Going the same way?"

"No, I am sorry to say! I have to get home over there" (he nodded indefinitely to the right), "and I feel as you do, that it is quite enough for my legs to do before bedtime."

The other had by this time finished the mead in the mug, after which, shaking hands heartily at the door, and wishing each other well, they went their several ways.

In the meantime the company of pursuers had reached the end of the hog's-back elevation which dominated this part of the down. They had decided on no particular plan of action; and, finding that the man of the baleful trade was no longer in their company, they seemed quite unable to form any such plan now. They descended in all directions down the hill, and straightway several of the party fell into the snare set by Nature for all misguided midnight ramblers over this part of the cretaceous formation. The "lanchets," or flint slopes, which belted the escarpment at intervals of a dozen yards, took the less cautious ones unawares, and losing their footing on the rubbly steep they slid sharply downwards, the lanterns rolling from their hands to the bottom, and there lying on their sides till the horn was scorched through.

When they had again gathered themselves together, the shepherd, as the man who knew the country best, took the lead, and guided them round these treacherous inclines. The lanterns, which seemed rather to dazzle their eyes and warn the fugitive than to assist them in the exploration, were extinguished, due silence was observed; and in this more rational order they plunged into the vale. It was a grassy, briery, moist defile, affording some shelter to any person who had sought it; but the party preambulated it in vain, and ascended on the other side. Here they wandered apart, and after an interval closed together again to report progress. At the second time of closing in they found themselves near a lonely ash, the single tree on this part of the coomb, probably sown there by a passing bird some fifty years before. And here, standing a little to one side of the trunk, as motionless as the trunk itself, appeared the man they were in quest of, his outline being well defined against the sky beyond. The band noiselessly drew up and faced him.

"Your money or your life!" said the constable sternly to the still figure.

"No, no," whispered John Pitcher. "'Tisn't our side ought to say that. That's the doctrine of vagabonds like him, and we be on the side of the law."

"Well, well," replied the constable impatiently; "I must say something, mustn't I? and if you had all the weight o' this undertaking upon your mind, perhaps you'd say the wrong thing too!—Prisoner at the bar, surrender, in the name of the Father—the Crown, I mane!"

The man under the tree seemed now to notice them for the first time, and, giving them no opportunity whatever for exhibiting their courage, he strolled slowly towards them. He was, indeed, the little man, the third stranger; but his trepidation had in a great measure gone.

"Well, travelers," he said, "did I hear ye speak to me?"

"You did: you've got to come and be our prisoner at once!" said the constable. "We arrest 'ee on the charge of not biding in Casterbridge jail in a decent proper manner to be hung tomorrow morning. Neighbors, do your duty, and seize the culpet!"

On hearing the charge, the man seemed

enlightened, and, saying not another word, resigned himself with preternatural civility to the search-party, who, with their staves in their hands, surrounded him on all sides, and marched him back towards the shepherd's cottage.

It was eleven o'clock by the time they arrived. The light shining from the open door, a sound of men's voices within, proclaimed to them as they approached the house that some new events had arisen in their absence. On entering they discovered the shepherd's living room to be invaded by two officers from the Casterbridge jail, and a well-known magistrate who lived at the nearest county-seat, intelligence of the escape having become generally circulated.

"Gentlemen," said the constable, "I have brought back your man—not without risk and danger; but every one must do his duty! He is inside this circle of able-bodied persons, who have lent me useful aid, considering their ignorance of Crown work. Men, bring forward your prisoner!" And the third stranger was led to the light.

"Who is this?" said one of the officials.

"The man," said the constable.

"Certainly not," said the turnkey; and the first corroborated his statement.

"But how can it be otherwise?" asked the constable. "Or why was he so terrified at sight o' the singing instrument of the law who sat there?" Here he related the strange behavior of the third stranger on entering the house during the hangman's song.

"Can't understand it," said the officer coolly. "All I know is that it is not the condemned man. He's quite a different character from this one; a gauntish fellow, with dark hair and eyes, rather good-looking, and with a musical bass voice that if you heard it once you'd never mistake as long as you lived."

"Why, souls—'twas the man in the chimney-corner!"

"Hey—what?" said the magistrate, coming forward after inquiring particulars from the shepherd in the background. "Haven't you got the man after all?"

"Well, sir," said the constable, "he's the man

we were in search of, that's true; and yet he's not the man we were in search of. For the man we were in search of was not the man we wanted, sir, if you understand my every-day way; for 'twas the man in the chimney-corner!"

"A pretty kettle of fish altogether!" said the magistrate. "You had better start for the other man at once."

The prisoner now spoke for the first time. The mention of the man in the chimney-corner seemed to have moved him as nothing else could do. "Sir," he said, stepping forward to the magistrate, "take no more trouble about me. The time is come when I may as well speak. I have done nothing; my crime is that the condemned man is my brother. Early this afternoon I left home at Shottsford to tramp it all the way to Casterbridge jail to bid him farewell. I was benighted, and called here to rest and ask the way. When I opened the door I saw before me the very man, my brother, that I thought to see in the condemned cell at Casterbridge. He was in this chimney-corner; and jammed close to him, so that he could not have got out if he had tried, was the executioner who'd come to take his life, singing a song about it and not knowing that it was his victim who was close by, joining in to save appearances. My brother looked a glance of agony at me, and I knew he meant, 'Don't reveal what you see; my life depends on it.' I was so terror-struck that I could hardly stand, and, not knowing what I did, I turned and hurried away."

The narrator's manner and tone had the stamp of truth, and his story made a great impression on all around. "And do you know where your brother is at the present time?" asked the magistrate.

"I do not. I have never seen him since I closed this door."

"I can testify to that, for we've been between ye ever since," said the constable.

"Where does he think to fly to?—what is his occupation?"

"He's a watch-and-clock-maker, sir."

"'A said 'a was a wheelwright—a wicked rogue," said the constable.

"The wheels of clocks and watches he meant, no doubt," said Shepherd Fennel. "I thought his hands were palish for's trade."

"Well, it appears to me that nothing can be gained by retaining this poor man in custody," said the magistrate; "your business lies with the other, unquestionably."

And so the little man was released off-hand; but he looked nothing the less sad on that account, it being beyond the power of magistrate or constable to raze out the written troubles in his brain, for they concerned another whom he regarded with more solicitude than himself. When this was done, and the man had gone his way, the night was found to be so far advanced that it was deemed useless to renew the search before the next morning.

Next day, accordingly, the quest for the clever sheep-stealer became general and keen, to all appearance at least. But the intended punishment was cruelly disproportioned to the transgression, and the sympathy of a great many country-folk in that district was strongly on the side of the fugitive. Moreover, his marvelous coolness and daring in hob-and-nobbing with the hangman, under the unprecedented circumstances of the shepherd's party, won their admiration. So that it may be questioned if all those who ostensibly made themselves so busy in exploring woods and fields and lanes were quite so thorough when it came to the private examination of their own lofts and outhouses. Stories were afloat of a mysterious figure being occasionally seen in some overgrown trackway or other, remote from turnpike roads; but when a search was instituted in any of these suspected quarters, nobody was found. Thus the days and weeks passed without tidings.

In brief, the bass-voiced man of the chimney-corner was never recaptured. Some said that he went across the sea, others that he did not, but buried himself in the depths of a populous city. At any rate, the gentleman in cinder-gray never did his morning's work at Casterbridge, nor met anywhere at all, for business purposes, the genial comrade with whom he had passed an hour of relaxation in the lonely house on the coomb.

The grass has long been green on the graves of Shepherd Fennel and his frugal wife; the guests who made up the christening party have mainly followed their entertainers to the tomb; the baby in whose honor they all had met is a matron in the sere and yellow leaf. But the arrival of the three strangers at the shepherd's that night, and the details connected therewith, is a story as well known as ever in the country about Higher Crowstairs.

JAMES THURBER

The Rabbits Who Caused All the Trouble

James Thurber (1894–1961), born in Columbus, Ohio, and educated at Ohio State University, began his literary career in journalism. From 1927 to 1933, he was on the staff of *The New Yorker,* to which he frequently contributed drawings and stories. Some of his best-known books are *Is Sex Necessary?* (in collaboration with E. B. White), 1929, a parody of books on sex education; *My Life and Hard Times,* 1933, an autobiography; *The Thurber Carnival,* 1945, a collection of his best work to that date; *The Beast in Me, and Other Animals,* 1948; *Thurber Country,* 1953; and *Lanterns and Lances,* 1961. In 1940 he collaborated with Elliott Nugent, who had been a fellow student at Ohio State, on a play, *The Male Animal,* a comedy about university life. Thurber also wrote a number of fairy tales and fables for children and adults which contain acute comments on present-day life.

From Aesop's time to the present, many writers have chosen to disguise the human character in animal fables. "The Rabbits Who Caused All the Trouble" illustrates Thurber's whimsy as well as the deftness of the fable form.

Within the memory of the youngest child there was a family of rabbits who lived near a pack of wolves. The wolves announced that they did not like the way the rabbits were living. (The wolves were crazy about the way they themselves were living, because it was the only way to live.) One night several wolves were killed in an earthquake and this was blamed on the rabbits, for it is well known that rabbits pound on the ground with their hind legs and cause earthquakes. On another night one of the wolves was killed by a bolt of lightning and this was also blamed on the rabbits, for it is well known that lettuce-eaters cause lightning. The wolves threatened to civilize the rabbits if they didn't behave, and the rabbits decided to run away to a desert island. But the other animals, who lived at a great distance, shamed them, saying, "You must stay where you are and be brave. This is no world for escapists. If the wolves attack you, we will come to your aid, in all probability." So the rabbits continued to live near the wolves and one day there was a terrible flood which drowned a great many wolves. This was blamed on the rabbits, for it is well known that carrot-nibblers with long ears cause floods. The wolves descended on the rabbits, for their own good, and imprisoned them in a dark cave, for their own protection.

When nothing was heard about the rabbits for some weeks, the other animals demanded to know what had happened to them. The wolves replied that the rabbits had been eaten and since they had been eaten the affair was a purely internal matter. But the other animals warned that they might possibly unite against the wolves unless some reason was given for the destruction of the rabbits. So the wolves gave them one. "They were trying to escape," said the wolves, "and, as you know, this is no world for escapists."

Moral: Run, don't walk, to the nearest desert island.

JOSEPH CONRAD

The Lagoon

Joseph Conrad (1857–1924) was born of Polish parents in the Ukraine and was named Jozef Teodor Konrad Nalecz Korzeniowski. He spent his childhood and early youth in Russia as an exile with his parents, who left him an orphan at the age of twelve to be brought up by his uncle in Cracow, Poland. As a boy, Conrad was fascinated by romantic tales of adventure at sea, and at seventeen he went to sea in the French merchant service. In 1878 he changed over to the British service; by 1884 he had become a ship's master, had taken on British citizenship, and had acquired an extraordinary command of English—the language in which he did all his writing. His first novel, *Almayer's Folly*, was begun in 1889 but not published until 1895. It was followed by *An Outcast of the Islands*, 1896; *The Nigger of the Narcissus*, 1897; *Lord Jim*, 1900; and many other novels, several collections of short stories, reminiscences, and literary essays.

In "The Lagoon," as in all of his writings, Conrad is preoccupied with man's need for fidelity, honor, and courage. Here, as elsewhere, he is a master both at creating an atmosphere through richly realistic settings and at probing deep into the moral and psychological motives of his characters.

The white man, leaning with both arms over the roof of the little house in the stern of the boat, said to the steersman—

THE LAGOON From *Tales of Unrest* by Joseph Conrad. Reprinted by permission of J. M. Dent & Sons Ltd., publishers.

"We will pass the night in Arsat's clearing. It is late."

The Malay only grunted, and went on looking fixedly at the river. The white man rested his chin on his crossed arms and gazed at the wake of the boat. At the end of the straight avenue of forests cut by the intense glitter of the river, the sun appeared unclouded and dazzling; poised low over the water that shown smoothly like a band of metal. The forests, somber and dull, stood motionless and silent on each side of the broad stream. At the foot of big, towering trees, trunkless nipa palms rose from the mud of the bank, in bunches of leaves enormous and heavy, that hung unstirring over the brown swirl of eddies. In the stillness of the air every tree, every leaf, every bough, every tendril of creeper and every petal of minute blossoms seemed to have been bewitched into an immobility perfect and final. Nothing moved on the river but the eight paddles that rose flashing regularly, dipped together with a single splash; while the steersman swept right and left with a periodic and sudden flourish of his blade describing a glinting semicircle above his head. The churned-up water frothed alongside with a confused murmur. And the white man's canoe, advancing upstream in the short-lived disturbance of its own making, seemed to enter the portals of a land from which the very memory of motion had forever departed.

The white man, turning his back upon the setting sun, looked along the empty and broad expanse of the sea-reach. For the last three miles of its course the wandering, hesitating river, as if enticed irresistibly by the freedom of an open horizon, flows straight into the sea, flows straight to the east—to the east that harbors both light and darkness. Astern of the boat the repeated call of some bird, a cry discordant and feeble, skipped along over the smooth water and lost itself, before it could reach the other shore, in the breathless silence of the world.

The steersman dug his paddle into the stream, and held hard with stiffened arms, his body thrown forward. The water gurgled aloud; and suddenly the long straight reach seemed to pivot on its center, the forests swung in a semicircle, and the slanting beams of sunset touched the broadside of the canoe with a fiery glow, throwing the slender and distorted shadows of its crew upon the streaked glitter of the river. The white man turned to look ahead. The course of the boat

had been altered at right-angles to the stream, and the carved dragon-head of its prow was pointing now at a gap in the fringing bushes of the bank. It glided through, brushing the overhanging twigs, and disappeared from the river like some slim and amphibious creature leaving the water for its lair in the forests.

The narrow creek was like a ditch: tortuous, fabulously deep; filled with gloom under the thin strip of pure and shining blue of the heaven. Immense trees soared up, invisible behind the festooned draperies of creepers. Here and there, near the glistening blackness of the water, a twisted root of some tall tree showed amongst the tracery of small ferns, black and dull, writhing and motionless, like an arrested snake. The short words of the paddlers reverberated loudly between the thick and somber walls of vegetation. Darkness oozed out from between the trees, through the tangled maze of the creepers, from behind the great fantastic and unstirring leaves; the darkness, mysterious and invincible; the darkness scented and poisonous of impenetrable forests.

The men poled in the shoaling water. The creek broadened, opening out into a wide sweep of a stagnant lagoon. The forests receded from the marshy bank, leaving a level strip of bright green, reedy grass to frame the reflected blueness of the sky. A fleecy pink cloud drifted high above, trailing the delicate coloring of its image under the floating leaves and the silvery blossoms of the lotus. A little house, perched on high poles, appeared black in the distance. Near it, two tall nibong palms, that seemed to have come out of the forests in the background, leaned slightly over the ragged roof, with a suggestion of sad tenderness and care in the droop of their leafy and soaring heads.

The steersman, pointing with his paddle, said, "Arsat is there. I see his canoe fast between the piles."

The polers ran along the sides of the boat, glancing over their shoulders at the end of the day's journey. They would have preferred to spend the night somewhere else than on this lagoon of weird aspect and ghostly reputation. Moreover, they disliked Arsat, first as a stranger, and also because he who repairs a ruined house, and dwells in it, proclaims that he is not afraid to live amongst the spirits that haunt the places abandoned by mankind. Such a man can disturb the course of fate by glances or words; while his familiar ghosts are not easy to propitiate by casual wayfarers upon whom they long to wreak the malice of their human master. White men care not for such things, being unbelievers and in league with the Father of Evil, who leads them unharmed through the invisible dangers of this world. To the warnings of the righteous they oppose an offensive pretense of disbelief. What is there to be done?

So they thought, throwing their weight on the end of their long poles. The big canoe glided on swiftly, noiselessly, and smoothly, towards Arsat's clearing, till, in a great rattling of poles thrown down, and the loud murmurs of "Allah be praised!" it came with a gentle knock against the crooked piles below the house.

The boatmen with uplifted faces shouted discordantly, "Arsat! O Arsat!" Nobody came. The white man began to climb the rude ladder giving access to the bamboo platform before the house. The juragan of the boat said sulkily, "We will cook in the sampan, and sleep on the water."

"Pass my blankets and the basket," said the white man, curtly.

He knelt on the edge of the platform to receive the bundle. Then the boat shoved off, and the white man, standing up, confronted Arsat, who had come out through the low door of his hut. He was a man young, powerful, with broad chest and muscular arms. He had nothing on but his sarong. His head was bare. His big, soft eyes stared eagerly at the white man, but his voice and demeanor were composed as he asked, without any words of greeting—

"Have you medicine, Tuan?"

"No," said the visitor in a startled tone. "No. Why? Is there sickness in the house?"

"Enter and see," replied Arsat, in the same calm manner, and turning short round, passed again through the small doorway. The white man, dropping his bundles, followed.

In the dim light of the dwelling he made out on a couch of bamboos a woman stretched on her back under a broad sheet of red cotton cloth. She lay still, as if dead; but her big eyes, wide open, glittered in the gloom, staring upwards at the slender rafters, motionless and unseeing. She was in a high fever, and evidently unconscious. Her cheeks were sunk slightly, her lips were partly open, and on the young face there was the ominous and fixed expression—the absorbed, contemplating expression of the unconscious who are going to die. The two men stood looking down at her in silence.

"Has she been long ill?" asked the traveler.

"I have not slept for five nights," answered the Malay, in a deliberate tone. "At first she heard voices calling her from the water and struggled against me who held her. But since the sun of today rose she hears nothing—she hears not me. She sees nothing. She sees not me—me!"

He remained silent for a minute, then asked softly—

"Tuan, will she die?"

"I fear so," said the white man, sorrowfully. He had known Arsat years ago, in a far country in times of trouble and danger, when no friendship is to be despised. And since his Malay friend had come unexpectedly to dwell in the hut on the lagoon with a strange woman, he had slept many times there, in his journeys up and down the river. He liked the man who knew how to keep faith in council and how to fight without fear by the side of his white friend. He liked him—not so much perhaps as a man likes his favorite dog—but still he liked him well enough to help and ask no questions, to think sometimes vaguely and hazily in the midst of his own pursuits, about the lonely man and the long-haired woman with audacious face and triumphant eyes, who lived together hidden by the forest—alone and feared.

The white man came out of the hut in time to see the enormous conflagration of sunset put out by the swift and stealthy shadows that, rising like a black and impalpable vapor above the tree-tops, spread over the heaven, extinguishing the crimson glow of floating clouds and the red brilliance of departing daylight.

In a few moments all the stars came out above the intense blackness of the earth and the great lagoon, gleaming suddenly with reflected lights, resembled an oval patch of night sky flung down into the hopeless and abysmal night of the wilderness. The white man had some supper out of the basket, then collecting a few sticks that lay about the platform, made up a small fire, not for warmth, but for the sake of the smoke, which would keep off the mosquitoes. He wrapped himself in the blankets and sat with his back against the reed wall of the house, smoking thoughtfully.

Arsat came through the doorway with noiseless steps and squatted down by the fire. The white man moved his outstretched legs a little.

"She breathes," said Arsat in a low voice, anticipating the expected question. "She breathes and burns as if with a great fire. She speaks not; she hears not—and burns!"

He paused for a moment, then asked in a quiet, incurious tone—

"Tuan . . . will she die?"

The white man moved his shoulders uneasily and muttered in a hesitating manner—

"If such is her fate."

"No, Tuan," said Arsat, calmly. "If such is my fate. I hear, I see, I wait. I remember . . . Tuan, do you remember the old days? Do you remember my brother?"

"Yes," said the white man. The Malay rose suddenly and went in. The other, sitting still outside, could hear the voice in the hut. Arsat said: "Hear me! Speak!" His words were succeeded by a complete silence. "O Diamelen!" he cried, suddenly. After that cry there was a deep sigh. Arsat came out and sank down again in his old place.

They sat in silence before the fire. There was no sound within the house, there was no sound near them; but far away on the lagoon they could hear the voices of the boatmen ringing fitful and distinct on the calm water. The fire in the bows of the sampan shone faintly in the distance with a hazy red glow. Then it died out. The voices ceased. The land and the water slept invisible, unstirring and mute. It was as though there had been nothing left in the world but the glitter of stars streaming, ceaseless and vain, through the black stillness of the night.

The white man gazed straight before him into the darkness with wide-open eyes. The fear and fascination, the inspiration and the wonder of death—of death near, unavoidable, and unseen, soothed the unrest of his race and stirred the most indistinct, the most intimate of his thoughts. The ever-ready suspicion of evil, the gnawing suspicion that lurks in our hearts, flowed out into the stillness round him—into the stillness profound and dumb, and made it appear untrustworthy and infamous, like the placid and impenetrable mask of an unjustifiable violence. In that fleeting and powerful disturbance of his being the earth enfolded in the starlight peace became a shadowy country of inhuman strife, a battlefield of phantoms terrible and charming, august or ignoble, struggling ardently for the possession of our helpless hearts. An unquiet and mysterious country of inextinguishable desires and fears.

A plaintive murmur rose in the night; a murmur saddening and startling, as if the great solitudes of surrounding woods had tried to whisper into his ear the wisdom of their immense and lofty indifference. Sounds hesitating and vague floated in the air around him, shaped themselves slowly into words; and at last flowed on gently in a murmuring stream of soft and monotonous sentences. He stirred like a man waking up and changed his position slightly. Arsat, motionless and shadowy, sitting with bowed head under the stars, was speaking in a low and dreamy tone—

". . . for where can we lay down the heaviness of our trouble but in a friend's heart? A man must speak of war and of love. You, Tuan, know what war is, and you have seen me in time of danger seek death as other men seek life! A writing may be lost; a lie may be written; but what the eye has seen is truth and remains in the mind!"

"I remember," said the white man, quietly. Arsat went on with mournful composure—

"Therefore I shall speak to you of love. Speak in the night. Speak before both night and love are gone—and the eye of day looks upon my sorrow and my shame; upon my blackened face; upon my burnt-up heart."

A sigh, short and faint, marked an almost imperceptible pause, and then his words flowed on, without a stir, without a gesture.

"After the time of trouble and war was over and you went away from my country in the pursuit of your desires, which we, men of the islands, cannot understand, I and my brother became again, as we had been before, the sword-bearers of the Ruler. You know we were men of family, belonging to a ruling race, and more fit than any to carry on our right shoulder the emblem of power. And in the time of prosperity Si Dendring showed us favor, as we, in time of sorrow, had showed to him the faithfulness of our courage. It was a time of peace. A time of deer-hunts and cock-fights; of idle talks and foolish squabbles between men whose bellies are full and weapons are rusty. But the sower watched the young rice-shoots grow up without fear, and the traders came and went, departed lean and returned fat into the river of peace. They brought news, too. Brought lies and truth mixed together, so that no man knew when to rejoice and when to be sorry. We heard from them about you also. They had seen you here and had seen you there. And I was glad to hear, for I remembered the stirring times, and I always remembered you, Tuan, till the time came when my eyes could see nothing in the past, because they had looked upon the one who is dying there—in the house."

He stopped to exclaim in an intense whisper, "O Mara bahia! O Calamity!" then went on speaking a little louder:

"There's no worse enemy and no better friend than a brother, Tuan, for one brother knows another, and in perfect knowledge is strength for good or evil. I loved my brother. I went to him and told him that I could see nothing but one face, hear nothing but one voice. He told me: 'Open your heart so that she can see what is in it—and wait. Patience is wisdom. Inchi Midah may die or our Ruler may throw off his fear of a woman!' . . . I waited! . . . You remember the lady with the veiled face, Tuan, and the fear of our Ruler before her cunning and temper. And

if she wanted her servant, what could I do? But I fed the hunger of my heart on short glances and stealthy words. I loitered on the path to the bath-houses in the daytime, and when the sun had fallen behind the forest I crept along the jasmine hedges of the women's courtyard. Unseeing, we spoke to one another through the scent of flowers, through the veil of leaves, through the blades of long grass that stood still before our lips; so great was our prudence, so faint was the murmur of our great longing. The time passed swiftly . . . and there were whispers amongst women—and our enemies watched—my brother was gloomy, and I began to think of killing and of a fierce death. . . . We are of a people who take what they want—like you whites. There is a time when a man should forget loyalty and respect. Might and authority are given to rulers, but to all men is given love and strength and courage. My brother said, 'You shall take her from their midst. We are two who are like one.' And I answered, 'Let it be soon, for I find no warmth in sunlight that does not shine upon her.' Our time came when the Ruler and all the great people went to the mouth of the river to fish by torchlight. There were hundreds of boats, and on the white sand, between the water and the forests, dwellings of leaves were built for the households of the Rajahs. The smoke of cooking-fires was like a blue mist of the evening, and many voices rang in it joyfully. While they were making the boats ready to beat up the fish, my brother came to me and said, 'Tonight!' I looked to my weapons, and when the time came our canoe took its place in the circle of boats carrying the torches. The lights blazed on the water, but behind the boats there was darkness. When the shouting began and the excitement made them like mad we dropped out. The water swallowed our fire, and we floated back to the shore that was dark with only here and there the glimmer of embers. We could hear the talk of slave-girls amongst the sheds. Then we found a place deserted and silent. We waited there. She came. She came running along the shore, rapid and leaving no trace, like a leaf driven by the wind into the sea. My brother said gloomily, 'Go and take her; carry her into our boat.' I lifted her in my arms. She panted. Her heart was beating against my breast. I said, 'I take you from those people. You came to the cry of my heart, but my arms take you into my boat against the will of the great!' 'It is right,' said my brother. 'We are men who take what we want and can hold it against many. We should have taken her in daylight.' I said, 'Let us be off'; for since she was in my boat I began to think of our Ruler's many men. 'Yes. Let us be off,' said my brother. 'We are cast out and this boat is our country now—and the sea is our refuge.' He lingered with his foot on the shore, and I entreated him to hasten, for I remembered the strokes of her heart against my breast and thought that two men cannot withstand a hundred. We left, paddling downstream close to the bank; and as we passed by the creek where they were fishing, the great shouting had ceased, but the murmur of voices was loud like the humming of insects flying at noonday. The boats floated, clustered together, in the red light of torches, under a black roof of smoke; and men talked of their sport. Men that boasted, and praised, and jeered—men that would have been our friends in the morning, but on that night were already our enemies. We paddled swiftly past. We had no more friends in the country of our birth. She sat in the middle of the canoe with covered face; silent as she is now; unseeing as she is now—and I had no regret at what I was leaving because I could hear her breathing close to me—as I can hear her now."

He paused, listened with his ear turned to the doorway, then shook his head and went on:

"My brother wanted to shout the cry of challenge—one cry only—to let the people know we were freeborn robbers who trusted our arms and the great sea. And again I begged him in the name of our love to be silent. Could I not hear her breathing close to me? I knew the pursuit would come quick enough. My brother loved me. He dipped his paddle without a splash. He only said, 'There is half a man in you now—the other half is in that woman. I can wait. When you are a whole man again, you will come back with me here to shout defiance. We are sons of the same mother.' I made no answer. All my strength and all my spirit were in my hands that held the paddle—for I longed to be with her in a safe place beyond the reach of men's anger and of women's spite. My love was so great, that I thought it could guide me to a country where death was unknown, if I could only escape from Inchi Midah's fury and from our Ruler's sword. We paddled with haste, breathing through our teeth. The blades bit deep into the smooth water. We passed out of the river; we flew in clear channels amongst the shallows. We skirted the black coast; we skirted the sand beaches where the sea speaks in whispers to the land; and the gleam of white sand flashed back past our boat, so swiftly she ran upon the water. We spoke not. Only once I said, 'Sleep, Diamelen, for soon you may want all your strength.' I heard the sweetness of her voice, but I never turned my head. The sun rose and still we went on. Water fell from my face like rain from a cloud. We flew in the light and heat. I never looked back, but I knew that my brother's eyes, behind me, were looking steadily ahead, for the boat went as straight as a bushman's dart, when it leaves the end of the sumpitan. There was no better paddler, no better steersman than my brother. Many times, together, we had won races in that canoe. But we never had put out our strength as we did then—then, when for the last time we paddled together! There was no braver or stronger man in our country than my brother. I could not spare the strength to turn my head and look at him, but every moment I heard the hiss of his breath getting louder behind me. Still he did not speak. The sun was high. The heat clung to my back like a flame of fire. My ribs were ready to burst, but I could no longer get enough air into my chest. And then I felt I must cry out with my last breath, 'Let us rest!' . . . 'Good!' he answered; and his voice was firm. He was strong. He was brave. He knew not fear and no fatigue . . . My brother!"

A murmur powerful and gentle, a murmur vast and faint; the murmur of trembling leaves, of stirring boughs, ran through the tangled depths of the forests, ran over the starry smoothness of the lagoon, and the water between the piles lapped the slimy timber once with a sudden splash. A breath of warm air touched the two men's faces and passed on with a mournful sound—a breath loud and short like an uneasy sigh of the dreaming earth.

Arsat went on in an even, low voice.

"We ran our canoe on the white beach of a little bay close to a long tongue of land that seemed to bar our road; a long wooded cape going far into the sea. My brother knew that place. Beyond the cape a river has its entrance, and through the jungle of that land there is a narrow path. We made a fire and cooked rice. Then we lay down to sleep on the soft sand in the shade of our canoe, while she watched. No sooner had I closed my eyes than I heard her cry of alarm. We leaped up. The sun was halfway down the sky already, and coming in sight in the opening of the bay we saw a prau manned by many paddlers. We knew it at once; it was one of our Rajah's praus. They were watching the shore, and saw us. They beat the gong, and turned the head of the prau into the bay. I felt my heart become weak within my breast. Diamelen sat on the sand and covered her face. There was no escape by sea. My brother laughed. He had the gun you had given him, Tuan, before you went away, but there was only a handful of powder. He spoke to me quickly: 'Run with her along the path. I shall keep them back, for they have no firearms, and landing in the face of a man with a gun is certain death for some. Run with her. On the other side of that wood there is a fisherman's house—and a canoe. When I have fired all the shots I will follow. I am a great runner, and before they can come up we shall be gone. I will hold out as long as I can, for she is but a woman—that can neither run nor fight, but she has your heart in her weak hands.' He dropped behind the canoe. The prau was coming. She and I ran, and as we rushed along the path I heard shots. My brother fired—once—twice—and the booming of the gong ceased. There was si-lence behind us. That neck of land is narrow. Before I heard my brother fire the third shot I saw the shelving shore, and I saw the water again; the mouth of a broad river. We crossed a grassy glade. We ran down to the water. I saw a low hut above the black mud, and a small canoe hauled up. I heard another shot behind me. I thought, 'This is his last charge.' We rushed down to the canoe; a man came running from the hut, but I leaped on him, and we rolled together in the mud. Then I got up, and he lay still at my feet. I don't know whether I had killed him or not. I and Diamelen pushed the canoe afloat. I heard yells behind me, and I saw my brother run across the glade. Many men were bounding after him. I took her in my arms and threw her into the boat, then leaped in myself. When I looked back I saw that my brother had fallen. He fell and was up again, but the men were closing round him. He shouted, 'I am coming!' The men were close to him. I looked. Many men. Then I looked at her. Tuan, I pushed the canoe! I pushed it into deep water. She was kneeling forward looking at me, and I said, 'Take your paddle,' while I struck the water with mine. Tuan, I heard him cry. I heard him cry my name twice; and I heard voices shouting, 'Kill! Strike!' I never turned back. I heard him calling my name again with a great shriek, as when life is going to-gether with the voice—and I never turned my head. My own name! . . . My brother! Three times he called—but I was not afraid of life. Was she not there in that canoe? And could I not with her find a country where death is for-gotten—where death is unknown!"

The white man sat up. Arsat rose and stood, an indistinct and silent figure above the dying embers of the fire. Over the lagoon a mist drifting and low had crept, erasing slowly the glittering images of the stars. And now a great expanse of white vapor covered the land: it flowed cold and gray in the darkness, eddied in noiseless whirls round the tree-trunks and about the platform of the house, which seemed to float upon a restless and impal-pable illusion of a sea. Only far away the tops of the trees stood outlined on the twinkle of heaven, like a somber and forbidding shore—a coast deceptive, pitiless and black.

Arsat's voice vibrated loudly in the profound peace. "I had her there! I had her! To get her I would have faced all mankind. But I had her—and—"

His words went out ringing into the empty distances. He paused, and seemed to listen to them dying away very far—beyond help and beyond recall. Then he said quietly—

"Tuan, I loved my brother."

A breath of wind made him shiver. High above his head, high above the silent sea of mist the drooping leaves of the palms rattled together with a mournful and expiring sound. The white man stretched his legs. His chin rested on his chest, and he murmured sadly without lifting his head—

"We all love our brothers."

Arsat burst out with an intense whispering violence—

"What did I care who died? I wanted peace in my own heart."

He seemed to hear a stir in the house—listened—then stepped in noiselessly. The white man stood up. A breeze was coming in fitful puffs. The stars shone paler as if they had retreated into the frozen depths of immense space. After a chill gust of wind there were a few seconds of perfect calm and absolute silence. Then from behind the black and wavy line of the forests a column of golden light shot up into the heavens and spread over the semicircle of the eastern horizon. The sun had risen. The mist lifted, broke into drifting patches, vanished into thin flying wreaths; and the unveiled lagoon lay, polished and black, in the heavy shadows at the foot of the wall of trees. A white eagle rose over it with a slanting and ponderous flight, reached the clear sunshine and appeared dazzlingly brilliant for a moment, then soaring higher, became a dark and motionless speck before it vanished into the blue as if it had left the earth forever. The white man, standing gazing upwards before the doorway, heard in the hut a confused and broken murmur of distracted words ending with a loud groan. Suddenly Arsat stumbled out with outstretched

hands, shivered, and stood still for some time with fixed eyes. Then he said—

"She burns no more."

Before his face the sun showed its edge above the treetops rising steadily. The breeze freshened; a great brilliance burst upon the lagoon, sparkled on the rippling water. The forests came out of the clear shadows of the morning, became distinct, as if they had rushed nearer—to stop short in a great stir of leaves, of nodding boughs, of swaying branches. In the merciless sunshine the whisper of unconscious life grew louder, speaking in an incomprehensible voice round the dumb darkness of that human sorrow. Arsat's eyes wandered slowly, then stared at the rising sun.

"I can see nothing," he said half aloud to himself.

"There is nothing," said the white man, moving to the edge of the platform and waving his hand to his boat. A shout came faintly over the lagoon and the sampan began to glide towards the abode of the friend of ghosts.

"If you want to come with me, I will wait all the morning," said the white man, looking away upon the water.

"No, Tuan," said Arsat, softly. "I shall not eat or sleep in this house, but I must first see my road. Now I can see nothing—see nothing! There is no light and no peace in the world; but there is death—death for many. We are sons of the same mother—and I left him in the midst of enemies; but I am going back now."

He drew a long breath and went on in a dreamy tone:

"In a little while I shall see clear enough to strike—to strike. But she has died, and . . . now . . . darkness."

He flung his arms wide open, let them fall along his body, then stood still with unmoved face and stony eyes, staring at the sun. The white man got down into his canoe. The polers ran smartly along the sides of the boat, looking over their shoulders at the beginning of a weary journey. High in the stern, his head muffled up in white rags, the juragan sat moody, letting his paddle trail in the water. The white man, leaning with both arms over the grass roof of the little cabin, looked back at the shining ripple of the boat's wake. Before the sampan passed out of the lagoon into the creek he lifted his eyes. Arsat had not moved. He stood lonely in the searching sunshine; and he looked beyond the great light of a cloudless day into the darkness of a world of illusions.

SHIRLEY JACKSON

After You, My Dear Alphonse

Shirley Jackson (1919–1966) was an essayist, novelist, and short-story writer, much of whose work originally appeared in *The New Yorker*. Her books include *The Road Through the Wall*, 1948; *The Lottery, or The Adventures of James Harris*, 1949; *Life Among the Savages*, 1953; *Raising Demons*, 1957; *The Haunting of Hill House*, 1959; and *We Have Always Lived in the Castle*, 1962.

Children not infrequently put their elders to shame. In this story, the innocent eye is at work with all of its resultant irony.

Mrs. Wilson was just taking the gingerbread out of the oven when she heard Johnny outside talking to someone.

"Johnny," she called, "you're late. Come in and get your lunch."

"Just a minute, Mother," Johnny said. "After you, my dear Alphonse."

"After *you*, my dear Alphonse," another voice said.

"No, after *you*, my dear Alphonse," Johnny said.

Mrs. Wilson opened the door. "Johnny," she said, "you come in this minute and get your lunch. You can play after you've eaten."

Johnny came in after her, slowly. "Mother,"

AFTER YOU, MY DEAR ALPHONSE Reprinted from *The Lottery* by Shirley Jackson, by permission of Farrar, Straus & Giroux, Inc. Copyright 1943, 1949 by Shirley Jackson. First published in *The New Yorker*.

he said, "I brought Boyd home for lunch with me."

"Boyd?" Mrs. Wilson thought for a moment. "I don't believe I've met Boyd. Bring him in, dear, since you've invited him. Lunch is ready."

"Boyd!" Johnny yelled. "Hey, Boyd, come on in!"

"I'm coming. Just got to unload this stuff."

"Well, hurry, or my mother'll be sore."

"Johnny, that's not very polite to either your friend or your mother," Mrs. Wilson said. "Come sit down, Boyd."

As she turned to show Boyd where to sit, she saw he was a Negro boy, smaller than Johnny but about the same age. His arms were loaded with split kindling wood. "Where'll I put this stuff, Johnny?" he asked.

Mrs. Wilson turned to Johnny. "Johnny," she said, "what is that wood?"

"Dead Japanese," Johnny said mildly. "We stand them in the ground and run over them with tanks."

"How do you do, Mrs. Wilson?" Boyd said.

"How do you do, Boyd? You shouldn't let Johnny make you carry all that wood. Sit down now and eat lunch, both of you."

"Why shouldn't he carry the wood, Mother? It's his wood. We got it at his place."

"Johnny," Mrs. Wilson said, "go on and eat your lunch."

"Sure," Johnny said. He held out the dish of scrambled eggs to Boyd. "After you, my dear Alphonse."

"After *you*, my dear Alphonse," Boyd said.

"After *you*, my dear Alphonse," Johnny said. They began to giggle.

"Are you hungry, Boyd?" Mrs. Wilson asked.

"Yes, Mrs. Wilson."

"Well, don't you let Johnny stop you. He always fusses about eating, so you just see that you get a good lunch. There's plenty of food here for you to have all you want."

"Thank you, Mrs. Wilson."

"Come on, Alphonse," Johnny said. He pushed half the scrambled eggs on to Boyd's plate. Boyd watched while Mrs. Wilson put a dish of stewed tomatoes beside his plate.

"Boyd don't eat tomatoes, do you, Boyd?" Johnny said.

"*Doesn't* eat tomatoes, Johnny. And just because you don't like them, don't say that about Boyd. Boyd will eat *anything*."

"Bet he won't," Johnny said, attacking his scrambled eggs.

"Boyd wants to grow up and be a big strong man so he can work hard," Mrs. Wilson said. "I'll bet Boyd's father eats stewed tomatoes."

"My father eats anything he wants to," Boyd said.

"So does mine," Johnny said. "Sometimes he doesn't eat hardly anything. He's a little guy, though. Wouldn't hurt a flea."

"Mine's a little guy, too," Boyd said.

"I'll bet he's strong, though," Mrs. Wilson said. She hesitated. "Does he . . . work?"

"Sure," Johnny said. "Boyd's father works in a factory."

"There, you see?" Mrs. Wilson said. "And

he certainly has to be strong to do that—all that lifting and carrying at a factory."

"Boyd's father doesn't have to," Johnny said. "He's a foreman."

Mrs. Wilson felt defeated. "What does your mother do, Boyd?"

"My mother?" Boyd was surprised. "She takes care of us kids."

"Oh. She doesn't work, then?"

"Why should she?" Johnny said through a mouthful of eggs. "You don't work."

"You really don't want any stewed tomatoes, Boyd?"

"No, thank you, Mrs. Wilson," Boyd said.

"No, thank you, Mrs. Wilson, no, thank you, Mrs. Wilson, no, thank you, Mrs. Wilson," Johnny said. "Boyd's sister's going to work, though. She's going to be a teacher."

"That's a very fine attitude for her to have, Boyd." Mrs. Wilson restrained an impulse to pat Boyd on the head. "I imagine you're all very proud of her?"

"I guess so," Boyd said.

"What about all your other brothers and sisters? I guess all of you want to make just as much of yourselves as you can."

"There's only me and Jean," Boyd said. "I don't know yet what I want to be when I grow up."

"We're going to be tank drivers, Boyd and me," Johnny said. "Zoom." Mrs. Wilson caught Boyd's glass of milk as Johnny's napkin ring, suddenly transformed into a tank plowed heavily across the table.

"Look, Johnny," Boyd said. "Here's a foxhole. I'm shooting at you."

Mrs. Wilson, with the speed born of long experience, took the gingerbread off the shelf and placed it carefully between the tank and the foxhole.

"Now eat as much as you want to, Boyd," she said. "I want to see you get filled up."

"Boyd eats a lot, but not as much as I do," Johnny said. "I'm bigger than he is."

"You're not much bigger," Boyd said. "I can beat you running."

Mrs. Wilson took a deep breath. "Boyd," she said. Both boys turned to her. "Boyd, Johnny has some suits that are a little too small for him, and a winter coat. It's not new, of course, but there's lots of wear in it still. And I have a few dresses that your mother or sister could probably use. Your mother can make them over into lots of things for all of you, and I'd be very happy to give them to you. Suppose before you leave I make up a big bundle and then you and Johnny can take it over to your mother right away . . ." Her voice trailed off as she saw Boyd's puzzled expression.

"But I have plenty of clothes, thank you," he said. "And I don't think my mother knows how to sew very well, and anyway I guess we buy about everything we need. Thank you very much though."

"We don't have time to carry that old stuff around, Mother," Johnny said. "We got to play tanks with the kids today."

Mrs. Wilson lifted the plate of gingerbread off the table as Boyd was about to take another piece. "There are many little boys like you, Boyd, who would be grateful for the clothes someone was kind enough to give them."

"Boyd will take them if you want him to, Mother," Johnny said.

"I didn't mean to make you mad, Mrs. Wilson," Boyd said.

"Don't think I'm angry, Boyd. I'm just disappointed in you, that's all. Now let's not say anything more about it."

She began clearing the plates off the table, and Johnny took Boyd's hand and pulled him to the door. "'Bye, Mother," Johnny said. Boyd stood for a minute, staring at Mrs. Wilson's back.

"After you, my dear Alphonse," Johnny said, holding the door open.

"Is your mother still mad?" Mrs. Wilson heard Boyd ask in a low voice.

"I don't know," Johnny said. "She's screwy sometimes."

"So's mine," Boyd said. He hesitated. "After *you*, my dear Alphonse."

ERNEST HEMINGWAY

After the Storm

Ernest Hemingway (1899–1961) was born in Oak Park, Illinois. During World War I he volunteered for service in an ambulance corps in France and later transferred to the Italian Army. After the war he became a newspaper correspondent in Paris, where he met Ezra Pound and Gertrude Stein who profoundly influenced his literary career.

Much of Hemingway's material was drawn from his personal experience. His short stories, collected in *The Short Stories of Ernest Hemingway,* 1954, are evidence of the variety and versatility of his writing. He is best known for his novels, the most prominent of which are *The Sun Also Rises,* 1926; *A Farewell to Arms,* 1929; *For Whom the Bell Tolls,* 1940; and *The Old Man and the Sea,* 1952. His last book was *A Moveable Feast,* published posthumously in 1964. He was awarded the Nobel Prize for Literature in 1954.

Hemingway's writings reflect his philosophy that man is a doomed creature whose only hope is to face the inevitable stoically. Edmund Wilson said that "with barometric accuracy" he seized "the real moral feeling of the moment" even though "his vision of life is one of perpetual annihilation." In his short stories and his novels there appears the famous Hemingway dialogue—short, clipped, and bare, the very essence of speech. "After the Storm" is characteristic of both his technique and his philosophy.

It wasn't about anything, something about making punch, and then we started fighting and I slipped and he had me down kneeling on my chest and choking me with both hands like he was trying to kill me and all the time I was trying to get the knife out of my pocket to cut him loose. Everybody was too drunk to pull him off me. He was choking me and hammering my head on the floor and I got the knife out and opened it up; and I cut the muscle right across his arm and he let go of me. He couldn't have held on if he wanted to. Then he rolled and hung onto that arm and started to cry and I said:

"What the hell you want to choke me for?"

I'd have killed him. I couldn't swallow for a week. He hurt my throat bad.

Well, I went out of there and there were plenty of them with him and some come out after me and I made a turn and was down by the docks and I met a fellow and he said somebody killed a man up the street. I said "Who killed him?" and he said "I don't know who killed him but he's dead all right," and it was dark and there was water standing in the street and no lights and windows broke and boats all up in the town and trees blown down and everything all blown and I got a skiff and went out and found my boat where I had her inside of Mango Key and she was all right only she was full of water. So I bailed her out and pumped her out and there was a moon but plenty of clouds and still plenty rough and I took it down along; and when it was daylight I was off Eastern Harbor.

Brother, that was some storm. I was the

first boat out and you never saw water like that was. It was just as white as a lye barrel and coming from Eastern Harbor to Sou'west Key you couldn't recognize the shore. There was a big channel blown right out through the middle of the beach. Trees and all blown out and a channel cut through and all the water white as chalk and everything on it; branches and whole trees and dead birds, and all floating. Inside the keys were all the pelicans in the world and all kinds of birds flying. They must have gone inside there when they knew it was coming.

I lay at Sou'west Key a day and nobody came after me. I was the first boat out and I seen a spar floating and I knew there must be a wreck and I started out to look for her. I found her. She was a three-masted schooner and I could just see the stumps of her spars out of water. She was in too deep water and I didn't get anything off of her. So I went on looking for something else. I had the start on all of them and I knew I ought to get whatever there was. I went on down over the sandbars from where I left that three-masted schooner and I didn't find anything and I went on a long way. I was way out toward the quicksands and I didn't find anything so I went on. Then when I was in sight of the Rebecca Light I saw all kinds of birds making over something and I headed over for them to see what it was and there was a cloud of birds all right.

I could see something looked like a spar up out of the water and when I got over close the birds all went up in the air and stayed all around me. The water was clear out there and there was a spar of some kind sticking out just above the water and when I come up close to it I saw it was all dark under water like a

long shadow and I came right over it and
there under water was a liner; just lying there
all under water as big as the whole world. I
drifted over her in the boat. She lay on her
side and the stern was deep down. The port
holes were all shut tight and I could see the
glass shine in the water and the whole of her;
the biggest boat I ever saw in my life laying
there and I went along the whole length of
her and then I went over and anchored and I
had the skiff on the deck forward and I shoved
it down into the water and sculled over with
the birds all around me.

I had a water glass like we use sponging
and my hand shook so I could hardly hold it.
All the port holes were shut that you could
see going along over her but way down below
near the bottom something must have been
open because there were pieces of things floating out all the time. You couldn't tell what
they were. Just pieces. That's what the birds
were after. You never saw so many birds.
They were all around me; crazy yelling.

I could see everything sharp and clear. I
could see her rounded over and she looked a
mile long under the water. She was lying on a
clear white bank of sand and the spar was a
sort of foremast or some sort of tackle that
slanted out of water the way she was laying
on her side. Her bow wasn't very far under.
I could stand on the letters of her name on
her bow and my head was just out of water.
But the nearest port hole was twelve feet
down. I could just reach it with the grains pole
and I tried to break it with that but I couldn't.
The glass was too stout. So I sculled back to
the boat and got a wrench and lashed it to
the end of the grains pole and I couldn't
break it. There I was looking down through
the glass at that liner with everything in her
and I was the first one to her and I couldn't
get into her. She must have had five million
dollars worth in her.

It made me shaky to think how much she
must have in her. Inside the port hole that was
closest I could see something but I couldn't
make it out through the water glass. I couldn't
do any good with the grains pole and I took
off my clothes and stood and took a couple of
deep breaths and dove over off the stern with

the wrench in my hand and swam down. I
could hold on for a second to the edge of the
port hole and I could see in and there was a
woman inside with her hair floating all out.
I could see her floating plain and I hit the
glass twice with the wrench hard and I heard
the noise clink in my ears but it wouldn't
break and I had to come up.

I hung onto the dinghy and got my breath
and then I climbed in and took a couple of
breaths and dove again. I swam down and
took hold of the edge of the port hole with my
fingers and held it and hit the glass as hard as
I could with the wrench. I could see the
woman floated in the water through the glass.
Her hair was tied once close to her head and
it floated all out in the water. I could see the
rings on one of her hands. She was right up
close to the port hole and I hit the glass twice
and I didn't even crack it. When I came up
I thought I wouldn't make it to the top before
I'd have to breathe.

I went down once more and I cracked the
glass, only cracked it, and when I came up my
nose was bleeding and I stood on the bow
of the liner with my bare feet on the letters
of her name and my head just out and rested
there and then I swam over to the skiff and
pulled up into it and sat there waiting for my
head to stop aching and looking down into
the water glass, but I bled so I had to wash
out the water glass. Then I lay back in the
skiff and held my hand under my nose to stop
it and I lay there with my head back looking
up and there was a million birds above and all
around.

When I quit bleeding I took another look
through the glass and then I sculled over to
the boat to try and find something heavier
than the wrench but I couldn't find a thing;
not even a sponge hook. I went back and the
water was clearer all the time and you could
see everything that floated out over that white
bank of sand. I looked for sharks but there
weren't any. You could have seen a shark a
long way away. The water was so clear and
the sand white. There was a grapple for an
anchor on the skiff and I cut it off and went
overboard and down with it. It carried me
right down and past the port hole and I

grabbed and couldn't hold anything and went on down and down, sliding along the curved side of her. I had to let go of the grapple. I heard it bump once and it seemed like a year before I came up through to the top of the water. The skiff was floated away with the tide and I swam over to her with my nose bleeding in the water while I swam and I was plenty glad there weren't sharks; but I was tired.

My head felt cracked open and I lay in the skiff and rested and then I sculled back. It was getting along in the afternoon. I went down once more with the wrench and it didn't do any good. That wrench was too light. It wasn't any good diving unless you had a big hammer or something heavy enough to do good. Then I lashed the wrench to the grains pole again and I watched through the water glass and pounded on the glass and hammered until the wrench came off and I saw it in the glass, clear and sharp, go sliding down along her and then off and down to the quicksand and go in. Then I couldn't do a thing. The wrench was gone and I'd lost the grapple so I sculled back to the boat. I was too tired to get the skiff aboard and the sun was pretty low. The birds were all pulling out and leaving her and I headed for Sou'west Key towing the skiff and the birds going on ahead of me and behind me. I was plenty tired.

That night it came on to blow and it blew for a week. You couldn't get out to her. They come out from town and told me the fellow I'd had to cut was all right except for his arm and I went back to town and they put me under five hundred dollar bond. It came out all right because some of them, friends of mine, swore he was after me with an ax, but by the time we got back out to her the Greeks had blown her open and cleaned her out. They got the safe out with dynamite. Nobody ever knows how much they got. She carried gold and they got it all. They stripped her clean. I found her and I never got a nickel out of her.

It was a hell of a thing all right. They say she was just outside of Havana harbor when the hurricane hit and she couldn't get in or the owners wouldn't let the captain chance coming in; they say he wanted to try; so she

had to go with it and in the dark they were running with it trying to go through the gulf between Rebecca and Tortugas when she struck on the quicksands. Maybe her rudder was carried away. Maybe they weren't even steering. But anyway they couldn't have known they were quicksands and when she struck the captain must have ordered them to open up the ballast tanks so she'd lay solid. But it was quicksand she'd hit and when they opened the tanks she went in stern first and then over on her beam ends. There were four hundred and fifty passengers and the crew on board of her and they must all have been aboard of her when I found her. They must have opened the tanks as soon as she struck and the minute she settled on it the quicksands took her down. Then her boilers must have burst and that must have been what made those pieces that came out. It was funny there weren't any sharks though. There wasn't a fish. I could have seen them on that clear white sand.

Plenty of fish now though; jewfish, the biggest kind. The biggest part of her's under the sand now but they live inside of her; the biggest kind of jewfish. Some weigh three to four hundred pounds. Sometime we'll go out and get some. You can see the Rebecca light from where she is. They've got a buoy on her now. She's right at the end of the quicksand right at the edge of the gulf. She only missed going through by about a hundred yards. In the dark in the storm they just missed it; raining the way it was they couldn't have seen the Rebecca. Then they're not used to that sort of thing. The captain of a liner isn't used to scudding that way. They have a course and they tell me they set some sort of a compass and it steers itself. They probably didn't know where they were when they ran with that blow but they come close to making it. Maybe they'd lost the rudder though. Anyway there wasn't another thing for them to hit till they'd get to Mexico once they were in that gulf. Must have been something though when they struck in that rain and wind and he told them to open her tanks. Nobody could have been on deck in that blow and rain. Everybody must have been below. They couldn't have lived on deck. There must have been some scenes inside all right because you know she settled fast. I saw that wrench go into the sand. The captain couldn't have known it was quicksand when she struck unless he knew these waters. He just knew it wasn't rock. He must have seen it all up in the bridge. He must have known what it was about when she settled. I wonder how fast she made it. I wonder if the mate was there with him. Do you think they stayed inside the bridge or do you think they took it outside? They never found any bodies. Not a one. Nobody floating. They float a long way with life belts too. They must have took it inside. Well, the Greeks got it all. Everything. They must have come fast all right. They picked her clean. First there was the birds, then me, then the Greeks, and even the birds got more out of her than I did.

EUDORA WELTY

A Worn Path

Eudora Welty (1909–   ) at present lives in Jackson, Mississippi, where she was born. She was educated at Mississippi State College for Women, the University of Wisconsin, where she took her A.B. degree, and Columbia University. After the publication of her first few short stories, mainly in the *Southern Review,* her stories began to appear in almost every reputable anthology. Her books include *A Curtain of Green,* 1941; *The Wide Net,* 1943; *Delta Wedding,* 1946; *The Golden Apples,* 1949; *The Ponder Heart,* 1954; *The Bride of the Innisfallen,* 1955; and *The Shoe Bird,* 1964, a children's story.

"A Worn Path," typically Welty in its Southern setting and its familiar-grotesque main character, is among her best short stories. The odyssey of Phoenix Jackson is a warm and moving story, because the difficulties of this frail old woman's life are transformed by her innocence and dignity into something close to joy.

It was December—a bright frozen day in the early morning. Far out in the country there was an old Negro woman with her head tied in a red rag, coming along a path through the pinewoods. Her name was Phoenix Jackson. She was very old and small and she

A WORN PATH   From *A Curtain of Green and Other Stories,* copyright, 1936, 1937, 1938, 1939, 1941, by Eudora Welty. Reprinted by permission of Harcourt, Brace & World, Inc.

walked slowly in the dark pine shadows, moving a little from side to side in her steps, with the balanced heaviness and lightness of a pendulum in a grandfather clock. She carried a thin, small cane made from an umbrella, and with this she kept tapping the frozen earth in front of her. This made a grave and persistent noise in the still air, that seemed meditative like the chirping of a solitary little bird.

She wore a dark striped dress reaching

down to her shoe tops, and an equally long apron of bleached sugar sacks, with a full pocket: all neat and tidy, but every time she took a step she might have fallen over her shoelaces, which dragged from her unlaced shoes. She looked straight ahead. Her eyes were blue with age. Her skin had a pattern all its own of numberless branching wrinkles and as though a whole little tree stood in the middle of her forehead, but a golden color ran underneath, and the two knobs of her cheeks were illumined by a yellow burning under the dark. Under the red rag her hair came down on her neck in the frailest of ringlets, still black, and with an odor like copper.

Now and then there was a quivering in the thicket. Old Phoenix said, "Out of my way, all you foxes, owls, beetles, jack rabbits, coons and wild animals! . . . Keep out from under these feet, little bob-whites. . . . Keep the big wild hogs out of my path. Don't let none of those come running my direction. I got a long way." Under her small black-freckled hand her cane, limber as a buggy whip, would switch at the brush as if to rouse up any hiding things.

On she went. The woods were deep and still. The sun made the pine needles almost too bright to look at, up where the wind rocked. The cones dropped as light as feathers. Down in the hollow was the mourning dove —it was not too late for him.

The path ran up a hill. "Seem like there is chains about my feet, time I get this far," she said, in the voice of argument old people keep to use with themselves. "Something always take a hold of me on this hill—pleads I should stay."

After she got to the top she turned and gave a full, severe look behind her where she had come. "Up through pines," she said at length. "Now down through oaks."

Her eyes opened their widest, and she started down gently. But before she got to the bottom of the hill a bush caught her dress.

Her fingers were busy and intent, but her skirts were full and long, so that before she could pull them free in one place they were caught in another. It was not possible to allow the dress to tear. "I in the thorny bush," she said. "Thorns, you doing your appointed work. Never want to let folks pass, no sir. Old eyes thought you was a pretty little *green* bush."

Finally, trembling all over, she stood free, and after a moment dared to stoop for her cane.

"Sun so high!" she cried, leaning back and looking, while the thick tears went over her eyes. "The time getting all gone here."

At the foot of this hill was a place where a log was laid across the creek.

"Now comes the trial," said Phoenix.

Putting her right foot out, she mounted the log and shut her eyes. Lifting her skirt, leveling her cane fiercely before her, like a festival figure in some parade, she began to march across. Then she opened her eyes and she was safe on the other side.

"I wasn't as old as I thought," she said.

But she sat down to rest. She spread her skirts on the bank around her and folded her hands over her knees. Up above her was a tree in a pearly cloud of mistletoe. She did not dare to close her eyes, and when a little boy brought her a plate with a slice of marble-cake on it she spoke to him. "That would be acceptable," she said. But when she went to take it there was just her own hand in the air.

So she left that tree, and had to go through a barbed-wire fence. There she had to creep and crawl, spreading her knees and stretching her fingers like a baby trying to climb the steps. But she talked loudly to herself: she could not let her dress be torn now, so late in the day, and she could not pay for having her arm or her leg sawed off if she got caught fast where she was.

At last she was safe through the fence and risen up out in the clearing. Big dead trees, like black men with one arm, were standing in the purple stalks of the withered cotton field. There sat a buzzard.

"Who you watching?"

In the furrow she made her way along.

"Glad this not the season for bulls," she said, looking sideways, "and the good Lord made his snakes to curl up and sleep in the winter. A pleasure I don't see no two-headed snake coming around that tree, where it come once. It took a while to get by him, back in the summer."

She passed through the old cotton and went into a field of dead corn. It whispered and shook and was taller than her head. "Through the maze now," she said, for there was no path.

Then there was something tall, black, and skinny there, moving before her.

At first she took it for a man. It could have been a man dancing in the field. But she stood still and listened, and it did not make a sound. It was as silent as a ghost.

"Ghost," she said sharply, "who be you the ghost of? For I have heard of nary death close by."

But there was no answer—only the ragged dancing in the wind.

She shut her eyes, reached out her hand, and touched a sleeve. She found a coat and inside that an emptiness, cold as ice.

"You scarecrow," she said. Her face lighted. "I ought to be shut up for good," she said with laughter. "My senses is gone. I too old. I the oldest people I ever know. Dance, old scarecrow," she said, "while I dancing with you."

She kicked her foot over the furrow, and with mouth drawn down, shook her head once or twice in a little strutting way. Some husks blew down and whirled in streamers about her skirts.

Then she went on, parting her way from side to side with the cane, through the whispering field. At last she came to the end, to a wagon track where the silver grass blew between the red ruts. The quail were walking around like pullets, seeming all dainty and unseen.

"Walk pretty," she said. "This the easy place. This the easy going."

She followed the track, swaying through the quiet bare fields, through the little strings of trees silver in their dead leaves, past cabins silver from weather, with the doors and windows boarded shut, all like old women under a spell sitting there. "I walking in their sleep," she said, nodding her head vigorously.

In a ravine she went where a spring was silently flowing through a hollow log. Old Phoenix bent and drank. "Sweet-gum makes the water sweet," she said, and drank more. "Nobody know who made this well, for it was here when I was born."

The track crossed a swampy part where the moss hung as white as lace from every limb. "Sleep on, alligators, and blow your bubbles." Then the track went into the road.

Deep, deep the road went down between the high green-colored banks. Overhead the live-oaks met, and it was as dark as a cave.

A black dog with a lolling tongue came up out of the weeds by the ditch. She was meditating, and not ready, and when he came at her she only hit him a little with her cane. Over she went in the ditch, like a little puff of milkweed.

Down there, her senses drifted away. A dream visited her, and she, reached her hand up, but nothing reached down and gave her a pull. So she lay there and presently went to talking. "Old woman," she said to herself, "that black dog come up out of the weeds to stall your off, and now there he sitting on his fine tail, smiling at you."

A white man finally came along and found her—a hunter, a young man, with his dog on a chain.

"Well, Granny!" he laughed. "What are you doing there?"

"Lying on my back like a June-bug waiting to be turned over, mister," she said, reaching up her hand.

He lifted her up, gave her a swing in the air, and set her down. "Anything broken, Granny?"

"No sir, them old dead weeds is springy enough," said Phoenix, when she had got her breath. "I thank you for your trouble."

"Where do you live, Granny?" he asked, while the two dogs were growling at each other.

"Away back yonder, sir, behind the ridge. You can't even see it from here."

"On your way home?"

"No sir, I going to town."

"Why, that's too far! That's as far as I walk when I come out myself, and I get something for my trouble." He patted the stuffed bag he carried, and there hung down a little closed claw. It was one of the bob-whites, with its beak hooked bitterly to show it was dead. "Now you go on home, Granny!"

"I bound to go to town, mister," said Phoenix. "The time come around."

He gave another laugh, filling the whole landscape. "I know you old colored people! Wouldn't miss going to town to see Santa Claus!"

But something held old Phoenix very still. The deep lines in her face went into a fierce and different radiation. Without warning, she had seen with her own eyes a flashing nickel fall out of the man's pocket onto the ground.

"How old are you, Granny?" he was saying.

"There is no telling, mister," she said, "no telling."

Then she gave a little cry and clapped her hands and said, "Git on away from here, dog! Look! Look at that dog!" She laughed as if in admiration. "He ain't scared of nobody. He a big black dog." She whispered, "Sic him!"

"Watch me get rid of that cur," said the man. "Sic him, Pete! Sic him!"

Phoenix heard the dogs fighting, and heard the man running and throwing sticks. She even heard a gunshot. But she was slowly bending forward by that time, further and further forward, the lids stretched down over her eyes, as if she were doing this in her sleep. Her chin was lowered almost to her knees. The yellow palm of her hand came out from the fold of her apron. Her fingers slid down and along the ground under the piece of money with the grace and care they would have in lifting an egg from under a setting hen. Then she slowly straightened up, she stood erect, and the nickel was in her apron pocket. A bird flew by. Her lips moved. "God watching me the whole time. I come to stealing."

The man came back, and his own dog panted about them. "Well, I scared him off that time," he said, and then he laughed and lifted his gun and pointed it at Phoenix.

She stood straight and faced him.

"Doesn't the gun scare you?" he said, still pointing it.

"No, sir, I seen plenty go off closer by, in my day, and for less than what I done," she said, holding utterly still.

He smiled, and shouldered the gun. "Well, Granny," he said, "you must be a hundred years old, and scared of nothing. I'd give you a dime if I had any money with me. But you take my advice and stay home, and nothing will happen to you."

"I bound to go on my way, mister," said Phoenix. She inclined her head in the red rag. Then they went in different directions, but she could hear the gun shooting again and again over the hill.

She walked on. The shadows hung from the oak trees to the road like curtains. Then she smelled wood-smoke, and smelled the river, and she saw a steeple and the cabins on their steep steps. Dozens of little black children whirled around her. There ahead was Natchez shining. Bells were ringing. She walked on.

In the paved city it was Christmas time. There were red and green electric lights strung and criss-crossed everywhere, and all turned on in the daytime. Old Phoenix would have been lost if she had not distrusted her eyesight and depended on her feet to know where to take her.

She paused quietly on the sidewalk where people were passing by. A lady came along in the crowd, carrying an armful of red-, green- and silver-wrapped presents; she gave off perfume like the red roses in hot summer, and Phoenix stopped her.

"Please, missy, will you lace up my shoe?" She held up her foot.

"What do you want, Grandma?"

"See my shoe," said Phoenix. "Do all right for out in the country, but wouldn't look right to go in a big building."

"Stand still then, Grandma," said the lady. She put her packages down on the sidewalk beside her and laced and tied both shoes tightly.

"Can't lace 'em with a cane," said Phoenix. "Thank you, missy, I doesn't mind asking a nice lady to tie up my shoe, when I gets out on the street."

Moving slowly and from side to side, she went into the big building, and into a tower of steps, where she walked up and around and around until her feet knew to stop.

She entered a door, and there she saw nailed up on the wall the document that had been stamped with the gold seal and framed in the gold frame, which matched the dream that was hung up in her head.

"Here I be," she said. There was a fixed and ceremonial stiffness over her body.

"A charity case, I suppose," said an attendant who sat at the desk before her.

But Phoenix only looked above her head. There was sweat on her face, the wrinkles in her skin shone like a bright net.

"Speak up, Grandma," the woman said. "What's your name? We must have your history, you know. Have you been here before? What seems to be the trouble with you?"

Old Phoenix only gave a twitch to her face as if a fly were bothering her.

"Are you deaf?" cried the attendant.

But then the nurse came in.

"Oh, that's just old Aunt Phoenix," she said. "She doesn't come for herself—she has a little grandson. She makes these trips just as regular as clockwork. She lives away back off the Old Natchez Trace." She bent down. "Well, Aunt Phoenix, why don't you just take a seat? We won't keep you standing after your long trip." She pointed.

The old woman sat down, bolt upright in the chair.

"Now, how is the boy?" asked the nurse.

Old Phoenix did not speak.

"I said, how is the boy?"

But Phoenix only waited and stared straight ahead, her face very solemn and withdrawn into rigidity.

"Is his throat any better?" asked the nurse. "Aunt Phoenix, don't you hear me? Is your grandson's throat any better since the last time you came for the medicine?"

With her hands on her knees, the old woman waited, silent, erect and motionless, just as if she were in armor.

"You musn't take up our time this way, Aunt Phoenix," the nurse said. "Tell us quickly about your grandson, and get it over. He isn't dead, is he?"

At last there came a flicker and then a flame of comprehension across her face, and she spoke.

"My grandson. It was my memory had left me. There I sat and forgot why I made my long trip."

"Forgot?" The nurse frowned. "After you came so far?"

Then Phoenix was like an old woman begging a dignified forgiveness for waking up frightened in the night. "I never did go to school, I was too old at the Surrender," she said in a soft voice. "I'm an old woman without an education. It was my memory fail me. My little grandson, he is just the same, and I forgot it in the coming."

"Throat never heals, does it?" said the nurse, speaking in a loud, sure voice to old Phoenix. By now she had a card with something written on it, a little list. "Yes. Swallowed lye. When was it?—January—two-three years ago—"

Phoenix spoke unasked now. "No, missy, he not dead, he just the same. Every little while his throat begin to close up again, and he not able to swallow. He not get his breath. He not able to help himself. So the time come around, and I go on another trip for the soothing medicine."

"All right. The doctor said as long as you came to get it, you could have it," said the nurse. "But it's an obstinate case."

"My little grandson, he sit up there in the house all wrapped up, waiting by himself," Phoenix went on. "We is the only two left in the world. He suffer and it don't seem to put him back at all. He got a sweet look. He going to last. He wear a little patch quilt and peep out holding his mouth open like a little bird. I remembers so plain now. I not going to forget him again, no, the whole enduring time. I could tell him from all the others in creation."

"All right." The nurse was trying to hush her now. She brought her a bottle of medicine. "Charity," she said, making a check mark in a book.

Old Phoenix held the bottle close to her eyes, and then carefully put it into her pocket.

"I thank you," she said.

"It's Christmas time, Grandma," said the

attendant. "Could I give you a few pennies out of my purse?"

"Five pennies is a nickel," said Phoenix stiffly.

"Here's a nickel," said the attendant.

Phoenix rose carefully and held out her hand. She received the nickel and then fished the other nickel out of her pocket and laid it beside the new one. She stared at her palm closely, with her head on one side.

Then she gave a tap with her cane on the floor.

"This is what come to me to do," she said. "I going to the store and buy my child a little windmill they sells, made out of paper. He going to find it hard to believe there such a thing in the world. I'll march myself back where he waiting, holding it straight up in this hand."

She lifted her free hand, gave a little nod, turned around, and walked out of the doctor's office. Then her slow step began on the stairs, going down.

FLANNERY O'CONNOR

A Late Encounter with the Enemy

Flannery O'Connor (1925–1964) was born in Georgia and educated at Georgia State College for Women and the State University of Iowa, where she received a master's degree in fine arts in 1947. Her first novel, *Wise Blood*, appeared in 1952. After publishing stories in the *Partisan Review, Harper's Bazaar, Mademoiselle*, and other magazines, she published a collection of ten stories, *A Good Man Is Hard to Find and Other Stories*, 1955. For her story "Greenleaf" she won first prize in the 1957 O. Henry Memorial Awards. Her last works are a novel, *The Violent Bear It Away*, 1960, and a collection of stories, *Everything That Rises Must Converge*, 1965.

"A Late Encounter with the Enemy" is typical of Miss O'Connor's work. In it, the reader finds bizarre, brutal, and often mindless characters who tend to be almost, but not quite, beyond the realm of one's experience.

General Sash was a hundred and four years old. He lived with his granddaughter, Sally Poker Sash, who was sixty-two years old and who prayed every night on her knees that he would live until her graduation from college.

lege. The General didn't give two slaps for her graduation but he never doubted he would live for it. Living had got to be such a habit with him that he couldn't conceive of any other condition. A graduation exercise was not exactly his idea of a good time, even if, as she said, he would be expected to sit on the stage in his uniform. She said there would be a long procession of teachers and students in

their robes but that there wouldn't be anything to equal *him* in his uniform. He knew
this well enough without her telling him, and
as for the damn procession, it could march to
hell and back and not cause him a quiver. He
liked parades with floats full of Miss Americas
and Miss Daytona Beaches and Miss Queen
Cotton Products. He didn't have any use for
processions and a procession full of school-
teachers was about as deadly as the River Styx
to his way of thinking. However, he was willing to sit on the stage in his uniform so that
they could see him.

Sally Poker was not as sure as he was that
he would live until her graduation. There had
not been any perceptible change in him for
the last five years, but she had the sense that
she might be cheated out of her triumph because she so often was. She had been going
to summer school every year for the past
twenty because when she started teaching,
there were no such things as degrees. In those
times, she said, everything was normal but
nothing had been normal since she was sixteen, and for the past twenty summers, when
she should have been resting, she had had to
take a trunk in the burning heat to the state
teacher's college; and though when she returned in the fall, she always taught in the
exact way she had been taught not to teach,
this was a mild revenge that didn't satisfy
her sense of justice. She wanted the General
at her graduation because she wanted to show
what she stood for, or, as she said, "what all
was behind her," and was not behind them.
This *them* was not anybody in particular. It
was just all the upstarts who had turned the
world on its head and unsettled the ways of
decent living.

She meant to stand on that platform in August with the General sitting in his wheel
chair on the stage behind her and she meant
to hold her head very high as if she were saying, "See him! See him! My kin, all you upstarts! Glorious upright old man standing for
the old traditions! Dignity! Honor! Courage!
See him!" One night in her sleep she screamed,
"See him! See him!" and turned her head and
found him sitting in his wheel chair behind
her with a terrible expression on his face and

with all his clothes off except the general's hat
and she had waked up and had not dared to
go back to sleep again that night.

For his part, the General would not have
consented even to attend her graduation if she
had not promised to see to it that he sit on
the stage. He liked to sit on any stage. He
considered that he was still a very handsome
man. When he had been able to stand up, he
had measured five feet four inches of pure
game cock. He had white hair that reached to
his shoulders behind and he would not wear
teeth because he thought his profile was more
striking without them. When he put on his
full-dress general's uniform, he knew well
enough that there was nothing to match him
anywhere.

This was not the same uniform he had worn
in the War between the States. He had not
actually been a general in that war. He had
probably been a foot soldier; he didn't remember what he had been; in fact, he didn't remember that war at all. It was like his feet,
which hung down now shriveled at the very
end of him, without feeling, covered with a
blue-gray afghan that Sally Poker had cro-
cheted when she was a little girl. He didn't
remember the Spanish-American War in which
he had lost a son; he didn't even remember
the son. He didn't have any use for history because he never expected to meet it again. To
his mind, history was connected with processions and life with parades and he liked
parades. People were always asking him if he
remembered this or that—a dreary black procession of questions about the past. There was
only one event in the past that had any significance for him and that he cared to talk
about: that was twelve years ago when he
had received the general's uniform and had
been in the premiere.

"I was in that preemy they had in Atlanta,"
he would tell visitors sitting on his front porch.
"Surrounded by beautiful guls. It wasn't a
thing local about it. It was nothing local about
it. Listen here. It was a nashnul event and
they had me in it—up onto the stage. There
was no bob-tails at it. Every person at it had
paid ten dollars to get in and had to wear his
tuxseeder. I was in this uniform. A beautiful

gul presented me with it that afternoon in a hotel room."

"It was in a suite in the hotel and I was in it too, Papa," Sally Poker would say, winking at the visitors. "You weren't alone with any young lady in a hotel room."

"Was, I'd a known what to do," the old General would say with a sharp look and the visitors would scream with laughter. "This was a Hollywood, California, gul," he'd continue. "She was from Hollywood, California, and didn't have any part in the pitcher. Out there they have so many beautiful guls that they don't need that they call them a extra and they don't use them for nothing but presenting people with things and having their pitchers taken. They took my pitcher with her. No, it was two of them. One on either side and me in the middle with my arms around each of them's waist and their waist ain't any bigger than a half a dollar."

Sally Poker would interrupt again. "It was Mr. Govisky that gave you the uniform, Papa, and he gave me the most exquisite corsage. Really, I wish you could have seen it. It was made with gladiola petals taken off and painted gold and put back together to look like a rose. It was exquisite. I wish you could have seen it, it was . . . ."

"It was as big as her head," the General would snarl. "I was tellin it. They gimme this uniform and they gimme this soward and they say, 'Now General, we don't want you to start a war on us. All we want you to do is march right up on that stage when you're innerduced tonight and answer a few questions. Think you can do that?' 'Think I can do it!' I say. 'Listen here. I was doing things before you were born,' and they hollered."

"He was the hit of the show," Sally Poker would say, but she didn't much like to remember the premier on account of what had happened to her feet at it. She had bought a new dress for the occasion—a long black crepe dinner dress with a rhinestone buckle and a bolero—and a pair of silver slippers to wear with it, because she was supposed to go up on the stage with him to keep him from falling. Everything was arranged for them. A real limousine came at ten minutes to eight and

took them to the theater. It drew up under the marquee at exactly the right time, after the big stars and the director and the author and the governor and the mayor and some less important stars. The police kept traffic from jamming and there were ropes to keep the people off who couldn't go. All the people who couldn't go watched them step out of the limousine into the lights. Then they walked down the red and gold foyer and an usherette in a Confederate cap and little short skirt conducted them to their special seats. The audience was already there and a group of UDC members began to clap when they saw the General in his uniform and that started everybody to clap. A few more celebrities came after them and then the doors closed and the lights went down.

A young man with blond wavy hair who said he represented the motion-picture industry came out and began to introduce everybody and each one who was introduced walked up on the stage and said how really happy he was to be here for this great event. The General and his granddaughter were introduced sixteenth on the program. He was introduced as General Tennessee Flintrock Sash of the Confederacy, though Sally Poker had told Mr. Govisky that his name was George Poker Sash and that he had only been a major. She helped him up from his seat but her heart was beating so fast she didn't know whether she'd make it herself.

The old man walked up the aisle slowly with his fierce white head high and his hat held over his heart. The orchestra began to play the Confederate Battle Hymn very softly and the UDC members rose as a group and did not sit down again until the General was on the stage. When he reached the center of the stage with Sally Poker just behind him guiding his elbow, the orchestra burst out in a loud rendition of the Battle Hymn and the old man, with real stage presence, gave a vigorous trembling salute and stood at attention until the last blast had died away. Two of the usherettes in Confederate caps and short skirts held a Confederate and a Union flag crossed behind them.

The General stood in the exact center of the

spotlight and it caught a weird moon-shaped slice of Sally Poker—the corsage, the rhinestone buckle and one hand clenched around a white glove and handkerchief. The young man with the blond wavy hair inserted himself into the circle of light and said he was *really* happy to have here tonight for this great event, one, he said, who had fought and bled in the battles they would soon see daringly re-acted on the screen, and "Tell me, General," he asked, "how old are you?"

"Niiiiiinnttty-two!" the General screamed.

The young man looked as if this were just about the most impressive thing that had been said all evening. "Ladies and gentlemen," he said, "let's give the General the biggest hand we've got!" and there was applause immediately and the young man indicated to Sally Poker with a motion of his thumb that she could take the old man back to his seat now so that the next person could be introduced; but the General had not finished. He stood immovable in the exact center of the spotlight, his neck thrust forward, his mouth slightly open, and his voracious gray eyes drinking in the glare and the applause. He elbowed his granddaughter roughly away. "How I keep so young," he screeched, "I kiss all the pretty guls!"

This was met with a great din of spontaneous applause and it was at just that instant that Sally Poker looked down at her feet and discovered that in the excitement of getting ready she had forgotten to change her shoes: two brown Girl Scout oxfords protruded from the bottom of her dress. She gave the General a yank and almost ran with him off the stage. He was very angry that he had not got to say how glad he was to be here for this event and on the way back to his seat, he kept saying as loud as he could, "I'm glad to be here at this preemy with all these beautiful guls!" but there was another celebrity going up the other aisle and nobody paid any attention to him. He slept through the picture, muttering fiercely every now and then in his sleep.

Since then, his life had not been very interesting. His feet were completely dead now, his knees worked like old hinges, his kidneys functioned when they would, but his heart persisted doggedly to beat. The past and the future were the same thing to him, one forgotten and the other not remembered; he had no more notion of dying than a cat. Every year on Confederate Memorial Day, he was bundled up and lent to the Capitol City Museum where he was displayed from one to four in a musty room full of old photographs, old uniforms, old artillery, and historic documents. All these were carefully preserved in glass cases so that children would not put their hands on them. He wore his general's uniform from the premiere and sat, with a fixed scowl, inside a small roped area. There was nothing about him to indicate that he was alive except an occasional movement in his milky gray eyes, but once when a bold child touched his sword, his arm shot forward and slapped the hand off in an instant. In the spring when the old homes were opened for pilgrimages, he was invited to wear his uniform and sit in some conspicuous spot and lend atmosphere to the scene. Some of these times he only snarled at the visitors but sometimes he told about the premiere and the beautiful girls.

If he had died before Sally Poker's graduation, she thought she would have died herself. At the beginning of the summer term, even before she knew if she would pass, she told the Dean that her grandfather, General Tennessee Flintrock Sash of the Confederacy, would attend her graduation and that he was a hundred and four years old and that his mind was still clear as a bell. Distinguished visitors were always welcome and could sit on the stage and be introduced. She made arrangements with her nephew, John Wesley Poker Sash, a Boy Scout, to come wheel the General's chair. She thought how sweet it would be to see the old man in his courageous gray and the young boy in his clean khaki—the old and the new, she thought appropriately—they would be behind her on the stage when she received her degree.

Everything went almost exactly as she had planned. In the summer while she was away at school, the General stayed with other relatives and they brought him and John Wesley, the Boy Scout, down to the graduation. A reporter came to the hotel where they stayed and took the General's picture with Sally Poker on one side of him and John Wesley on the other. The General, who had had his picture taken with beautiful girls, didn't think much of this. He had forgotten precisely what kind of event this was he was going to attend but he remembered that he was to wear his uniform and carry the sword.

On the morning of the graduation, Sally Poker had to line up in the academic procession with the B.S.'s in Elementary Education and she couldn't see to getting him on the stage herself—but John Wesley, a fat blond boy of ten with an executive expression, guaranteed to take care of everything. She came in her academic gown to the hotel and dressed the old man in his uniform. He was as frail as a dried spider. "Aren't you just thrilled, Papa?" she asked. "I'm just thrilled to death!"

"Put the soward acrost my lap, damm you," the old man said, "where it'll shine."

She put it there and then stood back looking at him. "You look just grand," she said.

"God damm it," the old man said in a slow monotonous certain tone as if he were saying it to the beating of his heart. "God damm every goddam thing to hell."

"Now, now," she said and left happily to join the procession.

The graduates were lined up behind the Science building and she found her place just as the line started to move. She had not slept much the night before and when she had, she had dreamed of the exercises, murmuring, "See him, see him?" in her sleep but waking up every time just before she turned her head to look at him behind her. The graduates had to walk three blocks in the hot sun in their black wool robes and as she plodded stolidly along she thought that if anyone considered this academic procession something impressive to behold, they need only wait until they saw that old General in his courageous gray and that clean young Boy Scout stoutly wheeling his chair across the stage with the sunlight catching the sword. She imagined that John Wesley had the old man ready now behind the stage.

The black procession wound its way up the two blocks and started on the main walk leading to the auditorium. The visitors stood on the grass, picking out their graduates. Men were pushing back their hats and wiping their foreheads and women were lifting their dresses slightly from the shoulders to keep them from sticking to their backs. The graduates in their heavy robes looked as if the last beads of ignorance were being sweated out of them. The sun blazed off the fenders of automobiles and beat from the columns of the buildings and pulled the eye from one spot of glare to another. It pulled Sally Poker's toward the big red Coca-Cola machine that had been set up by the side of the auditorium. Here she saw the General parked, scowling and hatless in his chair in the blazing sun while John Wesley, his blouse loose behind, his hip and cheek pressed to the red machine, was drinking a Coca-Cola. She broke from the line and galloped to them and snatched the bottle away. She shook the boy and thrust in his blouse and put the hat on the old man's head. "Now get him in there!" she said, pointing one rigid finger to the side door of the building.

For his part the General felt as if there were a little hole beginning to widen in the top of his head. The boy wheeled him rapidly down a walk and up a ramp and into a building and bumped him over the stage entrance and into position where he had been told and the General glared in front of him at heads that all seemed to flow together and eyes that moved from one face to another. Several figures in black robes came and picked up his hand and shook it. A black procession was flowing up each aisle and forming to stately music in a pool in front of him. The music seemed to be entering his head through the little hole and he thought for a second that the procession would try to enter it too.

He didn't know what procession this was but there was something familiar about it. It must be familiar to him since it had come to meet him, but he didn't like a black procession. Any procession that came to meet him, he thought irritably, ought to have floats with beautiful guls on them like the floats before the preemy. It must be something connected with history like they were always having. He had no use for any of it. What happened then wasn't anything to a man living now and he was living now.

When all the procession had flowed into the black pool, a black figure began orating in front of it. The figure was telling something about history and the General made up his mind he wouldn't listen, but the words kept seeping in through the little hole in his head. He heard his own name mentioned and his chair was shuttled forward roughly and the Boy Scout took a big bow. They called his name and the fat brat bowed. Goddam you, the old man tried to say, get out of my way, I can stand up!—but he was jerked back again before he could get up and take the bow. He supposed the noise they made was for him. If he was over, he didn't intend to listen to any more of it. If it hadn't been for the little hole in the top of his head, none of the words would have got to him. He thought of putting his finger up there into the hole to block them but the hole was a little wider than his finger and it felt as if it were getting deeper.

Another black robe had taken the place of the first one and was talking now and he heard his name mentioned again but they were not talking about him, they were still talking about history. "If we forget our past," the speaker was saying, "we won't remember our future and it will be as well for we won't have one." The General heard some of these words gradually. He had forgotten history and he didn't intend to remember it again. He had forgotten the name and face of his wife and the names and faces of his children or even if he had a wife and children, and he had forgotten the names of places and the places themselves and what had happened at them.

He was considerably irked by the hole in his head. He had not expected to have a hole in his head at this event. It was the slow black music that had put it there and though most of the music had stopped outside, there was still a little of it in the hole, going deeper and moving around in his thoughts, letting the words he heard into the dark places of his brain. He heard the words, Chickamauga, Shiloh, Johnston, Lee, and he knew he was inspiring all these words that meant nothing to him. He wondered if he had been a general

at Chickamauga or at Lee. Then he tried to see himself and the horse mounted in the middle of a float full of beautiful girls, being driven slowly through downtown Atlanta. Instead, the old words began to stir in his head as if they were trying to wrench themselves out of place and come to life.

The speaker was through with that war and had gone on to the next one and now he was approaching another and all his words, like the black procession, were vaguely familiar and irritating. There was a long finger of music in the General's head, probing various spots that were words, letting in a little light on the words and helping them to live. The words began to come toward him and he said, Dammit! I ain't going to have it! and he started edging backwards to get out of the way. Then he saw the figure in the black robe sit down and there was a noise and the black pool in front of him began to rumble and to flow toward him from either side to the black slow music, and he said, Stop dammit! I can't do but one thing at a time! He couldn't protect himself from the words and attend to the procession too and the words were coming at him fast. He felt that he was running backwards and the words were coming at him like musket fire, just escaping him but getting nearer and nearer. He turned around and began to run as fast as he could but he found himself running toward the words. He was running into a regular volley of them and meeting them with quick curses. As the music swelled toward him, the entire past opened up on him out of nowhere and he felt his body riddled in a hundred places with sharp stabs of pain and he fell down, returning a curse for every hit. He saw his wife's narrow face looking at him critically through her round gold-rimmed glasses; he saw one of his squinting bald-headed sons; and his mother ran toward him with an anxious look; then a succession of places—Chickamauga, Shiloh, Marthasville—rushed at him as if the past were the only future now and he had to endure it. Then suddenly he saw that the black procession was almost on him. He recognized it, for it had been dogging all his days. He made such a desperate effort to see over it and find out what comes after the past that his hand clenched the sword until the blade touched bone.

The graduates were crossing the stage in a long file to receive their scrolls and shake the president's hand. As Sally Poker, who was near the end, crossed, she glanced at the General and saw him sitting fixed and fierce, his eyes wide open, and she turned her head forward again and held it a perceptible degree higher and received her scroll. Once it was all over and she was out of the auditorium in the sun again, she located her kin and they waited together on a bench in the shade for John Wesley to wheel the old man out. That crafty scout had bumped him out the back way and rolled him at high speed down a flagstone path and was waiting now, with the corpse, in the long line at the Coca-Cola machine.

JOHN COLLIER

The Chaser

John Collier (1901–   ) is a widely read British short-story writer, currently residing in Hollywood, California. His stories have been especially popular with movie and television producers. Among his books are *His Monkey Wife, or Married to a Chimp*, 1930; *Full Circle*, 1933; *Defy the Foul Fiend*, 1934; *Presenting Moonshine*, 1941; *The Touch of Nutmeg*, 1943; and *Fancies and Goodnights*, 1951.

Mr. Collier is a master of the ironic and fantastic tale, but in his best stories, such as "The Chaser," the underlying commentary is on real people and real motives no matter how unreal the surface situation. Often compared to Saki, he is a consummate artist of the short short story.

Alan Austen, as nervous as a kitten, went up certain dark and creaky stairs in the neighborhood of Pell Street, and peered about for a long time on the dim landing before he found the name he wanted written obscurely on one of the doors.

He pushed open this door, as he had been told to do, and found himself in a tiny room, which contained no furniture but a plain kitchen table, a rocking-chair, and an ordinary chair. On one of the dirty buff-colored walls were a couple of shelves, containing in all perhaps a dozen bottles and jars.

An old man sat in the rocking-chair, reading a newspaper. Alan, without a word, handed him the card he had been given. "Sit down, Mr. Austen," said the old man very politely. "I am glad to make your acquaintance."

"Is it true," asked Alan, "that you have a certain mixture that has—er—quite extraordinary effects?"

"My dear sir," replied the old man, "my stock in trade is not very large—I don't deal in laxatives and teething mixtures—but such as it is, it is varied. I think nothing I sell has effects which could be precisely described as ordinary."

"Well, the fact is—" began Alan.

"Here, for example," interrupted the old man, reaching for a bottle from the shelf. "Here is a liquid as colorless as water, almost tasteless, quite imperceptible in coffee, milk, wine, or any other beverage. It is also quite imperceptible to any known method of autopsy."

"Do you mean it is a poison?" cried Alan, very much horrified.

"Call it a glove-cleaner if you like," said the old man indifferently. "Maybe it will clean gloves. I have never tried. One might call it a life-cleaner. Lives need cleaning sometimes."

"I want nothing of that sort," said Alan.

"Probably it is just as well," said the old man. "Do you know the price of this? For one teaspoonful, which is sufficient, I ask five thousand dollars. Never less. Not a penny less."

"I hope all your mixtures are not as expensive," said Alan apprehensively.

"Oh dear, no," said the old man. "It would be no good charging that sort of price for a love potion, for example. Young people who need a love potion very seldom have five thousand dollars. Otherwise they would not need a love potion."

"I am glad to hear that," said Alan.

"I look at it like this," said the old man. "Please a customer with one article, and he will come back when he needs another. Even if it *is* more costly. He will save up for it, if necessary."

"So," said Alan, "you really do sell love potions?"

"If I did not sell love potions," said the old man, reaching for another bottle, "I should not have mentioned the other matter to you. It is only when one is in a position to oblige that one can afford to be so confidential."

"And these potions," said Alan. "They are not just—just—er—"

"Oh, no," said the old man. "Their effects are permanent, and extend far beyond casual impulse. But they include it. Bountifully, insistently. Everlastingly."

"Dear me!" said Alan, attempting a look of scientific detachment. "How very interesting!"

"But consider the spiritual side," said the old man.

"I do, indeed," said Alan.

"For indifference," said the old man, "they substitute devotion. For scorn, adoration. Give one tiny measure of this to the young lady—its flavor is imperceptible in orange juice, soup, or cocktails—and however gay and giddy she is, she will change altogether. She will want nothing but solitude, and you."

"I can hardly believe it," said Alan. "She is so fond of parties."

"She will not like them any more," said the old man. "She will be afraid of the pretty girls you may meet."

"She will actually be jealous?" cried Alan in a rapture. "Of me?"

"Yes, she will want to be everything to you."

"She is, already. Only she doesn't care about it."

"She will, when she has taken this. She will care intensely. You will be her sole interest in life."

"Wonderful!" cried Alan.

"She will want to know all you do," said the old man. "All that has happened to you during the day. Every word of it. She will want to know what you are thinking about, why you smile suddenly, why you are looking sad."

"That is love!" cried Alan.

"Yes," said the old man. "How carefully she will look after you! She will never allow you to be tired, to sit in a draught, to neglect your food. If you are an hour late, she will be terrified. She will think you are killed, or that some siren has caught you."

"I can hardly imagine Diana like that!" cried Alan, overwhelmed with joy.

"You will not have to use your imagination," said the old man. "And, by the way, since there are always sirens, if by any chance you *should*, later on, slip a little, you need not worry. She will forgive you, in the end. She will be terribly hurt, of course, but she will forgive you—in the end."

"That will not happen," said Alan fervently.

"Of course not," said the old man. "But, if it did, you need not worry. She would never divorce you. Oh, no! And, of course, she herself will never give you the least, the very least, grounds for—uneasiness."

"And how much," said Alan, "is this wonderful mixture?"

"It is not as dear," said the old man, "as the glove-cleaner, or life-cleaner, as I sometimes call it. No. That is five thousand dollars, never a penny less. One has to be older than you are, to indulge in that sort of thing. One has to save up for it."

"But the love potion?" said Alan.

"Oh, that," said the old man, opening the drawer in the kitchen table, and taking out a tiny, rather dirty-looking phial. "That is just a dollar."

"I can't tell you how grateful I am," said Alan, watching him fill it.

"I like to oblige," said the old man. "Then customers come back, later in life, when they are rather better off, and want more expensive things. Here you are. You will find it very effective."

"Thank you again," said Alan. "Good-by."

"Au revoir," said the old man.

CARSON MC CULLERS

A Tree. A Rock. A Cloud.

Carson McCullers (1917–   ), was born in Columbus, Georgia, and began writing at an early age. Her first novel, *The Heart Is a Lonely Hunter*, 1940, was well received. Since then many other books have appeared: *Reflections in a Golden Eye*, 1941; *A Member of the Wedding*, a novel that was also produced as a play and a movie, 1946; *The Ballad of the Sad Cafe*, 1951; *Seven*, a volume of short stories, 1954; and *Clock Without Hands*, 1961.

This story presents, in a simple, direct, but moving way, the requirements for the growth of the emotion we call love.

It was raining that morning, and still very dark. When the boy reached the streetcar café he had almost finished his route and he went in for a cup of coffee. The place was an all-night café owned by a bitter and stingy man called Leo. After the raw, empty street the café seemed friendly and bright: along the

A TREE. A ROCK. A CLOUD. From *The Ballad of the Sad Cafe* by Carson McCullers. Reprinted by permission of the publisher, Houghton Mifflin Company.

counter there were a couple of soldiers, three spinners from the cotton mill, and in a corner a man who sat hunched over with his nose and half his face down in a beer mug. The boy wore a helmet such as aviators wear. When he went into the café he unbuckled the chin strap and raised the right flap up over his pink little ear; often as he drank his coffee someone would speak to him in a friendly way. But this morning Leo did not look into his face and none of the men were talking. He paid and was leaving the café when a voice called out to him:

"Son! Hey Son!"

He turned back and the man in the corner was crooking his finger and nodding to him. He had brought his face out of the beer mug and he seemed suddenly very happy. The man was long and pale, with a big nose and faded orange hair.

"Hey Son!"

The boy went toward him. He was an under-sized boy of about twelve, with one shoulder drawn higher than the other because of the weight of the paper sack. His face was shallow, freckled, and his eyes were round child eyes.

"Yeah Mister?"

The man laid one hand on the paper boy's shoulders, then grasped the boy's chin and turned his face slowly from one side to the other. The boy shrank back uneasily.

"Say! What's the big idea?"

The boy's voice was shrill; inside the café it was suddenly very quiet.

The man said slowly: "I love you."

All along the counter the men laughed. The boy, who had scowled and sidled away, did not know what to do. He looked over the counter at Leo, and Leo watched him with a weary, brittle jeer. The boy tried to laugh also. But the man was serious and sad.

"I did not mean to tease you, Son," he said. "Sit down and have a beer with me. There is something I have to explain."

Cautiously, out of the corner of his eye, the paper boy questioned the men along the counter to see what he should do. But they had gone back to their beer or their breakfast and did not notice him. Leo put a cup of coffee on the counter and a little jug of cream.

"He is a minor," Leo said.

The paper boy slid himself up onto the stool. His ear beneath the upturned flap of the helmet was very small and red. The man was nodding at him soberly. "It is important," he said. Then he reached in his hip pocket and brought out something which he held up in the palm of his hand for the boy to see.

"Look very carefully," he said.

The boy stared, but there was nothing to look at very carefully. The man held in his big, grimy palm a photograph. It was the face of a woman, but blurred, so that only the hat and the dress she was wearing stood out clearly.

"See?" the man asked.

The boy nodded and the man placed another picture in his palm. The woman was standing on a beach in a bathing suit. The suit made her stomach very big, and that was the main thing you noticed.

"Got a good look?" He leaned over closer and finally asked: "You ever seen her before?"

The boy sat motionless, staring slantwise at the man. "Not so I know of."

"Very well." The man blew on the photographs and put them back into his pocket. "That was my wife."

"Dead?" the boy asked.

Slowly the man shook his head. He pursed his lips as though about to whistle and answered in a long-drawn way: "Nuuu—" he said. "I will explain."

The beer on the counter before the man was in a large brown mug. He did not pick it up to drink. Instead he bent down and, putting his face over the rim, he rested there for a moment. Then with both hands he tilted the mug and sipped.

"Some night you'll go to sleep with your big nose in a mug and drown," said Leo. "Prominent transient drowns in beer. That would be a cute death."

The paper boy tried to signal to Leo. While the man was not looking he screwed up his face and worked his mouth to question soundlessly: "Drunk?" But Leo only raised his eyebrows and turned away to put some pink strips of bacon on the grill. The man pushed the mug away from him, straightened himself, and folded his loose crooked hands on the counter. His face was sad as he looked at the paper boy. He did not blink, but from time to time the lids closed down with delicate gravity over his pale green eyes. It was nearing dawn and the boy shifted the weight of the paper sack.

"I am talking about love," the man said. "With me it is a science."

The boy half slid down from the stool. But

the man raised his forefinger, and there was something about him that held the boy and would not let him go away.

"Twelve years ago I married the woman in the photograph. She was my wife for one year, nine months, three days, and two nights. I loved her. Yes . . . ." He tightened his blurred, rambling voice and said again: "I loved her. I thought also that she loved me. I was a railroad engineer. She had all home comforts and luxuries. It never crept into my brain that she was not satisfied. But do you know what happened?"

"Mgneeow!" said Leo.

The man did not take his eyes from the boy's face. "She left me. I came in one night and the house was empty and she was gone. She left me."

"With a fellow?" the boy asked.

Gently the man placed his palm down on the counter. "Why naturally, Son. A woman does not run off like that alone."

The café was quiet, the soft rain black and endless in the street outside. Leo pressed down the frying bacon with the prongs of his long fork. "So you have been chasing the floozie for eleven years. You frazzled old rascal!"

For the first time the man glanced at Leo. "Please don't be vulgar. Besides, I was not speaking to you." He turned back to the boy and said in a trusting and secretive undertone: "Let's not pay any attention to him. O.K.?"

The paper boy nodded doubtfully.

"It was like this," the man continued. "I am a person who feels many things. All my life one thing after another has impressed me. Moonlight. The leg of a pretty girl. One thing after another. But the point is that when I had enjoyed anything there was a peculiar sensation as though it was laying around loose in me. Nothing seemed to finish itself up or fit in with the other things. Women? I had my portion of them. The same. Afterwards laying around loose in me. I was a man who had never loved."

Very slowly he closed his eyelids, and the gesture was like a curtain drawn at the end of a scene in a play. When he spoke again his voice was excited and the words came fast— the lobes of his large, loose ears seemed to tremble.

"Then I met this woman. I was fifty-one years old and she always said she was thirty. I met her at a filling station and we were married within three days. And do you know what it was like? I just can't tell you. All I had ever felt was gathered together around this woman. Nothing lay around loose in me any more but was finished up by her."

The man stopped suddenly and stroked his long nose. His voice sank down to a steady and reproachful undertone: "I'm not explaining this right. What happened was this. There were these beautiful feelings and loose little pleasures inside me. And this woman was something like an assembly line for my soul. I run these little pieces of myself through her and I come out complete. Now do you follow me?"

"What was her name?" the boy asked.

"Oh," he said. "I called her Dodo. But that is immaterial."

"Did you try to make her come back?"

The man did not seem to hear. "Under the circumstances you can imagine how I felt when she left me."

Leo took the bacon from the grill and folded two strips of it between a bun. He had a gray face, with slitted eyes, and a pinched nose saddled by faint blue shadows. One of the mill workers signaled for more coffee and Leo poured it. He did not give refills on coffee free. The spinner ate breakfast there every morning, but the better Leo knew his customers the stingier he treated them. He nibbled his own bun as though he grudged it to himself.

"And you never got hold of her again?"

The boy did not know what to think of the man, and his child's face was uncertain with mingled curiosity and doubt. He was new on the paper route; it was still strange to him to be out in the town in the black, queer early morning.

"Yes," the man said. "I took a number of steps to get her back. I went around trying to locate her. I went to Tulsa where she had folks. And to Mobile. I went to every town she had ever mentioned to me, and I hunted down every man she had formerly been connected with. Tulsa, Atlanta, Chicago, Cheehaw, Memphis. . . . For the better part of two years I chased around the country trying to lay hold of her."

"But the pair of them had vanished from the face of the earth!" said Leo.

"Don't listen to him," the man said confidentially. "And also just forget those two years. They are not important. What matters is that around the third year a curious thing begun to happen to me."

"What?" the boy asked.

The man leaned down and tilted his mug to take a sip of beer. But as he hovered over the mug his nostrils fluttered slightly; he sniffed the staleness of the beer and did not drink. "Love is a curious thing to begin with. At first I thought only of getting her back. It was a kind of mania. But then as time went on I tried to remember her. But do you know what happened?"

"No," the boy said.

"When I laid myself down on a bed and tried to think about her my mind became a blank. I couldn't see her. I would take out her pictures and look. No good. Nothing doing. A blank. Can you imagine it?"

"Say Mac!" Leo called down the counter. "Can you imagine this bozo's mind a blank!"

Slowly, as though fanning away flies, the man waved his hand. His green eyes were concentrated and fixed on the shallow little face of the paper boy.

"But a sudden piece of glass on a sidewalk. Or a nickel tune in a music box. A shadow on a wall at night. And I would remember. It might happen in a street and I would cry or bang my head against a lamppost. You follow me?"

"A piece of glass . . ." the boy said.

"Anything. I would walk around and I had no power of how and when to remember her. You think you can put up a kind of shield. But remembering don't come to a man face forward—it corners around sideways. I was at the mercy of everything I saw and heard. Suddenly instead of me combing the coun-

tryside to find her she begun to chase me around in my very soul. *She* chasing *me*, mind you! And in my soul."

The boy asked finally: "What part of the country were you in then?"

"Ooh," the man groaned. "I was a sick mortal. It was like smallpox. I confess, Son, that I boozed. I fornicated. I committed any sin that suddenly appealed to me. I am loath to confess it but I will do so. When I recall that period it is all curdled in my mind, it was so terrible."

The man leaned his head down and tapped his forehead on the counter. For a few seconds he stayed bowed over in this position, the back of his stringy neck covered with orange furze, his hands with their long warped fingers held palm to palm in an attitude of prayer. Then the man straightened himself; he was smiling and suddenly his face was bright and tremulous and old.

"It was in the fifth year that it happened," he said. "And with it I started my science."

Leo's mouth jerked with a pale, quick grin. "Well none of we boys are getting any younger," he said. Then with sudden anger he balled up a dishcloth he was holding and threw it down hard on the floor. "You draggletailed old Romeo!"

"What happened?" the boy asked.

The old man's voice was high and clear: "Peace," he answered.

"Huh?"

"It is hard to explain scientifically, Son," he said. "I guess the logical explanation is that she and I had fleed around from each other for so long that finally we just got tangled up together and lay down and quit. Peace. A queer and beautiful blankness. It was spring in Portland and the rain came every afternoon. All evening I just stayed there on my bed in the dark. And that is how the science come to me."

The windows in the streetcar were pale blue with light. The two soldiers paid for their beers and opened the door—one of the soldiers combed his hair and wiped off his muddy puttees before they went outside. The three mill workers bent silently over their breakfasts. Leo's clock was ticking on the wall.

"It is this. And listen carefully. I meditated on love and reasoned it out. I realized what is wrong with us. Men fall in love for the first time. And what do they fall in love with?"

The boy's soft mouth was partly open and he did not answer.

"A woman," the old man said. "Without science, with nothing to go by, they undertake the most dangerous and sacred experience in God's earth. They fall in love with a woman. Is that correct, Son?"

"Yeah," the boy said faintly.

"They start at the wrong end of love. They begin at the climax. Can you wonder it is so miserable? Do you know how men should love?"

The old man reached over and grasped the boy by the collar of his leather jacket. He gave him a gentle little shake and his green eyes gazed down unblinking and grave.

"Son, do you know how love should be begun?"

The boy sat small and listening and still. Slowly he shook his head. The old man leaned closer and whispered:

"A tree. A rock. A cloud."

It was still raining outside in the street: a mild, gray, endless rain. The mill whistle blew for the six o'clock shift and the three spinners paid and went away. There was no one in the café but Leo, the old man, and the little paper boy.

"The weather was like this in Portland," he said. "At the time my science was begun. I meditated and I started very cautious. I would pick up something from the street and take it home with me. I bought a goldfish and I concentrated on the goldfish and I loved it. I graduated from one thing to another. Day by day I was getting this technique. On the road from Portland to San Diego—"

"Aw shut up!" screamed Leo suddenly. "Shut up! Shut up!"

The old man still held the collar of the boy's jacket; he was trembling and his face was earnest and bright and wild. "For six years now I have gone around by myself and built up my science. And now I am a master. Son. I can love anything. No longer do I have to think about it even. I see a street full of peo-ple and a beautiful light comes in me. I watch a bird in the sky. Or I meet a traveler on the road. Everything, Son. And anybody. All stranger and all loved! Do you realize what a science like mine can mean?"

The boy held himself stiffly, his hands curled tight around the counter edge. Finally he asked: "Did you ever really find that lady?"

"What? What say, Son?"

"I mean," the boy asked timidly. "Have you fallen in love with a woman again?"

The old man loosened his grasp on the boy's collar. He turned away and for the first time his green eyes had a vague and scattered look. He lifted the mug from the counter, drank down the yellow beer. His head was shaking slowly from side to side. Then finally he answered: "No, Son. You see that is the last step in my science. I go cautious. And I am not quite ready yet."

"Well!" said Leo. "Well well well!"

The old man stood in the open doorway. "Remember," he said. Framed there in the gray damp light of the early morning he looked shrunken and seedy and frail. But his smile was bright. "Remember I love you," he said with a last nod. And the door closed quietly behind him.

The boy did not speak for a long time. He pulled down the bangs on his forehead and slid his grimy little forefinger around the rim of his empty cup. Then without looking at Leo he finally asked:

"Was he drunk?"

"No," said Leo shortly.

The boy raised his clear voice higher. "Then was he a dope fiend?"

"No."

The boy looked up at Leo, and his flat little face was desperate, his voice urgent and shrill. "Was he crazy? Do you think he was a lunatic?" The paper boy's voice dropped suddenly with doubt. "Leo? Or not?"

But Leo would not answer him. Leo had run a night café for fourteen years, and he held himself to be a critic of craziness. There were the town characters and also the transients who roamed in from the night. He knew the manias of all of them. But he did not want to satisfy the questions of the waiting child. He tightened his pale face and was silent.

So the boy pulled down the right flap of his helmet and as he turned to leave he made the only comment that seemed safe to him, the only remark that could not be laughed down and despised:

"He sure has done a lot of traveling."

JOHN STEINBECK

The Chrysanthemums

John Steinbeck (1902–   ) was born in Salinas, California, and attended Stanford University. *Pastures of Heaven,* 1932, a collection of short stories about a rural community in the Salinas Valley, foreshadowed his later style. *Tortilla Flat,* 1935, first brought him attention as a writer, and this success was followed by *In Dubious Battle,* 1936; *Of Mice and Men,* 1937; and *The Grapes of Wrath,* 1939, for which he received the Pulitzer Prize. During World War II he was a war reporter for the New York *Herald Tribune.* In 1941, with Edward F. Ricketts, he wrote *Sea of Cortez,* a report of their explorations in the Gulf of California. *East of Eden,* 1952, was his first major novel after the war. This was followed by *The Winter of Our Discontent,* 1961; and *Travels with Charley,* 1962, an account of his journey across America. *America and Americans* appeared in 1966. In 1962 he was awarded the Nobel Prize for Literature and in 1964 he received the Presidential Medal of Freedom.

Mr. Steinbeck's short stories and novels tend to begin realistically and conclude symbolically. This tendency is vividly displayed in *The Grapes of Wrath.* It is also shown in "The Chrysanthemums," where the reader senses a strong conflict but, because of indirection in the telling of the story, must draw his own inference.

The high grey-flannel fog of winter closed off the Salinas Valley from the sky and from all the rest of the world. On every side it sat like a lid on the mountains and made of the great valley a closed pot. On the broad, level land floor the gang plows bit deep and left the black earth shining like metal where the shares had cut. On the foothill ranches across the Salinas River, the yellow stubble fields seemed to be bathed in pale cold sunshine, but there was no sunshine in the valley now in December. The thick willow scrub along the river flamed with sharp and positive yellow leaves.

It was a time of quiet and of waiting. The air was cold and tender. A light wind blew up from the southwest so that the farmers were mildly hopeful of a good rain before long; but fog and rain did not go together.

Across the river, on Henry Allen's foothill ranch there was little work to be done, for the hay was cut and stored and the orchards were plowed up to receive the rain deeply when it should come. The cattle on the higher slopes were becoming shaggy and rough-coated.

Elisa Allen, working in her flower garden, looked down across the yard and saw Henry, her husband, talking to two men in business suits. The three of them stood by the tractor shed, each man with one foot on the side of the little Fordson. They smoked cigarettes and studied the machine as they talked.

Elisa watched them for a moment and then went back to her work. She was thirty-five. Her face was lean and strong and her eyes were as clear as water. Her figure looked blocked and heavy in her gardening costume, a man's black hat pulled low down over her eyes, clod-hopper shoes, a figured print dress almost completely covered by a big corduroy apron with four big pockets to hold the snips, the trowel and scratcher, the seeds and the knife she worked with. She wore heavy leather gloves to protect her hands while she worked.

She was cutting down the old year's chrysanthemum stalks with a pair of short and powerful scissors. She looked down toward the men by the tractor shed now and then. Her face was eager and mature and handsome; even her work with the scissors was over-eager, over-powerful. The chrysanthemum stems seemed too small and easy for her energy.

She brushed a cloud of hair out of her eyes with the back of her glove, and left a smudge of earth on her cheek in doing it. Behind her stood the neat white farm house with red geraniums close-banked around it as high as the windows. It was a hard-swept looking little house, with hard-polished windows, and a clean mud-mat on the front steps.

Elisa cast another glance toward the tractor shed. The strangers were getting into their Ford coupe. She took off a glove and put her strong fingers down into the forest of new green chrysanthemum sprouts that were growing around the old roots. She spread the leaves and looked down among the close-growing stems. No aphids were there, no sowbugs or snails or cutworms. Her terrier fingers destroyed such pests before they could get started.

Elisa started at the sound of her husband's voice. He had come near quietly, and he leaned over the wire fence that protected her flower garden from cattle and dogs and chickens.

"At it again," he said. "You've got a strong new crop coming."

Elisa straightened her back and pulled on the gardening glove again. "Yes. They'll be strong this coming year." In her tone and on her face there was a little smugness.

"You've got a gift with things," Henry observed. "Some of those yellow chrysanthemums you had this year were ten inches across. I wish you'd work out in the orchard and raise some apples that big."

Her eyes sharpened. "Maybe I could do it, too. I've a gift with things, all right. My mother had it. She could stick anything in the ground and make it grow. She said it was having planters' hands that knew how to do it."

"Well, it sure works with flowers," he said.

"Henry, who were those men you were talking to?"

"Why, sure, that's what I came to tell you. They were from the Western Meat Company. I sold those thirty head of three-year-old steers. Got nearly my own price, too."

"Good," she said. "Good for you."

"And I thought," he continued, "I thought how it's Saturday afternoon, and we might go into Salinas for dinner at a restaurant, and then to a picture show—to celebrate, you see."

"Good," she repeated. "Oh, yes. That will be good."

Henry put on his joking tone. "There's fights tonight. How'd you like to go to the fights?"

"Oh, no," she said breathlessly. "No, I wouldn't like fights."

"Just fooling, Elisa. We'll go to a movie. Let's see. It's two now. I'm going to take Scotty and bring down those steers from the hill. It'll take us maybe two hours. We'll go in town about five and have dinner at the Cominos Hotel. Like that?"

"Of course I'll like it. It's good to eat away from home."

"All right, then. I'll go get up a couple of horses."

She said, "I'll have plenty of time to transplant some of these sets, I guess."

She heard her husband calling Scotty down by the barn. And a little later she saw the two men ride up the pale yellow hillside in search of the steers.

There was a little square sandy bed kept for rooting the chrysanthemums. With her trowel she turned the soil over and over, and smoothed it and patted it firm. Then she dug ten parallel trenches to receive the sets. Back at the chrysanthemum bed she pulled out the little crisp shoots, trimmed off the leaves of each one with her scissors and laid it on a small orderly pile.

A squeak of wheels and plod of hoofs came from the road. Elisa looked up. The country road ran along the dense bank of willows and cottonwoods that bordered the river, and up this road came a curious vehicle, curiously drawn. It was an old spring-wagon, with a round canvas top on it like the cover of a prairie schooner. It was drawn by an old bay horse and a little grey-and-white burro. A big stubble-bearded man sat between the cover flaps and drove the crawling team. Underneath the wagon, between the hind wheels, a lean and rangy mongrel dog walked sedately. Words were painted on the canvas in clumsy, crooked letters. "Pots, pans, knives, sisors, lawn mores, Fixed." Two rows of articles, and the triumphantly definitive "Fixed" below. The black paint had run down in little sharp points beneath each letter.

Elisa, squatting on the ground, watched to see the crazy, loose-jointed wagon pass by. But it didn't pass. It turned into the farm road in front of her house, crooked old wheels skirling and squeaking. The rangy dog darted from between the wheels and ran ahead. Instantly the two ranch shepherds flew out at him. Then all three stopped, and with stiff and quivering tails, with taut straight legs, with ambassadorial dignity, they slowly circled, sniffing daintily. The caravan pulled up to Elisa's wire fence and stopped. Now the newcomer dog, feeling outnumbered, lowered his tail and retired under the wagon with raised hackles and bared teeth.

The man on the wagon seat called out, "That's a bad dog in a fight when he gets started."

Elisa laughed. "I see he is. How soon does he generally get started?"

The man caught up her laughter and echoed it heartily. "Sometimes not for weeks and weeks," he said. He climbed stiffly down, over the wheel. The horse and the donkey drooped like unwatered flowers.

Elisa saw that he was a very big man. Although his hair and beard were greying, he did not look old. His worn black suit was wrinkled and spotted with grease. The laughter had disappeared from his face and eyes the moment his laughing voice ceased. His eyes were dark, and they were full of the brooding that gets in the eyes of teamsters and of sailors. The calloused hands he rested on the wire fence were cracked, and every crack was a black line. He took off his battered hat.

"I'm off my general road, ma'am," he said. "Does this dirt road cut over across the river to the Los Angeles highway?"

Elisa stood up and shoved the thick scissors in her apron pocket. "Well, yes, it does, but it winds around and then fords the river. I don't think your team could pull through the sand."

He replied with some asperity, "It might surprise you what them beasts can pull through."

"When they get started?" she asked.

He smiled for a second. "Yes. When they get started."

"Well," said Elisa, "I think you'll save time if you go back to the Salinas road and pick up the highway there."

He drew a big finger down the chicken wire and made it sing. "I ain't in any hurry, ma'am. I go from Seattle to San Diego and back every year. Takes all my time. About six months each way. I aim to follow nice weather."

Elisa took off her gloves and stuffed them

in the apron pocket with the scissors. She touched the under edge of her man's hat, searching for fugitive hairs. "That sounds like a nice kind of a way to live," she said.

He leaned confidentially over the fence. "Maybe you noticed the writing on my wagon. I mend pots and sharpen knives and scissors. You got any of them things to do?"

"Oh, no," she said quickly. "Nothing like that." Her eyes hardened with resistance.

"Scissors is the worst thing," he explained. "Most people just ruin scissors trying to sharpen 'em, but I know how. I got a special tool. It's a little bobbit kind of thing, and patented. But it sure does the trick."

"No. My scissors are all sharp."

"All right, then. Take a pot," he continued earnestly, "a bent pot, or a pot with a hole. I can make it like new so you don't have to buy no new ones. That's a saving for you."

"No," she said shortly. "I tell you I have nothing like that for you to do."

His face fell to an exaggerated sadness. His voice took on a whining undertone. "I ain't had a thing to do today. Maybe I won't have no supper tonight. You see I'm off my regular road. I know folks on the highway clear from Seattle to San Diego. They save their things for me to sharpen up because they know I do it so good and save them money."

"I'm sorry," Elisa said irritably. "I haven't anything for you to do."

His eyes left her face and fell to searching the ground. They roamed about until they came to the chrysanthemum bed where she had been working. "What's them plants, ma'am?"

The irritation and resistance melted from Elisa's face. "Oh, those are chrysanthemums, giant whites and yellows. I raise them every year, bigger than anybody around here."

"Kind of a long-stemmed flower? Looks like a quick puff of colored smoke?" he asked.

"That's it. What a nice way to describe them."

"They smell kind of nasty till you get used to them," he said.

"It's a good bitter smell," she retorted, "not nasty at all."

He changed his tone quickly. "I like the smell myself."

"I had ten-inch blooms this year," she said.

The man leaned farther over the fence. "Look. I know a lady down the road a piece, has got the nicest garden you ever seen. Got nearly every kind of flower but no chrysanthemums. Last time I was mending a copper-bottom washtub for her (that's a hard job but I do it good), she said to me, 'If you ever run acrost some nice chrysanthemums I wish you'd try to get me a few seeds.' That's what she told me."

Elisa's eyes grew alert and eager. "She couldn't have known much about chrysanthemums. You can raise them from seed, but it's much easier to root the little sprouts you see there."

"Oh," he said. "I s'pose I can't take none to her, then."

"Why yes you can," Elisa cried. "I can put some in damp sand, and you can carry them right along with you. They'll take root in the pot if you keep them damp. And then she can transplant them."

"She'd sure like to have some, ma'am. You say they're nice ones?"

"Beautiful," she said. "Oh, beautiful." Her eyes shone. She tore off the battered hat and shook out her dark pretty hair. "I'll put them in a flower pot, and you can take them right with you. Come into the yard."

While the man came through the picket fence Elisa ran excitedly along the geranium-bordered path to the back of the house. And she returned carrying a big red flower pot. The gloves were forgotten now. She kneeled on the ground by the starting bed and dug up the sandy soil with her fingers and scooped it into the bright new flower pot. Then she picked up the little pile of shoots she had prepared. With her strong fingers she pressed them into the sand and tamped around them with her knuckles. The man stood over her. "I'll tell you what to do," she said. "You remember so you can tell the lady."

"Yes, I'll try to remember."

"Well, look. These will take root in about a month. Then she must set them out, about a

foot apart in good rich earth like this, see?"
She lifted a handful of dark soil for him to
look at. "They'll grow fast and tall. Now remember this. In July tell her to cut them
down, about eight inches from the ground."

"Before they bloom?" he asked.

"Yes, before they bloom." Her face was tight
with eagerness. "They'll grow right up again.
About the last of September the buds will
start."

She stopped and seemed perplexed. "It's the
budding that takes the most care," she said
hesitantly. "I don't know how to tell you."
She looked deep into his eyes, searchingly.
Her mouth opened a little, and she seemed to
be listening. "I'll try to tell you," she said. "Did
you ever hear of planting hands?"

"Can't say I have, ma'am."

"Well, I can only tell you what it feels like.
It's when you're picking off the buds you don't
want. Everything goes right down into your
finger-tips. You watch your fingers work. They
do it themselves. You can feel how it is. They
pick and pick the buds. They never make a
mistake. They're with the plant. Do you see?
Your fingers and the plant. You can feel that,
right up your arm. They know. They never
make a mistake. You can feel it. When you're
like that you can't do anything wrong. Do you
see that? Can you understand that?"

She was kneeling on the ground looking up
at him. Her breast swelled passionately.

The man's eyes narrowed. He looked away
self-consciously. "Maybe I know," he said.
"Sometimes in the night in the wagon there—"

Elisa's voice grew husky. She broke in on
him. "I've never lived as you do, but I know
what you mean. When the night is dark—why,
the stars are sharp-pointed, and there's quiet.
Why, you rise up and up! Every pointed star
gets driven into your body. It's like that. Hot
and sharp and—lovely."

Kneeling there, her hand went out toward
his legs in the greasy black trousers. Her hesitant fingers almost touched the cloth. Then
her hand dropped to the ground. She
crouched low like a fawning dog.

He said, "It's nice, just like you say. Only
when you don't have no dinner, it ain't."

She stood up then, very straight, and her
face was ashamed. She held the flower pot
out to him and placed it gently in his arms.
"Here. Put it in your wagon, on the seat, where
you can watch it. Maybe I can find something
for you to do."

At the back of the house she dug in the
can pile and found two old and battered
aluminum saucepans. She carried them back
and gave them to him. "Here, maybe you can
fix these."

His manner changed. He became professional. "Good as new I can fix them." At the
back of his wagon he set a little anvil, and
out of an oily tool box dug a small machine
hammer. Elisa came through the gate to watch
him while he pounded out the dents in the
kettles. His mouth grew sure and knowing.
At a difficult part of the work he sucked his
under-lip.

"You sleep right in the wagon?" Elisa asked.

"Right in the wagon, ma'am. Rain or shine
I'm dry as a cow in there."

"It must be nice," she said. "It must be very
nice. I wish women could do such things."

"It ain't the right kind of a life for a
woman."

Her upper lip raised a little, showing her
teeth. "How do you know? How can you tell?"
she said.

"I don't know, ma'am," he protested. "Of
course I don't know. Now here's your kettles,
done. You don't have to buy no new ones."

"How much?"

"Oh, fifty cents'll do. I keep my prices down
and my work good. That's why I have all them
satisfied customers up and down the highway."

Elisa brought him a fifty-cent piece from
the house and dropped it in his hand. "You
might be surprised to have a rival some time.
I can sharpen scissors, too. And I can beat
the dents out of little pots. I could show you
what a woman might do."

He put his hammer back in the oily box and
shoved the little anvil out of sight. "It would
be a lonely life for a woman, ma'am, and a
scarey life, too, with animals creeping under
the wagon all night." He climbed over the
singletree, steadying himself with a hand on

the burro's white rump. He settled himself in the seat, picked up the lines. "Thank you kindly, ma'am," he said. "I'll do like you told me; I'll go back and catch the Salinas road."

"Mind," she called, "if you're long in getting there, keep the sand damp."

"Sand, ma'am? . . . Sand? Oh, sure. You mean around the chrysanthemums. Sure I will." He clucked his tongue. The beasts leaned luxuriously into their collars. The mongrel dog took his place between the back wheels. The wagon turned and crawled out the entrance road and back the way it had come, along the river.

Elisa stood in front of her wire fence watching the slow progress of the caravan. Her shoulders were straight, her head thrown back, her eyes half-closed, so that the scene came vaguely into them. Her lips moved silently, forming the words "Good-bye—good-bye." Then she whispered, "That's a bright direction. There's a glowing there." The sound of her whisper startled her. She shook herself free and looked about to see whether anyone had been listening. Only the dogs had heard. They lifted their heads toward her from their sleeping in the dust, and then stretched out their chins and settled asleep again. Elisa turned and ran hurriedly into the house.

In the kitchen she reached behind the stove and felt the water tank. It was full of hot water from the noonday cooking. In the bathroom she tore off her soiled clothes and flung them into the corner. And then she scrubbed herself with a little block of pumice, legs and thighs, loins and chest and arms, until her skin was scratched and red. When she had dried herself she stood in front of a mirror in her bedroom and looked at her body. She tightened her stomach and threw out her chest. She turned and looked over her shoulder at her back.

After a while she began to dress, slowly. She put on her newest underclothing and her nicest stockings and the dress which was the symbol of her prettiness. She worked carefully on her hair, pencilled her eyebrows and rouged her lips.

Before she was finished she heard the little thunder of hoofs and the shouts of Henry and his helper as they drove the red steers into the corral. She heard the gate bang shut and set herself for Henry's arrival.

His step sounded on the porch. He entered the house calling, "Elisa, where are you?"

"In my room, dressing. I'm not ready. There's hot water for your bath. Hurry up. It's getting late."

When she heard him splashing in the tub, Elisa laid his dark suit on the bed, and shirt and socks and tie beside it. She stood his polished shoes on the floor beside the bed. Then she went to the porch and sat primly and stiffly down. She looked toward the river road where the willow-line was still yellow with frosted leaves so that under the high grey fog they seemed a thin band of sunshine. This was the only color in the grey afternoon. She sat unmoving for a long time. Her eyes blinked rarely.

Henry came banging out of the door, shoving his tie inside his vest as he came. Elisa stiffened and her face grew tight. Henry stopped short and looked at her. "Why—why, Elisa. You look so nice!"

"Nice? You think I look nice? What do you mean by 'nice'?"

Henry blundered on. "I don't know. I mean you look different, strong and happy."

"I am strong? Yes, strong. What do you mean 'strong'?"

He looked bewildered. "You're playing some kind of a game," he said helplessly. "It's a kind of a play. You look strong enough to break a calf over your knee, happy enough to eat it like a watermelon."

For a second she lost her rigidity. "Henry! Don't talk like that. You didn't know what you said." She grew complete again. "I'm strong," she boasted. "I never knew before how strong."

Henry looked down toward the tractor shed, and when he brought his eyes back to her, they were his own again. "I'll get out the car. You can put on your coat while I'm starting."

Elisa went into the house. She heard him drive to the gate and idle down his motor, and then she took a long time to put on her hat. She pulled it here and pressed it there. When Henry turned the motor off she slipped into her coat and went out.

The little roadster bounced along on the dirt road by the river, raising the birds and driving the rabbits into the brush. Two cranes flapped heavily over the willow-line and dropped into the river-bed.

Far ahead on the road Elisa saw a dark speck. She knew.

She tried not to look as they passed it, but her eyes would not obey. She whispered to herself sadly, "He might have thrown them off the road. That wouldn't have been much trouble, not very much. But he kept the pot," she explained. "He had to keep the pot. That's why he couldn't get them off the road."

The roadster turned a bend and she saw the caravan ahead. She swung full around toward her husband so she could not see the little covered wagon and the mismatched team as the car passed them.

In a moment it was over. The thing was done. She did not look back. She said loudly, to be heard above the motor, "It will be good, tonight, a good dinner."

"Now you're changed again," Henry complained. He took one hand from the wheel and patted her knee. "I ought to take you in to dinner oftener. It would be good for both of us. We get so heavy out on the ranch."

"Henry," she asked, "could we have wine at dinner?"

"Sure we could. Say! That will be fine."

She was silent for a while; then she said, "Henry, at those prize fights, do the men hurt each other very much?"

"Sometimes a little, not often. Why?"

"Well, I've read how they break noses, and blood runs down their chests. I've read how the fighting gloves get heavy and soggy with blood."

He looked around at her. "What's the matter, Elisa? I didn't know you read things like that." He brought the car to a stop, then turned to the right over the Salinas River bridge.

"Do any women ever go to the fights?" she asked.

"Oh, sure, some. What's the matter, Elisa? Do you want to go? I don't think you'd like it, but I'll take you if you really want to go."

She relaxed limply in the seat. "Oh, no. No. I don't want to go. I'm sure I don't." Her face was turned away from him. "It will be enough if we can have wine. It will be plenty." She turned up her coat collar so he could not see that she was crying weakly—like an old woman.

FRIEDRICH DÜRRENMATT

The Tunnel

Friedrich Dürrenmatt (1921–   ), a Swiss writer of fiction and drama, combines comic real-life experiences with macabre imaginings to create expressionistic stories and plays. His best known story, later recast as a play, is "The Visit," 1958. A novel entitled *Traps* appeared in 1960. *Four Plays, 1957–1962* was published in 1965.

In "The Tunnel," published in the United States in 1961, Dürrenmatt creates a symbolic microcosm of an endless tunnel and a runaway train with its crew and passengers.

The young man who boarded his usual train that Sunday afternoon was twenty-four years old and fat. He was fat in order to protect himself, for anything he perceived out of the ordinary terrified him. Indeed, this clarity of vision was probably the only real ability he possessed, and even this was a burden to him. Although his fat gave a general protection to his body, he found it necessary to stuff every sort of hole in his body through which the terrifying influences might reach him. He smoked cigars (Ormond Brazil 10). He wore a pair of sunglasses over his ordinary glasses. He even stuffed his ears with wads of cotton wool. At twenty-four he was still dependent on his parents, a consequence of rather nebulous studies at the University. And the University was two hours away from home by train. Departure time five-fifty. Arrival at seven twenty-seven.

And so this student, fat and twenty-four years old, boarded his usual Sunday train to attend a seminar the following day. The fact that he had already decided to skip class was irrelevant. As he left his home town the afternoon sun shone from a cloudless summer sky. It was pleasant weather for a trip he knew almost by heart. The train's route lay between the Alps and the Juras, past rich villages and towns, over a river and, after some twenty minutes further travel, into a little tunnel just beyond Burgdorf. The train was overcrowded and he had entered at one of the front cars. With considerable difficulty he worked his way toward the rear. Perspiring, and with two pairs of glasses, he offered an oafish appearance. All the travellers were sitting closely packed, some even on suitcases. All the second-class compartments were occupied, and only the first-class compartments were relatively empty. The young man fought through the melee of families and recruits, students and lovers, falling against this one or that one as the train swayed, stumbling against stomachs and breasts until he came to

THE TUNNEL by Friedrich Dürrenmatt, translated by Carla Colter and Alison Scott, originally published in *Evergreen Review*, Volume 5, Number 17, March–April 1961. Copyright © 1961 by Evergreen Review, Inc.

a seat in the last car. At last he had found space enough to have a bench to himself, a pleasant surprise, since third-class coaches are seldom divided into compartments with benches. Opposite him, playing a solitary game of chess, he noted a man even fatter than himself, and on the same bench, near the corridor, sat a red-haired girl reading a novel. The young man gratefully chose the window seat on the empty bench. He had just lit an Ormond Brazil 10 when the train entered the little tunnel. Of course he had travelled this stretch many times before, almost every Saturday and Sunday throughout the past year, but he had never found the opportunity to examine the tunnel closely. He had, in fact, been only vaguely aware of it. Several times he had intended to give it his full attention, but each time he had been thinking of other matters, and each time the brief plunge into darkness had passed unnoticed, so fast was the train and so brief its plunge into the darkness of the little tunnel.

And even this time he had not been thinking of the tunnel and so had forgotten to take off his sunglasses. Outside the tunnel the sun had been shining with all its force, flooding the hills and woods and the distant chain of the Juras with golden evening light. Even the little houses of the town through which they had just passed had seemed built of gold. This abrupt passage from light to darkness must then be the reason why the tunnel seemed so much longer than usual. He waited patiently in the dark compartment for the return to daylight. At any moment the first pale shimmer of daylight would gleam on his window-pane, widen as quickly as a flash of lightning, then close in powerfully with its full yellow brightness. Nevertheless, the darkness lasted. He took off his sunglasses. At about the same time the girl lit a cigarette. As her match flared orange he thought he detected a grim annoyance in her face. No doubt she resented the interruption in her perusal of her novel. He looked at his wrist watch. The luminous dial said six-ten.

He leaned back, settling himself in the corner between window and compartment wall, and directed his thoughts to the com-

plications of his studies. No one really believed
he was studying at all. He thought of the
seminar he had to attend the next day, and
which he would not attend. Each of his activities seemed a pretext designed to achieve
order behind the façade of routine pursuits.
Perhaps what he sought was not order itself,
but only a semblance of order. The art of an
actor who used his fat, his cigars and his
cotton wool as make-up for a genteel comedy,
while all the while he knew himself to be a
part of some monstrous farce. When he next
looked at his watch the time was six-fifteen.
The train was still in the tunnel. He felt
confused. At last the light bulbs flickered and
the compartment brightened. The red-haired
girl returned to her novel and the fat gentleman resumed his solitary chess game. The
whole compartment now appeared reflected
in the window. But outside, on the other side
of the window, the tunnel was still there.

He stepped into the corridor in which a
tall man was walking up and down restlessly.
He observed the light raincoat and the black
scarf around the gentleman's neck. Surely
there was no need for a scarf in this weather?
A black scarf? He peered into the other
compartments in the rear coach. The passengers were reading their newspapers or
chatting. Normal. He returned to his corner
and sat down. The tunnel must come to an
end any minute now. At any second? His
wrist watch read six-twenty. He felt an obscure
annoyance with himself for not having paid
more attention to the tunnel on previous trips.
They had been in the tunnel for a quarter
of an hour now. And surely, allowing for the
speed of the train, it must be one of the
longest tunnels in Switzerland. Or perhaps
he had taken the wrong train. But he could
recall no other tunnel of such length and
importance within twenty minutes of his home.
On impulse he asked the fat chess player if
the train was indeed bound for Zurich. The
man confirmed this. The student ventured
again that he hadn't known that there was
such a long tunnel on this part of the journey.
The chess player was more than a little
annoyed to have his difficult considerations

interrupted a second time. He replied testily
that in Switzerland there were a great many
tunnels, in fact, an extraordinary number of
tunnels, that he was actually travelling in
Switzerland for the first time, but that an
affluence of tunnels was the first thing one
noticed about Switzerland, and indeed, his
statistical almanac confirmed the fact that no
country possessed such a positive abundance
of tunnels as Switzerland! And he added that
now he must excuse himself; he was very
sorry, really, but a most difficult chess problem in regard to the Nimzowitsch Defence
occupied his mind and he could afford no
further diversions. The last remark was polite,
but firm. It was evident that no further conversation could be expected from the chess
player and, in any event, he could be of little
use, since the route was new to him.

At that moment the conductor appeared,
and the student had high hopes that his ticket
would be refused. The official was pale and
scrawny. He gave an impression of nervousness as he remarked to the girl near the door
that she would have to change trains at
Olten. Although Olten was also a regular stop
on the Zurich run, the young man did not
give up hope of being on the wrong train,
so complete was his conviction that he had
mistaken trains in boarding. He didn't doubt
that he would have to pay extra fare, but
he accepted the expense with equanimity. The
return to daylight would be cheap at the
price. He therefore handed his ticket to the
conductor and said that his destination was
Zurich. He accomplished the speech without
once removing the Ormond Brazil 10 from his
mouth.

"But the gentleman is on the right train,"
replied the conductor as he inspected the
ticket.

"But we're going through a tunnel!" The
young man had spoken with considerable
anger. He was determined to put an end to
the confusion. The official replied that they
had just passed Herzogenbuchsee and would
soon approach Langenthal where the train
was due at six-twenty. The young man looked
at his watch. Six-twenty. But they had been

travelling through the tunnel for the past twenty minutes, he persisted. The conductor raised his brows.

"This is the Zurich train," he said, now looking for the first time toward the window. "Six-twenty," he said again, uneasily. "We'll be in Olten soon. Arrival time six thirty-seven. We must have gone into some bad weather suddenly. A storm. Yes. That's why it's dark."

The gentleman with the Nimzowitsch Defence problem entered the conversation now. He had been holding out his ticket (and holding up his game) for some time, but the conductor had not yet noticed him. "Nonsense," he interjected. "Nonsense! We're travelling through a tunnel. I can see the rock clearly. Looks like granite. Switzerland has more tunnels than all the rest of the world put together. Read it in a statistical almanac."

The conductor relieved him of his ticket, and repeated pleadingly that this was truly the Zurich train. Unmollified, the young man demanded to speak to the Chief Conductor. The ticket collector now felt his dignity to have been abused. He directed the student to the front of the train, but reiterated huffily that the train was going to Zurich, that the time was now six twenty-five, that in twelve minutes time (according to the summer schedule) the train would arrive in Olten, and that the young man should have no further doubts on that point. *He* travelled this train at least twelve times a month.

Nevertheless the young scholar set off to find the Chief Conductor. Movement through the crowded train now seemed even more difficult than before. The train must be travelling exceedingly fast. In any event, it was making a frightful racket. He stuffed the wads of cotton a little more firmly into his ears, for he had loosened them in order to speak to the ticket collector. The passengers were behaving calmly. This train was no different from any other Sunday afternoon train, and no one appeared worried. In the second-class compartments he came upon an Englishman standing by the corridor window. "Simplon," he was saying, as he tapped the pane with his pipe and beamed inanely.

Things were very much as usual in the dining car too. No seats were vacant, and neither waiters nor diners, occupied with Wiener Schnitzel and rice, made any comment on the tunnel. But there, near the exit of the dining car, he recognized the red bag of the Chief Conductor.

"What can I do for you, sir?" The Chief Conductor was a tall man, quiet behind a carefully groomed black mustache and neat rimless glasses.

"We have been in a tunnel for twenty-five minutes."

The Conductor did not look toward the windows, as the young man might have expected, but turned to a nearby waiter. "Give me a packet of Ormond 10," he said. "I smoke the same brand as the gentleman here." The waiter, however, indicated that the brand was not in stock, and the young man, glad of an opportunity for further conversation, proffered a Brazil.

"Thank you," returned the Conductor. "In Olten I shall hardly have time to buy any. You are doing me a great favor. Smoking is a most important business. Will you come this way, please?"

Mystified, the young man followed him into the freight car ahead of the diner.

"The next car is the locomotive," offered the official. "This is the front of the train."

A sickly yellow light burned amid the baggage. Most of the car lay in total darkness. The side doors were barred, as was the small window beside them, and through its irons the greater blackness of the tunnel seeped in. The trunks, many decorated with hotel stickers, the bicycles and the baby carriage that composed the cargo of the coach seemed haphazardly arranged. The Chief Conductor, an obviously precise man, hung his red bag on a nearby hook.

"What can I do for you?" he asked again, without, however, looking at the student. Instead, he began to enter neat columns in a book he had taken from his pocket.

"We have been in a tunnel since Burgdorf," answered the young man with determination. "There is no such enormous tunnel on this

line. I know. I travel back and forth every
week on this train."

The Chief Conductor continued to write.
"Sir," he said, stepping close to his inquisitor,
so close that their bodies almost touched, "sir,
I have little to tell you. I have no idea how
we got into this tunnel. I have no explanation
for it. But I ask you to consider this. We are
moving along on tracks: therefore this tunnel
leads somewhere. We have no reason whatever
to believe that anything is wrong with this
tunnel, except, of course, that there seems to
be no end to it." The Chief Conductor still
held the unlit Ormond Brazil 10 between his
lips. He had spoken extremely quietly, yet
with such dignity and clarity, and with such
assurance, that his words were audible despite
the increased noise of the baggage car.

"Then I must ask you to stop the train,"
said the young man impatiently. "I really
don't understand you. If there's something
wrong with this tunnel—and it seems you
can't explain even its existence—then your
duty is to stop this train at once."

"Stop the train?" returned the older man
slowly. It seemed he had already thought of
that, but, as he informed his companion, it
was a serious matter to stop a train. With
this, he shut the book and laid it in the red
bag which was swaying to and fro on its hook.
Then he carefully lit the Ormond 10. The
young man offered to pull the emergency
brake overhead, and was on the point of
releasing the lever, when suddenly he staggered forwards and was sent crashing against
the wall. At the same moment, the baby
carriage rolled toward him and several trunks
slid by. The Chief Conductor swayed strangely
and began to move, hands outstretched,
through the freight car.

"We are going downhill!" he announced as
he joined the young man now leaning against
the wall. But the expected crash of hurtling
train against granite tunnel did not occur.
There was no shattering of telescoped coaches.
Once again the train seemed to be running
on a level. The door opened at the other end
of the car. In the bright light of the diner,
until the door swung to again, they could see

the passengers merrily toasting one another's
health.

"Come into the locomotive." At this point
the Chief Conductor was peering thoughtfully,
almost menacingly at the student. He opened
the door nearby. As he did so a rush of
tempestuous heat-laden air struck the pair
with such force that they were driven back
against the wall. At the same moment a frightful clatter resounded through the almost empty
freight car.

"We'll have to climb over to the engine,"
he cried into the younger man's ear. Despite
his shouting, his voice was hardly audible. He
then disappeared through the right-angle of
the open doorway. The student followed
cautiously in the direction of the swaying and
brightly lit engine. He didn't know why he
was climbing, but at this point determination
had overcome reason. He found himself on
a pitching platform between the two cars, and
clung desperately to the iron rails on both
sides. Although the terrific draught moderated
but slightly as he inched his way up to the
locomotive, he dreaded the wind less than the
immediate nearness of the tunnel walls. They
were hidden from him in the blackness, but
were nevertheless frighteningly close. It was
necessary to focus all his attention on the
engine ahead, yet the pounding of the wheels
and the hissing vibrating push of air against
him gave him the feeling of careening, at the
speed of a falling star, into a world of stone.

A board just wide enough to walk on crossed
the gap between the cars and ran the length
of the engine. Above and parallel to it, a
curving metal rod served as railing. To reach
the plank he would have to make a jump of
nearly a yard. He braced himself, leapt, and
pushed himself along the board. His progress
was slow, since he had to press close to the
outside of the engine to keep his foothold.
It was not until he reached the long side of
the engine and was fully exposed to the roaring hurricane of wind and to the menacing
cliff walls now brilliantly illuminated by the
engine lights that he began to realize his fear.
But just then he was rescued by the Chief
Conductor who pulled him through a small

door into the engine. Exhausted, the young man lay against the wall. He was grateful for the sudden quiet. With the engine door shut, the steel walls of the giant locomotive deadened the noise almost completely.

"Well, we've lost the Ormond Brazil too," said the Conductor. "It wasn't a very sensible idea to light one before starting the climb, but they break so easily in one's pocket. It's their unusual length."

The young man was delighted to converse normally again. The close and terrifying rock walls had reminded him uncomfortably of his everyday world, of its ever similar days and years. The thought occurred to him that their boring similitude had perhaps been only a preparation for the present moment: that this was a moment of initiation, of truth, this departure from the surface of the earth and precipitous descent into the womb of the earth. He took another brown package from his right coat pocket and offered the Chief Conductor a new cigar. He took one himself, and carefully they lit their Brazils from the Conductor's lighter.

"I am very fond of these Ormonds," said the older man, "but one must pull very hard on them. Otherwise they go out so easily."

For some reason these words made the student suspicious. Was the Conductor as uncomfortable as he about the tunnel? For the tunnel still ran on interminably, and his mind persisted in the thought that surely the tunnel must stop, even as a dream can end, all of a sudden.

"Six-forty," he said, consulting his watch. "We should be in Olten now." Even as he spoke, he thought of the hills and woods radiant only a short while ago in the late golden sun. The thought could have been present in both their minds. Nevertheless, the two men stood and smoked and leaned against their wall.

"Keller is my name," announced the Conductor as he puffed at his Brazil.

The student refused to change the topic of conversation.

"The climb to the engine was very dangerous, didn't you think? At least it was for me.

I'm not used to that sort of thing. Anyway, I'd like to know why you've brought me here."

"I don't know," said Keller. "I wanted time to consider."

"Time to consider?"

"Yes," returned the Chief Conductor. "That's right." And he went on smoking. Just then the engine reeled over at a still steeper angle.

"We could go into the engineer's cabin," suggested Keller. He did not, however, leave his position against the wall. Annoyed by his companion's indecisiveness, the young man stepped briskly along the corridor to the driver's cabin, then abruptly stopped.

"Empty!" he said to the Conductor who had now moved up behind him. "The driver's seat is empty!" They went into the cabin. It was swaying too, for the engine was still tearing through the tunnel at enormous speed, bearing the train along with it, as though the weight of the coaches behind no longer counted.

"Allow me," said the Chief Conductor. He pressed some levers and pulled the emergency brake. There was no change. "We tried to stop the engine earlier. As soon as we noticed the alteration in the tracks. It didn't stop then either."

"It certainly isn't stopping now," said the other. He pointed to the speed indicator. "A hundred. Has the engine ever done a hundred before?"

"Good heavens! It has never gone so fast. Sixty-five at the most."

"Exactly. And the speed is increasing. Now the speedometer says a hundred and five. We must be falling." He went up to the window, but he couldn't keep his balance. He was pressed with his face against the glass, so fantastic was their speed. "The engine driver?" he shouted as he stared at the rock masses streaking towards him in the glare of the arc lights, disappearing above him and below him on either side of the engineer's cabin.

"He jumped off," Keller yelled back. He was now sitting on the floor, his back against the controls.

"When?" The student pursued the matter obstinately. Keller hesitated a while. He decided to relight his Ormond, an awkward task, for his legs were then at the same height as his head while the train continued its roll to one side.

"Five minutes after the switch. No use thinking to save him. Freight car man abandoned the train too."

"And you?" asked the student.

"I am in charge of this train. I, too, have always lived without hope."

"Without hope," repeated the young man. By then he was lying on the glass pane, face pressed against glass. Glass and engine and human flesh were pressed together above the abyss. "Back in the compartment," he thought, "we had entered the tunnel, but we didn't know that even then everything was already lost. We didn't think that anything had changed, and yet the shaft of the depths had already received us, and we had entered our abyss."

"I'll have to go to the rear," shouted the Chief Conductor. "The coaches will be in a panic. Everyone will be trying to get to the rear of the train."

"That's true." The student thought of the chessplayer and of the red-haired girl with her novel. He handed Keller his remaining packages of Ormond Brazil. "Take them. You'll lose your cigar again when you climb over."

"Aren't you coming?" The Conductor was once more on his feet and with difficulty he had begun to clamber up the funnel of the corridor. The student gazed at the useless instruments, at the useless ridiculous levers and switches shining silver-like in the glare of the cabin lights.

"A hundred and thirty," he called. "I don't think you'll be able to get to the coaches above us at this speed."

"It's my duty," shouted Keller over his shoulder.

"Certainly," returned the young man. He didn't bother turning his head to watch the other's senseless efforts.

"At least I have to try," yelled the Conductor. He was already far over the head of the fat young man. He braced elbows and thighs against slippery walls and seemed, indeed, to be making some progress. But just then the engine took a further turn downwards. It hurtled towards the interior of the earth, goal of all things, in its terrible plunge. Keller now was directly over his friend who lay face downwards on the silver gleaming window at the bottom of the driver's cabin. His strength gave. Suddenly he fell, crashed against the control panel and came to rest on the window beside his companion.

"What are we to do?" he cried, clinging to the young man's shoulders and shouting into his ear. The very fact that it was now necessary to shout alarmed him. The noise of the onrushing walls had destroyed even the quiet of the engine.

The younger man lay motionless on the pane of glass which separated him from the depths below. His fat body and weighty flesh were of no further use to him, no protection now.

"What are we to do?" persisted the Chief Conductor.

"Nothing," came the merciless reply. Merciless, yet not without a certain ghostly cheerfulness. Now, for the first time, his glasses were gone and his eyes were wide open. Greedily he sucked in the abyss through those wide-open eyes. Glass and metal splinters from the shattered control panel now studded his body. And still he refused to tear his thirsting eyes from the deadly spectacle below. As the first crack widened in the window beneath them, a current of air whistled into the cabin. It seized his two wads of cotton wool and swept them upwards like arrows into the corridor shaft overhead. He watched them briefly and spoke once more.

"Nothing. God let us fall. And now we'll come upon him."

FRANZ KAFKA

An Old Manuscript

Franz Kafka (1883–1924) was born in Prague of Czechoslovakian Jewish ancestry. He received a doctorate in jurisprudence from Karls-Ferdinand, a German university in Prague. A high-strung, sensitive individual, he continually sought new outlets for his intellectual interests and came under various influences—the Zionist Max Brod, Franz Werfel, Kierkegaard, and Pascal. With the encouragement of Brod, Kafka published his first books, *Observations* and *The Judgment,* in 1913. Thereafter he wrote steadily despite his ever-declining health. *Metamorphosis* was published in 1915; *The Trial* in 1925; *The Castle* in 1926—the last two posthumously. In the summer of 1923 he married and enjoyed a few months of contentment, during which he wrote *A Little Woman.* By Christmas of 1923, however, he was again very ill and in June 1924 he died of tuberculosis.

Kafka was a part of a movement known as existentialism, which views the world essentially as cosmic chaos, absurd and hostile to man. His writings are rich in symbols that communicate his despairing attitude toward civilization. Typical of this aspect of Kafka's art, "An Old Manuscript" involves more than the literal meaning conveys.

It looks as if much has been neglected in our country's system of defense. We have not concerned ourselves with it until now and have gone about our daily work; but things that have been happening recently begin to trouble us.

I have a cobbler's workshop in the square that lies before the Emperor's palace. Scarcely have I taken my shutters down, at the first glimpse of dawn, when I see armed soldiers already posted in the mouth of every street opening on the square. But these soldiers are not ours, they are obviously nomads from the North. In some way that is incomprehensible to me they have pushed right into the capital, although it is a long way from the frontier.

AN OLD MANUSCRIPT Reprinted by permission of Schocken Books Inc. from *The Penal Colony* by Franz Kafka. Copyright 1948 by Schocken Books Inc., New York. Translated by Willa and Edwin Muir.

At any rate, here they are; it seems that every morning there are more of them.

As is their nature, they camp under the open sky, for they abominate dwelling houses. They busy themselves sharpening swords, whittling arrows and practicing horsemanship. This peaceful square, which was always kept scrupulously clean, they have made literally into a stable. We do try every now and then to run out of our shops and clear away at least the worst of the filth, but this happens less and less often, for the labor is in vain and brings us besides into danger of falling under the hoofs of the wild horses or of being crippled with lashes from the whips.

Speech with the nomads is impossible. They do not know our language, indeed they hardly have a language of their own. They communicate with each other much as jackdaws do. A screeching of jackdaws is always in our ears. Our way of living and our institutions they neither understand nor care to understand. And so they are unwilling to make sense even out of our sign language. You can gesture at them till you dislocate your jaws and your wrists and still they will not have understood you and will never understand. They often make grimaces; then the whites of their eyes turn up and foam gathers on their lips, but they do not mean anything by that, not even a threat; they do it because it is their nature to do it. Whatever they need, they take. You cannot call it taking by force. They grab at something and you simply stand aside and leave them to it.

From my stock, too, they have taken many good articles. But I cannot complain when I see how the butcher, for instance, suffers across the street. As soon as he brings in any meat the nomads snatch it all from him and gobble it up. Even their horses devour flesh; often enough a horseman and his horse are lying side by side, both of them gnawing at the same joint, one at either end. The butcher is nervous and does not dare to stop his deliveries of meat. We understand that, however, and subscribe money to keep him going. If the nomads got no meat, who knows what they might think of doing; who knows anyhow what they may think of, even though they get meat every day.

Not long ago the butcher thought he might at least spare himself the trouble of slaughter-ing, and so one morning he brought along a live ox. But he will never dare to do that again. I lay for a whole hour flat on the floor at the back of my workshop with my head muffled in all the clothes and rugs and pillows I had, simply to keep from hearing the bellowing of that ox, which the nomads were leaping on from all sides, tearing morsels out of its living flesh with their teeth. It had been quiet for a long time before I risked coming out; they were lying overcome round the remains of the carcass like drunkards round a wine cask.

This was the occasion when I fancied I actually saw the Emperor himself at a window of the palace; usually he never enters these outer rooms but spends all of his time in the innermost garden; yet on this occasion he was standing, or so at least it seemed to me, at one of the windows, watching with bent head the ongoings before his residence.

"What is going to happen?" we all ask ourselves. "How long can we endure this burden and torment? The Emperor's palace has drawn the nomads here but does not know how to drive them away again. The gate stays shut; the guards, who used to be always marching out and in with ceremony, keep close behind barred windows. It is left to us artisans and tradesmen to save our country; but we are not equal to such a task; nor have we ever claimed to be capable of it. This is a misunderstanding of some kind; and it will be the ruin of us."

SYLVIA TOWNSEND WARNER

The Phoenix

Sylvia Townsend Warner (1893–   ) is an English writer who, since her first book *The Espalier*, 1925, has steadily continued to write novels and short stories. Her first two novels, *Lolly Willowes* (which was the first selection of the Book-of-the-Month Club in 1926) and *Mr. Fortune's Maggot* (an early choice of the Literary Guild), both out of print for years, were reprinted in 1966, the same year in which her latest collection of short stories, *Swans on an Autumn River,* was published. *The Cat's Cradle,* which included "The Phoenix," appeared in 1960.

In this story the classic phoenix takes proper revenge on his modern exploiters.

Lord Strawberry, a nobleman, collected birds. He had the finest aviary in Europe, so large that eagles did not find it uncomfortable, so well laid out that both humming-birds and snow-buntings had a climate that suited them perfectly. But for many years the finest set of apartments remained empty, with just a label saying: "PHOENIX. *Habitat: Arabia.*"

Many authorities on bird life had assured Lord Strawberry that the phoenix is a fabulous bird, or that the breed was long extinct. Lord Strawberry was unconvinced: his family had always believed in phoenixes. At intervals he received from his agents (together with statements of their expenses) birds which they declared were the phoenix but which turned out to be orioles, macaws, turkey buzzards dyed orange, etc., or stuffed cross-breeds, ingeniously assembled from various plumages. Finally Lord Strawberry went himself to Arabia, where, after some months, he found a phoenix, won its confidence, caught it, and brought it home in perfect condition.

It was a remarkably fine phoenix, with a charming character—affable to the other birds in the aviary and much attached to Lord Strawberry. On its arrival in England it made a great stir among ornithologists, journalists, poets, and milliners, and was constantly visited. But it was not puffed by these attentions, and when it was no longer in the news, and the visits fell off, it showed no pique or rancour. It ate well, and seemed perfectly contented.

It costs a great deal of money to keep up an aviary. When Lord Strawberry died he died penniless. The aviary came on the market.

THE PHOENIX From *The Cat's Cradle* by Sylvia Townsend Warner. Copyright 1940 by Sylvia Townsend Warner. Reprinted by permission of The Viking Press, Inc.

In normal times the rarer birds, and certainly the phoenix, would have been bid for by the trustees of Europe's great zoological societies, or by private persons in the U.S.A.; but as it happened Lord Strawberry died just after a world war, when both money and bird-seed were hard to come by (indeed the cost of bird-seed was one of the things which had ruined Lord Strawberry). The London *Times* urged in a leader that the phoenix be bought for the London Zoo, saying that a nation of bird-lovers had a moral right to own such a rarity; and a fund, called the Strawberry Phoenix Fund, was opened. Students, naturalists, and schoolchildren contributed according to their means; but their means were small, and there were no large donations. So Lord Strawberry's executors (who had the death duties to consider) closed with the higher offer of Mr. Tancred Poldero, owner and proprietor of Poldero's Wizard Wonderworld.

For quite a while Mr. Poldero considered his phoenix a bargain. It was a civil and obliging bird, and adapted itself readily to its new surroundings. It did not cost much to feed, it did not mind children; and though it had no tricks, Mr. Poldero supposed it would soon pick up some. The publicity of the Strawberry Phoenix Fund was now most helpful. Almost every contributor now saved up another half-crown in order to see the phoenix. Others, who had not contributed to the fund, even paid double to look at it on the five-shilling days.

But then business slackened. The phoenix was as handsome as ever, and as amiable; but, as Mr. Poldero said, it hadn't got Udge. Even at popular prices the phoenix was not really popular. It was too quiet, too classical. So people went instead to watch the antics of the baboons, or to admire the crocodile who had eaten the woman.

One day Mr. Poldero said to his manager, Mr. Ramkin:

"How long since any fool paid to look at the phoenix?"

"Matter of three weeks," replied Mr. Ramkin.

"Eating his head off," said Mr. Poldero. "Let alone the insurance. Seven shillings a week it costs me to insure that bird, and I might as well insure the Archbishop of Canterbury."

"The public don't like him. He's too quiet for them, that's the trouble. Won't mate nor nothing. And I've tried him with no end of pretty pollies, ospreys, and Cochin-Chinas, and the Lord knows what. But he won't look at them."

"Wonder if we could swap him for a livelier one," said Mr. Poldero.

"Impossible. There's only one of him at a time."

"Go on!"

"I mean it. Haven't you ever read what it says on the label?"

They went to the phoenix's cage. It flapped its wings politely, but they paid no attention. They read:

"PANSY. *Phoenix phoenixissima formosissima arabiana.* This rare and fabulous bird is UNIQUE. The World's Old Bachelor. Has no mate and doesn't want one. When old, sets fire to itself and emerges miraculously reborn. Specially imported from the East."

"I've got an idea," said Mr. Poldero. "How old do you suppose that bird is?"

"Looks in its prime to me," said Mr. Ramkin.

"Suppose," continued Mr. Poldero, "we could somehow get him alight? We'd advertise it beforehand, of course, work up interest. Then we'd have a new bird, and a bird with some romance about it, a bird with a life-story. We could sell a bird like that."

Mr. Ramkin nodded.

"I've read about it in a book," he said. "You've got to give them scented woods and what not, and they build a nest and sit down on it and catch fire spontaneous. But they won't do it till they're old. That's the snag."

"Leave that to me," said Mr. Poldero. "You get those scented woods, and I'll do the age-ing."

It was not easy to age the phoenix. Its allowance of food was halved, and halved again, but though it grew thinner its eyes were undimmed and its plumage glossy as ever. The heating was turned off; but it puffed out its feathers against the cold, and seemed none the worse. Other birds were put into its cage, birds of a peevish and quarrelsome nature. They pecked and chivied it; but the phoenix was so civil and amiable that after a day or two they lost their animosity. Then Mr. Poldero tried alley cats. These could not be won by manners, but the phoenix darted above their heads and flapped its golden wings in their faces, and daunted them.

Mr. Poldero turned to a book on Arabia, and read that the climate was dry. "Aha!" said he. The phoenix was moved to a small cage that had a sprinkler in the ceiling. Every night the sprinkler was turned on. The phoenix began to cough. Mr. Poldero had another good idea. Daily he stationed himself in front of the cage to jeer at the bird and abuse it.

When spring was come, Mr. Poldero felt justified in beginning a publicity campaign about the ageing phoenix. The old public favourite, he said, was nearing its end. Meanwhile he tested the bird's reactions every few days by putting a few tufts of foul-smelling straw and some strands of rusty barbed wire into the cage, to see if it were interested in nesting yet. One day the phoenix began turning over the straw. Mr. Poldero signed a contract for the film rights. At last the hour seemed ripe. It was a fine Saturday evening in May. For some weeks the public interest in the ageing phoenix had been working up, and the admission charge had risen to five shillings. The enclosure was thronged. The lights and the cameras were trained on the cage, and a loud-speaker proclaimed to the audience the rarity of what was about to take place.

"The phoenix," said the loud-speaker, "is the aristocrat of bird-life. Only the rarest and most expensive specimens of oriental wood, drenched in exotic perfumes, will tempt him to construct his strange love-nest."

Now a neat assortment of twigs and shavings, strongly scented, was shoved into the cage.

"The phoenix," the loud-speaker continued, "is as capricious as Cleopatra, as luxurious as la du Barry, as heady as a strain of wild gypsy music. All the fantastic pomp and passion of the ancient East, its languorous magic, its subtle cruelties . . . ."

"Lawks!" cried a woman in the crowd. "He's at it!"

A quiver stirred the dulled plumage. The phoenix turned its head from side to side. It descended, staggering, from its perch. Then wearily it began to pull about the twigs and shavings.

The cameras clicked, the lights blazed full on the cage. Rushing to the loud-speaker Mr. Poldero exclaimed:

"Ladies and gentlemen, this is the thrilling moment the world has breathlessly awaited. The legend of centuries is materializing before our modern eyes. The phoenix . . . ."

The phoenix settled on its pyre and appeared to fall asleep.

The film director said:

"Well, if it doesn't evaluate more than this, mark it instructional."

At that moment the phoenix and the pyre burst into flames. The flames streamed upwards, leaped out on every side. In a minute or two everything was burned to ashes, and some thousand people, including Mr. Poldero, perished in the blaze.

STEPHEN CRANE

The Open Boat

Stephen Crane (1871–1900), novelist, poet, journalist, and biographer, began his literary career by writing a startlingly realistic novel, *Maggie: A Girl of the Streets*, 1892. His second novel, *The Red Badge of Courage*, published in 1895, brought him fame. He was a war correspondent for Hearst's New York *Journal* during the Greco-Turkish War. After returning from Greece, Crane married and went to live in England, where he became a friend of Joseph Conrad. In 1898 he distinguished himself by his objective reporting from Cuba of the Spanish-American War. He contracted tuberculosis and died when he was only twenty-nine.

Crane's strongly realistic style did much to revolutionize the technique and style of American fiction. Carl and Mark Van Doren have commented, "Modern American fiction may be said to begin with Stephen Crane." H. G. Wells called "The Open Boat" the "finest short story in English." The story is based on an actual experience of Crane's, as indicated in the original subtitle—"A Fate Intended to Be After the Fact: Being the Experience of Four Men from the Sunk Steamer *Commodore*." Thoughtful readers will agree with Conrad, who commented, "The simple humanity of its presentation seems somehow to illustrate the essentials of life itself, like a symbolic tale."

None of them knew the color of the sky. Their eyes glanced level, and were fastened upon the waves that swept toward them. These waves were of the hue of slate, save for the tops, which were of foaming white, and all of the men knew the colors of the sea. The horizon narrowed and widened, and dipped and rose, and at all times its edge was jagged with waves that seemed thrust up in points like rocks.

Many a man ought to have a bath-tub larger than the boat which here rode upon the sea. These waves were most wrongfully and barbarously abrupt and tall, and each froth-top was a problem in small-boat navigation.

The cook squatted in the bottom and looked with both eyes at the six inches of gunwale which separated him from the ocean. His sleeves were rolled over his fat forearms, and the two flaps of his unbuttoned vest dangled as he bent to bail out the boat. Often he said: "Gawd! That was a narrow clip." As he remarked it he invariably gazed eastward over the broken sea.

The oiler, steering with one of the two oars in the boat, sometimes raised himself suddenly to keep clear of water that swirled in over the stern. It was a thin little oar and it seemed often ready to snap.

The correspondent, pulling at the other oar, watched the waves and wondered why he was there.

The injured captain, lying in the bow, was at this time buried in that profound dejection and indifference which comes, temporarily at least, to even the bravest and most enduring when, willy-nilly, the firm fails, the army loses, the ship goes down. The mind of the master of a vessel is rooted deep in the timbers of her, though he command for a day or a decade, and this captain had on him the stern impression of a scene in the grays of dawn of seven turned faces, and later a stump of a top-mast with a white ball on it that slashed to and fro at the waves, went low and lower, and down.

THE OPEN BOAT   From *Stephen Crane: An Omnibus*, edited by Robert Wooster Stallman, by permission of Alfred A. Knopf, Inc. Copyright 1952 by Alfred A. Knopf, Inc.

Thereafter there was something strange in his voice. Although steady, it was deep with mourning, and of a quality beyond oration or tears.

"Keep 'er a little more south, Billie," said he.

"A little more south, sir," said the oiler in the stern.

A seat in this boat was not unlike a seat upon a bucking bronco, and, by the same token, a bronco is not much smaller. The craft pranced and reared, and plunged like an animal. As each wave came, and she rose for it, she seemed like a horse making at a fence outrageously high. The manner of her scramble over these walls of water is a mystic thing, and, moreover, at the top of them were ordinarily these problems in white water, the foam racing down from the summit of each wave, requiring a new leap, and a leap from the air. Then, after scornfully bumping a crest, she would slide, and race, and splash down a long incline, and arrive bobbing and nodding in front of the next menace.

A singular disadvantage of the sea lies in the fact that after successfully surmounting one wave you discover that there is another behind it just as important and just as nervously anxious to do something effective in the way of swamping boats. In a ten-foot dinghy one can get an idea of the resources of the sea in the line of waves that is not probable to the average experience which is never at sea in a dinghy. As each slaty wall of water approached, it shut all else from the view of the men in the boat, and it was not difficult to imagine that this particular wave was the final outburst of the ocean, the last effort of the grim water. There was a terrible grace in the move of the waves, and they came in silence, save for the snarling of the crests.

In the wan light, the faces of the men must have been gray. Their eyes must have glinted in strange ways as they gazed steadily astern. Viewed from a balcony, the whole thing would doubtless have been weirdly picturesque. But the men in the boat had no time to see it, and if they had had leisure there were other things to occupy their minds. The sun swung steadily up the sky, and they knew it was broad day because the color of the sea changed from slate to emerald-green, streaked with amber lights, and the foam was like tumbling snow. The process of the breaking day was unknown to them. They were aware only of this effect upon the color of the waves that rolled toward them.

In disjointed sentences the cook and the correspondent argued as to the difference between a life-saving station and a house of refuge. The cook had said: "There's a house of refuge just north of the Mosquito Inlet Light, and as soon as they see us, they'll come off in their boat and pick us up."

"As soon as who see us?" said the correspondent.

"The crew," said the cook.

"Houses of refuge don't have crews," said the correspondent. "As I understand them, they are only places where clothes and grub are stored for the benefit of shipwrecked people. They don't carry crews."

"Oh, yes, they do," said the cook.

"No, they don't," said the correspondent.

"Well, we're not there yet, anyhow," said the oiler, in the stern.

"Well," said the cook, "perhaps it's not a house of refuge that I'm thinking of as being near Mosquito Inlet Light. Perhaps it's a life-saving station."

"We're not there yet," said the oiler, in the stern.

II

As the boat bounced from the top of each wave, the wind tore through the hair of the hatless men, and as the craft plopped her stern down again the spray slashed past them. The crest of each of these waves was a hill, from the top of which the men surveyed, for a moment, a broad tumultuous expanse, shining and wind-driven. It was probably splendid. It was probably glorious, this play of the free sea, wild with lights of emerald and white and amber.

"Bully good thing it's an on-shore wind," said the cook. "If not, where would we be? Wouldn't have a show."

"That's right," said the correspondent.

The busy oiler nodded his assent.

Then the captain, in the bow, chuckled in a way that expressed humor, contempt, tragedy, all in one. "Do you think we've got much of a show now, boys?" said he.

Whereupon the three were silent, save for a trifle of hemming and hawing. To express any particular optimism at this time they felt to be childish and stupid, but they all doubtless possessed this sense of the situation in their mind. A young man thinks doggedly at such times. On the other hand, the ethics of their condition was decidedly against any open suggestion of hopelessness. So they were silent.

"Oh, well," said the captain, soothing his children, "we'll get ashore all right."

But there was that in his tone which made them think, so the oiler quoth: "Yes! If this wind holds!"

The cook was bailing: "Yes! If we don't catch hell in the surf."

Canton flannel gulls flew near and far. Sometimes they sat down on the sea, near patches of brown seaweed that rolled over the waves with a movement like carpets on a line in a gale. The birds sat comfortably in groups, and they were envied by some in the dinghy, for the wrath of the sea was no more to them than it was to a covey of prairie chickens a thousand miles inland. Often they came very close and stared at the men with black bead-like eyes. At these times they were uncanny and sinister in their unblinking scrutiny, and the men hooted angrily at them, telling them to be gone. One came, and evidently decided to alight on the top of the captain's head. The bird flew parallel to the boat and did not circle, but made short sidelong jumps in the air in chicken-fashion. His black eyes were wistfully fixed upon the captain's head. "Ugly brute," said the oiler to the bird. "You look as if you were made with a jackknife." The cook and the correspondent swore darkly at the creature. The captain naturally wished to knock it away with the end of the heavy painter; but he did not dare do it, because anything resembling an emphatic gesture would have capsized this freighted boat, and so with his open hand, the captain gently and carefully waved the gull away. After it had been discouraged from the pursuit the captain breathed easier on account of his hair, and others breathed easier because the bird struck their minds at this time as being somehow gruesome and ominous.

In the meantime the oiler and the correspondent rowed. And also they rowed.

They sat together in the same seat, and each rowed an oar. Then the oiler took both oars; then the correspondent took both oars; then the oiler; then the correspondent. They rowed and they rowed. The very ticklish part of the business was when the time came for the reclining one in the stern to take his turn at the oars. By the very last star of truth, it is easier to steal eggs from under a hen than it was to change seats in the dinghy. First the man in the stern slid his hand along the thwart and moved with care, as if he were of Sèvres. Then the man in the rowing seat slid his hand along the other thwart. It was all done with the most extraordinary care. As the two sidled past each other, the whole party kept watchful eyes on the coming wave, and the captain cried: "Look out now! Steady there!"

The brown mats of seaweed that appeared from time to time were like islands, bits of earth. They were traveling, apparently, neither one way nor the other. They were, to all intents, stationary. They informed the men in the boat that it was making progress slowly toward the land.

The captain, rearing cautiously in the bow, after the dinghy soared on a great swell, said that he had seen the lighthouse at Mosquito Inlet. Presently the cook remarked that he had seen it. The correspondent was at the oars then, and for some reason he too wished to look at the lighthouse, but his back was toward the far shore and the waves were important, and for some time he could not seize an opportunity to turn his head. But at last there came a wave more gentle than the others, and when at the crest of it he swiftly scoured the western horizon.

"See it?" said the captain.

"No," said the correspondent slowly, "I didn't see anything."

"Look again," said the captain. He pointed. "It's exactly in that direction."

At the top of another wave, the correspond-

ent did as he was bid, and this time his eyes chanced on a small still thing on the edge of the swaying horizon. It was precisely like the point of a pin. It took an anxious eye to find a lighthouse so tiny.

"Think we'll make it, captain?"

"If this wind holds and the boat don't swamp, we can't do much else," said the captain.

The little boat, lifted by each towering sea, and splashed viciously by the crests, made progress that in the absence of seaweed was not apparent to those in her. She seemed just a wee thing wallowing, miraculously top up, at the mercy of five oceans. Occasionally, a great spread of water, like white flames, swarmed into her.

"Bail her, cook," said the captain serenely.

"All right, captain," said the cheerful cook.

III

It would be difficult to describe the subtle brotherhood of men that was here established on the seas. No one said that it was so. No one mentioned it. But it dwelt in the boat, and each man felt it warm him. They were a captain, an oiler, a cook, and a correspondent, and they were friends, friends in a more curiously iron-bound degree than may be common. The hurt captain, lying against the water-jar in the bow, spoke always in a low voice and calmly, but he could never command a more ready and swiftly obedient crew than the motley three of the dinghy. It was more than a mere recognition of what was best for the common safety. There was surely in it a quality that was personal and heartfelt. And after this devotion to the commander of the boat there was this comradeship that the correspondent, for instance, who had been taught to be cynical of men, knew even at the time was the best experience of his life. But no one said that it was so. No one mentioned it.

"I wish we had a sail," remarked the captain. "We might try my overcoat on the end of an oar and give you two boys a chance to rest." So the cook and the correspondent held the mast and spread wide the overcoat. The oiler steered, and the little boat made good way with her new rig. Sometimes the oiler had to scull sharply to keep a sea from breaking into the boat, but otherwise sailing was a success.

Meanwhile the lighthouse had been growing slowly larger. It had now almost assumed color, and appeared like a little gray shadow on the sky. The man at the oars could not be prevented from turning his head rather often to try for a glimpse of this little gray shadow.

At last, from the top of each wave the men in the tossing boat could see land. Even as the lighthouse was an upright shadow on the sky, this land seemed but a long black shadow on the sea. It certainly was thinner than paper. "We must be about opposite New Smyrna," said the cook, who had coasted this shore often in schooners. "Captain, by the way, I believe they abandoned that life-saving station there about a year ago."

"Did they?" said the captain.

The wind slowly died away. The cook and the correspondent were not now obliged to slave in order to hold high the oar. But the waves continued their old impetuous swooping at the dinghy, and the little craft, no longer under way, struggled woundily over them. The oiler or the correspondent took the oars again.

Shipwrecks are apropos of nothing. If men could only train for them and have them occur when the men had reached pink condition, there would be less drowning at sea. Of the four in the dinghy none had slept any time worth mentioning for two days and two nights previous to embarking in the dinghy, and in the excitement of clambering about the deck of a foundering ship they had also forgotten to eat heartily.

For these reasons, and for others, neither the oiler nor the correspondent was fond of rowing at this time. The correspondent wondered ingenuously how in the name of all that was sane could there be people who thought it amusing to row a boat. It was not an amusement; it was a diabolical punishment, and even a genius of mental aberrations could never conclude that it was anything but a horror to the muscles and a crime against the back. He mentioned to the boat in general how the amusement of rowing struck him, and the weary-faced oiler smiled in full sympathy. Previously to the foundering, by the way, the oiler had worked double-watch in the engine-room of the ship.

"Take her easy, now, boys," said the captain. "Don't spend yourselves. If we have to run a surf you'll need all your strength, because we'll sure have to swim for it. Take your time."

Slowly the land arose from the sea. From a black line it became a line of black and a line of white, trees and sand. Finally, the captain said that he could make out a house on the shore. "That's the house of refuge, sure," said the cook. "They'll see us before long, and come out after us."

The distant lighthouse reared high. "The keeper ought to be able to make us out now, if he's looking through a glass," said the captain. "He'll notify the life-saving people."

"None of those other boats could have got ashore to give word of the wreck," said the oiler, in a low voice. "Else the lifeboat would be out hunting us."

Slowly and beautifully the land loomed out of the sea. The wind came again. It had veered from the north-east to the south-east. Finally, a new sound struck the ears of the men in the boat. It was the low thunder of the surf on the shore. "We'll never be able to make the lighthouse now," said the captain. "Swing her head a little more north, Billie."

"A little more north, sir," said the oiler.

Whereupon the little boat turned her nose once more down the wind, and all but the oarsmen watched the shore grow. Under the influence of this expansion doubt and direful apprehension were leaving the minds of the men. The management of the boat was still most absorbing, but it could not prevent a quiet cheerfulness. In an hour, perhaps, they would be ashore.

Their backbones had become thoroughly used to balancing in the boat, and they now rode this wild colt of a dinghy like circus men. The correspondent thought that he had been drenched to the skin, but happening to feel in the top pocket of his coat, he found therein eight cigars. Four of them were soaked with sea-water; four were perfectly scatheless. After a search, somebody produced three dry matches, and thereupon the four waifs rode impudently in their little boat, and with an assurance of an impending rescue shining in their eyes, puffed at the big cigars and judged well and ill of all men. Everybody took a drink of water.

IV

"Cook," remarked the captain, "there don't seem to be any signs of life about your house of refuge."

"No," replied the cook. "Funny they don't see us!"

A broad stretch of lowly coast lay before the eyes of the men. It was of low dunes topped with dark vegetation. The oar of the surf was plain, and sometimes they could see the white lip of a wave as it spun up the beach. A tiny house was blocked out black upon the sky. Southward, the slim lighthouse lifted its little gray length.

Tide, wind, and waves were swinging the dinghy northward. "Funny they don't see us," said the men.

The surf's roar was here dulled, but its tone was, nevertheless, thunderous and mighty. As the boat swam over the great rollers, the men sat listening to this roar. "We'll swamp sure," said everybody.

It is fair to say here that there was not a life-saving station within twenty miles in either direction, but the men did not know this fact, and in consequence they made dark and op-probrious remarks concerning the eyesight of the nation's life-savers. Four scowling men sat in the dinghy and surpassed records in the invention of epithets.

"Funny they don't see us."

The light-heartedness of a former time had completely faded. To their sharpened minds it was easy to conjure pictures of all kinds of incompetency and blindness and, indeed, cowardice. There was the shore of the popu-lous land, and it was bitter and bitter to them that from it came no sign.

"Well," said the captain, ultimately, "I sup-pose we'll have to make a try for ourselves.

If we stay out here too long, we'll none of us have strength left to swim after the boat swamps."

And so the oiler, who was at the oars, turned the boat straight for the shore. There was a sudden tightening of muscles. There was some thinking.

"If we don't all get ashore—" said the cap-tain. "If we don't all get ashore, I suppose you fellows know where to send news of my finish?"

They then briefly exchanged some addresses and admonitions. As for the reflections of the men, there was a great deal of rage in them. Perchance they might be formulated thus: "If I am going to be drowned—if I am going to be drowned—if I am going to be drowned, why, in the name of the seven mad gods who rule the sea, was I allowed to come thus far and contemplate sand and trees? Was I brought here merely to have my nose dragged away as I was about to nibble the sacred cheese of life? It is preposterous. If this old ninny-woman, Fate, cannot do better than this, she should be deprived of the management of men's fortunes. She is an old hen who knows not her intention. If she has decided to drown me, why did she not do it in the beginning and save me all this trouble? The whole affair is absurd. . . . But no, she cannot mean to drown me. She dare not drown me. She cannot drown me. Not after all this work." Afterward the man might have had an impulse to shake his fist at the clouds: "Just you drown me, now, and then hear what I call you!"

The billows that came at this time were more formidable. They seemed always just about to break and roll over the little boat in a turmoil of foam. There was a preparatory and long growl in the speech of them. No mind unused to the sea would have concluded that the dinghy could ascend these sheer heights in time. The shore was still afar. The oiler was a wily surfman. "Boys," he said swiftly, "she won't live three minutes more, and we're too far out to swim. Shall I take her to sea again, captain?"

"Yes! Go ahead!" said the captain.

This oiler, by a series of quick miracles, and fast and steady oarsmanship, turned the boat in the middle of the surf and took her safely to sea again.

There was a considerable silence as the boat bumped over the furrowed sea to deeper water. Then somebody in gloom spoke. "Well, anyhow, they must have seen us from the shore by now."

The gulls went in slanting flight up the wind toward the gray desolate east. A squall, marked by dingy clouds, and clouds brick-red, like smoke from a burning building, appeared from the south-east.

"What do you think of those life-saving people? Ain't they peaches?"

"Funny they haven't seen us."

"Maybe they think we're out here for sport! Maybe they think we're fishin'. Maybe they think we're damned fools."

It was a long afternoon. A changed tide tried to force them southward, but wind and wave said northward. Far ahead, where coast-line, sea, and sky formed their mighty angle, there were little dots which seemed to indicate a city on the shore.

"St. Augustine?"

The captain shook his head. "Too near Mosquito Inlet."

And the oiler rowed, and then the correspondent rowed. Then the oiler rowed. It was a weary business. The human back can become the seat of more aches and pains than are registered in books for the composite anatomy of a regiment. It is a limited area, but it can become the theater of innumerable muscular conflicts, tangles, wrenches, knots, and other comforts.

"Did you ever like to row, Billie?" asked the correspondent.

"No," said the oiler. "Hang it."

When one exchanged the rowing-seat for a place in the bottom of the boat, he suffered a bodily depression that caused him to be careless of everything save an obligation to wiggle one finger. There was cold sea-water swashing to and fro in the boat, and he lay in it. His head, pillowed on a thwart, was within an inch of the swirl of a wave crest, and sometimes a particularly obstreperous sea came in-board and drenched him once more. But these matters did not annoy him. It is

almost certain that if the boat had capsized he would have tumbled comfortably out upon the ocean as if he felt sure that it was a great soft mattress.

"Look! There's a man on the shore!"

"Where?"

"There! See 'im? See 'im?"

"Yes, sure! He's walking along."

"Now he's stopped. Look! He's facing us!"

"He's waving at us!"

"So he is! By thunder!"

"Ah, now we're all right! Now we're all right! There'll be a boat out here for us in half an hour."

"He's going on. He's running. He's going up to that house there."

The remote beach seemed lower than the sea, and it required a searching glance to discern the little black figure. The captain saw a floating stick and they rowed to it. A bath-towel was by some weird chance in the boat, and, tying this on the stick, the captain waved it. The oarsman did not dare turn his head, so he was obliged to ask questions.

"What's he doing now?"

"He's standing still again. He's looking, I think. . . . There he goes again. Toward the house. . . . Now he stopped again."

"Is he waving at us?"

"No, not now! He was, though."

"Look! There comes another man!"

"He's running."

"Look at him go, would you!"

"Why, he's on a bicycle. Now he's met the other man. They're both waving at us. Look!"

"There comes something up the beach."

"What the devil is that thing?"

"Why, it looks like a boat."

"Why, certainly it's a boat."

"No, it's on wheels."

"Yes, so it is. Well, that must be the life-boat. They drag them along shore on a wagon."

"That's the life-boat, sure."

"No, by—, it's—it's an omnibus."

"I tell you it's a life-boat."

"It is not! It's an omnibus. I can see it plain. See? One of these big hotel omnibuses."

"By thunder, you're right. It's an omnibus, sure as fate. What do you suppose they are doing with an omnibus? Maybe they are going around collecting the life-crew, hey?"

"That's it, likely. Look! There's a fellow waving a little black flag. He's standing on the steps of the omnibus. There come those other two fellows. Now they're all talking together. Look at the fellow with the flag. Maybe he ain't waving it."

"That ain't a flag, is it? That's his coat. Why, certainly, that's his coat."

"So it is. It's his coat. He's taken it off and is waving it around his head. But would you look at him swing it."

"Oh, say, there isn't any life-saving station there. That's just a winter resort hotel omnibus that has brought over some of the boarders to see us drown."

"What's that idiot with the coat mean? What's he signaling, anyhow?"

"It looks as if he were trying to tell us to go north. There must be a life-saving station up there."

"No! He thinks we're fishing. Just giving us a merry hand. See? Ah, there, Billie."

"Well, I wish I could make something out of those signals. What do you suppose he means?"

"He don't mean anything. He's just playing."

"Well, if he'd just signal us to try the surf again, or to go to sea and wait, or go north, or go south, or go to hell—there would be some reason in it. But look at him. He just stands there and keeps his coat revolving like a wheel. The ass!"

"There come more people."

"Now there's quite a mob. Look! Isn't that a boat?"

"Where? Oh, I see where you mean. No, that's no boat."

"That fellow is still waving his coat."

"He must think we like to see him do that. Why don't he quit it? It don't mean anything."

"I don't know. I think he is trying to make us go north. It must be that there's a life-saving station there somewhere."

"Say, he ain't tired yet. Look at 'im wave."

"Wonder how long he can keep that up. He's been revolving his coat ever since he caught sight of us. He's an idiot. Why aren't they getting men to bring a boat out? A fish-

ing boat—one of those big yawls—could come out here all right. Why don't he do something?"

"Oh, it's all right, now."

"They'll have a boat out here for us in less than no time, now that they've seen us."

A faint yellow tone came into the sky over the low land. The shadows on the sea slowly deepened. The wind bore coldness with it, and the men began to shiver.

"Holy smoke!" said one, allowing his voice to express his impious mood, "if we keep on monkeying out here! If we've got to flounder out here all night!"

"Oh, we'll never have to stay here all night! Don't you worry. They've seen us now, and it won't be long before they'll come chasing out after us."

The shore grew dusky. The man waving a coat blended gradually into this gloom, and it swallowed in the same manner the omnibus and the group of people. The spray, when it dashed uproariously over the side, made the voyagers shrink and swear like men who were being branded.

"I'd like to catch the chump who waved that coat. I feel like soaking him one, just for luck."

"Why? What did he do?"

"Oh, nothing, but then he seemed so damned cheerful."

In the meantime the oiler rowed, and then the correspondent rowed, and then the oiler rowed. Gray-faced and bowed forward, they mechanically, turn by turn, plied the leaden oars. The form of the lighthouse had vanished from the southern horizon, but finally a pale star appeared, just lifting from the sea. The streaked saffron in the west passed before the all-merging darkness, and the sea to the east was black. The land had vanished, and was expressed only by the low and drear thunder of the surf.

"If I am going to be drowned—if I am going to be drowned—if I am going to be drowned, why, in the name of the seven mad gods who rule the sea, was I allowed to come thus far and contemplate sand and trees? Was I brought here merely to have my nose dragged away as I was about to nibble the sacred cheese of life?"

The patient captain, drooped over the water-jar, was sometimes obliged to speak to the oarsman.

"Keep her head up! Keep her head up!"

"'Keep her head up,' sir." The voices were weary and low.

This was surely a quiet evening. All save the oarsman lay heavily and listlessly in the boat's bottom. As for him, his eyes were just capable of noting the tall black waves that swept forward in a most sinister silence, save for an occasional subdued growl of a crest.

The cook's head was on a thwart, and he looked without interest at the water under his nose. He was deep in other scenes. Finally he spoke. "Billie," he murmured, dreamfully, "what kind of pie do you like best?"

V

"Pie," said the oiler and the correspondent, agitatedly. "Don't talk about those things, blast you!"

"Well," said the cook, "I was just thinking about ham sandwiches, and—"

A night on the sea in an open boat is a long night. As darkness settled finally, the shine of the light, lifting from the sea in the south, changed to full gold. On the northern horizon a new light appeared, a small bluish gleam on the edge of the waters. These two lights were the furniture of the world. Otherwise there was nothing but waves.

Two men huddled in the stern, and distances were so magnificent in the dinghy that the rower was enabled to keep his feet partly warmed by thrusting them under his companions. Their legs indeed extended far under the rowing-seat until they touched the feet of the captain forward. Sometimes, despite the efforts of the tired oarsman, a wave came piling into the boat, an icy wave of the night, and the chilling water soaked them anew. They would twist their bodies for a moment and groan, and sleep the dead sleep once more, while the water in the boat gurgled about them as the craft rocked.

The plan of the oiler and the correspondent was for one to row until he lost the ability, and then arouse the other from his sea-water couch in the bottom of the boat.

The oiler plied the oars until his head drooped forward, and the overpowering sleep blinded him. And he rowed yet afterward. Then he touched a man in the bottom of the boat, and called his name. "Will you spell me for a little while?" he said, meekly.

"Sure, Billie," said the correspondent, awakening and dragging himself to a sitting position. They exchanged places carefully, and the oiler, cuddling down in the sea-water at the cook's side, seemed to go to sleep instantly.

The particular violence of the sea had ceased. The waves came without snarling. The obligation of the man at the oars was to keep the boat headed so that the tilt of the rollers would not capsize her, and to preserve her from filling when the crests rushed past. The black waves were silent and hard to be seen in the darkness. Often one was almost upon the boat before the oarsman was aware.

In a low voice the correspondent addressed the captain. He was not sure that the captain was awake, although this iron man seemed to be always awake. "Captain, shall I keep her making for that light north, sir?"

The same steady voice answered him. "Yes. Keep it about two points off the port bow."

The cook had tied a life-belt around himself in order to get even the warmth which this clumsy cork contrivance could donate, and he seemed almost stove-like when a rower, whose teeth invariably chattered wildly as soon as he ceased his labor, dropped down to sleep.

The correspondent, as he rowed, looked down at the two men sleeping underfoot. The cook's arm was around the oiler's shoulders, and, with their fragmentary clothing and haggard faces, they were the babes of the sea, a grotesque rendering of the old babes in the wood.

Later he must have grown stupid at his work, for suddenly there was a growling of water, and a crest came with a roar and a swash into the boat, and it was a wonder that it did not set the cook afloat in his life-belt. The cook continued to sleep, but the oiler sat up, blinking his eyes and shaking with the new cold.

"Oh, I'm awful sorry, Billie," said the correspondent, contritely.

"That's all right, old boy," said the oiler, and lay down again and was asleep.

Presently it seemed that even the captain dozed, and the correspondent thought that he was the one man afloat on all the oceans. The wind had a voice as it came over the waves, and it was sadder than the end.

There was a long, loud swishing astern of the boat, and a gleaming trail of phosphorescence, like blue flame, was furrowed on the black waters. It might have been made by a monstrous knife.

Then there came a stillness, while the correspondent breathed with open mouth and looked at the sea.

Suddenly there was another swish and another long flash of bluish light, and this time it was alongside the boat, and might almost have been reached with an oar. The correspondent saw an enormous fin speed like a shadow through the water, hurling the crystalline spray and leaving the long glowing trail.

The correspondent looked over his shoulder at the captain. His face was hidden, and he seemed to be asleep. He looked at the babes of the sea. They certainly were asleep. So, being bereft of sympathy, he leaned a little way to one side and swore softly into the sea.

But the thing did not then leave the vicinity of the boat. Ahead or astern, on one side or the other, at intervals long or short, fled the long sparkling streak, and there was to be heard the *whiroo* of the dark fin. The speed and power of the thing was greatly to be admired. It cut the water like a gigantic and keen projectile.

The presence of this biding thing did not affect the man with the same horror that it would if he had been a picnicker. He simply looked at the sea dully and swore in an undertone.

Nevertheless, it is true that he did not wish to be alone with the thing. He wished one of his companions to awaken by chance and keep him company with it. But the captain hung motionless over the water-jar, and the oiler and the cook in the bottom of the boat were plunged in slumber.

VI

"If I am going to be drowned—if I am going to be drowned—if I am going to be drowned, why, in the name of the seven mad gods who rule the sea, was I allowed to come thus far and contemplate sand and trees?"

During this dismal night, it may be remarked that a man would conclude that it was really the intention of the seven mad gods to drown him, despite the abominable injustice of it. For it was certainly an abominable injustice to drown a man who had worked so hard, so hard. The man felt it would be a crime most unnatural. Other people had drowned at sea since galleys swarmed with painted sails, but still—

When it occurs to a man that nature does not regard him as important, and that she feels she would not maim the universe by disposing of him, he at first wishes to throw bricks at the temple, and he hates deeply the fact that there are no bricks and no temples. Any visible expression of nature would surely be pelleted with his jeers.

Then, if there be no tangible thing to hoot he feels, perhaps, the desire to confront a personification and indulge in pleas, bowed to one knee, and with hands supplicant, saying: "Yes, but I love myself."

A high cold star on a winter's night is the word he feels that she says to him. Thereafter he knows the pathos of his situation.

The men in the dinghy had not discussed these matters, but each had, no doubt, reflected upon them in silence and according to his mind. There was seldom any expression upon their faces save the general one of complete weariness. Speech was devoted to the business of the boat.

To chime the notes of his emotion, a verse mysteriously entered the correspondent's head. He had even forgotten that he had forgotten this verse, but it suddenly was in his mind.

A soldier of the Legion lay dying in Algiers,
There was lack of woman's nursing, there was
  dearth of woman's tears;
But a comrade stood beside him, and he took
  that comrade's hand,
And he said: "I shall never see my own, my native land."

In his childhood, the correspondent had been made acquainted with the fact that a soldier of the Legion lay dying in Algiers, but he had never regarded the fact as important. Myriads of his school-fellows had informed him of the soldier's plight, but the dinning had naturally ended by making him perfectly indifferent. He had never considered it his affair that a soldier of the Legion lay dying in Algiers, nor had it appeared to him as a matter for sorrow. It was less to him than the breaking of a pencil's point.

Now, however, it quaintly came to him as a human, living thing. It was no longer merely a picture of a few throes in the breast of a poet, meanwhile drinking tea and warming his feet at the grate; it was an actuality—stern, mournful, and fine.

The correspondent plainly saw the soldier. He lay on the sand with his feet out straight and still. While his pale left hand was upon his chest in an attempt to thwart the going of his life, the blood came between his fingers.

In the far Algerian distance, a city of low square forms was set against a sky that was faint with the last sunset hues. The correspondent, plying the oars and dreaming of the slow and slower movements of the lips of the soldier, was moved by a profound and perfectly impersonal comprehension. He was sorry for the soldier of the Legion who lay dying in Algiers.

The thing which had followed the boat and waited had evidently grown bored at the delay. There was no longer to be heard the slash of the cutwater, and there was no longer the flame of the long trail. The light in the north still glimmered, but it was apparently no nearer to the boat. Sometimes the boom of the surf rang in the correspondent's ears, and he turned the craft seaward then and rowed harder. Southward, someone had evidently built a watch-fire on the beach. It was too low and too far to be seen, but it made a shimmering, roseate reflection upon the bluff back of it, and this could be discerned from the boat. The wind came stronger, and sometimes a wave suddenly raged out like a mountain-cat, and there was to be seen the sheen and sparkle of a broken crest.

The captain, in the bow, moved on his water-jar and sat erect. "Pretty long night," he observed to the correspondent. He looked at the shore. "Those life-saving people take their time."

"Did you see that shark playing around?"

"Yes, I saw him. He was a big fellow, all right."

"Wish I had known you were awake."

Later the correspondent spoke into the bottom of the boat.

"Billie!" There was a slow and gradual disentanglement. "Billie, will you spell me?"

"Sure," said the oiler.

As soon as the correspondent touched the cold comfortable sea-water in the bottom of the boat and had huddled close to the cook's life-belt he was deep in sleep, despite the fact that his teeth played all the popular airs. This sleep was so good to him that it was but a moment before he heard a voice call his name in a tone that demonstrated the last stages of exhaustion. "Will you spell me?"

"Sure, Billie."

The light in the north had mysteriously vanished, but the correspondent took his course from the wide-awake captain.

Later in the night they took the boat farther out to sea, and the captain directed the cook to take one oar at the stern and keep the boat facing the seas. He was to call out if he should hear the thunder of the surf. This plan enabled the oiler and the correspondent to get respite together. "We'll give those boys a chance to get into shape again," said the captain. They curled down and, after a few preliminary chatterings and trembles, slept once more the dead sleep. Neither knew they had bequeathed to the cook the company of another shark, or perhaps the same shark.

As the boat caroused on the waves, spray occasionally bumped over the side and gave them a fresh soaking, but this had no power to break their repose. The ominous slash of the wind and the water affected them as it would have affected mummies.

"Boys," said the cook, with the notes of every reluctance in his voice, "she's drifted in pretty close. I guess one of you had better take her to sea again." The correspondent, aroused, heard the crash of the toppled crests.

As he was rowing, the captain gave him some whisky-and-water, and this steadied the chills out of him. "If I ever get ashore and anybody shows me even a photograph of an oar—"

At last there was a short conversation.

"Billie . . . Billie, will you spell me?"

"Sure," said the oiler.

VII

When the correspondent again opened his eyes, the sea and the sky were each of the gray hue of the dawning. Later, carmine and gold was painted upon the waters. The morning appeared finally, in its splendor, with a sky of pure blue, and the sunlight flamed on the tips of the waves.

On the distant dunes were set many little black cottages, and a tall white windmill reared above them. No man, nor dog, nor bicycle appeared on the beach. The cottages might have formed a deserted village.

The voyagers scanned the shore. A conference was held in the boat. "Well," said the captain, "if no help is coming, we might better try a run through the surf right away. If we stay out here much longer we will be too weak to do anything for ourselves at all." The others silently acquiesced in this reasoning. The boat was headed for the beach. The correspondent wondered if none ever ascended the tall wind-tower, and if then they never looked seaward. This tower was a giant, standing with its back to the plight of the ants. It represented in a degree, to the correspondent, the serenity of nature amid the struggles of the individual—nature in the wind, and nature in the vision of men. She did not seem cruel to him then, nor beneficent, nor treacherous, nor wise. But she was indifferent, flatly indifferent. It is, perhaps, plausible that a man in this situation, impressed with the unconcern of the universe, should see the innumerable flaws of his life, and have them taste wickedly in his mind and wish for another chance. A distinction between right and wrong seems absurdly clear to him, then, in this new ignorance of the grave-edge, and he understands that if he were given another oppor-

tunity he would mend his conduct and his words, and be better and brighter during an introduction or at a tea.

"Now, boys," said the captain, "she is going to swamp sure. All we can do is to work her in as far as possible, and then when she swamps, pile out and scramble for the beach. Keep cool now, and don't jump until she swamps sure."

The oiler took the oars. Over his shoulders he scanned the surf. "Captain," he said, "I think I'd better bring her about, and keep her head-on to the seas and back her in."

"All right, Billie," said the captain. "Back her in." The oiler swung the boat then and, seated in the stern, the cook and the correspondent were obliged to look over their shoulders to contemplate the lonely and indifferent shore.

The monstrous in-shore rollers heaved the boat high until the men were again enabled to see the white sheets of water scudding up the slanted beach. "We won't get in very close," said the captain. Each time a man could wrest his attention from the rollers, he turned his glance toward the shore, and in the expression of the eyes during this contemplation there was a singular quality. The correspondent, observing the others, knew that they were not afraid, but the full meaning of their glances was shrouded.

As for himself, he was too tired to grapple fundamentally with the fact. He tried to coerce his mind into thinking of it, but the mind was dominated at this time by the muscles, and the muscles said they did not care. It merely occurred to him that if he should drown it would be a shame.

There were no hurried words, no pallor, no plain agitation. The men simply looked at the shore. "Now, remember to get well clear of the boat when you jump," said the captain.

Seaward the crest of a roller suddenly fell with a thunderous crash, and the long white comber came roaring down upon the boat.

"Steady now," said the captain. The men were silent. They turned their eyes from the shore to the comber and waited. The boat slid up the incline, leaped at the furious top, bounced over it, and swung down the long back of the waves. Some water had been shipped and the cook bailed it out.

But the next crest crashed also. The tumbling boiling flood of white water caught the boat and whirled it almost perpendicular. Water swarmed in from all sides. The correspondent had his hands on the gunwale at this time, and when the water entered at that place he swiftly withdrew his fingers, as if he objected to wetting them.

The little boat, drunken with this weight of water, reeled and snuggled deeper into the sea.

"Bail her out, cook! Bail her out," said the captain.

"All right, captain," said the cook.

"Now, boys, the next one will do for us, sure," said the oiler. "Mind to jump clear of the boat."

The third wave moved forward, huge, furious, implacable. It fairly swallowed the dinghy, and almost simultaneously the men tumbled into the sea. A piece of life-belt had lain in the bottom of the boat, and as the correspondent went overboard he held this to his chest with his left hand.

The January water was icy, and he reflected immediately that it was colder than he had expected to find it off the coast of Florida. This appeared to his dazed mind as a fact important enough to be noted at the time. The coldness of the water was sad; it was tragic. This fact was somehow so mixed and confused with his opinion of his own situation that it seemed almost a proper reason for tears. The water was cold.

When he came to the surface he was conscious of little but the noisy water. Afterward he saw his companions in the sea. The oiler was ahead in the race. He was swimming strongly and rapidly. Off to the correspondent's left, the cook's great white and corked back bulged out of the water, and in the rear the captain was hanging with his one good hand to the keel of the overturned dinghy.

There is a certain immovable quality to a shore, and the correspondent wondered at it amid the confusion of the sea.

It seemed also very attractive, but the correspondent knew that it was a long journey, and he paddled leisurely. The piece of life-preserver lay under him, and sometimes he whirled down the incline of a wave as if he were on a hand-sled.

But finally he arrived at a place in the sea where travel was beset with difficulty. He did not pause swimming to inquire what manner of current had caught him, but there his progress ceased. The shore was set before him like a bit of scenery on a stage, and he looked at it and understood with his eyes each detail of it.

As the cook passed, much farther to the left, the captain was calling to him, "Turn over on your back, cook! Turn over on your back and use the oar."

"All right, sir." The cook turned on his back, and, paddling with an oar, went ahead as if he were a canoe.

Presently the boat also passed to the left of the correspondent with the captain clinging with one hand to the keel. He would have appeared like a man raising himself to look over a board fence, if it were not for the extraordinary gymnastics of the boat. The correspondent marveled that the captain could still hold to it.

They passed on, nearer to shore—the oiler, the cook, the captain—and following them went the water-jar, bouncing gaily over the seas.

The correspondent remained in the grip of this strange new enemy—a current. The shore, with its white slope of sand and its green bluff, topped with little silent cottages, was spread like a picture before him. It was very near to him then, but he was impressed as one who in a gallery looks at a scene from Brittany or Algiers.

He thought: "I am going to drown? Can it be possible? Can it be possible? Can it be possible?" Perhaps an individual must consider his own death to be the final phenomenon of nature.

But later a wave perhaps whirled him out of this small deadly current, for he found suddenly that he could again make progress toward the shore. Later still, he was aware that the captain, clinging with one hand to the keel of the dinghy, had his face turned away from the shore and toward him, and was call-ing his name. "Come to the boat! Come to the boat!"

In his struggle to reach the captain and the boat, he reflected that when one gets properly wearied, drowning must really be a comfort-able arrangement, a cessation of hostilities accompanied by a large degree of relief, and he was glad of it, for the main thing in his mind for some moments had been horror of the temporary agony. He did not wish to be hurt.

Presently he saw a man running along the shore. He was undressing with most remark-able speed. Coat, trousers, shirt, everything flew magically off him.

"Come to the boat," called the captain.

"All right, captain." As the correspondent paddled, he saw the captain let himself down to bottom and leave the boat. Then the corre-spondent performed his one little marvel of the voyage. A large wave caught him and flung him with ease and supreme speed com-pletely over the boat and far beyond it. It struck him even then as an event in gymnas-tics, and a true miracle of the sea. An over-turned boat in the surf is not a plaything to a swimming man.

The correspondent arrived in water that reached only to his waist, but his condition did not enable him to stand for more than a moment. Each wave knocked him into a heap, and the undertow pulled at him.

Then he saw the man who had been run-ning and undressing, and undressing and running, come bounding into the water. He dragged ashore the cook, and then waded toward the captain, but the captain waved him away, and sent him to the correspondent. He was naked, naked as a tree in winter, but a halo was about his head, and he shone like a saint. He gave a strong pull, and a long drag, and a bully heave at the correspondent's hand. The correspondent, schooled in the minor formulae, said: "Thanks, old man." But suddenly the man cried: "What's that?" He pointed a swift finger. The correspondent said: "Go."

In the shallows, face downward, lay the oiler. His forehead touched sand that was periodically, between each wave, clear of the sea.

The correspondent did not know all that transpired afterward. When he achieved safe ground he fell, striking the sand with each particular part of his body. It was as if he had dropped from a roof, but the thud was grate-ful to him.

It seems that instantly the beach was popu-lated with men, with blankets, clothes, and flasks, and women with coffee-pots and all the remedies sacred to their minds. The welcome of the land to the men from the sea was warm and generous, but a still and dripping shape was carried slowly up the beach, and the land's welcome for it could only be the differ-ent and sinister hospitality of the grave.

When it came night, the white waves paced to and fro in the moonlight, and the wind brought the sound of the great sea's voice to the men on shore, and they felt that they could then be interpreters.

FRANK O'CONNOR

Guests of the Nation

Frank O'Connor (1903–1966), whose real name was Michael O'Donovan, was born in Cork, Ireland, and attended the Christian Brothers School there. He was financially unable to pursue a university education, but he educated himself and developed his ability as a writer while he worked as a librarian. In 1931 his first book of short stories, *Guests of the Nation,* was published; it was followed by many volumes of short stories and verse, by plays, criticism, a history of Michael Collins and the Irish Revolution, and his autobiography, *An Only Child,* 1961.

"Guests of the Nation," like all of Mr. O'Connor's short stories, is noted for its technical skill. "Storytelling," he says, "is the nearest thing one can get to the quality of the pure lyric poem. It doesn't deal with problems; it doesn't have any solutions to offer; it just states the human condition."

At dusk the big Englishman, Belcher, would shift his long legs out of the ashes and say "Well, chums, what about it?" and Noble or me would say "All right, chum" (for we had picked up some of their curious expressions), and the little Englishman, Hawkins, would light the lamp and bring out the cards. Sometimes Jeremiah Donovan would come up and supervise the game and get excited over Hawkins's cards, which he always played badly, and shout at him as if he was one of our own "Ah, you divil, you, why didn't you play the trey?"

But ordinarily Jeremiah was a sober and contented poor devil like the big Englishman, Belcher, and was looked up to only because he was a fair hand at documents, though he was slow enough even with them. He wore a small cloth hat and big gaiters over his long pants, and you seldom saw him with his hands out of his pockets. He reddened when you talked to

GUESTS OF THE NATION   Reprinted from *More Stories* by Frank O'Connor, by permission of Alfred A. Knopf, Inc. Copyright, 1954 by Alfred A. Knopf, Inc.

him, tilting from toe to heel and back, and looking down all the time at his big farmer's feet. Noble and me used to make fun of his broad accent, because we were from the town.

I couldn't at the time see the point of me and Noble guarding Belcher and Hawkins at all, for it was my belief that you could have planted that pair down anywhere from this to Claregalway and they'd have taken root there like a native weed. I never in my short experience seen two men to take to the country as they did.

They were handed on to us by the Second Battalion when the search for them became too hot, and Noble and myself, being young, took over with a natural feeling of responsibility, but Hawkins made us look like fools when he showed that he knew the country better than we did.

"You're the bloke they calls Bonaparte," he says to me. "Mary Brigid O'Connell told me to ask you what you done with the pair of her brother's socks you borrowed."

For it seemed, as they explained it, that the

Second used to have little evenings, and some of the girls of the neighbourhood turned in, and, seeing they were such decent chaps, our fellows couldn't leave the two Englishmen out of them. Hawkins learned to dance "The Walls of Limerick," "The Siege of Ennis," and "The Waves of Tory" as well as any of them, though, naturally, we couldn't return the compliment, because our lads at that time did not dance foreign dances on principle.

So whatever privileges Belcher and Hawkins had with the Second they just naturally took with us, and after the first day or two we gave up all pretence of keeping a close eye on them. Not that they could have got far, for they had accents you could cut with a knife and wore khaki tunics and overcoats with civilian pants and boots. But it's my belief that they never had any idea of escaping and were quite content to be where they were.

It was a treat to see how Belcher got off with the old woman of the house where we were staying. She was a great warrant to scold, and cranky even with us, but before ever she had a chance of giving our guests, as I may call them, a lick of her tongue, Belcher had made her his friend for life. She was breaking sticks, and Belcher, who hadn't been more than ten minutes in the house, jumped up from his seat and went over to her.

"Allow me, madam," he says, smiling his queer little smile, "please allow me"; and he takes the bloody hatchet. She was struck too paralytic to speak, and after that, Belcher would be at her heels, carrying a bucket, a basket, or a load of turf, as the case might be. As Noble said, he got into looking before she leapt, and hot water, or any little thing she wanted, Belcher would have it ready for her. For such a huge man (and though I am five foot ten myself I had to look up at him) he had an uncommon shortness—or should I say lack?—of speech. It took us some time to get used to him, walking in and out, like a ghost, without a word. Especially because Hawkins talked enough for a platoon, it was strange to hear big Belcher with his toes in the ashes come out with a solitary "Excuse me, chum," or "That's right, chum." His one and only passion was cards, and I will say for him that he was a good card-player. He could have fleeced myself and Noble, but whatever we lost to him Hawkins lost to us, and Hawkins played with the money Belcher gave him.

Hawkins lost to us because he had too much old gab, and we probably lost to Belcher for the same reason. Hawkins and Noble would spit at one another about religion into the early hours of the morning, and Hawkins worried the soul out of Noble, whose brother was a priest, with a string of questions that would puzzle a cardinal. To make it worse, even in treating of holy subjects, Hawkins had a deplorable tongue. I never in all my career met a man who could mix such a variety of cursing and bad language into an argument. He was a terrible man, and a fright to argue. He never did a stroke of work, and when he had no one else to talk to, he got stuck in the old woman.

He met his match in her, for one day when he tried to get her to complain profanely of the drought, she gave him a great comedown by blaming it entirely on Jupiter Pluvius (a deity neither Hawkins nor I had ever heard of, though Noble said that among the pagans it was believed that he had something to do with the rain). Another day he was swearing at the capitalists for starting the German war when the old lady laid down her iron, puckered up her little crab's mouth, and said: "Mr. Hawkins, you can say what you like about the war, and think you'll deceive me because I'm only a simple poor countrywoman, but I know what started the war. It was the Italian Count that stole the heathen divinity out of the temple in Japan. Believe me, Mr. Hawkins, nothing but sorrow and want can follow the people that disturb the hidden powers."

A queer old girl, all right.

II

We had our tea one evening, and Hawkins lit the lamp and we all sat into cards. Jeremiah Donovan came in too, and sat down and watched us for a while, and it suddenly struck me that he had no great love for the two Englishmen. It came as a great surprise to me, because I hadn't noticed anything about him before.

Late in the evening a really terrible argument blew up between Hawkins and Noble, about capitalists and priests and love of your country.

"The capitalists," says Hawkins with an angry gulp, "pays the priests to tell you about the next world so as you won't notice what the bastards are up to in this."

"Nonsense, man!" says Noble, losing his temper. "Before ever a capitalist was thought of, people believed in the next world."

Hawkins stood us as though he was preaching a sermon.

"Oh, they did, did they?" he says with a sneer. "They believed all the things you believe, isn't that what you mean? And you believe that God created Adam, and Adam created Shem, and Shem created Jehoshophat. You believe all that silly old fairytale about Eve and Eden and the apple. Well, listen to me, chum. If you're entitled to hold a silly belief like that, I'm entitled to hold a silly belief—which is that the first thing your God created was a bleeding capitalist, with morality and Rolls-Royce complete. Am I right, chum?" he says to Belcher.

"You're right, chum," says Belcher with his amused smile, and got up from the table to stretch his long legs into the fire and stroke his moustache. So, seeing that Jeremiah Donovan was going, and that there was no knowing when the argument about religion would be over, I went out with him. We strolled down to the village together, and then he stopped and started blushing and mumbling and saying I ought to be behind, keeping guard on the prisoners. I didn't like the tone he took with me, and anyway I was bored with life in the cottage, so I replied by asking him what the hell we wanted guarding them at all for. I told him I'd talked it over with Noble, and that we'd both rather be out with a fighting column.

"What use are those fellows to us?" says I.

He looked at me in surprise and said: "I thought you knew we were keeping them as hostages."

"Hostages?" I said.

"The enemy have prisoners belonging to us," he says, "and now they're talking of shooting them. If they shoot our prisoners, we'll shoot theirs."

"Shoot them?" I said.

"What else did you think we were keeping them for?" he says.

"Wasn't it very unforeseen of you not to warn Noble and myself of that in the beginning?" I said.

"How was it?" says he. "You might have known it."

"We couldn't know it, Jeremiah Donovan," says I. "How could we when they were on our hands so long?"

"The enemy have our prisoners as long and longer," says he.

"That's not the same thing at all," says I.

"What difference is there?" says he.

I couldn't tell him, because I knew he wouldn't understand. If it was only an old dog that was going to the vet's, you'd try and not get too fond of him, but Jeremiah Donovan wasn't a man that would ever be in danger of that.

"And when is this thing going to be decided?" says I.

"We might hear tonight," he says. "Or tomorrow or the next day at latest. So if it's only hanging round here that's a trouble to you, you'll be free soon enough."

It wasn't the hanging round that was a trouble to me at all by this time. I had worse things to worry about. When I got back to the cottage the argument was still on. Hawkins was holding forth in his best style, maintaining that there was no next world, and Noble was maintaining that there was; but I could see that Hawkins had had the best of it.

"Do you know what, chum?" he was saying with a saucy smile. "I think you're just as big a bleeding unbeliever as I am. You say you believe in the next world, and you know just as much about the next world as I do, which is sweet damn-all. What's heaven? You don't know. Where's heaven? You don't know. You know sweet damn-all! I ask you again, do they wear wings?"

"Very well, then," says Noble, "they do. Is

that enough for you? They do wear wings."

"Where do they get them, then? Who makes them? Have they a factory for wings? Have they a sort of store where you hands in your chit and takes your bleeding wings?"

"You're an impossible man to argue with," says Noble. "Now, listen to—" And they were off again.

It was long after midnight when we locked up and went to bed. As I blew out the candle I told Noble what Jeremiah Donovan was after telling me. Noble took it very quietly. When we'd been in bed about an hour he asked me did I think we ought to tell the Englishmen. I didn't think we should, because it was more than likely that the English wouldn't shoot our men, and even if they did, the brigade officers, who were always up and down with the Second Battalion and knew the Englishmen well, wouldn't be likely to want them plugged. "I think so too," says Noble. "It would be great cruelty to put the wind up them now."

"It was very unforeseen of Jeremiah Donovan anyhow," says I.

It was next morning that we found it so hard to face Belcher and Hawkins. We went about the house all day scarcely saying a word. Belcher didn't seem to notice; he was stretched into the ashes as usual, with his usual look of waiting in quietness for something unforeseen to happen, but Hawkins noticed and put it down to Noble's being beaten in the argument of the night before.

"Why can't you take a discussion in the proper spirit?" he says severely. "You and your Adam and Eve! I'm a Communist, that's what I am. Communist or anarchist, it all comes to much the same thing." And for hours he went round the house, muttering when the fit took him. "Adam and Eve! Adam and Eve! Nothing better to do with their time than picking bleeding apples!"

III

I don't know how we got through that day, but I was very glad when it was over, the tea things were cleared away, and Belcher said in his peaceable way: "Well, chums, what about it?" We sat round the table and Haw-

kins took out the cards, and just then I heard Jeremiah Donovan's footstep on the path and a dark presentiment crossed my mind. I rose from the table and caught him before he reached the door.

"What do you want?" I asked.

"I want those two soldier friends of yours," he says, getting red.

"Is that the way, Jeremiah Donovan?" I asked.

"That's the way. There were four of our lads shot this morning, one of them a boy of sixteen."

"That's bad," I said.

At that moment Noble followed me out, and the three of us walked down the path together, talking in whispers. Feeney, the local intelligence officer, was standing by the gate.

"What are you going to do about it?" I asked Jeremiah Donovan.

"I want you and Noble to get them out; tell them they're being shifted again; that'll be the quietest way."

"Leave me out of that," says Noble under his breath.

Jeremiah Donovan looks at him hard.

"All right," he says. "You and Feeney get a few tools from the shed and dig a hole by the far end of the bog. Bonaparte and myself will be after you. Don't let anyone see you with the tools. I wouldn't like it to go beyond ourselves."

We saw Feeney and Noble go round to the shed and went in ourselves. I left Jeremiah Donovan to do the explanations. He told them that he had orders to send them back to the Second Battalion. Hawkins let out a mouthful of curses, and you could see that though Belcher didn't say anything, he was a bit upset too. The old woman was for having them stay in spite of us, and she didn't stop advising them until Jeremiah Donovan lost his temper and turned on her. He had a nasty temper, I noticed. It was pitch-dark in the cottage by this time, but no one thought of lighting the lamp, and in the darkness the two Englishmen fetched their topcoats and said good-bye to the old woman.

"Just as a man makes a home of a bleeding place, some bastard at headquarters thinks you're too cushy and shunts you off," says Hawkins, shaking her hand.

"A thousand thanks, madam," says Belcher. "A thousand thanks for everything"—as though he'd made it up.

We went round to the back of the house and down towards the bog. It was only then that Jeremiah Donovan told them. He was shaking with excitement.

"There were four of our fellows shot in Cork this morning and now you're to be shot as a reprisal."

"What are you talking about?" snaps Hawkins. "It's bad enough being mucked about as we are without having to put up with your funny jokes."

"It isn't a joke," says Donovan. "I'm sorry, Hawkins, but it's true," and begins on the usual rigmarole about duty and how unpleasant it is.

I never noticed that people who talk a lot about duty find it much of a trouble to them.

"Oh, cut it out!" says Hawkins.

"Ask Bonaparte," says Donovan, seeing that Hawkins isn't taking him seriously. "Isn't it true, Bonaparte?"

"It is," I say, and Hawkins stops.

"Ah, for Christ's sake, chum!"

"I mean it, chum," I say.

"You don't sound as if you meant it."

"If he doesn't mean it, I do," says Donovan, working himself up.

"What have you against me, Jeremiah Donovan?"

"I never said I had anything against you. But why did your people take out four of our prisoners and shoot them in cold blood?"

He took Hawkins by the arm and dragged him on, but it was impossible to make him understand that we were in earnest. I had the Smith and Wesson in my pocket and I kept fingering it and wondering what I'd do if they put up a fight for it or ran, and wishing to God they'd do one or the other. I knew if they did run for it, that I'd never fire on them. Hawkins wanted to know was Noble in it, and when we said yes, he asked us why Noble wanted to plug him. Why did any of us want to plug him? What had he done to us? Weren't we all chums? Didn't we understand him and didn't he understand us? Did we imagine for an instant that he'd shoot us for all the so-and-so officers in the so-and-so British Army?

By this time we'd reached the bog, and I was so sick I couldn't even answer him. We walked along the edge of it in the darkness, and every now and then Hawkins would call a halt and begin all over again, as if he was wound up, about our being chums, and I knew that nothing but the sight of the grave would convince him that we had to do it. And all the time I was hoping that something would happen; that they'd run for it or that Noble would take over the responsibility from me. I had the feeling that it was worse on Noble than on me.

IV

At last we saw the lantern in the distance and made towards it. Noble was carrying it, and Feeney was standing somewhere in the darkness behind him, and the picture of them so still and silent in the bogland brought it home to me that we were in earnest, and banished the last bit of hope I had.

Belcher, on recognizing Noble, said: "Hallo, chum," in his quiet way, but Hawkins flew at him at once, and the argument began all over again, only this time Noble had nothing to say for himself and stood with his head down, holding the lantern between his legs.

It was Jeremiah Donovan who did the answering. For the twentieth time, as though it was haunting his mind, Hawkins asked if anybody thought he'd shoot Noble.

"Yes, you would," says Jeremiah Donovan.

"No, I wouldn't, damn you!"

"You would, because you'd know you'd be shot for not doing it."

"I wouldn't, not if I was to be shot twenty times over. I wouldn't shoot a pal. And Belcher wouldn't—isn't that right, Belcher?"

"That's right, chum," Belcher said, but more by way of answering the question than of joining in the argument. Belcher sounded as though whatever unforeseen thing he'd always been waiting for had come at last.

"Anyway, who says Noble would be shot if I wasn't? What do you think I'd do if I was in his place, out in the middle of a blasted bog?"

"What would you do?" asks Donovan.

"I'd go with him wherever he was going, of course. Share my last bob with him and stick by him through thick and thin. No one can ever say of me that I let down a pal."

"We had enough of this," says Jeremiah Donovan, cocking his revolver. "Is there any message you want to send?"

"No, there isn't."

"Do you want to say your prayers?"

Hawkins came out with a cold-blooded remark that even shocked me and turned on Noble again.

"Listen to me, Noble," he says. "You and me are chums. You can't come over to my side, so I'll come over to your side. That show you I mean what I say? Give me a rifle and I'll go along with you and the other lads."

Nobody answered him. We knew that was no way out.

"Hear what I'm saying?" he says. "I'm through with it. I'm a deserter or anything else you like. I don't believe in your stuff, but it's no worse than mine. That satisfy you?"

Noble raised his head, but Donovan began to speak and he lowered it again without replying.

"For the last time, have you any messages to send?" says Donovan in a cold, excited sort of voice.

"Shut up, Donovan! You don't understand me, but these lads do. They're not the sort to make a pal and kill a pal. They're not the tools of any capitalist."

I alone of the crowd saw Donovan raise his Webley to the back of Hawkins's neck, and as he did so I shut my eyes and tried to pray. Hawkins had begun to say something else when Donovan fired, and as I opened my eyes at the bang, I saw Hawkins stagger at the knees and lie out flat at Noble's feet, slowly and as quiet as a kid falling asleep, with the lantern-light on his lean legs and bright farmer's boots. We all stood very still, watching him settle out in the last agony.

Then Belcher took out a handkerchief and began to tie it about his own eyes (in our excitement we'd forgotten to do the same for Hawkins), and, seeing it wasn't big enough, turned and asked for the loan of mine. I gave it to him and he knotted the two together and pointed with his foot at Hawkins.

"He's not quite dead," he says. "Better give him another."

Sure enough, Hawkins's left knee is beginning to rise. I bend down and put my gun to his head; then, recollecting myself, I get up again. Belcher understands what's in my mind.

"Give him his first," he says. "I don't mind. Poor bastard, we don't know what's happening to him now."

I knelt and fired. By this time I didn't seem to know what I was doing. Belcher, who was fumbling a bit awkwardly with the handkerchiefs, came out with a laugh as he heard the shot. It was the first time I heard him laugh and it sent a shudder down my back; it sounded so unnatural.

"Poor bugger!" he said quietly. "And last night he was so curious about it all. It's very queer, chums, I always think. Now he knows as much about it as they'll ever let him know, and last night he was all in the dark."

Donovan helped him to tie the handkerchiefs about his eyes. "Thanks, chum," he said. Donovan asked if there were any messages he wanted sent.

"No, chum," he says. "Not for me. If any of you would like to write to Hawkins's mother, you'll find a letter from her in his pocket. He and his mother were great chums. But my missus left me eight years ago. Went away with another fellow and took the kid with her. I like the feeling of a home, as you may have noticed, but I couldn't start again after that."

It was an extraordinary thing, but in those few minutes Belcher said more than in all the weeks before. It was just as if the sound of the shot had started a flood of talk in him and he could go on the whole night like that, quite happily, talking about himself. We stood round like fools now that he couldn't see us any longer. Donovan looked at Noble, and Noble shook his head. Then Donovan raised his Webley, and at that moment Belcher gives his queer laugh again. He may have thought we were talking about him, or perhaps he noticed the same thing I'd noticed and couldn't understand it.

"Excuse me, chums," he says. "I feel I'm talking the hell of a lot, and so silly, about my being so handy about a house and things like that. But this thing came on me suddenly. You'll forgive me, I'm sure."

"You don't want to say a prayer?" asks Donovan.

"No, chum," he says. "I don't think it would help. I'm ready, and you boys want to get it over."

"You understand that we're only doing our duty?" says Donovan.

Belcher's head was raised like a blind man's, so that you could only see his chin and the tip of his nose in the lantern-light.

"I never could make out what duty was myself," he said. "I think you're all good lads, if that's what you mean. I'm not complaining."

Noble, just as if he couldn't bear any more of it, raised his fist at Donovan, and in a flash Donovan raised his gun and fired. The big man went over like a sack of meal, and this time there was no need of a second shot.

I don't remember much about the burying, but that it was worse than all the rest because we had to carry them to the grave. It was all mad lonely with nothing but a patch of lantern-light between ourselves and the dark, and birds hooting and screeching all round, disturbed by the guns. Noble went through Hawkins's belongings to find the letter from his mother, and then joined his hands together. He did the same with Belcher. Then, when we'd filled in the grave, we separated from Jeremiah Donovan and Feeney and took our tools back to the shed. All the way we didn't speak a word. The kitchen was dark and cold as we'd left it, and the old woman was sitting over the hearth, saying her beads. We walked past her into the room, and Noble struck a match to light the lamp. She rose quietly and came to the doorway with all her cantankerousness gone.

"What did ye do with them?" she asked in a whisper, and Noble started so that the match went out in his hand.

"What's that?" he asked without turning round.

"I heard ye," she said.

"What did you hear?" asked Noble.

"I heard ye. Do ye think I didn't hear ye, putting the spade back in the houseen?"

Noble struck another match and this time the lamp lit for him.

"Was that what ye did to them?" she asked.

Then, by God, in the very doorway, she fell on her knees and began praying, and after looking at her for a minute or two Noble did the same by the fireplace. I pushed my way out past her and left them at it. I stood at the door, watching the stars and listening to the shrieking of the birds dying out over the bogs. It is so strange what you feel at times like that that you can't describe it. Noble says he saw everything ten times the size, as though there were nothing in the whole world but that little patch of bog with the two Englishmen stiffening into it, but with me it was as if the patch of bog where the Englishmen were was a million miles away, and even Noble and the old woman, mumbling behind me, and the birds and the bloody stars were all far away, and I was somehow very small and very lost and lonely like a child astray in the snow. And anything that happened to me afterwards, I never felt the same about again.

WILLIAM FAULKNER

Spotted Horses

William Faulkner (1897–1962) spent most of his life near Oxford, Mississippi, which is the "Jefferson" of his novels and short stories. During World War I he was enlisted in the Canadian Air Force. After the war he returned to Oxford, taking a few courses at the University of Mississippi and supporting himself by doing odd jobs. In 1959 he was appointed lecturer on writing at the University of Virginia.

Faulkner's early novels brought him critical acclaim but little or no popularity or financial remuneration. *Sartoris,* 1929, was the first of his many novels centering on the Sartoris family, patterned after his own wealthy Southern ancestors who had been reduced to genteel poverty after the Civil War. The Snopes family make their first appearance in this novel and began accumulating, by various rascalities, the wealth and power once held by the now degenerating aristocracy. In 1931 Faulkner published *Sanctuary,* which he said was deliberately made "horrific" in order to appeal to popular taste and earn enough money to support himself; in this aim he was successful. He wrote several other novels and many short stories; the latter were collected in a volume published in 1950. More recent publications are *The Town,* 1957; *The Long Hot Summer,* 1958, "a dramatic book" from *The Hamlet,* 1940; *The Mansion,* 1959, the third novel of the Snopes family; and *The Reivers,* 1962.

In 1939 Faulkner received the O. Henry Memorial Award; in 1949, after the publication in 1948 of *Intruder in the Dust,* he received the Nobel Prize for Literature "for his forceful and independently artistic contribution to modern American fiction," and in 1954 a Pulitzer Prize for *A Fable.* In all, Faulkner, along with Hemingway, has received greater critical acclaim than any other contemporary American novelist.

Few writers achieve so much intense dramatic activity in a story as William Faulkner. In "Spotted Horses," for instance, every detail vibrates with a life of its own and gives added life to other details—the wild, odd-eyed horses, which symbolize the folly of Henry Armstid and his kind; the meek and passive Mrs. Armstid, who objectifies the results of ignorance and rascality; the taciturn and sneaking Flem Snopes; and the calm, sensible Mrs. Littlejohn, who is never deluded by the folly and madness of her neighbors.

Yes sir. Flem Snopes has filled that whole country full of spotted horses. You can hear

folks running them all day and all night, whooping and hollering, and the horses running back and forth across them little wooden bridges ever now and then kind of like thunder. Here I was this morning pretty near halfway to town, with the team ambling along and me setting in the buckboard about half asleep, when all of a sudden something come swurging up outen the bushes and jumped the road clean, without touching hoof to it. It flew right over my team big as a billboard and flying through the air like a hawk. It taken me thirty minutes to stop my team and untangle the harness and the buckboard and hitch them up again.

That Flem Snopes. I be dog if he ain't a case, now. One morning about ten years ago the boys was just getting settled down on Varner's porch for a little talk and tobacco, when here come Flem out from behind the counter, with his coat off and his hair all parted, like he might have been clerking for Varner for ten years already. Folks all knowed him; it was a big family of them about five miles down the bottom. That year, at least. Share-cropping. They never stayed on any place over a year. Then they would move on to another place, with the chap or maybe the twins of that year's litter. It was a regular nest of them. But Flem. The rest of them stayed tenant farmers, moving ever year, but here come Flem one day, walking out from behind Jody Varner's counter like he owned it. And he wasn't there but a year or two before folks knowed that if him and Jody was both still in that store in ten years more it would be Jody clerking for Flem Snopes. Why, that fellow could make a nickel where it wasn't but four cents to begin with. He skun me in two trades myself, and the fellow that can do that, I just hope he'll get rich before I do; that's all.

All right. So here Flem was, clerking at Varner's, making a nickel here and there and not telling nobody about it. No, sir. Folks never knowed when Flem got the better of somebody lessen the fellow he beat told it. He'd just set there in the store-chair, chewing his tobacco and keeping his own business to hisself, until about a week later we'd find out it was somebody else's business he was keeping to hisself—provided the fellow he trimmed was mad enough to tell it. That's Flem.

We give him ten years to own ever thing Jody Varner had. But he never waited no ten years. I reckon you-all know that gal of Uncle Billy Varner's, the youngest one, Eula. Jody's sister. Ever Sunday ever yellow-wheeled

buggy and curried riding horse in that country would be hitched to Bill Varner's fence, and the young bucks setting on the porch, swarming around Eula like bees around a honey pot. One of these here kind of big, soft-looking gals that could giggle richer than plowed new-ground. Wouldn't none of them leave before the others, and so they would set there on the porch until time to go home, with some of them with nine and ten miles to ride and then get up tomorrow and go back to the field. So they would all leave together and they would ride in a clump down to the creek ford and hitch them curried horses and yellow-wheeled buggies and get out and fight one another. Then they would get in the buggies again and go on home.

Well, one day about a year ago, one of them yellow-wheeled buggies and one of them curried saddle-horses quit this country. We heard they was heading for Texas. The next day Uncle Billy and Eula and Flem come in to town in Uncle Bill's surrey, and when they come back, Flem and Eula was married. And on the next day we heard that two more of them yellow-wheeled buggies had left the country. They mought have gone to Texas, too. It's a big place.

Anyway, about a month after the wedding, Flem and Eula went to Texas, too. They was gone pretty near a year. Then one day last month, Eula come back, with a baby. We figgered up, and we decided that it was as well-growed a three-months-old baby as we ever see. It can already pull up on a chair. I reckon Texas makes big men quick, being a big place. Anyway, if it keeps on like it started, it'll be chewing tobacco and voting time it's eight years old.

And so last Friday here come Flem himself. He was on a wagon with another fellow. The other fellow had one of these two-gallon hats and a ivory-handled pistol and a box of gingersnaps sticking out of his hind pocket, and tied to the tail-gate of the wagon was about two dozen of them Texas ponies, hitched to one another with barbed wire. They was colored like parrots and they was quiet as doves, and ere a one of them would kill you quick as a rattlesnake. Nere a one of them had two eyes the same color, and nere a one of them had ever see a bridle, I reckon; and when that Texas man got down offen the wagon and walked up to them to show how gentle they was, one of them cut his vest clean offen him, same as with a razor.

Flem had done already disappeared; he had went on to see his wife, I reckon, and to see if that ere baby had done gone on to the field to help Uncle Billy plow, maybe. It was the Texas man that taken the horses on to Mrs. Littlejohn's lot. He had a little trouble at first, when they come to the gate, because they hadn't never see a fence before, and when he finally got them in and taken a pair of wire cutters and unhitched them and got them into the barn and poured some shell corn into the trough, they durn nigh tore down the barn. I reckon they thought that shell corn was bugs, maybe. So he left them in the lot and he announced that the auction would begin at sunup tomorrow.

That night we was setting on Mrs. Littlejohn's porch. You-all mind the moon was nigh full that night, and we could watch them spotted varmints swirling along the fence and back and forth across the lot same as minnows in a pond. And then now and then they would all kind of huddle up against the barn and rest themselves by biting and kicking one another. We would hear a squeal, and then a set of hoofs would go Bam! against the barn, like a pistol. It sounded just like a fellow with a pistol, in a nest of cattymounts, taking his time.

It wasn't ere a man knowed yet if Flem owned them things or not. They just knowed one thing: that they wasn't never going to know for sho if Flem did or not, or if maybe he didn't just get on that wagon at the edge of town, for the ride or not. Even Eck Snopes didn't know, Flem's own cousin. But wasn't nobody surprised at that. We knowed that Flem would skin Eck quick as he would ere a one of us.

They was there by sunup next morning, some of them come twelve and sixteen miles, with seed-money tied up in tobacco sacks in their overalls, standing along the fence, when the Texas man come out of Mrs. Littlejohn's after breakfast and clumb onto the gate post with that ere white pistol butt sticking outen

his hind pocket. He taken a new box of gingersnaps outen his pocket and bit the end offen it like a cigar and spit out the paper, and said the auction was open. And still they was coming up in wagons and a horse- and mule-back and hitching the teams across the road and coming to the fence. Flem wasn't nowhere in sight.

But he couldn't get them started. He begun to work on Eck, because Eck holp him last night to get them into the barn and feed them that shell corn. Eck got out just in time. He come outen that barn like a chip on the crest of a busted dam of water, and clumb into the wagon just in time.

He was working on Eck when Henry Armstid come up in his wagon. Eck was saying he was skeered to bid on one of them, because he might get it, and the Texas man says, "Them ponies? Them little horses?" He clumb down offen the gate post and went toward the horses. They broke and run, and him following them, kind of chirping to them, with his hand out like he was fixing to catch a fly, until he got three or four of them cornered. Then he jumped into them, and then we couldn't see nothing for a while because of the dust. It was a big cloud of it, and them blare-eyed, spotted things swoaring outen it twenty foot to a jump, in forty directions without counting up. Then the dust settled and there they was, that Texas man and the horse. He had its head twisted clean around like a owl's head. It's legs was braced and it was trembling like a new bride and groaning like a sawmill, and him holding its head wrung clean around on its neck so it was snuffing sky. "Look it over," he says, with his heels dug too and that white pistol sticking outen his pocket and his neck swole up like a spreading adder's until you could just tell what he was saying, cussing the horse and talking to us all at once: "Look him over, the fiddle-headed son of fourteen fathers. Try him, buy him; you will get the best—" Then it was all dust again, and we couldn't see nothing but spotted hide and mane, and that ere Texas man's boot-heels like a couple of walnuts on two strings, and after a while that two-gallon hat come sailing out like a fat old hen crossing a fence.

When the dust settled again, he was just

getting outen the far fence corner, brushing himself off. He come and got his hat and brushed it off and come and clumb onto the gate post again. He was breathing hard. The hammer-head horse was still running round and round the lot like a merry-go-round at a fair. That was when Henry Armstid come shoving up to the gate in them patched overalls and one of them dangle-armed shirts of hisn. Hadn't nobody noticed him until then. We was all watching the Texas man and the horses. Even Mrs. Littlejohn; she had done come out and built a fire under the wash-pot in her back yard, and she would stand at the fence a while and then go back into the house and come out again with a arm full of wash and stand at the fence again. Well, here come Henry shoving up, and then we see Mrs. Armstid right behind him, in that ere faded wrapper and sunbonnet and them tennis shoes. "Get on back to that wagon," Henry says.

"Henry," she says.

"Here, boys," the Texas man says; "make room for missus to git up and see. Come on Henry," he says; "here's your chance to buy that saddle-horse missus has been wanting. What about ten dollars, Henry?"

"Henry," Mrs. Armstid says. She put her hand on Henry's arm. Henry knocked her hand down.

"Git on back to that wagon, like I told you," he says.

Mrs. Armstid never moved. She stood behind Henry, with her hands rolled into her dress, not looking at nothing. "He hain't no more despair than to buy one of them things," she says. "And us not five dollars ahead of the pore house, he hain't no more despair." It was the truth, too. They ain't never made more than a bare living offen that place of theirs, and them with four chaps and the very clothes they wears she earns by weaving by the firelight at night while Henry's asleep.

"Shut your mouth and git on back to that wagon," Henry says. "Do you want I taken a wagon stake to you here in the big road?"

Well, that Texas man taken one look at her. Then he begun on Eck again, like Henry wasn't even there. But Eck was skeered. "I can git me a snapping turtle or a water moccasin for nothing. I ain't going to buy none."

So the Texas man said he would give Eck a horse. "To start the auction, and because you holp me last night. If you'll start the bidding on the next horse," he says, "I'll give you that fiddle-head horse."

I wish you could have seen them, standing there with their seed-money in their pockets, watching that Texas man give Eck Snopes a live horse, all fixed to call him a fool if he taken it or not. Finally Eck says he'll take it. "Only I just starts the bidding," he says. "I don't have to buy the next one lessen I ain't overtopped." The Texas man said all right, and Eck bid a dollar on the next one, with Henry Armstid standing there with his mouth already open, watching Eck and the Texas man like a mad-dog or something. "A dollar," Eck says.

The Texas man looked at Eck. His mouth was already open too, like he had started to say something and what he was going to say had up and died on him. "A dollar? You mean, *one* dollar, Eck?"

"Durn it," Eck says; "two dollars, then."

Well, sir, I wish you could a seen that Texas man. He taken out that gingersnap box and held it up and looked into it, careful, like it might have been a diamond ring in it, or a spider. Then he throwed it away and wiped his face with a bandanna. "Well," he says. "Well. Two dollars. Two dollars. Is your pulse all right, Eck?" he says. "Do you have ager-sweats at night, maybe?" he says. "Well," he says, "I got to take it. But are you boys going to stand there and see Eck get two horses at a dollar a head?"

That done it. I be dog if he wasn't nigh as smart as Flem Snopes. He hadn't no more than got the words outen his mouth before here was Henry Armstid, waving his hand. "Three dollars," Henry says. Mrs. Armstid tried to hold him again. He knocked her hand off, shoving up to the gate post.

"Mister," Mrs. Armstid says, "we got chaps in the house and not corn to feed the stock. We got five dollars I earned my chaps a-weaving after dark, and him snoring in the bed. And he hain't no more despair."

"Henry bid three dollars," the Texas man

says. "Raise him a dollar, Eck, and the horse is yours."

"Henry," Mrs. Armstid says.

"Raise him, Eck," the Texas man says.

"Four dollars," Eck says.

"Five dollars," Henry says, shaking his fist. He shoved up right under the gate post. Mrs. Armstid was looking at the Texas man too.

"Mister," she says, "if you take that five dollars I earned my chaps a-weaving for one of them things, it'll be a curse onto you and yourn during all the time of man."

But it wasn't no stopping Henry. He had shoved up, waving his fist at the Texas man. He opened it; the money was in nickels and quarters, and one dollar bill that looked like a cow's cud. "Five dollars," he says. "And the man that raises it'll have to beat my head off, or I'll beat hisn."

"All right," the Texas man says. "Five dollars is bid. But don't you shake your hand at me."

It taken till nigh sundown before the last one was sold. He got them hotted up once and the bidding got up to seven dollars and a quarter, but most of them went around three or four dollars, him setting on the gate post and picking the horses out one at a time by mouth-word, and Mrs. Littlejohn pumping up and down at the tub and stopping and coming to the fence for a while and going back to the tub again. She had done got done too, and the wash was hung on the line in the back yard, and we could smell supper cooking. Finally they was all sold; he swapped the last two and the wagon for a buckboard.

We was all kind of tired, but Henry Armstid looked more like a mad-dog than ever. When he bought, Mrs. Armstid had went back to the wagon, setting in it behind them two rabbit-sized, bone-pore mules, and the wagon itself looking like it would fall all to pieces soon as the mules moved. Henry hadn't even waited to pull it outen the road; it was still in the middle of the road and her setting in it, not looking at nothing, ever since this morning.

Henry was right up against the gate. He went up to the Texas man. "I bought a horse and I paid cash," Henry says. "And yet you

expect me to stand around here until they are all sold before I can get my horse. I'm going to take my horse outen that lot."

The Texas man looked at Henry. He talked like he might have been asking for a cup of coffee at the table. "Take your horse," he says.

Then Henry quit looking at the Texas man. He begun to swallow, holding onto the gate. "Ain't you going to help me?" he says.

"It ain't my horse," the Texas man says.

Henry never looked at the Texas man again, he never looked at nobody. "Who'll help me catch my horse?" he says. Never nobody said nothing. "Bring the plowline," Henry says. Mrs. Armstid got outen the wagon and brought the plowline. The Texas man got down offen the post. The woman made to pass him, carrying the rope.

"Don't you go in there, missus," the Texas man says.

Henry opened the gate. He didn't look back. "Come on here," he says.

"Don't you go in there, missus," the Texas man says.

Mrs. Armstid wasn't looking at nobody, neither, with her hands across her middle, holding the rope. "I reckon I better," she says. Her and Henry went into the lot. The horses broke and run. Henry and Mrs. Armstid followed.

"Get him into the corner," Henry says. They got Henry's horse cornered finally, and Henry taken the rope, but Mrs. Armstid let the horse get out. They hemmed it up again, but Mrs. Armstid let it get out again, and Henry turned and hit her with the rope. "Why didn't you head him back?" Henry says. He hit her again. "Why didn't you?" It was about that time I looked around and see Flem Snopes standing there.

It was the Texas man that done something. He moved fast for a big man. He caught the rope before Henry could hit the third time, and Henry whirled and made like he would jump at the Texas man. But he never jumped. The Texas man went and taken Henry's arm and led him outen the lot. Mrs. Armstid come behind them and the Texas man taken some money outen his pocket and he give it into Mrs. Armstid's hand. "Get him into the wagon and take him on home," the Texas man says, like he might have been telling them he enjoyed his supper.

Then here come Flem. "What's that for, Buck?" Flem says.

"Thinks he bought one of them ponies," the Texas man says. "Get him on away, missus."

But Henry wouldn't go. "Give him back that money," he says. "I bought that horse and I aim to have him if I have to shoot him."

And there was Flem, standing there with his hands in his pockets, chewing, like he had just happened to be passing.

"You take your money and I take my horse," Henry says. "Give it back to him," he says to Mrs. Armstid.

"You don't own no horse of mine," the Texas man says. "Get him on home, missus."

Then Henry seen Flem. "You got something to do with these horses," he says. "I bought one. Here's the money for it." He taken the bill outen Mrs. Armstid's hand. He offered it to Flem. "I bought one. Ask him. Here. Here's the money," he says, giving the bill to Flem.

When Flem taken the money, the Texas man dropped the rope he had snatched outen Henry's hand. He had done sent Eck Snopes's boy up to the store for another box of gingersnaps, and he taken the box outen his pocket and looked into it. It was empty and he dropped it on the ground. "Mr. Snopes will have your money for you tomorrow," he says to Mrs. Armstid. "You can get it from him tomorrow. He don't own no horse. You get him into the wagon and get him on home." Mrs. Armstid went back to the wagon and got in. "Where's that ere buckboard I bought?" the Texas man says. It was after sundown then. And then Mrs. Littlejohn come out on the porch and rung the supper bell.

I come on in and et supper. Mrs. Littlejohn would bring in a pan of bread or something, then she would go out to the porch a minute and come back and tell us. The Texas man had hitched his team to the buckboard he had swapped them last two horses for, and him and Flem had gone, and then she told that the rest of them that never had ropes had went back to the store with I. O. Snopes

to get some ropes, and wasn't nobody at the gate but Henry Armstid, and Mrs. Armstid setting in the wagon in the road, and Eck Snopes and that boy of hisn. "I don't care how many of them fool men gets killed by them things," Mrs. Littlejohn says, "but I ain't going to let Eck Snopes take that boy into that lot again." So she went down to the gate, but she come back without the boy or Eck neither.

"It ain't no need to worry about that boy," I says. "He's charmed." He was right behind Eck last night when Eck went to help feed them. The whole drove of them jumped clean over that boy's head and never touched him. It was Eck that touched him. Eck snatched him into the wagon and taken a rope and frailed the tar outen him.

So I had done et and went to my room and was undressing, long as I had a long trip to make next day; I was trying to sell a machine to Mrs. Bundren up past Whiteleaf; when Henry Armstid opened that gate and went in by hisself. They couldn't make him wait for the balance of them to get back with their ropes. Eck Snopes said he tried to make Henry wait, but Henry wouldn't do it. Eck said Henry walked right up to them and that when they broke, they run clean over Henry like a hay-mow breaking down. Eck said he snatched that boy of hisn out of the way just in time and that them things went through that gate like a creek flood and into the wagons and teams hitched side the road, busting wagon tongues and snapping harness like it was fishing-line, with Mrs. Armstid still setting in their wagon in the middle of it like something carved outen wood. Then they scattered, wild horses and tame mules with pieces of harness and singletrees dangling offen them, both ways up and down the road.

"There goes ourn, paw!" Eck said his boy said. "There it goes, into Mrs. Littlejohn's house." Eck says it run right up the steps and into the house like a boarder late for supper. I reckon so. Anyway, I was in my room, in my underclothes, with one sock on and one sock in my hand, leaning out the window when the commotion busted out, when I heard something run into the melodeon in the hall; it sounded like a railroad engine. Then the door to my room come sailing in like when you throw a tin bucket top into the wind and I looked over my shoulder and see something that looked like a fourteen-foot pinwheel a-blaring its eyes at me. It had to blare them fast, because I was already done jumped out the window.

I reckon it was anxious, too. I reckon it hadn't never seen barbed wire or shell corn before, but I know it hadn't never seen underclothes before, or maybe it was a sewing-machine agent it hadn't never seen. Anyway, it whirled and turned to run back up the hall and outen the house, when it met Eck Snopes and that boy just coming in, carrying a rope. It swirled again and run down the hall and out the back door just in time to meet Mrs. Littlejohn. She had just gathered up the clothes she had washed, and she was coming onto the back porch with a armful of washing in one hand and a scrubbing-board in the other, when the horse skidded up to her, trying to stop and swirl again. It never taken Mrs. Littlejohn no time a-tall.

"Git outen here, you son," she says. She hit it across the face with the scrubbing-board; that ere scrubbing-board split as neat as ere a axe could have done it, and when the horse swirled to run back up the hall, she hit it again with what was left of the scrubbing-board, not on the head this time. "And stay out," she says.

Eck and that boy was halfway down the hall by this time. I reckon that horse looked like a pinwheel to Eck too. "Git to hell outen here, Ad!" Eck says. Only there wasn't time. Eck dropped flat on his face, but the boy never moved. The boy was about a yard tall maybe, in overalls just like Eck's; that horse swoared over his head without touching a hair. I saw that, because I was just coming back up the front steps, still carrying that ere sock and still in my underclothes, when the horse come onto the porch again. It taken one look at me and swirled again and run to the end of the porch and jumped the banisters and the lot fence like a hen-hawk and lit in the lot running and went out the gate again

and jumped eight or ten upside-down wagons and went on down the road. It was a full moon then. Mrs. Armstid was still setting in the wagon like she had done been carved outen wood and left there and forgot.

That horse. It ain't never missed a lick. It was going about forty miles a hour when it come to the bridge over the creek. It would have had a clear road, but it so happened that Vernon Tull was already using the bridge when it got there. He was coming back from town; he hadn't heard about the auction; him and his wife and three daughters and Mrs. Tull's aunt, all setting in chairs in the wagon bed, and all asleep, including the mules. They waked up when the horse hit the bridge one time, but Tull said the first he knew was when the mules tried to turn the wagon around in the middle of the bridge and he seen that spotted varmint run right twixt the mules and run up the wagon tongue like a squirrel. He said he just had time to hit it across the face with his whip-stock, because about that time the mules turned the wagon around on that ere one-way bridge and that horse clumb across onto the bridge again and went on, with Vernon standing up in the wagon and kicking at it.

Tull said the mules turned in the harness and clumb back into the wagon too, with Tull trying to beat them out again, with the reins wrapped around his wrist. After that he says all he seen was overturned chairs and women-folks' legs and white drawers shining in the moonlight, and his mules and that spotted horse going on up the road like a ghost.

The mules jerked Tull outen the wagon and drug him a spell on the bridge before the reins broke. They thought at first that he was dead, and while they was kneeling around him, picking the bridge splinters outen him, here come Eck and that boy, still carrying the rope. They was running and breathing a little hard. "Where'd he go?" Eck said.

I went back and got my pants and shirt and shoes on just in time to go and help get Henry Armstid outen the trash in the lot. I be dog if he didn't look like he was dead, with his head hanging back and his teeth showing in the moonlight, and a little rim of white under his eye-lids. We could still hear them horses, here and there; hadn't none of them got more than four-five miles away yet, not knowing the country, I reckon. So we could hear them and folks yelling now and then: "Whooey. Head him!"

We toted Henry into Mrs. Littlejohn's. She was in the hall; she hadn't put down the armful of clothes. She taken one look at us, and she laid down the busted scrubbing-board and taken up the lamp and opened a empty door. "Bring him in here," she says.

We toted him in and laid him on the bed. Mrs. Littlejohn set the lamp on the dresser, still carrying the clothes. "I'll declare, you men," she says. Our shadows was way up the wall, tiptoeing too; we could hear ourselves breathing. "Better get his wife," Mrs. Littlejohn says. She went out, carrying the clothes.

"I reckon we had," Quick says. "Go get her, somebody."

"Whyn't you go?" Winterbottom says.

"Let Ernest git her," Durley says. "He lives neighbors with them."

Ernest went to fetch her. I be dog if Henry didn't look like he was dead. Mrs. Littlejohn come back, with a kettle and some towels. She went to work on Henry, and then Mrs. Armstid and Ernest come in. Mrs. Armstid come to the foot of the bed and stood there, with her hands rolled into her apron, watching what Mrs. Littlejohn was doing, I reckon.

"You men get outen the way," Mrs. Littlejohn says. "Git outside," she says. "See if you can't find something else to play with that will kill some more of you."

"Is he dead?" Winterbottom says.

"It ain't your fault if he ain't," Mrs. Littlejohn says. "Go tell Will Varner to come up here. I reckon a man ain't so different from a mule, come long come short. Except maybe a mule's got more sense."

We went to get Uncle Billy. It was a full moon. We could hear them, now and then, four miles away: "Whooey. Head him." The country was full of them, one on ever wooden bridge in the land, running across it like thunder: "Whooey. There he goes. Head him."

We hadn't got far before Henry begun to scream. I reckon Mrs. Littlejohn's water had brung him to; anyway, he wasn't dead. We went on to Uncle Billy's. The house was dark. We called to him, and after a while the window opened and Uncle Billy put his head out, peart as a peckerwood, listening. "Are they still trying to catch them durn rabbits?" he says.

He come down, with his britches on over his night-shirt and his suspenders dangling, carrying his horse-doctoring grip. "Yes, sir," he says, cocking his head like a woodpecker; "they're still a-trying."

We could hear Henry before we reached Mrs. Littlejohn's. He was going Ah-Ah-Ah. We stopped in the yard. Uncle Billy went on in. We could hear Henry. We stood in the yard, hearing them on the bridges, this-a-way and that: "Whooey. Whooey."

"Eck Snopes ought to caught hisn," Ernest says.

"Looks like he ought," Winterbottom said.

Henry was going Ah-Ah-Ah steady in the house; then he begun to scream. "Uncle Billy's started," Quick says. We looked into the hall. We could see the light where the door was. Then Mrs. Littlejohn come out.

"Will needs some help," she says. "You, Ernest. You'll do." Ernest went into the house.

"Hear them?" Quick said. "That one was on Four Mile bridge." We could hear them; it sounded like thunder a long way off; it didn't last long:

"Whooey."

We could hear Henry: "Ah-Ah-Ah-Ah-Ah."

"They are both started now," Winterbottom says. "Ernest too."

That was early in the night. Which was a good thing, because it taken a long night for folks to chase them things right and for Henry to lay there and holler, being as Uncle Billy never had none of this here chloryfoam to set Henry's leg with. So it was considerate in Flem to get them started early. And what do you reckon Flem's com-ment was?

That's right. Nothing. Because he wasn't there. Hadn't nobody see him since that Texas man left.

That was Saturday night. I reckon Mrs. Armstid got home about daylight, to see about the chaps. I don't know where they thought her and Henry was. But lucky the oldest one was a gal, about twelve, big enough to take care of the little ones. Which she did for the next two days. Mrs. Armstid would nurse Henry all night and work in the kitchen for hern and Henry's keep, and in the afternoon she would drive home (it was about four miles) to see to the chaps. She would cook up a pot of victuals and leave it on the stove, and the gal would bar the house and keep the little ones quiet. I would hear Mrs. Littlejohn and Mrs. Armstid talking in the kitchen. "How are the chaps making out?" Mrs. Littlejohn says.

"All right," Mrs. Armstid says.

"Don't they git skeered at night?" Mrs. Littlejohn says.

"Ina May bars the door when I leave," Mrs. Armstid says. "She's got the axe in bed with her. I reckon she can make out."

I reckon they did. And I reckon Mrs. Armstid was waiting for Flem to come back to town; hadn't nobody seen him until this morning; to get her money the Texas man said Flem was keeping for her. Sho. I reckon she was.

Anyway, I heard Mrs. Armstid and Mrs. Littlejohn talking in the kitchen this morning while I was eating breakfast. Mrs. Littlejohn had just told Mrs. Armstid that Flem was in town. "You can ask him for that five dollars," Mrs. Littlejohn says.

"You reckon he'll give it to me?" Mrs. Armstid says.

Mrs. Littlejohn was washing dishes, washing them like a man, like they was made out of iron. "No," she says. "But asking him won't do no hurt. It might shame him. I don't reckon it will, but it might."

"If he wouldn't give it back, it ain't no use to ask," Mrs. Armstid says.

"Suit yourself," Mrs. Littlejohn says. "It's your money."

I could hear the dishes.

"Do you reckon he might give it back to me?" Mrs. Armstid says. "That Texas man said he would. He said I could get it from Mr. Snopes later."

"Then go and ask him for it," Mrs. Littlejohn says.

I could hear the dishes.

"He won't give it back to me," Mrs. Armstid says.

"All right," Mrs. Littlejohn says. "Don't ask him for it, then."

I could hear the dishes; Mrs. Armstid was helping. "You don't reckon he would, do you?" she says. Mrs. Littlejohn never said nothing. It sounded like she was throwing the dishes at one another. "Maybe I better go and talk to Henry about it," Mrs. Armstid says.

"I would," Mrs. Littlejohn says. I be dog if it didn't sound like she had two plates in her hands, beating them together. "Then Henry can buy another five-dollar horse with it. Maybe he'll buy one next time that will out and out kill him. If I thought that, I'd give you back the money, myself."

"I reckon I better talk to him first," Mrs. Armstid said. Then it sounded like Mrs. Littlejohn taken up all the dishes and throwed them at the cook-stove, and I come away.

That was this morning. I had been up to Bundren's and back, and I thought that things would have kind of settled down. So after breakfast, I went up to the store. And there was Flem, setting in the store chair and whittling, like he might not have ever moved since he come to clerk for Jody Varner. I. O. was leaning in the door, in his shirt sleeves and with his hair parted too, same as Flem was before he turned the clerking job over to I. O. It's a funny thing about them Snopes: they all looks alike, yet there ain't ere a two of them that claims brothers. They're always just cousins, like Flem and Eck and Flem and I. O. Eck was there too, squatting against the wall, him and that boy, eating cheese and crackers outen a sack; they told me that Eck hadn't been home a-tall. And that Lon Quick hadn't got back to town, even. He followed his horse clean down to Samson's Bridge, with a wagon and a camp outfit. Eck finally caught one of hisn. It run into a blind lane at Freeman's and Eck and the boy taken and tied their rope across the end of the lane, about three foot high. The horse come to the end of the lane and whirled and run back without ever stopping. Eck says it never seen the rope a-tall. He says it looked just like one of these here Christmas pinwheels. "Didn't it try to run again?" I says.

"No," Eck says, eating a bite of cheese offen his knife blade. "Just kicked some."

"Kicked some?" I says.

"It broke its neck," Eck says.

Well, they was squatting there, about six of them, talking, talking at Flem; never nobody knowed yet if Flem had ere a interest in them horses or not. So finally I come right out and asked him. "Flem's done skun all of us so much," I says, "that we're proud of him. Come on, Flem," I says, "how much did you and that Texas man make offen them horses? You can tell us. Ain't nobody here but Eck that bought one of them; the others ain't got back to town yet, and Eck's your own cousin; he'll be proud to hear, too. How much did you-all make?"

They was all whittling, not looking at Flem, making like they was studying. But you could a heard a pin drop. And I. O. He had been rubbing his back up and down on the door, but he stopped now, watching Flem like a pointing dog. Flem finished cutting the sliver offen his stick. He spit across the porch, into the road. "Twarn't none of my horses," he says.

I. O. cackled, like a hen, slapping his legs with both hands. "You boys might just as well quit trying to get ahead of Flem," he said.

Well, about that time I see Mrs. Armstid come outen Mrs. Littlejohn's gate, coming up the road. I never said nothing. I says, "Well, if a man can't take care of himself in a trade, he can't blame the man that trims him."

Flem never said nothing, trimming at the stick. He hadn't seen Mrs. Armstid. "Yes, sir," I says. "A fellow like Henry Armstid ain't got nobody but hisself to blame."

"Course he ain't," I. O. says. He ain't seen her, either. "Henry Armstid's a born fool. Always is been. If Flem hadn't got his money, somebody else would."

We looked at Flem. He never moved. Mrs. Armstid come on up the road.

"That's right," I says. "But come to think of it, Henry never bought no horse." We looked at Flem; you could a heard a match drop. "That Texas man told her to get that five dollars back from Flem next day. I reckon Flem's done already taken that money to Mrs. Littlejohn's and give it to Mrs. Armstid."

We watched Flem. I. O. quit rubbing his back against the door again. After a while Flem raised his head and spit across the porch, into the dust. I. O. cackled, just like a hen. "Ain't he a beating fellow, now?" I. O. says.

Mrs. Armstid was getting closer, so I kept on talking, watching to see if Flem would look up and see her. But he never looked up. I went on talking about Tull, about how he was going to sue Flem, and Flem setting there, whittling his stick, not saying nothing else after he said they wasn't none of his horses.

Then I. O. happened to look around. He seen Mrs. Armstid. "Psssst!" he says. Flem looked up. "Here she comes!" I. O. says. "Go out the back. I'll tell her you done went in to town today."

But Flem never moved. He just sat there, whittling, and we watched Mrs. Armstid come up onto the porch, in that ere faded sunbonnet and wrapper and them tennis shoes that make a kind of hissing noise on the porch. She come onto the porch and stopped, her hands rolled into her dress in front, not looking at nothing.

"He said Saturday," she says, "that he wouldn't sell Henry no horse. He said I could get the money from you."

Flem looked up. The knife never stopped. It went on trimming off a sliver same as if he was watching it. "He taken that money off with him when he left," Flem says.

Mrs. Armstid never looked at nothing. We never looked at her, neither, except that boy of Eck's. He had a half-et cracker in his hand, watching her, chewing.

"He said Henry hadn't bought no horse," Mrs. Armstid says. "He said for me to get the money from you today."

"I reckon he forgot about it," Flem said. "He taken that money off with him Saturday." He whittled again. I. O. kept on rubbing his back, slow. He licked his lips. After a while the woman looked up the road, where it went on up the hill, toward the graveyard. She looked up that way for a while, with that boy of Eck's watching her and I. O. rubbing his back slow against the door. Then she turned back toward the steps.

"I reckon it's time to get dinner started," she says.

"How's Henry this morning, Mrs. Armstid?" Winterbottom says.

She looked at Winterbottom; she almost stopped. "He's resting, I thank you kindly," she says.

Flem got up, outen the chair, putting his knife away. He spit across the porch. "Wait a minute, Mrs. Armstid," he says. She stopped again. She didn't look at him. Flem went on into the store, with I. O. done quit rubbing his back now, with his head craned after Flem, and Mrs. Armstid standing there with her hands rolled into her dress, not looking at nothing. A wagon come up the road and passed; it was Freeman, on the way to town. Then Flem come out again, with I. O. still watching him. Flem had one of these little striped sacks of Jody Varner's candy; I bet he still owes Jody that nickel, too. He put the sack into Mrs. Armstid's hand, like he would have put it into a hollow stump. He spit

again across the porch. "A little sweetening for the chaps," he says.

"You're right kind," Mrs. Armstid says. She held the sack of candy in her hand, not looking at nothing. Eck's boy was watching the sack, the half-et cracker in his hand; he wasn't chewing now. He watched Mrs. Armstid roll the sack into her apron. "I reckon I better get on back and help with dinner," she says. She turned and went back across the porch. Flem set down in the chair again and opened his knife. He spit across the porch again, past Mrs. Armstid where she hadn't went down the steps yet. Then she went on, in that ere sunbonnet and wrapper all the same color, back down the road toward Mrs. Littlejohn's. You couldn't see her dress move, like a natural woman walking. She looked like a old snag still standing up and moving along on a high water. We watched her turn in at Mrs. Littlejohn's and go outen sight. Flem was whittling. I. O. begun to rub his back on the door. Then he begun to cackle, just like a durn hen.

"You boys might just as well quit trying," I. O. says. "You can't git ahead of Flem. You can't touch him. Ain't he a sight, now?"

I be dog if he ain't. If I had brung a herd of wild cattymounts into town and sold them to my neighbors and kinfolks, they would have lynched me. Yes, sir.

SHERWOOD ANDERSON

Sophistication

Sherwood Anderson (1876–1941) was born in Camden, Ohio, and spent his childhood in various southern Ohio towns. From his father, an itinerant harness-maker and sign-painter, he acquired the stock of tall tales that formed the basis of his first attempt at fiction writing, *Windy McPherson's Son*, 1916. Perhaps in reaction against his father's casual improvidence, Anderson became a successful businessman and advertising copy writer, despite his lack of formal education. Not until he was nearly forty did he abandon the commercial world to devote himself entirely to writing. With the sponsorship of such men as Theodore Dreiser, Ben Hecht, and Carl Sandburg, he was able to get his first works published. *Winesburg, Ohio,* 1919, brought him into public notice; then followed in rapid succession a number of novels, short stories, a book of verse, and an autobiography, *A Story Teller's Story,* 1924, in which he reveals the conflicts that beset him.

As a writer, Anderson was influenced by Gertrude Stein, who taught him the power of expression inherent in the simple sentence and the simple phrase. "Sophistication" is characteristic of Anderson's art not only in its insistence on the essential loneliness of human beings but in its sensitive revelation of deeply held emotions.

It was early evening of a day in the late fall and the Winesburg County Fair had brought crowds of country people into town. The day had been clear and the night came on warm and pleasant. On the Trunion Pike, where the road after it left town stretched away between berry fields now covered with dry brown leaves, the dust from passing wagons arose in clouds. Children, curled into little balls, slept on the straw scattered on wagon beds. Their hair was full of dust and their fingers were black and sticky. The dust rolled away over the fields and the departing sun set it ablaze with colors.

In the main street of Winesburg crowds filled the stores and the sidewalks. Night came on, horses whinnied, the clerks in the stores ran madly about, children became lost and cried lustily, an American town worked terribly at the task of amusing itself.

Pushing his way through the crowds in Main Street, young George Willard concealed himself in the stairway leading to Doctor Reefy's office and looked at the people. With feverish eyes he watched the faces drifting past under the store lights. Thoughts kept coming into his head and he did not want to think. He stamped impatiently on the wooden steps and looked sharply about. "Well, is she going to stay with him all day? Have I done all this waiting for nothing?" he muttered.

George Willard, the Ohio village boy, was fast growing into manhood and new thoughts had been coming into his mind. All that day,

amid the jam of people at the Fair, he had gone about feeling lonely. He was about to leave Winesburg to go away to some city where he hoped to get work on a city newspaper and he felt grown up. The mood that had taken possession of him was a thing known to men and unknown to boys. He felt old and a little tired. Memories awoke in him. To his mind his new sense of maturity set him apart, made of him a half-tragic figure. He wanted someone to understand the feeling that had taken possession of him after his mother's death.

There is a time in the life of every boy when he for the first time takes the backward view of life. Perhaps that is the moment when he crosses the line into manhood. The boy is walking through the street of his town. He is thinking of the future and of the figure he will cut in the world. Ambitions and regrets awake within him. Suddenly something happens; he stops under a tree and waits as for a voice calling his name. Ghosts of old things creep into his consciousness; the voices outside of himself whisper a message concerning the limitations of life. From being quite sure of himself and his future he becomes not at all sure. If he be an imaginative boy a door is torn open and for the first time he looks out upon the world, seeing, as though they marched in procession before him, the countless figures of men who before his time have come out of nothingness into the world, lived their lives and again disappeared into nothingness. The sadness of sophistication has come to the boy. With a little gasp he sees himself as merely a leaf blown by the wind through the streets of his village. He knows that in spite of all the stout talk of his fellows he must live and die in uncertainty, a thing blown by the winds, a thing destined like corn to wilt in the sun. He shivers and looks eagerly about. The eighteen years he has lived seem but a moment, a breathing space in the long march of humanity. Already he hears death calling. With all his heart he wants to come close to some other human, touch some-one with his hands, be touched by the hand of another. If he prefers that the other be a woman, that is because he believes that a woman will be gentle, that she will under-stand. He wants, most of all, understanding.

When the moment of sophistication came to George Willard his mind turned to Helen White, the Winesburg banker's daughter. Al-ways he had been conscious of the girl grow-ing into womanhood as he grew into man-hood. Once on a summer night when he was eighteen, he had walked with her on a country road and in her presence had given way to an impulse to boast, to make himself appear big and significant in her eyes. Now he wanted to see her for another purpose. He wanted to tell her of the new impulses that had come to him. He had tried to make her think of him as a man when he knew nothing of manhood and now he wanted to be with her and to try to make her feel the change he believed had taken place in his nature.

As for Helen White, she also had come to a period of change. What George felt, she in her young woman's way felt also. She was no longer a girl and hungered to reach into the grace and beauty of womanhood. She had come home from Cleveland, where she was at-tending college, to spend a day at the Fair. She also had begun to have memories. During the day she sat in the grand-stand with a young man, one of the instructors from the college, who was a guest of her mother's. The young man was of a pedantic turn of mind and she felt at once he would not do for her purpose. At the Fair she was glad to be seen in his com-pany as he was well dressed and a stranger. She knew that the fact of his presence would create an impression. During the day she was happy, but when night came on she began to grow restless. She wanted to drive the in-structor away, to get out of his presence. While they sat together in the grand-stand and while the eyes of former schoolmates were upon them, she paid so much attention to her escort that he grew interested. "A scholar needs money. I should marry a woman with money," he mused.

Helen White was thinking of George Wil-lard even as he wandered gloomily through the crowds thinking of her. She remembered the summer evening when they had walked together and wanted to walk with him again. She thought that the months she had spent in the city, the going to theatres and the see-ing of great crowds wandering in lighted thoroughfares, had changed her profoundly. She wanted him to feel and be conscious of the change in her nature.

The summer evening together that had left its mark on the memory of both the young man and woman had, when looked at quite sensibly, been rather stupidly spent. They had walked out of town along a country road. Then they had stopped by a fence near a field of young corn and George had taken off his coat and let it hang on his arm. "Well, I've stayed here in Winesburg—yes—I've not yet gone away but I'm growing up," he had said. "I've been reading books and I've been think-ing. I'm going to try to amount to something in life."

"Well," he explained, "that isn't the point. Perhaps I'd better quit talking."

The confused boy put his hand on the girl's arm. His voice trembled. The two started to walk back along the road toward town. In his desperation George boasted, "I'm going to be a big man, the biggest that ever lived here in Winesburg," he declared. "I want you to do something, I don't know what. Perhaps it is none of my business. I want you to try to be different from other women. You see the point. It's none of my business I tell you. I want you to be a beautiful woman. You see what I want."

The boy's voice failed and in silence the two came back into town and went along the street to Helen White's house. At the gate he tried to say something impressive. Speeches he had thought out came into his head, but they seemed utterly pointless. "I thought—I used to think—I had it in my mind you would marry Seth Richmond. Now I know you won't," was all he could find to say as she went through the gate and toward the door of her house.

On the warm fall evening as he stood in the stairway and looked at the crowd drifting through Main Street, George thought of the talk beside the field of young corn and was ashamed of the figure he had made of himself. In the street the people surged up and down like cattle confined in a pen. Buggies and wagons almost filled the narrow thoroughfare. A band played and small boys raced along the sidewalk, diving between the legs of men. Young men with shining red faces walked awkwardly about with girls on their arms. In a room above one of the stores, where a dance was to be held, the fiddlers tuned their instruments. The broken sounds floated down through an open window and out across the murmur of voices and the loud blare of the horns of the band. The medley of sounds got on young Willard's nerves. Everywhere, on all sides, the sense of crowding, moving life closed in about him. He wanted to run away by himself and think. "If she wants to stay with that fellow she may. Why should I care? What difference does it make to me?" he growled and went along Main Street and through Hern's grocery into a side street.

George felt so utterly lonely and dejected that he wanted to weep but pride made him walk rapidly along, swinging his arms. He came to Westley Moyer's livery barn and stopped in the shadows to listen to a group of men who talked of a race Westley's stallion, Tony Tip, had won at the Fair during the afternoon. A crowd had gathered in front of the barn and before the crowd walked Westley, prancing up and down and boasting. He held a whip in his hand and kept tapping the ground. Little puffs of dust arose in the lamplight. "Hell, quit your talking," Westley exclaimed. "I wasn't afraid, I knew I had 'em beat all the time. I wasn't afraid."

Ordinarily George Willard would have been intensely interested in the boasting of Moyer, the horseman. Now it made him angry. He turned and hurried away along the street. "Old wind-bag," he sputtered. "Why does he want to be bragging? Why don't he shut up?"

George went into a vacant lot and as he hurried along, fell over a pile of rubbish. A nail protruding from an empty barrel tore his trousers. He sat down on the ground and swore. With a pin he mended the torn place and then arose and went on. "I'll go to Helen White's house, that's what I'll do. I'll walk right in. I'll say that I want to see her. I'll walk right in and sit down, that's what I'll do," he declared, climbing over a fence and beginning to run.

On the veranda of Banker White's house Helen was restless and distraught. The instructor sat between the mother and daughter. His talk wearied the girl. Although he had also been raised in an Ohio town, the instructor began to put on the airs of the city. He wanted to appear cosmopolitan. "I like the chance you have given me to study the background out of which most of our girls come," he declared. "It was good of you, Mrs. White, to have me down for the day." He turned to Helen and laughed. "Your life is still bound up with the life of this town?" he asked. "There are people here in whom you are interested?" To the girl his voice sounded pompous and heavy.

Helen arose and went into the house. At the door leading to a garden at the back she stopped and stood listening. Her mother began to talk. "There is no one here fit to associate with a girl of Helen's breeding," she said.

Helen ran down a flight of stairs at the back of the house and into the garden. In the darkness she stopped and stood trembling. It seemed to her that the world was full of meaningless people saying words. Afire with eagerness she ran through a garden gate and turning a corner by the banker's barn, went into a little side street. "George! Where are you, George?" she cried, filled with nervous excitement. She stopped running, and leaned against a tree to laugh hysterically. Along the dark little street came George Willard, still saying words. "I'm going to walk right into her house. I'll go right in and sit down," he declared as he came up to her. He stopped and stared stupidly. "Come on," he said and took hold of her hand. With hanging heads they walked away along the street under the trees. Dry leaves rustled under foot. Now that he had found her George wondered what he had better do and say.

At the upper end of the fair ground, in Winesburg, there is a half decayed old grand-stand. It has never been painted and the boards are all warped out of shape. The fair ground stands on top of a low hill rising out of the valley of Wine Creek and from the grand-stand one can see at night, over a corn-field, the lights of the town reflected against the sky.

George and Helen climbed the hill to the fair ground, coming by the path past Water-works Pond. The feeling of loneliness and isolation that had come to the young man in the crowded streets of his town was both broken and intensified by the presence of Helen. What he felt was reflected in her.

In youth there are always two forces fight-ing in people. The warm unthinking little ani-mal struggles against the thing that reflects and remembers, and the older, the more so-phisticated thing had possession of George Willard. Sensing his mood, Helen walked be-side him filled with respect. When they got to the grand-stand they climbed up under the roof and sat down on one of the long bench-like seats.

There is something memorable in the ex-perience to be had by going into a fair ground that stands at the edge of a Middle Western town on a night after the annual fair has been held. The sensation is one never to be forgot-ten. On all sides are ghosts, not of the dead, but of living people. Here, during the day just passed, have come the people pouring in from the town and the country around. Farmers with their wives and children and all the peo-ple from the hundreds of little frame houses have gathered within these board walls. Young girls have laughed and men with beards have talked of the affairs of their lives. The place has been filled to overflowing with life. It has itched and squirmed with life and now it is

night and the life has all gone away. The si-lence is almost terrifying. One conceals one-self standing silently beside the trunk of a tree and what there is of a reflective tendency in his nature is intensified. One shudders at the thought of the meaninglessness of life while at the same instant, and if the people of the town are his people, one loves life so intensely that tears come into the eyes.

In the darkness under the roof of the grand-stand, George Willard sat beside Helen White and felt very keenly his own insignificance in the scheme of existence. Now that he had come out of town where the presence of the people stirring about, busy with a multitude of affairs, had been so irritating the irritation was all gone. The presence of Helen renewed and refreshed him. It was as though her woman's hand was assisting him to make some minute readjustment of the machinery of his life. He began to think of the people in the town where he had always lived with some-thing like reverence. He had reverence for Helen. He wanted to love and to be loved by her, but he did not want at the moment to be confused by her womanhood. In the darkness he took hold of her hand and when she crept close put a hand on her shoulder. A wind began to blow and he shivered. With all his strength he tried to hold and to under-stand the mood that had come upon him. In that high place in the darkness the two oddly sensitive human atoms held each other tightly and waited. In the mind of each was the same thought. "I have come to this lonely place and here is this other," was the substance of the thing felt.

In Winesburg the crowded day had run it-self out into the long night of the late fall. Farm horses jogged along lonely country roads pulling their portion of weary people. Clerks began to bring samples of goods in off the sidewalks and lock the doors of stores. In the Opera House a crowd had gathered to see a show and further down Main Street the fiddlers, their instruments tuned, sweated and worked to keep the feet of youth flying over a dance floor.

In the darkness in the grand-stand Helen White and George Willard remained silent.

Now and then the spell that held them was broken and they turned and tried in the dim light to see into each other's eyes. They kissed but that impulse did not last. At the upper end of the fair ground a half dozen men worked over horses that had raced during the afternoon. The men had built a fire and were heating kettles of water. Only their legs could be seen as they passed back and forth in the light. When the wind blew the little flames of the fire danced crazily about.

George and Helen arose and walked away into the darkness. They went along a path past a field of corn that had not yet been cut. The wind whispered among the dry corn blades. For a moment during the walk back into town the spell that held them was broken. When they had come to the crest of Waterworks Hill they stopped by a tree and George again put his hands on the girl's shoulders. She embraced him eagerly and then again they drew quickly back from that impulse. They stopped kissing and stood a little apart. Mutual respect grew big in them. They were both embarrassed and to relieve their embarrassment dropped into the animalism of youth. They laughed and began to pull and haul at each other. In some way chastened and purified by the mood they had been in they became, not man and woman, not boy and girl, but excited little animals.

It was so they went down the hill. In the darkness they played like two splendid young things in a young world. Once, running swiftly forward, Helen tripped George and he fell. He squirmed and shouted. Shaking with laughter, he rolled down the hill. Helen ran after him. For just a moment she stopped in the darkness. There is no way of knowing what woman's thoughts went through her mind but, when the bottom of the hill was reached and she came up to the boy, she took his arm and walked beside him in dignified silence. For some reason they could not have explained they had both got from their silent evening together the thing needed. Man or boy, woman or girl, they had for a moment taken hold of the thing that makes the mature life of men and women in the modern world possible.

PART FOUR

Drama

Drama has its genesis in several closely related human characteristics, most important of which perhaps are the urge to imitate and the love of make-believe. Such tendencies are everywhere apparent, in the games small children play—cowboys and Indians, or cops and robbers—and in the entertainments older people often enjoy—masquerades and costume parties. To lose oneself for a short time within the identity of some imagined creature—a Lone Ranger or a Queen of the Pirates—seems to answer a deeply felt need in the human heart. And both the urge to imitate and the love of make-believe culminate in drama—the impulse to make a story live through action.

The ancient Greeks, an agricultural people, met on semiannual feast days to honor the god Dionysus, who ruled over the harvest and wine press. At first, their worship of Dionysus seems to have been expressed in choral songs and dances performed by elaborately trained and costumed choruses; but with time, more and more of a dramatic element crept in. During an intermission, perhaps, the leader of the chorus would tell of some exploit in the life of Dionysus; later on he came to *represent* the god himself and tell his story in the first person. Finally, some minor member of the chorus answered the rhetorical utterances of Dionysus, and thus dramatic dialogue and impersonation came into being. To describe this activity, the word *drama*, derived from a Greek verb *dran* meaning *to act* or *to do,* was used. By its etymology, drama implies action, the essence of dramatic composition.

Greek comedy and tragedy both originated in seasonal festivals. From the broad jesting and burlesque natural to a rustic carnival developed comedy. From worship developed tragedy, which reached its culmination in three great writers—Aeschylus, Sophocles, and Euripides—all of whose works emphasize the Greek ideal of artistic restraint and balance.

During the Dark Ages, when Greek drama was forgotten, another form of drama emerged in western Europe—the morality plays of the medieval Christian Church. Everywhere confronted by ignorance and lack of schooling, the priests realized that the easiest way to tell the Christian story to the people was through dramatic representation of the Easter and Christmas stories in the cathedrals. What started as devices for religious instruction became so popular as entertainment that it was necessary to find a larger place for their presentation. Once outside the church, these plays soon fell into secular hands; the trade guilds in certain cities produced an elaborate series of pageants telling the Biblical story from the Creation to the Crucifixion and Resurrection.

Out of these religious plays of the late Middle Ages and out of the school and university revivals of long-neglected Greek and Roman dramas during the Renaissance grew the new drama of western Europe. In the English tradition this means pre-eminently the dramas of William Shakespeare; but there were many other playwrights in the sixteenth and seventeenth centuries who contributed their share toward making English drama worthy of comparison with drama anywhere in the world. After Oliver Goldsmith and Richard Brinsley Sheridan in the late eighteenth century, British drama went into a decline that lasted until Henrik Ibsen revolutionized the drama of all Europe. Profiting in part from this foreign influence, writers like George Bernard Shaw and Arthur Wing Pinero re-established British drama in the world's esteem, and so it has continued to our own day. In the United States powerful and original drama did not completely emerge until after World War I, when Eugene O'Neill began producing the plays that were to win for him the Nobel Prize for Literature in 1936. By this time such writers as Maxwell Anderson, Sidney Howard, Robert Sherwood, and Thornton Wilder had clearly demonstrated that American drama could take its place among the best contemporary drama found anywhere in the world. More recently, Tennessee Williams and Arthur Miller have affirmed the psychological power and lyricism of the American theater. And both in America and in Europe in the years during and since World War II an alliance has developed between drama and contemporary philosophy. Out of the interaction of naturalism, surrealism, and existentialism has come a new kind of drama known as "theater of the absurd." Writers working in this dramatic mode have continued to move from the representational, with concern for psychological motivation, to the presentational, with emphasis on situation. Albert Camus and Jean-Paul Sartre are writers identified with the early days of the movement; Eugene Ionesco, Samuel Beckett, and, in America, Edward Albee are the well-known figures in this new theater.

Both comedy and tragedy are likely to be built around a central figure involved in some kind of conflict of will—the wills of two persons who oppose each other, the will of a person to win out over unfavorable circumstances, or the internally conflicting emotions of a person torn between two irreconcilable desires. Generally speaking, if the central character is in the end defeated, the play is tragic; if he is triumphant, the play is comic. Aristotle, the ancient Greek philosopher, believed that tragedy must excite the emotions of pity and fear and that to accomplish this end, it must present a single, complete action, must present a reversal of fortune involving persons renowned and of superior attainments, and, finally, must be written in poetry of the highest sort.

Later writers have modified some of these requirements. According to Aristotle, the interest aroused in tragic conflict is proportionate to the impressiveness of character displayed by the central figure in the drama. Comedies can be written about trivial people, but a tragedy usually centers around a great personality going down in defeat before forces too great for him to master. It is doubtless this need for magnitude in the central character that long compelled dramatists to center their tragedies around people of exalted rank, such as kings and princesses. Shakespeare to some extent demonstrated that people of humbler station can be fit subjects for tragedy, and Ibsen set the example for modern dramatists not only by choosing tragic characters from common life but by utilizing prose instead of poetry as the language of tragedy.

In contrast with tragedy, comedy, by conventional definition at least, is light and amusing; where amusement is its end, it becomes farce or burlesque. But comedy at its best is scarcely less serious in purpose than tragedy and is equally exacting in plot, dialogue, and characterization. Since the comic effect derives primarily from the exposure of some kind of incongruity, comedy reveals to us absurd, illogical, or pretentious speech, action, or character. The function of comedy, as George Meredith observed, is to provoke thoughtful laughter, the sort that arises out of our realization of human foibles and inconsistencies. Consequently, comedy lends itself well to satire and becomes a means whereby the dramatist chastises the world for its vices and shortcomings.

The drama selections included here offer considerable variety in style and subject matter and represent characteristic plays by five great dramatists. Sophocles' *Antigonê* exemplifies the classic Greek tragedy. Edith Hamilton says in "The Idea of Tragedy" that three of the four great writers of tragedy are Greek—Sophocles, Euripides, and Aeschylus—and that it was the Greeks who created tragedy and perfected it. Arthur Miller's *The Crucible* is a tragedy set in the time of the Salem witchcraft trials but with intended application to social and psychological problems of modern times. *The Stronger* illustrates Strindberg's successful experimentation with simplifying the structure of drama and presenting psychological conflict solely through dialogue. This play has been said to mark the beginning of the modern one-act play. Modern comedy may assume the satiric, realistic form favored by Ben Jonson in the 1600's, which ridiculed the vices and follies of his contemporaries. So satirical and carefully drawn was Synge's portrait of the Irish in *The Playboy of the Western World* that its first audiences refused to allow the actors to be heard. Intense feelings of nationalism, together with the politics of the time, caused nightly disturbances at the Abbey Theatre in Dublin during the play's first week and were repeated when the play came to America. Jean Anouilh's drama of ideas, *Becket: or The Honor of God,* which was first performed in the United States at the St. James Theatre in New York in 1960 and won the Antoinette Perry Award ("Tony") as the best play of the 1960–61 season, comments on the vast question of the relations between church and state and on the personal conflict between one man and another.

Since most plays are written to be acted, the technique of play-reading is somewhat different from that of reading a short story or a novel; and the enjoyment of plays can therefore be increased greatly if one stops to consider some special problems that the reading of plays presents.

If plays are to be read successfully—that is, with the fullest degree of understanding and enjoyment—the reader is compelled to visualize with his own imagination, characters speaking, gesticulating, and moving about in a setting that playwrights, especially the modern ones, frequently describe in detail. From the cast of characters and from the stage directions, the reader can determine many things about the people of the play, particularly the main characters—what they look like, how old they are, what relationship exists among them, and what their special mannerisms and peculiarities imply. Another help to intelligent play-reading is to observe the play's structure. In the conventional play much of the first scene is devoted to getting the play under way. This portion—the "exposition" as it is technically called—should be read carefully in order to get one's bearings early. As soon as the exposition is finished, most playwrights start their main plot. In many modern dramas new scenes indicate the introduction of a new character or a new element in the story. The reader should watch for these developments.

SOPHOCLES

Antigonê

TRANSLATION BY DUDLEY FITTS AND ROBERT FITZGERALD

Sophocles (*c.* 496–406 B.C.), born near Athens, Greece, to a family of wealth and position, was a contemporary of the two other great Greek writers of tragedy, Aeschylus and Euripides. Only seven of his 123 plays have come down to us in complete form. His first successful tragedy was *Ajax. Antigonê* followed, then *Oedipus Rex* and *Electra.* Among the Greek dramatists of his time Sophocles was known for his innovations: increasing the size of the chorus, adding more actors, and introducing painted scenery.

Antigonê is the third and last play in Sophocles' Oedipus cycle, which also includes *Oedipus Rex* and *Oedipus at Colonus.* According to Greek legend, King Laios of Thebes and his descendants have been doomed by the god Apollo. Oedipus, supposedly killed as a baby, has survived in exile. Not knowing that he is the son of Laios and Iocastê, he kills his father. Several years later he solves the riddle of the Sphinx for the Thebans and becomes their king, marrying his mother, the widow Iocastê. When the truth is revealed, Oedipus, in horror, blinds himself and proclaims his own exile. His two sons, Eteoclês and Polyneicês, quarrel over the succession; the Thebans favor Eteoclês, and Polyneicês is driven from the city. He returns with an army, but he and Eteoclês kill each other in battle, and Creon, brother of Iocastê, succeeds to the throne. Antigonê and Ismenê, daughters of Oedipus, are discussing Creon's first official decree as the play opens.

Antigonê contains some of Sophocles' finest characterizations. The characters are more human than those in his other plays; they are governed less by the gods than by their own wills. Antigonê does not seem an unwitting victim of the gods; her tragedy arises from actions based on her own deep beliefs and emotions.

PERSONS REPRESENTED

ANTIGONÊ	A SENTRY	CREON	SERVANTS
ISMENÊ	A MESSENGER	HAIMON	GUARDS
EURYDICÊ	A BOY	TEIRESIAS	

CHORUS (*with a* CHORAGOS, *or Leader*)

SCENE

Before the palace of CREON, *King of Thebes.*
A central double door, and two lateral doors.
A platform extends the length of the façade,
and from this platform three steps lead down
into the orchestra, *or chorus-ground.*

   TIME: *Dawn of the day after the repulse of*
the Argive army from the assault on Thebes.

PROLOGUE

(ANTIGONÊ *and* ISMENÊ *enter from the cen-*
tral door of the Palace.)

ANTIGONÊ:
Ismenê, dear sister,
You would think that we had already suffered
   enough
For the curse on Oedipus:
I cannot imagine any grief
That you and I have not gone through. And
   now—
Have they told you of the new decree of our
   King Creon?

ISMENÊ:
I have heard nothing: I know
That two sisters lost two brothers, a double
   death
In a single hour; and I know that the Argive
   army
Fled in the night; but beyond this, nothing.

ANTIGONÊ:
I thought so. And that is why I wanted you
To come out here with me. There is something
   we must do.

ISMENÊ:
Why do you speak so strangely?

ANTIGONÊ:
Listen, Ismenê:
Creon buried our brother Eteoclês
With military honors, gave him a soldier's
   funeral,
And it was right that he should; but Poly-
   neicês,

ANTIGONÊ   *The Antigonê of Sophocles:* An English
Version by Dudley Fitts and Robert Fitzgerald, copyright, 1939, by Harcourt, Brace & World, Inc., and
reprinted with their permission.

Who fought as bravely and died as miser-
   ably,—
They say that Creon has sworn
No one shall bury him, no one mourn for him,
But his body must lie in the fields, a sweet
   treasure
For carrion birds to find as they search for
   food.
That is what they say, and our good Creon is
   coming here
To announce it publicly; and the penalty—
Stoning to death in the public square!
                              There it is,
And now you can prove what you are:
A true sister, or a traitor to your family.

ISMENÊ:
Antigonê, you are mad! What could I possibly
   do?

ANTIGONÊ:
You must decide whether you will help me or
   not.

ISMENÊ:
I do not understand you. Help you in what?

ANTIGONÊ:
Ismenê, I am going to bury him. Will you
   come?

ISMENÊ:
Bury him! You have just said the new law forbids it.

ANTIGONÊ:
He is my brother. And he is your brother, too.

ISMENÊ:
But think of the danger! Think what Creon
   will do!

ANTIGONÊ:
Creon is not strong enough to stand in my
   way.

ISMENÊ:
Ah sister!
Oedipus died, everyone hating him
For what his own search brought to light, his
   eyes
Ripped out by his own hand; and Iocastê died,
His mother and wife at once: she twisted the
   cords

That strangled her life; and our two brothers
died,
Each killed by the other's sword. And we are
left:
But oh, Antigonê,
Think how much more terrible than these
Our own death would be if we should go
against Creon
And do what he has forbidden! We are only
women,
We cannot fight with men, Antigonê!
The law is strong, we must give in to the law
In this thing, and in worse. I beg the Dead
To forgive me, but I am helpless: I must yield
To those in authority. And I think it is danger-
ous business
To be always meddling.

ANTIGONÊ:

　　　　　　　If that is what you think,
I should not want you, even if you asked to
come.
You have made your choice, you can be what
you want to be.
But I will bury him; and if I must die,
I say that this crime is holy: I shall lie down
With him in death, and I shall be as dear
To him as he to me.
　　　　　　　It is the dead,
Not the living, who make the longest de-
mands:
We die for ever . . .
　　　　　　　You may do as you like,
Since apparently the laws of the gods mean
nothing to you.

ISMENÊ:

They mean a great deal to me; but I have no
strength
To break laws that were made for the public
good.

ANTIGONÊ:

That must be your excuse, I suppose. But as
for me,
I will bury the brother I love.

ISMENÊ:

　　　　　　　Antigonê,
I am so afraid for you!

ANTIGONÊ:

　　　　　　You need not be:
You have yourself to consider, after all.

ISMENÊ:

But no one must hear of this, you must tell **no**
one!
I will keep it a secret, I promise!

ANTIGONÊ:

　　　　　　Oh tell it! Tell everyone!
Think how they'll hate you when it all comes
out
If they learn that you knew about it all the
time!

ISMENÊ:

So fiery! You should be cold with fear.

ANTIGONÊ:

Perhaps. But I am doing only what I must.

ISMENÊ:

But can you do it? I say that you cannot.

ANTIGONÊ:

Very well: when my strength gives out, I shall
do no more.

ISMENÊ:

Impossible things should not be tried at all.

ANTIGONÊ:

Go away, Ismenê:
I shall be hating you soon, and the dead will
too,
For your words are hateful. Leave me my
foolish plan:
I am not afraid of the danger; if it means
death,
It will not be the worst of deaths—death without honor.

ISMENÊ:

Go then, if you feel that you must.
You are unwise,
But a loyal friend indeed to those who love
you.

　　　(*Exit into the Palace.* ANTIGONÊ *goes off,*
　　　L. *Enter the* CHORUS.)

PÁRODOS

CHORUS: STROPHE 1

Now the long blade of the sun, lying
Level east to west, touches with glory
Thebes of the Seven Gates. Open, unlidded
Eye of golden day! O marching light
Across the eddy and rush of Dircê's stream,
Striking the white shields of the enemy
Thrown headlong backward from the blaze of
    morning!

CHORAGOS:

Polyneicês their commander
Roused them with windy phrases,
He the wild eagle screaming
Insults above our land,
His wings their shields of snow,
His crest their marshalled helms.

CHORUS: ANTISTROPHE 1

Against our seven gates in a yawning ring
The famished spears came onward in the
    night;
But before his jaws were sated with our blood,
Or pinefire took the garland of our towers,
He was thrown back; and as he turned, great
    Thebes—
No tender victim for his noisy power—
Rose like a dragon behind him, shouting war.

CHORAGOS:

For God hates utterly
The bray of bragging tongues;
And when he beheld their smiling,
Their swagger of golden helms,
The frown of his thunder blasted
Their first man from our walls.

CHORUS: STROPHE 2

We heard his shout of triumph high in the air
Turn to a scream; far out in a flaming arc
He fell with his windy torch, and the earth
    struck him.
And others storming in fury no less than his
Found shock of death in the dusty joy of battle.

CHORAGOS:

Seven captains at seven gates
Yielded their clanging arms to the god
That bends the battle-line and breaks it.

These two only, brothers in blood,
Face to face in matchless rage,
Mirroring each the other's death,
Clashed in long combat.

CHORUS: ANTISTROPHE 2

But now in the beautiful morning of victory
Let Thebes of the many chariots sing for joy!
With hearts for dancing we'll take leave of
    war:
Our temples shall be sweet with hymns of
    praise,
And the long night shall echo with our chorus.

SCENE I

CHORAGOS:

But now at last our new King is coming:
Creon of Thebes, Menoikeus' son.
In this auspicious dawn of his reign
What are the new complexities
That shifting Fate has woven for him?
What is his counsel? Why has he summoned
The old men to hear him?

*(Enter CREON from the Palace, C. He ad-
dresses the CHORUS from the top step.)*

CREON:

Gentlemen: I have the honor to inform you
that our Ship of State, which recent storms
have threatened to destroy, has come safely
to harbor at last, guided by the merciful wisdom of Heaven. I have summoned you here
this morning because I know that I can depend upon you: your devotion to King Laios
was absolute; you never hesitated in your duty
to our late ruler Oedipus; and when Oedipus
died, your loyalty was transferred to his children. Unfortunately, as you know, his two
sons, the princes Eteoclês and Polyneicês, have
killed each other in battle; and I, as the next
in blood, have succeeded to the full power of
the throne.

I am aware, of course, that no Ruler can
expect complete loyalty from his subjects until he has been tested in office. Nevertheless,
I say to you at the very outset that I have
nothing but contempt for the kind of Governor who is afraid, for whatever reason, to

follow the course that he knows is best for the State; and as for the man who sets private friendship above the public welfare,—I have no use for him, either. I call God to witness that if I saw my country headed for ruin, I should not be afraid to speak out plainly; and I need hardly remind you that I would never have any dealings with an enemy of the people. No one values friendship more highly than I; but we must remember that friends made at the risk of wrecking our Ship are not real friends at all.

These are my principles, at any rate, and that is why I have made the following decision concerning the sons of Oedipus: Eteoclês, who died as a man should die, fighting for his country, is to be buried with full military honors, with all the ceremony that is usual when the greatest heroes die; but his brother Polyneicês, who broke his exile to come back with fire and sword against his native city and the shrines of his fathers' gods, whose one idea was to spill the blood of his blood and sell his own people into slavery—Polyneicês, I say, is to have no burial: no man is to touch him or say the least prayer for him; he shall lie on the plain, unburied; and the birds and the scavenging dogs can do with him whatever they like.

This is my command, and you can see the wisdom behind it. As long as I am King, no traitor is going to be honored with the loyal man. But whoever shows by word and deed that he is on the side of the State, he shall have my respect while he is living, and my reverence when he is dead.

CHORAGOS:
If that is your will, Creon son of Menoikeus, You have the right to enforce it: we are yours.

CREON:
That is my will. Take care that you do your part.

CHORAGOS:
We are old men: let the younger ones carry it out.

CREON:
I do not mean that: the sentries have been appointed.

CHORAGOS:
Then what is it that you would have us do?

CREON:
You will give no support to whoever breaks this law.

CHORAGOS:
Only a crazy man is in love with death!

CREON:
And death it is; yet money talks, and the wisest
Have sometimes been known to count a few coins too many.

(*Enter* SENTRY *from L.*)

SENTRY:
I'll not say that I'm out of breath from running, King, because every time I stopped to think about what I have to tell you, I felt like going back. And all the time a voice kept saying, "You fool, don't you know you're walking straight into trouble?"; and then another voice: "Yes, but if you let somebody else get the news to Creon first, it will be even worse than that for you!" But good sense won out, at least I hope it was good sense, and here I am with a story that makes no sense at all; but I'll tell it anyhow, because, as they say, what's going to happen's going to happen, and—

CREON:
Come to the point. What have you to say?

SENTRY:
I did not do it. I did not see who did it. You must not punish me for what someone else has done.

CREON:
A comprehensive defense! More effective, perhaps,
If I knew its purpose. Come: what is it?

SENTRY:
A dreadful thing . . . I don't know how to put it—

CREON:
Out with it!

SENTRY:

Well, then;
The dead man—

Polyneicês—

(*Pause. The* SENTRY *is overcome, fumbles for words.* CREON *waits impassively.*)

out there—
someone,—

New dust on the slimy flesh!

(*Pause. No sign from* CREON.)

Someone has given it burial that way, and
Gone . . .

(*Long pause.* CREON *finally speaks with deadly control.*)

CREON:

And the man who dared do this?

SENTRY:

I swear I
Do not know! You must believe me!

Listen:

The ground was dry, not a sign of digging, no,
Not a wheeltrack in the dust, no trace of any-
one.
It was when they relieved us this morning:
and one of them,
The corporal, pointed to it.

There it was,
The strangest—

Look:

The body, just mounded over with light dust:
you see?
Not buried really, but as if they'd covered it
Just enough for the ghost's peace. And no sign
Of dogs or any wild animal that had been
there.

And then what a scene there was! Every man
of us
Accusing the other: we all proved the other
man did it,
We all had proof that we could not have done
it.
We were ready to take hot iron in our hands,
Walk through fire, swear by all the gods,
It was not I!
I do not know who it was, but it was not I!

(CREON's *rage has been mounting steadily,
but the* SENTRY *is too intent upon his story
to notice it.*)

And then, when this came to nothing, someone
said
A thing that silenced us and made us stare
Down at the ground: you had to be told the
news,
And one of us had to do it! We threw the dice,
And the bad luck fell to me. So here I am,
No happier to be here than you are to have
me:
Nobody likes the man who brings bad news.

CHORAGOS:

I have been wondering, King: can it be that
the gods have done this?

CREON (*furiously*):

Stop!
Must you doddering wrecks
Go out of your heads entirely? "The gods!"
Intolerable!
The gods favor this corpse? Why? How had
he served them?
Tried to loot their temples, burn their images,
Yes, and the whole State, and its laws with it!
Is it your senile opinion that the gods love to
honor bad men?
A pious thought!—

No, from the very beginning
There have been those who have whispered
together,
Stiff-necked anarchists, putting their heads together,
Scheming against me in alleys. These are the
men,
And they have bribed my own guard to do
this thing.

Money!

(*Sententiously*)

There's nothing in the world so demoralizing
as money.
Down go your cities,
Homes gone, men gone, honest hearts cor-
rupted,
Crookedness of all kinds, and all for money!

(*To* SENTRY)

But you—!
I swear by God and by the throne of God,

The man who has done this thing shall pay for
  it!
Find that man, bring him here to me, or your
  death
Will be the least of your problems: I'll string
  you up
Alive, and there will be certain ways to make
  you
Discover your employer before you die;
And the process may teach you a lesson you
  seem to have missed:
The dearest profit is sometimes all too dear:
That depends on the source. Do you under-
  stand me?
A fortune won is often misfortune.

SENTRY:
King, may I speak?

CREON:
                    Your very voice distresses me.

SENTRY:
Are you sure that it is my voice, and not your
  conscience?

CREON:
By God, he wants to analyze me now!

SENTRY:
It is not what I say, but what has been done,
  that hurts you.

CREON:
You talk too much.

SENTRY:
                    Maybe; but I've done nothing.

CREON:
Sold your soul for some silver: that's all you've
  done.

SENTRY:
How dreadful it is when the right judge judges
  wrong!

CREON:
Your figures of speech
May entertain you now; but unless you bring
  me the man,
You will get little profit from them in the end.
    (*Exit* CREON *into the Palace.*)

SENTRY:
"Bring me the man"—!
I'd like nothing better than bringing him the
  man!
But bring him or not, you have seen the last
  of me here.
At any rate, I am safe!
    (*Exit* SENTRY.)

ODE I

CHORUS: STROPHE 1
Numberless are the world's wonders, but none
More wonderful than man; the stormgray sea
Yields to his prows, the huge crests bear him
  high;
Earth, holy and inexhaustible, is graven
With shining furrows where his plows have
  gone
Year after year, the timeless labor of stallions.
                                      ANTISTROPHE 1
The lightboned birds and beasts that cling to
  cover,
The lithe fish lighting their reaches of dim
  water,
All are taken, tamed in the net of his mind;
The lion on the hill, the wild horse windy-
  maned,
Resign to him; and his blunt yoke has broken
The sultry shoulders of the mountain bull.
                                        STROPHE 2
Words also, and thought as rapid as air,
He fashions to his good use; statecraft is his,
And his the skill that deflects the arrows of
  snow,
The spears of winter rain: from every wind
He has made himself secure—from all but
  one:
In the late wind of death he cannot stand.
                                      ANTISTROPHE 2
O clear intelligence, force beyond all measure!
O fate of man, working both good and evil!
When the laws are kept, how proudly his city
  stands!
When the laws are broken, what of his city
  then?
Never may the anarchic man find rest at my
  hearth,
Never be it said that my thoughts are his
  thoughts.

SCENE II

(*Re-enter* SENTRY *leading* ANTIGONÊ.)

CHORAGOS:
What does this mean? Surely this captive woman
Is the Princess Antigonê. Why should she be taken?

SENTRY:
Here is the one who did it! We caught her
In the very act of burying him.—Where is Creon?

CHORAGOS:
Just coming from the house.

(*Enter* CREON, *C.*)

CREON:
What has happened?
Why have you come back so soon?

SENTRY (*expansively*):
O King,
A man should never be too sure of anything:
I would have sworn
That you'd not see me here again: your anger
Frightened me so, and the things you threatened me with;
But how could I tell then
That I'd be able to solve the case so soon?

No dice-throwing this time: I was only too glad to come!

Here is this woman. She is the guilty one:
We found her trying to bury him.
Take her, then; question her; judge her as you will.
I am through with the whole thing now, and glad of it.

CREON:
But this is Antigonê! Why have you brought her here?

SENTRY:
She was burying him, I tell you!

CREON (*severely*):
Is this the truth?

SENTRY:
I saw her with my own eyes. Can I say more?

CREON:
The details: come, tell me quickly!

SENTRY:
It was like this:
After those terrible threats of yours, King,
We went back and brushed the dust away from the body.
The flesh was soft by now, and stinking,
So we sat on a hill to windward and kept guard.
No napping this time! We kept each other awake.
But nothing happened until the white round sun
Whirled in the center of the round sky over us:
Then, suddenly,
A storm of dust roared up from the earth, and the sky
Went out, the plain vanished with all its trees
In the stinging dark. We closed our eyes and endured it.
The whirlwind lasted a long time, but it passed;
An then we looked, and there was Antigonê!
I have seen
A mother bird come back to a stripped nest, heard
Her crying bitterly a broken note or two
For the young ones stolen. Just so, when this girl
Found the bare corpse, and all her love's work wasted,
She wept, and cried on heaven to damn the hands
That had done this thing.
And then she brought more dust
And sprinkled wine three times for her brother's ghost.

We ran and took her at once. She was not afraid,
Not even when we charged her with what she had done.
She denied nothing.
And this was a comfort to me,
And some uneasiness: for it is a good thing
To escape from death, but it is no great pleasure
To bring death to a friend.
Yet I always say

There is nothing so comfortable as your own
  safe skin!

CREON (*slowly, dangerously*):
And you, Antigonê,
You with your head hanging, do you confess
  this thing?

ANTIGONÊ:
I do. I deny nothing.

CREON (*to* SENTRY):
                            You may go.

    (*Exit* SENTRY.)

    (*To* ANTIGONÊ)
Tell me, tell me briefly:
Had you heard my proclamation touching this
  matter?

ANTIGONÊ:
It was public. Could I help hearing it?

CREON:
And yet you dared defy the law.

ANTIGONÊ:
                            I dared.
It was not God's proclamation. That final
  Justice
That rules the world below makes no such
  laws.

Your edict, King, was strong,
But all your strength is weakness itself against
The immortal unrecorded laws of God.
They are not merely now: they were, and shall
  be,
Operative for ever, beyond man utterly.

I knew I must die, even without your decree:
I am only mortal. And if I must die
Now, before it is my time to die,
Surely this is no hardship: can anyone
Living, as I live, with evil all about me,
Think Death less than a friend? This death of
  mine
Is of no importance; but if I had left my
  brother
Lying in death unburied, I should have suf-
  fered.
Now I do not.

              You smile at me. Ah Creon,
Think me a fool, if you like; but it may well be
That a fool convicts me of folly.

CHORAGOS:
Like father, like daughter: both headstrong,
  deaf to reason!
She has never learned to yield.

CREON:
                        She has much to learn.
The inflexible heart breaks first, the toughest
  iron
Cracks first, and the wildest horses bend
  their necks
At the pull of the smallest curb.
                            Pride? In a slave?
This girl is guilty of a double insolence,
Breaking the given laws and boasting of it.
Who is the man here,
She or I, if this crime goes unpunished?
Sister's child, or more than sister's child,
Or closer yet in blood—she and her sister
Win bitter death for this!
    (*To* SERVANTS)
                        Go, some of you,
Arrest Ismenê. I accuse her equally.
Bring her: you will find her sniffling in the
  house there.

Her mind's a traitor: crimes kept in the dark
Cry for light, and the guardian brain shud-
  ders;
But how much worse than this
Is brazen boasting of barefaced anarchy!

ANTIGONÊ:
Creon, what more do you want than my death?

CREON:
                                        Nothing.
That gives me everything.

ANTIGONÊ:
                        Then I beg you: kill me.
This talking is a great weariness: your words
Are distasteful to me, and I am sure that mine
Seem so to you. And yet they should not seem
  so:
I should have praise and honor for what I have
  done.

All these men here would praise me
Were their lips not frozen shut with fear of
   you.
      (*Bitterly*)
Ah the good fortune of kings,
Licensed to say and do whatever they please!

CREON:
You are alone here in that opinion.

ANTIGONÊ:
No, they are with me. But they keep their
   tongues in leash.

CREON:
Maybe. But you are guilty, and they are not.

ANTIGONÊ:
There is no guilt in reverence for the dead.

CREON:
But Eteoclês—was he not your brother too?

ANTIGONÊ:
My brother too.

CREON:
                    And you insult his memory?

ANTIGONÊ (*softly*):
The dead man would not say that I insult it.

CREON:
He would: for you honor a traitor as much as
   him.

ANTIGONÊ:
His own brother, traitor or not, and equal in
   blood.

CREON:
He made war on his country. Eteoclês defended it.

ANTIGONÊ:
Nevertheless, there are honors due all the
   dead.

CREON:
But not the same for the wicked as for the just.

ANTIGONÊ:
Ah Creon, Creon,
Which of us can say what the gods hold
   wicked?

CREON:
An enemy is an enemy, even dead.

ANTIGONÊ:
It is my nature to join in love, not hate.

CREON (*finally losing patience*):
Go join them, then; if you must have your
   love,
Find it in hell!

CHORAGOS:
But see, Ismenê comes:

      (*Enter* ISMENÊ, *guarded.*)

Those tears are sisterly, the cloud
That shadows her eyes rains down gentle sorrow.

CREON:
You too, Ismenê,
Snake in my ordered house, sucking my blood
Stealthily—and all the time I never knew
That these two sisters were aiming at my
   throne!
                                          Ismenê,
Do you confess your share in this crime, or
   deny it?
Answer me.

ISMENÊ:
Yes, if she will let me say so. I am guilty.

ANTIGONÊ (*coldly*):
No, Ismenê. You have no right to say so.
You would not help me, and I will not have
   you help me.

ISMENÊ:
But now I know what you meant; and I am
   here
To join you, to take my share of punishment.

ANTIGONÊ:
The dead man and the gods who rule the dead
Know whose act this was. Words are not
   friends.

ISMENÊ:
Do you refuse me, Antigonê? I want to die
   with you:
I too have a duty that I must discharge to the
   dead.

ANTIGONÊ:
You shall not lessen my death by sharing it.

ISMENÊ:
What do I care for life when you are dead?

ANTIGONÊ:
Ask Creon. You're always hanging on his opinions.

ISMENÊ:
You are laughing at me. Why, Antigonê?

ANTIGONÊ:
It's a joyless laughter, Ismenê.

ISMENÊ:
                              But can I do nothing?

ANTIGONÊ:
Yes. Save yourself. I shall not envy you.
There are those who will praise you; I shall have honor, too.

ISMENÊ:
But we are equally guilty!

ANTIGONÊ:
                              No more, Ismenê.
You are alive, but I belong to Death.

CREON (to the CHORUS):
Gentlemen, I beg you to observe these girls:
One has just now lost her mind; the other,
It seems, has never had a mind at all.

ISMENÊ:
Grief teaches the steadiest minds to waver, King.

CREON:
Yours certainly did, when you assumed guilt with the guilty!

ISMENÊ:
But how could I go on living without her?

CREON:
                              You are.
She is already dead.

ISMENÊ:
                    But your own son's bride!

CREON:
There are places enough for him to push his plow.
I want no wicked women for my sons!

ISMENÊ:
O dearest Haimon, how your father wrongs you!

CREON:
I've had enough of your childish talk of marriage!

CHORAGOS:
Do you really intend to steal this girl from your son?

CREON:
No; Death will do that for me.

CHORAGOS:
                              Then she must die?

CREON (ironically):
You dazzle me.
                    —But enough of this talk!
     (To GUARDS)
You, there, take them away and guard them well:
For they are but women, and even brave men run
When they see Death coming.

          (Exeunt ISMENÊ, ANTIGONÊ, and GUARDS.)

ODE II

CHORUS: STROPHE 1
Fortunate is the man who has never tasted God's vengeance!
Where once the anger of heaven has struck, that house is shaken
For ever: damnation rises behind each child
Like a wave cresting out of the black northeast,
When the long darkness under sea roars up
And bursts drumming death upon the windwhipped sand.

                                        ANTISTROPHE 1
I have seen this gathering sorrow from time long past
Loom upon Oedipus' children: generation from generation
Takes the compulsive rage of the enemy god.
So lately this last flower of Oedipus' line
Drank the sunlight! but now a passionate word

And a handful of dust have closed up all its
   beauty.

STROPHE 2

What mortal arrogance
   Transcends the wrath of Zeus?
Sleep cannot lull him, nor the effortless long
   months
Of the timeless gods: but he is young for ever,
And his house is the shining day of high
   Olympos.
   And that is and shall be,
   And all the past, is his.
No pride on earth is free of the curse of
   heaven.

ANTISTROPHE 2

The straying dreams of men
   May bring them ghosts of joy:
But as they drowse, the waking embers burn
   them;
Or they walk with fixed eyes, as blind men
   walk.
But the ancient wisdom speaks for our own
   time:
   Fate works most for woe
   With Folly's fairest show.
Man's little pleasure is the spring of sorrow.

SCENE III

CHORAGOS:
But here is Haimon, King, the last of all your
   sons.
Is it grief for Antigonê that brings him here,
And bitterness at being robbed of his bride?

   (*Enter* HAIMON.)

CREON:
We shall soon see, and no need of diviners.
                                        —Son,
You have heard my final judgment on that girl:
Have you come here hating me, or have you
   come
With deference and with love, whatever I do?

HAIMON:
I am your son, father. You are my guide.
You make things clear for me, and I obey you.
No marriage means more to me than your con-
   tinuing wisdom.

CREON:
Good. That is the way to behave: subordinate
Everything else, my son, to your father's will.
This is what a man prays for, that he may get
Sons attentive and dutiful in his house,
Each one hating his father's enemies,
Honoring his father's friends. But if his sons
Fail him, if they turn out unprofitably,
What has he fathered but trouble for himself
And amusement for the malicious?
                           So you are right
Not to lose your head over this woman.
Your pleasure with her would soon grow cold,
   Haimon,
And then you'd have a hellcat in bed and else-
   where.
Let her find her husband in Hell!
Of all the people in this city, only she
Has had contempt for my law and broken it.

Do you want me to show myself weak before
   the people?
Or to break my sworn word? No, and I will
   not.
The woman dies.
I suppose she'll plead "family ties." Well, let
   her.
If I permit my own family to rebel,
How shall I earn the world's obedience?
Show me the man who keeps his house in
   hand,
He's fit for public authority.
                           I'll have no dealings
With law-breakers, critics of the government:
Whoever is chosen to govern should be
   obeyed—
Must be obeyed, in all things, great and small,
Just and unjust! O Haimon,
The man who knows how to obey, and that
   man only,
Knows how to give commands when the time
   comes.
You can depend on him, no matter how fast
The spears come: he's a good soldier, he'll
   stick it out.

Anarchy, anarchy! Show me a greater evil!
This is why cities tumble and the great houses
   rain down,
This is what scatters armies!

No, no: good lives are made so by discipline.
We keep the laws then, and the lawmakers,
And no woman shall seduce us. If we must lose,
Let's lose to a man, at least! Is a woman stronger than we?

CHORAGOS:
Unless time has rusted my wits,
What you say, King, is said with point and dignity.

HAIMON (*boyishly earnest*):
Father:
Reason is God's crowning gift to man, and you are right
To warn me against losing mine. I cannot say—
I hope that I shall never want to say!—that you
Have reasoned badly. Yet there are other men
Who can reason, too; and their opinions might be helpful.
You are not in a position to know everything
That people say or do, or what they feel:
Your temper terrifies them—everyone
Will tell you only what you like to hear.
But I, at any rate, can listen; and I have heard them
Muttering and whispering in the dark about this girl.
They say no woman has ever, so unreasonably,
Died so shameful a death for a generous act:
"She covered her brother's body. Is this indecent?
She kept him from dogs and vultures. Is this a crime?
Death?—She should have all the honor that we can give her!"

This is the way they talk out there in the city.

You must believe me:
Nothing is closer to me than your happiness.
What could be closer? Must not any son
Value his father's fortune as his father does his?
I beg you, do not be unchangeable:
Do not believe that you alone can be right.
The man who thinks that,
The man who maintains that only he has the power

To reason correctly, the gift to speak, the soul—
A man like that, when you know him, turns out empty.

It is not reason never to yield to reason!

In flood time you can see how some trees bend,
And because they bend, even their twigs are safe,
While stubborn trees are torn up, roots and all.
And the same thing happens in sailing:
Make your sheet fast, never slacken,—and over you go,
Head over heels and under: and there's your voyage.
Forget you are angry! Let yourself be moved!
I know I am young; but please let me say this:
The ideal condition
Would be, I admit, that men should be right by instinct;
But since we are all too likely to go astray,
The reasonable thing is to learn from those who can teach.

CHORAGOS:
You will do well to listen to him, King,
If what he says is sensible. And you, Haimon,
Must listen to your father.—Both speak well.

CREON:
You consider it right for a man of my years and experience
To go to school to a boy?

HAIMON:
                    It is not right
If I am wrong. But if I am young, and right,
What does my age matter?

CREON:
You think it right to stand up for an anarchist?

HAIMON:
Not at all. I pay no respect to criminals.

CREON:
Then she is not a criminal?

HAIMON:
The City would deny it, to a man.

CREON:
And the City proposes to teach me how to
   rule?

HAIMON:
Ah. Who is it that's talking like a boy now?

CREON:
My voice is the one voice giving orders in this
   City!

HAIMON:
It is no City if it takes orders from one voice.

CREON:
The State is the King!

HAIMON:
                              Yes, if the State is a desert.

   (*Pause.*)

CREON:
This boy, it seems, has sold out to a woman.

HAIMON:
If you are a woman: my concern is only for
   you.

CREON:
So? Your "concern"! In a public brawl with
   your father!

HAIMON:
How about you, in a public brawl with justice?

CREON:
With justice, when all that I do is within my
   rights?

HAIMON:
You have no right to trample on God's right.

CREON (*completely out of control*):
Fool, adolescent fool! Taken in by a woman!

HAIMON:
You'll never see me taken in by anything vile.

CREON:
Every word you say is for her!

HAIMON (*quietly, darkly*):
                              And for you.
And for me. And for the gods under the earth.

CREON:
You'll never marry her while she lives.

HAIMON:
Then she must die.—But her death will cause
   another.

CREON:
Another?
Have you lost your senses? Is this an open
   threat?

HAIMON:
There is no threat in speaking to emptiness.

CREON:
I swear you'll regret this superior tone of
   yours!
You are the empty one!

HAIMON:
                              If you were not my father,
I'd say you were perverse.

CREON:
You girlstruck fool, don't play at words with
   me!

HAIMON:
I am sorry. You prefer silence.

CREON.
                              Now, by God—!
I swear, by all the gods in heaven above us,
You'll watch it, I swear you shall!
   (*To the* SERVANTS)
                              Bring her out!
Bring the woman out! Let her die before his
   eyes!
Here, this instant, with her bridegroom beside
   her!

HAIMON:
Not here, no; she will not die here, King.
And you will never see my face again.
Go on raving as long as you've a friend to
   endure you.
   (*Exit* HAIMON.)

CHORAGOS:
Gone, gone.
Creon, a young man in a rage is dangerous!

CREON:
Let him do, or dream to do, more than a man
    can.
He shall not save these girls from death.

CHORAGOS:
                                    These girls?
You have sentenced them both?

CREON:
                            No, you are right.
I will not kill the one whose hands are clean.

CHORAGOS:
But Antigonê?

CREON (*somberly*):
                I will carry her far away
Out there in the wilderness, and lock her
Living in a vault of stone. She shall have food,
As the custom is, to absolve the State of her
    death.
And there let her pray to the gods of hell:
They are her only gods:
Perhaps they will show her an escape from
    death,
Or she may learn,
                though late,
That piety shown the dead is pity in vain.
    (*Exit* CREON.)

ODE III

CHORUS: STROPHE
Love, unconquerable
Waster of rich men, keeper
Of warm lights and all-night vigil
In the soft face of a girl:
Sea-wanderer, forest-visitor!
Even the pure Immortals cannot escape you,
And mortal man, in his one day's dusk,
Trembles before your glory.

                              ANTISTROPHE
Surely you swerve upon ruin
The just man's consenting heart,
As here you have made bright anger
Strike between father and son—
And none has conquered but Love!
A girl's glance working the will of heaven:
Pleasure to her alone who mocks us,
Merciless Aphroditê.

SCENE IV

CHORAGOS (*as* ANTIGONÊ *enters guarded*):
But I can no longer stand in awe of this,
Nor, seeing what I see, keep back my tears.
Here is Antigonê, passing to that chamber
Where all find sleep at last.

ANTIGONÊ: STROPHE 1
Look upon me, friends, and pity me
Turning back at the night's edge to say
Good-by to the sun that shines for me no
    longer;
Now sleepy Death
Summons me down to Acheron, that cold
    shore:
There is no bridesong there, nor any music.

CHORUS:
Yet not unpraised, not without a kind of honor,
You walk at last into the underworld;
Untouched by sickness, broken by no sword.
What woman has ever found your way to
    death?

ANTIGONÊ: ANTISTROPHE 1
How often I have heard the story of Niobê,
Tantalos' wretched daughter, how the stone
Clung fast about her, ivy-close: and they say
The rain falls endlessly
And sifting soft snow; her tears are never
    done.
I feel the loneliness of her death in mine.

CHORUS:
But she was born of heaven, and you
Are woman, woman-born. If her death is
    yours,
A mortal woman's, is this not for you
Glory in our world and in the world beyond?

ANTIGONÊ: STROPHE 2
You laugh at me. Ah, friends, friends,
Can you not wait until I am dead? O Thebes,
O men many-charioted, in love with Fortune,
Dear springs of Dircê, sacred Theban grove,
Be witnesses for me, denied all pity,
Unjustly judged! and think a word of love
For her whose path turns
Under dark earth, where there are no more
    tears.

CHORUS:
You have passed beyond human daring and
    come at last
Into a place of stone where Justice sits.
I cannot tell
What shape of your father's guilt appears in
    this.

ANTIGONÊ: ANTISTROPHE 2
You have touched it at last: that bridal bed
Unspeakable, horror of son and mother min-
    gling:
Their crime, infection of all our family!
O Oedipus, father and brother!
Your marriage strikes from the grave to murder
    mine.
I have been a stranger here in my own land:
All my life
The blasphemy of my birth has followed me.

CHORUS:
Reverence is a virtue, but strength
Lives in established law: that must prevail.
You have made your choice,
Your death is the doing of your conscious
    hand.

ANTIGONÊ: EPODE
Then let me go, since all your words are bitter,
And the very light of the sun is cold to me.
Lead me to my vigil, where I must have
Neither love nor lamentation; no song, but
    silence.

    (CREON interrupts impatiently.)

CREON:
If dirges and planned lamentations could put
    off death,
Men would be singing for ever.
    (To the SERVANTS)
                              Take her, go!
You know your orders: take her to the vault
And leave her alone there. And if she lives or
    dies,
That's her affair, not ours: our hands are clean.

ANTIGONÊ:
O tomb, vaulted bride-bed in eternal rock,
Soon I shall be with my own again
Where Persephonê welcomes the thin ghosts
    underground:

And I shall see my father again, and you,
    mother,
And dearest Polyneicês—
                              dearest indeed
To me, since it was my hand
That washed him clean and poured the ritual
    wine:
And my reward is death before my time!

And yet, as men's hearts know, I have done no
    wrong,
I have not sinned before God. Or if I have,
I shall know the truth in death. But if the guilt
Lies upon Creon who judged me, then, I pray,
May his punishment equal my own.

CHORAGOS:
                              O passionate heart,
Unyielding, tormented still by the same winds!

CREON:
Her guards shall have good cause to regret
    their delaying.

ANTIGONÊ:
Ah! That voice is like the voice of death!

CREON:
I can give you no reason to think you are
    mistaken.

ANTIGONÊ:
Thebes, and you my father's gods,
And rulers of Thebes, you see me now, the last
Unhappy daughter of a line of kings,
Your kings, led away to death. You will re-
    member
What things I suffer, and at what men's hands,
Because I would not transgress the laws of
    heaven.
    (To the GUARDS, simply)
Come: let us wait no longer.

    (Exit ANTIGONÊ, L., guarded.)

ODE IV

CHORUS: STROPHE 1
All Danaê's beauty was locked away
In a brazen cell where the sunlight could not
    come:
A small room, still as any grave, enclosed her.

Yet she was a princess too,
And Zeus in a rain of gold poured love upon
    her.
O child, child,
No power in wealth or war
Or tough sea-blackened ships
Can prevail against untiring Destiny!

ANTISTROPHE 1

And Dryas' son also, that furious king,
Bore the god's prisoning anger for his pride:
Sealed up by Dionysos in deaf stone,
His madness died among echoes.
So at the last he learned what dreadful power
His tongue had mocked:
For he had profaned the revels,
And fired the wrath of the nine
Implacable Sisters that love the sound of the
    flute.

STROPHE 2

And old men tell a half-remembered tale
Of horror done where a dark ledge splits the
    sea
And a double surf beats on the gray shores:
How a king's new woman, sick
With hatred for the queen he had imprisoned,
Ripped out his two sons' eyes with her bloody
    hands
While grinning Arês watched the shuttle
    plunge
Four times: four blind wounds crying for re-
    venge,

ANTISTROPHE 2

Crying, tears and blood mingled.—Piteously
    born,
Those sons whose mother was of heavenly
    birth!
Her father was the god of the North Wind
And she was cradled by gales,
She raced with young colts on the glittering
    hills
And walked untrammeled in the open light:
But in her marriage deathless Fate found
    means
To build a tomb like yours for all her joy.

SCENE V

(*Enter blind* TEIRESIAS, *led by a* BOY. *The
opening speeches of* TEIRESIAS *should be
in singsong contrast to the realistic lines
of* CREON.)

TEIRESIAS:
This is the way the blind man comes, Princes,
    Princes,
Lock-step, two heads lit by the eyes of one.

CREON:
What new thing have you to tell us, old
    Teiresias?

TEIRESIAS:
I have much to tell you: listen to the prophet,
    Creon.

CREON:
I am not aware that I have ever failed to
    listen.

TEIRESIAS:
Then you have done wisely, King, and ruled
    well.

CREON:
I admit my debt to you. But what have you to
    say?

TEIRESIAS:
This, Creon: you stand once more on the edge
    of fate.

CREON:
What do you mean? Your words are a kind of
    dread.

TEIRESIAS:
Listen, Creon:
I was sitting in my chair of augury, at the
    place
Where the birds gather about me. They were
    all a-chatter,
As is their habit, when suddenly I heard
A strange note in their jangling, a scream, a
Whirring fury; I knew that they were fighting,
Tearing each other, dying
In a whirlwind of wings clashing. And I was
    afraid.
I began the rites of burnt-offering at the altar,
But Hephaistos failed me: instead of bright
    flame,
There was only the sputtering slime of the fat
    thigh-flesh
Melting: the entrails dissolved in gray smoke,

The bare bone burst from the welter. And no
  blaze!

This was a sign from heaven. My boy described it,
Seeing for me as I see for others.

I tell you, Creon, you yourself have brought
This new calamity upon us. Our hearths and
  altars
Are stained with the corruption of dogs and
  carrion birds
That glut themselves on the corpse of Oedipus'
  son.
The gods are deaf when we pray to them, their
  fire
Recoils from our offering, their birds of omen
Have no cry of comfort, for they are gorged
With the thick blood of the dead.
                                        O my son,
These are no trifles! Think: all men make
  mistakes,
But a good man yields when he knows his
  course is wrong,
And repairs the evil. The only crime is pride.

Give in to the dead man, then: do not fight
  with a corpse—
What glory is it to kill a man who is dead?
Think, I beg you:
It is for your own good that I speak as I do.
You should be able to yield for your own
  good.

CREON:
It seems that prophets have made me their
  especial province.
All my life long
I have been a kind of butt for the dull arrows
Of doddering fortune-tellers!
                              No, Teiresias:
If your birds—if the great eagles of God him-
  self
Should carry him stinking bit by bit to heaven,
I would not yield. I am not afraid of pollution:
No man can defile the gods.
                            Do what you will,
Go into business, make money, speculate
In India gold or that synthetic gold from
  Sardis,
Get rich otherwise than by my consent to bury
  him.

Teiresias, it is a sorry thing when a wise man
Sells his wisdom, lets out his words for hire!

TEIRESIAS:
Ah Creon! Is there no man left in the world—

CREON:
To do what?—Come, let's have the aphorism!

TEIRESIAS:
No man who knows that wisdom outweighs
  any wealth?

CREON:
As surely as bribes are baser than any baseness.

TEIRESIAS:
You are sick, Creon! You are deathly sick!

CREON:
As you say: it is not my place to challenge a
  prophet.

TEIRESIAS:
Yet you have said my prophecy is for sale.

CREON:
The generation of prophets has always loved
  gold.

TEIRESIAS:
The generation of kings has always loved
  brass.

CREON:
You forget yourself! You are speaking to your
  King:

TEIRESIAS:
I know it. You are a king because of me.

CREON:
You have a certain skill; but you have sold out.

TEIRESIAS:
King, you will drive me to words that—

CREON:
                              Say them, say them!
Only remember: I will not pay you for them.

TEIRESIAS:
No, you will find them too costly.

CREON:
                              No doubt. Speak:
Whatever you say, you will not change my
  will.

TEIRESIAS:

Then take this, and take it to heart!

The time is not far off when you shall pay
    back

Corpse for corpse, flesh of your own flesh.

You have thrust the child of this world into
    living night,

You have kept from the gods below the child
    that is theirs:

The one in a grave before her death, the other,

Dead, denied the grave. This is your crime:

And the Furies and the dark gods of Hell

Are swift with terrible punishment for you.

Do you want to buy me now, Creon?

                           Not many days,

And your house will be full of men and women
    weeping,

And curses will be hurled at you from far

Cities grieving for sons unburied, left to rot

Before the walls of Thebes.

These are my arrows, Creon: they are all for
    you.

    (*To* BOY)

But come, child: lead me home.

Let him waste his fine anger upon younger
    men.

Maybe he will learn at last

To control a wiser tongue in a better head.

    (*Exit* TEIRESIAS.)

CHORAGOS:

The old man has gone, King, but his words

Remain to plague us. I am old, too,

But I cannot remember that he was ever false.

CREON:

That is true. . . . It troubles me.

Oh it is hard to give in! but it is worse

To risk everything for stubborn pride.

CHORAGOS:

Creon: take my advice.

CREON:

                What shall I do?

CHORAGOS:

Go quickly: free Antigonê from her vault

And build a tomb for the body of Polyneicês.

CREON:

You would have me do this?

CHORAGOS:

                      Creon, yes!

And it must be done at once: God moves

Swiftly to cancel the folly of stubborn men.

CREON:

It is hard to deny the heart! But I

Will do it: I will not fight with destiny.

CHORAGOS:

You must go yourself, you cannot leave it to
    others.

CREON:

I will go.

         —Bring axes, servants.

Come with me to the tomb. I buried her, I

Will set her free.

             Oh quickly!

My mind misgives—

The laws of the gods are mighty, and a man
    must serve them

To the last day of his life!

    (*Exit* CREON.)

PAEAN

CHORAGOS: STROPHE 1

God of many names

CHORUS:

                O Iacchos

                      son

of Kadmeian Sémelê

                O born of the Thunder!

Guardian of the West

                  Regent

of Eleusis' plain

          O Prince of maenad Thebes

and the Dragon Field by rippling Ismenos:

CHORAGOS: ANTISTROPHE 1

God of many names

CHORUS:

           the flame of torches

flares on our hills

          the nymphs of Iacchos

dance at the spring of Castalia:

from the vine-close mountain
>   come ah come in ivy:
Evohé evohé! sings through the streets of
  Thebes

CHORAGOS: STROPHE 2
God of many names

CHORUS:
>   Iacchos of Thebes
heavenly Child
>   of Sémelê bride of the Thunderer!
The shadow of plague is upon us:
>   come
with clement feet
>   oh come from Parnasos
down the long slopes
>   across the lamenting water

CHORAGOS: ANTISTROPHE 2
Iô Fire! Chorister of the throbbing stars!
O purest among the voices of the night!
Thou son of God, blaze for us!

CHORUS:
Come with choric rapture of circling Maenads
Who cry Iô Iacche!
>   *God of many names!*

ÉXODOS

(*Enter* MESSENGER, *L.*)

MESSENGER:
Men of the line of Kadmos, you who live
Near Amphion's citadel:
>   I cannot say
Of any condition of human life "This is fixed,
This is clearly good, or bad." Fate raises up,
And Fate casts down the happy and unhappy
  alike:
No man can foretell his Fate.
>   Take the case of Creon:
Creon was happy once, as I count happiness:
Victorious in battle, sole governor of the land,
Fortunate father of children nobly born.
And now it has all gone from him! Who can
  say
That a man is still alive when his life's joy
  fails?
He is a walking dead man. Grant him rich,

Let him live like a king in his great house:
If his pleasure is gone, I would not give
So much as the shadow of smoke for all he
  owns.

CHORAGOS:
Your words hint at sorrow: what is your news
  for us?

MESSENGER:
They are dead. The living are guilty of their
  death.

CHORAGOS:
Who is guilty? Who is dead? Speak!

MESSENGER:
>   Haimon.
Haimon is dead; and the hand that killed him
Is his own hand.

CHORAGOS:
>   His father's? or his own?

MESSENGER:
His own, driven mad by the murder his father
  had done.

CHORAGOS:
Teiresias, Teiresias, how clearly you saw it all!

MESSENGER:
This is my news: you must draw what conclusions you can from it.

CHORAGOS:
But look: Eurydicê, our Queen:
Has she overheard us?

(*Enter* EURYDICÊ *from the Palace, C.*)

EURYDICÊ:
I have heard something, friends:
As I was unlocking the gate of Pallas' shrine,
For I needed her help today, I heard a voice
Telling of some new sorrow. And I fainted
There at the temple with all my maidens
  about me.
But speak again: whatever it is, I can bear it:
Grief and I are no strangers.

MESSENGER:
>   Dearest Lady,
I will tell you plainly all that I have seen.
I shall not try to comfort you: what is the use,

Since comfort could lie only in what is not
  true?
The truth is always best.
                                    I went with Creon
To the outer plain where Polyneicês was lying,
No friend to pity him, his body shredded by
  dogs.
We made our prayers in that place to Hecatê
And Pluto, that they would be merciful. And
  we bathed
The corpse with holy water, and we brought
Fresh-broken branches to burn what was left
  of it,
And upon the urn we heaped up a towering
  barrow
Of the earth of his own land.
                                    When we were done, we ran
To the vault where Antigonê lay on her couch
  of stone.
One of the servants had gone ahead,
And while he was yet far off he heard a voice
Grieving within the chamber, and he came
  back
And told Creon. And as the King went closer,
The air was full of wailing, the words lost,
And he begged us to make all haste. "Am I a
  prophet?"
He said, weeping, "And must I walk this road,
The saddest of all that I have gone before?
My son's voice calls me on. Oh quickly,
  quickly!
Look through the crevice there, and tell me
If it is Haimon, or some deception of the
  gods!"

We obeyed; and in the cavern's farthest corner
We saw her lying:
She had made a noose of her fine linen veil
And hanged herself. Haimon lay beside her,
His arms about her waist, lamenting her,
His love lost under ground, crying out
That his father had stolen her away from him.

When Creon saw him the tears rushed to his
  eyes
And he called to him: "What have you done,
  child? Speak to me.
What are you thinking that makes your eyes
  so strange?
O my son, my son, I come to you on my knees!"

But Haimon spat in his face. He said not a
  word,
Staring—
            And suddenly drew his sword
And lunged. Creon shrank back, the blade
  missed; and the boy,
Desperate against himself, drove it half its
  length
Into his own side, and fell. And as he died
He gathered Antigonê close in his arms again,
Choking, his blood bright red on her white
  cheek.
And now he lies dead with the dead, and she
  is his
At last, his bride in the houses of the dead.

      (*Exit* EURYDICÊ *into the Palace.*)

CHORAGOS:
She has left us without a word. What can this
  mean?

MESSENGER:
It troubles me, too; yet she knows what is best,
Her grief is too great for public lamentation,
And doubtless she has gone to her chamber to
  weep
For her dead son, leading her maidens in his
  dirge.

CHORAGOS:
It may be so; but I fear this deep silence.

      (*Pause.*)

MESSENGER:
I will see what she is doing. I will go in.
      (*Exit* MESSENGER *into the Palace.*)

      (*Enter* CREON *with* ATTENDANTS, *bearing*
      HAIMON's *body.*)

CHORAGOS:
But here is the King himself: oh look at him,
Bearing his own damnation in his arms.

CREON:
Nothing you say can touch me any more.
My own blind heart has brought me
From darkness to final darkness. Here you see
The father murdering, the murdered son—
And all my civic wisdom!

Haimon my son, so young, so young to die,
I was the fool, not you; and you died for me.

CHORAGOS:

That is the truth; but you were late in learning it.

CREON:

This truth is hard to bear. Surely a god
Has crushed me beneath the hugest weight of
heaven,
And driven me headlong a barbaric way
To trample out the thing I held most dear.

The pains that men will take to come to pain!

(*Enter* MESSENGER *from the Palace.*)

MESSENGER:

The burden you carry in your hands is heavy,
But it is not all: you will find more in your
house.

CREON:

What burden worse than this shall I find there?

MESSENGER:

The Queen is dead.

CREON:

O port of death, deaf world,
Is there no pity for me? And you, Angel of
evil,
I was dead, and your words are death again.
Is it true, boy? Can it be true?
Is my wife dead? Has death bred death?

MESSENGER:

You can see for yourself.

(*The doors are opened, and the body of*
EURYDICÊ *is disclosed within.*)

CREON:

Oh pity!
All true, all true, and more than I can bear!
O my wife, my son!

MESSENGER:

She stood before the altar, and her heart
Welcomed the knife her own hand guided,
And a great cry burst from her lips for
Megareus dead,
And for Haimon dead, her sons; and her last
breath
Was a curse for their father, the murderer of
her sons.
And she fell, and the dark flowed in through
her closing eyes.

CREON:

O God, I am sick with fear.
Are there no swords here? Has no one a blow
for me?

MESSENGER:

Her curse is upon you for the deaths of both.

CREON:

It is right that it should be. I alone am guilty.
I know it, and I say it. Lead me in,
Quickly, friends.
I have neither life nor substance. Lead me in.

CHORAGOS:

You are right, if there can be right in so much
wrong.
The briefest way is best in a world of sorrow.

CREON:

Let it come,
Let death come quickly, and be kind to me.
I would not ever see the sun again.

CHORAGOS:

All that will come when it will; but we, meanwhile,
Have much to do. Leave the future to itself.

CREON:

All my heart was in that prayer!

CHORAGOS:

Then do not pray any more: the sky is deaf.

CREON:

Lead me away. I have been rash and foolish.
I have killed my son and my wife.
I look for comfort; my comfort lies here dead.
Whatever my hands have touched has come to
nothing.
Fate has brought all my pride to a thought of
dust.

(*As* CREON *is being led into the house, the*
CHORAGOS *advances and speaks directly to
the audience.*)

CHORAGOS:

There is no happiness where there is no wisdom;
No wisdom but in submission to the gods.
Big words are always punished,
And proud men in old age learn to be wise.

TRANSLATORS' COMMENTARY

Et quod propriè dicitur in idiomate Picardorum horrescit apud Burgundos, immò apud Gallicos viciniores; quanto igitur magis accidet hoc apud linguas diversas! Quapropter quod bene factum est in unâ linguâ non est possibile ut transferatur in aliam secundum ejus proprietatem quam habuerit in priori.

—ROGER BACON

I

In the Commentary appended to our version of Euripides' *Alcestis* we wrote:

Our object was to make the *Alcestis* clear and credible in English. Since it is a poem, it had to be made clear as a poem; and since it is a play, it had to be made credible as a play. We set for ourselves no fixed rules of translation or of dramatic verse: often we found the best English equivalent in a literalness which extended to the texture and rhythm of the Greek phrasing; at other times we were forced to a more or less free paraphrase in order to achieve effects which the Greek conveyed in ways impossible to English. Consequently, this version of the *Alcestis* is not a "translation" in the classroom sense of the word. The careful reader, comparing our text with the original, will discover alterations, suppressions, expansions—a word, perhaps, drawn out into a phrase, or a phrase condensed to a word: a way of saying things that is admittedly not Euripidean, if by Euripidean one means a translation *ad verbum expressa* of Euripides' poem. In defense we can say only that our purpose was to reach—and, if possible, to render precisely—the emotional and sensible meaning in every speech in the play; we could not follow the Greek word for word, where to do so would have been weak and therefore false.

We have been guided by the same principles in making this version of the *Antigonê*.

II

We have made cuts only when it seemed absolutely necessary. The most notable excision is that of a passage of sixteen lines beginning with 904 (Antigonê's long speech near the end

of Scene IV), which has been bracketed as spurious, either in whole or in part, by the best critics. Aristotle quotes two verses from it, which proves, as Professor Jebb points out, that if it is an interpolation it must have been made soon after Sophocles' death, possibly by his son Iophon. However that may be, it is dismal stuff. Antigonê is made to interrupt her lamentation by a series of limping verses whose sense is as discordant as their sound. We quote the Oxford translation, the style of which is for once wholly adequate to the occasion:

And yet, in the opinion of those who have just sentiments, I honoured you [Polyneicês] aright. For neither, though I had been the mother of children, nor though my husband dying, had mouldered away, would I have undertaken this toil against the will of the citizens. On account of what law do I say this? There would have been another husband for me if the first died, and if I lost my child there would have been another from another man! but my father and my mother being laid in the grave, it is impossible a brother should ever be born to me. On the principle of such a law, having preferred you, my brother, to all other considerations, I seemed to Creon to commit a sin, and to dare what was dreadful. And now, seizing me by force, he thus leads me away, having never enjoyed the nuptial bed, nor heard the nuptial lay, nor having gained the lot of marriage, nor of rearing my children; but thus I, an unhappy woman, deserted by my friends, go, while alive, to the cavern of the dead.

There are other excisions of less importance. Perhaps the discussion of one of them will serve to explain them all. Near the end of the *Éxodos*, Creon is told of his wife's suicide. The Messenger has five very graphic lines describing Eurydicê's suicide, to which Creon responds with an outburst of dread and grief; yet two lines later, as if he had not heard the first time, he is asking the Messenger how Eurydicê died. The Messenger replies that she stabbed herself to the heart. There is no evidence that the question and reply are interpolations: on the contrary, they serve the definite purpose of filling out the iambic interlude between two lyric strophes; but in a modern version which does not attempt to reproduce the strophic structure of this *Kommos* they merely clog the dialogue. Therefore we have skipped them; and the occasional suppression of short passages throughout the play is based upon similar considerations.

III

In a like manner, we have not hesitated to use free paraphrase when a literal rendering of the Greek would result in obscurity. Again, the discussion of a specific instance may illuminate the whole question.

After Antigonê has been led away to death, the Chorus, taking a hint from her having compared her own fate to that of Niobê, proceeds to elaborate the stories of mythological persons who have suffered similar punishment. The Fourth Ode cites Danaê, Lycurgos, the son of Dryas, and Cleopatra, the daughter of Boreas and wife of the Thracian king Phineus. Only Danaê is mentioned by name; the others are allusively identified. The difficulty arises from the allusive method. Sophocles' audience would be certain to recognize the allusions, but that is not true of ours. To what extent can we depend upon the audience's recognition in a day when, to quote Mr. I. A. Richards, "we can no longer refer with any confidence to any episode in the Bible or to any nursery tale or any piece of mythology"? We can assume that the story of Danaê is still current; but Lycurgos is forgotten now, and the sordid Phineus-Cleopatra-Eidothea affair no longer stirs so much as an echo. Nevertheless, Sophocles devotes two of his four strophes to this Cleopatra, and he does it in so oblique a manner that "translation" is out of the question. We have therefore rendered these strophes with such slight additions to the Greek sense as might convey an equivalent suggestion of fable to a modern audience.

IV

The Chorus is composed, says the Scholiast, of "certain old men of Thebes": leading citizens ("O men many-charioted, in love with Fortune") to whom Creon addresses his fatal decree, and from whom he later takes advice. Sophocles' Chorus numbered fifteen, including the Choragos, or Leader; its function was to chant the Odes and, in the person of the Choragos, to participate in the action. In a version designed for the modern stage certain changes are inevitable. It cannot be urged too strongly that the words of the Odes must be intelligible to the audience; and they are almost certain not to be intelligible if they are chanted in unison by so large a group, with or without musical accompaniment. It is suggested, then, that in producing this play no attempt be made to follow the ancient choric method. There should be no dancing. The *Párodos,* for example, should be a solemn but almost unnoticeable evolution of moving or still patterns accompanied by a drum-beat whose rhythm may be derived from the cadence of the Ode itself. The lines given to the Chorus in the Odes should probably be spoken by single voices. The only accompaniment should be percussion: we follow Allan Sly's score of the *Alcestis* in suggesting a large side drum, from which the snares have been removed, to be struck with two felt-headed tympani sticks, one hard, one soft.

V

A careful production might make successful use of masks. They should be of the Benda type used in the production of O'Neill's *The Great God Brown:* lifelike, closely fitting the contours of the face, and valuable only as they give the effect of immobility to character. On no account should there be any attempt to reproduce the Greek mask, which was larger than life size and served a function non-existent on the modern stage—the amplification of voice and mood for projection to the distant seats of the outdoor theater.

If masks are used at all, they might well be allotted only to those characters who are somewhat depersonalized by official position or discipline: Creon, Teiresias, the Chorus and Choragos, possibly the Messenger. By this rule, Antigonê has no mask; neither has Ismenê, Haimon, nor Eurydicê. If Creon is masked, we see no objection, in art or feeling, to the symbolic removal of his mask before he returns with the dead body of his son.

INDEX OF NAMES IN *Antigonê*

The transliteration of Greek names is an uncertain and—ultimately, perhaps—subjective matter. Certain of the entries below have more than one form, the first being that used in this translation.

ACHERON: a river of Hades

AMPHION: a prince of Orchomenos who married NIOBÊ, *q.v.*; hence, an ancestor of Oedipus

ANTIGONÊ: a daughter of Oedipus; in *Antigonê* affianced to HAIMON, *q.v.*

APHRODITÊ: goddess of love

APOLLO: god of the sun

ARÊS: god of war

ARGIVE: Greek

ARGOS: capital of Argolis, in the Peloponnesos

ARTEMIS: goddess of the hunt, sister of Apollo

ATHENA, ATHENÊ: daughter of Zeus, tutelary goddess of Athens

CASTALIA: a spring sacred to the Muses, on Mount Parnassos

CREON, KREON: brother of IOCASTÊ, *q.v.*; father of HAIMON and MEGAREUS, *qq.v.*; King of Thebes after the death of Polyneicês and Eteoclês

DANAÊ: a princess of Argos, confined by her father in a brazen chamber underground (or, some say, in a brazen tower), where she was seduced by Zeus in the form of a golden rain and bore him Perseus

DELPHI, DELPHOI: a city of Phokis, seat of a celebrated Oracle of Apollo

DEMÉTER: a sister of Zeus, goddess of agriculture

DIONYSOS, DIONYSUS: son of Zeus and SÉMELÊ, *q.v.*; god of wine

DIRCÊ, DIRKÊ: a spring near Thebes

DRYAS: a king of Thrace; father of Lykûrgos, who was driven mad by Dionysos

ELEUSIS: a city in Attica, sacred to Deméter and Persephonê; hence the adjective ELEUSINIAN

ETEOCLÊS, ETEOKLÊS: a son of Oedipus and Iocastê; brother of POLYNEICÊS, *q.v.*

EURYDICÊ, EURYDIKÊ: wife of CREON, *q.v.*

FURIES: the infernal spirits of Divine Vengeance

HAIMON, HAEMON: a son of Creon; affianced to Antigonê

HECATÊ: a goddess of the Titan race; identified with various other deities, as Selenê in heaven, Artemis on earth, and Persephonê in Hades; generally, a goddess of sorcery and witchcraft

HEPHAISTOS, HEPHAESTUS: god of fire

IACCHOS: a name for DIONYSOS, *q.v.*

IOCASTÊ, JOCASTA: wife of LAÏOS, *q.v.*; after Laïos' death, wife of Oedipus, and, by him, *mother of* ANTIGONÊ, ISMENÊ, POLYNEICÊS and ETEOCLÊS, *qq.v.*

ISMENÊ: a daughter of Oedipus and Iocastê; sister of Antigonê

ISMENOS: a river of Thebes, sacred to Apollo

KADMOS, CADMUS: the legendary founder of Thebes; father of SÉMELÊ, *q.v.*

LAÏOS, LAIUS: a king of Thebes; father of Oedipus, killed by him in fulfillment of an oracle

MAENAD: a priestess of DIONYSOS, *q.v.*

MEGAREUS: a son of CREON, *q.v.*; died during the assault of the Seven against Thebes

MENOIKEUS: father of CREON and IOCASTÊ, *qq.v.*

MUSES: nine daughters of Zeus and the nymph Mnemosynê, goddesses presiding over the arts and sciences

NIOBÊ: wife of AMPHION, *q.v.*; mother of fourteen children killed, because of her pride, by Apollo and Artemis; transformed into a rock on Mt. Sipylos

OEDIPUS: son of LAÏOS and IOCASTÊ, *qq.v.*

OLYMPOS, OLYMPUS: a Thessalian mountain, the seat of the gods

PALLAS: an epithet of ATHENA, *q.v.*

PARNASSOS, PARNASOS, PARNASSUS: a mountain sacred to Apollo; at its foot are Delphi and the Castalian Spring

PELOPS: a son of Tantalos; father of Atreus

PERSEPHONÊ: daughter of DEMÉTER, *q.v.*; Queen of Hades

PHOKIS: a kingdom on the Gulf of Corinth

PLUTO: brother of Zeus and Poseidon; King of Hades

POLYNEICÊS, POLYNEIKÊS: a son of Oedipus and Iocastê; killed by his brother Eteoclês, whom he killed at the same time, during the assault upon Thebes

SARDIS: a city in Lydia

SÉMELÊ: a daughter of KADMOS, *q.v.*; mother, by Zeus, of the god Dionysos

SPHINX: a riddling she-monster who killed herself when Oedipus solved her riddle

TANTALOS, TANTALUS: a king of Phrygia, father of PELOPS and NIOBÊ, *qq.v.*

TEIRESIAS, TIRESIAS: a blind prophet of Thebes, counsellor of Oedipus and Creon

ZEUS: father of gods and men

D.F.
R.F.

ARTHUR MILLER

The Crucible

Arthur Miller (1915–   ) was born to a middle-class Jewish family in the Harlem district of New York. While he was attending the University of Michigan, his talent for playwriting won him the Hopwood Prize for Drama in 1936. He won the Theatre Guild National Award in 1938, the year of his graduation.

In 1945 Miller wrote an ironic novel, *Focus*, about racial prejudice. His first successful play on Broadway was *All My Sons*, 1947, which deals with a father, who, during World War II, uses faulty parts in the airplane equipment that he supplies to the government. Like much of Miller's work, it is critical of a social evil—in this case, war profiteering. *Death of a Salesman*, 1949, has become one of the classics of the American theater. It has won five awards, including the New York Drama Critics' Circle Award and the Pulitzer Prize, and has been performed innumerable times by college drama departments and amateur little-theater groups. *Death of a Salesman* has grown in stature in the nearly two decades since its long Broadway run.

In 1950 Miller wrote an adaptation of Ibsen's *An Enemy of the People;* in 1953 he wrote *The Crucible*. In 1955 two one-act plays were produced under the title *A View from the Bridge*, which again won him the New York Drama Critics' Circle Award and the Pulitzer Prize. He then wrote and helped direct the successful movie *The Misfits*, 1961. Early in 1964 Miller's autobiographical drama *After the Fall* was the first play to be presented by the newly established Repertory Company of Lincoln Center in New York. In December 1964 Miller's most recent play *Incident at Vichy* was produced in New York. His newest work is *I Don't Need You Anymore*, 1967, a collection of short stories that includes "The Misfits," from which the screen play of the movie was developed.

A reader survey report in the London *Observer* in 1966 put *Death of a Salesman* and *The Crucible* on a list of twenty plays written since 1900 that show the main trends of the theater in this century.

The Crucible is a comparison of that dark period of the Salem witch trials in seventeenth-century New England with the so-called witch hunting of the post–World War II years, which was led by Senator Joseph McCarthy and which Miller sees as similar to the hysterical forces at work in Salem. The play is also a psychological and social dramatization of people destroyed by prejudice, guilt, and greed.

CAST OF CHARACTERS

REVEREND PARRIS	GILES COREY
BETTY PARRIS	REVEREND JOHN HALE
TITUBA	ELIZABETH PROCTOR
ABIGAIL WILLIAMS	FRANCIS NURSE
SUSANNA WALCOTT	EZEKIEL CHEEVER
MRS. ANN PUTNAM	MARSHAL HERRICK
THOMAS PUTNAM	JUDGE HATHORNE
MERCY LEWIS	DEPUTY
MARY WARREN	GOVERNOR DANFORTH
JOHN PROCTOR	SARAH GOOD
REBECCA NURSE	HOPKINS

A NOTE ON THE HISTORICAL
ACCURACY OF THIS PLAY

This play is not history in the sense in which the word is used by the academic historian. Dramatic purposes have sometimes required many characters to be fused into one; the number of girls involved in the "crying-out" has been reduced; Abigail's age has been raised; while there were several judges of almost equal authority, I have symbolized them all in Hathorne and Danforth. However, I believe that the reader will discover here the essential nature of one of the strangest and most awful chapters in human history. The fate of each character is exactly that of his historical model, and there is no one in the drama who did not play a similar—and in some cases exactly the same—role in history.

As for the characters of the persons, little is known about most of them excepting what may be surmised from a few letters, the trial record, certain broadsides written at the time, and references to their conduct in sources of varying reliability. They may therefore be taken as creations of my own, drawn to the best of my ability in conformity with their known behavior, except as indicated in the commentary I have written for this text.

ACT ONE
(AN OVERTURE)

A small upper bedroom in the home of REVEREND SAMUEL PARRIS, Salem, Massachusetts, in the spring of the year 1692.

There is a narrow window at the left. Through its leaded panes the morning sunlight streams. A candle still burns near the bed, which is at the right. A chest, a chair, and a small table are the other furnishings. At the back a door opens on the landing of the stairway to the ground floor. The room gives off an air of clean spareness. The roof rafters are exposed, and the wood colors are raw and unmellowed.

As the curtain rises, REVEREND PARRIS is discovered kneeling beside the bed, evidently in prayer. His daughter, BETTY PARRIS, aged ten, is lying on the bed, inert.

At the time of these events Parris was in his middle forties. In history he cut a villainous path, and there is very little good to be said for him. He believed he was being persecuted wherever he went, despite his best efforts to win people and God to his side. In meeting, he felt insulted if someone rose to shut the door without first asking his permission. He was a widower with no interest in children, or talent with them. He regarded them as young adults, and until this strange crisis he, like the rest of Salem, never conceived that the children were anything but thankful for being permitted to walk straight, eyes slightly lowered, arms at the sides, and mouths shut until bidden to speak.

His house stood in the "town"—but we today would hardly call it a village. The meeting house was nearby, and from this point outward—toward the bay or inland—there were a few small-windowed, dark houses snuggling against the raw Massachusetts winter. Salem had been established hardly forty years before. To the European world the whole province was a barbaric frontier inhabited by a sect of fanatics who, nevertheless, were shipping out products of slowly increasing quantity and value.

No one can really know what their lives were like. They had no novelists—and would not have permitted anyone to read a novel if one were handy. Their creed forbade anything resembling a theater or "vain enjoyment." They did not celebrate Christmas, and a holiday from work meant only that they must concentrate even more upon prayer.

Which is not to say that nothing broke into this strict and somber way of life. When a new farmhouse was built, friends assembled to "raise the roof," and there would be special foods cooked and probably some potent cider passed around. There was a good supply of ne'er-do-wells in Salem, who dallied at the shovelboard in Bridget Bishop's tavern. Probably more than the creed, hard work kept the morals of the place from spoiling, for the people were forced to fight the land like heroes for every grain of corn, and no man had very much time for fooling around.

That there were some jokers, however, is indicated by the practice of appointing a two-man patrol whose duty was to "walk forth in the time of God's worship to take notice of such as either lye about the meeting house, without attending to the word and ordinances, or that lye at home or in the fields without giving good account thereof, and to take the names of such persons, and to present them to the magistrates, whereby they may be accordingly proceeded against." This predilection for minding other people's business was time-honored among the people of Salem, and it undoubtedly created many of the suspicions which were to feed the coming madness. It was also, in my opinion, one of the things that a John Proctor would rebel against, for the time of the armed camp had almost passed, and since the country was reasonably—although not wholly—safe, the old disciplines were beginning to rankle. But, as in all such matters, the issue was not clearcut, for danger was still a possibility, and in unity still lay the best promise of safety.

The edge of the wilderness was close by. The American continent stretched endlessly west, and it was full of mystery for them. It stood, dark and threatening, over their shoulders night and day, for out of it Indian tribes marauded from time to time, and Reverend Parris had parishioners who had lost relatives to these heathen.

The parochial snobbery of these people was partly responsible for their failure to convert the Indians. Probably they also preferred to take land from heathens rather than from fellow Christians. At any rate, very few Indians were converted, and the Salem folk believed that the virgin forest was the Devil's last preserve, his home base and the citadel of his final stand. To the best of their knowledge the American forest was the last place on earth that was not paying homage to God.

For these reasons, among others, they carried about an air of innate resistance, even of persecution. Their fathers had, of course, been persecuted in England. So now they and their church found it necessary to deny any other sect its freedom, lest their New Jerusalem be defiled and corrupted by wrong ways and deceitful ideas.

They believed, in short, that they held in their steady hands the candle that would light the world. We have inherited this belief, and it has helped and hurt us. It helped them with the discipline it gave them. They were a dedicated folk, by and large, and they had to be to survive the life they had chosen or been born into in this country.

The proof of their belief's value to them may be taken from the opposite character of the first Jamestown settlement, farther south, in Virginia. The Englishmen who landed there were motivated mainly by a hunt for profit. They had thought to pick off the wealth of the new country and then return rich to England. They were a band of individualists, and a much more ingratiating group than the Massachusetts men. But Virginia destroyed them. Massachusetts tried to kill off the Puritans, but they combined; they set up a communal society which, in the beginning, was little more than an armed camp with an autocratic and very devoted leadership. It was, however, an autocracy by consent, for they were united from top to bottom by a commonly held ideology whose perpetuation was the reason and justification for all their sufferings. So their self-denial, their purposefulness, their suspicion of all vain pursuits, their hard-handed justice, were altogether perfect instruments for the conquest of this space so antagonistic to man.

But the people of Salem in 1692 were not quite the dedicated folk that arrived on the *Mayflower*. A vast differentiation had taken place, and in their own time a revolution had unseated the royal government and substituted a junta which was at this moment in power. The times, to their eyes, must have been out of joint, and to the common folk must have seemed as insoluble and complicated as do ours today. It is not hard to see how easily many could have been led to believe that the time of confusion had been brought upon them by deep and darkling forces. No hint of such speculation appears on the court record, but social disorder in any age breeds such mystical suspicions, and when, as in Salem, wonders are brought forth from below the social surface, it is too much to expect people to hold back very long from laying on the victims with all the force of their frustrations.

The Salem tragedy, which is about to begin in these pages, developed from a paradox. It is a paradox in whose grip we still live, and there is no prospect yet that we will discover its resolution. Simply, it was this: for good purposes, even high purposes, the people of Salem developed a theocracy, a combine of state and religious power whose function was to keep the community together, and to prevent any kind of disunity that might open it to destruction by material or ideological enemies. It was forged for a necessary purpose and accomplished that purpose. But all organization is and must be grounded on the idea of exclusion and prohibition, just as two objects cannot occupy the same space. Evidently the time came in New England when the repressions of order were heavier than seemed warranted by the dangers against which the order was organized. The witch-hunt was a perverse manifestation of the panic which set in among all classes when the balance began to turn toward greater individual freedom.

When one rises above the individual villainy displayed, one can only pity them all, just as we shall be pitied someday. It is still impossible for man to organize his social life without repressions, and the balance has yet to be struck between order and freedom.

The witch-hunt was not, however, a mere repression. It was also, and as importantly, a long overdue opportunity for everyone so inclined to express publicly his guilt and sins, under the cover of accusations against the victims. It suddenly became possible—and patriotic and holy—for a man to say that Martha Corey had come into his bedroom at night, and that, while his wife was sleeping at his side, Martha laid herself down on his chest and "nearly suffocated him." Of course it was her spirit only, but his satisfaction at confessing himself was no lighter than if it had been Martha herself. One could not ordinarily speak such things in public.

Long-held hatreds of neighbors could now be openly expressed, and vengeance taken, despite the Bible's charitable injunctions. Land-lust which had been expressed before by constant bickering over boundaries and deeds, could now be elevated to the arena of morality; one could cry witch against one's neighbor and feel perfectly justified in the bargain. Old scores could be settled on a plane of heavenly combat between Lucifer and the Lord; suspicions and the envy of the miserable toward the happy could and did burst out in the general revenge.

REVEREND PARRIS *is praying now, and, though we cannot hear his words, a sense of his confusion hangs about him. He mumbles, then seems about to weep; then he weeps, then prays again; but his daughter does not stir on the bed.*

The door opens, and his Negro slave enters. TITUBA *is in her forties.* PARRIS *brought her with him from Barbados, where he spent some years as a merchant before entering the ministry. She enters as one does who can no longer bear to be barred from the sight of her beloved, but she is also very frightened because her slave sense has warned her that, as always, trouble in this house eventually lands on her back.*

TITUBA (*already taking a step backward*): My Betty be hearty soon?

PARRIS: Out of here!

TITUBA (*backing to the door*): My Betty not goin' die . . .

PARRIS (*scrambling to his feet in a fury*): Out of my sight! (*She is gone.*) Out of my— (*He is overcome with sobs. He clamps his teeth against them and closes the door and leans against it, exhausted.*) Oh, my God! God help me! (*Quaking with fear, mumbling to himself through his sobs, he goes to the bed and gently takes* BETTY'*s hand.*) Betty. Child. Dear child. Will you wake, will you open up your eyes! Betty, little one . . .

(*He is bending to kneel again when his niece,* ABIGAIL WILLIAMS, *seventeen, enters— a strikingly beautiful girl, an orphan, with an endless capacity for dissembling. Now she is all worry and apprehension and propriety.*)

ABIGAIL: Uncle? (*He looks to her.*) Susanna Walcott's here from Doctor Griggs.

PARRIS: Oh? Let her come, let her come.

ABIGAIL (*leaning out the door to call to* SUSANNA, *who is down the hall a few steps*): Come in, Susanna.

(SUSANNA WALCOTT, *a little younger than* ABIGAIL, *a nervous, hurried girl, enters.*)

PARRIS (*eagerly*): What does the doctor say, child?

SUSANNA (*craning around* PARRIS *to get a look at* BETTY): He bid me come and tell you, reverend sir, that he cannot discover no medicine for it in his books.

PARRIS: Then he must search on.

SUSANNA: Aye, sir, he have been searchin' his books since he left you, sir. But he bid me tell you, that you might look to unnatural things for the cause of it.

PARRIS (*his eyes going wide*): No—no. There be no unnatural cause here. Tell him I have sent for Reverend Hale of Beverly, and Mr. Hale will surely confirm that. Let him look to medicine and put out all thought of unnatural causes here. There be none.

SUSANNA: Aye, sir. He bid me tell you. (*She turns to go.*)

ABIGAIL: Speak nothin' of it in the village, Susanna.

PARRIS: Go directly home and speak nothing of unnatural causes.

SUSANNA: Aye, sir. I pray for her. (*She goes out.*)

ABIGAIL: Uncle, the rumor of witchcraft is all about; I think you'd best go down and deny it yourself. The parlor's packed with people, sir. I'll sit with her.

PARRIS (*pressed, turns on her*): And what shall I say to them? That my daughter and my niece I discovered dancing like heathen in the forest?

ABIGAIL: Uncle, we did dance; let you tell them I confessed it—and I'll be whipped if I must be. But they're speakin' of witchcraft. Betty's not witched.

PARRIS: Abigail, I cannot go before the congregation when I know you have not opened with me. What did you do with her in the forest?

ABIGAIL: We did dance, uncle, and when you leaped out of the bush so suddenly, Betty was frightened and then she fainted. And there's the whole of it.

PARRIS: Child. Sit you down.

ABIGAIL (*quavering, as she sits*): I would never hurt Betty. I love her dearly.

PARRIS: Now look you, child, your punishment will come in its time. But if you trafficked with spirits in the forest I must know it now, for surely my enemies will, and they will ruin me with it.

ABIGAIL: But we never conjured spirits.

PARRIS: Then why can she not move herself since midnight? This child is desperate! (ABIGAIL *lowers her eyes.*) It must come out—my enemies will bring it out. Let me know what you done there. Abigail, do you understand that I have many enemies?

ABIGAIL: I have heard of it, uncle.

PARRIS: There is a faction that is sworn to drive me from my pulpit. Do you understand that?

ABIGAIL: I think so, sir.

PARRIS: Now then, in the midst of such disruption, my own household is discovered to be the very center of some obscene practice. Abominations are done in the forest—

ABIGAIL: It were sport, uncle!

PARRIS (*pointing at* BETTY): You call this sport? (*She lowers her eyes. He pleads.*) Abigail, if you know something that may help the doctor, for God's sake tell it to me. (*She is silent.*) I saw Tituba waving her arms over the fire when I came on you. Why was she doing that? And I heard a screeching and gibberish coming from her mouth. She were swaying like a dumb beast over that fire!

ABIGAIL: She always sings her Barbados songs, and we dance.

PARRIS: I cannot blink what I saw, Abigail, for my enemies will not blink it. I saw a dress lying on the grass.

ABIGAIL (innocently): A dress?

PARRIS (It is very hard to say.) Aye, a dress. And I thought I saw—someone naked running through the trees!

ABIGAIL (in terror): No one was naked! You mistake yourself, uncle!

PARRIS (with anger): I saw it! (He moves from her. Then, resolved.) Now tell me true, Abigail. And I pray you feel the weight of truth upon you, for now my ministry's at stake, my ministry and perhaps your cousin's life. Whatever abomination you have done, give me all of it now, for I dare not be taken unaware when I go before them down there.

ABIGAIL: There is nothin' more. I swear it, uncle.

PARRIS (studies her, then nods, half convinced): Abigail, I have fought here three long years to bend these stiff-necked people to me, and now, just now when some good respect is rising for me in the parish, you compromise my very character. I have given you a home, child, I have put clothes upon your back—now give me upright answer. Your name in the town—it is entirely white, is it not?

ABIGAIL (with an edge of resentment): Why, I am sure it is, sir. There be no blush about my name.

PARRIS (to the point): Abigail, is there any other cause than you have told me, for your being discharged from Goody Proctor's service? I have heard it said, and I tell you as I heard it, that she comes so rarely to the church this year for she will not sit so close to something soiled. What signified that remark?

ABIGAIL: She hates me, uncle, she must, for I would not be her slave. It's a bitter woman, a lying, cold, sniveling woman, and I will not work for such a woman!

PARRIS: She may be. And yet it has troubled me that you are now seven month out of their house, and in all this time no other family has ever called for your service.

ABIGAIL: They want slaves, not such as I. Let them send to Barbados for that. I will not black my face for any of them! (With ill-concealed resentment at him) Do you begrudge my bed, uncle?

PARRIS: No—no.

ABIGAIL (in a temper): My name is good in the village! I will not have it said my name is soiled! Goody Proctor is a gossiping liar!

(Enter MRS. ANN PUTNAM. She is a twisted soul of forty-five, a death-ridden woman, haunted by dreams.)

PARRIS (as soon as the door begins to open): No—no, I cannot have anyone. (He sees her, and a certain deference springs into him, although his worry remains.) Why, Goody Putnam, come in.

MRS. PUTNAM (full of breath, shiny-eyed): It is a marvel. It is surely a stroke of hell upon you.

PARRIS: No, Goody Putnam, it is—

MRS. PUTNAM (glancing at BETTY): How high did she fly, how high?

PARRIS: No, no, she never flew—

MRS. PUTNAM (very pleased with it): Why, it's sure she did. Mr. Collins saw her goin' over Ingersoll's barn, and come down light as a bird, he says!

PARRIS: Now, look you, Goody Putnam, she never—(Enter THOMAS PUTNAM, a well-to-do, hard-handed landowner, near fifty.) Oh, good morning, Mr. Putnam.

PUTNAM: It is a providence the thing is out now! It is a providence. (He goes directly to the bed.)

PARRIS: What's out, sir, what's—?

(MRS. PUTNAM goes to the bed.)

PUTNAM (looking down at Betty): Why, her eyes is closed! Look you, Ann.

MRS. PUTNAM: Why, that's strange. (To Parris) Ours is open.

PARRIS (shocked): Your Ruth is sick?

MRS. PUTNAM (with vicious certainty): I'd not call it sick; the Devil's touch is heavier than sick. It's death, y'know, it's death drivin' into them, forked and hoofed.

PARRIS: Oh, pray not! Why, how does Ruth ail?

MRS. PUTNAM: She ails as she must—she never waked this morning, but her eyes open and she walks, and hears naught, sees naught, and cannot eat. Her soul is taken, surely.

(PARRIS *is struck.*)

PUTNAM (*as though for further details*): They say you've sent for Reverend Hale of Beverly?

PARRIS (*with dwindling conviction now*): A precaution only. He has much experience in all demonic arts, and I—

MRS. PUTNAM: He has indeed; and found a witch in Beverly last year, and let you remember that.

PARRIS: Now, Goody Ann, they only thought that were a witch, and I am certain there be no element of witchcraft here.

PUTNAM: No witchcraft! Now look you, Mr. Parris—

PARRIS: Thomas, Thomas, I pray you, leap not to witchcraft. I know that you—you least of all, Thomas, would ever wish so disastrous a charge laid upon me. We cannot leap to witchcraft. They will howl me out of Salem for such corruption in my house.

A word about Thomas Putnam. He was a man with many grievances, at least one of which appears justified. Some time before, his wife's brother-in-law, James Bayley, had been turned down as minister at Salem. Bayley had all the qualifications, and a two-thirds vote into the bargain, but a faction stopped his acceptance, for reasons that are not clear.

Thomas Putnam was the eldest son of the richest man in the village. He had fought the Indians at Narragansett, and was deeply interested in parish affairs. He undoubtedly felt it poor payment that the village should so blatantly disregard his candidate for one of its more important offices, especially since he regarded himself as the intellectual superior of most of the people around him.

His vindictive nature was demonstrated long before the witchcraft began. Another former Salem minister, George Burroughs, had had to borrow money to pay for his wife's funeral, and, since the parish was remiss in his salary, he was soon bankrupt. Thomas and his brother John had Burroughs jailed for debts the man did not owe. The incident is important only in that Burroughs succeeded in becoming minister where Bayley, Thomas Putnam's brother-in-law, had been rejected; the motif of resentment is clear here. Thomas Putnam felt that his own name and the honor of his family had been smirched by the village, and he meant to right matters however he could.

Another reason to believe him a deeply embittered man was his attempt to break his father's will, which left a disproportionate amount to a stepbrother. As with every other public cause in which he tried to force his way, he failed in this.

So it is not surprising to find that so many accusations against people are in the handwriting of Thomas Putnam, or that his name is so often found as a witness corroborating the supernatural testimony, or that his daughter led the crying-out at the most opportune junctures of the trials, especially when—But we'll speak of that when we come to it.

PUTNAM (*At the moment he is intent upon getting* PARRIS, *for whom he has only contempt, to move toward the abyss.*) Mr. Parris, I have taken your part in all contention here, and I would continue; but I cannot if you hold back in this. There are hurtful, vengeful spirits layin' hands on these children.

PARRIS: But, Thomas, you cannot—

PUTNAM: Ann! Tell Mr. Parris what you have done.

MRS. PUTNAM: Reverend Parris, I have laid seven babies unbaptized in the earth. Believe me, sir, you never saw more hearty babies born. And yet, each would wither in my arms the very night of their birth. I have spoke nothin', but my heart has clamored intimations. And now, this year, my Ruth, my only— I see her turning strange. A secret child she has become this year, and shrivels like a sucking mouth were pullin' on her life too. And so I thought to send her to your Tituba—

PARRIS: To Tituba! What may Tituba—?

MRS. PUTNAM: Tituba knows how to speak to the dead, Mr. Parris.

PARRIS: Goody Ann, it is a formidable sin to conjure up the dead!

MRS. PUTNAM: I take it on my soul, but who else may surely tell us what person murdered my babies?

PARRIS (horrified): Woman!

MRS. PUTNAM: They were murdered, Mr. Parris! And mark this proof! Mark it! Last night my Ruth were ever so close to their little spirits; I know it, sir. For how else is she struck dumb now except some power of darkness would stop her mouth? It is a marvelous sign, Mr. Parris!

PUTNAM: Don't you understand it, sir? There is a murdering witch among us, bound to keep herself in the dark. (PARRIS turns to BETTY, a frantic terror rising in him.) Let your names make of it what they will, you cannot blink it more.

PARRIS (to ABIGAIL): Then you were conjuring spirits last night.

ABIGAIL (whispering): Not I, sir—Tituba and Ruth.

PARRIS (turns now, with new fear, and goes to BETTY, looks down at her, and then, gazing off): Oh, Abigail, what proper payment for my charity! Now I am undone.

PUTNAM: You are not undone! Let you take hold here. Wait for no one to charge you—declare it yourself. You have discovered witchcraft—

PARRIS: In my house? In my house, Thomas? They will topple me with this! They will make of it a—

(Enter MERCY LEWIS, the PUTNAMS' servant, a fat, sly, merciless girl of eighteen.)

MERCY: Your pardons. I only thought to see how Betty is.

PUTNAM: Why aren't you home? Who's with Ruth?

MERCY: Her grandma come. She's improved a little, I think—she give a powerful sneeze before.

MRS. PUTNAM: Ah, there's a sign of life!

MERCY: I'd fear no more, Goody Putnam. It were a grand sneeze; another like it will shake her wits together, I'm sure. (She goes to the bed to look.)

PARRIS: Will you leave me now, Thomas? I would pray a while alone.

ABIGAIL: Uncle, you've prayed since midnight. Why do you not go down and—

PARRIS: No—no. (To PUTNAM) I have no answer for that crowd. I'll wait till Mr. Hale arrives. (To get MRS. PUTNAM to leave) If you will, Goody Ann . . .

PUTNAM: Now look you, sir. Let you strike out against the Devil, and the village will bless you for it! Come down, speak to them—pray with them. They're thirsting for your word, Mister! Surely you'll pray with them.

PARRIS (swayed): I'll lead them in a psalm, but let you say nothing of witchcraft yet. I will not discuss it. The cause is yet unknown. I have had enough contention since I came; I want no more.

MRS. PUTNAM: Mercy, you go home to Ruth, d'y'hear?

MERCY: Aye, mum.

(MRS. PUTNAM goes out.)

PARRIS (to ABIGAIL): If she starts for the window, cry for me at once.

ABIGAIL: I will, uncle.

PARRIS (to PUTNAM): There is a terrible power in her arms today. (He goes out with PUTNAM.)

ABIGAIL (with hushed trepidation): How is Ruth sick?

MERCY: It's weirdish, I know not—she seems to walk like a dead one since last night.

ABIGAIL (turns at once and goes to BETTY, and now, with fear in her voice): Betty? (BETTY doesn't move. She shakes her.) Now stop this! Betty! Sit up now!

(BETTY doesn't stir. MERCY comes over.)

MERCY: Have you tried beatin' her? I gave Ruth a good one and it waked her for a minute. Here, let me have her.

ABIGAIL (holding MERCY back): No, he'll be comin' up. Listen, now; if they be questioning us, tell them we danced—I told him as much already.

MERCY: Aye. And what more?

ABIGAIL: He knows Tituba conjured Ruth's sisters to come out of the grave.

MERCY: And what more?

ABIGAIL: He saw you naked.

MERCY (clapping her hands together with a frightened laugh): Oh, Jesus!

(Enter MARY WARREN, breathless. She is seventeen, a subservient, naive, lonely girl.)

MARY WARREN: What'll we do? The village

is out! I just come from the farm; the whole country's talkin' witchcraft! They'll be callin' us witches, Abby!

MERCY (*pointing and looking at* MARY WARREN): She means to tell, I know it.

MARY WARREN: Abby, we've got to tell. Witchery's a hangin' error, a hangin' like they done in Boston two year ago! We must tell the truth, Abby! You'll only be whipped for dancin', and the other things!

ABIGAIL: Oh, *we'll* be whipped!

MARY WARREN: I never done none of it, Abby. I only looked!

MERCY (*moving menacingly toward* MARY): Oh, you're a great one for lookin', aren't you, Mary Warren? What a grand peeping courage you have!

(BETTY, *on the bed, whimpers.* ABIGAIL *turns to her at once.*)

ABIGAIL: Betty? (*She goes to* BETTY.) Now, Betty, dear, wake up now. It's Abigail. (*She sits* BETTY *up and furiously shakes her.*) I'll beat you, Betty! (BETTY *whimpers.*) My, you seem improving. I talked to your papa and I told him everything. So there's nothing to—

BETTY (*darts off the bed, frightened of* ABIGAIL, *and flattens herself against the wall*): I want my mama!

ABIGAIL (*with alarm, as she cautiously approaches* BETTY): What ails you, Betty? Your mama's dead and buried.

BETTY: I'll fly to Mama. Let me fly! (*She raises her arms as though to fly, and streaks for the window, gets one leg out.*)

ABIGAIL (*pulling her away from the window*): I told him everything; he knows now, he knows everything we—

BETTY: You drank blood, Abby! You didn't tell him that!

ABIGAIL: Betty, you never say that again! You will never—

BETTY: You did, you did! You drank a charm to kill John Proctor's wife! You drank a charm to kill Goody Proctor!

ABIGAIL (*smashes her across the face*): Shut it! Now shut it!

BETTY (*collapsing on the bed*): Mama, Mama! (*She dissolves into sobs.*)

ABIGAIL: Now look you. All of you. We danced. And Tituba conjured Ruth Putnam's dead sisters. And that is all. And mark this. Let either of you breathe a word, or the edge of a word, about the other things, and I will come to you in the black of some terrible night and I will bring a pointy reckoning that will shudder you. And you know I can do it; I saw Indians smash my dear parents' heads on the pillow next to mine, and I have seen some reddish work done at night, and I can make you wish you had never seen the sun go down! (*She goes to* BETTY *and roughly sits her up.*) Now, you—sit up and stop this!

(*But* BETTY *collapses in her hands and lies inert on the bed.*)

MARY WARREN (*with hysterical fright*): What's got her? (ABIGAIL *stares in fright at* BETTY.) Abby, she's going to die! It's a sin to conjure, and we—

ABIGAIL (*starting for* MARY): I say shut it, Mary Warren!

(*Enter* JOHN PROCTOR. *On seeing him,* MARY WARREN *leaps in fright.*)

Proctor was a farmer in his middle thirties. He need not have been a partisan of any faction in the town, but there is evidence to suggest that he had a sharp and biting way with hypocrites. He was the kind of man—powerful of body, even-tempered, and not easily led—who cannot refuse support to partisans without drawing their deepest resentment. In Proctor's presence a fool felt his foolishness instantly—and a Proctor is always marked for calumny therefore.

But as we shall see, the steady manner he displays does not spring from an untroubled soul. He is a sinner, a sinner not only against the moral fashion of the time, but against his own vision of decent conduct. These people had no ritual for the washing away of sins. It is another trait we inherited from them, and it has helped to discipline us as well as to breed hypocrisy among us. Proctor, respected and even feared in Salem, has come to regard himself as a kind of fraud. But no hint of this has yet appeared on the surface, and as he enters from the crowded parlor below it is a

man in his prime we see, with a quiet confidence and an unexpressed, hidden force.
Mary Warren, his servant, can barely speak
for embarrassment and fear.

MARY WARREN: Oh! I'm just going home,
Mr. Proctor.

PROCTOR: Be you foolish, Mary Warren? Be
you deaf? I forbid you leave the house, did
I not? Why shall I pay you? I am looking for
you more often than my cows!

MARY WARREN: I only come to see the great
doings in the world.

PROCTOR: I'll show you a great doin' on your
arse one of these days. Now get you home;
my wife is waitin' with your work! (*Trying to
retain a shred of dignity, she goes slowly out.*)

MERCY LEWIS (*both afraid of him and
strangely titillated*): I'd best be off. I have my
Ruth to watch. Good morning, Mr. Proctor.

(MERCY *sidles out. Since* PROCTOR's *entrance,*
ABIGAIL *has stood as though on tiptoe, absorbing his presence, wide-eyed. He glances at her
then goes to* BETTY *on the bed.*)

ABIGAIL: Gad. I'd almost forgot how strong
you are, John Proctor!

PROCTOR (*looking at* ABIGAIL *now, the faintest suggestion of a knowing smile on his face*):
What's this mischief here?

ABIGAIL (*with a nervous laugh*): Oh, she's
only gone silly somehow.

PROCTOR: The road past my house is a
pilgrimage to Salem all morning. The town's
mumbling witchcraft.

ABIGAIL: Oh, posh! (*Winningly she comes
a little closer, with a confidential, wicked air.*)
We were dancin' in the woods last night, and
my uncle leaped in on us. She took fright, is
all.

PROCTOR (*his smile widening*): Ah, you're
wicked yet, aren't y'! (*A thrill of expectant
laughter escapes her, and she dares come
closer, feverishly looking into his eyes.*) You'll
be clapped in the stocks before you're twenty.

(*He takes a step to go, and she springs into
his path.*)

ABIGAIL: Give me a word, John. A soft word.
(*Her concentrated desire destroys his smile.*)

PROCTOR: No, no, Abby. That's done with.

ABIGAIL (*tauntingly*): You come five mile to
see a silly girl fly? I know you better.

PROCTOR (*setting her firmly out of his path*):
I come to see what mischief your uncle's
brewin' now. (*With final emphasis*) Put it out
of mind, Abby.

ABIGAIL (*grasping his hand before he can
release her*): John—I am waitin' for you every
night.

PROCTOR: Abby, I never give you hope to
wait for me.

ABIGAIL (*now beginning to anger—she can't
believe it*): I have something better than hope,
I think!

PROCTOR: Abby, you'll put it out of mind.
I'll not be comin' for you more.

ABIGAIL: You're surely sportin' with me.

PROCTOR: You know me better.

ABIGAIL: I know how you clutched my back
behind your house and sweated like a stallion
whenever I come near! Or did I dream that?
It's she put me out, you cannot pretend it were
you. I saw your face when she put me out, and
you loved me then and you do now!

PROCTOR: Abby, that's a wild thing to say—

ABIGAIL: A wild thing may say wild things.
But not so wild, I think. I have seen you since
she put me out; I have seen you nights.

PROCTOR: I have hardly stepped off my
farm this seven-month.

ABIGAIL: I have a sense for heat, John, and
yours has drawn me to my window, and I have
seen you looking up, burning in your loneliness. Do you tell me you've never looked up
at my window?

PROCTOR: I may have looked up.

ABIGAIL (*now softening*): And you must.
You are no wintry man. I know you, John. I
know you. (*She is weeping.*) I cannot sleep
for dreamin'; I cannot dream but I wake and
walk about the house as though I'd find you
comin' through some door. (*She clutches him
desperately.*)

PROCTOR (*gently pressing her from him, with
great sympathy but firmly*): Child—

ABIGAIL (*with a flash of anger*): How do
you call me child!

PROCTOR: Abby, I may think of you softly
from time to time. But I will cut off my hand

before I'll ever reach for you again. Wipe it out of mind. We never touched, Abby.

ABIGAIL: Aye, but we did.

PROCTOR: Aye, but we did not.

ABIGAIL (*with a bitter anger*): Oh, I marvel how such a strong man may let such a sickly wife be—

PROCTOR (*angered—at himself as well*): You'll speak nothin' of Elizabeth!

ABIGAIL: She is blackening my name in the village! She is telling lies about me! She is a cold, sniveling woman, and you bend to her! Let her turn you like a—

PROCTOR (*shaking her*): Do you look for whippin'?

(*A psalm is heard being sung below.*)

ABIGAIL (*in tears*): I look for John Proctor that took me from my sleep and put knowledge in my heart! I never knew what pretense Salem was, I never knew the lying lessons I was taught by all these Christian women and their covenanted men! And now you bid me tear the light out of my eyes? I will not, I cannot! You loved me, John Proctor, and whatever sin it is, you love me yet! (*He turns abruptly to go out. She rushes to him.*) John, pity me, pity me!

(*The words "going up to Jesus" are heard in the psalm, and* BETTY *claps her ears suddenly and whines loudly.*)

ABIGAIL: Betty? (*She hurries to* BETTY, *who is now sitting up and screaming.* PROCTOR *goes to* BETTY *as* ABIGAIL *is trying to pull her hands down, calling "Betty!"*)

PROCTOR (*growing unnerved*): What's she doing? Girl, what ails you? Stop that wailing!

(*The singing has stopped in the midst of this, and now* PARRIS *rushes in.*)

PARRIS: What happened? What are you doing to her? Betty! (*He rushes to the bed, crying, "Betty, Betty!"* MRS. PUTNAM *enters, feverish with curiosity, and with her* THOMAS PUTNAM *and* MERCY LEWIS. PARRIS, *at the bed, keeps lightly slapping* BETTY's *face, while she moans and tries to get up.*)

ABIGAIL: She heard you singin' and suddenly she's up and screamin'.

MRS. PUTNAM: The psalm! The psalm! She cannot bear to hear the Lord's name!

PARRIS: No, God forbid. Mercy, run to the doctor! Tell him what's happened here! (MERCY LEWIS *rushes out.*)

MRS. PUTNAM: Mark it for a sign, mark it!

(REBECCA NURSE, *seventy-two, enters. She is white-haired, leaning upon her walking-stick.*)

PUTNAM (*pointing at the whimpering* BETTY): That is a notorious sign of witchcraft afoot, Goody Nurse, a prodigious sign!

MRS. PUTNAM: My mother told me that! When they cannot bear to hear the name of—

PARRIS (*trembling*): Rebecca, Rebecca, go to her, we're lost. She suddenly cannot bear to hear the Lord's—

(GILES COREY, *eighty-three, enters. He is knotted with muscle, canny, inquisitive, and still powerful.*)

REBECCA: There is hard sickness here, Giles Cory, so please to keep the quiet.

GILES: I've not said a word. No one here can testify I've said a word. Is she going to fly again? I hear she flies.

PUTNAM: Man, be quiet now!

(*Everything is quiet.* REBECCA *walks across the room to the bed. Gentleness exudes from her.* BETTY *is quietly whimpering, eyes shut.* REBECCA *simply stands over the child, who gradually quiets.*)

And while they are so absorbed, we may put a word in for Rebecca. Rebecca was the wife of Francis Nurse, who, from all accounts, was one of those men for whom both sides of the argument had to have respect. He was called upon to arbitrate disputes as thought he were an unofficial judge, and Rebecca also enjoyed the high opinion most people had for him. By the time of the delusion, they had three hundred acres, and their children were settled in separate homesteads within the same estate. However, Francis had originally rented the land, and one theory has it that, as he gradually paid for it and raised his social status, there were those who resented his rise.

Another suggestion to explain the systematic campaign against Rebecca, and inferentially against Francis, is the land war he fought with his neighbors, one of whom was a Putnam. This squabble grew to the proportions of a battle in the woods between partisans of both sides, and it is said to have lasted for two days. As for Rebecca herself, the general opinion of her character was so high that to explain how anyone dared cry her out for a witch—and more, how adults could bring themselves to lay hands on her—we must look to the fields and boundaries of that time.

As we have seen, Thomas Putnam's man for the Salem ministry was Bayley. The Nurse clan had been in the faction that prevented Bayley's taking office. In addition, certain families allied to the Nurses by blood or friendship, and whose farms were contiguous with the Nurse farm or close to it, combined to break away from the Salem town authority and set up Topsfield, a new and independent entity whose existence was resented by old Salemites.

That the guiding hand behind the outcry was Putnam's is indicated by the fact that, as soon as it began, this Topsfield-Nurse faction absented themselves from church in protest and disbelief. It was Edward and Jonathan Putnam who signed the first complaint against Rebecca; and Thomas Putnam's little daughter was the one who fell into a fit at the hearing and pointed to Rebecca as her attacker. To top it all, Mrs. Putnam—who is now staring at the bewitched child on the bed—soon accused Rebecca's spirit of "tempting her to iniquity," a charge that had more truth in it than Mrs. Putnam could know.

MRS. PUTNAM (astonished): What have you done?

(REBECCA, in thought, now leaves the bedside and sits.)

PARRIS (wondrous and relieved): What do you make of it, Rebecca?

PUTNAM (eagerly): Goody Nurse, will you go to my Ruth and see if you can wake her?

REBECCA (sitting): I think she'll wake in time. Pray calm yourselves. I have eleven children, and I am twenty-six times a grandma, and I have seen them all through their silly seasons, and when it comes on them they will run the Devil bowlegged keeping up with their mischief. I think she'll wake when she tires of it. A child's spirit is like a child, you can never catch it by running after it; you must stand

still, and, for love, it will soon itself come back.

PROCTOR: Aye, that's the truth of it, Rebecca.

MRS. PUTNAM: This is no silly season, Rebecca. My Ruth is bewildered, Rebecca; she cannot eat.

REBECCA: Perhaps she is not hungered yet. (To PARRIS) I hope you are not decided to go in search of loose spirits, Mr. Parris. I've heard promise of that outside.

PARRIS: A wide opinion's running in the parish that the Devil may be among us, and I would satisfy them that they are wrong.

PROCTOR: Then let you come out and call them wrong. Did you consult the wardens before you called this minister to look for devils?

PARRIS: He is not coming to look for devils!

PROCTOR: Then what's he coming for?

PUTNAM: There be children dyin' in the village, Mister!

PROCTOR: I see none dyin'. This society will not be a bag to swing around your head, Mr. Putnam. (To PARRIS.) Did you call a meeting before you—?

PUTNAM: I am sick of meetings; cannot the man turn his head without he have a meeting?

PROCTOR: He may turn his head, but not to Hell!

REBECCA: Pray, John, be calm. (Pause. He defers to her.) Mr. Parris, I think you'd best send Reverend Hale back as soon as he come. This will set us all to arguin' again in the society, and we thought to have peace this year. I think we ought rely on the doctor now, and good prayer.

MRS. PUTNAM: Rebecca, the doctor's baffled!

REBECCA: If so he is, then let us go to God for the cause of it. There is prodigious danger in the seeking of loose spirits. I fear it, I fear it. Let us rather blame ourselves and—

PUTNAM: How may we blame ourselves? I am one of nine sons; the Putnam seed have peopled this province. And yet I have but one child left of eight—and now she shrivels!

REBECCA: I cannot fathom that.

MRS. PUTNAM (with a growing edge of sarcasm): But I must! You think it God's work you should never lose a child, nor grandchild either, and I bury all but one? There are wheels within wheels in this village, and fires within fires!

PUTNAM (to PARRIS): When Reverend Hale comes, you will proceed to look for signs of witchcraft here.

PROCTOR (to PUTNAM): You cannot command Mr. Parris. We vote by name in this society, not by acreage.

PUTNAM: I never heard you worried so on this society, Mr. Proctor. I do not think I saw you at Sabbath meeting since snow flew.

PROCTOR: I have trouble enough without I come five mile to hear him preach only hellfire and bloody damnation. Take it to heart, Mr. Parris. There are many others who stay away from church these days because you hardly ever mention God any more.

PARRIS (now aroused): Why, that's a drastic charge!

REBECCA: It's somewhat true; there are many that quail to bring their children—

PARRIS: I do not preach for children, Rebecca. It is not the children who are unmindful of their obligations toward this ministry.

REBECCA: Are there really those unmindful?

PARRIS: I should say the better half of Salem village—

PUTNAM: And more than that!

PARRIS: Where is my wood? My contract provides I be supplied with all my firewood. I am waiting since November for a stick, and even in November I had to show my frostbitten hands like some London beggar!

GILES: You are allowed six pound a year to buy your wood, Mr. Parris.

PARRIS: I regard that six pound as part of my salary. I am paid little enough without I spend six pound on firewood.

PROCTOR: Sixty, plus six for firewood—

PARRIS: The salary is sixty-six pound, Mr. Proctor! I am not some preaching farmer with a book under my arm; I am a graduate of Harvard College.

GILES: Aye, and well instructed in arithmetic!

PARRIS: Mr. Corey, you will look far for a man of my kind at sixty pound a year! I am not used to this poverty; I left a thrifty business in the Barbados to serve the Lord. I do not fathom it, why am I persecuted here? I cannot offer one proposition but there be a howling riot of argument. I have often wondered if the Devil be in it somewhere; I cannot understand you people otherwise.

PROCTOR: Mr. Parris, you are the first minister ever did demand the deed to this house—

PARRIS: Man! Don't a minister deserve a house to live in?

PROCTOR: To live in, yes. But to ask ownership is like you shall own the meeting house itself; the last meeting I were at you spoke so long on deeds and mortgages I thought it were an auction.

PARRIS: I want a mark of confidence, is all! I am your third preacher in seven years. I do not wish to be put out like the cat whenever some majority feels the whim. You people seem not to comprehend that a minister is the Lord's man in the parish; a minister is not to be so lightly crossed and contradicted—

PUTNAM: Aye!

PARRIS: There is either obedience or the church will burn like Hell is burning!

PROCTOR: Can you speak one minute without we land in Hell again? I am sick of Hell!

PARRIS: It is not for you to say what is good for you to hear!

PROCTOR: I may speak my heart, I think!

PARRIS (in a fury): What, are we Quakers? We are not Quakers here yet, Mr. Proctor. And you may tell that to your followers!

PROCTOR: My followers!

PARRIS (Now he's out with it.) There is a party in this church. I am not blind; there is a faction and a party.

PROCTOR: Against you?

PUTNAM: Against him and all authority!

PROCTOR: Why, then I must find it and join it.

(There is shock among the others.)

REBECCA: He does not mean that.

PUTNAM: He confessed it now!

PROCTOR: I mean it solemnly, Rebecca; I like not the smell of this "authority."

REBECCA: No, you cannot break charity with your minister. You are another kind, John. Clasp his hand, make your peace.

PROCTOR: I have a crop to sow and lumber

to drag home. *(He goes angrily to the door and turns to* COREY *with a smile.)* What say you, Giles, let's find the party. He says there's a party.

GILES: I've changed my opinion of this man, John. Mr. Parris, I beg your pardon. I never thought you had so much iron in you.

PARRIS *(surprised)*: Why, thank you, Giles!

GILES: It suggests to the mind what the trouble be among us all these years. *(To all)* Think on it. Wherefore is everybody suing everybody else? Think on it now, it's a deep thing, and dark as a pit. I have been six time in court this year—

PROCTOR *(familiarly, with warmth, although he knows he is approaching the edge of* GILE's *tolerance with this)*: Is it the Devil's fault that a man cannot say you good morning without you clap him for defamation? You're old, Giles, and you're not hearin' so well as you did.

GILES *(He cannot be crossed.)* John Proctor, I have only last month collected four pound damages for you publicly sayin' I burned the roof off your house, and I—

PROCTOR *(laughing)*: I never said no such thing, but I've paid you for it, so I hope I can call you deaf without charge. Now come along, Giles, and help me drag my lumber home.

PUTNAM: A moment, Mr. Proctor. What lumber is that you're draggin', if I may ask you?

PROCTOR: My lumber. From out my forest by the riverside.

PUTNAM: Why, we are surely gone wild this year. What anarchy is this? That tract is in my bounds, it's in my bounds, Mr. Proctor.

PROCTOR: In your bounds! *(Indicating* RE-BECCA*)* I bought that tract from Goody Nurse's husband five months ago.

PUTNAM: He had no right to sell it. It stands clear in my grandfather's will that all the land between the river and—

PROCTOR: Your grandfather had a habit of willing land that never belonged to him, if I may say it plain.

GILES: That's God's truth; he nearly willed away my north pasture but he knew I'd break his fingers before he'd set his name to it.

Let's get your lumber home, John. I feel a sudden will to work coming on.

PUTNAM: You load one oak of mine and you'll fight to drag it home!

GILES: Aye, and we'll win too, Putnam—this fool and I. Come on! *(He turns to* PROCTOR *and starts out.)*

PUTNAM: I'll have my men on you, Corey! I'll clap a writ on you!

(Enter REVEREND JOHN HALE *of Beverly.)*

Mr. Hale is nearing forty, a tight-skinned, eager-eyed intellectual. This is a beloved errand for him; on being called here to ascertain witchcraft he felt the pride of the specialist whose unique knowledge has at last been publicly called for. Like almost all men of learning, he spent a good deal of his time pondering the invisible world, especially since he had himself encountered a witch in his parish not long before. That woman, however, turned into a mere pest under his searching scrutiny, and the child she had allegedly been afflicting recovered her normal behavior after Hale had given her his kindness and a few days of rest in his own house. However, that experience never raised a doubt in his mind as to the reality of the underworld or the existence of Lucifer's many-faced lieutenants. And his belief is not to his discredit. Better minds than Hale's were —and still are—convinced that there is a society of spirits beyond our ken. One cannot help noting that one of his lines has never yet raised a laugh in any audience that has seen this play; it is his assurance that "We cannot look to superstition in this. The Devil is precise." Evidently we are not quite certain even now whether diabolism is holy and not to be scoffed at. And it is no accident that we should be so bemused.

Like Reverend Hale and the others on this stage, we conceive the Devil as a necessary part of a respectable view of cosmology. Ours is a divided empire in which certain ideas and emotions and actions are of God, and their opposites are of Lucifer. It is as impossible for most men to conceive of a morality without sin as of an earth without "sky." Since 1692 a great but superficial change has wiped out God's beard and the Devil's horns, but the world is still gripped between two diametrically opposed absolutes. The concept of unity, in which positive and negative are attributes of the same force, in which good and evil are relative, ever-changing, and always joined to the same phenomenon—such a concept is still reserved to the physical sciences and to the few who have grasped the history of ideas. When it is recalled that until the Christian era the underworld was never regarded as a hostile area, that all gods were useful and essentially friendly to man despite occasional lapses; when we see the steady and methodical inculcation into humanity of the idea of man's worthlessness—until redeemed—the necessity of the Devil may become evident as a weapon, a weapon designed and used time and time again in every age to whip men into a surrender to a particular church or church-state.

Our difficulty in believing the—for want of a better word—political inspiration of the Devil is due in great part to the fact that he is called up and damned not only by our social antagonists but by our own side, whatever it may be. The Catholic Church, through its Inquisition, is famous for cultivating Lucifer as the arch-fiend, but the Church's enemies relied no less upon the Old Boy to keep the human mind enthralled. Luther was himself accused of alliance with Hell, and he in turn accused his enemies. To complicate matters further, he believed that he had had contact with the Devil and had argued theology with him. I am not surprised at this, for at my own university a professor of history—a Lutheran, by the way—used to assemble his graduate students, draw the shades, and commune in the classroom with Erasmus. He was never, to my knowledge, officially scoffed at for this, the reason being that the university officials, like most of us, are the children of a history which still sucks at the Devil's teats. At this writing, only England has held back before the temptations of contemporary diabolism. In the countries of the Communist ideology, all resistance of any import is linked to the totally malign capitalist succubi, and in

America any man who is not reactionary in his views is open to the charge of alliance with the Red hell. Political opposition, thereby, is given an inhumane overlay which then justifies the abrogation of all normally applied customs of civilized intercourse. A political policy is equated with moral right, and opposition to it with diabolical malevolence. Once such an equation is effectively made, society becomes a congerie of plots and counterplots, and the main role of government changes from that of the arbiter to that of the scourge of God.

The results of this process are no different now from what they ever were, except sometimes in the degree of cruelty inflicted, and not always even in that department. Normally the actions and deeds of a man were all that society felt comfortable in judging. The secret intent of an action was left to the ministers, priests, and rabbis to deal with. When diabolism rises, however, actions are the least important manifests of the true nature of a man. The Devil, as Reverend Hale said, is a wily one, and until an hour before he fell, even God thought him beautiful in Heaven.

The analogy, however, seems to falter when one considers that, while there were no witches then, there are Communists and capitalists now, and in each camp there is certain proof that spies of each side are at work undermining the other. But this is a snobbish objection and not at all warranted by the facts. I have no doubt that people *were* communing with, and even worshiping, the Devil in Salem, and if the whole truth could be known in this case, as it is in others, we should discover a regular and conventionalized propitiation of the dark spirit. One certain evidence of this is the confession of Tituba, the slave of Reverend Parris, and another is the behavior of the children who were known to have indulged in sorceries with her.

There are accounts of similar *klatches* in Europe, where the daughters of the towns would assemble at night and, sometimes with fetishes, sometimes with a selected young man, give themselves to love, with some bastardly results. The Church, sharp-eyed as it must be when gods long dead are brought to life, condemned these orgies as witchcraft and interpreted them, rightly, as a resurgence of the Dionysiac forces it had crushed long before. Sex, sin, and the Devil were early linked, and so they continued to be in Salem, and are today. From all accounts there are no more puritanical mores in the world than those enforced by the Communists in Russia, where women's fashions, for instance, are as prudent and all-covering as any American Baptist would desire. The divorce laws lay a tremendous responsibility on the father for the care of his children. Even the laxity of divorce regulations in the early years of the revolution was undoubtedly a revulsion from the nineteenth-century Victorian immobility of marriage and the consequent hypocrisy that developed from it. If for no other reasons, a state so powerful, so jealous of the uniformity of its citizens, cannot long tolerate the atomization of the family. And yet, in American eyes at least, there remains the conviction that the Russian attitude toward women is lascivious. It is the Devil working again, just as he is working within the Slav who is shocked at the very idea of a woman's disrobing herself in a burlesque show. Our opposites are always robed in sexual sin, and it is from this unconscious conviction that demonology gains both its attractive sensuality and its capacity to infuriate and frighten.

Coming into Salem now, Reverend Hale conceives of himself much as a young doctor on his first call. His painfully acquired armory of symptoms, catchwords, and diagnostic procedures are now to be put to use at last. The road from Beverly is unusually busy this morning, and he has passed a hundred rumors that make him smile at the ignorance of the yeomanry in this most precise science. He feels himself allied with the best minds of Europe—kings, philosophers, scientists, and ecclesiasts of all churches. His goal is light, goodness and its preservation, and he knows the exaltation of the blessed whose intelligence, sharpened by minute examinations of enormous tracts, is finally called upon to face what may be a bloody fight with the Fiend himself.

(He appears loaded down with half a dozen heavy books.)

HALE: Pray you, someone take these!

PARRIS *(delighted):* Mr. Hale! Oh! it's good to see you again! *(Taking some books)* My, they're heavy!

HALE *(setting down his books):* They must be; they are weighted with authority.

PARRIS *(a little scared):* Well, you do come prepared!

HALE: We shall need hard study if it comes to tracking down the Old Boy. *(Noticing* REBECCA*)* You cannot be Rebecca Nurse?

REBECCA: I am, sir. Do you know me?

HALE: It's strange how I knew you, but I suppose you look as such a good soul should. We have all heard of your great charities in Beverly.

PARRIS: Do you know this gentleman? Mr. Thomas Putnam. And his good wife Ann.

HALE: Putnam! I had not expected such distinguished company, sir.

PUTNAM *(pleased):* It does not seem to help us today, Mr. Hale. We look to you to come to our house and save our child.

HALE: Your child ails too?

MRS. PUTNAM: Her soul, her soul seems flown away. She sleeps and yet she walks . . .

PUTNAM: She cannot eat.

HALE: Cannot eat! *(Thinks on it. Then, to* PROCTOR *and* GILES COREY*)* Do you men have afflicted children?

PARRIS: No, no, these are farmers John Proctor—

GILES COREY: He don't believe in witches.

PROCTOR *(to* HALE*):* I never spoke on witches one way or the other. Will you come, Giles?

GILES: No—no, John, I think not. I have some few queer questions of my own to ask this fellow.

PROCTOR: I've heard you to be a sensible man, Mr. Hale. I hope you'll leave some of it in Salem.

*(*PROCTOR *goes.* HALE *stands embarrassed for an instant.)*

PARRIS *(quickly):* Will you look at my daughter, sir? *(Leads* HALE *to the bed.)* She has tried to leap out the window; we discovered her this morning on the highroad, waving her arms as though she'd fly.

HALE (*narrowing his eyes*): Tries to fly.

PUTNAM: She cannot bear to hear the Lord's name, Mr. Hale; that's a sure sign of witchcraft afloat.

HALE (*holding up his hands*): No, no. Now let me instruct you. We cannot look to superstition in this. The Devil is precise; the marks of his presence are definite as stone, and I must tell you all that I shall not proceed unless you are prepared to believe me if I should find no bruise of hell upon her.

PARRIS: It is agreed, sir—it is agreed—we will abide by your judgment.

HALE: Good then. (*He goes to the bed, looks down at* BETTY. *To* PARRIS) Now, sir, what were your first warning of this strangeness?

PARRIS: Why, sir—I discovered her—(*indicating* ABIGAIL)—and my niece and ten or twelve of the other girls, dancing in the forest last night.

HALE (*surprised*): You permit dancing?

PARRIS: No, no, it were secret—

MRS. PUTNAM (*unable to wait*): Mr. Parris's slave has knowledge of conjurin', sir.

PARRIS (*to* MRS. PUTNAM): We cannot be sure of that, Goody Ann—

MRS. PUTNAM (*frightened, very softly*): I know it, sir. I sent my child—she should learn from Tituba who murdered her sisters.

REBECCA (*horrified*): Goody Ann! You sent a child to conjure up the dead?

MRS. PUTNAM: Let God blame me, not you, not you, Rebecca! I'll not have you judging me any more! (*To* HALE) Is it a natural work to lose seven children before they live a day?

PARRIS: Sssh!

(REBECCA, *with great pain, turns her face away. There is a pause.*)

HALE: Seven dead in childbirth.

MRS. PUTNAM (*softly*): Aye. (*Her voice breaks; she looks up at him. Silence.* HALE *is impressed.* PARRIS *looks to him. He goes to his books, opens one, turns pages, then reads. All wait, avidly.*)

PARRIS (*hushed*): What book is that?

MRS. PUTNAM: What's there, sir?

HALE (*with a tasty love of intellectual pursuit*): Here is all the invisible world, caught, defined, and calculated. In these books the Devil stands stripped of all his brute disguises. Here are all your familiar spirits—your incubi and succubi; your witches that go by land, by air, and by sea; your wizards of the night and of the day. Have no fear now—we shall find him out if he has come among us, and I mean to crush him utterly if he has shown his face! (*He starts for the bed.*)

REBECCA: Will it hurt the child, sir?

HALE: I cannot tell, If she is truly in the Devil's grip we may have to rip and tear to get her free.

REBECCA: I think I'll go, then. I am too old for this. (*She rises.*)

PARRIS (*striving for conviction*): Why, Rebecca, we may open up the boil of all our troubles today!

REBECCA: Let us hope for that. I go to God for you, sir.

PARRIS (*with trepidation—and resentment*): I hope you do not mean to go to Satan here! (*Slight pause.*)

REBECCA: I wish I knew. (*She goes out; they feel resentful of her note of moral superiority.*)

PUTNAM (*abruptly*): Come, Mr. Hale, let's get on. Sit you here.

GILES: Mr. Hale, I have always wanted to ask a learned man—what signifies the readin' of strange books?

HALE: What books?

GILES: I cannot tell; she hides them.

HALE: Who does this?

GILES: Martha, my wife. I have waked at night many a time and found her in a corner, readin' of a book. Now what do you make of that?

HALE: Why, that's not necessarily—

GILES: It discomfits me! Last night—mark this—I tried and tried and could not say my prayers. And then she close her book and walks out of the house, and suddenly—mark this—I could pray again!

Old Giles must be spoken for, if only because his fate was to be so remarkable and so different from that of all the others. He was in his early eighties at this time, and was the most comical hero in the history. No man has ever been blamed for so much. If a cow was missed, the first thought was to look for her around Corey's house; a fire blazing up at night brought suspicion of arson to his door. He didn't give a hoot for public opinion, and only in his last years—after he had married Martha—did he bother much with the church. That she stopped his prayer is very probable, but he forgot to say that he'd only recently learned any prayers and it didn't take much to make him stumble over them. He was a crank and a nuisance, but withal a deeply innocent and brave man. In court, once, he was asked if it were true that he had been frightened by the strange behavior of a hog and had then said he knew it to be the Devil in an animal's shape. "What frighted you?" he was asked. He forgot everything but the word "frighted," and instantly replied, "I do not know that I ever spoke that word in my life."

HALE: Ah! The stoppage of prayer—that is strange. I'll speak further on that with you.

GILES: I'm not sayin' she's touched the Devil, now, but I'd admire to know what books she reads and why she hides them. She'll not answer me, y' see.

HALE: Aye, we'll discuss it. (*To all*) Now mark me, if the Devil is in her you will witness some frightful wonders in this room, so please to keep your wits about you. Mr. Putnam, stand close in case she flies. Now, Betty, dear, will you sit up? (PUTNAM *comes in closer, ready-handed.* HALE *sits* BETTY *up, but she hangs limp in his hands.*) Hmmm. (*He observes her carefully. The others watch breathlessly.*) Can you hear me? I am John Hale, minister of Beverly. I have come to help you, dear. Do you remember my two little girls in Beverly? (*She does not stir in his hands.*)

PARRIS (*in fright*): How can it be the Devil? Why would he choose my house to strike? We have all manner of licentious people in the village!

HALE: What victory would the Devil have to win a soul already bad? It is the best the Devil wants, and who is better than the minister?

GILES: That's deep, Mr. Parris, deep, deep!

PARRIS (*with resolution now*): Betty! Answer Mr. Hale! Betty!

HALE: Does someone afflict you, child? It need not be a woman, mind you, or a man. Perhaps some bird invisible to others comes to you—perhaps a pig, a mouse, or any beast at all. Is there some figure bids you fly? (*The child remains limp in his hands. In silence he lays her back on the pillow. Now, holding out his hands toward her, he intones.*) In nomine Domini Sabaoth sui filiique ite ad infernos. (*She does not stir. He turns to* ABIGAIL, *his eyes narrowing.*) Abigail, what sort of dancing were you doing with her in the forest?

ABIGAIL: Why—common dancing is all.

PARRIS: I think I ought to say that I—I saw a kettle in the grass where they were dancing.

ABIGAIL: That were only soup.

HALE: What sort of soup were in this kettle, Abigail?

ABIGAIL: Why, it were beans—and lentils, I think, and—

HALE: Mr. Parris, you did not notice, did you, any living thing in the kettle? A mouse, perhaps, a spider, a frog—?

PARRIS (*fearfully*): I—do believe there were some movement—in the soup.

ABIGAIL: That jumped in, we never put it in!

HALE (*quickly*): What jumped in?

ABIGAIL: Why, a very little frog jumped—

PARRIS: A frog, Abby!

HALE (*grasping* ABIGAIL): Abigail, it may be your cousin is dying. Did you call the Devil last night?

ABIGAIL: I never called him! Tituba, Tituba . . .

PARRIS (*blanched*): She called the Devil?

HALE: I should like to speak with Tituba.

PARRIS: Goody Ann, will you bring her up? (MRS. PUTNAM *exits.*)

HALE: How did she call him?

ABIGAIL: I know not—she spoke Barbados.

HALE: Did you feel any strangeness when she called him? A sudden cold wind, perhaps? A trembling below the ground?

ABIGAIL: I didn't see no Devil! (*Shaking* BETTY) Betty, wake up. Betty! Betty!

HALE: You cannot evade me, Abigail. Did your cousin drink any of the brew in that kettle?

ABIGAIL: She never drank it!

HALE: Did you drink it?

ABIGAIL: No, sir!

HALE: Did Tituba ask you to drink it?

ABIGAIL: She tried, but I refused.

HALE: Why are you concealing? Have you sold yourself to Lucifer?

ABIGAIL: I never sold myself! I'm a good girl! I'm a proper girl!

(MRS. PUTNAM *enters with* TITUBA, *and instantly* ABIGAIL *points at* TITUBA.)

ABIGAIL: She made me do it! She made Betty do it!

TITUBA (*shocked and angry*): Abby!

ABIGAIL: She makes me drink blood!

PARRIS: Blood!!

MRS. PUTNAM: My baby's blood?

TITUBA: No, no, chicken blood. I give she chicken blood!

HALE: Woman, have you enlisted these children for the Devil?

TITUBA: No, no, sir, I don't truck with no Devil!

HALE: Why can she not wake? Are you silencing this child?

TITUBA: I love me Betty!

HALE: You have sent your spirit out upon this child, have you not? Are you gathering souls for the Devil?

ABIGAIL: She sends her spirit on me in church; she makes me laugh at prayer!

PARRIS: She have often laughed at prayer!

ABIGAIL: She comes to me every night to go and drink blood!

TITUBA: You beg *me* to conjure! She beg *me* make charm—

ABIGAIL: Don't lie! (*To* HALE) She comes to me while I sleep; she's always making me dream corruptions!

TITUBA: Why you say that, Abby?

ABIGAIL: Sometimes I wake and find myself standing in the open doorway and not a stitch on my body! I always hear her laughing in my sleep. I hear her singing her Barbados songs and tempting me with—

TITUBA: Mister Reverend, I never—

HALE (*resolved now*): Tituba, I want you to wake this child.

TITUBA: I have no power on this child, sir.

HALE: You most certainly do, and you will free her from it now! When did you compact with the Devil?

TITUBA: I don't compact with no Devil!

PARRIS: You will confess yourself or I will take you out and whip you to your death, Tituba!

PUTNAM: This woman must be hanged! She must be taken and hanged!

TITUBA (*terrified, falls to her knees*): No, no, don't hang Tituba! I tell him I don't desire to work for him, sir.

PARRIS: The Devil?

HALE: Then you saw him! (*Tituba weeps.*) Now Tituba, I know that when we bind ourselves to Hell it is very hard to break with it. We are going to help you tear yourself free—

TITUBA (*frightened by the coming process*): Mister Reverend, I do believe somebody else be witchin' these children.

HALE: Who?

TITUBA: I don't know, sir, but the Devil got him numerous witches.

HALE: Does he! (*It is a clue.*) Tituba, look into my eyes. Come, look into me. (*She raises her eyes to his fearfully.*) You would be a good Christian woman, would you not, Tituba?

TITUBA: Aye, sir, a good Christian woman.

HALE: And you love these little children?

TITUBA: Oh, yes, sir, I don't desire to hurt little children.

HALE: And you love God, Tituba?

TITUBA: I love God with all my bein'.

HALE: Now, in God's holy name—

TITUBA: Bless Him. Bless Him. (*She is rocking on her knees, sobbing in terror.*)

HALE: And to His glory—

TITUBA: Eternal glory. Bless Him—bless God . . .

HALE: Open yourself, Tituba—open yourself and let God's holy light shine on you.

TITUBA: Oh, bless the Lord.

HALE: When the Devil comes to you does he ever come—with another person? (*She stares up into his face.*) Perhaps another person in the village? Someone you know.

PARRIS: Who came with him?

PUTNAM: Sarah Good? Did you ever see Sarah Good with him? Or Osburn?

PARRIS: Was it man or woman came with him?

TITUBA: Man or woman. Was—was woman.

PARRIS: What woman? A woman, you said. What woman?

TITUBA: It was black dark, and I—

PARRIS: You could see him, why could you not see her?

TITUBA: Well, they was always talking; they was always runnin' round and carryin' on—

PARRIS: You mean out of Salem? Salem witches?

TITUBA: I believe so, yes, sir.

(*Now* HALE *takes her hand. She is surprised.*)

HALE: Tituba. You must have no fear to tell us who they are, do you understand? We will protect you. The Devil can never overcome a minister. You know that, do you not?

TITUBA (*kisses* HALE's *hand*): Aye, sir, oh, I do.

HALE: You have confessed yourself to witchcraft, and that speaks a wish to come to Heaven's side. And we will bless you, Tituba.

TITUBA (*deeply relieved*): Oh, God bless you, Mr. Hale!

HALE (*with rising exaltation*): You are God's instrument put in our hands to discover the Devil's agent among us. You are selected, Tituba, you are chosen to help us cleanse our village. So speak utterly, Tituba, turn your back on him and face God—face God, Tituba, and God will protect you.

TITUBA (*joining with him*): Oh, God, protect Tituba!

HALE (*kindly*): Who came to you with the Devil? Two? Three? Four? How many?

(TITUBA *pants, and begins rocking back and forth again, staring ahead.*)

TITUBA: There was four. There was four.

PARRIS (*pressing in on her*): Who? Who? Their names, their names!

TITUBA (*suddenly bursting out*): Oh, how many times he bid me kill you, Mr. Parris!

PARRIS: Kill me!

TITUBA (*in a fury*): He say Mr. Parris must be kill! Mr. Parris no goodly man, Mr. Parris mean man and no gentle man, and he bid me rise out of my bed and cut your throat! (*They gasp.*) But I tell him, "No! I don't hate that man. I don't want kill that man." But he say, "You work for me, Tituba, and I make you free! I give you pretty dress to wear, and put you way high up in the air, and you gone fly back to Barbados!" And I say, "You lie, Devil, you lie!" And then he come one stormy night to me, and he say, "Look! I have *white* people belong to me." And I look—and there was Goody Good.

PARRIS: Sarah Good!

TITUBA (*rocking and weeping*): Aye, sir, and Goody Osburn.

MRS. PUTNAM: I knew it! Goody Osburn were midwife to me three times. I begged you, Thomas, did I not? I begged him not to call Osburn because I feared her. My babies always shriveled in her hands!

HALE: Take courage, you must give us all their names. How can you bear to see this child suffering? Look at her, Tituba. (*He is indicating* BETTY *on the bed.*) Look at her God-given innocence; her soul is so tender; we must protect her, Tituba; the Devil is out and preying on her like a beast upon the flesh of the pure lamb. God will bless you for your help.

(ABIGAIL *rises, staring as though inspired, and cries out.*)

ABIGAIL: I want to open myself! (*They turn to her, startled. She is enraptured, as though in a pearly light.*) I want the light of God, I want the sweet love of Jesus! I danced for the Devil; I saw him; I wrote in his book; I go back to Jesus; I kiss His hand. I saw Sarah Good with the Devil! I saw Goody Osburn with the Devil! I saw Bridget Bishop with the Devil!

(*As she is speaking,* BETTY *is rising from the bed, a fever in her eyes, and picks up the chant.*)

BETTY (*staring too*): I saw George Jacobs with the Devil! I saw Goody Howe with the Devil!

PARRIS: She speaks! (*He rushes to embrace* BETTY.) She speaks!

HALE: Glory to God! It is broken, they are free!

BETTY (*calling out hysterically and with great relief*): I saw Martha Bellows with the Devil!

ABIGAIL: I saw Goody Sibber with the Devil! (*It is rising to a great glee.*)

PUTNAM: The marshal, I'll call the marshal!

(PARRIS *is shouting a prayer of thanksgiving.*)

BETTY: I saw Alice Barrow with the Devil!

(*The curtain begins to fall.*)

HALE (*as* PUTNAM *goes out*): Let the marshal bring irons!

ABIGAIL: I saw Goody Hawkins with the Devil!

BETTY: I saw Goody Bibber with the Devil!

ABIGAIL: I saw Goody Booth with the Devil!

(*On their ecstatic cries the curtain falls.*)

ACT TWO

The common room of PROCTOR's *house, eight days later.*

At the right is a door opening on the fields outside. A fireplace is at the left, and behind it a stairway leading upstairs. It is the low, dark, and rather long living room of the time. As the curtain rises, the room is empty. From above, ELIZABETH *is heard softly singing to the children. Presently the door opens and* JOHN PROCTOR *enters, carrying his gun. He glances about the room as he comes toward the fireplace, then halts for an instant as he hears her singing. He continues on to the fireplace, leans the gun against the wall as he swings a pot out of the fire and smells it. Then he lifts out the ladle and tastes. He is not quite pleased. He reaches to a cupboard, takes a pinch of salt, and drops it into the pot. As he is tasting again, her footsteps are heard on the stair. He swings the pot into the fireplace and goes to a basin and washes his hands and face.* ELIZABETH *enters.*

ELIZABETH: What keeps you so late? It's almost dark.

PROCTOR: I were planting far out to the forest edge.

ELIZABETH: Oh, you're done then.

PROCTOR: Aye, the farm is seeded. The boys asleep?

ELIZABETH: They will be soon. (*And she goes to the fireplace, proceeds to ladle up stew in a dish.*)

PROCTOR: Pray now for a fair summer.

ELIZABETH: Aye.

PROCTOR: Are you well today?

ELIZABETH: I am. (*She brings the plate to the table, and, indicating the food*) It is a rabbit.

PROCTOR (*going to the table*): Oh, is it! In Jonathan's trap?

ELIZABETH: No, she walked into the house this afternoon; I found her sittin' in the corner like she come to visit.

PROCTOR: Oh, that's a good sign walkin' in.

ELIZABETH: Pray God. It hurt my heart to strip her, poor rabbit. (*She sits and watches him taste it.*)

PROCTOR: It's well seasoned.

ELIZABETH (*blushing with pleasure*): I took great care. She's tender?

PROCTOR: Aye. (*He eats. She watches him.*) I think we'll see green fields soon. It's warm as blood beneath the clods.

ELIZABETH: That's well.

(PROCTOR *eats, then looks up.*)

PROCTOR: If the crop is good I'll buy George Jacob's heifer. How would that please you?

ELIZABETH: Aye, it would.

PROCTOR (*with a grin*): I mean to please you, Elizabeth.

ELIZABETH (*It is hard to say.*) I know it, John.

(*He gets up, goes to her, kisses her. She receives it. With a certain disappointment, he returns to the table.*)

PROCTOR (*as gently as he can*): Cider?

ELIZABETH (*with a sense of reprimanding herself for having forgot*): Aye! (*She gets up and goes and pours a glass for him. He now arches his back.*)

PROCTOR: This farm's a continent when you go foot by foot droppin' seeds in it.

ELIZABETH (*coming with the cider*): It must be.

PROCTOR (*drinks a long draught, then, putting the glass down*): You ought to bring some flowers in the house.

ELIZABETH: Oh! I forgot! I will tomorrow.

PROCTOR: It's winter in here yet. On Sunday let you come with me, and we'll walk the farm together; I never see such a load of flowers on the earth. (*With good feeling he goes and looks up at the sky through the open doorway.*) Lilacs have a purple smell. Lilac is the smell of nightfall, I think. Massachusetts is a beauty in the spring!

ELIZABETH: Aye, it is.

(There is a pause. She is watching him from the table as he stands there absorbing the night. It is as though she would speak but cannot. Instead, now, she takes up his plate and glass and fork and goes with them to the basin. Her back is turned to him. He turns to her and watches her. A sense of their separation rises.)

PROCTOR: I think you're sad again. Are you?

ELIZABETH *(She doesn't want friction, and yet she must.)* You come so late I thought you'd gone to Salem this afternoon.

PROCTOR: Why? I have no business in Salem.

ELIZABETH: You did speak of going, earlier this week.

PROCTOR *(He knows what she means.)* I thought better of it since.

ELIZABETH: Mary Warren's there today.

PROCTOR: Why'd you let her? You heard me forbid her go to Salem any more!

ELIZABETH: I couldn't stop her.

PROCTOR *(holding back a full condemnation of her):* It is a fault, it is a fault, Elizabeth—you're the mistress here, not Mary Warren.

ELIZABETH: She frightened all my strength away.

PROCTOR: How may that mouse frighten you, Elizabeth? You—

ELIZABETH: It is a mouse no more. I forbid her go, and she raises up her chin like the daughter of a prince and says to me, "I must go to Salem, Goody Proctor; I am an official of the court!"

PROCTOR: Court! What court?

ELIZABETH: Aye, it is a proper court they have now. They've sent four judges out of Boston, she says, weighty magistrates of the General Court, and at the head sits the Deputy Governor of the Province.

PROCTOR *(astonished):* Why, she's mad.

ELIZABETH: I would to God she were. There be fourteen people in the jail now, she says. *(PROCTOR simply looks at her, unable to grasp it.)* And they'll be tried, and the court have power to hang them too, she says.

PROCTOR *(scoffing, but without conviction):* Ah, they'd never hang—

ELIZABETH: The Deputy Governor promise hangin' if they'll not confess, John. The town's gone wild, I think. She speak of Abigail, and I thought she were a saint, to hear her. Abigail brings the other girls into the court, and where she walks the crowd will part like the sea for Israel. And folks are brought before them, and if they scream and howl and fall to the floor—the person's clapped in the jail for bewitchin' them.

PROCTOR *(wide-eyed):* Oh, it is a black mischief.

ELIZABETH: I think you must go to Salem, John. *(He turns to her.)* I think so. You must tell them it is a fraud.

PROCTOR *(thinking beyond this):* Aye, it is, it is surely.

ELIZABETH: Let you go to Ezekiel Cheever—he knows you well. And tell him what she said to you last week in her uncle's house. She said it had naught to do with witchcraft, did she not?

PROCTOR *(in thought):* Aye, she did, she did. *(Now, a pause.)*

ELIZABETH *(quietly, fearing to anger him by prodding):* God forbid you keep that from the court, John. I think they must be told.

PROCTOR *(quietly, struggling with his thought):* Aye, they must, they must. It is a wonder they do believe her.

ELIZABETH: I would go to Salem now, John—let you go tonight.

PROCTOR: I'll think on it.

ELIZABETH *(with her courage now):* You cannot keep it, John.

PROCTOR *(angering):* I know I cannot keep it. I say I will think on it!

ELIZABETH *(hurt, and very coldly):* Good, then, let you think on it. *(She stands and starts to walk out of the room.)*

PROCTOR: I am only wondering how I may prove what she told me, Elizabeth. If the girl's a saint now, I think it is not easy to prove she's fraud, and the town gone so silly. She told it to me in a room alone—I have no proof for it.

ELIZABETH: You were alone with her?

PROCTOR *(stubbornly):* For a moment alone, aye.

ELIZABETH: Why, then, it is not as you told me.

PROCTOR *(his anger rising):* For a moment, I say. The others come in soon after.

ELIZABETH (*Quietly. She has suddenly lost all faith in him.*) Do as you wish, then. (*She starts to turn.*)

PROCTOR: Woman. (*She turns to him.*) I'll not have your suspicion any more.

ELIZABETH (*a little loftily*): I have no—

PROCTOR: I'll not have it!

ELIZABETH: Then let you not earn it.

PROCTOR (*with a violent undertone*): You doubt me yet?

ELIZABETH (*with a smile, to keep her dignity*): John, if it were not Abigail that you must go to hurt, would you falter now? I think not.

PROCTOR: Now look you—

ELIZABETH: I see what I see, John.

PROCTOR (*with solemn warning*): You will not judge me more, Elizabeth. I have good reason to think before I charge fraud on Abigail, and I will think on it. Let you look to your own improvement before you go to judge your husband any more. I have forgot Abigail, and—

ELIZABETH: And I.

PROCTOR: Spare me! You forget nothin' and forgive nothin'. Learn charity, woman. I have gone tiptoe in this house all seven month since she is gone. I have not moved from there to there without I think to please you, and still an everlasting funeral marches round your heart. I cannot speak but I am doubted, every moment judged for lies, as though I come into a court when I come into this house!

ELIZABETH: John, you are not open with me. You saw her with a crowd, you said. Now you—

PROCTOR: I'll plead my honesty no more, Elizabeth.

ELIZABETH (*Now she would justify herself.*) John, I am only—

PROCTOR: No more! I should have roared you down when first you told me your suspicion. But I wilted, and, like a Christian, I confessed. Confessed! Some dream I had must have mistaken you for God that day. But you're not, you're not, and let you remember it! Let you look sometimes for the goodness in me, and judge me not.

ELIZABETH: I do not judge you. The magistrate sits in your heart that judges you. I never thought you but a good man, John—(*with a smile*)—only somewhat bewildered.

PROCTOR (*laughing bitterly*): Oh, Elizabeth, your justice would freeze beer! (*He turns suddenly toward a sound outside. He starts for the door as* MARY WARREN *enters. As soon as he sees her, he goes directly to her and grabs her by the cloak, furious.*) How do you go to Salem when I forbid it? Do you mock me? (*Shaking her*) I'll whip you if you dare leave this house again!

(*Strangely, she doesn't resist him, but hangs limply by his grip.*)

MARY WARREN: I am sick, I am sick, Mr. Proctor. Pray, pray, hurt me not. (*Her strangeness throws him off, and her evident pallor and weakness. He frees her.*) My insides are all shuddery; I am in the proceedings all day, sir.

PROCTOR (*With draining anger—his curiosity is draining it.*) And what of these proceedings here? When will you proceed to keep this house, as you are paid nine pound a year to do—and my wife not wholly well?

(*As though to compensate,* MARY WARREN *goes to* ELIZABETH *with a small rag doll.*)

MARY WARREN: I made a gift for you today, Goody Proctor. I had to sit long hours in a chair, and passed the time with sewing.

ELIZABETH (*perplexed, looking at the doll*): Why, thank you, it's a fair poppet.

MARY WARREN (*with a trembling, decayed voice*): We must all love each other now, Goody Proctor.

ELIZABETH (*amazed at her strangeness*): Aye, indeed we must.

MARY WARREN (*glancing at the room*): I'll get up early in the morning and clean the house. I must sleep now. (*She turns and starts off.*)

PROCTOR: Mary. (*She halts.*) Is it true? There be fourteen women arrested?

MARY WARREN: No, sir. There be thirty-nine now—(*She suddenly breaks off and sobs and sits down, exhausted.*)

ELIZABETH: Why, she's weepin'! What ails you, child?

MARY WARREN: Goody Osburn—will hang!

(*There is a shocked pause, while she sobs.*)

PROCTOR: Hang! *(He calls into her face.)* Hang, y'say?

MARY WARREN *(through her weeping)*: Aye.

PROCTOR: The Deputy Governor will permit it?

MARY WARREN: He sentenced her. He must. *(To ameliorate it)* But not Sarah Good. For Sarah Good confessed, y'see.

PROCTOR: Confessed! To what?

MARY WARREN: That she—*(in horror at the memory)*—she sometimes made a compact with Lucifer, and wrote her name in his black book—with her blood—and bound herself to torment Christians till God's thrown down— and we all must worship Hell forevermore.

(Pause.)

PROCTOR: But—surely you know what a jabberer she is. Did you tell them that?

MARY WARREN: Mr. Proctor, in open court she near to choked us all to death.

PROCTOR: How, choked you?

MARY WARREN: She sent her spirit out.

ELIZABETH: Oh, Mary, Mary, surely you—

MARY WARREN *(with an indignant edge)*: She tried to kill me many times, Goody Proctor!

ELIZABETH: Why, I never heard you mention that before.

MARY WARREN: I never knew it before. I never knew anything before. When she come into the court I say to myself, I must not accuse this woman, for she sleep in ditches, and so very old and poor. But then—then she sit there, denying and denying, and I feel a misty coldness climbin' up my back, and the skin on my skull begin to creep, and I feel a clamp around my neck and I cannot breathe air; and then—*(entranced)*—I hear a voice, a screamin' voice, and it were my voice—and all at once I remembered everything she done to me!

PROCTOR: Why? What did she do to you?

MARY WARREN *(like one awakened to a marvelous secret insight)*: So many time, Mr. Proctor, she come to this very door, beggin' bread and a cup of cider—and mark this: whenever I turned her away empty, she *mumbled*.

ELIZABETH: Mumbled! She may mumble if she's hungry.

MARY WARREN: But *what* does she mumble?

You must remember, Goody Proctor. Last month—a Monday, I think—she walked away, and I thought my guts would burst for two days after. Do you remember it?

ELIZABETH: Why—I do, I think, but—

MARY WARREN: And so I told that to Judge Hathorne, and he asks her so. "Goody Osburn," says he, "what curse do you mumble that this girl must fall sick after turning you away?" And then she replies—*(mimicking an old crone)*—"Why, your excellence, no curse at all. I only say my commandments; I hope I may say my commandments," says she!

ELIZABETH: And that's an upright answer.

MARY WARREN: Aye, but then Judge Hathorne say, "Recite for us your commandments!"—*(leaning avidly toward them)*—and of all the ten she could not say a single one. She never knew no commandments, and they had her in a flat lie!

PROCTOR: And so condemned her?

MARY WARREN *(now a little strained, seeing his stubborn doubt)*: Why, they must when she condemned herself.

PROCTOR: But the proof, the proof!

MARY WARREN *(with greater impatience with him)*: I told you the proof. It's hard proof, hard as rock, the judges said.

PROCTOR *(pauses an instant, then)*: You will not go to court again, Mary Warren.

MARY WARREN: I must tell you, sir, I will be gone every day now. I am amazed you do not see what weighty work we do.

PROCTOR: What work you do! It's strange work for a Christian girl to hang old women!

MARY WARREN: But, Mr. Proctor, they will not hang them if they confess. Sarah Good will only sit in jail some time—*(recalling)*—and here's a wonder for you; think on this. Goody Good is pregnant!

ELIZABETH: Pregnant! Are they mad? The woman's near to sixty!

MARY WARREN: They had Doctor Griggs examine her, and she's full to the brim. And smokin' a pipe all these years, and no husband either! But she's safe, thank God, for they'll not hurt the innocent child. But be that not a marvel? You must see it, sir, it's God's work we do. So I'll be gone every day for some time. I'm—I am an official of the court, they say, and I—*(She has been edging toward offstage.)*

PROCTOR: I'll official you! *(He strides to the mantel, takes down the whip hanging there.)*

MARY WARREN *(terrified, but coming erect, striving for her authority):* I'll not stand whipping any more!

ELIZABETH *(hurriedly, as* PROCTOR *approaches):* Mary, promise you'll stay at home—

MARY WARREN *(backing from him, but keeping her erect posture, striving, striving for her way):* The Devil's loose in Salem, Mr. Proctor; we must discover where he's hiding!

PROCTOR: I'll whip the Devil out of you! *(With whip raised he reaches out for her, and she streaks away and yells.)*

MARY WARREN *(pointing at Elizabeth):* I saved her life today!

(Silence. His whip comes down.)

ELIZABETH *(softly):* I am accused?

MARY WARREN *(quaking):* Somewhat mentioned. But I said I never see no sign you ever sent your spirit out to hurt no one, and seeing I do live so closely with you, they dismissed it.

ELIZABETH: Who accused me?

MARY WARREN: I am bound by law, I cannot tell it. *(To* PROCTOR*)* I only hope you'll not be so sarcastical no more. Four judges and the King's deputy sat to dinner with us but an hour ago. I—I would have you speak civilly to me, from this out.

PROCTOR *(in horror, muttering in disgust at her):* Go to bed.

MARY WARREN *(with a stamp of her foot):* I'll not be ordered to bed no more, Mr. Proctor! I am eighteen and a woman, however single!

PROCTOR: Do you wish to sit up? Then sit up.

MARY WARREN: I wish to go to bed!

PROCTOR *(in anger):* Good night, then!

MARY WARREN: Good night. *(Dissatisfied, uncertain of herself, she goes out. Wide-eyed, both,* PROCTOR *and* ELIZABETH *stand staring.)*

ELIZABETH *(quietly):* Oh, the noose, the noose is up!

PROCTOR: There'll be no noose.

ELIZABETH: She wants me dead. I knew all week it would come to this!

PROCTOR *(without conviction):* They dismissed it. You heard her say—

ELIZABETH: And what of tomorrow? She will cry me out until they take me!

PROCTOR: Sit you down.

ELIZABETH: She wants me dead, John, you know it!

PROCTOR: I say sit down! *(She sits, trembling. He speaks quickly, trying to keep his wits.)* Now we must be wise, Elizabeth.

ELIZABETH *(with sarcasm, and a sense of being lost):* Oh, indeed, indeed!

PROCTOR: Fear nothing. I'll find Ezekiel Cheever. I'll tell him she said it were all sport.

ELIZABETH: John, with so many in the jail, more than Cheever's help is needed now, I think. Would you favor me with this? Go to Abigail.

PROCTOR *(his soul hardening as he senses . . .):* What have I to say to Abigail?

ELIZABETH *(delicately):* John—grant me this. You have a faulty understanding of young girls. There is a promise made in any bed—

PROCTOR *(striving against his anger):* What promise!

ELIZABETH: Spoke or silent, a promise is surely made. And she may dote on it now—I am sure she does—and thinks to kill me, then to take my place.

*(*PROCTOR's *anger is rising; he cannot speak.)*

ELIZABETH: It is her dearest hope, John, I know it. There be a thousand names; why does she call mine? There be a certain danger in calling such a name—I am no Goody Good that sleeps in ditches, nor Osburn, drunk and half-witted. She'd dare not call out such a farmer's wife but there be monstrous profit in it. She thinks to take my place, John.

PROCTOR: She cannot think it! *(He knows it is true.)*

ELIZABETH *("reasonably"):* John, have you ever shown her somewhat of contempt? She cannot pass you in the church but you will blush—

PROCTOR: I may blush for my sin.

ELIZABETH: I think she sees another meaning in that blush.

PROCTOR: And what see you? What see you, Elizabeth?

ELIZABETH *("conceding"):* I think you be

somewhat ashamed, for I am there, and she so close.

PROCTOR: When will you know me, woman? Were I stone I would have cracked for shame this seven month!

ELIZABETH: Then go and tell her she's a whore. Whatever promise she may sense—break it, John, break it.

PROCTOR (between his teeth): Good, then. I'll go. (He starts for his rifle.)

ELIZABETH (trembling, fearfully): Oh, how unwillingly!

PROCTOR (turning on her, rifle in hand): I will curse her hotter than the oldest cinder in hell. But pray, begrudge me not my anger!

ELIZABETH: Your anger! I only ask you—

PROCTOR: Woman, am I so base? Do you truly think me base?

ELIZABETH: I never called you base.

PROCTOR: Then how do you charge me with such a promise? The promise that a stallion gives a mare I gave that girl!

ELIZABETH: Then why do you anger with me when I bid you break it?

PROCTOR: Because it speaks deceit, and I am honest! But I'll plead no more! I see now your spirit twists around the single error of my life, and I will never tear it free!

ELIZABETH (crying out): You'll tear it free—when you come to know that I will be your only wife, or no wife at all! She has an arrow in you yet, John Proctor, and you know it well!

(Quite suddenly, as though from the air, a figure appears in the doorway. They start slightly. It is MR. HALE. He is different now—drawn a little, and there is a quality of deference, even of guilt, about his manner now.)

HALE: Good evening.

PROCTOR (still in his shock): Why, Mr. Hale! Good evening to you, sir. Come in, come in.

HALE (to ELIZABETH): I hope I do not startle you.

ELIZABETH: No, no, it's only that I heard no horse—

HALE: You are Goodwife Proctor.

PROCTOR: Aye; Elizabeth.

HALE (nods, then): I hope you're not off to bed yet.

PROCTOR (setting down his gun): No, no.

(HALE comes further into the room. And PROCTOR, to explain his nervousness) We are not used to visitors after dark, but you're welcome here. Will you sit you down, sir?

HALE: I will. (He sits.) Let you sit, Goodwife Proctor.

(She does, never letting him out of her sight. There is a pause as HALE looks about the room.)

PROCTOR (to break the silence): Will you drink cider, Mr. Hale?

HALE: No, it rebels my stomach; I have some further traveling yet tonight. Sit you down, sir. (PROCTOR sits.) I will not keep you long, but I have some business with you.

PROCTOR: Business of the court?

HALE: No—no, I come of my own, without the court's authority. Hear me. (He wets his lips.) I know not if you are aware, but your wife's name is—mentioned in the court.

PROCTOR: We know it, sir. Our Mary Warren told us. We are entirely amazed.

HALE: I am a stranger here, as you know. And in my ignorance I find it hard to draw a clear opinion of them that come accused before the court. And so this afternoon, and now tonight, I go from house to house—I come now from Rebecca Nurse's house and—

ELIZABETH (shocked): Rebecca's charged!

HALE: God forbid such a one be charged. She is, however—mentioned somewhat.

ELIZABETH (with an attempt at a laugh): You will never believe, I hope, that Rebecca trafficked with the Devil.

HALE: Woman, it is possible.

PROCTOR (taken aback): Surely you cannot think so.

HALE: This is a strange time, Mister. No man may longer doubt the powers of the dark are gathered in monstrous attack upon this village. There is too much evidence now to deny it. You will agree, sir?

PROCTOR (evading): I—have no knowledge in that line. But it's hard to think so pious a woman to be secretly a Devil's bitch after seventy year of such good prayer.

HALE: Aye. But the Devil is a wily one, you cannot deny it. However, she is far from accused, and I know she will not be. (Pause.) I thought, sir, to put some questions as to the

Christian character of this house, if you'll permit me.

PROCTOR (coldly, resentful): Why, we—have no fear of questions, sir.

HALE: Good, then. (He makes himself more comfortable.) In the book of record that Mr. Parris keeps, I note that you are rarely in the church on Sabbath Day.

PROCTOR: No, sir, you are mistaken.

HALE: Twenty-six time in seventeen month, sir. I must call that rare. Will you tell me why you are so absent?

PROCTOR: Mr. Hale, I never knew I must account to that man for I come to church or stay at home. My wife were sick this winter.

HALE: So I am told. But you, Mister, why could you not come alone?

PROCTOR: I surely did come when I could, and when I could not I prayed in this house.

HALE: Mr. Proctor, your house is not a church; your theology must tell you that.

PROCTOR: It does, sir, it does; and it tells me that a minister may pray to God without he have golden candlesticks upon the altar.

HALE: What golden candlesticks?

PROCTOR: Since we built the church there were pewter candlesticks upon the altar; Francis Nurse made them, y'know, and a sweeter hand never touched the metal. But Parris came, and for twenty week he preach nothin' but golden candlesticks until he had them. I labor the earth from dawn of day to blink of night, and I tell you true, when I look to heaven and see my money glaring at his elbows—it hurt my prayer, sir, it hurt my prayer. I think, sometimes, the man dreams cathedrals, not clapboard meetin' houses.

HALE (thinks, then): And yet, Mister, a Christian on Sabbath Day must be in church. (Pause.) Tell me—you have three children?

PROCTOR: Aye. Boys.

HALE: How comes it that only two are baptized?

PROCTOR (starts to speak, then stops, then, as though unable to restrain this): I like it not that Mr. Parris should lay his hand upon my baby. I see no light of God in that man. I'll not conceal it.

HALE: I must say it, Mr. Proctor; that is not for you to decide. The man's ordained, therefore the light of God is in him.

PROCTOR (flushed with resentment but trying to smile): What's your suspicion, Mr. Hale?

HALE: No, no, I have no—

PROCTOR: I nailed the roof upon the church, I hung the door—

HALE: Oh, did you! That's a good sign, then.

PROCTOR: It may be I have been too quick to bring the man to book, but you cannot think we ever desired the destruction of religion. I think that's in your mind, is it not?

HALE (not altogether giving way): I—have —there is a softness in your record, sir, a softness.

ELIZABETH: I think, maybe, we have been too hard with Mr. Parris. I think so. But sure we never loved the Devil here.

HALE (nods, deliberating this; then, with the voice of one administering a secret test): Do you know your Commandments, Elizabeth?

ELIZABETH (without hesitation, even eagerly): I surely do. There be no mark of blame upon my life, Mr. Hale. I am a covenanted, Christian woman.

HALE: And you, Mister?

PROCTOR (a trifle unsteadily): I—am sure I do, sir.

HALE (glances at her open face, then at JOHN, then): Let you repeat them, if you will.

PROCTOR: The Commandments.

HALE: Aye.

PROCTOR (looking off, beginning to sweat): Thou shalt not kill.

HALE: Aye.

PROCTOR (counting on his fingers): Thou shalt not steal. Thou shalt not covet thy neighbor's goods, nor make unto thee any graven image. Thou shalt not take the name of the Lord in vain; thou shalt have no other gods before me. (With some hesitation) Thou shalt remember the Sabbath Day and keep it holy. (Pause. Then) Thou shalt honor thy father and mother. Thou shalt not bear false witness. (He is stuck. He counts back on his fingers, knowing one is missing.) Thou shalt not make unto thee any graven image.

HALE: You have said that twice, sir.

PROCTOR (*lost*): Aye. (*He is flailing for it.*)

ELIZABETH (*delicately*): Adultery, John.

PROCTOR (*as though a secret arrow had pained his heart*): Aye. (*Trying to grin it away —to* HALE) You see, sir, between the two of us we do know them all. (HALE *only looks at* PROCTOR, *deep in his attempt to define this man.* PROCTOR *grows more uneasy.*) I think it be a small fault.

HALE: Theology, sir, is a fortress; no crack in a fortress may be accounted small. (*He rises; he seems worried now. He paces a little, in deep thought.*)

PROCTOR: There be no love for Satan in this house, Mister.

HALE: I pray it, I pray it dearly. (*He looks to both of them, an attempt at a smile on his face, but his misgivings are clear.*) Well, then —I'll bid you good night.

ELIZABETH (*unable to restrain herself*): Mr. Hale. (*He turns.*) I do think you are suspecting me somewhat? Are you not?

HALE (*obviously disturbed—and evasive*): Goody Proctor, I do not judge you. My duty is to add what I may to the godly wisdom of the court. I pray you both good health and good fortune. (*To* JOHN) Good night, sir. (*He starts out.*)

ELIZABETH (*with a note of desperation*): I think you must tell him, John.

HALE: What's that?

ELIZABETH (*restraining a call*): Will you tell him?

(*Slight pause.* HALE *looks questioningly at* JOHN.)

PROCTOR (*with difficulty*): I—I have no witness and cannot prove it, except my word be taken. But I know the children's sickness had naught to do with witchcraft.

HALE (*stopped, struck*): Naught to do—?

PROCTOR: Mr. Parris discovered them sportin' in the woods. They were startled and took sick.

(*Pause.*)

HALE: Who told you this?

PROCTOR (*hesitates, then*): Abigail Williams.

HALE: Abigail!

PROCTOR: Aye.

HALE (*his eyes wide*): Abigail Williams told you it had naught to do with witchcraft!

PROCTOR: She told me the day you came, sir.

HALE (*suspiciously*): Why—why did you keep this?

PROCTOR: I never knew until tonight that the world is gone daft with this nonsense.

HALE: Nonsense! Mister, I have myself examined Tituba, Sarah Good, and numerous others that have confessed to dealing with the Devil. They have *confessed* it.

PROCTOR: And why not, if they must hang for denyin' it? There are them that will swear to anything before they'll hang; have you never thought of that?

HALE: I have. I—I have indeed. (*It is his own suspicion, but he resists it. He glances at* ELIZABETH, *then at* JOHN.) And you—would you testify to this in court?

PROCTOR: I—had not reckoned with goin' into court. But if I must I will.

HALE: Do you falter here?

PROCTOR: I falter nothing, but I may wonder if my story will be credited in such a court. I do wonder on it, when such a steady-minded minister as you will suspicion such a woman that never lied, and cannot, and the world knows she cannot! I may falter somewhat, Mister; I am no fool.

HALE (*Quietly—it has impressed him.*) Proctor, let you open with me now, for I have a rumor that troubles me. It's said you hold no belief that there may even be witches in the world. Is that true, sir?

PROCTOR (*He knows this is critical, and is striving against his disgust with* HALE *and with himself for even answering.*) I know not what I have said, I may have said it. I have wondered if there be witches in the world— although I cannot believe they come among us now.

HALE: Then you do not believe—

PROCTOR: I have no knowledge of it; the Bible speaks of witches, and I will not deny them.

HALE: And you, woman?

ELIZABETH: I—I cannot believe it.

HALE (*shocked*): You cannot!

PROCTOR: Elizabeth, you bewilder him!

ELIZABETH (to HALE): I cannot think the Devil may own a woman's soul, Mr. Hale, when she keeps an upright way, as I have. I am a good woman, I know it; and if you believe I may do only good work in the world, and yet be secretly bound to Satan, then I must tell you, sir, I do not believe it.

HALE: But, woman, you do believe there are witches in—

ELIZABETH: If you think that I am one, then I say there are none.

HALE: You surely do not fly against the Gospel, the Gospel—

PROCTOR: She believe in the Gospel, every word!

ELIZABETH: Question Abigail Williams about the Gospel, not myself!

(HALE stares at her.)

PROCTOR: She do not mean to doubt the Gospel, sir, you cannot think it. This be a Christian house, sir, a Christian house.

HALE: God keep you both; let the third child be quickly baptized, and go you without fail each Sunday in to Sabbath prayer; and keep a solemn, quiet way among you. I think—

(GILES COREY appears in doorway.)

GILES: John!

PROCTOR: Giles! What's the matter?

GILES: They take my wife.

(FRANCIS NURSE enters.)

GILES: And his Rebecca!

PROCTOR (to FRANCIS): Rebecca's in the jail!

FRANCIS: Aye, Cheever come and take her in his wagon. We've only now come from the jail, and they'll not even let us in to see them.

ELIZABETH: They've surely gone wild now, Mr. Hale!

FRANCIS (going to HALE): Reverend Hale! Can you not speak to the Deputy Governor? I'm sure he mistakes these people—

HALE: Pray calm yourself, Mr. Nurse.

FRANCIS: My wife is the very brick and mortar of the church, Mr. Hale—(indicating Giles)—and Martha Corey, there cannot be a woman closer yet to God than Martha.

HALE: How is Rebecca charged, Mr. Nurse?

FRANCIS (with a mocking, half-hearted laugh): For murder, she's charged! (Mockingly quoting the warrant) "For the marvelous and supernatural murder of Goody Putnam's babies." What am I to do, Mr. Hale?

HALE (turns from FRANCIS, deeply troubled, then): Believe me, Mr. Nurse, if Rebecca Nurse be tainted, then nothing's left to stop the whole green world from burning. Let you rest upon the justice of the court; the court will send her home, I know it.

FRANCIS: You cannot mean she will be tried in court!

HALE (pleading): Nurse, though our hearts break, we cannot flinch; these are new times, sir. There is a misty plot afoot so subtle we should be criminal to cling to old respects and ancient friendships. I have seen too many frightful proofs in court—the Devil is alive in Salem, and we dare not quail to follow wherever the accusing finger points!

PROCTOR (angered): How may such a woman murder children?

HALE (in great pain): Man, remember, until an hour before the Devil fell, God thought him beautiful in Heaven.

GILES: I never said my wife were a witch, Mr. Hale; I only said she were reading books!

HALE: Mr. Corey, exactly what complaint were made on your wife?

GILES: That bloody mongrel Walcott charge her. Y'see, he buy a pig of my wife four or five year ago, and the pig died soon after. So he come dancin' in for his money back. So my Martha, she says to him, "Walcott, if you haven't the wit to feed a pig properly, you'll not live to own many," she says. Now he goes to court and claims that from that day to this he cannot keep a pig alive for more than four weeks because my Martha bewitch them with her books!

(Enter EZEKIEL CHEEVER. A shocked silence.)

CHEEVER: Good evening to you, Proctor.

PROCTOR: Why, Mr. Cheever. Good evening.

CHEEVER: Good evening, all. Good evening, Mr. Hale.

PROCTOR: I hope you come not on business of the court.

CHEEVER: I do, Proctor, aye. I am clerk of the court now, y'know.

(Enter MARSHAL HERRICK, *a man in his early thirties, who is somewhat shamefaced at the moment.)*

GILES: It's a pity, Ezekiel, that an honest tailor might have gone to Heaven must burn in Hell. You'll burn for this, do you know it?

CHEEVER: You know yourself I must do as I'm told. You surely know that, Giles. And I'd as lief you'd not be sending me to Hell. I like not the sound of it, I tell you; I like not the sound of it. *(He fears* PROCTOR, *but starts to reach inside his coat.)* Now believe me, Proctor, how heavy be the law, all its tonnage I do carry on my back tonight. *(He takes out a warrant.)* I have a warrant for your wife.

PROCTOR *(to* HALE*):* You said she were not charged!

HALE: I know nothin' of it. *(To* CHEEVER*)* When were she charged?

CHEEVER: I am given sixteen warrant tonight, sir, and she is one.

PROCTOR: Who charged her?

CHEEVER: Why, Abigail Williams charge her.

PROCTOR: On what proof, what proof?

CHEEVER *(looking about the room):* Mr. Proctor, I have little time. The court bid me search your house, but I like not to search a house. So will you hand me any poppets that your wife may keep here?

PROCTOR: Poppets?

ELIZABETH: I never kept no poppets, not since I were a girl.

CHEEVER *(embarrassed, glancing toward the mantel where sits* MARY WARREN'S *poppet):* I spy a poppet, Goody Proctor.

ELIZABETH: Oh! *(Going for it)* Why, this is Mary's.

CHEEVER *(shyly):* Would you please to give it to me?

ELIZABETH *(handing it to him, asks* HALE*):* Has the court discovered a text in poppets now?

CHEEVER *(carefully holding the poppet):* Do you keep any others in this house?

PROCTOR: No, nor this one either till tonight. What signifies a poppet?

CHEEVER: Why, a poppet—*(he gingerly turns the poppet over)*—a poppet may signify—Now, woman, will you please to come with me?

PROCTOR: She will not! *(To* ELIZABETH*)* Fetch Mary here.

CHEEVER *(ineptly reaching toward* ELIZABETH*):* No, no, I am forbid to leave her from my sight.

PROCTOR *(pushing his arm away):* You'll leave her out of sight and out of mind, Mister. Fetch Mary, Elizabeth. *(*ELIZABETH *goes upstairs.)*

HALE: What signifies a poppet, Mr. Cheever?

CHEEVER *(turning the poppet over in his hands):* Why, they say it may signify that she —*(He has lifted the poppet's skirt, and his eyes widen in astonished fear.)* Why, this, this—

PROCTOR *(reaching for the poppet):* What's there?

CHEEVER: Why—*(he draws out a long needle from the poppet)*—it is a needle! Herrick, Herrick, it is a needle!

*(*HERRICK *comes toward him.)*

PROCTOR *(angrily, bewildered):* And what signifies a needle!

CHEEVER *(his hands shaking):* Why, this go hard with her, Proctor, this—I had my doubts, Proctor, I had my doubts, but here's calamity. *(To* HALE, *showing the needle)* You see it, sir, it is a needle!

HALE: Why? What meanin' has it?

CHEEVER *(wide-eyed, trembling):* The girl, the Williams girl, Abigail Williams, sir. She sat to dinner in Reverend Parris's house tonight, and without word nor warnin' she falls to the floor. Like a struck beast, he says, and screamed a scream that a bull would weep to hear. And he goes to save her, and, stuck two inches in the flesh of her belly, he draw a needle out. And demandin' of her how she come to be so stabbed, she—*(to* PROCTOR *now)* —testify it were your wife's familiar spirit pushed it in.

PROCTOR: Why, she done it herself! *(To* HALE*):* I hope you're not takin' this for proof, Mister!

*(*HALE, *struck by the proof, is silent.)*

CHEEVER: 'Tis hard proof! *(To* HALE*)* I find here a poppet Goody Proctor keeps. I have found it, sir. And in the belly of the poppet a needle's stuck. I tell you true, Proctor, I never warranted to see such proof of Hell, and I bid you obstruct me not, for I—

(Enter ELIZABETH *with* MARY WARREN. PROCTOR, *seeing* MARY WARREN, *draws her by the arm to* HALE.)

PROCTOR: Here now! Mary, how did this poppet come into my house?

MARY WARREN *(frightened for herself, her voice very small):* What poppet's that, sir?

PROCTOR *(impatiently, points at the doll in* CHEEVER'S *hand):* This poppet, this poppet.

MARY WARREN *(evasively, looking at it):* Why, I—I think it is mine.

PROCTOR: It is your poppet, is it not?

MARY WARREN *(not understanding the direction of this):* It—is, sir.

PROCTOR: And how did it come into this house?

MARY WARREN *(glancing about at the avid faces):* Why—I made it in the court, sir, and—give it to Goody Proctor tonight.

PROCTOR *(to* HALE): Now, sir—do you have it?

HALE: Mary Warren, a needle have been found inside this poppet.

MARY WARREN *(bewildered):* Why, I meant no harm by it, sir.

PROCTOR *(quickly):* You stuck that needle in yourself?

MARY WARREN: I—I believe I did, sir, I—

PROCTOR *(to* HALE): What say you now?

HALE *(watching* MARY WARREN *closely):* Child, you are certain this be your natural memory? May it be, perhaps, that someone conjures you even now to say this?

MARY WARREN: Conjures me? Why, no, sir, I am entirely myself, I think. Let you ask Susanna Walcott—she saw me sewin' it in court. *(Or better still)* Ask Abby, Abby sat beside me when I made it.

PROCTOR *(to* HALE, *of* CHEEVER): Bid him begone. Your mind is surely settled now. Bid him out, Mr. Hale.

ELIZABETH: What signifies a needle?

HALE: Mary—you charge a cold and cruel murder on Abigail.

MARY WARREN: Murder! I charge no—

HALE: Abigail were stabbed tonight; a needle were found stuck into her belly—

ELIZABETH: And she charges me?

HALE: Aye.

ELIZABETH *(her breath knocked out):* Why—! The girl is murder! She must be ripped out of the world!

CHEEVER *(pointing at* ELIZABETH): You've heard that, sir! Ripped out of the world! Herrick, you heard it!

PROCTOR *(suddenly snatching the warrant out of* CHEEVER'S *hands):* Out with you.

CHEEVER: Proctor, you dare not touch the warrant.

PROCTOR *(ripping the warrant):* Out with you!

CHEEVER: You've ripped the Deputy Governor's warrant, man!

PROCTOR: Damn the Deputy Governor! Out of my house!

HALE: Now, Proctor, Proctor!

PROCTOR: Get y'gone with them! You are a broken minister.

HALE: Proctor, if she is innocent, the court—

PROCTOR: If *she* is innocent! Why do you never wonder if Parris may be innocent, or Abigail? Is the accuser always holy now? Were they born this morning as clean as God's fingers? I'll tell you what's walking Salem—vengeance is walking Salem. We are what we always were in Salem, but now the little crazy children are jangling the keys of the kingdom, and common vengeance writes the law! This warrant's vengeance! I'll not give my wife to vengeance!

ELIZABETH: I'll go, John—

PROCTOR: You will not go!

HERRICK: I have nine men outside. You cannot keep her. The law binds me, John, I cannot budge.

PROCTOR *(to* HALE, *ready to break him):* Will you see her taken?

HALE: Proctor, the court is just—

PROCTOR: Pontius Pilate! God will not let you wash your hands of this!

ELIZABETH: John—I think I must go with them. *(He cannot bear to look at her.)* Mary, there is bread enough for the morning; you will bake, in the afternoon. Help Mr. Proctor as you were his daughter—you owe me that, and much more. *(She is fighting her weeping. To* PROCTOR) When the children wake, speak nothing of witchcraft—it will frighten them. *(She cannot go on.)*

PROCTOR: I will bring you home. I will bring you soon.

ELIZABETH: Oh, John, bring me soon!

PROCTOR: I will fall like an ocean on that court! Fear nothing, Elizabeth.

ELIZABETH *(with great fear):* I will fear nothing. *(She looks about the room, as though to fix it in her mind.)* Tell the children I have gone to visit someone sick.

(She walks out the door, HERRICK and CHEEVER behind her. For a moment, PROCTOR watches from the doorway. The clank of chain is heard.)

PROCTOR: Herrick! Herrick, don't chain her! *(He rushes out the door. From outside)* Damn you, man, you will not chain her! Off with them! I'll not have it! I will not have her chained!

(There are other men's voices against his. HALE, in a fever of guilt and uncertainty, turns from the door to avoid the sight; MARY WARREN bursts into tears and sits weeping. GILES COREY calls to HALE.)

GILES: And yet silent, minister? It is fraud, you know it is fraud! What keeps you, man?

(PROCTOR is half braced, half pushed into the room by two deputies and HERRICK.)

PROCTOR: I'll pay you, Herrick, I will surely pay you!

HERRICK *(panting):* In God's name, John, I cannot help myself. I must chain them all. Now let you keep inside this house till I am gone! *(He goes out with his deputies.)*

(PROCTOR stands there, gulping air. Horses and a wagon creaking are heard.)

HALE *(in great uncertainty):* Mr. Proctor—

PROCTOR: Out of my sight!

HALE: Charity, Proctor, charity. What I have heard in her favor, I will not fear to testify in court. God help me, I cannot judge her guilty or innocent—I know not. Only this consider: the world goes mad, and it profit nothing you should lay the cause to the vengeance of a little girl.

PROCTOR: You are a coward! Though you be ordained in God's own tears, you are a coward now!

HALE: Proctor, I cannot think God be pro-voked so grandly by such a petty cause. The jails are packed—our greatest judges sit in Salem now—and hangin's promised. Man, we must look to cause proportionate. Were there murder done, perhaps, and never brought to light? Abomination? Some secret blasphemy that stinks to Heaven? Think on cause, man, and let you help me to discover it. For there's your way, believe it, there is your only way, when such confusion strikes upon the world. *(He goes to GILES and FRANCIS.)* Let you counsel among yourselves; think on your village and what may have drawn from heaven such thundering wrath upon you all. I shall pray God open up our eyes.

(HALE goes out.)

FRANCIS *(struck by HALE's mood):* I never heard no murder done in Salem.

PROCTOR *(He has been reached by HALE's words.)* Leave me, Francis, leave me.

GILES *(shaken):* John—tell me, are we lost?

PROCTOR: Go home now, Giles. We'll speak on it tomorrow.

GILES: Let you think on it. We'll come early, eh?

PROCTOR: Aye. Go now, Giles.

GILES: Good night, then.

(GILES COREY goes out. After a moment)

MARY WARREN *(in a fearful squeak of a voice):* Mr. Proctor, very likely they'll let her come home once they're given proper evidence.

PROCTOR: You're coming to the court with me, Mary. You will tell it in the court.

MARY WARREN: I cannot charge murder on Abigail.

PROCTOR *(moving menacingly toward her):* You will tell the court how that poppet come here and who stuck the needle in.

MARY WARREN: She'll kill me for sayin' that! *(PROCTOR continues toward her.)* Abby'll charge lechery on you, Mr. Proctor!

PROCTOR *(halting):* She's told you!

MARY WARREN: I have known it, sir. She'll ruin you with it, I know she will.

PROCTOR *(hesitating, and with deep hatred of himself):* Good. Then her saintliness is done with. *(MARY backs from him.)* We will slide together into our pit; you will tell the court what you know.

MARY WARREN (*in terror*): I cannot, they'll turn on me—

(PROCTOR *strides and catches her, and she is repeating, "I cannot, I cannot!"*)

PROCTOR: My wife will never die for me! I will bring your guts into your mouth but that goodness will not die for me!

MARY WARREN (*struggling to escape him*): I cannot do it, I cannot!

PROCTOR (*grasping her by the throat as though he would strangle her*): Make your peace with it! Now Hell and Heaven grapple on our backs, and all our old pretense is ripped away—make your peace! (*He throws her to the floor, where she sobs, "I cannot, I cannot . . ."* And now, half to himself, staring, and turning to the open door) Peace. It is a providence, and no great change; we are only what we always were, but naked now. (*He walks as though toward a great horror, facing the open sky.*) Aye, naked! And the wind, God's icy wind, will blow!

(*And she is over and over again sobbing, "I cannot, I cannot, I cannot," as the curtain falls.*)

ACT THREE

The vestry room of the Salem meeting house, now serving as the anteroom of the General Court.

As the curtain rises, the room is empty, but for sunlight pouring through two high windows in the back wall. The room is solemn, even forbidding. Heavy beams jut out, boards of random widths make up the walls. At the right are two doors leading into the meeting house proper, where the court is being held. At the left another door leads outside.

There is a plain bench at the left, and another at the right. In the center a rather long meeting table, with stools and a considerable armchair snugged up to it.

Through the partitioning wall at the right we hear a prosecutor's voice, JUDGE HA-THORNE'S, *asking a question; then a woman's voice,* MARTHA COREY'S, *replying.*

HATHORNE'S VOICE: Now, Martha Corey, there is abundant evidence in our hands to show that you have given yourself to the reading of fortunes. Do you deny it?

MARTHA COREY'S VOICE: I am innocent to a witch. I know not what a witch is.

HATHORNE'S VOICE: How do you know, then, that you are not a witch?

MARTHA COREY'S VOICE: If I were, I would know it.

HATHORNE'S VOICE: Why do you hurt these children?

MARTHA COREY'S VOICE: I do not hurt them. I scorn it!

GILES' VOICE (*roaring*): I have evidence for the court!

(*Voices of townspeople rise in excitement.*)

DANFORTH'S VOICE: You will keep your seat!

GILES' VOICE: Thomas Putnam is reaching out for land!

DANFORTH'S VOICE: Remove that man, Marshal!

GILES' VOICE: You're hearing lies, lies!

(*A roaring goes up from the people.*)

HATHORNE'S VOICE: Arrest him, excellency!

GILES' VOICE: I have evidence. Why will you not hear my evidence?

(*The door opens and* GILES *is half carried into the vestry room by* HERRICK.)

GILES: Hands off, damn you, let me go!

HERRICK: Giles, Giles!

GILES: Out of my way, Herrick! I bring evidence—

HERRICK: You cannot go in there, Giles! it's a court!

(*Enter* HALE *from the court.*)

HALE: Pray be calm a moment.

GILES: You, Mr. Hale, go in there and demand I speak.

HALE: A moment, sir, a moment.

GILES: They'll be hangin' my wife!

(JUDGE HATHORNE *enters. He is in his sixties, a bitter, remorseless Salem judge.*)

HATHORNE: How do you dare come roarin' into this court! Are you gone daft, Corey?

GILES: You're not a Boston judge, Hathorne. You'll not call me daft!

(*Enter* DEPUTY GOVERNOR DANFORTH *and, behind him,* EZEKIEL CHEEVER *and* PARRIS. *On his appearance, silence falls.* DANFORTH *is a grave man in his sixties, of some humor and sophistication that does not, however, interfere with an exact loyalty to his position and his cause. He comes down to* GILES, *who awaits his wrath.)*

DANFORTH *(looking directly at* GILES*):* Who is this man?

PARRIS: Giles Corey, sir, and a more contentious—

GILES *(to* PARRIS*):* I am asked the question, and I am old enough to answer it! *(To* DANFORTH, *who impresses him and to whom he smiles through his strain)* My name is Corey, sir, Giles Corey. I have six hundred acres, and timber in addition. It is my wife you be condemning now. *(He indicates the courtroom.)*

DANFORTH: And how do you imagine to help her cause with such contemptuous riot? Now be gone. Your old age alone keeps you out of jail for this.

GILES *(beginning to plead):* They be tellin' lies about my wife, sir, I—

DANFORTH: Do you take it upon yourself to determine what this court shall believe and what it shall set aside?

GILES: Your Excellency, we mean no disrespect for—

DANFORTH: Disrespect indeed! It is disruption, Mister. This is the highest court of the supreme government of this province, do you know it?

GILES *(beginning to weep):* Your Excellency, I only said she were readin' books, sir, and they come and take her out of my house for—

DANFORTH *(mystified):* Books! What books?

GILES *(through helpless sobs):* It is my third wife, sir; I never had no wife that be so taken with books, and I thought to find the cause of it, d'y'see, but it were no witch I blamed her for. *(He is openly weeping.)* I have broke charity with the woman, I have broke charity with her. *(He covers his face, ashamed.* DANFORTH *is respectfully silent.)*

HALE: Excellency, he claims hard evidence for his wife's defense. I think that in all justice you must—

DANFORTH: Then let him submit his evidence in proper affidavit. You are certainly aware of our procedure here, Mr. Hale. *(To* HERRICK*)* Clear this room.

HERRICK: Come now, Giles. *(He gently pushes* COREY *out.)*

FRANCIS: We are desperate, sir; we come here three days now and cannot be heard.

DANFORTH: Who is this man?

FRANCIS: Francis Nurse, Your Excellency.

HALE: His wife's Rebecca that were condemned this morning.

DANFORTH: Indeed! I am amazed to find you in such uproar. I have only good report of your character, Mr. Nurse.

HATHORNE: I think they must both be arrested in contempt, sir.

DANFORTH *(to* FRANCIS*):* Let you write your plea, and in due time I will—

FRANCIS: Excellency, we have proof for your eyes; God forbid you shut them to it. The girls, sir, the girls are frauds.

DANFORTH: What's that?

FRANCIS: We have proof of it, sir. They are all deceiving you.

*(*DANFORTH *is shocked, but studying* FRANCIS.*)*

HATHORNE: This is contempt, sir, contempt!

DANFORTH: Peace, Judge Hathorne. Do you know who I am, Mr. Nurse?

FRANCIS: I surely do, sir, and I think you must be a wise judge to be what you are.

DANFORTH: And do you know that near to four hundred are in the jails from Marblehead to Lynn, and upon my signature?

FRANCIS: I—

DANFORTH: And seventy-two condemned to hang by that signature?

FRANCIS: Excellency, I never thought to say it to such a weighty judge, but you are deceived.

(Enter GILES COREY *from left. All turn to see as he beckons in* MARY WARREN *with* PROCTOR. MARY *is keeping her eyes to the ground;* PROCTOR *has her elbow as though she were near collapse.)*

PARRIS *(on seeing her, in shock):* Mary Warren! *(He goes directly to bend close to her face.)* What are you about here?

PROCTOR *(pressing* PARRIS *away from her with a gentle but firm motion of protectiveness):* She would speak with the Deputy Governor.

DANFORTH *(shocked by this, turns to* HERRICK*):* Did you not tell me Mary Warren were sick in bed?

HERRICK: She were, Your Honor. When I go to fetch her to the court last week, she said she were sick.

GILES: She has been strivin' with her soul all week, Your Honor; she comes now to tell the truth of this to you.

DANFORTH: Who is this?

PROCTOR: John Proctor, sir. Elizabeth Proctor is my wife.

PARRIS: Beware this man, Your Excellency, this man is mischief.

HALE (excitedly): I think you must hear the girl, sir, she—

DANFORTH (who has become very interested in MARY WARREN and only raises a hand toward HALE): Peace. What would you tell us, Mary Warren?

(PROCTOR looks at her, but she cannot speak.)

PROCTOR: She never saw no spirits, sir.

DANFORTH (with great alarm and surprise, to MARY): Never saw no spirits!

GILES (eagerly): Never.

PROCTOR (reaching into his jacket): She has signed a deposition, sir—

DANFORTH (instantly): No, no, I accept no depositions. (He is rapidly calculating this; he turns from her to PROCTOR.) Tell me, Mr. Proctor, have you given out this story in the village?

PROCTOR: We have not.

PARRIS: They've come to overthrow the court, sir! This man is—

DANFORTH: I pray you, Mr. Parris. Do you know, Mr. Proctor, that the entire contention of the state in these trials is that the voice of Heaven is speaking through the children?

PROCTOR: I know that, sir.

DANFORTH (thinks, staring at PROCTOR, then turns to MARY WARREN): And you, Mary Warren, how came you to cry out people for sending their spirits against you?

MARY WARREN: It were pretense, sir.

DANFORTH: I cannot hear you.

PROCTOR: It were pretense, she says.

DANFORTH: Ah? And the other girls? Susanna Walcott, and—the others? They are also pretending?

MARY WARREN: Aye, sir.

DANFORTH (wide-eyed): Indeed. (Pause. He is baffled by this. He turns to study PROCTOR's face.)

PARRIS (in a sweat): Excellency, you surely cannot think to let so vile a lie be spread in open court.

DANFORTH: Indeed not, but it strike hard upon me that she will dare come here with such a tale. Now, Mr. Proctor, before I decide whether I shall hear you or not, it is my duty to tell you this. We burn a hot fire here; it melts down all concealment.

PROCTOR: I know that, sir.

DANFORTH: Let me continue. I understand well, a husband's tenderness may drive him to extravagance in defense of a wife. Are you certain in your conscience, Mister, that your evidence is the truth?

PROCTOR: It is. And you will surely know it.

DANFORTH: And you thought to declare this revelation in the open court before the public?

PROCTOR: I thought I would, aye—with your permission.

DANFORTH (his eyes narrowing): Now, sir, what is your purpose in so doing?

PROCTOR: Why, I—I would free my wife, sir.

DANFORTH: There lurks nowhere in your heart, nor hidden in your spirit, any desire to undermine this court?

PROCTOR (with the faintest faltering): Why, no, sir.

CHEEVER (clears his throat, awakening): I— Your Excellency.

DANFORTH: Mr. Cheever.

CHEEVER: I think it be my duty, sir—(Kindly, to PROCTOR) You'll not deny it, John. (To DANFORTH) When we come to take his wife, he damned the court and ripped your warrant.

PARRIS: Now you have it!

DANFORTH: He did that, Mr. Hale?

HALE (takes a breath): Aye, he did.

PROCTOR: It were a temper, sir. I knew not what I did.

DANFORTH (studying him): Mr. Proctor.

PROCTOR: Aye, sir.

DANFORTH (straight into his eyes): Have you ever seen the Devil?

PROCTOR: No, sir.

DANFORTH: You are in all respects a Gospel Christian?

PROCTOR: I am, sir.

PARRIS: Such a Christian that will not come to church but once in a month!

DANFORTH (*Restrained—he is curious.*) Not come to church?

PROCTOR: I—I have no love for Mr. Parris. It is no secret. But God I surely love.

CHEEVER: He plow on Sunday, sir.

DANFORTH: Plow on Sunday!

CHEEVER (*apologetically*): I think it be evidence, John. I am an official of the court, I cannot keep it.

PROCTOR: I—I have once or twice plowed on Sunday. I have three children, sir, and until last year my land give little.

GILES: You'll find other Christians that do plow on Sunday if the truth be known.

HALE: Your Honor, I cannot think you may judge the man on such evidence.

DANFORTH: I judge nothing. (*Pause. He keeps watching* PROCTOR, *who tries to meet his gaze.*) I tell you straight, Mister—I have seen marvels in this court. I have seen people choked before my eyes by spirits; I have seen them stuck by pins and slashed by daggers. I have until this moment not the slightest reason to suspect that the children may be deceiving me. Do you understand my meaning?

PROCTOR: Excellency, does it not strike upon you that so many of these women have lived so long with such upright reputation, and—

PARRIS: Do you read the Gospel, Mr. Proctor?

PROCTOR: I read the Gospel.

PARRIS: I think not, or you should surely know that Cain were an upright man, and yet he did kill Abel.

PROCTOR: Aye, God tells us that. (*To* DANFORTH) But who tells us Rebecca Nurse murdered seven babies by sending out her spirit on them? It is the children only, and this one will swear she lied to you.

(DANFORTH *considers, then beckons* HATHORNE *to him.* HATHORNE *leans in, and he speaks in his ear.* HATHORNE *nods.*)

HATHORNE: Aye, she's the one.

DANFORTH: Mr. Proctor, this morning, your wife send me a claim in which she states that she is pregnant now.

PROCTOR: My wife pregnant!

DANFORTH: There be no sign of it—we have examined her body.

PROCTOR: But if she say she is pregnant, then she must be! That woman will never lie, Mr. Danforth.

DANFORTH: She will not?

PROCTOR: Never, sir, never.

DANFORTH: We have thought it too convenient to be credited. However, if I should tell you now that I will let her be kept another month; and if she begin to show her natural signs, you shall have her living yet another year until she is delivered—what say you to that? (JOHN PROCTOR *is struck silent.*) Come now. You say your only purpose is to save your wife. Good, then, she is saved at least this year, and a year is long. What say you, sir? It is done now. (*In conflict,* PROCTOR *glances at* FRANCIS *and* GILES.) Will you drop this charge?

PROCTOR: I—I think I cannot.

DANFORTH (*now an almost imperceptible hardness in his voice*): Then your purpose is somewhat larger.

PARRIS: He's come to overthrow this court, Your Honor!

PROCTOR: These are my friends. Their wives are also accused—

DANFORTH (*with a sudden briskness of manner*): I judge you not, sir. I am ready to hear your evidence.

PROCTOR: I come not to hurt the court; I only—

DANFORTH (*cutting him off*): Marshal, go into the court and bid Judge Stoughton and Judge Sewall declare recess for one hour. And let them go to the tavern, if they will. All witnesses and prisoners are to be kept in the building.

HERRICK: Aye, sir. (*Very deferentially*) If I may say it, sir, I know this man all my life. It is a good man, sir.

DANFORTH (*It is the reflection on himself he resents.*) I am sure of it, Marshal. (HERRICK *nods, then goes out.*) Now, what deposition do you have for us, Mr. Proctor? And I beg you be clear, open as the sky, and honest.

PROCTOR (*as he takes out several papers*): I am no lawyer, so I'll—

DANFORTH: The pure in heart need no lawyers. Proceed as you will.

PROCTOR (*handing* DANFORTH *a paper*): Will you read this first, sir? It's a sort of testament. The people signing it declare their good opinion of Rebecca, and my wife, and Martha Corey. (DANFORTH *looks down at the paper.*)

PROCTOR (*to enlist* DANFORTH's *sarcasm*): Their good opinion! (*But* DANFORTH *goes on reading, and* PROCTOR *is heartened.*)

PROCTOR: These are all landholding farmers, members of the church. (*Delicately, trying to point out a paragraph*) If you'll notice, sir—they've known the women many years and never saw no sign they had dealings with the Devil.

(PARRIS *nervously moves over and reads over* DANFORTH's *shoulder.*)

DANFORTH (*glancing down a long list*): How many names are here?

FRANCIS: Ninety-one, Your Excellency.

PARRIS (*sweating*): These people should be summoned. (DANFORTH *looks up at him questioningly.*) For questioning.

FRANCIS (*trembling with anger*): Mr. Danforth, I gave them all my word no harm would come to them for signing this.

PARRIS: This is a clear attack upon the court!

HALE (*to* PARRIS, *trying to contain himself*): Is every defense an attack upon the court? Can no one—?

PARRIS: All innocent and Christian people are happy for the courts in Salem! These people are gloomy for it. (*To* DANFORTH *directly*) And I think you will want to know, from each and every one of them, what discontents them with you!

HATHORNE: I think they ought to be examined, sir.

DANFORTH: It is not necessarily an attack, I think. Yet—

FRANCIS: These are all covenanted Christians, sir.

DANFORTH: Then I am sure they may have nothing to fear. (*Hands* CHEEVER *the paper*) Mr. Cheever, have warrants drawn for all of these—arrest for examination. (*To* PROCTOR)

Now, Mister, what other information do you have for us? (FRANCIS *is still standing, horrified.*) You may sit, Mr. Nurse.

FRANCIS: I have brought trouble on these people; I have—

DANFORTH: No, old man, you have not hurt these people if they are of good conscience. But you must understand, sir, that a person is either with this court or he must be counted against it, there be no road between. This is a sharp time, now, a precise time—we live no longer in the dusky afternoon when evil mixed itself with good and befuddled the world. Now, by God's grace, the shining sun is up, and them that fear not light will surely praise it. I hope you will be one of those. (MARY WARREN *suddenly sobs.*) She's not hearty, I see.

PROCTOR: No, she's not, sir. (*To* MARY, *bending to her, holding her hand, quietly*) Now remember what the angel Raphael said to the boy Tobias. Remember it.

MARY WARREN (*hardly audible*): Aye.

PROCTOR: "Do that which is good, and no harm shall come to thee."

MARY WARREN: Aye.

DANFORTH: Come, man, we wait you.

(MARSHAL HERRICK *returns, and takes his post at the door.*)

GILES: John, my deposition, give him mine.

PROCTOR: Aye. (*He hands* DANFORTH *another paper.*) This is Mr. Corey's deposition.

DANFORTH: Oh? (*He looks down at it. Now* HATHORNE *comes behind him and reads with him.*)

HATHORNE (*suspiciously*): What lawyer drew this, Corey?

GILES: You know I never hired a lawyer in my life, Hathorne.

DANFORTH (*finishing the reading*): It is very well phrased. My compliments. Mr. Parris, if Mr. Putnam is in the court, will you bring him in? (HATHORNE *takes the deposition, and walks to the window with it.* PARRIS *goes into the court.*) You have no legal training, Mr. Corey?

GILES (*very pleased*): I have the best, sir—I am thirty-three time in court in my life. And always plaintiff, too.

DANFORTH: Oh, then you're much put-upon.

GILES: I am never put-upon; I know my

rights, sir, and I will have them. You know, your father tried a case of mine—might be thirty-five year ago, I think.

DANFORTH: Indeed.

GILES: He never spoke to you of it?

DANFORTH: No, I cannot recall it.

GILES: That's strange, he give me nine pound damages. He were a fair judge, your father. Y'see, I had a white mare that time, and this fellow come to borrow the mare—(*Enter* PARRIS *with* THOMAS PUTNAM. *When he sees* PUTNAM, GILES' *ease goes; he is hard.*) Aye, there he is.

DANFORTH: Mr. Putnam, I have here an accusation by Mr. Corey against you. He states that you coldly prompted your daughter to cry witchery upon George Jacobs that is now in jail.

PUTNAM: It is a lie.

DANFORTH (*turning to* GILES): Mr. Putnam states your charge is a lie. What say you to that?

GILES (*furious, his fists clenched*): A fart on Thomas Putnam, that is what I say to that!

DANFORTH: What proof do you submit for your charge, sir?

GILES: My proof is there! (*Pointing to the paper*) If Jacobs hangs for a witch he forfeit up his property—that's law! And there is none but Putnam with the coin to buy so great a piece. This man is killing his neighbors for their land!

DANFORTH: But proof, sir, proof.

GILES (*pointing at his deposition*): The proof is there! I have it from an honest man who heard Putnam say it! The day his daughter cried out on Jacobs, he said she'd given him a fair gift of land.

HATHORNE: And the name of this man?

GILES (*taken aback*): What name?

HATHORNE: The man that give you this information.

GILES (*hesitates, then*): Why, I—I cannot give you his name.

HATHORNE: And why not?

GILES (*hesitates, then bursts out*): You know well why not! He'll lay in jail if I give his name!

HATHORNE: This is contempt of the court, Mr. Danforth!

DANFORTH (*to avoid that*): You will surely tell us the name.

GILES: I will not give you no name. I mentioned my wife's name once and I'll burn in hell long enough for that. I stand mute.

DANFORTH: In that case, I have no choice but to arrest you for contempt of this court, do you know that?

GILES: This is a hearing; you cannot clap me for contempt of a hearing.

DANFORTH: Oh, it is a proper lawyer! Do you wish me to declare the court in full session here? Or will you give me good reply?

GILES (*faltering*): I cannot give you no name, sir, I cannot.

DANFORTH: You are a foolish old man. Mr. Cheever, begin the record. The court is now in session. I ask you, Mr. Corey—

PROCTOR (*breaking in*): Your Honor—he has the story in confidence, sir, and he—

PARRIS: The Devil lives on such confidences! (*To* DANFORTH) Without confidences there could be no conspiracy, Your Honor!

HATHORNE: I think it must be broken, sir.

DANFORTH (*to* GILES): Old man, if your informant tells the truth let him come here openly like a decent man. But if he hide in anonymity I must know why. Now sir, the government and central church demand of you the name of him who reported Mr. Thomas Putnam a common murderer.

HALE: Excellency—

DANFORTH: Mr. Hale.

HALE: We cannot blink it more. There is a prodigious fear of this court in the country—

DANFORTH: Then there is a prodigious guilt in the country. Are *you* afraid to be questioned here?

HALE: I may only fear the Lord, sir, but there is fear in the country nevertheless.

DANFORTH (*angered now*): Reproach me not with the fear in the country; there is fear in the country because there is a moving plot to topple Christ in the country!

HALE: But it does not follow that everyone accused is part of it.

DANFORTH: No uncorrupted man may fear this court, Mr. Hale! None! (*To* GILES): You are under arrest in contempt of this court. Now sit you down and take counsel with yourself, or you will be set in the jail until you decide to answer all questions.

(GILES COREY *makes a rush for* PUTNAM. PROCTOR *lunges and holds him.*)

PROCTOR: No, Giles!

GILES (*over* PROCTOR'S *shoulder at* PUTNAM): I'll cut your throat, Putnam, I'll kill you yet!

PROCTOR (*forcing him into a chair*): Peace, Giles, peace. (*Releasing him.*) We'll prove ourselves. Now we will. (*He starts to turn to* DANFORTH.)

GILES: Say nothin' more, John. (*Pointing at* DANFORTH) He's only playin' you! He means to hang us all!

(MARY WARREN *bursts into sobs.*)

DANFORTH: This is a court of law, Mister. I'll have no effrontery here!

PROCTOR: Forgive him, sir, for his old age. Peace, Giles, we'll prove it all now. (*He lifts up* MARY'S *chin.*) You cannot weep, Mary. Remember the angel, what he say to the boy. Hold to it, now; there is your rock. (MARY *quiets. He takes out a paper, and turns to* DANFORTH.) This is Mary Warren's deposition. I—I would ask you remember, sir, while you read it, that until two week ago she were no different than the other children are today. (*He is speaking reasonably, restraining all his fears, his anger, his anxiety.*) You saw her scream, she howled, she swore familiar spirits choked her; she even testified that Satan, in the form of women now in jail, tried to win her soul away, and then when she refused—

DANFORTH: We know all this.

PROCTOR: Aye, sir. She swears now that she never saw Satan; nor any spirit, vague or clear, that Satan may have sent to hurt her. And she declares her friends are lying now.

(PROCTOR *starts to hand* DANFORTH *the deposition, and* HALE *comes up to* DANFORTH *in a trembling state.*)

HALE: Excellency, a moment. I think this goes to the heart of the matter.

DANFORTH (*with deep misgivings*): It surely does.

HALE: I cannot say he is an honest man; I know him little. But in all justice, sir, a claim so weighty cannot be argued by a farmer. In God's name, sir, stop here; send him home and let him come again with a lawyer—

DANFORTH (*patiently*): Now look you, Mr. Hale—

HALE: Excellency, I have signed seventy-two death warrants; I am a minister of the Lord, and I dare not take a life without there be a proof so immaculate no slightest qualm of conscience may doubt it.

DANFORTH: Mr. Hale, you surely do not doubt my justice.

HALE: I have this morning signed away the soul of Rebecca Nurse, Your Honor. I'll not conceal it, my hand shakes yet as with a wound! I pray you, sir, *this* argument let lawyers present to you.

DANFORTH: Mr. Hale, believe me; for a man of such terrible learning you are most bewildered—I hope you will forgive me. I have been thirty-two year at the bar, sir, and I should be confounded were I called upon to defend these people. Let you consider, now— (*To* PROCTOR *and the others*) And I bid you all do likewise. In an ordinary crime, how does one defend the accused? One calls up witnesses to prove his innocence. But witchcraft is *ipso facto*, on its face and by its nature, an invisible crime, is it not? Therefore, who may possibly be witness to it? The witch and the victim. None other. Now we cannot hope the witch will accuse herself; granted? Therefore, we must rely upon her victims—and they do testify, the children certainly do testify. As for the witches, none will deny that we are most eager for all their confessions. Therefore, what is left for a lawyer to bring out? I think I have made my point. Have I not?

HALE: But this child claims the girls are not truthful, and if they are not—

DANFORTH: That is precisely what I am about to consider, sir. What more may you ask of me? Unless you doubt my probity?

HALE (*defeated*): I surely do not, sir. Let you consider it, then.

DANFORTH: And let you put your heart to rest. Her deposition, Mr. Proctor.

(PROCTOR *hands it to him.* HATHORNE *rises, goes beside* DANFORTH, *and starts reading.* PARRIS *comes to his other side.* DANFORTH *looks at* JOHN PROCTOR, *then proceeds to read.* HALE *gets up, finds position near the* JUDGE, *reads too.* PROCTOR *glances at* GILES. FRANCIS *prays silently, hands pressed together.* CHEEVER *waits placidly, the sublime official, dutiful.* MARY WARREN *sobs once.* JOHN PROCTOR *touches her head reassuringly. Presently* DANFORTH *lifts his eyes, stands up, takes out a kerchief and blows his nose. The others stand aside as he moves in thought toward the window.)*

PARRIS *(hardly able to contain his anger and fear):* I should like to question—

DANFORTH *(his first real outburst, in which his contempt for* PARRIS *is clear):* Mr. Parris, I bid you be silent! *(He stands in silence, looking out the window. Now, having established that he will set the gait)* Mr. Cheever, will you go into the court and bring the children here?* (CHEEVER *gets up and goes out upstage.* DANFORTH *now turns to* MARY.) Mary Warren, how came you to this turnabout? Has Mr. Proctor threatened you for this deposition?

MARY WARREN: No, sir.

DANFORTH: Has he ever threatened you?

MARY WARREN *(weaker):* No, sir.

DANFORTH *(sensing a weakening):* Has he threatened you?

MARY WARREN: No, sir.

DANFORTH: Then you tell me that you sat in my court, callously lying, when you knew that people would hang by your evidence? *(She does not answer.)* Answer me!

MARY WARREN *(almost inaudibly):* I did, sir.

DANFORTH: How were you instructed in your life? Do you not know that God damns all liars? *(She cannot speak.)* Or is it now that you lie?

MARY WARREN: No, sir—I am with God now.

DANFORTH: You are with God now.

MARY WARREN: Aye, sir.

DANFORTH *(containing himself):* I will tell you this—you are either lying now, or you were lying in the court, and in either case you have committed perjury and you will go to jail for it. You cannot lightly say you lied, Mary. Do you know that?

MARY WARREN: I cannot lie no more. I am with God, I am with God.

(But she breaks into sobs at the thought of it, and the right door opens, and enter SUSANNA WALCOTT, MERCY LEWIS, BETTY PAR-

RIS, *and finally* ABIGAIL. CHEEVER *comes to* DANFORTH.)*

CHEEVER: Ruth Putnam's not in the court, sir, nor the other children.

DANFORTH: These will be sufficient. Sit you down, children. *(Silently they sit.)* Your friend, Mary Warren, has given us a deposition. In which she swears that she never saw familiar spirits, apparitions, nor any manifest of the Devil. She claims as well that none of you have seen these things either. *(Slight pause.)* Now, children, this is a court of law. The law, based upon the Bible, and the Bible, writ by Almighty God, forbid the practice of witchcraft, and describe death as the penalty thereof. But likewise, children, the law and Bible damn all bearers of false witness. *(Slight pause.)* Now then. It does not escape me that this deposition may be devised to blind us; it may well be that Mary Warren has been conquered by Satan, who sends her here to distract our sacred purpose. If so, her neck will break for it. But if she speak true, I bid you now drop your guile and confess your pretense, for a quick confession will go easier with you. *(Pause.)* Abigail Williams, rise. *(Abigail slowly rises.)* Is there any truth in this?

ABIGAIL: No, sir.

DANFORTH *(thinks, glances at* MARY, *then back to* ABIGAIL*):* Children, a very augur bit will now be turned into your souls until your honesty is proved. Will either of you change your positions now, or do you force me to hard questioning?

ABIGAIL: I have naught to change, sir. She lies.

DANFORTH *(to* MARY*):* You would still go on with this?

MARY WARREN *(faintly):* Aye, sir.

DANFORTH *(turning to Abigail):* A poppet were discovered in Mr. Proctor's house, stabbed by a needle. Mary Warren claims that you sat beside her in the court when she made it, and that you saw her make it and witnessed how she herself stuck the needle into it for safe-keeping. What say you to that?

ABIGAIL *(with a slight note of indignation):* It is a lie, sir.

DANFORTH *(after a slight pause):* While you

worked for Mr. Proctor, did you see poppets in that house?

ABIGAIL: Goody Proctor always kept poppets.

PROCTOR: Your Honor, my wife never kept no poppets. Mary Warren confesses it was her poppet.

CHEEVER: Your Excellency.

DANFORTH: Mr. Cheever.

CHEEVER: When I spoke with Goody Proctor in that house, she said she never kept no poppets. But she said she did keep poppets when she were a girl.

PROCTOR: She has not been a girl these fifteen years, Your Honor.

HATHORNE: But a poppet will keep fifteen years, will it not?

PROCTOR: It will keep if it is kept, but Mary Warren swears she never saw no poppets in my house, nor anyone else.

PARRIS: Why could there not have been poppets hid where no one ever saw them?

PROCTOR (furious): There might also be a dragon with five legs in my house, but no one has ever seen it.

PARRIS: We are here, Your Honor, precisely to discover what no one has even seen.

PROCTOR: Mr. Danforth, what profit this girl to turn herself about? What may Mary Warren gain but hard questioning and worse?

DANFORTH: You are charging Abigail Williams with a marvelous cool plot to murder, do you understand that?

PROCTOR: I do, sir. I believe she means to murder.

DANFORTH (pointing at ABIGAIL, incredulously): This child would murder your wife?

PROCTOR: It is not a child. Now hear me, sir. In the sight of the congregation she were twice this year put out of this meetin' house for laughter during prayer.

DANFORTH (shocked, turning to ABIGAIL): What's this? Laughter during—!

PARRIS: Excellency, she were under Tituba's power at that time, but she is solemn now.

GILES: Aye, now she is solemn and goes to hang people!

DANFORTH: Quiet, man.

HATHORNE: Surely it have no bearing on the question, sir. He charges contemplation of murder.

DANFORTH: Aye. (He studies ABIGAIL for a moment. Then) Continue, Mr. Proctor.

PROCTOR: Mary. Now tell the Governor how you danced in the woods.

PARRIS (instantly): Excellency, since I come to Salem this man is blackening my name. He—

DANFORTH: In a moment, sir. (To MARY WARREN, sternly, and surprised) What is this dancing?

MARY WARREN: I—(She glances at ABIGAIL, who is staring down at her remorselessly. Then, appealing to PROCTOR) Mr. Proctor—

PROCTOR (taking it right up): Abigail leads the girls to the woods, Your Honor, and they have danced there naked—

PARRIS: Your Honor, this—

PROCTOR (at once): Mr. Parris discovered them himself in the dead of night! There's the "child" she is!

DANFORTH (It is growing into a nightmare, and he turns, astonished, to PARRIS.) Mr. Parris—

PARRIS: I can only say, sir, that I never found any of them naked, and this man is—

DANFORTH: But you discovered them dancing in the woods? (Eyes on Parris, he points at ABIGAIL.) Abigail?

HALE: Excellency, when I first arrived from Beverly, Mr. Parris told me that.

DANFORTH: Do you deny it, Mr. Parris?

PARRIS: I do not, sir, but I never saw any of them naked.

DANFORTH: But she have danced?

PARRIS (unwillingly): Aye, sir.

(DANFORTH, as though with new eyes, looks at ABIGAIL.)

HATHORNE: Excellency, will you permit me? (He points at MARY WARREN.)

DANFORTH (with great worry): Pray, proceed.

HATHORNE: You say you never saw no spirits, Mary, were never threatened or afflicted by any manifest of the Devil or the Devil's agents.

MARY WARREN (very faintly): No, sir.

HATHORNE (with a gleam of victory): And

yet, when people accused of witchery confronted you in court, you would faint, saying their spirits came out of their bodies and choked you—

MARY WARREN: That were pretense, sir.

DANFORTH: I cannot hear you.

MARY WARREN: Pretense, sir.

PARRIS: But you did turn cold, did you not? I myself picked you up many times, and your skin were icy. Mr. Danforth, you—

DANFORTH: I saw that many times.

PROCTOR: She only pretended to faint, Your Excellency. They're all marvelous pretenders.

HATHORNE: Then can she pretend to faint now?

PROCTOR: Now?

PARRIS: Why not? Now there are no spirits attacking her, for none in this room is accused of witchcraft. So let her turn herself cold now, let her pretend she is attacked now, let her faint. (He turns to MARY WARREN.) Faint!

MARY WARREN: Faint?

PARRIS: Aye, faint. Prove to us how you pretended in the court so many times.

MARY WARREN (looking to PROCTOR): I—cannot faint now, sir.

PROCTOR (alarmed, quietly): Can you not pretend it?

MARY WARREN: I—(She looks about as though searching for the passion to faint.) I—have no sense of it now, I—

DANFORTH: Why? What is lacking now?

MARY WARREN: I—cannot tell, sir, I—

DANFORTH: Might it be that here we have no afflicting spirit loose, but in the court there were some?

MARY WARREN: I never saw no spirits.

PARRIS: Then see no spirits now, and prove to us that you can faint by your own will, as you claim.

MARY WARREN (stares, searching for the emotion of it, and then shakes her head): I—cannot do it.

PARRIS: Then you will confess, will you not? It were attacking spirits made you faint!

MARY WARREN: No, sir, I—

PARRIS: Your Excellency, this is a trick to blind the court!

MARY WARREN: It's not a trick! (She stands.)

I—I used to faint because I—I thought I saw spirits.

DANFORTH: *Thought* you saw them!

MARY WARREN: But I did not, Your Honor.

HATHORNE: How could you think you saw them unless you saw them?

MARY WARREN: I—I cannot tell how, but I did. I—I heard the other girls screaming, and you, Your Honor, you seemed to believe them, and I—It were only sport in the beginning, sir, but then the whole world cried spirits, spirits, and I—I promise you, Mr. Danforth, I only thought I saw them but I did not.

(DANFORTH peers at her.)

PARRIS (smiling, but nervous because DANFORTH seems to be struck by MARY WARREN's story): Surely Your Excellency is not taken by this simple lie.

DANFORTH (turning worriedly to Abigail): Abigail. I bid you now search your heart and tell me this—and beware of it, child, to God every soul is precious and His vengeance is terrible on them that take life without cause. Is it possible, child, that the spirits you have seen are illusion only, some deception that may cross your mind when—

ABIGAIL: Why, this—this—is a base question, sir.

DANFORTH: Child, I would have you consider it—

ABIGAIL: I have been hurt, Mr. Danforth; I have seen my blood runnin' out! I have been near to murdered every day because I done my duty pointing out the Devil's people—and this is my reward? To be mistrusted, denied, questioned like a—

DANFORTH (weakening): Child, I do not mistrust you—

ABIGAIL (in an open threat): Let *you* beware, Mr. Danforth. Think you to be so mighty that the power of Hell may not turn *your* wits? Beware of it! There is—(Suddenly, from an accusatory attitude, her face turns, looking into the air above—it is truly frightened.)

DANFORTH (apprehensively): What is it, child?

ABIGAIL (looking about in the air, clasping her arms about her as though cold): I—I know not. A wind, a cold wind, has come. *(Her eyes fall on* MARY WARREN.*)*

MARY WARREN *(terrified, pleading):* Abby!

MERCY LEWIS *(shivering):* Your Honor, I freeze!

PROCTOR: They're pretending!

HATHORNE *(touching* ABIGAIL's *hand):* She is cold, Your Honor, touch her!

MERCY LEWIS *(through chattering teeth):* Mary, do you send this shadow on me?

MARY WARREN: Lord, save me!

SUSANNA WALCOTT: I freeze, I freeze!

ABIGAIL *(shivering visibly):* It is a wind, a wind!

MARY WARREN: Abby, don't do that!

DANFORTH *(himself engaged and entered by* ABIGAIL*):* Mary Warren, do you witch her? I say to you, do you send your spirit out?

(With a hysterical cry MARY WARREN *starts to run.* PROCTOR *catches her.)*

MARY WARREN *(almost collapsing):* Let me go, Mr. Proctor, I cannot, I cannot—

ABIGAIL *(crying to Heaven):* Oh, Heavenly Father, take away this shadow!

(Without warning or hesitation, PROCTOR *leaps at* ABIGAIL *and, grabbing her by the hair, pulls her to her feet. She screams in pain.* DAN-FORTH, *astonished, cries, "What are you about?" and* HATHORNE *and* PARRIS *call, "Take your hands off her!" and out of it all comes* PROCTOR's *roaring voice.)*

PROCTOR: How do you call Heaven! Whore! Whore!

*(*HERRICK *breaks* PROCTOR *from her.)*

HERRICK: John!

DANFORTH: Man! Man, what do you—

PROCTOR *(breathless and in agony):* It is a whore!

DANFORTH *(dumfounded):* You charge—?

ABIGAIL: Mr. Danforth, he is lying!

PROCTOR: Mark her! Now she'll suck a scream to stab me with, but—

DANFORTH: You will prove this! This will not pass!

PROCTOR *(trembling, his life collapsing about him):* I have known her, sir. I have known her.

DANFORTH: You—you are a lecher?

FRANCIS *(horrified):* John, you cannot say such a—

PROCTOR: Oh, Francis, I wish you had some evil in you that you might know me! *(To* DAN-FORTH*)* A man will not cast away his good name. You surely know that.

DANFORTH *(dumfounded):* In—in what time? In what place?

PROCTOR *(his voice about to break, and his shame great):* In the proper place—where my beasts are bedded. On the last night of my joy, some eight months past. She used to serve me in my house, sir. *(He has to clamp his jaw to keep from weeping.)* A man may think God sleeps, but God sees everything. I know it now. I beg you, sir, I beg you—see her what she is. My wife, my dear good wife, took this girl soon after, sir, and put her out on the highroad. And being what she is, a lump of vanity, sir—*(He is being overcome.)* Excellency, forgive me, forgive me. *(Angrily against himself, he turns away from the governor for a moment.)* *(Then, as though to cry out is his only means of speech left)* She thinks to dance with me on my wife's grave! And well she might, for I thought of her softly. God help me, I lusted, and there *is* a promise in such sweat. But it is a whore's vengeance, and you must see it; I set myself entirely in your hands. I know you must see it now.

DANFORTH *(blanched, in horror, turning to* ABIGAIL*):* You deny every scrap and tittle of this?

ABIGAIL: If I must answer that, I will leave and I will not come back again!

*(*DANFORTH *seems unsteady.)*

PROCTOR: I have a bell of my honor! I have rung the doom of my good name—you will believe me, Mr. Danforth! My wife is innocent, except she knew a whore when she saw one!

ABIGAIL *(stepping up to* DANFORTH*):* What look do you give me? *(*DANFORTH *cannot speak.)* I'll not have such looks! *(She turns and starts for the door.)*

DANFORTH: You will remain where you are! *(*HERRICK *steps into her path. She comes up short, fire in her eyes.)* Mr. Parris, go into the court and bring Goodwife Proctor out.

PARRIS *(objecting):* Your Honor, this is all a—

DANFORTH *(sharply to* PARRIS*):* Bring her out! And tell her not one word of what's been spoken here. And let you knock before you enter. (PARRIS *goes out.*) Now we shall touch the bottom of this swamp. *(To* PROCTOR*)* Your wife, you say, is an honest woman.

PROCTOR: In her life, sir, she have never lied. There are them that cannot sing, and them that cannot weep—my wife cannot lie. I have paid much to learn it, sir.

DANFORTH: And when she put this girl out of your house, she put her out for a harlot?

PROCTOR: Aye, sir.

DANFORTH: And knew her for a harlot?

PROCTOR: Aye, sir, she knew her for a harlot.

DANFORTH: Good then. *(To* ABIGAIL*)* And if she tell me, child, it were for harlotry, may God spread His mercy on you! *(There is a knock. He calls to the door.)* Hold! *(To* ABIGAIL*)* Turn your back. Turn your back. *(To* PROCTOR*)* Do likewise. *(Both turn their backs* —ABIGAIL *with indignant slowness.)* Now let neither of you turn to face Goody Proctor. No one in this room is to speak one word, or raise a gesture aye or nay. *(He turns toward the door, calls.)* Enter! *(The door opens.* ELIZABETH *enters with* PARRIS. PARRIS *leaves her. She stands alone, her eyes looking for* PROCTOR.*)* Mr. Cheever, report this testimony in all exactness. Are you ready?

CHEEVER: Ready, sir.

DANFORTH: Come here, woman. (ELIZABETH *comes to him, glancing at* PROCTOR's *back.)* Look at me only, not at your husband. In my eyes only.

ELIZABETH *(faintly)*: Good, sir.

DANFORTH: We are given to understand that at one time you dismissed your servant, Abigail Williams.

ELIZABETH: That is true, sir.

DANFORTH: For what cause did you dismiss her? *(Slight pause. Then* ELIZABETH *tries to glance at* PROCTOR.*)* You will look in my eyes only and not at your husband. The answer is in your memory and you need no help to give it to me. Why did you dismiss Abigail Williams?

ELIZABETH *(not knowing what to say, sensing a situation, wetting her lips to stall for time)*: She—dissatisfied me. *(Pause.)* And my husband.

DANFORTH: In what way dissatisfied you?

ELIZABETH: She were—*(She glances at* PROCTOR *for a cue.)*

DANFORTH: Woman, look at me? (ELIZABETH *does.)* Were she slovenly? Lazy? What disturbance did she cause?

ELIZABETH: Your Honor, I—in that time I were sick. And I—My husband is a good and righteous man. He is never drunk as some are, nor wastin' his time at the shovelboard, but always at his work. But in my sickness—you see, sir, I were a long time sick after my last baby, and I thought I saw my husband somewhat turning from me. And this girl—*(She turns to* ABIGAIL.*)*

DANFORTH: Look at me.

ELIZABETH: Aye, sir. Abigail Williams—*(She breaks off.)*

DANFORTH: What of Abigail Williams?

ELIZABETH: I came to think he fancied her. And so one night I lost my wits, I think, and put her out on the highroad.

DANFORTH: Your husband—did he indeed turn from you?

ELIZABETH *(in agony)*: My husband—is a goodly man, sir.

DANFORTH: Then he did not turn from you.

ELIZABETH *(starting to glance at Proctor)*: He—

DANFORTH *(reaches out and holds her face, then)*: Look at me! To your own knowledge, has John Proctor ever committed the crime of lechery? *(In a crisis of indecision she cannot speak.)* Answer my question! Is your husband a lecher!

ELIZABETH *(faintly)*: No, sir.

DANFORTH: Remove her, Marshal.

PROCTOR: Elizabeth, tell the truth!

DANFORTH: She has spoken. Remove her!

PROCTOR *(crying out)*: Elizabeth, I have confessed it!

ELIZABETH: Oh, God! *(The door closes behind her.)*

PROCTOR: She only thought to save my name!

HALE: Excellency, it is a natural lie to tell; I beg you, stop now before another is condemned! I may shut my conscience to it no more—private vengeance is working through this testimony! From the beginning this man has struck me true. By my oath to Heaven, I believe him now, and I pray you call back his wife before we—

DANFORTH: She spoke nothing of lechery, and this man has lied!

HALE: I believe him! (*Pointing at* ABIGAIL) This girl has always struck me false! She has—

(ABIGAIL, *with a weird, wild, chilling cry, screams up to the ceiling.*)

ABIGAIL: You will not! Begone! Begone, I say!

DANFORTH: What is it, child? (*But* ABIGAIL, *pointing with fear, is now raising up her frightened eyes, her awed face, toward the ceiling—the girls are doing the same—and now* HATHORNE, HALE, PUTNAM, CHEEVER, HERRICK, *and* DANFORTH *do the same.*) What's there? (*He lowers his eyes from the ceiling, and now he is frightened; there is real tension in his voice.*) Child! (*She is transfixed—with all the girls, she is whimpering open-mouthed, agape at the ceiling.*) Girls! Why do you—?

MERCY LEWIS (*pointing*): It's on the beam! Behind the rafter!

DANFORTH (*looking up*): Where!

ABIGAIL: Why—? (*She gulps.*) Why do you come, yellow bird?

PROCTOR: Where's a bird? I see no bird!

ABIGAIL (*to the ceiling*): My face? My face?

PROCTOR: Mr. Hale—

DANFORTH: Be quiet!

PROCTOR (*to* HALE): Do you see a bird?

DANFORTH: Be quiet!!

ABIGAIL (*to the ceiling, in a genuine conversation with the "bird," as though trying to talk it out of attacking her*): But God made my face; you cannot want to tear my face. Envy is a deadly sin, Mary.

MARY WARREN (*on her feet with a spring, and horrified, pleading*): Abby!

ABIGAIL (*unperturbed, continuing to the "bird"*): Oh, Mary, this is a black art to change your shape. No, I cannot, I cannot stop my mouth; it's God's work I do.

MARY WARREN: Abby, I'm *here!*

PROCTOR (*frantically*): They're pretending, Mr. Danforth!

ABIGAIL (*Now she takes a backward step, as though in fear the bird will swoop down momentarily.*) Oh, please, Mary! Don't come down.

SUSANNA WALCOTT: Her claws, she's stretching her claws!

PROCTOR: Lies, lies.

ABIGAIL (*backing further, eyes still fixed above*): Mary, please don't hurt me!

MARY WARREN (*to* DANFORTH): I'm not hurting her!

DANFORTH (*to* MARY WARREN): Why does she see this vision?

MARY WARREN: She sees nothin'!

ABIGAIL (*now staring full front as though hypnotized, and mimicking the exact tone of* MARY WARREN's *cry*): She sees nothin'!

MARY WARREN (*pleading*): Abby, you mustn't!

ABIGAIL AND ALL THE GIRLS (*all transfixed*): Abby, you mustn't!

MARY WARREN (*to all the girls*): I'm here, I'm here!

GIRLS: I'm here, I'm here!

DANFORTH (*horrified*): Mary Warren! Draw back your spirit out of them!

MARY WARREN: Mr. Danforth!

GIRLS (*cutting her off*): Mr. Danforth!

DANFORTH: Have you compacted with the Devil? Have you?

MARY WARREN: Never, never!

GIRLS: Never, never!

DANFORTH (*growing hysterical*): Why can they only repeat you?

PROCTOR: Give me a whip—I'll stop it!

MARY WARREN: They're sporting. They—!

GIRLS: They're sporting!

MARY WARREN (*turning on them all hysterically and stamping her feet*): Abby, stop it!

GIRLS (*stamping their feet*): Abby, stop it!

MARY WARREN: Stop it!

GIRLS: Stop it!

MARY WARREN (*screaming it out at the top of her lungs, and raising her fists*): Stop it!!

GIRLS (*raising their fists*): Stop it!!

(MARY WARREN, *utterly confounded, and becoming overwhelmed by* ABIGAIL's—*and the girls'—utter conviction, starts to whimper, hands half raised, powerless, and all the girls begin whimpering exactly as she does.*)

DANFORTH: A little while ago you were

afflicted. Now it seems you afflict others; where did you find this power?

MARY WARREN (*staring at* ABIGAIL): I—have no power.

GIRLS: I have no power.

PROCTOR: They're gulling you, Mister!

DANFORTH: Why did you turn about this past two weeks? You have seen the Devil, have you not?

HALE (*indicating* ABIGAIL *and the girls*): You cannot believe them!

MARY WARREN: I—

PROCTOR (*sensing her weakening*): Mary, God damns all liars!

DANFORTH (*pounding it into her*): You have seen the Devil, you have made compact with Lucifer, have you not?

PROCTOR: God damns liars, Mary!

(MARY *utters something unintelligible, staring at* ABIGAIL, *who keeps watching the "bird" above.*)

DANFORTH: I cannot hear you. What do you say? (MARY *utters again unintelligibly.*) You will confess yourself or you will hang? (*He turns her roughly to face him.*) Do you know who I am? I say you will hang if you do not open with me!

PROCTOR: Mary, remember the angel Raphael—do that which is good and—

ABIGAIL (*pointing upward*): The wings! Her wings are spreading! Mary, please, don't, don't—!

HALE: I see nothing, Your Honor!

DANFORTH: Do you confess this power! (*He is an inch from her face.*) Speak!

ABIGAIL: She's going to come down! She's walking the beam!

DANFORTH: Will you speak!

MARY WARREN (*staring in horror*): I cannot!

GIRLS: I cannot!

PARRIS: Cast the Devil out! Look him in the face! Trample him! We'll save you, Mary, only stand fast against him and—

ABIGAIL (*looking up*): Look out! She's coming down!

(*She and all the girls run to one wall, shielding their eyes. And now, as though cornered, they let out a gigantic scream, and* MARY, *as though infected, opens her mouth and screams*

with them. Gradually ABIGAIL *and the girls leave off, until only* MARY *is left there, staring up at the "bird," screaming madly. All watch her, horrified by this evident fit.* PROCTOR *strides to her.*)

PROCTOR: Mary, tell the Governor what they—(*He has hardly got a word out, when, seeing him coming for her, she rushes out of his reach, screaming in horror.*)

MARY WARREN: Don't touch me—don't touch me! (*At which the girls halt at the door.*)

PROCTOR (*astonished*): Mary!

MARY WARREN (*pointing at* PROCTOR): You're the Devil's man!

(*He is stopped in his tracks.*)

PARRIS: Praise God!

GIRLS: Praise God!

PROCTOR (*numbed*): Mary, how—?

MARY WARREN: I'll not hang with you! I love God, I love God.

DANFORTH (*to* MARY): He bid you do the Devil's work?

MARY WARREN (*hysterically, indicating* PROCTOR): He come at me by night and every day to sign, to sign, to—

DANFORTH: Sign what?

PARRIS: The Devil's book? He come with a book?

MARY WARREN (*hysterically, pointing at* PROCTOR, *fearful of him*): My name, he want my name. "I'll murder you," he says, "if my wife hangs! We must go and overthrow the court," he says!

(DANFORTH'S *head jerks toward* PROCTOR, *shock and horror in his face.*)

PROCTOR (*turning, appealing to* HALE): Mr. Hale!

MARY WARREN (*her sobs beginning*): He wake me every night, his eyes were like coals and his fingers claw my neck, and I sign, I sign . . .

HALE: Excellency, this child's gone wild!

PROCTOR (*as* DANFORTH'S *wide eyes pour on him*): Mary, Mary!

MARY WARREN (*screaming at him*): No, I love God; I go your way no more. I love God, I bless God. (*Sobbing, she rushes to* ABIGAIL.) Abby, Abby, I'll never hurt you more! (*They all watch, as* ABIGAIL, *out of her* infinite charity, *reaches out and draws the sobbing* MARY *to her, and then looks up to* DANFORTH.)

DANFORTH (*to* PROCTOR): What are you? (PROCTOR *is beyond speech in his anger.*) You are combined with anti-Christ, are you not? I have seen your power; you will not deny it! What say you, Mister?

HALE: Excellency—

DANFORTH: I will have nothing from you, Mr. Hale! (*To* PROCTOR) Will you confess yourself befouled with Hell, or do you keep that black allegiance yet? What say you?

PROCTOR (*his mind wild, breathless*): I say— I say—God is dead!

PARRIS: Hear it, hear it!

PROCTOR (*laughs insanely, then*): A fire, a fire is burning! I hear the boot of Lucifer, I see his filthy face! And it is my face, and yours, Danforth! For them that quail to bring men out of ignorance, as I have quailed, and as you quail now when you know in all your black hearts that this be fraud—God damns our kind especially, and we will burn, we will burn together.

DANFORTH: Marshal! Take him and Corey with him to the jail!

HALE (*starting across to the door*): I denounce these proceedings!

PROCTOR: You are pulling Heaven down and raising up a whore!

HALE: I denounce these proceedings, I quit this court! (*He slams the door to the outside behind him.*)

DANFORTH (*calling to him in a fury*): Mr. Hale! Mr. Hale!

(*The curtain falls.*)

ACT FOUR

A cell in Salem jail, that fall.

At the back is a high barred window; near it, a great, heavy door. Along the walls are two benches.

The place is in darkness but for the moon-light seeping through the bars. It appears empty. Presently footsteps are heard coming down a corridor beyond the wall, keys rattle, and the door swings open. MARSHAL HERRICK enters with a lantern.

He is nearly drunk, and heavy-footed. He goes to a bench and nudges a bundle of rags lying on it.

HERRICK: Sarah, wake up! Sarah Good! (*He then crosses to the other bench.*)

SARAH GOOD (*rising in her rags*): Oh, Majesty! Comin', comin'! Tituba, he's here, His Majesty's come!

HERRICK: Go to the north cell; this place is wanted now. (*He hangs his lantern on the wall.* TITUBA *sits up.*)

TITUBA: That don't look to me like His Majesty; look to me like the marshal.

HERRICK (*taking out a flask*): Get along with you now, clear this place. (*He drinks, and* SARAH GOOD *comes and peers up into his face.*)

SARAH GOOD: Oh, is it you, Marshal! I thought sure you be the devil comin' for us. Could I have a sip of cider for me goin'-away?

HERRICK (*handing her the flask*): And where are you off to, Sarah?

TITUBA (*as* SARAH *drinks*): We goin' to Barbados, soon the Devil gits here with the feathers and the wings.

HERRICK: Oh? A happy voyage to you.

SARAH GOOD: A pair of bluebirds wingin' southerly, the two of us! Oh, it be a grand transformation, Marshal! (*She raises the flask to drink again.*)

HERRICK (*taking the flask from her lips*): You'd best give me that or you'll never rise off the ground. Come along now.

TITUBA: I'll speak to him for you, if you desires to come along, Marshal.

HERRICK: I'd not refuse it, Tituba; it's the proper morning to fly into Hell.

TITUBA: Oh, it be no Hell in Barbados. Devil, him be pleasureman in Barbados, him be singin' and dancin' in Barbados. It's you folks—you riles him up 'round here; it be too cold 'round here for that Old Boy. He freeze his soul in Massachusetts, but in Barbados he just as sweet and—(*A bellowing cow is heard, and* TITUBA *leaps up and calls to the window.*) Aye, sir! That's him, Sarah!

SARAH GOOD: I'm here, Majesty! (*They hur-*

riedly pick up their rags as HOPKINS, *a guard, enters.)*

HOPKINS: The Deputy Governor's arrived.

HERRICK *(grabbing* TITUBA*):* Come along, come along.

TITUBA *(resisting him):* No, he comin' for me. I goin' home!

HERRICK *(pulling her to the door):* That's not Satan, just a poor old cow with a hatful of milk. Come along now, out with you!

TITUBA *(calling to the window):* Take me home, Devil! Take me home!

SARAH GOOD *(following the shouting* TITUBA *out):* Tell him I'm goin', Tituba! Now you tell him Sarah Good is goin' too!

(In the corridor outside TITUBA *calls on—"Take me home, Devil; Devil take me home!" and* HOPKINS' *voice orders her to move on.* HERRICK *returns and begins to push old rags and straw into a corner. Hearing footsteps, he turns, and enter* DANFORTH *and* JUDGE HATHORNE. *They are in greatcoats and wear hats against the bitter cold. They are followed in by* CHEEVER, *who carries a dispatch case and a flat wooden box containing his writing materials.)*

HERRICK: Good morning, Excellency.

DANFORTH: Where is Mr. Parris?

HERRICK: I'll fetch him. *(He starts for the door.)*

DANFORTH: Marshal. *(*HERRICK *stops.)* When did Reverend Hale arrive?

HERRICK: It were toward midnight, I think.

DANFORTH *(suspiciously):* What is he about here?

HERRICK: He goes among them that will hang, sir. And he prays with them. He sits with Goody Nurse now. And Mr. Parris with him.

DANFORTH: Indeed. That man have no authority to enter here, Marshal. Why have you let him in?

HERRICK: Why, Mr. Parris command me, sir. I cannot deny him.

DANFORTH: Are you drunk, Marshal?

HERRICK: No, sir; it is a bitter night, and I have no fire here.

DANFORTH *(containing his anger):* Fetch Mr. Parris.

HERRICK: Aye, sir.

DANFORTH: There is a prodigious stench in this place.

HERRICK: I have only now cleared the people out for you.

DANFORTH: Beware hard drink, Marshal.

HERRICK: Aye, sir. *(He waits an instant for further orders. But* DANFORTH, *in dissatisfaction, turns his back on him, and* HERRICK *goes out. There is a pause.* DANFORTH *stands in thought.)*

HATHORNE: Let you question Hale, Excellency; I should not be surprised he have been preaching in Andover lately.

DANFORTH: We'll come to that; speak nothing of Andover. Parris prays with him. That's strange. *(He blows on his hands, moves toward the window, and looks out.)*

HATHORNE: Excellency, I wonder if it be wise to let Mr. Parris so continuously with the prisoners. *(*DANFORTH *turns to him, interested.)* I think, sometimes, the man has a mad look these days.

DANFORTH: Mad?

HATHORNE: I met him yesterday coming out of his house, and I bid him good morning—and he wept and went his way. I think it is not well the village sees him so unsteady.

DANFORTH: Perhaps he have some sorrow.

CHEEVER *(stamping his feet against the cold):* I think it be the cows, sir.

DANFORTH: Cows?

CHEEVER: There be so many cows wanderin' the highroads, now their masters are in the jails, and much disagreement who they will belong to now. I know Mr. Parris be arguin' with farmers all yesterday—there is great contention, sir, about the cows. Contention make him weep, sir; it were always a man that weep for contention. *(He turns, as do* HATHORNE *and* DANFORTH, *hearing someone coming up the corridor. Danforth raises his head as* PARRIS *enters. He is gaunt, frightened, and sweating in his greatcoat.)*

PARRIS *(to* DANFORTH, *instantly):* Oh, good morning, sir, thank you for coming. I beg your pardon wakin' you so early. Good morning, Judge Hathorne.

DANFORTH: Reverend Hale have no right to enter this—

PARRIS: Excellency, a moment. *(He hurries back and shuts the door.)*

HATHORNE: Do you leave him alone with the prisoners?

DANFORTH: What's his business here?

PARRIS *(prayerfully holding up his hands):* Excellency, hear me. It is a providence. Reverend Hale has returned to bring Rebecca Nurse to God.

DANFORTH *(surprised):* He bids her confess?

PARRIS *(sitting):* Hear me. Rebecca have not given me a word this three month since she came. Now she sits with him, and her sister and Martha Corey and two or three others, and he pleads with them, confess their crimes and save their lives.

DANFORTH: Why—this is indeed a providence. And they soften, they soften?

PARRIS: Not yet, not yet. But I thought to summon you, sir, that we might think on whether it be not wise, to—*(He dares not say it.)* I had thought to put a question, sir, and I hope you will not—

DANFORTH: Mr. Parris, be plain, what troubles you?

PARRIS: There is news, sir, that the court—the court must reckon with. My niece, sir, my niece—I believe she has vanished.

DANFORTH: Vanished!

PARRIS: I had thought to advise you of it earlier in the week, but—

DANFORTH: Why? How long is she gone?

PARRIS: This be the third night. You see, sir, she told me she would stay a night with Mercy Lewis. And next day, when she does not return, I send to Mr. Lewis to inquire. Mercy told him she would sleep in *my* house for a night.

DANFORTH: They are both gone?!

PARRIS *(in fear of him):* They are, sir.

DANFORTH *(alarmed):* I will send a party for them. Where may they be?

PARRIS: Excellency, I think they be aboard a ship. *(DANFORTH stands agape.)* My daughter tells me how she heard them speaking of ships last week, and tonight I discover my—my strongbox is broke into. *(He presses his fingers against his eyes to keep back tears.)*

HATHORNE *(astonished):* She have robbed you?

PARRIS: Thirty-one pound is gone. I am penniless. *(He covers his face and sobs.)*

DANFORTH: Mr. Parris, you are a brainless man! *(He walks in thought, deeply worried.)*

PARRIS: Excellency, it profit nothing you should blame me. I cannot think they would run off except they fear to keep in Salem any more. *(He is pleading.)* Mark it, sir, Abigail had close knowledge of the town, and since the news of Andover has broken here—

DANFORTH: Andover is remedied. The court returns there on Friday, and will resume examinations.

PARRIS: I am sure of it, sir. But the rumor here speaks rebellion in Andover, and it—

DANFORTH: There is no rebellion in Andover!

PARRIS: I tell you what is said here, sir. Andover have thrown out the court, they say, and will have no part of witchcraft. There be a faction here, feeding on that news, and I tell you true, sir, I fear there will be riot here.

HATHORNE: Riot! Why at every execution I have seen naught but high satisfaction in the town.

PARRIS: Judge Hathorne—it were another sort that hanged till now. Rebecca Nurse is no Bridget that lived three year with Bishop before she married him. John Proctor is not Isaac Ward that drank his family to ruin. *(To DANFORTH)* I would to God it were not so, Excellency, but these people have great weight yet in the town. Let Rebecca stand upon the gibbet and send up some righteous prayer, and I fear she'll wake a vengeance on you.

HATHORNE: Excellency, she is condemned a witch. The court have—

DANFORTH *(in deep concern, raising a hand to HATHORNE):* Pray you. *(To PARRIS)* How do you propose, then?

PARRIS: Excellency, I would postpone these hangin's for a time.

DANFORTH: There will be no postponement.

PARRIS: Now Mr. Hale's returned, there is hope, I think—for if he bring even one of these to God, that confession surely damns the others in the public eye, and none may doubt more that they are all linked to Hell. This way, unconfessed and claiming innocence, doubts are multiplied, many honest people will weep for them, and our good purpose is lost in their tears.

DANFORTH (*after thinking a moment, then going to* CHEEVER): Give me the list.

(CHEEVER *opens the dispatch case, searches.*)

PARRIS: It cannot be forgot, sir, that when I summoned the congregation for John Proctor's excommunication there were hardly thirty people come to hear it. That speak a discontent, I think, and—

DANFORTH (*studying the list*): There will be no postponement.

PARRIS: Excellency—

DANFORTH: Now, sir—which of these in your opinion may be brought to God? I will myself strive with him till dawn. (*He hands the list to* PARRIS, *who merely glances at it.*)

PARRIS: There is not sufficient time till dawn.

DANFORTH: I shall do my utmost. Which of them do you have hope for?

PARRIS (*not even glancing at the list now, and in a quavering voice, quietly*): Excellency —a dagger—(*He chokes up.*)

DANFORTH: What do you say?

PARRIS: Tonight, when I open my door to leave my house—a dagger clattered to the ground. (*Silence.* DANFORTH *absorbs this. Now* PARRIS *cries out.*) You cannot hang this sort. There is danger for me. I dare not step outside at night!

(REVEREND HALE *enters. They look at him for an instant in silence. He is steeped in sorrow, exhausted, and more direct than he ever was.*)

DANFORTH: Accept my congratulations, Reverend Hale; we are gladdened to see you returned to your good work.

HALE (*coming to* DANFORTH *now*): You must pardon them. They will not budge.

(HERRICK *enters, waits.*)

DANFORTH (*conciliatory*): You misunderstand, sir; I cannot pardon these when twelve are already hanged for the same crime. It is not just.

PARRIS (*with failing heart*): Rebecca will not confess?

HALE: The sun will rise in a few minutes. Excellency, I must have more time.

DANFORTH: Now hear me, and beguile yourselves no more. I will not receive a single plea for pardon or postponement. Them that will not confess will hang. Twelve are already executed; the names of these seven are given out, and the village expects to see them die this morning. Postponement now speaks a floundering on my part; reprieve or pardon must cast doubt upon the guilt of them that died till now. While I speak God's law, I will not crack its voice with whimpering. If retaliation is your fear, know this—I should hang ten thousand that dared to rise against the law, and an ocean of salt tears could not melt the resolution of the statutes. Now draw yourselves up like men and help me, as you are bound by Heaven to do. Have you spoken with them all, Mr. Hale?

HALE: All but Proctor. He is in the dungeon.

DANFORTH (*to* HERRICK): What's Proctor's way now?

HERRICK: He sits like some great bird; you'd not know he lived except he will take food from time to time.

DANFORTH (*after thinking a moment*): His wife—his wife must be well on with child now.

HERRICK: She is, sir.

DANFORTH: What think you, Mr. Parris? You have closer knowledge of this man; might her presence soften him?

PARRIS: It is possible, sir. He have not laid eyes on her these three months. I should summon her.

DANFORTH (*to* HERRICK): Is he yet adamant? Has he struck at you again?

HERRICK: He cannot, sir, he is chained to the wall now.

DANFORTH (*after thinking on it*): Fetch Goody Proctor to me. Then let you bring him up.

HERRICK: Aye, sir. (HERRICK *goes. There is silence.*)

HALE: Excellency, if you postpone a week and publish to the town that you are striving for their confessions, that speak mercy on your part, not faltering.

DANFORTH: Mr. Hale, as God have not empowered me like Joshua to stop this sun from rising, so I cannot withhold from them the perfection of their punishment.

HALE *(harder now):* If you think God wills you to raise rebellion, Mr. Danforth, you are mistaken!

DANFORTH *(instantly):* You have heard rebellion spoken in the town?

HALE: Excellency, there are orphans wandering from house to house; abandoned cattle bellow on the highroads, the stink of rotting crops hangs everywhere, and no man knows when the harlots' cry will end his life—and you wonder yet if rebellion's spoke? Better you should marvel how they do not burn your province!

DANFORTH: Mr. Hale, have you preached in Andover this month?

HALE: Thank God they have no need of me in Andover.

DANFORTH: You baffle me, sir. Why have you returned here?

HALE: Why, it is all simple. I come to do the Devil's work. I come to counsel Christians they should belie themselves. *(His sarcasm collapses.)* There is blood on my head! Can you not see the blood on my head!!

PARRIS: Hush! *(For he has heard footsteps. They all face the door.* HERRICK *enters with* ELIZABETH. *Her wrists are linked by heavy chain, which* HERRICK *now removes. Her clothes are dirty; her face is pale and gaunt.* HERRICK *goes out.)*

DANFORTH *(very politely):* Goody Proctor. *(She is silent.)* I hope you are hearty?

ELIZABETH *(as a warning reminder):* I am yet six months before my time.

DANFORTH: Pray be at your ease, we come not for your life. We—*(uncertain how to plead, for he is not accustomed to it)* Mr. Hale, will you speak with the woman?

HALE: Goody Proctor, your husband is marked to hang this morning.

(Pause.)

ELIZABETH *(quietly):* I have heard it.

HALE: You know, do you not, that I have no connection with the court? *(She seems to doubt it.)* I come of my own, Goody Proctor. I would save your husband's life, for if he is taken I count myself his murderer. Do you understand me?

ELIZABETH: What do you want of me?

HALE: Goody Proctor, I have gone this three month like our Lord into the wilderness. I have sought a Christian way, for damnation's doubled on a minister who counsels men to lie.

HATHORNE: It is no lie, you cannot speak of lies.

HALE: It is a lie! They are innocent!

DANFORTH: I'll hear no more of that!

HALE *(continuing to* ELIZABETH*):* Let you not mistake your duty as I mistook my own. I came into this village like a bridegroom to his beloved, bearing gifts of high religion; the very crowns of holy law I brought, and what I touched with my bright confidence, it died; and where I turned the eye of my great faith, blood flowed up. Beware, Goody Proctor—cleave to no faith when faith brings blood. It is mistaken law that leads you to sacrifice. Life, woman, life is God's most precious gift; no principle, however glorious, may justify the taking of it. I beg you, woman, prevail upon your husband to confess. Let him give his lie. Quail not before God's judgment in this, for it may well be God damns a liar less than he that throws his life away for pride. Will you plead with him? I cannot think he will listen to another.

ELIZABETH *(quietly):* I think that be the Devil's argument.

HALE *(with a climactic desperation):* Woman, before the laws of God we are as swine! We cannot read His will!

ELIZABETH: I cannot dispute with you, sir; I lack learning for it.

DANFORTH *(going to her):* Goody Proctor, you are not summoned here for disputation. Be there no wifely tenderness within you? He will die with the sunrise. Your husband. Do you understand it? *(She only looks at him.)* What say you? Will you contend with him? *(She is silent.)* Are you stone? I tell you true, woman, had I no other proof of your unnatural life, your dry eyes now would be sufficient evidence that you delivered up your soul to Hell! A very ape would weep at such calamity! Have the devil dried up any tear of pity in you? *(She is silent.)* Take her out. It profit nothing she should speak to him!

ELIZABETH *(quietly):* Let me speak with him, Excellency.

PARRIS (*with hope*): You'll strive with him? (*She hesitates.*)

DANFORTH: Will you plead for his confession or will you not?

ELIZABETH: I promise nothing. Let me speak with him.

(*A sound—the sibilance of dragging feet on stone. They turn. A pause.* HERRICK *enters with* JOHN PROCTOR. *His wrists are chained. He is another man, bearded, filthy, his eyes misty as though webs had overgrown them. He halts inside the doorway, his eye caught by the sight of* ELIZABETH. *The emotion flowing between them prevents anyone from speaking for an instant. Now* HALE, *visibly affected, goes to* DANFORTH *and speaks quietly.*)

HALE: Pray, leave them, Excellency.

DANFORTH (*pressing* HALE *impatiently aside*): Mr. Proctor, you have been notified, have you not? (PROCTOR *is silent, staring at* ELIZABETH.) I see light in the sky, Mister; let you counsel with your wife, and may God help you turn your back on Hell. (PROCTOR *is silent, staring at* ELIZABETH.)

HALE (*quietly*): Excellency, let—

(DANFORTH *brushes past* HALE *and walks out.* HALE *follows.* CHEEVER *stands and follows,* HATHORNE *behind.* HERRICK *goes.* PARRIS, *from a safe distance, offers:*)

PARRIS: If you desire a cup of cider, Mr. Proctor, I am sure I—(PROCTOR *turns an icy stare at him, and he breaks off.* PARRIS *raises his palms toward* PROCTOR.) God lead you now. (PARRIS *goes out.*)

(*Alone.* PROCTOR *walks to her, halts. It is as though they stood in a spinning world. It is beyond sorrow, above it. He reaches out his hand as though toward an embodiment not quite real, and as he touches her, a strange soft sound, half laughter, half amazement, comes from his throat. He pats her hand. She covers his hand with hers. And then, weak, he sits. Then she sits, facing him.*)

PROCTOR: The child?

ELIZABETH: It grows.

PROCTOR: There is no word of the boys?

ELIZABETH: They're well. Rebecca's Samuel keeps them.

PROCTOR: You have not seen them?

ELIZABETH: I have not. (*She catches a weakening in herself and downs it.*)

PROCTOR: You are a—marvel, Elizabeth.

ELIZABETH: You—have been tortured?

PROCTOR: Aye. (*Pause. She will not let herself be drowned in the sea that threatens her.*) They come for my life now.

ELIZABETH: I know it.

(*Pause.*)

PROCTOR: None—have yet confessed?

ELIZABETH: There be many confessed.

PROCTOR: Who are they?

ELIZABETH: There be a hundred or more, they say. Goody Ballard is one; Isaiah Goodkind is one. There be many.

PROCTOR: Rebecca?

ELIZABETH: Not Rebecca. She is one foot in Heaven now; naught may hurt her more.

PROCTOR: And Giles?

ELIZABETH: You have not heard of it?

PROCTOR: I hear nothin', where I am kept.

ELIZABETH: Giles is dead.

(*He looks at her incredulously.*)

PROCTOR: When were he hanged?

ELIZABETH (*quietly, factually*): He were not hanged. He would not answer aye or nay to his indictment; for if he denied the charge they'd hang him surely, and auction out his property. So he stand mute, and died Christian under the law. And so his sons will have his farm. It is the law, for he could not be condemned a wizard without he answer the indictment, aye or nay.

PROCTOR: Then how does he die?

ELIZABETH (*gently*): They press him, John.

PROCTOR: Press?

ELIZABETH: Great stones they lay upon his chest until he plead aye or nay. (*With a tender smile for the old man*) They say he give them but two words. "More weight," he says. And died.

PROCTOR (*numbed—a thread to weave into his agony*): "More weight."

ELIZABETH: Aye. It were a fearsome man, Giles Corey.

(*Pause.*)

PROCTOR (*with great force of will, but not quite looking at her*): I have been thinking I would confess to them, Elizabeth. (*She shows nothing.*) What say you? If I give them that?

ELIZABETH: I cannot judge you, John. *(Pause.)*

PROCTOR *(simply—a pure question):* What would you have me do?

ELIZABETH: As you will, I would have it. *(Slight pause)* I want you living, John. That's sure.

PROCTOR *(pauses, then with a flailing of hope):* Giles' wife? Have she confessed?

ELIZABETH: She will not. *(Pause.)*

PROCTOR: It is a pretense, Elizabeth.

ELIZABETH: What is?

PROCTOR: I cannot mount the gibbet like a saint. It is a fraud. I am not that man. *(She is silent.)* My honesty is broke, Elizabeth; I am no good man. Nothing's spoiled by giving them this lie that were not rotten long before.

ELIZABETH: And yet you've not confessed till now. That speak goodness in you.

PROCTOR: Spite only keeps me silent. It is hard to give a lie to dogs. *(Pause. For the first time he turns directly to her.)* I would have your forgiveness, Elizabeth.

ELIZABETH: It is not for me to give, John, I am—

PROCTOR: I'd have you see some honesty in it. Let them that never lied die now to keep their souls. It is pretense for me, a vanity that will not blind God nor keep my children out of the wind. *(Pause.)* What say you?

ELIZABETH *(upon a heaving sob that always threatens):* John, it come to naught that I should forgive you, if you'll not forgive yourself. *(Now he turns away a little, in great agony.)* It is not my soul, John, it is yours. *(He stands, as though in physical pain, slowly rising to his feet with a great immortal longing to find his answer. It is difficult to say, and she is on the verge of tears.)* Only be sure of this, for I know it now: Whatever you will do, it is a good man does it. *(He turns his doubting, searching gaze upon her.)* I have read my heart this three month, John. *(Pause.)* I have sins of my own to count. It needs a cold wife to prompt lechery.

PROCTOR *(in great pain):* Enough, enough—

ELIZABETH *(now pouring out her heart):* Better you should know me!

PROCTOR: I will not hear it! I know you!

ELIZABETH: You take my sins upon you, John—

PROCTOR *(in agony):* No, I take my own, my own!

ELIZABETH: John, I counted myself so plain, so poorly made, no honest love could come to me! Suspicion kissed you when I did; I never knew how I should say my love. It were a cold house I kept! *(In fright, she swerves, as HATHORNE enters.)*

HATHORNE: What say you, Proctor? The sun is soon up.

(PROCTOR, his chest heaving, stares, turns to ELIZABETH. She comes to him as though to plead, her voice quaking.)

ELIZABETH: Do what you will. But let none be your judge. There be no higher judge under Heaven than Proctor is! Forgive me, forgive me, John—I never knew such goodness in the world! *(She covers her face, weeping.)*

(PROCTOR turns from her to HATHORNE; he is off the earth, his voice hollow.)

PROCTOR: I want my life.

HATHORNE *(electrified, surprised):* You'll confess yourself?

PROCTOR: I will have my life.

HATHORNE *(with a mystical tone):* God be praised! It is a providence! *(He rushes out the door, and his voice is heard calling down the corridor.)* He will confess! Proctor will confess!

PROCTOR *(with a cry, as he strides to the door):* Why do you cry it? *(In great pain he turns back to her.)* It is evil, is it not? It is evil.

ELIZABETH *(in terror, weeping):* I cannot judge you, John, I cannot!

PROCTOR: Then who will judge me? *(Suddenly clasping his hands)* God in Heaven, what is John Proctor, what is John Proctor? *(He moves as an animal, and a fury is riding in him, a tantalized search.)* I think it is honest, I think so; I am no saint. *(As though she had denied this he calls angrily at her.)* Let Rebecca go like a saint; for me it is fraud!

(Voices are heard in the hall, speaking together in suppressed excitement.)

ELIZABETH: I am not your judge, I cannot be. *(As though giving him release)* Do as you will, do as you will!

PROCTOR: Would you give them such a lie?

Say it. Would you ever give them this? *(She cannot answer.)* You would not; if tongs of fire were singeing you you would not! It is evil. Good, then—it is evil, and I do it!

(HATHORNE enters with DANFORTH, and, with them, CHEEVER, PARRIS, and HALE. It is a businesslike, rapid entrance, as though the ice had been broken.)

DANFORTH *(with great relief and gratitude):* Praise to God, man, praise to God; you shall be blessed in Heaven for this. *(CHEEVER has hurried to the bench with pen, ink, and paper. PROCTOR watches him.)* Now then, let us have it. Are you ready, Mr. Cheever?

PROCTOR *(with a cold, cold horror at their efficiency):* Why must it be written?

DANFORTH: Why, for the good instruction of the village, Mister; this we shall post upon the church door! *(To PARRIS, urgently)* Where is the marshal?

PARRIS *(runs to the door and calls down the corridor):* Marshal! Hurry!

DANFORTH: Now, then, Mister, will you speak slowly, and directly to the point, for Mr. Cheever's sake. *(He is on record now, and is really dictating to CHEEVER, who writes.)* Mr. Proctor, have you seen the Devil in your life? *(PROCTOR's jaws lock.)* Come, man, there is light in the sky; the town waits at the scaffold; I would give out this news. Did you see the Devil?

PROCTOR: I did.

PARRIS: Praise God!

DANFORTH: And when he come to you, what were his demand? *(PROCTOR is silent. DANFORTH helps.)* Did he bid you to do his work upon the earth?

PROCTOR: He did.

DANFORTH: And you bound yourself to his service? *(DANFORTH turns, as REBECCA NURSE enters, with HERRICK helping to support her. She is barely able to walk.)* Come in, come in, woman!

REBECCA *(brightening as she sees PROCTOR):* Ah, John! You are well, then, eh?

(PROCTOR turns his face to the wall.)

DANFORTH: Courage, man, courage—let her witness your good example that she may come to God herself. Now hear it, Goody Nurse! Say on, Mr. Proctor. Did you bind yourself to the Devil's service?

REBECCA *(astonished):* Why, John!

PROCTOR *(through his teeth, his face turned from REBECCA):* I did.

DANFORTH: Now, woman, you surely see it profit nothin' to keep this conspiracy any further. Will you confess yourself with him?

REBECCA: Oh, John—God send his mercy on you!

DANFORTH: I say, will you confess yourself, Goody Nurse?

REBECCA: Why, it is a lie, it is a lie; how may I damn myself? I cannot, I cannot.

DANFORTH: Mr. Proctor. When the Devil came to you did you see Rebecca Nurse in his company? *(PROCTOR is silent.)* Come, man, take courage—did you ever see her with the Devil?

PROCTOR *(almost inaudibly):* No.

(DANFORTH, now sensing trouble, glances at JOHN and goes to the table, and picks up a sheet—the list of condemned.)

DANFORTH: Did you ever see her sister, Mary Easty, with the Devil?

PROCTOR: No, I did not.

DANFORTH *(his eyes narrow on PROCTOR):* Did you ever see Martha Corey with the Devil?

PROCTOR: I did not.

DANFORTH *(realizing, slowly putting the sheet down):* Did you ever see anyone with the Devil?

PROCTOR: I did not.

DANFORTH: Proctor, you mistake me. I am not empowered to trade your life for a lie. You have most certainly seen some person with the Devil. *(Proctor is silent.)* Mr. Proctor, a score of people have already testified they saw this woman with the Devil.

PROCTOR: Then it is proved. Why must I say it?

DANFORTH: Why "must" you say it! Why, you should rejoice to say it if your soul is truly purged of any love for Hell!

PROCTOR: They think to go like saints. I like not to spoil their names.

DANFORTH *(inquiring, incredulous):* Mr. Proctor, do you think they go like saints?

PROCTOR *(evading):* This woman never thought she done the Devil's work.

DANFORTH: Look you, sir. I think you mistake your duty here. It matters nothing what she thought—she is convicted of the unnatural murder of children, and you for sending your spirit out upon Mary Warren. Your soul alone is the issue here, Mister, and you will prove its whiteness or you cannot live in a Christian country. Will you tell me now what persons conspired with you in the Devil's company? (PROCTOR *is silent.*) To your knowledge was Rebecca Nurse ever—

PROCTOR: I speak my own sins; I cannot judge another. (*Crying out, with hatred*) I have no tongue for it.

HALE (*quickly to* DANFORTH): Excellency, it is enough he confess himself. Let him sign it, let him sign it.

PARRIS (*feverishly*): It is a great service, sir. It is a weighty name; it will strike the village that Proctor confess. I beg you, let him sign it. The sun is up, Excellency!

DANFORTH (*considers; then with dissatisfaction*): Come, then, sign your testimony. (*To* CHEEVER) Give it to him. (CHEEVER *goes to* PROCTOR, *the confession and a pen in hand.* PROCTOR *does not look at it.*) Come, man, sign it.

PROCTOR (*after glancing at the confession*): You have all witnessed it—it is enough.

DANFORTH: You will not sign it?

PROCTOR: You have all witnessed it; what more is needed?

DANFORTH: Do you sport with me? You will sign your name or it is no confession, Mister! (*His breast heaving with agonized breathing,* PROCTOR *now lays the paper down and signs his name.*)

PARRIS: Praise be to the Lord!

(PROCTOR *has just finished signing when* DANFORTH *reaches for the paper. But* PROCTOR *snatches it up, and now a wild terror is rising in him, and a boundless anger.*)

DANFORTH (*perplexed, but politely extending his hand*): If you please, sir.

PROCTOR: No.

DANFORTH (*as though* PROCTOR *did not understand*): Mr. Proctor, I must have—

PROCTOR: No, no. I have signed it. You have seen me. It is done! You have no need for this.

PARRIS: Proctor, the village must have proof that—

PROCTOR: Damn the village! I confess to God, and God has seen my name on this! It is enough!

DANFORTH: No, sir, it is—

PROCTOR: You came to save my soul, did you not? Here! I have confessed myself; it is enough!

DANFORTH: You have not con—

PROCTOR: I have confessed myself! Is there no good penitance but it be public? God does not need my name nailed upon the church! God sees my name; God knows how black my sins are! It is enough!

DANFORTH: Mr. Proctor—

PROCTOR: You will not use me! I am no Sarah Good or Tituba, I am John Proctor! You will not use me! It is no part of salvation that you should use me!

DANFORTH: I do not wish to—

PROCTOR: I have three children—how may I teach them to walk like men in the world, and I sold my friends?

DANFORTH: You have not sold your friends—

PROCTOR: Beguile me not! I blacken all of them when this is nailed to the church the very day they hang for silence!

DANFORTH: Mr. Proctor, I must have good and legal proof that you—

PROCTOR: You are the high court, your word is good enough! Tell them I confessed myself; say Proctor broke his knees and wept like a woman; say what you will, but my name cannot—

DANFORTH (*with suspicion*): It is the same, is it not? If I report it or you sign to it?

PROCTOR (*He knows it is insane.*) No, it is not the same! What others say and what I sign to is not the same!

DANFORTH: Why? Do you mean to deny this confession when you are free?

PROCTOR: I mean to deny nothing!

DANFORTH: Then explain to me, Mr. Proctor, why you will not let—

PROCTOR (*with a cry of his whole soul*): Because it is my name! Because I cannot have another in my life! Because I lie and sign myself to lies! Because I am not worth the dust on the feet of them that hang! How may I live without my name? I have given you my soul; leave me my name!

DANFORTH (*pointing at the confession in* PROCTOR's *hand*): Is that document a lie? If it is a lie I will not accept it! What say you? I will not deal in lies, Mister! (PROCTOR *is motionless.*) You will give me your honest confession in my hand, or I cannot keep you from the rope. (PROCTOR *does not reply.*) Which way do you go, Mister?

(*His breast heaving, his eyes staring,* PROCTOR *tears the paper and crumples it, and he is weeping in fury, but erect.*)

DANFORTH: Marshal!

PARRIS (*hysterically, as though the tearing paper were his life*): Proctor, Proctor!

HALE: Man, you will hang! You cannot!

PROCTOR (*his eyes full of tears*): I can. And there's your first marvel, that I can. You have made your magic now, for now I do think I see some shred of goodness in John Proctor. Not enough to weave a banner with, but white enough to keep it from such dogs. (ELIZABETH, *in a burst of terror, rushes to him and weeps against his hand.*) Give them no tear! Tears pleasure them! Show honor now, show a stony heart and sink them with it! (*He has lifted her, and kisses her now with great passion.*)

REBECCA: Let you fear nothing! Another judgment waits us all!

DANFORTH: Hang them high over the town! Who weeps for these, weeps for corruption! (*He sweeps out past them.* HERRICK *starts to lead* REBECCA, *who almost collapses, but* PROCTOR *catches her, and she glances up at him apologetically.*)

REBECCA: I've had no breakfast.

HERRICK: Come, man.

(HERRICK *escorts them out,* HATHORNE *and* CHEEVER *behind them.* ELIZABETH *stands staring at the empty doorway.*)

PARRIS (*in deadly fear, to* ELIZABETH): Go to him, Goody Proctor! There is yet time!

(*From outside a drumroll strikes the air.* PARRIS *is startled.* ELIZABETH *jerks about toward the window.*)

PARRIS: Go to him! (*He rushes out the door, as though to hold back his fate.*) Proctor! Proctor!

(*Again, a short burst of drums.*)

HALE: Woman, plead with him! (*He starts to rush out the door, and then goes back to her.*) Woman! It is pride, it is vanity. (*She avoids his eyes, and moves to the window. He drops to his knees.*) Be his helper!—What profit him to bleed? Shall the dust praise him? Shall the worms declare his truth? Go to him, take his shame away!

ELIZABETH (*supporting herself against collapse, grips the bars of the window, and with a cry*): He have his goodness now. God forbid I take it from him!

(*The final drumroll crashes, then heightens violently.* HALE *weeps in frantic prayer, and the new sun is pouring in upon her face, and the drums rattle like bones in the morning air. The curtain falls.*)

JEAN ANOUILH

Becket: or The Honor of God

TRANSLATION BY LUCIENNE HILL

Jean Anouilh (1910–   ), born in Bordeaux, France, moved to Paris while still young. He attended the Collège Chaptal and studied at the University of Paris. After brief employment in an advertising firm, he became secretary to Louis Jouvet's company, at the Comédie des Champs Élysées, 1931–35. Anouilh has written or adapted some two dozen plays, many of which have been translated and produced outside of France. Perhaps best known among these many works are *Le Voyageur sans bagages* (*Traveler Without Baggage*), 1937; *Le Bal des voleurs* (*Thieves' Carnival*), 1938; *Léocadia* (*Time Remembered*), 1939; *Antigone*, 1944; *L'Invitation au château* (*Ring Round the Moon*), 1947; *La Valse des toreadors* (*The Waltz of the Toreadors*), 1951; *L'Alouette* (*The Lark*), 1953; and *Becket ou l'Amour de Dieu* (*Becket: or The Honor of God*), 1959. In addition, Anouilh has written many scripts for French films, including a version of Tolstoy's *Anna Karenina*.

The subtitle of this play—*The Honor of God*—signals the vast difference between King Henry II and his minister. The two were fun-loving roisterers in their youth and pledged eternal affection; but their relationship becomes strained when Becket is appointed Archbishop of Canterbury. Prior to his elevation, Becket is portrayed as a witty, carefree Saxon courtier—one who cannot experience a deep love for anything. But when he becomes the head of the Church of England, he finds something to believe in, to honor. Becket, taking his duties seriously, adheres to the principles of his ecclesiastic office and becomes King Henry's implacable enemy.

Anouilh takes a careful look at the powerful king and seeks some of the reasons for Becket's death. King Henry never loses his great affection for Becket despite his later bitterness, for he cannot find anyone to replace his former friend. Becket, who never again enjoys the king's favor, finds a replacement—he gives his love to God.

INTRODUCTION

I am not a serious man, I wrote *Becket* by chance. I had bought on the quays of the Seine—where, in curious little stalls set up on the parapet, old gentlemen of another age sell old books to other old gentlemen and to the very young—*The Conquest of England by the Normans*, by Augustin Thierry, an historian of the Romantic school, forgotten today and scrapped; for history, too, has its fashions.

I did not expect to read this respectable work, which I assumed would be boring. I had bought it because it had a pretty green binding and I needed a spot of green on my shelves. All the same, when I returned home I skimmed through the book (I am well-mannered with old books) and I happened upon the chapters that tell the story of Becket, some thirty pages, which one might have taken to be fiction except that the bottom of the pages were jammed with references in Latin from the chroniclers of the twelfth century.

I was dazzled. I had expected to find a saint—I am always a trifle distrustful of saints, as I am of great theatre stars—and I found a man.

The idea of writing a play about it skirted my mind, as the idea to become a fencing champion had done in my childhood. Just as I was reminding myself that I was not a serious man and that probably this was not for me, the telephone rang. I began to exchange the latest news about a family that held for me not the faintest glimmer of interest; then I was told that dinner was served and at the same time I would have to take strong measures against my son who had just laid low both his sisters with his bare fists; I was reminded at the same time of the evening mail, which contained letters from two spongers and three actresses (the three who were miraculously destined to play all the feminine leads in my plays); then came a sinister gray envelope, a note from my tax collector . . . I completely forgot about Becket.

The following winter, green decidedly did not look well on my shelves in Paris and I bought an admirable red Balzac, first edition; I took *The Conquest of England by the Normans* to a mountain chalet where the shelves were a little empty.

One evening I was playing a game of solitaire, a game that for twenty years I have failed to bring off: my young wife, wearied by the endless spectacle of my failures, the extent of which she is only partially aware, decided to go up to bed and asked me for a book with which to read herself to sleep. I removed one of the green volumes on the shelves behind me and told her, "Read the story of Becket, it is beautiful," and I continued to fail at my solitaire, a gauge of my serenity and

self-confidence. (The day that I succeed, the shock will be so great that I will probably have to be locked up in a psychiatric ward.)

An hour passed by the tick-tock of the Swiss cuckoo clock I have taught to play mischief with time; and I was in a state of remorse over that extra shot of whiskey and those last cigarettes of the day; the ones that will probably kill you in the end, which in fact no longer give you any pleasure. My wife appeared at the top of the stairs in her pajamas. She had tears in her eyes.

I was about to defend myself when I realized the tears had actually nothing to do with me. She simply told me (and I can still recall the emotion expressed in her face at that moment), "Oh, how beautiful it is! Why don't you make a play of it? It's absolutely you!"

I muttered something; I went up to bed and the next day at 8 o'clock I started, without a plan, to write the first word. Everything was marshaled in my mind. It was already written, I had only to copy it out. In fifteen happy days I finished the first part.

Then I returned to Paris, where I have never written anything, except my first play, necessitated by poverty, and that play, incidentally, provided me with the means for writing my second one in the country.

In the meantime, life went on as usual in Paris; rehearsals for another play; the doubt came back. The second part of Becket was undoable. The troubles between the Pope and the king of France; this undercurrent conflict that lasted through seven years of exile, ending in the sham reconciliation on the plain at Ferté-Bernard and finally death in the cathedral, a subject already magnificently treated by Eliot. This was certainly not for me.

The following summer, having left Paris, I started a short play, *The Fair at Empoigne*, which will be produced this winter by Jean-Louis Barrault. I completed it very easily. I felt myself in good form, my appetite whetted rather than satiated by the work. Talent is like a faucet; while it is open, one must write. Inspiration is a farce that poets have invented to give themselves importance. It was still

only the middle of the summer and it was
absolutely necessary that I write something
else.

My wife reappeared, this time smiling, on
the threshold of the bottom of the garden of
a house we had rented on a beach in the
Landes. She said to me simply but firmly:
"You are ridiculous; finish *Becket*."

I have always feared ridicule; and for this
specific reason and, incidentally, to please her,
I started the very next day on the second part
of the play, a scene with some facile comedy
lines that I habitually write to give myself
courage and to prove to myself that the work
is, after all, not as important as one would
like to pretend. Things fell into their place of
themselves, and in fifteen days I finished
Becket.

Altogether shamefaced at the idea of having
written an historical play, I gave it to an
historian friend of mine to read, and he roared
with laughter, saying: "Are you unaware that
history, like everything else on this earth,
makes progress? In Augustin Thierry's time
one could believe that Becket was of Saxon
origin; but for over fifty years we have had
proof that he was a good Norman. He was
from the vicinity of Rouen and was in fact
called Bequet."

A large part of the subject of my play was
based on the fact that Becket was of the
vanquished race. A serious man at this point
would have torn out his hair; then he would
have rewritten his play on a more exact historical basis.

I decided that if history in the next fifty
years should go on making progress it will
perhaps rediscover that Becket was indubi-
tably of Saxon origin; in any case, for this
drama of friendship between two men, between the king and his friend, his companion
in pleasure and in work (and this is what
had gripped me about the story), this friend
whom he could not cease to love though he
became his worst enemy the night he was
named archbishop—for this drama it was a
thousand times better that Becket remained
a Saxon.

I changed nothing; I had the play performed three months later in Paris. It had a

great success and I noticed that no one except
my historian friend was aware of the progress
of history.

All this was part and parcel of my increasingly involved technique for unsuccessful
solitaire, which has been protecting me for
close to thirty years against the extreme
hazards of this profession.

JEAN ANOUILH

CAST OF CHARACTERS

HENRY II	1ST ENGLISH BARON
THOMAS BECKET	2ND ENGLISH BARON
ARCHBISHOP OF	3RD ENGLISH BARON
CANTERBURY	4TH ENGLISH BARON
GILBERT FOLLIOT	QUEEN MOTHER
BISHOP OF YORK	THE QUEEN
SAXON PEASANT	LOUIS, KING OF
HIS SON	FRANCE
GWENDOLEN	THE POPE
THE CARDINAL	

ACT ONE

*An indeterminate set, with pillars. We are
in the cathedral. Center stage:* BECKET's *tomb;
a stone slab with a name carved on it. Two*
SENTRIES *come in and take up their position
upstage. Then the* KING *enters from the back.
He is wearing his crown, and is naked under
a big cloak. A* PAGE *follows at a distance. The*
KING *hesitates a moment before the tomb;
then removes his cloak with a swift movement
and the* PAGE *takes it away. He falls to his
knees on the stone floor and prays, alone,
naked, in the middle of the stage. Behind the
pillars, in the shadows, one senses the disquieting presence of unseen lookers-on.*

KING: Well, Thomas Becket, are you satisfied? I am naked at your tomb and your monks
are coming to flog me. What an end to our
story! You, rotting in this tomb, larded with
my barons' dagger thrusts, and I, naked,
shivering in the draughts, and waiting like
an idiot for those brutes to come and thrash
me. Don't you think we'd have done better to
understand each other?

(BECKET *in his Archbishop's robes, just as he was on the day of his death, has appeared on the side of the stage, from behind a pillar. He says softly*)

BECKET: Understand each other? It wasn't possible.

KING: I said, "In all save the honor of the realm." It was you who taught me that slogan, after all.

BECKET: I answered you, "In all save the honor of God." We were like two deaf men talking.

KING: How cold it was on that bare plain at La Ferté-Bernard, the last time we two met! It's funny, it's always been cold, in our story. Save at the beginning, when we were friends. We had a few fine summer evenings together, with the girls . . . (*He says suddenly.*) Did you love Gwendolen, Archbishop? Did you hate me, that night when I said, "I am the King," and took her from you? Perhaps that's what you never could forgive me for?

BECKET (*quietly*): I've forgotten.

KING: Yet we were like two brothers, weren't we—you and I? That night it was a childish prank—a lusty lad shouting "I am the King!" . . . I was so young . . . And every thought in my head came from you, you know that.

BECKET (*gently, as if to a little boy*): Pray, Henry, and don't talk so much.

KING (*irritably*): If you think I'm in the mood for praying at the moment . . .

(BECKET *quietly withdraws into the darkness and disappears during the* KING's *next speech.*) I can see them through my fingers, spying on me from the aisles. Say what you like, they're an oafish lot, those Saxons of yours! To give oneself over naked to those ruffians! With my delicate skin . . . Even you'd be afraid. Besides, I'm ashamed. Ashamed of this whole masquerade. I need them though, that's the trouble. I have to rally them to my cause, against my son, who'll gobble up my kingdom if I let him. So I've come to make my peace with their Saint. You must admit it's funny. You've become a Saint and here am I, the King, desperately in need of that great amorphous mass which could do nothing, up till now, save lie inert beneath its own enormous weight, cowering under blows, and which is all-powerful now. What use are conquests, when you stop to think? They are England now, because of their vast numbers, and the rate at which they breed—like rabbits, to make good the massacres. But one must always pay the price—that's another thing you taught me, Thomas Becket, when you were still advising me . . . You taught me everything . . . (*dreamily*) Ah, those were happy times . . . At the peep of dawn—well, our dawn that is, around noon, because we always went to bed very late—you'd come into my room, as I was emerging from the bathhouse, rested, smiling, debonair, as fresh as if we'd never spent the entire night drinking and whoring through the town. (*He says a little sourly.*) That's another thing you were better at than me . . .

(*The* PAGE *has come in. He wraps a white towel around the* KING *and proceeds to rub him down. Off stage is heard for the first time —we will hear it often—the gay, ironical Scottish marching song which* BECKET *is always whistling.*

The lighting changes. We are still in the empty cathedral. Then, a moment or so later, BECKET *will draw aside a curtain and reveal the* KING's *room. Their manner, his and the* KING's, *faraway at first, like a memory relived, will gradually become more real.*

THOMAS BECKET, *dressed as a nobleman, elegant, young, charming, in his short doublet and pointed, upturned shoes, comes in blithely and greets the* KING.)

BECKET: My respects, my Lord!

KING (*his face brightening*): Oh, Thomas . . . I thought you were still asleep.

BECKET: I've already been for a short gallop to Richmond and back, my Lord. There's a divine nip in the air.

KING (*his teeth chattering*): To think you actually like the cold! (*To the* PAGE) Rub harder, pig!

(*Smiling,* BECKET *pushes the* PAGE *aside and proceeds to rub the* KING *himself.*)
(*To the* PAGE) Throw a log on the fire and get out. Come back and dress me later.

BECKET: My prince, I shall dress you myself.
(*The* PAGE *goes.*)

KING: Nobody rubs me down the way you do. Thomas, what would I do without you?

You're a nobleman, why do you play at being my valet? If I asked my barons to do this, they'd start a civil war!

BECKET (*smiling*): They'll come round to it in time, when Kings have learnt to play their role. I am your servant, my prince, that's all. Helping you to govern or helping you get warm again is part of the same thing to me. I like helping you.

KING (*with an affectionate little gesture*): My little Saxon! At the beginning, when I told them I was taking you into my service, do you know what they all said? They said you'd seize the chance to knife me in the back one day.

BECKET (*smiling as he dresses him*): Did you believe them, my prince?

KING: N . . . no. I was a bit scared at first. You know I scare easily . . . But you looked so well brought up, beside those brutes. However did you come to speak French without a trace of an English accent?

BECKET: My parents were able to keep their lands by agreeing to "collaborate," as they say, with the King your father. They sent me to France as a boy to acquire a good French accent.

KING: To France? Not to Normandy?

BECKET (*still smiling*): That was their one patriotic conceit. They loathed the Norman accent.

KING (*distinctly*): Only the accent?

BECKET (*lightly and inscrutably*): My father was a very severe man. I would never have taken the liberty of questioning him on his personal convictions while he was alive. And his death shed no light on them, naturally. He managed, by collaborating, to amass a considerable fortune. As he was also a man of rigid principles, I imagine he contrived to do it in accordance with his conscience. That's a little piece of sleight of hand that men of principle are very skillful at in troubled times.

KING: And you?

BECKET (*feigning not to understand the question*): I, my Lord?

KING (*putting a touch of contempt into his voice, for despite his admiration for* THOMAS *or perhaps because of it, he would like to score a point against him occasionally*): The sleight of hand, were you adept at it too?

BECKET (*still smiling*): Mine was a different problem. I was a frivolous man, you'll agree? In fact, it never came up at all. I adore hunting and only the Normans and their protégés had the right to hunt. I adore luxury and luxury was Norman. I adore life and the Saxons' only birthright was slaughter. I'll add that I adore honor.

KING (*with faint surprise*): And was honor reconciled with collaboration too?

BECKET (*lightly*): I had the right to draw my sword against the first Norman nobleman who tried to lay hands on my sister. I killed him in single combat. It's a detail, but it has its points.

KING (*a little slyly*): You could always have slit his throat and fled into the forest, as so many did.

BECKET: That would have been uncomfortable, and not a lot of use. My sister would immediately have been raped by some other Norman baron, like all the Saxon girls. Today, she is respected. (*Lightly*) My Lord, did I tell you?—My new gold dishes have arrived from Florence. Will my Liege do me the honor of christening them with me at my house?

KING: Gold dishes! You lunatic!

BECKET: I'm setting a new fashion.

KING: I'm your King and I eat off silver!

BECKET: My prince, your expenses are heavy and I have only my pleasures to pay for. The trouble is I'm told they scratch easily. Still, we'll see. I received two forks as well—

KING: Forks?

BECKET: Yes. It's a new instrument, a devilish little thing to look at—and to use too. It's for pronging meat with and carrying it to your mouth. It saves you dirtying your fingers.

KING: But then you dirty the fork?

BECKET: Yes. But it's washable.

KING: So are your fingers. I don't see the point.

BECKET: It hasn't any, practically speaking. But it's refined, it's subtle. It's very un-Norman.

KING (*with sudden delight*): You must order me a dozen! I want to see my great fat barons' faces, at the first court banquet, when I present them with that! We won't tell them what they're for. We'll have no end of fun with them.

BECKET (*laughing*): A dozen! Easy now, my Lord! Forks are very expensive you know! My prince, it's time for the Privy Council.

KING (*laughing too*): They won't make head nor tail of them! I bet you they'll think they're a new kind of dagger. We'll have a hilarious time!

(*They go out, laughing, behind the curtain, which draws apart to reveal the same set, with the pillars. The Council Chamber. The Councilors stand waiting. The* KING *and* BECKET *come in, still laughing.*)

KING (*sitting in a chair*): Gentlemen, the Council is open. I have summoned you here today to deal with this refusal of the clergy to pay the absentee tax. We really must come to an understanding about who rules this kingdom, the Church—

(*The* ARCHBISHOP *tries to speak.*)

just a moment, Archbishop—or me! But before we quarrel, let us take the good news first. I have decided to revive the office of Chancellor of England, keeper of the Triple Lion Seal, and to entrust it to my loyal servant and subject Thomas Becket.

(BECKET *rises in surprise, the color draining from his face.*)

BECKET: My Lord . . . !

KING (*roguishly*): What's the matter, Becket? Do you want to go and piss already? True, we both had gallons to drink last night! (*He looks at him with delight.*) Well, that's good! I've managed to surprise you for once, little Saxon.

BECKET (*dropping on one knee, says gravely*): My Liege, this is a token of your confidence of which I fear I may not be worthy. I am very young, frivolous perhaps—

KING: I'm young too. And you know more than all of us put together. (*To the others*) He's read books, you know. It's amazing the amount he knows. He'll checkmate the lot of you! Even the Archbishop! As for his frivolity, don't let him fool you! He drinks strong wine, he likes to enjoy himself, but he's a lad who thinks every minute of the time! Sometimes it embarrasses me to feel him thinking away beside me. Get up, Thomas. I never did anything without your advice anyway. Nobody knew it, now everybody will, that's all. (*He bursts out laughing, pulls something out of his pocket and gives it to* BECKET.) There. That's the Seal. Don't lose it. Without the Seal, there's no more England and we'll all have to go back to Normandy. Now, to work!

(*The* ARCHBISHOP *rises, all smiles, now the first shock is over.*)

ARCHBISHOP: May I crave permission to salute, with my Lord's approval, my young and learned archdeacon here? For I was the first—I am weak enough to be proud of pointing it out—to notice him and take him under my wing. The presence at this Council, with the preponderant title of Chancellor of England, of one of our brethren—our spiritual son in a sense—is a guarantee for the Church of this country, that a new era of agreement and mutual understanding is dawning for us all and we must now, in a spirit of confident cooperation—

KING (*interrupting*): Etc., etc. . . . Thank you, Archbishop! I knew this nomination would please you. But don't rely too much on Becket to play your game. He is my man. (*He turns to* BECKET, *beaming.*) Come to think of it, I'd forgotten you were a deacon, little Saxon.

BECKET (*smiling*): So had I, my prince.

KING: Tell me—I'm not talking about wenching, that's a venial sin—but on the odd occasions when I've seen you fighting, it seems to me you have a mighty powerful sword arm, for a priest! How do you reconcile that with the Church's commandment forbidding a priest to shed blood?

BISHOP OF OXFORD (*prudently*): Our young friend is only a deacon, he has not yet taken all his vows, my Lord. The Church in its wisdom knows that youth must have its day and that—under the sacred pretext of a war—a holy war, I mean, of course, young men are permitted to—

KING (*interrupting*): All wars are holy wars, Bishop! I defy you to find me a serious belligerent who doesn't have Heaven on his side, in theory. Let's get back to the point.

ARCHBISHOP: By all means, your Highness.

KING: Our customs demand that every landowner with sufficient acreage to maintain one must send a man-at-arms to the quarterly review of troops, fully armed and shield in hand, or pay a tax in silver. Where is my tax?

BISHOP OF OXFORD: *Distingo,* your Highness.

KING: Distinguish as much as you like. I've made up my mind. I want my money. My purse is open, just drop it in. (*He sprawls back in his chair and picks his teeth. To* BECKET) Thomas, I don't know about you, but I'm starving. Have them bring us something to eat.

(BECKET *makes a sign to the* SENTRY *who goes out. A pause. The* ARCHBISHOP *rises.*)

ARCHBISHOP: A layman who shirks his duty to the State, which is to assist his Prince with arms, should pay the tax. Nobody will question that.

KING (*jovially*): Least of all the clergy!

ARCHBISHOP (*continuing*): A churchman's duty to the State is to assist his Prince in his prayers, and in his educational and charitable enterprises. He cannot therefore be liable to such a tax unless he neglects those duties.

BISHOP OF OXFORD: Have we refused to pray?

KING (*rising in fury*): Gentlemen! Do you seriously think that I am going to let myself be swindled out of more than two thirds of my revenues with arguments of that sort? In the days of the Conquest, when there was booty to be had, our Norman abbots tucked up their robes all right. And lustily too! Sword in fist, hams in the saddle, at cockcrow or earlier! "Let's go to it, Sire! Out with the Saxon scum! It's God's will! It's God's will!" You had to hold them back then! And on the odd occasions when you wanted a little Mass, they never had the time. They'd mislaid their vestments, the churches weren't equipped—any excuse to put it off, for fear they'd miss some of the pickings while their backs were turned!

ARCHBISHOP: Those heroic days are over. It is peacetime now.

KING: Then pay up! I won't budge from that.

(*Turning to* BECKET) Come on, Chancellor, say something! Has your new title caught your tongue?

BECKET: May I respectfully draw my Lord Archbishop's attention to one small point?

KING (*grunting*): Respectfully, but firmly. You're the Chancellor now.

BECKET (*calmly and casually*): England is a ship.

KING (*beaming*): Why, that's neat! We must use that, sometime.

BECKET: In the hazards of seafaring, the instinct of self-preservation has always told men that there must be one and only one master on board ship. Mutinous crews who drown their captain always end up, after a short interval of anarchy, by entrusting themselves body and soul to one of their number, who then proceeds to rule over them, more harshly sometimes than their drowned captain.

ARCHBISHOP: My Lord Chancellor—my young friend—there is in fact a saying—the captain is sole master after God. (*He thunders suddenly, with a voice one did not suspect from that frail body*) After God!

(*He crosses himself. All the* BISHOPS *follow suit. The wind of excommunication shivers through the Council. The* KING, *awed, crosses himself too and mumbles, a little cravenly.*)

KING: Nobody's trying to question God's authority, Archbishop.

BECKET (*who alone has remained unperturbed*): God steers the ship by inspiring the captain's decisions. But I never heard tell that He gave His instructions directly to the helmsman.

(GILBERT FOLLIOT, *Bishop of London, rises. He is a thin-lipped, venomous man.*)

FOLLIOT: Our young Chancellor is only a deacon—but he is a member of the Church. The few years he has spent out in the tumult of the world cannot have made him forget so soon that it is through His Church Militant and more particularly through the intermediary of our Holy Father the Pope and his Bishops—his qualified representatives—that God dictates His decisions to men!

BECKET: There is a chaplain on board every ship, but he is not required to determine the size of the crew's rations, nor to take the vessel's bearings. My Reverend Lord the Bishop of London—who is the grandson of a sailor they tell me—cannot have forgotten that point either.

FOLLIOT *(yelping):* I will not allow personal insinuations to compromise the dignity of a debate of this importance! The integrity and honor of the Church of England are at stake!

KING *(cheerfully):* No big words, Bishop. You know as well as I do that all that's at stake is its money. I need money for my wars. Will the Church give me any, yes or no?

ARCHBISHOP *(cautiously):* The Church of England has always acknowledged that it was its duty to assist the King, to the best of its ability, in all his needs.

KING: There's a fine speech. But I don't like the past tense, Archbishop. There's something so nostalgic about it. I like the present. And the future. Are you going to pay up?

ARCHBISHOP: Your Highness, I am here to defend the privileges which your illustrious forefather William granted to the Church of England. Would you have the heart to tamper with your forefather's work?

KING: May he rest in peace. His work is inviolable. But where he is now he doesn't need money. I'm still on earth unfortunately, and I do.

FOLLIOT: Your Highness, this is a question of principle!

KING: I'm levying troops, Bishop! I have sent for 1,500 German foot soldiers, and three thousand Swiss infantry to help fight the King of France. And nobody has ever paid the Swiss with principles.

BECKET *(rises suddenly and says incisively):* I think, your Highness, that it is pointless to pursue a discussion in which neither speaker is listening to the other. The law and custom of the land give us the means of coercion. We will use them.

FOLLIOT *(beside himself):* Would you dare—you whom she raised from the obscurity of your base origins—to plunge a dagger in the bosom of your Mother Church?

BECKET: My Lord and King has given me his Seal with the Three Lions to guard. My mother is England now.

FOLLIOT *(frothing, and slightly ridiculous):*

A deacon! A miserable deacon nourished in our bosom! Traitor! Little viper! Libertine! Sycophant! Saxon!

KING: My Reverend friend, I suggest you respect my Chancellor, or else I'll call my guards.

(He has raised his voice a little toward the end of this speech. The GUARDS *come in.)*

(Surprised) Why, here they are! Oh, no, it's my snack. Excuse me, gentlemen, but around noon I need something to peck at or I tend to feel weak. And a King has no right to weaken, I needn't tell you that. I'll have it in my chapel, then I can pray directly afterwards. Come and sit with me, son.

(He goes out taking BECKET *with him. The three prelates have risen, deeply offended. They move away, murmuring to one another, with sidelong glances in the direction in which the* KING *went out.)*

FOLLIOT: We must appeal to Rome! We must take a firm line!

YORK: My Lord Archbishop, you are the Primate of England. Your person is inviolate and your decisions on all matters affecting the Church are law in this country. You have a weapon against such intransigence: excommunication.

BISHOP OF OXFORD: We must not use it save with a great deal of prudence, Reverend Bishop. The Church has always triumphed over the centuries, but it has triumphed prudently. Let us bide our time. The King's rages are terrible, but they don't last. They are fires of straw.

FOLLIOT: The little self-seeker he has at his elbow now will make it his business to kindle them. And I think, like the Reverend Bishop, that only the excommunication of that young libertine can reduce him to impotence.

(BECKET comes in.)

BECKET: My Lords, the King has decided to adjourn his Privy Council. He thinks that a night of meditation will inspire your Lordships with a wise and equitable solution—which he authorizes you to come and submit to him tomorrow.

FOLLIOT *(with a bitter laugh):* You mean it's time for the hunt.

BECKET *(smiling):* Yes, my Lord Bishop, to

be perfectly frank with you, it is. Believe me, I am personally most grieved at this difference of opinion and the brutal form it has taken. But I cannot go back on what I said as Chancellor of England. We are all bound, laymen as well as priests, by the same feudal oath we took to the King as our Lord and Sovereign; the oath to preserve his life, limbs, dignity and honor. None of you, I think, has forgotten the words of that oath?

ARCHBISHOP *(quietly):* We have not forgotten it, my son. No more than the other oath we took, before that—the oath to God. You are young, and still uncertain of yourself, perhaps. Yet you have, in those few words, taken a resolution the meaning of which has not escaped me. Will you allow an old man, who is very close to death, and who, in this rather sordid argument, was defending more perhaps than you suspect—to hope, as a father, that you will never know the bitterness of realizing, one day, that you made a mistake.

(He holds out his ring and BECKET kisses it.) I give you my blessing, my son.

(BECKET has knelt. Now he rises and says lightly)

BECKET: An unworthy son, Father, alas. But when is one worthy? And worthy of what? *(He pirouettes and goes out, insolent and graceful as a young boy.)*

FOLLIOT *(violently):* Such insults to your Grace cannot be tolerated! This young rake's impudence must be crushed!

ARCHBISHOP *(thoughtfully):* He was with me for a long time. His is a strange, elusive nature. Don't imagine he is the ordinary libertine that outward appearances would suggest. I've had plenty of opportunity to observe him, in the bustle of pleasure and daily living. He is as it were detached. As if seeking his real self.

FOLLIOT: Break him, my Lord, before he finds it! Or the clergy of this country will pay dearly.

ARCHBISHOP: We must be very circumspect. It is our task to see into the hearts of men. And I am not sure that this one will always be our enemy.

(The ARCHBISHOP and the three BISHOPS go out. The KING is heard calling off stage.)

KING: Well, son, have they gone? Are you coming hunting?

(Trees come down from the flies. The black velvet curtain at the back opens on a clear sky, transforming the pillars into the leafless trees of a forest in winter. Bugles. The lights have gone down. When they go up again, the KING and BECKET are on horseback, each with a hawk on his gauntleted wrist. Torrential rain is heard.)

KING: Here comes the deluge. *(Unexpectedly)* Do you like hunting this way, with hawks?

BECKET: I don't much care to delegate my errands. I prefer to feel a wild boar on the end of my spear. When he turns and charges there's a moment of delicious personal contact when one feels, at last, responsible for oneself.

KING: It's odd, this craving for danger. Why are you all so hell-bent on risking your necks for the most futile reasons?

BECKET: One has to gamble with one's life to feel alive.

KING: Or dead! You make me laugh. *(To his hawk)* Quiet, my pretty, quiet! We'll take your hood off in a minute. You couldn't give much of a performance under all these trees. I'll tell you one creature that loves hawking anyway, and that's a hawk! It seems to me we've rubbed our backsides sore with three hours' riding, just to give them this royal pleasure.

BECKET *(smiling):* My Lord, these are Norman hawks. They belong to the master race. They have a right to it.

KING *(suddenly, as he reins his horse):* Do you love me, Becket?

BECKET: I am your servant, my prince.

KING: Did you love me when I made you Chancellor? I wonder sometimes if you're capable of love. Do you love Gwendolen?

BECKET: She is my mistress, my prince.

KING: Why do you put labels onto everything to justify your feelings?

BECKET: Because, without labels, the world would have no shape, my prince.

KING: Is it so important for the world to have a shape?

BECKET: It's essential, my prince, otherwise we can't know what we're doing.

(Bugles in the distance.)
The rain is getting heavier, my Lord! Come, let us shelter in that hut over there.

(He gallops off. After a second of confused indecision, the KING *gallops after him, holding his hawk high and shouting)*

KING: Becket! You didn't answer my question!

(He disappears into the forest. Bugles again. The four BARONS *cross the stage, galloping after them, and vanish into the forest. Thunder. Lightning. A hut has appeared to one side of the stage.* BECKET *is heard shouting)*

BECKET: Hey there! You! Fellow! Can we put the horses under cover in your barn? Do you know how to rub down a horse? And have a look at the right forefoot of messire's horse. I think the shoe is loose. We'll sit out the storm under your roof.

(After a second, the KING *enters the hut, followed by a hairy Saxon who, cap in hand, bows repeatedly, in terrified silence.)*

KING *(shaking himself):* What a soaking! I'll catch my death! *(He sneezes.)* All this just to keep the hawks amused! *(Shouting at the man)* What are you waiting for? Light a fire, dog! It's freezing cold in this shack.

(The MAN, *terror-stricken, does not move. The* KING *sneezes again. To* BECKET)
What is he waiting for?

BECKET: Wood is scarce, my Lord. I don't suppose he has any left.

KING: What—in the middle of the forest?

BECKET: They are entitled to two measures of dead wood. One branch more and they're hanged.

KING *(astounded):* Really? And yet people are always complaining about the amount of dead wood in the forests. Still, that's a problem for my intendants, not me. *(Shouting at the* MAN) Run and pick up all the wood you can carry and build us a roaring fire! We won't hang you this time, dog!

(The peasant, terrified, dares not obey. BECKET *says gently)*

BECKET: Go, my son. Your King commands it. You've the right.

(The MAN *goes out, trembling, bowing to the ground, repeatedly.)*

KING: Why do you call that old man your son?

BECKET: Why not? You call him dog, my prince.

KING: It's a manner of speaking. Saxons are always called "dog." I can't think why, really. One could just as well have called them "Saxon"! But that smelly old ragbag your son! *(Sniffing)* What on earth can they eat to make the place stink so—dung?

BECKET: Turnips.

KING: Turnips—what are they?

BECKET: Roots.

KING *(amused):* Do they eat roots?

BECKET: Those who live in the forests can't grow anything else.

KING: Why don't they move out into the open country then?

BECKET: They would be hanged if they left their area.

KING: Oh, I see. Mark you, that must make life a lot simpler, if you know you'll be hanged at the least show of initiative. You must ask yourself far fewer questions. They don't know their luck! But you still haven't told me why you called the fellow your son?

BECKET *(lightly):* My prince, he is so poor and so bereft and I am so strong beside him, that he really is my son.

KING: We'd go a long way with that theory!

BECKET: Besides, my prince, you're appreciably younger than I am and you call me "son" sometimes.

KING: That's got nothing to do with it. It's because I love you.

BECKET: You are our King. We are all your sons and in your hands.

KING: What, Saxons too?

BECKET *(Lightly, as he strips off his gloves):* England will be fully built, my prince, on the day the Saxons are your sons as well.

KING: You are a bore today! I get the feeling that I'm listening to the Archbishop. And I'm dying of thirst. Hunt around and see if you can't find us something to drink. Go on, it's your son's house!

(BECKET starts looking, and leaves the room after a while. The KING *looks around too, examining the hut with curiosity, touching things with grimaces of distaste. Suddenly he*

notices a kind of trap door at the foot of a wall. He opens it, thrusts his hand in and pulls out a terrified GIRL. *He shouts)*
Hey, Thomas! Thomas!

*(*BECKET *comes in.)*

BECKET: Have you found something to drink, Lord?

KING *(holding the* GIRL *at arm's length):* No. Something to eat. What do you say to that, if it's cleaned up a bit?

BECKET *(coldly):* She's pretty.

KING: She stinks a bit, but we could wash her. Look, did you ever see anything so tiny? How old would you say it was—fifteen, sixteen?

BECKET *(quietly):* It can talk, my Lord. *(Gently, to the* GIRL*)*
How old are you?

(The GIRL *looks at them in terror and says nothing.)*

KING: You see? Of course it can't talk!

(The MAN *has come back with the wood and stops in the doorway, terrified.)*
How old is your daughter, dog?

(The MAN *trembles like a cornered animal and says nothing.)*
He's dumb as well, that son of yours. How did you get him—with a deaf girl? It's funny the amount of dumb people I meet the second I set foot out of my palace. I rule over a kingdom of the dumb. Can you tell me why?

BECKET: They're afraid, my prince.

KING: I know that. And a good thing too. The populace must live in fear, it's essential. The moment they stop being afraid they have only one thought in mind—to frighten other people instead. And they adore doing that! Just as much as we do! Give them a chance to do it and they catch up fast, those sons of yours! Did you never see a peasants' revolt? I did once, in my father's reign, when I was a child. It's not a pretty sight. *(He looks at the* MAN, *exasperated.)* Look at it, will you? It's tongue-tied, it's obtuse, it stinks and the country is crawling with them! *(He seizes the* GIRL *who was trying to run away.)* Stay here, you! *(To* BECKET*)* I ask you, what use is it?

BECKET *(smiling):* It scratches the soil, it makes bread.

KING: Pooh, the English eat so little of it

. . . At the French Court, yes, I daresay—they fairly stuff it down! But here!

BECKET *(smiling):* The troops have to be fed. For a King without troops . . .

KING *(struck by this):* True enough! Yes, that makes sense. There must be some sort of reason in all these absurdities. Well well, you little Saxon philosopher, you! I don't know how you do it, but you'll turn me into an intelligent man yet! The odd thing is, it's so ugly and yet it makes such pretty daughters. How do you explain that, you who can explain it all?

BECKET: At twenty, before he lost his teeth and took on that indeterminate age the common people have, that man may have been handsome. He may have had one night of love, one minute when he too was a King, and shed his fear. Afterwards, his pauper's life went on, eternally the same. And he and his wife no doubt forgot it all. But the seed was sown.

KING *(dreamily):* You have such a way of telling things . . . *(He looks at the* GIRL.) Do you think she'll grow ugly too?

BECKET: For sure.

KING: If we made her a whore and kept her at the palace, would she stay pretty?

BECKET: Perhaps.

KING: Then we'd be doing her a service, don't you think?

BECKET *(coldly):* No doubt.

(The MAN *stiffens. The* GIRL *cowers, in terror. The* BROTHER *comes in, somber-faced, silent, threatening.)*

KING: Would you believe it? They understand every word, you know! Who's that one there?

BECKET *(taking in the situation at a glance):* The brother.

KING: How do you know?

BECKET: Instinct, my Lord. *(His hand moves to his dagger.)*

KING *(bawling suddenly):* Why are they staring at me like that? I've had enough of this! I told you to get something to drink, dog!

(Terrified, the MAN *scuttles off.)*

BECKET: Their water will be brackish. I have a gourd of juniper juice in my saddlebag. *(to the* BROTHER*)* Come and give me a hand, you! My horse is restive.

(He seizes the boy roughly by the arm and hustles him out into the forest, carelessly whistling his little marching song. Then, all of a sudden, he hurls himself onto him. A short silent struggle. BECKET *gets the boy's knife away; he escapes into the forest.* BECKET *watches him go for a second, holding his wounded hand. Then he walks around the back of the hut. The* KING *has settled himself on a bench, with his feet up on another, whistling to himself. He lifts the* GIRL's *skirts with his cane and examines her at leisure.)*

KING *(in a murmur):* All my sons! . . . *(He shakes himself.)* That Becket! He wears me out. He keeps making me think! I'm sure it's bad for the health.

(He gets up, BECKET *comes in followed by the* MAN.)
What about the water? How much longer do I have to wait?

BECKET: Here it is, my Lord. But it's muddy. Have some of this juniper juice instead.

KING: Drink with me. *(He notices* BECKET's *hand, wrapped in a bloodstained cloth.)* What's the matter? You're wounded!

BECKET *(Hiding his hand):* No doubt about it, that horse of mine is a nervous brute. He can't bear his saddle touched. He bit me.

KING *(with a hearty, delighted laugh):* That's funny! Oh, that's very funny! Milord is the best rider in the Kingdom! Milord can never find a stallion with enough spirit for him! Milord makes us all look silly at the jousts, with his fancy horsemanship, and when he goes to open his saddlebags he gets himself bitten! Like a page! *(He is almost savagely gleeful. Then suddenly, his gaze softens.)* You're white as a sheet, little Saxon . . . Why do I love you? . . . It's funny, I don't like to think of you in pain. Show me that hand. A horse bite can turn nasty. I'll put some of that juniper gin on it.

BECKET *(snatching his hand away):* I already have, my Lord, it's nothing.

KING: Then why do you look so pale? Show me your hand.

BECKET *(with sudden coldness):* It's an ugly wound and you know you hate the sight of blood.

KING *(steps back a little, then exclaims with delight):* All this just to fetch me a drink! Wounded in the service of the King! We'll tell the others you defended me against a wild boar and I'll present you with a handsome gift this evening. What would you like?

BECKET *(softly):* This girl. *(He adds after a pause)* I fancy her.

(A pause.)

KING *(his face clouding over):* That's tiresome of you. I fancy her too. And where that's concerned, friendship goes by the board. *(A pause. His face takes on a cunning look.)* All right, then. But favor for favor. You won't forget, will you?

BECKET: No, my prince.

KING: Favor for favor; do you give me your word as a gentleman?

BECKET: Yes, my prince.

KING *(draining his glass, suddenly cheerful):* Done! She's yours. Do we take her with us or shall we have her sent?

BECKET: I'll send two soldiers to fetch her. Listen. The others have caught up.

(A troop of men-at-arms have come riding up behind the shack during the end of the scene.)

KING *(To the* MAN*):* Wash your daughter, dog, and kill her fleas. She's going to the palace. For Milord here, who's a Saxon too. You're pleased about that, I hope? *(To* BECKET *as he goes)* Give him a gold piece. I'm feeling generous this morning.

(He goes out. The MAN *looks at* BECKET *in terror.)*

BECKET: No one will come and take your daughter away. Keep her better hidden in future. And tell your son to join the others, in the forest, he'll be safer there, now. I think one of the soldiers saw us. Here!

(He throws him a purse and goes out. When he has gone, the MAN *snatches up the purse, then spits venomously, his face twisted with hate.)*

MAN: God rot your guts! Pig!

GIRL *(unexpectedly):* He was handsome, that one. Is it true he's taking me to the palace?

MAN: You whore! You Norman's trollop!

(He hurls himself onto her and beats her

savagely. The KING, BECKET *and the* BARONS *have galloped off, amid the sound of bugles. The hut and the forest backcloth disappear. We are in* BECKET'S *palace.*

FOOTMEN *push on a kind of low bed-couch, with cushions and some stools. Upstage, between two pillars, a curtain behind which can be seen the shadows of banqueting guests. Singing and roars of laughter. Downstage, curled up on the bed,* GWENDOLEN *is playing a string instrument. The curtain is drawn aside,* BECKET *appears. He goes to* GWENDOLEN *while the banqueting and the laughter, punctuated by hoarse incoherent snatches of song, go on upstage.* GWENDOLEN *stops playing.)*

GWENDOLEN: Are they still eating?

BECKET: Yes. They have an unimaginable capacity for absorbing food.

GWENDOLEN *(softly, beginning to play again):* How can my Lord spend his days and a large part of his nights with such creatures?

BECKET *(crouching at her feet and caressing her):* If he spent his time with learned clerics debating the sex of angels, your Lord would be even more bored, my kitten. They are as far from the true knowledge of things as mindless brutes.

GWENDOLEN *(gently, as she plays):* I don't always understand everything my Lord condescends to say to me . . . What I do know is that it is always very late when he comes to see me.

BECKET *(caressing her):* The only thing I love is coming to you. Beauty is one of the few things which don't shake one's faith in God.

GWENDOLEN: I am my Lord's war captive and I belong to him body and soul. God has willed it so, since He gave the Normans victory over my people. If the Welsh had won the war I would have married a man of my own race, at my father's castle. God did not will it so.

BECKET *(quietly):* That belief will do as well as any, my kitten. But, as I belong to a conquered race myself, I have a feeling that God's system is a little muddled. Go on playing.

(GWENDOLEN *starts to play again. Then she says suddenly)*

GWENDOLEN: I'm lying. You are my Lord,

God or no God. And if the Welsh had been victorious, you could just as easily have stolen me from my father's castle. I should have come with you.

(She says this gravely. BECKET *rises abruptly and moves away. She looks up at him with anguished eyes and stops playing.)*
Did I say something wrong? What is the matter with my Lord?

BECKET. Nothing. I don't like being loved. I told you that.

(The curtain opens. The KING *appears.)*

KING *(a little drunk):* Well, son, have you deserted us? It worked! I told you! They've tumbled to it! They're fighting with your forks! They've at last discovered that they're for poking one another's eyes out. They think it's a most ingenious little invention. You'd better go in, son, they'll break them in a minute.

*(*BECKET *goes behind the curtain to quieten his guests. He can be heard shouting)*
Gentlemen, gentlemen! No, no, they aren't little daggers. No, truly—they're for pronging meat . . . Look, let me show you again.

(Huge roars of laughter behind the curtain. The KING *has moved over to* GWENDOLEN. *He stares at her.)*

KING: Was that you playing, while we were at table?

GWENDOLEN *(with a deep curtsy):* Yes, my Lord.

KING: You have every kind of accomplishment, haven't you? Get up.

(He lifts her to her feet, caressing her as he does so. She moves away, ill at ease. He says with a wicked smile)

KING: Have I frightened you, my heart? We'll soon put that right. *(He pulls the curtain aside.)* Hey there, Becket! That's enough horseplay, my fat lads! Come and hear a little music. When the belly's full, it's good to elevate the mind a bit. *(To* GWENDOLEN*)* Play!

(The four BARONS, *bloated with food and drink, come in with* BECKET. GWENDOLEN *has taken up her instrument again. The* KING *sprawls on the bed, behind her. The* BARONS, *with much sighing and puffing, unclasp their belts and sit down on stools, where they soon*

fall into a stupor. BECKET *remains standing.)*
Tell her to sing us something sad. I like sad
music after dinner, it helps the digestion. *(He
hiccups.)* You always feed us far too well,
Thomas. Where did you steal that cook of
yours?

BECKET: I bought him, Sire. He's a Frenchman.

KING: Really? Aren't you afraid he might
poison you? Tell me, how much does one pay
for a French cook?

BECKET: A good one, like him, costs almost
as much as a horse, my Lord.

KING *(genuinely outraged):* It's outrageous!
What is the country coming to! No man is
worth a horse! If I said "favor for favor"—remember?—and I asked you to give him to me,
would you?

BECKET: Of course, my Lord.

KING *(with a smile, gently caressing* GWEN-
DOLEN*):* Well, I won't. I don't want to eat too
well every day; it lowers a man's morale. Sadder, sadder, my little doe. *(He belches.)* Oh,
that venison! Get her to sing that lament they
composed for your mother, Becket. It's my
favorite song.

BECKET: I don't like anyone to sing that lament, my Lord.

KING: Why not? Are you ashamed of being
a Saracen girl's son? That's half your charm,
you fool! There must be some reason why
you're more civilized than all the rest of us
put together! I adore that song.

*(*GWENDOLEN *looks uncertainly at* BECKET.
There is a pause. Then the KING *says coldly)*
That's an order, little Saxon.

BECKET *(inscrutably, to* GWENDOLEN*):* Sing.
(She strikes a few opening chords, while the
KING *makes himself comfortable beside her,
belching contentedly. She begins)*

GWENDOLEN *(singing):*
> Handsome Sir Gilbert
> Went to the war
> One fine morning in May
> To deliver the heart
> Of Lord Jesus our Saviour,
> From the hands of the Sara-
>   cens.
> Woe! Woe! Heavy is my heart
> At being without love!

> Woe! Woe! Heavy is my heart
> All the livelong day!

KING *(singing):*
> All the livelong day! Go on!

GWENDOLEN: As the battle raged
> He swung his mighty sword
> And many a Moor fell dead
> But his trusty charger
> Stumbled in the fray
> And Sir Gilbert fell.
> Woe! Woe! Heavy is my heart!
> At being without love!
> Woe Woe! Heavy is my heart
> All the livelong day.

> Wounded in the head
> Away Gilbert was led
> To the Algiers market
> Chained hand and foot
> And sold there as a slave.

KING *(singing, out of tune):*
> All the livelong day!

GWENDOLEN: A Saracen's daughter
> Lovely as the night
> Lost her heart to him
> Swore to love him always
> Vowed to be his wife.

> Woe! Woe! Heavy is my heart
> At being without love!
> Woe! Woe! Heavy is my heart
> All the livelong day—

KING *(interrupting):* It brings tears to my
eyes, you know, that story. I look a brute but
I'm soft as swansdown really. One can't
change one's nature. I can't imagine why you
don't like people to sing that song. It's wonderful to be a love child. When I look at my
august parents' faces, I shudder to think what
must have gone on. It's marvelous to think of
your mother helping your father to escape and
then coming to join him in London with you
inside her. Sing us the end, girl. I adore the
end.

GWENDOLEN *(softly):*
> Then he asked the holy Father
> For a priest to baptize her
> And he took her as his wife
> To cherish with his life
> Giving her his soul
> To love and keep alway.

Gay! Gay! Easy is my heart
At being full of love
Gay! Gay! Easy is my heart
To be loved alway.

KING (*dreamily*): Did he really love her all his life? Isn't it altered a bit in the song?

BECKET: No, my prince.

KING (*getting up, quite saddened*): Funny, it's the happy ending that makes me feel sad . . . Tell me, do you believe in love, Thomas?

BECKET (*coldly*): For my father's love for my mother, Sire, yes.

(*The* KING *has moved over to the* BARONS *who are now snoring on their stools. He gives them a kick as he passes.*)

KING: They've fallen asleep, the hogs. That's their way of showing their finer feelings. You know, my little Saxon, sometimes I have the impression that you and I are the only sensitive men in England. We eat with forks and we have infinitely distinguished sentiments, you and I. You've made a different man of me, in a way . . . What you ought to find me now, if you loved me, is a girl to give me a little polish. I've had enough of whores. (*He has come back to* GWENDOLEN. *He caresses her a little and then says suddenly*) Favor for favor—do you remember?

(*A pause.*)

BECKET (*pale*): I am your servant, my prince, and all I have is yours. But you were also gracious enough to say I was your friend.

KING: That's what I mean! As one friend to another it's the thing to do! (*A short pause. He smiles maliciously, and goes on caressing* GWENDOLEN, *who cowers, terrified.*) You care about her then? Can you care for something? Go on, tell me, tell me if you care about her?

(BECKET *says nothing. The* KING *smiles.*) You can't tell a lie. I know you. Not because you're afraid of lies—I think you must be the only man I know who isn't afraid of anything —not even Heaven—but because it's distasteful to you. You consider it inelegant. What looks like morality in you is nothing more than esthetics. Is that true or isn't it?

BECKET (*meeting his eyes, says softly*): It's true, my Lord.

KING: I'm not cheating if I ask for her, am I? I said "favor for favor" and I asked you for your word of honor.

BECKET (*icily*): And I gave it to you.

(*A pause. They stand quite still. The* KING *looks at* BECKET *with a wicked smile.* BECKET *does not look at him. Then the* KING *moves briskly away.*)

KING: Right. I'm off to bed. I feel like an early night tonight. Delightful evening, Becket. You're the only man in England who knows how to give your friends a royal welcome. (*He kicks the slumbering* BARONS.) Call my guards and help me wake these porkers.

(*The* BARONS *wake with sighs and belches as the* KING *pushes them about, shouting*) Come on, Barons, home! I know you're connoisseurs of good music, but we can't listen to music all night long. Happy evenings end in bed, eh Becket?

BECKET (*stiffly*): May I ask your Highness for a brief moment's grace?

KING: Granted! Granted! I'm not a savage. I'll wait for you both in my litter. You can say good night to me downstairs.

(*He goes out, followed by the* BARONS. BECKET *stands motionless for a while under* GWENDOLEN's *steady gaze. Then he says quietly*)

BECKET: You will have to go with him, Gwendolen.

GWENDOLEN (*composedly*): Did my Lord promise me to him?

BECKET: I gave him my word as a gentleman that I would give him anything he asked for. I never thought it would be you.

GWENDOLEN: If he sends me away tomorrow, will my Lord take me back?

BECKET: No.

GWENDOLEN: Shall I tell the girls to put my dresses in the coffer?

BECKET: He'll send over for it tomorrow. Go down. One doesn't keep the King waiting. Tell him I wish him a respectful good night.

GWENDOLEN (*laying her viol on the bed*): I shall leave my Lord my viol. He can almost play it now. (*She asks, quite naturally*) My Lord cares for nothing, in the whole world, does he?

BECKET: No.

GWENDOLEN (*moves to him and says gently*): You belong to a conquered race too. But through tasting too much of the honey of life, you've forgotten that even those who have been robbed of everything have one thing left to call their own.

BECKET (*inscrutably*): Yes, I daresay I had forgotten. There is a gap in me where honor ought to be. Go now.

GWENDOLEN *goes out.* BECKET *stands quite still. Then he goes to the bed, picks up the viol, looks at it, then throws it abruptly away. He pulls off the fur coverlet and starts to unbutton his doublet.*

A GUARD *comes in, dragging the* SAXON GIRL *from the forest, whom he throws down in the middle of the room. The* KING *appears.*)

KING (*hilariously*): Thomas, my son! You'd forgotten her! You see how careless you are! Luckily I think of everything. It seems they had to bully the father and the brother a tiny bit to get her, but anyway, here she is. You see?—I really am a friend to you, and you're wrong not to love me. You told me you fancied her. I hadn't forgotten that, you see. Sleep well, son!

(*He goes out, followed by the* GUARD. *The* GIRL, *still dazed, looks at* BECKET *who has not moved. She recognizes him, gets to her feet and smiles at him. A long pause, then she asks with a kind of sly coquetry*)

GIRL: Shall I undress, my Lord?

BECKET (*who has not moved*): Of course.

(*The* GIRL *starts to undress.* BECKET *looks at her coldly, absent-mindedly whistling a few bars of his little march. Suddenly he stops, goes to the* GIRL, *who stands there dazed and half naked, and seizes her by the shoulders.*) I hope you're full of noble feelings and that all this strikes you as pretty shabby?

(*A* SERVANT *runs in wildy and halts in the doorway spechless. Before he can speak, the* KING *comes stumbling in.*)

KING (*soberly*): I had no pleasure with her, Thomas. She let me lay her down in the litter, limp as a corpse, and then suddenly she pulled out a little knife from somewhere. There was blood everywhere . . . I feel quite sick.

(BECKET *has let go of the* GIRL. *The* KING *adds, haggard*):
She could easily have killed me instead! (*A pause. He says abruptly*): Send that girl away. I'm sleeping in your room tonight. I'm frightened.

(BECKET *motions to the* SERVANT, *who takes away the half-naked* GIRL. *The* KING *has thrown himself fully dressed, onto the bed with an animal-like sigh.*)
Take half the bed.

BECKET: I'll sleep on the floor, my prince.

KING: No. Lie down beside me. I don't want to be alone tonight. (*He looks at him and murmurs*): You loathe me, I shan't even be able to trust you now . . .

BECKET: You gave me your Seal to keep, my prince. And the Three Lions of England which are engraved on it keep watch over me too. (*He snuffs out the candles, all save one. It is almost dark.*)

KING (*his voice already thick with sleep*): I shall never know what you're thinking . . .

(BECKET *has thrown a fur coverlet over the* KING. *He lies down beside him and says quietly*)

BECKET: It will be dawn soon, my prince. You must sleep. Tomorrow we are crossing to the Continent. In a week we will face the King of France's army and there will be simple answers to everything at last.

(*He has lain down beside the* KING. *A pause, during which the* KING's *snoring gradually increases. Suddenly, the* KING *moans and tosses in his sleep.*)

KING (*crying out*): They're after me! They're after me! They're armed to the teeth! Stop them! Stop them!

(BECKET *sits up on one elbow. He touches the* KING, *who wakes up with a great animal cry.*)

BECKET: My prince . . . my prince . . . sleep in peace. I'm here.

KING: Oh . . . Thomas, it's you . . . They were after me.

(*He turns over and goes back to sleep with a sigh. Gradually he begins to snore again, softly.* BECKET *is still on one elbow. Almost tenderly, he draws the coverlet over the* KING.)

BECKET: My prince . . . If you were my true prince, if you were one of my race, how simple everything would be. How tenderly I would love you, my prince, in an ordered world. Each of us bound in fealty to the other, head, heart and limbs, with no further questions to ask of oneself, ever.

(A pause. The KING's *snores grow louder.*
BECKET *sighs and says with a little smile)*
But I cheated my way, a twofold bastard, into
the ranks, and found a place among the conquerors. You can sleep peacefully though,
my prince. So long as Becket is obliged to improvise his honor, he will serve you. And if
one day, he meets it face to face . . . *(A short
pause)* But where is Becket's honor?

(He lies down with a sigh, beside the KING.
The KING's *snores grow louder still. The can-
dle sputters. The lights grow even dimmer
. . . The curtain falls.)*

ACT TWO

*The curtain rises on the same set of arching
pillars, which now represents a forest in
France. The* KING's *tent, not yet open for the
day, is set up among the trees. A* SENTRY *stands
some way off.*

*It is dawn. Crouched around a campfire,
the four* BARONS *are having their morning
meal, in silence. After a while, one of them
says:*

1ST BARON: This Becket then, who is he?
*(A pause. All four are fairly slow in their
reactions.)*

2ND BARON *(surprised at the question):* The
Chancellor of England.

1ST BARON: I know that! But who is he,
exactly?

2ND BARON: The Chancellor of England, I
tell you! The Chancellor of England is the
Chancellor of England! I don't see what else
there is to inquire into on that score.

1ST BARON: You don't understand. Look,
supposing the Chancellor of England were
some other man. Me, for instance . . .

2ND BARON: That's plain idiotic.

1ST BARON: I said supposing. Now, I would
be Chancellor of England but I wouldn't be
the same Chancellor of England as Becket is.
You can follow that, can you?

2ND BARON *(guardedly):* Yes . . .

1ST BARON: So, I *can* ask myself the question.

2ND BARON: What question?

1ST BARON: Who is this man Becket?

2ND BARON: What do you mean, who is this
man Becket? He's the Chancellor of England.

1ST BARON: Yes. But what I'm asking myself is who is he, as a man?

2ND BARON *(looks at him and says sorrowfully):* Have you got a pain?

1ST BARON: No, why?

2ND BARON: A Baron who asks himself questions is a sick Baron. Your sword—what's that?

1ST BARON: My sword?

2ND BARON: Yes.

1ST BARON *(putting his hand to the hilt):* It's
my sword! And anyone who thinks different—

2ND BARON: Right. Answered like a nobleman. We peers aren't here to ask questions.
We're here to give answers.

1ST BARON: Right then. Answer me.

2ND BARON: Not to questions! To orders.
You aren't asked to think in the army. When
you're face to face with a French man-at-arms,
do you ask yourself questions?

1ST BARON: No.

2ND BARON: Does he?

1ST BARON: No.

2ND BARON: You just fall to and fight. If you
started asking each other questions like a pair
of women, you might as well bring chairs onto
the battlefield. If there are any questions to
be asked you can be sure they've been asked
already, higher up, by cleverer heads than
yours.

1ST BARON *(vexed):* I meant I didn't like
him, that's all.

2ND BARON: Why couldn't you say so then?
That we'd have understood. You're entitled
not to like him. I don't like him either, come
to that. To begin with, he's a Saxon.

1ST BARON: To begin with!

3RD BARON: One thing you can't say though.
You can't say he isn't a fighter. Yesterday when
the King was in the thick of it, after his squire
was killed, he cut his way right through the
French, and he seized the King's banner and
drew the enemy off and onto himself.

1ST BARON: All right! He's a good fighter!

3RD BARON *(to* 2ND BARON): Isn't he a good
fighter?

2ND BARON *(stubbornly):* Yes. But he's a
Saxon.

1ST BARON (*to the* 4TH BARON, *who has so far said nothing*): How about you, Regnault? What do you think of him?

4TH BARON (*placidly, swallowing his mouthful of food*): I'm waiting.

1ST BARON: Waiting for what?

4TH BARON: Till he shows himself. Some sorts of game are like that: you follow them all day through the forest, by sounds, or tracks, or smell. But it wouldn't do any good to charge ahead with drawn lance; you'd just spoil everything because you don't know for sure what sort of animal it is you're dealing with. You have to wait.

1ST BARON: What for?

4TH BARON: For whatever beast it is to show itself. And if you're patient it always does in the end. Animals know more than men do, nearly always, but a man has something in him that an animal hasn't got: he knows how to wait. With this man Becket—I'll wait.

1ST BARON: For what?

4TH BARON: For him to show himself. For him to break cover. (*He goes on eating.*) The day he does, we'll know who he is.

(BECKET's *little whistled march is heard off stage.* BECKET *comes in, armed.*)

BECKET: Good morning to you, Gentlemen. (*The four* BARONS *rise politely, and salute.*) Is the King still asleep?

1ST BARON (*stiffly*): He hasn't called yet.

BECKET: Has the camp marshal presented his list of losses?

1ST BARON: No.

BECKET: Why not?

2ND BARON (*surlily*): He was part of the losses.

BECKET: Oh?

1ST BARON: I was nearby when it happened. A lance knocked him off his horse. Once on the ground, the foot soldiers dealt with him.

BECKET: Poor Beaumont. He was so proud of his new armor.

2ND BARON: There must have been a chink in it then. They bled him white. On the ground. French swine!

BECKET (*with a slight shrug*): That's war.

1ST BARON: War is a sport like any other. There are rules. In the old days, they took you

for ransom. A Knight for a Knight. That was proper fighting!

BECKET (*smiling*): Since one has taken to sending the foot soldiery against the horses with no personal protection save a cutlass, they're a little inclined to seek out the chink in the armor of any Knight unwise enough to fall off his horse. It's repulsive, but I can understand them.

1ST BARON: If we start understanding the common soldiery war will be butchery plain and simple.

BECKET: The world is certainly tending towards butchery, Baron. The lesson of this battle, which has cost us far too much, is that we will have to form platoons of cutthroats too, that's all.

1ST BARON: And a soldier's honor, my Lord Chancellor, what of that?

BECKET (*dryly*): A soldier's honor, Baron, is to win victories. Let us not be hypocritical. The Norman nobility lost no time in teaching those they conquered that little point. I'll wake the King. Our entry into the city is timed for eight o'clock and the *Te Deum* in the cathedral for a quarter past nine. It would be bad policy to keep the French Bishop waiting. We want these people to collaborate with a good grace.

1ST BARON (*grunting*): In my day, we slaughtered the lot and marched in afterwards.

BECKET: Yes, into a dead city! I want to give the King living cities to increase his wealth. From eight o'clock this morning, I am the French people's dearest friend.

1ST BARON: What about England's honor, then?

BECKET (*quietly*): England's honor, Baron, in the final reckoning, has always been to succeed.

(*He goes into the* KING's *tent smiling. The four* BARONS *look at each other, hostile.*)

1ST BARON (*muttering*): What a mentality!

4TH BARON (*sententiously*): We must wait for him. One day, he'll break cover.

(*The four* BARONS *move away.* BECKET *lifts the tent flap and hooks it back. The* KING *is revealed, in bed with a girl.*)

KING (*yawning*): Good morning, son. Did you sleep well?

BECKET: A little memento from the French on my left shoulder kept me awake, Sire. I took the opportunity to do some thinking.

KING (*worriedly*): You think too much. You'll suffer for it, you know! It's because people think that there are problems. One day, if you go on like this, you'll think yourself into a dilemma, your big head will present you with a solution and you'll jump feet first into a hopeless mess—which you'd have done far better to ignore, like the majority of fools, who know nothing and live to a ripe old age. What do you think of my little French girl? I must say, I adore France.

BECKET (*smiling*): So do I, Sire, like all Englishmen.

KING: The climate's warm, the girls are pretty, the wine is good. I intend to spend at least a month here every winter.

BECKET: The only snag is, it's expensive! Nearly 2,000 casualties yesterday.

KING: Has Beaumont made out his total?

BECKET: Yes. And he added himself to the list.

KING: Wounded?

(BECKET *does not answer. The* KING *shivers. He says somberly*)
I don't like learning that people I know have died. I've a feeling it may give Death ideas.

BECKET: My prince, shall we get down to work? We haven't dealt with yesterday's dispatches.

KING: Yesterday we were fighting! We can't do everything.

BECKET: That was a holiday! We'll have to work twice as hard today.

KING: Does it amuse you—working for the good of my people? Do you mean to say you love all those folk? To begin with they're too numerous. One can't love them, one doesn't know them. Anyway, you're lying, you don't love anything or anybody.

BECKET (*tersely*): There's one thing I do love, my prince, and that I'm sure of. Doing what I have to do and doing it well.

KING (*grinning*): Always the es—es . . . What's your word again? I've forgotten it.

BECKET: Esthetics?

KING: Esthetics! Always the esthetic side, eh?

BECKET: Yes, my prince.

KING (*slapping the* GIRL's *rump*): And isn't that esthetic too? Some people go into ecstasies over cathedrals. But this is a work of art too! Look at that—round as an apple . . . (*Quite naturally, as if he were offering him a sweetmeat*) Want her?

BECKET (*smiling*): Business, my Lord!

KING (*Pouting like a schoolboy*): All right. Business. I'm listening. Sit down.

(BECKET *sits down on the bed, beside the* KING, *with the* GIRL *like a fascinated rabbit in between them.*)

BECKET: The news is not good, my prince.

KING (*with a careless wave of the hand*): News never is. That's a known fact. Life is one long web of difficulties. The secret of it— and there is one, brought to perfection by several generations of worldly-wise philosophers—is to give them no importance whatever. In the end one difficulty swallows up the other and you find yourself ten years later still alive with no harm done. Things always work out.

BECKET: Yes. But badly. My prince, when you play tennis, do you simply sit back and let things work out? Do you wait for the ball to hit your racket and say "It's bound to come this way eventually"?

KING: Ah, now just a minute. You're talking about things that matter. A game of tennis is important, it amuses me.

BECKET: And suppose I were to tell you that governing can be as amusing as a game of tennis? Are we going to let the others smash the ball into our court, my prince, or shall we try to score a point, both of us, like two good English sportsmen?

KING (*suddenly roused by his sporting instinct*): The point, Begod, the point! You're right! On the court, I sweat and strain, I fall over my feet, I half kill myself, I'll cheat if need be, but I never give up the point!

BECKET: Well then, I'll tell you what the score is, so far. Piecing together all the information I have received from London since we've been on the Continent, one thing strikes me, and that is: that there exists in England a power which has grown until it almost rivals yours, my Lord. It is the power of your clergy.

KING: We did get them to pay the tax. That's something!

BECKET: Yes, it's a small sum of money. And they know that Princes can always be pacified with a little money. But those men are past masters at taking back with one hand what they were forced to give with the other. That's a little conjuring trick they've had centuries of practice in.

KING (to the GIRL): Pay attention, my little sparrow. Now's your chance to educate yourself. The gentleman is saying some very profound things!

BECKET (in the same flippant way): Little French sparrow, suppose you educate us instead. When you're married—if you do marry despite the holes in your virtue—which would you prefer, to be mistress in your own house or to have your village priest laying down the law there?

(The KING, a little peeved, gets up on his knees on the bed and hides the bewildered GIRL under an eiderdown.)

KING: Talk sense, Becket! Priests are always intriguing, I know that. But I also know that I can crush them any time I like.

BECKET: Talk sense, Sire. If you don't do the crushing now, in five years' time there will be two Kings in England, the Archbishop of Canterbury and you. And in ten years' time there will be only one.

KING (a bit shamefaced): And it won't be me?

BECKET (coldly): I rather fear not.

KING (with a sudden shout): Oh, yes, it will! We Plantagenets hold on to our own! To horse, Becket, to horse! For England's glory! War on the faithful! That will make a change for us!

(The eiderdown starts to toss. The GIRL emerges, disheveled, and red in the face.)

GIRL (pleadingly): My Lord! I can't breathe!

(The KING looks at her in surprise. He had clearly forgotten her. He bursts out laughing.)

KING: What are you doing there? Spying for the clergy? Be off. Put your clothes on and go home. Give her a gold piece, Thomas.

(The GIRL picks up her rags and holds them up in front of her.)

GIRL: Am I to come back to the camp tonight, my Lord?

KING (exasperated): Yes. No. I don't know! We're concerned with the Archbishop now, not you! Be off.

(The GIRL disappears into the back portion of the tent. The KING cries)
To horse, Thomas! For England's greatness! With my big fist and your big brain we'll do some good work, you and I! (With sudden concern) Wait a second. You can never be sure of finding another one as good in bed. (He goes to the rear of the tent and cries) Come back tonight, my angel! I adore you! You have the prettiest eyes in the world! (He comes downstage and says confidentially to BECKET) You always have to tell them that, even when you pay for it, if you want real pleasure with them. That's high politics, too! (Suddenly anxious, as his childish fear of the clergy returns) What will God say to it all, though? After all, they're His Bishops!

BECKET (with an airy gesture): We aren't children. You know one can always come to some arrangement with God, on this earth. Make haste and dress, my prince. We're going to be late.

KING (hurrying out): I'll be ready in a second. Do I have to shave?

BECKET (smiling): It might be as well, after two days' fighting.

KING: What a fuss for a lot of conquered Frenchmen! I wonder sometimes if you aren't a bit too finicky, Thomas.

(He goes out. BECKET closes the tent just as two SOLDIERS bring on a YOUNG MONK, with his hands tied.)

BECKET: What is it?

SOLDIER: We've just arrested this young monk, my Lord. He was loitering round the camp. He had a knife under his robe. We're taking him to the Provost.

BECKET: Have you got the knife?

(The SOLDIER hands it to him. BECKET looks at it, then at the little MONK.)
What use do you have for this in your monastery?

MONK: I cut my bread with it!

BECKET (amused): Well, well. (To the SOLDIERS) Leave him to me. I'll question him.

SOLDIER: He's turbulent, my Lord. He struggled like a very demon. It took four of us to get his knife away and tie him up. He wounded the Sergeant. We'd have finished him there and then, only the Sergeant said there might be some information to be got out of him. That's why we're taking him to the Provost. *(He adds)* That's just to tell you he's a spiteful devil.

BECKET *(who has not taken his eyes off the little* MONK): Very well. Stand off.

(The SOLDIERS *move out of earshot.* BECKET *goes on looking at the boy, and playing with the knife.)*

What are you doing in France? You're a Saxon.

MONK *(crying out despite himself):* How do you know?

BECKET: I can tell by your accent. I speak Saxon very well, as well as you speak French. Yes, you might almost pass for a Frenchman—to unpracticed ears. But I'd be careful. In your predicament, you'd do as well to be taken for a Frenchman as a Saxon. It's less unpopular.

(A pause.)

MONK *(abruptly):* I'm prepared to die.

BECKET *(smiling):* After the deed. But before, you'll agree it's stupid. *(He looks at the knife which he is still holding between two fingers.)* Where are you from?

MONK *(venomously):* Hastings!

BECKET: Hastings. And who was this kitchen implement intended for?

(No answer.)

You couldn't hope to kill more than one man with a weapon of this sort. You didn't make the journey for the sake of an ordinary Norman soldier, I imagine.

(The little MONK *does not answer.)*

(Tersely) Listen to me, my little man. They're going to put you to the torture. Have you ever seen that? I'm obliged to attend professionally from time to time. You think you'll have the necessary strength of spirit, but they're terribly ingenious and they have a knowledge of anatomy that our imbecilic doctors would do well to emulate. One always talks. Believe me, I know. If I can vouch that you've made a full confession, it will go quicker for you. That's worth considering.

(The MONK *does not answer.)*

Besides, there's an amusing detail to this affair. You are directly under my jurisdiction.

The King gave me the deeds and livings of all the abbeys in Hastings when he made me Chancellor.

MONK *(stepping back):* Are you Becket?

BECKET: Yes. *(He looks at the knife with faint distaste.)* You didn't only use it to cut your bread. Your knife stinks of onion, like any proper little Saxon's knife. They're good, aren't they, the Hastings onions? *(He looks at the knife again with a strange smile.)* You still haven't told me who it was for.

(The MONK *says nothing.)*

If you meant it for the King, there was no sense in that, my lad. He has three sons. Kings spring up again like weeds! Did you imagine you could liberate your race single-handed?

MONK: No. *(He adds dully)* Not my race. Myself.

BECKET: Liberate yourself from what?

MONK: My shame.

BECKET *(with sudden gravity):* How old are you?

MONK: Sixteen.

BECKET *(quietly):* The Normans have occupied the island for a hundred years. Shame is an old vintage. Your father and your grandfather drank it to the dregs. The cup is empty now.

MONK *(shaking his head):* No.

(A shadow seems to cross BECKET's *eyes. He goes on, quietly)*

BECKET: So, one fine morning, you woke in your cell to the bell of the first offices, while it was still dark. And it was the bells that told you, a boy of sixteen, to take the whole burden of shame onto yourself?

MONK *(with the cry of a cornered animal):* Who told you that?

BECKET *(softly):* I told you I was a polyglot. *(Indifferently)* I'm a Saxon too, did you know that?

MONK *(stonily):* Yes.

BECKET *(smiling):* Go on. Spit. You're dying to.

(The MONK *looks at him, a little dazed, and then spits.)*

BECKET *(smiling):* That felt good, didn't it? *(Tersely)* The King is waiting. And this conversation could go on indefinitely. But I want to keep you alive, so we can continue it one of these days. *(He adds lightly)* It's pure selfishness, you know. Your life hasn't any sort of importance for me, obviously, but it's very rare for Fate to bring one face to face with one's own ghost, when young. *(Calling)* Soldier!

(The SOLDIER *comes back and springs clanking to attention.)*

Fetch me the Provost. Run!

(The SOLDIER *runs out.* BECKET *comes back to the silent* YOUNG MONK.*)*

Delightful day, isn't it? This early-morning sun, hot already under this light veil of mist . . . A beautiful place, France. But I'm like you, I prefer the solid mists of the Sussex downs. Sunshine is luxury. And we belong to a race which used to despise luxury, you and I.

(The PROVOST MARSHAL *of the camp comes in, followed by the* SOLDIER. *He is an important personage, but* BECKET *is inaccessible, even for a* PROVOST MARSHAL, *and the man's behavior shows it.)*

Sir Provost, your men have arrested this monk who was loitering round the camp. He is a lay brother from the convent of Hastings and he is directly under my jurisdiction. You will make arrangements to have him sent back to England and taken to the convent, where his Abbot will keep him under supervision until my return. There is no specific charge against him, for the moment. I want him treated without brutality, but very closely watched. I hold you personally responsible for him.

PROVOST: Very good, my Lord.

(He motions to the SOLDIERS. *They surround the little* MONK *and take him away without a further glance from* BECKET. *Left alone,* BECKET *looks at the knife, smiles, wrinkles his nose and murmurs, with faint distaste)*

BECKET: It's touching, but it stinks, all the same. *(He flings the knife away, and whistling his little march goes toward the tent. He goes in, calling out lightheartedly)* Well, my prince, have you put on your Sunday best? It's time to go. We mustn't keep the Bishop waiting!

A sudden joyful peal of bells. The tent disappears as soon as BECKET *has gone in. The set changes. A backcloth representing a street comes down from the flies. The permanent* pillars are there, but the SOLDIERS *lining the route have decorated them with standards. The* KING *and* BECKET *advance into the city, on horseback, preceded by two* TRUMPETERS; *the* KING *slightly ahead of* BECKET *and followed by the four* BARONS. *Acclamations from the crowd. Bells, trumpets throughout the scene.*

KING *(beaming as he waves):* Listen to that! They adore us, these French!

BECKET: It cost me quite a bit. I had money distributed among the populace this morning. The prosperous classes are at home, sulking, of course.

KING: Patriots?

BECKET: No. But they would have cost too much. There are also a certain number of your Highness' soldiers among the crowd, in disguise, to encourage any lukewarm elements.

KING: Why do you always make a game of destroying my illusions? I thought they loved me for myself! You're an amoral man, Becket. *(Anxiously)* Does one say amoral or immoral?

BECKET *(smiling):* It depends what one means.

KING: She's pretty, look—the girl on the balcony to the right there. Suppose we stopped a minute . . .

BECKET: Impossible. The Bishop is waiting in the cathedral.

KING: It would be a lot more fun than going to see a Bishop!

BECKET: My Lord, do you remember what you have to say to him?

KING *(waving to the crowd):* Yes, yes, yes! As if it mattered what I say to a French Bishop, whose city I've just taken by force!

BECKET: It matters a great deal. For our future policy.

KING: Am I the strongest or am I not?

BECKET: You are, today. But one must never drive one's enemy to despair. It makes him strong. Gentleness is better politics. It saps virility. A good occupational force must not crush, it must corrupt.

KING *(waving graciously):* What about my pleasure then? Where does that enter into your scheme of things? Suppose I charged into this heap of frog-eaters now instead of acting the goat at their *Te Deum*? I can indulge in a bit of pleasure, can't I? I'm the conqueror.

BECKET: That would be a fault. Worse, a failing. One can permit oneself anything, Sire, but one must never indulge.

KING: Yes, Papa, right, Papa. What a bore you are today. Look at that little redhead there, standing on the fountain! Give orders for the procession to follow the same route back.

(*He rides on, turning his horse to watch the girl out of sight. They have gone by, the four* BARONS *bringing up the rear. Organ music. The standards disappear, together with the* SOLDIERS. *We are in the cathedral. The stage is empty.*

The organ is heard. Swelling chords. The organist is practicing in the empty cathedral. Then a sort of partition is pushed on, which represents the sacristy.

The KING, *attired for the ceremony, the* BARONS, *an unknown* PRIEST *and a* CHOIRBOY *come in. They seem to be waiting for something. The* KING *sits impatiently on a stool.*)

KING: Where's Becket? And what are we waiting for?

1ST BARON: He just said to wait, my Lord. It seems there's something not quite in order.

KING (*pacing about ill-humoredly*): What a lot of fuss for a French Bishop! What do I look like, I ask you, hanging about in this sacristy like a village bridegroom!

4TH BARON: I quite agree, my Lord! I can't think why we don't march straight in. After all, it's your cathedral now. (*Eagerly*) What do you say, my Lord? Shall we just draw our swords and charge?

KING (*going meekly back to his stool with a worried frown*): No. Becket wouldn't like it. And he's better than we are at knowing the right thing to do. If he told us to wait, there must be a good reason.

(BECKET *hurries in.*)
Well, Becket, what's happening? We're freezing to death in here! What do the French think they're at, keeping us moldering in this sacristy?

BECKET: The order came from me, Sire. A security measure. My police are certain that a French rising was to break out during the ceremony.

(*The* KING *has risen. The* 2ND BARON *has*
drawn his sword. The other three follow suit.*)

2ND BARON: God's Blood!

BECKET: Put up your swords. The King is safe in here. I have put guards on all the doors.

2ND BARON: Have we your permission to go in and deal with it, my Lord? We'll make short work of it!

3RD BARON: Just say the word, Sire! Shall we go?

BECKET (*curtly*): I forbid you. There aren't enough of us. I am bringing fresh troops into the city and having the cathedral evacuated. Until that is done, the King's person is in your keeping, gentlemen. But sheathe your swords. No provocation, please. We are at the mercy of a chance incident and I still have no more than the fifty escort men-at-arms in the city.

KING (*tugging at* BECKET's *sleeve*): Becket! Is that priest French?

BECKET: Yes. But he is part of the Bishop's immediate entourage. And the Bishop is our man.

KING: You know how reliable English Bishops are! So I leave you to guess how far we can trust a French one! That man has a funny look in his eyes.

BECKET: Who, the Bishop?

KING: No. That priest.

BECKET (*glances at the* PRIEST *and laughs*): Of course, my prince, he squints! I assure you that's the only disturbing thing about him! It would be tactless to ask him to leave. Besides, even if he had a dagger, you have your coat of mail and four of your Barons. I must go and supervise the evacuation of the nave.

(*He starts to go. The* KING *runs after him.*)

KING: Becket!

(BECKET *stops.*)
The choirboy?

BECKET (*laughing*): He's only so high!

KING: He may be a dwarf. You never know with the French. (*Drawing* BECKET *aside*) Becket, we talked a little flippantly this morning. Are you sure God isn't taking his revenge?

BECKET (*smiling*): Of course not. I'm afraid it's simply my police force taking fright and being a little overzealous. Policemen have a slight tendency to see assassins everywhere. They only do it to make themselves important. Bah, what does it matter? We'll hear the *Te Deum* in a deserted church, that's all.

KING *(bitterly):* And there was I thinking those folk adored me. Perhaps you didn't give them enough money.

BECKET: One can only buy those who are for sale, my prince. And those are just the ones who aren't dangerous. With the others, it's wolf against wolf. I'll come back straightaway and set your mind at rest.

(He goes out. The KING *darts anxious looks on the* PRIEST *as he paces up and down muttering his prayers.)*

KING: Baron!

(The 4TH BARON *is nearest the* KING. *He steps forward.)*

4TH BARON *(bellowing as usual):* My Lord?

KING: Shush! Keep an eye on that man, all four of you, and at the slightest move, leap on him.

(There follows a little comic dumbshow by the KING *and the* PRIEST, *who is beginning to feel uneasy too. A sudden violent knocking on the sacristy door. The* KING *starts.)* Who is it?

(A SOLDIER *comes in.)*

SOLDIER: A messenger from London, my Lord. They sent him on here from the camp. The message is urgent.

KING *(worried):* I don't like it. Regnault, you go and see.

(The 4TH BARON *goes out and comes back again, reassured.)*

4TH BARON: It's William of Corbeil, my Lord. He has urgent letters.

KING: You're sure it *is* him? It wouldn't be a Frenchman in disguise? That's an old trick.

4TH BARON *(roaring with laughter):* I know him, Sire! I've drained more tankards with him than there are whiskers on his face. And the old goat has plenty!

(The KING *makes a sign. The* 4TH BARON *admits the* MESSENGER, *who drops on one knee and presents his letters to the* KING.)*

KING: Thank you. Get up. That's a fine beard you have, William of Corbeil. Is it well stuck on?

MESSENGER *(rising bewildered):* My beard, Sire?

(The 4TH BARON *guffaws and slaps him on the back.)*

4TH BARON: You old porcupine you!

(The KING *has glanced through the letters.)*

KING: Good news, gentlemen! We have one enemy less.

*(BECKET *comes in. The* KING *cries joyfully)* Becket!

BECKET: Everything is going according to plan, my prince. The troops are on their way. We've only to wait here quietly, until they arrive.

KING *(cheerfully):* You're right, Becket, everything is going according to plan. God isn't angry with us. He has just recalled the Archbishop.

BECKET *(in a murmur):* That little old man . . . How could that feeble body contain so much strength?

KING: Now, now, now! Don't squander your sorrow, my son. I personally consider this an excellent piece of news!

BECKET: He was the first Norman who took an interest in me. He was a true father to me. God rest his soul.

KING: He will! After all the fellow did for Him, he's gone to Heaven, don't worry. Where he'll be definitely more use to God than he was to us. So it's definitely for the best. *(He pulls* BECKET *to him.)* Becket! My little Becket, I think the ball's in our court now! This is the time to score a point. *(He seizes his arm, tense and quite transformed.)* An extraordinary idea is just creeping into my mind, Becket. A master stroke! I can't think what's got into me this morning, but I suddenly feel extremely intelligent. It probably comes of making love with a French girl last night. I am subtle, Becket, I am profound! So profound it's making my head spin. Are you sure it isn't dangerous to think too hard? Thomas, my little Thomas! Are you listening to me?

BECKET *(smiling at his excitement):* Yes, my prince.

KING *(as excited as a little boy):* Are you listening carefully? Listen, Thomas! You told me once that the best ideas are the stupidest ones, but the clever thing is to think of them! Listen, Thomas! Tradition prevents me from touching the privileges of the Primacy. You follow me so far?

BECKET: Yes, my prince . . .

KING: But what if the Primate is my man? If the Archbishop of Canterbury is for the King, how can his power possibly incommodate me?

BECKET: That's an ingenious idea, my prince, but you forget that his election is a free one.

KING: No! You're forgetting the Royal Hand! Do you know what that is? When the candidate is displeasing to the Throne the King sends his Justicer to the Conclave of Bishops and it's the King who has the final say. That's an old custom too, and for once, it's in my favor! It's fully a hundred years since the Conclave of Bishops has voted contrary to the wishes of the King!

BECKET: I don't doubt it, my Lord. But we all know your Bishops. Which one of them could you rely on? Once the Primate's miter is on their heads, they grow dizzy with power.

KING: Are you asking me, Becket? I'll tell you. Someone who doesn't know what dizziness means. Someone who isn't even afraid of God. Thomas, my son, I need your help again and this time it's important. I'm sorry to deprive you of French girls and the fun of battle, my son, but pleasure will come later. You are going over to England.

BECKET: I am at your service, my prince.

KING: Can you guess what your mission will be?

(*A tremor of anguish crosses* BECKET's *face at what is to come.*)

BECKET: No, my prince.

KING: You are going to deliver a personal letter from me to every Bishop in the land. And do you know what those letters will contain, my Thomas, my little brother? My royal wish to have you elected Primate of England.

(BECKET *has gone deathly white. He says with a forced laugh*)

BECKET: You're joking, of course, my Lord. Just look at the edifying man, the saintly

man whom you would be trusting with these holy functions! (*He has opened his fine coat to display his even finer doublet.*) Why, my prince, you really fooled me for a second!

(*The* KING *bursts out laughing.* BECKET *laughs too, rather too loudly in his relief.*) A fine Archbishop I'd have made! Look at my new shoes! They're the latest fashion in Paris. Attractive, that little upturned toe, don't you think? Quite full of unction and compunction, isn't it, Sire?

KING (*suddenly stops laughing*): Shut up about your shoes, Thomas! I'm in deadly earnest. I shall write those letters before noon. You will help me.

(BECKET, *deathly pale, stammers*)

BECKET: But my Lord, I'm not even a priest!

KING (*tersely*): You're a deacon. You can take your final vows tomorrow and be ordained in a month.

BECKET: But have you considered what the Pope will say?

KING (*brutally*): I'll pay the price!

(BECKET, *after an anguished pause, murmurs*)

BECKET: My Lord, I see now that you weren't joking. Don't do this.

KING: Why not?

BECKET: It frightens me.

KING (*his face set and hard*): Becket, this is an order!

(BECKET *stands as if turned to stone. A pause. He murmurs*)

BECKET (*gravely*): If I become Archbishop, I can no longer be your friend.

(*A burst of organ music in the cathedral. Enter an* OFFICER.)

OFFICER: The church is now empty, my Lord. The Bishop and his clergy await your Highness' good pleasure.

KING (*roughly to* BECKET): Did you hear that, Becket? Pull yourself together. You have an odd way of taking good news. Wake up! They say we can go in now.

(*The procession forms with the* PRIEST *and the* CHOIRBOY *leading.* BECKET *takes his place, almost reluctantly, a pace or so behind the* KING.)

BECKET (*in a murmur*): This is madness,

my Lord. Don't do it. I could not serve both God and you.

KING (*looking straight ahead, says stonily*): You've never disappointed me, Thomas. And you are the only man I trust. You will leave tonight. Come, let's go in.

(*He motions to the* PRIEST. *The procession moves off and goes into the empty cathedral, as the organ swells.*

A moment's darkness. The organ continues to play. Then a dim light reveals BECKET's *room. Open chests into which two* SERVANTS *are piling costly clothes.*)

2ND SERVANT (*who is the younger of the two*): The coat with the sable trimming as well?

1ST SERVANT: Everything! You heard what he said!

2ND SERVANT (*grumbling*): Sables! To beggars! Who'll give them alms if they beg with that on their backs! They'll starve to death!

1ST SERVANT (*cackling*): They'll eat the sables! Can't you understand, you idiot! He's going to sell all this and give them the money!

2ND SERVANT: But what will he wear himself? He's got nothing left at all!

(BECKET *comes in, wearing a plain gray dressing gown.*)

BECKET: Are the chests full? I want them sent over to the Jew before tonight. I want nothing left in this room but the bare walls. Gil, the fur coverlet!

1ST SERVANT (*regretfully*): My Lord will be cold at night.

BECKET: Do as I say.

(*Regretfully, the* 1ST SERVANT *takes the coverlet and puts it in the chest.*)
Has the steward been told about tonight's meal? Supper for forty in the great hall.

1ST SERVANT: He says he won't have enough gold plate, my Lord. Are we to mix it with the silver dishes?

BECKET: Tell him to lay the table with the wooden platters and earthenware bowls from the kitchens. The plate has been sold. The Jew will send over for it late this afternoon.

1ST SERVANT (*dazed*): The earthenware bowls and the wooden platters. Yes, my Lord. And the steward says could he have your list of invitations fairly soon, my Lord. He only has three runners and he's afraid there won't be time to—

BECKET: There are no invitations. The great doors will be thrown open and you will go out into the street and tell the poor they are dining with me tonight.

1ST SERVANT (*appalled*): Very good, my Lord.

(*He is about to go.* BECKET *calls him back.*)

BECKET: I want the service to be impeccable. The dishes presented to each guest first, with full ceremony, just as for princes. Go now.

(*The two* SERVANTS *go out.* BECKET, *left alone, casually looks over one or two articles of clothing in the chests. He murmurs*)
I must say it was all very pretty stuff. (*He drops the lid and bursts out laughing.*) A prick of vanity! The mark of an upstart. A truly saintly man would never have done the whole thing in one day. Nobody will ever believe it's genuine. (*He turns to the jeweled crucifix above the bed and says simply*) I hope You haven't inspired me with all these holy resolutions in order to make me look ridiculous, Lord. It's all so new to me. I'm setting about it a little clumsily perhaps. (*He looks at the crucifix and with a swift gesture takes it off the wall.*) And you're far too sumptuous too. Precious stones around your bleeding Body . . . I shall give you to some poor village church. (*He lays the crucifix on the chest. He looks around the room, happy, lighthearted, and murmurs*) It's like leaving for a holiday. Forgive me, Lord, but I never enjoyed myself so much in my whole life. I don't believe You are a sad God. The joy I feel in shedding all my riches must be part of Your divine intentions.

(*He goes behind the curtain into the antechamber where he can be heard gaily whistling an old English marching song. He comes back a second later, his bare feet in sandals, and wearing a monk's coarse woolen robe. He draws the curtain across again and murmurs*)

BECKET: There. Farewell, Becket. I wish there had been something I had regretted parting with, so I could offer it to You. *(He goes to the crucifix and says simply)* Lord, are You sure You are not tempting me? It all seems far too easy. *(He drops to his knees and prays. Curtain.)*

ACT THREE

A room in the KING's *palace. The two* QUEENS, *the* QUEEN MOTHER *and the* YOUNG QUEEN, *are on stage, working at their tapestry. The* KING's *two* SONS, *one considerably older than the other, are playing in a corner, on the floor. The* KING *is in another corner, playing at cup-and-ball. After several unsuccessful attempts to catch the ball in the cup, he throws down the toy and exclaims irritably*

KING: Forty beggars! He invited forty beggars to dinner!

QUEEN MOTHER: The dramatic gesture, as usual! I always said you had misplaced your confidence, my son.

KING *(pacing up and down)*: Madam, I am very particular where I place my confidence. I only ever did it once in my whole life and I am still convinced I was right. But there's a great deal we don't understand! Thomas is ten times more intelligent than all of us put together.

QUEEN MOTHER *(reprovingly)*: You are talking about royalty, my son.

KING *(grunting)*: What of it? Intelligence has been shared out on a different basis.

YOUNG QUEEN: It seems he has sold his gold plate and all his rich clothes to a Jew. He wears an ordinary homespun habit now.

QUEEN MOTHER: I see that as a sign of ostentation, if nothing worse! One can become a saintly man, certainly, but not in a single day. I've never liked the man. You were insane to make him so powerful.

KING *(crying out)*: He is my friend!

QUEEN MOTHER *(acidly)*: More's the pity.

YOUNG QUEEN: He is your friend in debauchery. It was he who lured you away from your duty towards me. It was he who first took you to the whorehouses!

KING *(furious)*: Rubbish, Madam! I didn't need anybody to lure me away from my duty towards you. I made you three children, very conscientiously. Phew! My duty is done for a while.

YOUNG QUEEN *(stung)*: When that libertine loses the evil influence he has on you, you will come to appreciate the joys of family life again. Pray Heaven he disobeys you!

KING: The joys of family life are limited, Madam. To be perfectly frank, you bore me. You and your eternal backbiting, over your everlasting tapestry, the pair of you! That's no sustenance for a man! *(He trots about the room, furious, and comes to a halt behind their chairs.)* If at least it had some artistic merit. My ancestress Mathilda, while she was waiting for her husband to finish carving out his kingdom, now *she* embroidered a masterpiece —which they left behind in Bayeux, more's the pity. But that! It's beyond belief it's so mediocre.

YOUNG QUEEN *(nettled)*: We can only use the gifts we're born with.

KING: Yes. And yours are meager. *(He glances out of the window once more to look at the time, and says with a sigh)* I've been bored to tears for a whole month. Not a soul to talk to. After his nomination, not wanting to seem in too indecent a hurry, I leave him alone to carry out his pastoral tour. Now, back he comes at last, I summon him to the palace and he's late. *(He looks out of the window again and exclaims)* Ah! Someone at the sentry post! *(He turns away, disappointed.)* No, it's only a monk. *(He wanders about the room, aimlessly. He goes over to join the children, and watches them playing for a while. Sourly)* Charming babes. Men in the making. Sly and obtuse already. And to think one is expected to be dewy-eyed over creatures like that, merely because they aren't yet big enough to be hated or despised. Which is the elder of you two?

ELDER BOY *(rising)*: I am, Sir.

KING: What's your name again?

ELDER BOY: Henry III.

KING *(sharply)*: Not yet, Sir! Number II is in the best of health. *(To the* QUEEN*)* You've brought them up well! Do you think of your-

self as Regent already? And you wonder that
I shun your bedchamber? I don't care to make
love with my widow.

(An OFFICER comes in.)

OFFICER: A messenger from the Archbishop,
my Lord.

KING *(beside himself with rage):* A messenger! A messenger! I summoned the Archbishop Primate in person! *(He turns to the
women, suddenly uneasy, almost touching.)*
Perhaps he's ill? That would explain everything.

QUEEN MOTHER *(bitterly):* That's too much
to hope for.

KING *(raging):* You'd like to see him dead,
wouldn't you, you females—because he loves
me? If he hasn't come, it's because he's dying!
Send the man in, quickly! O my Thomas . . .

*(The OFFICER goes and admits the MONK.
The KING hurries over to him.)*

Who are you? Is Becket ill?

MONK *(falling on one knee):* My Lord, I
am William son of Etienne, secretary to his
Grace the Archbishop.

KING: Is your master seriously ill?

MONK: No, my Lord. His Grace is in good
health. He has charged me to deliver this
letter with his deepest respects—and to give
your Highness this. *(He bows lower and hands
something to the KING.)*

KING *(stunned):* The Seal? Why has he sent
me back the Seal? *(He unrolls the parchment
and reads it in silence. His face hardens. He
says curtly, without looking at the MONK)* You
have carried out your mission. Go.

(The MONK rises and turns to go.)

MONK: Is there an answer from your Highness for his Grace the Archbishop?

KING *(harshly):* No!

*(The MONK goes out. The KING stands still
a moment, at a loss, then flings himself onto
his throne, glowering. The women exchange
a conspiratorial look. The QUEEN MOTHER rises
and goes to him.)*

QUEEN MOTHER *(insidiously):* Well, my son,
what does your friend say in his letter?

KING *(bawling):* Get out! Get out, both of
you! And take your royal vermin with you!
I am alone!

(Frightened, the QUEENS hurry out with the

children. The KING stands there a moment,
reeling a little, as if stunned by the blow.
Then he collapses onto the throne and sobs
like a child.)*

(Moaning) O my Thomas!

*(He remains a moment prostrate, then col-
lects himself and sits up. He looks at the Seal
in his hand and says between clenched teeth)*
You've sent me back the Three Lions of
England, like a little boy who doesn't want
to play with me any more. You think you
have God's honor to defend you now! I would
have gone to war with all England's might
behind me, and against England's interests,
to defend you, little Saxon. I would have given
the honor of the Kingdom laughingly . . .
for you . . . Only I loved you and you didn't
love me . . . that's the difference. *(His face
hardens. He adds between clenched teeth)*
Thanks all the same for this last gift as you
desert me. I shall learn to be alone.

*(He goes out. The lights dim. SERVANTS re-
move the furniture. When the lights go up
again, the permanent set, with the pillars, is
empty.*

*A bare church; a man half hidden under a
dark cloak is waiting behind a pillar. It is the
KING. Closing chords of organ music. Enter
GILBERT FOLLIOT, Bishop of London, followed
by his CLERGY. He has just said Mass. The KING
goes to him.)*

Bishop . . .

FOLLIOT *(stepping back):* What do you
want, fellow?

*(His acolytes are about to step between
them, when he exclaims)*

The King!

KING: Yes.

FOLLIOT: Alone, without an escort, and
dressed like a common squire?

KING: The King nevertheless. Bishop, I
would like to make a confession.

FOLLIOT *(with a touch of suspicion):* I am
the Bishop of London. The King has his own
Confessor. That is an important Court appointment and it has its prerogatives.

KING: The choice of priest for Holy Confession is open, Bishop, even for a King.

*(FOLLIOT motions to his CLERGY, who draw
away.)*

Anyway, my confession will be short, and I'm not asking for absolution. I have something much worse than a sin on my conscience, Bishop: a mistake. A foolish mistake.

(FOLLIOT *says nothing.*)

I ordered you to vote for Thomas Becket at the Council of Clarendon. I repent of it.

FOLLIOT *(inscrutably):* We bowed before the Royal Hand.

KING: Reluctantly, I know. It took me thirteen weeks of authority and patience to crush the small uncrushable opposition of which you were the head, Bishop. On the day the Council met you looked green. They told me you fell seriously ill afterwards.

FOLLIOT *(impenetrably):* God cured me.

KING: Very good of Him. But He is rather inclined to look after His own, to the exclusion of anyone else. He let me fall ill without lifting a finger! And I must cure myself without divine intervention. I have the Archbishop on my stomach. A big hard lump I shall have to vomit back. What does the Norman clergy think of him?

FOLLIOT *(reserved):* His Grace seems to have the reins of the Church of England well in hand. Those who are in close contact with him even say that he behaves like a holy man.

KING *(with grudging admiration):* It's a bit sudden, but nothing he does ever surprises me. God knows what the brute is capable of, for good or for evil. Bishop, let us be frank with each other. Is the Church very interested in holy men?

FOLLIOT *(with the ghost of a smile):* The Church has been wise for so long, your Highness, that she could not have failed to realize that the temptation of saintliness is one of the most insidious and fearsome snares the devil can lay for her priests. The administration of the realm of souls, with the temporal difficulties it carries with it, chiefly demands, as in all administrations, competent administrators. The Roman Catholic Church has its Saints, it invokes their benevolent intercession, it prays to them. But it has no need to create others. That is superfluous. And dangerous.

KING: You seem to be a man one can talk to, Bishop. I misjudged you. Friendship blinded me.

FOLLIOT *(still impenetrable):* Friendship is a fine thing.

KING *(suddenly hoarse):* It's a domestic animal, a living tender thing. It seems to be all eyes, forever gazing at you, warming you. You don't see its teeth. But it's a beast with one curious characteristic. It is only after death that it bites.

FOLLIOT *(prudently):* Is the King's friendship for Thomas Becket dead, your Highness?

KING: Yes, Bishop. It died quite suddenly. A sort of heart failure.

FOLLIOT: A curious phenomenon, your Highness, but quite frequent.

KING *(taking his arm suddenly):* I hate Becket now, Bishop. There is nothing more in common between that man and me than this creature tearing at my guts. I can't bear it any more. I shall have to turn it loose on him. But I am the King; what they conventionally call my greatness stands in my way. I need somebody.

FOLLIOT *(stiffening):* I do not wish to serve anything but the Church.

KING: Let us talk like grown men, Bishop. We went in hand in hand to conquer, pillage and ransom England. We quarrel, we try to cheat each other of a penny or two, but Heaven and Earth still have one or two common interests. Do you know what I have just obtained from the Pope? His blessing to go and murder Catholic Ireland, in the name of the Faith. Yes, a sort of crusade to impose Norman barons and clergy on the Irish, with our swords and standards solemnly blessed as if we were off to give the Turks a drubbing. The only condition: a little piece of silver per household per year, for St. Peter's pence, which the native clergy of Ireland is loath to part with and which I have undertaken to make them pay. It's a mere pittance. But at the end of the year it will add up to a pretty sum. Rome knows how to do her accounts.

FOLLIOT *(terror-stricken):* There are some things one should never say, your Highness: one should even try not to know about them, so long as one is not directly concerned with them.

KING *(smiling):* We are alone, Bishop, and the church is empty.

FOLLIOT: The church is never empty. A little red lamp burns in front of the High Altar.

KING (*impatiently*): Bishop, I like playing games, but only with boys of my own age! Do you take me for one of your sheep, holy pastor? The One whom that little red lamp honors read into your innermost heart and mine a long time ago. Of your cupidity and my hatred, He knows all there is to know.

(FOLLIOT *withdraws into his shell. The* KING *cries irritably*)

If that's the way you feel you must become a monk, Bishop! Wear a hair shirt on your naked back and go and hide yourself in a monastery to pray! The Bishopric of London, for the purehearted son of a Thames waterman, is too much, or too little!

(*A pause.*)

FOLLIOT (*impassively*): If, as is my duty, I disregard my private feelings, I must admit that his Grace the Archbishop has so far done nothing which has not been in the interests of Mother Church.

KING (*eying him, says jovially*): I can see your game, my little friend. You mean to cost me a lot of money. But I'm rich—thanks to Becket, who has succeeded in making you pay the Absentee Tax. And it seems to me eminently ethical that a part of the Church's gold should find its way, via you, back to the Church. Besides, if we want to keep this on a moral basis, Holy Bishop, you can tell yourself that as the greatness of the Church and that of the State are closely linked, in serving me, you will in the long run be working for the consolidation of the Catholic Faith.

FOLLIOT (*contemplating him with curiosity*): I had always taken your Highness for a great adolescent lout who cared only for his pleasure.

KING: One can be wrong about people, Bishop. I made the same mistake. (*With a sudden cry*) O my Thomas . . .

FOLLIOT (*fiercely*): You love him, your Highness! You still love him! You love that mitered hog, that impostor, that Saxon bastard, that little guttersnipe!

KING (*seizing him by the throat*): Yes, I love him! But that's my affair, priest! All I confided to you was my hatred. I'll pay you to rid me

of him, but don't ever speak ill of him to me. Or we'll fight it out as man to man!

FOLLIOT: Highness, you're choking me!

KING (*abruptly releasing him*): We will meet again tomorrow, my Lord Bishop, and we'll go over the details of our enterprise together. You will be officially summoned to the palace on some pretext or other—my good works in your London Diocese, say—where I am your chief parishioner. But it won't be the poor and needy we'll discuss. My poor can wait. The Kingdom they pin their hopes on is eternal.

(*The* KING *goes out.* GILBERT FOLLIOT *remains motionless. His* CLERGY *join him timidly. He takes his crook and goes out with dignity, but not before one of his Canons has discreetly adjusted his miter, which was knocked askew in the recent struggle. They have gone out.*

The lighting changes. Curtains between the pillars. The episcopal palace.

Morning. A PRIEST *enters, leading two* MONKS *and the* YOUNG MONK *from the convent of Hastings.*

PRIEST: His Grace will receive you here.

(*The two* MONKS *are impressed. They push the* YOUNG MONK *about a little.*)

1ST MONK: Stand up straight. Kiss his Grace's ring and try to answer his questions with humility, or I'll tan your backside for you!

2ND MONK: I suppose you thought he'd forgotten all about you? The great never forget anything. And don't you act proud with him or you'll be sorry.

(*Enter* BECKET, *wearing a coarse monk's robe.*)

BECKET: Well, brothers, is it fine over in Hastings?

(*He gives them his ring to kiss.*)

1ST MONK: Foggy, my Lord.

BECKET (*smiling*): Then it's fine in Hastings. We always think fondly of our Abbey there and we intend to visit it soon, when our new duties grant us a moment's respite. How has this young man been behaving? Has he given our Abbot much trouble?

2ND MONK: A proper mule, my Lord. Father Abbot tried kindness, as you recommended, but he soon had to have recourse to the dungeon and bread and water, and even to the whip. Nothing has any effect. The stubborn little wretch is just the same; all defiance and insults. He has fallen into the sin of pride. Nothing I know of will pull him out of that!

1ST MONK: Save a good kick in the rump perhaps—if your Grace will pardon the expression. *(To the boy)* Stand up straight.

BECKET *(to the boy):* Pay attention to your brother. Stand up straight. As a rule the sin of pride stiffens à man's back. Look me in the face.

(The YOUNG MONK *looks at him.)*
Good. (BECKET *looks at the boy for a while, then turns to the* MONKS.*)* You will be taken to the kitchens where you can refresh yourselves before you leave, brothers. They have orders to treat you well. Don't spurn our hospitality; we relieve you, for today, of your vows of abstinence, and we fondly hope you will do honor to our bill of fare. Greet your father Abbot in Jesus on our behalf.

2ND MONK *(hesitantly):* And the lad?

BECKET: We will keep him here.

1ST MONK: Watch out for him, your Grace. He's vicious.

BECKET *(smiling):* We are not afraid.

(The MONKS *go out.* BECKET *and the* YOUNG MONK *remain, facing each other.)*
Why do you hold yourself so badly?

YOUNG MONK: I don't want to look people in the face any more.

BECKET: I'll teach you. That will be your first lesson. Look at me.

(The boy gives him a sidelong glance.)
Better than that.

(The boy looks at him.)
Are you still bearing the full weight of England's shame alone? Is it that shame which bends your back like that?

YOUNG MONK: Yes.

BECKET: If I took over half of it, would it weigh less heavy? *(He motions to the* PRIEST.*)* Show in their Lordships the Bishops. You'll soon see that being alone is not a privilege reserved entirely for you.

(The BISHOPS *come in.* BECKET *leads the* YOUNG MONK *into a corner.)*
You stay here in the corner and hold my tablets. I ask only one thing. Don't leap at their

throats; you'd complicate everything. *(He motions to the* BISHOPS *who remain standing.)*

FOLLIOT: Your Grace, I am afraid this meeting may be a pointless one. You insisted—against our advice—on attacking the King openly. Even before the three excommunications which you asked us to sanction could be made public, the King has hit back. His Grand Justicer Richard de Lacy has just arrived in your antechamber and is demanding to see you in the name of the King. He is the bearer of an official order summoning you to appear before his assembled Council within twenty-four hours and there to answer the charges made against you.

BECKET: Of what is the King accusing me?

FOLLIOT: Prevarication. Following the examination of accounts by his Privy Council, his Highness demands a considerable sum still outstanding on your administration of the Treasury.

BECKET: When I resigned the Chancellorship I handed over my ledgers to the Grand Justicer who acquitted me of all subsequent dues and claims. What does the King demand?

OXFORD: Forty thousand marks in fine gold.

BECKET *(smiling):* I don't believe there was ever as much money in all the coffers of all England in all the time I was Chancellor. But a clever clerk can soon change that . . . The King has closed his fist and I am like a fly inside it. *(He smiles and looks at him.)* I have the impression, gentlemen, that you must be feeling something very akin to relief.

YORK: We advised you against open opposition.

BECKET: William of Aynsford, incited by the King, struck down the priest I had appointed to the Parish of his Lordship's See, on the pretext that his Highness disapproved of my choice. Am I to look on while my priests are murdered?

FOLLIOT: It is not for you to appoint a priest to a free fief! There is not a Norman, layman or cleric, who will ever concede that. It would mean reviewing the entire legal system of the Conquest. Everything can be called into question in England except the fact that it was conquered in 1066. England is the land of law and of the most scrupulous respect for the law; but the law begins at that date only, or England as such ceases to exist.

BECKET: Bishop, must I remind you that we are men of God and that we have an Honor to defend, which dates from all eternity?

OXFORD (quietly): This excommunication was bad policy, your Grace. William of Aynsford is a companion of the King.

BECKET (smiling): I know him very well. He's a charming man. I have drained many a tankard with him.

YORK (yelping): And his wife is my second cousin!

BECKET: That is a detail I deplore, my Lord Bishop, but he has killed one of my priests. If I do not defend my priests, who will? Gilbert of Clare has indicated before his court of justice a churchman who was under our exclusive jurisdiction.

YORK: An interesting victim I must say! He deserved the rope a hundred times over. The man was accused of rape and murder. Wouldn't it have been clever to let the wretch hang—and have peace?

BECKET: "I bring not peace but the sword." Your Lordship must I'm sure have read that somewhere. I am not interested in what this man is guilty of. If I allow my priests to be tried by a secular tribunal; if I let Robert de Vere abduct our tonsured clerics from our monasteries, as he has just done, on the grounds that the man was one of his serfs who had escaped land bondage, I don't give much for our freedom and our chances of survival in five years' time, my Lord. I have excommunicated Gilbert of Clare, Robert de Vere and William of Aynsford. The Kingdom of God must be defended like any other Kingdom. Do you think that Right has only to show it's handsome face for everything to drop in its lap? Without Might, its old enemy, Right counts for nothing.

YORK: What Might? Let us not indulge in empty words. The King is Might and he is the law.

BECKET: He is the written law, but there is another, unwritten law, which always makes Kings bend the neck eventually. (He looks at them for a moment and smiles.) I was a profligate, gentlemen, perhaps a libertine, in any case, a wordly man. I loved living and I laughed at all these things. But you passed the burden on to me and now I have to carry it. I have rolled up my sleeves and taken it on my back and nothing will ever make me set it down again. I thank your Lordships. The council is adjourned and I have made my decision. I shall stand by these three excommunications. I shall appear tomorrow before the King's supreme court of Justice.

(The BISHOPS look at one another in surprise, then bow and go out. BECKET turns to the YOUNG MONK)

Well, does the shame weigh less heavy now?

YOUNG MONK: Yes.

BECKET (leading him off and laughing): Then stand up straight!

(The drapes close. Distant trumpets. The KING comes out from behind the curtains and turns to peep through them at something. A pause. Then GILBERT FOLLIOT comes hurrying in.)

KING: What's happening? I can't see a thing from up here.

FOLLIOT: Legal procedure is taking its course, your Highness. The third summons has been delivered. He has not appeared. In a moment he will be condemned in absentia. Once prevarication is established, our Dean the Bishop of Chichester will go to see him and communicate according to the terms of the ancient Charter of the Church of England, our corporated repudiation of allegiance, absolving us of obedience to him—and our intention to report him to our Holy Father the Pope. I shall then, as Bishop of London, step forward and publicly accuse Becket of having celebrated, in contempt of the King, a sacrilegious Mass at the instigation of the Evil Spirit.

KING (anxiously): Isn't that going rather far?

FOLLIOT: Of course. It won't fool anyone, but it always works. The assembly will then go out to vote, in order of precedence, and return a verdict of imprisonment. The sentence is already drawn up.

KING: Unanimously?

FOLLIOT: We are all Normans. The rest is your Highness' concern. It will merely be a matter of carrying out the sentence.

KING (*staggering suddenly*): O my Thomas!

FOLLIOT (*impassively*): I can still stop the machine, your Highness.

KING (*hesitates a second then says*): No. Go.

(FOLLIOT *goes out. The* KING *goes back to his place, behind the curtain.*

The two QUEENS *come into the room, and join the* KING. *All three stand and peer through the curtain. A pause.*)

YOUNG QUEEN: He's doomed, isn't he?

KING (*dully*): Yes.

YOUNG QUEEN: At last!

(*The* KING *turns on her, his face twisted with hate.*)

KING: I forbid you to gloat!

YOUNG QUEEN: At seeing your enemy perish—why not?

KING (*frothing*): Becket is my enemy, but in the human balance, bastard as he is, and naked as his mother made him, he weighs a hundred times more than you do, Madam, with your crown and all your jewels and your august father the Emperor into the bargain. Becket is attacking me and he has betrayed me. I am forced to fight him and crush him, but at least he gave me, with open hands, everything that is at all good in me. And you have never given me anything but your carping mediocrity, your everlasting obsession with your puny little person and what you thought was due to it. That is why I forbid you to smile as he lies dying!

YOUNG QUEEN: I gave you my youth! I gave you your children!

KING (*shouting*): I don't like my children! And as for your youth—that dusty flower pressed in a hymnbook since you were twelve years old, with its watery blood and its insipid scent—you can say farewell to that without a tear. With age, bigotry and malice may perhaps give some spice to your character. Your body was an empty desert, Madam!— which duty forced me to wander in alone. But you have never been a wife to me! And Becket was my friend, red-blooded, generous and full of strength! (*He is shaken by a sob.*) O my Thomas!

(*The* QUEEN MOTHER *moves over to him.*)

QUEEN MOTHER (*haughtily*): And I, my son, I gave you nothing either, I suppose?

KING (*recovers his composure, glares at her and says dully*): Life. Yes. Thank you. But after that I never saw you save in a passage, dressed for a Ball, or in your crown and ermine mantle, ten minutes before official ceremonies, where you were forced to tolerate my presence. I have always been alone, and no one on this earth has ever loved me except Becket!

QUEEN MOTHER (*bitterly*): Well, call him back! Absolve him, since he loves you! Give him supreme power then! But do something!

KING: I am. I'm learning to be alone again, Madam. As usual.

(*A* PAGE *comes in, breathless.*)

Well? What's happening? How far have they got?

PAGE: My Liege, Thomas Becket appeared just when everyone had given him up; sick, deathly pale, in full pontifical regalia and carrying his own heavy silver cross. He walked the whole length of the hall without anyone daring to stop him, and when Robert Duke of Leicester, who was to read out his sentence, began the consecrated words, he stopped with a gesture and forbade him, in God's name, to pronounce judgment against him, his spiritual Father. Then he walked back through the crowd, which parted for him in silence. He has just left.

KING (*unable to hide his delight*): Well played, Thomas! One point to you. (*He checks himself, embarrassed, and then says*) And what about my Barons?

PAGE: Their hands flew to their swords with cries of "Traitor! Perjurer! Arrest him! Miserable wretch! Hear your sentence!" But not one of them dared move, or touch the sacred ornaments.

KING (*with a roar*): The fools! I am surrounded by fools and the only intelligent man in my Kingdom is against me!

PAGE (*continuing his story*): Then, on the threshold, he turned, looked at them coldly as they shouted in their impotence, and he said that not so long ago he could have answered their challenge sword in hand. Now he could no longer do it, but he begged them to remember that there was a time when he met strength with strength.

KING (*jubilantly*): He could beat them all! All, I tell you! On horseback, on foot, with a mace, with a lance, with a sword! In the lists they fell to him like ninepins!

PAGE: And his eyes were so cold, and so ironic—even though all he had in his hand was his episcopal crook—that one by one, they fell silent. Only then did he turn and go out. They say he has given orders to invite all the beggars of the city to sup at his house tonight.

KING (*somberly*): And what about the Bishop of London, who was going to reduce him to powder? What about my busy friend Gilbert Folliot?

PAGE: He had a horrible fit of rage trying to incite the crowd, he let out a screech of foul abuse and then he fainted. They are bringing him round now.

(*The* KING *suddenly bursts into a shout of irrepressible laughter, and, watched by the two outraged* QUEENS, *collapses into the* PAGE's *arms, breathless and helpless with mirth.*)

KING: It's too funny! It's too funny!

QUEEN MOTHER (*coldly*): You will laugh less heartily tomorrow, my son. If you don't stop him, Becket will reach the coast tonight, ask asylum of the King of France and jeer at you, unpunished, from across the Channel.

(*She sweeps out with the* YOUNG QUEEN. *Suddenly, the* KING *stops laughing and runs out.*

The light changes. Curtains part. We are at the Court of LOUIS, KING OF FRANCE. *He is sitting in the middle of the courtroom, very erect on his throne. He is a burly man with intelligent eyes.*)

LOUIS (*to his* BARONS): Gentlemen, we are in France and a fart on England's King—as the song goes.

1ST BARON: Your Majesty cannot *not* receive his Ambassadors Extraordinary!

LOUIS: Ordinary, or extraordinary, I am at home to all ambassadors. It's my job. I shall receive them.

1ST BARON: They have been waiting in your Majesty's anteroom for over an hour, Sire.

LOUIS: Let them wait. That's *their* job. An ambassador is made for pacing about an ante-chamber. I know what they are going to ask me.

2ND BARON: The extradition of a felon is a courtesy due from one crowned head to another.

LOUIS: My dear man, crowned heads can play the little game of courtesy but nations owe each other none. My right to play the courteous gentleman stops where France's interests begin. And France's interests consist in making things as difficult as possible for England—a thing England never hesitates to do to us. The Archbishop is a millstone round Henry Plantagenet's neck. Long live the Archbishop! Anyway, I like the fellow.

2ND BARON: My gracious sovereign is master. And so long as our foreign policy permits us to expect nothing of King Henry—

LOUIS: For the time being, it is an excellent thing to stiffen our attitude. Remember the Montmirail affair. We only signed the peace treaty with Henry on condition that he granted to spare the lives of the refugees from Brittany and Poitou whom he asked us to hand over to him. Two months later all of them had lost their heads. That directly touched my personal honor. I was not strong enough at the time, so I had to pretend I hadn't heard of these men's execution. And I continued to lavish smiles on my English cousin. But praise God our affairs have taken a turn for the better. And today *he* needs *us*. So I will now proceed to remember my honor. Show in the ambassadors.

(*Exit* 1ST BARON. *He comes back with* FOLLIOT *and the* DUKE OF ARUNDEL.)

1ST BARON: Permit me to introduce to your Majesty the two envoys extraordinary from his Highness Henry of England; his Grace the Bishop of London and the Duke of Arundel.

LOUIS (*with a friendly wave to the* DUKE): Greetings to you, Milord. I have not forgotten your amazing exploits at the last tournament at Calais. Do you still wield a lance as mightily as you did, Milord?

ARUNDEL (*with a gratified bow*): I hope so, Sire.

LOUIS: We hope that our friendly relations with your gracious master will allow us to appreciate your jousting skill again before long, on the occasion of the forthcoming festivities.

(FOLLIOT has unrolled a parchment.)
Bishop, I see you have a letter for us from your master. We are listening.

FOLLIOT *(bows again and starts to read):* "To my Lord and friend Louis, King of the French; Henry, King of England, Duke of Normandy, Duke of Aquitaine and Count of Anjou: Learn that Thomas, former Archbishop of Canterbury, after a public trial held at my court by the plenary assembly of the Barons of my realm has been found guilty of fraud, perjury and treason towards me. He has forthwith fled my Kingdom as a traitor, and with evil intent. I therefore entreat you not to allow this criminal, nor any of his adherents, to reside upon your territories, nor to permit any of your vassals to give help, support or counsel to this my greatest enemy. For I solemnly declare that your enemies or those of your Realm would receive none from me or my subjects. I expect you to assist me in the vindication of my honor and the punishment of my enemy, as you would wish me to do for you, should the need arise."

(A pause. FOLLIOT bows very low and hands the parchment to the KING who rolls it up casually and hands it to one of the BARONS.)

LOUIS: Gentlemen, we have listened attentively to our gracious cousin's request and we take good note of it. Our chancellery will draft a reply which will be sent to you tomorrow. All we can do at the moment, is express our surprise. No news had reached us of the presence of the Archbishop of Canterbury on our domains.

FOLLIOT *(tersely):* Sire, the former Archbishop has taken refuge at the Abbey of St. Martin, near Saint-Omer.

LOUIS *(still gracious):* My Lord Bishop, we flatter ourselves that there is some order in our Kingdom. If he were there, we would certainly have been informed.

(He makes a gesture of dismissal. The Ambassadors bow low and go out backwards, ushered out by the 1ST BARON. Immediately, LOUIS says to the 2ND BARON)
Show in Thomas Becket and leave us.

(The 2ND BARON goes out and a second later admits THOMAS, dressed in a monk's robe. THOMAS drops onto one knee. The BARON goes out.)

(Kindly) Rise, Thomas Becket. And greet us as the Primate of England. The bow is enough —and if I know my etiquette, you are entitled to a slight nod of the head from me. There, that's done. I would even be required to kiss your ring, if your visit were an official one. But I have the impression that it isn't, am I right?

BECKET *(with a smile):* No, Sire. I am only an exile.

LOUIS *(graciously):* That too is an important title, in France.

BECKET: I am afraid it is the only one I have left. My property has been seized and distributed to those who served the King against me; letters have been sent to the Duke of Flanders and all his Barons enjoining them to seize my person. John, Bishop of Poitiers, who was suspected of wanting to grant me asylum, has just been poisoned.

LOUIS *(smiling):* In fact you are a very dangerous man.

BECKET: I'm afraid so.

LOUIS *(unperturbed):* We like danger, Becket. And if the King of France started being afraid of the King of England, there would be something sadly amiss in Europe. We grant you our royal protection on whichever of our domains it will please you to choose.

BECKET: I humbly thank your Majesty. I must, however, tell you that I cannot buy this protection with any act hostile to my country.

LOUIS: You do us injury. That was understood. You may be sure we are practiced enough in the task of Kingship not to make such gross errors in our choice of spies and traitors. The King of France will ask nothing of you. But . . . There is always a but, as I'm sure you are aware, in politics.

(BECKET looks up. The KING rises heavily onto his fat legs, goes to him and says familiarly)
I am only responsible for France's interests, Becket. I really can't afford to shoulder those of Heaven. In a month or a year I can summon you back here and tell you, just as blandly,

that my dealings with the King of England have taken a different turn and that I am obliged to banish you. *(He slaps him affably on the back, his eyes sparkling with intelligence and asks, with a smile)* I believe you have dabbled in politics too, Archbishop?

BECKET *(smiling):* Yes, Sire. Not so very long ago.

LOUIS *(jovially):* I like you very much. Mark you, had you been a French Bishop, I don't say I wouldn't have clapped you in prison myself. But in the present circumstances, you have a right to my royal protection. Do you value candor, Becket?

BECKET: Yes, Sire.

LOUIS: Then we are sure to understand each other. Do you intend to go to see the Holy Father?

BECKET: Yes, Sire, if you give me your safe conduct.

LOUIS: You shall have it. But a word in your ear—as a friend. (Keep this to yourself, won't you?—don't go and stir up trouble for me with Rome.) Beware of the Pope. He'll sell you for thirty pieces of silver. The man needs money.

(The lights dim. A curtain closes. Two small rostrums, bearing the POPE and the CARDINAL, are pushed on stage, to a light musical accompaniment.

The POPE is a thin, fidgety little man with an atrocious Italian accent. The CARDINAL is swarthy, and his accent is even worse. The whole effect is a little grubby, among the gilded splendor.)

POPE: I don't agree, Zambelli! I don't agree at all! It's a very bad plan altogether. We will forfeit our honor all for 3,000 silver marks.

CARDINAL: Holy Father, there is no question of forfeiting honor, but merely of taking the sum offered by the King of England and thereby gaining time. To lose that sum and give a negative answer right away would solve neither the problems of the Curia, nor those of Thomas Becket—nor even, I am afraid, those of the higher interests of the Church. To accept the money—the sum is meager, I agree, and cannot be viewed as a factor in our decision—is merely to make a gesture of appeasement in the interests of peace in Europe.

Which has always been the supreme duty of the Holy See.

POPE *(concerned):* If we take money from the King, I cannot possibly receive the Archbishop, who has been waiting here in Rome for a whole month for me to grant him an audience.

CARDINAL: Receive the money from the King, Very Holy Father, and receive the Archbishop too. The one will neutralize the other. The money will remove all subversive taint from the audience you will grant the Archbishop and on the other hand, the reception of the Archbishop will efface whatever taint of humiliation there may have been in accepting the money.

POPE *(gloomily):* I don't want to receive him at all. I gather he is a sincere man. I am always disconcerted by people of that sort. They leave me with a bad taste in my mouth.

CARDINAL: Sincerity is a form of strategy, just like any other, Holy Father. In certain very difficult negotiations, when matters are not going ahead and the usual tactics cease to work, I have been known to use it myself. The great pitfall, of course, is if your opponent starts being sincere at the same time as you. Then the game becomes horribly confusing.

POPE: You know what they say Becket's been meaning to ask me?—in the month he's spent pacing about my antechamber?

CARDINAL *(innocently):* No, Holy Father.

POPE *(impatiently):* Zambelli! Don't play the fox with me! It was you who told me!

CARDINAL *(caught out):* I beg your pardon, Holy Father, I had forgotten. Or rather, as your Holiness asked me the question, I thought you had forgotten and so I took a chance and—

POPE *(irritably):* Zambelli, if we start outmaneuvering each other to no purpose, we'll be here all night!

CARDINAL *(in confusion):* Force of habit, your Holiness. Excuse me.

POPE: To ask me to relieve him of his rank and functions as Archbishop of Canterbury— that's the reason Becket is in Rome! And do you know why he wants to ask me that?

CARDINAL *(candidly for once):* Yes, Holy Father.

POPE *(irritably):* No, you do not know! It was your enemy Rapallo who told me!

CARDINAL *(modestly):* Yes, but I knew it just the same, because I have a spy in Rapallo's palace.

POPE *(with a wink):* Culograti?

CARDINAL: No. Culograti is only my spy in his master's eyes. By the man I have spying on Culograti.

POPE *(cutting short the digression):* Becket maintains that the election of Clarendon was not a free one, that he owes his nomination solely to the royal whim and that consequently the honor of God, of which he has now decided he is the champion, does not allow him to bear this usurped title any longer. He wishes to be nothing more than an ordinary priest.

CARDINAL *(after a moment's thought):* The man is clearly an abyss of ambition.

POPE: And yet he knows that we know that his title and functions are his only safeguard against the King's anger. I don't give much for his skin wherever he is, when he is no longer Archbishop!

CARDINAL *(thoughtfully):* He's playing a deep game. But I have a plan. Your Holiness will pretend to believe in his scruples. You will receive him and relieve him of his titles and functions as Primate, then, immediately after, as a reward for his zeal in defending the Church of England, you will reappoint him Archbishop, in right and due form this time. We thus avert the danger, we score a point against him—and at the same time a point against the King.

POPE: That's a dangerous game. The King has a long arm.

CARDINAL: We can cover ourselves. We will send secret letters to the English court explaining that this new nomination is a pure formality and that we herewith rescind the excommunications pronounced by Becket; on the other hand, we will inform Becket of the existence of these secret letters, swearing him to secrecy and begging him to consider them as null and void.

POPE *(getting muddled):* In that case, perhaps there isn't much point in the letters being secret?

CARDINAL: Yes, there is. Because that will allow us to maneuver with each of them as if the other was ignorant of the contents, while taking the precaution of making it known to them both. The main thing is for them not to know that we know they know. It's so simple a child of twelve could grasp it!

POPE: But Archbishop or no, what are we going to do with Becket?

CARDINAL *(with a lighthearted wave of his hand):* We will send him to a convent. A French convent, since King Louis is protecting him—to the Cistercians say, at Pontigny. The monastic rule is a strict one. It will do that onetime dandy a world of good! Let him learn real poverty! That will teach him to be the comforter of the poor!

POPE: That sounds like good advice, Zambelli. Bread and water and nocturnal prayers are an excellent remedy for sincerity.

(He muses a moment.)

The only thing that puzzles me, Zambelli, is why you should want to give me a piece of good advice . . .

(The CARDINAL looks a little embarrassed.

The little rostra go as they came and the curtain opens revealing a small, bare cell, center stage.

BECKET *is praying before a humble wooden crucifix. Crouching in a corner, the* YOUNG MONK *is playing with a knife.)*

BECKET: Yet it would be simple enough. Too simple perhaps. Saintliness is a temptation too. Oh, how difficult it is to get an answer from You, Lord! I was slow in praying to You, but I cannot believe that others, worthier than I, who have spent years asking You questions, have been better than myself at deciphering Your real intentions. I am only a beginner and I must make mistake after mistake, as I did in my Latin translations as a boy, when my riotous imagination made the old priest roar with laughter. But I cannot believe that one learns Your language as one learns any human tongue, by hard studying, with a dictionary, a grammar and a set of idioms. I am sure that to the hardened sinner, who drops to his knees for the first time and murmurs Your name, marveling, You tell him all Your secrets, straightaway, and that he understands.

I have served You like a dilettante, surprised that I could still find my pleasure in Your service. And for a long time I was on my guard because of it. I could not believe this pleasure would bring me one step nearer You. I could not believe that the road could be a happy one. Their hair shirts, their fasting, their bells in the small hours summoning one to meet You, on the icy paving stones, in the sick misery of the poor ill-treated human animal—I cannot believe that all these are anything but safeguards for the weak. In power and in luxury, and even in the pleasures of the flesh, I shall not cease to speak to You, I feel this now. You are the God of the rich man and the happy man too, Lord, and therein lies Your profound justice. You do not turn away Your eyes from the man who was given everything from birth. You have not abandoned him, alone in his ensnaring facility. And he may be Your true lost sheep. For Your scheme of things, which we mistakenly call Justice, is secret and profound and You plumb the hidden depths of poor men's puny frames as carefully as those of Kings. And beneath those outward differences, which blind us, but which to You are barely noticeable; beneath the diadem or the grime, You discern the same pride, the same vanity, the same petty, complacent preoccupation with oneself. Lord, I am certain now that You meant to tempt me with this hair shirt, object of so much vapid self-congratulation! this bare cell, this solitude, this absurdly endured winter cold—and the conveniences of prayer. It would be too easy to buy You like this, at so low a price. I shall leave this convent, where so many precautions hem You round. I shall take up the miter and the golden cope again, and the great silver cross, and I shall go back and fight in the place and with the weapons it has pleased You to give me. It has pleased You to make me Archbishop and to set me, like a solitary pawn, face to face with the King, upon the chessboard. I shall go back to my place, humbly, and let the world accuse me of pride, so that I may do what I believe is my life's work. For the rest, Your will be done.

(He crosses himself.

The YOUNG MONK *is still playing with his knife. Suddenly he throws it and watches as it quivers, embedded in the floor. The curtain falls.)*

ACT FOUR

The King of France's Court.

*(*KING LOUIS *comes in, holding* BECKET *familiarly by the arm.)*

LOUIS: I tell you, Becket, intrigue is an ugly thing. You keep the smell about you for ages afterwards. There is a return of good understanding between the Kingdom of England and Ourselves. Peace in that direction assures me of a great advantage in the struggle which I will shortly have to undertake against the Emperor. I must protect my rear by a truce with Henry Plantagenet, before I march towards the East. And, needless to say, you are one of the items on the King's bill of charges. I can even tell you, that apart from yourself, his demands are negligible. *(musingly)* Curious man. England's best policy would have been to take advantage of the Emperor's aggressive intentions and close the other jaw of the trap. He is deliberately sacrificing this opportunity for the pleasure of seeing you driven out. He really hates you, doesn't he?

BECKET *(simply)*: Sire, we loved each other and I think he cannot forgive me for preferring God to him.

LOUIS: Your King isn't doing his job properly, Archbishop. He is giving way to passion. However! He has chosen to score a point against you, instead of against me. You are on his bill, I have to pay his price and banish you. I do not do so without a certain shame. Where are you thinking of going?

BECKET: I am a shepherd who has remained too long away from his flock. I intend to go back to England. I had already made my decision before this audience with your Majesty.

LOUIS *(surprised)*: You have a taste for martyrdom? You disappoint me. I thought you more healthy-minded.

BECKET: Would it be healthy-minded to walk the roads of Europe, and beg a refuge where my carcass would be safe? Besides, where would I be safe? I am a Primate of Eng-

land. That is a rather showy label on my back.
The honor of God and common sense, which
for once coincide, dictate that instead of risking the knife thrust of some hired assassin, on
the highway, I should go and have myself
killed—if killed I must be—clad in my golden
cope, with my miter on my head and my silver
cross in my hand, among my flock in my own
cathedral. That place alone befits me.

(A pause.)

LOUIS: I daresay you're right. *(He sighs.)*
Ah, what a pity it is to be a King, sometimes,
when one has the surprise of meeting a man!
You'll tell me, fortunately for me, that men are
rare. Why weren't you born on this side of the
Channel, Becket? *(He smiles.)* True, you
would no doubt have been a thorn in *my* side
then! The honor of God is a very cumbersome
thing. *(He muses for a moment and then says
abruptly)* Who cares, I'll risk it! I like you too
much. I'll indulge in a moment's humanity. I
am going to try something, even if your
master does seize on the chance to double his
bill. After all, banishing you would merely
have cost me a small slice of honor . . . I am
meeting Henry in a day or two, at La Ferté-
Bernard, to seal our agreement. I shall try to
persuade him to make his peace with you.
Should he agree, will you be willing to talk
with him?

BECKET: Sire, ever since we stopped seeing
each other, I have never ceased to talk to him.

*(Blackout. Prolonged blare of trumpets. The
set is completely removed. Nothing remains
but the cyclorama around the bare stage. A
vast, arid plain, lashed by the wind. Trumpets
again.*

Two SENTRIES *are on stage, watching something in the distance.)*

SENTRY: Open those eyes of yours, lad! And
drink it all in. You're new to the job, but you
won't see something like this every day! This
a historic meeting!

YOUNG SENTRY: I daresay, but it's perishing
cold! How long are they going. to keep us
hanging about?

SENTRY: We're sheltered by the wood here,
but you can bet they're even colder than we
are, out there in the plain.

YOUNG SENTRY: Look! They've come up to

each other! I wonder what they're talking
about?

SENTRY: What do you think they're talking
about, muttonhead? Inquiring how things are
at home? Complaining about their chilblains?
The fate of the world, that's what they're
arguing about! Things you and I won't ever
understand. Even the words those bigwigs use
—why, you wouldn't even know what they
meant!

(They go off. The lights go up. BECKET *and
the* KING, *on horseback, are alone in the middle of the plain, facing each other.*

*Throughout the scene, the winter blizzard
wails like a shrill dirge beneath their words.
And during their silences, only the wind is
heard.)*

KING: You look older, Thomas.

BECKET: You too, Highness. Are you sure
you aren't too cold?

KING: I'm frozen stiff. You love it of course!
You're in your element, aren't you? And you're
barefooted as well!

BECKET *(smiling)*: That's my latest affecta-
tion.

KING: Even with these fur boots on, my chilblains are killing me. Aren't yours, or don't
you have any?

BECKET *(gently)*: Of course.

KING *(cackling)*: You're offering them up to
God, I hope, holy monk?

BECKET *(gravely)*: I have better things to
offer Him.

KING *(with a sudden cry)*: If we start
straightaway, we're sure to quarrel! Let's talk
about trivial things. You know my son is fourteen? He's come of age.

BECKET: Has he improved at all?

KING: He's a little idiot and sly like his
mother. Becket, don't you ever marry!

BECKET *(smiling)*: The matter has been taken
out of my hands. By you, Highness! It was you
who had me ordained!

KING *(with a cry)*: Let's not start yet, I tell
you! Talk about something else!

BECKET *(lightly)*: Has your Highness done
much hunting lately?

KING *(snarling)*: Yes, every day! And it
doesn't amuse me any more.

BECKET: Have you any new hawks?

KING (*furiously*): The most expensive on the market! But they don't fly straight.

BECKET: And your horses?

KING: The Sultan sent me four superb stallions for the tenth anniversary of my reign. But they throw everyone! Nobody has managed to mount one of them, yet!

BECKET (*smiling*): I must see what I can do about that some day.

KING: They'll throw you too! And we'll see your buttocks under your robe! At least, I hope so, or everything would be too dismal.

BECKET (*after a pause*): Do you know what I miss most, Sire? The horses.

KING: And the women?

BECKET (*simply*): I've forgotten.

KING: You hypocrite. You turned into a hypocrite when you became a priest. (*Abruptly*) Did you love Gwendolen?

BECKET: I've forgotten her too.

KING: You did love her! That's the only way I can account for it.

BECKET (*gravely*): No, my prince, in my soul and conscience, I did not love her.

KING: Then you never loved anything, that's worse! (*Churlishly*) Why are you calling me your prince, like in the old days?

BECKET (*gently*): Because you have remained my prince.

KING (*crying out*): Then why are you doing me harm?

BECKET (*gently*): Let's talk about something else.

KING: Well, what? I'm cold.

BECKET: I always told you, my prince, that one must fight the cold with the cold's own weapons. Strip naked and splash yourself with cold water every morning.

KING: I used to when you were there to force me into it. I never wash now. I stink. I grew a beard at one time. Did you know?

BECKET (*smiling*): Yes. I had a hearty laugh over it.

KING: I cut it off because it itched. (*He cries out suddenly, like a lost child*) Becket, I'm bored!

BECKET (*gravely*): My prince. I do so wish I could help you.

KING: Then what are you waiting for? You can see I'm dying for it!

BECKET (*quietly*): I'm waiting for the honor of God and the honor of the King to become one.

KING: You'll wait a long time then!

BECKET: Yes. I'm afraid I will.

(*A pause. Only the wind is heard.*)

KING (*suddenly*): If we've nothing more to say to each other, we might as well go and get warm!

BECKET: We have everything to say to each other, my prince. The opportunity may not occur again.

KING: Make haste, then. Or there'll be two frozen statues on this plain making their peace in a frozen eternity! I am your King, Becket! And so long as we are on this earth you owe me the first move! I'm prepared to forget a lot of things but not the fact that I am King. You yourself taught me that.

BECKET (*gravely*): Never forget it, my prince. Even against God. You have a different task to do. You have to steer the ship.

KING: And you—what do you have to do?

BECKET: Resist you with all my might, when you steer against the wind.

KING: Do you expect the wind to be behind me, Becket? No such luck! That's the fairytale navigation! God on the King's side? That's never happened yet! Yes, once in a century, at the time of the Crusades, when all Christendom shouts "It's God's will!" And even then! You know as well as I do what private greeds a Crusade covers up, in nine cases out of ten. The rest of the time, it's a head-on wind. And there must be somebody to keep the watch!

BECKET: And somebody else to cope with the absurd wind—and with God. The tasks have been shared out, once and for all. The pity of it is that it should have been between us two, my prince—who were friends.

KING (*crossly*): The King of France—I still don't know what he hopes to gain by it—preached at me for three whole days for me to make my peace with you. What good would it do you to provoke me beyond endurance?

BECKET: None.

KING: You know that I am the King, and that I must act like a King! What do you expect of me? Are you hoping I'll weaken?

BECKET: No. That would prostrate me.

KING: Do you hope to conquer me by force then?

BECKET: You are the strong one.

KING: To win me round?

BECKET: No. Not that either. It is not for me to win you round. I have only to say no to you.

KING: But you must be logical, Becket!

BECKET: No. That isn't necessary, my Liege. We must only do—absurdly—what we have been given to do—right to the end.

KING: Yet I know you well enough, God knows. Ten years we spent together, little Saxon! At the hunt, at the whorehouse, at war; carousing all night long the two of us; in the same girl's bed, sometimes . . . and at work in the Council Chamber too. Absurdly. That word isn't like you.

BECKET: Perhaps. I am no longer like my-self.

KING (derisively): Have you been touched by grace?

BECKET (gravely): Not by the one you think. I am not worthy of it.

KING: Did you feel the Saxon in you coming out, despite Papa's good collabo-rator's sentiments?

BECKET: No. Not that either.

KING: What then?

BECKET: I felt for the first time that I was being entrusted with something, that's all—there in that empty cathedral, somewhere in France, that day when you ordered me to take up this burden. I was a man without honor. And suddenly I found it—one I never imagined would ever become mine—the honor of God. A frail, incomprehensible honor, vulnerable as a boy-King fleeing from danger.

KING (roughly): Suppose we talked a little more precisely, Becket, with words I under-stand? Otherwise we'll be here all night. I'm cold. And the others are waiting for us on the fringes of this plain.

BECKET: I am being precise.

KING: I'm an idiot then! Talk to me like an idiot! That's an order. Will you lift the excommunication which you pronounced on William of Aynsford and others of my liege-men?

BECKET: No, Sire, because that is the only weapon I have to defend this child, who was given, naked, into my care.

KING: Will you agree to the twelve pro-posals which my Bishops have accepted in your absence at Northampton, and notably to forego the much-abused protection of Saxon clerics who get themselves tonsured to escape land bondage?

BECKET: No, Sire. My role is to defend my sheep. And they are my sheep. (A pause) Nor will I concede that the Bishops should forego the right to appoint priests in their own dioceses, nor that churchmen should be subject to any but the Church's jurisdiction. These are my duties as a pastor—which it is not for me to relinquish. But I shall agree to the nine other articles in a spirit of peace, and because I know that you must remain King—in all save the honor of God.

(A pause.)

KING (coldly): Very well. I will help you defend your God, since that is your new vocation, in memory of the companion you once were to me—in all save the honor of the Realm. You may come back to England, Thomas.

BECKET: Thank you, my prince. I meant to go back in any case and give myself up to your power, for on this earth, you are my King. And in all that concerns this earth, I owe you obedience.

(A pause.)

KING (ill at ease): Well, let's go back now. We've finished. I'm cold.

BECKET (dully): I feel cold too, now.

(Another pause. They look at each other. The wind howls.)

KING (suddenly): You never loved me, did you, Becket?

BECKET: In so far as I was capable of love, yes, my prince, I did.

KING: Did you start to love God? (He cries out) You mule! Can't you ever answer a simple question?

BECKET (quietly): I started to love the honor of God.

KING (somberly): Come back to England.

I give you my royal peace. May you find yours. And may you not discover you were wrong about yourself. This is the last time I shall come begging to you. *(He cries out)* I should never have seen you again! It hurts too much. *(His whole body is suddenly shaken by a sob.)*

BECKET *(goes nearer to him; moved)*: My prince—

KING *(yelling)*: No! No pity! It's dirty. Stand away from me! Go back to England! It's too cold out here!

(BECKET turns his horse and moves nearer to the KING.)

BECKET *(gravely)*: Farewell, my prince. Will you give me the kiss of peace?

KING: No! I can't bear to come near you! I can't bear to look at you! Later! Later! When it doesn't hurt any more!

BECKET: I shall set sail tomorrow. Farewell, my prince. I know I shall never see you again.

KING *(his face twisted with hatred)*: How dare you say that to me after I gave you my royal word? Do you take me for a traitor?

(BECKET looks at him gravely for a second longer, with a sort of pity in his eyes. Then he slowly turns his horse and rides away. The wind howls.)

KING: Thomas!

(But BECKET has not heard. The KING does not call a second time. He spurs his horse and gallops off in the other direction. The lights fade. The wind howls.

The lights change. Red curtains fall. BECKET's *whistled march is heard off stage during the scene change.*

The curtains open. Royal music. KING HENRY's *palace somewhere in France. The two* QUEENS, *the* BARONS *and* HENRY's *son are standing around the dinner table, waiting. The* KING, *his eyes gleaming maliciously, looks at them and then exclaims)*

KING: Today, gentlemen, I shall not be the first to sit down! *(To his* SON, *with a comic bow)* You are the King, Sir. The honor belongs to you. Take the high chair. Today I shall wait on *you!*

QUEEN MOTHER *(with slight irritation)*: My son!

KING: I know what I'm doing, Madam! *(With a sudden shout)* Go on, you great loon, look sharp! You're the King, but you're as stupid as ever!

(The boy flinches to avoid the blow he was expecting and goes to sit in the KING's *chair, sly and rather ill at ease.)*

Take your places, gentlemen! I shall remain standing. Barons of England, here is your second King. For the good of our vast domains, a kingly colleague had become a necessity. Reviving an ancient custom, we have decided to have our successor crowned during our lifetime and to share our responsibilities with him. We ask you now to give him your homage and to honor him with the same title as Ourself.

(He makes a sign. Two SERVANTS *have brought in a haunch of venison on a silver charger. The* KING *serves his* SON.)

YOUNG QUEEN *(to her* SON): Sit up straight! And try to eat properly for once, now that you've been raised to glory!

KING *(grunting as he serves him)*: He hasn't the face for it! He's a little slyboots and dim-witted at that. However, he'll be your King in good earnest one day, so you may as well get used to him. Besides, it's the best I had to offer.

QUEEN MOTHER *(indignantly)*: Really, my son! This game is unworthy of you and of us. You insisted on it—against my advice—at least play it with dignity!

KING *(rounding on her in fury)*: I'll play the games that amuse me, Madam, and I'll play them the way I choose! This mummery, gentlemen, which is, incidentally, without any importance at all—(if your new King fidgets, let me know, I'll give him a good kick up his train)—will at the very least have the appreciable result of showing our new friend, the Archbishop, that we can do without him. If there was one ancient privilege the Primacy clung to, tooth and nail, it was its exclusive right to anoint and consecrate the Kings of this realm. Well, it will be that old toad the Archbishop of York—with letters from the Pope authorizing him to do so—I paid the price!—who, tomorrow, will crown our son in the cathedral! What a joke that's going to be! *(He roars with laughter amid the general silence.)* What a tremendous, marvelous joke! I'd give anything to see that Archbishop's face when he has to swallow that! *(To his* SON*)* Get down from there, you imbecile! Go back to the bottom of the table and take your victuals with you! You aren't officially crowned until tomorrow.

(The boy picks up his plate and goes back to his place, casting a cowed, smoldering look at his father.)

(Watching him, says jovially) What a look! Filial sentiments are a fine thing to see, gentlemen! You'd like to be the real King, wouldn't you, you young pig? You'd like that number III after your name, eh, with Papa good and stiff under his catafalque! You'll have to wait a bit! Papa is well. Papa is very well indeed!

QUEEN MOTHER: My son, God knows I criticized your attempts at reconciliation with that wretch, who has done us nothing but harm . . . God knows I understand your hatred of him! But do not let it drag you into making a gesture you will regret, merely for the sake of wounding his pride. Henry is still a child. But you were not much older when you insisted on reigning by yourself, and in opposition to me. Ambitious self-seekers—and there is never any scarcity of those around Princes—can advise him, raise a faction against you and avail themselves of this hasty coronation to divide the Kingdom! Think it over, there is still time.

KING: We are still alive, Madam, and in control! And nothing can equal my pleasure in imagining my proud friend Becket's face when he sees the fundamental privilege of the Primacy whisked from under his nose! I let him cheat me out of one or two articles the other day, but I had something up my sleeve for him!

QUEEN MOTHER: Henry! I bore the weight of state affairs longer than you ever have. I have been your Queen and I am your mother. You are answerable for the interests of a great Kingdom, not for your moods. You already gave far too much away to the King of France, at La Ferté-Bernard. It is

England you must think of, not your hatred —or disappointed love—for that man.

KING *(in a fury):* Disappointed love—disappointed love? What gives you the right, Madam, to meddle in my loves and hates?

QUEEN MOTHER: You have a rancor against the man which is neither healthy nor manly. The King your father dealt with his enemies faster and more summarily than that. He had them killed and said no more about it. If Thomas Becket were a faithless woman whom you still hankered after, you would act no differently. Sweet Jesu, tear him out of your heart once and for all! *(She bawls suddenly)* Oh, if I were a man!

KING *(grinning):* Thanks be to God, Madam, he gave you dugs. Which I never personally benefited from. I suckled a peasant girl.

QUEEN MOTHER *(acidly):* That is no doubt why you have remained so lumpish, my son.

YOUNG QUEEN: And haven't I a say in the matter? I tolerated your mistresses, Sir, but do you expect me to tolerate everything? Have you ever stopped to think what kind of woman I am? I am tired of having my life encumbered with this man. Becket! Always Becket! Nobody ever talks about anything else here! He was almost less of a hindrance when you loved him. I am a woman. I am your wife and your Queen. I refuse to be treated like this! I shall complain to my father, the Duke of Aquitaine! I shall complain to my uncle, the Emperor! I shall complain to all the Kings of Europe, my cousins! I shall complain to God!

KING *(shouting rather vulgarly):* I should start with God! Be off to your private chapel, Madam, and see if He's at home. *(He turns to his mother, fuming.)* And you, the other Madam, away to your chamber with your secret councilors and go and spin your webs! Get out, both of you! I can't stand the sight of you! I retch with boredom whenever I set eyes on you! And young Henry III too! Go on, get out! *(He chases him out with kicks, yelling)* Here's my royal foot in your royal buttocks! And to the devil with my whole family, if he'll have you! Get out, all of you! Get out! Get out! Get out!

(The QUEENS *scurry out, with a great rustling of silks. He turns to the* BARONS *who all stand watching him, terror-stricken.)*
(More calmly) Let us drink, gentlemen. That's about all one can do in your company. Let us get drunk, like men, all night; until we roll under the table, in vomit and oblivion. *(He fills their glasses and beckons them closer.)* Ah, my four idiots! My faithful hounds! It's warm beside you, like being in a stable. Good sweat! Comfortable nothingness! *(He taps their skulls.)* Not the least little glimmer inside to spoil the fun. And to think that before he came I was like you! A good fat machine for belching after drink, for pissing, for mounting girls and punching heads. What the devil did you put into it, Becket, to stop the wheels from going round? *(Suddenly to the* 2ND BARON*)* Tell me, do you think sometimes, Baron?

2ND BARON: Never, Sire. Thinking has never agreed with an Englishman. It's unhealthy. Besides, a gentleman has better things to do.

KING *(sitting beside them, suddenly quite calm):* Drink up, gentlemen. That's always been considered a healthy thing to do. *(He fills the goblets.)* Has Becket landed? I'm told the sea has been too rough to cross these last few days.

1ST BARON *(somberly):* He has landed, Sire, despite the sea.

KING: Where?

1ST BARON: On a deserted stretch of coast, near Sandwich.

KING: So God did not choose to drown him?

1ST BARON: No.

KING *(he asks in his sly, brutish way):* Was nobody there waiting for him? There must be one or two men in England whom he can't call his friends!

1ST BARON: Yes. Gervase, Duke of Kent, Regnouf de Broc and Regnault de Garenne were waiting for him. Gervase had said that if he dared to land he'd cut off his head with his own hands. But the native Englishmen from all the coastal towns had armed themselves to form an escort for the Arch-bishop. And the Dean of Oxford went to meet the Barons and charged them not to cause bloodshed and make you look a traitor, seeing that you had given the Archbishop a safe conduct.

KING *(soberly):* Yes, I gave him a safe conduct.

1ST BARON: All along the road to Canterbury, the peasants, the artisans and the small shopkeepers came out to meet him, cheering him and escorting him from village to village. Not a single rich man, not a single Norman, showed his face.

KING: Only the Saxons?

1ST BARON: Poor people armed with make-shift shields and rusty lances. Riffraff. Swarms of them though, all camping around Canterbury, to protect him. *(Gloomily)* Who would have thought there were so many people in England!

(The KING *has remained prostrate without uttering a word. Now he suddenly jumps up and roars)*

KING: A miserable wretch who ate my bread! A man I raised up from nothing! A Saxon! A man loved! *(Shouting like a madman)* I loved him! Yes, I loved him! And I believe I still do! Enough, O God! Enough! Stop, stop, O God, I've had enough!

(He flings himself down on the couch, sobbing hysterically; tearing at the horsehair mattress with his teeth, and eating it. The BARONS, *stupified, go nearer to him.)*

1ST BARON *(timidly):* Your Highness . . .

KING *(moaning, with his head buried in the mattress):* I can do nothing! Nothing! I'm as limp and useless as a girl! So long as he's alive, I'll never be able to do a thing. I tremble before him astonished. And I am the King! *(With a sudden cry)* Will no one rid me of him? A priest! A priest who jeers at me and does me injury! Are there none but cowards like myself around me? Are there no men left in England? Oh, my heart! My heart is beating too fast to bear!

(He lies, still as death on the torn mattress. The four BARONS *stand around speechless. Suddenly, on a percussion instrument, there rises a rhythmic beating, a sort of muffled*

tom-tom which is at first only the agitated heartbeats of the KING, *but which swells and grows more insistent. The four* BARONS *look at each other. Then they straighten, buckle their sword belts, pick up their helmets and go slowly out, leaving the* KING *alone with the muffled rhythm of the heartbeats, which will continue until the murder. The* KING *lies there prostrate, among the upturned benches, in the deserted hall. A torch splutters and goes out. He sits up, looks around, sees they have gone and suddenly realizes why. A wild, lost look comes into his eyes. A moment's pause then he collapses on the bed with a long broken moan.)*

KING: O my Thomas!

(A second torch goes out. Total darkness. Only the steady throb of the heartbeats is heard. A dim light. The forest of pillars again. Canterbury Cathedral. Upstage a small altar, with three steps leading up to it, half screened by a grill. In a corner downstage BECKET, *and the* YOUNG MONK, *who is helping him on with his vestments. Nearby, on a stool, the Archbishop's miter. The tall silver cross is leaning against a pillar.)*

BECKET: I must look my best today. Make haste.

(The MONK *fumbles with the vestments. The muffled tom-tom is heard distantly at first, then closer.)*

MONK: It's difficult with all those little laces. It wants a girl's hands.

BECKET *(softly):* A man's hands are better, today. Never mind the laces. The alb, quickly. And the stole. And then the cope.

MONK *(conscientiously):* If it's worth doing it's worth doing well.

BECKET: You're quite right. If it's worth doing it's worth doing well. Do up all the little laces, every one of them. God will give us time.

(A pause. The boy struggles manfully on, putting out his tongue in concentration. The throbbing grows louder.)

(Smiling) Don't pull your tongue out like that! *(He watches the boy as he works away.)*

MONK *(sweating but content):* There. That's all done. But I'd rather have cleaned out our pigsty at home! It's not half such hard work!

BECKET: Now the alb. *(A pause.)* Were you fond of your pigs?

MONK *(his eyes lighting up):* Yes, I was.

BECKET: At my father's house, we had some pigs too, when I was a child. *(Smiling)* We're two rough lads from Hastings, you and I! Give me the chasuble. (BECKET *kisses the chasuble and slips it over his head. He looks at the boy and says gently)* Do you miss your knife?

MONK: Yes. *(Pause.)* Will it be today?

BECKET *(gravely):* I think so, my son. Are you afraid?

MONK: Oh, no. Not if we have time to fight. All I want is the chance to strike a few blows first; so I shan't have done nothing but receive them all my life. If I can kill one Norman first—just one, I don't want much—one for one, that will seem fair and right enough to me.

BECKET *(with a kindly smile):* Are you so very set on killing one?

MONK: One for one. After that, I don't much care if I *am* just a little grain of sand in the machine. Because I know that by putting more and more grains of sand in the machine, one day it will come grinding to a stop.

BECKET *(gently):* And on that day, what then?

MONK: We'll set a fine, new, well-oiled machine in the place of the old one and this time we'll put the Normans into it instead. *(He asks, quite without irony)* That's what justice means, isn't it?

*(*BECKET *smiles and does not answer him.)*

BECKET: Fetch me the miter. *(He says quietly, as the boy fetches it)* O Lord, You forbade Peter to strike a blow in the Garden of Olives. But I shall not deprive him of that joy. He has had too few joys in his short span on earth. *(To the boy)* Now give me my silver cross. I must hold it.

MONK *(passing it to him):* Lord, it's heavy! A good swipe with that and they'd feel it! My word, I wish I could have it!

BECKET *(stroking his hair):* Lucky little

Saxon! This black world will have been in order to the end, for you. *(He straightens, grave once more.)* There. I'm ready, all adorned for Your festivities, Lord. Do not, in this interval of waiting, let one last doubt enter my soul.

(During this scene, the throbbing has grown louder. Now it mingles with a loud knocking on the door. A PRIEST *runs in wildly.)*

PRIEST: Your Grace! There are four armed men outside! They say they must see you on behalf of the King. I've barricaded the door but they're breaking it in! They've got hatchets! Quickly! You must go into the back of the church and have the choir gates closed! They're strong enough, they'll hold!

BECKET *(calmly)*: It is time for Vespers, William. Does one close the choir gates during Vespers? I never heard of such a thing.

PRIEST *(nonplused)*: I know, but . . .

BECKET: Everything must be the way it should be. The choir gates will remain open. Come, boy, let us go up to the altar. This is no place to be.

(He goes toward the altar, followed by the YOUNG MONK. *A great crash. The door has given way. The four* BARONS *come in, in their helmets. They fling down their hatchets and draw their swords.* BECKET *turns to face them, grave and calm, at the foot of the altar. They stop a moment, uncertain and disconcerted; four statues, huge and threatening. The tom-tom has stopped. There is nothing now but a heavy silence.* BECKET *says simply)*

Here it comes. The supreme folly. This is its hour.

(He holds their eyes. They dare not move. He says coldly:)

One does not enter armed into God's house. What do you want?

1ST BARON *(thickly)*: Your death.

(A pause.)

2ND BARON *(thickly)*: You bring shame to the King. Flee the country or you're a dead man.

BECKET *(softly)*: It is time for the service.

(He turns to the altar and faces the tall crucifix without paying any further attention to them. The throbbing starts again, muffled. The four men close in like automata. The YOUNG MONK *suddenly leaps forward brandishing the heavy silver cross in order to protect* BECKET, *but one of the* BARONS *swings his sword and fells him to the ground.* BECKET *murmurs, as if in reproach)*

Not even one! It would have given him so much pleasure, Lord. *(With a sudden cry)* Oh how difficult You make it all! And how heavy Your honor is to bear! *(He adds, very quietly)* Poor Henry.

(The four men hurl themselves onto him. He falls at the first blow. They hack at his body, grunting like woodcutters. The PRIEST *has fled with a long scream, which echoes in the empty cathedral.*

Blackout.

On the same spot. The KING, *naked, on bended knees at* BECKET's *tomb, as in the first scene. Four* MONKS *are whipping him with ropes, almost duplicating the gestures of the* BARONS *as they killed* BECKET.)

KING *(crying out)*: Are you satisfied now, Becket? Does this settle our account? Has the honor of God been washed clean?

(The four MONKS *finish beating him, then kneel down and bow their heads. The* KING *mutters—one feels it is part of the ceremony)* Thank you. Yes, yes, of course, it was agreed, I forgive you. Many thanks.

(The PAGE *comes forward with a vast cloak, which the* KING *wraps around himself. The* BARONS *surround the* KING *and help him to dress, while the* BISHOPS *and the* CLERGY, *forming a procession, move away solemnly upstage to the strains of the organ. The* KING *dresses hurriedly, with evident bad temper, aided by his* BARONS. *He grimaces ill-humoredly and growls)* The pigs! The Norman Bishops just went through the motions, but those little Saxon monks—my word, they had their money's worth!

(A BARON *comes in. A joyful peal of bells is heard.)*

BARON: Sire, the operation has been successful! The Saxon mob is yelling with enthusiasm outside the cathedral, acclaiming your Majesty's name in the same breath as Becket's! If the Saxons are on our side now, Prince Henry's followers look as though they have definitely lost the day.

KING (*with a touch of hypocritical majesty beneath his slightly loutish manner*): The honor of God, gentlemen, is a very good thing, and taken all in all, one gains by having it on one's side. Thomas Becket, who was our friend, used to say so. England will owe her ultimate victory over chaos to him, and it is our wish that, henceforward, he should be honored and prayed to in this Kingdom as a saint. Come, gentlemen. We will determine, tonight, in Council, what posthumous honors to render him and what punishment to deal out to his murderers.

1ST BARON (*imperturbably*): Sire, they are unknown.

KING (*impenetrably*): Our justice will seek them out, Baron, and you will be specially entrusted with this inquiry, so that no one will be in any doubt as to our Royal desire to defend the honor of God and the memory of our friend from this day forward.

(*The organ swells triumphantly, mingled with the sound of the bells and the cheering of the crowds as they file out. Curtain.*)

JOHN MILLINGTON SYNGE

The Playboy of the Western World

John Millington Synge (1871–1910), was born in Dublin, attended Trinity College, Dublin, and studied for six years in Paris. In 1899 he returned to Ireland, partly at the persuasion of the poet W. B. Yeats. He was to live as one of the Aran Islanders, learn their peasant dialect, and write of their experiences. He brought with him, however, the balancing effect of a sound classical education and extensive travel and study on the Continent.

Synge's first prose work, *The Aran Islands,* recounts his journeys to the four islands that lie off the west coast of Ireland; his second, not completed, is a series of essays about the surrounding countryside. His first play, *In the Shadow of the Glen,* 1903, with a theme similar to that of Ibsen's *A Doll House,* renders a story he had heard and recounted in *The Aran Islands.* It was followed by the five plays on which his reputation as a playwright rests: *Riders to the Sea,* 1904, a story of fate and the implacable sea; *The Well of the Saints,* 1905, his first three-act drama; *The Playboy of the Western World,* 1907; *The Tinker's Wedding,* 1908, not produced in Dublin during the poet's lifetime because of its controversial nature; and the unfinished *Deirdre of the Sorrows,* 1910, his first play based on Irish legendary material. In a reader survey reported in the London *Observer* in 1966, *The Playboy of the Western World* was included as one of the twenty plays written since 1900 in which the main trends of the theater in this century could be most clearly discerned.

The Playboy of the Western World is based on a story Synge heard in the Aran Islands. Deceptively simple, the story clearly demonstrates his dramatic theory: that one must listen to and use the imaginative language of the people; that "one must have reality, and one must have joy."

PREFACE

In writing *The Playboy of the Western World,* as in my other plays, I have used one or two words only that I have not heard among the country people of Ireland, or spoken in my own nursery before I could read the newspapers. A certain number of the phrases I employ I have heard also from herds and fishermen along the coast from Kerry to Mayo, or from beggarwomen and ballad singers near Dublin; and I am glad to acknowledge how much I owe to the folk imagination of these fine people. Anyone who has lived in real intimacy with the Irish peasantry will know that the wildest sayings and ideas in this play are tame indeed, compared with the fancies one may hear in any little hillside cabin in Geesala, or Carraroe, or Dingle Bay. All art is a collaboration! and there is little doubt that in the happy ages of literature, striking and beautiful phrases were as ready to the story-teller's or the playwright's hand, as the rich cloaks and dresses of his time. It is probable that when the Elizabethan dramatist took his inkhorn and sat down to his work he used many phrases that he had just heard, as he sat at dinner, from his mother or his children. In Ireland, those of us who know the people have the same privilege. When I was writing *The Shadow of the Glen,* some years ago, I got more aid than any learning could have given me from a chink in the floor of the old Wicklow house where I was staying, that let me hear what was being said by the servant girls in the kitchen. This matter, I think, is of importance, for in countries where the imagination of the people, and the language they use, is rich and living, it is possible for a writer to be rich and copious in his words, and at the same time to give the reality, which is the root of all poetry, in a comprehensive and natural form. In the modern literature of towns, however, richness is found only in sonnets, or prose poems, or in one or two elaborate books that are far away from the profound and common interests of life. One has, on one side, Mallarmé and Huysmans [1] producing this literature; and, on the other, Ibsen and Zola dealing with the reality of life in joyless and pallid words. On the stage one must have reality, and one must have joy; and that is why the intellectual modern drama has failed, and people have grown sick of the false joy of the musical comedy that has been given them in place of the rich joy found only in what is superb and wild in reality. In a good play every speech should be as fully flavored as a nut or apple, and such speeches cannot be written by anyone who works among people who have shut their lips on poetry. In Ireland, for a few years more, we have a popular imagination that is fiery and magnificent, and tender; so that those who wish to write start with a chance that is not given to writers in places where the springtime of the local life has been forgotten, and the harvest is a memory only, and the straw has been turned into bricks.

1907

---

[1] Joris Karl Huysmans (1848–1907), French novelist and poet, most famous for *Against the Grain.*

CAST OF CHARACTERS

CHRISTOPHER MAHON

OLD MAHON, *his father—a squatter*

MICHAEL JAMES FLAHERTY, *called* MICHAEL JAMES, *a publican*

MARGARET FLAHERTY, *called* PEGEEN MIKE, *his daughter*

WIDOW QUIN, *a woman of about thirty*

SHAWN KEOGH, *her cousin, a young farmer*

PHILLY CULLEN *and* JIMMY FARRELL, *small farmers*

SARA TANSEY, SUSAN BRADY, *and* HONOR BLAKE, *village girls*

A BELLMAN

SOME PEASANTS

The action takes place near a village, on a wild coast of Mayo. The first act passes on an evening of autumn, the other two acts on the following day.

ACT ONE

SCENE

Country public-house or shebeen, very rough and untidy. There is a sort of counter on the right with shelves, holding many bottles and jugs, just seen above it. Empty barrels stand near the counter. At back, a little to left of counter, there is a door into the open air, then, more to the left, there is a settle with shelves above it, with more jugs, and a table beneath a window. At the left there is a large open fireplace, with turf fire, and a small door into inner room. PEGEEN, *a wild-looking but fine girl, of about twenty, is writing at table. She is dressed in the usual peasant dress.*

PEGEEN (*slowly as she writes*): Six yards of stuff for to make a yellow gown. A pair of lace boots with lengthy heels on them and brassy eyes. A hat is suited for a wedding day. A fine tooth comb. To be sent with three barrels of porter in Jimmy Farrell's creel cart on the evening of the coming Fair to Mister Michael James Flaherty. With the best compliments of this season. Margaret Flaherty.

SHAWN KEOGH (*a fat and fair young man,*

comes in as she signs, looks round awkwardly, when he sees she is alone): Where's himself?

PEGEEN *(without looking at him):* He's coming. *(She directs the letter)* To Mister Sheamus Mulroy, Wine and Spirit Dealer, Castlebar.

SHAWN *(uneasily):* I didn't see him on the road.

PEGEEN: How would you see him *(licks stamp and puts it on letter)* and it dark night this half hour gone by?

SHAWN *(turning towards the door again):* I stood a while outside wondering would I have a right to pass on or to walk in and see you, Pegeen Mike *(comes to fire),* and I could hear the cows breathing, and sighing in the stillness of the air, and not a step moving any place from this gate to the bridge.

PEGEEN *(putting letter in envelope):* It's above at the cross-roads he is, meeting Philly Cullen; and a couple more are going along with him to Kate Cassidy's wake.

SHAWN *(looking at her blankly):* And he's going that length in the dark night?

PEGEEN *(impatiently):* He is surely, and leaving me lonesome on the scruff of the hill. *(She gets up and puts envelope on dresser, then winds clock.)* Isn't it long the nights are now, Shawn Keogh, to be leaving a poor girl with her own self counting the hours to the dawn of day?

SHAWN *(with awkward humor):* If it is, when we're wedded in a short while you'll have no call to complain, for I've little will to be walking off to wakes or weddings in the darkness of the night.

PEGEEN *(with rather scornful good humor):* You're making mighty certain, Shaneen, that I'll wed you now.

SHAWN: Aren't we after making a good bargain, the way we're only waiting these days on Father Reilly's dispensation from the bishops, or the Court of Rome.

PEGEEN *(looking at him teasingly, washing up at dresser):* It's a wonder, Shaneen, the Holy Father'd be taking notice of the likes of you; for if I was him I wouldn't bother with this place where you'll meet none but Red Linahan, has a squint in his eye, and Patcheen is lame in his heel, or the mad Mulrannies were driven from California and they lost in their wits. We're a queer lot these times to go troubling the Holy Father on his sacred seat.

SHAWN *(scandalized):* If we are, we're as good this place as another, maybe, and as good these times as we were for ever.

PEGEEN *(with scorn):* As good, is it? Where now will you meet the like of Daneen Sullivan knocked the eye from a peeler, or Marcus Quin, God rest him, got six months for maiming ewes, and he a great warrant to tell stories of holy Ireland till he'd have the old women shedding down tears about their feet. Where will you find the like of them, I'm saying?

SHAWN *(timidly):* If you don't, it's a good job, maybe; for *(with peculiar emphasis on the words)* Father Reilly has small conceit to have that kind walking around and talking to the girls.

PEGEEN *(impatiently, throwing water from basin out of the door):* Stop tormenting me with Father Reilly *(imitating his voice)* when I'm asking only what way I'll pass these twelve hours of dark, and not take my death with the fear. *(Looking out of door.)*

SHAWN *(timidly):* Would I fetch you the Widow Quin, maybe?

PEGEEN: Is it the like of that murderer? You'll not, surely.

SHAWN *(going to her, soothingly):* Then I'm thinking himself will stop along with you when he sees you taking on, for it'll be a long night-time with great darkness, and I'm after feeling a kind of fellow above in the furzy ditch, groaning wicked like a maddening dog, the way it's good cause you have, maybe, to be fearing now.

PEGEEN *(turning on him sharply):* What's that? Is it a man you seen?

SHAWN *(retreating):* I couldn't see him at all; but I heard him groaning out, and breaking his heart. It should have been a young man from his words speaking.

PEGEEN *(going after him):* And you never went near to see was he hurted or what ailed him at all?

SHAWN: I did not, Pegeen Mike. It was a dark, lonesome place to be hearing the like of him.

PEGEEN: Well, you're a daring fellow, and

if they find his corpse stretched above in the dews of dawn, what'll you say then to the peelers, or the Justice of the Peace?

SHAWN (*thunderstruck*): I wasn't thinking of that. For the love of God, Pegeen Mike, don't let on I was speaking of him. Don't tell your father and the men is coming above; for if they heard that story, they'd have great blabbing this night at the wake.

PEGEEN: I'll maybe tell them, and I'll maybe not.

SHAWN: They are coming at the door. Will you whisht, I'm saying?

PEGEEN: Whisht yourself.

(*She goes behind counter.* MICHAEL JAMES, *fat jovial publican, comes in followed by* PHILLY CULLEN, *who is thin and mistrusting, and* JIMMY FARRELL, *who is fat and amorous, about forty-five.*)

MEN (*together*): God bless you. The blessing of God on this place.

PEGEEN: God bless you kindly.

MICHAEL (*to men who go to the counter*): Sit down now, and take your rest. (*Crosses to* SHAWN *at the fire*) And how is it you are, Shawn Keogh? Are you coming over the sands to Kate Cassidy's wake?

SHAWN: I am not, Michael James. I'm going home the short cut to my bed.

PEGEEN (*speaking across the counter*): He's right too, and have you no shame, Michael James, to be quitting off for the whole night, and leaving myself lonesome in the shop?

MICHAEL (*good-humoredly*): Isn't it the same whether I go for the whole night or a part only? and I'm thinking it's a queer daughter you are if you'd have me crossing backward through the Stooks of the Dead Women, with a drop taken.

PEGEEN: If I am a queer daughter, it's a queer father'd be leaving me lonesome these twelve hours of dark, and I piling the turf with the dogs barking, and the calves mooing, and my own teeth rattling with the fear.

JIMMY (*flatteringly*): What is there to hurt you, and you a fine, hardy girl would knock the head of any two men in the place?

PEGEEN (*working herself up*): Isn't there the harvest boys with their tongues red for drink, and the ten tinkers is camped in the east glen, and the thousand militia—bad cess to them!—walking idle through the land. There's lots surely to hurt me, and I won't stop alone in it, let himself do what he will.

MICHAEL: If you're that afeard, let Shawn Keogh stop along with you. It's the will of God, I'm thinking, himself should be seeing to you now.

(*They all turn on* SHAWN.)

SHAWN (*in horrified confusion*): I would and welcome, Michael James, but I'm afeard of Father Reilly; and what at all would the Holy Father and the Cardinals of Rome be saying if they heard I did the like of that?

MICHAEL (*with contempt*): God help you! Can't you sit in by the hearth with the light lit and herself beyond in the room? You'll do that surely, for I've heard tell there's a queer fellow above, going mad or getting his death, maybe, in the gripe of the ditch, so she'd be safer this night with a person here.

SHAWN (*with plaintive despair*): I'm afeard of Father Reilly, I'm saying. Let you not be tempting me, and we near married itself.

PHILLY (*with cold contempt*): Lock him in the west room. He'll stay then and have no sin to be telling to the priest.

MICHAEL (*to* SHAWN, *getting between him and the door*): Go up now.

SHAWN (*at the top of his voice*): Don't stop me, Michael James. Let me out of the door, I'm saying, for the love of the Almighty God. Let me out. (*Trying to dodge past him*) Let me out of it, and may God grant you His indulgence in the hour of need.

MICHAEL (*loudly*): Stop your noising, and sit down by the hearth. (*Gives him a push and goes to counter laughing.*)

SHAWN (*turning back, wringing his hands*): Oh, Father Reilly and the saints of God, where will I hide myself to-day? Oh, St. Joseph and St. Patrick and St. Brigid, and St. James, have mercy on me now!

(SHAWN *turns round, sees door clear, and makes a rush for it.*)

MICHAEL (*catching him by the coat tail*): You'd be going, is it?

SHAWN (*screaming*): Leave me go, Michael James, leave me go, you old Pagan, leave me go, or I'll get the curse of the priests on you,

and of the scarlet-coated bishops of the courts
of Rome.

*(With a sudden movement he pulls himself
out of his coat, and disappears out of the door,
leaving his coat in* MICHAEL'*s hands.)*

MICHAEL *(turning round, and holding up
coat):* Well, there's the coat of a Christian
man. Oh, there's sainted glory this day in the
lonesome west; and by the will of God I've
got you a decent man, Pegeen, you'll have no
call to be spying after if you've a score of
young girls, maybe, weeding in your fields.

PEGEEN *(taking up the defence of her property):* What right have you to be making game
of a poor fellow for minding the priest, when
it's your own the fault is, not paying a penny
pot-boy to stand along with me and give me
courage in the doing of my work? *(She snaps
the coat away from him, and goes behind
counter with it.)*

MICHAEL *(taken aback):* Where would I get
a pot-boy? Would you have me send the bellman screaming in the streets of Castlebar?

SHAWN *(opening the door a chink and putting in his head, in a small voice):* Michael
James!

MICHAEL *(imitating him):* What ails you?

SHAWN: The queer dying fellow's beyond
looking over the ditch. He's come up, I'm
thinking, stealing your hens. *(Looks over his
shoulder)* God help me, he's following me now
(he runs into room), and if he's heard what I
said, he'll be having my life, and I going home
lonesome in the darkness of the night.

*(For a perceptible moment they watch the
door with curiosity. Some one coughs outside.
Then* CHRISTY MAHON, *a slight young man,
comes in very tired and frightened and dirty.)*

CHRISTY *(in a small voice):* God save all
here!

MEN: God save you kindly.

CHRISTY *(going to the counter):* I'd trouble
you for a glass of porter, woman of the house.
(He puts down coin.)

PEGEEN *(serving him):* You're one of the
tinkers, young fellow, is beyond camped in the
glen?

CHRISTY: I am not; but I'm destroyed walking.

MICHAEL *(patronizingly):* Let you come up

then to the fire. You're looking famished with
the cold.

CHRISTY: God reward you. *(He takes up his
glass and goes a little way across to the left,
then stops and looks about him.)* Is it often
the police do be coming into this place, master
of the house?

MICHAEL: If you'd come in better hours,
you'd have seen "Licensed for the sale of Beer
and Spirits, to be consumed on the premises,"
written in white letters above the door, and
what would the polis want spying on me, and
not a decent house within four miles, the way
every living Christian is a bona fide, saving
one widow alone?

CHRISTY *(with relief):* It's a safe house, so.

*(He goes over to the fire, sighing and moan-
ing. Then he sits down, putting his glass beside
him and begins gnawing a turnip, too miserable to feel the others staring at him with
curiosity.)*

MICHAEL *(going after him):* Is it yourself is
fearing the polis? You're wanting, maybe?

CHRISTY: There's many wanting.

MICHAEL: Many surely, with the broken
harvest and the ended wars. *(He picks up
some stockings, etc., that are near the fire,
and carries them away furtively.)* It should be
larceny, I'm thinking?

CHRISTY *(dolefully):* I had it in my mind
it was a different word and a bigger.

PEGEEN: There's a queer lad. Were you
never slapped in school, young fellow, that
you don't know the name of your deed?

CHRISTY *(bashfully):* I'm slow at learning, a
middling scholar only.

MICHAEL: If you're a dunce itself, you'd
have a right to know that larceny's robbing
and stealing. Is it for the like of that you're
wanting?

CHRISTY *(with a flash of family pride):* And
I the son of a strong farmer *(with a sudden
qualm),* God rest his soul, could have bought
up the whole of your old house a while since,
from the butt of his tailpocket, and not have
missed the weight of it gone.

MICHAEL *(impressed):* If it's not stealing,
it's maybe something big.

CHRISTY *(flattered):* Aye, it's maybe something big.

JIMMY: He's a wicked-looking young fellow. Maybe he followed after a young woman on a lonesome night.

CHRISTY (shocked): Oh, the saints forbid, mister; I was all times a decent lad.

PHILLY (turning on JIMMY): You're a silly man, Jimmy Farrell. He said his father was a farmer a while since, and there's himself now in a poor state. Maybe the land was grabbed from him, and he did what any decent man would do.

MICHAEL (to CHRISTY, mysteriously): Was it bailiffs?

CHRISTY: The divil a one.

MICHAEL: Agents?

CHRISTY: The divil a one.

MICHAEL: Landlords?

CHRISTY (peevishly): Ah, not at all, I'm saying. You'd see the like of them stories on any little paper of a Munster town. But I'm not calling to mind any person, gentle, simple, judge or jury, did the like of me.

(They all draw nearer with delighted curiosity.)

PHILLY: Well, that lad's a puzzle-the-world.

JIMMY: He'd beat Dan Davies' circus, or the holy missioners making sermons on the villainy of man. Try him again, Philly.

PHILLY: Did you strike golden guineas out of solder, young fellow, or shilling coins itself?

CHRISTY: I did not, mister, not sixpence nor a farthing coin.

JIMMY: Did you marry three wives maybe? I'm told there's a sprinkling have done that among the holy Luthers of the preaching north.

CHRISTY (shyly): I never married with one, let alone with a couple or three.

PHILLY: Maybe he went fighting for the Boers, the like of the man beyond, was judged to be hanged, quartered and drawn. Were you off east, young fellow, fighting bloody wars for Kruger and the freedom of the Boers?

CHRISTY: I never left my own parish till Tuesday was a week.

PEGEEN (coming from counter): He's done nothing, so. (To CHRISTY) If you didn't commit murder or a bad, nasty thing, or false coining, or robbery, or butchery, or the like of them, there isn't anything that would be worth your troubling for to run from now. You did nothing at all.

CHRISTY (his feelings hurt): That's an unkindly thing to be saying to a poor orphaned traveller, has a prison behind him, and hanging before, and hell's gap gaping below.

PEGEEN (with a sign to the men to be quiet): You're only saying it. You did nothing at all. A soft lad the like of you wouldn't slit the windpipe of a screeching sow.

CHRISTY (offended): You're not speaking the truth.

PEGEEN (in mock rage): Not speaking the truth, is it? Would you have me knock the head of you with the butt of the broom?

CHRISTY (twisting round on her with a sharp cry of horror): Don't strike me. I killed my poor father, Tuesday was a week, for doing the like of that.

PEGEEN (with black amazement): Is it killed your father?

CHRISTY (subsiding): With the help of God I did surely, and that the Holy Immaculate Mother may intercede for his soul.

PHILLY (retreating with JIMMY): There's a daring fellow.

JIMMY: Oh, glory be to God!

MICHAEL (with great respect): That was a hanging crime, mister honey. You should have had good reason for doing the like of that.

CHRISTY (in a very reasonable tone): He was a dirty man, God forgive him, and he getting old and crusty, the way I couldn't put up with him at all.

PEGEEN: And you shot him dead?

CHRISTY (shaking his head): I never used weapons. I've no license, and I'm a law-fearing man.

MICHAEL: It was with a hilted knife maybe? I'm told, in the big world it's bloody knives they use.

CHRISTY (loudly, scandalized): Do you take me for a slaughter-boy?

PEGEEN: You never hanged him, the way Jimmy Farrell hanged his dog from the license, and had it screeching and wriggling three hours at the butt of a string, and himself swearing it was a dead dog, and the peelers swearing it had life?

CHRISTY: I did not then. I just riz the loy

and let fall the edge of it on the ridge of his skull, and he went down at my feet like an empty sack, and never let a grunt or groan from him at all.

MICHAEL (*making a sign to* PEGEEN *to fill* CHRISTY'*s glass*): And what way weren't you hanged, mister? Did you bury him then?

CHRISTY (*considering*): Aye. I buried him then. Wasn't I digging spuds in the field?

MICHAEL: And the peelers never followed after you the eleven days that you're out?

CHRISTY (*shaking his head*): Never a one of them, and I walking forward facing hog, dog, or divil on the highway of the road.

PHILLY (*nodding wisely*): It's only with a common week-day kind of a murderer them lads would be trusting their carcase, and that man should be a great terror when his temper's roused.

MICHAEL: He should then. (*To* CHRISTY): And where was it, mister honey, that you did the deed?

CHRISTY (*looking at him with suspicion*): Oh, a distant place, master of the house, a windy corner of high, distant hills.

PHILLY (*nodding with approval*): He's a close man, and he's right, surely.

PEGEEN: That'd be a lad with a sense of Solomon to have for a pot-boy, Michael James, if it's the truth you're seeking one at all.

PHILLY: The peelers is fearing him, and if you'd that lad in the house there isn't one of them would come smelling around if the dogs itself were lapping poteen from the dung-pit of the yard.

JIMMY: Bravery's a treasure in a lonesome place, and a lad would kill his father, I'm thinking, would face a foxy divil with a pitch-pike on the flags of hell.

PEGEEN: It's the truth they're saying, and if I'd that lad in the house, I wouldn't be fearing the looséd kharki cut-throats, or the walking dead.

CHRISTY (*swelling with surprise and triumph*): Well, glory be to God!

MICHAEL (*with deference*): Would you think well to stop here and be pot-boy, mister honey, if we gave you good wages, and didn't destroy you with the weight of work?

SHAWN (*coming forward uneasily*): That'd be a queer kind to bring into a decent quiet household with the like of Pegeen Mike.

PEGEEN (*very sharply*): Will you whisht? Who's speaking to you?

SHAWN (*retreating*): A bloody-handed murderer the like of . . .

PEGEEN (*snapping at him*): Whisht I am saying: we'll take no fooling from your like at all. (*To* CHRISTY *with a honeyed voice*) And you, young fellow, you'd have a right to stop, I'm thinking, for we'd do our all and utmost to content your needs.

CHRISTY (*overcome with wonder*): And I'd be safe in this place from the searching law?

MICHAEL: You would, surely. If they're not fearing you, itself, the peelers in this place is decent droughty poor fellows, wouldn't touch a cur dog and not give warning in the dead of night.

PEGEEN (*very kindly and persuasively*): Let you stop a short while anyhow. Aren't you destroyed walking with your feet in bleeding blisters, and your whole skin needing washing like a Wicklow sheep.

CHRISTY (*looking round with satisfaction*): It's a nice room, and if it's not humbugging me you are, I'm thinking that I'll surely stay.

JIMMY (*jumps up*): Now, by the grace of God, herself will be safe this night, with a man killed his father holding danger from the door, and let you come on, Michael James, or they'll have the best stuff drunk at the wake.

MICHAEL (*going to the door with men*): And begging your pardon, mister, what name will we call you, for we'd like to know?

CHRISTY: Christopher Mahon.

MICHAEL: Well, God bless you, Christy, and a good rest till we meet again when the sun'll be rising to the noon of day.

CHRISTY: God bless you all.

MEN: God bless you.

(*They go out except* SHAWN, *who lingers at door.*)

SHAWN (*to* PEGEEN): Are you wanting me to stop along with you to keep you from harm?

PEGEEN (*gruffly*): Didn't you say you were fearing Father Reilly?

SHAWN: There'd be no harm staying now, I'm thinking, and himself in it too.

PEGEEN: You wouldn't stay when there was need for you, and let you step off nimble this time when there's none.

SHAWN: Didn't I say it was Father Reilly . . .

PEGEEN: Go on, then, to Father Reilly (in a jeering tone), and let him put you in the holy brotherhoods, and leave that lad to me.

SHAWN: If I meet the Widow Quin . . .

PEGEEN: Go on, I'm staying, and don't be waking this place with your noise. (She hustles him out and bolts the door.) That lad would wear the spirits from the saints of peace. (Bustles about, then takes off her apron and pins it up in the window as a blind. CHRISTY watching her timidly. Then she comes to him and speaks with bland good humor.) Let you stretch out now by the fire, young fellow. You should be destroyed travelling.

CHRISTY (shyly again, drawing off his boots): I'm tired, surely, walking wild eleven days, and waking fearful in the night. (He holds up one of his feet, feeling his blisters, and looking at them with compassion.)

PEGEEN (standing beside him, watching him with delight): You should have had great people in your family, I'm thinking, with the little, small feet you have, and you with a kind of a quality name, the like of what you'd find on the great powers and potentates of France and Spain.

CHRISTY (with pride): We were great surely, with wide and windy acres of rich Munster land.

PEGEEN: Wasn't I telling you, and you a fine, handsome young fellow with a noble brow?

CHRISTY (with a flash of delighted surprise): Is it me?

PEGEEN: Aye. Did you never hear that from the young girls where you come from in the west or south?

CHRISTY (with venom): I did not then. Oh, they're bloody liars in the naked parish where I grew a man.

PEGEEN: If they are itself, you've heard it these days, I'm thinking, and you walking the world telling out your story to young girls or old.

CHRISTY: I've told my story no place till this night, Pegeen Mike, and it's foolish I was here, maybe, to be talking free, but you're decent people, I'm thinking, and yourself a kindly woman, the way I wasn't fearing you at all.

PEGEEN (filling a sack with straw): You've said the like of that, maybe, in every cot and cabin where you've met a young girl on your way.

CHRISTY (going over to her, gradually raising his voice): I've said it nowhere till this night, I'm telling you, for I've seen none the like of you the eleven long days I am walking the world, looking over a low ditch or a high ditch on my north or my south, into stony scattered fields, or scribes of bog, where you'd see young, limber girls, and fine prancing women making laughter with the men.

PEGEEN: If you weren't destroyed travelling, you'd have as much talk and streeleen, I'm thinking, as Owen Roe O'Sullivan or the poets of the Dingle Bay, and I've heard all times it's the poets are your like, fine fiery fellows with great rages when their temper's roused.

CHRISTY (drawing a little nearer to her): You've a power of rings, God bless you, and would there be any offense if I was asking are you single now?

PEGEEN: What would I want wedding so young?

CHRISTY (with relief): We're alike, so.

PEGEEN (She puts sack on settle and beats it up.): I never killed my father. I'd be afeard to do that, except I was the like of yourself with blind rages tearing me within, for I'm thinking you should have had great tussling when the end was come.

CHRISTY (expanding with delight at the first confidential talk he has ever had with a woman): We had not then. It was a hard woman was come over the hill, and if he was always a crusty kind when he'd a hard woman setting him on, not the divil himself or his four fathers could put up with him at all.

PEGEEN (with curiosity): And isn't it a great wonder that one wasn't fearing you?

CHRISTY (very confidentially): Up to the day I killed my father, there wasn't a person in Ireland knew the kind I was, and I there drinking, waking, eating, sleeping, a quiet, simple poor fellow with no man giving me heed.

PEGEEN *(getting a quilt out of the cupboard and putting it on the sack)*: It was the girls were giving you heed maybe, and I'm thinking it's most conceit you'd have to be gaming with their like.

CHRISTY *(shaking his head, with simplicity)*: Not the girls itself, and I won't tell you a lie. There wasn't anyone heeding me in that place saving only the dumb beasts of the field. *(He sits down at fire.)*

PEGEEN *(with disappointment)*: And I thinking you should have been living the like of a king of Norway or the Eastern world. *(She comes and sits beside him after placing bread and mug of milk on the table.)*

CHRISTY *(laughing piteously)*: The like of a king, is it? And I after toiling, moiling, digging, dodging from the dawn till dusk with never a sight of joy or sport saving only when I'd be abroad in the dark night poaching rabbits on hills, for I was a devil to poach, God forgive me, *(very naïvely)* and I near got six months for going with a dung fork and stabbing a fish.

PEGEEN: And it's that you'd call sport, is it, to be abroad in the darkness with yourself alone?

CHRISTY: I did, God help me, and there I'd be as happy as the sunshine of St. Martin's Day, watching the light passing the north or the patches of fog, till I'd hear a rabbit starting to screech and I'd go running in the furze. Then when I'd my full share I'd come walking down where you'd see the ducks and geese stretched sleeping on the highway of the road, and before I'd pass the dunghill, I'd hear himself snoring out, a loud lonesome snore he'd be making all times, the while he was sleeping, and he a man 'd be raging all times, the while he was waking, like a gaudy officer you'd hear cursing and damning and swearing oaths.

PEGEEN: Providence and Mercy, spare us all!

CHRISTY: It's that you'd say surely if you seen him and he after drinking for weeks, rising up in the red dawn, or before it maybe, and going out into the yard as naked as an ash tree in the moon of May, and shying clods against the visage of the stars till he'd put the fear of death into the banbhs and the screeching sows.

PEGEEN: I'd be well-nigh afeard of that lad myself, I'm thinking. And there was no one in it but the two of you alone?

CHRISTY: The divil a one, though he'd sons and daughters walking all great states and territories of the world, and not a one of them, to this day, but would say their seven curses on him, and they rousing up to let a cough or sneeze, maybe, in the deadness of the night.

PEGEEN *(nodding her head)*: Well, you should have been a queer lot. I never cursed my father the like of that, though I'm twenty and more years of age.

CHRISTY: Then you'd have cursed mine, I'm telling you, and he a man never gave peace to any, saving when he'd get two months or three, or be locked in the asylums for battering peelers or assaulting men *(with depression)* the way it was a bitter life he led me till I did up a Tuesday and halve his skull.

PEGEEN *(putting her hand on his shoulder)*: Well, you'll have peace in this place, Christy Mahon, and none to trouble you, and it's near time a fine lad like you should have your good share of the earth.

CHRISTY: It's time surely, and I a seemly fellow with great strength in me and bravery of . . .

(Someone knocks.)

CHRISTY *(clinging to PEGEEN)*: Oh, glory! it's late for knocking, and this last while I'm in terror of the peelers, and the walking dead.

(Knocking again.)

PEGEEN: Who's there?

VOICE *(outside)*: Me.

PEGEEN: Who's me?

VOICE: The Widow Quin.

PEGEEN *(jumping up and giving him the bread and milk)*: Go on now with your supper, and let on to be sleepy, for if she found you were such a warrant to talk, she'd be stringing gabble till the dawn of day.

(He takes bread and sits shyly with his back to the door.)

PEGEEN *(opening door, with temper)*: What ails you, or what is it you're wanting at this hour of the night?

WIDOW QUIN (*coming in a step and peering at* CHRISTY): I'm after meeting Shawn Keogh and Father Reilly below, who told me of your curiosity man, and they fearing by this time he was maybe roaring, romping on your hands with drink.

PEGEEN (*pointing to* CHRISTY): Look now is he roaring, and he stretched away drowsy with his supper and his mug of milk. Walk down and tell that to Father Reilly and to Shaneen Keogh.

WIDOW QUIN (*coming forward*): I'll not see them again, for I've their word to lead that lad forward for to lodge with me.

PEGEEN (*in blank amazement*): This night, is it?

WIDOW QUIN (*going over*): This night. "It isn't fitting," says the priesteen, "to have his likeness lodging with an orphaned girl." (*To* CHRISTY) God save you, mister!

CHRISTY (*shyly*): God save you kindly.

WIDOW QUIN (*looking at him with half-amazed curiosity*): Well, aren't you a little smiling fellow? It should have been great and bitter torments did arouse your spirits to a deed of blood.

CHRISTY (*doubtfully*): It should, maybe.

WIDOW QUIN: It's more than "maybe" I'm saying, and it'd soften my heart to see you sitting so simple with your cup and cake, and you fitter to be saying your catechism than slaying your da.

PEGEEN (*at counter, washing glasses*): There's talking when any'd see he's fit to be holding his head high with the wonders of the world. Walk on from this, for I'll not have him tormented and he destroyed travelling since Tuesday was a week.

WIDOW QUIN (*peaceably*): We'll be walking surely when his supper's done, and you'll find we're great company, young fellow, when it's of the like of you and me you'd hear the penny poets singing in an August Fair.

CHRISTY (*innocently*): Did you kill your father?

PEGEEN (*contemptuously*): She did not. She hit himself with a worn pick, and the rusted poison did corrode his blood the way he never overed it, and died after. That was a sneaky kind of murder did win small glory with the boys itself. (*She crosses to* CHRISTY'S *left.*)

WIDOW QUIN (*with good humor*): If it didn't, maybe all knows a widow woman has buried her children and destroyed her man is a wiser comrade for a young lad than a girl, the like of you, who'd go helter-skeltering after any man would let you a wink upon the road.

PEGEEN (*breaking out into wild rage*): And you'll say that, Widow Quin, and you gasping with the rage you had racing the hill beyond to look on his face.

WIDOW QUIN (*laughing derisively*): Me, is it? Well, Father Reilly has cuteness to divide you now. (*She pulls* CHRISTY *up.*) There's great temptation in a man did slay his da, and we'd best be going, young fellow; so rise up and come with me.

PEGEEN (*seizing his arm*): He'll not stir. He's pot-boy in this place, and I'll not have him stolen off and kidnabbed while himself's abroad.

WIDOW QUIN: It'd be a crazy pot-boy'd lodge him in the shebeen where he works by day, so you'd have a right to come on, young fellow, till you see my little houseen, a perch off on the rising hill.

PEGEEN: Wait till morning, Christy Mahon. Wait till you lay eyes on her leaky thatch is growing more pasture for her buck goat than her square of fields, and she without a tramp itself to keep in order her place at all.

WIDOW QUIN: When you see me contriving in my little gardens, Christy Mahon, you'll swear the Lord God formed me to be living lone, and that there isn't my match in Mayo for thatching, or mowing, or shearing a sheep.

PEGEEN (*with noisy scorn*): It's true the Lord God formed you to contrive indeed. Doesn't the world know you reared a black lamb at your own breast, so that the Lord Bishop of Connaught felt the elements of a Christian, and he eating it after in a kidney stew? Doesn't the world know you've been seen shaving the foxy skipper from France for a threepenny bit and a sop of grass tobacco would wring the liver from a mountain goat you'd meet leaping the hills?

WIDOW QUIN (*with amusement*): Do you hear her now young fellow? Do you hear the way she'll be rating at your own self when a week is by?

PEGEEN (to CHRISTY): Don't heed her. Tell her to go into her pigsty and not plague us here.

WIDOW QUIN: I'm going; but he'll come with me.

PEGEEN (shaking him): Are you dumb, young fellow?

CHRISTY (timidly, to WIDOW QUIN): God increase you; but I'm pot-boy in this place, and it's here I'd liefer stay.

PEGEEN (triumphantly): Now you have heard him, and go on from this.

WIDOW QUIN (looking round the room): It's lonesome this hour crossing the hill, and if he won't come along with me, I'd have a right maybe to stop this night with yourselves. Let me stretch out on the settle, Pegeen Mike; and himself can lie by the hearth.

PEGEEN (short and fiercely): Faith, I won't. Quit off or I will send you now.

WIDOW QUIN (gathering her shawl up): Well, it's a terror to be aged a score. (To CHRISTY) God bless you now, young fellow, and let you be wary, or there's right torment will await you here if you go romancing with her like, and she waiting only, as they bade me say, on a sheepskin parchment to be wed with Shawn Keogh of Killakeen.

CHRISTY (going to PEGEEN as she bolts the door): What's that she's after saying?

PEGEEN: Lies and blather, you've no call to mind. Well, isn't Shawn Keogh an impudent fellow to send up spying on me? Wait till I lay hands on him. Let him wait, I'm saying.

CHRISTY: And you're not wedding him at all?

PEGEEN: I wouldn't wed him if a bishop came walking for to join us here.

CHRISTY: That God in glory may be thanked for that.

PEGEEN: There's your bed now. I've put a quilt upon you I'm after quilting a while since with my own two hands, and you'd best stretch out now for your sleep, and may God give you a good rest till I call you in the morning when the cocks will crow.

CHRISTY (as she goes to inner room): May God and Mary and St. Patrick bless you and

reward you, for your kindly talk. (She shuts the door behind her. He settles his bed slowly, feeling the quilt with immense satisfaction.) Well, it's a clean bed and soft with it, and it's great luck and company I've won me in the end of time—two fine women fighting for the likes of me—till I'm thinking this night wasn't I a foolish fellow not to kill my father in the years gone by.

ACT TWO

SCENE

As before. Brilliant morning light. CHRISTY, looking bright and cheerful, is cleaning a girl's boots.

CHRISTY (to himself, counting jugs on dresser): Half a hundred beyond. Ten there. A score that's above. Eighty jugs. Six cups and a broken one. Two plates. A power of glasses. Bottles, a school-master'd be hard set to count, and enough in them. I'm thinking, to drunken all the wealth and wisdom of the County Clare. (He puts down the boot carefully.) There's her boots now, nice and decent for her evening use, and isn't it grand brushes she has? (He puts them down and goes by degrees to the looking-glass.) Well, this'd be a fine place to be my whole life talking out with swearing Christians, in place of my old dogs and cat, and I stalking around, smoking my pipe and drinking my fill, and never a day's work but drawing a cork an odd time, or wiping a glass, or rinsing out a shiny tumbler for a decent man. (He takes the looking-glass from the wall and puts it on the back of a chair; then sits down in front of it and begins washing his face.) Didn't I know rightly I was handsome, though it was the divil's own mirror we had beyond, would twist a squint across an angel's brow; and I'll be growing fine from this day, the way I'll have a soft lovely skin on me and won't be the like of the clumsy young fellows do be ploughing all times in the earth and dung. (He starts.) Is she coming again? (He looks out.) Stranger girls. God help me, where'll I hide myself away and my long neck naked to the world?

(He looks out.) I'd best go to the room maybe till I'm dressed again. *(He gathers up his coat and the looking-glass, and runs into the inner room. The door is pushed open, and* SUSAN BRADY *looks in, and knocks on door.)*

SUSAN: There's nobody in it. *(Knocks again.)*

NELLY *(pushing her in and following her, with* HONOR BLAKE *and* SARA TANSEY*):* It'd be early for them both to be out walking the hill.

SUSAN: I'm thinking Shawn Keogh was making game of us and there's no such man in it at all.

HONOR *(pointing to straw and quilt):* Look at that. He's been sleeping there in the night. Well, it'll be a hard case if he's gone off now, the way we'll never set our eyes on a man killed his father, and we after rising early and destroying ourselves running fast on the hill.

NELLY: Are you thinking them's his boots?

SARA *(taking them up):* If they are, there should be his father's track on them. Did you never read in the papers the way murdered men do bleed and drip?

SUSAN: Is that blood there, Sara Tansey?

SARA *(smelling it):* That's bog water, I'm thinking, but it's his own they are surely, for I never seen the like of them for whity mud, and red mud, and turf on them, and the fine sands of the sea. That man's been walking, I'm telling you. *(She goes down right, putting on one of his boots.)*

SUSAN *(going to window):* Maybe he's stolen off to Belmullet with the boots of Michael James, and you'd have a right so to follow after him, Sara Tansey, and you the one yoked the ass cart and drove ten miles to set your eyes on the man bit the yellow lady's nostril on the northern shore. *(She looks out.)*

SARA *(running to window with one boot on):* Don't be talking, and we fooled today *(putting on other boot.)* There's a pair do fit me well, and I'll be keeping them for walking to the priest, when you'd be ashamed this place, going up winter and summer with nothing worth while to confess at all.

HONOR *(who has been listening at the door):* Whisht! there's someone inside the room. *(She pushes door a chink open.)* It's a man.

*(*SARA *kicks off boots and puts them where*

they were. They all stand in a line looking through chink.)*

SARA: I'll call him. Mister! Mister! *(He puts in his head.)* Is Pegeen within?

CHRISTY *(coming in as meek as a mouse, with the looking-glass held behind his back):* She's above on the cnuceen, seeking the nanny goats, the way she'd have a sup of goat's milk for to color my tea.

SARA: And asking your pardon, is it you's the man killed his father?

CHRISTY *(sidling toward the nail where the glass was hanging):* I am, God help me!

SARA *(taking eggs she has brought):* Then my thousand welcomes to you, and I've run up with a brace of duck's eggs for your food today. Pegeen's ducks is no use, but these are the real rich sort. Hold out your hand and you'll see it's no lie I'm telling you.

CHRISTY *(coming forward shyly, and holding out his left hand):* They're a great and weighty size.

SUSAN: And I run up with a pat of butter, for it'd be a poor thing to have you eating your spuds dry, and you after running a great way since you did destroy your da.

CHRISTY: Thank you kindly.

HONOR: And I brought you a little cut of cake, for you should have a thin stomach on you, and you that length walking the world.

NELLY: And I brought you a little laying pullet—boiled and all she is—was crushed at the fall of night by the curate's car. Feel the fat of that breast, mister.

CHRISTY: It's bursting, surely. *(He feels it with the back of his hand, in which he holds the presents.)*

SARA: Will you pinch it? Is your right hand too sacred for to use at all? *(She slips round behind him.)* It's a glass he has. Well, I never seen to this day a man with a looking-glass held to his back. Them that kills their fathers is a vain lot surely.

(Girls giggle.)

CHRISTY *(smiling innocently and piling presents on glass):* I'm very thankful to you all today. . . .

WIDOW QUIN *(coming in quickly, at door):* Sara Tansey, Susan Brady, Honor Blake!

What in glory has you here at this hour of day?

GIRLS (*giggling*): That's the man killed his father.

WIDOW QUIN (*coming to them*): I know well it's the man; and I'm after putting him down in the sports below for racing, leaping, pitching, and the Lord knows what.

SARA (*exuberantly*): That's right, Widow Quin. I'll bet my dowry that he'll lick the world.

WIDOW QUIN: If you will, you'd have a right to have him fresh and nourished in place of, nursing a feast. (*Taking presents.*) Are you fasting or fed, young fellow?

CHRISTY: Fasting, if you please.

WIDOW QUIN (*loudly*): Well, you're the lot. Stir up now and give him his breakfast. (*To* CHRISTY) Come here to me (*she puts him on bench beside her while the girls make tea and get his breakfast*) and let you tell us your story before Pegeen will come, in place of grinning your ears off like the moon of May.

CHRISTY (*beginning to be pleased*): It's a long story; you'd be destroyed listening.

WIDOW QUIN: Don't be letting on to be shy, a fine, gamey, treacherous lad the like of you. Was it in your house beyond you cracked his skull?

CHRISTY (*shy but flattered*): It was not. We were digging spuds in his cold, sloping stony, divil's patch of a field.

WIDOW QUIN: And you went asking money of him, or making talk of getting a wife would drive him from his farm?

CHRISTY: I did not, then; but there I was, digging and digging, and "You squinting idiot," says he, "let you walk down now and tell the priest you'll wed the Widow Casey in a score of days."

WIDOW QUIN: And what kind was she?

CHRISTY (*with horror*): A walking terror from beyond the hills, and she two score and two hundredweights and five pounds in the weighing scales, with a limping leg on her, and a blinded eye, and she a woman of noted misbehavior with the old and young.

GIRLS (*clustering round him, serving him*): Glory be.

WIDOW QUIN: And what did he want driving you to wed with her? (*She takes a bit of the chicken.*)

CHRISTY (*eating with growing satisfaction*): He was letting on I was wanting a protector from the harshness of the world, and he without a thought the whole while but how he'd have her hut to live in and her gold to drink.

WIDOW QUIN: There's maybe worse than a dry hearth and a widow woman and your glass at night. So you hit him then?

CHRISTY (*getting almost excited*): I did not. "I won't wed her," says I, "when all know she did suckle me for six weeks when I came into the world, and she a hag this day with a tongue on her has the crows and seabirds scattered, the way they wouldn't cast a shadow on her garden with the dread of her curse."

WIDOW QUIN (*teasingly*): That one should be right company.

SARA (*eagerly*): Don't mind her. Did you kill him then?

CHRISTY: "She's too good for the like of you," says he, "and go on now or I'll flatten you out like a crawling beast has passed under a dray." "You will not if I can help it," says I. "Go on," says he, "or I'll have the divil making garters of your limbs tonight." "You will not if I can help it," says I. (*He sits up, brandishing his mug.*)

SARA: You were right surely.

CHRISTY (*impressively*): With that the sun came out between the cloud and the hill, and it shining green in my face. "God have mercy on your soul," says he, lifting a scythe; "or on your own," says I, raising the loy.

SUSAN: That's a grand story.

HONOR: He tells it lovely.

CHRISTY (*flattered and confident, waving bone*): He gave a drive with the scythe, and I gave a lep to the east. Then I turned around with my back to the north, and I hit a blow on the ridge of his skull, laid him stretched out, and he split to the knob of his gullet. (*He raises the chicken bone to his Adam's apple.*)

GIRLS (*together*): Well, you're a marvel! Oh, God bless you! You're the lad surely!

SUSAN: I'm thinking the Lord God sent him this road to make a second husband to the

Widow Quin, and she with a great yearning to be wedded, though all dread her here. Lift him on her knee, Sara Tansey.

WIDOW QUIN: Don't tease him.

SARA (*going over to dresser and counter very quickly, and getting two glasses and porter*): You're heroes surely, and let you drink a supeen with your arms linked like the outlandish lovers in the sailor's song. (*She links their arms and gives them the glasses.*) There now. Drink a health to the wonders of the western world, the pirates, preachers, poteen-makers, with the jobbing jockies; parching peelers, and the juries fill their stomachs selling judgments of the English law. (*Brandishing the bottle.*)

WIDOW QUIN: That's a right toast, Sara Tansey. Now Christy.

(*They drink with their arms linked, he drinking with his left hand, she with her right. As they are drinking,* PEGEEN MIKE *comes in with a milk can and stands aghast. They all spring away from* CHRISTY. *He goes down left.* WIDOW QUIN *remains seated.*)

PEGEEN (*angrily, to* SARA): What is it you're wanting?

SARA (*twisting her apron*): A ounce of tobacco.

PEGEEN: Have you tuppence?

SARA: I've forgotten my purse.

PEGEEN: Then you'd best be getting it and not fooling us here. (*To the* WIDOW QUIN, *with more elaborate scorn*) And what is it you're wanting, Widow Quin?

WIDOW QUIN (*insolently*): A penn'orth of starch.

PEGEEN (*breaking out*): And you without a white shift or a shirt in your whole family since the drying of the flood. I've no starch for the like of you, and let you walk on now to Killamuck.

WIDOW QUIN (*turning to* CHRISTY, *as she goes out with the girls*): Well, you're mighty huffy this day, Pegeen Mike, and, you young fellow, let you not forget the sports and racing when the noon is by.

(*They go out.*)

PEGEEN (*imperiously*): Fling out that rubbish and put them cups away. (CHRISTY *tidies away in great haste.*) Shove in the bench by the wall. (*He does so.*) And hang that glass on the nail. What disturbed it at all?

CHRISTY (*very meekly*): I was making myself decent only, and this a fine country for young lovely girls.

PEGEEN (*sharply*): Whisht your talking of girls. (*Goes to counter—right.*)

CHRISTY: Wouldn't any wish to be decent in a place . . .

PEGEEN: Whisht I'm saying.

CHRISTY (*Looks at her face for a moment with great misgivings, then as a last effort, takes up a loy, and goes towards her, with feigned assurance.*) It was with a loy the like of that I killed my father.

PEGEEN (*still sharply*): You've told me that story six times since the dawn of day.

CHRISTY (*reproachfully*): It's a queer thing you wouldn't care to be hearing it and them girls after walking four miles to be listening to me now.

PEGEEN (*turning round astonished*): Four miles.

CHRISTY (*apologetically*): Didn't himself say there were only four bona fides living in this place?

PEGEEN: It's bona fides by the road they are, but that lot came over the river lepping the stones. It's not three perches when you go like that, and I was down this morning looking on the papers the post-boy does have in his bag. (*With meaning and emphasis*) For there was great news this day, Christopher Mahon. (*She goes into room left.*)

CHRISTY (*suspiciously*): Is it news of my murder?

PEGEEN (*inside*): Murder, indeed.

CHRISTY (*loudly*): A murdered da?

PEGEEN (*coming in again and crossing right*): There was not, but a story filled half a page of the hanging of a man. Ah, that should be a fearful end, young fellow, and it worst of all for a man who destroyed his da, for the like of him would get small mercies, and when it's dead he is, they'd put him in a narrow grave, with cheap sacking wrapping him round, and pour down quicklime on his head, the way you'd see a woman pouring any frish-frash from a cup.

CHRISTY (*very miserably*): Oh, God help me. Are you thinking I'm safe? You were saying at the fall of night, I was shut of jeopardy and I here with yourselves.

PEGEEN (*severely*): You'll be shut of jeopardy no place if you go talking with a pack of wild girls the like of them do be walking abroad with the peelers, talking whispers at the fall of night.

CHRISTY (*with terror*): And you're thinking they'd tell?

PEGEEN (*with mock sympathy*): Who knows, God help you.

CHRISTY (*loudly*): What joy would they have to bring hanging to the likes of me?

PEGEEN: It's queer joys they have, and who knows the thing they'd do, if it'd make the green stones cry itself to think of you swaying and swiggling at the butt of a rope, and you with a fine, stout neck, God bless you! the way you'd be a half an hour, in great anguish, getting your death.

CHRISTY (*getting his boots and putting them on*): If there's that terror of them, it'd be best, maybe, I went on wandering like Esau or Cain and Abel on the sides of Neifin or the Erris plain.

PEGEEN (*beginning to play with him*): It would, maybe, for I've heard the Circuit Judges this place is a heartless crew.

CHRISTY (*bitterly*): It's more than Judges this place is a heartless crew. (*Looking up at her*) And isn't it a poor thing to be starting again and I a lonesome fellow will be looking out on women and girls the way the needy fallen spirits do be looking on the Lord?

PEGEEN: What call have you to be that lonesome when there's poor girls walking Mayo in their thousands now?

CHRISTY (*grimly*): It's well you know what call I have. It's well you know it's a lonesome thing to be passing small towns with the lights shining sideways when the night is down, or going in strange places with a dog noising before you and a dog noising behind, or drawn to the cities where you'd hear a voice kissing and talking deep love in every shadow of the ditch, and you passing on with an empty, hungry stomach failing from your heart.

PEGEEN: I'm thinking you're an odd man, Christy Mahon. The oddest walking fellow I ever set my eyes on to this hour today.

CHRISTY: What would any be but odd men and they living lonesome in the world?

PEGEEN: I'm not odd, and I'm my whole life with my father only.

CHRISTY (*with infinite admiration*): How would a lovely handsome woman the like of you be lonesome when all men should be thronging around to hear the sweetness of your voice, and the little infant children should be pestering your steps I'm thinking, and you walking the roads.

PEGEEN: I'm hard set to know what way a coaxing fellow the like of yourself should be lonesome either.

CHRISTY: Coaxing?

PEGEEN: Would you have me think a man never talked with the girls would have the words you've spoken today? It's only letting on you are to be lonesome, the way you'd get around me now.

CHRISTY: I wish to God I was letting on; but I was lonesome all times, and born lonesome, I'm thinking, as the moon of dawn. (*Going to door.*)

PEGEEN (*puzzled by his talk*): Well, it's a story I'm not understanding at all why you'd be worse than another, Christy Mahon, and you a fine lad with the great savagery to destroy your da.

CHRISTY: It's little I'm understanding myself, saving only that my heart's scalded this day, and I going off stretching out the earth between us, the way I'll not be waking near you another dawn of the year till the two of us do arise to hope or judgment with the saints of God, and now I'd best be going with my wattle in my hand, for hanging is a poor thing (*turning to go*), and it's little welcome only is left me in this house today.

PEGEEN (*sharply*): Christy! (*He turns round.*) Come here to me. (*He goes towards her.*) Lay down that switch and throw some sods on the fire. You're pot-boy in this place, and I'll not have you mitch off from us now.

CHRISTY: You were saying I'd be hanged if I stay.

PEGEEN (*quite kindly at last*): I'm after going down and reading the fearful crimes of Ireland for two weeks or three, and there wasn't a word of your murder. (*Getting up and going over to the counter*) They've likely not found the body. You're safe so with ourselves.

CHRISTY (*astonished, slowly*): It's making game of me you were (*following her with fearful joy*), and I can stay so, working at your side, and I not lonesome from this mortal day.

PEGEEN: What's to hinder you from staying, except the widow woman or the young girls would inveigle you off?

CHRISTY (*with rapture*): And I'll have your words from this day filling my ears, and that look is come upon you meeting my two eyes, and I watching you loafing around in the warm sun, or rinsing your ankles when the night is come.

PEGEEN (*kindly, but a little embarrassed*): I'm thinking you'll be a loyal young lad to have working around, and if you vexed me a while since with your leaguing with the girls, I wouldn't give a thraneen for a lad hadn't a mighty spirit in him and a gamey heart.

(SHAWN KEOGH *runs in carrying a cleeve on his back, followed by the* WIDOW QUIN.)

SHAWN (*to* PEGEEN): I was passing below, and I seen your mountainy sheep eating cabbages in Jimmy's field. Run up or they'll be bursting surely.

PEGEEN: Oh, God mend them! (*She puts a shawl over her head and runs out.*)

CHRISTY (*looking from one to the other. Still in high spirits*): I'd best go to her aid maybe. I'm handy with ewes.

WIDOW QUIN (*closing the door*): She can do that much, and there is Shaneen has long speeches for to tell you now. (*She sits down with an amused smile.*)

SHAWN (*taking something from his pocket and offering it to* CHRISTY): Do you see that, mister?

CHRISTY (*looking at it*): The half of a ticket to the Western States!

SHAWN (*trembling with anxiety*): I'll give it to you and my new hat (*pulling it out of hamper*); and my breeches with the double

seat (*pulling it off*); and my new coat is woven from the blackest shearings for three miles around (*giving him the coat*); I'll give you the whole of them, and my blessing, and the blessing of Father Reilly itself, maybe, if you'll quit from this and leave us in the peace we had till last night at the fall of dark.

CHRISTY (*with a new arrogance*): And for what is it you're wanting to get shut of me?

SHAWN (*looking to the* WIDOW *for help*): I'm a poor scholar with middling faculties to coin a lie, so I'll tell you the truth, Christy Mahon I'm wedding with Pegeen beyond, and I don't think well of having a clever fearless man the like of you dwelling in her house.

CHRISTY (*almost pugnaciously*): And you'd be using bribery for to banish me?

SHAWN (*in an imploring voice*): Let you not take it badly mister honey, isn't beyond the best place for you where you'll have golden chains and shiny coats and you riding upon hunters with the ladies of the land. (*He makes an eager sign to the* WIDOW QUIN *to come to help him.*)

WIDOW QUIN (*coming over*): It's true for him, and you'd best quit off and not have that poor girl setting her mind on you, for there's Shaneen thinks she wouldn't suit you though all is saying that she'll wed you now.

(CHRISTY *beams with delight.*)

SHAWN (*in terrified earnest*): She wouldn't suit you, and she with the divil's own temper the way you'd be strangling one another in a score of days. (*He makes the movement of strangling with his hands.*) It's the like of me only that she's fit for, a quiet simple fellow wouldn't raise a hand upon her if she scratched itself.

WIDOW QUIN (*putting* SHAWN's *hat on* CHRISTY): Fit them clothes on you anyhow, young fellow, and he'd maybe loan them to you for the sports. (*Pushing him towards inner door*) Fit them on and you can give your answer when you have them tried.

CHRISTY (*beaming, delighted with the clothes*): I will then. I'd like herself to see me in them tweeds and hat. (*He goes into room and shuts the door.*)

SHAWN (*in great anxiety*): He'd like herself

to see them. He'll not leave us, Widow Quin. He's a score of divils in him the way it's well nigh certain he will wed Pegeen.

WIDOW QUIN (jeeringly): It's true all girls are fond of courage and do hate the like of you.

SHAWN (walking about in desperation): Oh, Widow Quin, what'll I be doing now? I'd inform again him, but he'd burst from Kilmainham and he'd be sure and certain to destroy me. If I wasn't so God-fearing, I'd near have courage to come behind him and run a pike into his side. Oh, it's a hard case to be an orphan and not to have your father that you're used to, and you'd easy kill and make yourself a hero in the sight of all. (Coming up to her) Oh, Widow Quin, will you find me some contrivance when I've promised you a ewe?

WIDOW QUIN: A ewe's a small thing, but what would you give me if I did wed him and did save you so?

SHAWN (with astonishment): You?

WIDOW QUIN: Aye. Would you give me the red cow you have and the mountainy ram, and the right of way across your rye path, and a load of dung at Michaelmas, and turbary upon the western hill?

SHAWN (radiant with hope): I would surely, and I'd give you the wedding ring I have, and the loan of a new suit, the way you'd have him decent on the wedding day. I'd give you two kids for your dinner, and a gallon of poteen, and I'd call the piper on the long car to your wedding from Crossmolina or from Ballina. I'd give you . . .

WIDOW QUIN: That'll do so, and let you whisht, for he's coming now again.

(CHRISTY comes in very natty in the new clothes. WIDOW QUIN goes to him admiringly.)

WIDOW QUIN: If you seen yourself now, I'm thinking you'd be too proud to speak to us at all, and it'd be a pity surely to have your like sailing from Mayo to the Western World.

CHRISTY (as proud as a peacock): I'm not going. If this is a poor place itself, I'll make myself contented to be lodging here.

(WIDOW QUIN makes a sign to SHAWN to leave them.)

SHAWN: Well, I'm going measuring the race-course while the tide is low, so I'll leave you the garments and my blessing for the sports today. God bless you! (He wriggles out.)

WIDOW QUIN (admiring CHRISTY): Well, you're mighty spruce, young fellow. Sit down now while you're quiet till you talk with me.

CHRISTY (swaggering): I'm going abroad on the hillside for to seek Pegeen.

WIDOW QUIN: You'll have time and plenty for to seek Pegeen, and you heard me saying at the fall of night the two of us should be great company.

CHRISTY: From this out I'll have no want of company when all sorts is bringing me their food and clothing (he swaggers to the door, tightening his belt), the way they'd set their eyes upon a gallant orphan cleft his father with one blow to the breeches belt. (He opens door, then staggers back.) Saints of glory! Holy angels from the throne of light!

WIDOW QUIN (going over): What ails you?

CHRISTY: It's the walking spirit of my murdered da?

WIDOW QUIN (looking out): Is it that tramper?

CHRISTY (wildly): Where'll I hide my poor body from that ghost of hell?

(The door is pushed open, and old MAHON appears on threshold. CHRISTY darts in behind door.)

WIDOW QUIN (in great amusement): God save you, my poor man.

MAHON (gruffly): Did you see a young lad passing this way in the early morning or the fall of night?

WIDOW QUIN: You're a queer kind to walk in not saluting at all.

MAHON: Did you see the young lad?

WIDOW QUIN (stiffly): What kind was he?

MAHON: An ugly young streeler with a murderous gob on him, and a little switch in his hand. I met a tramper seen him coming this way at the fall of night.

WIDOW QUIN: There's harvest hundreds do be passing these days for the Sligo boat. For what is it you're wanting him, my poor man?

MAHON: I want to destroy him for breaking the head on me with the clout of a loy. (He takes off a big hat, and shows his head in a *mass of bandages and plaster, with some pride.)* It was he did that, and amn't I a great wonder to think I've traced him ten days with that rent in my crown?

WIDOW QUIN *(taking his head in both hands and examining it with extreme delight):* That was a great blow. And who hit you? A robber maybe?

MAHON: It was my own son hit me, and he the divil a robber, or anything else, but a dirty, stuttering lout.

WIDOW QUIN *(letting go his skull and wiping her hands in her apron):* You'd best be wary of a mortified scalp, I think they call it, lepping around with that wound in the splendor of the sun. It was a bad blow surely, and you should have vexed him fearful to make him strike that gash in his da.

MAHON: Is it me?

WIDOW QUIN *(amusing herself):* Aye. And isn't it a great shame when the old and hardened do torment the young?

MAHON *(raging):* Torment him is it? And I after holding out with the patience of a martyred saint till there's nothing but destruction on, and I'm driven out in my old age with none to aid me.

WIDOW QUIN *(greatly amused):* It's a sacred wonder the way that wickedness will spoil a man.

MAHON: My wickedness, is it? Amn't I after saying it is himself has me destroyed, and he a liar on walls, a talker of folly, a man you'd see stretched the half of the day in the brown ferns with his belly to the sun.

WIDOW QUIN: Not working at all?

MAHON: The divil a work, or if he did itself, you'd see him raising up a haystack like the stalk of a rush, or driving our last cow till he broke her leg at the hip, and when he wasn't at that he'd be fooling over little birds he had—finches and felts—or making mugs at his own self in the bit of a glass we had hung on the wall.

WIDOW QUIN *(looking at* CHRISTY*):* What way was he so foolish? It was running wild after the girls may be?

MAHON *(with a shout of derision):* Running wild, is it? If he seen a red petticoat coming swinging over the hill, he'd be off to hide in the sticks, and you'd see him shooting out his sheep's eyes between the little twigs and the leaves, and his two ears rising like a hare looking out through a gap. Girls, indeed!

WIDOW QUIN: It was drink maybe?

MAHON: And he a poor fellow would get drunk on the smell of a pint. He'd a queer rotten stomach, I'm telling you, and when I gave him three pulls from my pipe a while since, he was taken with contortions till I had to send him in the ass cart to the females' nurse.

WIDOW QUIN *(clasping her hands):* Well, I never till this day heard tell of a man the like of that!

MAHON: I'd take a mighty oath you didn't surely, and wasn't he the laughing joke of every female woman where four baronies meet, the way the girls would stop their weeding if they seen him coming the road to let a roar at him, and call him the looney of Mahon's.

WIDOW QUIN: I'd give the world and all to see the like of him. What kind was he?

MAHON: A small low fellow.

WIDOW QUIN: And dark?

MAHON: Dark and dirty.

WIDOW QUIN *(considering):* I'm thinking I seen him.

MAHON *(eagerly):* An ugly young blackguard.

WIDOW QUIN: A hideous, fearful villain, and the spit of you.

MAHON: What way is he fled?

WIDOW QUIN: Gone over the hills to catch a coasting steamer to the north or south.

MAHON: Could I pull up on him now?

WIDOW QUIN: If you'll cross the sands below where the tide is out, you'll be in it as soon as himself, for he had to go round ten miles by the top of the bay. *(She points to the door.)* Strike down by the head beyond and then follow on the roadway to the north and east.

*(*MAHON *goes abruptly.)*

WIDOW QUIN *(shouting after him):* Let you give him a good vengeance when you come up with him, but don't put yourself in the power of the law, for it'd be a poor thing to see a judge in his black cap reading out his sentence on a civil warrior the like of you. *(She swings the door to and looks at* CHRISTY, *who is cowering in terror, for a moment, then she bursts into a laugh.)*

WIDOW QUIN: Well, you're the walking Playboy of the Western World, and that's the poor man you had divided to his breeches belt.

CHRISTY *(looking out: then, to her):* What'll Pegeen say when she hears that story? What'll she be saying to me now?

WIDOW QUIN: She'll knock the head of you, I'm thinking, and drive you from the door. God help her to betaking you for a wonder, and you a little schemer making up the story you destroyed your da.

CHRISTY *(turning to the door, nearly speechless with rage, half to himself):* To be letting on he was dead, and coming back to his life, and following after me like an old weasel tracing a rat, and coming in here laying desolation between my own self and the fine women of Ireland, and he a kind of carcase that you'd fling upon the sea . . .

WIDOW QUIN *(more soberly):* There's talking for a man's one only son.

CHRISTY *(breaking out):* His one son, is it? May I meet him with one tooth and it aching, and one eye to be seeing seven and seventy divils in the twists of the road, and one old timber leg on him to limp into the scalding grave. *(Looking out)* There he is now crossing the strands, and that the Lord God would send a high wave to wash him from the world.

WIDOW QUIN *(scandalized):* Have you no shame? *(Putting her hand on his shoulder and turning him round)* What ails you? Near crying, is it?

CHRISTY *(in despair and grief):* Amn't I after seeing the love-light of the star of knowledge shining from her brow, and hearing words would put you thinking on the holy Brigid speaking to the infant saints, and now she'll be turning again, and speaking hard words to me, like an old woman with a spavindy ass she'd have, urging on a hill.

WIDOW QUIN: There's poetry talk for a girl you'd see itching and scratching, and she with a stale stink of poteen on her from selling in the shop.

CHRISTY *(impatiently):* It's her like is fitted to be handling merchandise in the heavens above, and what'll I be doing now, I ask you, and I a kind of wonder was jilted by the heavens when a day was by.

(There is a distant noise of girls' voices. WIDOW QUIN *looks from window and comes to him, hurriedly.)*

WIDOW QUIN: You'll be doing like myself, I'm thinking, when I did destroy my man, for I'm above many's the day, odd times in great spirits, abroad in the sunshine, darning a stocking or stitching a shift; and odd times again looking out on the schooners, hookers, trawlers is sailing the sea, and I thinking on the gallant hairy fellows are drifting beyond, and myself long years living alone.

CHRISTY *(interested):* You're like me, so.

WIDOW QUIN: I am your like, and it's for that I'm taking a fancy to you, and I with my little houseen above where there'd be myself to tend you, and none to ask were you a murderer or what at all.

CHRISTY: And what would I be doing if I left Pegeen?

WIDOW QUIN: I've nice jobs you could be doing, gathering shells to make a whitewash for our hut within, building up a little goosehouse, or stretching a new skin on an old curragh I have, and if my hut is far from all sides, it's there you'll meet the wisest old men, I tell you, at the corner of my wheel, and it's there yourself and me will have great times whispering and hugging. . . .

VOICES *(outside, calling far away):* Christy! Christy Mahon! Christy!

CHRISTY: Is it Pegeen Mike?

WIDOW QUIN: It's the young girls, I'm thinking, coming to bring you to the sports below, and what is it you'll have me to tell them now?

CHRISTY: Aid me for to win Pegeen. It's herself only that I'm seeking now. *(*WIDOW QUIN *gets up and goes to window.)* Aid me for to win her, and I'll be asking God to stretch a hand to you in the hour of death, and lead you short cuts through the Meadows of Ease, and up the floor of Heaven to the Footstool of the Virgin's Son.

WIDOW QUIN: There's praying.

VOICES *(nearer):* Christy! Christy Mahon!

CHRISTY *(with agitation):* They're coming. Will you swear to aid and save me for the love of Christ?

WIDOW QUIN *(looks at him for a moment):* If I aid you, will you swear to give me a right of way I want, and a mountainy ram, and a load of dung at Michaelmas, the time that you'll be master here?

CHRISTY: I will, by the elements and stars of night.

WIDOW QUIN: Then we'll not say a word of the old fellow, the way Pegeen won't know your story till the end of time.

CHRISTY: And if he chances to return again?

WIDOW QUIN: We'll swear he's a maniac and not your da. I could take an oath I seen him raving on the sands today.

(Girls run in.)

SUSAN: Come on to the sports below. Pegeen says you're to come.

SARA TANSEY: The lepping's beginning, and we've a jockey's suit to fit upon you for the mule race on the sands below.

HONOR: Come on, will you?

CHRISTY: I will then if Pegeen's beyond.

SARA TANSEY: She's in the boreen making game of Shaneen Keogh.

CHRISTY: Then I'll be going to her now. *(He runs out followed by the girls.)*

WIDOW QUIN: Well, if the worst comes in the end of all, it'll be great game to see there's none to pity him but a widow woman, the like of me, has buried her children and destroyed her man. *(She goes out.)*

ACT THREE

SCENE

As before. Later in the day. JIMMY comes in, slightly drunk.

JIMMY *(calls):* Pegeen! *(Crosses to inner door.)* Pegeen Mike! *(Comes back again into the room.)* Pegeen! *(PHILLY comes in in the same state.) (To PHILLY)* Did you see herself?

PHILLY: I did not; but I sent Shawn Keogh with the ass cart for to bear him home. *(Trying cupboards which are locked)* Well, isn't he a nasty man to get into such staggers at a morning wake? and isn't herself the divil's daughter for locking, and she so fussy after that young gaffer, you might take your death with drought and none to heed you?

JIMMY: It's little wonder she'd be fussy, and he after bringing bankrupt ruin on the roulette man, and the trick-o'-the-loop man, and breaking the nose of the cockshot-man, and winning all in the sports below, racing, lepping, dancing, and the Lord knows what! He's right luck, I'm telling you.

PHILLY: If he has, he'll be rightly hobbled yet, and he not able to say ten words without making a brag of the way he killed his father, and the great blow he hit with the loy.

JIMMY: A man can't hang by his own informing, and his father should be rotten by now.

(OLD MAHON passes window slowly.)

PHILLY: Supposing a man's digging spuds in that field with a long spade, and supposing he flings up the two halves of that skull, what'll be said then in the papers and the courts of law?

JIMMY: They'd say it was an old Dane, maybe, was drowned in the flood. *(OLD MAHON comes in and sits down near door listening.)* Did you never hear tell of the skulls they have in the city of Dublin, ranged out like blue jugs in a cabin of Connaught?

PHILLY: And you believe that?

JIMMY *(pugnaciously):* Didn't a lad see them and he after coming from harvesting in the Liverpool boat? "They have them there," says he, "making a show of the great people there was one time walking the world. White skulls and black skulls and yellow skulls, and some with full teeth, and some haven't only but one."

PHILLY: It was no lie, maybe, for when I was a young lad there was a graveyard beyond the house with the remnants of a man who had thighs as long as your arm. He was a horrid man, I'm telling you, and there was many a fine Sunday I'd put him together for fun, and he with shiny bones, you wouldn't meet the like of these days in the cities of the world.

MAHON (*getting up*): You wouldn't, is it? Lay your eyes on that skull, and tell me where and when there was another the like of it, is splintered only from the blow of a loy.

PHILLY: Glory be to God! And who hit you at all?

MAHON (*triumphantly*): It was my own son hit me. Would you believe that?

JIMMY: Well, there's wonders hidden in the heart of man!

PHILLY (*suspiciously*): And what way was it done?

MAHON (*wandering about the room*): I'm after walking hundreds and long scores of miles, winning clean beds and the fill of my belly four times in the day, and I doing nothing but telling stories of that naked truth. (*He comes to them a little aggressively.*) Give me a supeen and I'll tell you now.

(WIDOW QUIN *comes in and stands aghast behind him. He is facing* JIMMY *and* PHILLY, *who are on the left.*)

JIMMY: Ask herself beyond. She's the stuff hidden in her shawl.

WIDOW QUIN (*coming to* MAHON *quickly*): You here, is it? You didn't go far at all?

MAHON: I seen the coasting steamer passing, and I got a drought upon me and a cramping leg, so I said, "The divil go along with him," and turned again. (*Looking under her shawl*) And let you give me a supeen, for I'm destroyed travelling since Tuesday was a week.

WIDOW QUIN (*getting a glass, in a cajoling tone*): Sit down then by the fire and take your ease for a space. You've a right to be destroyed indeed, with your walking, and fighting, and facing the sun (*giving him poteen from a stone jar she has brought in*). There now is a drink for you, and may it be to your happiness and length of life.

MAHON (*taking glass greedily and sitting down by fire*): God increase you!

WIDOW QUIN (*taking men to the right stealthily*): Do you know what? That man's raving from his wound today, for I met him a while since telling a rambling tale of a tinker had him destroyed. Then he heard of Christy's deed, and he up and says it was his son had cracked his skull. O isn't madness a fright, for he'll go killing someone yet, and he thinking it's the man has struck him so?

JIMMY (*entirely convinced*): It's a fright, surely. I knew a party was kicked in the head by a red mare, and he went killing horses a great while, till he eat the insides of a clock and died after.

PHILLY (*with suspicion*): Did he see Christy?

WIDOW QUIN: He didn't. (*With a warning gesture*) Let you not be putting him in mind of him, or you'll be likely summoned if there's murder done. (*Looking round at* MAHON) Whisht! He's listening. Wait now till you hear me taking him easy and unravelling all. (*She goes to* MAHON.) And what way are you feeling, mister? Are you in contentment now?

MAHON (*slightly emotional from his drink*): I'm poorly only, for it's a hard story the way I'm left today, when it was I did tend him from his hour of birth, and he a dunce never reached his second book, the way he'd come from school, many's the day, with his legs lamed under him, and he blackened with his beatings like a tinker's ass. It's a hard story, I'm saying, the way some do have their next and nighest raising up a hand of murder on them, and some is lonesome getting their death with lamentation in the dead of night.

WIDOW QUIN (*not knowing what to say*): To hear you talking so quiet, who'd know you were the same fellow we seen pass today?

MAHON: I'm the same surely. The wrack and ruin of three score years; and it's a terror to live that length, I tell you, and to have your sons going to the dogs against you, and you wore out scolding them, and skelping them, and God knows what.

PHILLY (*to* JIMMY): He's not raving. (*To* WIDOW QUIN) Will you ask him what kind was his son?

WIDOW QUIN (*to* MAHON, *with a peculiar look*): Was your son that hit you a lad of one year and a score maybe, a great hand at racing and lepping and licking the world?

MAHON (*turning on her with a roar of rage*): Didn't you hear me say he was the fool of men, the way from this out he'll know the orphan's lot with old and young making game of him and they swearing, raging, kicking at him like a mangy cur.

(*A great burst of cheering outside, some way off.*)

MAHON (*putting his hands to his ears*): What in the name of God do they want roaring below?

WIDOW QUIN (*with the shade of a smile*): They're cheering a young lad, the champion Playboy of the Western World.

(*More cheering.*)

MAHON (*going to window*): It'd split my heart to hear them, and I with pulses in my brain-pan for a week gone by. Is it racing they are?

JIMMY (*looking from door*): It is then. They are mounting him for the mule race will be run upon the sands. That's the playboy on the winkered mule.

MAHON (*puzzled*): That lad, is it? If you said it was a fool he was, I'd have laid a mighty oath he was the likeness of my wandering son (*uneasily, putting his hand to his head*). Faith, I'm thinking I'll go walking for to view the race.

WIDOW QUIN (*stopping him, sharply*): You will not. You'd best take the road to Belmullet, and not be dilly-dallying in this place where there isn't a spot you could sleep.

PHILLY (*coming forward*): Don't mind her. Mount there on the bench and you'll have a view of the whole. They're hurrying before the tide will rise, and it'd be near over if you went down the pathway through the crags below.

MAHON (*mounts on bench,* WIDOW QUIN *beside him*): That's a right view again the edge of the sea. They're coming now from the point. He'd leading. Who is he at all?

WIDOW QUIN: He's the champion of the world, I tell you, and there isn't a hop'orth isn't falling lucky to his hands today.

PHILLY (*looking out, interested in the race*): Look at that. They're pressing him now.

JIMMY: He'll win it yet.

PHILLY: Take your time, Jimmy Farrell. It's too soon to say.

WIDOW QUIN (*shouting*): Watch him taking the gate. There's riding.

JIMMY (*cheering*): More power to the young lad!

MAHON: He's passing the third.

JIMMY: He'll lick them yet!

WIDOW QUIN: He'd lick them if he was running races with a score itself.

MAHON: Look at the mule he has, kicking the stars.

WIDOW QUIN: There was a lep! (*Catching hold of* MAHON *in her excitement*) He's fallen! He's mounted again! Faith, he's passing them all!

JIMMY: Look at him skelping her!

PHILLY: And the mountain girls hooshing him on!

JIMMY: It's the last turn! The post's cleared for them now!

MAHON: Look at the narrow place. He'll be into the bogs! (*With a yell*) Good rider! He's through it again!

JIMMY: He neck and neck!

MAHON: Good boy to him! Flames, but he's in!

(*Great cheering, in which all join.*)

MAHON (*with hesitation*): What's that? They're raising him up. They're coming this way. (*With a roar of rage and astonishment*) It's Christy! by the stars of God! I'd know his way of spitting and he astride the moon.

(*He jumps down and makes for the door, but* WIDOW QUIN *catches him and pulls him back.*)

WIDOW QUIN: Stay quiet, will you. That's not your son. (*To* JIMMY) Stop him, or you'll get a month for the abetting of manslaughter and be fined as well.

JIMMY: I'll hold him.

MAHON (*struggling*): Let me out! Let me out, the lot of you! till I have my vengeance on his head today.

WIDOW QUIN (*shaking him, vehemently*): That's not your son. That's a man is going to make a marriage with the daughter of this house, a place with fine trade, with a license, and with poteen too.

MAHON (*amazed*): That man marrying a decent and a moneyed girl! Is it mad yous are? Is it in a crazy house for females that I'm landed now?

WIDOW QUIN: It's mad yourself is with the blow upon your head. That lad is the wonder of the Western World.

MAHON: I seen it's my son.

WIDOW QUIN: You seen that you're mad.

(Cheering outside.) Do you hear them cheering him in the zig-zags of the road? Aren't you after saying that your son's a fool, and how would they be cheering a true idiot born?

MAHON *(getting distressed):* It's maybe out of reason that that man's himself. *(Cheering again.)* There's none surely will go cheering him. Oh, I'm raving with a madness that would fright the world! *(He sits down with his hand to his head.)* There was one time I seen ten scarlet divils letting on they'd cork my spirit in a gallon can; and one time I seen rats as big as badgers sucking the life blood from the butt of my lug; but I never till this day confused that dribbling idiot with a likely man. I'm destroyed surely.

WIDOW QUIN: And who'd wonder when it's your brain-pan that is gaping now?

MAHON: Then the blight of the sacred drought upon myself and him, for I never went mad to this day, and I not three weeks with the Limerick girls drinking myself silly, and parlatic from the dusk to dawn. *(To* WIDOW QUIN, *suddenly)* Is my visage astray?

WIDOW QUIN: It is then. You're a sniggering maniac, a child could see.

MAHON *(getting up more cheerfully):* Then I'd best be going to the union beyond, and there'll be a welcome before me, I tell you *(with great pride)*, and I a terrible and fearful case, the way that there I was one time, screeching in a straitened waistcoat, with seven doctors writing out my sayings in a printed book. Would you believe that?

WIDOW QUIN: If you're a wonder itself, you'd best be hasty, for them lads caught a maniac one time and pelted the poor creature till he ran out, raving and foaming, and was drowned in the sea.

MAHON *(with philosophy):* It's true mankind is the divil when your head's astray. Let me out now and I'll slip down the boreen, and not see them so.

WIDOW QUIN *(showing him out):* That's it. Run to the right, and not a one will see.

(He runs off.)

PHILLY *(wisely):* You're at some gaming, Widow Quin; but I'll walk after him and give him his dinner and a time to rest, and I'll see then if he's raving or as sane as you.

WIDOW QUIN *(annoyed):* If you go near that lad, let you be wary of your head, I'm saying. Didn't you hear him telling he was crazed at times?

PHILLY: I heard him telling a power; and I'm thinking we'll have right sport, before night will fall. *(He goes out.)*

JIMMY: Well, Philly's a conceited and foolish man. How could that madman have his senses and his brain-pan slit? I'll go after them and see him turn on Philly now.

(He goes; WIDOW QUIN *hides poteen behind counter. Then hubbub outside.)*

VOICES: There you are! Good jumper! Grand lepper! Darlint boy! He's the racer! Bear him on, will you!

*(*CHRISTY *comes in, in Jockey's dress, with* PEGEEN MIKE, SARA, *and other girls, and men.)*

PEGEEN *(to crowd):* Go on now and don't destroy him and he drenching with sweat. Go along, I'm saying, and have your tug-of-warring till he's dried his skin.

CROWD: Here's his prizes! A bagpipes! A fiddle was played by a poet in the years gone by! A flat and three-thorned blackthorn would lick the scholars out of Dublin town!

CHRISTY *(taking prizes from the men):* Thank you kindly, the lot of you. But you'd say it was little only I did this day if you'd seen me a while since striking my one single blow.

TOWN CRIER *(outside, ringing a bell):* Take notice, last event of this day! Tug-of-warring on the green below! Come on, the lot of you! Great achievements for all Mayo men!

PEGEEN: Go on, and leave him for to rest and dry. Go on, I tell you, for he'll do no more.

(She hustles crowd out; WIDOW QUIN *following them.)*

MEN *(going):* Come on then. Good luck for the while!

PEGEEN *(radiantly, wiping his face with her shawl):* Well, you're the lad, and you'll have great times from this out when you could win that wealth of prizes, and you sweating in the heat of noon!

CHRISTY *(looking at her with delight):* I'll have great times if I win the crowning prize I'm seeking now, and that's your promise that you'll wed me in a fortnight, when our banns is called.

PEGEEN *(backing away from him):* You're

right daring to go ask me that, when all knows you'll be starting to some girl in your own townland, when your father's rotten in four months, or five.

CHRISTY (*indignantly*): Starting from you, is it? (*He follows her.*) I will not, then, and when the airs is warming in four months, or five, it's then yourself and me should be pacing Neifin in the dews of night, the times sweet smells do be rising, and you'd see a little shiny new moon, maybe, sinking on the hills.

PEGEEN (*looking at him playfully*): And it's that kind of a poacher's love you'd make, Christy Mahon, on the sides of Neifin, when the night is down?

CHRISTY: It's little you'll think if my love's a poacher's, or an earl's itself, when you'll feel my two hands stretched around you, and I squeezing kisses on your puckered lips, till I'd feel a kind of pity for the Lord God is all ages sitting lonesome in his golden chair.

PEGEEN: That'll be right fun, Christy Mahon, and any girl would walk her heart out before she'd meet a young man was your like for eloquence, or talk, at all.

CHRISTY (*encouraged*): Let you wait, to hear me talking, till we're astray in Erris, when Good Friday's by, drinking a sup from a well, and making mighty kisses with our wetted mouths, or gaming in a gap or sunshine, with yourself stretched back onto your necklace, in the flowers of the earth.

PEGEEN (*in a lower voice, moved by his tone*): I'd be nice so, is it?

CHRISTY (*with rapture*): If the mitred bishops seen you that time, they'd be the like of the holy prophets, I'm thinking, do be straining the bars of Paradise to lay eyes on the Lady Helen of Troy, and she abroad, pacing back and forward, with a nosegay in her golden shawl.

PEGEEN (*with real tenderness*): And what is it I have, Christy Mahon, to make me fitting entertainment for the like of you, that has such poet's talking, and such bravery of heart?

CHRISTY (*in a low voice*): Isn't there the light of seven heavens in your heart alone, the way you'll be an angel's lamp to me from this out, and I abroad in the darkness, spearing salmons in the Owen, or the Carrowmore?

PEGEEN: If I was your wife, I'd be along with you those nights, Christy Mahon, the way you'd see I was a great hand at coaxing bailiffs, or coining funny nick-names for the stars of night.

CHRISTY: You, is it? Taking your death in the hailstones, or in the fogs of dawn.

PEGEEN: Yourself and me would shelter easy in a narrow bush (*with a qualm of dread*), but we're only talking, maybe, for this would be a poor, thatched place to hold a fine lad is the like of you.

CHRISTY (*putting his arm around her*): If I wasn't a good Christian, it's on my naked knees I'd be saying my prayers and paters to every jackstraw you have roofing your head, and every stony pebble is paving the laneway to your door.

PEGEEN (*radiantly*): If that's the truth, I'll be burning candles from this out to the miracles of God that have brought you from the south today, and I, with my gowns bought ready, the way that I can wed you, and not wait at all.

CHRISTY: It's miracles, and that's the truth. Me there toiling a long while, and walking a long while, not knowing at all I was drawing all times nearer to this holy day.

PEGEEN: And myself, a girl, was tempted often to go sailing the seas till I'd marry a Jew-man, with ten kegs of gold, and I not knowing at all there was the like of you drawing nearer, like the stars of God.

CHRISTY: And to think I'm long years hearing women talking that talk, to all bloody fools, and this the first time I've heard the like of your voice talking sweetly for my own delight.

PEGEEN: And to think it's me is talking sweetly, Christy Mahon, and I the fright of seven townlands for my biting tongue. Well, the heart's a wonder; and, I'm thinking, there won't be our like in Mayo, for gallant lovers, from this hour, today. (*Drunken singing is heard outside.*) There's my father coming from the wake, and when he's had his sleep we'll tell him, for he's peaceful then.

(*They separate.*)

MICHAEL (*singing outside*):

The jailor and the turnkey
They quickly ran us down,
And brought us back as prisoners
Once more to Cavan town.

(He comes in supported by SHAWN.*)*

There we lay bewailing
All in a prison bound. . . .

(He sees CHRISTY. *Goes and shakes him drunkenly by the hand, while* PEGEEN *and* SHAWN *talk on the left.)*

MICHAEL *(to* CHRISTY*):* The blessing of God and the holy angels on your head, young fellow. I hear tell you're after winning all in the sports below; and wasn't it a shame I didn't bear you along with me to Kate Cassidy's wake, a fine, stout lad, the like of you, for you'd never see the match of it for flows of drink, the way when we sunk her bones at noonday in her narrow grave, there were five men, aye, and six men, stretched out retching speechless on the holy stones.

CHRISTY *(uneasily, watching* PEGEEN*):* Is that the truth?

MICHAEL: It is then, and aren't you a louty schemer to go burying your poor father unbeknownst when you'd a right to throw him on the crupper of a Kerry mule and drive him westwards, like holy Joseph in the days gone by, the way we could have given him a decent burial, and not have him rotting beyond, and not a Christian drinking a smart drop to the glory of his soul?

CHRISTY *(gruffly):* It's well enough he's lying, for the likes of him.

MICHAEL *(slapping him on the back):* Well, aren't you a hardened slayer? It'll be a poor thing for the household man where you go sniffing for a female wife; and *(pointing to* SHAWN*)* look beyond at that shy and decent Christian I have chosen for my daughter's hand, and I after getting the gilded dispensation this day for to wed them now.

CHRISTY: And you'll be wedding them this day, is it?

MICHAEL *(drawing himself up):* Aye. Are you thinking, if I'm drunk itself, I'd leave my daughter living single with a little frisky rascal is the like of you?

PEGEEN *(breaking away from* SHAWN*):* Is it the truth the dispensation's come?

MICHAEL *(triumphantly):* Father Reilly's after reading it in gallous Latin, and "It's come in the nick of time," says he; "so I'll wed them in a hurry, dreading that young gaffer who'd capsize the stars."

PEGEEN *(fiercely):* He's missed his nick of time, for it's that lad, Christy Mahon, that I'm wedding now.

MICHAEL *(loudly with horror):* You'd be making him a son to me, and he wet and crusted with his father's blood?

PEGEEN: Aye. Wouldn't it be a bitter thing for a girl to go marrying the like of Shaneen, and he a middling kind of a scarecrow, with no savagery or fine words in him at all?

MICHAEL *(gasping and sinking on a chair):* Oh, aren't you a heathen daughter to go shaking the fat of my heart, and I swamped and drowned with the weight of drink? Would you have them turning on me the way that I'd be roaring to the dawn of day with the wind upon my heart? Have you not a word to aid me, Shaneen? Are you not jealous at all?

SHAWN *(in great misery):* I'd be afeard to be jealous of a man did slay his da.

PEGEEN: Well, it'd be a poor thing to go marrying your like. I'm seeing there's a world of peril for an orphan girl, and isn't it a great blessing I didn't wed you, before himself came walking from the west or south?

SHAWN: It's a queer story you'd go picking a dirty tramp up from the highways of the world.

PEGEEN *(playfully):* And you think you're a likely beau to go straying along with, the shiny Sundays of the opening year, when it's sooner on a bullock's liver you'd put a poor girl thinking than on the lily or the rose?

SHAWN: And have you no mind of my weight of passion, and the holy dispensation, and the drift of heifers I am giving, and the golden ring?

PEGEEN: I'm thinking you're too fine for the like of me, Shawn Keogh of Killakeen, and let you go off till you'd find a radiant lady with droves of bullocks on the plains of Meath, and herself bedizened in the diamond jewelleries of Pharaoh's ma. That'd be your match,

Shaneen. So God save you now! *(She retreats behind* CHRISTY.*)*

SHAWN: Won't you hear me telling you . . . ?

CHRISTY *(with ferocity):* Take yourself from this, young fellow, or I'll maybe add a murder to my deeds today.

MICHAEL *(springing up with a shriek):* Murder is it? Is it mad yous are? Would you go making murder in this place, and it piled with poteen for our drink tonight? Go on to the foreshore if it's fighting you want, where the rising tide will wash all traces from the memory of man. *(Pushing* SHAWN *towards* CHRISTY.*)*

SHAWN *(shaking himself free, and getting behind* MICHAEL*):* I'll not fight him, Michael James. I'd liefer live a bachelor, simmering in passions to the end of time, than face a lepping savage the like of him has descended from the Lord knows where. Strike him yourself, Michael James, or you'll lose my drift of heifers and my blue bull from Sneem.

MICHAEL: Is it me fight him, when it's father-slaying he's bred to now? *(Pushing* SHAWN*)* Go on you fool and fight him now.

SHAWN *(coming forward a little):* Will I strike him with my hand?

MICHAEL: Take the loy is on your western side.

SHAWN: I'd be afeard of the gallows if I struck him with that.

CHRISTY *(taking up the loy):* Then I'll make you face the gallows or quit off from this.

*(*SHAWN *flies out of the door.)*

CHRISTY: Well, fine weather be after him, *(going to* MICHAEL, *coaxingly):* and I'm thinking you wouldn't wish to have that quaking blackguard in your house at all. Let you give us your blessing and hear her swear her faith to me, for I'm mounted on the springtide of the stars of luck, the way it'll be good for any to have me in the house.

PEGEEN *(at the other side of* MICHAEL*):* Bless us now, for I swear to God I'll wed him, and I'll not renege.

MICHAEL *(standing up in the center, holding on to both of them):* It's the will of God, I'm thinking, that all should win an easy or a cruel end, and it's the will of God that all

should rear up lengthy families for the nurture of the earth. What's a single man, I ask you, eating a bit in one house and drinking a sup in another, and he with no place of his own, like an old braying jackass strayed upon the rocks? *(To* CHRISTY*)* It's many would be in dread to bring your like into their house for to end them, maybe, with a sudden end; but I'm a decent man of Ireland, and I liefer face the grave untimely and I seeing a score of grandsons growing up little gallant swearers by the name of God, than go peopling my bedside with puny weeds the like of what you'd breed, I'm thinking, out of Shaneen Keogh. *(He joins their hands.)* A daring fellow is the jewel of the world, and a man did split his father's middle with a single clout, should have the bravery of ten, so may God and Mary and St. Patrick bless you, and increase you from this mortal day.

CHRISTY *and* PEGEEN: Amen, O Lord!

(Hubbub outside. OLD MAHON *rushes in, followed by all the crowd, and* WIDOW QUIN. *He makes a rush at* CHRISTY, *knocks him down, and begins to beat him.)*

PEGEEN *(dragging back his arm):* Stop that, will you. Who are you at all?

MAHON: His father, God forgive me!

PEGEEN *(drawing back):* Is it rose from the dead?

MAHON: Do you think I look so easy quenched with the tap of a loy? *(Beats* CHRISTY *again.)*

PEGEEN *(glaring at* CHRISTY*):* And it's lies you told, letting on you had him slitted, and you nothing at all.

CHRISTY *(catching* MAHON's *stick):* He's not my father. He's a raving maniac would scare the world. *(Pointing to* WIDOW QUIN*)* Herself knows it is true.

CROWD: You're fooling Pegeen! The Widow Quin seen him this day, and you likely knew! You're a liar!

CHRISTY *(dumbfounded):* It's himself was a liar, lying stretched out with an open head on him, letting on he was dead.

MAHON: Weren't you off racing the hills before I got my breath with the start I had seeing you turn on me at all?

PEGEEN: And to think of the coaxing glory

we had given him, and he after doing nothing but hitting a soft blow and chasing northward in a sweat of fear. Quit off from this.

CHRISTY (*piteously*): You've seen my doings this day, and let you save me from the old man; for why would you be in such a scorch of haste to spur me to destruction now?

PEGEEN: It's there your treachery is spurring me, till I'm hard set to think you're the one I'm after lacing in my heart-strings half-an-hour gone by. (*To* MAHON) Take him on from this, for I think bad the world should see me raging for a Munster liar, and the fool of men.

MAHON: Rise up now to retribution, and come on with me.

CROWD (*jeeringly*): There's the playboy! There's the lad thought he'd rule the roost in Mayo. Slate him now, mister.

CHRISTY (*getting up in shy terror*): What is it drives you to torment me here, when I'd asked the thunders of the might of God to blast me if I ever did hurt to any saving only that one single blow.

MAHON (*loudly*): If you didn't, you're a poor good-for-nothing, and isn't it by the like of you the sins of the whole world are committed?

CHRISTY (*raising his hands*): In the name of the Almighty God. . . .

MAHON: Leave troubling the Lord God. Would you have him sending down droughts, and fevers, and the old hen and the cholera morbus?

CHRISTY (*to* WIDOW QUIN): Will you come between us and protect me now?

WIDOW QUIN: I've tried a lot, God help me, and my share is done.

CHRISTY (*looking round in desperation*): And I must go back into my torment is it, or run off like a vagabond straying through the Unions with the dusts of August making mud-stains in the gullet of my throat, or the winds of March blowing on me till I'd take an oath I felt them making whistles of my ribs within?

SARA: Ask Pegeen to aid you. Her like does often change.

CHRISTY: I will not then, for there's torment in the splendor of her like, and she a girl any moon of midnight would take pride to meet, facing southwards on the heaths of Keel. But what did I want crawling forward to scorch my understanding at her flaming brow?

PEGEEN (*to* MAHON, *vehemently, fearing she will break into tears*): Take him on from this or I'll set the young lads to destroy him here.

MAHON (*going to him, shaking his stick*): Come on now if you wouldn't have the company to see you skelped.

PEGEEN (*half laughing, through her tears*): That's it, now the world will see him pandied, and he an ugly liar was playing off the hero, and the fright of men.

CHRISTY (*to* MAHON, *very sharply*): Leave me go!

CROWD: That's it. Now Christy. If them two set fighting, it will lick the world.

MAHON (*making a grab at* CHRISTY): Come here to me.

CHRISTY (*more threateningly*): Leave me go, I'm saying.

MAHON: I will maybe, when your legs is limping, and your back is blue.

CROWD: Keep it up, the two of you. I'll back the old one. Now the playboy.

CHRISTY (*in low and intense voice*): Shut your yelling, for if you're after making a mighty man of me this day by the power of a lie, you're setting me now to think if it's a poor thing to be lonesome, it's worse maybe to go mixing with the fools of earth.

(MAHON *makes a movement towards him.*)

CHRISTY (*almost shouting*): Keep off . . . lest I do show a blow unto the lot of you would set the guardian angels winking in the clouds above. (*He swings round with a sudden rapid movement and picks up a loy.*)

CROWD (*half frightened, half amused*): He's going mad! Mind yourselves! Run from the idiot!

CHRISTY: If I am an idiot, I'm after hearing my voice this day saying words would raise the topknot on a poet in a merchant's town. I've won your racing, and your lepping, and . . .

MAHON: Shut your gullet and come on with me.

CHRISTY: I'm going, but I'll stretch you first.

(*He runs at old* MAHON *with the loy, chases him out of the door, followed by* CROWD *and*

WIDOW QUIN. *There is a great noise outside, then a yell, and dead silence for a moment.* CHRISTY *comes in, half dazed, and goes to fire.)*

WIDOW QUIN *(coming in, hurriedly, and going to him):* They're turning again you. Come on, or you'll be hanged, indeed.

CHRISTY: I'm thinking, from this out, Pegeen'll be giving me praises the same as in the hours gone by.

WIDOW QUIN *(impatiently):* Come by the back door. I'd think bad to have you stifled on the gallows tree.

CHRISTY *(indignantly):* I will not, then. What good'd be my life-time, if I left Pegeen?

WIDOW QUIN: Come on, and you'll be no worse than you were last night; and you with a double murder this time to be telling to the girls.

CHRISTY: I'll not leave Pegeen Mike.

WIDOW QUIN *(impatiently):* Isn't there the match of her in every parish public, from Binghamstown unto the plain of Meath? Come on, I tell you, and I'll find you finer sweethearts at each waning moon.

CHRISTY: It's Pegeen I'm seeking only, and what'd I care if you brought me a drift of chosen females, standing in their shifts itself, maybe, from this place to the Eastern World?

SARA *(runs in, pulling off one of her petticoats):* They're going to hang him. *(Holding out petticoat and shawl)* Fit these upon him, and let him run off to the east.

WIDOW QUIN: He's raving now; but we'll fit them on him, and I'll take him, in the ferry, to the Achill boat.

CHRISTY *(struggling feebly):* Leave me go, will you? When I'm thinking of my luck today, for she will wed me surely, and I a proven hero in the end of all.

(They try to fasten petticoat round him.)

WIDOW QUIN: Take his left hand, and we'll pull him now. Come on, young fellow.

CHRISTY *(suddenly starting up):* You'll be taking me from her? You're jealous, is it, of her wedding me? Go on from this. *(He snatches up a stool, and threatens them with it.)*

WIDOW QUIN *(going):* It's in the mad-house they should put him, not in jail, at all. We'll go by the back door, to call the doctor, and we'll save him so.

(She goes out, with SARA, *through inner room. Men crowd in the doorway.* CHRISTY *sits down again by the fire.)*

MICHAEL *(in a terrified whisper):* Is the old lad killed surely?

PHILLY: I'm after feeling the last gasps quitting his heart.

(They peer in at CHRISTY.)

MICHAEL *(with a rope):* Look at the way he is. Twist a hangman's knot on it, and slip it over his head, while he's not minding at all.

PHILLY: Let you take it, Shaneen. You're the soberest of all that's here.

SHAWN: Is it me to go near him, and he the wickedest and worst with me? Let you take it, Pegeen Mike.

PEGEEN: Come on, so.

(She goes forward with the others, and they drop the double hitch over his head.)

CHRISTY: What ails you?

SHAWN *(triumphantly, as they pull the rope tight on his arms):* Come on to the peelers, till they stretch you now.

CHRISTY: Me!

MICHAEL: If we took pity on you, the Lord God would, maybe, bring us ruin from the law today, so you'd best come easy, for hanging is an easy and a speedy end.

CHRISTY: I'll not stir. *(To* PEGEEN) And what is it you'll say to me, and I after doing it this time in the face of all?

PEGEEN: I'll say, a strange man is a marvel, with his mighty talk; but what's a squabble in your back yard, and the blow of a loy, have taught me that there's a great gap between a gallous story and a dirty deed. *(To* MEN) Take him on from this, or the lot of us will be likely put on trial for his deed today.

CHRISTY *(with horror in his voice):* And it's yourself will send me off, to have a horny-fingered hangman hitching his bloody slip-knots at the butt of my ear.

MEN *(pulling rope):* Come on, will you? *(He is pulled down on the floor.)*

CHRISTY *(twisting his legs round the table):* Cut the rope, Pegeen, and I'll quit the lot of you, and live from this out, like the madmen of Keel, eating muck and green weeds, on the faces of the cliffs.

PEGEEN: And leave us to hang, is it, for a saucy liar, the like of you? *(To* MEN*)* Take him on, out from this.

SHAWN: Pull a twist on his neck, and squeeze him so.

PHILLY: Twist yourself. Sure he cannot hurt you, if you keep your distance from his teeth alone.

SHAWN: I'm afeard of him. *(To* PEGEEN*)* Lift a lighted sod, will you, and scorch his leg.

PEGEEN *(blowing the fire, with a bellows):* Leave go now, young fellow, or I'll scorch your shins.

CHRISTY: You're blowing for to torture me. *(His voice rising and growing stronger)* That's your kind, is it? Then let the lot of you be wary, for, if I've to face the gallows, I'll have a gay march down, I tell you, and shed the blood of some of you before I die.

SHAWN *(in terror):* Keep a good hold, Philly. Be wary, for the love of God. For I'm thinking he would liefest wreak his pains on me.

CHRISTY *(almost gaily):* If I do lay my hands on you, it's the way you'll be at the fall of night, hanging as a scarecrow for the fowls of hell. Ah, you'll have a gallous jaunt I'm saying, coaching out through Limbo with my father's ghost.

SHAWN *(to* PEGEEN*):* Make haste, will you? Oh, isn't he a holy terror, and isn't it true for Father Reilly, that all drink's a curse that has the lot of you so shaky and uncertain now?

CHRISTY: If I can wring a neck among you, I'll have a royal judgment looking on the trembling jury in the courts of law. And won't there be crying out in Mayo the day I'm stretched upon the rope with ladies in their silks and satins snivelling in their lacy kerchiefs, and they rhyming songs and ballads on the terror of my fate? *(He squirms round on the floor and bites* SHAWN's *leg.)*

SHAWN *(shrieking):* My leg's bit on me. He's the like of a mad dog, I'm thinking, the way that I will surely die.

CHRISTY *(delighted with himself):* You will then, the way you can shake out hell's flags of welcome for my coming in two weeks or

three, for I'm thinking Satan hasn't many have killed their da in Kerry, and in Mayo too.

*(*OLD MAHON *comes in behind on all fours and looks on unnoticed.)*

MEN *(to* PEGEEN*):* Bring the sod, will you?

PEGEEN *(coming over):* God help him so. *(Burns his leg.)*

CHRISTY *(kicking and screaming):* O, glory be to God!

(He kicks loose from the table, and they all drag him towards the door.)

JIMMY *(seeing old* MAHON*):* Will you look what's come in?

(They all drop CHRISTY *and run left.)*

CHRISTY *(scrambling on his knees face to face with old* MAHON*):* Are you coming to be killed a third time, or what ails you now?

MAHON: For what is it they have you tied?

CHRISTY: They're taking me to the peelers to have me hanged for slaying you.

MICHAEL *(apologetically):* It is the will of God that all should guard their little cabins from the treachery of law, and what would my daughter be doing if I was ruined or was hanged itself?

MAHON *(grimly, loosening* CHRISTY*):* It's little I care if you put a bag on her back, and went picking cockles till the hour of death; but my son and myself will be going our own way, and we'll have great times from this out telling stories of the villainy of Mayo, and the fools is here. *(To* CHRISTY, *who is freed)* Come on now.

CHRISTY: Go with you, is it? I will then, like a gallant captain with his heathen slave. Go on now and I'll see you from this day stewing my oatmeal and washing my spuds, for I'm master of all fights from now. *(Pushing* MAHON*)* Go on, I'm saying.

MAHON: Is it me?

CHRISTY: Not a word out of you. Go on from this.

MAHON *(walking out and looking back at* CHRISTY *over his shoulder):* Glory be to God! *(With a broad smile)* I am crazy again! *(Goes.)*

CHRISTY: Ten thousand blessings upon all that's here, for you've turned me a likely gaffer in the end of all, the way I'll go romancing through a romping lifetime from this hour to the drawing of the judgment day. *(He goes out.)*

MICHAEL: By the will of God, we'll have peace now for our drinks. Will you draw the porter, Pegeen?

SHAWN *(going up to her):* It's a miracle Father Reilly can wed us in the end of all, and we'll have none to trouble us when his vicious bite is healed.

PEGEEN *(hitting him a box on the ear):* Quit my sight. *(Putting her shawl over her head and breaking out into wild lamentations)* Oh my grief, I've lost him surely. I've lost the only Playboy of the Western World.

AUGUST STRINDBERG

The Stronger

TRANSLATION BY ANTS ORAS

August Strindberg (1849–1912) was one of the most influential dramatists of the late nineteenth century. Born in Stockholm, Sweden, he was the fourth in a family of eleven children, and his life, from the beginning, was filled with poverty, hardship, and fear. In 1867 he spent a term at the University of Upsala; then he briefly attended the University of Stockholm, left to try teaching and acting, but soon returned to study literature and science. Finally King Charles XV of Sweden gave him a financial reward for one of his plays, and he left the university for a writing career. Although his first full-length play, *Master Olof*, was rejected by publishers, he received for it an appointment to the Royal Library, where he read, studied Chinese, and wrote his first novel. Many short stories, novels, and plays followed. Among his most influential plays are *The Father*, 1887; *Miss Julie*, 1888; *There Are Crimes and Crimes*, 1898; and *A Dream Play*, 1902.

Although Strindberg began by writing realistic drama, he moved to the naturalistic and finally to the symbolistic. He became preoccupied with innovation in the structure of drama, reducing the amount of exposition included, relying more and more on dialogue to present the psychological conflict, and abolishing the division of the play into acts.

The Stronger, 1889, which represents a breaking away from the conventional dramatic form, displays Strindberg's concern with the presentation of psychological conflict through dialogue alone and with the reduction of a play's structure to its simplest form, the brief monologue.

PERSONS

MME. X, *actress, married*
MLLE. Y, *actress, single*
A WAITRESS

A corner in a ladies' café; two small iron tables, a red velvet sofa and some chairs. MME. X *enters in winter clothing, wearing a hat and a cloak and carrying a fine Japanese basket on her arm.* MLLE. Y *sits with a half-empty beer*

THE STRONGER   Reprinted by permission of Ants Oras.

bottle in front of her, reading an illustrated paper, then changing it for another.

MME. X: How are you, little Amelie?—You're sitting alone here on Christmas Eve like a disconsolate old bachelor.

(MLLE. Y *looks up from the paper, nods, goes on reading.*)

MME. X: You know, I am heartily sorry to see you like this, alone, all alone in a café on Christmas Eve. I feel quite as sorry as that evening in a Paris restaurant when I saw a bridal party, with the bride sitting and reading a comic paper and the groom playing billiards with the witnesses. Goodness, I thought, with such a beginning how is this to continue and to end!

He played billiards on his wedding evening! —Yes, and she read a comic paper! Well, but that is hardly the same situation as here.

(The WAITRESS *enters, places a cup of hot chocolate before* MME. X *and goes out.)*

MME. X: I tell you what, Amelie! Now I really believe you would have done better to have kept him. Remember, I was the first to urge you "Forgive him!" Don't you recall it?— You could have been married to him, with a home of your own. Don't you remember last Christmas, how happy you felt out in the country with your fiancé's parents; how you praised the happiness of a home and how you longed to get away from the theater?—Yes, darling Amelie, a home is the best of all things—next to the theater—a home and some brats too— but that you wouldn't understand.

*(*MLLE. Y *looks contemptuous.)*

MME. X *(drinks a few spoonfuls from her cup, opens her basket and shows her Christmas presents):* Now you'll see what I've bought for my piglets. *(Shows a doll)* Look at this. This is for Lisa. Look how it rolls its eyes and turns its neck. There! And here is Maja's pop gun. *(Loads it and shoots at* MLLE. Y.)

*(*MLLE. Y *makes a scared gesture.)*

MME. X: Did this startle you? Did you fear I'd shoot you? What?—Good heavens, I don't believe you could possibly have thought that. I'd be less surprised if you were shooting me, since I got in your way—I know you can't forget that—although I was completely innocent. You still believe I eased you out of the theater with my intrigues, but I didn't! I didn't, even though you think I did!—But what is the use of telling you, for you still believe I did it. *(Takes out a pair of embroidered slippers)* And these are for my old man. With tulips embroidered by myself—I abhor tulips, you understand, but he wants tulips on everything.

*(*MLLE. Y *looks up from her paper, ironically and with some curiosity.)*

MME. X *(puts a hand in each slipper):* Look how small Bob's feet are. Well? And you ought to see how daintily he walks. You've never seen him in his slippers.

*(*MLLE. Y *laughs aloud.)*

MME. X: Look, I'll show you. *(Makes the slippers walk along the table.)*

*(*MLLE. Y *laughs aloud.)*

MME. X: Now look, and when he is out of sorts he stamps with his foot like this. "What! Damn those servants, they'll never learn how to make coffee! Goodness! Now those morons haven't clipped the lamp wick properly." And then there's a draught from the floor and his feet freeze: "Blast it, how cold it is, and these unspeakable idiots can't keep the fire going." *(Rubs one slipper's sole against the other's upper.)*

*(*MLLE. Y *bursts out laughing.)*

MME. X: And then he comes home and has to search for his slippers, which Marie has put under the chiffonier . . . Oh, but it is sinful to sit thus and make a fool of one's old man. Whatever he is, he is nice, a decent little fellow—you ought to've had such a husband, Amelie.—Why are you laughing? Why? Why? —And look here, I know he is faithful to me; yes, I do know that, for he told me himself . . . What are you grinning at? . . . When I was on my Norway tour, that nasty Frédérique came and tried to seduce him— Could you imagine such an infamy? *(Pause.)* But I'd have scratched out her eyes if she'd come near me after my return! *(Pause.)* What a good thing Bob told me about it himself rather than let me hear it through gossip! *(Pause.)* But Frédérique was not the only one, believe me! I don't know why, but the women are positively crazy about my husband—perhaps they think he has some say about theater engagements because he is in the government department!—Who knows but you yourself may have been chasing him!—I never trusted you more than just so much—but now I do know he doesn't care for you, and I always thought you were bearing him some grudge.

(Pause. They view each other, both embarrassed.)

MME. X: Come to see us in the evening, Amelie, and show you aren't cross with us, at least not with me! I don't know why, but it is so uncomfortable to be at loggerheads with you, of all people. Possibly because I got in your way that time—*(rallentando)* or—I just don't know why in particular!

(Pause. MLLE. Y *gazes curiously at* MME. X.*)*

MME. X *(pensively):* Our acquaintance was such an odd one—when I first saw you I was afraid of you, so afraid that I couldn't risk letting you out of my sight; whenever I came or went I was always near you—I couldn't afford to have you for an enemy, so I became your friend. But there was always something discordant in the air when you came to our home, for I saw my husband couldn't stand you—it all felt somehow awkward, like ill-fitting clothes—and I did what I could to make him take to you but to no purpose—until you got yourself engaged to be married! Then a violent friendship flared up so that for a moment it looked as though the two of you had only now ventured to show your real feelings because you were safe—and so what?—What happened?—I wasn't jealous—how queer!—And I recall the christening when you stood godmother to our baby—I made Bob kiss you—and he did, but you were so confused—that is to say, I didn't notice at the time—haven't thought about it since—not once until—this moment. *(Gets up furiously.)*

Why are you silent? You haven't said a word all this time, you've only let me sit and talk. You've been sitting and staring and making me unwind all these thoughts which lay like raw silk in their cocoon—thoughts—maybe suspicious ones—let me see.—Why did you break off your engagement? Why haven't you been to our house since that happened? Why aren't you coming to see us tonight?

*(*MLLE. Y *seems on the point of speaking.)*

MME. X: Be quiet! You needn't say a word, for now I grasp it all myself. It was because—because—because!—Yes indeed!—Every bit of it falls into its place! That's it!—Shame! Shame! I won't sit at the same table with you. *(Moves her things to the other table.)*

So that was why I had to embroider tulips on his slippers although I hate tulips—because you like them! That was why—*(throws the slippers on the floor)*—that was why we had to spend the summer on Lake Mälar—because you couldn't bear the sea at Saltsiö; that was

why my son had to be christened Eskil—because such was the name of your father; that was why I had to wear your colors, read your authors, eat your favorite dishes, drink your drinks—your chocolate, for example; that was why—Oh, my God—this is frightful to think of, frightful!—Everything came from you to me, even your passions and addictions!—Your soul slithered into mine like a worm into an apple, eating and eating, digging and digging, until all that was left was a rind with some black, messy substance inside! I wanted to escape from you but couldn't; you lay like a snake bewitching me with your black eyes—I felt how my wings rose only to drag me down; I lay with tied feet in the water, and the harder my hands struck out, the more I worked myself down, down right to the bottom where you lay like an enormous crab in order to grip me with your claws—and this is where I now am.

Shame, shame! How I hate you, how I hate you, how I hate you! Yet you only sit, silent, calm, uncaring; not caring whether the moon is waxing or waning, whether it is Christmas or New Year's, whether people are happy or unhappy; incapable of love or hatred; rigid like a stork over a mousehole—unable to grab your quarry, unable to chase it, yet well able to wait until it comes into your clutches. Here you sit in your corner—do you know that it is because of you that it's called the Rat-trap?—Here you scan your paper to find out whether anybody has got into trouble or is wretched or must give up the theater; here you sit, watching out for victims, calculating your chances like a pilot planning a shipwreck, and collecting your tribute!

Poor Amelie, do you know that I pity you because you are unhappy, unhappy like a hurt beast and full of malice because you are hurt?—I can't feel angry with you although I would like to—you are the cornered one after all—well yes, that affair with Bob, why should I bother about it?—In what way does it harm me?—And whether it was you or somebody else who taught me to drink chocolate, what of it? *(Drinks a spoonful from her cup; knowingly)* After all, chocolate is good for one's health. And if I learned from you how to dress

*—tant mieux—*that only strengthened my husband's affection for me—and so you lost what I won—Yes, there are indications that you really have lost him. Yet of course you intended me to fade out of the picture—as you have done, sitting here as you do and regretting what you did—but look here, I just won't do it!—We shan't be petty, don't you agree? And why should I take only what no one else wants!

Perhaps, all things considered, I may indeed be the stronger—for you never got anything out of me, you only gave—and now I am like that thief—as you woke up you found I had all the things you missed.

How else could it come about that everything turned worthless and barren in your hand? With all your tulips and fine affections you never managed to keep a man's love—as I have done; you never learned the art of living from your writers, as I did; nor did you ever get any little Eskil of your own, even though Eskil is the name of your father!

And why are you always silent, silent, silent? Yes, I mistook this for strength; but perhaps all it meant was that you hadn't anything to say—that you never were able to think a thought. *(Gets up and takes the slippers from the floor)* Now I'm going home—with the tulips—*your* tulips! You were unable to learn anything from people—unable to bend—and so you snapped like a dry stalk—but I won't snap.

Thanks ever so much, Amelie, for all your kind lessons; thanks for teaching my husband how to love! Now I'm going home to love him. *(Goes.)*

PART FIVE

Poetry

Poetry is a form of literature that many readers hold in a special kind of affectionate admiration. From the earliest times, probably even before the time of recorded language, poets have been the oracles and prophets of their peoples. Poets have always reflected the temper of the ages in which they live: Homer epitomizes a glorious epoch in Greek history, as Hardy epitomizes the perplexity and despair of late Victorian England.

The nature of poetry. Poetry cannot be precisely defined, but some of its distinguishing characteristics can be described. Poetry deals in matters beyond direct statement—in meanings conditioned by emotional attitudes—and its intention is to evoke the full flavor and impact of experience. Poetry often achieves its effects by the selection of words that are suggestive not only of sensory experience but of emotional attitudes, by the use of figurative comparisons, and by rime and rhythm. Finally, the most distinctive feature of poetry is the organic quality achieved by the close organization of its component parts. The poet in a sense is a maker of experiences. (The Old English word for poet is *scop*, "the maker.") Life is so cluttered with detail that to most of us it often seems chaotic. Like other artists, the poet discards the confusing detail, selects and arranges the remainder to communicate his impression, and thereby creates a meaningful experience for his reader.

What one receives from a poem, then, is an experience. I. A. Richards, perhaps the most stimulating of the contemporary critics of poetry, has pointed out that a poem has a "Total Meaning" which is a blend of the poet's *sense* (what the poem is apparently about), his *feeling* (the poet's attitude toward his subject matter), his *tone* (attitude toward his reader), and his *intention* (aim, or effect). A poet is more or less aware of this fact and, as he writes, expresses all the meanings as fully as his ability and his medium will permit. The reader, in turn, will profit by considering all of them when trying to arrive at a full realization of a poem.

Consider, for example, the following occasional poem by Thomas Hardy, "On an Invitation to the United States." [1]

---

[1] Reprinted with permission of the publisher from *Collected Poems* by Thomas Hardy. Copyright 1925 by The Macmillan Company.

1

My ardours for emprize nigh lost
Since life has bared its bones to me,
I shrink to seek a modern coast
Whose riper times have yet to be;
For, wonning in these ancient lands,
Enchased and lettered as a tomb,
And scored with prints of perished hands,
And chronicled with dates of doom,

2

Where the new regions claim them free
From that long drip of human tears
Which peoples old in tragedy
Have left upon the centuried years.
Though my own Being bear no bloom
I trace the lives such scenes enshrine,
Give past exemplars present room,
And their experience count as mine.

Obviously, the poem is about Hardy's declining an invitation to visit the United States —his reaction to an invitation to come to a land with a more promising future but a less historic past. But statement of the *sense* of the poem is not the equivalent of the poem. In fact, even the following full paraphrase of the sense of the poem falls far short of the poem itself: "I have almost lost my taste for adventure since I discovered how grim life is; I hesitate to seek a new country that has not yet reached full fruition, and has not had a tragic-storied past. Living in this old land, which is much like a tombstone with its inscriptions, I—even though I do not prosper personally—study the lives of the great people of England's history and consider their experience as mine."

For full comprehension we need to absorb the poet's *feeling* about the material. Hardy presents that feeling by implying a contrast between the pasts of the United States and England and by suggesting a relationship between his own past and that of his country. He hints some mild doubt of the United States—a country raw and untried by a long history of adversities and tribulations, though perhaps with a promising future. Just as indirectly he communicates, without sentimentality, his love of England by imagery that pictures her long and tragic history, full of adversities, trials, and struggles; and he makes clear his desire to share what he feels is England's unhappy lot.

We need also to grasp his *tone*, or his attitude toward his reader. His tone, like his feeling, is complex, for, though he is addressing himself particularly to the people of the United States, the people who extended to him the invitation that occasioned the poem, in the background he includes among his audience English compatriots. With neither condescension to the inviters nor depreciation of the worth of their regard, he courteously declines. Though he reminds his background audience, the English, of their mournful history, and indirectly rededicates them as well as himself to his resolve to endure and to be proud of enduring, he steers as widely clear of national conceit and chauvinism as he does of a defensive attitude that would be uncomfortable to English and American alike.

Hardy's full poetic *intention* is to comment feelingly on the individual's relation to his country's history and on his goal in life. Furthermore, he intends to imply the judgment that to assume a share of the unhappy human lot may be a greater act than to achieve purely personal well-being—the attitude of a true pessimist.

The total meaning of "On an Invitation to the United States," therefore, depends on its *sense, feeling, tone,* and *intention.* Briefly, Hardy says that he cannot accept the invitation, acknowledges the favorable prospects of America and expresses his love of England, shows to those who invited him a courteous but not deferential appreciation, and takes the opportunity to comment on the value of tradition. In other words, the communication of this complex meaning provides an experience for the reader, an experience which *is* the poem.

The method of poetry. As "On an Invitation to the United States" reveals, there is more to a poem than the *sense* which can be translated into direct prose statement or paraphrase. Poets characteristically communicate by suggestion or implication; that is, they say more than their words and word combinations literally mean. Perhaps *indirection* is the best term to summarize the way by which poets say so much in so few words.

DICTION. The words of poetry are for the most part the same words that people use to carry on the plain business of living. Individually those words stand for about the same things and have approximately the same sounds in poems as they have in everyday speech. But in poetry words are used more precisely and are ordered more carefully than in conversation. Moreover, a poem does not depend solely upon denotative meanings of words; what the words suggest—their connotative rather than their denotative values—may be even more important to its effect. Consider the implications of some of the words in "On an Invitation to the United States": *modern, riper, emprize, wonning,* In context *modern* has just a slightly unfavorable overtone; it suggests, though faintly, that Hardy had in mind an overmodernity, an excessive degree of modernity. Much the same is true of the word *riper* in its context here: Hardy seems to imply that the United States is presently lacking the maturity he cherishes in England. *Emprize* and *wonning* are also highly implicative words. Their effect here is to promote, by supplying atmosphere, Hardy's intention of getting the reader to understand and approve his cherishing of the past. Both are archaic—*emprize* having been supplanted by the modern form *enterprise* or *adventure;* and *wonning,* by *dwelling, residing, living.* By using these archaisms along with such other words as *old, centuried, ancient, chronicled, dates of doom,* Hardy reminds the reader of Norse and Norman invaders, the Anglo-Saxon Chronicle, Alfred and Harold, the Domesday Book, and Runnymede and Magna Charta.

IMAGERY. The selection of language in poetry is governed primarily by the poet's desire to give his reader sensory experience—as Coleridge says, "to instill that energy into the mind, which compels the imagination to produce the picture." By appealing to one or more of the physical senses, the poet arouses both the mind and the emotion of the reader so that he in a measure experiences physical sensation. These things imaginatively sensed are collectively known as *imagery.*

THE CONCRETE WORD. Doubtless the simplest device to evoke imagery is the single concrete word, a word such as *scored* or *chronicled* in Hardy's poem. Hardy might have written *marked* "with prints of perished hands" instead of "*scored* with prints of perished hands." But he chose *scored* because it supplies to the reader's imagination the image Hardy desired, that of signs much deeper and more permanent than mere surface "marks." So with *chronicled.* Hardy chose a word to suggest a whole complex of meaning, the Anglo-Saxon Chronicle and even England's whole history.

FIGURATIVE LANGUAGE. Another device poets use to create imagery is figurative language. Basically, most figures are comparisons, expressed or implied, of things not ordinarily thought of as being alike—comparisons that do not on the surface seem logical but that on closer inspection prove illuminating. For instance, Hardy says "life has bared its bones to me." He is using a *metaphor* here, an implied comparison that not only suggests his interpretation of the true character of life, but vividly reveals Hardy's state of mind. Again, Hardy, in a *simile*, directly compares England to a tomb—"ancient lands,/Enchased and lettered as a tomb." Thus he suggests to the reader the richness of England's past—the multitude of deeds and personages that make up England's history. As the inscriptions on tombs record the deeds and exploits (as well as the vital statistics) of the persons buried in the tombs, so England is filled with places and covered with monuments and shrines that recall the richness of her past.

RHYTHM AND RIME. Another kind of indirection prominent in the method of poetry is the use of sound effects to intensify meaning. Along with the attempt to communicate his total meaning by choosing words and images which convey his sense, feeling, and tone, the poet attempts to organize his words into a pattern of sound that is a part of that total meaning. The sound of poetry, then, like the diction and the imagery, is to be considered only in relation to the total design of the poem.

Sound effects are the products of organized repetitions. *Rhythm* is the result of systematically *stressing* or *accenting* words and syllables, whereas *rime* repeats similar sounds in some apparent scheme. Both rhythm and rime arouse interest in the reader, for as soon as he grasps their pattern he unconsciously expects them to continue. Expecting their continuation, he is more attentive not only to the sound itself but to the sense, feeling, and tone of the poet.

Different rhythms tend to arouse different emotions.

> Scots, wha hae wi' Wallace bled,
> Scots, wham Bruce has aften led,
> Welcome to your gory bed,
>   Or to victory!
>
> Now's the day, and now's the hour:
> See the front o' battle lour;
> See approach proud Edward's power—
>   Chains and slavery! [2]

The rhythmic beat here, along with the sense of the words, sounds a grim, determined battle cry and stirs the reader to a quicker beating of the blood.

> They sat them down upon the yellow sand,
> Between the sun and moon upon the shore;
> And sweet it was to dream of Fatherland,
> Of child, and wife, and slave; but evermore
> Most weary seemed the sea, weary the oar,
> Weary the wandering fields of barren foam.
> Then some one said, "We will return no more;"
> And all at once they sang, "Our island home
> Is far beyond the wave; we will no longer roam." [3]

Here the rhythm, aided by the heavy frequency of liquids and nasals, helps to induce in the reader a sense of the dreaminess and lack of ambition that, according to the myth, characterized all those who ate the lotus.

Rhythms exist for the full gamut of emotions, since the only limitation upon the

[2] From "Scots, Wha Hae wi' Wallace Bled" by Robert Burns.
[3] From "The Lotos-Eaters" by Alfred, Lord Tennyson. See pages 661–62.

variety of rhythms is that which word-meaning imposes. Thus rhythms can easily be found for those quieter emotions accompanying meditation and reflection:

> "A cold coming we had of it,
> Just the worst time of the year
> For a journey, and such a long journey:
> The ways deep and the weather sharp,
> The very dead of winter."
> And the camels galled, sore-footed, refractory,
> Lying down in the melting snow.[4]

This rhythm is less patterned than the preceding two. The poet here has departed from a strict rhythmic movement much more frequently and prominently than has either of the two preceding poets. These departures, while preserving a reflective mood, make for informality and a conversational tone. Variation from a rigid metrical pattern is often found in poetry, especially in modern poetry.

Rime—a patterned recurrence of like or similar sounds—also functions indirectly to intensify meaning. It is a further impressing of design upon material in order to achieve an intention in sense, feeling, and tone. It serves as a binding and unifying element and lends continuity. It may also be used for emphasis, especially when, as often occurs, the rime word at the end of a line concludes a phrase or clause. And rime, like rhythm, affords pleasure at the fulfillment of a pattern the reader has unconsciously recognized. When Tennyson writes

> They sat them down upon the yellow sand,

the reader recognizes the likelihood that Tennyson will somewhere, perhaps in the very next line, come back to a sound similar to the one on which he stopped the first, and is pleased when he finds that expectation fulfilled:

> They sat them down upon the yellow sand,
> Between the sun and moon upon the shore;
> And sweet it was to dream of Fatherland.

Closely allied to metrical and rime pattern are a number of textural devices—devices that are similar to rime in that they involve correspondence of sounds. These devices tend to occur within the line unit of poetry but affect the total sound pattern. *Alliteration, assonance, consonance* give ease and speed to pronunciation, stepping up melody and tempo. Such pleasantness of sound is called euphony. Not always, however, is euphony desirable. In fact, cacophony, its opposite, may better achieve the poet's intention. For instance, in Eliot's line

> And the camels galled, sore-footed, refractory

the last three words, *galled, sore-footed, refractory,* cause a sense of strain and slowing of tempo appropriate to the experience he is describing.

The nature of poetry and the method of poetry are so dependent upon each other that one cannot be conceived without the other. Their relationship is organic; it is not a mere mechanical association. In other words, the way of saying a thing is a large part of what is said. A poem does much more than say or state. It transmutes sense, feeling, tone, and intention into experience, into being itself.

[4] From "Journey of the Magi" by T. S. Eliot. See pages 650–51 for the full text.

THE POET AS STORYTELLER

ANONYMOUS

Brennan on the Moor

It's of a fearless highwayman a story now I'll tell:
His name was Willie Brennan, and in Ireland he did dwell;
'Twas on the Limerick mountains he commenced his wild career,
Where many a wealthy gentleman before him shook with fear.
    Brennan on the moor, Brennan on the moor,
    Bold and yet undaunted stood young Brennan on the moor.

A brace of loaded pistols he carried night and day,
He never robb'd a poor man upon the King's highway;
But what he'd taken from the rich, like Turpin and Black Bess,
He always did divide it with the widow in distress.   10

One night he robbed a packman, his name was Pedlar Bawn;
They travelled on together, till day began to dawn;
The pedlar seeing his money gone, likewise his watch and chain,
He at once encountered Brennan and robbed him back again.

When Brennan saw the pedlar was as good a man as he,
He took him on the highway, his companion for to be;
The pedlar threw away his pack without any more delay,
And proved a faithful comrade until his dying day.

One day upon the highway Willie he sat down,
He met the Mayor of Cashel, a mile outside the town;   20
The Mayor he knew his features, "I think, young man," said he,
"Your name is Willie Brennan, you must come along with me."

As Brennan's wife had gone to town provisions for to buy,
When she saw her Willie, she began to weep and cry;
He says, "Give me that tenpence;" as soon as Willie spoke,
She handed him the blunderbuss from underneath her cloak.

Then with his loaded blunderbuss, the truth I will unfold,
He made the Mayor to tremble, and robbed him of his gold;
One hundred pounds was offered for his apprehension there,
And with his horse and saddle to the mountains did repair.   30

Then Brennan being an outlaw upon the mountain high,
Where cavalry and infantry to take him they did try,
He laughed at them with scorn, until at length, it's said,
By a false-hearted young man he was basely betrayed.

In the County of Tipperary, in a place they called Clonmore,
Willie Brennan and his comrade that day did suffer sore;
He lay among the fern which was thick upon the field,
And nine wounds he had received before that he did yield.

Then Brennan and his companion knowing they were betrayed,
He with the mounted cavalry a noble battle made;   40
He lost his foremost finger, which was shot off by a ball;
So Brennan and his comrade they were taken after all.

So they were taken prisoners, in irons they were bound,
And conveyed to Clonmel jail, strong walls did them surround;
They were tried and found guilty, the judge made this reply,
"For robbing on the King's highway you are both condemned to die."

Farewell unto my wife, and to my children three,
Likewise my aged father, he may shed tears for me,
And to my loving mother, who tore her gray locks and cried,
Saying, "I wish, Willie Brennan, in your cradle you had died."   50

ANONYMOUS

The Three Ravens

There were three ravens sat on a tree,
    Downe a downe, hay downe, hay downe.
There were three ravens sat on a tree,
    With a downe.

There were three ravens sat on a tree,
They were as blacke as they might be.
    With a downe derrie, derrie, derrie, downe,
        downe.

The one of them said to his mate,
"Where shall we our breakfast take?"

"Downe in yonder greene field,   10
There lies a knight slain under his shield.

"His hounds they lie downe at his feete,
So well they can their master keepe.

"His haukes they flie so eagerly,
There's no fowle dare him come nie."

Downe there comes a fallow doe,
As great with yong as she might goe.

She lift up his bloudy hed,
And kist his wounds that were so red.

She got him up upon her backe,   20
And carried him to earthen lake.[1]

She buried him before the prime,
She was dead herselfe ere euen-song time.

God send every gentleman,
Such haukes, such hounds, and such a leman.[2]

ANONYMOUS

The Twa Corbies

As I was walking all alane,
I heard twa corbies making a mane;[3]
The tane[4] unto the t'other say,
"Where sall we gang[5] and dine today?"

"In behint yon auld fail dyke,[6]
I wot[7] there lies a new slain knight;
And naebody kens[8] that he lies there
But his hawk, his hound, and lady fair.

[1] pit.   [2] lover.   [3] moan.   [4] one.   [5] go.
[6] turf wall.   [7] know.   [8] knows.

"His hound is to the hunting gane,
His hawk to fetch the wild-fowl hame,   10
His lady's ta'en another mate,
So we may mak our dinner sweet.

"Ye'll sit on his white hause-bane,[9]
And I'll pike out his bonny blue een;
Wi ae lock o' his gowden hair
We'll theek[10] our nest when it grows bare.

"Mony a one for him makes mane,
But nane sall ken where he is gane;
O'er his white banes, when they are bare,
The wind sall blaw for evermair."   20

EZRA POUND

Ballad of the Goodly Fere

*Simon Zelotes speaketh it somewhile
after the Crucifixion.*

Ha' we lost the goodliest fere o' all
For the priests and the gallows tree?
Aye, lover he was of brawny men,
O' ships and the open sea.

When they came wi' a host to take Our Man
His smile was good to see;
"First let these go!" quo' our Goodly Fere,
"Or I'll see ye damned," says he.

Aye, he sent us out through the crossed high
        spears,
And the scorn of his laugh rang free;   10
"Why took ye not me when I walked about
Alone in the town?" says he.

Oh, we drunk his "Hale" in the good red wine
When we last made company;
No capon priest was the Goodly Fere
But a man o' men was he.

I ha' seen him drive a hundred men
Wi' a bundle o' cords swung free,
That they took the high and holy house
For their pawn and treasury.   20

[9] neckbone.   [10] thatch.

BALLAD OF THE GOODLY FERE   From Ezra Pound,
Personae. Copyright 1926 by Ezra Pound. Reprinted
by permission of New Directions Publishing Corporation.

They'll no' get him a' in a book I think,
Though they write it cunningly;
No mouse of the scrolls was the Goodly Fere
But aye loved the open sea.

If they think they ha' snared our Goodly Fere
They are fools to the last degree.
"I'll go to the feast," quo' our Goodly Fere,
"Though I go to the gallows tree."

"Ye ha' seen me heal the lame and blind,
And wake the dead," says he;   30
"Ye shall see one thing to master all:
'Tis how a brave man dies on the tree."

A son of God was the Goodly Fere
That bade us his brothers be.
I ha' seen him cow a thousand men.
I have seen him upon the tree.

He cried no cry when they drave the nails
And the blood gushed hot and free;
The hounds of the crimson sky gave tongue
But never a cry cried he.   40

I ha' seen him cow a thousand men
On the hills o' Galilee;
They whined as he walked out calm between,
Wi' his eyes like the grey o' the sea,

Like the sea that brooks no voyaging
With the winds unleashed and free,
Like the sea that he cowed at Genseret
Wi' twey words spoke' suddently.

A master of men was the Goodly Fere,
A mate of the wind and sea;   50
If they think they ha' slain our Goodly Fere
They are fools eternally.

I ha' seen him eat o' the honey-comb
Sin' they nailed him to the tree.

JOHN CROWE RANSOM

Captain Carpenter

Captain Carpenter rose up in his prime
Put on his pistols and went riding out
But had got wellnigh nowhere at that time
Till he fell in with ladies in a rout.

CAPTAIN CARPENTER   Reprinted from *Selected Poems*
by John Crowe Ransom, by permission of Alfred A.
Knopf, Inc. Copyright, 1924 by Alfred A. Knopf, Inc.
Renewed, 1952 by John Crowe Ransom.

It was a pretty lady and all her train
That played with him so sweetly but before
An hour she'd taken a sword with all her main
And twined him of his nose for evermore.

Captain Carpenter mounted up one day
And rode straightway into a stranger rogue   10
That looked unchristian but be that as may
The Captain did not wait upon prologue.

But drew upon him out of his great heart
The other swung against him with a club
And cracked his two legs at the shinny part
And let him roll and stick like any tub.

Captain Carpenter rode many a time
From male and female took he sundry harms
He met the wife of Satan crying "I'm
The she-wolf bids you shall bear no more
      arms."   20

Their strokes and counters whistled in the wind
I wish he had delivered half his blows
But where she should have made off like a hind
The bitch bit off his arms at the elbows.

And Captain Carpenter parted with his ears
To a black devil that used him in this wise
O Jesus ere his threescore and ten years
Another had plucked out his sweet blue eyes.

Captain Carpenter got up on his roan
And sallied from the gate in hell's despite   30
I heard him asking in the grimmest tone
If any enemy yet there was to fight?

"To any adversary it is fame
If he risk to be wounded by my tongue
O burnt in two beneath my red heart's flame
Such are the perils he is cast among.

"But if he can he has a pretty choice
From an anatomy with little to lose
Whether he cut my tongue and take my voice
Or whether it be my round red heart he
      choose."   40

It was the neatest knave that ever was seen
Stepping in perfume from his lady's bower
Who at this word put in his merry mien
And fell on Captain Carpenter like a tower.

I would not knock old fellows in the dust
But there lay Captain Carpenter on his back
His weapons were the old heart in his bust
And a blade shook between rotten teeth alack.

The rogue in scarlet and grey soon knew his mind
He wished to get his trophy and depart   50
With gentle apology and touch refined
He pierced him and produced the Captain's heart.

God's mercy rest on Captain Carpenter now
I thought him Sirs an honest gentleman
Citizen husband soldier and scholar enow
Let jangling kites eat of him if they can.

But God's deep curses follow after those
That shore him of his goodly nose and ears
His legs and strong arms at the two elbows
And eyes that had not watered seventy years.   60

The curse of hell upon the sleek upstart
That got the Captain finally on his back
And took the red red vitals of his heart
And made the kites to whet their beaks clack clack.

JOHN MANIFOLD

The Griesly [1] Wife

"Lie still, my newly married wife,
    Lie easy as you can.
You're young and ill accustomed yet
    To sleeping with a man."

The snow lay thick, the moon was full
    And shone across the floor.
The young wife went with never a word
    Barefooted to the door.

He up and followed sure and fast,
    The moon shone clear and white.   10
But before his coat was on his back
    His wife was out of sight.

He trod the trail wherever it turned
    By many a mound and scree,
And still the barefoot track led on,
    And an angry man was he.

He followed fast, he followed slow,
    And still he called her name,
But only the dingoes of the hills
    Yowled back at him again.   20

[1] ghastly, grisly, uncanny

His hair stood up along his neck,
    His angry mood was gone,
For the track of the two bare feet gave out
    And a four-foot track went on.

Her nightgown lay upon the snow
    As it might upon the sheet,
But the track that led from where it lay
    Was never of human feet.

His heart turned over in his chest,
    He looked from side to side,   30
And he thought more of his gumwood fire
    Than he did of his griesly bride.

And first he started walking back
    And then began to run,
And his quarry wheeled at the end of her track
    And hunted him in turn.

Oh, long the fire may burn for him
    And open stand the door,
And long the bed may wait empty:
    He'll not be back any more.   40

T. S. ELIOT

Journey of the Magi

"A cold coming we had of it,
Just the worst time of the year
For a journey, and such a long journey:
The ways deep and the weather sharp,
The very dead of winter."
And the camels galled, sore-footed, refractory,
Lying down in the melting snow.
There were times we regretted
The summer palaces on slopes, the terraces,
And the silken girls bringing sherbet.   10
Then the camel men cursing and grumbling
And running away, and wanting their liquor and
    women,
And the night-fires going out, and the lack of
    shelters,
And the cities hostile and the towns unfriendly
And the villages dirty and charging high prices:
A hard time we had of it.
At the end we preferred to travel all night,
Sleeping in snatches,

With the voices singing in our ears, saying
That this was all folly.   20

Then at dawn we came down to a temperate
  valley,
Wet, below the snow line, smelling of vegetation;
With a running stream and a water-mill beating
  the darkness,
And three trees on the low sky,
And an old white horse galloped away in the
  meadow.
Then we came to a tavern with vine-leaves over
  the lintel,
Six hands at an open door dicing for pieces of
  silver,
And feet kicking the empty wine-skins.
But there was no information, and so we con-
  tinued
And arrived at evening, not a moment too
  soon   30
Finding the place; it was (you may say) satis-
  factory.

All this was a long time ago, I remember,
And I would do it again, but set down
This set down
This: were we led all that way for
Birth or Death? There was a Birth, certainly,
We had evidence and no doubt. I had seen birth
  and death,
But had thought they were different; this Birth
  was
Hard and bitter agony for us, like Death, our
  death.
We returned to our places, these Kingdoms,   40
But no longer at ease here, in the old dispensation,
With an alien people clutching their gods.
I should be glad of another death.

A. E. HOUSMAN

Hell Gate

  Onward led the road again
Through the sad uncoloured plain
Under twilight brooding dim,
And along the utmost rim
Wall and rampart risen to sight
Cast a shadow not of night,

And beyond them seemed to glow
Bonfires lighted long ago.
And my dark conductor broke
Silence at my side and spoke,   10
Saying, "You conjecture well:
Yonder is the gate of hell."

  Ill as yet the eye could see
The eternal masonry,
But beneath it on the dark
To and fro there stirred a spark.
And again the sombre guide
Knew my question, and replied:
"At hell gate the damned in turn
Pace for sentinel and burn."   20

  Dully at the leaden sky
Staring, and with idle eye
Measuring the listless plain,
I began to think again.
Many things I thought of then,
Battle, and the loves of men,
Cities entered, oceans crossed,
Knowledge gained and virtue lost,
Cureless folly done and said,
And the lovely way that led   30
To the slimepit and the mire
And the everlasting fire.
And against a smoulder dun
And a dawn without a sun
Did the nearing bastion loom,
And across the gate of gloom
Still one saw the sentry go,
Trim and burning, to and fro,
One for women to admire
In his finery of fire.   40
Something, as I watched him pace,
Minded me of time and place,
Soldiers of another corps
And a sentry known before.

  Ever darker hell on high
Reared its strength upon the sky,
And our football on the track
Fetched the daunting echo back.
But the soldier pacing still
The insuperable sill,   50
Nursing his tormented pride,
Turned his head to neither side,
Sunk into himself apart
And the hell-fire of his heart.
But against our entering in
From the drawbridge Death and Sin
Rose to render key and sword
To their father and their lord.

And the portress foul to see
Lifted up her eyes on me   60
Smiling, and I made reply:
"Met again, my lass," said I.
Then the sentry turned his head,
Looked, and knew me, and was Ned.

WILLIAM MORRIS

The Haystack in the Floods

Had she come all the way for this,
To part at last without a kiss?
Yea, had she borne the dirt and rain
That her own eyes might see him slain
Beside the haystack in the floods?

Along the dripping, leafless woods,
The stirrup touching either shoe,
She rode astride as troopers do;
With kirtle kilted to her knee,
To which the mud splashed wretchedly;   10
And the wet dripped from every tree
Upon her head and heavy hair,
And on her eyelids broad and fair;
The tears and rain ran down her face.

By fits and starts they rode apace,
And very often was his place
Far off from her; he had to ride
Ahead, to see what might betide
When the roads crossed; and sometimes, when
There rose a murmuring from his men,   20
Had to turn back with promises.
Ah me! she had but little ease;
And often for pure doubt and dread
She sobbed, made giddy in the head
By the swift riding; while, for cold,
Her slender fingers scarce could hold
The wet reins; yea, and scarcely, too,
She felt the foot within her shoe
Against the stirrup: all for this,
To part at last without a kiss   30
Beside the haystack in the floods.

For when they neared that old soaked hay,
They saw across the only way
That Judas, Godmar, and the three
Red running lions dismally
Grinned from his pennon, under which
In one straight line along the ditch,
They counted thirty heads.

                              So then
While Robert turned round to his men,
She saw at once the wretched end,   40
And, stooping down, tried hard to rend
Her coif the wrong way from her head,
And hid her eyes; while Robert said,
"Nay, love, 'tis scarcely two to one;
At Poictiers where we made them run
So fast—why, sweet my love, good cheer,
The Gascon frontier is so near,
Naught after us."

                    But: "O!" she said,
"My God; my God! I have to tread
The long way back without you; then   50
The court at Paris; those six men;
The gratings of the Chatelet;
The swift Seine on some rainy day
Like this, and people standing by,
And laughing, while my weak hands try
To recollect how strong men swim.
All this, or else a life with him,
For which I should be damned at last;
Would God that this next hour were past!"

He answered not, but cried his cry,   60
"St. George for Marny!" cheerily;
And laid his hand upon her rein.
Alas! no man of all his train
Gave back that cheery cry again;
And, while for rage his thumb beat fast
Upon his sword-hilt, someone cast
About his neck a kerchief long,
And bound him.

                    Then they went along
To Godmar; who said: "Now, Jehane,
Your lover's life is on the wane   70
So fast, that, if this very hour
You yield not as my paramour,
He will not see the rain leave off;
Nay, keep your tongue from gibe and scoff,
Sir Robert, or I slay you now."

She laid her hand upon her brow,
Then gazed upon the palm, as though
She thought her forehead bled, and "No!"
She said, and turned her head away,
As there was nothing else to say,   80
And everything was settled; red
Grew Godmar's face from chin to head—
"Jehane, on yonder hill there stands
My castle, guarding well my lands;
What hinders me from taking you,

And doing that I list to do
To your fair willful body, while
Your knight lies dead?"

     A wicked smile
Wrinkled her face, her lips grew thin,
A long way out she thrust her chin: 90
"You know that I should strangle you
While you were sleeping; or bite through
Your throat, by God's help; ah!" she said,
"Lord Jesus, pity your poor maid!
For in such wise they hem me in,
I cannot choose but sin and sin,
Whatever happens; yet I think
They could not make me eat or drink,
And so should I just reach my rest."
"Nay, if you do not my behest,   100
O Jehane! though I love you well,"
Said Godmar, "would I fail to tell
All that I know?" "Foul lies," she said.
"Eh? lies, my Jehane? by God's head,
At Paris folks would deem them true!
Do you know, Jehane, they cry for you:
'Jehane the brown! Jehane the brown!
Give us Jehane to burn or drown!'
Eh!—gag me Robert!—sweet my friend,
This were indeed a piteous end   110
For those long fingers, and long feet,
And long neck, and smooth shoulders sweet;
An end that few men would forget
That saw it. So, an hour yet—
Consider, Jehane, which to take
Of life or death!"

    So, scarce awake,
Dismounting, did she leave that place,
And totter some yards; with her face
Turned upward to the sky she lay,
Her head on a wet heap of hay,   120
And fell asleep; and while she slept,
And did not dream, the minutes crept
Round to the twelve again; but she,

Being waked at last, sighed quietly,
And strangely childlike came, and said:
"I will not." Straightway Godmar's head,
As though it hung on strong wires, turned
Most sharply round, and his face burned.

For Robert, both his eyes were dry—
He could not weep—but gloomily   130
He seemed to watch the rain; yea, too,
His lips were firm; he tried once more
To touch her lips; she reached out, sore
And vain desire so tortured them,
The poor gray lips, and now the hem
Of his sleeve brushed them.

     With a start
Up Godmar rose, thrust them apart;
From Robert's throat he loosed the bands
Of silk and mail; with empty hands
Held out, she stood and gazed, and saw,   140
The long bright blade without a flaw
Glide out from Godmar's sheath, his hand
In Robert's hair; she saw him bend
Back Robert's head; she saw him send
The thin steel down; the blow told well—
Right backward the knight Robert fell,
And moaned as dogs do, being half dead,
Unwitting, as I deem; so then
Godmar turned grinning to his men,
Who ran, some five or six, and beat   150
His head to pieces at their feet.

Then Godmar turned again and said:
"So, Jehane, the first fitte is read!
Take note, my lady, that your way
Lies backward to the Chatelet!"
She shook her head and gazed awhile
At her cold hands with a rueful smile,
As though this thing had made her mad.

This was the parting that they had
Beside the haystack in the floods.   160

WILLIAM BUTLER YEATS

For Anne Gregory

"Never shall a young man,
Thrown into despair
By those great honey-coloured
Ramparts at your ear,
Love you for yourself alone
And not your yellow hair."

"But I can get hair-dye
And set such colour there,
Brown, or black, or carrot,
That young men in despair   10
May love me for myself alone
And not my yellow hair."

"I heard an old religious man
But yesternight declare
That he had found a text to prove
That only God, my dear,
Could love you for yourself alone
And not your yellow hair."

WILLIAM BUTLER YEATS

Down by the Salley Gardens

Down by the salley gardens my love and I did
meet;
She passed the salley gardens with little snow-
white feet.
She bid me take love easy, as the leaves grow on
the tree;
But I, being young and foolish, with her would
not agree.

In a field by a river my love and I did stand,
And on my leaning shoulder she laid her snow-
white hand.
She bid me take life easy, as the grass grows on
the weirs
But I was young and foolish, and now am full of
tears.

ANDREW MARVELL

To His Coy Mistress *8 syllables Landih vattamana*

Had we but world enough, and time,
This coyness, Lady, were no crime.
We would sit down and think which way
To walk and pass our long love's day.
Thou by the Indian Ganges' side
Shouldst rubies find; I by the tide
Of Humber would complain. I would
Love you ten years before the Flood,
And you should, if you please, refuse
Till the conversion of the Jews.   10
My vegetable love would grow
Vaster than empires, and more slow;
An hundred years would go to praise
Thine eyes and on thy forehead gaze;
Two hundred to adore each breast,

FOR ANNE GREGORY   Reprinted with permission of the publisher from *Collected Poems* by William Butler Yeats. Copyright 1933 by The Macmillan Company, renewed 1961 by Bertha Georgie Yeats.
DOWN BY THE SALLEY GARDENS   Reprinted with permission of the publisher from *Collected Poems* by William Butler Yeats. Copyright 1906 by The Macmillan Company, renewed 1934 by William Butler Yeats.

But thirty thousand to the rest;
An age at least to every part,
And the last age should show your heart.
For, Lady, you deserve this state,
Nor would I love at lower rate. 20

But at my back I always hear
Time's wingèd chariot hurrying near;
And yonder all before us lie
Deserts of vast eternity.
Thy beauty shall no more be found,
Nor, in thy marble vault, shall sound
My echoing song; then worms shall try
That long preserved virginity,
And your quaint honor turn to dust,
And into ashes all my lust: 30
The grave's a fine and private place,
But none, I think, do there embrace.

Now therefore, while the youthful hue
Sits on thy skin like morning dew,
And while thy willing soul transpires
At every pore with instant fires,
Now let us sport us while we may,
And now, like amorous birds of prey
Rather at once our time devour
Than languish in his slow-chapped power. 40
Let us roll all our strength and all
Our sweetness up into one ball,
And tear our pleasures with rough strife
Thorough the iron gates of life:
Thus, though we cannot make our sun
Stand still, yet we will make him run.

ROBERT HERRICK

Upon Julia's Clothes

Whenas in silks my Julia goes,
Then, then, methinks, how sweetly flows
The liquefaction of her clothes.

Next, when I cast mine eyes, and see
That brave vibration, each way free,
Oh, how that glittering taketh me!

EDNA ST. VINCENT MILLAY

I Know I Am But Summer

I know I am but summer to your heart,
And not the full four seasons of the year;
And you must welcome from another part
Such noble moods as are not mine, my dear.

No gracious weight of golden fruits to sell
Have I, nor any wise and wintry thing;
And I have loved you all too long and well
To carry still the high sweet breast of Spring.
Wherefore I say: O love, as summer goes,
I must be gone, steal forth with silent drums, 10
That you may hail anew the bird and rose
When I come back to you, as summer comes.
Else will you seek, at some not distant time,
Even your summer in another clime.

WILLIAM SHAKESPEARE

*Shakespearean:
Sonnet a 3 quatrain
Couplet*

Let Me Not to the Marriage of True Minds

Let me not to the marriage of true minds
Admit impediments. Love is not love
Which alters when it alteration finds,
Or bends with the remover to remove.
O, no! it is an ever-fixèd mark *mas.*
That looks on tempests and is never shaken. *fem.*
It is the star to every wand'ring bark, *mas.*
Whose worth's unknown, although his height be
taken. *fem.*
Love's not Time's fool, though rosy lips and cheeks
Within his bending sickle's compass come. *approx 10*
Love alters not with his brief hours and weeks,
But bears it out even to the edge of doom. *approx*
   If this be error and upon me proved,
   I never writ, nor no man ever loved.

ELINOR WYLIE

I Hereby Swear That to Uphold Your House

I hereby swear that to uphold your house
I would lay my bones in quick destroying lime
Or turn my flesh to timber for all time;
Cut down my womanhood; lop off the boughs
Of that perpetual ecstasy that grows
From the heart's core; condemn it as a crime
If it be broader than a beam, or climb
Above the stature that your roof allows.

I am not the hearthstone nor the cornerstone
Within this noble fabric you have builded;   10
Not by my beauty was its cornice gilded;
Not on my courage were its arches thrown:
My lord, adjudge my strength, and set me where
I bear a little more than I can bear.

JOHN CIARDI

Men Marry What They Need.
I Marry You

Men marry what they need. I marry you,
morning by morning, day by day, night by night,
and every marriage makes this marriage new.

In the broken name of heaven, in the light
that shatters granite, by the spitting shore,
in air that leaps and wobbles like a kite,

I marry you from time and a great door
is shut and stays shut against wind, sea, stone,
sunburst, and heavenfall. An home once more

inside our walls of skin and struts of bone,   10
man-woman, woman-man, and each the other,
I marry you by all dark and all dawn

and learn to let time spend. Why should I bother
the flies about me? Let them buzz and do.
Men marry their queen, their daughter, or their
    mother

by names they prove, but that thin buzz whines
    through:
when reason falls to reasons, cause is true.
Men marry what they need. I marry you.

E. E. CUMMINGS   *Sonnet*

if i have made, my lady, intricate

if i have made, my lady, intricate
imperfect various things chiefly which wrong
your eyes (frailer than most deep dreams are frail)
songs less firm than your body's whitest song
upon my mind—if i have failed to snare
the glance too shy—if through my singing slips
the very skillful strangeness of your smile

MEN MARRY WHAT THEY NEED. I MARRY YOU   Copyright, 1955, by the Trustees of Rutgers College in New Jersey. From *I Marry You*, 1958, by John Ciardi. Reprinted by permission of the author.

the keen primeval silence of your hair
—let the world say "his most wise music stole
nothing from death"—
            you only will create   10
(who are so perfectly alive) my shame:
lady through whose profound and fragile lips
the sweet small clumsy feet of April came

into the ragged meadow of my soul.

CARL SANDBURG

For You

The peace of great doors be for you.
Wait at the knobs, at the panel oblongs.
Wait for the great hinges.

The peace of great churches be for you,
Where the players of lofty pipe organs
Practice old lovely fragments, alone.

The peace of great books be for you,
Stains of pressed clover leaves on pages,
Bleach of the light of years held in leather.

The peace of great prairies be for you.   10
Listen among windplayers in cornfields,
The wind leaning over its oldest music.

The peace of great seas be for you.
Wait on a hook of land, a rock footing
For you, wait in the salt wash.

The peace of great mountains be for you,
The sleep and the eyesight of eagles,
Sheet mist shadows and the long look across.

The peace of great hearts be for you,
Valves of the blood of the sun,   20
Pumps of the strongest wants we cry.

The peace of great silhouettes be for you,
Shadow dancers alive in your blood now,
Alive and crying, "Let us out, let us out."

The peace of great changes be for you.
Whispers, Oh beginners in the hills.
Tumble, Oh cubs—tomorrow belongs to you.

IF I HAVE MADE, MY LADY, INTRICATE   Copyright, 1926, by Horace Liveright; renewed, 1954, by E. E. Cummings. Reprinted from his *Poems 1923–1954* by permission of Harcourt, Brace & World, Inc.
FOR YOU   From *Smoke and Steel* by Carl Sandburg, copyright, 1920, by Harcourt, Brace & World, Inc.; copyright 1948, by Carl Sandburg. Reprinted by permission of the publisher.

The peace of great loves be for you.
Rain, soak these roots; wind, shatter the dry rot.
Bars of sunlight, grips of the earth, hug these. 30

The peace of great ghosts be for you,
Phantoms of night-gray eyes, ready to go
To the fog-star dumps, to the fire-white doors.

Yes, the peace of great phantoms be for you,
Phantom iron men, mothers of bronze,
Keepers of the lean clean breeds.

ANONYMOUS

The Maidens Came

The maidens came
When I was in my mother's bower:
I had all that I would.
The bailey [1] beareth the bell away:
The lily, the rose, the rose I lay.

The silver is white, red is the gold:
The robes they lay in fold.
The bailey beareth the bell away:
The lily, the rose, the rose I lay.

And through the glass window shines the sun. 10
How should I love, and I so young?
The bailey beareth the bell away:
The lily, the lily, the rose I lay.

ANONYMOUS

Back and Side Go Bare

Back and side go bare, go bare,
   Both foot and hand go cold;
But, belly, God send thee good ale enough,
   Whether it be new or old.

I cannot eat but little meat,
   My stomach is not good;
But sure I think that I can drink
   With him that wears a hood.
Though I go bare, take ye no care,
   I am nothing a-cold; 10
I stuff my skin so full within
   Of jolly good ale and old.

Back and side go bare, &c.

[1] bailiff or steward.

I love no roast but a nutbrown toast,
   And a crab laid in the fire;
A little bread shall do me stead,
   Much bread I not desire. 20
No frost nor snow, no wind, I trow,
   Can hurt me if I would,
I am so wrapped, and thoroughly lapped
   Of jolly good ale and old.

Back and side go bare, &c.

Now let them drink, till they nod and wink,
   Even as good fellows should do; 30
They shall not miss to have the bliss
   Good ale doth bring men to;
And all poor souls that have scoured bowls
   Or have them lustily trolled,
God save the lives of them and their wives,
   Whether they be young or old.

Back and side go bare, go bare,
   Both foot and hand go cold;
But, belly, God send thee good ale enough,
   Whether it be new or old. 40

WALT WHITMAN

The Commonplace

The commonplace I sing;
How cheap is health! how cheap nobility!
Abstinence, no falsehood, no gluttony, lust;
The open air I sing, freedom, toleration,
(Take here the mainest lesson—less from books—
      less from the schools,)
The common day and night—the common earth
      and waters,
Your farm—your work, trade, occupation,
The democratic wisdom underneath, like solid
      ground for all.

THOM GUNN

On the Move

"Man, you gotta Go."

The blue jay scuffling in the bushes follows
Some hidden purpose, and the gust of birds
That spurts across the field, the wheeling swallows,
Have nested in the trees and undergrowth.

ON THE MOVE From *The Sense of Movement* by
Thom Gunn. Reprinted by permission of Faber and
Faber Ltd.

Seeking their instinct, or their poise, or both,
One moves with an uncertain violence
Under the dust thrown by a baffled sense
Or the dull thunder of approximate words.

On motorcycles, up the road, they come:
Small, black, as flies hanging in heat, the Boys,   10
Until the distance throws them forth, their hum
Bulges to thunder held by calf and thigh.
In goggles, donned impersonality,
In gleaming jackets trophied with the dust,
They strap in doubt—by hiding it, robust—
And almost hear a meaning in their noise.

Exact conclusion of their hardiness
Has no shape yet, but from known whereabouts
They ride, direction where the tires press.
They scare a flight of birds across the field: 20
Much that is natural, to the will must yield.
Men manufacture both machine and soul,
And use what they imperfectly control
To dare a future from the taken routes.

It is a part solution, after all.
One is not necessarily discord
On earth; or damned because, half animal,
One lacks direct instinct, because one wakes
Afloat on movement that divides and breaks.
One joins the movement in a valueless world,   30
Choosing it, till, both hurler and the hurled,
One moves as well, always toward, toward.

A minute holds them, who have come to go:
The self-defined, astride the created will
They burst away; the towns they travel through
Are home for neither bird nor holiness,
For birds and saints complete their purposes.
At worst, one is in motion; and at best,
Reaching no absolute, in which to rest,
One is always nearer by not keeping still.   40

ROBERT FROST

A Soldier

He is that fallen lance that lies as hurled,
That lies unlifted now, come dew, come rust,
But still lies pointed as it plowed the dust.

If we who sight along it round the world,
See nothing worthy to have been its mark,
It is because like men we look too near,
Forgetting that as fitted to the sphere,
Our missiles always make too short an arc.
They fall, they rip the grass, they intersect
The curve of earth, and striking, break their
    own;   10
They make us cringe for metal-point on stone.
But this we know, the obstacle that checked
And tripped the body, shot the spirit on
Further than target ever showed or shone.

ROBERT FROST

In Hardwood Groves

The same leaves over and over again!
They fall from giving shade above
To make one texture of faded brown
And fit the earth like a leather glove.

Before the leaves can mount again
To fill the trees with another shade,
They must go down past things coming up,
They must go down into the dark decayed.

They *must* be pierced by flowers and put
Beneath the feet of dancing flowers.   10
However it is in some other world
I know that this is the way in ours.

WALLACE STEVENS

Domination of Black

At night, by the fire,
The colors of the bushes
And of the fallen leaves,
Repeating themselves,
Turned in the room,

Like the leaves themselves
Turning in the wind.
Yes: but the color of the heavy hemlocks
Came striding.
And I remembered the cry of the peacocks.   10

The colors of their tails
Were like the leaves themselves
Turning in the wind,
In the twilight wind.
They swept over the room,
Just as they flew from the boughs of the hemlocks
Down to the ground.
I heard them cry—the peacocks.
Was it a cry against the twilight
Or against the leaves themselves   20
Turning in the wind,
Turning as the flames
Turned in the fire,
Turning as the tails of the peacocks
Turned in the loud fire,
Loud as the hemlocks
Full of the cry of the peacocks?
Or was it a cry against the hemlocks?

Out of the window,
I saw how the planets gathered   30
Like the leaves themselves
Turning in the wind.
I saw how the night came,
Came striding like the color of the heavy hem-
   locks
I felt afraid.
And I remembered the cry of the peacocks.

WALTER DE LA MARE

Silver

Slowly, silently, now the moon
Walks the night in her silver shoon;
This way, and that, she peers, and sees
Silver fruit upon silver trees;
One by one the casements catch
Her beams beneath the silvery thatch;
Couched in his kennel, like a log,
With paws of silver sleeps the dog;

SILVER   From *Collected Poems*, 1920, by Walter de la Mare. Reprinted by permission of The Literary Trustees of Walter de la Mare and The Society of Authors as their representative.

From their shadowy cote the white breasts peep
Of doves in a silver-feathered sleep;   10
A harvest mouse goes scampering by,
With silver claws, and silver eye;
And moveless fish in the water gleam,
By silver reeds in a silver stream.

ROBERT P. TRISTRAM COFFIN

Strange Holiness

There is strange holiness around
Our common days on common ground.
I have heard it in the birds
Whose voices reach above all words,
Going upward, bars on bars,
Until they sound as high as stars.
I have seen it in the snake,
A flowing jewel in the brake.
It has sparkled in my eyes
In luminous breath of fireflies.   10
I have come upon its track
Where trilliums curled their petals back.
I have seen it flash in under
The towers of the midnight thunder.
Once, I met it face to face
In a fox pressed by the chase.
He came down the road on feet,
Quiet and fragile, light as heat.
He had a fish still wet and bright
In his slender jaws held tight.   20
His ears were conscious whetted darts,
His eyes had small flames in their hearts.
The preciousness of life and breath
Glowed through him as he outran death.
Strangeness and secrecy and pride
Ran rippling down his golden hide.
His beauty was not meant for me,
With my dull eyes, so close to see.
Unconscious of me, rapt, alone,
He came, and then stopped still as stone.   30
His eyes went out as in a gust,
His beauty crumbled into dust.
There was but a ruin there,
A hunted creature, stripped and bare.
Then he faded at one stroke,
Like a dingy, melting smoke.
But there his fish lay like a key
To the bright lost mystery.

STRANGE HOLINESS   Reprinted with permission of the publisher from *Collected Poems* by Robert P. Tristram Coffin. Copyright 1935 by The Macmillan Company.

CONRAD AIKEN

Morning Song from Senlin

It is morning, Senlin says, and in the morning
When the light drips through the shutters like the
    dew,
I arise, I face the sunrise,
And do the things my fathers learned to do.
Stars in the purple dusk above the rooftops
Pale in a saffron mist and seem to die,
And I myself on a swiftly tilting planet
Stand before a glass and tie my tie.

Vine leaves tap my window,
Dew-drops sing to the garden stones,   10
The robin chirps in the chinaberry tree
Repeating three clear tones.

It is morning. I stand by the mirror
And tie my tie once more.
While waves far off in a pale rose twilight
Crash on a coral shore.
I stand by a mirror and comb my hair:
How small and white my face!—
The green earth tilts through a sphere of air
And bathes in a flame of space.   20

There are houses hanging above the stars
And stars hung under a sea.
And a sun far off in a shell of silence
Dapples my walls for me.

It is morning, Senlin says, and in the morning
Should I not pause in the light to remember god?
Upright and firm I stand on a star unstable,
He is immense and lonely as a cloud.
I will dedicate this moment before my mirror
To him alone, for him I will comb my hair.   30
Accept these humble offerings, cloud of silence!
I will think of you as I descend the stair.

Vine leaves tap my window,
The snail-track shines on the stones,
Dew-drops flash from the chinaberry tree
Repeating two clear tones.

It is morning, I awake from a bed of silence,
Shining I rise from the starless waters of sleep.
The walls are about me still as in the evening,
I am the same, and the same name still I keep   40
The earth revolves with me, yet makes no motion,
The stars pale silently in a coral sky.
In a whistling void I stand before my mirror,
Unconcerned, and tie my tie.

There are horses neighing on far-off hills
Tossing their long white manes,
And mountains flash in the rose-white dusk,
Their shoulders black with rains.
It is morning. I stand by the mirror
And surprise my soul once more;   50
The blue air rushes above my ceiling,
There are suns beneath my floor.

. . . It is morning, Senlin says, I ascend from
    darkness
And depart on the winds of space for I know not
    where,
My watch is wound, a key is in my pocket,
And the sky is darkened as I descend the stair.
There are shadows across the windows, clouds in
    heaven,
And a god among the stars; and I will go
Thinking of him as I might think of daybreak
And humming a tune I know.   60

Vine leaves tap at the window,
Dew-drops sing to the garden stones,
The robin chirps in the chinaberry tree
Repeating three clear tones.

W. H. AUDEN

Look, Stranger, on This Island Now

Look, stranger, on this island now
The leaping light for your delight discovers,
Stand stable here
And silent be,
That through the channels of the ear
May wander like a river
The swaying sound of the sea.

Here at the small field's ending pause
When the chalk wall falls to the foam and its tall
    ledges
Oppose the pluck   10
And knock of the tide,
And the shingle scrambles after the sucking surf,
And the gull lodges
A moment on its sheer side.

Far off like floating seeds the ships
Diverge on urgent voluntary errands,
And the full view
Indeed may enter
And move in memory as now these clouds do,
That pass the harbour mirror   20
And all the summer through the water saunter.

A. E. HOUSMAN

Loveliest of Trees

Loveliest of trees, the cherry now
Is hung with bloom along the bough,
And stands about the woodland ride
Wearing white for Eastertide.

Now, of my threescore years and ten,
Twenty will not come again,
And take from seventy springs a score,
It only leaves me fifty more.

And since to look at things in bloom
Fifty springs are little room,   10
About the woodlands I will go
To see the cherry hung with snow.

ELINOR WYLIE

August

Why should this Negro insolently stride
Down the red noonday on such noiseless feet?
Piled in his barrow, tawnier than wheat,
Lie heaps of smoldering daisies, somber-eyed,
Their copper petals shriveled up with pride,
Hot with a superfluity of heat,
Like a great brazier borne along the street
By captive leopards, black and burning pied.
Are there no water-lilies, smooth as cream,
With long stems dripping crystal? Are there
    none   10
Like those white lilies, luminous and cool,

LOVELIEST OF TREES   From *A Shropshire Lad,* Authorized Edition, from *Complete Poems* by A. E. Housman. Copyright © 1959 by Holt, Rinehart and Winston, Inc. Reprinted by permission of Holt, Rinehart
and Winston, Inc.
AUGUST   Reprinted from *Collected Poems* by Elinor
Wylie, by permission of Alfred A. Knopf, Inc. Copyright, 1921 by Alfred A. Knopf, Inc. Renewed, 1949
by William Rose Benét.

Plucked from some hemlock-darkened northern
    stream
By fair-haired swimmers, diving where the sun
Scarce warms the surface of the deepest pool?

ALFRED, LORD TENNYSON

from The Lotos-Eaters

"Courage!" he said, and pointed toward the land,
"This mounting wave will roll us shoreward soon."
In the afternoon they came unto a land
In which it seemèd always afternoon.
All round the coast the languid air did swoon,
Breathing like one that hath a weary dream.
Full-faced above the valley stood the moon;
And, like a downward smoke, the slender stream
Along the cliff to fall and pause and fall did seem.

A land of streams! some, like a downward
    smoke,   10
Slow-drooping veils of thinnest lawn, did go;
And some through wavering lights and shadows
    broke,
Rolling a slumbrous sheet of foam below.
They saw the gleaming river seaward flow
From the inner land; far off, three mountain-tops,
Three silent pinnacles of aged snow,
Stood sunset-flushed; and, dewed with showery
    drops,
Up-clomb the shadowy pine above the woven
    copse.

The charmèd sunset lingered low adown
In the red West; through mountain clefts the
    dale   20
Was seen far inland, and the yellow down
Bordered with palm, and many a winding vale
And meadow, set with slender galingale;
A land where all things always seemed the same!
And round about the keel with faces pale,
Dark faces pale against that rosy flame,
The mild-eyed melancholy Lotos-eaters came.

Branches they bore of that enchanted stem,
Laden with flowers and fruit, whereof they
    gave
To each, but whoso did receive of them   30
And taste, to him the gushing of the wave
Far far away did seem to mourn and rave
On alien shores; and if his fellow spake,
His voice was thin, as voices from the grave;
And deep-asleep he seemed, yet all awake.
And music in his ears his beating heart did make.

They sat them down upon the yellow sand,
Between the sun and moon upon the shore;
And sweet it was to dream of Fatherland,
Of child, and wife, and slave; but evermore   40
Most weary seemed the sea, weary the oar,
Weary the wandering fields of barren foam.
Then some one said, "We will return no more";
And all at once they sang, "Our island home
Is far beyond the wave; we will no longer roam."

C. DAY LEWIS

Nearing Again the Legendary Isle

Nearing again the legendary isle
Where sirens sang and marines were skinned,
We wonder now what was there to beguile
That such stout fellows left their bones behind.

Those chorus-girls are surely past their prime,
Voices grow shrill and paint is wearing thin,
Lips that sealed up the sense from gnawing time
Now beg the favor with a graveyard grin.

We have no flesh to spare and they can't bite,
Hunger and sweat have stripped us to the bone;
A skeleton crew we toil upon the tide   11
And mock the theme-song meant to lure us on:

No need to stop the ears, avert the eyes
From purple rhetoric of evening skies.

G. K. CHESTERTON

The Donkey

When fishes flew and forests walked
    And figs grew upon thorn,
Some moment when the moon was blood,
    Then surely I was born;

With monstrous head and sickening cry
    And ears like errant wings,
The devil's walking parody
    On all four-footed things.

NEARING AGAIN THE LEGENDARY ISLE   Copyright by
C. Day Lewis. Reprinted by permission of Harold
Matson Company, Inc., from Collected Poems of C.
Day Lewis, 1935.
THE DONKEY   From the book The Wild Knight and
Other Poems, 1900, by G. K. Chesterton. Published
by E. P. Dutton & Co., Inc., and reprinted with their
permission.

The tattered outlaw of the earth,
    Of ancient crooked will;   10
Starve, scourge, deride me: I am dumb;
    I keep my secret still.

Fools! For I also had my hour;
    One far, fierce hour and sweet.
There was a shout about my ears,
    And palms before my feet.

EMILY DICKINSON

I Never Saw a Moor

I never saw a moor,
I never saw the sea;
Yet know I how the heather looks,
And what a wave must be.

I never spoke with God,
Nor visited in heaven;
Yet certain am I of the spot
As if the chart were given.

JOHN DONNE

Death Be Not Proud

Death be not proud, though some have called
    thee
Mighty and dreadful, for, thou are not soe,
For, those, whom thou think'st, thou dost
    overthrow,
Die not, poore Death, nor yet canst thou kill mee;
From rest and sleepe, which but thy pictures bee,
Much pleasure, then from thee, much more must
    flow,
And soonest our best men with thee doe goe,
Rest of their bones, and soules deliverie.
Thou art slave to Fate, chance, kings, and
    desperate men,
And dost with poyson, warre, and sicknesse
    dwell,   10
And poppie, or charmes can make us sleepe
    as well,
And better than thy stroake; why swell'st thou
    then?
One short sleepe past, wee wake eternally,
And Death shall be no more, Death thou shalt
    die.

I NEVER SAW A MOOR   From The Complete Poems of
Emily Dickinson, Little, Brown and Company, 1960.

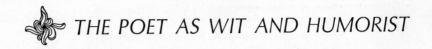

ROBERT HOGAN

After Sending Freshmen to Describe a Tree

Twenty inglorious Miltons looked at a tree and saw God,
Noted its "clutching fingers groping in the sod,"
Heard "Zephyr's gentle breezes wafting through her hair,"
Saw "a solemn statue," heard "a growing woody prayer,"
Saw "dancing skirts" and "the Lord's design,"
"Green arrows to God" instead of pine,
Saw symbols in squirrels, heard musings in bees;
Not one of the Miltons saw any trees.

If you must see a tree, clean, clear, and bright,
For God's sake and mine, look *outside* your heart and write.   10

PHYLLIS MC GINLEY

Girl's-Eye View of Relatives

FIRST LESSON

The thing to remember about fathers is, they're men.
A girl has to keep it in mind.
They are dragon-seekers, bent on improbable rescues.
Scratch any father, you find
Someone chock-full of qualms and romantic terrors,
Believing change is a threat—
Like your first shoes with heels on, like your first bicycle
It took such months to get.

Walk in strange woods, they warn you about the snakes there.
Climb, and they fear you'll fall.   10
Books, angular boys, or swimming in deep water—
Fathers mistrust them all.
Men are the worriers. It is difficult for them
To learn what they must learn:
How you have a journey to take and very likely,
For a while, will not return.

HILAIRE BELLOC

Epitaph on the Politician

Here, richly, with ridiculous display,
The Politician's corpse was laid away.
While all of his acquaintance sneered and slanged,
I wept: for I had longed to see him hanged.

FREDERICK WINSOR

Little Jack Horner

Little Jack Horner
Sits in a corner
Extracting cube roots to infinity,
    An assignment for boys
    This will minimize noise
And produce a more peaceful vicinity.

ARTHUR GUITERMAN

On the Vanity of Earthly Greatness

The tusks that clashed in mighty brawls
Of mastodons, are billiard balls.

The sword of Charlemagne the Just
Is ferric oxide, known as rust.
The grizzly bear whose potent hug
Was feared by all, is now a rug.
Great Caesar's bust is on the shelf,
And I don't feel so well myself!

EPITAPH ON THE POLITICIAN   Reprinted by permission of A. D. Peters, for the estate of Hilaire Belloc.
LITTLE JACK HORNER   From *The Space Child's Mother Goose* by Frederick Winsor. Reprinted by permission of Simon and Schuster. Copyright, 1956, 1957, 1958 by Frederick Winsor and Marian Parry.
ON THE VANITY OF EARTHLY GREATNESS   From the book *Gaily the Troubadour* by Arthur Guiterman. Copyright, 1936, by E. P. Dutton & Co., Inc. Reprinted by permission of the publishers.

ANONYMOUS

The Modern Hiawatha

He killed the noble Mudjokivis.
Of the skin he made him mittens,
Made them with the fur side inside,
Made them with the skin side outside;
He, to get the warm side inside,
Put the inside skin side outside;
He, to get the cold side outside,
Put the warm side fur side inside.
That's why he put the fur side inside,
Why he put the skin side outside,   10
Why he turned them inside outside.

MORRIS BISHOP

$E = mc^2$

What was our trust, we trust not,
    What was our faith, we doubt;
Whether we must or must not
    We may debate about.
The soul perhaps is a gust of gas
    And wrong is a form of right—
But we know that Energy equals Mass
    By the Square of the Speed of Light.

What we have known, we know not,
    What we have proved, abjure.   10
Life is a tangled bow-knot,
    But one thing still is sure.
Come, little lad; come, little lass,
    Your docile creed recite:
"We know that Energy equals Mass
    By the Square of the Speed of Light."

E = MC²   Reprinted from *A Bowl of Bishop* by Morris Bishop. Copyright 1954 by Morris Bishop and used with the permission of the publisher, The Dial Press, Inc.

ROBERT FROST

The Hardship of Accounting

Never ask of money spent
Where the spender thinks it went.
Nobody was ever meant
To remember or invent
What he did with every cent.

ROBERT FROST

Forgive, O Lord

Forgive, O Lord, my little jokes on Thee
And I'll forgive Thy great big one on me.

ROBERT GRAVES

Traveller's Curse After Misdirection

(from the Welsh)

May they stumble, stage by stage
On an endless pilgrimage,
Dawn and dusk, mile after mile,
At each and every step, a stile;
At each and every step withal
May they catch their feet and fall;
At each and every fall they take
May a bone within them break;
And may the bone that breaks within
Not be, for variation's sake,   10
Now rib, now thigh, now arm, now shin,
But always, without fail THE NECK.

JAMES STEPHENS

A Glass of Beer

The lanky hank of a she in the inn over there
Nearly killed me for asking the loan of a glass of beer;
May the devil grip the whey-faced slut by the hair,
And beat bad manners out of her skin for a year.

That parboiled ape, with the toughest jaw you will see
On virtue's path, and a voice that would rasp the dead,
Came roaring and raging the minute she looked at me,
And threw me out of the house on the back of my head!

If I asked her master he'd give me a cask a day;
But she, with the beer at hand, not a gill would arrange!   10
May she marry a ghost and bear him a kitten, and may
The High King of Glory permit her to get the mange.

LOUIS SIMPSON

The Custom of the World

O, we loved long and happily, God knows!
The ocean danced, the green leaves tossed, the
    air
Was filled with petals, and pale Venus rose
When we began to kiss. Kisses brought care,
And closeness caused the taking off of clothes.
O, we loved long and happily, God knows!

"The watchdogs are asleep, the doormen
    doze. . . ."
We huddled in the corners of the stair,
And then we climbed it. What had we to lose?
What would we gain? The best way to
    compare   10
And quickest, was by taking off our clothes.
O, we loved long and happily, God knows!

Between us two a silent treason grows,
Our pleasures have been changed into despair.
Wild is the wind, from a cold country blows,
In which these tender blossoms disappear.
And did this come of taking off our clothes?
O, we loved long and happily, God knows!

Mistress, my song is drawing to a close.
Put on your rumpled skirt and comb your
    hair,   20
And when we meet again let us suppose
We never loved or ever naked were.
For though this nakedness was good, God knows
The custom of the world is wearing clothes.

LUCIAN

On Magical Whiskers

Translation by Willis Barnstone

If by growing a goatee you hope to come upon
    wisdom,
then, O wise friend, any smelly goat in
                             a handsome beard
is at once Plato.

OGDEN NASH

Mother Isn't Well

I do not like the sound of "additive,"
The current video pitchman's fadditive.
From scrutiny of a thousand screens
I've now decided what it means:
You add a syllable, as in "moderen,"
"Prince Charels," "westeren," or "squaderon."
The additive, as a matter of factitive,
Logically leads to the subtractitive,
By eminent announcers endorsed,
In which the forest becomes the forst.   10
When I hear an orange called an ornch
I feel forgotten and forlornch—

Yet whom am I to cavil thus?
My own faults are preposterous.
I've caught me, even without imbibery,
Referring to my reference libary.
Occasionally, if still you follow me,
I prefer to pronounce the "P" in Ptolemy.
I also admit that almost half the
Time I omit the "h" in naphtha.   20

EDWIN ARLINGTON ROBINSON

Mr. Flood's Party aman petemia

Old Eben Flood, climbing alone one night
Over the hill between the town below
And the forsaken upland hermitage
That held as much as he should ever know
On earth again of home, paused warily.
The road was his with not a native near;
And Eben, having leisure, said aloud,
For no man else in Tilbury Town to hear:

"Well, Mr. Flood, we have the harvest moon
Again, and we may not have many more;   10
The bird is on the wing, the poet says,
And you and I have said it here before.
Drink to the bird." He raised up to the light
The jug that he had gone so far to fill,
And answered huskily: "Well, Mr. Flood,
Since you propose it, I believe I will."

Alone, as if enduring to the end
A valiant armor of scarred hopes outworn,
He stood there in the middle of the road
Like Roland's ghost winding a silent horn.   20
Below him, in the town among the trees,
Where friends of other days had honored him,
A phantom salutation of the dead
Rang thinly till old Eben's eyes were dim.

Then, as a mother lays her sleeping child
Down tenderly, fearing it may awake,
He set the jug down slowly at his feet
With trembling care, knowing that most things
  break;

And only when assured that on firm earth
It stood, as the uncertain lives of men   30
Assuredly did not, he paced away,
And with his hand extended paused again:

"Well, Mr. Flood, we have not met like this
In a long time; and many a change has come
To both of us, I fear, since last it was
We had a drop together. Welcome home!"
Convivially returning with himself,
Again he raised the jug up to the light;
And with an acquiescent quaver said:
"Well, Mr. Flood, if you insist, I might.   40

"Only a very little, Mr. Flood—
For auld lang syne. No more, sir; that will do."
So, for the time, apparently it did,
And Eben evidently thought so too;
For soon amid the silver loneliness
Of night he lifted up his voice and sang,
Secure, with only two moons listening,
Until the whole harmonious landscape rang—

"For auld lang syne." The weary throat gave out,
The last word wavered; and the song being done,
He raised again the jug regretfully   51
And shook his head, and was again alone.
There was not much that was ahead of him,
And there was nothing in the town below—
Where strangers would have shut the many doors
That many friends had opened long ago.

E. E. CUMMINGS

"next to of course god america i

"next to of course god america i
love you land of the pilgrims' and so forth oh
say can you see by the dawn's early my
country 'tis of centuries come and go
and are no more what of it we should worry
in every language even deafanddumb
thy sons acclaim your glorious name by gorry
by jingo by gee by gosh by gum
why talk of beauty what could be more beautiful than these heroic happy dead   10
who rushed like lions to the roaring slaughter
they did not stop to think they died instead
then shall the voice of liberty be mute?"

He spoke. And drank rapidly a glass of water

EMILY DICKINSON

He Preached upon "Breadth"

He preached upon "breadth" till it argued him
    narrow,—
The broad are too broad to define;
And of "truth" until it proclaimed him a liar,—
The truth never flaunted a sign.

Simplicity fled from his counterfeit presence
As gold the pyrites would shun.
What confusion would cover the innocent Jesus
To meet so enabled a man!

PHYLLIS MC GINLEY

Simeon Stylites

On top of a pillar Simeon sat.
He wore no mantle,
He had no hat,
But bare as a bird
Sat night and day.
And hardly a word
Did Simeon say.

Under the sun of the desert sky
He sat on a pillar
Nine feet high   10
When Fool and his brother
Came round to admire,
He raised it another
Nine feet high'r.

The seasons circled about his head.
He lived on water
And crusts of bread
(Or so one hears)
From pilgrims' store,
For thirty years   20
And a little more.

And why did Simeon sit like that,
Without a garment,
Without a hat,
In a holy rage
For the world to see?
It puzzles the age,
It puzzles me.
It puzzled many
A Desert Father.   30
And I think it puzzled the Good Lord,
    rather.

ROBERT BROWNING

Soliloquy of the Spanish Cloister

Gr-r-r—there go, my heart's abhorrence!
    Water your damned flower-pots, do!
If hate killed men, Brother Lawrence,
    God's blood, would not mine kill you!
What? your myrtle-bush wants trimming?
    Oh, that rose has prior claims—
Needs its leaden vase filled brimming?
    Hell dry you up with its flames!

At the meal we sit together:
    Salve tibi! I must hear   10
Wise talk of the kind of weather,
    Sort of season, time of year:
*Not a plenteous cork-crop: scarcely
    Dare we hope oak-galls, I doubt:*
What's the Latin name for "parsley"?
    What's the Greek name for Swine's Snout?

Whew! We'll have our platter burnished,
    Laid with care on our own shelf!
With a fire-new spoon we're furnished,
    And a goblet for ourself,   20
Rinsed like something sacrificial
    Ere 'tis fit to touch our chaps—
Marked with L for our initial!
    (He-he! There his lily snaps!)

Saint, forsooth! While brown Dolores
    Squats outside the Convent bank
With Sanchicha, telling stories,
    Steeping tresses in the tank,
Blue-black, lustrous, thick like horse-hairs,
    —Can't I see his dead eye glow,   30
Bright as 'twere a Barbary corsair's?
    (That is, if he'd let it show!)

When he finishes refection,
    Knife and fork he never lays
Cross-wise, to my recollection,
    As do I, in Jesu's praise.
I the Trinity illustrate,
    Drinking watered orange-pulp—
In three sips the Arian frustrate;
    While he drains his at one gulp.   40

Oh, those melons! If he's able
    We're to have a feast! so nice!
One goes to the Abbot's table,
    All of us get each a slice.

How go on your flowers? None double?
    Not one fruit-sort can you spy?
Strange!—And I, too, at such trouble
    Keep them close-nipped on the sly!

There's a great text in Galatians,
    Once you trip on it, entails   50
Twenty-nine distinct damnations,
    One sure, if another fails:
If I trip him just a-dying,
    Sure of heaven as sure can be,
Spin him round and send him flying
    Off to hell, a Manichee! → heresy (evil & good live side by side) not created by God & thee.

Or, my scrofulous French novel
    On gray paper with blunt type!
Simply glance at it, you grovel
    Hand and foot in Belial's gripe: 60
If I double down its pages
    At the woeful sixteenth print,
When he gathers his greengages,
    Ope a sieve and slip it in't?

Or, there's Satan! one might venture
    Pledge one's soul to him, yet leave
Such a flaw in the indenture
    As he'd miss till, past retrieve,
Blasted lay that rose-acacia
    We're so proud of! *Hy, Zy, Hine* . . .   70
'St, there's Vespers! *Plena gratia,*
    Ave, Virgo! Gr-r-r—you swine!

CARL SANDBURG

Limited

I am riding on a limited express, one of the crack trains of the nation.
Hurtling across the prairie into blue haze and dark air go fifteen all-steel coaches holding a thousand people.
(All the coaches shall be scrap and rust and all the men and women laughing in the diners and sleepers shall pass to ashes.)
I ask a man in the smoker where he is going and he answers: "Omaha."

ALAN DUGAN

Morning Song

Look, it's morning, and a little water gurgles in the tap.
I wake up waiting, because it's Sunday, and turn twice more
than usual in bed, before I rise to cereal and comic strips.
I have risen to the morning danger and feel proud,
and after shaving off the night's disguises, after searching
close to the bone for blood, and finding only a little,
I shall walk out bravely into the daily accident.

WILLIAM BUTLER YEATS

That the Night Come

She lived in storm and strife,
Her soul had such desire
For what proud death may bring
That it could not endure
The common good of life,
But lived as 'twere a king
That packed his marriage day
With banneret and pennon,
Trumpet and kettle drum,
And the outrageous cannon   10
To bundle time away
That the night come.

ROBERT FROST

The Silken Tent

She is as in a field a silken tent
At midday when a sunny summer breeze
Has dried the dew and all its ropes relent,
So that in guys it gently sways at ease,
And its supporting central cedar pole,
That is its pinnacle to heavenward
And signifies the sureness of the soul,
Seems to owe naught to any single cord,
But strictly held by none, is loosely bound
By countless silken ties of love and thought   10
To everything on earth the compass round,
And only by one's going slightly taut
In the capriciousness of summer air
Is of the slightest bondage made aware.

HENRY REED

Lessons Of War: Judging Distances

Not only how far away, but the way that you say it
Is very important. Perhaps you may never get
The knack of judging a distance, but at least you know
How to report on a landscape: the central sector,
The right of arc and that, which we had last Tuesday,
        And at least you know

That maps are of time, not place, so far as the army
Happens to be concerned—the reason being,
Is one which need not delay us. Again, you know
There are three kinds of tree, three only, the fir and the poplar,   10
And those which have bushy tops too; and lastly
        That things only seem to be things.

A barn is not called a barn, to put it more plainly,
Or a field in the distance, where sheep may be safely grazing.
You must never be over-sure. You must say, when reporting:
At five o'clock in the central sector is a dozen
Of what appear to be animals; whatever you do,
        Don't call the bleeders *sheep.*

I am sure that's quite clear; and suppose, for the sake of example,
The one at the end, asleep, endeavours to tell us   20
What he sees over there to the west, and how far away,
After first having come to attention. There to the west,
On the fields of summer the sun and the shadows bestow
    Vestments of purple and gold.

The still white dwellings are like a mirage in the heat,
And under the swaying elms a man and a woman
Lie gently together. Which is, perhaps, only to say
That there is a row of houses to the left of arc,
And that under some poplars a pair of what appears to be humans
    Appear to be loving.   30

Well that, for an answer, is what we might rightly call
Moderately satisfactory only, the reason being,
Is that two things have been omitted, and those are important.
The human beings, now: in what direction are they,
And how far away, would you say? And do not forget
    There may be dead ground in between.

There may be dead ground in between; and I may not have got
The knack of judging a distance; I will only venture
A guess that perhaps between me and the apparent lovers,
(Who, incidentally, appear by now to have finished,)   40
At seven o'clock from the houses, is roughly a distance
    Of about one year and a half.

JOHN FREDERICK NIMS

Love Poem

My clumsiest dear, whose hands shipwreck vases,
At whose quick touch all glasses chip and ring,
Whose palms are bulls in china, burs in linen,
And have no cunning with any soft thing

Except all ill-at-ease fidgeting people:
The refugee uncertain at the door
You make at home; deftly you steady
The drunk clambering on his undulant floor.

Unpredictable dear, the taxi drivers' terror,
Shrinking from far headlights pale as a dime   10
Yet leaping before red apoplectic streetcars—
Misfit in any space. And never on time.

A wrench in clocks and the solar system. Only
With words and people and love you move at ease.
In traffic of wit expertly manoeuvre
And keep us, all devotion, at your knees.

Forgetting your coffee spreading on our flannel,
Your lipstick grinning on our coat,
So gayly in love's unbreakable heaven
Our souls on glory of spilt bourbon float.   20

Be with me, darling, early and late. Smash glasses—
I will study wry music for your sake.
For should your hands drop white and empty
All the toys of the world would break.

JOANNE CHILDERS

Children in an Empty House

Children with wet red boots and frozen faces
Went where they had never been before,
Into the empty house whose disrepair
Stared lazily from blank and broken spaces.

Children who added up dried nests of birds,
Dead matches, bits of paper, shards of glass,
Were certain they at last had found their place,
Themselves most silent at their echoing words.

Though they had beds to fill before the night,
They lay on straw and read the half-burnt letters   10
Of nameless men, and by the banging shutters
They guessed the haunts were sightless to their sight.

They guessed the lovers here by intimation,
Lurking like shadows in dark shadows hidden.
They guessed the tramps, the coupling cats unbidden
In phantom vacancy of habitation.

Because they loved the life they barely found
They knew full ownership of emptiness
In matters which could tempt them to a sense
Of unseen shadow and of unheard sound.   20

THEODORE ROETHKE

I Knew a Woman

I knew a woman, lovely in her bones,
When small birds sighed, she would sigh back at them;
Ah, when she moved, she moved more ways than one:
The shapes a bright container can contain!
Of her choice virtues only gods should speak,
Or English poets who grew up on Greek
(I'd have them sing in chorus, cheek to cheek).

How well her wishes went! She stroked my chin,
She taught me Turn, and Counter-turn, and Stand;
She taught me Touch, that undulant white skin;   10
I nibbled meekly from her proffered hand;
She was the sickle; I, poor I, the rake,
Coming behind her for her pretty sake
(But what prodigious mowing we did make).

Love likes a gander, and adores a goose:
Her full lips pursed, the errant note to seize;
She played it quick, she played it light and loose;
My eyes, they dazzled at her flowing knees;
Her several parts could keep a pure repose,
Or one hip quiver with a mobile nose   20
(She moved in circles, and those circles moved).

Let seed be grass, and grass turn into hay:
I'm martyr to a motion not my own;
What's freedom for? To know eternity.
I swear she cast a shadow white as stone.
But who would count eternity in days?
These old bones live to learn her wanton ways:
(I measure time by how a body sways).

KARL SHAPIRO

The Bourgeois Poet Closes the Door

The bourgeois poet closes the door of his study
and lights his pipe. Why am I in this box, he
says to himself (although it is exactly as he
planned). The bourgeois poet sits down at his
inoffensive desk—a door with legs, a door
turned table—and almost approves the careful
disarray of books, papers, magazines and such
artifacts as thumbtacks. The bourgeois poet is
already out of matches and gets up. It is too
early in the morning for any definite emotion
and the B.P. smokes. It is beautiful in the mid-
lands: green fields and tawny fields, sorghum
the color of red morocco bindings, distant new
neighborhoods, cleanly and treeless, and the
Veterans Hospital fronted with a shimmering
Indian Summer tree. The Beep feels seasonal,
placid as a melon, neat as a child's football
lying under the tree, waiting for whose hands
to pick it up.

ROBERT SWARD

Grandma Refreshed!

Grandma was out
upon the porch,
sipping catsup
through a straw.

The catsup
was made
with pineapple:
and distilled vinegar.

My sister, absorbed
in the pineapple, sucked   10
sometimes, at grandma's tight-
round, yellow-sour hair.

Poor grandma!
the first thing we said
to her was:
Where's grandpa?

Grandma wasn't one
for lipstick, nor for
grandpa; however,
she looked as if she were.   20

A shirt, a pair of pants
and socks
were lying there
beside the hamburger-buns.

Now, then, will anyone
have a pickle?
Grandma accepted one
herself, and smacked her lips.

Hot-damn! Grandpa's dead!! Yes,
evidently, said my mother.   30
And there was grandma, in her
little black bikini, sipping coke.

JOHN CIARDI

Elegy Just in Case

Here lie Ciardi's pearly bones
In their ripe organic mess.
Jungle blown, his chromosomes
Breed to a new address.

Progenies of orchids seek
The fracture's white spilled lymph.
And his heart's red valve will leak
Fountains for a protein nymph.

Was it bullets or a wind
Or a rip-cord fouled on Chance?   10
Artifacts the natives find
Decorate them when they dance.

Here lies the sgt.'s mortal wreck
Lily spiked and termite kissed,
Spiders pendant from his neck
And a beetle on his wrist.

Bring the tick and southern flies
Where the land crabs run unmourning
Through a night of jungle skies
To a climeless morning.   20

And bring the chalked eraser here
Fresh from rubbing out his name.
Burn the crew-board for a bier.
(Also Colonel what's-his-name.)

ELEGY JUST IN CASE From *As If, Poems New and
Selected* by John Ciardi. Reprinted by permission of
the author. Copyright, 1955, by the Trustees of Rutgers College in New Jersey.

Let no dice be stored and still.
Let no poker deck be torn.
But pour the smuggled rye until
The barracks threshold is outworn.

File the papers, pack the clothes,
Send the coded word through air— 30
"We regret and no one knows
Where the sgt. goes from here."

"Missing as of inst. oblige,
Deepest sorrow and remain—"
Shall I grin at persiflage?
Could I have my skin again

Would I choose a business form
Stilted mute as a giraffe,
Or a pinstripe unicorn
On a cashier's epitaph? 40

Darling, darling, just in case
Rivets fail or engines burn,
I forget the time and place
But your flesh was sweet to learn.

In the grammar of not yet
Let me name one verb for chance,
Scholarly to one regret:
That I leave your mood and tense.

Swift and single as a shark
I have seen you churn my sleep; 50
Now if beetles hunt my dark
What will beetles find to keep?

Fractured meat and open bone—
Nothing single or surprised.
Fragments of a written stone,
Undeciphered but surmised.

It is a Sestrina
Written in
Terza Rima

EMILY DICKINSON

This Quiet Dust

This quiet dust was gentlemen and ladies,
And lads and girls;
Was laughter and ability and sighing,
And frocks and curls.

This passive place a summer's nimble mansion,
Where bloom and bees
Exist an oriental circuit,
Then cease, like these.

EMILY DICKINSON

Because I Could Not Stop for Death

Because I could not stop for Death,
He kindly stopped for me;
The carriage held but just ourselves
And Immortality.

We slowly drove; he knew no haste,
And I had put away
My labor and my leisure too,
For his civility.

We passed the school, where children strove,
At recess, in the ring,   10
We passed the fields of gazing grain,
We passed the setting sun.

Or rather, he passed us;
The dews drew quivering and chill;
For only gossamer, my gown;
My tippet, only tulle.

We paused before a house that seemed
A swelling of the ground;
The roof was scarcely visible,
The cornice, in the ground.   20

Since then, 'tis centuries, and yet
Feels shorter than the day
I first surmised the horses' heads
Were toward eternity.

DYLAN THOMAS

Do Not Go Gentle into That Good Night

Do not go gentle into that good night,
Old age should burn and rave at close of day;
Rage, rage against the dying of the light.

Though wise men at their end know dark is right,
Because their words had forked no lightning they
Do not go gentle into that good night.

Good men, the last wave by, crying how bright
Their frail deeds might have danced in a green bay,
Rage, rage against the dying of the light.

Wild men who caught and sang the sun in flight,   10
And learn, too late, they grieved it on its way,
Do not go gentle into that good night.

Grave men, near death, who see with blinding sight
Blind eyes could blaze like meteors and be gay,
Rage, rage against the dying of the light.

And you, my father, there on the sad height,
Curse, bless, me now with your fierce tears, I pray.
Do not go gentle into that good night.
Rage, rage against the dying of the light.

A. E. HOUSMAN

Epitaph on an Army of Mercenaries

These, in the day when heaven was falling,
    The hour when earth's foundations fled,
Followed their mercenary calling
    And took their wages and are dead.

Their shoulders held the sky suspended;
    They stood, and earth's foundations stay;
What God abandoned, these defended,
    And saved the sum of things for pay.

WILLIAM WORDSWORTH

A *Slumber Did My Spirit Seal*

A slumber did my spirit seal;
  I had no human fears:
She seemed a thing that could not feel
  The touch of earthly years.

No motion has she now, no force;
  She neither hears nor sees;
Rolled round in earth's diurnal course,
  With rocks, and stones, and trees.

JOHN CROWE RANSOM

Bells for John Whiteside's Daughter

There was such speed in her little body,
And such lightness in her footfall,
It is no wonder her brown study
Astonishes us all.

Her wars were bruited in our high window.
We looked among orchard trees and beyond,
Where she took arms against her shadow,
Or harried unto the pond

The lazy geese, like a snow cloud
Dripping their snow on the green grass,   10
Tricking and stopping, sleepy and proud,
Who cried in goose, Alas,

For the tireless heart within the little
Lady with rod that made them rise
From their noon apple-dreams and scuttle
Goose-fashion under the skies!

But now go the bells, and we are ready,
In one house we are sternly stopped
To say we are vexed at her brown study,
Lying so primly propped.   20

W. H. AUDEN

In Memory of W. B. Yeats

1

He disappeared in the dead of winter:
The brooks were frozen, the airports almost deserted,
The snow disfigured the public statues;
The mercury sank in the mouth of the dying day.
O all the instruments agree
The day of his death was a dark cold day.

Far from his illness
The wolves ran on through the evergreen forests,
The peasant river was untempted by the fashionable quays;
By mourning tongues   10
The death of the poet was kept from his poems.

But for him it was his last afternoon as himself,
An afternoon of nurses and rumors;
The provinces of his body revolted,
The squares of his mind were empty,
Silence invaded the suburbs,
The current of his feeling failed: he became his admirers.

Now he is scattered among a hundred cities
And wholly given over to unfamiliar affections;
To find his happiness in another kind of wood   20
And be punished under a foreign code of conscience.
The words of a dead man
Are modified in the guts of the living.

But in the importance and noise of tomorrow
When the brokers are roaring like beasts on the floor of the Bourse,
And the poor have the sufferings to which they are fairly accustomed,
And each in the cell of himself is almost convinced of his freedom;
A few thousand will think of this day
As one thinks of a day when one did something slightly unusual.

O all the instruments agree   30
The day of his death was a dark cold day.

2

You were silly like us: your gift survived it all;
The parish of rich women, physical decay,
Yourself; mad Ireland hurt you into poetry.
Now Ireland has her madness and her weather still,
For poetry makes nothing happen: it survives
In the valley of its saying where executives
Would never want to tamper; it flows south
From ranches of isolation and the busy griefs,

Raw towns that we believe and die in; it survives,   40
A way of happening, a mouth.

                    3

Earth, receive an honored guest;
William Yeats is laid to rest:
Let the Irish vessel lie
Emptied of its poetry.

Time that is intolerant
Of the brave and innocent,
And indifferent in a week
To a beautiful physique,

Worships language and forgives   50
Everyone by whom it lives;
Pardons cowardice, conceit,
Lays its honors at their feet.

Time that with this strange excuse
Pardoned Kipling and his views,
And will pardon Paul Claudel,
Pardons him for writing well.

In the nightmare of the dark
All the dogs of Europe bark,
And the living nations wait,   60
Each sequestered in its hate;

Intellectual disgrace
Stares from every human face,
And the seas of pity lie
Locked and frozen in each eye.

Follow, poet, follow right
To the bottom of the night,
With your unconstraining voice
Still persuade us to rejoice;

With the farming of a verse   70
Make a vineyard of the curse,
Sing of human unsuccess
In a rapture of distress;

In the deserts of the heart
Let the healing fountain start,
In the prison of his days
Teach the free man how to praise.

GROUNDHOG From *Collected Poems 1930–1960* by
Richard Eberhart. © 1960 by Richard Eberhart. Reprinted by permission of Oxford University Press, Inc.

RICHARD EBERHART

The Groundhog

In June, amid the golden fields,
I saw a groundhog lying dead.
Dead lay he; my senses shook,
And mind outshot our naked frailty.
There lowly in the vigorous summer
His form began its senseless change,
And made my senses waver dim
Seeing nature ferocious in him.
Inspecting close his maggots' might
And seething cauldron of his being,   10
Half with loathing, half with a strange love,
I poked him with an angry stick.
The fever rose, became a flame
And Vigour circumscribed the skies,
Immense energy in the sun,
And through my frame a sunless trembling.
My stick had done nor good nor harm.
Then stood I silent in the day
Watching the object, as before;
And kept my reverence for knowledge   20
Trying for control, to be still,
To quell the passion of the blood;
Until I had bent down on my knees
Praying for joy in the sight of decay.
And so I left; and I returned
In Autumn strict of eye, to see
The sap gone out of the groundhog,
But the bony sodden hulk remained.
But the year had lost its meaning,
And in intellectual chains   30
I lost both love and loathing,
Mured up in the wall of wisdom.
Another summer took the fields again
Massive and burning, full of life,
But when I chanced upon the spot
There was only a little hair left,
And bones bleaching in the sunlight
Beautiful as architecture;
I watched them like a geometer,
And cut a walking stick from a birch.   40
It has been three years, now.
There is no sign of the groundhog.
I stood there in the whirling summer,
My hand capped a withered heart,
And thought of China and of Greece,
Of Alexander in his tent;
Of Montaigne in his tower,
Of Saint Theresa in her wild lament.

THOMAS HARDY

Afterwards

When the Present has latched its postern behind my tremulous stay,
   And the May month flaps its glad green leaves like wings,
Delicate-filmed as new-spun silk, will the neighbors say,
   "He was a man who used to notice such things"?

If it be in the dusk when, like an eyelid's soundless blink,
   The dewfall-hawk comes crossing the shades to alight
Upon the wind-warped upland thorn, a gazer may think,
   "To him this must have been a familiar sight."

If I pass during some nocturnal blackness, mothy and warm,
   When the hedgehog travels furtively over the lawn.   10
One may say, "He strove that such innocent creatures should come to no harm,
   But he could do little for them; and now he is gone."

If, when hearing that I have been stilled at last, they stand at the door,
   Watching the full-starred heavens that winter sees,
Will this thought rise on those who will meet my face no more,
   "He was one who had an eye for such mysteries"?

And will any say when my bell of quittance is heard in the gloom,
   And a crossing breeze cuts a pause in its outrollings,
Till they rise again, as they were a new bell's boom,
   "He hears it not now, but used to notice such things"?   20

PERCY BYSSHE SHELLEY

Ozymandias

I met a traveler from an antique land
Who said: Two vast and trunkless legs of stone
Stand in the desert. Near them, on the sand,
Half sunk, a shattered visage lies, whose frown,
And wrinkled lip, and sneer of cold command,
Tell that its sculptor well those passions read
Which yet survive, stamped on these lifeless things,
The hand that mocked them, and the heart that fed.
And on the pedestal these words appear:
"My name is Ozymandias, king of kings;   10
Look on my works, ye Mighty, and despair!"
Nothing beside remains. Round the decay
Of that colossal wreck, boundless and bare,
The lone and level sands stretch far away.

RANDALL JARRELL

The Death of the Ball Turret Gunner

From my mother's sleep I fell into the State,
And I hunched in its belly till my wet fur froze.
Six miles from earth, loosed from its dream of life,
I woke to black flak and the nightmare fighters.
When I died they washed me out of the turret
    with a hose.

THE DEATH OF THE BALL TURRET GUNNER   From *Little Friend, Little Friend,* 1945, by Randall Jarrell. Reprinted by permission of the author.

RANDALL JARRELL

Hope

The spirit killeth, but the letter giveth life.

The week is dealt out like a hand
That children pick up card by card.
One keeps getting the same hand.
One keeps getting the same card.

HOPE   From *The Seven-League Crutches* by Randall Jarrell, copyright, 1951, by Harcourt, Brace & World, Inc.

But twice a day—except on Saturday—
But every day—except on Sunday—
The wheel stops, there is a catch in Time:
With a hiss of soles, a rattle of tin,
My own gray Daemon pauses on the stair,
My own bald Fortune lifts me by the hair.   10

Woe's me! Woe's me! In Folly's mailbox
Still laughs the postcard, Hope:
Your uncle in Australia
Has died and you are Pope.
For many a soul has entertained
A Mailman unawares—
And as you cry, "Impossible,"
A step is on the stairs.

One keeps getting the same dream
Delayed, marked Postage Due,   20
The bill that one has paid
Delayed, marked Payment Due,

Twice a day, in a rotting mailbox,
The white grubs are new:
And Faith once more is mine
Faithfully, but Charity
Writes hopefully about a new
Asylum—but Hope is as good as new.

Woe's me! Woe's me! In Folly's mailbox
Still laughs the postcard, Hope: 30
Your uncle in Australia
Has died and you are Pope.
For many a soul has entertained
A Mailman unawares—
And as you cry, "Impossible,"
A step is on the stairs.

ROBINSON JEFFERS

The Bloody Sire

It is not bad. Let them play.
Let the guns bark and the bombing-plane
Speak his prodigious blasphemies.
It is not bad, it is high time,
Stark violence is still the sire of all the world's
        values.
What but the wolf's tooth whittled so fine
The fleet limbs of the antelope?
What but fear winged the birds, and hunger
Jeweled with such eyes the great goshawk's head?
Violence has been the sire of all the world's
        values.   10
Who would remember Helen's face
Lacking the terrible halo of spears?
Who formed Christ but Herod and Caesar,
The cruel and bloody victories of Caesar?
Violence, the bloody sire of all the world's values.

Never weep, let them play,
Old violence is not too old to beget new values.

THE BLOODY SIRE   Reprinted from *Be Angry at the Sun and Other Poems*, by Robinson Jeffers. Copyright 1941 by Robinson Jeffers. Reprinted by permission of Random House, Inc.
SCIENCE   Copyright 1925 and renewed 1953 by Robinson Jeffers. Reprinted from *The Selected Poetry of Robinson Jeffers* by permission of Random House, Inc.

ROBINSON JEFFERS

Science

Man, introverted man, having crossed
In passage and but a little with the nature of things this latter century
Has begot giants; but being taken up
Like a maniac with self-love and inward conflicts cannot manage his hybrids.
Being used to deal with edgeless dreams,
Now he's bred knives on nature turns them also inward: they have thirsty points though.
His mind forebodes his own destruction;
Actaeon who saw the goddess naked among leaves and his hounds tore him.
A little knowledge, a pebble from the shingle,
A drop from the oceans: who would have dreamed this infinitely little too much?   10

octameter couplet [handwritten]

A. E. HOUSMAN

written in couplets / 8 syllables long [handwritten]

"Terence, This Is Stupid Stuff. . ."

"Terence, this is stupid stuff:
You eat your victuals fast enough;
There can't be much amiss, 'tis clear,
To see the rate you drink your beer.
But oh, good Lord, the verse you make,
It gives a chap the belly-ache.
The cow, the old cow, she is dead;
It sleeps well, the horned head:
We poor lads, 'tis our turn now
To hear such tunes as killed the cow.   10
Pretty friendship 'tis to rhyme
Your friends to death before their time
Moping melancholy mad: *— illiteration?* [handwritten]
Come, pipe a tune to dance to, lad."

Why, if 'tis dancing you would be,
There's brisker pipes than poetry.
Say, for what were hop-yards meant,
Or why was Burton built on Trent?
Oh many a peer of England brews
Livelier liquor than the Muse,   20
And malt does more than Milton can
To justify God's ways to man.
Ale, man, ale's the stuff to drink
For fellows whom it hurts to think:
Look into the pewter pot
To see the world as the world's not.
And faith, 'tis pleasant till 'tis past:
The mischief is that 'twill not last.
Oh I have been to Ludlow fair
And left my necktie God knows where,   30
And carried half-way home, or near,
Pints and quarts of Ludlow beer:
Then the world seemed none so bad,
And I myself a sterling lad;
And down in lovely muck I've lain,
Happy till I woke again.
Then I saw the morning sky:
Heigho, the tale was all a lie;
The world, it was the old world yet,
I was I, my things were wet,   40
And nothing now remained to do
But begin the game anew.

Therefore, since the world has still
Much good, but much less good than ill,
And while the sun and moon endure
Luck's a chance, but trouble's sure,

I'd face it as a wise man would,
And train for ill and not for good.
'Tis true, the stuff I bring for sale
Is not so brisk a brew as ale: 50
Out of a stem that scored the hand
I wrung it in a weary land.
But take it: if the smack is sour,
The better for the embittered hour;
It should do good to heart and head
When your soul is in my soul's stead;
And I will friend you, if I may,
In the dark and cloudy day.

There was a king reigned in the East:
There, when kings will sit to feast,   60
They get their fill before they think
With poisoned meat and poisoned drink.
He gathered all that springs to birth
From the many-venomed earth;
First a little, thence to more,
He sampled all her killing store;
And easy, smiling, seasoned sound
Sate the king when healths went round.
They put arsenic in his meat
And stared aghast to watch him eat;   70
They poured strychnine in his cup
And shook to see him drink it up:
They shook, they stared as white's their shirt:
Them it was their poison hurt.
—I tell the tale that I heard told.
Mithridates, he died old.

MATTHEW ARNOLD

Dover Beach

The sea is calm tonight,
The tide is full, the moon lies fair
Upon the straits;—on the French coast the light
Gleams and is gone; the cliffs of England stand,
Glimmering and vast, out in the tranquil bay.
Come to the window, sweet is the night-air!
Only, from the long line of spray
Where the sea meets the moon-blanched land,
Listen! you hear the grating roar
Of pebbles which the waves draw back, and
  fling,   10
At their return, up the high strand,
Begin, and cease, and then again begin,
With tremulous cadence slow, and bring
The eternal note of sadness in.

Sophocles long ago
Heard it on the Aegean, and it brought
Into his mind the turbid ebb and flow
Of human misery; we
Find also in the sound a thought,
Hearing it by this distant northern sea.   20

The Sea of Faith
Was once, too, at the full, and round earth's shore
Lay like the folds of a bright girdle furled.
But now I only hear
Its melancholy, long, withdrawing roar,

Retreating, to the breath
Of the night-wind, down the vast edges drear
And naked shingles of the world.

Ah, love, let us be true
To one another! for the world, which seems   30
To lie before us like a land of dreams,
So various, so beautiful, so new,
Hath really neither joy, nor love, nor light,
Nor certitude, nor peace, nor help for pain;
And we are here as on a darkling plain
Swept with confused alarms of struggle and flight,
Where ignorant armies clash by night.

DYLAN THOMAS

Fern Hill

Now as I was young and easy under the apple boughs
About the lilting house and happy as the grass was green,
        The night above the dingle starry,
            Time let me hail and climb
        Golden in the heydays of his eyes,
And honoured among wagons I was prince of the apple towns
And once below a time I lordly had the trees and leaves
            Trail with daisies and barley
        Down the rivers of the windfall light.

And as I was green and carefree, famous among the barns   10
About the happy yard and singing as the farm was home,
        In the sun that is young once only,
            Time let me play and be
        Golden in the mercy of his means,
And green and golden I was huntsman and herdsman, the calves
Sang to my horn, the foxes on the hills barked clear and cold,
            And the sabbath rang slowly
        In the pebbles of the holy streams.

All the sun long it was running, it was lovely, the hay-
Fields high as the house, the tunes from the chimneys, it was air   20
        And playing, lovely and watery
            And fire green as grass.
        And nightly under the simple stars
As I rode to sleep the owls were bearing the farm away,
All the moon long I heard, blessed among stables, the night-jars
            Flying with the ricks, and the horses
                Flashing into the dark.

And then to awake, and the farm, like a wanderer white
With the dew, come back, the cock on his shoulder: it was all
        Shining, it was Adam and maiden,   30
            The sky gathered again
        And the sun grew round that very day.

So it must have been after the birth of the simple light
In the first, spinning place, the spellbound horses walking warm
    Out of the whinnying green stable
      On to the fields of praise.

And honoured among foxes and pheasants by the gay house
Under the new made clouds and happy as the heart was long,
    In the sun born over and over,
      I ran my heedless ways,   40
    My wishes raced through the house-high hay
And nothing I cared, at my sky blue trades, that time allows
In all his tuneful turnings so few and such morning songs
    Before the children green and golden
      Follow him out of grace.

Nothing I cared, in the lamb white days, that time would take me
Up to the swallow thronged loft by the shadow of my hand,
    In the moon that is always rising,
      Nor that riding to sleep
    I should hear him fly with the high fields   50
And wake to the farm forever fled from the childless land.
Oh as I was young and easy in the mercy of his means,
      Time held me green and dying
    Though I sang in my chains like the sea.

DYLAN THOMAS

In My Craft or Sullen Art

In my craft or sullen art
Exercised in the still night
When only the moon rages
And the lovers lie abed
With all their griefs in their arms,
I labour by singing light
Not for ambition or bread
Or the strut and trade of charms
On the ivory stages
But for the common wages   10
Of their most secret heart.
Not for the proud man apart
From the raging moon I write
On these spindrift pages
Not for the towering dead
With their nightingales and psalms
But for the lovers, their arms
Round the griefs of the ages,
Who pay no praise or wages
Nor heed my craft or art.   20

ROBERT FROST

I Could Give All to Time

To Time it never seems that he is brave
To set himself against the peaks of snow
To lay them level with the running wave,
Nor is he overjoyed when they lie low,
But only grave, contemplative and grave.

What now is inland shall be ocean isle,
Then eddies playing round a sunken reef
Like the curl at the corner of a smile;
And I could share Time's lack of joy or grief
At such a planetary change of style.   10

I could give all to Time except—except
What I myself have held. But why declare
The things forbidden that while the Customs slept
I have crossed to Safety with? For I am There,
And what I would not part with I have kept.

ROBERT FROST

Sand Dunes

Sea waves are green and wet,
But up from where they die,
Rise others vaster yet,
And those are brown and dry.

They are the sea made land
To come at the fisher town,
And bury in solid sand
The men she could not drown.

She may know cove and cape,
But she does not know mankind   10
If by any change of shape,
She hopes to cut off mind.

Men left her a ship to sink:
They can leave her a hut as well;
And be but more free to think
For the one more cast off shell.

EDWIN ARLINGTON ROBINSON

Karma

Christmas was in the air and all was well
With him, but for a few confusing flaws
In divers of God's images. Because
A friend of his would neither buy nor sell,
Was he to answer for the axe that fell?
He pondered; and the reason for it was,
Partly, a slowly freezing Santa Claus
Upon the corner, with his beard and bell.

Acknowledging an improvident surprise,
He magnified a fancy that he wished   10
The friend whom he had wrecked were here again.
Not sure of that, he found a compromise;
And from the fullness of his heart he fished
A dime for Jesus who had died for men.

COUNTEE CULLEN

Ultimatum

I hold not with the fatalist creed
Of what must be must be;
There is enough to meet my need
In this most meagre me.

These two slim arms were made to rein
My steed, to ward and fend;
There is more gold in this small brain
Than I can ever spend.

The seed I plant is chosen well;
Ambushed by no sly sweven,   10
I plant it if it droops to hell,
Or if it blooms to heaven.

WILLIAM CARLOS WILLIAMS

Tract

I will teach you my townspeople
how to perform a funeral
for you have it over a troop
of artists—
unless one should scour the world—
you have the ground sense necessary.

See! the hearse leads.
I begin with a design for a hearse.
For Christ's sake not black—
nor white either—and not polished!   10
Let it be weathered—like a farm wagon—
with gilt wheels (this could be
applied fresh at small expense)
or no wheels at all:
a rough dray to drag over the ground.

Knock the glass out!
My God—glass, my townspeople!
For what purpose? Is it for the dead
to look out or for us to see
how well he is housed or to see   20

the flowers or the lack of them—
or what?
To keep the rain and snow from him?
He will have a heavier rain soon:
pebbles and dirt and what not.
Let there be no glass—
and no upholstery, phew!
and no little brass rollers
and small easy wheels on the bottom—
my townspeople what are you thinking of?   30

A rough plain hearse then
with gilt wheels and no top at all.
On this the coffin lies
by its own weight.

        No wreaths please—
especially no hot house flowers.
Some common memento is better,
something he prized and is known by:
his old clothes—a few books perhaps—
God knows what! You realize   40
how we are about these things
my townspeople—
something will be found—anything
even flowers if he had come to that.
So much for the hearse.

For heaven's sake though see to the driver!
Take off the silk hat! In fact
that's no place at all for him—
up there unceremoniously
dragging our friend out to his own dignity!   50
Bring him down—bring him down!
Low and inconspicuous! I'd not have him ride
on the wagon at all—damn him—
the undertaker's understrapper!
Let him hold the reins
and walk at the side
and inconspicuously too!

Then briefly as to yourselves:
Walk behind—as they do in France,
seventh class, or if you ride   60
Hell take curtains! Go with some show
of inconvenience; sit openly—
to the weather as to grief.
Or do you think you can shut grief in?
What—from us? We who have perhaps
nothing to lose? Share with us
share with us—it will be money
in your pockets.
        Go now
I think you are ready.   70

WILLIAM CARLOS WILLIAMS

Poem

As the cat
climbed over
the top of

the jamcloset
first the right
forefoot

carefully
then the hind
stepped down

into the pit of   10
the empty
flowerpot

WILLIAM CARLOS WILLIAMS

The Term

A rumpled sheet
of brown paper
about the length

and apparent bulk
of a man was
rolling with the

wind slowly over
and over in
the street as

a car drove down   10
upon it and
crushed it to

the ground. Unlike
a man it rose
again rolling

with the wind over
and over to be as
it was before.

HART CRANE

Voyages I

Above the fresh ruffles of the surf
Bright striped urchins flay each other with sand.
They have contrived a conquest for shell shucks,
And their fingers crumble fragments of baked weed
Gaily digging and scattering.

And in answer to their treble interjections
The sun beats lightning on the waves,
The waves fold thunder on the sand;
And could they hear me I would tell them:

O brilliant kids, frisk with your dog,   10
Fondle your shells and sticks, bleached
By time and the elements; but there is a line
You must not cross nor ever trust beyond it
Spry cordage of your bodies to caresses
Too lichen-faithful from too wide a breast.
The bottom of the sea is cruel.

EMILY DICKINSON

Success Is Counted Sweetest

Success is counted sweetest
By those who ne'er succeed.
To comprehend a nectar
Requires sorest need.

Not one of all the purple host
Who took the flag today
Can tell the definition,
So clear of victory

As he, defeated—dying—
On whose forbidden ear   10
The distant strains of triumph
Burst agonized and clear!

EMILY DICKINSON

Split the Lark and You'll Find the Music

Split the lark and you'll find the music,
    Bulb after bulb, in silver rolled,
Scantily dealt to the summer morning,
    Saved for your ear when lutes be old.

Loose the flood, you shall find it patent,
    Gush after gush, reserved for you;
Scarlet experiment! sceptic Thomas,
    Now, do you doubt that your bird was true?

HENRY WADSWORTH LONGFELLOW

Nature

As a fond mother, when the day is o'er,
Leads by the hand her little child to bed,
Half willing, half reluctant to be led
And leave his broken playthings on the floor,
Still gazing at them through the open door,
Nor wholly reassured and comforted
By promises of others in their stead,
Which, though more splendid, may not please
    him more:
So Nature deals with us, and takes away
Our playthings one by one, and by the hand   10
Leads us to rest so gently that we go
Scarce knowing if we wish to go or stay,
Being too full of sleep to understand
How far the unknown transcends the what we
    know.

SUCCESS IS COUNTED SWEETEST From *The Complete Poems of Emily Dickinson*, Little, Brown and Company, 1960.
SPLIT THE LARK AND YOU'LL FIND THE MUSIC From *The Complete Poems of Emily Dickinson*, Little, Brown and Company, 1960.

VOYAGES I From *The Complete Poems & Selected Letters & Prose of Hart Crane*. By permission of Liveright, Publishers, N. Y. Copyright © 1966, by Liveright Publishing Corp.

JOHN MILTON   *Petrachen*

On His Blindness

When I consider how my light is spent
  Ere half my days in this dark world and wide,
  And that one talent which is death to hide
Lodged with me useless, though my soul more
    bent
To serve therewith my Maker, and present
  My true account, lest He returning chide,
  "Doth God exact day-labor, light denied?"
I fondly ask. But Patience, to prevent
That murmur, soon replies, "God doth not need
  Either man's work or his own gifts. Who best
  Bear His mild yoke, they serve Him best. His
    state   11
Is kingly: thousands at His bidding speed
  And post o'er land and ocean without rest;
  They also serve who only stand and wait."

THOMAS HARDY

The Oxen   *modified Ballad*

Christmas Eve, and twelve of the clock.
  "Now they are all on their knees,"
An elder said as we sat in a flock
  By the embers in hearthside ease.

We pictured the meek mild creatures where
  They dwelt in their strawy pen,
Nor did it occur to one of us there
  To doubt they were kneeling then.

So fair a fancy few would weave
  In these years! Yet, I feel,   10
If someone said on Christmas Eve,
  "Come; see the oxen kneel,

"In the lonely barton by yonder coomb
  Our childhood used to know,"
I should go with him in the gloom,
  Hoping it might be so.

THOMAS HARDY

The Convergence of the Twain

(*Lines on the loss of the* Titanic)

  In a solitude of the sea
  Deep from human vanity,
And the Pride of Life that planned her, stilly
    couches she.

  Steel chambers, late the pyres
  Of her salamandrine fires,
Cold currents thrid, and turn to rhythmic tidal
    lyres.

  Over the mirrors meant
  To glass the opulent
The sea-worm crawls—grotesque, slimed, dumb,
    indifferent.

  Jewels in joy designed   10
  To ravish the sensuous mind
Lie lightless, all their sparkles bleared and black
    and blind.

  Dim moon-eyed fishes near
  Gaze at the gilded gear
And query: "What does this vaingloriousness
    down here?" . . .

  Well: while was fashioning
  This creature of cleaving wing,
The Immanent Will that stirs and urges everything

  Prepared a sinister mate
  For her—so gaily great—   20
A Shape of Ice, for the time far and dissociate.

  And as the smart ship grew
  In stature, grace, and hue,
In shadowy silent distance grew the Iceberg too.

  Alien they seemed to be:
  No mortal eye could see
The intimate welding of their later history,

  Or sign that they were bent
  By paths coincident
On being anon twin halves of one august event, 30

  Till the Spinner of the Years
  Said "Now!" And each one hears,
And consummation comes, and jars two hemi-
    spheres.

THOMAS HARDY Quatrains

Hap

If but some vengeful god would call to me
From up the sky, and laugh: "Thou suffering
  thing,
Know that thy sorrow is my ecstasy,
That thy love's loss is my hate's profiting!"

Then would I bear it, clench myself, and die,
Steeled by the sense of ire unmerited;
Half-eased in that a Powerfuller than I
Had willed and meted me the tears I shed.

But not so. How arrives it joy lies slain,
And why unblooms the best hope ever sown?   10
—Crass Casualty obstructs the sun and rain,
And dicing Time for gladness casts a moan. . . .
These purblind Doomsters had as readily strown
Blisses about my pilgrimage as pain.

HAP Reprinted with permission of the publisher from
Collected Poems by Thomas Hardy. Copyright 1925
by The Macmillan Company.
THE MAN HE KILLED Reprinted with permission of
the publisher from *Collected Poems* by Thomas
Hardy. Copyright 1925 by The Macmillan Company.

THOMAS HARDY

The Man He Killed

Had he and I but met
  By some old ancient inn,
We should have sat us down to wet
  Right many a nipperkin!

But ranged as infantry,
  And staring face to face,
I shot at him as he at me,
  And killed him in his place.

I shot him dead because—
  Because he was my foe,   10
Just so: my foe of course he was;
  That's clear enough; although

He thought he'd 'list, perhaps
  Off-hand-like—just as I—
Was out of work—had sold his traps—
  No other reason why.

Yes; quaint and curious war is!
  You shoot a fellow down
You'd treat if met where any bar is,
  Or help to half-a-crown.   20

HAROLD WITT

Certainty

Certainty seems to be this person
at work on the roof,
who sped up the ladder as agilely urgent
as if in a circus,
and kneels there wearing a yellow helmet;
his pliers of purpose

flash as he grips them, and twists—just enough—
mysterious wires.
He's wristed with cleverness, belted with tools,
a lineman of light
who knows what he's doing (though we may be fools)   10
and does it right.

If only all darkness had such perfect workmen
risking the task—
to catch the tossed cable that can bring brightness
and nimbly attach
power where it's best to, then step down lithely,
without a scratch.

CERTAINTY By Harold Witt, from the *Saturday Review,* June 12, 1965. Reprinted by permission of the author and the publisher.

RICHARD WILBUR

Year's End

Now winter downs the dying of the year,
And night is all a settlement of snow;
From the soft street the rooms of houses show
A gathered light, a shapen atmosphere,
Like frozen-over lakes whose ice is thin
And still allows some stirring down within.

I've known the wind by water banks to shake
The late leaves down, which frozen where they
    fell
And held in ice as dancers in a spell
Fluttered all winter long into a lake;   10
Graved on the dark in gestures of descent,
They seemed their own most perfect monument.

There was perfection in the death of ferns
Which laid their fragile cheeks against the stone
A million years. Great mammoths overthrown
Composedly have made their long sojourns,
Like palaces of patience, in the gray
And changeless lands of ice. And at Pompeii

The little dog lay curled and did not rise
But slept the deeper as the ashes rose   20
And found the people incomplete, and froze
The random hands, the loose unready eyes
Of men expecting yet another sun
To do the shapely thing they had not done.

These sudden ends of time must give us pause.
We fray into the future, rarely wrought
Save in the tapestries of afterthought.
More time, more time. Barrages of applause
Come muffled from a buried radio.
The New-year bells are wrangling with the
    snow.   30

RICHARD WILBUR

Ceremony

A striped blouse in a clearing by Bazille
Is, you may say, a patroness of boughs
Too queenly kind toward nature to be kin.
But ceremony never did conceal,
Save to the silly eye, which all allows,
How much we are the woods we wander in.

YEAR'S END   First published in the *New Yorker* and
reprinted from *Ceremony and Other Poems*, copyright, 1948, 1949, 1950, by Richard Wilbur, by permission of Harcourt, Brace & World, Inc.

Let her be some Sabrina fresh from stream,
Lucent as shallows slowed by wading sun,
Bedded on fern, the flowers' cynosure:
Then nymph and wood must nod and strive to
    dream   10
That she is airy earth, the trees, undone,
Must ape her languor natural and pure.

Ho-hum. I am for wit and wakefulness,
And love this feigning lady by Bazille.
What's lightly hid is deepest understood,
And when with social smile and formal dress
She teaches leaves to curtsey and quadrille,
I think there are most tigers in the wood.

RICHARD WILBUR

Lamarck Elaborated

"The environment creates the organ"

The Greeks were wrong who said our eyes have
    rays;
Not from these sockets or these sparkling poles
Comes the illumination of our days.
It was the sun that bored these two blue holes.

It was the song of doves begot the ear
And not the ear that first conceived of sound:
That organ bloomed in vibrant atmosphere,
As music conjured Ilium from the ground.

The yielding water, the repugnant stone,
The poisoned berry and the flaring rose   10
Attired in sense the tactless finger-bone
And set the taste-buds and inspired the nose.

Out of our vivid ambiance came unsought
All sense but that most formidably dim.
The shell of balance rolls in seas of thought.
It was the mind that taught the head to swim.

Newtonian numbers set to cosmic lyres
Whelmed us in whirling worlds we could not
    know,
And by the imagined floods of our desires
The voice of Sirens gave us vertigo.   20

CEREMONY   From *Ceremony and Other Poems*, copyright, 1948, 1949, 1950, by Richard Wilbur. Reprinted by permission of Harcourt, Brace & World,
Inc.
LAMARCK ELABORATED   From *Things of This World*,
© 1956, by Richard Wilbur. Reprinted by permission
of Harcourt, Brace & World, Inc.

MARIANNE MOORE

Silence

My father used to say,
"Superior people never make long visits,
have to be shown Longfellow's grave
or the glass flowers at Harvard.
Self-reliant like the cat—
that takes its prey to privacy,
the mouse's limp tail hanging like a shoelace from
    its mouth—
they sometimes enjoy solitude,
and can be robbed of speech
by speech which has delighted them.   10
The deepest feeling always shows itself in silence;
not in silence, but restraint."
Nor was he insincere in saying, "Make my house
    your inn."
Inns are not residences.

MARIANNE MOORE

Poetry

I, too, dislike it: there are things that are important beyond all this fiddle.
    Reading it, however, with a perfect contempt for it, one discovers in
    it, after all, a place for the genuine.
        Hands that can grasp, eyes
        that can dilate, hair that can rise
           if it must, these things are important not because a

high-sounding interpretation can be put upon them but because they are
    useful. When they become so derivative as to become unintelligible,
    the same thing may be said for all of us, that we
        do not admire what   10
        we cannot understand: the bat
           holding on upside down or in quest of something to

eat, elephants pushing, a wild horse taking a roll, a tireless wolf under
    a tree, the immovable critic twitching his skin like a horse that feels a flea, the base-
    ball fan, the statistician—
        nor is it valid
           to discriminate against 'business documents and

school-books'; all these phenomena are important. One must make a distinction
    however: when dragged into prominence by half poets, the result is not poetry,
    nor till the poets among us can be   20
        'literalists of
        the imagination'—above
           insolence and triviality and can present

for inspection, imaginary gardens with real toads in them, shall we have
    it. In the meantime, if you demand on the one hand,
    the raw material of poetry in
        all its rawness and
        that which is on the other hand
           genuine, then you are interested in poetry.

JOHN BETJEMAN

Senex

Oh would I could subdue the flesh
  Which sadly troubles me!
And then perhaps could view the flesh
As though I never knew the flesh
  And merry misery.

To see the golden hiking girl
  With wind about her hair,
The tennis-playing, biking girl,
The wholly-to-my-liking girl,
  To see and not to care.   10

At sundown on my tricycle
  I tour the Borough's edge,
And icy as an icicle
See bicycle by bicycle
  Stacked waiting in the hedge.

Get down from me! I thunder there,
  You spaniels! Shut your jaws!
Your teeth are stuffed with underwear,
Suspenders torn asunder there
  And buttocks in your paws!   20

Oh whip the dogs away, my Lord,
  They make me ill with lust.
Bend bare knees down to pray, my Lord,
Teach sulky lips to say, my Lord,
  That flaxen hair is dust.

EDNA ST. VINCENT MILLAY

Sonnet to Gath

Country of hunchbacks!—where the strong,
    straight spine,
Jeered at by crooked children, makes his way
Through by-streets at the kindest hour of day,
Till he deplore his stature, and incline
To measure manhood with a gibbous line;
Till out of loneliness, being flawed with clay,
He stoop into his neighbour's house and say,
"Your roof is low for me—the fault is mine."

SENEX From *John Betjeman's Collected Poems,* Houghton Mifflin Company, 1959. Reprinted by permission of John Murray Ltd.
SONNET TO GATH From *Collected Poems* of Edna St. Vincent Millay, Harper & Row. Copyright 1921, 1928, 1948, 1955 by Edna St. Vincent Millay and Norma Millay Ellis. Reprinted by permission of Norma Millay Ellis.

Dust in an urn long since, dispersed and dead
Is great Apollo; and the happier he;   10
Since who amongst you all would lift a head
At a god's radiance on the mean door-tree,
Saving to run and hide your dates and bread,
And cluck your children in about your knee?

RALPH WALDO EMERSON

The Rhodora: On Being Asked,
Whence Is the Flower?

In May, when sea-winds pierced our solitudes,
I found the fresh Rhodora in the woods,
Spreading its leafless blooms in a damp nook,
To please the desert and the sluggish brook.
The purple petals, fallen in the pool,
Made the black water with their beauty gay;
Here might the red-bird come his plumes to cool,
And court the flower that cheapens his array.
Rhodora! if the sages ask thee why
This charm is wasted on the earth and sky,   10
Tell them, dear, that if eyes were made for seeing,
Then Beauty is its own excuse for being:
Why thou wert there, O rival of the rose!
I never thought to ask, I never knew;
But, in my simple ignorance, suppose
The self-same Power that brought me there
  brought you.

T. S. ELIOT

Animula

"Issues from the hand of God, the simple soul"
To a flat world of changing lights and noise,
To light, dark, dry or damp, chilly or warm;
Moving between the legs of tables and of chairs,
Rising or falling, grasping at kisses and toys,
Advancing boldly, sudden to take alarm,
Retreating to the corner of arm and knee,
Eager to be reassured, taking pleasure
In the fragrant brilliance of the Christmas tree,
Pleasure in the wind, the sunlight and the sea; 10
Studies the sunlit pattern on the floor
And running stags around a silver tray;
Confounds the actual and the fanciful,
Content with playing-cards and kings and queens,
What the fairies do and what the servants say.

ANIMULA From *Collected Poems of T. S. Eliot,* copyright 1936, by Harcourt, Brace & World, Inc., and reprinted with their permission.

The heavy burden of the growing soul
Perplexes and offends more, day by day;
Week by week, offends and perplexes more
With the imperatives of "is and seems"
And may and may not, desire and control.   20
The pain of living and the drug of dreams
Curl up the small soul in the window seat
Behind the *Encyclopaedia Britannica.*
Issues from the hand of time the simple soul
Irresolute and selfish, misshapen, lame,
Unable to fare forward or retreat,
Fearing the warm reality, the offered good,
Denying the importunity of the blood,
Shadow of its own shadows, spectre in its own
    gloom,
Leaving disordered papers in a dusty room;   30
Living first in the silence after the viaticum.

Pray for Guiterriez, avid of speed and power,
For Boudin, blown to pieces,
For this one who made a great fortune,
And that one who went his own way.
Pray for Floret, by the boarhound slain between
    the yew trees,
Pray for us now and at the hour of our birth.

THEODORE ROETHKE

The Waking

I wake to sleep, and take my waking slow.
I feel my fate in what I cannot fear.
I learn by going where I have to go.

We think by feeling. What is there to know?
I hear my being dance from ear to ear.
I wake to sleep, and take my waking slow.

Of those so close beside me, which are you?
God bless the ground! I shall walk softly there,
And learn by going where I have to go.

Light takes the tree; but who can tell us how?   10
The lowly worm climbs up a winding stair;
I wake to sleep, and take my waking slow.

Great Nature has another thing to do
To you and me; so take the lively air,
And, lovely, learn by going where to go.

This shaking keeps me steady. I should know.
What falls away is always. And is near.
I wake to sleep, and take my waking slow.
I learn by going where I have to go.

WALLACE STEVENS

Anecdote of the Jar

I placed a jar in Tennessee,
And round it was, upon a hill.
It made the slovenly wilderness
Surround that hill.

The wilderness rose up to it,
And sprawled around, no longer wild.
The jar was round upon the ground
And tall and of a port in air.

It took dominion everywhere.
The jar was gray and bare.   10
It did not give of bird or bush,
Like nothing else in Tennessee.

WALLACE STEVENS

The Glass of Water

That the glass would melt in heat,
That the water would freeze in cold,
Shows that this object is merely a state,
One of many, between two poles. So,
In the metaphysical, there are these poles.

Here in the centre stands the glass. Light
Is the lion that comes down to drink. There
And in that state, the glass is a pool.
Ruddy are his eyes and ruddy are his claws
When light comes down to wet his frothy jaws   10

And in the water winding weeds move round.
And there and in another state—the refractions,
The *metaphysica*, the plastic parts of poems
Crash in the mind—But, fat Jocundus, worrying
About what stands here in the center, not in the
    glass,

But in the centre of our lives, this time, this day,
It is a state, this spring among the politicians
Playing cards. In a village of the indigenes,
One would have still to discover. Among the dogs
   and dung,
One would continue to contend with one's
   ideas.   20

RICHARD EBERHART

Rumination

When I can hold a stone within my hand
And feel time make it sand and soil, and see
The roots of living things grow in this land,
Pushing between my fingers flower and tree,
Then I shall be as wise as death,
For death has done this and he will
Do this to me, and blow his breath
To fire my clay, when I am still.

WILLIAM BUTLER YEATS

Crazy Jane Talks with the Bishop

I met the Bishop on the road
And much said he and I.
"Those breasts are flat and fallen now,
Those veins must soon be dry;
Live in a heavenly mansion,
Not in some foul sty."

"Fair and foul are near of kin,
And fair needs foul," I cried.
"My friends are gone, but that's a truth
Nor grave nor bed denied,   . 10
Learned in bodily lowliness
And in the heart's pride.

"A woman can be proud and stiff
When on love intent;
But Love has pitched his mansion in
The place of excrement;
For nothing can be sole or whole
That has not been rent."

WILLIAM BUTLER YEATS

The Second Coming

Turning and turning in the widening gyre
The falcon cannot hear the falconer;
Things fall apart; the centre cannot hold;
Mere anarchy is loosed upon the world,
The blood-dimmed tide is loosed, and everywhere
The ceremony of innocence is drowned;
The best lack all conviction, while the worst
Are full of passionate intensity.

Surely some revelation is at hand;
Surely the Second Coming is at hand.   10
The Second Coming! Hardly are those words out
When a vast image out of *Spiritus Mundi*
Troubles my sight: somewhere in sands of the
   desert
A shape with lion body and the head of a man,
A gaze blank and pitiless as the sun,
Is moving its slow thighs, while all about it
Reel shadows of the indignant desert birds.
The darkness drops again; but now I know
That twenty centuries of stony sleep
Were vexed to nightmare by a rocking cradle, 20
And what rough beast, its hour come round at last,
Slouches towards Bethlehem to be born?

JOSEPHINE MILES

Government Injunction Restraining Harlem Cosmetic Co.

They say La Jac Brite Pink Skin Bleach avails not,
They say its Orange Beauty Glow does not glow,
Nor the face grow five shades lighter nor the heart
Five shades lighter. They say no.

They deny good luck, love, power, romance, and inspiration
From La Jac Brite ointment and incense of all kinds,
And condemn in writing skin brightening and whitening
And whitening of minds.

There is upon the federal trade commission a burden of glory
So to defend the fact, so to impel   10
The plucking of hope from the hand, honor from the complexion,
Sprite from the spell.

HOWARD NEMEROV

Writing

The cursive crawl, the squared-off characters,
these by themselves delight, even without
a meaning, in a foreign language, in
Chinese, for instance, or when skaters curve
all day across the lake, scoring their white
records in ice. Being intelligible,
these winding ways with their audacities
and delicate hesitations, they become
miraculous, so intimately, out there
at the pen's point or brush's tip, do world   10
and spirit wed. The small bones of the wrist
balance against great skeletons of stars
exactly; the blind bat surveys his way
by echo alone. Still, the point of style
is character. The universe induces
a different tremor in every hand, from the
check-forger's to that of the Emperor
Hui Tsung, who called his own calligraphy
the 'Slender Gold.' A nervous man
writes nervously of a nervous world, and so on.   20

Miraculous. It is as though the world
were a great writing. Having said so much,
let us allow there is more to the world
than writing; continental faults are not
bare convoluted fissures in the brain.
Not only must the skaters soon go home;
also the hard inscription of their skates
is scored across the open water, which long
remembers nothing, neither wind nor wake.

E. E. CUMMINGS

pity this busy monster,manunkind

pity this busy monster,manunkind,

not. Progress is a comfortable disease:
your victim(death and life safely beyond)

plays with the bigness of his littleness
—electrons deify one razorblade
into a mountainrange;lenses extend

unwish through curving wherewhen till unwish
returns on its unself.
                    A world of made
is not a world of born—pity poor flesh

and trees,poor stars and stones,but never this   10
fine specimen of hypermagical

ultraomnipotence. We doctors know

a hopeless case if—listen:there's a hell
of a good universe next door;let's go

WRITING   From *New and Selected Poems* by Howard
Nemerov. Reprinted by permission of Margot John-
son Agency.
PITY THIS BUSY MONSTER,MANUNKIND   Copyright
1944, by E. E. Cummings. Reprinted from his volume
Poems 1923–1954 by permission of Harcourt, Brace
& World, Inc.

GERARD MANLEY HOPKINS

Petrachen Sonnet [handwritten]

I Wake and Feel the Fell of Dark

heart [handwritten]

I wake and feel the fell of dark, not day.
What hours, O what black hoürs we have spent
This night! what sights you, heart, saw; ways you went!
And more must, in yet longer light's delay.
   With witness I speak this. But where I say
Hours I mean years, mean life. And my lament
Is cries countless, cries like dead letters sent
To dearest him that lives alas! away.

same bitter [handwritten]

   I am gall, I am heartburn. God's most deep decree
Bitter would have me taste: my taste was me;   10
Bones built in me, flesh filled, blood brimmed the curse.
Selfyeast of spirit a dull dough sours. I see
The lost are like this, and their scourge to be
As I am mine, their sweating selves; but worse.

The mind knew me. The more I am bitter [handwritten, left margin]

GERARD MANLEY HOPKINS

dead meat [handwritten]

Carrion Comfort

Not, I'll not, carrion comfort, Despair, not feast on thee;   *I will not feast on despair / despair* [handwritten]
Not untwist—slack they may be—these last strands of man
In me ór, most weary, cry *I can no more*. I can;
Can something, hope, wish day come, not choose not to be.
But ah, but O thou terrible, why wouldst thou rude on me   *you be rude* [handwritten]
Thy wring-world right foot rock? lay a lionlimb against me? scan
With darksome devouring eyes my bruisèd bones? and fan,
O in turns of tempest, me heaped there; me frantic to avoid thee and flee?

   Why? That my chaff might fly; my grain lie, sheer and clear.   *Leave me bare* [handwritten]
Nay in all that toil, that coil, since (seems) I kissed the rod,   10
Hand rather, my heart lo! lapped strength, stole joy, would laugh, chéer.
Cheer whom though? the hero whose heaven-handling flung me, fóot tród
Me? or me that fought him? O which one? is it each one? That night, that year
Of now done darkness I wretch lay westling with (my God!) my God.

GERARD MANLEY HOPKINS

No Worst, There Is None

No worst, there is none. Pitched past pitch of grief,
More pangs will, schooled at forepangs, wilder wring.
Comforter, where, where is your comforting?
Mary, mother of us, where is your relief?
My cries heave, herds-long; huddle in a main, a chief
Woe, world-sorrow; on an age-old anvil wince and sing—
Then lull, then leave off. Fury had shrieked "No ling-
ering! Let me be fell: Force I must be brief."

  O the mind, mind has mountains; cliffs of fall
Frightful, sheer, no-man-fathomed. Hold them cheap   10
May who ne'er hung there. Nor does long our small
Durance deal with that steep or deep. Here! creep,
Wretch, under a comfort serves in a whirlwind: all
Life death does end and each day dies with sleep.

ROBERT LOWELL

Salem

In Salem seasick spindrift drifts or skips
To the canvas flapping on the seaward panes
Until the knitting sailor stabs at ships
Nosing like sheep of Morpheus through his brain's
Asylum. Seaman, seaman, how the draft
Lashes the oily slick about your head,
Beating up whitecaps! Seaman, Charon's raft
Dumps its damned goods into the harbor-bed,—
There sewage sickens the rebellious seas.
Remember, seaman, Salem fishermen   10
Once hung their nimble fleets on the Great Banks.
Where was it that New England bred the men
Who quartered the Leviathan's fat flanks
And fought the British Lion to his knees?

ARCHIBALD MAC LEISH

You, Andrew Marvell

And here face down beneath the sun
And here upon earth's noonward height
To feel the always coming on
The always rising of the night

To feel creep up the curving east
The earthly chill of dusk and slow
Upon those under lands the vast
And ever-climbing shadow grow

And strange at Ecbatan the trees
Take leaf by leaf the evening strange   10
The flooding dark about their knees
The mountains over Persia change

And now at Kermanshah the gate
Dark empty and the withered grass
And through the twilight now the late
Few travelers in the westward pass

And Baghdad darken and the bridge
Across the silent river gone
And through Arabia the edge
Of evening widen and steal on   20

And deepen on Palmyra's street
The wheel rut in the ruined stone
And Lebanon fade out and Crete
High through the clouds and overblown

And over Sicily the air
Still flashing with the landward gulls
And loom and slowly disappear
The sails above the shadowy hulls

And Spain go under and the shore
Of Africa the gilded sand
And evening vanish and no more   30
The low pale light across that land

Nor now the long light on the sea—

And here face downward in the sun
To feel how swift how secretly
The shadow of the night comes on . . .

DELMORE SCHWARTZ

The Heavy Bear

"The withness of the body"—WHITEHEAD

The heavy bear who goes with me,
A manifold honey to smear his face,
Clumsy and lumbering here and there,
The central ton of every place,
The hungry beating brutish one
In love with candy, anger, and sleep,
Crazy factotum, dishevelling all,
Climbs the building, kicks the football,
Boxes his brother in the hate-ridden city.

Breathing at my side, that heavy animal,   10
That heavy bear who sleeps with me,
Howls in his sleep for a world of sugar,
A sweetness intimate as the water's clasp,
Howls in his sleep because the tight-rope
Trembles and shows the darkness beneath.

—The strutting show-off is terrified,
Dressed in his dress-suit, bulging his pants,
Trembles to think that his quivering meat
Must finally wince to nothing at all.

That inescapable animal walks with me,   20
Has followed me since the black womb held,
Moves where I move, distorting my gesture,
A caricature, a swollen shadow,
A stupid clown of the spirit's motive,
Perplexes and affronts with his own darkness,
The secret life of belly and bone,
Opaque, too near, my private, yet unknown,
Stretches to embrace the very dear
With whom I would walk without him near,
Touches her grossly, although a word   30
Would bare my heart and make me clear,
Stumbles, flounders, and strives to be fed
Dragging me with him in his mouthing care,
Amid the hundred million of his kind,
The scrimmage of appetite everywhere.

JACQUES PRÉVERT

To Paint the Portrait of a Bird

Translation by John Dixon Hunt

Paint first a cage
with an open door
paint then
something pretty
something simple
something handsome
something useful
for the bird
then place the canvas against a tree
in a garden   10
in a wood
or in a forest
hide behind the tree
silently
motionless
Sometimes the bird arrives at once
but it may also take many years
before making up its mind
Do not be discouraged
wait   20
wait if need be many years
a speedy or a delayed arrival

bears no relation
to the success of the portrait
When the bird arrives
if it arrives
observe the most profound silence
wait until the bird enters the cage
and when it has entered
close the door gently with a stroke of the brush
then   31
paint out one by one all the bars of the cage
taking care to touch none of the bird's feathers
Paint then the portrait of a tree
choosing the loveliest of its branches
for the bird

paint too the green foliage and the fresh wind
the dust of the sun
and the noise of insects in the grass in the summer
    heat
and then wait for the bird to sing   40
If the bird does not sing
it is a bad sign
a sign that the picture is bad
but if it sings it is a good sign
a sign that you can sign
So you pluck gently then
one of the bird's feathers
and you write your name in a corner of the
    portrait.

PABLO PICASSO

give tear twist and kill

give tear twist and kill I traverse illuminate and
burn caress and lick embrace and look I sound at
every flight and bells till they bleed frightening
the pigeons and I make them fly around the dovecot
till they fall to earth already dead of weariness
I will raze all the windows and doors to the earth
and with your hair I will hang all the birds that are
singing and cut down all the flowers I will take the lamp
in my arms and give it my breast to eat and will
go to sleep alongside the song of my solitude   10
by *Soleares* and I will etch the fields of wheat and
hay and I shall see them die supine with their faces
to the sun and I will wrap the flowers in the newspaper and
I will fling them through the window
in the gutterstream that is hurrying by with all its
sins on its back but laughing all the same to make
its nest in the sewer and I will break the music of
the woodlands against the rocks of the waves of the
sea and I will bite the lion on the cheek and I
will make the wolf cry for tender pity in front   20
of the portrait of the water which is letting its arms
fall slackly into the wash-hand basin.

WILLIAM BLAKE

The Scoffers

Mock on, Mock on, Voltaire, Rousseau;
Mock on, Mock on; 'tis all in vain!
You throw the sand against the wind,
And the wind blows it back again.

And every sand becomes a Gem
Reflected in the beams divine;
Blown back they blind the mocking eye,
But still in Israel's paths they shine.

The Atoms of Democritus
And Newton's Particles of light   10
Are sands upon the Red sea shore,
Where Israel's tents do shine so bright.

GLOSSARY OF POETIC TERMS

ACCENT: Stress or emphasis given to a poetic syllable. *See* Prosody.

ALLEGORY: A narrative in which objects and persons stand for meanings outside the narrative itself; an elaborated metaphor. *See* Figurative Language.

ALLITERATION: The repetition of initial consonant sounds or of accented consonant sounds. *See* Rime; Texture.

ALLUSION: A reference to something outside the primary content of the poem, often used figuratively.

ANALOGY: A comparison, bordering on metaphor, of particular points of resemblance between obviously different things.

ANAPEST: *See* Meter; Prosody.

APOSTROPHE: Direct address to a person, object, or abstract idea, often treating the dead as living, the nonhuman as human, and the absent as present. *See* Figurative Language.

ASSONANCE: Repetition of vowel sounds that are not followed, as in rime, by similar consonants. *See* Rime; Texture.

BALLAD: In its original form a simple, highly concentrated verse-story, often sung. The more recent literary ballad is a consciously artistic imitation. *See* Narrative; Types of Poetry.

BLANK VERSE: Unrimed iambic pentameter. *See* Prosody; Stanza; Verse Paragraphs.

CACOPHONY: Harsh, unpleasant sound. *See* Euphony; Texture.

CADENCE: Rhythmic, though not regularly metrical, flow of language. Cadence is influenced by many of the factors that determine rhythm. *See* Rhythm.

CAESURA: A sense pause within a line of poetry. *See* Prosody.

CONSONANCE: Identity of the pattern of consonants (*deer, door*); unlike rime in that the vowels involved differ. *See* Rime; Texture.

COUPLET: The form of verse with two successive lines riming. *See* Stanza.

DACTYL: *See* Meter; Prosody.

DIMETER: *See* Line; Meter; Prosody.

DRAMATIC: That one of the three main types of poetry which uses methods that resemble the methods of drama. *See* Types of Poetry.

DRAMATIC MONOLOGUE: Poem that is the speech of one character.

ELEGY: A subjective, meditative poem, usually expressing emotions associated with grief or death. *See* Lyric; Types of Poetry.

END-STOPPED LINE: Line whose end coincides with a pause in meaning. *See* Prosody.

ENVOY: A short stanza in the nature of a postscript at the end of a poem.

EPIC: A long narrative poem in elevated style dealing with heroic personalities and great actions. *See* Narrative; Types of Poetry.

EUPHONY: Sound combinations, consonant or vowel, which are pleasing to the ear. *See* Cacophony; Texture.

EYE-RIME: A terminal pairing of words or syllables that appear from the spelling to rime but in pronunciation do not (*yea, tea*).

FIGURATIVE LANGUAGE: Words used out of their literal sense to convey a special effect and meaning. Many figures of speech are based upon comparison or intensification. The more common figures are simile and metaphor, which are based on comparison. Other figurative comparisons are symbol and allegory. Some figures based on intensification are per-

700

sonification, apostrophe, hyperbole, litotes or understatement, and irony.

FOOT: A metrical unit composed of one accented syllable and one or more unaccented syllables. *See* Meter; Prosody.

FREE VERSE: Verse with loose or irregular rhythm. *See* Stanza.

HEPTAMETER: *See* Line; Meter; Prosody.

HEXAMETER: *See* Line; Meter; Prosody.

HYPERBOLE: Figure of speech using an exaggerated statement not intended to be taken literally; overstatement. *See* Understatement; Figurative Language.

IAMB: *See* Meter; Prosody.

IMAGERY: The representation of sensory experience by use of allusions and figurative language. *See* Allusion; Figurative Language.

INTERNAL RIME: Rime occurring within a single line of poetry. *See* Rime.

IRONY: An implication opposite to the literal meaning of the words used; a situation or effect opposite to the expected and the normally appropriate one. *See* Figurative Language.

ITALIAN SONNET: *See* Sonnet.

LINE: A typographical unit of one metrical foot in verse. The poetic line is described by the predominant kind of foot and the number of feet it contains. *See* Foot; Meter; Prosody.

LYRIC: A poem meant to be sung, or an especially musical or highly subjective poem; one of the three main types of poetry. *See* Types of Poetry.

METAPHOR: Narrowly, the figure of speech expressing by implication—not using *as* or *like*—a resemblance of an object in one class to an object in another class. Broadly, figurative language in general. *See* Figurative Language; Simile.

METER: The relationship of accented and unaccented syllables. Used both to designate the kind of metrical foot and the number of feet in a line of verse. The common kinds of meter in English are anapestic, dactylic, trochaic, iambic. The spondee, a metrical foot of two accented syllables, is only approximated in English prosody. Common line lengths (reckoned in number of metrical feet) are monometer, dimeter, trimeter, tetrameter, pentameter, hexameter, heptameter. *See* Line; Rhythm; Prosody.

MONOMETER: *See* Line; Meter; Prosody.

NARRATIVE: A story, or a connected series of events; one of the three main types of poetry. *See* Types of Poetry.

OCTAVE: Stanza of eight lines, or the first eight lines of a sonnet. *See* Sonnet.

ODE: Usually a serious formal poem that follows a set, complicated metrical pattern and is written for a special purpose and occasion. *See* Lyric; Types of Poetry.

ONOMATOPOEIA: Words formed in imitation of the natural sounds they name. *See* Texture.

PARODY: An imitation of the language, style, and ideas of another work for comic or critical effect.

PASTORAL: Broadly, a type of classical poetry, or, narrowly, any favorable treatment of rural life. *See* Lyric; Types of Poetry.

PENTAMETER: *See* Line; Meter; Prosody.

PERSONIFICATION: Figure of speech in which human qualities are given to nonhuman objects or abstractions. *See* Figurative Language.

PETRARCHAN SONNET: *See* Sonnet.

PROSODY: Art of metrical composition, or a special theory or practice in metrics. See fuller discussion of prosody, pages 702–04.

QUATRAIN: Four-line stanza in any of a number of end-rime schemes. *See* Prosody; Stanza.

RHYTHM: Literally, the measured motion of language. Rhythm is primarily a product of the relationship of accented and unaccented syllables or sounds, though pitch, tempo, syllabic length, and sentence structure are other influential factors. Often rhythm refers to regular metrical pattern. *See* Meter.

RIME: Usually refers to end rime, the similarity or correspondence of the terminal sounds of words; but, in general, rime is any degree of correspondence of sound combinations whether terminal or internal (within a line). Slant or partial rime is an approximate correspondence of sounds. Textural effects—assonance, consonance, alliteration—are themselves forms of rime. *See* Internal Rime; Texture.

RIME SCHEME: The patterns of end rime in a stanza. Small letters are ordinarily used to indicate this pattern, thus: couplet, *aa*; ballad quatrain, *abcb*; envelope quatrain, *abba*; Rubáiyát quatrain, *aaba*; Spenserian stanza, *ababbcbcc*. *See* Stanza.

RUN-ON LINE: A line in which the sense is not concluded but continues into the next line without pause. *See* Prosody; End-stopped Line.

SCANSION: The determining of the relationship between accented and unaccented syllables in verse. *See* Prosody.

SESTET: Stanza of six lines, or the last six lines of a sonnet. *See* Sonnet.

SHAKESPEAREAN SONNET: *See* Sonnet.

SIMILE: The figure of speech expressing with *as* or *like* a resemblance in one or more points of an object of one class to an object of another class. *See* Figurative Language; Metaphor.

SLANT RIME: Loose or approximate rime (*run*, *tone*). *See* Rime.

SONNET: A poem of fourteen lines in iambic pentameter. The Petrachan or Italian sonnet commonly divides itself into an octave riming *abbaabba*, in which the theme is presented, and a sestet riming *cdecde*, or sometimes more freely, in which the conclusion to the theme is presented. The Shakespearean sonnet, riming *ababcdcdefefgg*, commonly develops the theme in three quatrains and concludes it in a couplet.

SPONDEE: See Meter; Prosody.

STANZA: A pattern of lines and rimes in verse. Stanzas are identified on the basis of the type of meter, number of metrical feet in each line, number of lines, and the pattern of rime when rime is employed. Many stanzaic patterns have been long established and have conventional names—for example, couplet, ballad quatrain, Spenserian. Blank verse (unrimed iambic pentameter) and other non-stanzaic verse forms (like free verse) may be broken into verse paragraphs, which are determined more by content than by form. *See* Prosody.

SYMBOL: In the broadest sense, something that suggests or stands for an idea, quality, or conception larger than itself, as the lion is the symbol of courage, the cross the symbol of Christianity. In poetic usage, a symbol is a more central and pervasive comparison than either simile or metaphor, often providing the basic imagery of an entire poem. It represents a step beyond metaphor in that the first term of the comparison is not supplied. *See* Figurative Language.

TEMPO: Rate of articulation or delivery of words and syllables. *See* Rhythm.

TETRAMETER: *See* Line; Meter; Prosody.

TEXTURE: As applied to poetry, texture is the general relationship of sounds, generally not including the more exact forms of rime. Important textural devices are cacophony, euphony, onomatopeia, alliteration, assonance, consonance. *See* Rime.

TRIMETER: *See* Line; Meter; Prosody.

TROCHEE: *See* Meter; Prosody.

TYPES OF POETRY: Generally, poetry is divided into three main types: the narrative, which is the story poem; the dramatic, which uses many of the methods of the drama itself; and the lyric, which is highly musical, emotional, subjective. Some common types of dramatic poetry are the dramatic monologue and the verse-drama. Some common types of lyric are the descriptive lyric, the didactic lyric, the elegy, the hymn, the sonnet, the ode, the pastoral, the reflective or philosophical lyric, and the satiric lyric. *See* Dramatic; Lyric; Narrative.

UNDERSTATEMENT: Popular designation of the figure of speech classically known as *litotes*. Understatement is the saying less about an occasion than might normally be expected. *See* Figurative Language.

VERSE: A single line of a poem. A literary composition with a systematic metrical pattern as opposed to prose. Sometimes *verse* is used disparagingly in reference to such compositions as attain only the outward and mechanical features and not the high quality of poetry.

VERSE PARAGRAPHS: Thought divisions in non-stanzaic verse forms such as blank verse and free verse. *See* Stanza.

PROSODY

Prosody, generally defined as the "science of versification," rises above mere attention to the mechanical considerations of metrical structure to become an art of communication in which the sound furthers the sense and in which the sense intensifies the sound. Since English verse is primarily accentual and not quantitative (that is, primarily dependent upon emphasis given a syllable rather than on length of syllable), English prosody is much a matter of studying the occurrence of accents.

The prosodic structure of a stanza is analyzed by a process known as *scansion*. In scanning, one examines (1) the prevailing metrical foot; (2) the line length; (3) the placement of pauses; and (4) the number of lines and, if the verse is rimed, the pattern of end rime.

1. METRICAL FEET

Iamb: Unaccented syllable, accented syllable (a-go).

Trochee: Accented syllable, unaccented syllable (dwel-ling).

Anapest: Two unaccented syllables, accented syllable (of the sun).

Dactyl: Accented syllable, two unaccented syllables (mér-ri-ly).

Spondee: A fifth kind of metrical foot, in which two consecutive accented syllables from different metrical feet occur or in which a primary and secondary accent occur consecutively (pláy-hóuse).

2. LINE

The line length in metrical feet is *monometer* if the line has one foot, *dimeter* if two feet, *trimeter* if three, *tetrameter* if four, *pentameter* if five, *hexameter* (*Alexandrine*) if six, *heptameter* if seven, *octameter* if eight. In theory there may be more than eight feet in a line, but in practice a line longer than heptameter tends to break up into two or more lines.

3. PAUSES

Also important, especially in blank verse, alliterative verse, and the heroic couplet, is the location of pauses ending sense units—phrases, clauses, sentences—within the line. A main pause, known as the *caesura,* and secondary pauses are common. (In scansion they are indicated by the symbols // and /.) A line is termed *end-stopped* when it ends with a sense pause, *run-on* when the sense extends into the next line.

Little verse is metrically perfect, for metrical perfection does not permit the flexibility necessary to combine sense and sound most fittingly. Nearly all English verse is iambic, but substitution of another type of foot is common and substantial passages of trochee, dactyl, and anapest can be found.

4. PATTERN OF LINES AND RIMES

The number of lines and the rime pattern are described as *couplet* (*aa*); *tercet* or *triplet* (*terza rima, aba-bcb-cdc,* etc.); *quatrain* (*ballad, abcb; Rubáiyát, aaba; In Memoriam, abba*); *octave;* and so forth.

Following are metrical descriptions of some common verse patterns.

Blank verse: Iambic pentameter unrimed.

The wórld | was áll | befóre | them, // whére | to choóse

Their pláce | of rést, | // and Próv | idénce | their guíde.

They, / hánd | in hánd, | // with wán | dering stéps | and slów,

Through É | den toók | their sól | itár | y wáy.

Heroic couplet: Iambic pentameter rimed (*aa*); first couplet below is run-on, second couplet end-stopped.

Of áll | the cáus | es whích | conspíre | to blínd

Man's ér | ring júdg | ment, and | misguíde | the mínd,

Whát the | weák heád | with stróng | est bí | as rúles,

Is Príde, // the név | er faíl | ing více | of foóls.

Ballad measure: Iambic, first and third lines tetrameter, second and fourth lines trimeter, and second and fourth lines riming (i.e., iambic, 4-3-4-3, *abcb*).

And soón | I heárd | a roár | ing wínd;

It díd | not cóme | anéar;

But wíth | its soúnd | it shoók | the saíls

That wére | so thín | and seár.

Rubáiyát quatrain: Iambic pentameter rimed *aaba.*

Come, fíll | the cúp, | // and ín | the fíre | of Spríng

Your Wín | ter-gár | ment óf | Repén | tance flíng.

The Bírd | of Tíme | has bút | a lít | tle wáy

To flút | ter // —and | the Bírd | is ón | the Wíng.

Spenserian stanza: Iambic pentameter rimed *ababbcbcc,* the last line being hexameter (Alexandrine).

And stíll | she slépt | an áz | ure-líd | ded sleép,

In blán | chèd lín | en, / smoóth, | and láv | endéred,

While hé | from fórth | the clós | et broúght | a heáp

Of cán | died áp | ple, quínce, | and plúm, | and
gourd;
With jél | lies soóth | er than | the creám | y
curd,
And lú | cent sýr | ops, // tínct | with cín | na-
mon;

Mánna | and dátes, | in ar | gosý | transferred
From Féz; | and spíc | èd dáin | ties, év | ery
one,
From síl | ken Sám | arcánd | to cé | dared Léb |
anón.

CONRAD AIKEN (1889–   ), born in Savannah, Georgia, is an American poet, anthologist, and critic. A leader among American poets who wrote immediately after World War I, he was, from 1917 to 1919, a contributing editor to *The Dial,* a distinguished literary magazine that gave staunch support to new artistic movements and published the works of new authors. In 1930 he was awarded a Pulitzer Prize for his *Selected Poems,* and in 1950–51 he served as consultant on poetry to the Library of Congress. His poetry, musical but occasionally obscure, records his deep probing of the human spirit.

MATTHEW ARNOLD (1822–1888), an English poet and critic greatly interested in social and religious topics, was strongly affected by the science of his day. In both his poetry and his prose he revealed wide learning and a deep respect for culture, which he defined as "the best that has been thought and said in the world."

W. H. AUDEN (1907–   ), an English-born, Oxford-educated poet, now a naturalized American citizen, was, in the 1930's, a leader of a group of young English poets who wrote about the political and social problems of their time. More recently, Mr. Auden's verse has shown a religious and philosophical outlook. His latest collection of poems is *About the House,* 1965. In 1967 he was awarded the National Medal for Literature.

HILAIRE BELLOC (1870–1953), born in Paris and educated at Oxford University, wrote essays, historical pieces, novels, and poetry. He became a British subject in 1902 and was at one time a member of the House of Commons. He was one of the most prolific and versatile of English writers, and his poems are characterized by brilliance, wit, and careful craftsmanship.

JOHN BETJEMAN (1906–   ), an English poet, was educated at Oxford University. He writes on architectural subjects with the same polish and wit that appear in his poetry. He has been a book critic for the *Daily Telegraph,* a weekly columnist for the *Spectator,* a prep-school master, an essayist, a radio and television performer, and the author of guidebooks.

MORRIS BISHOP (1893–   ) was educated at Cornell University. After serving in the United States Infantry during World War I, engaging in business, and holding various government positions, he returned to Cornell. He is now Kappa Alpha Professor of Romance Literature, Emeritus. *A Bowl of Bishop,* 1954, was his twelfth book.

WILLIAM BLAKE (1757–1827), the self-educated son of a London tradesman, was a rare combination of poet and painter. In his lyrics and in his highly original paintings, notably those for *The Book of Job,* he expressed a mystical awareness of the Divine.

ROBERT BROWNING (1812–1889), English poet of the Victorian period, wrote for many years without attracting public attention or critical approval, but he lived to become a hero in the literary world, with cults founded solely to study his works. He is especially known for his employment of the dramatic verse monologue to reveal character and personality.

G. K. CHESTERTON (1874–1936), often called the master of paradox, began his literary career as a critic of art books. A versatile writer, he published fiction (he is best remembered in this field as the creator of Father Brown, a whimsical priest-detective), biography, criticism, poetry, essays, and plays.

JOANNE CHILDERS (1926–   ), born in Cincinnati, Ohio, is a graduate of the University of Cincinnati and holds a master's degree in modern European history from the University of Florida. Besides writing poetry, which has appeared in many magazines and journals, she is acting director of social services at a state institution for mentally retarded children.

JOHN CIARDI (1916–   ), a major American poet and critic, was born in Massachusetts, educated at Bates College in Maine, at Tufts College in Massachusetts, and at the University of Michigan, where he took an M.A. and won a major poetry award. He has taught at Kansas City University, Harvard University, and Rutgers University and has lectured at the Salzburg Seminar in American Studies. He translated Dante's *Inferno* and *Purgatorio* and made a study of methods of teaching poetry for the Fund for the Advancement of Education.

ROBERT P. TRISTRAM COFFIN (1892–1955), a scholar whose special field of interest was English and classical literature, was a prolific nature poet and historian of Maine, his native state. He spent much time lecturing and giving poetry recitations, and conducted a number of writers' conferences.

HART CRANE (1899–1932) was an American poet who began writing verse at thirteen. In 1926 he published the best of his early poems in *White Buildings;* in 1930 *The Bridge* appeared —a group of fifteen poems unified by a symbolic use of the Brooklyn Bridge. Crane wrote from his experience, using bold symbols and showing mystical insight; his poetry is becoming increasingly significant to the American literary scene. His early suicide followed great personal difficulties and a belief that his best creative years were over.

COUNTEE CULLEN (1903–1946), a Negro poet who was popular during the twenties and thirties, wrote seven volumes of verse (*Color*, 1925, was the first; *On These I Stand*, 1947, the last), largely about the feelings and aspirations of Negroes.

E. E. CUMMINGS (1894–1962), was born in Cambridge, Massachusetts, and was educated at Harvard University. He published many volumes of verse and prose. The unconventional punctuation and form of his poetry are technical devices which indicate the way the poem should be read and which he felt gave purer

and clearer expression of his thought. His *73 Poems* was published in 1963.

WALTER DE LA MARE (1873–1956), English novelist and poet, wrote verse for children and adults. It is marked by music and mystery.

EMILY DICKINSON (1830–1886), now considered one of America's greatest poets, spent most of her life in self-imposed seclusion. She published only four poems in her lifetime and won no wide audience until the 1920's. Though her poems are all brief, they show close observation, intensity, and illuminating, often whimsical, metaphor.

JOHN DONNE (1572–1631), who, after an intense spiritual struggle, became the most famous Anglican preacher of his day, won his lasting reputation not so much for his *Sermons* as for two groups of poems, the love lyrics of his youth and the religious lyrics of his maturity.

ALAN DUGAN (1923–   ) was born in Brooklyn, attended Olivet College and Mexico City College, and served in the U.S. Air Force in World War II. He received his first award for poetry in 1946. Since then he has received the National Book Award for Poetry in 1961, the Pulitzer Prize for Poetry in 1962, and a Guggenheim Fellowship in 1963–64. He has published *Poems*, 1961, and *Poems 2*, 1963.

RICHARD EBERHART (1904–   ) is an American poet, playwright, and teacher. In 1930 he published *A Bravery of Earth;* since then several other volumes of his poems have appeared, including *Collected Poems*, 1960. His poetry is about simple things and situations from which he draws intricate truths about life.

T. S. ELIOT (1888–1965), an American-born critic and poet who became a British citizen, influenced a whole generation of writers, particularly through his long poem *The Waste Land*. His major theme is the frustration and the consequent spiritual inadequacy of our times.

RALPH WALDO EMERSON (1803–1882), clergyman, philosopher, poet, and essayist, was born in Concord, Massachusetts, educated at Harvard University, and became one of the major literary figures in America. He was the leader of the Transcendentalist movement, which was based on his philosophical doctrine of the relation of the soul to nature.

ROBERT FROST (1874–1963), though born in San Francisco, is identified with the New England of his forebears. As a young man, he taught, farmed, and wrote poetry there—all with little initial success. Not until he went to England for the years 1912–15 did he come to the attention of critics and public. After his return to New England, his reputation grew steadily—he won the Pulitzer Prize four times and is considered one of the greatest American poets.

ROBERT GRAVES (1895–   ), an English novelist, poet and critic, was elected to the Chair of Poetry at Oxford University, in 1961. Both as poet and as novelist, he displays a wide, thorough scholarship and an active imagination. His poetry often does not seem to be in either the American or British tradition. His books, which number over a hundred, and his manuscripts are on permanent exhibition at Lockwood Memorial Library, Buffalo, New York.

ARTHUR GUITERMAN (1871–1943), an American lecturer and magazine editor, wrote light verse with wry humor and unexpected twists.

THOM GUNN (1929–   ) is an English poet whose verse often deals with the violence in the contemporary scene. He is a graduate of Cambridge University and has taught at the University of California at Berkeley. His third book of poems, *My Sad Captains,* appeared in 1961.

THOMAS HARDY (1840–1928), one of the two or three English writers who have produced both great poetry and great novels, was trained as an architect. His earliest writings were poems; about 1870 he turned to the novel and wrote all his novels in the succeeding twenty-six years. In 1896, discouraged by harsh criticism of *Jude the Obscure,* which he had written a year earlier, he returned to poetry. In this final period of his work he wrote *The Dynasts,* 1904–08, a great epic drama in verse and the most ambitious of his poems.

ROBERT HERRICK (1591–1674), the most popular of the Cavalier poets, was, like Donne, a churchman as well as a poet. Like Donne, too, he is best known for his love lyrics and religious lyrics. His graceful, light secular poems usually treat of the simple pleasures of life and of love.

ROBERT HOGAN (1930–   ) is a teacher, critic, and poet. He has published poems, several articles on the theater and on Sean O'Casey's plays, and a book, *The Experiments of Sean O'Casey,* 1960.

GERARD MANLEY HOPKINS (1844–1889), a brilliant Oxford graduate, became converted to Roman Catholicism and entered the priesthood. His poetry, which was experimental in its imagery and rhythm, was not known until 1918, when Robert Bridges published a volume of his verse.

A. E. HOUSMAN (1859–1936), English scholar and poet, was not a prolific writer; he produced only three small volumes of lyrics. But the simplicity, irony, and flawlessness of these lyrics place him among the chief English poets.

RANDALL JARRELL (1914–1965), American poet, has taught at several universities; in 1956–58 he was poetry consultant to the Library of Congress. His poetry, greatly influenced by his experiences in World War II, shows his deep reaction to the tragedies of life and to the courage of many who face those tragedies.

ROBINSON JEFFERS (1887–1962) has been called American poetry's apostle of negation. Jeffers' poetic line resembles Whitman's in length, vigor, and rhythm, but the philosophies of the two poets are at opposite poles. Jeffers' creed is the renunciation of humanity and the glorification of unspoiled nature.

CECIL DAY LEWIS (1904–   ) was born in Ireland and educated at Oxford University, where he became one of the post-World War I group of writers which included Stephen Spender and W. H. Auden. He has written serious novels and criticism as well as poetry; under the pseudonym of Nicholas Blake he published some sixteen crime and detective novels. He has been active in political as well as literary matters.

HENRY WADSWORTH LONGFELLOW (1807–1882) was born in Maine and educated at Bowdoin College, where he was a classmate of Nathaniel Hawthorne. Later he was professor of modern languages at Bowdoin and Harvard University. He is best known for his long poems "Evangeline" and "Hiawatha" and for "Paul Revere's Ride."

ROBERT LOWELL (1917–   ) is an American poet who writes much about New England, commemorating his ancestors who settled there and became influential in American life; he is a great-grandnephew of James Russell Lowell. In 1940 he converted to Catholicism, and many of his poems written since then reflect his religious thinking. He was awarded the Pulitzer Prize in 1947 for his volume of poetry *Lord Weary's Castle.* Lowell's more recent work includes *The Old Glory,* 1964—three plays based on stories by Hawthorne and Melville—and a volume of poetry, *Near the Ocean,* published in 1967.

LUCIAN (*c.* 120–*c.* 200), Greek poet, satirist, and wit, came to literary notice after the Roman Empire had expanded to include Greece. He is considered the first classical writer to have composed satirical dialogue. His writing has been compared to that of Swift and Voltaire.

PHYLLIS MC GINLEY (1905–   ), a suburban housewife, is a writer of light verse. She has published several volumes and contributed widely to national magazines.

ARCHIBALD MAC LEISH (1892–   ), an important public figure as well as a literary man, has been Librarian of Congress and an Undersecretary of State. In 1949, he was awarded the Boylston Professorship of Rhetoric and Oratory at Harvard University.

JOHN MANIFOLD (1915–   ), poet and musicologist, was born in Australia and educated at Cambridge University. Though he uses a variety of poetic forms, he shows a mature control of them; his poetry stresses action and lyricism. His *Selected Verse* was published in 1946.

ANDREW MARVELL (1621–1678) was educated at Cambridge University and became in 1657 assistant to John Milton, who was Latin secretary to the Council of State. His poetry at first was chiefly lyrical. Later he turned to political satire in verse.

JOSEPHINE MILES (1911–   ) is a poet, scholar, and educator. She received her undergraduate degree from the University of California at Los Angeles and two advanced degrees from the University of California at Berkeley. She has taught at Berkeley since 1940. She has published several volumes of poems, including *Poems 1936–60*, and has done much scholarly and critical writing.

EDNA ST. VINCENT MILLAY (1892–1950), Pulitzer Prize winner for poetry in 1923, was born in Rockland, Maine, attended school at Vassar College, and, after a varied career as journalist, actress, dramatist, and libretto writer, devoted the remainder of her life to writing poetry. Her verse is distinguished by its passionate zest for life, its revolt against Victorian prudery, and its intense emotions. *Renascence and Other Poems*, published in 1917, established her reputation among the brilliant young poets of her generation.

JOHN MILTON (1608–1674), one of the greatest poets of the late Renaissance, was educated at Christ's College, Cambridge. He served as Latin secretary to the Council of State under Oliver Cromwell, during which time he became blind. The Restoration of Charles II brought both political and financial reverses to Milton, who was an ardent Puritan and a champion of political freedom. Though he is best known as the author of the epic *Paradise Lost,* he was also an important sonnet writer.

MARIANNE MOORE (1887–   ) is noted for the effective imagery and keen wit of her poems. Her first book of verse, *Poems,* 1921, was published by her friends without her assistance. Since then she has published several collections of poetry and a highly praised translation of La Fontaine's *Fables,* 1954. Her most recent work is *Tell Me, Tell Me,* 1966.

WILLIAM MORRIS (1834–1896) was an English poet, artist, decorator, and manufacturer, who influenced Victorian England greatly through his furniture designs and his ideas about interior decoration. He was deeply interested in preserving old buildings of historical or architectural significance. In addition to writing poetry, he translated Greek, Latin, and Icelandic poetry into English.

OGDEN NASH (1902–   ), master of light verse, uses irregular rhythm and intriguingly clever rime in his poetic commentaries on the modern scene. Nash's collections of verse include *The Bad Parent's Garden of Verse,* 1936; *The Private Dining Room,* 1953; *Everyone But Thee and Me,* 1962; *Animal Garden,* 1965.

HOWARD NEMEROV (1920–   ) is an American writer of poetry, short stories, and novels. He has published several volumes beginning in 1947 with a book of poems, *The Image and the Law.* His more recent works include *New and Selected Poems,* 1960; *Next Room of the Dream,* 1963; *Journal of the Fictive Life,* 1965.

JOHN FREDERICK NIMS (1913–   ) is an American poet and teacher. He uses both traditional and modern verse forms and derives his symbols from the harshness and violence of the present-day scene.

PABLO PICASSO (1881–   ) is a renowned painter who was born in Málaga, Spain. He founded the Cubist school of painting, designed for the Diaghilev Ballet, and for a few years directed the Prado Museum in Madrid. He has lived in France since 1903. His poetry shows his interest in creating verbal images that are transformations of the colors and materials of his visual images.

EZRA POUND (1885–   ), an expatriate American, published his first poetry in 1909. Though not widely popular, his work—chiefly the long series, the *Cantos*—has rivaled that of Eliot in its influence upon other poets. He is also a translator and critic of considerable significance. *Selected Poems,* 1957, has perhaps the greatest interest for the general reader.

JACQUES PRÉVERT (1900–   ) is a French poet much influenced by modern politics and esthetics and thus reminiscent of the manner of E. E. Cummings in his craftsmanship and choice of topics. His poetry includes much that is humorous and satirical. Prévert is also a writer of film scripts.

JOHN CROWE RANSOM (1888–   ), a native Tennessean, was educated at Vanderbilt and Oxford universities. He is now Carnegie Professor of Poetry, Emeritus, at Kenyon College. Until 1958 he was editor of the *Kenyon Review*, which he began in 1939. He is one of the leading literary critics in America. Among his books are *Chills and Fever*, 1924, *Two Gentlemen in Bonds*, 1927, and *Selected Poems of John Crowe Ransom*, 1945.

HENRY REED (1914–   ) is an English poet and a script writer for various of the communications media. His first poems satirized bureaucracy during World War II.

EDWIN ARLINGTON ROBINSON (1869–1935), three-time Pulitzer Prize winner, is in the first rank of American poets. He wrote character studies in verse, revealing the inner triumphs and outward failures of man.

THEODORE ROETHKE (1908–1963), born in Michigan and educated at the University of Michigan and Harvard University, was a public relations counsel and a tennis coach, then a teacher of English at the University of Washington. His poetry was first published in 1930; later he held Guggenheim fellowships and received the Pulitzer Prize for Poetry in 1953.

CARL SANDBURG (1878–1967), poet, Lincoln biographer, and authority on American folk songs, worked as a barber, a dishwasher, and a harvest hand, among other jobs, before his thoughts turned to literature during his college days. This background equipped him well to write about the vitality and variety of American life. In 1940 Sandburg was awarded the Pulitzer Prize for History for *Abraham Lincoln: The War Years*. His volumes of poetry include *Smoke and Steel*, 1920; *Slabs of the Sunburnt West*, 1922; *The People, Yes*, 1936; *Honey and Salt*, 1963. In 1951 his *Complete Poems* won the Pulitzer Prize for Poetry. In line, language, and subject matter he extends the Whitman tradition.

DELMORE SCHWARTZ (1913–1966), born in Brooklyn and educated at the University of Wisconsin, New York University, and Harvard, was a poet, translator, critic, and fiction writer. He was editor of *Partisan Review* and poetry editor of the *New Republic*. Among his publications are a translation of Arthur Rimbaud's *A Season in Hell*, 1939; *The Imitation of Life and Other Problems of Literary Criticism*, 1941; *Summer Knowledge: New and Selected Poems 1938–58*, 1959; *Successful Love and Other Stories*, 1961.

WILLIAM SHAKESPEARE (1564–1616), England's, and perhaps the world's, greatest dramatic poet, produced some thirty plays, many of which contain memorable short songs. Apart from his plays, his chief work was a sonnet sequence.

KARL SHAPIRO (1913–   ) published two books of poetry while stationed in the Pacific during World War II (*Person, Place and Thing*, 1942, and *V-Letter and Other Poems*, 1944). From 1950 to 1956 he was editor of *Poetry* magazine. Among his books are *Poems 1940–1953*, 1953; *In Defense of Ignorance*, 1960, which is a collection of essays about modern poetry; *The Bourgeois Poet*, 1964; *Primer for Poets*, 1965. Like many other contemporary poets, Shapiro is a teacher.

PERCY BYSSHE SHELLEY (1792–1822), English Romantic poet, was an idealist who revolted against tyranny in all forms—political, social, and moral—and who led an unconventional life in accordance with his ideals. His major theme is the possibility of human perfection.

LOUIS SIMPSON (1923–   ) is an American poet and novelist who migrated from the British West Indies to the United States in 1940. He is known for his editorial work on the two volumes of *New Poets of England and America*, 1957, and for several volumes of his own poetry. He has also written a novel and several critical works.

GEORGE STARBUCK (1931–   ) was born in Columbus, Ohio. He has been a Fellow at the American Academy in Rome; *Bone Thoughts*, 1960, is a collection of his poems. His poetry appears frequently in the *New Yorker* and in other magazines.

JAMES STEPHENS (1882–1950), Irish poet and storyteller, was born in Dublin and spent his childhood in extreme poverty. He began work as a clerk but turned to writing both prose and poetry and to collecting and retelling old Irish legends. A prose work, *Crock of Gold*, 1912, brought his first recognition. His *Collected Poems* appeared in 1926.

WALLACE STEVENS (1879–1955) studied law at Harvard University and New York Law School and made his career in insurance, becoming vice president of the Hartford Accident and

Indemnity Company. At the same time he was steadily publishing his poetry and gaining literary stature. He won a Pulitzer Prize in the last year of his life and is considered one of America's important poets.

ROBERT SWARD (1933–   ), a veteran of the Korean War, is a teacher and poet. His poems have appeared frequently in magazines and journals. His first volume of poetry, *Uncle Dog,* was published in England in 1962. Mr. Sward's use of the blatant, shocking image reminds the reader of the strong visual symbolism of many contemporary Italian film directors.

ALFRED, LORD TENNYSON (1809–1892) is in many ways the poet who best represents the spirit of Victoria's England. After an early period of neglect and adverse criticism, he won great public favor, which he held to his death. He became poet laureate in 1850.

DYLAN THOMAS (1914–1953), considered by many the greatest lyric poet of the younger generation of his time, was born in the Welsh seaport of Swansea. He was early steeped in Welsh lore and poetry and in the Bible, all of which left their mark on his rich, startling imagery and driving rhythm. He made his living by radio broadcasting, scenario writing, storytelling, and readings of his poetry. His first book, *Eighteen Poems,* was published when he was twenty. His *Collected Poems, 1934–1952* contains in the poet's own words, "all, up to the present year, that I wish to preserve."

WALT WHITMAN (1819–1892) created the free verse form. His *Leaves of Grass,* published in 1855, was a revolutionary book. In it Whitman spoke as the prophet of democracy and a worshiper of the common man. His technique has influenced two generations of later poets, including Sandburg, MacLeish, and Jeffers.

RICHARD WILBUR (1921–   ) was born in New York City, grew up in New Jersey, attended Amherst College and Harvard University, served in World War II in Italy and Germany, and taught at Harvard. He has received a Gug-

genheim Fellowship, the Prix de Rome of the American Academy of Arts and Sciences, and, in 1957, a Pulitzer Prize.

WILLIAM CARLOS WILLIAMS (1883–1963), born in New Jersey and trained as a physician at the University of Pennsylvania and in Europe, combined the writing of poetry with the practice of medicine. His ability to find concrete images that convey his ideas and attitudes puts him in the first rank of American poets. His poetry achieves a clear artistic unity of idea and form.

FREDERICK WINSOR (1900–   ) is an architect and a writer of witty verse. *The Space Child's Mother Goose,* 1963, is his rewriting of the traditional Mother Goose poems for the reader in the Space Age.

HAROLD WITT (1923–   ) was born in California and attended the University of California at Berkeley and the University of Michigan. He is a librarian and writer who has published several volumes and contributes frequently to the *Saturday Review* and the *New Yorker.* In 1947 he was given the Hopwood Prize for Poetry, and in 1960 the Phelan Award for Narrative Poetry.

WILLIAM WORDSWORTH (1770–1850), English Romantic poet, found most of his subjects in nature and the life of simple people. He had the genius to see and record the beauty and wonder of the familiar.

ELINOR WYLIE (1885–1928), whose poems are always controlled, exact, and brilliant, was in her personal life a rebel against social convention. Her peak of popularity came in the early 1920's when, as the wife of William Rose Benét, she took an active part in the literary life of New York City.

WILLIAM BUTLER YEATS (1865–1939), foremost figure of the Irish literary renaissance and one of the great poets of our century, was also an editor, folklorist, and playwright and took an active interest in politics. His best poetry is sinewy, conversational, and musical.

BOOK TWO

Fundamentals
of Speaking, Listening,
and Writing

PART SIX

Speaking and Listening

Fundamentals of Speaking

The person who learns to use the spoken language effectively is adapting the skills of an ancient tradition to the context of modern times. Before writing systems were developed, men were totally dependent upon the spoken language to disseminate information and news, to preserve their history, and to perpetuate their culture. Certain individuals specialized in being the spokesmen for their people; they were the news reporters and the storytellers. There is no evidence that these men followed a formal training program to learn the skills for their jobs, but there can be no doubt that they developed special techniques for organizing and presenting their material.

As writing systems were developed, the ways of using language changed. Organizational principles, of necessity, had to be different. New techniques in presentation evolved. Repetition, an effective device in speech, lost much of its value in written discourse, because a reader could always return to a written statement if his memory was unreliable. Also, writing had its own special requirements for attention-getting.

In time the principles that governed writing affected the way of using spoken language for public statement. The interaction between the older principles of effective speaking and the newer principles of effective writing begot

oratory, which ultimately became a highly specialized activity. In the period of classical oratory, great orators were influential men because they made skillful use of the spoken language to present significant ideas.

Subsequently oratory fell into disrepute because the techniques of speaking were over-emphasized at the expense of thoughtful content. For a period of time, study of the spoken language was chiefly concerned with such matters as enunciation, artistic use of the voice, and studiedly graceful bodily movement. Oratory had a special and limited place in the lives of men. It became a performing art rather than an act of communication.

In our own time technical and social changes have influenced the purpose and method of public speaking. Man's achievements in communications have put purposeful speaking into a position somewhat similar to the one it held prior to the advent of writing. Because motion pictures, radio, and television play a prominent part in everyday life, the spoken language has once more become an important medium for disseminating information and news, for recording history, and for perpetuating the culture.

Electronic devices have created a new relationship between speaker and audience. They have given us the illusion that the speaker enters our lives personally. One individual is communicating with another individual. The effect is like conversation. The listener seems to have a more active and responsible part in the communication. The responsible speaker is constantly aware of the reactions of his listeners. Electronic devices have also provided the basis for new speaking techniques: the speaker who can depend on electricity to project his voice can concentrate his energy on projecting his personality and his ideas. The result is a mode of speaking that has come to prevail in all speaking situations. Today's effective speaker is aware that a good speech means involving an audience in a sincere presentation of his best thoughts on a topic in which he has a genuine interest.

Modern Occasions for Public Speaking

In a country where meetings of one kind or another are a part of daily life, everyone finds that he is a potential public speaker. A single edition of a newspaper may report that speeches have recently been made by an engineer, a beautician, an accountant, a teacher, a police officer, a housewife, a librarian, a football coach, a musician, an astronaut.

Speeches are made for a variety of purposes. A superficially informative speech has become a popular feature of club programs. Profoundly informative and productively persuasive speeches are the main fare at professional meetings. Over and above the possible speaking opportunities that may come to an individual in his professional and social life, there is the insistent demand for a citizen in a democratic society to be both enlightened and articulate. Good citizens have a responsibility to learn about crucial issues so that they can take a stand. They have a further obligation to speak out for their convictions.

Since speaking is of vital importance to the welfare of both the individual and society, the prospect of making a speech should be looked upon as an opportunity. Students indicate that this is their conclusion when they express a desire for speech instruction and practice. Yet some, when faced with the opportunity, are reluctant to stand up and speak to an audience —even to a classroom audience.

If you lack confidence as a speaker, you should attempt to assess for yourself the specific aspects of speaking that worry you. Only after you have identified the sources of your trouble can you concentrate on ways to gain confidence. Any speaking problem can be overcome without the aid of special inborn talent. Good speakers are made, not born. Both the good speaker and the good speech are the results of good preparation.

Preparation of the Speaker

Students often say, "I have to prepare a speech," but how often do they say, "I have to prepare myself to give a speech"? The preparation of a speech is a specific activity for a specific occasion; yet the preparation of the speaker can and should be in constant process. (Although the speaker and his speech are not actually separable, consideration of the speech itself can be delayed momentarily.)

You might begin by determining the qualities of a good speaker that you must develop. Think about speakers whom you have heard. Why did they impress you as being good?

You might start your analysis with this summary statement: a good speaker has something to say, and he says it well. A speaker says things well when his manner communicates directness, sincerity, and liveliness. These qualities are carried over from good conversation.

The conversational mode. A good speech is very much like conversation. It differs in only two ways: while making a speech a person talks for an extended period of time without interruption, and he is talking to more than two or three people. The latter difference is not significant, however, when we recall that one effect of modern devices for communication has been to bring the speaker and his listeners into a closer relationship. For this reason, present-day audiences respond favorably to naturalness and ease. As a group, they listen with interest just as they would listen as individuals to the natural flow of good, spontaneous conversation.

An analysis of your own conversational manner will be of value in your preparation as a speaker. Is your daily conversation marked by directness, genuineness, and liveliness?

When conversation is direct, we feel that the speaker is personally concerned with us and with our reaction. He gives us his full attention. He probably looks at us, inclines his head in our direction, possibly emphasizes a point with a gesture. No barrier, real or imagined, is between us.

The second characteristic of conversation at its best is genuineness. The participants are being themselves. The artificial social manner crumbles in real conversation. People are speaking sincerely because they want to share their thoughts with each other.

Good conversation is also lively. It moves along with an undercurrent of eagerness to participate. It may take on the aspect of a game of tennis when a volley is in progress: the conversational ball goes back and forth from one participant to the other with a rapidity of exchange that may make it difficult to follow. But liveliness should not be confused with speed of utterance; it isn't speaking rate but rather inherent interest that makes for liveliness. This interest frequently reveals itself in the bodily set and the radiant glow of enjoyment that suffuses the speaker.

Every conversation that you engage in can be used as a laboratory for you as a student of speaking. Do people often ask you to repeat? You probably need to make an effort to speak more clearly. Do not label yourself a mumbler and give up. Mumbling is an acquired habit, not an inborn trait. When you are conversing with people, do you pay attention to what you are saying? Do you try to phrase your statements with some care so that other people can follow your thought?

Are you constantly aware of the way your listener reacts to what you are saying? Can you read understanding, puzzlement, agreement, disagreement, interest, lack of interest in his face? How do you respond to these reactions? If he seems puzzled, do you find another way to express your ideas? Do you add new evidence to stimulate agreement in the place of disagreement? Do you seek to enliven what you are saying by illustration, by varying the pitch or volume of your voice to gain interest where there seems to be little or none?

All these adaptations are requisite also to being a good speaker. The individuals in a conversation have a good opportunity to speak, observe, and react immediately to what they observe. The speaker on the platform must be able to do the same, but he must observe and react to a larger group. Even though an audience is made up of many individuals who represent a variety of interests and responses, its members tend to present a uniform reaction. It is that to which a speaker needs to sensitize himself. It is also true that audiences, except in very special situations, want a speaker to succeed. Speaker and audience are involved in a common experience. The audience enters into its silent partnership in the conversation with a spirit of cooperativeness.

Personal appearance. Another part of your general preparation as a speaker is to subject your personal mannerisms to a critical review. Your appearance and your actions are a reflection of the personality which you present to an audience. They are, furthermore, the first things that an audience reacts to. You will make a good initial impression if you are dressed neatly and tastefully. The audience's attention will not be distracted if your hands and feet are under control.

Posture is of major importance. If you are afraid that you will not stand properly, you are probably reflecting an awareness of your own poor posture. Unnatural posture on the platform will be uncomfortable for you and unpleasantly obvious to an audience. You should, then, try to improve your posture constantly. Good posture should be habitual. Movement will contribute to your comfort, but it needs to be spontaneous, the kind you use naturally in conversation.

You can find your own way of presenting yourself successfully to an audience by becoming aware of how you conduct yourself in everyday oral communication. After an experiment has proved successful, you can start working to create a new habit. Once you stand before an audience, you need to be able to rely on well-developed speech habits. You cannot make a good speech if you are preoccupied with trying to remember not to do some things which you habitually do, while at the same time you are trying to remember to do things which you never do at any other time.

Making the body aid in speaking. Speaking involves the entire body. This is more obvious in some people than it is in others. When some people talk, they talk all over. Many people use their hands so much that they prompt the well-worn comment, "If you cut off his hands, he wouldn't be able to say a word." Uninhibited movement of this kind is a part of the animation that goes with a speaker's real desire to communicate.

If you would be an effective speaker, you must learn to capitalize on the natural movements which are a normal part of your everyday speaking habits. The best speaking has a foundation in feeling. As a speaker who feels that what he is saying is worth saying well, is worth listening to, is a matter of importance, you must use all your resources, including bodily activity, to infect your audience with your own feeling about your subject. Attitudes are contagious; so display clear symptoms of enthusiasm, indignation, concern, or whatever feeling motivates you. Give physical vent to your feelings, not in a wild, unrestrained fashion, but like a sensible, cultured person.

Sometimes, when you feel tense, this tension expresses itself in a physical rigidity. The more tense you become physically, the tighter you become emotionally, and vice versa. The best way to free yourself from the effects of this circular response pattern is through bodily action. Even before you get up to speak, move your fingers and your hands, wiggle your toes, start working off the excessive bodily tensions. When it is time for you to speak, move forward without hesitation. Before you actually start speaking, it may even be advisable to busy your hands for a few moments arranging your notes. Use physical action to free yourself from tensions.

It is a commonplace that a speaker's action should aid him in conveying meaning. A bit of descriptive hand movement may help an audience to visualize the shape of something mentioned in a speech. In argumentative speaking you may wish to drive home a good point with action that serves to emphasize the idea. In practically all speaking situations bodily action aids not only in conveying mean-ing but in providing a sense of immediacy. Spontaneous movements by the speaker help him to make his subject come alive before the audience's eyes.

Sometimes, beginning speakers have the notion that they can improve their use of action by planning and practicing definite movements. Nothing could be further from the truth. Prearranged bodily activity—such as planning at certain points in a talk to move one or two steps to the right or left, or to raise the right hand, or to thrust out the forefinger of the left hand—is mechanical and distracting. Such gestures are artificial; they do not spring from a genuine desire to communicate; they may actually become amusing to the audience.

Animation, one of the requisites of good action, simply means showing signs of life. The speaker who employs effective action has taken the first step toward making a lively presentation. The sparkle in his eyes, his way of walking, the alertness of his entire body—all these things say to the observer that this person is "alive." You should constantly remember that, as a speaker, you must be alert physically as well as mentally.

Preparation of the Speech

When you are to make a speech, your task is a specific one. You will prepare a particular speech for a particular occasion. As a student, for example, you plan a speech so that it will be appropriate for a designated assignment and significant for the classroom audience. The method that you find useful for this specific situation should provide a pattern for the preparation of all your speeches.

Choosing a topic. The first step is to choose a topic. In doing so, consider yourself. Always, regardless of the speaking situation that may confront you, choose a subject—or some phase of an assigned subject—that interests you, one about which you have some knowledge and to which you have given thought. You should, moreover, be willing to extend your knowledge as a part of your speech preparation. Your own interest in the topic is of primary importance because an interested person is one who knows what he is talking about and enjoys the challenge a speaking situation affords.

Your interests have been formed by your experiences throughout your life. Search your memory for things that have been important to you. Examine your daily conversation for topic ideas. What do you get excited about when talking with your friends? Perhaps you have been in an accident at some time and the experience has caused you to think carefully about traffic regulations. You believe some of them should be changed, or you believe that there should be more rigid enforcement of some traffic laws. A speech assignment provides an excellent opportunity for you to develop and organize your ideas on the subject.

Do not shy away from a topic because you feel that you are not an authority. *Authority* is a frightening word because it seems to connote one who knows everything about something. Actually, there are degrees of authority. No one expects a person to know more than his experience and learning could warrant at any given time in his development. We can, however, expect a speaker to talk about something that he has considered in great detail for a fairly extended period of time and about which he has further informed himself as much as possible for the purpose of his speech. Above all, we can expect a speaker to be aware of the extent of his own authority, and we can expect him to build his speech within those limitations. We can also expect him not to talk on a topic that he knows about only from a recent reading of an article or two. Choose your subject after a careful survey of your own interests. Then spend some time compiling what you know and think about it. Supplement your own material with that of recognized authorities.

College students are generally bombarded with so many new ideas and experiences that they tend to forget or reject many things that were important and interesting to them in their precollege days. But you need to reach back as far as possible to find the foundations upon which your new ideas are being built. You are unique; everything you have experienced up to this moment combines to make

you so. It is important for a speaker to communicate this subtle uniqueness.

Controversial topics are always good sources for speech subjects, but only if you choose one in which you have an absorbing interest, one that you spend time talking and reading about for reasons other than that you have an assignment to do.

Establishing a purpose. After you have chosen a topic, your next step is to establish a purpose for this specific speech. You do this with the audience in mind. You want a particular audience to share your interest in your subject; you want them to feel fortunate to have heard about the subject in terms that apply directly to them. To achieve these goals you will need to think about the variety of individuals who will make up your audience, and you will need to state your purpose so that your audience can identify themselves with it.

Purpose and audience are very closely related, for any declared purpose must be developed in terms of the reaction desired from the audience. There are, however, some general things to be said about the purposes for speaking. They can be divided into five categories: to inform, to entertain, to stimulate, to convince, and to actuate. These purposes are not mutually exclusive; they may and do overlap. Certainly most speeches need some elements of entertainment. These should be provided through illustrative anecdotes, original material, and lively language. Elaborate attempts at humor should be avoided. Overlapping occurs among the other categories, too. A speech to convince, one to stimulate, or one to actuate will have to provide some information. But every speech must have one major purpose toward which the other elements contribute. If you make a speech with the purpose of convincing your classmates that clothing regulations on your campus should be changed, you want them to carry away a strong feeling for the issue. However, you might include so much detailed information about various types of clothing that their overwhelming reaction would be that of having acquired interesting new fashion data.

It is important to remember that if your

speaking is to be effective, you must have in mind a definite purpose expressed in terms of audience reaction. For example, your aim might be to persuade a particular audience, twenty men and women, that people who live on an allowance from their parents should avoid buying expensive luxury items on the installment plan. Without a purpose or central idea, you are almost certain to fail; with it, you have provided one of the essentials of effective speaking.

Audience analysis. Since purpose and audience are so closely related, you should get as much information as possible about the people who will be listening to you. You cannot hope to have full biographical information about all the people who will be in the audience, but you can get a general idea about them. Your classroom audience will possibly have both men and women students; they will range in age from eighteen to twenty; they are college students; some of them will belong to social organizations; some of them may have done military service; they are majoring in various subjects. Do not use this information only to find the common denominator of the audience and then to scale your speech to that level; instead, take cognizance of differences within the audience and address some of your remarks to the special interests of individuals.

Using source materials. Once you have chosen your topic and decided upon your purpose, consider what sources of material are available. Presumably you explored your personal resources when you were selecting your topic. Keep your own experience as the core of your speech and turn to other sources for supplementary material. The most obvious place to find further information is the library. Newspapers, magazines, and books are always available to the student.

Most audiences are not interested in hearing a summary of what you have read, but they *are* interested in your opinion of it. Your talk should spring from, and not consist of, the content of your reading. You should ask yourself what you have to contribute to the topic. Remember that your audience expects you to keep your speech within your own

limitations, and they have every right to expect you, out of your uniqueness, to say something that nobody else has said in exactly the same way. It is difficult to be original, to present in a fresh way a topic that many people are writing and talking about. It is not sufficient just to summarize another person's fresh thoughts on a subject. You will find that your originality is displayed by the reasons you have for holding your opinions. If you feel that your opinions are simply the result of powerful arguments by recognized authorities, search deeper. Why did those arguments appeal to you? Something in your own background and experience made you receptive to them, made you feel that you could substantiate them. The basis for your convictions is what you have to offer to an audience.

In many instances the college student has an unusual opportunity to secure information from members of the faculty who can qualify as experts. Though not necessarily exhaustively informed on that aspect of the subject about which a student is seeking additional information, some faculty member probably has a grasp of the underlying principles involved.

Whatever sources you use, people or printed materials, should be given credit if they supply you with new ideas. Do not present the ideas of others as if they were your own.

Organization. You have selected a topic, decided on a purpose, and obtained material for your talk. You turn now to the problem of organization. Good talks, like good written papers, must have order. They must have a progression of thought which an audience can follow. In most talks the material can be organized in outline form, which aids the speaker in presenting his material and his audience in following his thought. The most useful outline forms are the complete sentence outline and the topical outline. The first of these serves best in the preparation of a talk; the second is preferable for use in presenting a talk.

In preparing your outline you should set aside the introduction and conclusion and concentrate on the body of your speech. As you plan the body, you should give particular attention to matters of main points and subordination. Be sure that all your main points are equally important and that they have a logical relationship to one another. If, for example, you are dealing with a topic in which chronology is significant, you should move in a consistent pattern from past to present or, perhaps, from present to past. This kind of arrangement will be helpful to both you and the audience: you will find it easy to remember, and your audience will find it easy to follow.

To continue with the example of a chronologically significant subject, keep your time references consistent with regard to the periods covered in each main point. Do not let one deal with the entire eighteenth century, another with a decade in the nineteenth century, and a third with 1925. Neither should you allow your main points to overlap. Do not, for example, establish one main point as the eighteenth century and then follow with a second major division which consists of the period from 1780 to 1806.

Some topics lend themselves to an organizational pattern based on cause and effect. Others deal with matters of contrast or comparison. You may choose to develop a central idea by the process of deduction or induction. In any case, you should treat the various parts of equal rank in a similar manner, with supporting material divided among them as evenly as possible.

For the body of a speech to be developed properly, each main point must have supporting details. These should be clearly planned as subordinate parts of the speech. The main points should be beacon lights of which the audience never loses sight.

Transition devices have speical importance in speeches. An audience is dependent upon its ears and its memory. The memory does not have a long time in which to record because the speaker is moving on through his speech. The speaker needs, therefore, to help his listeners by repeating key words and by explicitly stating the relationships he wants to establish. For example, *my first point, next, then,* and *finally* would help an audience follow a four-point speech.

In addition to organizing the material for the body of your speech, you have to give careful thought to the way you will begin and end. A stimulating introduction pushes a speech toward success. In simple terms the aim of an introduction is to secure the attention of the audience, to arouse an interest in the subject, to show the relevance of the subject to the occasion, and to establish a favorable relationship between speaker and audience. In view of this you will not want to start any speech on the dead level of mediocrity. You should, therefore, avoid such trite expressions as "I'm going to talk about . . ." or "I'm reminded of a story . . . ." Start with a statement that is carefully phrased to reflect your individuality and to establish the tone of your speech. The well-known criminal lawyer Clarence Darrow did this in a speech on crime and criminals:

> If I looked at jails and crimes and prisoners in the way the ordinary person does, I should not speak on this subject to you. The reason I talk to you on the question of crime, its cause and cure, is because I really do not in the least believe in crime.

If you choose to begin with a story, let it be one that leads into your topic. In opening a speech on morality, C. S. Lewis began,

> There is a story about a schoolboy who was asked what he thought God was like. He replied that, as far as he could make out, God was "The sort of person who is always snooping round to see if anyone is enjoying himself and then trying to stop it." And I am afraid that is the sort of idea that the word Morality raises in a good many people's minds: something that interferes, something that stops your having a good time.

Both of these introductions stimulate curiosity, and that is a very good way to begin a speech.

A good speech must be good to the last word: it should conclude rather than merely stop. The conclusion rounds off the talk, summarizes the material, and makes a final appeal to the audience. It is not merely a recapitulation; it provides the best opportunity for dramatic emphasis. William Faulkner made the most of this opportunity in the closing sentences of his acceptance speech for the 1949 Nobel Prize for literature:

The poet's, the writer's, duty is to write about these things. It is his privilege to help man endure by lifting his heart, by reminding him of the courage and honor and hope and pride and compassion and pity and sacrifice which have been the glory of his past. The poet's voice need not merely be the record of men; it can be one of the props, the pillars to help him endure and prevail.

Memorable words such as these linger in an audience's ears after the final applause has ended.

A Final Note

A study of the principles underlying good speaking is only the first step toward successful speaking. To apply them is important. But the application of the principles may not make you a good speaker. A good speaker is, first of all, one who, when he calls upon himself, finds somebody at home. Or, to paraphrase Emerson, one should strive to be not merely a good speaker but a good man speaking effectively. In the final analysis, your speaking will be a reflection of your character.

This is a day of high specialization. Standards are prescribed for those engaged in every occupation and profession—barbers, plumbers, lawyers, doctors, teachers, engineers. One of the earliest professional codes originated about 2,500 years ago when Hippocrates, a famous physician of ancient Greece, gave the medical profession an admirable code of ethics. To this date, the Hippocratic oath is administered to those about to enter the practice of medicine. In a democracy, where public speaking plays so large a part in molding public opinion, citizens would no doubt profit greatly by some improved standards for speakers. To this end, Professor William Norwood Brigance suggests, in his book *Speech Communication,* that each person who wishes to make public addresses, after having passed a prescribed test, be certified to speak in public only after he has taken a required Hippocratic oath for speakers, pledging that he will never speak in public unless he has prepared himself with something worth saying and has put it in a form that can be comprehended; that whenever he appears before an audience he will think of its welfare and not of his own pride; that he will not mumble or fidget or otherwise evade or shirk his duty; and that he will present his ideas with such sincerity, earnestness, and consideration for the audience that none can fail to hear and comprehend.

Reading Aloud

Because the written language is so much a part of our everyday lives and because of a natural impulse to share ideas and stories, every literate person will find himself reading aloud at times. Members of the family and close friends may be the most frequent audience for the majority of us, but there will be times when members of a club or some segment of the public at large will compose the audience. Whoever they may be, they prefer to hear a person read well. Reading aloud is a thoroughly enjoyable activity for both the reader and his listeners if it is well done. If it is not, it is a thoroughly painful experience for everyone concerned. Learning a few basic principles of effective oral reading is a preventive measure against the latter sad ordeal.

Language conventions. Since the language in which ideas are expressed is what actually guides a reader, a part of learning to read aloud well is to gain some understanding of the way in which we respond to the system of language as we read. The oral reader lets his eyes run ahead of what he is saying so that he quickly grasps the significance of the language conventions before he orally interprets them for his listeners.

What are the language conventions to which the oral reader responds and which he translates into familiar speech patterns? Perhaps the most significant convention for the reader is the grouping of words into meaningful relationships. The unit of thought is the word group; it is not the separate word. In speech, word groups are distinguished one from another by patterns of pitch, stress, and pause. We employ these devices automatically and naturally in conversation. They are an inseparable part of the meaning that a speaker wants to convey.

In spontaneous conversation we are not consciously aware of the groupings we make in a statement such as "We/might/have/won—if/ Joe/hadn't/dropped/the/ball." The oral reader who comes upon this sentence is not formulating thought and creating an appropriate language pattern simultaneously. He is interpreting an already existing pattern. Before he starts to read the sentence aloud, he must recognize in less than a split second that all the words from *we* through *won* must come together in one vocal pattern. Otherwise his reading will communicate ineffectively because he has violated a convention of the spoken language. The example given here is based on the relatively simple patterns of ordinary conversation. The problem for the oral reader, especially in reading literary material, is the necessity of sorting out with lightning speed the word groups in long sentences which spin out complex ideas.

Although some help in apprehending word groups may be afforded by punctuation, these little marks are not infallible guides. The least reliable of them all is the comma. Consider the following sentence: "Oh, no, Joe, you're not going to try that, too?" The four commas here might lead a reader who slavishly follows punctuation to have four breaks or short pauses. A quick trial of that kind of reading will demonstrate the folly of putting blind faith in commas as indicators of spoken word groups. In a natural reading there would be but one break: "Oh/no/Joe—you're/not/going/to/try/that/too?"

On the other hand, there are times when a break must occur even though no punctuation of any kind can appear to suggest it. For example, "The minister and his friends were drinking in the happy atmosphere." A slight break should come after *in* so that the activity referred to is clearly appropriate to the people engaged in it. Of course, the alternative meaning would definitely be indicated if a break occurred before *in.*

The breaks, or pauses, which might be used in the sentence above would be accompanied by distinctive stress patterns to reinforce the intended meaning. A pause after *in* would be accompanied by a stress on *in;* a pause before *in* would be accompanied by a stress on *drink-*

ing. Stress, then, is another convention of the spoken language which the reader must determine quickly in his mind and supply for his listeners.

Because we are accustomed in our everyday use of speech to responding at an almost subconscious level to the frequent occurrence of little words, such as *on, by, and, for, so,* and *the,* we do not usually stress words of that kind. We do stress the less frequently occurring ones that identify the details of a particular situation. Words of this kind are "idea words"; they include nouns, verbs, adverbs, and adjectives.

Even though you need to follow conversational patterns when reading aloud, you should at the same time realize that reading aloud is a more deliberate act than carrying on a conversation. You must, therefore, give careful thought to the ways in which you can use your voice to impart all kinds of meaning. You must be aware that you can achieve emphasis through pauses, or that pauses can indicate suspense, lapse of time, change of scene, or reflection. Loudness, slowness, a sharp change in the tone of your voice can all be used for emphasis. You should constantly beware of using devices which emphasize material that should not be emphasized. Things that deserve emphasis are key idea words, contrasting ideas, startling details, sharp changes in thought.

Techniques of body and voice. Reading aloud, like making a speech, is not the same as giving a dramatic performance. A reader is *not* an actor who creates an array of fully developed characters. A reader maintains his own identity and serves largely as an interpreter. As such he should use his voice and body to convey not only the surface meaning but what he understands to be the underlying mood of what he is reading. The effective oral reader creates a harmonious whole by blending his voice and body with the thought and language of an author.

In reading aloud, you will find that the use of your body is restricted by the physical circumstances of your needing to stay close to a manuscript or book. If you are reading in public, you will probably have a speaker's stand on which to rest your material. Under those conditions it will not be feasible for you to go walking about in front of your audience. Your movement will be limited to gestures of the hands and arms and head. These gestures should be spontaneous rather than planned. They should, moreover, be suggestive rather than uninhibitedly descriptive, and they should contribute in a definite way to the meaning of your material without violating its mood.

One way of indicating the mood of the selection you are reading is through facial expression. For most material your usual mien plus the natural movements of speech will suffice. If there are times when a smile or a frown will contribute to your interpretation, you should use it, but it should not be exaggerated. Remember, you are not acting—you are suggesting an attitude or a mood.

Although eye contact is not a part of gesture or facial expression, it does involve a kind of movement which is a special problem in reading aloud. When you are reading, you must keep your place on the page and at the same time maintain eye contact with your audience. The solution to this problem is a kind of compromise. Follow the manuscript until you are sure of the words ahead, and then look at the audience while completing the thought. Keeping your place should not be a serious problem if you have made adequate preparation for a public reading appearance, for adequate preparation includes previewing the material you are to read. You can also help yourself by moving your hand unobstrusively along the margin of a page as you are reading.

Any concern that you may feel about gestures, facial expression, and eye contact should be overriden by your eagerness to share the meaning of what you are reading. You need to show that the meaning on the page you hold has had an impact on you. Interest begets interest. Your own interest should be directed toward the audience, as well as toward the material being read. Your listeners should get the feeling that it is important for them to be interested, too. Your dual concern

for both audience and material will manifest itself in enthusiasm, or vitality, an essential quality in good oral reading.

Vitality will make itself apparent in both your body and your voice. Your posture will reflect your enthusiasm by assuming what we might call optimum tension—a condition comfortably between relaxation and nervous stiffness. The body is under control but remains poised to react to the mood and meaning of the language before your eyes.

Your voice will show vitality in volume, melody, and rate of speech. If you really want an audience to hear what you are reading, you will not make them strain in order to catch words too softly spoken. Neither will you set them to the task of puzzling out recognizable words from a mass of indistinctly muttered sounds. Nor will you assault their ears with such a rapid series of vibrations that they cannot find time to hear words. In short, you will make the physical act of listening as easy as possible for them.

As you read, you should be constantly on the alert for clues as to what variation in pitch, rhythm, and stress you need to employ. You will find these clues in the words selected by the author and in the sentence patterns into which he has cast his thoughts. Notice the contrasts indicated by the language of the following two passages from Joseph Conrad's short story "The Lagoon" (pages 388–96). The first contains the words *stillness, immobility, memory of motion*. These words, along with the long sentences, repetitious phrasing, and attention to minute details, suggest a quiet and steadily rhythmic reading.

> In the stillness of the air every tree, every leaf, every bough, every tendril of creeper and every petal of minute blossoms seemed to have been bewitched into an immobility perfect and final. . . . And the white man's canoe, advancing upstream in the short-lived disturbance of its own making, seemed to enter the portals of a land from which the very memory of motion had forever departed.

The second passage is in marked contrast to this one. Words like *rushed, running, leaped,* and *bounding* suggest vigor and speed. This suggestion is reinforced by the short, uncluttered clauses.

> We rushed down to the canoe; a man came running from the hut, but I leaped on him, and we rolled together in the mud. Then I got up, and he lay still at my feet. I don't know whether I had killed him or not. I and Diamelen pushed the canoe afloat. I heard yells behind me, and I saw my brother run across the glade. Many men were bounding after him.

Once you have learned to use the skills described here, reading aloud becomes a particularly satisfying thing to do. The reader who has learned how to translate the printed page into familiar speech patterns feels a pleasant sense of discovery. Because of his special ability to appreciate the potential sound of the written language, he gives an author's work a new dimension and becomes a creator in his own right.

Fundamentals of Listening

The Importance of Listening

One way to measure the importance of listening is to find out how much time one spends each day in the role of a listener. One group of college freshmen kept a daily log of the time they spent reading, writing, speaking, and listening, dividing conversation and discussion time equally between listening and speaking. The results were as follows: listening, 42 per cent; speaking, 25 per cent; writing, 18 per cent; and reading, 15 per cent. Results of similar experiments in other colleges varied somewhat, but in every case listening consumed the greatest amount of time. Apparently, you spend more time listening than you do speaking, reading, or writing. Although it does not follow that listening is three times as important as reading and twice as important as writing, it is evident that an activity that takes up so much time warrants consideration and study.

It might be worthwhile for you to take a closer look at your listening activities. A daily record of time spent listening in conversation, listening in the classroom, listening to radio, television, and motion pictures, and listening to formal talks, announcements, and directions would give you some information on the relative frequency of various kinds of listening situations.

Most of what you know and believe you have learned by listening. From the beginning of school through college more of your education is acquired by listening to teachers and students than by any other means. The grades you get in most of your classes depend upon your skill as a listener as much as or more than they do upon your skill as a reader or writer.

One study of the relative importance of reading and listening in college classes by college freshmen indicated that they considered listening more important than reading in 41 per cent of their courses. In 43 per cent of their courses they considered listening and reading equally important, and in only 16 per cent did they rate reading as more important than listening. The explanations they gave for their judgments revealed that many teachers spend much time explaining and illustrating the main ideas of the course in the classroom and base their tests largely upon these ideas.

Radio, television, and motion pictures are an important part of your daily life. Through these media you are constantly being bombarded with words intended to stir your emotions and shape your opinions. Accurate and critical listening is essential to intelligent response to these media.

The Prevalence of Poor Listening

Evidence and observation indicate that most college students are poor listeners. They jumble directions, distort ideas, remember unimportant details, misunderstand opinions, misjudge evidence, take inadequate notes, and are unable to find the central idea, all because they do not know how to listen.

A recent survey revealed that only 27 per cent of a group of freshman students could identify the main points in a lecture, and only 18 per cent could locate the inferences correctly. When these freshmen answered questions about stories to which they had listened, 75 per cent of them responded correctly to 33 per cent or less of the items. No more than half of a freshman group could identify the point of view expressed in a short controversial statement.

If you are a poor listener, it may be because you have never given the matter any consideration. You may never have studied listening in school, and you have probably assumed that listening just happens whenever words are being spoken, that it is an involuntary process like breathing. A look at some of the listening experiences in your daily life will reveal how false these assumptions are.

Have you ever suddenly become conscious that you are not listening to someone who is speaking to you—that your mind is occupied with irrelevant thoughts or that you are watching the movement of his lips or the way he squints his eyes? It is an embarrassing awareness, and you probably give yourself a mental shake and concentrate on tuning in the speaker. Perhaps he finishes talking and you become aware that you have not the slightest notion of what to say in response.

Do you ever deliberately affect attention in conversation, smiling and nodding your head while impatiently waiting for the speaker to finish? Perhaps you have learned the trick of reliving in your imagination some exciting experience you have had; the interest on your face and the sparkle in your eye encourage the speaker without subjecting you to the tedium of listening. Are you quickly bored by conversation unless it is about you or your special interests? If you are frequently guilty of these faults—and everyone is sometimes—you are a poor listener.

What happens in class when the teacher is talking? Do you take notes? What do you put down, and how do you decide what to put down? Do you think about what the teacher is saying before putting his words on paper? Do you take the same kind of notes in all classes? How useful are the notes weeks later; are they a jumbled mass of details, topics, generalizations, and meaningless words? If they are, you are a poor listener.

When the speaker tells you the way he thinks about a problem, what do you do? Do you get angry and excited if he attacks your ideas? Do you criticize his delivery or the color and design of his tie? Are you bored by any serious talk about any subject beyond your immediate world of personal concerns? If so, you are a poor listener.

Poor listening is common and is probably the undetected cause of much misunderstanding, unhappiness, and conflict. The quarrel with your roommate, the falling out with your girl or boy friend, angry words with your parents, the *F* you received in biology—all may be due, in part at least, to faulty listening.

The Process of Listening

If you want to become a better listener, the first thing you must do is to become aware of the importance of listening and your own need for improvement. Then you are ready to examine the process of listening.

Hearing is the first phase of the process of listening. Your ears receive the sound waves created by the spoken utterance and transform them into auditory impulses. Interestingly enough, it appears that one need not have perfect hearing in order to be a good listener. Experiments seem to indicate that some hearing loss does not significantly diminish listening ability but rather that persons who have some hearing loss and who are aware of it listen better because they try harder.

As the paragraph above points out, hearing may occur without listening. *Attention* is necessary for listening. When the speaker says, "May I have your attention, please?" he is recognizing that unless you try to listen, his words will be spoken in vain. Attention is a mental readiness to receive the message and is accompanied by a physical alertness. You are "at-tension," for you are exerting mental and physical energy as you direct your thinking toward understanding and interpreting the incoming message. Attention operates like a "make-and-break" electrical circuit; brief periods of attention alternate with brief periods of rest or recovery. Attention is tiring; there seem to be definite limits to the length of time an adult can listen to a single source of stimulation, such as a speaker. It has been estimated that 75 per cent of the average adult audience can give adequate attention during the first fifteen minutes of a talk, but only 50 per cent maintain a high level of attention during the next fifteen minutes. Only 25 per cent continue to give optimum attention throughout a forty-five-minute talk, and any remarks beyond forty-five minutes are so much wasted energy on the part of the speaker.

Perception is the process by which the listener "decodes" the message he is getting from the speaker. It happens so rapidly as to be apparently instantaneous, but probably a process of identification and recognition goes on. Let us look at a simple example on a nonverbal level. At ten o'clock each morning in our town the whistle at the power plant is blown, not only to indicate the hour but to predict the weather. When I hear the sound, I identify it as the sound of a whistle, and because of its particular loudness and timbre, I recognize it as the power-plant whistle. I also understand that it is now ten o'clock, and I set my watch accordingly. If my knowledge also includes acquaintance with the code, I am able to understand what the particular kind of blast means. Three short blasts indicate rainy and colder weather ahead, and one long blast indicates that it will be fair and warmer. By an analogous process you recognize words, phrases, and sentences. You search for the meaning of the words and units of thought by relating the speaker's ideas to similar ideas in your past experience. You try to create in your own mind a reasonable facsimile of the idea that was in the speaker's mind.

Listening is complicated by the fact that meaning is conveyed not only by the spoken words themselves but by how they are spoken, and when and where and to whom they are spoken. Therefore, as in the case of the whistle, perception probably occurs at various levels, depending upon the knowledge and experience of the listener and his ability to discern the implications of all the factors involved.

Evaluation is the stage of listening that involves the application of judgment to the ideas perceived. You are not content to understand. You also make a judgment about the adequacy of the evidence, the value of the information, the validity of the conclusion. In other words, you decide whether the idea is good or bad, whether it is one to remember or forget, whether it should be put in your notes or discarded.

Response or reaction is an inevitable outcome in the process of listening, whether implicit or explicit, immediate or delayed. In conversation the listener's reaction is likely to be immediate; in listening to a lecture it is likely to be delayed. In a sense, you talk to yourself about what the speaker is saying, you formulate questions you would like to ask, you plan the reply you would like to make, or you store away certain ideas to be contemplated at your leisure.

In other words, successful listening is a complex process requiring energy and skill. It does not simply happen when you are quiet and another person is talking. It is neither passive, like receiving a blow on the head, nor automatic, like the operation of a vending machine when a coin is put in the slot. You listen because you want to listen, and you listen effectively when you know how to get the most out of what you hear.

Visual cues are important not only as helps in determining meaning but as a means of focusing attention. One does not actually need to observe the color of the speaker's tie or his mannerisms and features. To do so is distracting. But seeing the speaker or at least looking in his direction seems to make listening more effective.

Factors That Influence Listening Effectiveness

Let us examine some of the many factors that influence listening effectiveness. The good listener is conscious of these factors. He knows that some of them provide cues to the meaning of what is said or motivate his listening; others are distractions which impede listening.

The speaker. We are generally conscious of delivery factors in the speaking-listening situation; in fact, we are probably too sensitive to them. We become speech critics rather than listeners seeking information and ideas. The physical appearance, mannerisms, and dress of the speaker can be distractions; the poor listener dwells on them and the good listener ignores them.

The rate of speaking becomes a distraction when it is much slower or much faster than normal. Inflection, emphasis, pauses, and gestures usually help you get the intended meaning of the message; however, overuse or exaggeration of any technique of delivery makes it a distraction, diverting the listener's attention from the ideas being expressed to the techniques being used.

The better the speaker, the better the listening is likely to be, but the well-motivated, trained listener gets the message regardless of the quality of the speaking. In fact, it is reassuring to know that the skill of the speaker does not make a great deal of difference if you know how to listen. The world is full of poor speakers who have interesting ideas and useful information to share with us.

The speech. In what is said as well as in how it is said lie roadblocks to understanding or aids to listening. If the words are unfamiliar, if the phrases are trite, or if the ideas are vague, the good listener has difficulty, and the poor listener is lost. Attention to the speaker's use of transitional expressions, to his repetition of important points, illustrations of main ideas, and enumeration of reasons makes listening easier, as these factors help the listener to reconstruct the speaker's thought structure.

The subject of a speech does not seem to make much difference to the listener, but he is strongly influenced by its difficulty. You can read and understand more difficult material than you can listen to effectively. Material which, as a junior in high school, you could read and understand with some difficulty is equally difficult for you now when presented as listening material.

The situation. Listening often occurs at a time and place and in circumstances not of the listener's choosing; therefore, most listening situations contain real and imagined distractions, which the poor or reluctant listener seizes upon as excuses for not listening.

Sitting where you can see and hear the speaker without strain makes it easier to pay attention and therefore helps your listening. The people about you may encourage you by their interest and attention, or they may make listening almost impossible by their noise and restlessness.

Other possible sources of irritation in the listening situation may be ventilation, temperature, outside noises, humidity, seats, lighting, time of day, weather, acoustics, and even the decoration and architecture of the room. Consciousness of any of these factors may easily block your listening, especially if you are disinclined to listen.

The listener. Less obvious and most powerful are the factors in you, the listener. Personal worries and concerns will claim your attention the moment you cease to direct your thinking toward the incoming message. A practice group of college freshmen reported that they were diverted from listening by thoughts of "vacation, marriage, French test last hour, research paper to be written, letters, lake, coming week end, illness of father." The good listener is able to set aside such personal concerns while listening. Other factors in the listener identified by the practice group as causes of poor listening were: "not interested in the subject, prejudices, previous ideas, previous experiences, questioned statement, statement made me angry, wondered about application to me, heard it before."

The Principles of Effective Listening

Your listening will be more effective if you know the principles of good listening and how to apply them.

The listening experience begins when you first know that you are to be in a listening situation and continues beyond the listening act itself as long as you reflect upon or discuss what you have heard. Probably you have never stopped to observe that the success of your listening in your class is influenced by your attitudes and actions before you come to class and that the "proof of the pudding" is in what you subsequently do with what you hear.

Preparing to listen. The good listener gets ready to listen by finding out something about the speaker and the subject or by calling to mind what he has previously read and heard about them. He tries to sit where he can see and hear the speaker easily, and he does what he can to eliminate or adjust to the obvious distractions about him. He sets aside any negative or indifferent attitudes toward the speaker or the subject matter. In other words, he listens with an open mind. If the situation requires, he is ready to take notes.

Understanding the ideas of the speaker. The primary task in most listening situations is to find or to formulate the central idea, which embraces the meaning and purpose of what is being said. Some of the clues to the central idea are structural. It is often presented as a thesis in the introduction and restated in the conclusion. It may be repeated in various ways during the talk and may be prefaced by such phrases as: "You can see from all that I have said that . . . ." Often the speaker will help the listener by emphasizing the central idea or by pausing before and after it.

After determining the speaker's central idea, the good listener tries to find the main supporting ideas. They may be enumerated, stated in question form, anticipated by leading remarks, or stated as topic sentences beginning parts of the talk. Voice volume, intensity, and pauses may help to identify these main ideas. Try always to distinguish what is relevant from what is irrelevant to the general purpose of the talk, fact from opinion, and detail from generalization.

Some listeners reconstruct the speaker's outline in their minds by identifying the introduction, the main divisions of the talk, and the conclusion. The danger in this approach is that the result may be, like many a student outline, a list of topics rather than statements of ideas.

Equally as important as the main ideas but less easily detected are the implicit meanings in a speech: the speaker's purpose (frequently not stated), the inferences to be drawn from his remarks, and the significance of what he leaves unsaid. At this point we can only try to make intelligent guesses based on what seems to lie behind the words or is hinted in voice and manner.

Evaluating the ideas of the speaker. The good listener seeks first to understand and then to evaluate. He asks himself such questions as these: Are the speaker's facts accurate and complete? Is his reasoning sound? Is his opinion based upon evidence and is the evidence adequate? Do the facts he gives support his conclusion? Do the details he presents support his generalizations?

The good listener checks the opinions and assertions of the speaker against his past knowledge and experience in an effort to judge their soundness and accuracy. The poor listener tends to accept the speaker's statements as true or false on the basis of whether he agrees with them rather than on the basis of the evidence presented and the logic employed. He is inclined to be quite sure of their truth if the speaker states them emphatically and with dramatic appeal. He unquestioningly accepts facts and conclusions because of the way they are said or the reputation of the speaker. When the speech is over, he cannot decide whether what was said was worthwhile or not.

Responding to the ideas of the speaker. The good listener responds to what he hears. Response may be in the form of notes. Good notes are the product of an understanding-evaluating process, not a matter of writing down exactly what the speaker says. Notes should be a record of the ideas—generalizations and significant details—which you, the listener, have understood and judged to be important. They should be in sentence form and should use familiar words, not in unrelated topics or meaningless phrases. Probably the best notes are those which are reworked soon after the listening experience, although few students seem to find time for reorganization and restudying of the notes they take in class.

The poor listener tries to write down what the speaker says without thinking about the ideas, asks no questions, is unresponsive during listening, and is unable to discuss or restate the ideas of the speaker afterwards. The pattern of response by the poor listener begins like this: "I enjoyed the talk," "Wasn't it awful?" or "Isn't he a handsome man?" In response to the question of what was said he continues, "Oh, he talked about China," "He told a good story," or "He didn't say anything new." We ask for one main idea—just one—and this is what he says: "Oh, I can't remember," "He told us many interesting things," or "I don't know, but he was a good speaker."

Applying the Principles of Effective Listening

Poor listeners can become good listeners, and good listeners can become better listeners by applying the principles of effective listening in their daily listening experiences. Here are some things which you can do to become a better listener:

In general. Make an analysis of your listening habits. When and where are you a listener, and what do you do when you listen? How frequent and important is your listening in conversations, in the classroom, at speeches, and in radio–television–motion-picture situations?

In conversations.

1. Find a reason for listening that is strong enough to sustain your attention.

2. Watch the speaker, trying not to think about his appearance, his mannerisms, or your feelings about him.

3. Before responding to a statement of opinion, restate it in your own words and ask the speaker if you have understood him correctly. Do not give your opinion on the issue until you have satisfied him that you understand his point of view.

4. Show the speaker that you are listening, both by your actions while listening and by your subsequent reply. React to what he says with appropriate facial expressions, head movements, and encouraging words.

5. Relate your response to the remark just made in words and content. Introductory phrases such as "That's right," "I see what you mean, but . . . ," or "I agree with you that . . ." indicate that you have been listening. Help to build the conversation by relating your remark to the one before it.

6. Try writing down a conversation word for word. Examine it for evidences of poor listening, such as disconnected remarks and obvious misunderstandings.

7. If the conversation involves directions and specific details which are to be acted upon, repeat them and ask the speaker to correct any inaccuracy.

In the classroom.

1. If note-taking is in order, take down significant details and important generalizations. State them in your own words and in complete sentences. Compare your notes with those of another student in the same class; discuss the differences. Suit the method to the course; probably in biology most of the notes will be details, and in history most of the notes will be generalizations. Rework your notes soon after class, omitting details which in light of the entire lecture are not significant and formulating additional generalizations in accordance with the details.

2. If at all possible, ask questions and make comments to check on your understanding of the ideas and to practice restating them in your own words. Mulling over the ideas with the teacher and your classmates helps your comprehension.

3. Listen to your classmates' questions and comments. If one of the other students has not made his point clear, try putting the same ideas in your own words. In class discussion, talking and listening among students are often

more fruitful than talking and listening to the teacher.

At a speech.

1. Find a strong personal reason for listening to the speaker—one that will hold you to your job as a listener for the duration of a long talk.

2. When practical, take notes on your listening problems in a speaker-audience situation. When your mind wanders, put down where and why. When you react to an emotional word, idea, or mannerism, put down the circumstances and your reaction.

3. Prepare a listening-experience report on the speech. Include a statement of the central idea, main supporting ideas, and your reactions to the ideas. If possible, have the speaker check your report.

4. Summarize the talk for persons who have not heard it; write about it in a letter. Concentrate on stating ideas and your reactions to them, not on the speaker and how you liked or disliked him.

5. Discuss the speech with friends who have also heard it. Compare your understanding of the central idea with theirs. Try to arrive, as a group, at a statement of the central idea and the supporting main ideas, and at a consensus as to the validity and significance of what was said.

6. Listen to many kinds of speakers, in many different situations, talking on many different subjects. Make reports on these speaking situations.

Radio, television, and motion pictures.

1. Listen to discussion programs of various kinds—news commentators, newscasters, interview programs, and forums.

2. Compare the analysis of the same news events by different news commentators. Listen for motive, inference, and use of emotional language.

3. Discuss the ideas in a radio or television commentary or a serious movie. Use one such program or movie as a basis for group discussion.

PART SEVEN

Rhetorical Guidelines

Good writing, like good speaking, is the effective communication of thoughts and feelings. All written communication is effective (1) when the writer knows what he has to say, that is, when he knows his subject; (2) when the writer knows how to give structure to his ideas; and (3) when the writer knows how to express himself well, that is, when he is in command of an appropriate style.

Good writing does not come easily. One may recognize good writing and state the basic principles that underlie it without being able to produce it. But behind every good writer lie many years of experience in observing the various facets of human life, in exploring ideas in the realms of science, literature, and philosophy, and in thinking a subject through to its essential meaning.

Hence a beginning student needs to be patient with himself. He cannot suddenly know all he should in order to write well about a book, an author, a philosophical idea, or any other important subject. He must study a subject carefully, listen, read, and think. He must begin over again, read more widely, revise his thoughts, rearrange his plans, and constantly correct his language. Good writing is based on continuous growth in knowledge, reflection, and writing.

But we cannot wait to write until we are experts on a subject. Writing itself is a means by which we come to know a subject, evaluate our knowledge of it, and refine our style. Indeed, good writing is an *end;* writing as well as we can is a *means* to that end.

Two of the best ways of achieving good writing are made available to the student in *College English.* The first is the analysis of effective prose on subjects within his range of interest and ability. To carefully read the essays in Book One is to discover the principles that underlie the choice of a particular subject, the type of analysis used in explanation and reasoning, the arrangement of the various parts of the whole piece in relation to a central theme, and the use of a particular style. In other words, these essays, together with the biographies and fiction, may be analyzed in order to see how they are composed. This analytic process develops one's knowledge of the art of writing.

The second way of becoming a good writer also involves analysis, but here the analysis is a step in planning one's own composition. It is the process of determining the parts and the relationship of parts that constitute the whole theme that a writer proposes to present.

Obviously, composition is the more pressing task for the beginning writer. In analyzing the work of another writer, the beginner studies a work that is already composed. A reasonable amount of application enables him to discover the purpose of the work, its central idea, its method of development, and its meshing of thought and style. But in composing his own thoughts on a subject of his own choice the beginning writer climbs uphill all the way. Unless a topic is assigned by an instructor, the beginning writer starts with such preliminary questions as "What should I write about?" "How long should my composition be?" "What do I intend to say?" After that he must construct some kind of outline. Finally, he has the difficult job of putting his sentences in a logical order and of choosing the most exact and vivid words to make his purpose, or central idea, plain.

Just as the readings in *College English* help the student to cultivate the habit of analyzing the work of others, so this rhetoric section of the book, including its writing lessons, and the *Harbrace College Handbook* help him to plan and write his own compositions. The basic rules are presented—what to do and what not to do with the word, the sentence, the paragraph, and the whole composition. If you wish to improve your writing, make full use of all the directions and suggestions afforded you in these sections.

"Rhetorical Guidelines," moreover, attempts to show how the principles of good writing may be applied to the four forms of discourse and to the specializations of these forms that most college students and graduates are expected to use in their academic, social, and professional lives.

The Forms of Discourse

Theoretically, prose composition may be divided into four forms of discourse—exposition, argument, description, and narration. Is this division a mere convenience? Does it really conform to the practice of good writers today?

For instance, many of the essays in Book One contain two or more forms of discourse. George Orwell's "Shooting an Elephant" (pages 167–71) is descriptive and narrative as well as explanatory. In "Machinery, Magic, and Art" (pages 241–47) T. K. Whipple explains his subject and then attempts to convince his readers that artists must return to utilitarian purposes if they are to regain their social stature. In fiction, too, in Stephen Crane's "The Open Boat" (pages 437–50), for example, the descriptive element is just as important as the narrative element. *Antigonê* (pages 478–503) contains some dialogue that is expository or argumentative rather than narrative or dramatic in character. It is true that writers rarely employ one form of discourse exclusively. But, for the following reasons, the student should understand the separate forms of discourse.

First, most effective compositions have a single dominant shape or character; they are primarily expository, argumentative, descriptive, or narrative—that is, good writing has a specific *purpose* or *intention*. Good writing explains an idea (exposition), or convinces the reader of the truth of a proposition or thesis (argument), or depicts in words the realities that strike the senses (description), or relates a series of incidents (narrative). When a writer intermingles one form of discourse with another, as able writers do, his specific aim—his governing purpose—compels him to emphasize one form of discourse rather than another. If he failed to do so, his essay or article would lack unity of purpose and hence unity of impression. It would not be effective writing.

The second reason emerges from the first. In order to combine several forms of discourse successfully, a writer must know what each form is meant to do. A good writer, conscious of his main purpose, chooses that form of discourse that is the proper vehicle of his purpose.

In Marshall McLuhan's "Sight, Sound, and

the Fury" (pages 206–211) the main purpose is to explain the unusual potentialities of the sight and sound media. McLuhan does not explicitly argue for or against these media. He knows that argument is not meant to explain an idea or a subject, but to convince the reader of the truth or falsity of a proposition. He uses the form which best enables his readers to understand the potentialities of the media and to draw their own conclusions as to how closely the operation of the sight and sound media should be guarded.

To illustrate a mistaken use of the forms of discourse, let us say that I propose to *convince* someone (argument) that college athletics contribute to the intellectual growth of the student. This proposition is debatable. To prove it I must define the terms *college athletics* and *intellectual growth* and then give reasons for the truth of my proposition. Suppose that, instead of following this procedure, I choose to relate my own personal experiences as a football player (narration). Even if, in the course of my personal narrative, I recount football incidents that were related to my intellectual growth, it is extremely unlikely that I would convince my listener of the truth of the proposition. He might believe my story; he might even be interested in it. But it would remain at best only a single testimony. Its effect would be less to convince him than it would be to arouse his interest or feelings. I would have aimed at conviction and achieved something else. Such confusion of purpose produces writing that is effective by accident, if at all.

The third reason for study and practice of the various forms of discourse is perhaps the most important. Each form of discourse has its own appropriate structure and style. In each the general principles of structure—unity, coherence, and emphasis—are applied in a slightly different way. In argument, for instance, unity is determined by the logical process of reasoning, whereas in literary description unity proceeds from the dominant impression the author wishes to convey, and in fictitious narrative from the effect the writer aims to produce. The principle is the same, but the application is different.

There is, too, a marked difference in the tone and style of the various forms of discourse. A writer of exposition normally views his subject calmly and objectively and speaks primarily to the reason. On the other hand, a writer who argues to influence the decision or conduct of his reader frequently writes in a style made vivid by his convictions and his feelings.

To sum up, we study and practice the four forms of discourse because we thereby help ourselves (1) to clarify the purpose of writing and thus to attain the chief end of rhetoric, effective writing, and (2) to adapt the general principles of structure and style to the different forms of written and spoken discourse.

We shall now study in order exposition, argument, description, and narration.

Exposition—Writing to Inform

Exposition is a form of discourse that explains. Its purpose is to clarify a subject. Writing directed to this purpose is often called *informative* writing. The subject may be an idea, such as T. K. Whipple's belief that art must be useful; a historical fact, such as society's growing dependence upon computers; a significant aspect of character, such as the imperviousness of the Townsends ("The Pound Party"), an operation, such as the digging of a trunkback turtle's nest; or a process, such as making a bookcase. Indeed anything that needs clarification is a proper subject of exposition.

Exposition is the most widely used form of discourse. It is the mode of speech adopted in most lectures and textbooks, in encyclopedia articles, and in informative writing in general. The questions proposed in final examinations almost always demand exposition: "Explain the circumstances that led up to the War of 1812." "Discuss the effect of the frontier on American life." "Show how the characters in Hawthorne's *The Scarlet Letter* are related to the main theme." All these questions call for information.

Obviously a writer cannot explain what he does not know. He might be a first-rate writer in the sense that he employs good grammar, commands a wide vocabulary, and has a knack of stringing sentences together. But this skill does not guarantee that he can write anything worthwhile about a subject with which he is unfamiliar. The essential condition of good exposition, then, is knowledge of the subject. (To check on the means of investigating a subject, consult the *Harbrace College Handbook*, Section 33.)

Of equal importance, however, is the ability to analyze a subject that one has chosen or has been directed to explain. A mass of facts, even when neatly recorded on index cards under various heads, does not organize itself into a clear, purposeful composition. Facts must be weighed, sifted, and analyzed if the writer is to discover their true value, just as an assayer weighs, sifts, and refines mineral ore to determine the proportion of copper, silver, or gold it contains. Method, as well as matter, is important.

METHODS OF DEVELOPMENT

But what methods of analysis should be used? How is a subject made clear? There are many possible methods, six of which will be briefly considered here—classification or division, definition, exemplification, cause and effect, comparison and contrast, and process.

Classification or division is a separating of the parts that together compose some whole thing (the subject). This method of analysis is prominently used in such essays as Lancelot Law Whyte's "Where Do Those Bright Ideas Come From?" (pages 87–92) General David Sarnoff's "No Life Untouched" (pages 124–27), and Charles Frankel's "The Morality of Civil Disobedience" (pages 177–81). In this method the parts are logically identified as to kind and degree of importance. The outline is a means for graphically presenting the complete classification or division. (See Section 32b of the *Harbrace College Handbook*.) A classification should meet certain standards. If it is to be logical, a single, consistent principle of division must be used throughout to determine the parts. If, for example, the books of a library are being classified as to subject matter, the writer should not without proper notice shift to a principle of division based upon the age, condition, cost, or

size of the books. Furthermore, the classification must be complete, that is, account for all the items involved. There should be a bracket for each subject dealt with in the books of the library under study. Of course, if the subject is complex, more than one classification may be used, but the writer must complete his first classification, announce his shift to another, and keep each classification clear and distinct. In any classification the principle of division should be an important one. A classification of college students, for example, should deal with such matters as field of study, class, or academic record instead of such trivial matters as weight, height, or color of hair.

Frequently, in analysis by classification the writer's purpose or the demands of his over-all writing situation make it not only necessary but advisable that he use a selective division instead of attempting a complete one. If, for example, he were discussing the attractions of his home town, he might well limit his subject and entitle his paper "The Main Attractions of My Home Town" or "The Recreational Attractions of My Home Town." He would then be able to develop his ideas adequately and would not waste his reader's time with relatively insignificant or random matters.

Definition. A writer makes a subject clear by *defining* its terms, the words that contain the main ideas of the subject. A scientific definition of a term sets it apart from other terms by stating the class to which it belongs and the special characteristics that distinguish it from other members of its class. Thus, for example, a student in a contemporary civilization course may well be asked to explain the term *empiricism*. As a first step in his exposition he might say that *empiricism* (the term to be defined) is a philosophical doctrine (the class) that all knowledge is derived from experience (the difference that distinguishes empiricism from all other philosophical doctrines).

This definition of empiricism may, of course, be expanded in a number of ways. The writer may tell when empiricism began, or he may identify individual authors associated with the doctrine, and so on. Indeed many essays are really extended definitions. Often the writer begins his essay with a strict definition and then expands this definition by developing his ideas according to one or more of the methods listed below. For example, in "The Language Line" (pages 20–24) Susanne K. Langer first defines what she means by a *symbol*, a *sign*, and a *thing*, the main terms in her essay, and then modifies and distinguishes the meanings of these terms in her subsequent discussion. Her essay is an extended definition.

Exemplification is a specific, concrete illustration or proof of a general principle or idea. It is perhaps the most frequent method of analysis in expository discourse. In exposition concrete, specific objects are more often described than explained. But a general principle, such as the psychological law of association or the idea of a democracy, normally requires explanation. These general, or abstract, subjects are rarely understood even when they are strictly defined. The reader needs to see how the principle works out in practice or how the idea manifests itself in actual life—he needs examples. Hence, we typically say, "democracy, for example, the form of government practiced in the United States," or "a lyric poem, such as Shelley's 'Ode to the West Wind.'"

A good example is *direct* and *cogent*. It is *direct* when the details of a subject are clearly perceived: "No tropical beach is fun to walk on at cloudless, windless midday," writes Archie Carr in "The Black Beach" (pages 325–32). This general statement is immediately supported by specific references to the softness and heat of the sand and to the tangled wilderness of great driftwood logs.

An example is *cogent* or compelling when, in itself or as a link in a series of examples, it tends to prove the truth of a given statement. In "Where Do Those Bright Ideas Come From?" (pages 87–92) Lancelot Law Whyte supports his statement—that "all truly creative activity" depends upon the unconscious—by quoting a good single instance from Richard Wagner:

> The rush and roar soon took musical shape within my brain as the chord of E-flat major, surging incessantly in broken chords. . . . Yet the pure triad of E-flat major never changed, but seemed by its steady persistence to impart infinite significance to the element in which I was sinking. I awoke from my half-sleep in terror, feeling as though the waves were rushing high above my head. I at once recognized that the orchestral prelude to the "Rhinegold," which for a long time I must have carried about within me, yet had never been able to fix definitely, had at last come to being within me; and I quickly understood the very essence of my own nature: the stream of life was not to flow to me from without, but from within.

In many situations, however, a single example is insufficient to indicate the truth of a statement. The writer must adduce a series of instances, all interconnected, to demonstrate his general statement. Accordingly, in "Art and Society" (pages 227–37), Kenneth Clark attempts to prove that image art confirms and maintains a philosophic system by citing some seven examples of artifacts that embody one doctrine or another.

Underlying the method of exemplification is the logical relationship of the genus and species. A genus is a whole or class consisting of two or more species or parts which, though distinct, are united because of their common, that is, generic, qualities. Thus, the term *science* is a genus that comprises the species *physics, biology,* and *chemistry*. What we say of the genus or whole must be true of its species or parts. For example, if we say that science is a body of organized knowledge, it must also be true that physics, biology, and chemistry are, individually, bodies of organized knowledge. A good example, then, is a species of its genus or a specific illustration of a general statement.

Cause and effect. We frequently hear the words "Why?" and "What are the results?" A student may say, "I understand what Leslie Fiedler means by 'Mass Culture' and I recognize his specific allusions (exemplifications), but why do most people prefer the second-rate in art? I should like to know the reasons for this state of affairs." Or we might hear it said on the same subject, "What are the results of this preference?"

The questions "Why?" and "What are the results?" are simply common-sense references to the method of analysis known as cause and effect. We sometimes analyze a subject by discovering its causes, or by describing its effects, or by doing both because both methods help to show us just what our subject is.

A *cause* is the reason why something exists. The subject *White House,* for instance, is the result of a number of factors. Most important are the so-called *efficient* causes. The architect or designer James Hoban was chiefly responsible for the official residence of the President of the United States. Cooperating with him were various artisans and laborers. Their work, together with that of their successors, contributed to the total effect. Hoban, the artisans, and the laborers were the efficient causes.

But the White House is also made up of material things—wood, brick, and plaster—materials given a special *form,* design, or shape by the architect and the artisans. Hence, among the many causal factors are the *material* and the *formal* causes. Moreover, the artisans used certain instruments in constructing the White House. Surely the tools they used are at least secondary, or *instrumental,* causes. Then, too, the White House would never have existed unless it had a purpose, unless the people of the United States through their Congress had communicated to the architect their desire for a presidential residence at once worthy of the national dignity and simple enough for republican tastes. The knowledge of these and other factors that make up the total cause of the effect—the *White House*—are helpful ways of understanding and explaining the subject.

Another example of causal analysis is found in T. K. Whipple's "Machinery, Magic, and Art" (pages 241–47). Here the author investigates the factors that cause art to seem unimportant to most people. He concludes that the causes lie in our artists' having forsaken their essential function of conveying psychological power.

We may describe a subject in terms of its effects. Some subjects, for instance, sorrow, laughter, joy, and fear, are frequently too complex for causal analysis alone. We are compelled, therefore, to show what they do, what effect they produce. In this manner Edith Hamilton in "The Idea of Tragedy" (page 267) defines the true nature of tragedy:

> For tragedy is nothing less than pain . . . changed into, or, let us say, charged with, exaltation. It would seem that tragedy is a strange matter. There is indeed none stranger. A tragedy shows us pain and gives us pleasure thereby. The greater the suffering depicted, the more terrible the events, the more intense our pleasure. The most monstrous and appalling deeds life can show are those the tragedian chooses, and by the spectacle he thus offers us, we are moved to a very passion of enjoyment. There is food for wonder here. . . .

Sometimes both cause and effect are employed together. One of the most famous instances of this occurs in Edmund Burke's *Bristol Oration,* in which he shows that the Repeal of the Act of 1699 was good both in its causes and in its effects. After describing the particular features of this act Burke presents his cause-and-effect analysis in the manner described in the table below. Note that the subject is at once the effect of good causes—hence good for that reason—and in itself the cause of good effects—hence good for another reason.

CAUSES →	SUBJECT →	EFFECT
1. Excellence of men who made the law	Repeal of the Act of 1699	1. Good effects in England
a. Sponsor: Sir George Saville		2. Good effects in Ireland
b. Seconder: Mr. Dunning		3. Good effects abroad
c. Ratifiers: King, both houses, all clergy of all sects		
2. Noble purpose of the bill		
3. Justice of its provisions		
4. Expedience of its provisions		

Comparison and contrast. You can show

A subject in its form and fit
By setting it against its opposite;
Jack is more or less like Jim
And Tom's the contrary of Tim:
Comparison the likeness shows;
Unlikeness in the contrast glows

We often explain our views to others by putting our subject side by side with other subjects that are in the same class. In ordinary conversation we are continually saying something like this: "You've never been to Atlantic City. . . . Well, it's something like Coney Island. . . ."

The purpose of stressing the likeness or unlikeness of a subject with subjects that are closely related to it is to sharpen understanding. What makes a good comparison or contrast? A good *comparison* or *contrast,* like a good example, is either an illustration or a proof. It illustrates when it explains a relatively unfamiliar idea by virtue of its similarity, or dissimilarity, to a relatively familiar idea. Thus in "The Language Line" (pages 20–24) Susanne K. Langer illustrates her ideas on the animal mind (the unfamiliar idea) by comparing it to a telephone exchange (the familiar idea).

The animal mind is like a telephone exchange; it receives stimuli from outside through the sense organs and sends out appropriate responses through the nerves that govern muscles, glands, and other parts of the body. The organism is constantly interacting with its surroundings, receiving messages and acting on the new state of affairs that the messages signify.

In the next paragraph the author contrasts the human mind with the animal mind by turning her metaphor in another direction. Note how she first denies the validity of the comparison between the human mind and the telephone exchange and then affirms a second comparison between the human mind (the less familiar idea) and a great projector (the more familiar idea).

But the human mind is not a simple transmitter like a telephone exchange. It is more like a great projector; for instead of merely mediating between an event in the outer world and a creature's responsive action, it transforms or, if you will, distorts the event into an image to be looked at, retained, and contemplated. For the images of things that we remember are not exact and faithful transcriptions even of our actual sense impressions. They are made as much by what we think as by what we see. It is a well-known fact that if you ask several people the size of the moon's disk as they look at it, their estimates will vary from the area of a dime to that of a barrel top. Like a magic lantern, the mind projects its ideas on things on the screen of what we call "memory"; but like all projections, these ideas are transformations of actual things. They are, in fact, *symbols* of reality, not pieces of it.

Comparison and contrast may be used to reason, as well as to illustrate. In "The Mass Mind: Our Favorite Folly" (pages 203–06) Joyce Cary argues that education promotes individuality. As proof he contrasts the intractability of a committee of professors to the conformism of a council of African tribal chiefs, finding the professors much harder to regiment.

Process. Classification places a subject in a category, or class; definition explains what a subject is; exemplification sets forth specific details about a subject; cause and effect answer the questions "Why?" and "What are the results?"; comparison and contrast show how a subject is like and unlike subjects in the same class. *Process* is a method of analysis that answers the question "How does something work?"

This method is particularly valuable when a subject is dynamic rather than static. The practical operation of a general idea (how democracy works), the development of a historical concept (how the middle classes rose), the analysis of events that led up to a problem (how the Suez crisis of 1956 came about) are best treated by tracing each successive step in the development.

Process is sometimes used by itself but is often used with other methods of analysis. In a composition entitled "How to Hang a Door" the writer should be exclusively concerned with explaining how to trim the door to fit the jamb, how to mortise for and set the hinges on the door and jamb, and how to install the lock. In "Technology and the Claims of Community," on the other hand, Richard H. Rovere intermingles process with causal analysis as he explains the competing claims of privacy and community.

Good process analysis accounts for all the essential steps in the making or operating of something, in the development of an idea, in the application of a principle, or in the meaning of an event. It will put the steps into their proper order and give each a clear presentation proportioned to the importance or complexity of the step.

Combining methods of analysis. We have just sketched six methods of analysis frequently employed by writers in exposition. Except in short compositions, however, these methods are rarely used alone. Most subjects require virtually all the methods, for one leads to another. Classification often makes definition necessary. Definitions are supported by examples, comparisons suggest contrasts, causes and effects are classified and exemplified. The essays in Book One employ whatever methods are most likely to make the subject clear to a given audience. This judicious combining of methods should also be used by students. (Some of the writing lessons included in this rhetoric section intentionally direct students to combine methods of development.)

Argument—Writing to Persuade

Argument, or persuasive writing, is a form of discourse that aims to convince the reader of the truth of a given proposition. Exposition sometimes is indirectly argumentative: it does not always merely state and explain facts; it occasionally reasons from one statement to another. "If what I have just explained is true, then, it follows . . . ." Some such language is an inescapable element in even the purest exposition.

In argument, however, the desire to convince is the primary, distinctive element. "I want you to believe that John Smith is a good husband, because, as I shall show, he is faithful, generous, and forgiving." That sentence differs sharply from explanatory remarks on the same subject, such as, "John invariably goes and comes from home at regular hours, provides for his family generously, and rarely grows sullen under the pressures of domestic life." The first sentence gives reasons, and promises to develop those reasons, for believing the statement that John Smith is a good husband. The second sentence merely states facts that are not necessarily proposed as reasons or means of convincing the reader that John is a good husband.

A good argument is one that provides convincing reasons—reasons that serve as proof. When we argue convincingly, we make our reader agree with us. To do this honestly, we must get the facts straight, produce our evidence, make our theory plain, and introduce pertinent authorities or witnesses. For the fact, or theory, or evidence that provides the *content* of argument is not taken for granted. We do not argue about the obvious. It goes without saying, then, that the first condition of good argument is the reliability of our evidence.

Furthermore, as in exposition, the subject must be examined and organized in keeping with the various methods of analysis, and the reasons must be made clear.

In this form of discourse two kinds of presentation are distinguishable. The first may be termed *formal argument* and the other *informal persuasion.* There is no exact distinction between them. Since they aim at the same objective—to convince—they are dependent for their effects upon much the same qualities. There are, nevertheless, some characteristics that differentiate them.

Formal argument has taken on certain rather rigid, conventional structures, such as those in formal debates and in the closing or rebuttal speeches of lawyers in trials and hearings. Because it recognizes—or assumes—a strong and articulate opposition, it tends not only to fixed patterns of organization but to formidable arrays of evidence (proofs) and to reasoning that is logically invulnerable. T. K. Whipple's "Machinery, Magic, and Art" (pages 241–47), Charles Frankel's "The Morality of Civil Disobedience" (pages 177–81), and Henry M.

Pachter's "In Defense of Television" (pages 190–95) lean heavily toward formal argument, at least in certain sections.

Informal persuasion is typically found in critical reviews of books, movies, and art exhibitions and even in evaluative accounts of sports events. Much of the writing of magazine editors and columnists, including those who are popular because of their humor, falls into this class. It seems less aware than formal argument does of the existence of any solidified, thoughtful opposition, and it seems less urgently motivated by an intense desire to convince. In order to achieve this relaxing of tone, writers of informal persuasion use less rigid and conventional structures. They tend toward reasoning that deliberately or instinctively avoids or disguises displays of inflexible, formidable logic. They present less evidence and less directly emphatic evidence. Finally, informal persuasion characteristically features language that strikes a note of familiarity, even friendliness, with the reader. It frequently suggests that the reader is an ally instead of an opponent. Throughout, it is likely to make skillful use of emotionally toned words.

A word of caution is perhaps necessary here. Informal persuasion is not ineffective formal argument. A decision to present a point of view by informal persuasion instead of by formal argument is no license to indulge in random opinion expressed in riotously emotional terms and unsupported by facts and logic. Informal persuasion is quite often the more effective level in that it better achieves the primary purpose of convincing the reader. E. M. Forster's "What I Believe" (pages 172–77) and George Orwell's "Shooting an Elephant" (pages 167–71) are extremely persuasive. Consider the high success that John Galsworthy has in "A Novelist's Allegory" (pages 275–81), where he completely abandons formal argument. The success of his "allegory" lies in his indirect presentation of his view of the function of the fiction writer.

In formal argument the arguments or proofs are organized in two different ways—by deduction and induction. In *deduction* we reason from premises to conclusion, that is, from two statements, one general and one particular,

so connected that a third statement or conclusion necessarily follows. Algebraically, deduction is expressed this way:

$$A = B$$
$$C = A$$
$$C = B$$

Note that the third statement, or conclusion, follows from the two preceding statements. Or, to put it in the form of a syllogism:

All animals (A) require food (B).
A fox (C) is an animal (A).
Therefore a fox (C) requires food (B).

In *induction* we argue from a series of particular statements *sufficient in number and in cogency* to establish reasonable grounds for a general statement or conclusion. T. H. Huxley illustrates this principle:

Suppose you go into a fruiterer's shop, wanting an apple—you take one up, and, on biting it, you find it is sour; you look at it, and see that it is hard and green. You take up another one and that too is hard, green, and sour. The shopman offers you a third; but, before biting it, you examine it, and find that it is hard and green, and you immediately say that you will not have it, as it must be sour, like those that you have already tried.

Nothing can be more simple than that, you think, but if you will take the trouble to analyse and trace out into its logical elements what has been done by the mind, you will be greatly surprised. In the first place, you have performed the operation of induction. You found, that, in two experiences, hardness and greenness in apples went together with sourness. It was so in the first case, and it was confirmed by the second. True, it is a very small basis, but still it is enough to make an induction from; you generalize the facts, and you expect to find sourness in apples where you get hardness and greenness. You found upon that a general law, that all hard and green apples are sour; and that, so far as it goes, is a perfect induction.[1]

In both deductive and inductive argument reasons are given for a conclusion. In deductive argument the conclusion derives from the

[1] From Letter III, *On Our Knowledge of the Causes of the Phenomena of Organic Nature*, 1863.

logical connection between two premises; in inductive argument the conclusion derives from the strength of the evidence contained in the particular facts.

As Huxley observes, deduction and induction are not totally separate methods of reasoning. Frequently the conclusion of an induction becomes the basis of a deduction, as he demonstrates below:

> Well, having got your natural law in this way when you are offered another apple which you find is hard and green, you say, "All hard and green apples are sour; this apple is hard and green, therefore this apple is sour." That train of reasoning is what logicians call a syllogism and has all its various parts and terms—its major premise, its minor premise, and its conclusion. And, by the help of further reasoning which, if drawn out, would have to be exhibited in two or three other syllogisms, you arrive at your final determination. "I will not have that apple." So that, you see, you have, in the first place, established a law by induction and upon that you have founded a deduction and reasoned out the special conclusion of the particular case.

The same reciprocal relationship between deduction and induction may be observed in the speech "The Ancient Classics in a Modern Democracy" (pages 740–44). Here, Samuel Eliot Morison aims to convince his audience that the ancient classics, Greek and Latin, have a place in a democracy. His argument, chiefly deductive, may be expressed formally in complete syllogisms, although Morison, like most argumentative writers, does not explicitly state his major premises. One such deduction is this:

Whatever is needed to develop the intellect (A) deserves a place in modern democracy (B). (This general statement, or major premise, is implied.)

Latin and Greek (C) are needed to develop the intellect (A). (This minor premise is stated.)

Therefore Latin and Greek (C) deserve a place in a modern democracy (B). (This is the conclusion.)

You will note, however, that the minor premise in this deductive process—Latin and Greek are needed to develop the intellect—is supported by five particular statements. (See sentence outline, pages 739–40.)

Fallacies in argument. A fallacy is a flaw in the reasoning process. In deduction, for example, it is essential to establish the connection between two propositions ($A = B$; $B = C$) so that the conclusion ($A = C$) is necessarily implied. If we said $A = B$, $C = D$, we could not say $A = D$. There is no such connection between A and D in the second example as there is between A and C in the first by virtue of their common identification in the middle term, B. Note how the figures below explain this point.

A and C are connected by their common *situation* within the compass of B.

Note the difference, however, in this figure:

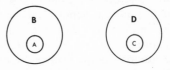

A is connected with B and C with D; but there is no connection between the pairs A, B and C, D. Hence, to say that $A = D$ is to assert a *non sequitur*, that which does not follow.

There are many possible fallacies in deductive reasoning, but all of them have this in common—the conclusion does not follow (*non sequitur*) from the premises that are given as reasons. The error may be in the use of one or all of the three terms (ambiguity, for instance) or in the specious connection between the terms, as has been shown above.

In induction the essence of reasoning is to establish a general truth by an examination of the particular truths that make it up. Thus, to prove that poetry in general is characterized by exceptionally vivid language, a person might show how this characteristic is present in Shakespeare, in Milton, in Keats, and so on. But he may err here if he states exceptional cases rather than representative particulars, or if his individual examples do not converge on the same general point, or if he does not use a sufficient number of examples to establish the probability of the general statement.

The external form of argument. Argument, then, differs from exposition in its outward form, in the way it is usually presented. The more formal the argument, the stricter the form.

Each element in an argumentative essay or speech is shaped to achieve the central purpose—conviction or persuasion. Hence, the *beginning*, especially in formal argument, is likely to be more elaborate than the beginning of an exposition. Here a writer explains his purpose, introduces his subject, defines his terms, and sets forth his central thesis or proposition. When the argument is long, he frequently announces the main divisions or headings that he will develop.

The *middle* section of an argument contains the proof of his proposition. This proof is normally set forth in the clearest, most coherent, and most emphatic order—often concluding, as in the climax of a drama, with the most forceful argument. Frequently the writer follows the positive proof with a refutation (denial, distinction, or retort) of the principal objections against his proposition.

The *end* of an argument not only sums up the main points but appeals directly for the audience's consent to the proposition or even for its decision to act in accordance with the author's views.

Thus argument, from beginning to end, attempts to change the audience's mind. Good argument is organized to accomplish this purpose and to make clear the connections between its several assertions.

Let us see how Samuel Eliot Morison arranged his material in his commencement address at Wooster College on the important subject "The Ancient Classics in a Modern Democracy."

The sentence outline below indicates the general line of the development. Read this outline first. In the marginal comment on the speech (pages 740–44) the special characteristics of the argument are stressed.

SENTENCE OUTLINE OF "THE ANCIENT CLASSICS IN A MODERN DEMOCRACY"

Beginning: Statement of Purpose and Central Concept

I. The classics, Latin and Greek, deserve a place in a modern democracy. (1–18)
   A. The classics will make for true democracy—a leveling up.
   B. The classics formed Thomas Jefferson, an ideal democrat.
   C. The classics have a practical value.

Middle: Development of Argument

II. Latin and Greek are needed to develop the intellect. (19–34)
   A. Latin develops conciseness of thought and expression.
   B. Greek aids precise expression of complicated thought.
   C. Latin and Greek are logical in contrast to uninflected languages.
   D. Latin and Greek help the modern American to organize his speech into literature.
   E. Latin and Greek, with Mathematics, are unrivaled in the training of youthful minds in accurate and original thought.
III. Latin and Greek are vital to the understanding of the best of English and modern European literature. (35–39)
IV. Latin and Greek are important to future scientists. (40–44)
V. Latin and Greek are useful to students of the social sciences. (45–53)
   A. Latin classics help us to know history by revealing the significance of the Roman Empire, which in turn reveals the significance of medieval and modern history.
   B. Greek historians, such as Thucydides, help us to know ourselves.
      1. They warn of the consequences of power politics and demagoguery.
      2. Greek history, as well as Roman history, was a guide of our forefathers.
VI. The classical training of our early leaders (along with their religious faith and their political heritage from Great Britain) ac-

counts for the amazing success of the young American Republic. (54–71)

A. Their classical background helped our early leaders to know what they were doing.

B. It was partly responsible for the phenomenal accomplishments of our early leaders.

C. A majority of the signers of the Declaration of Independence and of the framers of the Federal Constitution were classically trained men.

D. These men were governed by the ideal of Greek virtue and Roman honor.

End: Summary of Argument

VII. The classics are necessary in America today. (72–81)

A. America needs an intellectual aristocracy in a political democracy.

B. The classics, working hand in hand with Christianity, provide the only means of cultivating an intellectual aristocracy.

THE ANCIENT CLASSICS IN A MODERN DEMOCRACY

Samuel Eliot Morison

1. It is often said that the classics are all very well for an aristocratic society, but are not to be cultivated in a democracy, because other things are more important for the average boy, and because their acquisition marks off those so educated as a separate caste. 2. Now, let us admit at once that other things are more important nowadays for the average American, who will end his formal education at the age of sixteen or eighteen. . . . 3. But it seems to me a perverted logic to deny the classics to *some* because they *are* beyond attainment for *all*. 4. Yet that is what many progressive educators today advocate. 5. They would keep school studies so easy, so elementary, that no child in full possession of his faculties would fail . . . , while providing nothing to challenge the admiration and stimulate the ability of a gifted young person. 6. This leveling down is the inversion of true democracy, which implies a leveling up.

Morison challenges the logic of progressive educators and prepares the ground for his own position.

7. Thomas Jefferson never expected education to produce equality; on the contrary: "It becomes expedient for the publick happiness," he wrote, "that those persons, whom nature hath endowed with genius and virtue should be rendered by a liberal education worthy to receive, and able to guard the sacred deposit of the rights and liberties of their fellow citizens; and that they should be called to that charge without regard to wealth, birth or other accidental condition or circumstance." 8. In other words, Jefferson's educational object was to create an intellectual aristocracy, by taking the most gifted young men, irrespective of their parents' wealth or social station, and giving them a liberal education—an education of which the classics and ancient history were the core—that they might be the more fit to govern America, to embellish her cities with beautiful buildings, and to write a national literature. 9. And in all his schemes of education, the classics were central. 10. He himself was an excellent classical scholar. 11. At the age of fifty-six, when Vice-President of the United States, he wrote, "to read the Latin and Greek authors in their original, is a sublime luxury. . . . I thank on my knees, Him who directed my early education, for having put into my possession this rich source of delight; and I would not exchange it for anything which I could then have acquired, and have

Jefferson is cited in favor of the speaker's view.

not since acquired." 12. A young man who visited Jefferson at Monticello when the sage was eighty-two years old recorded that he rode horseback ten or twelve miles a day, spent several hours on the business of the University, and passed his leisure reading Greek. 13. Jefferson is a good enough democrat for me!

14. Yet I am aware that if the classics are to be retained as an investment of democracy, some immediate return, some palpable dividend must be promised. 15. If thus valued, the classics ask for no more than a fair comparison with rival subjects. 16. Is it not a generous estimate to assume that less than five per cent of the boys and girls who are now learning algebra in school will ever find any "use" for it? 17. French is as much a dead language for the average high-school graduate as Latin. 18. He will never hear it spoken or read a page of it again; but let us waive that, and apply the practical test to the ancient languages and literatures.

19. In several different ways, Latin and Greek are superb instruments for developing the human intellect. 20. Latin is so concise, and the words so packed with meaning, that it cannot even be translated into another language with equal brevity. 21. That is why the study of Latin helps one to write clear, concise, forceful English prose. 22. And Greek is the most magnificent instrument so far invented for the precise expression of complicated thought, by the human mind. 23. It combines simplicity with flexibility and sensitiveness—the qualities attained in the best English poetry. 24. Both languages are organic, not slipshod like the uninflected modern languages, where so much depends on idiom, or the order of words. 25. A Greek poem, or a passage of good Latin prose, is articulated, functional, and inevitable, like the steel skeleton of a skyscraper; everything is there that is structurally necessary. . . . 26. This logical quality of the ancient languages is such that the very act of translation is an intellectual discipline of the highest order, helping one to counteract the tendency of English to gain emphasis by mere repetition, and to check the sloppiness in which writers not educated in the classical tradition, like Charles Dickens and Gertrude Stein, are prone to indulge. 27. Just as musical theory and counterpoint enable a musician to compose melodies, concertos, and symphonies out of his national folk-song; so Latin and Greek enable an American to organize the common speech of his countryside into enduring literature. 28. Of this I have an example that will surprise you. 29. It was Ernest L. Thayer, one who took A's and B's in his classics course, a graduate *magna cum laude* of my own university, who wrote that classic on the great American game, "Casey at the Bat"!

30. Latin, Greek, and Mathematics are instruments unrivaled by anything invented in twenty centuries of educational experience for the training of youthful minds in accurate and original thought. 31. The analysis involved in translating Latin or Greek into English provides an unconscious training in logic. 32. If in after life your job be to think, four years or more of Latin is the best training you can possibly have. 33. You are learning logic, the art of thinking, without knowing it. 34. And the art of thinking is the key to creative work in science and statesmanship, as in philosophy.

35. For understanding the best English literature and modern European literature, the classics are vital. 36. The ancient world was implicit in the writings of Dante, of Chaucer, of Montaigne, of Milton, and of Goethe, to name only a few. 37. They cannot become explicit to us, unless we grasp in some measure the background of their thought. 38. How wretched are those school texts of Milton, with every god and goddess and classical allusion annotated! 39. If we cannot teach our pupils a little Greek

Here Morison is leading up to his central proposition. He does not state the division of his points. (For the actual division, see outline, pages 739–40.)

The speaker does not quote specimens of Latin and Greek poetry. Does this lessen the force of his argument? The method of proof here is cause and effect.

Note the transition from causal analysis to contrast in sentence 26, to comparison in sentence 27, and then to example in sentences 28–29.

Morison resumes his proof from cause and effect.

Argument from specific examples to prove necessity of classics in understanding English literature. Note the exclamatory style of sentence 38, the irony in sentence 39.

and Roman mythology first, better give up Milton and Dryden, Keats and Shelley, and start English poetry with Walt Whitman.

40. For future scientists, the ancient languages are important not merely as a mental discipline, and as a means of recreation, but as the basis of all scientific terminology. 41. After a man has made up his mind to choose a career in medicine, enginering, or applied science, it is usually too late to get a fundamental grounding in Latin. 42. One result of engineers' and scientists' neglecting the classics is a purely parrot-knowledge of their basic terminology, and a blatant misuse of it both in speech and writing. 43. The style of the average American scientific paper nowadays is often so bad that even specialists in the writer's own field cannot tell what he is trying to say. 44. Indeed, the only worse English to be found nowadays is written by those "Progressive Educators" who have done their best to kill the classics, and who write dissertations on high-school plumbing in a jargon that may best be described as Pedagese English.

Argument from contrast: what happens when scientists neglect the classics. Note, too, how the speaker ridicules the writing of the scientist— an indirect form of refutation.

45. Again, the ancient classics are of use as an introduction to the social sciences, and a running interpretation of them. 46. They open a window to your mind from these times to other times, and from this place to all other places. 47. The Roman Empire is a bottle-neck through which the vintage of the past has flowed into modern life. 48. To comprehend in some manner the mentality of Rome is the key to medieval and modern history; and in ancient history you will find many of the current questions of today threshed out in a clean-cut fashion that will help you to comprehend your own age. 49. What a terrible warning Thucydides gives of the consequences of war and power politics and demagoguery! 50. And it will enable you to get under the skin of American history, too. 51. The fathers of our Revolution, the framers of our federal and state constitutions, and the great Senators (note the term) of the nineteenth century were steeped in Roman and Greek History. 52. Antique liberty was a phrase often on their lips, and ever in their hearts. 53. They were closer to the ancients in spirit, Americans as they were, than we are to them.

Sentences 46 and 47 contain metaphors that are persuasive as well as explanatory.

54. Those men, the founders of our Republic, seemed to know what they were doing, and where they were going, whilst "The *merely modern* man never knows what he is about." 55. Our forefathers were not *merely modern,* even in their own day. 56. Behind them, in the backs of their minds, and before them as a goal there was always the supreme achievement of Judaea in religion, the supreme achievement of Hellas in the good life, and the supreme achievement of Rome in statecraft. 57. They knew what they wanted, in terms of the attainable. 58. Most of our present leaders don't know what they want, except that they want very much to get in power if they are out, or stay in power if they are in.

59. No generation of Americans has ever accomplished so much of permanent good for this country as the generation of 1770. 60. Thirty years saw independence won, a colonial policy—the Northwest Ordinance— worked out, the gateways to the West opened, state constitutions adopted, the Federal Constitution drafted and ratified, federal government placed in successful operation on a scale hitherto unknown, the war debt liquidated, American credit placed higher than that of most European countries, the bases of American foreign policy laid, and finally, a peaceful revolution (the election of Jefferson) effected by the ballot. 61. No American can look back upon the achievements of that generation without pride; and, when we contemplate the mess the world is in today, we can look back not only with pride but with wonder at those men who pledged to the cause of Independence their lives, their fortunes, and their sacred honor.

An appeal to patriotic pride

62. Where did they acquire the political maturity that enabled them to perform so admirably these almost superhuman tasks? 63. Partly, no doubt, from the experience in self-government that they had enjoyed as part of [Great Britain]. 64. That nation had a long tradition in self-government, from which we benefited and the ripe experience of which went into our constitutions, our bills of rights, and our political tolerance. 65. Yet, partly, the achievement of our heroic age must be ascribed to the fact that America was a Christian nation, that far from regarding the State as the be-all and end-all of political existence, an entity that could do no wrong, its interest was the supreme good; our founders believed that citizens individually were responsible to God for the acts of the state, that righteousness exalteth a people, and sin is a reproach to any nation.

The proof from cause and effect is again resumed. In sentences 63–65, the speaker admits that other causes helped to produce the political wisdom and philosophical maturity of the founding fathers.

66. And partly, too, the amazing success of the young republic was due to the classical training of her leaders. 67. A majority of the signers of the Declaration of Independence and of the framers of the Federal Constitution were classically trained college men; and most of the remainder had studied in school more classics than most Americans nowadays learn in college. 68. Our Revolutionary leaders were *not* fitted for responsibility by courses in civics, sociology, and psychology. 69. It was by Plutarch's Lives, the orations of Cicero and Demosthenes, and by Thucydides that the young men of the 1760's learned the wisdom to deal with other men and with great events in the 1770's and 80's. 70. American Revolutionary leaders both North and South, the Adamses and Trumbulls of New England; Hamilton, John Jay, the Morrises and Stocktons of the Middle States; Madison, Mason, and Jefferson of Virginia; and the Rutledges and Pickneys of South Carolina were prepared for their unexpected tasks by a study of classical culture that broadened their mental horizon, sharpened their intellectual powers, stressed *virtus* and promoted *areté*, the civic qualities appropriate to a Republican. 71. It was of Greek virtue and Roman honor that Thomas Jefferson was thinking when he concluded the immortal declaration, "We mutually pledge to each other our lives, our fortunes, and our sacred honor."

Proof through example of the effects of classical training.

72. And so I come to this final argument, that we need the classics because our country needs the intelligent leadership and disinterested service of an intellectual aristocracy—not a plutocracy, or a hereditary ruling caste, but an intellectual élite recruited from the people, as Thomas Jefferson said, "without regard to wealth, birth or other accidental condition or circumstance." 73. It was just such an aristocracy of brains and character that won the United States independence, that secured by diplomacy our free access to the West, that founded our colleges and universities. 74. And it was want of it, in business and in politics, that led to the great depression. 75. Now that we all know that slough in which materialism, unrestrained greed, and untrained leaders brought us, it would seem logical to return to the noble American tradition of Thomas Jefferson: an intellectual aristocracy in a political democracy. . . .

Note the deductive reasoning. The classics produce intelligent leaders; we need intelligent leaders; therefore we need the classics.

76. If educated people simply drift with the current, reject responsibility, and adopt the protective coloring of the mediocre, America may well drift into the gangster state . . . , the negation of democracy, or, at best, will aim no higher than to provide for the needs and desires of the average. 77. Without a leadership imbued with the standards of antique virtue, and trained in the classical tradition, our civilization threatens to become the mirror where the common man contemplates himself, and is pleased at the sight of his imperfections. 78. Now, the only base on which to rebuild an intellectual aristocracy, so far as I can see, is the civilization of the ancient world, working hand in hand with Christianity, as it has

Note the abridged syllogism in sentence 76. Major: If educated people in America drift . . . Minor (implied): But educated people in America are drifting . . . Conclusion: America may well . . . .

Summary of main arguments

done in the universities of Europe and America these six hundred years.
79. Let the autocracies of today . . . , if they wish, delude themselves
into believing that they can establish a completely new order divorced
from the past, unblessed by God. 80. We, I trust, are wiser than they, and
will hold fast to that which is good. 81. To cut loose from our classical
background would be to sever the main nerve of modern civilization, to
attenuate and impoverish life, and to leave some of man's noblest capacities unused.

This speech was delivered in 1939, when Russia and Germany were temporarily allies.

The metaphors, the parallel constructions, the climax, the periodic structure—all contribute to the vigor and suspense of this concluding passage.

Description and Narration—
Writing to Present Experience

Thus far, two primary intentions that may guide a writer have been distinguished—to inform (exposition) or to convince (argument or persuasion). However, much writing exists for neither of these purposes. We rarely read a short story, for example, for some stray bit of information we may incidentally glean from it or for a direct proof it affords us for supporting or changing our positions in some controversy. We recognize that we read (and writers write) to fulfill some other intention. Unless we are pressed, we may not stop to identify or define that intention closely. Such articulate essays as John Galsworthy's "A Novelist's Allegory" (pages 275–81) and John Ciardi's ". . . an ulcer, gentlemen, is an unwritten poem" (pages 271–75) are rarities, in that they attempt to identify for us that something for which almost all of us read, that something beyond and above information and evidence. Most of us are content to say, rather vaguely, that it is "escape," "pleasure," "entertainment," or "a way of passing time."

Perhaps we can identify the intention of this third kind of writing, and our reason for reading it, by saying that it affords us *experience.* *Experiential* writing sets before us in words the objects and conditions of life itself. It pictures for us the scenes of life and tells us of the activities of the natural universe and humankind. The scenes and activities may already be at least partially familiar to us. If so, we get satisfaction out of re-experiencing them, just as we sometimes turn through old photograph albums to renew acquaintance with the familiar. More often, however, we find that the familiar is presented with a deeper or broader, or at least different, view than we

had taken. This new vision or interpretation to some degree creates experience new to us and thus gives us pleasure. Sometimes the scenes and activities are unfamiliar. If so, our pleasure comes largely from the extension of our experience beyond what real life has so far put before us or beyond what we have taken in. This kind of writing gives us the pleasure of recognizing and reliving experience or of expanding and intensifying experience.

Like informative and persuasive writing, experiential writing has certain specializations of materials and techniques, though they are harder to segregate and define. This type of writing is conventionally divided into two traditional subclasses—*description* and *narration.* Each division has certain distinguishing characteristics.

DESCRIPTION

Descriptive writing presents the sensory qualities of a subject—a person, a place, or an object. Two different purposes may be served by presenting such qualities. Each purpose produces a distinct kind of description. First, often for utilitarian purposes we wish merely to identify a thing closely enough that the reader will recognize it when he encounters it. Second, we may want to give the reader an experience in sensation, an experience that he will get only from material that does far more than merely identify. We want to give him an intense impression of something, an impression that stimulates him—as well as words can—into feeling that he is actually confronting and perceiving the thing itself. Sometimes we want to go so far as to suggest something of its inner nature, or at least of what our perception apparatus and emotional and mental "set" tell us its inner nature is.

Description of the first, more simple level is usually called *expository* description. Its chief aim is to give identifying information. Within itself as a kind of description it has considerable range. At one end of the scale it is applied in daily life to supply useful information: "To get to John Smith's house, you go out North Main, which has a curve in it about a mile from here. Three blocks beyond the curve, you turn onto a narrow, unpaved street. Stay on it until you see a new subdivision—it has houses under construction all over it. Watch the street markers—they're concrete posts about three feet high, placed at intersections. Turn left onto 23rd Street. The house you're trying to find is the second one on the right. It is of yellow concrete block with red brick trim, and the lawn has just been seeded." Dictionary definitions are compressed expository descriptions, for example, "bun' ga·low . . . *n*. . . . A dwelling of a type first developed in India, usually one-storied, with low sweeping lines and a wide veranda." [2] At the other end of the scale is highly scientific or technical description. An object is described with extreme precision, perhaps made possible only with instrumentation, to distinguish it from objects closely like it. For instance, if a surgeon were writing an article for a medical journal about a strange growth he had removed from a patient's lungs, he would be likely to use an exactness and completeness expressed in technical, professional terminology that would be almost meaningless to the layman.

The intention of the second kind of description—*artistic* or *literary* description—is to do more than give the minimum of physical characteristics that together serve as a reliable identification. We frequently want to induce in the reader the sensory and emotional and mental experience we have had and that he therefore might have if he were to encounter the thing described.

Let us examine a passage from Eudora Welty's "A Worn Path" (pages 402–07) that can be used not only as an example of literary description in general but as a basis for later

remarks upon the nature of effective literary description.

> Far out in the country there was an old Negro woman with her head tied in a red rag, coming along a path through the pinewoods. Her name was Phoenix Jackson. She was very old and small and she walked slowly in the dark pine shadows, moving a little from side to side in her steps, with the balanced heaviness and lightness of a pendulum in a grandfather clock. She carried a thin, small cane made from an umbrella, and with this she kept tapping the frozen earth in front of her. This made a grave and persistent noise in the still air, that seemed meditative like the chirping of a solitary little bird.
>
> She wore a dark striped dress reaching down to her shoe tops, and an equally long apron of bleached sugar sacks, with a full pocket: all neat and tidy, but every time she took a step she might have fallen over her shoelaces, which dragged from her unlaced shoes. She looked straight ahead. Her eyes were blue with age. Her skin had a pattern all its own of numberless branching wrinkles and as though a whole little tree stood in the middle of her forehead, but a golden color ran underneath, and the two knobs of her cheeks were illumined by a yellow burning under the dark. Under the red rag her hair came down on her neck in the frailest of ringlets, still black, and with an odor like copper.

This description serves not merely to identify Phoenix Jackson so that we might recognize her, but, more important, it tends to make us feel that we see her and know and understand a great deal about her. It prompts our memory to recall somewhat parallel real-life experiences we have had and in a way re-creates experience for us.

Now let us examine the passage more closely in order to isolate some of the features prominent in descriptive writing and some of the qualities that make description effective.

First, this description is obviously a fragment lifted from its context—in this case a short story. This depiction of Phoenix contributes to Eudora Welty's larger purpose of telling us a story in which Phoenix is the main character. The same principle applies in the examples of expository description we have

[2] From *Webster's New Collegiate Dictionary*.

given earlier, the only difference being that in them the descriptions are used to supply information, not experience. Except for instructor-motivated or self-imposed practice, then, description is written mainly as a supporting part of a larger structure such as a narrative or exposition. Since description is not self-contained, it follows that it has an introduction and a conclusion, in only a very limited sense. They are made unnecessary, or are substituted for by the immediately preceding and following parts of the larger fabric to which the description itself is but a contributing element.

Not so obvious, but nevertheless detectable, is its structure. That is, description has an ordering of its details. It is not a collection of random items. The progression of details here reveals that the describer sees Phoenix as she approaches from some distant position to a closer one. In other words, a consistent *point of view* is established and maintained.

One aspect of point of view—the simpler one—is the location in space and time of the observer who is supplying the description and the location of the thing being described. Many systematic spatial relationships are familiar to us. We describe in patterns of far-to-near or near-to-far, top-to-bottom or bottom-to-top, left-to-right or right-to-left, clockwise or counterclockwise, and so forth. Sometimes we may present the features of a place in consistent relationship to its focal feature. For instance, if a room were dominated by a huge coffee table we might well report the other features of the room according to their distance and direction from that table. Sometimes we find an accurate and meaningful comparison to reveal spatial relationships. We say, for example, "Approached from the north, the valley lay like a huge horseshoe opened toward us. On the right tip. . . ."

Location in time is also important. Notice that in the opening sentence of her story (page 402) Miss Welty says, "a bright frozen day in the early morning." Just as a reader would be confused by a description that did not maintain proper perspective, so he would be confused if a scene were inconsistently described as it appeared at high noon, dawn,

and sunset. Different times of day and different qualities of light affect the appearance of things. Trees cast little shade at noon, and leaves are black, not green, at night.

Consistency of physical point of view in space and time is imperative for effective description. This requirement, however, is not a limitation upon the possible relationships between the describer and the thing described. A stationary observer may describe a stationary object or a shifting object. An observer may report the appearance of an object as the passage of time or the waxing or waning of light reveals different features of it. He has many alternatives so long as he is consistent in his presentation.

Point of view involves a second, more subtle and complex consideration than space and time relationships. What is the character of the describer, and what is the nature of his relationship (other than in space and time) to the object being described? Though this aspect of point of view is especially significant in narration, it also is important in description.

A critical inspection of the Welty passage reveals two areas within this second aspect of point of view. In addition to making indirectly apparent her space and time relationship to Phoenix, Miss Welty implies her own attitude toward the old woman. We thereby learn something of the quality of Miss Welty's mind, or something of the nature and mood of the "voice" that is presenting this picture. We detect a certain detachment, a certain esthetic distance. There is feeling, but not sentimentality. Miss Welty deals largely with observable facts.

But the word *largely* is a very significant qualification. Miss Welty does not deal *strictly* with the facts for two very good reasons. First, she could not have, even if she had wished to. Second, she did not wish to.

This is because Miss Welty, like the rest of us, is equipped by birth and training with a unique perception apparatus. Some of the things her eyes and ears report to her are not "real." The testimony of the human senses is not reliable even among those in the best physical condition. There are at least three reasons for this unreliability. First, each of us has a perception apparatus that is to a considerable degree a product of the use he has made of it and the training he has had. We therefore perceive little or much, accurately or inaccurately. Second, as L. A. G. Strong points out in his excellent study of reality, "The Poetic Approach to Reality" (pages 99–102), even a simple object is an extremely complex thing with many qualities that no one can perceive with the unaided human senses. This factor, of course, contributes to the unreliability of human perceptions. As Strong says, "The reality apparent to our senses *must always be an interpretation.*" An interpretation, then, is inevitably a distortion. Third, it is almost impossible for us to encounter an object, scene, or person without some frame of reference. Our earlier experiences with it and knowledge of it, or of similar objects or of objects present along with it, do much to determine what we perceive in it. Our interests in it—specific and general—result in perceptions that are to some degree distorted. For example, it would be virtually impossible for a timber cruiser to see a tree in the same way as, say, a big-game hunter sees it.

But the matter has a further complication. Our mood at the moment of perception intrudes to color and warp the testimony of our senses. If that mood largely determines what we perceive, if it distorts the material aspects of things perceived, we are yielding to what is called *subjectivity.* Its opposite—*objectivity*—is the perceiving accurately, with proper emphases, of only the qualities actually residing in an object. Complete objectivity is, of course, superhuman. We cannot empty ourselves of feeling. Even if we could, the inherent character of language would make it impossible for us to express this superhuman neutrality.[3] (We might switch to the symbols of the mathematician and scientist and get this neutrality, but the result, though intentional, would be an extremely specialized distortion in which only the fully initiated could recognize anything familiar.)

Most of us are ordinarily unaware of our

subjectivity. We are like the freshman Robert Hogan talks about in "After Sending Freshmen to Describe a Tree" (page 663). But the artist often consciously uses subjectivity to serve his purpose. For example, Miss Welty wishes to give the reader one dominant impression of Phoenix: the infirmity of the old Negress. To a greater degree than immediately strikes the eye, Miss Welty is therefore subjective.

The relative subjectivity or objectivity of a description is produced by a combination of three factors—the character of the exact details selected, the arrangement of the details, and the language in which they are presented. By her choice, arrangement, and wording of details Miss Welty achieves just the degree of subjectivity needed to convey a vivid impression of Phoenix' frailness—a trait central to the intention of the story. In the first place, she makes a calculated *selection* of details. We can safely assume that many other details were present which Miss Welty did not perceive or, more likely, did not choose to present. As we have said, she wished to give enough accurate physical particulars to enable us to visualize Phoenix, but these particulars were chosen to make us see Phoenix as frail. The details she presents tend to emphasize the weakness of extreme age. She spotlights Phoenix' weaving steps and near blindness. (If you have questioned the need of requiring the phrase "the whole truth" in the legal oath, you should now understand the justification for a court's emphasizing the difference between "telling the truth" and "telling the *whole* truth." One may build up a favorable or an unfavorable picture by selecting only those items that point in the desired direction.)

Like Miss Welty, the student who writes descriptive passages should do more than array a series of accurate particulars. He should determine the central impression produced by the salient features of the object he is describing (objectivity). Or he should contrive from certain of those features an impression that serves some special purpose he had for describing the object (subjectivity). In either case, he should present only those details that

---

[3] For explanations of this characteristic of language see Section 20a of the *Harbrace College Handbook.*

contribute to the desired impression. This statement applies whether he is being relatively objective (that is, being led primarily by the physical qualities of the object itself) or relatively subjective (that is, being led by a special view of things determined by the kind of person he is, the mood he wishes to establish, or the dominant impression he wants to convey). Having made the proper selection, he should fuse those details into a meaningful whole.

Miss Welty does just this. She imposes an *arrangement* upon the details. Simultaneously with preserving her spatial order of far-to-near, she moves us nearer to the dominant impression she is attempting—from figure and movement to a close-up of the face, a close-up that, in a sort of climax, puts Phoenix' extreme agedness beyond the shadow of a doubt.

Several possible arrangements exist. A writer may, like Miss Welty, begin by a rather direct thematic statement: "She was very old. . . ." He then should follow with the supporting details. To do this, he may use a meaningful comparison. If he says "The hill was like a tower," he should then specify the significant points of similarity between the two things. He may choose some kind of climactic progression. If so, he should put his details in the order of their increasing contributions to his central impression.

Finally, Miss Welty deftly manipulates the *language* of her details so that it promotes the effect she is seeking. Knowing that we might get no impression whatsoever of Phoenix if we had no physical image to pin it to, she uses concrete words—words that, by appealing to our physical senses, create mental images in us. Consider the effect of such phrases as "thin, small cane made from an umbrella" and "apron of bleached sugar sacks." Both items put definite, intense pictures in our minds. She also uses several figures of speech. Such figures add concreteness by giving us an image that reinforces one already supplied by literal terms. For instance, to her direct statement that Phoenix moved "a little from side to side in her steps," Miss Welty adds "with the balanced heaviness and lightness of a pendulum in a grandfather clock."

Still another aspect of her choice of language adds to the success of the description. She is deliberately repetitive: "old Negro woman," "very old," and "eyes . . . blue with age." This repetition extends beyond the use of the same word or a synonym for it. Words like "grandfather," "grave," "meditative," "solitary," "unlaced shoes," and "frailest of ringlets" indirectly impel the reader to sense the extreme age of Phoenix. Image-creating words are the heart of effective description. All good description rests ultimately on a choice of language that results in the reader's recalling or reliving sense experience. Whether it is Miss Welty's description of old Phoenix, or Archie Carr's description of his noonday walk on a Caribbean beach (pages 325–32), or Joseph Conrad's description of the mouth of a Pacific river (pages 388–96), the reader is immersed in sights, sounds, and other sensations. Like Carr, he feels the sand burning his shanks, or, like Conrad, he feels the absence of motion, the heavy weight of silence, and the lack of breeze upon his skin. Though appeals to our visual sense are by far the most prominently used, even by professional writers, the beginning writer should do more than develop his sense of sight and expand his vocabulary of concrete terms representing visual images. He should, as well, consciously observe the effects an object makes upon his other senses and try to reproduce these for his reader, since it is generally agreed that olfactory and tactile sensations often have the longest lasting, most intense effects upon people.

In her selection and arrangement of detail and in her choice of language, then, Miss Welty is shaping the nature of her reader's experience to her purpose, to one dominant impression in thought and feeling. In this respect and to this degree she is being consciously subjective. But her subjectivity is unobtrusive. Unlike Hogan's freshmen describing trees, she keeps before the reader the solid substratum of concrete, objective details that enable him to visualize Phoenix clearly. Only after this basic requirement has been well met does she artfully move him further toward the impression she desires by slipping in an occasional subjective word such as "grave" and "meditative" or a subjective comparison such as "like the chirping of a solitary little bird."

In addition to her careful attention to the three important matters of selecting, arranging, and expressing details, Miss Welty employs still other good descriptive devices. For example, we should note that she conveys to us one of Phoenix' most important characteristics by using action, not outright description. How do we know that Phoenix was near-blind? We know as a result of Miss Welty's reporting that Phoenix tottered from side to side, tapped her cane persistently before her, and looked straight ahead. Often the reporting of action is more communicative than direct description. Instead of saying, "The ax was very dull," one might say, "He had to sharpen the ax before he could cut the log with it." Descriptions of people, especially, should include more than details of physical appearance. Other significant features can be conveyed by demonstration. A trait of character such as honesty, for example, would best be communicated by showing a person performing an honest act such as returning change that a sales clerk has given him by mistake. Exact indications of the properties a person chooses to surround himself with and the typical activities he chooses to spend time on are highly revealing of character. Dialogue is useful in description since not only what a person says but how he says it helps to individualize him. And through dialogue, too, we may detect the reactions of other people to the character being portrayed. Finally, many good character portrayals let us at least glimpse what the person is like inside, sometimes by the use of some stream-of-consciousness material. Miss Welty uses all these devices in her story. In the paragraph following the quoted passage, on page 403, she has Phoenix talk to herself so that we learn not only the quality of the old woman's speech but something of the nature of her mind.

We should also be aware that although Miss Welty uses many adjectives, she is not overly dependent upon them. In fact, some of her sentences have few adjectives. Even the most cursory inspection of the outstanding poems in "The Poet as Portrayer of Character" section (pages 667–74) will show that the best of poets put little reliance upon the ability of the adjective to describe—poets like Robinson, Dickinson, Browning, Yeats, Frost, and Auden. Like Miss Welty, they do not need to indulge in riotous adjectivitis, for they have successfully combined more effective devices.

Finally, though Miss Welty uses the degree and kind of subjectivity needed to establish the dominant impression intended, she keeps the reader's attention on her subject, Phoenix Jackson, not on Eudora Welty. She does not tell us how and why she got to the spot from which she viewed Phoenix on that early morning of a frozen December day. Nor does she say "As the little old woman drew near, I could see. . . ." She does not announce her intentions of describing. She has no statement that directs attention away from the image of Phoenix and to the fact that there is a perceiving and interpreting consciousness on hand and at work. She does not say "I saw . . . ," much less "It seemed to me that . . ." or "From my observation I would say that. . . ." And she makes no useless, amateurish declarations as to the unusual or spectacular nature of her subject. She has no statements like "She (it) was so unique (or arresting, moving, vivid, memorable, and so forth) a person (scene) that I will never forget her (it) as long as I live."

Such material as Miss Welty presents in this descriptive passage is memorable not because she says it is but because she makes it memorable. By her control of details, choice of language, and use of devices that indirectly describe, she puts a vivid, dynamic character before us. The result is the essence of literary art—experience.

NARRATION

Narration is like description in its intent to create or re-create experience for the reader. Like description, it is aimed at man's whole complex of thought and feeling. In keeping with its breadth of aim, it has a number of basic ingredients. It has (1) a sequence of related actions. This sequence leads to (2) some end. It presents (3) a character or characters who engage in and are affected by these actions. These characters perform in (4) some particular setting of space and time. It unfolds its actions in (5) a particular time sequence.

For example, in W. Somerset Maugham's "Appointment in Samarra" (page 367) the sequence of related actions is as follows: the servant goes to the market, sees Death's gesture, reports this incident to his master, and asks for a horse. The master gives him the horse, and the servant leaves town. The master goes to the market place, sees Death there, and hears Death's explanation of her gesture toward the servant. Note that these events not only flow from the first to the second to the third, and so forth, but that they come to one result or end. Three characters are involved in these events, and the fortune of one is at stake. There is a particular scene of action. The reader is told not merely that the action took place in Bagdad but that the specific events that constitute the action occurred in the market place and at the home of the merchant. Even the town to which the servant fled is named. The events are reported in the order in which they took place, and that order is communicated by such modifying expressions as "and in a little while," "just now," and "then."

Writers and readers of narrative may become immersed in a particular aspect of experience or in some combination of aspects. A narrative, or story, may focus attention on the inner life of one or more of the characters, with the author probing their motivations and reactions, as Sherwood Anderson does with George Willard in "Sophistication" (pages 469–73). It may call attention to the environmental influences of time, place, family, and social and economic class, as Flannery O'Connor's "A Late Encounter with the Enemy" (pages 407–13) and Joseph Conrad's "The Lagoon" (pages 388–96) tend to do. It may concern itself with a philosophical question such as the nature of nature, as Stephen Crane's "The Open Boat" (pages 437–50) does, or whether man's fate is a product of his making or of some cosmic design or whimsy, as does, to some degree, W. Somerset Maugham's "Appointment in Samarra." Or it may center itself on the sheer

ingenuity or rapidity or violence of the incidents that constitute its action, as does Thomas Hardy's "The Three Strangers" (pages 375–87).

Two uses of narrative. The chief use of pure narrative is to create vicarious experience. For example, "Appointment in Samarra" captures the terrifying realization that the very steps taken to ensure a certain conclusion turn out irrevocably to be the very steps that result in its opposite—as when we reduce the speed of an automobile so that we can control it better, only to cause it to skid and go completely out of our control.

Narration is sometimes used for a different and larger purpose than to re-create experience (much as description is almost always used to support an explanation or a story). Very often writers choose to accomplish their primary purpose of explaining something by telling a story that, by itself or with the addition of direct explanatory comment, clarifies the matter. The second use of narrative, then, is to supplement or substitute for exposition. In expository narrative, though the form and features of narrative are preserved, the primary intention is to give information. For example, Dylan Thomas' "A Visit to America" (pages 223–26) and George Orwell's "Shooting an Elephant" (pages 167–71) are narratives subordinated to the primary purpose of explaining the private judgments of each author on his subject. The details of the actions reported clarify the judgments made. In this respect narrative is one of the methods of developing expository material. In fact, it is essentially a sustained exemplification.

The kinds of narrative. These two uses or purposes of narrative become the basis for dividing it into two broad classes: *informative* or *expository* or *factual* narrative, and *experiential* or *literary* or *artistic* narrative. Several subclasses of each of these two kinds are customarily given, though only some of them have been satisfactorily defined and distinguished. No single principle of division into subclasses has been discovered or devised to cover either informative or experiential narrative. This difficulty in logically classifying narrative arises out of the nature of narrative—its varieties of forms and purposes—and is, in a way, a tribute to its versatility.

Informative or expository narrative may be classified in a number of ways, though it is difficult to divide it into mutually exclusive categories. First, it may be classified according to the narrator's relationship to his material. If he tells the story from his own point of view—that is, if he uses the outright first person or the third person that conceals the fact that he is telling about himself—he is producing autobiography. Generally, autobiography emphasizes the teller's involvement in the action. For example, George Orwell in "Shooting an Elephant" (pages 167–71), uses the first person and figures as the central character. But a narrator may assume some other relationship to his material and have some subject other than himself. His material may be centered upon the life of another person, in which case the writing is biography. It may be centered upon some occurrence in nature or a historic event that is only incidentally autobiographical or biographical.

Second, informative narrative may be classified according to its subject matter. Thus a narrative may be given such a designation as travel, adventure, or human interest.

A third classification of informative narrative, though by no means a complete one, is based on form. Certain types have solidified into somewhat standard forms. Within this classification are such types as the anecdote—for example, the short, illustrative incidents in Marjorie Kinnan Rawlings' "The Pound Party" (pages 332–35); reportage—news accounts like Murray Kempton and James Ridgeway's "Romans" (pages 336–39); and history—like the more general passages in Sir Arthur Bryant's "The Holy Blissful Martyr" (pages 347–60).

Although such terms as short story, novella, and novel are freely used, classification of experiential or literary narrative involves many of the same problems encountered in classifying informative narrative. Only one of the forms of literary narrative—the short story—has been closely defined, and some critics take exception to the standard definition of it. (See the introduction to "The Short Story" (pages 361–66) and Bonaro Overstreet's "Little Story, What Now?" (pages 263–66).) To some degree length is a dividing factor. A short story is short. But it is difficult to determine what shortness is, and we know that mere brevity does not necessarily result in a short story. About all that can be safely said is that a short story is a comparatively short, fictitious, prose story with comparatively great tension (the degree of reader involvement in a story); a simple narrative is a comparatively short prose story with comparatively little tension and is perhaps more factual than a short story; a novel is a comparatively long, fictitious, prose story; and stories in verse are narrative poems.

Perhaps at this point it should be noted that, although we rather automatically categorize as informative a narrative that is true, much narrative of either kind contains factual *and* fictional material. Expository narrative frequently embellishes fact if the teller is anything of an artist, and many short stories and novels have a highly factual basis, for instance, the novels of Thomas Wolfe and historical fiction, at least that produced by sound historical research.

There are, of course, other methods of classifying narratives. For example, narratives differ in the degree of unity achieved, in the degree of tension maintained, and in the regularity or irregularity of the patterns of language used; that is, they may be written in prose or verse.

But, fortunately, all these classifications are of perhaps minor importance to the student or amateur writer. The qualities of good narrative in general are of far greater consequence.

The qualities of good narrative. The mere incorporation into a story of all the basic ingredients of narrative (defined and illustrated on pages 749–50) will result in recognizable narrative. It will not necessarily result in good narrative. Good narrative manipulates its basic ingredients of setting, action, and character in such a way as to produce often intense vicarious experience, not just understanding. Good narrative has order, focus, tension, movement, and credibility.

ORDER. All true narrative is told in one of two kinds of time order. Straightforward chronological order relates events in the exact order of their occurrence from beginning to end, as in Ernest Hemingway's "After the Storm" (pages 398–402). Interrupted time order plunges the reader into the middle of things, into an important event from the middle of the action, and follows with an account of what led up to this event. (This background material, or antecedent action, is called the *exposition* whether it comes first, as in straightforward time order, or follows the first crucial event, as in interrupted time order.) In long narrative works, such as novels, this technique may be extended so that the bulk of the story is told by flashbacks, that is, by scenes from the past inserted into the action of the present.

But time order is not the only order necessary to good narrative. The definition of narrative emphasizes the fact that the series of events must be *connected* or *related*. The meaning of a series of events is not necessarily revealed by time order alone. There must be a causal connection among the events. Take, for example, this news item: "The Prime Minister left the hospital at 9:00 A.M. He flew to London, arriving at 11:00 A.M. Crowds welcomed him at the airport." This account does tell a story, but far more meaning is apparent in: "Cured of the heart ailment that has disabled him for the past month, the Prime Minister left the hospital at 9:00 A.M. He flew to London, arriving at 11:00 A.M. Glad that he was well enough to return to active duty, crowds greeted him at the airport." This causal order is, of course, concomitant with time order, not in any way in conflict with it, and is often implied rather than stated. It is this causal connection more than the time one that is the basis for dividing a story into a beginning, a middle, and an end. The beginning presents the initial cause of an action, the middle demonstrates that cause in operation, and the end signifies the result of the action.

These problems of order are so entangled with each other that they must be considered and resolved simultaneously. The writer must choose between telling his story in a straightforward time sequence or in some interrupted time scheme. He can scarcely make this choice without identifying the causal connection among events and thereby clarifying for himself the beginning, middle, and end of his story.

In the simple narrative the student writer probably should use straightforward time order. Readers find it easy to follow. This order presents the problem of achieving an interesting but self-explanatory opening. But if the student writer begins with some exciting event in the middle of his story he faces as substantial a problem in preventing a sagging of reader attention when he drops back to relate the action antecedent to that event. If he is attempting a short story the choice is less easy to make. Length, the nature of the material, and point of view must be considered. There is an inviting simplicity in the straightforward time order of John Cheever's "The Swimmer" (pages 368–74), but a richer, longer story, such as William Faulkner's "Spotted Horses" (pages 458–68), may artfully move forward and backward in time in keeping with the character of the narrator.

Perhaps more positive and helpful advice can be given the student writer on two problems bearing on order. He should begin his story as close as possible to its first significant action, no matter which order he uses. Whether writing a simple narrative or a short story, the student should be sure that he starts at the true beginning instead of at some unnecessary earlier moment or with some unnecessary matter.

From "A Worn Path" the writer can learn two further lessons about this problem of beginning. First, he can strip his exposition to the minimum absolutely vital to his story. Eudora Welty manages to put her extremely significant background material into the first five or six sentences. Second, he can achieve this desired minimum as Miss Welty does, by confining himself to causal explanation. A cursory inspection of stories that feature the flashback technique, such as "The Lagoon" and "Spotted Horses," shows that authors tend to restrict the flashbacks to material that clarifies the motives of characters—to material that deals with causes of action.

FOCUS. In addition to being unified by presenting only a limited action or a series of incidents constituting an overall action, good narrative has focus. Some particular aspect of events must be singled out for attention.

Principles applicable to order in a story also have a bearing on focus. Establishing a causal relationship as well as a time order; having a structure with a definite beginning, middle, and end; and starting as close as possible to the first essential incident all contribute to focus. But some other matters contribute heavily.

First, focus governs the selection of events. For example, if a student writes either an informative autobiographical narrative or a simple narrative based on the events that occurred on the day his family moved from one city to another, some sustained strand of interest more definite than a mere progression of events in time order should bind these events together. The student should concentrate on some special interest. Perhaps there was a series of delays that cumulatively made the members of the family irritable. Perhaps there was a series of pleasant experiences unanticipated by the family. Whichever the case, he should present only the items that contribute to the special interest. In "The Pound Party" (pages 332–35) Marjorie Kinnan Rawlings focuses on the baffling nature of the Townsends and limits herself to material that bears on that nature.

Another way to get this point of concentration is to confine attention to the fortune of a single character. This method is generally the primary way of getting focus in autobiographical and biographical writings.

In much narrative, point of view largely determines the focus. The quality of the consciousness of the narrator—his comparative involvement in or detachment from events and the characters figuring in these events—has much to do with focus, as does his location in space and time. (In the discussion of description on pages 744–49 this matter is given considerable attention.) Though other devices that give focus are used, too, the quality of mind and the special attitudes of the narrators are most important to the effects produced in such stories as Ernest Hemingway's "After the Storm" (pages 398–402) and Marjorie Kinnan Rawlings' "The Pound Party" (pages 332–35).

TENSION is the degree of reader involvement established and maintained in a story. It is a product of well-organized, or plotted, conflict. The intention of narrative is to create for the reader an experience to which he responds emotionally as well as intellectually. Good narrative causes him to take sides with one or more of the characters and to suffer or rejoice at every turn of fortune of that character or those characters. Good narrative captures this involvement early and sustains it until the end. (For a presentation of the general matters of action and tension, the student should consult the passage on action in the short story introduction on pages 361–66.)

Specifically, there are four problems of immediate concern to a beginning writer that must be taken into consideration: What tension should be sought? How is tension established? How is it maintained? How is it broken so that the conflict is resolved and the story ended?

First, in good narrative there should be some tension. Narrative without tension is more or less a contradiction in terms. The degree of tension sought should be determined by the nature of the material and the writer's purpose in telling the story. Informational and reminiscent material may produce little tension because there was little conflict involved in the situation reported. But even such a reminiscent account as "The Pound Party" has background conflicts that are the very heart of the author's material: should Mrs. Rawlings lend the Townsend's money, give them clothes, arrange for schooling and medical care of the children? Should she tolerate weaknesses in them that she does not tolerate in herself? The student should likewise be led by his material and purpose. If he is reporting an action, such as going on a journey, that had only subdued conflicts in it, he should remain "true" to the material. Even if his purpose with that material is to reveal that conflict is always present in normal, commonplace life, he should not overtly strain or falsify the material for intense effects.

Tension is established by opening with a situation in which conflict between opposing forces is apparent. A scenic incident, usually involving dialogue that indirectly indicates this conflict, is doubtless the most effective beginning in this respect. A student might well start his story with at least a brief scene. That scene should have in it either dialogue or action or both to reveal the fact that opposing forces are in conflict. Depending upon the exact character of his story and upon his purpose with it, he may expose a good deal about the degree of intensity, the nature, and the motivation of the conflict. If he is writing factual, expository narrative, he may directly state that the scene is used to exemplify the existence of conflict and may comment at length upon features of the conflict that the scene has demonstrated. If the student is attempting a literary narrative, he should probably begin more indirectly, that is, make the conflict apparent through particulars of the action and through a selection of dialogue calculated to expose that conflict. This is Eudora Welty's method in "A Worn Path" (pages 402–07). With the first pitting of Phoenix Jackson's physical frailty and indomitable spirit against a particular real or imaginary obstacle on her path, we see the character of the opposing forces. Thus a literary craftsman makes the story self-sufficient and does not have to insert interpretive comment to give it meaning or to add to its meaning.

If tension is established early, the story is well begun. Then the problem is to maintain that tension or suspense. The solution is to select or invent further incidents or new phases or areas of action in which the opposing forces clash, with sometimes one force prevailing and sometimes the other. The suspense in "A Worn Path" is preserved because, having realized the full extent of Phoenix' handicaps as a result of the author's vivid description, we are not led to assume that Phoenix will surmount the next obstacle just because she surmounted the last one. When she falls and cannot get to her feet, the obstacle temporarily prevails. The accidental appearance of the hunter overcomes this obstacle, but not without planting a doubt in our minds: what of the next time she falls, as she is most likely to do? In fact, we feel that she is pushing her luck too far, that the odds are bound to catch up with her, that with each victory of hers the more likely is the coming defeat. The trick, then, is to plan a series of incidents in which first one force, then the other seems to be prevailing. *Seems* here is a very important word, for in this section of the story each incident should leave a seed of doubt as to whether winning this one battle means winning the war.

The final problem is to break the tension with a resolution of the conflict—a resolution that somehow stabilizes the situation in favor of one of the contending forces. Only then can an end be put to the story and the characters returned to the enveloping action of their normal lives. In most stories the seesawing of action culminates in some sort of crucial incident that signifies the victor. Therefore the writer must have this culmination sharply in mind as he selects and arranges his events. In factual narrative one has merely to follow actual events and conclude with what was in fact the decisive incident. In fiction one must contrive the decisive incident.

In a story based heavily upon external conflict this crucial incident may involve some overtly strong or violent act, such as the execution of the prisoners in Frank O'Connor's "Guests of the Nation" (pages 451–57). But the beginning writer should cultivate the ability to reveal a significant triumphing of one force over the other without having to resort to murder. He can learn a lesson from Marjorie Kinnan Rawlings' "The Pound Party" (page 335). Mrs. Townsend's comment, "You can't trust nothin' is free," is sufficient to signal Mrs. Rawlings' defeat. In fact, it is not always necessary to have one especially decisive incident. At the end of Eudora Welty's "A Worn Path" (page 407) we find that though Phoenix has yet to face the arduous trip home, we now have no fears for her. For the obstacles she faces on the way home will probably be of the same nature as those she overcame on her way to town, and we know that Phoenix' unquenchable inner strength will see her safely through.

Once the tension in a story is broken the story is over except for as gracefully brief an ending as one can manage. For example, William Faulkner finds it necessary to use only a half-dozen lines—a comment by a bystander and the narrator's silent agreement with it— to conclude "Spotted Horses" (page 468).

MOVEMENT in narrative refers to the pace in which the sequence of connected incidents makes headway toward its predetermined end. Except when the writer is held to a given space or word limit, movement should be governed by the nature of the material. For example, Stephen Crane's "The Open Boat" (pages 437–50) moves slowly, in keeping with the doubtful progress of the ten-foot boat on a rough sea.

Three factors combine to give a story its movement. The first is selection. Marjorie Kinnan Rawlings' "The Pound Party" moves briskly because she chooses to report to the reader only four or five of the more significant encounters she had with the Townsends. The student writer also can hasten the movement of his story by choosing relatively few of the many incidents that actually happened or that he invented. He should choose incidents that are significant both in themselves and to the overall action. In John Cheever's "The Swimmer" (pages 368–74) each encounter Neddy has with his neighbors moves the story forward toward its resolution. Furthermore, the incidents chosen should imply what happened in the stretches of time between them, thus clarifying their connection with each other. William Faulkner is especially skillful in having the narrator in "Spotted Horses" (pages 458–68) reveal Flem Snopes' background by suggesting the connections between the incidents in the story. Finally, these carefully selected incidents should be so presented that they carry their own weight, that is, they should not be dependent upon intrusive explanations or evaluations by the writer. When Archie Carr, in "The Black Beach" (page 331), recounts Mrs. Ybarra's hilarity at the sight of her egg-beplastered horse and gear, he does not belabor the obvious by writing another paragraph to point out that she had a ready sense of humor.

The second important factor that influences the movement of a story is the relative amount of space or development each of the incidents is given. The good writer gives an incident significance or emphasis by presenting it in fuller detail than he uses for less significant matters. In fact, critical incidents are generally presented in a scene, with each character's words given in dialogue and with each particular action fully reported. Comparatively unimportant events are hurried over in summary treatment, as Frank O'Connor hurries over them in this passage from "Guests of the Nation" (page 454): "I don't know how we got through that day, but I was very glad when it was over." Thus in one sentence he covers the events of a full day, though elsewhere he spends two pages on the events of a few minutes.

To some degree movement is a product of style. Vivid, image-creating words give vigor and thrust to an action. Variations of sentence patterns reinforce the movement appropriate to a given passage in a story. And sentence rhythms may be used to stimulate the movement. Take, for example, this sentence from Stephen Crane's "The Open Boat" (page 438): "There was a terrible grace in the move of the waves, and they came in silence, save for the snarling of the crests."

CREDIBILITY is the believability a story has for the reader. Because readers can get no vicarious experience from a story that creates no belief in them, any kind of story must establish its credibility. Readers have a general willingness not to disbelieve, and few of them hesitate to give at least temporary belief to a story that offers the kind and degree of "truthfulness" in keeping with the nature and the purpose of the story. Consciously or unconsciously, they accept the fact that the "events" in a story are only representations of events, not events themselves. They know that a reporter's eyewitness, factual account of a hurricane is not the hurricane. Narrative's whole stock in trade is representation or illusion. Readers demand only that a writer offer them the illusion of reality—an "artistic" truth of some intensity. Paradoxically, the wildest fantasy can successfully be used for purposes as far to the extreme of each other as purposes can be—sheer momentary entertainment, such as that in John Manifold's narrative poem "The Griesly Wife" (page 650), and high ethical or philosophical insight, such as that in James Thurber's "Many Moons" (pages 67–73). Or a factual story can fail both to entertain and to communicate an ethical concern because it rings false.

In fact or fiction, realism or fantasy, credibility is dependent mainly upon the writer's being faithful in two matters. He must present the circumstances, the particulars of scene and action, and he must make the motives behind the actions probable motives.

John Collier's "The Chaser" (pages 413–15) immediately establishes the necessary illusion by packing into the first two paragraphs a dozen or so particulars, such as "dark and creaky stairs in the neighborhood of Pell Street." Joseph Conrad, in the first few paragraphs of "The Lagoon" (pages 388–96), richly pictures the isolated and ominous character of Arsat's clearing. We are prepared, therefore, in each story to believe in the strange and unusual events that will follow.

Similarly, we expect the motives to be recognizably human. Even if the story has Ray Bradbury's Martians or George Orwell's pigs as characters, we unconsciously translate them into human beings and their actions into human concerns. We reject as false any cause for action that a human being would not have *if he were put into the shoes of a Martian or a pig.* We, of course, do make proper allowances. We probably would not act and react exactly as Arsat does in "The Lagoon" (pages 388–96), but we do acknowledge that his behavior is recognizably human in that time and place. Sometimes our view of reality is the product of literary tradition and convention. Few of us have had any direct observation of kings. But we accept the king in James Thurber's "Many Moons" (pages 67–73) because he fits the role established for kings in countless other stories of the same kind. We recognize in him the attitudes those other literary kings have demonstrated, and credibility is thus established.

The student writer should try especially hard to create the necessary illusion, for student narrative tends to be deficient in this quality. This lack is needless for two reasons. First, most students can easily grasp that the seeming truthfulness of any report of an event is based on the degree to which its main outline is bulwarked by supporting details. These details enable readers to visualize the scene, the action, and the characters. Even irrelevant details tend to create belief. For example, a witness is asked by the prosecuting attorney, "Are you sure that it was 10:00 P.M. when you saw John Doe?" The witness answers, "Yes, it was about ten. I had to stop to put on my topcoat after I stepped out of the theater—it had gotten much colder. I looked at my watch then. It was a minute or two after nine-thirty. I walked the five or six blocks to Smith's Drugstore, window-shopping some but not losing much time. I ordered coffee and pie—banana, it was; they don't often have banana. I'd about finished the pie and coffee when John came in. It'd have to be about ten."

Students can recognize that they would give this report credence because it is highly circumstantial. They can see something of the method that establishes this credibility: if a person can remember a marginal, even irrelevant, detail, such as the kind of pie he had on a given night, he probably can be trusted to remember a more important matter, such as the time his watch showed when he checked it. Of course, it is the circumstantiality, not the irrelevancy, that convinces.

This lack of credibility is needless also because the student writer almost always knows all the circumstantial details. Like the witness, he can easily summon the facts if he is pressed to do so. If he is to write good narrative he must realize that the reader needs details and that the writer must supply them.

Now and then a student remains dubious of the contribution made by circumstantial details. He says details bore him and therefore will bore the reader. This viewpoint is unsound. Details interest the reader. *Every narrative in this book—regardless of its form and length and whether it is fact or fiction—is circumstantial, and it is this circumstantiality that creates the reader's interest, for he will*

*have no interest in something in which he does
not believe.*

Postscript

Throughout the discussion of the forms of
discourse it has repeatedly been emphasized
that, though there are values to be gained
from studying the purposes and techniques of
the separate forms, most writing is a skillful
combination of these forms. That whole will
be dominated by one primary purpose but will
use a variety of forms and devices to develop
its material. Most of the writing lessons (pages
764–789) are designed to keep this fact alive
in the mind of the student writer. Though
some of the lessons are closely limited to
exercise in some special technique of a given
form, the underlying assumption is that, once
that particular skill is gained, the technique
will be put to use wherever and whenever it
can contribute something of value to a larger
pattern or purpose.

The Rhetoric of the Sentence

A sentence may be grammatically sound,
clearly stated, and adequately punctuated—
that is, it may meet all the conventional standards of correctness—without serving its purpose well. Rhetorically, a sentence is good
only to the degree that the idea in it is given
meaning and impact. A study of the rhetoric
of the sentence is a study of the features or
devices that a good writer uses, consciously
or unconsciously, to make his sentences effective. This level of rhetoric is best understood
as the manipulation of the grammatical elements, the words, and the sounds within the
sentence unit.

The following sentence, on page 438 of
Stephen Crane's "The Open Boat," demonstrates three major aspects of sentence rhetoric
and an accomplished integration of them:
"There was a terrible grace in the move of the
waves, and they came in silence, save for the
snarling of the crests." A close consideration
of this sentence reveals that its structure, its
diction, and its sound effects conspire to make
it unusually effective.

Several features of structure contribute here.
First, the sentence is compounded. This compounding gives length. Length is necessary
since the sentence has two climaxes—"terrible
grace" and "snarling of the crests." Climax
can hardly be achieved without building toward it with less consequential matter. Furthermore, the length of this sentence expresses a fact about the nature of waves that
serves not only the need of the passage from
which the sentence comes but the needs of the
whole story—that is, the fact that the waves
are endless. The compounding also expresses
this vital character of the waves; to some degree it indicates that they come with little or
no pause between them. Second, the sentence
is loosely constructed in that its modifiers are
placed near the ends of the two statements.
This positioning of modifiers, supported by the
compounding, makes the sentence natural and
conversational. A third notable feature of
structure is the delayed subject pattern in the
first clause. Without it, the first clause could
not achieve its climactic effect, that is, the
special emphasis on "terrible grace." This delayed subject pattern is the variation that keeps
the sentence from being balanced, or parallel
in construction. This variation keeps the two
independent clauses from having the same
weight or emphasis; it tends to subordinate
the second clause to the first in a manner suggesting that the silence of the waves constitutes a part of their terribleness.

The diction of this sentence has much to do

with its effect. Though the individual words are of only average concreteness, a visual and auditory image arises out of the combination of "move of the waves," "silence," "snarling," and "crests." Of far more consequence, however, is the figurative cast of the diction. Although we are momentarily shocked by the oxymoron "terrible grace," our imaginations quickly leap to a proper appreciation of it, especially when it is reinforced by the image of the snarling crests. Grace, we realize, *is* terrible when it is embodied in Blake's tiger or Crane's relentless waves. We perhaps end with a profound understanding of something that, previously, we may have grasped only dimly, if at all. In another respect "terrible grace" is of special interest. It is the most significant, most illuminating expression in the sentence—the meaning of the sentence rides more upon it than upon any other single element. Such an expression might be called a "pivot" or "key" expression. As its name indicates there can be only one such expression in a clause, for a pivot is executed gracefully only when weight is concentrated at one point. The names also suggest that the expression must be comparatively brief—sometimes a single word and rarely more than a brief, organic phrase.

As impressive as structure and diction are in Crane's sentence, its sound effects contribute even more to its effectiveness. These sound effects fall into two major classes: movement, or rhythm, and texture. As indicated in the "Glossary of Poetic Terms" (pages 700–04), rhythm is to some degree influenced by pause, pitch, and syllabic length. But rhythm is mainly established by the relationship of unaccented and accented syllables, or the comparative stresses a natural intonation would give the syllables. The rhythms of this sentence wed themselves to the sense or meaning of the idea. The sentence opens with a series of five anapests—unstressed syllable, unstressed syllable, stressed syllable. The five metric units—"was a tér/ri ble gráce/in the móve/of the wáves,/and they cáme"—simulate the repetitive motion of the body of waves.

The second section of the sentence switches to a more irregular pattern of stresses and hastens the tempo because in it Crane is calling attention to a different aspect of the waves, to their noisy, quick-breaking crests. The comma after "silence" signals a meaningful, lengthy pause in keeping with a wave's long gathering of force before it breaks.

In addition to rhythm a second kind of sound effect is involved in rhetoric. This is a relationship of sounds themselves apart from the rhythmic factors of stress, pitch, pause, and length. Texture, the product of this second kind of relationship, is largely a matter of playing upon the similarities or dissimilarities of sounds. The texture of a sentence is its combination of like and unlike sounds. Crane's sentence has a particularly successful texture. A significant part of its unity is produced by its use of two positive textural devices—the assonance, or repetition of the same vowel sound, in the long *a* of "grace," "waves," "they," "came," and "save"; and the alliteration, or repetition of the same initial sound in stressed syllables, in the *s* of "silence," "save," and "snarling" and in the *k* sound of "came" and "crests." The assonance also makes euphonious, or pleasant-sounding, the section of the sentence in which it occurs. The euphony, like the rhythm, is appropriate to the sense of that section. But, again like the rhythm, the euphony is abandoned in the phrase "the snarling of the crests" in favor of a combination of harsh sounds, or cacophony, that parallels the unpleasant character of the crests. Another important textural device here is the onomatopoeia in "snarling," a word formed in imitation of the action it names, which is vividly image-creating as well as harsh. Finally, this sentence is full of sibilants; the words "was," "grace," "waves," "silence," "save," "snarling," and "crests" have a hissing sound. This sibilance is in tune with the surge and swell of the sea.

The analysis of the rhetorical aspects of this sentence has been lengthy, but by no means exhaustive, for it has so far been categorical. No rhetorical analysis that stops with an examination of only the separate features of structure, diction, and sound can be complete. The fact that analysis deals with one matter at a time leads inevitably to the false impression that rhetoric consists of single features with individual, isolable effects. The reverse is true: all these features are blended and exert their influence simultaneously in a way that no analysis can convey very accurately. The most powerful single rhetorical consideration in any sentence is the degree of success it has in its overall integration of structure, diction, and sound.

The categorical analysis has, in passing, suggested that structure, diction, and sound reinforce one another. It is in order here to examine more pointedly some of the areas in which a structure is adapted to diction or sound, and vice versa.

Opening a sentence with "There was" is generally wasteful and tends to create a static effect. But Crane uses it not only to get a meaningful variation from parallel structure (as pointed out in the discussion of the structure of this sentence) but to launch the undulant movement that the series of anapests creates. This structure gets the proper rhythm under way more successfully than would "The waves had a terrible grace. . . ." Another adaptation involves choosing the less usual noun form "move" rather than "movement" so that the rhythm can continue uninterrupted.

Finally, the contrasts, or antitheses, in this sentence are so much a product of the blending of structure, diction, and rhythm that it is impossible to do them justice in categorical analysis. Some of the impact of the antithesis in the pivotal "terrible grace" comes from its early though not initial position. The antitheses between "grace" and "silence" and "snarling" are also sharpened by the placement of those terms. The second great climax of this sentence, "snarling of the crests," is accomplished by structure, diction, and sound. The structure puts it in the emphatic final position. Its diction is the most intensively concrete of the entire sentence, besides being figurative in the word "snarling." And its sound pattern varies in several respects from the norm set in the first four-fifths of the sentence. The rhythm

has been broken. An imitative sound word is used not only for the first time but as the first word in this unit. Cacophony is used for the first time, not only in "snarling," the first word of this unit, but in "crests," the last word in the sentence.

It is this integration, then, that accounts for the great impact of the sentence. The separate rhetorical devices are disguised in the easy, natural, conversational surface. The purpose of the sentence has been served with high distinction without calling attention to techniques. The whole art of rhetoric is, in fact, to keep attention on the idea conveyed, not on the way it is conveyed. To adorn or to leave the machinery exposed distracts, and distraction weakens the effect.

Is all the intricacy ascribed to Crane's sentence really there? Yes, and perhaps more. Then why is one not conscious of it as one reads "The Open Boat" and encounters that sentence? There are two or three answers: Any sentence of this length is intricate whether or not the composer or reader is aware of that intricacy. It is so inherent in the character of communication that we usually give no more thought to it than we do to the basic principles of the internal-combustion engine when we step on the accelerator. Second, this intricacy is not a superficial aggregation of tricks veneering a basic sentence. It *is* the sentence—from one point of view, a sentence no more distinctive than any other sentence with its particular combination (successful or not) of word meaning, sound, and structure. Crane drew his combination from a storehouse of techniques open to and used by all. That he drew a successful combination is part of the difference between him, one of the world's great writers, and those who have written nothing worthy of publication. Furthermore, most readers rarely pause to marvel at individual sentences; they quite properly move on to follow the story.

A related and perhaps more important question arises: Was Crane conscious of all the rhetorical features and effects ascribed to the sentence? Probably not. But we are on unsure ground here. The working manuscripts of many authors, particularly poets, indicate an astonishing number of trial versions both in sentences and even in the choice of single words. It seems somewhat presumptuous to insist that a great writer did not know what he was doing. It is doubtful that success is largely a matter of divine inspiration, that most effects are fortuitous. Probably the most satisfactory answer is that any artist as great as Crane reaches a stage in which his art operates on only a half-conscious level. He is aware of the comparative success or failure in the overall effect. If he is satisfied, he moves on. If he is dissatisfied, he stops for a conscious reconsideration and revision.

How hard should a beginning writer strain for effects? The answer is that he should always stop short of the appearance of strain. He doubtless should cultivate an awareness of effects and an understanding of how they are produced. In time his conscious attention will grow toward an unconscious, or only half-conscious, sensitivity that will result in more effective sentences.

Though the integration of all its devices determines the rhetorical effectiveness of a sentence, many sentences depend primarily for their effect upon some one striking feature of structure, diction, or sound. The writer who is making a conscious effort to improve the effectiveness of his sentences might best confine his attention for a while to the individual devices and effects. After he has gained reasonable facility with individual features, he will be in a better position to adapt and blend them in sentences that achieve rhetorical impact without strain or unnaturalness.

To help the writer gain this needed understanding of basic devices—what they are and for what effect they may be used—is the object of the remaining discussion of sentence rhetoric. In each of the sentences used as examples attention will be directed solely to the one device of structure, diction, or sound effects that seems the most striking feature of the given sentence, though other features of rhetorical consequence are, of course, actively present. Admittedly, this special attention to one device is justifiable only to the degree that clarifying the individual device will lead the writer to an overall improvement in sentence effectiveness.

Structure

The outstanding feature of the Biblical sentence "The wolf also shall dwell with the lamb, and the leopard shall lie down with the kid" is its *balance;* that is, the same grammatical construction is used in both independent clauses. This casting of ideas of the same rank into like grammatical constructions is called *parallelism.* The main distinction between the two terms is that balance refers to the more obvious and extended uses of parallel structure, especially to its use in the subject-verb-complement patterns in successive clauses. By repetition of the structure this sentence emphasizes that the ideas of the two clauses are basically the same; in fact, the two statements have one underlying idea: the time will come when peace will prevail.

Sometimes balance is used to mark a progression of ideas that pursues some natural relationship, such as past, present, and future time:

> One sees the past better than it was; one finds the present worse than it is; one hopes for a future happier than it will be.

Sometimes the balance depends upon the repetition of an "understood" basic pattern:

> But you shall never beat the fly from the candle though he burn, nor the quail from the hemlock though it be poison, nor the lover from the company of his lady though it be perilous.

Though the balanced sentence often secures emphasis for one idea by repeating variant wordings of it in the same grammatical pattern, it may work just as successfully for the emphasis of contrasting ideas. The contrast of ideas is actually sharpened by the likeness of the structures into which those ideas have been put:

> He prostrated himself in the dust before his Maker, but he set his boot upon the neck of his King.

Parallelism, of course, may be used in many varieties of less extensive structures:

The Townsends were in their Sunday best, fresh-scrubbed and uncomfortable.

But the quality of the imagination is to flow, and not to freeze.

The Puritans hated bear-baiting, not because it gave pain to the bear, but because it gave pleasure to the spectators.

A second important area of structure has to do not with the repetition of the grammatical pattern used but with the positioning of modifiers within the sentence. At one extreme is the *loose* sentence—one in which the modifiers tend to follow the main grammatical elements of subject, verb, and complement. At the other is the *periodic* sentence—one in which the modifiers are pushed forward so that the main grammatical elements appear immediately ahead of the period. These two sentences illustrate loose and periodic structures, respectively:

For Pope was merely repeating St. Thomas, who had written twenty volumes to reassure a world on the verge of doubt—twenty volumes to say that it was really right that things should be wrong. God only knows why.

And then, in the deep stillness of the desert air—unbroken by falling stream, or note of bird, or tramp of beast, or cry of man—came an eerie whisper.

In the first sentence, which is an example of the loose sentence normal to English, the modifiers containing the qualifying and explanatory details appear in what seems to be a natural grouping, as if they had been added as they came to the author's mind. This sentence could have been stopped at any one of three other places without producing a fragment; and yet it is, as it stands, a unified sentence. The modifiers at the end of most loose sentences—prepositional and verbal phrases, subordinate clauses—are needed for the full meaning of the sentence but unlike the verb, subject, or object, they are not absolutely essential. The loose sentence gives a casual and conversational flavor to writing, which is often highly desirable; certainly the term *loose* is not used in a disparaging sense.

The second sentence, like all other periodic sentences, is built on the principle of suspense. The words or phrases expressing the main idea are delayed until the end, or near the end, while the effect is prepared for by the addition of details—ideas, conditions, circumstances.

The effect of the periodic sentence, in serious composition, is to give weight and dignity; if the subject is light, it gives an impression of neatness and finish. But the use of the periodic sentence must be judicious. Since it is deliberately organized so as to place the focal point near the end, it, like the balanced sentence, seems artificial to many modern readers. It is best adapted to formal prose but may be used effectively in ordinary prose when some concentrated effect is desired.

There is, of course, no reason to strive to make either loose or periodic sentences dominant. One is just as amenable to artistic finish and effective use as the other. It is true, however, that, since most sentences are loose, an occasional periodic sentence, with the full meaning suspended until the end, is likely to give variety to a paragraph and to emphasize the idea expressed in it. It is especially true that an occasional periodic sentence is extremely attractive if it gets a periodic effect without being mechanically a true periodic sentence or if it gets some of its emphasis from brevity instead of depending upon a long build-up of initial modifiers:

The stars are the apexes of what triangles!

To the wounded heart, silence and shadow.

It should be noted that the deliberate fragmentation of the second sentence is appropriate to the sense of the sentence.

Diction

Most effective sentences use enough concrete words to establish an image in the reader's mind. This image may be the product of a single, exact, literal word or it may be the product of a combination of such words:

In his faded gray sweatshirt and his unpressed flannels and his grass-stained tennis shoes, he seemed like an intellectual oarsman.

This is not to say that abstract and general words have no place. They also serve a purpose. In the following sentence the idea is illuminated by image-creating words, but it is first stated, fittingly enough, as a principle expressed in abstract and general terms. The writer, probably a foreign observer, cannily wishes to remain somewhat vague as to what qualities constitute prettiness and charm. He is willing only to put the reader on the right track with the hint incorporated in the concretely worded addition to his general statement:

> American girls are pretty and charming—little oases of pretty unreasonableness in a vast desert of practical common sense.

As we have mentioned earlier a sentence may contain a "pivot" or "key" expression—a word or word cluster which carries the main force of the idea. Such expressions are often memorable and deft, sometimes almost summaries. They are usually, though not always, image-producing. They often are figurative but are not necessarily so.

> The poet was a *rag of a man*—dark, little, and lean, with hollow cheeks and thin black locks.

> Words, as is well known, are the great *foes of reality*.

> Marriage is the first *refuge of mediocrity*.

Many sentences achieve their effectiveness through use of a revealing figure of speech. The figure may reside in a single word, as in the first example below. Or it may run throughout the sentence with attention to it reinforced by words that develop it further, as in the second example.

> The heart of man is by turns a sanctuary and a cesspool.

> I can reason or deny everything, except this perpetual belly; feed he must and will, and I cannot make him respectable.

Not infrequently the figure creates a contrast—an antithesis—as it does in the two preceding sentences and as it does in the opposing words "satellite" and "system" in this sentence:

> I had better never see a book than to be warped by its attraction clean out of my own orbit, and made a satellite instead of a system.

Figures that are sustained are especially communicative. Their development in further terms brings into view more aspects of the likeness of the two things compared. But the images created by the figure must be consistent and unmixed. A writer must avoid a mixing or shifting of images that will result in obscurity or amusement. In the following three sentences the figures should have been sustained consistently or the writer should have abandoned figurative language in favor of literal language:

> It leapt and ran in the first act, walked in the second, and in the third was insufferably tedious.

> The Red Herrings our Democratic leaders scoffed at are now coming home to roost.

> Like a big cat the right end struck while the iron was hot and chopped the passer down for a twelve-yard loss.

Sound Effects

The movement—the rhythm and tempo—and the texture of a sentence greatly influence its overall effect. It is in the nature of language that the reader's inward ear hears, at least unconsciously, the patterning the sounds would take if the words were read aloud. Stresses, tempos, repetition of similar sounds, and other devices can be manipulated to serve two main purposes. They can be made to indicate the emphases the writer desires and they can be varied to support the sense or meaning. The rhythm of each of these two passages serves both purposes.

> In the stillness of the air every tree, every leaf, every bough, every tendril of creeper and every petal of minute blossoms seemed to have been bewitched into an immobility perfect and final.

> He [the captain] must have seen it all up in the bridge. He must have known what it was about when she the [wrecked ship] settled. I wonder how fast she made it. I wonder if the mate was there with him. Do you think the

mate was there with him? Do you think they stayed inside the bridge or do you think they took it outside? They never found any bodies. Not a one. Nobody floating.

Since rhythm is not obvious to the eye, the lack of appropriate rhythm often goes undetected by the beginning writer unless he reads his sentence aloud. An oral reading of the following sentence reveals that it is unfortunate in two respects. It has a rhythm that sing-songs its way past meaning, and, even more obvious, its rimes distract attention from its meaning.

That hope is today either shattered or put away in storage against a better day.

The texture of a sentence, that is, the qualities of its sounds apart from stress and tempo, may likewise create emphases and reinforce meaning. In addition, some textural devices tend to unify a sentence. For example, in the following sentence the assonance in the *i* in the accented syllables and in the *a* of "penetrating" and "entangled" subtly intensifies and unifies the statement:

Wit is the gift of penetrating things without becoming entangled in them.

This next sentence couples assonance with onomatopoeic words to achieve its success:

The churned-up water frothed alongside with a confused murmur.

Onomatopoeia, assonance, and the numerous liquid and nasal sounds of the following sentence support its sense well:

He was lulled by the hum and buzz of the summer afternoon.

Both of the immediately preceding sentences are composed of sounds easy to make and pleasant to hear, for euphony is in keeping with the simplicity of the ideas. But sometimes the idea is gnarled and intricate. If such is the case, the sound pattern may appropriately be made harsh and dissonant by the use of consonant combinations that cause strain in pronunciation and therefore a slowing down or irregularity of rhythm:

But love cannot make smart
Again this year his heart
Who no heart hath.

Indiscriminate euphonies and cacophonies should of course be avoided.

All the devices of internal, partial rime—assonance, consonance, alliteration—should be used judiciously in prose, for prose seems unnatural if its sound effects are closely and tightly patterned. Alliteration especially seems to be overattractive to beginning writers. Any such sentence as "The car skidded, slid, and slammed across the sleety surface of the street onto the sidewalk" calls entirely too much amused attention to its choice of words and therefore jeopardizes its meaning.

Writing Lessons

CONTENTS

A PREFATORY NOTE

This series of exercises confronts the student with problems characteristic of each of the forms of discourse. Each exercise is a self-contained unit. Each defines a limited number of objectives and offers suggestions for achieving them. The lessons progress loosely from the elementary to the more complex. Many are designed to give the student guided practice in mixing forms of discourse. Overall, they form a skeletal program for a first-year college composition course. It is assumed that the instructor will supplement and adapt the individual lessons according to the needs of his particular class.

LESSON 1

The Autobiographical Sketch

In many colleges and universities the first assignment given the student in freshman English is to write an autobiographical sketch. Writing is a highly personal activity; this autobiographical essay, then, serves to introduce the student to his instructor.

A well-written autobiographical essay should not be a chronological listing of facts. Rather, it should emphasize the student's interests, the meaningful experiences that he has had, the influences that have molded his thinking and his personality, and the incidents that may have changed the course of his life. The student's main problem is selecting the significant forces in his life and finding a suitable organizational pattern.

Assignment: Write a 600–800-word autobiographical essay in which you discuss several of the controlling forces in your life.

One of the first things to do is to list the influences that you believe have had the most profound impact upon your development. First, list these without organizing them. Then rank the influences in order of importance, using the rankings as the basis for a logical outline. Discover whether travel, the influence of a parent or friend, some prevailing interests or hobby, an incident in your life, or some reading you have done has made a deep impression upon you. When you have decided which three or four influences were strongest, you will be able to limit your material more easily. In the opening paragraph explain how and why you selected these particular influences. In the body of the essay treat each of them in a well-developed paragraph. In the concluding sections you may wish to mention briefly other forces that have influenced your development but that did not fit your essay's pattern of organization. But keep the emphasis upon rounding out—possibly summarizing—those you have discussed. A good ending to any essay, even an autobiographical one, must achieve a sense of finality and completeness. The reader must feel that you have said what you intended to say and that you have finished.

This essay may well give your instructor his first impression of you as a person and as a writer. You should therefore write it with as attractive a style as you can and proofread it carefully for possible errors in spelling, punctuation, grammar, and diction.

LESSON 2

The Parts of an Essay

An essay must be a unified composition containing a beginning, a middle, and an end. The beginning, or introductory, paragraph establishes a kind of contract with the reader by telling him what he can expect from the essay. It prepares him to think about the central idea or thesis. The writer of an essay must always introduce the reader to the particular treatment its topic will receive. The middle of the essay is a detailed discussion of the parts or subdivisions of the central idea. The main paragraphs, considered together, should enable the reader to understand the validity of the central idea.

Assume, for instance, that the central idea for an essay is this sentence: "The age for voting should be lowered to eighteen because that is more defensible as an age for voting than is twenty-one." Then assume that the topic sentences of the three main paragraphs are these: (1) "The eighteen-year-old may own property, must serve in the armed forces if he is physically fit, and must pay taxes on income that he earns"; (2) "He is now permitted to vote in some states, and some very prominent persons in public affairs have urged that he be allowed to vote in all states"; and (3) "He is better educated and more widely informed today, because of the great advances in public education, than was a twenty-one-year-old several generations ago." Each of these sentences, elaborated upon in a well-planned paragraph, would give the reader sufficient evidence to judge the validity of the central idea in the introductory paragraph.

The final paragraph should either summarize the main paragraphs and echo the central idea or state the writer's specific conclusion and urge acceptance of his thesis. In some instances the final paragraph, in addition to giving a conclusion, may include a proposal for a course of action. Whatever type of final paragraph is needed, the writer must remember that a reader relies heavily on the first and last paragraphs to help him understand and remember the essay. A final paragraph based on the central idea and topic sentences used as examples above must state a specific conclusion and suggest a course of action. If the central idea had not been argumentative, the writer could have used a summary paragraph rather than one presenting a conclusion.

Assignment: Compose a sentence containing the central idea for an argumentative essay. Write the introductory paragraph, giving close attention to what the reader will need to know at the outset to follow the arguments in the main paragraphs. Make a two-level sentence outline to show what the main paragraphs will contain, but do not compose the paragraphs. Use this form:

FIRST MAIN PARAGRAPH
   I. Topic Sentence
     A.
     B.
     C.

SECOND MAIN PARAGRAPH
  II. Topic Sentence
     A.
     B.
     C.

THIRD MAIN PARAGRAPH
 III. Topic Sentence
     A.
     B.
     C.

The sentence outline of these paragraphs should show their content clearly. Compose a final paragraph which states the specific conclusion you wish to be drawn from the evidence given and which asks the reader to follow a course of action that you recommend.

This assignment is designed to emphasize the essential organization of the essay and the importance of carefully written opening and closing paragraphs. It is suggested that you concentrate on writing the introductory and concluding paragraphs and that you submit a sentence outline only to show what the body of the essay will contain.

LESSON 3

The Process Essay

One basic kind of writing is that which explains how something is accomplished. There is much need in our time for detailed explanation of processes. Such writing is a primary source of information for many readers, and any magazine that advertises do-it-yourself articles on its front cover will be widely read. Students often have to write essays and answer questions on examinations that require skill at setting down the method by which something is created. Process writing ranges from directions for assembling the Christmas toy to technical manuals that translate the scientist's knowledge into the foreman's terms so that rockets can be launched.

Assignment: Select a process. You might best choose one with which you are familiar. Analyze it into its parts or steps to see how one would proceed if one were learning the process. Determine what happens from step to step and why it happens. Write a 600-word paper giving in detail the steps in the process and an explanation of each step.

In the introductory paragraph tell what is to be produced or accomplished, why one might want to know about the process, and what tools or materials are needed. Allot one main paragraph for each of the steps. If there are many intricate steps, you will need to group several related steps so that they can be treated together in one paragraph. In the last paragraph summarize the steps and make a final comment on the process.

This essay may be centered on any process by which a product is made or a result effected—for example, the process by which a swimming pool is built or one's spelling is improved. The process need not be a current one or one you know well. If you were to take time to do some careful research, you might, for instance, write about how the pyramids were built or how a bill is dealt with in your state legislature. Be sure your essay will interest and inform the reader. Do not select a process which is likely to be common knowledge.

LESSON 4

The Expository Narrative

One of the most frequently used patterns in communication is to begin with a long, illustrative story and to follow with an explanation of its meaning. If George Orwell had omitted the first two paragraphs and the first two sentences of the third paragraph of "Shooting an Elephant" (pages 167–71), his essay would be a pure example of this pattern.

Assignment: Write a paper, about 800 words long, in which you begin with a fully developed incident. Present it dramatically, using a little dialogue and giving particular, concrete details of action and scene. Then explain the significance of this incident.

This composition has two main objectives. First, you are to try to make the story interesting in and of itself, at the same time selecting or designing it for the purpose of the explanation which will follow. Second, you are to try to generalize skillfully from the one specific instance that your story provides.

The major problem of organization has been solved for you by the terms of the assignment itself. Your paper will have two clear-cut sections, one narrative and one expository. What, then, are the problems?

First, what kind of incident should you select? Examine your own experience and draw from it an actual incident (actual at least in its basic outline) in which you took part or which you observed and from which you learned a valuable lesson. That lesson could be an insight into character—your own or another person's. It could be a discovery of the true nature or effect of some social phenomenon. It could be anything that made you see a situation with new eyes and caused you to reconsider your values or standards.

Second, your narrative must have enough circumstantiality to give it interest but also enough selectivity or focus to enable it to serve its larger purpose as the basis of your explanatory generalization. You will have to state that generalization for yourself before you begin; otherwise, you will have no principle for selecting the details you will use to develop your story. Do as Orwell does in "Shooting an Elephant." His generalization, or central idea—when he had to shoot a valuable, innocent elephant to "save face," he learned that imperialism corrupts the imperialist as well as the subjugated—caused him to emphasize by use of rich detail the pressure exerted upon him by the hostile crowd of natives. In this same way, you must select details that directly or indirectly support your generalization.

A further problem may arise. Should the opening narrative contain any explanatory or interpretive comments? The answer is "No." Keep the narrative pure. Make it a story that is interesting in and of itself, independent of the purpose to which you will put it. The significance of some of your narrative details may not be grasped by the reader until he reads your explanation. But, since a large part of your job here is to write narrative that will give the reader vicarious experience, do not risk turning his attention to direct information in this section.

There are, of course, other organizational patterns for presenting these same materials. If your instructor prefers, you can use one of the following patterns:

1. You can open and close with exposition, inserting your illustrative narrative in the middle.

2. You can interweave your explanatory comment throughout the narrative as you unfold the story.

3. You can use narrative throughout and suggest the underlying generalization only by the indirect means of choosing details that

point toward it and of using highly implicative language. Well done, this method would result in a short story.

Presenting Character—The Use of Incident

Both the expository and the narrative writer depend heavily upon character presentation. In any explanation of a human situation the writer must be able to identify and make clear the human traits that are basic in creating or perpetuating that situation. For example, in the first paragraph of "The Black Beach" (page 326), Archie Carr indicates that he wishes to explain why Mrs. Ybarra left a deep impression upon him. To do so he must present the traits that made her impressive to him; thus he is using characterization to support explanation.

Assignment: In a 500–800-word composition explain a situation primarily in terms of the human character traits that have created it. Present the traits in action. Take as a model paragraphs 15–108 of "The Black Beach" (from "Mrs. Ybarra no doubt took . . ." on page 328 through "'Adios, pues,' she said" on page 331).

Let us assume that you have chosen as your title, "I've Got to Reform My Roommate." (You may choose a parallel topic, or your instructor may assign one.)

What are some of the main problems?

First, you must limit your subject. Keep clearly in mind that you are to explain why you do not get along well with your roommate. You think the explanation lies in certain things about him. If so, your job is to make those things clear to your reader.

Why is it that you do not get along well with him?

"Well," you say, "he has traits that I don't like: he's irresponsible; he's opinionated; he's snobbish; he's noisy; he's pessimistic; he's . . ." Exactly. And this is your subject— these traits that you don't like, the ones that cause you trouble. Forget about those traits

you do like. Furthermore, for the purpose of this paper, forget all but two or three of his most troublesome traits. (You haven't a week to spend writing this paper. Even if you had, the reader mightn't have an hour to spend reading it. And, anyway, Joe really isn't so snobbish, come to think of it—he has never objected to having you as a roommate.)

If you are inclined to feel that you must deal with all the little areas of difficulty between you and your roommate, note that Archie Carr contents himself with presenting only those characteristics of Mrs. Ybarra that manifested themselves to him in his one brief encounter with her.

At this stage express the substance of your proposed paper in one sentence: "My trouble with my roommate lies in his being an irresponsible, pessimistic, and opinionated person." In this sentence—a statement of your central idea—you have limited your subject to significant matters and established the major divisions of your discussion.

Your second problem is to determine an effective method of developing your materials.

Stop and think for a minute. How did you discover that, for example, Joe is irresponsible?

Let's see, there was that time he forgot and left your scooter parked overnight in front of the Empress Theatre and made you late to class the next morning, and you were lucky that it wasn't stolen. That just goes to show you, doesn't it?

Yes. It showed you. It shows me. It will show any reader.

In fact, you would never have discovered Joe's irresponsibility if he hadn't demonstrated it in some specific act. It is doubtful that you would have been much disturbed by Joe's having some inward trait that never manifested itself in any overt way. It follows that your reader may not recognize, much less be concerned about, Joe's irresponsibility unless you give him some telling instance of it.

The use of action is perhaps, for common purposes, the most effective way to present character (and therefore to present a situation that rests upon the traits of some person) because this method tends to compel understanding and belief. There is no doubt in the reader's mind, not even a subconscious doubt, that the character actually has the traits he displays.

Verify the promised effectiveness of this method by reinspecting Carr's presentation of Mrs. Ybarra's good humor. Carr does not say that she had a sense of humor; he demonstrates it in a specific incident.

This is to be your method here. Recall the most convincing and interesting incident that illustrates each of the character defects you charge Joe with having. Then, episode by episode, present each trait at work in a lively story that has a minimum of direct analysis of the trait.

Finally, how should you begin? Since your basic purpose in this paper is to explain a situation, you probably should open with direct statements that indicate the seriousness of the situation. If you are on the point of punching Joe in the eye or of moving out, say so. You may then state your central idea and plunge without delay into your presentation of an incident that exemplifies in action one of Joe's major defects.

LESSON 6

Classification

Some of your writing, especially in reports and on examinations, will require you to study a body of information, classify it, and draw conclusions which can then be supported by specific facts and figures.

Assignment: Write a paper of 600 or more words, in which you use as the central idea one of the conclusions you arrive at after an analysis of the data in the table Public School Expenditures and Per Capita Income (pages 770–71). This assignment has two main objectives: (1) to give you practice in analyzing and interpreting a set of data and (2) to give you an opportunity to report in writing some of your findings and their meaning to you.

In making an analysis begin by putting each of the four columns of figures in order by rank and state from 1st to 50th. Then link each state from column to column to see where it stands in one column in relation to its standing in each other column. As you manipulate the states and their figures in various ways, you will begin to arrive at some tentative conclusions suggested by the rankings. Continue the analysis by comparing the figures for each state (or groups of states by region) with the national average given at the top of the table. In addition, reflect on the following figures, which show total amounts spent in the United States for various purposes and the lowest, average, and highest expenditures per pupil from the chart:

	1960–61	1965–66
Expenditure for public schools (percentage of national wealth: 3%–4%)	$15 billion	$25 billion
Military defense	47 billion	60 billion
Recreation	17 billion	26 billion
Automobiles	30 billion	60 billion
Alcohol and tobacco	15 billion	20 billion
Lowest expenditure per pupil	$217	$317
Average expenditure per pupil	$390	$532
Highest expenditure per pupil	$585	$876

After you have studied the table carefully, comparing and classifying the data in many ways, select one of the most striking conclusions you have reached and use it as the central idea for your paper. List three or four statements that will give adequate support to your main conclusion. Then from the table and from other sources (the library will have more recent data than the table provides) select specific facts and figures that will give your reader detailed evidence that your conclusion is valid. *Assume that your reader has no access to the table of data or to other specific information.* That is, repeat the information; do not refer your reader to your sources.

Public School Expenditures and Per Capita Income

	Expenditure Per Pupil 1965–66	Income Per Capita 1965	Percentage of Personal Income Spent 1965–66	Increase in Expenditure Per Pupil 1960–61 and 1965–66
UNITED STATES [National Average]	$532	$2,724	4.8%	36.4%
Alabama	355 (48)	1,910 (47)	4.8 (26)	63.1 (1)
Alaska	775 (2)	3,375 (2)	5.5 (15)	34.0 (31)
Arizona	514 (23)	2,310 (35)	5.8 (8)	31.7 (37)
Arkansas	376 (44)	1,781 (49)	5.5 (15)	55.3 (8)
California	582 (7)	3,196 (8)	5.8 (8)	17.8 (50)
Colorado	513 (24)	2,706 (19)	6.6 (4)	26.0 (45)
Connecticut	637 (4)	3,390 (1)	3.9 (47)	51.6 (10)
Delaware	580 (8)	3,335 (3)	4.7 (31)	26.0 (45)
Florida	439 (37)	2,420 (28)	5.1 (21)	41.6 (16)
Georgia	384 (42)	2,156 (40)	4.5 (34)	62.7 (2)
Hawaii	515 (22)	2,906 (12)	4.9 (24)	34.3 (29)
Idaho	400 (41)	2,338 (34)	4.8 (26)	40.3 (17)
Illinois	591 (6)	3,245 (5)	3.9 (47)	29.3 (41)
Indiana	512 (25)	2,827 (14)	4.5 (34)	37.3 (21)
Iowa	548 (18)	2,595 (24)	5.5 (15)	37.0 (22)
Kansas	511 (26)	2,692 (20)	4.7 (31)	33.0 (33)
Kentucky	375 (45)	2,043 (43)	4.2 (42)	36.3 (24)
Louisiana	481 (31)	2,061 (41)	5.6 (13)	30.0 (39)
Maine	410 (40)	2,245 (37)	4.8 (26)	25.7 (47)
Maryland	552 (16)	3,014 (10)	7.5 (2)	33.0 (33)
Massachusetts	530 (19)	3,023 (9)	3.5 (49)	28.3 (44)
Michigan	523 (21)	3,009 (11)	5.0 (23)	23.3 (48)
Minnesota	577 (10)	2,625 (23)	5.8 (8)	39.0 (19)
Mississippi	317 (50)	1,566 (50)	5.6 (13)	40.2 (18)
Missouri	485 (30)	2,628 (22)	4.0 (45)	28.3 (44)
Montana	567 (13)	2,409 (29)	6.0 (7)	32.7 (35)
Nebraska	419 (39)	2,573 (25)	4.3 (40)	30.9 (38)
Nevada	528 (20)	3,289 (4)	4.2 (42)	57.3 (6)
New Hampshire	479 (33)	2,570 (26)	4.5 (34)	31.9 (36)
New Jersey	662 (3)	3,242 (6)	4.3 (40)	29.2 (43)
New Mexico	578 (9)	2,227 (39)	7.61 (1)	58.3 (3)
New York	876 (1)	3,242 (6)	5.2 (20)	49.9 (12)
North Carolina	379 (43)	2,028 (44)	4.1 (44)	57.9 (5)
North Dakota	460 (34)	2,304 (36)	5.4 (19)	33.3 (32)
Ohio	503 (29)	2,816 (16)	4.5 (34)	29.6 (40)
Oklahoma	481 (31)	2,236 (38)	5.5 (15)	50.3 (11)
Oregon	612 (5)	2,794 (17)	5.8 (8)	36.6 (23)
Pennsylvania	565 (14)	2,728 (18)	4.0 (45)	34.1 (30)
Rhode Island	576 (11)	2,817 (15)	3.5 (49)	38.1 (20)

Public School Expenditures and Per Capita Income—Continued

	Expenditure Per Pupil 1965–66	Income Per Capita 1965	Percentage of Personal Income Spent 1965–66	Increase in Expenditure Per Pupil 1960–61 and 1965–66
UNITED STATES [National Average]	$532	$2,724	4.8%	36.4%
South Carolina	349 (49)	1,838 (48)	5.1 (21)	56.5 (7)
South Dakota	504 (28)	2,055 (42)	6.2 (5)	44.0 (14)
Tennessee	361 (47)	1,992 (46)	4.6 (33)	58.3 (3)
Texas	449 (36)	2,346 (31)	4.9 (24)	36.0 (27)
Utah	459 (35)	2,340 (32)	7.5 (2)	35.0 (28)
Vermont	507 (27)	2,340 (32)	4.8 (26)	49.5 (13)
Virginia	424 (38)	2,392 (30)	4.4 (38)	54.1 (9)
Washington	556 (15)	2,864 (13)	5.7 (12)	29.3 (41)
West Virginia	367 (46)	2,007 (45)	4.4 (38)	43.9 (15)
Wisconsin	575 (12)	2,682 (21)	4.8 (26)	36.2 (26)
Wyoming	551 (17)	2,479 (27)	6.2 (5)	21.3 (49)

LESSON 7

Evaluating Written Composition

In most composition courses the student is expected to proofread his papers before he submits them and may be expected to revise them in part or in full after his instructor's evaluation. But often, because of the other demands upon the student and upon class time, these efforts are random and thus less effectual than they could be. The chief problems of composition recur, and practice in solving them can be gained in each new composition attempted. But unless the student has developed the ability to evaluate and criticize his own work he will not know what his problems are. Developing this ability is primarily a matter of learning the approach that a reader would take. If a writer can reliably spot in the first drafts of his paper the questions a reader would be apt to ask, he can probably eliminate those difficulties from his finished paper.

A good way to discover the questions a reader would ask is to be the reader in real situations. In many composition classrooms students are occasionally asked to read and discuss a classmate's paper. But for the discussion to have value for the group, all students must read the same paper, and, for them to do so conveniently, many copies of the paper have to be made. This lesson is intended to give the class, in convenient form, the materials needed for an evaluation project. It should help the student develop a systematic approach to revisions of his own work. It should enlarge his critical sense in general and should have some carry-over value in all his reading. In addition, it should give him valuable insight into the nature of his instructor's job and perhaps help him see many matters not as deficiencies in his instructor but as difficulties inherent in the complex task of criticism.

Assignment: Using the following student theme and the rating sheet on pages 773–74, evaluate the theme, assign a letter grade, and be prepared to defend your judgments. Using the same system your instructor employs to designate errors in your compositions, point out the errors in this student's theme. At your instructor's discretion, rewrite the paper to avoid or correct its weaknesses.

The paper reproduced below is an actual theme submitted by a freshman. Paragraph numbers have been added for easier identification of features that call for discussion.

HER ROYAL HIGHNESS: MRS. JONES

1. In this beloved country, that hates tyranny so much, there is a tyrant who demands and is getting the devotion and attention of a large segment of our people. The name of the dictator is "Mrs. Jones" and many frustrated women bend their knees to her demands. She is the gauge of social success and we have placed social success as an imperative to mortal life.

2. There are many possibilities for the existence of this peculiar sense of values that have been adopted by our culture. One of the most probable is our general gullibility in response to advertising via the many mass media we are continually exposed to. This competitive economy we have established in our country by mass production has stimulated the role of the advertising profession in the business world. The advertiser in turn must create markets and prospects for the increased production. This has lead to even creating false markets and the establishment of apparent needs in individuals, families and societies, where need actually did not exist. We have, in turn, geared our ideals of success and accomplishment to equal or excel "Mrs. Jones." We are then, subjecting ourselves to the will of a monster that has no apparent sense of appeasement and an ungodly appetite.

3. In a news release this past week, it was noted that men, not women, are the largest consumers of perfumes and deodorants in this nation. And, it wouldn't be surprising to find that perhaps daddy likes to be seen in a new car; rejuventated and reduced, as much as mother. However, whoever is actually the victim, male or female, the problem exist that we do maintain a warped sense of success and value.

4. There are many ramifications concerning the inevitable results of such devotion to "Mrs. Jones." One bearing comment upon being the effect on our new generations. It seems that we are developing in them too much of a realism that the only things that are really important are sensual things. We are to judge Mrs. Jones by what she appears to be, her dress, her brand of cigarettes, the way she holds her liquor, her home (physical and not moral or spiritual) her automobile and where she holds her club memberships. We want our children to be social successes. They must attend college and here success is dependent upon which fraternity or sorority makes them a bid, and whether or not their adopted chums come from the right social stock.

5. It is not confined to the upper or middle brackets of society; this keeping up with "Mrs. Jones." Finance Companies and banks get rich from all most everyone's futile attempt at being modern. Here is where it really hurts. When people allow themselves to become over-committed in their finances, the results can be unhappy and even broken homes.

6. The only real and permanent solution must be a return to what is truly worthwhile in this life. A little review and perhaps an inspection tour down our individual "department of the interior." We would have to admit that the

real, lasting values are the unseeable, untouchable, undefinable, spiritual developments in our ethics; This is the true barometer with which we should judge ourselves and others. It would caste out all kinds of prejudices and make "Mrs. Jones" take on a new sense of social correctness.

A TYPICAL RATING SHEET FOR FRESHMAN COMPOSITION

	A	B	C	D	E
ORGANIZATION					

Central idea or purpose made clear
Approach or procedure made clear
Order appropriate to material and purpose
Management of transitions
Beginning and ending appropriate
Paragraph—unity and coherence
Meaningful proportions

	A	B	C	D	E
CONTENT					

Commonplace topic or treatment of topic
Level of discussion adapted to reader
Adequacy of development of supporting ideas
Emphasis by means other than flat statement
Factual accuracy
Management of source materials
Relevance

	A	B	C	D	E
MECHANICS					

Capitalization, abbreviations, numbers, italics, manuscript form
Punctuation other than that of compound sentence
Spelling and syllabication
Agreement and reference
Tense
Case

	A	B	C	D	E
SENTENCE STRUCTURE					

Punctuation of compound sentence
Fragmentation
Management of modifiers
Subordination
Obscurity/point of view
Parallelism
Variety and emphasis

DICTION

Gross errors
Exactness
Wordiness
Level of usage appropriate and consistent
Idiom

TOTAL EVALUATION

LESSON 8

The Interpretive or Critical Essay

An essay may interpret or criticize the idea contained in a quotation. If the writer is to interpret a quotation, he will choose to write an expository essay. However, if he wishes to be critical, the essay will probably take the form of argument. Tests and essay examinations frequently require the composing of this kind of interpretive or critical essay. Sometimes the treatment is indicated, but often the writer must decide what form he will use. Experience with this writing problem can prepare a writer to work simply but effectively when time is an important factor.

Assignment: Choose one of the following quotations (or one from another selection that you have read) and write a 500-word essay.

1. "If I had to choose between betraying my country and betraying my friend, I hope I should have the guts to betray my country." (Forster, "What I Believe")
2. "It is modern man, *Homo sapiens,* 'the wise' as he styles himself, who is now the secret nightmare of man." (Eiseley, "An Evolutionist Looks at Modern Man")
3. "Every age, they say, has its special bit of nonsense." (Cary, "The Mass Mind: Our Favorite Folly")
4. "Television turns reality into news; writers make news into reality." (Judith Wheeler, "The Electronic Age")
5. "Little by little, however we dislike it, we are forced to the conclusion that what our senses tell us is only an interpretation." (Strong, "The Poetic Approach to Reality")

6. "At its best education is a series of private conversations . . ." (Taylor, "The Private World of the Man with a Book")

After selecting the quotation to use as the central idea or thesis for your paper, underline the key words that must be considered. Then decide whether you will organize an expository or argumentative paper. You will want in either case to compose an introductory paragraph that gives the quotation or paraphrases it, three or four main paragraphs, and a final paragraph that either summarizes or states a conclusion. From the quotation you must derive three or four statements to serve as topic sentences for the main paragraphs.

Assume, for example, that the quotation given you said, "Civilization is only a thin coat which sometimes clothes man's barbarism." Probably you would almost immediately agree or disagree. If you agreed you would want to reinforce the validity of the generalization with evidence that occurs to you. One possible way of organizing your written reply would be to plan three paragraphs—one on war, one on crime, and one on prejudice—which would show that man's barbarism was still easily discernible. If you disagreed you would want to marshal evidence to disprove the statement. You might possibly compose three paragraphs that would show that education, humanitarianism, and democratic ideas are so prevalent that man is clearly removed from savagery. Bear in mind that any quotation will allow many interpretations. Your interpretation, reaction, and experience will govern the treatment you give. The main concern in an assignment of this kind is that the quotation serve as a springboard to a well-composed essay.

LESSON 9

Persuasion

The presentation of a well-supported point of view on a controversial topic is an important kind of basic writing. The purpose of the argumentative paper is to persuade the reader to accept a point of view by presenting convincing reasons. Too often the oral expression of support for one side of an issue is built on emotional reaction rather than on valid evidence. However, expressing one's point of view in writing requires thinking about one's arguments and the reasons for them. Careful analysis of the reasons for holding a point of view will show whether one's arguments need clarification or strengthening. For example, suppose the issue were whether there should be a reduction of federal income taxes without a reduction of federal spending. To begin, the issue being considered as a topic for a paper should be put into question form: "Should federal income taxes be reduced without a planned reduction in federal spending?" Both the writer and the reader can react to this statement with either "Yes" or "No." Once a side is taken, the reasons to support it and their order of importance as persuasive statements must be determined. Then the reasons that the opposing side may use must be considered. You must assume the possibility that your reader will oppose your ideas until you can convince him. Put the three or four most cogent reasons into sentences to be used as topic sentences for the main paragraphs.

Assignment: Write a 600-word essay expressing strong support for one side of a current controversial issue about which you have been talking, reading, and thinking. Choose a topic about which you have strong feeling or conviction.

Your opening paragraph should contain a statement of the issue and the point of view that you will take. Then carefully define the key terms in the question so that the reader may understand how they are used in your essay.

Before writing further list the main points you are going to develop, making certain that you have material that will sufficiently prove them. In argument or persuasion such as you are attempting, there must not be a loophole in the logic of your position. A weakness anywhere in an argument tends to invalidate the rest of the reasoning. In presenting your position, try to anticipate what reaction your reader may have so that you can try to confirm or refute his point before he raises it.

A statement of the issue and your point of view should be included in the introductory paragraph. A restatement of the issue and a strong conclusion should appear in the final paragraph.

LESSON 10

Cause and Effect

Writers often use the cause-and-effect relationship as the basis for essays. Much historical, biographical, scientific, and critical writing deals with the causes that produced certain effects or the effects that were the results of certain causes. The human mind searches for causal relationships; such searching is the center of scientific investigation.

If one asks "Why?" one wants to find the reasons for the existence of an effect and the reasons the effect is what it is. If one asks "What?" one wants to know the effect that will be produced by a certain set of causes. In determining causes one must be sure that the effect can clearly be traced back to the cause. Further, one must prove that that cause is really necessary to that effect. When you wrote an autobiographical essay you tried to show that certain strong influences (causes) in your life produced the person you now are (the effect). If you wrote about some of the ill effects that science and technology have had on contemporary society, you would attempt to show what causes produced those ill effects. A critical essay on a poem might center on the poem as the effect and attempt to show what techniques of language created it.

Assignment: Write a 600-word paper using cause and effect as the basis for your thinking and organization. Select an effect (a result, situation, product, or answer) whose direct causes you feel you can isolate.

In the introductory paragraph tell what the effect is, why you believe you can give the causes, and what your interest in the relationship is. Each cause or group of causes should be treated in one of the main paragraphs. The final paragraph should summarize the causes and explain generally why you feel you have provided valid evidence of the causal relationship.

Careful analysis and logical thinking are necessary to establish a justifiable relationship between cause and effect. Many times the relationship seems apparent, but on close examination the linking of a certain cause to an effect turns out to be inappropriate. Your choice of an effect to use for this paper seems limitless. Many of the courses you are taking are essentially concerned with cause and effect: psychology, history, economics, literature, linguistics, chemistry, physics, biology, and statistics, to name some. Every day is filled with a sequence of causes and effects. You should select an effect whose causes you are concerned about. It may be close to you—why you are in college—or further removed—what makes man want to land on the moon. The aim of this paper should be to derive and present accurate causes for an effect.

LESSON 11

Extended Definition

Since higher education is chiefly concerned with ideas, the student is expected to become increasingly familiar with abstractions and to move with increasing ease among them. He will be called upon in classroom recitations and in oral reports and written compositions to explain the meaning of such terms as *liberal education, universality, propaganda,*

obsolescence, and *nationalism.* In the usual freshman writing course the student may spend much of his time explaining the nature of abstract ideas that are a direct or indirect part of the content not only of his English course but of the other courses he is taking.

Ideas are abstract, intangible. They are unlike real, concrete objects. When a person is discussing a process, such as the building of a hi-fi cabinet, he has mental images to help him. With minimum word skill he can arouse those images in the mind of his reader. He can even use a sketch of a necessary tool, piece of material, or operation. Abstract ideas, however, cannot be so pictured. They are more difficult to deal with, for they have no exact combination of physical properties to which he can refer and orient himself and his reader.

Yet an abstraction is not fully explained until it has been given sufficient concreteness to enable readers to apply it in actual or theoretical situations.

Assignment: Write a 400–600-word extended definition of some abstraction assigned by your instructor or listed later in this exercise. Begin with the general and abstract idea and work through to a particular, concrete presentation of it. For the indirect help of models, read Edward Sapir's "Language Defined" (pages 10–19) and Susanne K. Langer's "The Language Line" (pages 20–24). Study the following brief explanation of the process of extending a definition.

You cannot explain an abstract idea until you know what that idea is. Therefore, begin with a central definition that, so far as it goes, is accurate.

Your initial definition, though accurate in general, is not likely to be self-sufficient. Your definition will contain some key terms that are themselves abstract or obscure. You will solve this difficulty only by extending the definition—that is, by doing two main things. You must analyze the idea, or break it into its essential elements. Then you will have to clarify each element by one or more of several methods. You may define it. You may compare it with or contrast it to similar but not identical elements with which it might be confused. You may give its causes and effects in a way that illuminates it. You may present it in examples or illustrations—an especially communicative way to clarify abstract material.

An extended definition, then, generally involves at least three methods of developing expository material: (1) definition; (2) classification or division; and (3) comparison and contrast, or cause and effect, or exemplification, or a combination of the three.

Subjects for extended definition: sportsmanship, liberal education, savoir-faire, conservatism, philanthropy, good citizenship, the public interest.

LESSON 12

Objective and Concrete Literary Description

Description is an extremely important supporting element in both explanatory and narrative writing. In exposition it is used for the businesslike purpose of making identifications. But even though the purpose is utilitarian, and intellectual understanding is the object, the avenue to that understanding is the play of the physical senses. The identification is made accurate by a procession of images. Literary description differs from expository description in two main respects. First, not content with giving merely identifying images, literary description intends to induce the full vicarious experience of confronting the thing described —the receiving and reacting simultaneously to its full battery of sensations. Second, literary description often attempts to create an attitude toward the thing described or a mood or atmosphere that will support the intention of the story to which the description is subordinated.

The basis of all effective description is the image stimulated by concrete words. One's first effort in descriptive writing should be to produce images. It should be to present the physical qualities of an object or scene in their proper emphases. The student should come to see that the attitude, mood, or atmosphere he wishes to induce can be reliably created by an objective presentation of the appropriate succession of physical images untainted by his inner feelings or state of mind. Oversimplified,

this means that an accumulation of concrete, objective phrases such as "gray skies," "chill drip of rain," and "motionless air" will do more to establish the gloominess of a day than will a corresponding number of abstract, subjective terms such as "gloomy," "dreary," and "depressing." Only after the student has gained considerable success in communicating objective images should he attempt subjective description, for there is grave danger that the amateur writer's subjectivity will reveal much more about the state of his soul at the time than it does of the character of the object it pretends to picture.

Assignment: Write a 500–800-word literary description that presents the main features of a scene in an orderly pattern and with proper emphases. Use objective, sensory language that will give readers a reliable and intense experience of the scene, not just an understanding of it.

A few observations about writing literary description may assist in the preparation of this assignment. First, the simpler or the more self-contained the scene chosen, the easier it will be to perceive and reproduce its main features. Do not attempt so large or complex a canvas that you will be led toward merely cataloguing a host of elements, many of which make no real contribution in that they would not attract the attention of even an alert observer.

Second, the more fixed your physical point of view, the easier it is to get the orderly pattern and proper emphases (perspective) desired. If this is your first serious attempt at description, you probably should describe a fixed scene from a fixed position in space. Also, select and maintain one point of view in time. Different qualities and strengths of light change the aspect of things, as any painter knows. Attempt to picture what you can "see" in one split instant of a stationary scene from some one stationary position.

Third, your vivid memory of the scene is often a more reliable guide to what you should picture than is a close reinspection and study of that scene pointedly directed at writing a description. The ingredients of effective description are the features of a scene that make themselves intensely felt without the observer's having to unearth them by some studied approach.

Next, keep yourself out of the picture. A reader expects to see the scene without having to push you from his line of vision. Avoid explaining how or why you got there. Do not directly refer to your movements. Furthermore, you are to assume that the reader is not interested in the state of your soul. Scrutinize your paper to be sure that it contains no avoidable subjectivity.

Use nouns and verbs and verbals. Do not depend too heavily upon modifiers. Modifiers are ineffective much of the time. Take a hint from paragraph 7 of Archie Carr's "The Black Beach." Note that Carr uses relatively few adjectives and adverbs.

Consider only the appearances of things, not their causes. The reader wants images, not explanations. Remember that in description the appearance is the thing. Do not distinguish between what the thing is and what it looks like. It is, for your purpose here, the thing it looks like and cannot be anything else. If a fist appears to be as big as a ham, call it a ham instead of saying that it seems to be as big as a ham.

Finally, use concrete words. No description can succeed without this foundation of concreteness. For example, create images as George Orwell does in his description of the native the elephant had trampled (page 169):

> This was the rainy season and the ground was soft, and his face had scored a trench a foot deep and a couple of yards long. He was lying on his belly with arms crucified and head sharply twisted to one side. His face was coated with mud, the eyes wide open, the teeth bared and grinning with an expression of unendurable agony. . . . The friction of the great beast's foot had stripped the skin from his back as neatly as one skins a rabbit.

LESSON 13

Description—Dominant Impression

Good description must go beyond the mere presentation of facts: it must interpret. If it is the description of a place, a scene, or a person, the details chosen must give a central, unified effect. Like all creative art, description, to be successful, must leave a dominant impression —it must reveal the outstanding attribute of the object: its odor, appearance, sound, taste, feeling, or some other quality. Poets make excellent use of this technique. For example, when Walter de la Mare wrote his poem "Silver," every image—"silver shoon," "silver fruit upon silver trees," "silvery thatch," "paws of silver," and many more—contributed to the impression of a silvery sheen. When Keats wished to create an atmosphere of bitter cold in "The Eve of St. Agnes," he used such details as these: "The owl, for all his feathers, was a-cold; / The hare limped trembling through the frozen grass, / And silent was the flock in woolly fold: / Numb were the Beadsman's fingers while he told / His rosary . . . ."

Every person or thing has some salient feature that distinguishes it from others like it. Successful description captures this uniqueness. The dominant impression may center in such qualities as ugliness or beauty, happiness or sorrow, movement or stillness, calm or tempest, or any one of innumerable other features.

Assignment: Choose one of the following central ideas and write a 400-word description, giving special attention to the creation of a dominant impression.

1. There was plenty of life here.
2. Mrs. Jones sat, enduring the winter.
3. Everything was deathly still.
4. She had the makings of a goddess.
5. There is no finer apple (orange, peach, etc.).
6. The captain's cabin was immaculate.
7. The heat was intense.
8. He had been on skid row too long.
9. He was all eyes.

You will, of course, need to choose both tangible and intangible characteristics to achieve the desired singleness of effect. Every detail must contribute to the total picture. Seek, then, to present a few vivid details rather than a large number of heterogeneous items, since too many images and details keep the reader from getting a unified impression.

If details are chosen well to produce a singleness of effect, unity will naturally follow. However, the organization, the arrangement of details, should be planned. You might start by giving the reader a whole impression and following with supporting details, or you might present the items in some order, such as near to far or far to near, or you might arrange them in some climactic order. Regardless of how you organize your selected details, they must produce one single, dominant impression.

LESSON 14

The Simple Narrative

A simple narrative is a story of a connected series of events which the writer himself experienced or has intimate, first-hand knowledge of. Its order is straightforward chronology. Its purpose is to afford the reader a vicarious experience.

Assignment: In 600–800 words write a narrative account of something that happened to you or that you observed closely in the life of an acquaintance. Use a factual basis, but feel free to depart from fact if fictional touches serve the purpose.

Your success with simple narrative will depend to a large extent upon how well you solve certain basic problems, such as those raised in the following paragraphs.

First, though the simple narrative is usually not rigidly plotted or artistically unified as some short stories are, you must select your material so that reader attention will be centered upon the one strand of interest you wish to develop. To select relevant material, you must first have defined rather exactly for yourself what that one strand is. If you intend to tell the story of your changing attitude in your senior year of high school toward the desirability of going to college, you will select a few events that present the growth of this new attitude and will omit all other events of that year, no matter how interesting they may have been. If you are going to relate the story of a friend's accident-proneness, you will present only events in which it figures. Only by the selection of pertinent material can you give your story unity and develop events in interesting detail.

Second, you should put the events you select into a meaningful progression. In the simple narrative, the writer follows chronology, but the events should be so presented that one leads logically to the next; that is, the causal connections should be made or suggested. In many cases you may need to use a direct transition, such as "On the very next day a similar situation arose."

Next, you should give these events proper proportions. Devote space and full development to each event according to the contribution it makes to the overall story. The more significant events should often be presented in scenes, and the less important ones should be given summary treatment.

Finally, a word on the related matters of conflict and completeness. The simple narrative does not necessarily demand emphatic conflict and great tension, but reader interest is much easier to maintain if you select events that represent some instability or that put at least mildly opposing forces into play. By making use of conflict, you afford yourself a beginning and end more satisfying than such common, mechanical ones as the start and close of a day or of a summer vacation. Even a mild conflict enables you to begin with the event in which that conflict came to light and to close with the event in which it was resolved.

LESSON 15

Presenting Character— Other Dramatic Methods

Though human character is perhaps best demonstrated by a person's actions, especially where the actions are also part of a story, many character sketches depend chiefly upon other methods of revealing character. The main purpose of the character sketch is to reveal the subject, independent of his actions.

Assignment: In 600–800 words write a character sketch using a combination of the methods of portraying character presented below. Do not use action prominently.

All the methods discussed here may contribute to an accurate and vivid picture of the subject if they are skillfully used. But some may communicate more penetrating insights than others, for some tend to deal with more superficial matters—matters more of appearance than of inner traits.

First, you may describe the person's physical features. Readers are interested in what a character looks like and try to get a visual image of him. But this method must be cautiously and sparingly used, for several reasons. Physical appearance is not a reliable index to character. There are some literary stereotypes—the brunette villain, the temperamental redhead, the aggressive runt, the jolly fat man. But most readers know that these are often misleading associations of physical features with character traits. Furthermore, you can describe a person in minute physical detail and still not really convey the desired impression of beauty, strength, or agility. If you are going to use physical description, you will achieve your best effects by confining yourself to physical features that affect your subject's inner qualities. Physical handicaps and blemishes or unusual physical charms often have psychological effects upon their possessor, effects that you can develop by other methods of character presentation. Second, present the physical features indirectly. It is more effective to say that your subject had a "rodent-like face" than to say he had a "receding chin." Whatever details of physical appearance you use should be made pertinent and congruous with the rest of your presentation and should be such that you can reinforce or develop them through your use of other devices.

Much more revealing than directly described items of physical appearance are certain little betraying physical mannerisms. Nailbiting, the fingering of a necktie or a necklace, the smacking of lips at the end of a statement, and the continual polishing of eyeglasses can be made to express something significant in terms of character.

Present the external circumstances of your subject's life. His occupation tells much about him. The properties a person surrounds himself with and spends his money and time on most truly signify what he is. What is the appearance or character of his home, dress, manners, and recreation? What is his family background? Who are his associates? What are his social and economic brackets?

Use dialogue. What a person says, especially in his natural, unguarded moments, does much to reveal what he is. Though people can and do mislead others by what they say, a substantial bit of speech generally betrays the real self: for example, study a dramatic monologue such as Browning's "Soliloquy of the Spanish Cloister" or "My Last Duchess." Do not overlook the significance of speech mannerisms. *How* something is said, as well as what is said, affords insight to the reader—the tune, as Mark Twain called it, as well as the words. What, for example, is your own reaction to the person who naturally says *buy* but then immediately changes it to *purchase?*

Show the reactions of other people to the person you are portraying. If these are demonstrated clearly to the reader, he can better detect and understand the traits of your subject that cause those reactions. Many of the famed beauties in literature are not physically described, but readers think of them as having extreme beauty because of the effects these women had on men. For instance, Helen launched a thousand ships and caused the burning of Troy, but we do not know whether she was blonde or brunette, much less her girth of chest or length of leg.

A final method of presenting character—one to be used most cautiously by beginning writers—is stream of consciousness. Expertly handled, a fifteen-second span of a person's private, uncensored, inner thoughts, the exact nature of which he himself is unconscious, is the most reliable indication of his true self. Readers know the main character (the narrator) in E. B. White's "The Door" (pages 118–21) because they are, by this stream-of-consciousness technique, let into his intimate thoughts and feelings. But if you attempt this technique, be careful not to leave contradictions that will confuse the reader, and be careful to preserve some kind of purposeful psychological continuity. This material has to be selected, unified, and made coherent, despite its surface appearance of fragmentation and lack of direction.

All these devices, including the presentation of action, can be pulled together in a scene. Combining makes them more effective and takes less space than if you used them piecemeal. Two or three skillful scenes may give the reader all he wishes or needs to know about your subject.

LESSON 16

Explication of a Poem

Perhaps the first step you should take toward fulfilling this assignment successfully is to reconsider the nature of the poetic experience. The poem does not lie in the printed, tangible, mechanical version that is presented on the page. The poem is the happening of what the poet intended to happen to you as a result of your reading it. If nothing happens, no poem exists as far as you are concerned. If the printed version merely sets you off into a welter of fuzzy ideas and uncontrolled emotions, you are not having a legitimate experience. The experience you have must be recognizably one that arises out of the organic union of material and techniques the poet has used in the particular poem concerned. Depending upon the poem, some variations of produced experience are allowable, but they exist only where the poet has seen fit to leave a point or area open for individual interpretation. In general, however, you are to assume that he has intended a rather tightly controlled, focused, particularized experience. *You can legitimately claim as poetic experience only that experience which you can explain as having its origin in identifiable features of the poem in question.*

Assignment: In 600–1000 words explicate a short poem, preferably one from this book. Select one that contains some words and figurative language you do not immediately understand, but that intrigues you with ideas and feelings similar to some that you have had but have never been able to express.

An explication is an ordered and comprehensive interpretation of the meaning of a statement, especially of a statement that communicates partly by implication or indirection. For a fuller understanding of what is involved, read the poetry introduction (pages 641–45), and for a model study the interpretation presented there of Hardy's "On an Invitation to the United States."

A sound explication will explore all the compressed riches that constitute a poem. It should give adequate attention to all kinds of meaning that, working together, result in a "Total Meaning," as I. A. Richards calls it. (See page 641).

To make your work easier and more effective, you should consider the following procedures and responsibilities:

Read the poem over silently *as a whole* several times. Follow its punctuation—its phrasing and pausing. Try to grasp its theme. Note major aspects of its order, pattern, progression.

Read it aloud until you have refined and made more meaningful its sense units, rhythms, and stresses.

Consider the parts or features of the poem one by one, looking for meanings that you have not fully grasped. Consider the connotations of words carefully. For example, the word "flat" in the second line of Eliot's "Animula" (page 692) has at least a half-dozen meanings, all applicable and significant. Perceive the imagery. Help it to take hold of you as it takes hold of perceptive and imaginative human beings. Penetrate the figures of speech by defining for yourself the points of likeness the poet had in mind in his saying that A is B when in fact A is not B as we well know.

Heed form. Understand that form includes all aspects of organization, not just the obvious mechanics of meter and rime. What steps or parts other than stanza exist along with or without stanzaic pattern? How do they function? Is there a logical progression as in Marvell's "To His Coy Mistress" (pages 664–65), which is developed in the common if-but-so progression? Does the poem begin in abstraction and generality and develop by supporting concreteness and specifics, or does it follow the reverse order? Pursue the matter of form through various levels below that of the overall poem. What repetitions—exact or variant— exist and for what effect? Do rimes support emphases? Do stresses put attention on key words? Are rhythms meaningfully chosen to reinforce sense? Are textural devices like alliteration merely "pretty" or significant as they are in Robinson's "Karma" (page 685), in which "fullness" and "fished" and "dime" and "died" are intensified as opposites by their alliterative form?

Do not overlook the obvious. Give special attention to what seem to be obscure and crucial passages, but try to be sure that the full meaning of seemingly simple passages is understood.

Finally, have reasonably clear and convincing evidence to support your interpretation. Draw upon precise words and passages and upon the poem as a whole to give a coherent, plausible explanation.

LESSON 17

Slanting Materials

Outside the classroom most writing is either literature or a highly purposeful kind of informative and persuasive expression where the writer has, directly or indirectly, some sort of personal ax to grind. The forms of self-serving are many and subtle. If we had the time and opportunity to unearth the motivations behind the great flood of nonliterary material we subject ourselves to in our daily reading, we probably would conclude that nine tenths of it is intended to propagate an idea or to sell a product. And, of course, literature is generally persuasive. Many great writers, such as George Bernard Shaw, have insisted that literature must have a didactic or moral purpose, must sell ideas and beliefs. Language is a potent instrument of social control. The skillful user of it can incline others to his way of thinking and acting.

That, in a moral sense, there are both good and bad uses of language as social control is not the question here. The problem here is to understand how language can be manipulated to one's advantage. The exercise that follows is intended to help the student understand the devices used to *slant* material to serve the writer's purpose. The student's practice with these devices will help him more effectively to influence others and to defend himself against those who would so influence him.

Assignment: Rewrite the following sketch of Miss Badengood to present as favorable or as unfavorable an account of her as possible. Do not omit or add to the basic facts supplied. Make use of all the devices for slanting that are discussed later in this lesson.

MISS BADENGOOD

Miss Badengood, an unmarried woman about sixty years old, lives by herself in our neighborhood. Her next-door neighbors to the east, the Hardins, will not speak to her. She likes dogs; in fact, she occasionally raises a litter of registered puppies for sale. She keeps the dogs penned. Neighbors three blocks away say they can hear the dogs barking at feeding time. She has an aversion to cats and has been seen out under her three pecan trees banging on a pan to scare the squirrels away. She keeps a late-model car, never one over two years old, but rarely uses it. The drugstore delivery scooter is seen weekly in her driveway. She is very active in her yard, mowing the grass weekly and trimming her trees and shrubs herself. She also has been seen on a tall ladder, painting the gables of her two-story house, a wooden structure built twenty years ago. Now and then, when the younger children of the neighbors are in her yard, she shows them the puppies and gives them each one cookie. But she sends them home at meal time or her nap time with, "Go home *now*." Older children do not visit her. Her hair is unusually dark. Her everyday clothes are starched cottons of solid pastels. She is rarely seen without a flower in her hair. She arises at 6:00 A.M. and waits for the paper boy. She also waits for the postman and often gets an armload of mail. She has gone to the Sunday church service for six years straight but never attends any other services. About twice a year she is visited by out-of-town relatives or friends. On occasion some of these visitors stay in a nearby motel. According to the motel owner, one of these visitors told him that she had put him through college. Repairmen say that three rooms in the house are kept securely locked but that the rest of the house is well furnished and maintained and that she reads *Fortune* and Ellery Queen.

If your effort is to be successful, you must understand the most important principle involved in effective slanting: *the slanting must be slanting,* not a complete upsetting or reversing. Extremes should be avoided. Slanting is made acceptable by the unavoidable human defects in observers. Because no two out of one hundred people who witness an event can give identical accounts of it, you are allowed considerable leeway for interpretation. But, for now, content yourself with making black gray instead of attempting to make it white. The devices must be concealed to the casual inspection. Your appeals to the emotional and irrational must be dressed in the garments of the rational. The point is not so much that there are laws of libel and slander as it is that open evasions of fact and logic not only nullify themselves but also corrupt your whole case. You must be able to defend your presentation by having some basis for your statements. Those statements must seem plausible, given your frame of reference, no matter how tenuous or remote their bases.

What are the devices? What can you do with a stubborn fact to advance your case positively or to nullify or at least reduce its potency against your case? First, you can omit it or ignore it. But that is hardly effective, for there will always be someone who insists upon putting it back into the picture. Therefore, abandon that head-in-the-sand approach.

Second, you can offset it with another fact to which you can plausibly give an interpretation favorable to your viewpoint. Facts, especially those about people, are notoriously contradictory. John Doe may pay cash for his car but charge his groceries. In this exercise you must remember that you are not permitted to present new facts. There is, however, a related technique available. You can de-emphasize or minimize the significance of a fact that runs counter to your case. By giving it an unemphatic location, by burying it among numerous facts in the middle of a long paragraph, you may blur its importance. Save the climactic final section of the paragraph for the presentation of the statements most favorable to your case.

Another way to slant through controlling the order of your remarks is to juxtapose two facts so that a relationship is implied that would not be inferred if they were not adjacent to one another. That John drinks milk and has a stomach ulcer proves neither that milk causes nor that it cures an ulcer, but one or the other is plausibly suggested, for it is human habit to interpret matters in cause-and-effect relationships. Well handled, this device is very effective, in that the writer can point to his exact wording and, if pressed, can insist that the violation of logic was the reader's, not his.

One of the best ways to de-emphasize an unfavorable fact is to subordinate it in a sentence. For example, consider the effects of these two statements: "Though John is a liar, he lies pleasantly." "Though John lies pleasantly, he is a liar." The principle works both ways, of course. You can give prominence to favorable facts by putting them into main statements.

The most frequently used method of slanting, however, is to choose words with connotations that will lure the reader into seeing matters as you wish him to. By playing upon connotations you can turn a neutral or even unfavorable item to your advantage or can increase the effect of items that already favor you. If a person is sixty years old, his age can be referred to as either "dotage" or "ripeness of age," depending upon the impression you wish to leave. A teacher can be called either a pedant or a scholar. Of course here, as well as in your use of the other devices for slanting, you should exercise care and avoid extremes that are indefensible. Instead of depending upon the use of a few words that are highly charged with pleasant or unpleasant associations, slant many of your words temperately and rely upon the cumulative effect. You do not have to condemn violently; you can ridicule subtly. You do not have to praise extravagantly; you can admire modestly. Finally, by generalizing a fact, you can often communicate the effect you are after. Refusal to buy an item that would violate one's budget can be interpreted either as stinginess or prudence. Qualifying a given statement with "I think" can be considered either as uncertainty or open-mindedness. Abstract and general terms lend themselves to slanting. They have no fully agreed-upon denotative meanings verifiable by reference to physical things, for no physical referents for them exist. Thus their obscurity can be used to your purpose.

LESSON 18

Beginning the Composition

Study the first paragraph of each of the selections listed below. Match the title of each with the description of opening technique that most adequately fits it. The various techniques are presented in the following Key List.

KEY LIST

A. A positive, bold assertion that is set forth as the true state of affairs
B. An assertion followed by a direct or indirect appeal to the reader to judge for himself from the evidence that will be presented
C. A statement calling attention to a presently confused or misunderstood state of affairs
D. The presentation of a striking contrast, one element of which is to be investigated in some respect
E. A statement asserting that a deplorable situation exists and that it has such and such factor or factors as its cause

AUTHOR / SELECTION	OPENING TECHNIQUE
1. Whyte, "Where Do Those Bright Ideas Come From?"	_____
2. Carr, "The Black Beach"	_____
3. Langer, "The Language Line"	_____
4. Cary, "The Mass Mind: Our Favorite Folly"	_____
5. O'Casey, "The Harp in the Air Still Sings"	_____
6. Orwell, "Shooting an Elephant"	_____
7. Ciardi, ". . . an ulcer, gentlemen, is an unwritten poem"	_____

Let us see whether we can deduce from these examples the qualities of an effective opening. The first and most important quality, if we are to judge by its presence in *all* the examples, is directness. Without exception, the authors of these selections have chosen to disclose their central intention without preamble or hesitation. There is no slow lead-up, no circuitousness, no obliqueness. Second, a stark relevance marks these beginnings. Nothing remote or marginal is used. Third, most of these openings are in one way or another attractive, that is, intriguing, provocative, challenging. The importance of the subject matter, the depth of the writer's insight, the intensity of his feeling—something of this kind is suggested. Finally, some of these openings directly or indirectly try to establish a common ground with the reader.

It cannot be overemphasized that nothing is gained by elaborate introductions. They tend always to be overelaborate, out of proportion to the space devoted to the development of the central matter itself. Elaborate introductions tend to introduce irrelevancies that confuse and mislead the reader, setting up expectations that are never fulfilled. The essay openings examined here introduce comparatively long and intensively developed essays; yet these openings introduce their subjects immediately and tersely.

If the professional writer uses only fifty words to introduce his five-thousand-word essay, how many should you use to introduce your five-hundred-word composition?

Assignment: Write three brief composition introductions in which you intend to discuss a disturbing campus or local situation and what you consider to be its chief cause. Try to achieve in each introduction the qualities that make an opening effective. Use different approaches to each introduction. Refer to the Key List for suggestions.

LESSON 19

The Critical Review

The critical review attempts to pass judgment upon such a subject as a magazine article, book, play, story, or movie. Such reviews serve a useful purpose in directing readers to what is good and in sparing them from wasting time and energy on something they might find trivial and worthless.

A good review must be factual and informative, but also it should give evaluative comment, favorable and unfavorable. A good portion of a literary review should provide an analysis of what the author has said—a concise summary shorn of all unimportant details. The heart of such a review is its discussion of the relevancy of the issues the author has raised and the validity of their content. To discuss these matters the reviewer must have a firmer grasp of and greater insight into the subject matter of the work than the ordinary reader possesses. Otherwise his evaluation may be prejudicial and impressionistic.

Assignment: Write a 400–500-word critical review of a magazine article dealing with a subject about which you are thoroughly knowledgeable. If you do not have readily at hand an article appropriate for review, consult the *Readers' Guide to Periodical Literature* for assistance in finding one.

This paper should follow a general pattern dominant in most critical reviews. In the beginning of the review summarize briefly what the author has said, making certain you cover all the salient points. Omit inconsequential details in order to center your summary on the significant features.

Next, determine the author's purpose in writing the article. Is the purpose worthwhile? Does the author present a hackneyed point of view? Has he failed or succeeded in accomplishing his goal? At this point it is possible—and valuable—to make comparisons with other authors' works on the same subject.

In making a final appraisal, the reviewer of an article may consider a number of questions:

1. How does this article differ from others on the subject?
2. Does the author deal fairly with his material, or has he slanted it to enforce his own preconceptions?
3. Is the article well written? What are its stylistic qualities, and how effective are they?
4. Is the article worthy of serious consideration by the prospective reader?

One final word. The reviewer must capture the essence of the article, think clearly about its real meaning, and evaluate it fairly. And he must write well himself.

LESSON 20

Literary Criticism

Literary men have always written about their art. Sometimes they defend themselves against critics; sometimes they criticize other writers. Sometimes they define the province of their art, or jest about their insensitive readers. Such writing usually is called literary criticism. To read literary criticism—whether it is about an author, an individual piece of writing, or a whole literary movement—makes the reader more sensitive to a writer and his purpose. In this text a number of selections make critical judgments on literature and its function in our lives. In this assignment you are asked to react to certain writers' points of view about their art.

Assignment: Select from the following titles a poem, an essay, or a short story, or some grouping of them, and write a 400–600-word essay in which you summarize related comments about literature made by one or more of these writers and then give your reaction to those comments:

1. Ciardi, ". . . an ulcer, gentlemen, is an unwritten poem"

2. Galsworthy, "A Novelist's Allegory"
3. Bonaro Overstreet, "Little Story, What Now?"
4. Marianne Moore, "Poetry"
5. Thomas, "In My Craft or Sullen Art"
6. O'Casey, "The Harp in the Air Still Sings"
7. Edith Hamilton, "The Idea of Tragedy"
8. Housman, "'Terence, This Is Stupid Stuff'. . ."

The success of this assignment will depend upon your careful reading of the selections and your reaction to what the writers say.

To begin your essay, you might make clear your understanding of what is said about literature in the chosen items. You need next to take a position agreeing or disagreeing with these ideas and to support your conviction with substantial logic. For instance, you may agree or disagree with Galsworthy that the novelist's purpose in writing is to shed light upon the evils in society. Or you may think that O'Casey is too critical of modern dramatists and wish to write a rejoinder in their behalf, taking as your point of departure what O'Casey says about them. The problem is not only to present what the writer says in order to focus attention upon his ideas but also to evaluate in terms of your own supported judgment the validity of what the author has said about poetry, the novel, the short story, or the drama.

Your conclusion should be the result of the evidence presented or the logical deductions that you can make. Make certain to present enough evidence to persuade the reader to your point of view—whether you think the author is right or wrong, and why.

LESSON 21

Literary Similarity and Contrast

In the study of language and literature, it is essential that a student learn to associate and compare the ideas in several works. For example, a reading *in sequence* of Orwell's "Shooting an Elephant," Forster's "What I Believe," O'Connor's "Guests of the Nation," and Hardy's "The Man He Killed" will demonstrate how opposed Orwell's and Forster's

ideas are and how closely O'Connor can be related to Forster and Hardy.

Assignment: Write a paper of 500–600 words setting forth the association of ideas you have made between several literary works and commenting on the conflicts among the authors and between you and some or all of the authors.

Proceed carefully from each author's ideas to the relation of all their ideas and how they compare with your own. You might use the four authors listed above; or you might find three or four in your own reading experience; or you might try one of the groups that follow:

1. Fromm's "The Marketing Orientation" (pages 132–37)
   Marjorie Kinnan Rawlings' "The Pound Party" (pages 332–35)
   Thurber's "The Rabbits Who Caused All the Trouble" (pages 387–88)
   Arnold's "Dover Beach" (pages 682–83)
2. Overstreets' "Making Psychic Space for One Another" (pages 151–59)
   Carson McCullers' "A Tree. A Rock. A Cloud." (pages 415–20)
   Picasso's "give tear twist and kill" (page 699)
   Anderson's "Sophistication" (pages 467–73)
   Strindberg's "The Stronger" (pages 637–40)
3. Strong's "The Poetic Approach to Reality" (pages 99–102)
   Galsworthy's "A Novelist's Allegory" (pages 275–81)
   Chase's "Words and the World View" (pages 24–29)
   Prévert's "To Paint the Portrait of a Bird" (pages 698–99)

LESSON 22

Ethical Insight in Literature

Among the rewards of reading good literature is an increased insight into truth. Quite often this awareness comes in a poem, or in a novel, or in a short story. But the writer, sensitive about life and its meaning, may speak, through any genre, of truth or falsehood, honor or dishonor, loyalty or betrayal, right versus wrong, love versus hate, and a host of other ethical considerations.

Assignment: Choose some idea that has ethical considerations and select three or four of the literary selections that deal with the idea. Then prepare a 600-word essay in which you show the relationships among the various ethical insights you find in the selected pieces. For instance, Anouilh's "Becket: or The Honor of God" (pages 560–606); Sophocles' "Antigonê" (pages 478–503); Conrad's "The Lagoon" (pages 388–96); and O'Connor's "Guests of the Nation" (pages 451–57) focus attention upon some aspect of loyalty. Anderson's "Sophistication" (pages 469–73), Eudora Welty's "A Worn Path" (pages 402–07), Herrick's "Upon Julia's Clothes" (page 665), Browning's "Soliloquy of the Spanish Cloister" (pages 668–69), Shelley's "Ozymandias" (page 680), Yeats' "Crazy Jane Talks with the Bishop" (page 694), and Simpson's "The Custom of the World" (page 666) treat some aspect of love or hate. Schwartz's "The Heavy Bear" (page 698), Marjorie Kinnan Rawlings' "The Pound Party" (pages 332–35), Shirley Jackson's "After You, My Dear Alphonse" (pages 396–98), Thurber's "The Rabbits Who Caused All the Trouble" (pages 387–88), Collier's "The Chaser" (pages 413–15), Miller's "The Crucible" (pages 504–59), Faulkner's "Spotted Horses" (pages 458–68), and Steinbeck's "The Chrysanthemums" (pages 420–26) highlight still other ethical considerations.

After you have selected one of the groupings of ideas listed above or have chosen a group of your own, construct an opening paragraph in which you make some generalization about the theme, or elaborate upon the idea that good literature is one of the most valuable sources from which to secure insight into life. Then mention the various aspects of the theme your literary selections will illustrate. Now you are ready to analyze your selections, pointing out what insight the materials give, how the author achieves his desired end, and, possibly, what relationship exists between the various authors' treatment of the theme.

Do not try to summarize the selection; rather, try to utilize the overall comment the author makes concerning some truth about life. Your concluding paragraph ought to pull all the threads together with some broad generalization covering the insight.

LESSON 23

The Documented Idea

Note to Instructor: *This assignment should be made only after the class has read and discussed selections on which it is based and after Writing Lessons 20 and 21 have been completed.*

You are to use *College English* as a sourcebook for the materials you will be asked to deal with in this composition. Discussion of certain readings has doubtless brought to your attention the fact that one dominant idea may underlie and tie together many selections. Loosely put, the idea that you will be concerned with here is that men live by a hierachy of loyalties and that the chief conflicts of life—both external and internal—arise when two of these loyalties collide. For example, the question of whether one's first loyalty is owed to one's country (patriotism) or to the whole community of man (humanitarianism or friendship) is central in E. M. Forster's "What I Believe" (pages 172–77), Frank O'Connor's "Guests of the Nation" (pages 451–57), and Thomas Hardy's "The Man He Killed" (page 689).

Assignment: In a 1200–2000-word composition, treat the concept of loyalties in the following manner:

1. Define with considerable precision this concept or premise as it is used as a point of departure or controlling theme by a representative cross section of authors. [Your instructor should define for you "a representative cross section" by (a) indicating the number of variations on the basic theme he wishes you to deal with, (b) designating the number of types of literature that are to be considered, or (c) stipulating the number of authors he wishes you to examine.]

2. Analyze and demonstrate each author's application of this basic theme in a particular work by him.

3. Document throughout in acceptable form all references to the selections under study. (Consult Section 33 of the *Harbrace College Handbook* for the conventions of documentation.)

Your first task will be to make clear to your reader what this underlying premise is and to show him that it is fundamental in the group of selections you deal with. From your acquaintance with your selected group of readings as a whole you are to arrive at and state an abstract concept or generalization. This generalization, of course, will be to the effect that all selections do operate on the same basic assumption that men erect the same or different scales of values, which results in clashes between men (external conflict) when their codes disagree. It should also take into account the fact that two nearly equal loyalties may compete with each other within the mind and heart of one man (internal conflict). Finally, this generalization should point out that an author in a given selection is usually interested not in a general clash of codes but in one special conflict between two firmly held and perhaps nearly equal loyalties.

Your other job, the particularization and differentiation of the various ideas on loyalties—that is, determining which loyalty should have precedence over another—suggests the use of comparison and contrast as well as of examples and illustrations. This section of your paper should proceed from one set of opposing loyalties to another set. With each set you should consider all pertinent readings—those that feature this particular conflict—and by documentation reveal which view each supports.

An incomplete but suggested list of loyalty conflicts should include (1) country versus friends or humankind in general, (2) state versus church or religion, (3) love versus honor, (4) individual versus group (institution or society), (5) idealism versus practicality, (6) love versus convention.

An incomplete but representative list of *College English* selections that pose some aspect of loyalty conflicts includes

1. Expositions like Erich Fromm's "The Marketing Orientation" (pages 132–37), Richard H. Rovere's "Technology and the Claims of Community" (pages 137–42), Clarence Henry Faust's "The Search for Answers" (pages 144–51), George Orwell's "Shooting an Elephant" (pages 167–71), E. M. Forster's "What I Believe" (pages 172–77), and Charles Frankel's "The Morality of Civil Disobedience" (pages 177–81)

2. The factual historical narrative by Sir Arthur Bryant, "The Holy Blissful Martyr" (pages 347–60)

3. The dramas of Sophocles, *Antigonê* (pages 478–502), and Jean Anouilh, *Becket* (pages 560–606)

4. Such short stories as Joseph Conrad's "The Lagoon" (pages 388–96) and Frank O'Connor's "Guests of the Nation" (pages 451–57)

5. Poems like T. S. Eliot's "Journey of the Magi" (pages 650–51), William Morris' "Haystack in the Floods" (pages 652–53), Dylan Thomas' "Do Not Go Gentle into That Good Night" (page 676), William Butler Yeats' "Crazy Jane Talks to the Bishop" (page 694), and Thomas Hardy's "The Man He Killed" (page 689).

Here is a final suggestion that should help you master the reading material on which you are to base your work. Writers present their ideas in many direct and indirect ways and combinations of ways. Be on the alert to spot the writer's direct statements as to what his ideas are. Though direct statement is particularly the method of the expository writer, it is occasionally used in other types. Grasp the direct statements of the writer's spokesman or "mouthpiece" (technically known as the *persona*), that is, some character who seems to serve as the medium for the author's ideas. Follow the ideas as they are made explicit in dialogue among the characters and try to determine which of these ideas the author is advocating and which he is against. Last, and most important in literary works, consolidate for yourself one total impression given you by the selection. What ideas, stated or unstated, are produced by the total involvement of events and characters?

LESSON 24

Test Composition: The Critical Reaction

These writing assignments have given you experience in using the several forms of discourse. The importance of an organization appropriate to the kind of writing has been stressed. You have learned that a single topic may be treated in various ways, according to the central purpose of the writer. This final assignment will give you a chance to select a topic and its treatment. All that is required is that you now show what you can do when you are free to make most of the decisions.

Assignment: Write an essay of 400–600 words using as your central idea a significant statement from a poem, short story, or play you have read in this course. The statement should probably be one that impressed you as being either unusually acceptable or unusually debatable. Plan your treatment and organization as your purpose dictates. Consider what will make this your best piece of writing. Refer to past assignments and to the critical comments you have received on your earlier papers. Below your title give the statement you have selected, and indicate its source.

The major questions are these: (1) What significant statement will serve as a good thesis? (2) Basically, what type of discourse will be suitable? (3) What organizational scheme will present the ideas most satisfactorily to the reader?

Next, compose the first draft, which will help you to appraise the soundness of your decisions. The writing experience you have had should now enable you to continue or to redirect your efforts to achieve the best paper that you have written in this course.

JOHN C. HODGES

Late of the University of Tennessee

and **MARY E. WHITTEN**

North Texas State University

PART EIGHT

HARBRACE COLLEGE HANDBOOK

6th edition

To the Instructor

The *Harbrace College Handbook* is both a guide for the individual writer and a text for use in class. It presents its subject matter in a readily usable form and thus lightens the instructor's task for reading student papers. Although the rhetoric sections of the Sixth Edition have been strengthened, other sections have been carefully shortened to keep the book compact and convenient to use.

Numbers. The book contains only thirty-five major sections, or numbers, referring to the principles of effective writing. These include (as has been shown by a comprehensive examination of student writing) everything to which instructors normally refer in marking papers. But the principles less frequently needed have not been overlooked. They are subordinated logically to the thirty-five primary numbers and may be found readily by reference to the back endpapers or to the detailed index. If an instructor wishes to have any of these subordinate principles conveniently before his students, he can have them added in the blanks provided on the chart inside the front cover. Some college students may need Sections **1-18** only for review or for occasional reference.

Symbols. Instead of the simplified list of numbers, the instructor may, if he prefers, use the corresponding symbols. Most of these symbols are well known to English teachers; they are entered on both front and back charts.

General Plan. The sections on **Sentence Sense (1)** and **Grammatical Terms (35)** are general sections. The former may be used, whenever needed, as an introduction to the other sections; the latter should be used throughout as a glossary of terms. For corrections of specific errors, students will normally be referred to Sections **2-34.** Some instructors may wish to begin with Section **32, Planning and Writing the Whole Composition.** Others may prefer beginning with Section **31, The Paragraph,** or with Sections **19-30.** Emphasis from the start on good subject matter, clarity of organization, and effective style will help the student keep in mind the primary objectives of his writing.

Sentence Patterns. The Sixth Edition makes extensive use of sentence patterns, which many students find more helpful than diagrams. For those who prefer diagrams, a brief explanation is given in Section **35, Grammatical Terms.**

Drill Materials. Exercises are provided both for the major sections and for many of the subsections. Many of these exercises consist of lively paragraphs instead of conventional lists of unrelated sentences. Many of the exercises are of a positive type, in which the student is asked not to correct errors but to give reasons why sentences are correct, to drill orally so that correct forms will sound right, or to compose good sentences to illustrate the principle being studied. Some classes may need very little of the drill materials; others may need all of them, or even additional exercises such as those in the *Harbrace College Workbook*, Form 6A (keyed to the *Harbrace College Handbook*, Sixth Edition).

Recent Language Studies. Any English handbook such as this owes a great debt to all scholars, past and present, who have increased our understanding of the language. The authors of this handbook have endeavored to make full use of those linguistic principles—both new and old—that have definite practical value in college composition courses. These selected principles have been thoroughly tested in freshman English classes.

Acknowledgments. Among the many individuals who have generously offered suggestions for making this handbook more usable are Professors Ben H. Adelson (Los Angeles Pierce College), Donald L. Cross (Upsala College), David F. Finnigan (Oregon State University), George D. Hendricks (North Texas State University), John McKiernan (College of St. Thomas), John W. Morris (Wisconsin State University), and Bain Tate Stewart and others on the Freshman Staff (University of Tennessee). For important contributions to Section **33, Library Paper,** the authors are grateful to Miss Eleanor Goehring, of the Library Staff (University of Tennessee), and to Miss Barbara J. Reid (University of Tennessee). To Professor Roy F.

Montgomery (Spring Hill College) is due continuing appreciation for his help with the exercises.

Sections **19-32** still owe a great deal to the genius of the late Francis X. Connolly, whose untimely death is a great loss to the teaching profession.

The authors are especially indebted to Miss Audrey Ann Welch of Denton, Texas, who assisted in revising the manuscript and who wrote new exercise materials.

To the Student

Contemporary Usage; Authority. This Sixth Edition of the *Harbrace College Handbook* attempts to describe the usual practice of good contemporary writers and to state that practice as simply as possible. The "rules" in boldface are to be interpreted as descriptions derived from usage, and they have authority only to the extent that they describe usage. In your reading you should observe the practice of good writers so that you may eventually gain the confidence that comes from first-hand knowledge of what good writing is.

Numbers or Symbols. A number or a symbol written in the margin of your paper indicates a need for correction or improvement and calls for revision. If a number is used, turn directly to the corresponding number at the top of the page in the handbook. If a symbol is used, first consult the alphabetical list of symbols inside the front cover to find the number to which you should turn.

Ordinary References. The ordinary reference will be to the number or symbol (**2** or **frag, 9** or **cap, 18** or **sp, 28** or **ref**) standing at the head of one of the thirty-five sections of the handbook. The statement in large boldface at the beginning of each section covers the section as a whole. One of the statements in smaller boldface within the section will usually be needed to solve your problem. Study the section to which you have been referred—the whole of the section if necessary—and master the specific part of the section that explains your difficulty.

Specific References. Whenever your instructor wishes to refer you to a specific part of a section, he will add the appropriate letter to the number or symbol.

EXAMPLES **2c** (OR **frag-c**), **9a** (OR **cap-a**), **18b** (OR **sp-b**), **28d** (OR **ref-d**). A still more specific reference might be **9a(4)** or **cap-a(4)**.

General References. At times your instructor may give you a very general reference from which you are to determine and correct your error. For example, the symbol **gr** will refer you to the whole division on GRAMMAR, including Sections 1–7; the symbol **m** to the division on MECHANICS, including Sections 8–11; the symbol **p** to the division on PUNCTUATION, Sections 12–17; and so forth. An obvious error may be called to your attention by the symbol **x**, and general awkwardness by the symbol **k**.

Additional Help. Some of the principles treated in English handbooks can be mastered only by students who understand the fundamentals of the sentence. A well-developed "sentence sense" is especially helpful in the mastery of Sections **2** (**Sentence Fragment**), **3** (**Comma Splice**), **5** (**Case**), **6** (**Agreement**), **12** (**The Comma**), **14** (**The Semicolon**), **21** (**Wordiness**), **23** (**Unity**), **24** (**Subordination**), **25** (**Coherence**), **26** (**Parallelism**), and **30** (**Variety**). If you have difficulty in understanding these sections, you should first master the fundamentals of the sentence treated in Section **1** (**Sentence Sense**) and then turn again to the principle immediately involved. If you fail to understand any grammatical term used in the handbook, consult the alphabetical list in Section **35** (**Grammatical Terms**).

Correction and Revision. After you have mastered the principle underlying the correction of each error called to your attention, you should make careful revision of your paper in the manner recommended by your instructor. One method of revision is explained and illustrated in Section **8** (**Manuscript Form and Revision**), pages 821–24. To prove that you have found the specific principle needed for the revision, your instructor may ask you to write the appropriate letter (**a, b, c,** etc.) after the number or symbol he has supplied. An **x** written by the instructor after a number or symbol calls for the writing out of the appropriate exercise.

Contents

SPELLING AND DICTION

DICTION

EFFECTIVE SENTENCES

GRAMMAR

Sentence Sense

1

Master the essentials of the sentence as an aid to clear thinking and effective writing.

Acquiring sentence sense means developing the ability to recognize what *makes* a sentence. An understanding of the grammar of English sentences is prerequisite to good writing.

As you study grammar, you should always be aware of the fact that English is a living, changing language. It has been evolving for some fifteen centuries. What we now call Old English prevailed in England from about 450 A.D. to about 1100 A.D. This Old English, derived from West Germanic, contained many inflections.

OLD ENGLISH

Sē þe wæs ǣrur rīce   cyng and maniges landes
He that was before powerful king and of many lands
hlāford, hē næfde þā   ealles landes būton seofon fōt mǣl.
lord,   he had not then of all land   but   seven foot space.
— FROM THE *Anglo-Saxon Chronicle*

Middle English dates from about the twelfth century to the end of the fifteenth century.

MIDDLE ENGLISH

Thenne within two yeres king Uther felle seke of a grete maladye. And in the meane whyle hys enemyes usurpped upon hym, and dyd a grete bataylle upon his men, and slewe many of his peple.   — FROM MALORY'S *Morte d'Arthur*

The English in use from 1500 to the present is called Modern English. As it has emerged, nearly all the old inflections have been lost, and the order of words in the sentence has become more fixed. See also **19a** (4).

A study of Sections 1 through 7 of this textbook should help you understand how words are related to one another, why their forms change, and what order they take in sentence patterns of Modern English.

1a

Learn to recognize verbs.

Words such as *drank, organizes, falsify,* and *reoccurred* function as verbs. The verb is the heart of the sentence; without a verb no group of words is grammatically a sentence. You can recognize a verb by (1) its form and (2) its meaning.

Form   When converted from the present to the past tense, nearly all verbs change form (*eat-ate*). In the present tense, all verbs change form to indicate a singular subject in the third person (I *eat*-he *eats*); all verbs in the progressive tense end in *-ing* (*is eating*).

PRESENT	I *play*. It *plays*.	We *eat* early. He *eats* early.
PAST	Leonard *played* well.	All of them *ate* here today.
PROGRESSIVE	He *is playing*.	They *were eating* breakfast.

Meaning   Often defined as a predicator or as a word expressing action or a state of being, a verb is used to make a statement, to ask a question, or to give a command or direction.

Charles *slept* well.   *Leave* the computer alone!
Was it necessary?   *Turn* left at Akard Street.

Verb phrases   A verb consisting of more than one word is often referred to as a verb phrase (or cluster). A verb phrase comprises the verb together with the auxiliary words.

will endanger, may be studying, ought to rest

Words commonly used as auxiliaries are *has, have, had, am, is, are, was, were, be, been, do, does, did, used to, may, might, must, have to, has to, had to, shall, will, am* (*is, are,* etc.) *going to, am* (*is, are,* etc.) *about to, would, should, ought to, can,* and *could.*

The words that make up a verb phrase are often separated.

A gentleman *may,* of course, *become* angry at times.
He *does* not often *show* his anger.

Note: A verb may be combined with the adverb *not* or with a contraction of *not.*

He *cannot leave* now.   *Doesn't* it *matter?*

▶ EXERCISE 1   Write sentences using the first five words below as verbs. Then write sentences using the second five words in verb phrases.

1. up   3. long   5. yellow   7. record   9. question
2. tree   4. bone   6. down   8. signal   10. experiment

▶ EXERCISE 2   Underline the fifteen verbs and seven verb phrases in the following sentences.

[1] Jim angrily called himself a fool, as he had been doing all the way through the woods.   [2] Why had he listened to Fred's mad idea?   [3] What were ghosts and family legends to him, in this year of grace and nuclear fission?   [4] He had mysteries enough of his own, of a highly complex electronic sort, which would occupy him through the rest of a lifetime.   [5] But now he was plodding along here, like the Mississippi schoolboy that he had been a dozen years

before; this ghost chase in the middle of the night was preposterous. [6] It was an outrage to all that he represented; it was lunacy. [7] It was—he swallowed the truth like a bitter pill—frightful! [8] The legend and the ghost had been a horror to him as a child; and they were a horror still. [9] As he stood at the edge of the weed-choked, briar-tangled slope, on the top of which the decayed mansion waited evilly, he felt almost sick. [10] The safe, sure things of every day had become distant, childish fantasies. [11] This grotesque night and whatever, ghoulish and monstrous, inhabited it were clammily and horribly real.

1b

Learn to recognize subjects and objects of verbs.

Nearly every grammatically complete sentence has a verb and a subject; the only exception is the command, or imperative, which omits the subject, often considered as implied. In the following sentences the subjects are in **boldface** and the verbs are in *italics*.

> The **ambassador** *arrived* shortly before noon.
> There *will be* a formal **reception** tonight.
> *Fasten* your safety belt. [Imperative]

The subject of a sentence that asks a question (an interrogative sentence) is more readily located when the sentence is recast in the form of a statement.

> *Has* the **last** of the deserters *surrendered?*
> The **last** of the deserters *has surrendered.*

The *complete subject* is the subject and words associated with it; the *complete predicate* is the verb and words associated with it.

Complete subject	Complete predicate
The stewardess on Flight 118	often smiled during the storm.

Many sentences require objects of the verb to complete their meaning. In the following sentences the objects are in SMALL CAPITALS.

> **Frank** *has met* HELEN.
> **I** *laid* the PLIERS on that shelf.
> One **man** in the crowd *raised* his VOICE in protest.

One test for an object is that it can be made the subject of a passive verb: "Helen was met by Frank."

You can learn to recognize subjects and objects by observing (1) their form, (2) their meaning, and (3) their position.

Form Nouns and noun substitutes (sometimes called *substantives* or *nominals*) are used as subjects and objects of verbs. The most frequently used subject or object of the verb is the noun or pronoun.

Forms of pronouns (*I, you, he,* etc.) are easy to recognize; see the list on page 813. Most nouns (words used to name persons, places, things, ideas, or actions) change their form to indicate number (*movement, movements; city, cities; woman, women*) and the possessive case (*John's* car, the *boys'* dogs, the *men's* job). Such suffixes as *-ance, -ation, -ence, -ment, -ness,* and *-ship* frequently indi-

cate that a word is a noun: *appearance, atonement, boldness, determination, hardship, reference.* The articles *a, an,* and *the* are sometimes called "noun indicators" or "noun determiners" because they regularly point to a following noun: "a *chair,*" "an *activity,*" "the last *race.*"

Meaning In order to find the subject, simply ask, in connection with the verb, "Who or what?"

> The **actor,** after a long flight from South America, happily *greets* the REPORTERS at the Miami airport. [*Who* or *what* greets? The *actor* greets.][1]

Ordinarily an object receives, or is in some way affected by, the action of the verb. To find the object, ask, in connection with the subject and verb, "Whom or what?" For example, in the sentence about the actor, "The actor greets *whom?*" *Reporters,* the answer, is the direct object.

Some verbs (such as *give, offer, bring, take, lend, send, buy,* and *sell*) may have both an indirect object and a direct object. To find the indirect object, ask, "*To whom* or *for whom* is something done?"

> **Dad** *gave* HARRY a BOAT. [Dad gave a boat (direct object) *to whom? Harry* is the indirect object.]

Position A third way to recognize subjects and objects is to become thoroughly aware of the meaningfulness of English word order, normally SUBJECT—VERB—OBJECT. As you study carefully the following commonly used sentence patterns, observe the importance of word order (especially in Pattern 2) in determining meaning.

1. SUBJECT—VERB.

   Coyotes howl in the distance.
   Diseases of the blood *are* often *caused* by bacteria.

2. SUBJECT—VERB—OBJECT.

   Elephants frighten mice.
   Mice frighten elephants.
   Sparrows in our yard *eat* all the *seed* in the feeder.

3. SUBJECT—VERB—INDIRECT OBJECT—DIRECT OBJECT.

   Mary baked Fred a cake.
   Candidates often rashly *promise voters* lower *taxes.*

4. There[2]—VERB—SUBJECT.

   There have been no *objections.*
   There are nearly forty national *parks* in America.

For patterns with subject complements, see **4b.**

The preceding patterns are patterns of statements, or declarative sentences. Notice the changes that take place when these patterns are transformed into questions:

5. AUXILIARY—SUBJECT—VERB?

   Do coyotes howl in the distance?
   Are diseases of the blood *caused* by bacteria?

---

[1]It is sometimes helpful to make a diagram, or to form a mental picture, of the subject and its verb; see **Diagraming,** Section **35.**

[2]*There* used as an introductory word or filler is an expletive, which is never the subject.

6. AUXILIARY—SUBJECT—VERB—OBJECT?

Have mice ever *frightened elephants?*
Would sparrows eat all the *seed* in the feeder?

7. AUXILIARY—SUBJECT—VERB—INDIRECT OBJECT—
DIRECT OBJECT?

Will Mary bake Fred a *cake?*
Had the candidates promised voters lower *taxes?*

8. OBJECT—AUXILIARY—SUBJECT—VERB?

What did the *mice frighten?*
Which seeds in the feeder *will* the *sparrows eat?*

9. VERB—there—SUBJECT?

Were there any *objections?*
Are there forty national *parks* in America?

10. AUXILIARY—there—VERB—SUBJECT?

Has there been any *objection?*
Should there be only forty national *parks* in America?

The common patterns of commands, or imperative sentences, are derived from the first three patterns of statements. Notice, however, that the imperative sentences in the examples below have no expressed subjects.

Sell now.   Sell the car now.   Sell him the car now.

Many exclamatory sentences are also derived from patterns of statements:

There have been a hundred objections!
Mary baked Fred a cake!

Such sentences as the following, however, usually take an exclamation point because the word order is not that of an ordinary statement, question, or command:

How many objections there were!
What a cake Mary baked Fred!

Depending upon the writer's intention, a sentence pattern such as the following may be a statement, a question, or an exclamation:

What is said about the subj [handwritten margin note]

Mice frighten elephants.
Mice frighten elephants?
Mice frighten elephants!

For other sentence patterns, see **1d, 3a, 4b, 5f, 12a, 12b, 14a,** and **30b.**

Note: Subjects, verbs, and objects may be compound.

The high *wheeler* and the safety *bicycle* were popular in the late nineteenth century. [Compound subject]
A capable student *can face* and *solve* his *problems* or *difficulties.* [Compound verb and compound object]

▶ EXERCISE 3   Make a list of the twelve verbs, the nine subjects, and the nine objects, direct and indirect, in the paragraph below. Be prepared for a class discussion of the sentence patterns used.

¹ On New Year's Eve, I joined the happy throng at Times Square.   ² Between eleven and twelve o'clock, the noisy mob celebrated the death of the old year.   ³ Many people leaned against boarded-up store windows, milled in the streets, or blew ear-splitting horns.   ⁴ Others formed snake lines and whipped their way through the crowd. ⁵ A few fighting ragamuffins gave the police trouble. ⁶ Confetti filled the air.   ⁷ Airplanes roared overhead. ⁸ Subways thundered.   ⁹ Television cameras flashed the spectacular hubbub across the nation.

▶ EXERCISE 4   Write two sentences of your own to illustrate each one of the ten patterns on pages 801–02.

1c

Learn to recognize all the parts of speech.

Words are usually grouped into eight classes or "parts of speech": *verbs, nouns, pronouns, adjectives, adverbs, prepositions, conjunctions,* and *interjections.* Verbs, nouns, adjectives, and adverbs are sometimes called *vocabulary words* because they make up more than ninety-nine percent of all words listed in the dictionary. But pronouns, prepositions, and conjunctions—though small in number—are important because they are used over and over in our speaking and writing. Prepositions and conjunctions, often called *function words,* connect and relate vocabulary words and pronouns. Of the eight word classes, only three—prepositions, conjunctions, and interjections—do not change their form.

For a summary of the form changes of verbs, nouns, pronouns, adjectives, and adverbs, see Section 35, under **Inflection.**

Carefully study the forms, meanings, and functions of each of the eight parts of speech listed below.

VERBS   *notify, notifies, notified, are notifying*
        write, writes, wrote, has written, is writing

Verbs function as predicators in sentences:

The dean *notified* Brad's parents.

NOUNS   *neighbor, neighbors (neighbor's, neighbors')*
        kindness, kindnesses, prudence, the *money,* an
        understanding

In sentences, nouns function as subjects, complements, objects, appositives; they are also used in direct address and absolute phrases. Nouns may name persons, places, things, ideas, animals, qualities, actions.

Edward paid the *men* for the *work.*

PRONOUNS   *I, me, my, mine, myself, they, you, him, it*
           one, ones (one's), both, everybody, anyone
           who, whose, whom, which, that, these, this

Pronouns take the positions of nouns in sentences.

He paid *them* for *it. Everyone* knows *this.*

ADJECTIVES   *young, younger, youngest, a, an, the, this* day
              three men, *a sturdy* chair, *the only* one

Adjectives modify or qualify nouns and pronouns. Generally adjectives are placed near the words they modify. A *predicate adjective*, however, is nearly always separated from the word modified. A predicate adjective helps to complete the meaning of a linking verb (*am, is, are, was, were, be, been, taste, smell*, etc.) and modifies the subject. See **4b**.

> The poems of E. E. Cummings look *different*.

Adjectives may precede or follow the words they modify.

> *The weary* driver, *alone* and *sleepy*, was *glad* to see *the familiar* streets of home.

ADVERBS   *slowly* walking, *very* short, *almost never* wins
           too, not, sometimes, soon, sooner, soonest

Adverbs usually modify verbs, adjectives, or other adverbs. They may also modify a verbal, a whole phrase or clause, or the rest of the sentence in which they appear.

> *Honestly*, she *nearly always* lies about her age.

PREPOSITIONS   *at* times, *between* us, *because of* rain
                to the door, *by* them, *before* class

Other words commonly used as prepositions are *across, after, as, for, from, in, in front of, in regard to, like, of, on, over, through, together with, under, until, up, with*. A preposition, a function word, always has an object, which is usually a noun or a pronoun; the preposition with its object (and any modifiers) is called a *prepositional phrase*.

> These poems express *with* great force the poet's love *of* liberty.

The preposition may follow, rather than precede, the noun or noun substitute, and be placed at the end of the sentence. At times a sentence is most idiomatic or emphatic with the preposition at the end.

UNNATURAL   *For* what are you waiting?
NATURAL   What are you waiting *for*?
NATURAL   We live *by* faith.
NATURAL (*and more emphatic*)   Faith is what we live *by*.

Note: Words like *up, off, on, out, in, over* may be used as prepositions, as adverbs, or as parts of verb-adverb combinations (verb equivalents).

Prepositions	Adverbs	Verb-adverb combinations
up the ladder	Look *up*.	*Look up* (Find) George.
a mile *off* shore	He marched *off*.	I *put off* (delayed) the work.

CONJUNCTIONS   eat *and* sleep, Carl *or* Helen, long *but*
                witty, rested *while* it rained, a spot
                where we meet

Conjunctions function as connectors. They fall into two classes: (1) the coordinating conjunctions (*and, but, or, nor, for*, and sometimes *so* and *yet*), used to connect words or phrases, or clauses that are of equal rank; and (2) the subordinating conjunctions (such as *after, because, if, since, till, when, where, while*), used to connect subordinate clauses with main clauses.

> According to one biographer, Bacon did not look at friends *when* he talked with them, *for* he was concerned chiefly with ideas, not people.

INTERJECTIONS   *Ouch! Oh*, pardon me.

Interjections are exclamations, which may be followed by an exclamation point or a comma.

The dictionary shows the word class (often the several word classes) in which a given word may be used, but the actual classification of any word is dependent upon its use in the sentence. Notice how the classification of *round* varies in accordance with its use in the following sentences:

> The second *round* was tiring. [Noun]
> Any *round* table will do. [Adjective]
> Some drivers *round* corners too rapidly. [Verb]
> The sound goes *round* and *round*. [Adverb]
> He lives *round* the corner. [Preposition]

▶ **EXERCISE 5** As you fill in the blanks below with appropriate parts of speech to make logical sentences, note how word order, inflectional endings, and function words determine your choices. Above each word you add, write its part of speech.

1. The _____ have _____ed a _____.
2. _____ were _____ ing in the _____.
3. _____ly the _____ are not _____.
4. A very _____ _____ may _____.
5. _____ of the _____ on the _____ looked _____.
6. Did _____ and _____ _____ their _____?
7. A _____ boy was _____ing _____ly on the _____.
8. Either _____ or _____ ought to _____ the _____.
9. _____ _____ not _____ a _____ or a _____.
10. During the _____ _____, _____ _____ed for _____.

▶ **EXERCISE 6** Give the part of speech of each of the italicized words below.

The sea, of course, is never [1] *silent*. I have [2] *often* thought that if our ear [3] *were* finer, [4] *it* would catch the soft, smooth friction [5] *between* the glassy wave top and the resisting air. [6] *Even* far out, [7] *when* a still day lies like [8] *metal* [9] *on* the oily surface, and the lazy [10] *patches* of the sun dilate between imperceptible [11] *rises*, a little wave will suddenly [12] *raise* its head out of nothingness with a [13] *plop* and subside into [14] *nothingness* again: and yet when [15] *those* days have fulfilled [16] *us* with their long, empty hours, and in spite of the interrupted [17] *but* fairly [18] *continuous* rap of canvas against a mast, the feeling we take home is [19] *that* of silence, the thing we have [20] *never* known.

—FREYA STARK[3]

[3] From "On Silence," *Holiday*, December, 1965. By permission of the author.

1d

Learn to recognize phrases and subordinate clauses.

Phrases

A phrase is a group of related words, without subject and predicate, functioning as a verb, a noun, an adjective, or an adverb. Phrases are generally classified as:

VERB PHRASES   The rose *has wilted*. *Did* you *see* it? Mr. Kelly *may run* up the bill. The roof *used to leak*.

PREPOSITIONAL PHRASES   A special program *on the growth of flowers* fascinated audiences everywhere. *In fact*, the timed photography was spectacular.

PARTICIPIAL PHRASES   A person *seeing an accident* should stay on the scene. *Seeing the accident*, a man stopped. *Seen by three men*, the accident was reported at once.

GERUND PHRASES   *Riding a horse* takes skill. I prefer *riding a bicycle*.

INFINITIVE PHRASES   Does James like *to swim in the ocean*? That is the problem *to be solved now*.

Notice in the examples above that the gerund *riding*, like the present participle *seeing*, ends in *-ing* and that the two are to be distinguished only by their use in the sentence: the participle is the adjective and the gerund is the noun.

Participles, gerunds, and infinitives are derived from verbs and are therefore called *verbals*. (See also Section **35**.) They are much like verbs in that they have different tenses, can take subjects and objects, and can be modified by adverbs. But they are not verbs, for they cannot serve as the heart of a sentence: they cannot make a statement, ask a question, or give a command.

(1) Phrases used as nouns

Gerund phrases are always used as nouns. Infinitive phrases are often used as nouns (though they may also function as modifiers). Occasionally a prepositional phrase functions as a noun.

NOUNS	PHRASES USED AS NOUNS
The *decision* is important.	*Choosing a major* is important. [Gerund phrase—subject]
Sandra likes the *job*.	Sandra likes *to do the work*. [Infinitive phrase—object]

NOUNS	PHRASES USED AS NOUNS
His *action* prompted the *change*.	*His leaving the farm* caused her to seek a job in town. [Gerund phrase—subject; infinitive phrase—object]
That *hour* is too late.	*After supper* is too late. [Prepositional phrase—subject]

▶ EXERCISE 7   Make a list of the five gerund phrases and five infinitive phrases used as nouns in the following sentences (selected from *Time*).

1. Successfully merchandising a product is creative.
2. Great wealth seems to produce a security and mobility that usually enable the rich to grow richer.

3. They prefer instead to hear counterpoint, to hear the architecture of the music.
4. "We just want to take some of the blindness out of blind dates," explains the founder of Operation Match.
5. He insisted on calling every play from the bench; he tried installing a radio receiver in his quarterback's helmet, and when other teams started tuning in on his broadcast, he switched to shuttling "messenger guards" back and forth with his orders.

(2) Phrases used as modifiers

Prepositional phrases nearly always function as adjectives or adverbs. Infinitive phrases are also used as adjectives or adverbs. Participial phrases are used as adjectives.

ADJECTIVES	PHRASES USED AS ADJECTIVES
It is a *significant* discovery.	It is a discovery *of significance*. [Prepositional phrase]
Appropriate language is important.	Language *to suit the occasion* is important. [Infinitive phrase]

ADJECTIVES	PHRASES USED AS ADJECTIVES
Destructive storms lashed the Midwest.	Storms, *destroying many crops of corn and oats*, lashed the Midwest. [Participial phrase containing prepositional phrase used as adjective]
The *icy* bridge was dangerous.	*Covered with ice*, the bridge was dangerous. [Participial phrase modified by prepositional phrase]

ADVERBS	PHRASES USED AS ADVERBS
Drive *carefully*.	Drive *with care on slick streets*. [Prepositional phrases]
Certainly Mary Ann lacks self-confidence.	*To be sure*, Mary Ann lacks self-confidence. [Infinitive phrase]

The examples on this page show how phrases function in the same way as single-word modifiers. Remember, however, that phrases are not merely substitutes for single words. Many times phrases express more than can be packed into a single word.

> The gas gauge fluttered *from empty to full*.
> He telephoned his wife *to tell her of his arrival*.
> *Walking down Third Avenue*, I noticed many new buildings.

▶ EXERCISE 8   Each italicized phrase below is used as a modifier. First classify each phrase as prepositional, participial, or infinitive; then state whether the phrase functions as an adjective or as an adverb. (These sentences were selected from *Life*.)

The open road, the freedom [1] *to move on*, these are among the most treasured American traditions.

[2] *Reading the piece and looking at the pictures*, I was overwhelmed [3] *by conscience*.

[4] *On the mist-shrouded moors* [5] *of northern England*, men poked sticks [6] *into the mushy peat* and then held the

stick ends [7] *to their noses,* [8] *seeking—and fearing—the smell* [9] *of death.*

She is too shy [10] *to employ the hustle and muscle necessary* [11] *to win the honor.*

[12] *Working like a sculptor,* José Limon molds large groups [13] *of dancers* [14] *into heroic units,* [15] *telling intensely dramatic stories* [16] *like* <u>Othello</u> and <u>The Emperor Jones.</u>

[17] *Cradled in his mother's arms,* a skinny monkey baby [18] *with a forlorn face* made his debut [19] *at the San Diego Zoo.* The infant is a rare proboscis monkey, the first of its kind [20] *born in captivity.*

Subordinate Clauses

A clause is a group of related words which contains both a verb and its subject. Unlike a *main clause* (which can either stand alone as a sentence or function with other clauses in complex and compound sentences—see **1e**), a *subordinate clause* functions as a noun, an adjective, or an adverb and is therefore only part of a sentence. Subordinating conjunctions (such as *after, although, as, because, before, if, since, until, when, while*) and relative pronouns (such as *who, which, that*) are called "subordinate clause markers" because they introduce subordinate clauses and make them dependent.

MAIN CLAUSES   *Money had been stolen,* and *I called the police.* [Two main clauses in a compound sentence]

SUBORDINATE CLAUSES   The police knew *that the money had been stolen.* [Noun clause, object of the verb *knew*] The money *which had been stolen* was found. [Adjective clause modifying *money*] *Because money had been stolen,* I called the police. [Adverb clause preceding main clause]

(1) Subordinate clauses used as nouns

NOUNS	NOUN CLAUSES
The newspaper *accounts* may be false.	*What the newspapers say* may be false. [Subject]
I do not remember his *name.*	I do not remember *what his name is.* [Object]
Give the tools to *Paul.*	Give the tools to *whoever can use them.* [Object of the preposition *to*]

▶ EXERCISE 9   Bracket the noun clauses in the following sentences and explain the use of each clause.

[1] The repairman said that he would have to take the typewriter into the shop.   [2] What it needed most of all was to be junked.   [3] But he remembered that his customer had a sentimental fondness for this old machine. [4] And he had long ago learned that a battered, used-up piece of machinery could be to some people what politics, wife, or religion was to others.   [5] What one man loved, other men had to pretend to respect.   [6] The repairman wondered whether that saying was in the Bible.   [7] He thought that it might well be.

(2) Subordinate clauses used as modifiers

Two types of subordinate clauses, the adjective clause and the adverb clause, are used as modifiers.

ADJECTIVE	ADJECTIVE CLAUSE
The *golden* window reflects the sun.	The window, *which looks like solid gold,* reflects the sun.

ADVERB	ADVERB CLAUSE
The work stops *then.*	The work stops *when it rains.*

Adjective clauses   Any clause that modifies a noun or a pronoun is an adjective clause. An adjective clause may also modify a gerund. Adjective clauses, which nearly always follow the words modified, are most frequently introduced by a relative pronoun, which often is the subject or object in the subordinate clause.

A man *who knows the truth* is fortunate. [The relative pronoun *who* is the subject of *knows* in the adjective clause.]
He is a man *whom I have always admired.* [The relative pronoun *whom* is the object of *have admired.*]

Other words (for example, conjunctions and adverbs) may introduce adjective clauses: "a time *when all things went well for him,*" "the reason *why I changed my mind.*"

Note: If not used as a subject, the word introducing an adjective or a noun clause may sometimes be omitted. (See also **22a.**)

He is a man [*whom* or *that*] I have always admired.
I know [*that*] she is right.

Adverb clauses   An adverb clause may modify a verb, an adjective, an adverb, a verbal, a prepositional phrase, or even a whole clause.

An adverb clause often precedes or follows the main clause:

ADVERB CLAUSE, MAIN CLAUSE.

When Bill decided to leave, everyone expressed regret. [An adverb clause in this position is usually followed by a comma. See **12b.**]

MAIN CLAUSE ADVERB CLAUSE.

Everyone expressed regret when Bill decided to leave. [An adverb clause in this position is usually not set off by a comma. See **12b.**]

An adverb clause may also interrupt a main clause.

I can, *if you wish,* help you paint the woodwork. [A parenthetical adverb clause set off by commas. See **12d.**]

The position of the adverb clause depends on its relative importance in the sentence. See **29a–b.**

▶ EXERCISE 10   Bracket the five adjective clauses in the following sentences.

[1] William was not at the corner where he usually took the bus.   [2] The bus driver, who knew all his regular passengers, commented about it to one of those getting on. [3] The passenger remembered something that William had said one day about beginning his vacation in the middle of the week.   [4] That sounded reasonable to the driver, who after all had a schedule to maintain.   [5] Edging the big bus back into the traffic that was streaming by, he mentally put William on his "absent with leave" list for the next two weeks.

▶ EXERCISE 11 Bracket the eleven adverb clauses in the following paragraph.

¹ While Mr. Baker was shaving, he thought of the day ahead. ² He always began his day's work before he arrived at the office. ³ After he got on the train, he nearly always started planning his day. ⁴ Sometimes he began before the train arrived if it was a minute or two late. ⁵ But this morning, as he was shaving the tender place under his chin, details of the day's work clicked through his mind. ⁶ Since he had first been made head accountant, he couldn't remember having brought the job home with him. ⁷ Whenever anything was not the usual routine with him, he naturally wondered. ⁸ Suddenly he remembered; while he was rinsing his razor under the hot water, he smiled cheerfully. ⁹ Today, unless the state auditors broke a long habit, they would show up. ¹⁰ And because this time he had worked extra carefully to have the books ready for them, he could look forward happily to their coming.

1e

Learn to recognize main clauses and the various types of sentences.

As we have already noted in **1d,** a main clause has both a subject and a verb and can stand alone as a sentence. And as we observed in **1b,** nearly every grammatically complete sentence (all except commands or imperatives) has a subject and verb expressed.

A sentence is a unit of expression that can stand alone grammatically, though it may require other sentences to complete its meaning. It is followed in speaking by a full stop and in writing by a period, a question mark, or an exclamation point.

> He refused the offer. [Statement—followed by a period]
> Refuse the offer. [Command—followed by a period]
> Did he refuse the offer? [Question—followed by a question mark]
> How absurd the offer was! [Exclamation—followed by an exclamation point]

Sentences are classified, according to the number and kind of clauses they contain, as (1) simple, (2) compound, (3) complex, or (4) compound-complex.

A simple sentence (with the exception of the imperative) is made up of one main clause; see various patterns of the simple sentence on pages 801–02.

SIMPLE SENTENCES One part of the TV screen carried the football game. The other part showed the launching countdown.

A compound sentence has two or more main clauses.

COMPOUND SENTENCE One part of the TV screen carried the football game, and the other part showed the launching countdown.

Except when joined by one of the coordinating conjunctions (*and, but, or, nor, for*), main clauses are separated by a semicolon. See Section **14.**

> One part of the TV screen carried the football game; the other part showed the launching countdown.

A complex sentence has one main clause and at least one subordinate clause.

COMPLEX SENTENCE While one part of the TV screen carried the football game, the other part showed the launching countdown.

A compound-complex sentence is made up of two or more main clauses and at least one subordinate clause.

COMPOUND-COMPLEX SENTENCE The Saturday afternoon program was like a two-ring circus; while one part of the TV screen carried the football game, the other part showed the launching countdown.

▶ EXERCISE 12 Classify each of the following sentences (selected from the *New Yorker*) as (1) simple, (2) compound, (3) complex, or (4) compound-complex. Be prepared to justify your classification by analysis of the sentence.

1. On distant hillsides, whole stands of trees lay pointing in the same direction, like combed hair.
2. She was a chameleon, a restless, untrammeled creature dappled with sunlight and shadow.
3. Just why Bruckner's Sixth Symphony has always been the most neglected of his works has always been a puzzle to me.
4. I was happy in my own world of snow, as if I were living inside one of those glass paperweights that snow when you shake them, and I went back to sleep easily.
5. Time and again we are led through one or another of Conrad's works, detail by detail, to reach the startling conclusion that what Conrad put into the story is still there and that the story means what he said it meant.
6. Once, the stone floor of the portico must have rung with the sound of iron wheels and shod hoofs; now it is silent and the doors of the stables are shut.
7. The harvests are scanty, for the clay sheds the rain, and, with no trees to hold it, the water rushes to the valley, carrying seeds with it and carving great, gray, gutterlike channels.
8. As part of our program to promote clean and efficient business methods, we spent many years developing a copying paper that would eliminate the need for carbons.
9. His face faintly suggested mumps, and he once tipped the theatre-ticket girl in the lobby of the Hotel New Yorker three cents for getting him four tickets to a show that was sold out for a month in advance.
10. The crowd moved through the two anterooms into the Great Hall, where, from their portraits on the wall, mayors, presidents, and justices looked down with the complacent rosiness of those who have dined and died.

▶ EXERCISE 13 Compose ten sentences and classify each sentence as (1) simple, (2) complex, (3) compound, or (4) compound-complex. Write at least two sentences of each type.

▶ EXERCISE 14   Analyze the following sentences of the Gettysburg Address as directed by the instructor.

1. Fourscore and seven years ago our fathers brought forth on this continent a new nation, conceived in liberty, and dedicated to the proposition that all men are created equal.
2. Now we are engaged in a great civil war, testing whether that nation, or any nation so conceived and so dedicated, can long endure.
3. We are met on a great battlefield of that war.
4. We have come to dedicate a portion of that field as a final resting place for those who here gave their lives that that nation might live.
5. It is altogether fitting and proper that we should do this.
6. But in a larger sense we cannot dedicate, we cannot consecrate, we cannot hallow this ground.
7. The brave men, living and dead, who struggled here, have consecrated it far above our power to add or detract.
8. The world will little note, nor long remember, what we say here, but it can never forget what they did here.
9. It is for us, the living, rather to be dedicated here to the unfinished work which they who fought here have thus far so nobly advanced.
10. It is rather for us to be here dedicated to the great task remaining before us, that from these honored dead we take increased devotion to that cause for which they gave the last full measure of devotion; that we here highly resolve that these dead shall not have died in vain; that this nation, under God, shall have a new birth of freedom, and that government of the people, by the people, for the people shall not perish from the earth.

Sentence Fragment

2

Do not carelessly write a sentence fragment —a phrase or a subordinate clause—as if it were a complete sentence.

Both sentences and nonsentences begin with capitals and end with periods in such writing as the following:

> He wasn't a gorilla. *Just the cutest little baboon.* And the garbage wasn't garbage. It was ice cream. *A genuine strawberry and fish-guts sundae.*   —ALDOUS HUXLEY

Fragments (nonsentences) such as those italicized above are sometimes used intentionally and effectively by professional writers, especially in fiction. Even in formal exposition, grammatically incomplete sentences such as those in the left column below are considered standard.

NONSENTENCES	SENTENCES
How undemocratic!	How undemocratic it is!
By raising prices? No.	No, do not raise prices.

College students are usually advised, however, to learn the fundamentals of English composition before permitting themselves to take liberties with the accepted patterns of the complete sentence. (See pages 801–02.) Make it a practice, therefore, to avoid fragments; do not set off a phrase or a subordinate clause as if it were a complete sentence. The fragment should be either (1) included in the preceding or following sentence—that is, attached to the main clause—or (2) rewritten to form a sentence by itself.

FRAGMENT   He registered for the summer session. Hoping thus to graduate ahead of his class. [We have here one sentence and one fragment, a participial phrase.]

REVISED   He registered for the summer session, hoping thus to graduate ahead of his class. [Participial phrase included in the sentence]

He registered for the summer session. By this means he hoped to graduate ahead of his class. [Participial phrase made into a sentence]

FRAGMENT   He registered for the summer session. Because he hoped thus to graduate ahead of his class. [We have here one sentence and one fragment, a subordinate clause.]

REVISED   He registered for the summer session because he hoped thus to graduate ahead of his class. [Subordinate clause included in the sentence]

TESTS FOR SENTENCE COMPLETENESS

A sentence fragment may be obvious to the student who reads it aloud in context. If he reads the fragment properly, he will find that either it is not preceded by a full stop or else it is not followed by one. That is, the fragment belongs with the preceding sentence or with the following one.

Sentence completeness may also be tested (1) by searching for the verb and its subject and (2) by determining whether this verb and subject are introduced by a subordinating conjunction or relative pronoun. If the supposed sentence does not have a verb and its subject, it may be identified at once as a phrase. *Hoping thus to graduate ahead of his class,* for example, has neither verb nor subject. *Hoping* is a participle and *to graduate* is an infinitive. Even when both verb and subject are present, they may be introduced by a subordinating conjunction or relative pronoun and thus constitute a subordinate clause. *Because he hoped to graduate ahead of his class* has the verb *hoped* and the subject *he.* But since these words are introduced by the subordinating conjunction *because,* the group of words is a subordinate clause—still a sentence fragment.

If you unintentionally write fragments, carefully proofread your compositions. Form a mental picture of the core of each of your sentences after you have reviewed the sentence patterns on pages 801–02.

▶ EXERCISE 1   Find the seven fragments in the following paragraphs. Revise each fragment by attaching it logically to a main clause or by rewriting the fragment so that it will stand by itself as a sentence.

[1] As a weather watcher, I am often amused by official forecasts. [2] Or, rather, by occasional prophecies made by weather men who seldom bother to glance out the window. [3] For example, one day last spring when heavy rain and large hail lashed the city. [4] I promptly telephoned the weather bureau. [5] To ask about the possibility of a tornado. [6] A confident voice replied glibly, "Oh, don't worry about a tornado; we're not even in an alert area."

[7] Relieved, I turned on the radio, found a chair near a window, and watched the angry clouds. [8] Amazingly enough, I soon saw a swirling funnel emerge from a black cloud and reach for the ground. [9] Just north of the city, about five miles away. [10] Of course, I immediately notified the weather bureau.

[11] A short time later. [12] An important message interrupted the jazz on the radio: "The weather bureau has issued a warning that a tornado may strike north of here." [13] I smiled as I repeated the words "may strike." [14] Knowing that the official prophets were vigilant. [15] As they busily observed falling barometers and erratic wind gauges instead of paying attention to the turbulent weather itself.

2a

Do not carelessly write a phrase (participial, prepositional, or infinitive) as a complete sentence.

FRAGMENT   I made little progress. *Finally giving up all my efforts.* [Participial phrase]

REVISED   I made so little progress that I finally gave up all my efforts. [Fragment included in the sentence]

         I made little progress. Finally I gave up all my efforts. [Fragment made into a sentence]

FRAGMENT   Soon I began to work for the company. *First in the rock pit and later on the highway.* [Prepositional phrases]

REVISED   Soon I began to work for the company, first in the rock pit and later on the highway. [Fragment included in the sentence]

FRAGMENT   He will have an opportunity to visit his home town. *And to talk with many of his old friends.* [Infinitive phrase]

REVISED   He will have an opportunity to visit his home town and to talk with many of his old friends. [Fragment included in the sentence]

▶ **EXERCISE 2**   Eliminate each fragment below by including it in a sentence or by making it into a sentence.

1. We had a wonderful time at the lake. Swimming near the dock and fishing on the barge.
2. I spray the shrubbery twice a year. Once in the late spring and again in the early fall.
3. The pampered Dennis finally left home. Earnestly seeking to become an individual in his own right.
4. He was once a beautiful child. With curly black hair and bright blue eyes.
5. I want to make high grades. To succeed not only as an athlete but also as a scholar.
6. In high school I was a "discipline problem." In more ways than one.
7. My grandmother is a delightful conversationalist. Often

speaking of the "days of her youth," during what she calls the "Renaissance period."
8. I think that it is wise to ignore his sarcasm. Or to make a quick exit.
9. Squinting her eyes, the gossip leaned forward. To whisper this question in my ear: "Have you seen that mangy little thug she dates?"
10. Bill smiled self-consciously. Like a politician posing before a television camera.

2b

Do not carelessly write a subordinate clause as a complete sentence.

FRAGMENT   A railway control board should be constructed with care. *Because from this board trains are moved through a system of tracks and switches.* [Subordinate clause]

REVISED   A railway control board should be constructed with care because from this board trains are moved through a system of tracks and switches. [Fragment included in the sentence]

FRAGMENT   I was trying to read the directions. *Which were confusing and absurd.* [Subordinate clause]

REVISED   I was trying to read the directions, which were confusing and absurd. [Fragment included in the sentence]

         I was trying to read the directions. They were confusing and absurd. [Fragment made into a sentence]

▶ **EXERCISE 3**   Some of the following numbered word groups contain fragments; others do not. Write *F* after each fragment; write *S* after each sentence.

F 1. I stopped trying to read my assignment. As soon as he started imitating my favorite comedian by doing the tango with a lamp shade on his head.
C 2. The little thief was almost sick from fright. And the sheriff believed that he could handle his prisoner alone.
C 3. My hobby is oil painting. In fact, that is my pride, my joy, and my dependable moneymaker.
F 4. Mr. Adams did not insist on my buying insurance. Which is more than I can say for the last agent we had here.
C 5. Then she would fail. This was the nightmare that haunted her, the dread of the inevitable surrender to defeat.
F 6. Grandmother was proud of her Indian pudding. Especially when several of the guests asked for second helpings.
C 7. I do not believe the printed label. As a rule, it takes all night for the paint to harden.
F 8. The adjuster had no trouble last time. Although I know, of course, that this is an entirely different situation.
F 9. Mrs. Gayle never speaks about her travels abroad. As if she knew everything and we were all ignoramuses.
F 10. The *Titanic* rammed into an iceberg. Which took place on April 15, 1912.

2c

Do not carelessly write as a complete sentence any other fragment, such as an appositive (noun or noun substitute) or a member of a compound predicate.

FRAGMENT   My father was born in Cartersville. *A little country town where everyone knows everyone else.* [Appositive modified by a subordinate clause]

REVISED   My father was born in Cartersville, a little country town where everyone knows everyone else.

FRAGMENT   William was elected president of his class. *And was made a member of the National Honor Society.* [Detached member of a compound predicate]

REVISED   William was elected president of his class and was made a member of the National Honor Society.

▶ EXERCISE 4   Attach each fragment below to the preceding sentence or make the fragment into an independent sentence.

1. Fred received an invitation to my wedding. And acknowledged it by sending me a sympathy card.
2. You should work when you are young and enthusiastic. And should leave dreams to old men.
3. I am often told to do things I do not like. Such as getting out of bed.
4. The hydraulic lift raises the plows out of the ground. And lowers them again.
5. I had a feeling that some sinister spirit of evil brooded over the place. A feeling that I could not analyze.

▶ EXERCISE 5   Identify each fragment; determine whether it falls under the rule for **2a, 2b,** or **2c**; then make the appropriate correction. Write *C* after each numbered item which contains no fragment.

1. I knew that he was asking for trouble. As soon as I heard of his buying that motorcycle.
2. He let me believe that I had first chance at the job. But without definitely committing himself.
3. He was still angry with me. His eyes glaring fiercely.
4. He killed three ducks with one shot. Against the law of averages but possible.
5. She dressed exactly like the Hollywood starlets. Since she wanted to become one of them herself.
6. To watch Dempsey in the ring was to watch a perfectly engineered machine operated with exact precision.
7. To anyone who knew him in 1840, it would have seemed ridiculous beyond belief. To predict that one day this rawboned frontier lawyer would be President of the United States.
8. The festival beginning on the twentieth of June and continuing through the month of July.
9. Early in life he decided upon a simple philosophy. From which grew all his subsequent opinions.
10. Doc Potter is exactly what you said he would be. A thoroughly profane and entertaining old reprobate.

▶ EXERCISE 6   Attach each fragment below to an existing sentence or make it into an independent sentence.

[1] Very late in *The Merry Wives of Windsor,* Shakespeare introduces an incident which is altogether extraneous to either of the plot lines in the play.   [2] And which advances the action in no way whatsoever.   [3] Bardolph in a very brief scene with the Host announces that "the Germans" desire three of the Host's horses.   [4] So that they may go to meet "the Duke," who is to be at court on the next day.   [5] The Host seems to know so little of these Germans that he must ask if they speak English.   [6] A highly improbable ignorance on his part, for in his next lines he states that they have been already a week at his tavern.   [7] But he lets them have the horses.   [8] Insisting, however, that they must pay for them.   [9] Two scenes later Bardolph returns to the tavern with the report that the villainous Germans have handled him roughly on the road.   [10] Thrown him into a puddle, and run off with the horses.   [11] Immediately on his heels, in come first Sir Hugh and then Dr. Caius.   [12] With rumors confirming Bardolph's assurance of the evil character of the Germans.   [13] So that the Host is at last alarmed.   [14] He is convinced now that the Germans have indeed cozened him of a week's board bill.   [15] And stolen his horses in the bargain.

Comma Splice and Fused Sentence

3

Do not carelessly link two main clauses with only a comma between them (comma splice) or run main clauses together without any punctuation (fused sentence).

COMMA SPLICE   The current was swift, he could not swim to shore. [Two main clauses linked only by a comma]

FUSED SENTENCE   The current was swift he could not swim to shore. [Omission of all punctuation between main clauses]

If you cannot recognize main clauses and distinguish them from subordinate clauses, study Section 1, Sentence Sense, as you apply the following instructions to your writing.

3a

Correct either comma splices or fused sentences by one of the following methods:

(1) By subordinating one of the main clauses—usually the best method. (See also Section **24.**)

COMMA SPLICE   The current was swift, he could not swim to shore.

REVISED   Since the current was swift, he could not swim to shore. [First main clause changed to a subordinate clause]

PATTERN   SUBORDINATE CLAUSE, MAIN CLAUSE.

(2) By making each main clause into a sentence.

FUSED   The current was swift he could not swim to shore.

REVISED   The current was swift. He could not swim to shore.

(3) By joining main clauses with a semicolon.

REVISED   The current was swift; he could not swim to shore.

PATTERN   MAIN CLAUSE; MAIN CLAUSE.

(4) By joining the main clauses with a comma plus a coordinating conjunction.

REVISED   The current was swift, and he could not swim to shore.

PATTERN
    MAIN CLAUSE, *and* (or *but, or, nor, for*) MAIN CLAUSE.

Some exceptions: Short coordinate clauses in series, parallel in form and unified in thought, may be separated by commas.

I came, I saw, I conquered.

The comma is also used to separate a statement from an echo question.

You can come, can't you? [Statement echoed by question]

Main clauses separated only by commas are fairly common in some informal types of writing. Occasionally examples are found in more formal writing, chiefly when there is a balance or contrast between the clauses.

They trundle mobile baskets at the A&P, they sit under driers at the hairdressers, they sweep their porches and set out bulbs and stitch up slip covers.   —PHYLLIS MC GINLEY

The student learning to write formal papers in college will do well, however, to make sure that main clauses in his sentences are separated (1) by a comma plus a coordinate conjunction or (2) by a semicolon.

3b

Caution: Do not let a conjunctive adverb, a transitional phrase, or a divided quotation trick you into making a comma splice. (See also 14a.)

Unlike coordinating conjunctions, which have a fixed position when they link main clauses, conjunctive adverbs and transitional phrases do not have a fixed position: they may join main clauses or be used parenthetically. A semicolon or a comma before a conjunctive adverb or transitional phrase is therefore an important signal to the reader, telling him whether or not to expect a main clause to follow.

I do not like ice cream, *but* I sometimes eat it at parties. [Coordinating conjunction with fixed position]
I do not like ice cream; *however,* I sometimes eat it at parties. [Conjunctive adverb with semicolon introducing a main clause]
I do not like ice cream; I sometimes eat it, *however,* at parties. [Parenthetical *however* set off by commas]

Remember that **conjunctive adverbs** (such as *accordingly, also, anyhow, besides, consequently, furthermore, hence, henceforth, however, indeed, instead, likewise, meanwhile, moreover, nevertheless, otherwise, still, then, therefore, thus*) and **transitional phrases** (such as *for example, in fact, on the contrary, on the other hand, that is*) connecting main clauses are always preceded by a semicolon.

Divided quotations

COMMA SPLICE   "Your answer is wrong," he said, "correct it."
REVISED   "Your answer is wrong," he said. "Correct it."
COMMA SPLICE   "What are you looking for?" she asked, "may I help you?"
REVISED   "What are you looking for?" she asked. "May I help you?"

EXERCISES ON BUILDING SENTENCES
AND OBSERVING SENTENCE PATTERNS
(TO AVOID THE COMMA SPLICE)

▶ **EXERCISE 1**   Write two sentences to illustrate each construction specified below.

1. Main clause; main clause.
2. Main clause, *coordinating conjunction* main clause.
3. Main clause; *conjunctive adverb* (,) main clause.

▶ **EXERCISE 2**   All of the following sentences (selected from *Harper's Magazine*) are correctly punctuated. Identify the pattern or construction of each sentence.

1. The forest became a dancing pattern of light and shade, and a pathway of light fell before me on the ground.
2. The other day a police car shot past me at about 150 miles an hour, and I did not even crunch my toes.
3. He may haggle fiercely over details, but he also has a magnificent detachment and an almost saintly freedom from any sense of grievance toward his detractors.
4. In ancient times, fats were the hallmark of affluence; they still are in some cultures.
5. Chris thinks scholarship is a matter for the young, and he's ravenous for it as a sort of intellectual hamburger.
6. But policemen are scarce in the country districts; besides, the Moustheni Explorers planned to work at night.
7. The first cars are very long; hence there are correspondingly long intervals between the flashes of daylight you see between them.
8. She wore her hair in a bun to seem mature, but the blue jeans necessary for climbing among the rafters took ten years off her age.
9. Both James and Dreiser had a profound feeling for the femininity of cities, but they had revealingly different attitudes toward it.
10. The villas drip with wooden fringe; they support cornices that are sunbursts of frilly lattice and balconies that seem to be squeezed from pastry tubes.

▶ **EXERCISE 3**   Determine which of the following sentences contain comma splices. (As an aid to your analysis, you may wish to bracket each subordinate clause and to underline the subject and verb of each main clause.) Write C after each sentence that needs no revision. Correct each comma splice in the most appropriate way.

1. Mary Queen of Scots' death warrant was written on a playing card, the nine of diamonds; therefore this card is sometimes called "the curse of Scotland."
2. If Jay's batting average had been better, for example, he would have been the best baseball player in the league.

3. "Rate the entries," he said, "Interview the applicants, and study their recommendations."
4. Irving exploited local legends; he helped to start American folklore by writing "Rip Van Winkle."
5. Typhus used to kill more soldiers than actual warfare did; however the disease is rarely heard of now.
6. Fred was lucky in his choice of rooms; although they were small, they were close to his work.
7. Liechtenstein postage stamps are especially beautiful; stamp collectors eagerly buy special issues.
8. To be a baby sitter, one should know something of child care; for example, one should know how to warm a bottle and to burp a baby.
9. The western world is indebted to the Saracens for paper. It was the Saracens, moreover, who built Europe's first paper mill.
10. Frogs swallow moving objects; as a matter of fact, they will die of hunger rather than strike a motionless insect.

▶ EXERCISE 4 Revise each comma splice (or fused sentence) by some method of subordination. Write *C* after any sentence that needs no revision.

1. Frantically I wound and jerked the starting cord a tow of gravel barges was bearing directly down upon me.
2. Sheila has her mind made up, nothing you can say will change it.
3. We have enough bricks we can build a barbecue pit.
4. I spoke of the Rufus Kane matter to Chief Kelly, he recalled the case quite clearly.
5. The plaster hardens rapidly it should not be mixed in large quantities.
6. When you come to a red brick church across from a filling station, turn left and go exactly one block.
7. There is a roadside market on the Maryville highway you can buy all the berries you want there.
8. At farrowing, her pigs weighed slightly over three pounds apiece, this is a little above average weight.
9. We do not plan to come back in the fall, therefore we are giving up our apartment.
10. One man was digging at the bottom of the well, and the other stayed at the top to haul up the loose dirt.

Adjectives and Adverbs

4

Distinguish between adjectives and adverbs and use the appropriate forms.

Adjectives and adverbs are modifiers. That is, they qualify or limit, make clearer or more specific, other words in the sentence. Any word modifying a noun or a pronoun functions as an adjective; an adjective may also modify a gerund or a noun phrase. Any word modifying a verb, an adjective, or another adverb functions as an adverb; an adverb may also modify verbals (gerunds, infinitives, participles) or even whole clauses. In the following examples, arrows indicate modification; brackets enclose modified groups of words.

NO MODIFIERS Lobbyists advocated laws. (Noun—verb—noun.)

ADJECTIVES *Many* lobbyists advocated *severe* [*blue* laws].

ADVERBS *Honestly,* [*too* many lobbyists *very deceitfully* advocated *unduly* severe blue laws].

Forms of Adjectives and Adverbs

As a rule, suffixes such as *-al, -ish, -ive, -ly, -like,* and *-ous* make adjectives out of nouns:

NOUNS a *nation,* my *friend,* a *boy,* the *danger*
ADJECTIVES *national* bank, *friendly* cat, *boyish* prank, *dangerous* work

The *-ly* ending nearly always converts adjectives to adverbs:

ADJECTIVES *formal* dress, a *quick* turn, a *real* gem, *sure* thing
ADVERBS *formally* dressed, *quickly* turning, *really* valuable, *surely* is

Note: A few words ending in *-ly* (such as *only, early, cowardly*) may be either adjectives or adverbs, and the same is true for a considerable number of common words not ending in *-ly* (such as *far, fast, late, little, near, right, straight, well*). For the comparative and superlative forms of adjectives and adverbs, see **4c.**

A good dictionary shows the appropriate form for adjective or adverb, but only the use to which the word is put in the sentence determines whether the adjective or the adverb form is required.

▶ EXERCISE 1 Identify each italicized word below as an adjective or an adverb and explain why it is appropriately used.

1. We took a *leisurely* drive. We drove *leisurely.*
2. He is *sure* of victory. He will *surely* win.
3. The Boy Scouts did *good* work. The Boy Scouts did the work *well.*
4. The silence in the catacombs was *awful.* It was *awfully* silent in the catacombs.
5. The patient expressed *real* gratitude. He was *really* grateful.

4a

Use the adverb form for modifiers of verbs, adjectives, and other adverbs.

(1) Modifiers of verbs

NONSTANDARD His clothes fit him perfect. [The adjective *perfect* misused to modify the verb *fit*]
STANDARD His clothes fit him *perfectly.*
NONSTANDARD He ran good for the first half mile. [The adjective *good* misused to modify the verb *ran*]
STANDARD He ran *well* for the first half mile.

(2) **Modifiers of adjectives**

NONSTANDARD The farmer has a reasonable secure future. [The adjective *reasonable* misused to modify the adjective *secure*]
STANDARD The farmer has a *reasonably* secure future.

NONSTANDARD The plane was a special built fighter.
STANDARD The plane was a *specially* built fighter.

(3) **Modifiers of adverbs**

INFORMAL Only by working real hard can I pass the course.
FORMAL Only by working *really* hard can I pass the course.

▶ **EXERCISE 2** Choose the standard form of the modifier within parentheses appropriate to formal writing. If necessary, use your dictionary to distinguish between formal and informal usage.

1. If you study (consistent, consistently) and (regular, regularly), you should overcome (most, almost) any handicap.
2. The wind blew (fierce, fiercely), and the snow fell (continuous, continuously) all the long night.
3. The next few weeks passed very (rapid, rapidly).
4. I am afraid that the good woman is (some, somewhat) confused.
5. Dave is (uncommon, uncommonly) light on his feet for such a (heavy, heavily) built man.
6. It was a (fair, fairly), warm day in April.
7. It was a (fair, fairly) warm day in April.
8. Mr. Porter was so excited that he could not play his part (good, well).
9. I want someone who can do the work (prompt and efficient, promptly and efficiently) and still behave (courteous, courteously) toward the customers.
10. Do you realize how (bad, badly) your grades may suffer if you do not work (steady, steadily) or (serious, seriously) enough?

4b

Use adjectives rather than adverbs as subject complements.

As subject complements, adjectives always modify the subject. Subject complements usually follow but sometimes precede linking verbs. *Be, am, are, is, was, were, been, seem, become,* and their equivalents, as well as such verbs as *feel, look, smell, sound,* and *taste* are commonly used to link subjects and complements.

SUBJECT—LINKING VERB—SUBJECT COMPLEMENT.

The name sounds *familiar.* [*Familiar* name]
Still waters run (OR are) *deep.* [*Deep* waters]
This cake does not taste very *fresh.* [*Fresh* cake]

Apparent exception: The modifier should be an adverb when it refers to the action of the verb. In that case the verb is not used as a linking verb.

The blind beggar felt *cautiously* along the wall. [The adverb *cautiously* qualifies the verb *felt.*]
The woman looked *angrily* at him. [The adverb *angrily* qualifies the verb *looked.*]

Note: A modifier following a verb and its direct object is an adjective when it refers to the object rather than to the action of the verb.

PATTERN   SUBJECT—VERB—OBJECT—COMPLEMENT.

The boy dug the hole *deep.* [*Deep* hole]

▶ **EXERCISE 3** Using adjectives as subject complements, write five sentences that illustrate the following pattern:

SUBJECT—LINKING VERB—SUBJECT COMPLEMENT.

4c

Use the appropriate forms for the comparative and the superlative.

In general the shorter adjectives (and a few adverbs) form the comparative degree by adding *-er* and the superlative by adding *-est;* the longer adjectives and most adverbs form the comparative by the use of *more (less)* and the superlative by the use of *most (least).* A few modifiers have an irregular comparison.

Positive	*Comparative*	*Superlative*
warm	warmer	warmest
warmly	more warmly	most warmly
helpful	less helpful	least helpful
good, well	better	best
bad, badly	worse	worst

(1) **Use the comparative degree for two persons or things.**

Was Monday or Tuesday *warmer?*
James was the *taller* of the two boys. [The superlative is occasionally used in such sentences, especially in informal speaking and writing.]

(2) **Use the superlative degree for three or more persons or things.**

Today is the *warmest* day of the year.
William was the *tallest* of the three boys.

4d

Avoid any awkward or ambiguous use of a noun form as an adjective.

Although many noun forms (*boat* race, *show* business, *opera* tickets, etc.) are used effectively as adjectives, especially when appropriate adjectives are not available, such forms should be avoided when they are either awkward or ambiguous.

AWKWARD I sometimes forget basic mathematics principles.
BETTER I sometimes forget basic mathematical principles. OR:
     I sometimes forget principles of basic mathematics.

▶ **EXERCISE 4** Revise the following sentences to provide the proper adjectives or adverbs in accordance with formal English usage. Write *C* after each sentence that needs no revision.

1. Don's explanation, the clearest of the two, indicates that he will do good at teaching.

2. Mr. Hawkins takes life entirely too serious.
3. If you want to catch him, you had better be quick about it.
4. We felt certain that we had walked long enough.
5. If Edna expects a passing grade, she had better study a reasonably amount of time.
6. So vivid does the author picture the meeting that the reader sure feels as if he is present.
7. Karen gets along with her professors, but she is not real smart.
8. When the truck stopped so sudden, Herb's car rammed into it.
9. Although this desk is probably some cheaper than that, it is not so well built.
10. I sure hope I can pronounce that French title correctly.

▶ **EXERCISE 5** Compose sentences containing these constructions:

1. *good* as a subject complement
2. *well* modifying a verb
3. *surely* modifying a verb
4. an adjective used as subject complement after *looked*
5. an adverb modifying *looked*
6. an adjective following and modifying a direct object
7. an adverb following a direct object and modifying the verb
8. the superlative form of *bad*
9. the comparative form of *good*
10. a clear, effective noun form used as an adjective

Case

5

Use the proper case form to show the function of pronouns or nouns in sentences.

The pronouns *I*, *me*, *my*, and *mine* all refer to the one who is speaking or writing. The change in form to indicate function is called *case*. *I* is in the subjective or nominative case; *me*, in the objective case; and *my* and *mine*, in the possessive case. Nouns and some indefinite pronouns (*anyone*, *someone*, *everyone*, etc.) have a distinctive case form only for the possessive (the *boy's* book, the *boys'* mother; see **15a**), but six of our common pronouns have distinctive forms in all three cases and must be used with care.

FORMS

SUBJECTIVE	I	we	he, she	they	who
POSSESSIVE	my	our	his, her	their	whose
	(mine)	(ours)	(hers)	(theirs)	
OBJECTIVE	me	us	him, her	them	whom

Note: The personal pronouns *it* and *you* change form only to indicate the possessive—*its*, *your* (*yours*).

USES

SUBJECTIVE   *He* and *I* traveled together in France. [Subjects]
             It was *she* who paid the bill. [*She* used as subject complement, and *who* as subject of *paid*]
POSSESSIVE   That is *your* gift, not *mine*. [Possessors]
             Carl approved of *his* amending the motion. [Before the gerund]
OBJECTIVE   Frances has already met *him*. [Direct object]
             Give *them* our best regards. [Indirect object]
             The task was hard for *us*. [Object of preposition]
             Our guest did not expect *us* to entertain *him*. [*Us* is subject of the infinitive; *him*, the object. See also **5e**.]

5a

Take special care with pronouns in apposition and in compound constructions.

(1) Appositives

An appositive takes the same case as the noun or pronoun with which it is in apposition.

We—John and I (not *me*)—are responsible for the damage. [*I* is in the subjective case since it is in apposition with the subject *we*.]
Let's you and *me* (not *I*) go together. Let us—you and *me*—go together. [*Me* and *us* are in the same case]
Two boys—John and I (not *me*)—represented our class. [*I* is in the subjective case since it is in apposition with the subject *boys*.]
Our class was represented by two boys, John and *me* (not *I*). [*Me* is in the objective case since it is in apposition with *boys*, object of the preposition *by*.]

Note: Do not let an appositive following a pronoun trick you into making a mistake with case.

We boys often study together. [*We* is the subject of *study*: *We study*. No one would say *Us often study*.]
He would not let *us* girls do any of the hard work. [Since *us* is the subject of the infinitive (*to*) *do*, it is in the objective case. See **5e**.]

(2) Compound constructions

My brother and I (not *me*) share expenses. [*I* is a subject of the verb *share*.]
Everyone but Hazel and *her* (not *she*) signed the petition. [*Her* is an object of the preposition *but*.]
Last summer my father hired Tom and *me* (not *I*). [*Me* is an object of the verb *hired*.]

Note: In formal writing, *myself* is usually avoided as a substitute for *I* or *me*. See **19i**. The *-self* pronouns (such as *myself*, *himself*, *ourselves*, *themselves*) are ordinarily used either as reflexive or intensive pronouns.

REFLEXIVE   James hurt *himself*.
INTENSIVE   James *himself* was hurt.

▶ **EXERCISE 1** Compose brief sentences correctly using five of the following compound elements as appositives and five as subjects or objects.

1. Bill and he   3. you or I
2. Bill and him   4. you or me

5. her sister and her
6. her sister and she
7. Ann and she
8. her and Ann
9. they or we
10. them or us

5b

Determine the case of each pronoun by its use in its own clause.

(1) Pronoun as subject of a clause.

The subject of a clause always takes the subjective case, even when the whole clause is the object of a verb or a preposition.

> He will employ *whoever* is willing to work. [*Whoever* is the subject of *is willing.* The whole clause *whoever is willing to work* is the object of *will employ.*]
> He has respect for *whoever* is in power. [The complete clause *whoever is in power,* not merely the pronoun *whoever,* is the object of the preposition *for.*]

(2) Pronoun followed by a parenthetical *I think, he says,* etc.

Such parenthetical expressions as *I think; he says, we know* often cause the subjective *who* (*whoever, whosoever*) to be incorrectly changed to *whom* (*whomever, whomsoever*).

> Henry is a person *who* (not *whom*) I think will prove worthy of every trust. [*Who* is the subject of *will prove.*]
> Jones is a man *who* (not *whom*) we know is dependable.

(3) Pronoun following *than* or *as.*

A pronoun following *than* or *as* takes the subjective or objective case according to whether the pronoun is subject or object of an implied verb.

> He is older than *I* [am].
> He is as wise as *they* [are].
> He likes you better than *I* [like you].
> He likes you as much as *I* [like you].
> He likes you better than [he likes] *me.*
> He likes you as much as [he likes] *me.*

5c

In formal writing use *whom* for all objects.

EXAMPLES   For *whom* did you vote? [Good usage, formal or informal, calls for the objective *whom* when the pronoun immediately follows a preposition.]
The artist *whom* she loved has gone away. [*Whom* is the object of *loved.*]-

Informal English tends to avoid the use of the objective *whom* unless it comes immediately after a preposition.

FORMAL   *Whom* did you vote for?
INFORMAL   *Who* did you vote for? [*Who* may be used in an informal situation to begin any question.]

Both informal and formal English may avoid *whom* by omitting it in sentences such as the following:

> The artist she loved has gone away.

▶ EXERCISE 2   First underline each subordinate clause below and determine the use of the relative pronoun in its own clause; then choose the correct pronoun within the parentheses.

1. Mary Todd, (who, whom) historians say was socially ambitious, married a country lawyer.
2. Daniel Boone is the hero (who, whom) I most admire.
3. The author is a local woman to (who, whom) a Pulitzer prize was awarded.
4. (Whoever, Whomever) designed the August cover is a clever cartoonist.
5. Do you know the name of the Frenchman (who, whom) it is said made a helicopter as long ago as 1784?
6. Fran, (who, whom) the boys think is a poor dancer, won the figure skating championship.
7. He is an orator (who, whom), I believe, has a golden tongue.
8. Are these the astronauts (who, whom) your father talked about?
9. (Who, Whom) will be his opponent is not yet known.
10. (Who, Whom) he will fight is not yet known.

5d

A pronoun immediately before the gerund (verbal noun) is usually in the possessive case.

EXAMPLES   *His* leaving the farm was a surprise.
Mother approved of *my* (*our, his, her, your, their*) going to the fair.

Note: Since the gerund (verbal noun) and the present participle (verbal adjective) both end in *-ing,* they are sometimes difficult to distinguish. See **Verbals,** Section **35.** When the emphasis is on the noun or pronoun preceding the verbal, the verbal may be interpreted as a participle modifying the noun or pronoun. Then the noun or pronoun is not used in the possessive case.

PARTICIPLE (VERBAL ADJECTIVE)	GERUND (VERBAL NOUN)
We caught *John* running away.	*John's* running away was unexpected.
We could not think of *him* acting the part.	*His* acting was surprisingly good.

5e

Use the objective case for subject, object, or complement of an infinitive.

EXAMPLES   He asked *me* to help *him.* [*Me* is the subject and *him* is the object of the infinitive *to help. Me to help him* is the object of the verb *asked.*]
We expected *him* to be *her.* [*Him* is the subject and *her* is the complement of the infinitive *to be.*]

Note: In formal writing the complement of the infinitive *to be* is in the subjective case when the infinitive *to be* has no subject.

> I would like to be *he.*

5f

Use the subjective case for the complement of the verb *be.*

PATTERN   SUBJECT—LINKING VERB *BE*—COMPLEMENT.

That	may be	she.
It	was	they.

Note: Informal usage accepts *It is me* (*It's me*).

▶ **EXERCISE 3**   Give the reason why each italicized noun or pronoun below is correct by pointing out its function. If any sentence sounds wrong to you, read it aloud several times so that you will become accustomed to saying and hearing correct case forms.

1. Just between you and *me*, both her sister and *she* are in love with the same man.
2. The losers, you and *he*, deserve this booby prize.
3. It is Doris and *she whom* he blames.
4. He blames Doris and *her*, not you and *me*.
5. *Jack's* teasing did not annoy Tom or *me*.
6. Since Marian eats a great deal more than *I*, I do not weigh as much as *she*.
7. Let's you and *me* send an invitation to Kate and *him*.
8. The professor asked *us* students to write a composition about someone *whom* we particularly admired.
9. He introduced me to Ruth and *her*, *who* I think are his sisters.
10. *We* boys always cooperate with our coach, *whom* we respect and *who* respects us.

▶ **EXERCISE 4**   Find and correct all case errors in the following sentences. Write *C* after each sentence that needs no revision.

1. Van objected to me buying Hogarth's *The Shrimp Girl*.
2. He wanted us—Luke, you, and I—to choose *Calais Gate* instead.
3. Whom do you think is the best pitcher in the league?
4. Between you and I, I prefer Japanese wood-block prints.
5. It was I who made the mistake.
6. My sister, who I have told you of, collects Grant Wood paintings.
7. Us boys all landed at Kennedy Airport yesterday.
8. Jorge can do the trimming and spraying as well as me.
9. Sheriff Comstock, to who I had introduced myself, had records of three men who he believed were capable of committing a burglary such as that in East Dover Heights.
10. Whom does your professor consider is the best modern composer?

Agreement

6

Make a verb agree in number with its subject; make a pronoun agree in number with its antecedent.

Singular subjects require singular verbs; plural subjects require plural verbs.[1] Pronouns agree with their antecedents

[1] Although verbs have no number, it is customary to use the terms *singular verbs* for verb forms used with singular subjects and *plural verbs* for those used with plural subjects.

(the words to which they refer) in the same way. Note that in the subject the *-s* ending is the sign of the plural, that in the verb it is the sign of the third person singular.

> The *risk* of the workers *seems* great. [Singular subject—singular verb]
> The *risks* of the workers *seem* great. [Plural subject—plural verb]
> The *woman* washes *her* own clothes. [Singular antecedent—singular pronoun]
> The *women* wash *their* own clothes. [Plural antecedent—plural pronoun]

Single out each subject and its verb and connect them mentally (*risk seems, risks seem*). Do the same with each antecedent and its pronoun (*woman ← her, women ← their*). This practice will make it easy to avoid errors in agreement. If you find it difficult to distinguish verbs and relate them to their subjects, review **1a** and **1b**.

6a

Make a verb agree in number with its subject.

(1) Do not be misled (a) by nouns or pronouns intervening between the subject and the verb or (b) by subjects and verbs with endings difficult to pronounce.

> The *recurrence* of like sounds *helps* (not *help*) to stir the emotions.
> Every *one* of you *is* (not *are*) invited to the panel discussion.
> The *scientist asks* (not *ask*) pertinent questions.

The number of the subject is not changed by the addition of parenthetical expressions introduced by such words as *with, together with, as well as, no less than, including, accompanied by.*

> *John*, together with James and William, *was drafted* into the Army.
> *Thomas*, like his two brothers, *was* often in debt.

(2) Subjects joined by *and* are usually plural.

> A hammer and a saw *are* useful tools.
> Mary, Jane, and I *were* tired after our morning's work.

Exceptions: A compound subject referring to a single person, or to two or more things considered as a unit, is singular.

> My best friend and adviser *has gone*. [A single individual was both friend and adviser.]
> The tumult and the shouting *dies*.—KIPLING. [Two nouns considered a single entity]

Each or *every* preceding singular subjects joined by *and* calls for a singular verb.

> Each boy and each girl *is* to work independently.
> Every boy and girl *has been urged* to attend the play.

(3) Singular subjects joined by *or, nor, either . . . or, neither . . . nor* usually take a singular verb.

> Neither the boy nor the girl *is* to blame for the accident.
> Either the man or his wife *knows* the exact truth of the matter.

When the meaning is felt to be plural, informal English occasionally uses the plural verb: "Neither she nor I *were* dancing, for we felt tired."

If one subject is singular and one plural, the verb usually agrees with the nearer.

> Neither teacher nor pupils *are* invited.
> Neither pupils nor teacher *is* invited.
> Either you or I *am* mistaken.

Many writers prefer to recast such sentences and thus avoid the problem:

> The invitation included neither teacher nor pupils.
> Either you are mistaken or I am. OR One of us is mistaken.

(4) **When the subject follows the verb (as in sentences beginning with *there is, there are*) special care is needed to determine the subject and to make sure that it agrees with the verb.**

> According to the rules, there *are* to be at least three *contestants* for each prize. [Contestants—are]
> There *are* many possible *candidates*.
> There *is* only one good *candidate*.

Before a compound subject the first member of which is singular, a singular verb is sometimes used: "In the basement there *is* a restaurant, which serves delicious food, and a poolroom and two barber shops."

Note: The expletive *it* is always followed by a singular verb: "It *is* the *woman* who suffers." "It *is* the *women* who suffer."

(5) **A relative pronoun used as a subject takes a plural or singular verb to accord with its antecedent.**

> *Boys* who *work* . . . . A *boy* who *works* . . . .
> Mary is among the *students* who *have* done honor to the college. [*Students* is the antecedent of *who*.]
> Mary is the only *one* of our students who *has achieved* national recognition. [*One*, not *students*, is the antecedent of *who*. The sentence means, "Of all our students Mary is the only *one* who *has achieved* national recognition."]

(6) **When used as subjects, *each, either, neither, another, anyone, anybody, anything, someone, somebody, something, one, everyone, everybody, everything, nobody, nothing* regularly take singular verbs.**

> Each *takes* his turn at rowing.
> Neither *likes* the friends of the other.
> Someone *is* likely to hear the signal.
> Everyone *has* his prejudices.
> Nobody *cares* to listen to worries.

None is plural or singular, depending upon the other words in the sentence or in the immediately surrounding sentences (the context) which condition its meaning.

> None *are* so blind as those who will not see.
> None *is* so blind as he who will not see.

(*Any, all, more, most,* and *some* are used with plural or singular verbs in much the same way as *none*.)

(7) **Collective nouns (and numbers denoting fixed quantity) usually take singular verbs because the group or quantity is usually regarded as a unit.**

The whole family *is* concerned. [The common use: *family* regarded as a unit]
The family *have* gone about their several duties. [Less common: individuals of the family regarded separately]
A thousand bushels *is* a good yield. [A unit]
A thousand bushels *were* crated. [Individual bushels]
The number of students *was* small. [*The number* is regularly taken as a unit.]
A number of students *were* sick. [*A number* refers to individuals.]

(8) **A verb agrees with its subject, not with its predicate noun.**

> His chief support *is* his brother and sister.
> His brother and sister *are* his chief support.

But such sentences are often better recast so as to avoid the disagreement in number between subject and predicate noun.

BETTER   His support came chiefly from his brother and sister.

(9) **Nouns plural in form but singular in meaning usually take singular verbs. In all doubtful cases a good dictionary should be consulted.**

Regularly singular: aesthetics, civics, economics, genetics, linguistics, mathematics, measles, mumps, news, physics, semantics
Regularly plural: environs, trousers

Some nouns ending in *-ics* (such as *athletics, acoustics,* and *statistics*) are considered singular when referring to an organized body of knowledge and plural when referring to activities, qualities, or individual facts.

> Athletics [activity in games] *is required* of every student.
> Athletics [various games] *provide* good recreation.

> Acoustics *is* an interesting study.
> The acoustics of the hall *are* good.

> Statistics *is* a science.
> The statistics *were* easily *assembled*.

(10) **A title of a single work or a word spoken of as a word, even when plural in form, takes a singular verb.**

> *Twice-Told Tales was written* by Hawthorne.
> The New York *Times has* a wide circulation.
> *They is* a pronoun.

▶ EXERCISE 1   Read the following correct sentences aloud, stressing the italicized words. If any sentence sounds wrong to you, read it aloud as many times as necessary for the verb form to sound right.

1. After the lecture, *everybody* in the group *is* invited to meet the speaker.
2. The *farmer*, as well as his sons, *grows* wheat.
3. *Each* of those lawyers *has* won many suits.
4. One of the *men who were* fishing on the pier caught a stingaree.
5. He was the *only one* in the group *who was* bored.
6. A *dictionary* and a *thesaurus are* lying on my desk.
7. Doyle's *"The Five Orange Pips" is* a fascinating story.
8. There *are* a few *cookies* and potato *chips* left.
9. Here *come* the *clowns*!
10. Every *one* of the *boys who belong* to the organization *is* planning to help build and decorate the float.

▶ **EXERCISE 2** Choose the correct form of the verb within parentheses in each of the following sentences.

1. Taste in magazines (differ, <u>differs</u>) greatly.
2. There (is, <u>are</u>) ever so many men needed to fill the quota.
3. Each of the awards (<u>carries</u>, carry) several guarantees.
4. (<u>Is</u>, Are) either of the novels likely to become a best seller?
5. The cat or her kittens (<u>are</u>, is) to blame for turning over the Christmas tree.
6. Those buttermilk clouds (presage, <u>presages</u>) a storm.
7. Everyone in the stands (were, <u>was</u>) unusually quiet.
8. Almost every illustration in these folios (<u>has</u>, have) been done by an amateur.
9. (<u>Is</u>, Are) neither of those clever floats to be awarded a prize?
10. A rustic lodge with tall pines and fishing waters close by (<u>was</u>, were) what we wanted.

▶ **EXERCISE 3** In the following sentences, find each verb and relate it to its subject. If subject and verb do not agree, change the verb to secure agreement. Justify every change. Write *C* after each sentence that needs no revision.

1. Neither rain nor sleet stop our postman.
2. Do either of you really understand the extent of your obligations?
3. Neither of you appreciates my sense of humor.
4. Everybody we met in town were excitedly talking about Mr. Zello's speech.
5. A simple majority are sufficient to elect Gene class secretary.
6. His aging parents and the provision he might make for them were his one principal concern.
7. There comes to my mind now the two or three men who were most influential in my life.
8. The significance of words is learned by breaking them up into suffixes, prefixes, and roots.
9. A study of the many contrasts in the poetry of Browning and Tennyson seem a good research topic.
10. Has each and every one of the figures been checked on that account sheet?

▶ **EXERCISE 4** Rewrite the following *correct* sentences as directed. Change verbs to secure agreement and make any additional changes required for good sentence sense.

¹ Certain portions of our collection are kept in an underground, air-conditioned vault and are never placed on exhibit. [Insert *One* before *Certain*.] ² Each piece in the exhibit has to be carefully dusted and polished once a day and then put back in place. [Change *Each piece* to *The pieces*.] ³ I might mention that this particular specimen has a distinguished place in history. [Change *this* to *these*.] ⁴ Our staff takes great pride in the efficient cataloging system which we have developed here. [Insert *members* after *staff*.] ⁵ In this room is my assistant, who is cataloging a newly arrived shipment. [Change *assistant* to *assistants*.] ⁶ One of our research parties has just returned from the field and is to be meeting with the directors during the remainder of the week. [Change *One* to *Two*.] ⁷ A detachment of four men has been left behind to maintain a permanent camp at the excavation site. [Omit *A detachment of*.] ⁸ Eaton Murray, the leader of the expedition and an especially capable man, is among the four. [Insert *John Wade* after *and*.] ⁹ Neither of the others is known to us here. [Change *is known* to *are unknown*.] ¹⁰ Both, however, were selected for particular abilities which they have shown. [Change *they* to *he*.]

6b

Make a pronoun agree in number with its antecedent.

A singular antecedent (one which would take a singular verb) is referred to by a singular pronoun; a plural antecedent (one which would take a plural verb) is referred to by a plural pronoun.

(1) In formal English, use a singular pronoun to refer to such antecedents as *man, woman, person, one, anyone, anybody, someone, somebody, everyone, everybody, each, kind, sort, either, neither, no one, nobody.* See also **6a(6)**.

> An outstanding trait of primitive *man* was *his* (NOT *their*) belief in superstitions.

In informal English, plural pronouns are sometimes used after such antecedents when the sense is clearly plural.

> Each of the boys had planned to follow *his* father's occupation. [Formal]
> Each of the boys had planned to follow *their* father's occupation. [Informal]

Note: Avoid illogical sentences that may result from strict adherence to this rule.

ILLOGICAL   Since every one of the patients seemed discouraged, I told a joke to cheer him up.
LOGICAL   Since all the patients seemed discouraged, I told a joke to cheer *them* up.

(2) Two or more antecedents joined by *and* are referred to by a plural pronoun; two or more singular antecedents joined by *or* or *nor* are referred to by a singular pronoun. If one of two antecedents joined by *or* is singular and one plural, the pronoun usually agrees with the nearer. See also **6a(2),(3)**.

Henry and James have completed *their* work.
Neither *Henry nor James* has completed *his* work.

Neither the *master* nor the *servants* were aware of *their* danger. [The plural *servants* is the nearer antecedent.]
Neither the *servants* nor the *master* was aware of *his* danger. [If the danger is to the master rather than the servants, the subjects can be reversed.]

Note: Avoid clumsy sentences that may result from strict adherence to the rule.

CLUMSY   When a *boy or girl* enters college, *he or she* finds it different from high school.
BETTER   When *boys and girls* enter college, *they* find it different from high school.

(3) Collective nouns are referred to by singular or plural pronouns depending on whether the collective noun is considered singular or plural. See also **6a(7)**.

Special care should be taken to avoid making a collective noun *both* singular and plural within the same sentence.

INCONSISTENT | The group is writing their own music. [The *group* is first considered singular because of the choice of *is* and then plural because of *their*.]
CONSISTENT | The *group is* writing *its* own music. [Singular]
CONSISTENT | The *group are* writing *their* own music. [Plural]

▶ **EXERCISE 5** Compose brief sentences using each antecedent and pronoun listed below.

EXAMPLE type ← its
That *type* of battery soon loses *its* power.

1. everybody ← he
2. neither ← she
3. each ← his
4. a person ← him
5. committee ← they
6. committee ← its
7. none ← those
8. none ← he
9. boy or his sisters ← they
10. girls or their brother ← he

▶ **EXERCISE 6** Write *C* after each correct sentence below. If a sentence contains a pronoun that does not agree with its antecedent in number, eliminate the error by substituting a correct pronoun form.

1. According to G. B. Shaw, a woman delights in wounding a man's ego, though a man takes most pleasure in gratifying hers.
2. An author like Shaw, however, seldom captures the whole truth with their generalizations.
3. A generalization is frequently only partially true, though a person may quote it and think they wholly believe it.
4. For example, nearly everyone, to express their appreciation, has said with great conviction, "A friend in need is a friend indeed."
5. At the same time, probably no one will deny that far too often a successful man avoids the very shoulders that they have climbed upon or despises the hands that once fed them.
6. Each of these quotations contains its grain of truth, but not the whole truth: (1) "As a rule man is a fool." (2) "What a piece of work is a man! how noble in reason!"
7. That these quotations are contradictory anyone in their right mind can see.
8. Though contradictory, each of the quotations may be true if they are applied to specific persons in particular circumstances.
9. A great satirist like Swift or Mark Twain in their works may often depict man as a fool.
10. Yet every reader who thinks for himself knows that the satirist—by pointing out man's foibles and follies—strives to reform man by showing him the value of making good use of his reason for lofty purposes.

▶ **EXERCISE 7** In the following sentences select the pronoun in parentheses that agrees with its antecedent in accordance with formal English usage. Note any pronouns that would be acceptable in conversation or familiar writing but not in formal writing.

¹ The foreman unlocked the shed and everybody went in and got (his, their) tools. ² Each man, and Charlie too, left (his, their) lunch pail inside. ³ Roy and Dave were tearing out concrete forms, and (he, each, they) took a section apiece and went to work. ⁴ One or another would yell for help to clear away the salvage lumber (he was, they were) tearing out. ⁵ The helpers were supposed to pile the lumber outside the foundation, where Andy was cleaning (it, them) up and stacking (it, them) for reuse. ⁶ Every few minutes someone would call out for the water boy to bring (him, them) a drink. ⁷ The crew was small, but (its, their) thirst was large. ⁸ Charlie, the water boy, had all he could do to keep (it, them) satisfied. ⁹ "If anybody here ever drank water when (he was, they were) off the job," he grumbled, "I'd be proud to shake (him, them) by the hand." ¹⁰ But nobody volunteered (his, their) hand to be shaken. ¹¹ Every minute, instead, somebody new would be yelling for water, and Charlie would trudge off toward (him, them). ¹² It was either Roy or Dave who was whooping for (his, their) ninetieth drink when the noon whistle blew. ¹³ Nobody was so ready to stop where (he was, they were) as Charlie. ¹⁴ "Whoever wants a drink knows where (he, they) can get it," he let it be known, and emptied his bucket out on the ground.

▶ **EXERCISE 8** In Exercise 7 make each change as directed below and then complete the sentence so as to secure agreement of pronoun with its antecedent. In Sentence 1, change *everybody* to *the workmen*. In 4, change *One or another* to *Both*. In 9, change *anybody here* to *these men*. In 11, change *somebody new* to *two or three more*.

Tense and Mood

7

Use the appropriate form of the verb.

Verbs have more inflections than any other part of speech. All verbs have at least three forms: the form in the dictionary, the *-s* form, and the *-ing* form.

set, sets, setting   hurt, hurts, hurting

Most verbs have four forms. All regular verbs (those which take the endings *-d*, *-ed*, or *-t*) have four forms.

REGULAR VERBS believe, believes, believing, believed
repeat, repeats, repeating, repeated
sweep, sweeps, sweeping, swept

Some irregular verbs (those not taking the endings *-d*, *-ed*, or *-t*) have four forms; others have five; a few, three. *Be*, the most irregular verb in the language, has eight forms.

IRREGULAR VERBS become, becomes, becoming, became
choose, chooses, choosing, chose, chosen
burst, bursts, bursting
be, am, is, are, was, were, being, been

It is very important that you learn not only how to recognize verbs but also how to use appropriate verb forms in your speaking and writing.

Tense relates to *time*. Verb forms indicate time and therefore have tense. Actually, there are three main divisions of time: past, present, and future. But actual time and grammatical tense do not always agree. Some grammarians (basing their classification upon form changes of single-word verbs) designate only two tenses: present and past. Other grammarians (considering both auxiliaries and single-word form changes) describe the following six tenses. Notice that the six tenses in the following examples are built on three forms of the verb *see*, called the *principal parts*. (See the list of principal parts of verbs on page 820.)

PRESENT TENSE   *see*—used with all subjects except third-person singular ones
                 sees—used only with third-person singular subjects

He *sees* me daily. [Habitual action]
Tomorrow I *see* my lawyer. [Used for future]
The Spaniards *see* their Armada defeated. [Historical present]
Men *see* that death is inevitable. [Universal truth]

PAST TENSE   *saw*

He *saw* me yesterday. [Past action at a specific time stated or implied]

FUTURE TENSE   *will see, shall see*

Tomorrow he *will see* his lawyer.

PRESENT PERFECT   *have seen*—used with all subjects except third-person singular
                   has seen—used with third-person singular subjects

Have you ever *seen* a mermaid? [Past action at any time before now]
Myra *has seen* the fair. [Before now]

PAST PERFECT   *had seen*

I *had seen* him before the game started. [Past action completed before another past action]

FUTURE PERFECT (rarely used)   *shall have seen, will have seen*

By tomorrow evening I *will have seen* the report. [Action completed before a set future time]

Other auxiliaries (in addition to *will, shall, has, have,* and *had*) also express time:

I *used to* see him every day. [Past]
We *are going to* see much progress. [Future]
He *is about to* see defeat. [Immediate future]

In the indicative mood, both active and passive verbs have all these six tense forms. (See the conjugation of the verb *see* under **Conjugation** in Section 35. See this section also for definitions of such terms as **Mood** and **Voice**.)

In addition to the simple verb forms illustrated by the conjugation, English uses a progressive form (the *-ing* form—*is seeing*) to show action in progress and a *do* form (*do see, does see, did see*) for (1) emphatic statements, (2) questions, or (3) negations. The *do* form is used only in the present and the past.

EMPHATIC   I *did see* a mirage.
QUESTION   *Did* you *see* that picture?
NEGATION   He *does* not *see* her often.

Below is a summary of the forms of *see*—the simple forms and the progressive forms, both active and passive voice.

PRESENT   he sees, is seen, is seeing, is being seen
PAST   he saw, was seen, was seeing, was being seen
FUTURE   he will see, will be seen, will be seeing, will be being seen
PRESENT PERFECT   he has seen, has been seen, has been seeing, has been being seen
PAST PERFECT   he had seen, had been seen, had been seeing, had been being seen
FUTURE PERFECT   he will have seen, will have been seen, will have been seeing, will have been being seen

In the imperative mood, verbs have only present tense: *See. Be seen.* For forms of the subjunctive, see **7c**. See also **Conjugation** in Section 35.

Verbals also have tense, but not all six tenses:

INFINITIVES   to see, to be seen, to be seeing [Present tense]
               to have seen, to have been seen, to have been seeing [Present perfect]
PARTICIPLES   seeing, being seen [Present tense]
               seen [Past tense]
               having seen, having been seen [Present perfect]
GERUNDS   seeing, being seen [Present tense]
           having seen, having been seen [Present perfect]

7a

Avoid confusing similar verbs or misusing principal parts of verbs.

Confused Verbs

The forms of transitive verbs such as *lay* and *set* are sometimes confused with intransitive verbs such as *lie* and *sit*. A verb with an object is a *transitive* verb; the object can ordinarily be made into the subject of the same verb made passive. Master the principal parts of the following verbs, observing in the examples that (1) forms of the intransitive verbs *lie* and *sit* do not have objects and are not passive, and (2) forms of the transitive verbs *lay* and *set* either have an object or are in the passive. Also observe the meanings of these verbs.

Present stem (infinitive)	Past tense	Past participle	Present participle
lie (to recline)	lay	lain	lying
lay (to cause to lie)	laid	laid	laying
sit (to be seated)	sat	sat	sitting
set (to place or put)	set	set	setting

Lie down. Yesterday he *lay* asleep in Ward 20. *Has* it *lain* there long? Papers *are lying* on the porch.
Lay it down. Yesterday he *laid* bricks. They *are laying* plans now. A foundation *was laid* last week.

Sit down. Helen *sat* up straight. *Have* you *sat* here long? A flowerpot *was sitting* on the window ledge.

Set that down. *Will* you *set* the time? They *were setting* the table. A date *has been set*.

▶ EXERCISE 1   Oral Drill. Respond to each of the following commands (1) in the present progressive tense, (2) in the past tense, and (3) in the present perfect tense. For example, the responses to *Sit down* would be: *I am sitting down; I sat down; I have sat down.*

1. Sit in the rocking chair.
2. Lay the facts in front of him.
3. Set that vase on the mantelpiece.
4. Lie down for a few minutes.
5. Set the tray where he can reach it.
6. Lay a little money aside each pay day.
7. Sit where you can see well.
8. Set a bowl of fruit in the middle of the table.
9. Lie in wait for him.
10. Lay your coat over a chair.

Misused Principal Parts

If you do not know the verb form needed to express a given tense, you can determine the correct form by consulting your dictionary for the principal parts of the verb. In the dictionary every irregular verb is listed by its infinitive or present stem—for example, *see*. Then follow the past tense (*saw*), the past participle (*seen*), and the present participle (*seeing*). *See, saw,* and *seen* are the principal parts from which you can readily derive the proper form for any of the six tenses. For regular verbs (such as *use*) the past tense and the past participle, when not given, are understood to be formed by adding *-d* or *-ed*.

NONSTANDARD	The boy seen where the bullet had entered. [Past tense needed; the dictionary gives *saw* as the correct form.]
STANDARD	The boy *saw* where the bullet had entered.
NONSTANDARD	I use to live in the country. [Past tense needed]
STANDARD	I *used* to live in the country.

▶ EXERCISE 2   Make your own SPECIAL LIST OF PRINCIPAL PARTS of verbs which you need to study and review. Include from the following list any verbs whose principal parts are not thoroughly familiar to you, and add all verbs that you have used incorrectly in your writing. Master your SPECIAL LIST and compose sentences to illustrate the correct use of each principal part.

Present stem	Past tense	Past participle
bear	bore	borne
begin	began	begun
bite	bit	bitten, bit
blow	blew	blown
break	broke	broken
bring	brought	brought
burst	burst	burst
catch	caught	caught
choose	chose	chosen
come	came	come
dive	dived, dove	dived
do	did	done
drag	dragged	dragged
draw	drew	drawn
drink	drank	drunk
drive	drove	driven
eat	ate	eaten
fall	fell	fallen
fly	flew	flown
forbid	forbade, forbad	forbidden
freeze	froze	frozen
get	got	got, gotten
give	gave	given
go	went	gone
grow	grew	grown
know	knew	known
lead	led	led
lose	lost	lost
raise	raised	raised
ride	rode	ridden
ring	rang	rung
rise	rose	risen
run	ran	run
shake	shook	shaken
shrink	shrank, shrunk	shrunk, shrunken
sing	sang, sung	sung
sink	sank, sunk	sunk
speak	spoke	spoken
spring	sprang, sprung	sprung
steal	stole	stolen
swear	swore	sworn
swim	swam	swum
swing	swung	swung
take	took	taken
tear	tore	torn
throw	threw	thrown
wear	wore	worn
wring	wrung	wrung
write	wrote	written

7b

Use logical tense forms in sequence, focusing upon the tense of the main or governing verb.

(1) Verbs in clauses

Make the tense of a verb in a subordinate clause relate logically and naturally to the tense of the verb in the main clause.

> The audience *rose* as the speaker *entered*. [The past *entered* follows the past *rose*.]
> I *have ceased* worrying because I *have heard* no more rumors. [The present perfect follows the present perfect.]
> When I *had been* at camp four weeks, I *received* word that my father *had died*. [The past perfect *had been* or *had died* indicates a time prior to that of the main verb *received*.]
> If Bill *had attended* (NOT *attended*) classes regularly, he *could have passed* the final examination.

(2) Infinitives

Use the present infinitive to express action contemporaneous with, or later than, that of the governing verb; use the perfect infinitive for action prior to that of the governing verb.

> I hoped *to go* (NOT *to have gone*). I hope *to go*. [Present infinitives. At the time indicated by the verbs I was still hoping *to go*, not *to have gone*.]

I would like *to have lived* in Shakespeare's time. [Perfect infinitive—expressing time prior to that of the governing verb. *Simpler:* I wish I had lived in Shakespeare's time.]

I would have liked *to live* (NOT *to have lived*) in Shakespeare's time. [Present infinitive—for time contemporaneous with that of the governing verb]

(3) Participles

Use the present participle to express action contemporaneous with that of the governing verb; use the perfect participle for action prior to that of the governing verb.

Walking along the streets, he met many old friends. [The walking and the meeting were contemporaneous.]

Having walked all the way home, he found himself tired. [The walking was prior to the finding.]

▶ **EXERCISE 3** Choose the verb form inside parentheses that is the logical tense form in sequence.

1. When the fire sale (ended, had ended), the store displayed new merchandise.
2. Fans cheered as the touchdown (had been made, was made).
3. The freshmen hope (to celebrate, to have celebrated) tomorrow.
4. We should have agreed (to have chartered, to charter) a bus.
5. (Having finished his test, Finishing his test), James left the room.
6. (Having bought the tickets, Buying the tickets), Mr. Selby took the children to the circus.
7. The chairman had left the meeting before it (had adjourned, adjourned).
8. It is customary for ranchers (to brand, to have branded) their cattle.
9. Phoebe had not expected (to see, to have seen) her cousin in the shop.
10. The pond has begun freezing because the temperature (dropped, has dropped).

7c

Use the subjunctive mood in the few types of expressions in which it is still regularly used.

Distinctive forms for the subjunctive occur only (1) in the present and past tenses of *be* and (2) in the present tense of other verbs used with third-person singular subjects.

INDICATIVE I *am*, you *are*, he *is*, others *are* [Present]
            I *was*, you *were*, he *was*, others *were* [Past]

SUBJUNCTIVE (with all subjects): *be* [Present], *were* [Past]

INDICATIVE he *sees*, others *see* [Present]

SUBJUNCTIVE (that) he *see*, (that) others *see* [Present]

See also **Conjugation**, Section 35.

Although the subjunctive mood has been largely displaced by the indicative, the subjunctive is still used in a few structures, such as the following:

As Steinberg once remarked, it was as if he *were* guided by an ouija board.   —OLIVER LA FARGE

Such a school demands from the teacher that he *be* a kind of artist in his province.   —ALBERT EINSTEIN

The subjunctive is required (1) in *that* clauses of motions, resolutions, recommendations, orders, or demands and (2) in a few idiomatic expressions.

I move that the report *be* approved.
Resolved, that dues for the coming year *be* doubled.
I recommend (order, demand) that the prisoner *see* his lawyer.
I demand (request, insist) that the messenger *go* alone.
If need *be*.... *Suffice* it to say.... *Come* what may....
[Fixed subjunctive in idiomatic expressions]

Many writers prefer the subjunctive in contrary-to-fact conditions.

INFORMAL   If the apple was ripe, it would be good. [Indicative form]
PREFERRED If the apple *were* ripe, it would be good. [Subjunctive]
INFORMAL   I wish that he was here now. [Indicative form]
PREFERRED I wish that he *were* here now. [Subjunctive]

▶ **EXERCISE 4** Underline all subjunctive verb forms used in the following sentences. Write *R* after those sentences containing *required* subjunctives; write *P* after those containing subjunctives preferred by many writers. Write *I* after sentences with verb forms that would be labeled *informal*.

1. If Lena was here, she'd explain everything.
2. We insist that he be punished.
3. I wish that peace were possible.
4. Americans now speak of Spain as though it were just across the river.
5. Present-day problems demand that we be ready for any emergency.
6. If there was time, I could finish my report.
7. Come what may, we will never choose anarchy.
8. I demand that he make amends.
9. If I were you, I would apply tomorrow.
10. The man acts as though he were the owner.

▶ **EXERCISE 5** Compose five sentences in which the subjunctive is required. Compose three other sentences in which either the subjunctive or the indicative may be used, giving the indicative (informal) form in parentheses.

7d

Avoid needless shifts in tense or mood.

SHIFT   He came to the river and pays a man to ferry him across. [Inconsistent use of tenses within one sentence]

IMPROVED He *came* to the river and *paid* a man to ferry him across.

INCONSISTENT It is necessary to restrain an occasional foolhardy park visitor lest a mother bear *mistake* his friendly intentions and *supposes* him a menace to her cubs. [Mood shifts improperly from subjunctive to indicative within the compound predicate.] But females with cubs *were* only one of the dangers. [A correct enough sentence if standing alone, but here inconsistent with present tense of preceding one, and therefore misleading] One *has* to remember that all bears *were* wild animals and not domesticated pets. [Inconsistent and misleading shift of tense from present in main clause to past in subordinate clause] Though a bear *may* seem altogether peaceable and harmless, he *might* not remain peaceable, and he is never harmless. [Tense shifts improperly from present in introductory clause to past in main clause.] It *is* therefore an important part of the park ranger's duty *to watch* the tourists, and above all *don't* let anybody try to feed the bears. [Inconsistent. Mood shifts needlessly from indicative to imperative.]

IMPROVED   It is necessary to restrain an occasional foolhardy park visitor lest a mother bear *mistake* his friendly intentions and *suppose* him a menace to her cubs. But females with cubs *are* only one of the dangers. One *has* to remember that all bears *are* wild animals and not domesticated pets. Though a bear *may* seem altogether peaceable and harmless, he *may* not remain peaceable, and he is never harmless. It *is* therefore an important part of the park ranger's duty *to watch* the tourists and above all not *to let* anybody try to feed the bears.

See also **27a** and **27b.**

▶ **EXERCISE 6**   In the following passage correct all errors and inconsistencies in tense and mood and any other errors in verb usage. Write *C* after any sentence which is satisfactory as it stands.

¹ Across the Thames from Shakespeare's London lay the area known as the Bankside, probably as rough and unsavory a neighborhood as ever laid across the river from any city.   ² And yet it was to such a place that Shakespeare and his company had to have gone to build their new theater.   ³ For the Puritan government of the City had set up all sorts of prohibitions against theatrical entertainment within the city walls.   ⁴ When it became necessary, therefore, for the Company to have moved their playhouse from its old location north of the city, they obtain a lease to a tract on the Bankside.   ⁵ Other theatrical companies had went there before them, and it seemed reasonable to have supposed that Shakespeare and his partners would prosper in the new location.   ⁶ Apparently the Puritans of the City had no law against anyone's moving cartloads of lumber through the public streets.   ⁷ There is no record that the Company met with difficulty while the timbers of the dismantled playhouse are being hauled to the new site.   ⁸ One difficulty the partners had foresaw and forestalled, and that is the effort that their old landlord might make to have stopped their removing the building.   ⁹ Lest his presence complicate their task and would perhaps defeat its working altogether, they waited until he had gone out of town.   ¹⁰ And when he came back, his lot was bare; the building's timbers were all in stacks on the far side of the river; and the theater is waiting only to be put together.   ¹¹ It is a matter of general knowledge that on the Bankside Shakespeare continued his successful career as a showman and went on to enjoy even greater prosperity after he had made the move than before.

7e

Observe such distinctions as exist among *should*, *would*, *shall*, and *will*.

(1) Use *should* in all persons to express an obligation (in the sense "ought to") or a condition.

> I (You, He, We, They) *should* (*ought to*) help the needy.
> If I (you, he, we, they) *should* resign, the program would not be continued.

(2) Use *would* in all persons to express a wish or a customary action.

> *Would* that I (you, he, we, they) had received the message!
> I (You, He, We, They) *would* spend hours by the seashore during the summer months.

Caution: Do not use *would have* as a substitute for *had*.

> If you *had* (not *would have*) arrived earlier, you would have seen the President.

Shall is generally used for the first person in asking questions (*Shall* I go first?), and it is often used in all persons for special emphasis. Except for these uses of *shall*, and for the use of *should* to express an obligation or condition, informal English tends to use *will* and *would* in all persons.

A few writers still distinguish between *shall* and *will*:

(a) By using *shall* in the first person and *will* in the second and third to express the simple future or expectation (I *shall* plan to stay; he *will* probably stay).

(b) By using *will* in the first person and *shall* in the second and third to express determination, threat, command, prophecy, promise, or willingness (I *will* stay; you and he *shall* stay).

▶ **EXERCISE 7**   Revise those sentences below which contain any incorrect verb form; write *C* after those needing no revision. Be prepared to justify each revision.

1. Has spring training began yet?
2. If he would have registered later, he would have had Saturday classes.
3. Start the engine, and then you should release the brake.
4. If you set up too late, you may wish to lay in bed till noon next day.
5. If Mary enrolled in the class at the beginning, she could have made good grades.
6. It has been said that a rolling stone gathers no moss.
7. A stone lying in one position for a long time may gather moss.
8. The members recommended that all delinquents be fined.
9. It was reported that there use to be very few delinquents.
10. After Mr. Norwood entered the room, he sat down at the desk and begins to write rapidly.
11. Until I received your letter, I was hoping to have had a visit from you.
12. We attend religious services to learn how we would conduct ourselves toward our fellows.
13. Follow the main road for a mile; then you need to take the next road on the left.
14. The beggar could not deny that he had stole the purse.
15. I should have liked to have been with the team on the trip to New Orleans.

MECHANICS

Manuscript Form and Revision; Syllabication

8

Put your manuscript in acceptable form. Make revisions with care.

8a
Use the proper materials.

(1) **Paper.**   Unless you are given other instructions, use standard theme paper, size 8½ by 11 inches, with lines about half an inch apart, and write only on the ruled side of the paper. (The usual notebook paper, even if it is the standard size, should not be used because the narrow spaces between lines make for hard reading and allow insufficient space for corrections.) For type-written manuscripts use the unruled side of theme paper; or, if you prefer, regular weight typewriter paper (not onion skin), size 8½ by 11 inches.

(2) **Ink.**   Use black or blue-black ink.

(3) **Typewriter.**   Unless otherwise instructed, submit type-written papers only if you do your own typewriting. Use a black ribbon and make sure that the type is clean.

8b
Arrange your writing in clear and orderly fashion on the page. Divide a word at the end of a line only between syllables.

(1) **Margins.**   Leave sufficient margins—about an inch and a half at the left and top, an inch at the right and bottom—to prevent a crowded appearance. The ruled lines on theme paper indicate the proper margins at the left and top.

(2) **Indention.**   Indent the first lines of paragraphs uniformly, about an inch in longhand and five spaces in typewritten copy.

(3) **Paging.**   Use Arabic numerals—without parentheses or period—in the upper right-hand corner to mark all pages after the first.

(4) **Title.**   *Do not put quotation marks around the title or underline it* (unless it is a quotation or the title of a book), and use no period after the title. Center the title on the page about an inch and a half from the top or on the first ruled line. Leave the next line blank and begin the first paragraph on the third line. In this way the title will stand off from the text. Capitalize the first and last word of the title and all other words except articles, short conjunctions, and short prepositions.

(5) **Poetry.**   Quoted lines of poetry should be arranged and indented as in the original. (See also **16a.**)

(6) **Punctuation.**   Never begin a line with a comma, a colon, a semicolon, or a terminal mark of punctuation; never end a line with opening quotation marks, bracket, or parenthesis.

(7) **Endorsement.**   Papers are endorsed in the way prescribed by the instructor to facilitate handling. Usually papers carry the name of the student and the course, the date, and the number of the assignment.

(8) **Word Division at End of Line.**   You will seldom need to divide words, especially short ones, if you leave a reasonably wide right-hand margin. The reader will object less to an uneven margin than to a number of broken words. When division is necessary, remember to divide words carefully between syllables. Whenever you are uncertain about the proper syllabication of a word, consult a good dictionary.

    ig-ni-tion, sen-ti-nel, te-na-cious, in-con-gru-ous

Double consonants are usually divided except when they come at the end of a simple word.

    can-ning, com-mit-ting, *but* kill-ing

Do not divide a word so that a single letter is on either line (*e-vade, man-y*); a single letter on the first line is too small a saving of space to justify the break, and a single letter on the second line is no saving at all, for it could use the space on the first line needed for the hyphen. Do not confuse the reader by setting off an -*ed* pronounced as part of the preceding syllable (*enjoy-ed, gleam-ed*). Divide hyphenated words only where the hyphen comes in the regular spelling (*mass-produced* or *Pre-Raphaelite*).

▶ EXERCISE With the aid of your dictionary write out the following words by syllables, grouping (1) those that may properly be divided at the end of a line, and (2) those that may not be divided:

affection	levy	through	veiled
against	looked	tolerate	walked
alone	nature	transient	weary
combed	omit	treaty	willing
decadent	rainy	tròller	willow

8c

Write legibly, so that your writing may be read easily and accurately.

(1) Spacing for Legibility. Adequate space between lines and between the words in the line is essential to easy reading. In typewritten copy use double space between lines. Single-spaced copy is difficult for the instructor to read and even more difficult for the student to revise. Leave one space after a comma or semicolon, one or two after a colon, and two or three after a period, a question mark, or an exclamation point. In longhand make each word a distinct unit: join all the letters of a word and leave adequate space in the line before beginning the next word.

(2) Shaping for Legibility. Shape each letter distinctly. Avoid flourishes. Many pages of manuscript, though artistic and attractive to the eye, are almost illegible. Dot the *i*, not some other letter nearby. Cross the *t*, not the adjoining *h* or some other letter. Make dots and periods real dots, not small circles. Let all capitals stand out distinctly as capitals and keep all small letters down to the average of other small letters. Remember that you will not be present to tell the reader which letters you intend for capitals, which for small letters.

8d

Revise the manuscript with care.[1]

(1) Revise the paper before submitting it to the instructor.

If time permits, the writer should put the paper aside for a day or more after completing his first draft. Then he will be able to read the paper more objectively, to see what parts need to be expanded, what to be excised. After he has revised his paper, he should make a completely new copy to submit to the instructor. If slight revisions are needed in this final copy or if the student is writing in class, the paper may be handed in—after corrections have been made—without re-writing. The changes should be made as follows:

[1]For marks used in correcting proofs for the printer see *Standard College Dictionary*, pp. 1604–06; *Webster's Seventh New Collegiate Dictionary*, pp. 1051–52; or *The American College Dictionary*, p. xxxv.

(a) Draw one line horizontally through any word to be deleted. Do not put it in parentheses or make an unsightly erasure.

(b) In case of a short addition of one line or less, place a caret ($_\wedge$) in the line where the addition comes and write just above the caret the word or words to be added.

CHECK LIST FOR REVISION

1. Have I stated my central idea clearly, and have I developed it adequately in effective paragraphs? (See Sections **31–32**.)
2. Is the paper correct in
   (a) manuscript form? (See Section **8**.)
   (b) grammar and mechanics? (See Sections **1–7, 9–11**.)
   (c) punctuation? (See Sections **12–17**.)
   (d) spelling? (See Section **18**.)
3. Is the diction standard, exact, concise? (See Sections **19–22**.)
4. Are the sentences as effective as possible? (See Sections **23–30**.)
5. What do my answers to the foregoing questions show my chief difficulties to be? (Review intensively the sections of this book which deal with your defects. Later, after the paper has been read and returned by the instructor, observe the same procedure for additional defects noted by your instructor.)

(2) Revise the paper after the instructor has criticized it.

The best way to learn the mechanics of writing is by correcting one's own errors. Corrections made by another are of comparatively little value. Therefore the instructor points out the errors but *allows the student to make the actual revision for himself.*

The instructor usually indicates a necessary correction by a number or a symbol from the handbook marked in the margin of the paper opposite the error. For example, if he finds a fragmentary sentence, he will write either the number **2** or the symbol **frag.** The student should then find in the text the specific part (**a, b,** or **c**) of Section **2** that deals with his error, correct the error in red (or as the instructor directs), and write the appropriate letter after the instructor's number or symbol in the margin. (See the example paragraph marked by the instructor and then corrected by the student on page 825.)

The comma After the number **12** in the margin the student should take special care to supply the appropriate letter (**a, b, c,** or **d**) to show why the comma is needed. The act of inserting a comma teaches little; understanding why it is required in a particular situation is a definite step toward mastery of the comma.

The following pages reproduce a paragraph from a student paper and show, on the first page, the instructor's markings (for grammar and other details) and, on the second page, the same paragraph after it has been corrected by the student. These corrections should be in a different color to make them stand out distinctly from the original paragraph and the markings of the instructor.

Give special attention to the instructor's comments on content and organization, which are even more important than details of grammar and mechanics.

Marked by the Instructor—with Numbers

3   Making photographs for newspapers is hard work,

12   it is not the romantic carefree adventure glorified

in motion pictures and fiction books. For every

18   great moment recorded by the stareing eye of the

camera, there are twenty routine assignments that

28   must be handled in the same efficient manner. He

must often overcome great hardships. The work con-

24   tinues for long hours. It must meet the deadline.

At times he is called upon to risk his own life to

2   secure a picture. To the newspaper photographer,

getting his picture being the most important thing.

Corrected by the Student

3a   Making photographs for newspapers is hard work/;

12c   it is not the romantic, carefree adventure glorified

in motion pictures and fiction books. For every

18d   great moment recorded by the ~~stareing~~ *staring* eye of the

camera, there are twenty routine assignments that

28c   must be handled in the same efficient manner. ~~He~~ *The*
newspaper photographer must often overcome great
~~must often overcome great hardships. The work con-~~ *hardships and work long hours to meet the deadline.*

24a   ~~tinues for long hours. It must meet the deadline.~~

At times he is called upon to risk his own life to

2a   secure a picture. To the newspaper photographer,
is
getting his picture ~~being~~ the most important thing.

Marked by the Instructor—with Symbols

cs   Making photographs for newspapers is hard work,

9/   it is not the romantic carefree adventure glorified

in motion pictures and fiction books. For every

sp   great moment recorded by the stareing eye of the

camera, there are twenty routine assignments that

ref   must be handled in the same efficient manner. He

must often overcome great hardships. The work con-

sub   tinues for long hours. It must meet the deadline.

At times he is called upon to risk his own life to

frag   secure a picture. To the newspaper photographer,

getting his picture being the most important thing.

Corrected by the Student

cs a   Making photographs for newspapers is hard work/;

9/c   it is not the romantic, carefree adventure glorified

in motion pictures and fiction books. For every

sp d   great moment recorded by the ~~stareing~~ *staring* eye of the

camera, there are twenty routine assignments that

ref c   must be handled in the same efficient manner. ~~He~~ *The*
newspaper photographer must often overcome great
~~must often overcome great hardships. The work con-~~ *hardships and work long hours to meet the deadline.*

sub a   ~~tinues for long hours. It must meet the deadline.~~

At times he is called upon to risk his own life to

frag a   secure a picture. To the newspaper photographer,
is
getting his picture ~~being~~ the most important thing.

8e

Keep a record to check the improvement in your writing.

A clear record on a single notebook page will show at a glance the progress you are making from paper to paper. As you write each paper, try to avoid mistakes already pointed out. Master the correct spelling of each word you have misspelled. *Be sure that you have made every correction and have considered every comment on your last paper before you write the next.* If you follow this plan consistently throughout the year, your writing will show marked improvement.

One simple but useful way to record your errors is to write them down in the order in which they occur in each paper, grouping them in columns according to the seven major divisions of the handbook as illustrated below. In the spaces for Paper Number 1 are recorded the errors from the student paragraph on the preceding page. In the spelling column appears the correct spelling of the misspelled word, and in other columns the section number with the letter to indicate the specific error made. You may wish to add on your record sheet other columns for date, grade, and instructor's comments.

RECORD OF ERRORS

Paper No.	Grammar 1-7	Mechanics 8-11	Punctuation 12-17	Words Misspelled 18	Diction 19-22	Effective- ness 23-30	Larger Elements 31-34
1	3 b 2 a			staring		28 c 24 a	
2							

Capitals

9

Capitalize words in accordance with standard conventions. Avoid unnecessary capitals.[1]

Capitalization of individual words may be checked in a good dictionary, such as *The American College Dictionary, Standard College Dictionary, Webster's New World Dictionary,* or *Webster's Seventh New Collegiate Dictionary.* Words regularly capitalized begin with capital letters in dictionary entries.

9a

Capitalize proper names, words used as an essential part of proper names, and usually derivatives of proper names and abbreviations of them.

Proper names begin with capitals, but not names of classes of persons, places, or things: *Churchill, England, Broadway—man, country, street.*

(1) Proper Names

Capitalize names of specific persons, places, and things; organizations and institutions; historical periods and events; members of national, political, racial, and religious groups; calendar items; and words pertaining to the Deity and Holy Scripture.

Milton, Abraham Lincoln, Mary, George the First, America, Arabia, Texas, London, Mount McKinley, the Statue of Liberty, a Winchester, Young Men's Christian Association, Federal Bureau of Investigation, the Second World War,

the Middle Ages, the Alamo, Negro, Episcopalian, Memorial Day, the Lord, Christ and His followers, the Old Testament.

(2) Words Used as Essential Parts of Proper Names

Such words as *college, high school, club, lake, river, park, building, street, pike, county, railroad,* and *society* are (except in newspapers) usually capitalized when they are an essential part of a proper name, but not when used alone as a substitute for the name: *the Statue of Liberty, a statue; Central High School, the high school; Madison Street, the street; the Pennsylvania Railroad, the railroad.*

(3) Derivatives

Words derived from proper names are usually capitalized: *Miltonic, Marian, Georgian, American, Arabian, Texan, Londoner, Southerner.*

(4) Abbreviations

In general, abbreviations are capitalized or not according to the capitalization of the word abbreviated: *Y.M.C.A., FBI, m.p.h. (miles per hour).* One important exception is *No.* for *number.* (See also Section **11.**)

Note: Proper names and their derivatives sometimes lose significance as names of particulars and thus become common names of a general class and are no longer capitalized. For example, *quixotic* is derived from *Don Quixote; malapropism, Mrs. Malaprop; quisling, Major Vidkun Quisling.*

Caution: Some words may be used correctly as either common nouns or as proper names: "the *God* of Moses," "a *god* of the pagans"; "a *democratic* system," "the *Democratic* Party." Words denoting family relationship (*father, mother, brother, aunt, cousin*) are generally capitalized when used as titles or alone in place of the name, but not when preceded by a possessive: *Brother William; Sister Mary*[2]*; Mary, my sister; my brother; my uncle;*

[1]For a more detailed discussion of capitalization of words and abbreviations see the *Style Manual* of the United States Government Printing Office, 1959, pp. 21–56, or *A Manual of Style,* University of Chicago Press, 1949, pp. 23–45.

[2]This rule also applies to names of members of religious orders.

a trip with Father; a trip with my father; a letter from Mother; a letter from my mother.

9b

Capitalize titles preceding, but usually not following, a proper name.

EXAMPLES   Mr. Brown, Judge White, King George, Aunt Mary

Titles immediately following the name, or used alone as a substitute for the name, are capitalized only to indicate preeminence or high distinction: *Lyndon B. Johnson, President of the United States; the President of the United States; the President.* On the other hand, ordinary titles are usually not capitalized: *William Smith, president of the First National Bank; the president of the bank.*

9c

In titles of books, plays, student papers, etc., capitalize the first and last word and all other words except articles (*a, an, the*), short conjunctions, and short prepositions.

EXAMPLES   *Crime and Punishment, To the Lighthouse, Midnight on the Desert, The Man Without a Country, What Men Live By* [A conjunction or preposition of five or more letters (*Without*) is usually capitalized.]

9d

Capitalize the pronoun *I* and the interjection *O* (but not *oh* except when it begins a sentence).

EXAMPLE   If *I* forget thee, *O* Jerusalem, let my right hand forget her cunning.   —PSALMS

9e

Capitalize the first word of every sentence (including quoted sentences and direct questions within sentences).

EXAMPLES
We were late.
My friend said, "*We* are late," and added, "very late."
My friend said that we were "very late." [A fragmentary quotation does not begin with a capital.]
The question is, Will others be late, too?
We both had one worry: What explanation could we give our host? [After the colon, complete sentences usually begin with a capital, but not always unless they are quoted.]

9f

Avoid unnecessary capitals.

Many students err in using too many rather than too few capitals. If you have a tendency to overuse capitals, you should study the five principles treated above (**9a, b, c, d, e**) and use a capital letter only when you can justify it. You should also carefully study the following STYLE SHEET.

STYLE SHEET FOR CAPITALIZATION

CAPITALS	NO CAPITALS
Proper Names and Derivatives	*Names of Classes of Persons, Places, Things*
Demosthenes	the famous orator
Chicago, Cook County	a city in that county
Texas, Alaska	a big state, a new state
Proper Names and Derivatives	*Names of Classes of Persons, Places, Things*
Boston College, Cisco High School	a college, in high school
the Amazon River, Lake Erie	a large river, a wide lake
Fifth Avenue, Highway 40	a busy street, the new highway
the President of Chile	the president of the bank
flowers for Mother and a book for Cousin Elizabeth	flowers for my mother and a book for my cousin
the First Presbyterian Church	the first church built
the French Revolution	a revolution in design
a Communist	communistic ideas
General Electric Company	an insurance company
the Physics Club	the society
a Baptist	baptism
the Medal of Honor	a medal for bravery
the Lord God	the lord of the manor, the Greek gods
Labor Day	the holiday weekend
a Rolls Royce	a limousine
the Freshman-Sophomore Prom	a freshman and two sophomores
Marxism	socialism
Titles Before	*Titles After*
Lieutenant William Jones	William Jones, the lieutenant
President C. B. Jones	C. B. Jones, president of the company
Specific Courses	*General Courses or Subjects*
Chemistry B, Geology 100, History 2	courses in chemistry, geology, and history
to take Mathematics A	to study mathematics
Specific Sections	*Directions*
the West	to fly west
the South	a wind from the south, a southerly wind
in the East, an Eastern rite, an Easterner	to the east, an eastern college
Months, Days	*Seasons*
May, July, Friday, Sunday	summer, fall, winter, spring

▶ EXERCISE 1   Supply capitals wherever needed in the following sentences. Be prepared to give a reason for the use of each capital.

1. In america, candidates for president frequently make promises to minority groups—such as southern democrats, negroes, farmers, laborers, westerners, and alaskans—because, if united, the minorities can determine the outcome of an election.

2. During the easter vacation, after window shopping on fifth avenue and seeing the sights on broadway, I went to bedloe's island, climbed up into the crown of the statue of liberty, and took pictures of new york harbor.

3. Senator redwine, a republican, spoke on our campus and strongly advocated prohibition in hunt county.

4. We invited judge green to meet uncle henry at the cosmos club to make plans for the annual community chest drive.

5. Before the end of the summer, perhaps during july, the president of the united states will take a vacation in florida.

6. The pacific ocean was discovered in 1513 by a spaniard named balboa.

7. Many americans in the northwest are of polish or scandinavian descent.

8. The battle of new orleans, which made general jackson famous, took place *after* the signing of the peace treaty at ghent.

9. The minister stressed not only the importance of obeying god's laws as set forth in the bible but also the need for trusting in his infinite mercy.

10. The west offers grand sights for tourists: the carlsbad caverns, the grand canyon, yellowstone national park —not to mention the attractions of hollywood, las vegas, and salt lake city.

11. Many new englanders go south for part of the winter, but usually they turn back north before easter.

▶ EXERCISE 2   Supply capitals wherever needed in the following paragraphs. Be prepared to give the reason for the use of each capital.

¹ Laying aside gilbert highet's *the art of teaching*, helen, my roommate, sighed and mumbled, "this book doesn't solve my problems as a student teacher at elmwood elementary school."
² "Since mother is a teacher," I responded, "and often tells me about her discipline problems, maybe I can help you out. ³ Now that my english assignment is finished, I've got plenty of time to listen to your troubles."
⁴ "I'm so discouraged," moaned helen, "because my pupils are either stupid or hard of hearing. ⁵ For instance, after teaching vowels and consonants for days, I gave a test friday. ⁶ One child put this title on his paper: 'what i know about valves and constants.'"
⁷ "oh," I laughed, "my mother has a big collection of similar boners made by her students at madison high school."
⁸ Too absorbed in serious thought to be cheered by a pollyanna roommate, helen continued, "I wish I could read a book called *how to win students and influence parents.* ⁹ Maybe its advice would help me on days like last monday, when beverly atkins whimpered for hours. ¹⁰ Desperate, I asked dr. jones, principal of elmwood, what to do; he suggested the threat of spanking, which served only to make beverly cry even louder.
¹¹ "On the telephone early tuesday morning, beverly's mother gave me what she called 'the perfect solution to the problem.' ¹² She advised, 'just spank a child sitting near my beverly, who'll then get scared and stop crying.'"

▶ EXERCISE 3   Write brief sentences correctly using each of the following: (1) *freshman*, (2) *Freshman*, (3) *college*, (4) *College*, (5) *south*, (6) *South*, (7) *avenue*, (8) *Avenue*, (9) *algebra*, (10) *Algebra*, (11) *theater*, (12) *Theater*.

Italics

10

Italicize (underline) titles of publications, foreign words, names of ships, titles of works of art, and words spoken of as words. Use italics sparingly for emphasis.

In longhand or typewritten papers, italics are indicated by underlining. The printer sets all underlined words in italic type.

TYPEWRITTEN
In <u>David Copperfield</u> Dickens writes of his own boyhood.

PRINTED
   In *David Copperfield* Dickens writes of his own boyhood.

10a

Titles of separate publications—such as books, bulletins, magazines, newspapers, musical works—are italicized (underlined) when mentioned in writing.

EXAMPLES   Many people still enjoy Mark Twain's *Roughing It.* [Note that the author's name is not italicized.]
     We read *The Comedy of Errors,* which is based on the *Menaechmi* of Plautus. [An initial *a, an,* or *the* is capitalized and italicized only when it belongs to the title.]
     Mozart's *Don Giovanni;* Beethoven's *Fifth Symphony*
     He pored over *Time,* the *Atlantic Monthly,* the *Saturday Evening Post,* and the *New York Times* (OR: New York *Times*). [Italics are not commonly used for articles standing first in the titles of periodicals, and sometimes not used for the name of the city in the titles of newspapers.]

Occasionally quotation marks are used instead of italics for titles of separate publications. The usual practice, however, reserves quotation marks for short stories, short poems, one-act plays, articles from periodicals, and subdivisions of books. See **16b.**

David Copperfield opens with a chapter entitled "I Am Born."

Exception: Neither italics nor quotation marks are used in references to the Bible and its parts.

   The first part of the Bible, the Old Testament, begins with Genesis.

▶ EXERCISE 1   Underline all words below that should be italicized.

1. While waiting in the dentist's office, I thumbed through an old issue of Sports Illustrated and scanned an article entitled "Girls on the Go-Go-Go."
2. My father reads the editorials in the San Francisco Chronicle and the comic strips in the Chicago Tribune.
3. A performance of Verdi's opera La Traviata was reviewed in the Fort Worth Star Telegram.
4. Huxley's Brave New World differs greatly from Plato's Republic and More's Utopia.
5. Ivanhoe is a character in the novel Ivanhoe.

10b

Foreign words and phrases not yet Anglicized are usually italicized (underlined).

Such words are indicated in *Webster's New World Dictionary* by a double dagger (‡) immediately before the word; in *Standard College Dictionary* and *The American College Dictionary,* by the italicized name of the foreign language immediately after the word.

> If I ever heard a *faux pas,* Ann's remark was one.
> Mexico is sometimes called the land of *mañana.*
> We heartily wish him *bon voyage.*

▶ **EXERCISE 2**   With the aid of your dictionary, list and underline five foreign words or phrases that are generally written in italics. List five other foreign words or phrases (such as "apropos," "bona fide," "ex officio") that no longer require italics.

10c

Names of ships, trains, and aircraft and titles of motion pictures and works of art are italicized (underlined).

EXAMPLES   The *Queen Mary* and the *Queen Elizabeth* sailed from New York.
From Chicago we took the *Denver Zephyr* across the plains to Colorado.
Rodin's *The Thinker* stands in one of the Parisian gardens.
On Halloween I enjoy seeing motion pictures like *The Walking Dead.*

10d

Words, letters, or figures spoken of as such or used as illustrations are usually italicized (underlined).

EXAMPLES   The article *the* has lost much of its demonstrative force.
In England *elevators* are called *lifts.* [Sometimes quotation marks ("the," "elevators," "lifts") are used instead of italics. See **16c.**]
The final *e* in *stone* is silent.
The first *3* and the final *0* of the serial number are barely legible.

10e

As a rule do not use italics (underlining) to give special emphasis to a word or a group of words. Do not underline the title of your own paper.

Frequent use of italics for emphasis defeats its own purpose and becomes merely an annoyance to the reader. This use of italics has been largely abandoned by good contemporary writers. Emphasis on a given word or phrase is usually best secured by careful arrangement of the sentence. See Section **29.**

A title is not italicized when it stands at the head of a book or an article. Accordingly, a student should not italicize (underline) the title standing at the head of his own paper (unless the title happens to be also the title of a book). See also **8b(4).**

▶ **EXERCISE 3**   Underline all words below that should be italicized.

1. My handwriting is difficult to read because each o looks like an a and each 9 resembles a 7.
2. In the early 1920's, Rudolph Valentino starred as "the great lover" in The Sheik.
3. To Let was completed in September, 1920, before Galsworthy sailed from Liverpool on the Empress of France to spend the winter in America.
4. Galsworthy's novels have been reviewed in such periodicals as Harper's Magazine and the Saturday Review and such newspapers as the New York Herald Tribune.
5. According to Greenough and Kittredge, in their book entitled Words and Their Ways in English Speech, "it is more natural for us to say divide (from L. divido) than cleave (from A.S. cleofan)."
6. A Manual of Style, published by the University of Chicago Press, recommends that such Latin words or abbreviations as vide, idem, ibid., and op. cit. be italicized when used in literary references.
7. In the Spirit of St. Louis, Charles A. Lindbergh made the first solo nonstop transatlantic flight from New York to Paris.
8. The original of Benjamin West's Penn's Treaty with the Indians is in the Pennsylvania Academy of Fine Arts in Philadelphia.
9. The embassy aide was declared persona non grata and asked to leave the country at once.
10. There are two acceptable ways to spell such words as judgment, catalogue, and gruesome.
11. Stevenson is said to have revised the first chapter of Treasure Island no fewer than thirty-seven times.
12. Michelangelo's Battle of the Centaurs and his Madonna of the Steps are among the world's finest sculptures.

▶ **EXERCISE 4**   Copy the following passage, underlining all words that should be italicized.

[1] I was returning home on the America when I happened to see a copy of Euripides' Medea.   [2] The play was of course in translation, by Murray, I believe; it was reprinted in Riley's Great Plays of Greece and Rome. [3] I admire Medea the play and Medea the woman. [4] Both of them have a quality of atrocitas which our contemporary primitivism misses.   [5] Characters in modern plays are neurotic; Medea was sublimely and savagely mad.

Abbreviations and Numbers

11

In ordinary writing avoid abbreviations (with a few well-known exceptions), and write out numbers that can be expressed in one or two words.

Abbreviations

11a

In ordinary writing spell out all titles except Mr., Messrs., Mrs., Mmes., Dr., and St. (saint, not street). Spell out even these titles when not followed by proper names.

INAPPROPRIATE	The Dr. made his report to the Maj.
APPROPRIATE	The doctor (OR Dr. Smith) made his report to the major (OR to Major Brown).

Note: *Hon.* and *Rev.* may be used before the surname when it is preceded by the first name or initials, never before the surname alone.

INAPPROPRIATE	Hon. Smith, Rev. Jones
APPROPRIATE	Hon. George Smith, Hon. G. E. Smith, Rev. Thomas Jones, Rev. T. E. Jones
MORE FORMAL	The Honorable George Edward Smith, the Reverend Thomas Everett Jones, the Reverend Mr. Jones

For forms of address in writing or speaking to officials and other dignitaries of church and state, see "Forms of Address" in *Webster's New World Dictionary*, pp. 1717–19, and *Webster's Seventh New Collegiate Dictionary*, pp. 1173–76.

11b

In ordinary writing spell out names of states, countries, months, days of the week, and units of measurement.

INAPPROPRIATE	He left Ia. on the last Sun. in Jul.
APPROPRIATE	He left Iowa on the last Sunday in July.
INAPPROPRIATE	On Oct. 15 James arrived in Mex.
APPROPRIATE	On October 15 James arrived in Mexico.
INAPPROPRIATE	Only five ft. tall, Susan weighs about a hundred lbs.
APPROPRIATE	Only five feet tall, Susan weighs about a hundred pounds.

11c

In ordinary writing spell out Street, Road, Park, Company, and similar words used as part of a proper name.

EXAMPLE	The procession moved down Lee Street between Central Park and the neon signs of the Ford Motor Company.

Note: Avoid the use of & (for *and*) and such abbreviations as *Bros.* or *Inc.* except in copying official titles: *A & P; Goldsmith Bros.; Best & Co., Inc.; Doubleday & Company, Inc.*

11d

In ordinary writing spell out the words *volume, chapter,* and *page* and the names of subjects.

INAPPROPRIATE	The notes on chem. are taken from ch. 9, p. 46.
APPROPRIATE	The notes on chemistry are taken from chapter 9, page 46.

11e

In ordinary writing spell out first names.

INAPPROPRIATE	Jas. Smith, Geo. White
APPROPRIATE	James Smith, George White

Permissible abbreviations: In addition to the abbreviations mentioned in **11a**, the following are permissible and usually desirable.

1. *After proper names:* Jr., Sr., Esq., and degrees such as D.D., Ph.D., M.A., M.D.

   Mr. Sam Jones, Sr.; Sam Jones, Jr.; Thomas Jones, M.D.

2. *With dates or numerals:* A.D., B.C., A.M., P.M. (OR a.m., p.m.), No., $

APPROPRIATE	In 450 B.C.; at 9:30 A.M.; in room No. 6; for $365
INAPPROPRIATE	Early this A.M. he asked the No. of your room. [The abbreviations are appropriate only with the numerals.]
APPROPRIATE	Early this morning he asked the number of your room.

3. *For names of organizations and government agencies usually referred to by their initials:* DAR, GOP, FBI, AMA, NASA, UN, FHA

4. *For certain common Latin expressions, although the English term is often spelled out in formal writing, as indicated in parentheses:* i.e. (*that is*), e.g. (*for example*), viz. (*namely*), cf. (*compare*), etc. (*and so forth*), vs. (*versus*)

Note: Use *etc.* sparingly. Never write *and etc.* The abbreviation comes from *et cetera*, of which *et* means *and*.

Special exceptions: Many abbreviations are desirable in footnotes, in tabulations, and in certain types of technical writing. In such special writing the student should follow the practice of the better publications in the field. If he has any doubt regarding the spelling or capitalization of any abbreviation, he should consult a good dictionary such as the *Standard College Dictionary* or *Webster's New World Dictionary* (in the main vocabulary).

▶ EXERCISE 1   Decide which form in each of the following items is appropriate in ordinary writing, and check the letter (*a* or *b*) of the correct form. If both forms are permissible, check both *a* and *b*. Use each appropriate form in a sentence.

1. a. in the U. S.
   b. in the United States
2. a. Rev. H. E. McGill
   b. The Reverend H. E. McGill
3. a. on Hickory St.
   b. on Hickory Street
4. a. etc.
   b. and etc.
5. a. FBI
   b. Federal Bureau of Investigation
6. a. on August 15
   b. on Aug. 15
7. a. for Jr.
   b. for John Evans, Jr.
8. a. e.g.
   b. for example
9. a. at 6:15 A.M.
   b. early in the A.M.
10. a. in Bangor, Me.
    b. in Bangor, Maine

Numbers

11f

Although usage varies, writers tend to spell out numbers that require only one or two words; they regularly use figures for other numbers.

EXAMPLES   after twenty years; only thirty-four dollars; more than four million votes; two thirds of the voters
after 124 years; only $34.15; exactly 4,568,305 votes [Note the commas used to separate millions, thousands, hundreds.]

Special usage regarding numbers:

1. *Use figures for dates.*

   May 1, 1967; 1 May 1967; July 12, 1763

   Such endings as *-st, -nd, -rd, -th* should not be added to the day of the month when the year follows; they need not be added even when the year is omitted.

   August 2, 1967; August 2

   Ordinal numbers to designate the day of the month may be written out or expressed in figures. The year is never written out except in very formal social announcements or invitations.

   the fifth (*or* 5th) of May, June first

2. *Use figures for street numbers, for pages and divisions of a book, for decimals and percentages, and for the hour of the day when used with* A.M. *or* P.M.

26 Main Avenue, 460 Fourth Street
The quotation is from page 80.
The bar is .63 of an inch thick.
She gets 10½ percent of the profits.
He arrived at 4:30 P.M.

3. *Be consistent in spelling out or using figures. Normally use figures for a series of numbers.*

   The garden plot was 125 feet long and 50 feet wide and contained an asparagus bed 12 feet square.

4. *Normally spell out any numeral at the beginning of a sentence. If necessary, recast the sentence.*

   INAPPROPRIATE   25 boys made the trip.
   APPROPRIATE   Twenty-five boys made the trip.

   INAPPROPRIATE   993 freshmen entered the college last year.
   APPROPRIATE   Last year 993 freshmen entered the college.

5. *The practice of repeating in parentheses a number that is spelled out (now generally reserved for legal and commercial writing) should be used correctly if at all.*

   I enclose twenty (20) dollars.   I enclose twenty dollars ($20).

▶ EXERCISE 2   Correct all errors in the use of numbers in the following sentences. Write *C* after each sentence that needs no correction.

1. The Thanksgiving holidays begin at one p.m.
2. On June 27th, 1959, Hawaiians voted 18 to 1 for statehood.
3. 500 freshmen are expected at the bonfire tonight.
4. On September 15 I wrote a check for $35.40.
5. On the fifteenth of September I wrote a check for thirty-five dollars.
6. Lex enjoyed the nineteen sixty Olympics.
7. At the age of 14 I spent 12 days hunting and fishing with a group of Boy Scouts in the Ozarks.
8. The reception, to be held at 27 Jackson Street, will begin about 8 o'clock.
9. 18,000 fans watched the Eagles win their 7th victory of the season.
10. The Tigers gained only 251 yards on the ground and 35 in the air.

▶ EXERCISE 3   Correct all errors in the use of abbreviations and numbers in the following sentences.

1. My father moved to Cal. about 10 years ago.
2. He is now living at sixty-five Sandusky St. in Frisco.
3. Geo. Washington, our first Pres., was born in seventeen hundred and thirty-two.
4. When he was 20 years old, he inherited Mt. Vernon from his half bro.
5. He assumed command of the Continental armies in Cambridge, Mass., on Jul. 3, 1775.
6. 125 men were stationed in the mts. to serve as guides.
7. These one hundred and twenty-five men have been in service for nearly 5 years.
8. Our class in math. did not meet last Wed.
9. Do you know the No. of the prof.'s office?
10. Rev. Williams will preach next Sun.

PUNCTUATION

The Comma

12

Use the comma (which ordinarily indicates a pause and a variation in voice pitch) where it is required by the structure of the sentence.

Punctuation helps to clarify the meaning of the written sentence. The writer must supply, as well as he can with marks of punctuation, what the speaker does naturally with his stops and pauses and with his voice variations or pitch. Read the following sentences aloud, noticing how commas indicate differences in the way sentences are spoken:

When I tried to help Ben, I failed at first.
When I tried to help, Ben, I failed at first.

The starter does not function properly, however the mechanic repairs it.
The starter does not function properly; however, the mechanic repairs it.

It is evident that the sound of the spoken sentence can serve as a guide in the punctuation of the written sentence.

But the principles governing punctuation can be stated most exactly in terms of the structure of the sentence. Anyone who understands this structure can master with comparative ease the very few principles governing the different uses of the comma. (If you cannot readily distinguish main clauses, subordinate clauses, and the various kinds of phrases, review Section 1, Sentence Sense.) These principles, which cover the normal practice of the best contemporary writers, are adequate for the needs of the average college student. He may note that skilled writers sometimes employ the comma in unusual ways to express delicate shades of meaning. Such variations can safely be made by the writer who has first learned to apply the following major principles:

Use commas

a. To separate main clauses joined by *and, but, or, nor,* or *for.*
b. To set off certain introductory elements.
c. To separate items in a series (including coordinate adjectives).
d. To set off nonrestrictive and other parenthetical elements.

Main Clauses

12a

Main clauses joined by one of the coordinating conjunctions (*and, but, or, nor, for*)[1] are separated by a comma.

PATTERN   MAIN CLAUSE, $\left\{\begin{array}{l} \text{and} \\ \text{but} \\ \text{or} \\ \text{nor} \\ \text{for} \end{array}\right\}$ MAIN CLAUSE.

We were sitting before the fire in the big room at Twin Farms, and Lewis had rudely retired behind a newspaper.
—DOROTHY THOMPSON

It was not actually raining, but the air had the heavy smell of ozone produced by the lightning of the previous night.
—JEREMY BERNSTEIN

Justice stands upon Power, or there is no justice.
—WILLIAM S. WHITE

The peoples of the Sahara have never been united, nor have they even considered uniting in any common cause.
—JAMES R. NEWMAN

Note: A comma precedes a coordinating conjunction joining the main clauses of a compound-complex sentence (which has at least two main clauses and one subordinate clause).

I was glad to agree, for I feel that showing live animals arouses people's interest in their local fauna and its preservation.
—GERALD DURRELL

Caution: Do not confuse the compound sentence (two main clauses) with the simple sentence (one main clause) containing a compound predicate.

COMPOUND SENTENCE   On the steppe one is electrified, and one can feel one's life burn faster.   —V. S. PRITCHETT

COMPOUND PREDICATE   On the steppe one is electrified and can feel one's life burn faster. [No comma before *and*]

At times professional writers use the comma to set off what seems to be merely the second part of a compound element, especially in long sentences. Closer examination usually discloses, however, that the material following the comma is actually a regular main clause with some words "understood"; the use of the comma emphasizes the distinction between the principal ideas in the sentence. Note

---

[1] *Yet* is occasionally used as a coordinating conjunction equivalent to *but.* Informal writing frequently uses *so* as a coordinating conjunction, but careful writers usually avoid the *so*-sentence by subordinating one of the clauses.

the following sentences, in which the implied matter is inserted in brackets:

> There is no other way for the world's living standards to be raised to anything like our level, and [there is] no other way to link or merge the economies of the free nations. —FORTUNE

> The number of high school graduates has been increasing since 1890 about thirteen times as fast as the population, and the number of college graduates [has been increasing] six times as fast. —THE ATLANTIC MONTHLY

Exceptions to 12a

1. *Omission of the comma:*

When the main clauses are short, the comma is frequently omitted before *and* or *or*. Before the conjunctions *but* and *for*, the comma is usually needed to prevent confusion with the prepositions *but* and *for*. Sometimes, especially in narrative writing, the comma is omitted even when the clauses are long.

> The next night the wind shifted and the thaw began.
> —RACHEL L. CARSON

> This was met with a great din of spontaneous applause and it was at just that instant that Sally Poker looked down at her feet and discovered that in the excitement of getting ready she had forgotten to change her shoes: two brown Girl Scout oxfords protruded from the bottom of her dress.
> —FLANNERY O'CONNOR

2. *Use of the semicolon instead of the comma:*

Sometimes the coordinating conjunction is preceded by a semicolon instead of the usual comma, especially when the main clauses have internal punctuation or reveal a striking contrast. See also **14a**.

> It was childish, of course; for any disturbance, any sudden intruding noise, would make the creatures stop.
> —ALDOUS HUXLEY

> Doormen grow rich blowing their whistles for cabs; and some doormen belong to no door at all—merely wander about through the streets, opening cabs for people as they happen to find them. —E. B. WHITE

▶ **EXERCISE 1**   Use a comma (or a semicolon) where required in the following sentences. Write *C* after any sentence which needs no further punctuation.

1 In college a smug freshman receives a kind of shock treatment for professors often use surprising facts to pry open complacent or closed minds. 2 For example, a history professor may consider William Wirt a greater hero than Patrick Henry or an English teacher may say that a double negative like "don't have no money" does not really make the meaning of a sentence positive. 3 A freshman should not become rebellious nor should he be unduly alarmed when new information threatens old, cherished opinions. 4 An intelligent student may question surprising facts but he never doubts the value of opening his mind to new ideas. 5 Moreover, he expects to be confused, at least part of the time, in the college classroom for he, like John Ciardi, the poet, knows that a person who is not confused probably has not yet asked the right questions.

6 The governor announced that the water supply was dangerously low and he proclaimed that a state of civil emergency existed. 7 The days passed and the drought grew steadily worse. 8 The state fire marshal ordered all parks closed but forest fires broke out in spite of all precautions. 9 City-dwellers watched their gardens shrivel and die and industrial workers were laid off as electric-power output failed. 10 But perhaps the worst afflicted were the farmers for there was no hope of saving their crops and even their livestock had to be sold on a glutted market or else left to die in the fields.

▶ **EXERCISE 2**   Write eight sentences to illustrate **12a** and two sentences to illustrate the exceptions to it. Be sure to use all five coordinating conjunctions. If necessary, refer to the pattern and examples on page 832.

Introductory Elements

12b
Introductory elements such as adverb clauses, long phrases, transitional expressions, and interjections are usually set off by commas.

To set off an introductory element is to put a comma after it. See also **12d**.

(1) Introductory adverb clauses

PATTERN   ADVERB CLAUSE, MAIN CLAUSE.

> Whenever I tried to put chains on a tire, the car would maliciously wrap them around a rear axle. —JAMES THURBER

> If any college man will work intelligently, I guarantee his success. —HARDIN CRAIG

Many writers omit the comma after short introductory clauses, and sometimes after longer ones, when the omission does not make for difficult reading. In the following sentences the commas may be used or omitted at the option of the writer:

> If we leave(,) he will be offended.
> When *he* comes to the end of the lane(,) *he* should turn to the left. [When the subject of the introductory clause is repeated in the main clause, the comma is usually unnecessary.]

Note: When the adverb clause *follows* the main clause, there is usually no pause and no need for a comma.

PATTERN   MAIN CLAUSE ADVERB CLAUSE.

> I waited there until he returned.
> Ben arrived before the train did.

Such adverb clauses, however, are set off by a comma if they are parenthetical or loosely connected with the rest of the sentence, especially if the subordinating conjunction seems equivalent to a coordinating conjunction (or if a distinct pause is required in the reading).

> Henry is now in good health, although he has been an invalid most of his life. [*Although* is equivalent to *but*.]
> With children and young people his magic never fails, whether he is doing bottle tricks for three-year-olds or counseling teen-agers about courses or careers. —ALICE KIMBALL SMITH

(2) Long introductory phrases

> *In two years of acting in cowboy films,* W. S. Hart earned
> $900,000.   —H. A. OVERSTREET
>
> *At the critical moments in this sad history,* there have been
> men worth listening to who warned the people against their
> mistakes.   —WALTER LIPPMANN

Introductory phrases containing a gerund, a participle,
or an infinitive, even though short, must often be followed
by a comma to prevent misreading.

> *Before leaving,* the soldiers demolished the fort.
> *Because of his effort to escape,* his punishment was increased.

Short introductory prepositional phrases, except when
they are distinctly parenthetical expressions (as *in fact* or
for example), are seldom followed by commas.

> *At ninety* she was still active.
> *During the night* he heard many noises.

(3) Transitional expressions and interjections

Interjections as well as transitional expressions (such as
*for example, in fact, on the other hand, in the second
place*) are generally considered parenthetical. See **12d(3)**.
When used as introductory elements, they are usually
followed by commas.

> *In fact,* I hope to leave tomorrow.
> *For example,* most boys enjoy fishing.
> *Well,* just to stand up and face life's problems takes courage.

▶ **EXERCISE 3** In each of the following sentences find the
main clause and identify the preceding element as a subordinate clause or a phrase. Then determine whether to
use or omit a comma after the introductory element.
Justify your decision.

¹ In order to pay his way through college George worked
at night in an iron foundry. ² During this time he became acquainted with all the company's operations. ³ At
the end of four years' observation of George's work, the
foundry owner offered George a position as manager.
⁴ Although George had planned to attend medical school
and enter his father's profession, he found now that the kind
of work he had been doing had a far greater appeal for him.
⁵ In fact, he accepted the offer without hesitation.

Items in Series

12c

**Words, phrases, or clauses in a series (including coordinate
adjectives) are separated by commas.**

(1) Words, phrases, or clauses in a series

> The room is *bright, clean, quiet.* [Form *a, b, c*]
> The room is *bright, clean,* and *quiet.* [Form *a, b,* and *c*]
> The room is *bright* and *clean* and *quiet.* [Form *a* and *b* and *c.*
>   Commas are omitted when *and* is used throughout the
>   series.]
> He walked *up the steps, across the porch,* and *through the
>   doorway.* [Phrases in a series]

> We protested *that the engine used too much oil, that the
> brakes were worn out,* and *that the tires were dangerous.*
> [Subordinate clauses in a series]
> *We rang the bell, we knocked on the door,* and *we shouted
> until we were hoarse.* [Main clauses in a series]

The final comma is often omitted, especially by newspapers, when the series takes the form *a, b,* and *c.* But
students are usually advised to follow the practice of the
more conservative books and periodicals in using the
comma throughout the series, if only because the comma
is sometimes needed to prevent confusion.

CONFUSING The natives ate beans, onions, rice and honey. [Was
           the rice and honey a mixture?]
CLEAR   The natives ate beans, onions, rice, and honey. OR
           The natives ate beans, onions, and rice and honey.

(2) Coordinate adjectives

Adjectives are coordinate when they modify the same
word or word group. Notice in the following examples that
the pauses between coordinate adjectives are indicated by
commas.

> a clean, quiet room [A *clean* and *quiet* room—both adjectives
>   modify the word *room.*]
> a clean, quiet public dining room [*Clean* and *quiet* modify the
>   word group *public dining room,* which is pronounced as a
>   unit.]

Coordinate adjectives ordinarily have a reversible word
order; adjectives which are not coordinate do not.

COORDINATE   colorful, expensive scarves [*Logical:* expensive, color-
              ful scarves]
NOT COORDINATE many colorful scarves [*Illogical:* colorful many
              scarves]

▶ **EXERCISE 4** In the following sentences distinguish each
series and each group of coordinate adjectives, inserting
commas where needed. Justify each comma used.

¹ Do you remember Pete Moore and that old battered
lunch pail he used to carry? ² He would go past our
house every morning wait on the corner for his ride hand
his lunch pail up to one of the men on the truck climb up
himself and go rolling away. ³ Year after year—spring
summer, fall and winter—Pete and his lunch pail would
wait on that corner. ⁴ And every year they both got a
little older a little more battered a little nearer used up.
⁵ My brothers my sisters and I used to make bets about
which would wear out first. ⁶ Then one awful day we
heard the blast at the plant saw the sky black with smoke
and watched the streets fill with frightened hurrying
people. ⁷ That day was the end of old Pete, of his
battered lunch pail and of the jokes we made about him.

▶ **EXERCISE 5** Using necessary commas, supply coordinate
adjectives to modify each of the following.

EXAMPLE old fogy—an arrogant, aggressive old fogy

1. office boy   5. salad dressing
2. oil painting   6. motion picture
3. stock market   7. crab grass
4. best man   8. mountain lion

Parenthetical Elements

12d

Nonrestrictive clauses (or phrases) and other parenthetical elements ("interrupters") are set off by commas. Restrictive clauses (or phrases) are not set off.

Use a comma after a parenthetical element at the beginning of a sentence, before a parenthetical element at the end, and both before and after one within a sentence.

> *My friends,* we have no alternative.
> We have no alternative, *my friends.*
> We have, *my friends,* no alternative.
>
> *He said,* "The story has been told."
> "The story has been told," *he said.*
> "The story," *he said,* "has been told."

Caution: When two commas are needed to set off a parenthetical element within the sentence, do not forget the second comma. To use one comma but not the second makes reading more difficult than the omission of both commas.

CONFUSING   Ours is, of course a democratic country.
CLEAR   Ours is, of course, a democratic country. OR Ours is of course a democratic country.

CONFUSING   Ours is, we are told a democratic country.
CLEAR   Ours is, we are told, a democratic country. [The marked pauses in speaking show that commas are needed.]

(1) Nonrestrictive clauses and phrases are set off by commas. Restrictive clauses and phrases are not set off.

Adjective clauses and phrases are nonrestrictive (set off by commas) when they merely add information about a word already identified. Such modifiers are parenthetical; they are not essential to the meaning of the main clause and may be omitted.

> Henry Smith, *who is lazy,* will lose his job. ["Henry will lose his job" is true without the nonessential *who is lazy.*]
> Venice, *which he visited next,* was then torn by rival factions.
> Venice, *visited next,* was then torn by rival factions.

Adjective clauses and phrases are restrictive (not set off by commas) when they are needed for identification of the word they modify. Such clauses limit or restrict the meaning of the sentence.

> A boy *who is lazy* deserves to lose his job. ["A boy deserves to lose his job" is true only with the essential *who is lazy.*]
> The city *that he visited next* was Venice.
> The city *visited next* was Venice.

Adjective clauses beginning with *that* are restrictive. Adjective clauses beginning with *who* (*whom, whose*) and *which* may be restrictive or nonrestrictive.

Your voice can help you distinguish between restrictive and nonrestrictive modifiers. As you read the following sentences aloud, note that you neither pause nor lower the pitch of your voice for the italicized (restrictive) passages.

RESTRICTIVE   A mother *who does not love her children* is unnatural.
RESTRICTIVE   The girl *sitting near the window* laughed at me.

When reading aloud the sentences below, you naturally "set off" the italicized nonrestrictive modifiers (1) by using definite pauses and (2) by lowering the pitch of your voice. (Note also that a nonrestrictive modifier can be omitted without changing the meaning of the main clause.)

NONRESTRICTIVE   My mother, *who loves her children,* is an ideal parent.
NONRESTRICTIVE   Martha Thompson, *sitting near the window,* smiled knowingly.

Study the meaning of the sentences on the next page. Also read each one aloud, and let your voice help you distinguish between restrictive and nonrestrictive clauses and phrases.

NONRESTRICTIVE CLAUSE   Our newest boat, *which is painted red and white,* has sprung a leak. [The *which* clause, adding information about a boat already identified, is parenthetical. It is not essential to the main clause, *Our newest boat has sprung a leak.*]
NONRESTRICTIVE PHRASE   Our newest boat, *painted red and white,* has sprung a leak.
RESTRICTIVE CLAUSE (NO COMMAS)   A boat *that leaks* is of little use. [The clause *that leaks* is essential to the meaning of the main clause.]
RESTRICTIVE PHRASE (NO COMMAS)   A boat *with a leak* is of little use.
NONRESTRICTIVE CLAUSE   My new car, *which is parked across the street,* is ready. [Clause adding information about a car already identified; pauses and change in voice pitch marked by commas.]
NONRESTRICTIVE PHRASE   My new car, *parked across the street,* is ready.
RESTRICTIVE CLAUSE (NO COMMAS)   The car *which is parked across the street* is ready. [Clause essential to the identification]
RESTRICTIVE PHRASE (NO COMMAS)   The car *parked across the street* is ready.

Sometimes a clause (or phrase) may be either restrictive or nonrestrictive; the writer signifies his meaning by the proper use of the comma.

NONRESTRICTIVE   He spent hours caring for the Indian guides, *who were sick with malaria.* [He cared for all the Indian guides. All of them were sick with malaria.]
RESTRICTIVE (NO COMMA)   He spent hours caring for the Indian guides *who were sick with malaria.* [Some of the Indian guides were sick with malaria. He cared for the sick ones.]

▶ **EXERCISE 6** In the following sentences determine whether each clause (or phrase) is restrictive or nonrestrictive. Set off only the nonrestrictive clauses (or phrases).

R 1. The James Lee who owns the bank is a grandson of the one who founded it.
N 2. James Lee who owns this bank and five others is one of the wealthiest men in the state.
N 3. The coach called out to Higgins, who got up from the bench and trotted over to him.
R N 4. The coach who chewed on cigars but never lighted them threw one away and reached for another.
R 5. Anyone who saw him could tell that something was troubling him.

R6. All banks which fail to report will be closed.

R7. All banks failing to report will be closed.

R8. Henry betrayed the man who had helped him build his fortune.

N9. James White, who had helped Henry build his fortune, died yesterday.

N10. My father, hoping that I would remain at home, offered me a share in his business.

▶ **EXERCISE 7** Compose and punctuate five sentences containing nonrestrictive clauses or phrases. Compose five sentences containing restrictive clauses or phrases and underline the restrictive elements.

(2) Nonrestrictive appositives, contrasted elements, geographical names, and items in dates and addresses are set off by commas.

Note that most appositives may be readily expanded into nonrestrictive clauses. In other words, the principle underlying the use of commas to set off nonrestrictive clauses also applies here; see page 835.

APPOSITIVES AND CONTRASTED ELEMENTS

Jesse, *the caretaker*, is a good fellow. [The appositive *caretaker* is equivalent to the nonrestrictive clause *who is the caretaker*. Note the distinct pauses and change in voice pitch.]

Sandburg, *the biographer of Lincoln*, was awarded the Pulitzer Prize. [The appositive is equivalent to the nonrestrictive clause *who is the biographer of Lincoln*.]

My companions were James White, *Esq.*, William Smith, *M.D.*, and Rufus L. Black, *Ph.D.* [Abbreviated titles after a name are treated as appositives.]

The cook, *not the caretaker*, will assist you. [The contrasted element is a sort of negative appositive.]

Our failures, *not our successes*, will be remembered.

Trade comes with peace, *not with war*.

Appositives are usually nonrestrictive (parenthetical), merely adding information about a person or thing already identified. Such appositives are set off by commas, which mark distinct pauses and change in voice pitch. But when an appositive is restrictive, commas are usually omitted.

The poet Sandburg has written a biography. [*Sandburg* restricts the meaning, telling what poet has written a biography.]

His son James is sick. [*James*, not his son *William*]

William the Conqueror invaded England in 1066. [An appositive that is part of a title is restrictive.]

The word *malapropism* is derived from Sheridan's *The Rivals*.

Do you refer to Samuel Butler the poet or to Samuel Butler the novelist?

▶ **EXERCISE 8** Use commas to set off contrasted elements and nonrestrictive appositives in the following paragraph. Underline restrictive appositives.

[1] Years ago, I read *The Marks of an Educated Man*, an interesting book by Albert Wiggam. [2] According to Wiggam, one outstanding characteristic of the educated man is that he "links himself with a great cause" one that requires selfless service. [3] Certainly many famous men whether scientists or artists or philosophers have dedicated their lives to the cause of serving others. [4] For example,

Louis Pasteur, the famous French chemist, devoted his life to the study of medicine to benefit mankind. [5] And the artist Michelangelo served humanity by creating numerous works of lasting beauty. [6] Francis of Assisi, a saint of the twelfth century, was also devoted to a great cause. [7] His life was the mirror of his creed, a reflection of his ardent love for others. [8] Among twentieth-century philosophers was Albert Schweitzer, a well-known missionary and physician. [9] Schweitzer, a person who worked for both peace and brotherhood, was like Pasteur, Michelangelo, and St. Francis because he linked himself with a great cause, not with transitory, selfish aims. [10] I think that the author, Wiggam, should use the adjective *great* not *educated* to describe the man who devotes himself to a noble cause.

▶ **EXERCISE 9** Compose ten sentences to illustrate the punctuation of appositives and contrasted elements.

GEOGRAPHICAL NAMES,
ITEMS IN DATES AND ADDRESSES

Pasadena, California, is the site of the Rose Bowl. [*California* may be thought of as equivalent to the nonrestrictive clause *which is in California*.]

Address the letter to Mr. J. L. Karnes, Clayton, Delaware 19938. [The zip code is not separated by a comma from the name of the state.]

Tuesday, May 8, 1967, in Chicago; 8 May 1967; May, 1967, in Boston OR May 1967 in Boston. [Commas are often omitted when the day of the month is not given, or when the day of the month precedes rather than follows the month. Students are usually advised not to follow the less conservative practice of dropping the comma after the year, as in "May 8, 1967 in Chicago."]

▶ **EXERCISE 10** Copy the following sentences, inserting commas where they are needed.

1. The letter was sent to a special agent at 6222 North Central Expressway Dallas Texas 75206.
2. Their son was born on Friday June 18 1954 at Baptist Hospital Knoxville Tennessee.
3. He was inducted into the army at Fort Oglethorpe Georgia on 30 September 1942.
4. William Congreve was born in Bardsey England on January 24 1670.
5. The accident occurred in De Soto Parish Louisiana on Saturday January 1 1966.
6. Please send all communications to 757 Third Avenue New York New York 10017.
7. Pearl Harbor Hawaii was bombed on December 7 1941.

(3) Parenthetical words, phrases, or clauses (inserted expressions), words in direct address, and absolute elements are set off by commas.

PARENTHETICAL EXPRESSIONS

As a matter of fact, the term "parenthetical" is correctly applied to everything discussed under **12d;** but the term is more commonly applied to such expressions as *on the other hand, in the first place, in fact, to tell the truth, however, that is, for example, I hope, I report, he says.*

The term would apply equally well to expressions inserted in dialogue: *he said, he observed, he protested,* etc. Expressions that come at the beginning of a sentence are treated both by **12b** and by **12d**.

> You will, *then,* accept our offer?
> *To tell the truth,* we anticipated bad luck.
> The work is, *on the whole,* very satisfactory.
> "We believe," *he replied,* "that you are correct."
> We believe, *however,* that you should go. [When *however* means "nevertheless," it is usually set off by commas. But when *however* means "no matter how," it is not a parenthetical word but a subordinator: "The trip will be hard, *however* you go."]

Some parenthetical expressions causing little if any pause in reading are frequently not set off by commas: *also, too, indeed, perhaps, at least, likewise,* etc. The writer must use his judgment.

> I am *also* of that opinion.
> He is *perhaps* the best swimmer on the team.
> Your efforts will *of course* be appreciated. OR, Your efforts will, *of course,* be appreciated.

DIRECT ADDRESS

> Come here, *Mary,* and help us.
> I refuse, *sir,* to believe the report.
> This, *my friends,* is the whole truth.

ABSOLUTE ELEMENTS

> *Win or lose,* play by rule. [Absolute phrase]
> I fear the encounter, *his temper being what it is.* [Nominative absolute]
> *Well,* let him try if he insists. [Mild interjection]
> Leslie doesn't play the tuba, *does she?* [Echo question]

12e

Note: Occasionally a comma, though not called for by any of the major principles already discussed, may be needed to prevent misreading.

Use **12e** sparingly to justify your commas. In a general sense, nearly all commas are used to prevent misreading or to make reading easier. Your mastery of the comma will come through the application of the more specific major principles (**a, b, c, d**) to the structure of your sentences.

CONFUSING   Inside the room was gaily decorated. [*Inside* may be at first mistaken for the preposition.]

CLEAR   Inside, the room was gaily decorated. [*Inside* is clearly an adverb.]

CONFUSING   After all the conquest of malaria is a fascinating story.

CLEAR   After all, the conquest of malaria is a fascinating story.

▶ **EXERCISE 11**   All commas in the following passage are correctly used. Justify each comma by referring to **12a** (main clauses joined by a coordinating conjunction), **12b** (introductory elements), **12c** (a series or coordinate adjectives), or **12d** (parenthetical elements).

[1] In the cold months there are few visitors, for northern Minnesota is not a winter playground.   [2] And yet the intrepid traveler would be well rewarded by the natural beauty surrounding him.   [3] The skies and the undulating fields merge as one; unreality assails the mind and the eye.   [4] The sun swings in a low arc, and at sunrise and sunset it is not hard to imagine what the world may be like in many distant aeons when ice and snow envelop the earth, while the sun, cooled to the ruddy glow of bittersweet, lingeringly touches the clouds with warm colors of apricot, tangerine, lavender, and rose.   [5] Night skies may be indescribably clear.   [6] The stars are sharp and brilliant, pricking perception; the northern constellations diagramed with utmost clarity upon the blackest of skies.   [7] There is no illusion here that they are hung like lanterns just beyond reach.   [8] The vast distances of space are as clear to see as the barbed points of light.   [9] When the aurora borealis sweeps in to dominate the night, it elicits a quite different and emotional reaction, not unlike the surging, impressive sight itself.   [10] If the luminous, pulsing scarves of light were tangible streamers, certainly it would be possible to become entangled in and absorbed into the celestial kaleidoscope.

—FRANCES GILLIS[2]

▶ **EXERCISE 12**   Insert commas where needed in the following sentences (selected and adapted from the *New Yorker*). Be prepared to justify each comma used.

1. He was in truth slightly bowlegged but he concealed the flaw by standing with one knee bent.
2. What living American has had a mountain a bird a fish a spider a lizard and a louse named after him?
3. A teacup balanced on a chair tumbled to the floor and immediately our attention turned to poltergeists.
4. A black cloud crossed the city flashed two or three fierce bolts rumbled halfheartedly and passed on.
5. When Miss Meltzer reminded Feder that there existed neither sufficiently powerful lamps nor properly designed fixtures for the project he said "Of course they don't exist Meltzer. We're going to create them."
6. He dies of pneumonia shortly afterward but returns as a robust ghost to steal the overcoats off the backs of half the citizens in the city triumphantly righting one wrong with a dozen wrongs.
7. Although histoplasmosis is now established as a disease of nearly universal distribution it appears to be most prevalent in the United States.
8. Still something had to be done and Mother and Aunt Berta not being inventive decided to do what all the world was doing.
9. For a week suspended in air we had given thought to becoming engaged—I more than she perhaps for she was engaged already.
10. Clara collapsed into laughter gasping her two hands thrust to her face in a spasm.
11. Two girls one of them with pert buckteeth and eyes as black as vest buttons the other with white skin and flesh-colored hair like an underdeveloped photograph of a redhead came and sat on my right.

[2] From "Winter North of the Mississippi" by Frances Gillis, reprinted from the *Atlantic Monthly,* March, 1961. By permission of the author.

12. After officials have measured the jump the result is flashed on the bulletin board but that isn't as satisfactory as seeing the high-jump bar tremble and then stay up or fall.

Superfluous Commas

13

Do not use superfluous commas.

Necessary commas indicate appropriate pauses and voice pitch and thus help to clarify the meaning of a sentence. Unnecessary or misplaced commas, however, are false or awkward signals that often confuse the reader. Compare the punctuation of the following sentences.

> The boys, go to the gymnasium, at two o'clock. [Unnecessary commas]
> The boys go to the gymnasium at two o'clock. [No commas needed]
> Boys, go to the gymnasium at two o'clock. [Comma needed to indicate direct address—see 12d]
> Helen enjoys tennis but, she cannot play well. [Misplaced comma]
> Helen enjoys tennis, but she cannot play well. [Comma *before* coordinating conjunction—see 12a]

If you tend to use superfluous commas, consider the need for every comma you are tempted to use and omit it unless you can justify it by Section 12.

13a

Do not use a comma to separate the subject from its verb, the verb from its object, or an adjective from the noun it precedes.

In the following sentences the encircled commas should be omitted:

> Rain at frequent intervals⊙ is productive of mosquitoes. [Needless separation of subject and verb]
> He learned at an early age⊙ the necessity of economizing. [Needless separation of verb and object]
> The book says⊙ that members of the crew deserted. [Indirect discourse: needless separation of verb and object]
> He was a bad, deceitful, unruly⊙ boy. [Incorrect separation of adjective and its noun]

Note: A comma before the verb sometimes makes for clarity when the subject is heavily modified.

> Rain coming at frequent intervals and in sufficient amounts to fill the ponds, the cisterns, and the many small containers near the house, is productive of mosquitoes.

13b

Do not use a comma to separate two words or two phrases joined by a coordinating conjunction.

In the following sentences the encircled commas should be omitted:

The poem has nobility of sentiment⊙ and dignity of style.
The players work together⊙ and gain a victory. [Compound predicate: *and* joins two verbs.]
He had decided to work⊙ and to save his money. [*And* joins two infinitive phrases.]

13c

Do not use commas to set off words or short phrases (especially introductory ones) that are not parenthetical or that are very slightly so.

In the following sentences the encircled commas should be omitted:

> Last Monday⊙ I went to a baseball game⊙ too.
> Maybe⊙ he had a better reason for leaving.
> Yet⊙ it is easy to talk⊙ by wire⊙ to any continent.

13d

Do not use commas to set off restrictive (necessary) clauses, restrictive phrases, or restrictive appositives.

In the following sentences the encircled commas should be omitted:

> A man⊙ *who hopes to succeed*⊙ must work hard. [Restrictive clause]
> Any man⊙ *willing to work*⊙ can make a living there. [Restrictive phrase]
> Only in ancient Spanish was *k* used, and the letter⊙ *w*⊙ has never had a place in the Spanish alphabet. [Restrictive appositive]

13e

Do not put a comma before the first item of a series, after the last item of a series, or after a coordinating conjunction.

In the following sentences the encircled commas should be omitted:

> I enjoy the study of⊙ history, geography, and geology. [Needless comma before the first item of a series. A colon here would also be needless since there is no formal introduction. See 17d.]
> History, geography, and geology⊙ are interesting subjects.
> I enjoy these subjects, but⊙ for others I have less appreciation.
> Field work is required in a few sciences, such as⊙ botany and geology.

▶ EXERCISE 1   Some of the following sentences contain commas that would usually be omitted in good contemporary writing. Draw a circle around each unnecessary comma. Be prepared to justify each comma that you allow to stand.

1. I gave the note to Helen, and George asked her to read it aloud.
2. I gave the note to Helen, and asked her to read it aloud.
3. Any teacher, who is enthusiastic, deserves a lively class.
4. Professor Brown, who is enthusiastic, has a lively class.
5. One of the debaters, had apparently read Castell's *College Logic*.

6. My brother, one of the debaters, had never heard of the poet, Sandburg.

7. I like to celebrate Christmas quietly, but, my family prefers parties, and fireworks.

8. An old proverb states, that love and a cough are difficult to hide.

9. Remembering a line, from Pascal, I replied, "Noble deeds that are concealed are most esteemed."

10. During the half, we drank coffee, and talked about the close, exciting, football game, especially crucial plays, such as, the pass interference, the untimely fumbles, and the surprising, field goal.

▶ EXERCISE 2 In the following sentences (adapted from Thoreau) draw a circle around each superfluous comma and be prepared to justify each needed comma.

[1] We admire Chaucer, for his sturdy, English wit. [2] The easy height, he speaks from, in his "Prologue," to the *Canterbury Tales*, as if he were equal to any of the company there assembled, is as good as any particular excellence in it. [3] But, though it is full of good sense, and humanity, it is not transcendent poetry. [4] For picturesque descriptions, of persons, it is, perhaps, without a parallel in English poetry. [5] Yet, it is, essentially, humorous, as the loftiest genius never is. [6] Humor, however broad and genial, takes a narrower view than enthusiasm. [7] To his own finer vein, he added all the common wit, and wisdom, of his time, and everywhere in his works, his remarkable knowledge of the world, and nice perception of character, his rare, common sense, and proverbial wisdom, are apparent . . . . [8] The lover learns at last, that there is no person quite transparent and trustworthy, but every one has a devil in him, that is capable of any crime, in the long run. [9] Yet, as an oriental philosopher has said, "Although friendship between good men, is interrupted, their principles remain unaltered. [10] The stalk of the lotus, may be broken, and the fibers remain connected."

The Semicolon

14

Use the semicolon (a) between two main clauses not joined by *and*, *but*, *or*, *nor*, or *for* and (b) between coordinate elements containing commas. (Use the semicolon only between parts of equal rank.)

The pause in speaking required for the semicolon is almost as full as that for the period; in fact, the semicolon may be called a weak period. (Read the preceding sentence aloud, noting the very distinct pause marked by the semicolon and the lesser pause marked by the comma.)

The pause test can help you place the semicolon as well as the comma, but you should rely chiefly on your knowl-edge of the structure of the sentence. If you can distinguish between phrases and clauses, between main and subordinate clauses (see Section **1d** and **1e**), you should have little trouble using the semicolon.

14a

Use the semicolon between two main clauses not joined by one of the coordinating conjunctions (*and*, *but*, *or*, *nor*, *for*).

PATTERN MAIN CLAUSE; MAIN CLAUSE. [Compound sentence]

> We didn't abolish truth; even we couldn't do that.
> —WILLIAM FAULKNER

> Essentially the form of art is an imitation of reality; it holds the mirror up to nature.   —WILL DURANT

> I had great anxiety and no means of relieving it; I had vehement convictions and small power to give effect to them.
> —WINSTON CHURCHILL

Note: The semicolon also separates main clauses not joined by a coordinating conjunction in compound-complex sentences.

> No society can survive if everything changes but its institutions; no society can stay sane if no one is to innovate except the technologists.   —BARBARA WARD

[Main clause subordinate clause; main clause subordinate clause.]

Conjunctive adverbs (e.g., *accordingly, also, anyhow, besides, consequently, furthermore, hence, however, indeed, instead, likewise, moreover, nevertheless, still, then, therefore, thus*) and such transitional phrases as *for example, in fact, in other words, on the contrary, on the other hand*, and *that is* are not grammatically equivalent to coordinating conjunctions. See **3b**. Therefore, use a semicolon before these conjunctive adverbs and transitional phrases when they connect main clauses.

PATTERN

	CONJUNCTIVE ADVERB	
MAIN CLAUSE;	*or*	MAIN CLAUSE.
	TRANSITIONAL PHRASE,	

> Kon-Tiki, on his original voyage across the sea, had no asphalt or hermetically sealed tins; nevertheless he had no serious food problems.   —THOR HEYERDAHL

> The organism gets a chance to function according to its own laws; in other words, it gets a chance to realize such good as it is capable of.   —ALDOUS HUXLEY

Note that a comma follows the transitional phrase *in other words* but not the conjunctive adverb *nevertheless*. After transitional phrases the pause in reading is usually sufficient to require a comma but often not so after conjunctive adverbs. The pause test is the best guide. See also **12b**.

Caution: Do not overwork the semicolon. Often compound sentences are better revised according to the principles of subordination. See Section **24** and also **14c**.

Exception to 14a: Coordinating conjunctions between main clauses are often preceded by a semicolon (instead of the usual comma) if the clauses have internal punctuation or reveal a striking contrast. See also **12a**.

American education may be sometimes slapdash and fantastic, with its short-story and saxophone courses, its strange fraternities and sororities, its musical-comedy co-ed atmosphere, its heavily solemn games departments; but at least it has never departed from the fine medieval tradition of the poor scholar.   —J. B. PRIESTLEY

14b

The semicolon is used to separate a series of equal elements which themselves contain commas.

This use of the semicolon makes for clarity, showing the reader at a glance the main divisions, which would be more difficult to distinguish if only commas were used throughout the sentence.

> I came to this conclusion after talking in Moscow last spring with three kinds of people concerned: foreign diplomats, students, and correspondents; the new Rector of Friendship University; and the harried Afro-Asian students themselves.
> —PRISCILLA JOHNSON

> The challenge of facing a large audience, expectant but unaroused; the laughter that greets a sally at the outset, then the stillness as the power of imagery and ideas takes hold; the response that flows, audibly or inaudibly, from the audience to the speaker; the fresh extemporizing without which a lecture is dead; the tension and timing as the talk nears the hour; and the unexpected conclusion—this is what every professional speaker comes to know.   —EDWARD WEEKS

14c

Caution: **Use the semicolon between parts of equal rank only, not between a clause and a phrase or a main clause and a subordinate clause.**

PARTS OF EQUAL RANK

A bitter wind swept the dead leaves along the street; it cast them high in the air and against the buildings. [Two main clauses]

I hope to spend my vacation in Canada; I enjoy the fishing there.

PARTS OF UNEQUAL RANK

A bitter wind swept the dead leaves along the street, casting them high in the air and against the buildings. [Main clause and phrase, separated by a comma]

I hope to spend my vacation in Canada, where I enjoy the fishing. [Main clause and subordinate clause, separated by a comma]

Note: At times a semicolon is apparently used between parts of unequal rank. However, closer examination usually reveals that the semicolon is in reality a mark of coordination: following the semicolon is a group of words which, with "understood" words carried over from the preceding clause, constitutes a main clause.

> Popularization is one thing; dedicated music-making [is] another.
> —HARPER'S MAGAZINE

> The theory applied equally well to Mrs. Kerr's case; perhaps [the theory applied] even better since it also confirmed the deep-rooted public conviction that no woman really knows what a car is for.   —IBID.

▶ **EXERCISE 1**   In the following sentences (selected from the *Atlantic Monthly*), all semicolons are used correctly. Be prepared to give the reason for the use of each semicolon.

1. The narrow windows and the steeply sloping roof oppressed me; I wished to turn away and go back.
2. Even stillness is a positive factor; it is to motion what silence is to sound.
3. We are not as careful or cherishing of our artists as Europeans; nevertheless, what with television, movies, and shows, it is possible for outstanding dancers to make a living, while choreographers, directors, and dancing actors can make fortunes.
4. The rhymes are filled with fun and good humor; the music, arranged by Cecil Sharp, is a fine accompaniment; but the superb part of the book is the hilarious array of pictures in rainbow colors.
5. Beyond this are the three objectives of the American space program: "to understand the nature of the control exerted by the sun over events on the earth; to learn the nature and origin of the universe, including the solar system; and to search for the origin of life and its presence outside the earth."
6. Everybody was confused; no one knew what to do.
7. "As a historian," wrote De Voto, "I have interested myself in the growth among the American people of the feeling that they were properly a single nation between two oceans; in the development of what I have called the continental mind."
8. Treitschke confirmed him in his belief in blood and iron; Nietzsche in his veneration for the Aryan "blond beast," the superman who would conquer and decimate the subject races.
9. It is beyond possibility to mention all the outstanding books; however, some of the highlights are suggested in the chronological list that follows.
10. It was an inland country, with the forlorn look of all unloved things; winter in this part of the South is a moribund coma, not the Northern death sleep with the sure promise of resurrection.

▶ **EXERCISE 2**   In the following sentences insert semicolons where they are needed. Remove semicolons standing between parts of unequal rank. Write *C* after each sentence that needs no revision.

1. Although I did my best to explain why I had failed; my parents scolded me for failing the history test.
2. Mac goes around in par now, he has trimmed several strokes off his game since we played together last.
3. I hear it said by the people hereabouts that the old mansion is haunted, in fact, there are some who swear that it is.
4. Hank had dismantled his motor; intending to give it a complete overhaul for the following week's races.
5. He is fairly even-tempered most of the time, and you should have no difficulty getting along with him but whatever you do, don't ever let him get you into a political argument.
6. He lamented that he had no suggestions to offer, however, he spent the next forty minutes offering them.

7. It's all right for you to be here, I crashed this party myself.
8. I went to the address you gave me; if your brother lives there, he lives upstairs over a vacant lot.
9. In our unit at that time there were Lieutenant Holmes, a criminologist by profession and a university lecturer on penology, Captain Sturm, in peacetime a U.S. Steel executive, two old majors, previously retired and now still writing their memoirs, and Lieutenant Colonel Beale, a Mississippi cotton planter.
10. If you expect me to be here in time, or even to get back at all; you had better send somebody to help me.

▶ EXERCISE 3   From your reading, copy any five sentences in which the semicolon is properly used. Explain the reason for each semicolon.

▶ EXERCISE 4   Compose five sentences to illustrate the proper use of the semicolon.

[*See also the general exercises immediately following and the general exercises following Section 17.*]

GENERAL EXERCISES ON THE COMMA
AND THE SEMICOLON

▶ EXERCISE 5   Commas are used correctly in the following sentences. Explain each comma by writing above it the appropriate letter from Section 12: a, b, c, or d.

1. After crossing the river we built no more fires, for we were now in hostile Indian country.
2. Having nothing very important to do, I simply did nothing at all.
3. If he says he'll be there, he'll be there.
4. The smith straightened up, the horse's hoof still between his knees, and then he bent back to his work.
5. Although there are a few adjustments yet to be made, the main part of the work is finished, and the next few days should see it completed altogether.
6. The panting, tormented bull lowered his head for another charge.
7. The kit contains cement, balsa, paper, and instructions for assembly.
8. You will, I suppose, be back tomorrow.
9. The old opera house, which has stood unused for years, will finally be torn down.
10. It was a long, hot, tiresome trip, and I was sorry that I had promised to go.

▶ EXERCISE 6   Insert all necessary commas and semicolons in the following sentences. Above each mark of punctuation write the appropriate rule number.

1. If I were in your position however I would be extremely cautious about believing what I heard.
2. Taking everything into consideration I believe that Robinson should have a better season this year than ever before however you understand that this is only an opinion and that I reserve the right to amend it after I have seen him work out a few times.
3. After we wash the dishes we must wash the towels.
4. Two or three scrawny mangy-looking hounds lay sprawled in the shade of the cabin.
5. While Frank was unpacking the cooking gear and

Gene was chopping firewood I began to put up our shelter.
6. Phil meanwhile had gone down to the lake to try to get a few bass for our supper.
7. After perhaps an hour or so of waiting they may go away but don't expect them to go far and don't think they aren't still watching.
8. Bales of cotton hogsheads of sugar and salted meats barrels of flour and cases and crates of goods of every kind imaginable crowded the busy landing as far up and down the river as the eye could reach.
9. In complete disregard of the machine-gun bullets that were nipping through the grass tops all around us Jerry wriggled on his belly all the way out to where I was put a tourniquet on my leg and then began dragging me back to the shelter of the ditch.
10. If I am expected to arrive by eleven o'clock someone should volunteer to wake me up otherwise I shall probably sleep until noon.

The Apostrophe

15

Use the apostrophe to indicate the possessive case (except for personal pronouns), to mark omissions, and to form certain plurals.

15a

Do not carelessly omit the apostrophe in the possessive case of nouns and indefinite pronouns.

The apostrophe indicates a relationship that may be otherwise expressed by the substitution of an *of* phrase or a similar modifier.

> The girls' mother (the mother of the girls); Ted's dog (the dog owned by Ted); tomorrow's assignment (the assignment for tomorrow); no one's fault (the fault of no one); everybody's friend (the friend of everybody)

For inanimate objects the *of* phrase is more commonly used than the *'s: the back of the chair, the top of the desk.*

(1) If the ending (either singular or plural) is not in an s or z sound, add the apostrophe and s.

> The man's hat; the boy's shoes; a dollar's worth; today's problems [Singular]
> The men's hats; the women's dresses; the children's playground [Plural]
> One's hat; another's coat; someone's shirt; anybody's room [Indefinite pronouns—singular]

(2) If the plural ends in an s or z sound, add only the apostrophe.

> Ladies' hats (hats for ladies); boys' shoes (shoes for boys); the Joneses' boys (the boys of the Joneses); three dollars' worth; Farmers' (OR Farmers) Cooperative Society [The names of organizations frequently omit the apostrophe, as in *Ball State Teachers College.*]

(3) If the singular ends in an *s* or *z* sound, add the apostrophe and *s* for words of one syllable. Add only the apostrophe for words of more than one syllable unless you expect the pronunciation of the second *s* or *z* sound.

> James's book; Moses' law; Xerxes' army; Hortense's coat

(4) Compounds or nouns in joint possession show the possessive in the last word only. But if there is individual (or separate) possession, each noun takes the possessive form.

> My brother-in-law's house; my brothers-in-law's houses; someone else's hat
> Helen and Mary's piano [Joint ownership]
> Helen's and Mary's clothes [Individual ownership]

▶ **EXERCISE 1** Copy the following, inserting apostrophes to indicate the possessive case:

1. the girls (*sing.*) coat
2. the girls (*pl.*) coats
3. a months pay
4. two months pay
5. everybodys business
6. everyone elses clothes
7. the childs mother
8. the childrens mother
9. babys toys
10. babies toys

▶ **EXERCISE 2** Rewrite the following as possessives with the apostrophe:

1. the home of my neighbor
2. homes of my neighbors
3. a book for a boy
4. books for boys
5. the car of my sister
6. the cars of my sisters
7. the ideas of a woman
8. the ideas of women
9. the boat of Robert and Jim
10. the boats of Robert and Jim (individual possession)
11. the hat of the lady
12. the hats of the ladies

15b

Do not use the apostrophe with the pronouns *his, hers, its, ours, yours, theirs, whose* or with plural nouns not in the possessive case.

EXAMPLES He is a friend of *yours* and *theirs*.
He makes *hats* for *ladies*. (BUT He makes *ladies'* hats.)

Do not confuse the possessive pronoun *its* with the contraction *it's*, which means *it is*, or the possessive pronoun *whose* with the contraction *who's*, which means *who is*.

POSSESSIVE The bird returned to *its* nest.
CONTRACTION *It's* a small, well-hidden nest.
POSSESSIVE There is the man *whose* son has been elected to Congress.
CONTRACTION There is the man *who's* going to be our new congressman.

15c

Use an apostrophe to mark omissions in contracted words or numerals.

EXAMPLES Can't; didn't; he's (he is); it's (it is); you're (you are); o'clock (of the clock); the class of '70 (1970)

Caution: Place the apostrophe exactly where the omission occurs: *isn't, haven't* [NOT *is'nt, have'nt*].

15d

Use the apostrophe and *s* to form the plural of letters, figures, symbols, and words referred to as words.

EXAMPLES Congreve seldom crossed his *t*'s, his *7*'s looked like *9*'s, and his *and*'s were usually *&*'s.

Note: This apostrophe is sometimes omitted when there is no danger of ambiguity: the 1930's, or the 1930s; two *B*'s and three *C*'s, or two *Bs* and three *Cs*.

▶ **EXERCISE 3** Write brief sentences correctly using (a) the possessive singular, (b) the plural, and (c) the possessive plural of each of the following words.

EXAMPLE
1. *student*
   a. A student's attitude is important.
   b. Several students dropped the course.
   c. The students' parents were invited.

1. woman
2. father
3. other
4. family
5. lawyer
6. jockey
7. sailor
8. goose
9. brother-in-law
10. genius
11. army
12. Brooks

▶ **EXERCISE 4** Copy the following sentences, inserting necessary apostrophes and omitting needless or faulty ones. Underline each possessive once and each contraction twice.

1. Who's going to do the dishes? Who's turn is it?
2. The choice is our's to make, not your's.
3. Shes writing copy for a new program on one of the local station's.
4. On Thursday's the childrens' department does'nt open.
5. That boys one of the worlds' worst. Whats he doing now?
6. Its a dogs' life—jeweled collars, T-bone steaks, and fur wraps!
7. *Ifs, buts,* and *maybes* wont satisfy a young swains ardent proposal.
8. They have'nt said the property is theirs'.
9. I did'nt go to sleep until after two oclock.
10. Its a mans right to see that he gets his dollars worth.
11. Theyre not coming to see Freds' new house.
12. The books format is it's best feature.

Quotation Marks (and Quotations)

16

Use quotation marks to set off all direct quotations, some titles, and words used in a special sense. Place other marks of punctuation in proper relation to quotation marks.

Quotations usually consist of (1) passages borrowed from the written work of others or (2) the direct speech of individuals, especially in conversation (dialogue).

QUOTED WRITING   John Ciardi has written: "Dante is a supreme master because he entered the activity of his life-imagination at a heat of passion beyond most men, yet saw through diamond eyes: he could burn and still see." [The words and punctuation within quotation marks are exactly as they appear in "The Relevance of Dante," in *Saturday Review*, May 22, 1965, p. 53.]

QUOTED SPEECH   "My husband won't let me watch TV programs about doctors and hospitals," Donna explained. "As soon as I hear of a disease or even a symptom, I get sick!" [Within quotation marks are the exactly recorded words of the speaker; the punctuation is supplied by the writer.]

Notice above that quotation marks are used in pairs: the first set marks the beginning of the quotation, and the second set marks the end. Be careful not to omit or misplace the second set. Also remember that the verb of saying and the speaker (such as *Donna explained*) should never be within the quotation marks.

16a

Use double quotation marks to enclose direct (but not indirect) quotations; use single marks to enclose a quotation within a quotation.

EXAMPLES

He said, "I have no intention of staying." [Direct quotation—the exact words spoken]
He said that he had "no intention of staying." [Direct quotation of a fragment of the speech]
He said that he had not intended to stay. [Indirect quotation—no quotation marks]

Notice in the example below that the quotation within a quotation is enclosed by single quotation marks; one within that, by double marks.

"It took courage," the speaker said, "for a man to affirm in those days: 'I endorse every word of Patrick Henry's sentiment, "Give me liberty or give me death!" ' "
                                              —WILLIAM LEWIN

(1) **Long quotations (not dialogue).**   In printed matter, small type usually sets off quoted material of ten or more lines.[1] No quotation marks are used, unless the original carries quotation marks. In typewritten papers, such quoted passages are single-spaced and indented from both sides five spaces.[2] The first line is indented ten spaces when it marks a paragraph beginning.

In an interesting essay entitled "The Growing Power of Admen," Vance Packard has this to say about American buyers:

Happily for the marketers, Americans by nature seem to relish learning to want new things. We are a restless people who like continually to hear of new things to do and buy. (Note the recent popularity of bejeweled fly swatters and mousetraps.) Emerson commented on this trait in Americans when he said that they, unlike Europeans, exhibit "an uncalculated, headlong expenditure." This makes them the world's prize consumers.

Recently the president of the Institute for Motivational Research (which conducts psychological studies for marketers) noted with satisfaction "our increasing willingness to give vent to our whims and desires" and offered the opinion that America is "experiencing a revolution in self-indulgence."[3]

(2) **Poetry.**   A single line of poetry or less is usually handled like other short quotations, run in with the text and enclosed in quotation marks. Longer passages should be set off from the text, indented, and quoted line by line exactly as they appear in the original.

The last part of "The Leaden Echo," by Gerard Manley Hopkins, offers no hope to those who would like to stay young and beautiful:

Be beginning; since, no, nothing can be done
To keep at bay
Age and age's evils—hoar hair,
Ruck and wrinkle, drooping, dying, death's worst, winding sheets,
     tombs and worms, and tumbling to decay;
So be beginning, be beginning to despair.
Oh, there's none—no, no, no, there's none:
     Be beginning to despair, to despair,
     Despair, despair, despair, despair.

In the companion poem, "The Golden Echo," however, Hopkins presents a cure for despair, one that is "Only not within seeing of the sun."

(3) **Dialogue (conversation).**   Written dialogue represents the directly quoted speech of two or more persons talking together. Standard practice is to write each person's speech, no matter how short, as a separate paragraph. Verbs of saying, as well as closely related bits of narrative, are included in the paragraph along with the speech.

"You remember Kate Stoddard, Mother?" Georgia asked. "This is Kate to pay us a little visit."
Mrs. Stanton rocked and closed her eyes. "What's everybody shouting for?" she asked.
"Sit down, Kate," Georgia said.
Mrs. Stoddard pulled a chair close to Mrs. Stanton. "Well, I will, but I can't stay. I came for a reason."
"We paid our yearly dues," Georgia said.
"I don't know what makes you say that," Mrs. Stoddard said. "I don't think you've ever known me to solicit *personally*. I came about quite another matter. I wanted you to look at this." She fished in her bag and brought out the diary, which she held out rather grudgingly to Georgia. "Be careful of it! It's quite old!"
                                              —SALLY BENSON[4]

In the last paragraph, note that although a narrative passage interrupts the dialogue, the speaker is Mrs. Stoddard throughout.

(4) **Punctuation of dialogue.**   Note that such expressions as "he said," when introducing a *short* speech, are usually followed by a comma; that they are set off by

---

[1] Recommended by "The MLA Style Sheet," Revised Edition, 1959, p. 8, reprinted from *Publications of the Modern Language Association of America*.
[2] When quotation marks—instead of the usual smaller type or indention—are used for a passage of two or more paragraphs, the quotation marks come before each paragraph and at the end of the last; they do not come at the end of intermediate paragraphs.

[3] Copyright © by The Atlantic Monthly Company, Boston, Massachusetts. Reprinted with permission.
[4] From "Spirit of '76" by Sally Benson. Originally published in the *New Yorker*, December 25, 1954.

commas when interpolated (see 12d[3]); that they are preceded by a comma when added at the end of a speech (unless the speech is a question or an exclamation, when the question mark or the exclamation point replaces the comma). Such expressions as "he said" before *longer* speeches are usually followed by a colon (see 17d[1]).

▶ EXERCISE 1   Compose five sentences to illustrate the proper use of double and single quotation marks.

16b

Use quotation marks for minor titles (short stories, essays, one-act plays, short poems, songs, articles from magazines) and for subdivisions of books.

EXAMPLES

The January 3, 1966, issue of *Sports Illustrated* contains a lively article entitled "A Snook Hunt on the Spanish Main."
In this book are numerous short poems and stories, such as "The Raven" and "The Fall of the House of Usher."
Last summer I read "L'Allegro," a short lyric, and parts of *Paradise Lost*.
Stevenson's *Treasure Island* is divided into six parts, the last of which, called "Captain Silver," opens with a chapter entitled "In the Enemy's Camp."

Note: Quotation marks are sometimes used to enclose titles of books, magazines, and newspapers, but italics are usually preferred. See 10a.

▶ EXERCISE 2   Compose five sentences showing use of quotation marks with minor titles and subdivisions of books.

16c

Words used in a special sense are sometimes enclosed in quotation marks.

EXAMPLES

The printer must see that quotation marks are "cleared"— that is, kept within the margins.
"Sympathy" means "to suffer with." [OR: *Sympathy* means *to suffer with*. Sympathy means "to suffer with." See also 10d.]

16d

Do not overuse quotation marks.

Do not use quotation marks to enclose titles of themes or to mark bits of humor. In general do not enclose in quotation marks common nicknames, technical terms, and trite or well-known expressions. Instead of placing slang and colloquialisms inside quotation marks, use formal English. Above all, do not use quotation marks for emphasis.

NEEDLESS PUNCTUATION   "Old Hickory" was wrought up over the loss of his friend.
BETTER   Old Hickory was wrought up over the loss of his friend.
INAPPROPRIATE IN FORMAL WRITING   He must have been "nuts." The tiny pink telephone is "as cute as a bug's ear."
APPROPRIATE   He must have been insane. The tiny pink telephone is an attractive novelty.

16e

In using marks of punctuation with quoted words, phrases, or sentences, follow the arbitrary printers' rules by placing:

(1) The period and the comma always within the quotation marks.
(2) The colon and the semicolon always outside the quotation marks.
(3) The dash, the question mark, and the exclamation point within the quotation marks when they apply to the quoted matter only; outside when they refer to the whole sentence.

"I will go," he insisted. "I am needed." [Comma and period always inside quotation marks]
He spoke of his "old log house"; he might have called it a mansion. [Semicolon (and colon) always outside quotation marks]
He asked, "When did you arrive?" [Here the question mark applies only to the part of the sentence within quotation marks.]
Why did he ask, "When did you arrive?" [A second question mark does not follow the quotation.]
What is the meaning of "the open door"? [Here the question mark applies to the whole sentence.]
The captain shouted, "Halt!" [Here the exclamation point applies only to the quotation.]
Save us from his "mercy"! [Here the exclamation point applies to the whole sentence.]

▶ EXERCISE 3   Add correctly placed quotation marks where needed in the following sentences.

1. Surely, I replied facetiously, you know the difference between prose and poetry.
2. Dan asked, Did you accept Beverly's invitation?
3. Have you read the short poem To an Athlete Dying Young?
4. One angry spectator yelled, That blockhead!
5. Who is the author of the line A spark disturbs our clod?
6. Thomas Gray did write 'Tis folly to be wise; however, he qualified the statement with Where ignorance is bliss.
7. How he enjoyed reading the short story The Luck of Roaring Camp!
8. Only one main character appears in Poe's short story The Tell-Tale Heart: the mad murderer.
9. Was it Knox or a Hebrew writer who asked Why is man, mere earth and ashes, proud?
10. The lip of truth shall be established forever, states an ancient proverb, but a lying tongue is but for a moment.

▶ EXERCISE 4   After you have studied 16a(3), giving special attention to the punctuation of the dialogue on page 149, and have reviewed 16e, write a short, original dialogue of approximately two hundred words. Place all quotation marks properly.

▶ EXERCISE 5   Insert quotation marks where they are needed in the following sentences.

1. Campus fads come and go, I commented to Carl as we sat down to lunch in the cafeteria. But, as far as your

friend Helen is concerned, this current fad of acting like Mrs. Malaprop will probably never die.

2. "Be patient with Helen!" Carl snapped as he unrolled his napkin and sorted his silverware. I actually like Helen's bad jokes. Her word play—

3. "Please pass the salt," I interrupted.

4. Ignoring my frown, Carl continued, "I'll grant you that Helen's puns are usually as old and as clever as the joke ending with Squawbury Shortcake; but here she comes. Let's change the subject pronto.

5. Clearing my throat pretentiously, I took his advice and said, "Perhaps your parents should buy a perambulator".

6. "A perambulator!" Helen happily took up my cue as she plopped down in the chair near Carl. "My parents bought me an eight-cup perambulator for my birthday. Just plug it in, and coffee is ready in four minutes!"

7. "Aren't you thinking of a percolator?" I asked her in mock seriousness. "An electric percolator heats quickly."

8. "Yeah," Helen replied, winking at Carl. "It's the same thing as an incubator."

9. "You don't mean *incubator!*" I barked sharply and then added a bit of my own nonsense. "You mean *incinerator.*" After a moment of silence, I yawned and said, "Incinerator bombs are really fiery weapons. They cause much perturbation."

10. This time Helen had no ready answer. Admitting defeat at her own ridiculous word game, she grinned and announced, "Repartee like this is for immature freshmen who like the Malaprop fad—not for me."

The Period and Other Marks

17

Use the period, the question mark, the exclamation point, the colon, the dash, parentheses, and brackets in accordance with standard usage.

End marks indicate those pitches and stops of the voice which help to reveal the meanings of sentences.

No man is an island. [Statement]
No man is an island? [Question]
No man is an island! [Exclamation]

Dashes, colons, parentheses, and brackets are signals for pauses or voice variations which usually indicate degrees of emphasis within a sentence.

Man is a piece of the continent — not an island.
Consider this idea: no man is an island.
John Donne (1573–1631) said that man is not an island.
The metaphor closes with "because I [John Donne] am involved in mankind."

The Period (.)

17a

Use the period after declarative and mildly imperative sentences, after indirect questions, and after most abbreviations. Use the ellipsis mark (three spaced periods) to indicate omissions from quoted passages.

(1) Use the period to mark the end of a declarative sentence, a mildly imperative sentence, or an indirect question.

DECLARATIVE   They changed the rules.
MILDLY IMPERATIVE   Change the rules. Let's change the troublesome rules.
INDIRECT QUESTION   He asked whether the rules had been changed.

(2) Use periods to follow most abbreviations.

Mr., Mrs., Dr., Jr., Ph.D., etc., B.C., A.D.   R.S.V.P. or r.s.v.p., C.O.D. or c.o.d., A.M. or a.m., P.M. or p.m.

Frequently current usage omits periods after many abbreviations, especially of organizations and national or international agencies.

TV, CBS, CIO, ROTC, VA, FBI, USN, FHA, UN

If you have any doubt about the punctuation of a given abbreviation, consult a good college dictionary.

Caution: Do not use periods to indicate that such words as *I've, can't, 2nd, 15th,* and *gym* are contractions or abbreviations.

(3) Use the ellipsis mark (three spaced periods) to indicate an omission of one or more words within a quoted passage.

If the omission ends with a period, use four spaced periods (one to mark the end of the sentence and three to show the omission).

QUOTATION
No man is an island, entire of itself; every man is a piece of the continent, a part of the main. If a clod be washed away by the sea, Europe is the less, as well as if a promontory were, as well as if a manor of thy friend's or of thine own were. Any man's death diminishes me because I am involved in mankind, and therefore never send to know for whom the bell tolls; it tolls for thee.   —JOHN DONNE

QUOTATION WITH ELLIPSES
No man is an island . . . every man is a piece of the continent, a part of the main. . . . Any man's death diminishes me because I am involved in mankind . . . .   —JOHN DONNE

The Question Mark (?)

17b

Use the question mark to follow direct (but not indirect) questions.

EXAMPLES
Who started the riot?
Did he ask who started the riot? [The sentence as a whole is a direct question despite the indirect question at the end.]

"Who started the riot?" he asked.
He asked, "Who started the riot?"
You started the riot? [Question in the form of a declarative sentence]
You told me—did I hear you correctly?—that you started the riot. [Interpolated question]
Did you hear him say, "What right have you to ask about the riot?" [Double direct question followed by a single question mark]
Did he plan the riot, employ assistants, and give the signal to begin?
Did he plan the riot? employ assistants? give the signal to begin? [Question marks used between the parts of the series cause full stops and throw emphasis on each part.]

Caution: Do not use the question mark to indicate the end of an indirect question. See also **17a(1).**

He asked who started the riot. To ask why the riot started is unnecessary. I want to know what the cause of the riot was. How foolish it is to ask what caused the riot!

OTHER USES OF THE QUESTION MARK

A question mark (within parentheses) is used to express the writer's uncertainty as to the correctness of the preceding word, figure, or date: "Chaucer was born in 1340(?) and died in 1400." But the question mark is not a desirable means of expressing the author's wit or sarcasm.

QUESTIONABLE   This kind (?) proposal caused Gulliver to take refuge in nearby Blefuscu. [Omit the question mark. If the context does not make the irony clear, either revise your sentence or give up your attempt to strike an ironic note.]

Courtesy questions common to business letters may be followed by question marks but are usually followed by periods: "Will you (= Please) write me again if I can be of further service."

Caution: Do not use a comma or a period after a question mark.

"Are you ready?" he asked.
He asked, "Are you ready?"

The Exclamation Point (!)
17c

Use the exclamation point after an emphatic interjection and after a phrase, clause, or sentence to express a high degree of surprise, incredulity, or other strong emotion.

EXAMPLES
What! I cannot believe it! How beautiful! [*What* and *how* often begin exclamations.]
Oh! You have finally come! (OR: Oh, you have finally come!)
March! Halt! Get out of this house! [Sharp commands—vigorous imperatives]

Forbid it, Almighty God! I know not what course others may take, but as for me, give me liberty, or give me death!
—PATRICK HENRY

Caution 1: Avoid overuse of the exclamation point. Use a comma after mild interjections, and end mildly exclamatory sentences with a period.

Well, you are to be congratulated.
Oh, I cannot do that.

Caution 2: Do not use a comma or a period after the exclamation point.

"Halt!" shouted the corporal.
The corporal shouted, "Halt!"

▶ **EXERCISE 1**   Illustrate the chief uses of the period, the question mark, and the exclamation point by composing and correctly punctuating brief sentences as directed below.

EXAMPLE
a declarative sentence containing a quoted direct question
"Is Fred a ventriloquist?" she asked.

1. a declarative sentence containing a quoted exclamation
2. a direct question
3. an indirect question
4. a double direct question
5. a declarative sentence containing an interpolated question
6. a vigorous imperative
7. a mild imperative
8. a direct question having the form of a declaration
9. an ellipsis at the beginning of a quoted sentence
10. an ellipsis at the end of a quoted sentence

▶ **EXERCISE 2**   Correctly punctuate the following sentences by supplying needed periods, question marks, and exclamation points. Be prepared to give a reason for each mark you add. (*In this exercise* place all end marks that appear together with quotation marks *inside* the quotation marks; see **16c**.)

1. Frank asked me why I did not take Ellen to the dance
2. Frank asked, "Why didn't you take Ellen to the dance"
3. Did Frank ask you why I did not take Ellen to the dance
4. "What will you sell that wreck for" Mr. Lacy asked.
5. Stumbling toward the telephone, I wondered who could be calling me after 11:30 PM
6. The joker on the other end of the line chirped softly, "Honey, how many hours each week do you watch TV"
7. After a short silence, the voice asked me what channel I was watching then
8. What a surprise that was
9. On April 15th I arrived in Washington, DC
10. Members of the YMCA smiled when the speaker was introduced; his name was Dr. A. J. Byrd

The colon precedes a list only if the sentence ## The Colon (:) *is complete*
17d   *without it.*

Use the colon after a formal introductory statement to direct attention to what is to follow. Avoid needless colons.

The colon and the semicolon, notwithstanding the similarity of the names, differ greatly in use. The semicolon (see Section 14) is a strong *separator* almost equal to a period, and is used only between equal parts. The colon after a statement or a main clause is a formal *introducer*, calling attention to something that is to follow. The colon usually means *as follows*.

(1) **The colon may direct attention to an appositive (or a series of appositives) at the end of a sentence, to a formal list or explanation, or to a long quotation.**

All her thoughts were centered on one objective: marriage. [A dash or a comma, which might be used instead of the colon, would be less formal.]

We may divide poems into three classes: narrative, lyric, and dramatic. [A dash might be used instead of the colon; because of the series a comma would be confusing.]

Competition in the steel industry is described by one of the Corporation's competitors as follows: "Your ability to win when competition for business gets tough comes in the entire setup of your operation, the quality of your management . . . and so on. You have to play a judgment game. This is no 2-cent poker." —FORTUNE

(2) **The colon may separate two main clauses when the second clause explains or amplifies the first.**

The scientific value of even the most recent contributions to this literature, however, is seriously qualified: The sole witness to the dream is the dreamer himself. —SCIENTIFIC AMERICAN

There is something like a Puritan's restraint in the scientist who seeks truth: he keeps away from anything voluntaristic or emotional. —ALBERT EINSTEIN

Note: After the colon a quoted sentence regularly begins with a capital, but other sentences (as the examples above show) may begin with either a capital or a small letter.

(3) **Use the colon after the salutation of a business letter, between a title and a subtitle, between figures indicating the chapter and verse of a Biblical reference or the hour and minute of a time reference.**

Dear Sir:
Creative Pattern Practice: A New Approach to Writing
according to Matthew 6:10   exactly at 10:35 P.M.

(4) **Avoid needless colons.**

When there is no formal introduction or summarizing word, the colon is usually a needless interruption of the sentence.

NEEDLESS   All her thoughts were centered on: marriage.
BETTER   All her thoughts were centered on marriage.
NEEDLESS   Three kinds of poems are: narratives, lyrics, and dramas. [Awkward separation of verb and its complement]
BETTER   Three kinds of poems are narratives, lyrics, and dramas.

▶ **EXERCISE 3**   Punctuate the following sentences by adding appropriate colons or semicolons. When deciding whether a colon or a semicolon should separate two main clauses, use the colon only when the second main clause explains or amplifies the first. Write *C* after any sentence that needs no change.

1. Within two hours we had a strange variety of weather: rain, hail, sleet, snow.
2. Promptly at 8:15 P.M. the minister began his sermon by quoting John 20:21.
3. Two questions well worth asking yourself every day are these: What must I do? Have I done it?
4. The conference had only one purpose: agreement upon a suitable topic for a research paper.
5. Professor Boaz smiled a quick greeting; I sat down and tried to look like an intelligent sophomore.
6. My roommate has a simple formula for looking like a sophomore: Act depressed.
7. At first I merely looked gloomy; later, however, I had good reason to feel depressed.
8. Professor Boaz started suggesting fantastic subjects: "Causes of the Korean War," "An Analysis of the 1961 Recession," "Early Poetry of W. B. Yeats."
9. I then dared to mention that the only interests I have are cars, sports, and girls.
10. At the end of the conference I acted like the freshman that I am; ironically enough, it was the professor who looked as depressed as an intelligent sophomore.

The Dash (—)

17e

Use the dash to mark a sudden break in thought, to set off a summary, or to set off a parenthetical element that is very abrupt or that has commas within it.

On the typewriter the dash is made by two hyphens without spacing before, between, or after. In handwriting the dash is an unbroken line about the length of two or three hyphens.

PUNCTUATION OF PARENTHETICAL MATTER

Dashes, parentheses, commas—all are used to set off parenthetical matter. Dashes set off parenthetical elements sharply and therefore tend to emphasize them:

Rifle cartridges and shotgun shells — measured by today's prices — were cheap in 1905. —DAVID L. COHN

Parentheses tend to minimize the importance of the parts thus set off:

Rifle cartridges and shotgun shells (measured by today's prices) were cheap in 1905.

Commas are the mildest, most commonly used separators and tend to leave the parts more closely connected with the sentence. Dashes and parentheses should be used sparingly, only when commas will not serve equally well. (For the use of the comma to set off parenthetical matter, see **12d;** for the use of parentheses, see **17f.**)

(1) **Use the dash to mark a sudden break in thought.**

"It is hard to explain—" he said, and paused as they composed themselves. —LIONEL TRILLING

Can I — I mean, where do you get a saw like that? —GERALD WARNER BRACE

In fact, she was always right — in a way. —J. F. POWERS

(2) **Use the dash to set off a brief summary or appositive.**

The German borrowings are also homely and everyday— wieners, pretzels, hunk, and dunk. —BERGEN EVANS

The long neck, the small head, the knickers whose cuffs were worn down near his ankles — all these points, often observed by caricaturists, were visible in the flesh.   —JOHN UPDIKE

(3) **Use dashes to set off a parenthetical element that is very abrupt or that has commas within it.**

A telltale suggestion of relief — or was it gratitude? — brightened their eyes.   —JOHN MASON BROWN

He stood up — small, frail, and tense — staring toward things in his homeland.   —NORA WALN

I was mediocre at drill, certainly — that is, until my senior year.   —JAMES THURBER

Caution: The dash should be used carefully in formal writing. It is more in keeping with an informal style, but even there it becomes ineffective when overused.

Parentheses ( )

17f

Use parentheses (1) to enclose figures, as in this rule, and (2) to set off parenthetical, supplementary, or illustrative matter.

EXAMPLES

Dashes are used (1) to mark breaks, (2) to set off summaries, and (3) to set off parenthetical elements. [Parentheses enclose figures used to enumerate items.]

Mr. Brown's horses (the best, no doubt, in the whole state) were exhibited at the fair. [Dashes would be used if the writer wished to emphasize the parenthetical matter.]

It is strange (as one reviews all the memories of that good friend and master) to think that there is now a new generation beginning at Haverford that will never know his spell.   —CHRISTOPHER MORLEY

When the sentence demands other marks of punctuation with the parenthetical matter, these marks are placed after the second parenthesis. The comma is never used before the first parenthesis. If a whole sentence beginning with a capital is in parentheses, the period or other terminal mark is placed inside the second parenthesis. A parenthetical statement not beginning with a capital is not followed by a period within the parentheses.

Brackets [ ]

17g

Use brackets to set off editorial corrections or interpolations in quoted matter.

EXAMPLES

At the office he found a note from the janitor: "Last night i [*sic*] found the door unlocked." [A bracketed *sic* (meaning *thus*) tells the reader that the error appears in the original— is not merely a misprint.]

Every man who loved our vanished friend [Professor Gummere] must know with what realization of shamed incapacity one lays down the tributary pen.   —CHRISTOPHER MORLEY

▶ EXERCISE 4   Correctly punctuate each of the following sentences by supplying commas, dashes, parentheses, or brackets. Be prepared to justify all marks you add, especially those you choose to set off parenthetical matter.

1. Gordon Gibbs or is it his twin brother? plays left tackle.
2. Joseph who is Gordon's brother is a guard on the second string.
3. "Dearest" his voice broke; he could say no more.
4. This organization needs more of everything more money, brains, initiative.
5. Some of my courses for example, French and biology demand a great deal of work outside the classroom.
6. A penalty clipping cost the Steers fifteen yards.
7. This ridiculous sentence appeared in the school paper: "Because of a personal fool *sic* the Cougars failed to cross the goal line during the last seconds of the game."
8. The word *Zipper* a trade-mark like Kodak is now used frequently without the initial capital as a common noun.
9. Rugged hills, rich valleys, beautiful lakes these things impress the tourist in Connecticut.
10. Our course embraced these projects: 1 the close reading of *Hamlet,* 2 the writing of critiques on various aspects of this tragedy, and 3 the formation of a tentative theory of tragedy.

▶ EXERCISE 5   Punctuate the following sentences (selected and adapted from the *Atlantic Monthly*) by supplying appropriate end marks, commas, colons, dashes, and parentheses. Do not use unnecessary punctuation. Be prepared to justify each mark you add, especially when you have a choice of correct marks (e.g., commas, dashes, or parentheses).

1. Emily formerly Mrs Goyette caught McAndless' sleeve where no one could see and tugged it briefly but urgently
2. "Do they still have good food at the Automat" he asked
3. "Oh I know" Granny exclaimed "Let me think about it"
4. "I know" I said "But that's not the real bed what happened to it"
5. For forty-eight years 1888–1936 he taught at Harvard
6. I tell you again What is alive and young and throbbing with historic current in America is musical theatre
7. Louise had then she has it still something near to genius for making improbable persons, places, and situations sound attractive
8. *Good and* can mean *very* "I am good and mad" and "a hot cup of coffee" means that the coffee not the cup is to be hot
9. At last she had become what she had always wished to be a professional dancer
10. Prestige call it status if you like is in great demand these days
11. At last Marvin stood up, uneasily. "You you think we'd better take him to the vet"
12. There are three essential qualities for vulture country a rich supply of unburied corpses, high mountains, a strong sun

13. They failed forgivably! to see the less happy results of their enthusiasm
14. A significant little adage which circulates in Michigan athletic circles says in effect that there are three aspects of college life at Michigan intellectual, social, and athletic but that the student has time for only two
15. Women sit in their corner discussing items out of their exclusively feminine world children, servants, gardens, gossip
16. An older law was operating at the box office if you try
to please everybody, you don't please anybody
17. As one man put it "Rose Bowl, Sugar Bowl, Orange Bowl all are gravy bowls"
18. Industrialization of Red China with German machines and German technology what a prize
19. We are told and we believe women more than men that to win love but more imperatively to retain love we must be beautiful
20. There is a democratic process the box office that determines the success and eminence of an artist

SPELLING AND DICTION

Spelling

18

Spell every word according to established usage as shown by a good dictionary.[1]

If you are the typical college student, you will misspell about fifty words as you write your freshman English papers. And of these fifty, only two or three will be found in another student's list of fifty misspellings. Thus it is evident that spelling is a highly individual problem, to be solved by attention to one's own particular difficulties. By writing down in your INDIVIDUAL SPELLING LIST (see the model at the end of this section) all the words you misspell during your first college year, and by analyzing and mastering these words as they are called to your attention, you can make steady improvement in your spelling.

In college you cannot count upon much class time devoted to spelling. But by following independently the program outlined in this section, you can improve your spelling tremendously. *Ignorance of the correct spelling of ordinary words is now, and will probably continue to be, the one universally accepted sign of the uneducated man.*

As aids in fixing the correct spelling of the word in your memory, use chiefly the EAR and the EYE.

THE EAR—FOR WORDS SPELLED AS PRONOUNCED Pronounce the word aloud several times, clearly and distinctly, in accordance with the pronunciation shown by the dictionary. Be careful not to omit, add, change, or transpose any letter or syllable. Then write the word down in your INDIVIDUAL SPELLING LIST.

THE EYE—FOR WORDS NOT SPELLED AS PRONOUNCED Look carefully at the word (1) as it appears in the dictionary and (2) as you write it *correctly* in your INDIVIDUAL SPELLING LIST. Note the differences between pronunciation and spelling. Photograph the word with your eye so that you can visualize it later.

SPELLING RULES Use a few spelling rules if you find them helpful. See 18d and 18e. (For more detailed rules see the section entitled "Orthography" in *Webster's New International Dictionary*, Second Edition, or "Spelling" in *Webster's Third New International Dictionary* or *Webster's Seventh New Collegiate Dictionary*.)

18a

Do not allow mispronunciation to cause misspelling. (The ear is especially helpful in overcoming such misspelling.)

At least two problems arise when one uses pronunciation as a guide to correct spelling. First, the spellings of many words reflect the pronunciations used two or three hundred years ago because changes in pronunciation take place more rapidly than changes in spelling. Second, one spelling may symbolize a half dozen sounds (like *ough* in *though, rough, through*, etc.), and one sound may have numerous spellings (like *sh* in *ration, tissue, ocean*.)[2] In spite of these problems, however, mispronunciation can and does cause the misspelling of words such as those in the following lists.

▶ EXERCISE 1   Find in the following four lists the words you tend to mispronounce—and to misspell.

(1) Careless omission

Pronounce this first list distinctly, making it a point *not to omit* the sound represented by the italicized letters.

cand*i*date	libr*a*ry	quan*t*ity
environ*m*ent	lit*e*rature	recogn*i*ze
ever*y*body	occasiona*l*ly	su*r*prise
gen*e*rally	prob*a*bly	us*u*ally

(2) Careless addition

Pronounce this second list distinctly, making it a point *not to add* any syllable or letter.

athlete	entrance	lightning
disastrous	grievous	mischievous

---

[1] Careful study of Section 18 will help to eliminate one of the two most common errors in the average student paper.

[2] See Mario Pei, "The Problem of Spelling Reform," *The Story of English*, J. B. Lippincott Co., Philadelphia, 1952.

drowned	height	remembrance
elm	hindrance	umbrella

(3) Careless change

Pronounce this third list distinctly, making it a point *not to change* letters, particularly letters in italics.

accum*u*late	int*ro*duce	partic*u*lar
accu*r*ate	opt*i*mistic	pre*j*udice

(4) Careless transpositions of letters

Pronounce this fourth list distinctly, making it a point *not to transpose* italicized letters.

ca*v*alry	ir*r*ele*v*ant	p*r*efer
child*r*en	pe*r*haps	p*r*escription
hund*r*ed	pe*r*spiration	p*r*eserve

Add to your INDIVIDUAL SPELLING LIST any of the words in the four lists that you have a tendency to misspell. Follow the model spelling list at the end of this section.

18b

Distinguish between words of similar sound and spelling, and use the spelling demanded by the meaning. (The eye is the chief aid in avoiding such misspelling.)

▶ **EXERCISES 2–7** Study the following list, ten word groups at a time, to improve your ability to select the word needed to express your meaning. With the aid of your dictionary compose a sentence to illustrate the correct use of each word. Add to your INDIVIDUAL SPELLING LIST any word that you misspell.

[2]

accent, ascent, assent	forth, fourth
accept, except	freshman, freshmen
advice, advise	hear, here
affect, effect	holy, wholly
all ready, already	instance, instants
all together, altogether	irrelevant, irreverent
allusive, elusive, illusive	[5]
altar, alter	
berth, birth	its, it's
born, borne	know, no
	later, latter
[3]	lead, led
capital, capitol	lessen, lesson
choose, chose	lose, loose
cite, sight, site	moral, morale
coarse, course	of, off
complement, compliment	passed, past
conscience, conscious	peace, piece
council, counsel, consul	
decent, descent, dissent	[6]
desert, dessert	personal, personnel
device, devise	plain, plane
	precede, proceed
[4]	presence, presents
dual, duel	principal, principle
dyeing, dying	prophecy, prophesy
fair, fare	quiet, quite, quit
formally, formerly	respectfully, respectively

right, rite, wright, write
sense, since

[7]

shone, shown	there, their, they're
stationary, stationery	threw, through
than, then	to, too, two
	weak, week
	weather, whether
	whose, who's
	your, you're

18c

Distinguish between the prefix and the root.

The root is the base to which prefix or suffix is added. Take care not to double the last letter of the prefix (as in *disappear*) when it is different from the first letter of the root or to drop the last letter of the prefix when the root begins with the same letter (as in *immortal* and *unnecessary*.)

dis- (prefix)	+	appear (root)	=	disappear
grand-	+	daughter	=	granddaughter
im-	+	mortal	=	immortal
un-	+	necessary	=	unnecessary

18d

Apply the rules for spelling in adding suffixes.

(1) Drop final e before a suffix beginning with a vowel but not before a suffix beginning with a consonant

Drop final *e* before a suffix beginning with a vowel.

bride	+	-al	=	bridal
combine	+	-ation	=	combination
come	+	-ing	=	coming
fame	+	-ous	=	famous
plume	+	-age	=	plumage
precede	+	-ence	=	precedence
prime	+	-ary	=	primary

Retain final *e* before a suffix beginning with a consonant.

care	+	-ful	=	careful
care	+	-less	=	careless
entire	+	-ly	=	entirely
place	+	-ment	=	placement
rude	+	-ness	=	rudeness
stale	+	-mate	=	stalemate
state	+	-craft	=	statecraft
sure	+	-ty	=	surety

Some Exceptions: *due, duly; true, truly; awe, awful; hoe, hoeing, singe, singeing.* After *c* or *g* the final *e* is retained before suffixes beginning with *a* or *o*: *notice, noticeable; courage, courageous.* Note that pronunciation will help you with this rule; "soft" *c* and *g* are followed by *e* before *a* and *o*, while "hard" *c* and *g* are not. Compare *noticeable* and *despicable, courageous* and *analogous.*

▶ **EXERCISE 8** For each word below cite the rule governing dropping or retaining final *e*.

1. confine	+	-ing		6. love	+	-ly	
2. confine	+	-ment		7. peruse	+	-al	
3. arrange	+	-ing		8. like	+	-ness	
4. arrange	+	-ment		9. like	+	-ing	
5. love	+	-ing		10. like	+	-ly	

(2) Double a final single consonant before a suffix beginning with a vowel (a) if the consonant ends a word of one syllable or an accented syllable and (b) if the consonant is preceded by a single vowel. Otherwise, do not double the consonant.

drop, dropping [In a word of one syllable preceded by a single vowel. But preceded by a double vowel: *droop, drooping.*]

admit, admitted [In accented syllable preceded by a single vowel. But in unaccented syllable: *benefit, benefited.*]

▶ EXERCISE 9   Note the importance of the last rule in forming the present participle and the past tense of verbs. Example: *regret, regretting, regretted.* Supply the present participle for each of the following verbs, justifying the spelling by the rule: *appear, compel, differ, happen, occur, plan, profit, refer, remit, scoop.*

(3) Except before *ing*, final *y* is usually changed to *i*.

defy	+	-ance	=	defiance
happy	+	-ness	=	happiness
mercy	+	-ful	=	merciful
modify	+	-er	=	modifier
modify	+	-ing	=	modifying [Not changed before *ing*]

Note: Verbs ending in *y* preceded by a vowel do not change the *y* to form the third person singular of the present tense or the past participle: *array, arrays, arrayed.* Exceptions: *lay, laid; pay, paid; say, said.*

▶ EXERCISE 10   Cite the rule to justify retaining or dropping final *y* before the suffixes of the following words: *alloys, craftiness, employed, employs, fanciful, fancying, studied, studying, volleys, volleying.*

(4) Form the plural by adding *s* to the singular, but by adding *es* if the plural makes an extra syllable.

boy, boys; cap, caps; radio, radios
bush, bushes; match, matches [The plural makes an extra syllable.]

Exceptions:

a. If the noun ends in *y* preceded by a consonant, change the *y* to *i* and add *es: sky, skies; comedy, comedies.* But after final *y* preceded by a vowel, *y* is retained and only *s* is added: *joy, joys.*

b. If the noun ends in *fe*, change the *fe* to *ve* and add *s: knife, knives.*

c. A few nouns ending in *o* take the *-es* plural, although the plural does not make an extra syllable: *potato, potatoes; Negro, Negroes.*

d. For plurals of compound words such as *father-in-law* usually add the *-s* to the chief word, not the modifier: *fathers-in-law, maids of honor.*

For other plurals formed irregularly, consult your dictionary.

Note: Add *'s* to form the plurals of letters, signs, and figures. See also **15d.**

▶ EXERCISE 11   Supply plural forms for words listed below. If words are not covered by the rules given under **18d,** consult your dictionary.

cup	army	foot	passer-by
wife	cameo	son-in-law	room
box	marsh	valley	leaf
child	ox	alumnus	goose
key	sheep	radius	mouse

18e

Apply the rules for spelling to avoid confusion of *ei* and *ie*.

When the sound is *ee*, write *ie* (except after *c*, in which case write *ei*).

				(after *c*)	
chief	grief	pierce	wield	ceiling	deceive
field	niece	relief	yield	conceit	perceive

When the sound is other than *ee*, usually write *ei*.

eight	height	heir	reign	sleigh	vein
foreign	deign	neighbor	feign	weigh	stein

Exceptions: Fiery, financier, leisure, seize, species, weird.

▶ EXERCISE 12   Write out the following words, filling out the blanks with *ei* or *ie*. Justify your choice for each word.

bes—ge	dec—t	fr—ght	r—gned	s—ve
conc—ve	f—nd	pr—st	s—ne	th—f

Hyphenated Words

18f

Hyphenate words chiefly to express a unit idea or to avoid ambiguity. (For division of words at the end of a line, see **8b.**)

A hyphenated word may be either two words still in the process of becoming one word or a new coinage made by the writer to fit the occasion. In the former case a recent dictionary will assist in determining current usage. Many words now written as one were originally separate words and later hyphenated in the transitional stage. For example, *post man* first became *post-man* and then *postman.* More recently *basket ball* has passed through the transitional *basket-ball* to *basketball.* The use of the hyphen in compounding is in such a state of flux that authorities often disagree. Some of the more generally accepted uses are listed below.

(1) The hyphen may be used to join two or more words serving as a single adjective before a noun.

[The dictionary ordinarily cannot help with this use of the hyphen. The writer joins recognized words to coin a new unit idea to fit the occasion.]

A know-it-all expression, a bluish-green dress

But the hyphen is omitted when the first word of the compound is an adverb ending in *-ly* or when the words follow the noun.

A slightly elevated walk, a gently sloping terrace
His expression suggested that he knew it all.
The dress was a bluish green.

(2) The hyphen is used with compound numbers from twenty-one to ninety-nine.

twenty-two, forty-five, ninety-eight

Note: Hyphenate a fraction when it functions as an adjective and is placed before the word modified.

A *two-thirds* vote is needed. [*Two-thirds* is an adjective modifying *vote.*]
Two thirds of the voters endorsed the amendment. [*Two thirds* is the subject, not an adjective.]

(3) The hyphen is used to avoid ambiguity or an awkward union of letters or syllables between prefix or suffix and root.

His re-creation of the setting was perfect. [BUT Fishing is good recreation.]
He re-covered the leaky roof. [BUT He recovered his health.]
Micro-organism, re-enter, semi-independent, shell-like, thrill-less, sub-subcommittee.

(4) The hyphen is used with the prefixes ex- (meaning "former"), *self-, all-,* and the suffix *-elect.*

ex-governor, self-made, all-American, mayor-elect

EXERCISES ON SPELLING

The general list of words most frequently misspelled is made up of 654 (651 + *it's, too, two*) common words that everyone needs in his business and social life. The list is drawn, by kind permission of Dean Thomas Clark Pollock, from his study of 31,375 misspellings in the written work of college students.[3] In the list as given below the words *its, it's* and *to, too, two* are treated as word groups; all other words are listed individually, usually omitting any word that is spelled the same as a part of a longer word. For example, the list includes *definitely* but not *definite, existence* but not *exist, performance* but not *perform.* Each of the first hundred words in the general list below was misspelled more than forty-three times (or more than an *average* of forty-three times in the case of words grouped in Dean Pollock's report).

▶ EXERCISES 13–25   With the aid of your dictionary study the words in the general list in units of fifty words at a time until you feel sure (1) of the meaning and (2) of the spelling of each word. Then without the aid of your dictionary test yourself by writing sentences in which each word is correctly used and spelled. Add to your INDIVIDUAL SPELLING LIST each word that you misspell.

GENERAL SPELLING LIST

I. The Hundred Words Most Frequently Misspelled[4]

[13]
1. accommodate
2. achi*e*vement
3. ac*qu*ire
4. al*l* right
5. am*o*ng
6. ap*par*ent
7. ar*gu*ment
8. ar*gu*ing

[3] See Thomas Clark Pollock, "Spelling Report," *College English,* XVI (November, 1954), 102–09; and Thomas Clark Pollock and William D. Baker, *The University Spelling Book,* Prentice-Hall, Inc., Englewood Cliffs, N. J., 1955, pp. 6–12.

[4] An asterisk indicates the most frequently misspelled words among the first hundred. The most troublesome letters for all 651 words are indicated by italics.

9. belief°
10. believe°
11. beneficial
12. benefited
13. category
14. coming
15. comparative
16. conscious
17. controversy
18. controversial
19. definitely
20. definition
21. define
22. describe
23. description
24. disastrous
25. effect
26. embarrass
27. environment
28. exaggerate
29. existence°
30. existent°
31. experience
32. explanation
33. fascinate
34. height
35. interest
36. its (it's)
37. led
38. lose
39. losing
40. marriage

41. mere
42. necessary
43. occasion°
44. occurred
45. occurring
46. occurrence
47. opinion
48. opportunity
49. paid
50. particular

[14]
51. performance
52. personal
53. personnel
54. possession
55. possible
56. practical
57. precede°
58. prejudice
59. prepare
60. prevalent
61. principal
62. principle
63. privilege°
64. probably
65. proceed
66. procedure
67. professor
68. profession
69. prominent
70. pursue

71. quiet
72. receive°
73. receiving°
74. recommend
75. referring°
76. repetition
77. rhythm
78. sense
79. separate°
80. separation°
81. shining
82. similar°
83. studying
84. succeed
85. succession
86. surprise
87. technique
88. than
89. then
90. their°
91. there°
92. they're°
93. thorough
94. to° (too,° two°)
95. transferred
96. unnecessary
97. villain
98. woman
99. *write*
100. writing

II. The Next 551 Words Most Frequently Misspelled

[15]
101. absence
102. abundance
103. abundant
104. academic
105. academically
106. academy
107. acceptable
108. acceptance
109. accepting
110. accessible
111. accidental
112. accidentally
113. acclaim
114. accompanied
115. accompanies
116. accompaniment
117. accompanying
118. accomplish
119. accuracy
120. accurate
121. accurately
122. accuser
123. accuses
124. accusing
125. accustom
126. acquaintance
127. across
128. actuality
129. actually
130. adequately
131. admission
132. admittance

133. adolescence
134. adolescent
135. advantageous
136. advertisement
137. advertiser
138. advertising
139. advice
140. advise
141. affect
142. afraid
143. against
144. aggravate
145. aggressive
146. alleviate
147. allotted
148. allotment
149. allowed
150. allows

[16]
151. already
152. altar
153. all together
154. altogether
155. amateur
156. amount
157. analysis
158. analyze
159. and
160. another
161. annually
162. anticipated
163. apologetically

164. apologized
165. apology
166. apparatus
167. appearance
168. applies
169. applying
170. appreciate
171. appreciation
172. approaches
173. appropriate
174. approximate
175. area
176. arise
177. arising
178. arouse
179. arousing
180. arrangement
181. article
182. atheist
183. athlete
184. athletic
185. attack
186. attempts
187. attendance
188. attendant
189. attended
190. attitude
191. audience
192. authoritative
193. authority
194. available
195. bargain
196. basically

197. basis
198. beauteous
199. beautified
200. beautiful

[17]

201. beauty
202. become
203. becoming
204. before
205. began
206. beginner
207. beginning
208. behavior
209. bigger
210. biggest
211. boundary
212. breath
213. breathe
214. brilliance
215. brilliant
216. Britain
217. Britannica
218. burial
219. buried
220. bury
221. business
222. busy
223. calendar
224. capitalism
225. career
226. careful
227. careless
228. carried
229. carrier
230. carries
231. carrying
232. cemetery
233. certainly
234. challenge
235. changeable
236. changing
237. characteristic
238. characterized
239. chief
240. children
241. Christian
242. Christianity
243. choice
244. choose
245. chose
246. cigarette
247. cite
248. clothes
249. commercial
250. commission

[18]

251. committee
252. communist
253. companies
254. compatible
255. competition
256. competitive
257. competitor
258. completely
259. concede
260. conceivable

261. conceive
262. concentrate
263. concern
264. condemn
265. confuse
266. confusion
267. connotation
268. connote
269. conscience
270. conscientious
271. consequently
272. considerably
273. consistency
274. consistent
275. contemporary
276. continuous(ly)
277. controlled
278. controlling
279. convenience
280. convenient
281. correlate
282. council
283. counselor
284. countries
285. create
286. criticism
287. criticize
288. cruelly
289. cruelty
290. curiosity
291. curious
292. curriculum
293. dealt
294. deceive
295. decided
296. decision
297. dependent
298. desirability
299. desire
300. despair

[19]

301. destruction
302. detriment
303. devastating
304. device
305. difference
306. different
307. difficult
308. dilemma
309. diligence
310. dining
311. disappoint
312. disciple
313. discipline
314. discrimination
315. discussion
316. disease
317. disgusted
318. disillusioned
319. dissatisfied
320. divide
321. divine
322. doesn't
323. dominant
324. dropped
325. due
326. during

327. eager
328. easily
329. efficiency
330. efficient
331. eighth
332. eliminate
333. emperor
334. emphasize
335. encourage
336. endeavor
337. enjoy
338. enough
339. enterprise
340. entertain
341. entertainment
342. entirely
343. entrance
344. equipment
345. equipped
346. escapade
347. escape
348. especially
349. etc.
350. everything

[20]

351. evidently
352. excellence
353. excellent
354. except
355. excitable
356. exercise
357. expense
358. experiment
359. extremely
360. fallacy
361. familiar
362. families
363. fantasies
364. fantasy
365. fashions
366. favorite
367. fictitious
368. field
369. finally
370. financially
371. financier
372. foreigners
373. forty
374. forward
375. fourth
376. friendliness
377. fulfill
378. fundamentally
379. further
380. gaiety
381. generally
382. genius
383. government
384. governor
385. grammar
386. grammatically
387. group
388. guaranteed
389. guidance
390. guiding
391. handled
392. happened

393. happiness
394. hear
395. here
396. heroes
397. heroic
398. heroine
399. hindrance
400. hopeless

[21]

401. hoping
402. hospitalization
403. huge
404. humorist
405. humorous
406. hundred
407. hunger
408. hungrily
409. hungry
410. hypocrisy
411. hypocrite
412. ideally
413. ignorance
414. ignorant
415. imaginary
416. imagination
417. imagine
418. immediately
419. immense
420. importance
421. incidentally
422. increase
423. indefinite
424. independence
425. independent
426. indispensable
427. individually
428. industries
429. inevitable
430. influence
431. influential
432. ingenious
433. ingredient
434. initiative
435. intellect
436. intelligence
437. intelligent
438. interference
439. interpretation
440. interrupt
441. involve
442. irrelevant
443. irresistible
444. irritable
445. jealousy
446. knowledge
447. laboratory
448. laborer
449. laboriously
450. laid

[22]

451. later
452. leisurely
453. lengthening
454. license
455. likelihood
456. likely

457. likeness
458. listener
459. literary
460. literature
461. liveliest
462. livelihood
463. liveliness
464. lives
465. loneliness
466. lonely
467. loose
468. loss
469. luxury
470. magazine
471. magnificence
472. magnificent
473. maintenance
474. management
475. maneuver
476. manner
477. manufacturers
478. material
479. mathematics
480. matter
481. maybe
482. meant
483. mechanics
484. medical
485. medicine
486. medieval
487. melancholy
488. methods
489. miniature
490. minutes
491. mischief
492. moral
493. morale
494. morally
495. mysterious
496. narrative
497. naturally
498. Negroes
499. ninety
500. noble

[23]

501. noticeable
502. noticing
503. numerous
504. obstacle
505. off
506. omit
507. operate
508. oppose
509. opponent
510. opposite
511. optimism
512. organization
513. original
514. pamphlets
515. parallel
516. parliament
517. paralyzed
518. passed
519. past
520. peace
521. peculiar
522. perceive

523. permanent
524. permit
525. persistent
526. persuade
527. pertain
528. phase
529. phenomenon
530. philosophy
531. physical
532. piece
533. planned
534. plausible
535. playwright
536. pleasant
537. politician
538. political
539. practice
540. predominant
541. preferred
542. presence
543. prestige
544. primitive
545. prisoners
546. propaganda
547. propagate
548. prophecy
549. psychoanalysis
550. psychology

[24]

551. psychopathic
552. psychosomatic
553. quantity
554. really
555. realize
556. rebel
557. recognize
558. regard
559. relative
560. relieve
561. religion
562. remember
563. reminisce
564. represent
565. resources
566. response
567. revealed
568. ridicule
569. ridiculous
570. roommate
571. sacrifice
572. safety
573. satire
574. satisfied
575. satisfy
576. scene
577. schedule
578. seize
579. sentence
580. sergeant
581. several
582. shepherd
583. significance
584. simile
585. simple
586. simply
587. since
588. sincerely

589. sociology
590. sophomore
591. source
592. speaking
593. speech
594. sponsor
595. stabilization
596. stepped
597. stories
598. story
599. straight
600. strength

[25]

601. stretch
602. strict
603. stubborn
604. substantial
605. subtle
606. sufficient
607. summary
608. summed

609. suppose
610. suppress
611. surrounding
612. susceptible
613. suspense
614. swimming
615. symbol
616. synonymous
617. temperament
618. tendency
619. themselves
620. theories
621. theory
622. therefore
623. those
624. thought
625. together
626. tomorrow
627. tragedy
628. tremendous
629. tried
630. tries

631. tyranny
632. undoubtedly
633. unusually
634. useful
635. useless
636. using
637. vacuum
638. valuable
639. varies
640. various
641. view
642. vengeance
643. warrant
644. weather
645. weird
646. where
647. whether
648. whole
649. whose
650. yield
651. you're

INDIVIDUAL SPELLING LIST

▶ EXERCISE 26   No doubt you have been keeping your INDIVIDUAL SPELLING LIST from the beginning of the course and have been mastering each misspelled word as it has come to your attention. If by any chance you have not, begin now by listing, in the form shown below, all words that you have misspelled thus far in your written work. These should be in the spelling column of your "Record of Errors." (See page 826 at the end of Section 8.) Add to these all words misspelled as you have worked through Exercises 1–25 of this section. Continue throughout the course to add to your LIST every misspelled word that is called to your attention.

In the first column, write the word (correctly spelled); in the second, write the word by syllables, with accent marked; and in the third, show what you consider the best method for mastering the spelling of the word. Study the words in your LIST from time to time to make sure that you do not misspell any of them again.

MODEL FORM FOR SPELLING LIST

Word (correctly spelled)	Word (spelled by syllables)	Best Method for Mastery of Spelling
candidate	can'di date	Ear—letter omitted in pronunciation
prejudice	prej'u dice	Ear—letter changed in pronunciation
its	its	Eye—confused with it's
athlete	ath'lete	Ear—letter added in pronunciation
bridal	brid'al	Rule—drop final e before vowel
perspiration	per spi ra'tion	Ear—letters transposed in pronunciation
principal	prin'ci pal	Eye—confused with principle
accidentally	ac ci den'tal ly	Ear—letters omitted in pronunciation
merciful	mer'ci ful	Rule—change final y to i except before ing

Good Use—Glossary

19

Use a good dictionary to help you select the words best suited to express your ideas.

A dictionary is a storehouse of words. It is a good storehouse to the extent that it brings together words used in the English language and gives the reliable information you need about those words.

19a

Use only a good dictionary, and be sure to use it intelligently.

A good English dictionary is based upon the scientific examination of the writing and speaking habits of the English-speaking world; it records the origin, development, and changing use of words. Any dictionary is reliable only to the extent that it is soundly based on usage. But even the best dictionary cannot be perfect, as Dr. Johnson observed long ago.

The "unabridged" dictionaries, those that try to include the half million words in the language, must run to several thousand pages in a single volume or to a number of volumes. Among these large dictionaries, the following are especially useful.

New Standard Dictionary. New York: Funk & Wagnalls Company, Inc., 1959. 2815 pages.
Webster's New International Dictionary. Second Edition. Springfield, Massachusetts: G. & C. Merriam Company, 1934. 3194 pages.
Webster's Third New International Dictionary. Springfield, Massachusetts: G. & C. Merriam Company, 1961. 2662 pages.
A Dictionary of American English on Historical Principles. 4 volumes. Chicago: University of Chicago Press, 1936–44.
The Oxford English Dictionary. 12 volumes and Supplement. Oxford: Clarendon Press, 1933. (A corrected reissue of *A New English Dictionary on Historical Principles*, 10 volumes and Supplement, 1888–1928)—Abbreviated *OED* or *NED*.

Most students must consult these large dictionaries in the library. But even if a student owns a large dictionary, he will need one of the smaller dictionaries on the college or adult level, such as the following:

American College Dictionary (1947).—*ACD*
Standard College Dictionary (1963).—*SCD*
Webster's New World Dictionary (1953).—*NWD*
Webster's Seventh New Collegiate Dictionary (1963).—*NCD*

Note: Dictionaries are usually kept up to date by frequent slight revisions, sometimes with supplementary pages for new words. The last thorough revision of each dictionary listed above is shown by the date in parentheses.

Intelligent use of a dictionary requires some knowledge of its plan and special abbreviations as given in the introductory matter. This knowledge will help you understand a typical entry, such as that for *expel*.

(1) Spelling, Pronunciation   (2) Parts of Speech, Inflected Forms

(3) Meanings

(4) Origin
Synonyms

ex·pel (ik·spel′) *v.t.* **·pelled, ·pel·ling 1.** To drive out by force; force out; eject: to *expel* something from the mouth. **2.** To force by decision of the proper authorities to end attendance at a school, etc., or to terminate membership in an organization, etc.; oust. [< L *expellere* < *ex-* out + *pellere* to drive, thrust] — **ex·pel′la·ble** *adj.*
— **Syn.** *Expel, eject, dislodge, evict, oust,* and *dismiss* mean to send away forcibly. A school *expels* an unruly pupil; water in the lungs must be promptly *expelled.* A rifle *ejects* a shell automatically; a squid *ejects* an inky fluid. To *dislodge* is to move something heavy or resisting from its place; an avalanche may *dislodge* a large boulder. A man is *evicted* from his house; an official is *ousted* from office; an employee is *dismissed* from his job.

By permission from *Funk & Wagnalls Standard® College Dictionary,* copyright 1966 by Funk & Wagnalls, A Division of Reader's Digest Books, Inc.

(1) Spelling and pronunciation. The spelling of *expel* (by syllables separated by a dot) is given first, with pronunciation indicated (within parentheses) immediately following. The sound of each letter is shown by the short key to pronunciation at the bottom of the page (and by the detailed key in the front introductory matter). The accent in *expel,* as shown by the mark (′), falls on the last syllable.

(2) Parts of speech and inflected forms come next: *v. t.* classifies *expel* as a "verb, transitive"; the words in boldface give the inflected forms for the past participle and the present participle; another part of speech formed from the base word (the adjective *expellable*) is given in the last line of the entry.

(3) Meanings (including synonyms). Two separate meanings of *expel* are shown after the numbers *1* and *2.* In the *NCD* and in the *NWD* such definitions are arranged in the historical order of development, thus enabling the reader to see at a glance something of the history of the word. *But he should note that the meaning which developed first, and is consequently placed first, may no longer be the most common.* For example, the *NCD* and the *NWD,* in defining *prevent,* begin with the original but obsolete meaning "to anticipate" and come later to the present meaning "to keep from happening." The *SCD* and *ACD,* which put the most common meaning first, begin with "to keep from happening" and come later to the obsolete meaning. With *expel,* as with many words, the meaning that first developed is still the most common.

The meaning is made clearer by comparing the word to other words of similar meaning (synonyms, abbreviated **Syn.**). Note the special paragraph in which *expel* and five synonyms are differentiated.

For more detailed information about *expel* the student may consult one of the unabridged dictionaries in the library. In *Webster's New International Dictionary,* Second Edition, the entry for this word is more than twice as long as that in the shorter dictionaries and includes a quotation from Spenser. In *Webster's Third New International Dictionary* the entry is nearly four times as long and gives nine quotations to illustrate the various uses of the word. *The Oxford English Dictionary,* the most detailed of all dictionaries of the English language, quotes some fifty English writers of the past five or six hundred years to show the exact meaning of *expel* at each stage of its history.

(4) Origin: development of the language. The origin of the word—also called its *derivation* or *etymology*—is shown

in square brackets: [< L *expellere* < *ex-* out + *pellere* to drive, thrust]. This bracketed information means that *expel* is derived from (<) the Latin (L) word *expellere,* which is made up of *ex-,* meaning "out," and the combining form *pellere,* meaning "to drive or thrust." Breaking up a word, when possible, into prefix and combining form, as in the case of *expel,* (and also suffix, if any) will often help to get at the basic meaning of a word.

	Prefix		Combining Form		Suffix
circumvention	*circum-,* around	+	*venire,* to come	+	*-ion,* act of
dependent	*de-,* down	+	*pendere,* to hang	+	*-ent,* one who
intercede	*inter-,* between	+	*cedere,* to pass		
preference	*pre-,* before	+	*ferre,* to carry	+	*-ence,* state of
transmit	*trans-,* across	+	*mittere,* to send		

The bracketed information given by a good dictionary is especially rich in meaning when associated with the historical development of our language. English is one of the Indo-European (IE.)[1] languages, a group of languages apparently derived from a common source. Within this group of languages, many of the more familiar words are remarkably alike. Our word *mother,* for example, is *mater* in Latin (L), *meter* in Greek (Gk.), and *matar* in the ancient Persian and in the Sanskrit (Skt.) of India. Our pronoun *me* is exactly the same in Latin, in Greek, in Persian, and in Sanskrit. Words in different languages which apparently go back to a common parent language are called *cognates.* The large number of cognates and the many correspondences in sounds and structures indicate that most of the languages of Europe and some of the languages of Asia are derived from a common language, called by linguists Indo-European, which was spoken in the east-central region of Europe about five thousand years ago. By the opening of the Christian era the speakers of this language had spread themselves over most of Europe and as far east as India. Of the eight or nine language groups into which they had developed (see the inside back cover of the *NWD,* the entry "Indo-European" and "A Brief History of the English Language" in *SCD,* or "Indo-European languages" in *NCD*), English is chiefly concerned with the Greek (Hellenic) on the eastern Mediterranean, with the Latin (Italic) on the central and western Mediterranean, and with the Germanic in northwestern Europe. English is descended from the Germanic.

Two thousand years ago the Greek, the Latin, and the Germanic each comprised a more or less unified language group. After the fall of the Roman Empire in the fifth century, the several Latin-speaking divisions developed independently into the modern Romance languages, chief of which are Italian, French, and Spanish. Long before the fall of Rome the Germanic group was breaking up into three groups: (1) East Germanic, represented by the Goths, who were to play a large part in the last century of the Roman Empire before losing themselves in its

---

[1]The parenthetical abbreviations for languages here and on the next few pages are those commonly used in the bracketed derivations in dictionaries.

ruins; (2) North Germanic, or Old Norse (ON.), from which we have modern Danish (Dan.) and Swedish (Swed.), Norwegian (Norw.) and Icelandic (Icel.); and (3) West Germanic, the direct ancestor of English, Dutch (D.), and German (G.).

The English language may be said to have begun about the middle of the fifth century, when the West Germanic Angles and Saxons began the conquest of what is now England and either absorbed or drove out the Celtic-speaking inhabitants. The next six or seven hundred years are known as the Old English (OE.) or Anglo-Saxon (AS.) period of the English language. The fifty or sixty thousand words then in the language were chiefly Anglo-Saxon, with a small mixture of Old Norse words as a result of the Danish (Viking) conquests of England beginning in the eighth century. But the Old Norse words were so much like the Anglo-Saxon that they cannot always be distinguished.

The transitional period—about 1100 to 1500—from Old English to Modern English is known as Middle English (ME.). Changes already under way were accelerated by the Norman Conquest beginning in 1066. The Normans or "Northmen" had settled in northern France during the Viking invasions and had adopted the Old French (OF.) in place of their native Old Norse. The Normans, coming over to England by thousands, made French the language of the King's court in London and of the ruling classes (both French and English) throughout the land, while the masses continued to speak English. Only toward the end of the fifteenth century did English become once more the common language of all classes. But the language that emerged had lost most of its Anglo-Saxon inflections[2] and had taken on thousands of French words (derived originally from Latin). It was, however, still basically English, not French, in its structure.

A striking feature of Modern English (that is, English since 1500) is its immense vocabulary. As already noted, Old English used some fifty or sixty thousand words, very largely native Anglo-Saxon; Middle English used perhaps a hundred thousand, many taken through the French from Latin and others directly from Latin; and now our unabridged dictionaries list over four times as many. To make up this tremendous word hoard, we have borrowed most heavily from the Latin, but we have drawn some words from almost every known language. English writers of the sixteenth century were especially eager to interlard their works with words from Latin authors; and as Englishmen pushed out to colonize and to trade in many parts of the globe, they brought home new words as well as goods. Modern science and technology have drawn heavily from the Greek. The result of all this borrowing is that English has become the richest, most cosmopolitan of all languages.

In the process of enlarging our vocabulary we have lost most of our original Anglo-Saxon words. But those that are left make up the most familiar, most useful part of our vocabulary. Practically all of our simple verbs, our articles, conjunctions, prepositions, and pronouns are native Anglo-Saxon; and so are many of our familiar nouns, adjectives, and adverbs. Every speaker and writer uses these native

[2] See p. 1.

words over and over, much more frequently than the borrowed words. If every word is counted every time it is used, the percentage of native words runs very high, usually between 70 and 90 percent. Milton's percentage was 81, Tennyson's 88, Shakespeare's about 90, and that of the King James Bible about 94. English has been enriched by its extensive borrowings without losing its individuality; it is still fundamentally the *English* language.

▶ EXERCISE 1   Note the origins of the words on a typical page (or on several typical pages) of your dictionary. Copy examples of words derived from (1) Anglo-Saxon; (2) Old French or Latin through Old French; (3) Latin directly; (4) Greek through Latin; (5) Greek directly; (6) other languages.

(5) Dictionary labels—levels of usage. See also pages 857–58, 859–60.) Most dictionaries use such labels as *Informal* (OR *Colloquial*), *Slang, Dialect, Obsolete* (OR *Archaic*), and *Illiterate* (OR *Substandard*). Labeled words, or labeled meanings of words, should be used with appropriate care, as treated further under **19b-h.**

The labeling or classification of words is often difficult, for the language is constantly changing and many words are on the borderline between the formal (or general) and the informal (or colloquial), between colloquial and slang, between slang and dialect, and between dialectal words and illiterate (or substandard) ones. There are no clearly marked boundaries between the various classes, and naturally even the best dictionaries will not always agree. Although classes of words are often referred to as "levels of usage," we are not to think of one class as always higher or better than another. Any one may be appropriate for a given occasion. Technical language that might not be generally understood is often the clearest and most economical for speech and writing addressed to those in one's profession. The occasion and the purpose of the writer or speaker will determine the best words to select. The unlabeled words, or word meanings (for many words are labeled for one meaning but not for another), which make up the bulk of the English vocabulary, are usually best for general (formal) writing and, along with colloquialisms, for conversation and the more informal types of writing. But it should be noted that *Webster's Third International Dictionary,* followed by the *NCD,* has discontinued the label *Colloquial,* thus leaving to the writer's judgment the problem of avoiding many unlabeled words that would be inappropriate in the usual expository prose. Words commonly unlabeled by dictionaries range from the very learned words appropriate in the most formal situations to the very simple words that are used in both the most dignified and the most informal styles.

▶ EXERCISE 2   The ten words in the *Standard College Dictionary* beginning with *grind* may be classified as indicated below. *Italics* indicate that a word belongs in the class in respect to one or more of its meanings but not all. Note that all ten of the words are unlabeled for at least one meaning.

FORMAL or GENERAL (not labeled)   *grind,* grindelia, *grinder,*
    grindery, grindstone, gringo, *grip*[1], *grip*[2], *gripe,* grippe
INFORMAL or COLLOQUIAL   *grind, grinder, gripe*

SLANG *grind*
BRITISH *grindery* (also FORMAL because in general use throughout one country)
UNITED STATES *grip*[1] (also FORMAL because in general use throughout one country)
ARCHAIC *gripe*

Classify according to the labels in your dictionary the ten words (exclusive of proper names) beginning with *grating*. Note that most of the ten words are unlabeled for at least one meaning.

▶ **EXERCISE 3** Classify according to the labels in your dictionary the ten words beginning with *knock*. Note that nearly all these words are unlabeled for at least one meaning.

FURTHER EXERCISES ON THE USE OF THE DICTIONARY

▶ **EXERCISE 4** What are the etymologies of the following words?

adjective	conjunction	dialogue	monarchy
aristocracy	democracy	emperor	oligarchy

▶ **EXERCISE 5** If a copy of the *Oxford English Dictionary* is available, determine the first English meanings of the following words. What meanings developed later?

doom	inspiration	prevent	sanguine
gallery	knave	proper	silly

▶ **EXERCISE 6** List synonyms for each of the following words. (For synonyms and antonyms you may find that your dictionary should be supplemented by a book of synonyms such as *Roget's International Thesaurus*, New York, 1965, which is available also in a pocketbook size.)

act	change	fight	see
anger	eat	go	think

▶ **EXERCISE 7** List antonyms for each of the following words.

awkward	clever	gallantry	quiet
clear	fast	greed	study

▶ **EXERCISE 8** Study the following pairs of words in your dictionary (in the special paragraphs, if any, that compare and contrast the pairs) and write sentences to illustrate the shades of difference in meaning.

cause—reason	help—aid	push—shove
freedom—liberty	position—situation	valid—sound

▶ **EXERCISE 9** Determine the most common American spelling of the following words: *connexion, gypsy, labour.* Which of the following words should be written separately, which should be written solid, and which should be hyphenated?

cropeared	girlscout	heartfelt	postoffice
cubbyhole	heartbroken	heartfree	vestpocket

▶ **EXERCISE 10** Determine the pronunciation for each of the following words. Which of the words change the accent to indicate a change in grammatical function?

absent	exquisite	Montaigne	vehement
contest	impious	object	Vietnam

▶ **EXERCISE 11** Classify each of the following words as a verb (transitive or intransitive), a noun, an adjective, an adverb, a preposition, or a conjunction. Give the principal parts of each verb, the plural (or plurals) of each noun, and the comparative and superlative of each adjective or adverb. (Note that some words are used as two or more parts of speech.)

bad	drag	often	since	stratum
bite	into	sheep	sing	tomato

▶ **EXERCISE 12** Which of the following words are usually capitalized? Which are capitalized only for certain meanings?

easter	italic	platonic	spanish
italian	liberian	roman	stoical

▶ **EXERCISE 13** Divide the following words into syllables.

analytic	industrious	liberty	vindictive
indistinguishable	laboriously	supplement	vocabulary

▶ **EXERCISE 14** Get from your dictionary specific information about each of the following. Note the source of information as (a) general vocabulary, (b) list of abbreviations, (c) gazetteer, (d) biographical list, or (e) appendix.

Annam	Esau	Melpomene	*vive le roi*
Attila	Escorial	Louis Pasteur	WAC

19b

Avoid informal (colloquial) words in the more formal types of writing.

Words or expressions labeled *Informal* or *Colloquial* in most dictionaries are appropriate to conversation and to informal writing. For these purposes colloquialisms often give a desirable tone of informality. But colloquial expressions tend to bring a discordant note into expository or other formal types of writing.

INFORMAL The repeated *phone* calls only *aggravated* me but made my sister *plenty mad.*
FORMAL The repeated *telephone* calls only *annoyed* me but made my sister *very angry.*

INFORMAL I *got away with it* then, but it's *plumb no go* now.
FORMAL I *was not discovered* then, but I *could not do* it now.

Contracted forms (*won't, I'd, he'll, hasn't*) are proper for informal writing and equally proper for all but the most extremely formal speech. In formal expository writing, such contractions are normally written out—*will not, I would* or *I should, he will, has not.*

INFORMAL It's really too bad that *he's* been held up and *can't* be here for the opening.
FORMAL It is unfortunate that he *has been* detained and *cannot* be here for the opening.

▶ **EXERCISE 15** Consult your dictionary for informal meanings of the following words: *brass, dig, fizzle, kick, way.* For each word compose a sentence in which the word is used with an informal meaning. Then in each sentence substitute a formal word with the same meaning.

19c
Use slang only when appropriate; in general, avoid jargon.

(See **19g** for technical words.)

Slang is defined by the *Standard College Dictionary* as "language, words, or phrases of a vigorous, colorful, facetious, or taboo nature, invented for specific occasions or uses, or derived from the unconventional use of the standard vocabulary." Some slang words have a pungent quality: *goon* and *moocher* may soon join *van, sham, mob,* and *banter* as standard words of the English language. Such slang may be effective on certain informal occasions.

But much slang is trite and tasteless, and is used in an ineffective attempt to mask an inadequate vocabulary. For some people everything disapproved of is "lousy," when they could be more exact with "contemptible," "unfair," "mean," or "worthless." Most of the objection to slang, then, is based not upon arbitrary *don'ts* but upon slang's habitual alliance with lazy thinking. Slang is the sluggard's way of avoiding the search for the exact, meaningful word.

Perhaps more objectionable than slang are certain types of jargon—language which is meaningless, or at least very confusing except to a special group. Almost every trade or occupation has its own jargon. A man with recent military experience might write the following jargon about his first day in college:

The mustering-in was snafu.

This sentence would be easily understood by his army friends; other readers might require a formal statement:

The registration was confused.

A particularly confusing type of jargon is found in much government writing. (See also **21a, Wordiness.**)

BUREAUCRATIC JARGON   All personnel functioning in the capacity of clerks will indicate that they have had opportunity to take due cognizance of this notice by transmitting signed acknowledgment of receipt of same.
IMPROVED   All clerks will acknowledge in writing the receipt of this notice.
COMMERCIAL JARGON   Allow us to express our appreciation of your esteemed favor.
IMPROVED   Thank you for your letter.

Note: Jargon in the sense of technical terms used by the learned professions can be very useful. See **19g.**

19d
Dialectal words should be used appropriately.

Dialectal words (also called *localisms* or *provincialisms*) should normally be avoided in speaking and writing outside the limited region where they are current. Speakers and writers may, however, safely use dialectal words known to the audience they are addressing.

DIALECT   I *reckon* he filled the *poke* with apples.
STANDARD   I *suppose* he filled the *bag* with apples.

19e
Illiteracies and improprieties should be avoided.

Illiteracies (also called *vulgarisms*) are the *nonstandard* expressions of uneducated people and are usually not listed in the dictionary.

NONSTANDARD   The boys *ain't* going. *They's* no use asking them.
STANDARD   The boys *are not* going. *There's* no use asking them.

An *impropriety* is a good word used with the wrong sense or function.

WRONG SENSE   I *except* your invitation. [Wrong meaning]
RIGHT WORD   I *accept* your invitation.
QUESTIONABLE   She sang *good.* [Wrong function—adjective used as adverb]
STANDARD   She sang *well.*

19f
Obsolete, archaic, or obsolescent words should be avoided.

All dictionaries list words (and meanings for words) that have long since passed out of general use. Such words as *ort* (fragment of food) and *yestreen* (last evening) are still found in dictionaries because these words, once the standard vocabulary of great authors, occur in our older literature and must be defined for the modern reader.

Some archaic words—like *wight, methinks,* and *quoth*—have been used for purposes of humor. Modern practice tends to label such usage as juvenile.

19g
Technical words should be used only when appropriate to the audience.

When you are writing for the general reader, avoid all unnecessary technical language. Since the ideal of the good writer is to make his thought clear to as many people as possible, he will not describe an apple tree as a *Malus pumila* or a high fever as *hyperpyrexia.* (Of course technical language, with its greater precision, is highly desirable when one is addressing an audience that can understand it, as when a physician addresses a group of physicians.)

Whenever technical terms come to be generally understood, as they often do (*phosphate* and *atomic energy,* for example), they may be used, of course, as freely as the unlabeled words in the dictionary.

19h
Avoid (1) "fine writing," (2) "poetic" expressions, and (3) unpleasing combinations of sound or overuse of alliteration.

(1) Avoid "fine writing." "Fine writing" is the unnecessary use of ornate words and expressions. It is generally fuzzy and repetitious; it tends to emphasize words rather than ideas. A simple, direct statement like "From childhood I have looked forward to a journey" can become by fine writing something like this: "From the halcyon days

of early youth I have always anticipated with eagerness and pleasure the exciting vistas of distant climes and mysterious horizons."

(2) **Avoid "poetic" expressions.** Genuine poetry has its very proper place, and the vivid language of simile and metaphor enriches even colloquial prose. But the sham poetry of faded imagery (*eye of night* for *moon*) and inappropriate expressions like *oft, eftsoons, 'twas,* and *'neath* are misplaced in the usual prose style.

(3) **Avoid unpleasing combinations of sound or overuse of alliteration.** Good prose has rhythm, but it does not rhyme. If you write, "In foreign relations, the western nations are subject to dictation," you distract the reader's attention from your meaning. Equally offensive to the average reader is the overuse of alliteration (repetition of the same consonant sound), as in "Some people *s*hun the *s*eashore."

OTHER EXERCISES ON USAGE

▶ **EXERCISE 16** In the following list put *C* after any sentence that requires no revision, even for formal writing. Write *Inf.* for each sentence approved for informal use only. Label each violation of good usage. Then rewrite all sentences (except those marked *C*) to make them conform to formal English. You may find the **Glossary of Usage** (**19i**) helpful in determining some inappropriate usages.

1. If I had of known you was coming, I would of waited longer.
2. Everyone suspicioned the old man of stealing our apples.
3. The ad in the paper was sort of hazy.
4. The sifting snow screened our view of the highway.
5. George was not dumb, though he looked like he was.
6. The profs dished out more than we could take.
7. Has your neighbor done sold his house?
8. The boy had a keen desire to win the game.
9. You do things different from anybody I know.
10. We filled the bucket with H_2O.
11. The poor man was in a sad fix.
12. I suppose that your findings are correct.
13. "You are batty," I yelled. "Now scram!"
14. I am terribly aggravated with your doings.
15. Ten miles is all the farther that I can live away from my store.
16. Where do you live at now?
17. The general was completely sold on the private who had some spunk.
18. 'Twas a clear, cool eve, and the moon shed an effulgent glow.
19. A first-rate farmer raises heaps of farm produce.
20. I am kind of late today, for I do not feel so good.
21. He took and snatched the parcel from her hands although he knew that he hadn't ought.
22. Since Richard hopes to become a musician, he is taking piano lessons.
23. Because of the depression he lost considerable in his business.
24. Her folks live in the country ten miles outside the city limits.
25. He calculated he could win out in the election.

▶ **EXERCISE 17** Rewrite the following passages of bureaucratic, legal, or academic jargon in simple formal English.[3]

1. It is obvious from the difference in elevation with relation to the short depth of the property that the contour is such as to preclude any reasonable developmental potential for active recreation.
2. Verbal contact with Mr. Blank regarding the attached notification of promotion has elicited the attached representation intimating that he prefers to decline the assignment.
3. Voucherable expenditures necessary to provide adequate dental treatment required as adjunct to medical treatment being rendered a pay patient in in-patient status may be incurred as required at the expense of the Public Health Service.
4. I hereby give and convey to you, all and singular, my estate and interests, right, title, claim and advantages of and in said orange, together with all rind, juice, pulp and pits, and all rights and advantages therein.
5. I prefer an abbreviated phraseology, distinguished for its lucidity.
6. Realization has grown that the curriculum or the experiences of learners change and improve only as those who are most directly involved examine their goals, improve their understandings and increase their skill in performing the tasks necessary to reach newly defined goals.

Glossary of Usage

19i

Consult the following glossary to determine the standing of a word or phrase and its appropriateness to your purpose.

The glossary below can include only a few of the words likely to cause difficulty. If the word you are looking for is not included, or if you need more information about any word in the list, consult a good recent college dictionary, remembering that dictionaries do not always agree. The following list does not represent the usage of any one dictionary, but justification for each usage label can usually be found in at least two of the leading dictionaries.

This glossary follows the *Standard College Dictionary* (page xxiii) in classifying all English words as STANDARD or NONSTANDARD.

STANDARD words are those in general use throughout the English-speaking world, or in one country (with such dictionary labels as *U.S.* or *Brit.*), or at least in a large section of a country (with such labels as *Western U.S.*). A relatively few standard words, or word meanings, are labeled *Informal* or *Colloquial* by most dictionaries to distinguish words better suited for conversation and familiar writing than for more formal expository writing, such as

[3]Quoted, by permission, from Stuart Chase's *Power of Words*, Harcourt, Brace & World, New York, 1953, pp. 250–53.

that usually expected in college. (See also **19b.**) These standard but "colloquial" words are called INFORMAL in this glossary to distinguish them from all other standard words, a much larger group called FORMAL. This term, as here used, has almost the meaning "general" since FORMAL includes both our most learned words and also such simple words as *boy, cat, dog, go, see, come, good, bad* and our pronouns, prepositions, conjunctions, and articles (*a, an, the*).

NONSTANDARD is the term applied to all other words in the dictionary—that is, to all words not classified as STANDARD. These "nonstandard" words, for one reason or another, have only a limited use. They make up but a minor part of words listed and generally have such dictionary labels as the following (some of which are used in this glossary):

SLANG. Vivid, recently coined, highly colloquial words. See also **19c.**

DIALECT. Words common to a very limited region. See also **19d.**

OBSOLETE or ARCHAIC. Words not in current use. See also **19f.**

LAW, MEDICINE, etc. Technical terms not generally understood. See also **19g.**

ILLITERATE, SUBSTANDARD, or VULGAR. Substandard words used in dialogue to illustrate the speech of the uneducated. See also **19e.**

Note that some meanings of a word may be STANDARD while other meanings of the same word have a NONSTANDARD label.

a, an Use *a* before a consonant sound, *an* before a vowel sound.

a heavy load   *a* nap   *a* uniform   *a* one-man show
an honest boy   *an* ape   *an* umpire   *an* only child

accept, except The verb *accept* means "to give an affirmative answer to" or "to receive." The verb *except*, seldom used, means "to exclude"; as a preposition, *except* means "with the exclusion of."

Mary *accepted* the invitation to dinner.
They *excepted* Mary from the invitation.
All the boys *accept* John as their leader.
All the boys *except* John are leaders.

accidentally, incidentally When using these adverbs, remember that *-ly* is added to the adjective forms *accidental* and *incidental*, not to the noun forms *accident* and *incident*.

NONSTANDARD Mr. Kent accidently overheard the report.
STANDARD Mr. Kent *accidentally* overheard the report.

ad, exam, gym, math Informal shortening of *advertisement, examination, gymnasium,* and *mathematics.* Formal writing requires the full word.

advice, advise Pronounced and spelled differently, *advice* is a noun, *advise* a verb.

Patients should follow their doctors' *advice*.
Patients should do what their doctors *advise*.

affect, effect *Affect*, meaning "to influence," is a verb only. *Effect* may function as a verb or a noun. The verb *effect* means "to bring about" or "to achieve"; the noun *effect* means "the result."

The reforms *affected* many citizens.
The citizens *effected* a few reforms.

He said that wars *affect* the economy.
He stressed the *effect* of wars on the economy.

aggravate Formally *aggravate* means "to make worse or intensify." Informally it means "to provoke or annoy."

INFORMAL The children's noise aggravated Mrs. Faber.
FORMAL Lack of water aggravated the suffering.

ain't A nonstandard contraction avoided by the educated, unless used for humorous effect.

alibi Informal for *excuse*. In formal English, used only with the legal meaning.

all the farther, all the faster Nonstandard substitutes for *as far as, as fast as.*

NONSTANDARD A mile is all the farther we can walk.
STANDARD A mile is *as far as* we can walk.

allusion, illusion Do not confuse *allusion*, "an indirect reference," with *illusion*, "an unreal image or false impression."

Timothy made an *allusion* to the Trojans.
The Trojan horse was no optical *illusion*.

almost, most *Most* is informal when used as a substitute for *almost*.

INFORMAL Most all referees strive to be fair.
FORMAL *Almost* all referees strive to be fair.

a lot, lots Informal for "very much," "a great deal," or "many." *Alot* is a misspelling of *a lot.*

already, all ready *Already* means "before or by the time specified." *All ready* means "completely prepared."

The theater was *already* full by seven o'clock.
The cast was *all ready* for the curtain call.

all right *Alright* is still an unacceptable spelling of *all right.*

altogether, all together *Altogether* means "wholly, thoroughly." *All together* means "in a group."

That type of rule is *altogether* unnecessary.
They were *all together* in the lobby.

alumnus, alumna *Alumnus*, a male graduate; *alumni*, two or more male graduates. *Alumna*, a female graduate; *alumnae*, two or more female graduates. *Alumni*, male and female graduates grouped together.

A.M., P.M. (also **a.m., p.m.**). Use only with figures. "He came at 10:00 A.M. (*not* in the A.M.) and left at 4:00 P.M." "He came in the morning and left in the afternoon (*not* in the P.M.)."

among, between *Among* always implies more than two, a group; *between* literally implies only two. *Between*, however, is now often used for three or more when each is regarded individually.

What honor was there *among* the forty thieves?
What is the difference *between* a thief and a robber?
"This secret," said Uncle Rex, "is *between* you and me and the gate post."

amount, number Use *amount* to refer to things in bulk or mass; *number* refers to the countable.

A large *amount* of rice is consumed annually.
A large *number* of disgruntled men barred the entrance.

an, a See **a, an.**

and etc. Never place *and* before *etc.* The *and* is redundant since *etc.* is an abbreviation of *et* (and) + *cetera* (other things).

anyone, any one *Anyone* means "any person at all." *Any one* singles out one person or thing in a group. Similarly with *everyone, every one, someone, some one.*

Anyone can wax a floor.
Any one of those maids can wax a floor.

anyways, anywheres   Dialectal for *anyway, anywhere.*

DIALECTAL	Janice cannot drive anywheres.
STANDARD	Janice cannot drive *anywhere*.

as   Avoid using *as* instead of *because, for, since, that, which, who,* or *whether.*

DIALECTAL	I do not know as I should go.
STANDARD	I do not know *whether* I should go.
AMBIGUOUS	As it was snowing, we played basketball.
PRECISE	*While* it was snowing, we played basketball.
PRECISE	*Because* it was snowing, we played basketball.

In negative statements some writers prefer *so . . . as* to *as . . . as:* The poet is not *so* popular *as* he once was. See also **like, as, as if.**

as to   A vague substitute for *about.*

She spoke to me about (*not as to*) her plans.

at   Although *from* after *where* is standard, *at* after *where* is not standard.

NONSTANDARD	Where did the Brownings live at?
STANDARD	Where did they live? Where were they from?

at about   *About* is preferable.

WORDY	He arrived at about noon.
BETTER	He arrived about noon.

awful, awfully   *Awful* in the sense of "very great, bad, ugly," as well as *awfully* in the sense of "extremely," is not only informal but trite.

INFORMAL	That costume jewelry looks awful.
FORMAL	That costume jewelry looks ostentatious.
INFORMAL	The price of the car is awfully high.
FORMAL	The price of the car is extremely high.

awhile, a while   Distinguish between the adverb *awhile* and the article and noun *a while.*

Rest *awhile* before you leave.
Rest for *a while* before you leave.

bad, badly   Although either *bad* or *badly* is now standard in the sense of "ill, sorry," writers usually prefer *bad* after such verbs as *feel* or *look.*

STANDARD	Charles feels *bad*. Charles feels *badly*.

bank on   Informal expression for *rely on.*

because   See **reason is because.**

being as, being that   Nonstandard for *since, because.*

beside, besides   When meaning "except," *beside* and *besides* are interchangeable prepositions. Distinguish, however, between *beside* meaning "by the side of" and *besides* meaning "in addition to."

STANDARD	I sat *beside* the window.
STANDARD	Herbert has income *besides* his salary.

Notice the difference in the meaning below:

He owns the car *beside* the house.
He owns the car *besides* the house.

better   See **had better, had rather, would rather.**

between, among   See **among, between.**

bursted, bust, busted   The obsolete *bursted* is not standard usage; *bust* and *busted* are slang. The principal parts of *burst* are *burst, burst, burst.*

but, hardly, scarcely   "Can't help but" is now standard, both formally and informally, but such negatives as "can't hardly" and "don't scarcely" are still nonstandard.

STANDARD	I *couldn't help but* laugh. OR I *couldn't help* laughing.
NONSTANDARD	I couldn't hardly read his handwriting.
STANDARD	I *could hardly* read his handwriting.

but what   Informal for *that* in negative expressions.

INFORMAL	Brad has no doubt but what the Lions will win.
FORMAL	Brad has no doubt *that* the Lions will win.

calculate   Dialectal for *think* or *expect.*

can, may   Informal usage substitutes *can* for *may* in questions and negations. Formal usage still requires that *can* be used to denote ability to perform and *may* to denote permission to do.

INFORMAL	*Can* I use your class notes?
FORMAL	*May* I use your class notes?

can't hardly   A double negative in implication. Use *can hardly.* See **but, hardly, scarcely.**

case, line   Often used in wordy expressions.

WORDY	In the case of Jones there were good intentions.
CONCISE	Jones had good intentions.
WORDY	Buy something in the line of fruit.
CONCISE	Buy some fruit.

complected   Dialectal for *complexioned.*

DIALECT	They are light-complected children.
STANDARD	They are light-*complexioned* children (OR children of light complexion).

considerable   Used formally as an adjective, informally as a noun. Nonstandard as an adverb.

NONSTANDARD	Prices have dropped considerable.
INFORMAL	Considerable has been donated to the civic fund.
FORMAL	A *considerable* amount has been donated.

contact   Frequently overused for more exact words or phrases such as *ask, consult, inform, query, talk with, telephone, write to.*

continual, continuous   *Continual* implies "occurring in steady, rapid but not unbroken succession"; *continuous* means "complete absence of interruption."

Continual interruptions delayed the rehearsal.
The *continuous* roar of the waterfall was disturbing.

could of   Nonstandard for *could have.*

data, criteria, phenomena   Plurals of *datum* (rarely used), *criterion, phenomenon. Criterion* and *phenomenon* have alternate plurals: *criterions, phenomenons.* The plural *data* is often construed as a collective noun: "This *data* has been verified."

deal   Informal for "business transaction." Frequently overworked for more exact words such as *sale, agreement, plan, secret agreement.*

definitely   Often overused as a vague intensifier.

differ from, differ with   *Differ from* means "to stand apart because of unlikeness." *Differ with* means "to disagree."

Poe's stories *differ from* those of Hemingway.
On that point I *differ with* you.

different from   In America, the preferred preposition after *different* is *from.* But *different than* is accepted by many writers if the expression is followed by a clause.

The Stoic philosophy is *different from* the Epicurean.

The outcome was *different from* what I expected (OR, more informally, *different than I had expected*).

done Standard as an adjective and as the past participle of the verb *do*. Nonstandard as an adverb and as a substitute for *did*.

NONSTANDARD The bread is done sold.
STANDARD The bread is *already* sold. The bread is *done*.
NONSTANDARD Do the police know who done it?
STANDARD Do the police know who *did* it? Who *has* done it?

don't A contraction for *do not* rather than for *does not*.

NONSTANDARD He don't smoke. (He do not smoke.)
STANDARD *He doesn't* smoke. (He *does* not smoke.)

each other, one another Used interchangeably. Some writers prefer *each other* when referring to only two, and *one another* when referring to more than two.

effect, affect See **affect, effect.**

either, neither Used to refer to one or the other of two. (As subjects, the words are singular.)

Either a bicycle or a car will please him.
Neither of the paintings is finished.

emigrate, immigrate *Emigrate* means "to leave a place of abode for residence in another country." *Immigrate* means "to come for permanent residence into a country of which one is not a native."

Conrad *emigrated* from Poland.
He *immigrated* to England.

enthuse, enthused Informal as a verb for "to show enthusiasm" and as a synonym for *enthusiastic.*

INFORMAL We were all enthused about the new club.
FORMAL We were all *enthusiastic* about the new club.

etc. See **and etc.**

everyone, every one See **anyone, any one.**

everywheres Dialectal for *everywhere.*

except, accept See **accept, except.**

expect Informal if used for *suppose* or *think.*

INFORMAL I expect James voted yesterday.
FORMAL I *suppose* James voted yesterday.

farther, further Although these words are often used interchangeably to express geographic distance, some writers prefer *farther. Further* is used to express additional time, degree, or quantity.

Denver is *farther* north than Dallas.
Will there be *further* improvements in city government?

faze Informal for "disturb, worry, disconcert." Not related to the noun *phase*, standard English for *aspect* or *stage.*

fewer, less Informally, interchangeable. Formal English makes this distinction: *less* refers to value, degree, or amount; *fewer* refers to number, to the countable.

INFORMAL Less children are born during a depression.
FORMAL *Fewer* children are born during a depression.

fine Informal when used as an adverb meaning "well, excellently." *Fine* is a vague, overused adjective; choose a more exact expression.

flunk Informal for *fail.*

folks Informal for *parents, relatives.*

former Refers to the first named of two.

The Folger and the Huntington are two famous libraries; the *former* is in Washington, D.C., and the latter is in California. [If three items are referred to, do not use *former* or *latter* but *first* and *last*.]

funny Informal for *strange, queer, odd.* In general usage *funny* means "amusing."

further, farther See **farther, further.**

gentleman, lady Generally preferable: *man, woman.* Use *gentleman, lady* when your purpose is to distinguish persons of refinement and culture from the ill-bred. Use the plural forms in addressing an audience: "Ladies and Gentlemen."

get, got The verb *to get* is one of the most useful words in standard English. It is common in such good idioms as *get along with* (someone), *get the better of* (someone), *get at* (information), *get up* (a dance), *get on* (a horse), or *get over* (an illness). Avoid, however, *get* or *got* in expressions considered slang or too informal.

INFORMAL I do not get the professor half the time.
FORMAL I do not *understand* the professor half the time.

good Nearly always used as an adjective. Generally considered informal when used as an adverb.

INFORMAL Mrs. Nevins cooks good.
FORMAL Mrs. Nevins cooks *good* meals. She cooks *well.*

gotten Past participle of *get*, the principal parts of which are *get* (present), *got* (past), *got*, or *gotten* (past participle). In England *gotten* is now old-fashioned, but in the United States both *got* and *gotten* are in general use.

grand A vague, trite adjective. Describe what you mean with more specific words.

guy Informal for *man* or *boy.*

had better, had rather, would rather Good idioms used to express advisability (with *better*) or preference (with *rather*). *Better* is an informal shortening of *had better.*

INFORMAL Members better pay their dues.
FORMAL Members *had better* pay their dues.

had of, had ought Nonstandard for *had, ought.*

half a, a half, a half a Use *half a* or *a half*, but avoid the redundant *a half a.*

REDUNDANT He worked a half a day.
STANDARD He worked *half a* day.
STANDARD He worked *a half* day. [Perhaps more formal and more specific]

hanged, hung Informally, the distinction between *hanged* and *hung* is often no longer made, but formal usage still makes a distinction: *hanged* is used in referring to executions; *hung*, to objects.

The outlaw was *hanged.*
The lodge is *hung* with African trophies.

hardly See **but, hardly, scarcely.**

have, of See **of, have.**

healthful, healthy Although both *healthful* and *healthy* are standard words meaning "conducive to health," *healthy* is most frequently used to mean "having health"; *healthful*, "giving health."

That is a *healthful* (OR *healthy*) climate.
Healthy (NOT healthful) pets are sold in that shop.

himself, myself   See **myself, himself.**

hisself   Nonstandard for *himself.*

Honorable, Reverend   See **Reverend, Honorable.**

if, whether   Some writers prefer *whether* to *if* after such verbs as *say, learn, know, understand, doubt,* especially when followed by *or.*

Forecasters did not know *whether* it would rain or snow.

illusion, allusion   See **allusion, illusion.**

immigrate, emigrate   See **emigrate, immigrate.**

imply, infer   The writer or speaker *implies;* the reader or listener *infers. Imply* means "to suggest without stating"; *infer* means "to reach a conclusion based upon evidence." Often used interchangeably in informal English.

His statement *implies* that he will resign.
From his statement I *infer* that he will resign.

in, into   Do not confuse. *In* indicates "location within." "He was *in* the room." *Into* indicates "motion or direction to a point within." "He came *into* the room." Compare the meaning of these sentences:

We flew *in* another jet.
We flew *into* another jet.

in back of, in behind, in between   Wordy for *back of, behind, between.*

incidentally, accidentally   See **accidentally, incidentally.**

incredible, incredulous   *Incredible* means "too extraordinary to admit of belief." *Incredulous* means "inclined not to believe on slight evidence."

The hunters told *incredible* stories.
The hunters' stories made me *incredulous.*

individual, party, person   *Individual* refers to a single thing, animal, or person. In legal writing, *party* may refer to a group of people or to a single person, but in other formal writing, *party* designates a group only. *Person* is preferred for general reference to a human being.

INFORMAL   Paul is the only interested party.
FORMAL   Paul is the only interested *person.*

infer, imply   See **imply, infer.**

inferior than   Nonstandard. Use *inferior to* or *worse than.*

ingenious, ingenuous   *Ingenious* means "clever, resourceful," as "an ingenious device." *Ingenuous* means "open, frank, artless," as "ingenuous actions."

The electric can opener is an *ingenious* device.
Don's *ingenuous* smile disarms the critics.

in regards to   Use either of the correct idioms, *in regard to* or *as regards.*

inside of, outside of   The *of* is often unnecessary. *Inside of* is informal for *within. Outside of* is informal for *except, besides.*

FORMAL   We live *inside* the city limits.
FORMAL   The job will be finished *within* (NOT inside of) ten days.

into, in   See **in, into.**

invite   Slang when used as a substitute for *invitation.*

irregardless   Nonstandard for *regardless.*

its, it's   *Its* is a possessive pronoun; *it's* is a contraction of *it is* or *it has.*

just   Informal for *truly, very, accurately.* Choose an exact word.

INFORMAL   The earthquake was just dreadful.
FORMAL   The earthquake was unbelievably dreadful.

kind, sort   Singular forms, which may be modified by *that* or *this.* Use *those* or *these* to modify only plural forms, such as *these kinds.*

INFORMAL   Mr. Pratt prefers these kind.
FORMAL   Mr. Pratt prefers *this kind.*

kind of, sort of   Informal when used as an adverb meaning "somewhat, rather, after a fashion."

INFORMAL   The kitchen floor seems kind of uneven.
FORMAL   The kitchen floor seems *somewhat* uneven.

kind of a   Omit the *a* in your formal writing.

lady, gentleman   See **gentleman, lady.**

later, latter   Referring to time, *later* is the comparative form of *late. Latter* refers to the last named of two. If more than two are named, use *last,* not *latter.*

lay, lie   Do not confuse these verbs. See 7a, pages 819–20.

learn, teach   *Learn* means "to acquire knowledge"; *teach* means "to impart knowledge."

STANDARD   Miss Evans *taught* Earl only one week, but he *learned* how to study during that time.

leave, let   Do not use *leave* for *let. Leave* means "to depart from"; *let* means "to permit." But "Leave (*or* Let) me alone" is a standard idiom.

NONSTANDARD   I will not leave you go today.
STANDARD   I will not *let* you go today.

less, fewer   See **fewer, less.**

let's us   Redundant for *let's,* which is the contraction of *let us.*

lie, lay   Do not confuse. See 7a, pages 819–20.

like, as, as if   Informal English uses *like* either as a preposition or as a conjunction: "Work like a man." "This tastes like it should." Formal written English still prefers *as* or *as if* for the conjunction: "This tastes *as* it should." "He eats *as if* he were starving.

likely, liable   Informally, *liable* is substituted for *likely.* Formally, *likely* means "probable, to be expected," but *liable* means "susceptible to something unpleasant" or "legally responsible."

INFORMAL   My favorite program is liable to win an award.
FORMAL   My favorite program is *likely* to win an award.
FORMAL   John is *liable* to cut his foot with the ax.

line, case   See **case, line.**

locate   Informal for "settle, to make one's residence."

INFORMAL   He located in Texas.
FORMAL   He *settled* in Texas; he *located* his factory there.

lose, loose   Do not confuse. *Lose* means "to cease having." *Loose* (verb) means "to set free." *Loose* (adjective) means "free, not fastened."

lots, lots of, a lot   Informal for *many, much, a great deal.*

lovely   Informal for *delightful, highly pleasing.* Choose the exact word to fit your meaning.

mad   Still considered informal for *angry, furious.*

math   Informal for *mathematics.*

may be, maybe   Distinguish between the verb form *may be* and the adverb *maybe,* meaning "perhaps."

> April *may be* the best time for a vacation.
> *Maybe* the family will take a vacation in April.

may, can   See **can, may.**

mighty   Informally used for *very, exceedingly.*

> INFORMAL   The Wards are mighty good neighbors.
> FORMAL   In Rhodes stood the *mighty* statue of Colossus.

moral, morale   The noun *moral* means "lesson, maxim"; the adjective *moral* means "pertaining to right conduct, ethical." *Morale,* a noun, refers to "a cheerful, confident state of mind."

> What is the *moral* of Thurber's fable?
> Has the *morale* of the team improved?

most   See **almost, most.**

myself, himself, yourself   Properly intensive or reflexive pronouns. "I *myself* will go; I will see for myself." In general *myself* is not a proper substitute for *I* or *me;* but it is substituted informally (1) for *I* after comparisons with *than* or *as* ("Everyone worked as well as myself") or (2) for *me* when it is the second member of a compound object ("He allowed my brother and myself to go home.").

nice   Overworked as a vague word of approval. Find an exact word.

nohow   Nonstandard for *not at all.*

nowheres   Dialectal for *nowhere.*

number   See **amount, number.**

of, have   The preposition *of* is nonstandard when substituted in writing for the verb form *have.*

> NONSTANDARD   Mary could of (would of, may of, might of, must of, ought to of) done that last week.
> STANDARD   Mary could *have* (would *have,* may *have,* might *have,* must *have,* ought to *have*) done that last week.

off of   Informal for *off.*

> INFORMAL   The clock fell off of the desk.
> FORMAL   The clock fell *off* the desk.

OK, O.K., okay   All three are accepted as standard forms expressing general approval. A more specific word, however, usually replaces *OK* in formal writing.

one another, each other   See **each other, one another.**

ought   See **had ought.**

outside of   See **inside of, outside of.**

party, person, individual   See **individual, party, person.**

per   Careful writers generally avoid *per,* except in business English or in Latin phrases.

phenomena   Plural of *phenomenon.* See **data, criteria, phenomena.**

phone   Informal for *telephone.* Formally, use the full word.

photo   Informal shortening of *photograph.* Use the full word in your formal writing.

plenty   Informal as an adverb meaning *very.*

> INFORMAL   The chemistry test was plenty hard.
> FORMAL   The chemistry test was *very* hard.

P.M., A.M.   See **A.M., P.M.**

practical, practicable   *Practical* means "useful, sensible, not theoretical." *Practicable* means "feasible, capable of being put into practice."

> The sponsors are *practical,* and their plans are *practicable.*

principal, principle   Distinguish between *principal,* an adjective or noun meaning "chief" or "chief official," and the noun *principle,* meaning "fundamental truth."

prof   Informal for *professor.* Use the full word in your formal writing.

quite   An adverb meaning "entirely, positively." Used informally to mean "very, to a great extent, noticeably."

> INFORMAL   The lake is quite near.
> FORMAL   His guess was *quite* wrong.

raise, rise   See **rise, raise.**

real   Informal for *very, extremely.*

> INFORMAL   The victorious team was real tired.
> FORMAL   The victorious team was *extremely* tired.

reason is because   Formal English usually completes the construction *The reason is (was)* with a *that* clause or recasts the sentence.

> INFORMAL   The reason why he missed his class was because (*or* on account of) he overslept.
> FORMAL   The reason why he missed his class was *that* he overslept.
> FORMAL   He missed his class because he overslept.

reckon   Informal or dialectal for *guess, suppose, think.*

respectfully, respectively   *Respectfully* means "in a manner showing respect." *Respectively* means "each in the order given."

> Tom rose *respectfully* when Mrs. Hughes entered.
> The President commended the Army, Navy, and Air Force, *respectively.*

Reverend, Honorable   To be followed not only by the surname but also by the initials or some other title (such as *Mr.*) of the person referred to.

> The *Honorable Mr. Wilson* presided.
> The next speaker was *Rev. J. C. Boyle.*

right along   Informal for "without interruption, continuously."

> INFORMAL   Road construction moved right along.
> FORMAL   Road construction moved forward without interruption.

rise, raise   An intransitive verb, *rise* (*rose, risen*) means "to move upward." A transitive verb, *raise* (*raised*) means "to cause to move upward, to place erect."

> Franklin *rises* promptly at seven.
> Franklin *raises* his hand often in English class.

same, said, such   Except in legal documents, questionable substitutes for *it, this, that, before-mentioned.*

says, said   Not interchangeable. *Says* is present tense; *said,* past.

> NONSTANDARD   Allen dashed into the cafeteria and says, "Helen won the essay contest."
> STANDARD   Allen dashed into the cafeteria and *said,* "Helen won the essay contest."

scarcely   See **but, hardly, scarcely.**

seldom ever, seldom or ever   Use *seldom if ever, hardly ever.*

sit, set   See **Section 7, pages 819–20.**

so, so that *So* is an overworked word. Do not overwork *so* to join main clauses. In clauses denoting purpose, *so that* is usually preferred to *so*.

AMBIGUOUS	Ralph left so I could study.
CLEAR	Ralph left *so that* I could study.
CLEAR	Ralph left; *therefore,* I could study.

some Informal for *remarkable, striking, extraordinary.*

| INFORMAL | The St. Bernard is some dog! |
| FORMAL | The St. Bernard is a *remarkable* dog! |

someone, some one See **anyone, any one.**

somewheres Dialectal for *somewhere.*

sort, sort of, sort of a See **kind, kind of, kind of a.**

speak, speech The verb *speak* means "to talk"; the noun *speech* is "the act of speaking."

> Hamlet told the actors to *"speak the speech* trippingly on the tongue."

such Note carefully the formal uses of *such* listed in the dictionary. Avoid the vague, weak use of *such* or *such a.* When *such* is completed by a result clause, it should be followed by *that.*

INFORMAL	Twain has such a remarkable sense of humor.
FORMAL	Twain has a remarkable sense of humor.
FORMAL	There was *such* a rain *that* we could not drive.

See also **same, said, such.**

sure Informal for *surely* or *certainly.*

| INFORMAL | The sunrise sure was beautiful. |
| FORMAL | The sunrise *surely* was beautiful. |

sure and Informal for *sure to.*

suspicion Dialectal when used as a verb in place of *suspect.*

| DIALECTAL | I did not suspicion anything. |
| STANDARD | I did not *suspect* anything. |

take In your formal writing, avoid such informal expressions as *take it out on, to take up with, take in a movie.* Choose instead expressions such as *vent one's anger on, be friendly with, attend a movie.*

teach See **learn, teach.**

terrible, terribly *Terrible* is informal for *unpleasant, very bad. Terribly* is informal in the sense of *extremely, exceedingly.*

than, then *Than* and *then* are not interchangeable. Do not confuse the conjunction *than* with the adverb or adverbial conjunction *then,* which relates to time.

> Nylon wears better *than* rayon.
> First it snowed; *then* it sleeted.

their, there, they're Do not confuse. *Their* is a possessive pronoun; *there* is an adverb or an expletive; *they're* is the contraction of *they are.*

> *There* is no explanation for *their* refusal.
> *They're* installing a traffic light *there.*

theirself, theirselves Nonstandard for *themselves.*

these kind, these sort See **kind, sort.**

this here, that there, these here, them there Nonstandard expressions. Use *this, that, these, those.*

to, too, two Distinguish the preposition *to* ("*to* the store") from the adverb *too* ("*too* cold") and the numeral *two* ("*two* apples").

try and Informal for *try to.*

type of Do not omit the *of* in expressions such as "that type of film" or "that type of hero."

used to, supposed to Be sure to add the *-d* to *use* and *suppose* when writing, although the *-d* is often dropped in speech.

> Horses *used to* be indispensable.
> James was *supposed to* be in charge.

used to could Nonstandard or facetious for *used to be able.*

wait on Means *to attend, to serve.* Informal for *wait for.*

| FORMAL | I *waited for* the lecturer to begin. |

want Nonstandard if a *that* clause is its object.

| NONSTANDARD | I want that he should have a chance. |
| STANDARD | I want him to have a chance. |

want in, out, down, up, off, through. Informal or dialectal for *want to come in* or *get in, out, down, up, off, through.*

ways Informal for *way* referring to distance.

| INFORMAL | It's a long ways to Chicago. |
| FORMAL | It is a long *way* to Chicago. |

where Informal for *that.*

| INFORMAL | I saw in the newspaper where the strike had been settled. |
| FORMAL | I saw in the newspaper *that* the strike had been settled. |

where . . . at Redundant. Omit the *at.*

which, who Use *who* or *that* instead of *which* to refer to persons.

while Do not overuse as a substitute for *and* or *but.* The conjunction *while* usually refers to time.

who, which See **which, who.**

worst way *In the worst way* is slang for *very much.*

| NONSTANDARD | Mrs. Simmons wanted a color TV in the worst way. |
| STANDARD | Mrs. Simmons wanted a color TV *very much.* |

would of Nonstandard for *would have.*

would rather See **had better, had rather, would rather.**

you Avoid the awkward use of *you* as an indefinite pronoun.

| AWKWARD | When a person eats too much before bedtime, you may have nightmares. |
| BETTER | A person who eats too much before bedtime may have nightmares. |

you all A standard plural, now used generally in various sections of the United States, particularly in the South. Unacceptable if used to indicate the singular *you.*

you was Nonstandard for *you were.*

Exactness

20

Select words that are exact, idiomatic, and fresh.

Especially when writing, you should strive to choose words which express your ideas exactly, precise words which convey the emotional suggestions you intend. The choice of a right word will depend on your purpose, your point of view, and your reader.

If you can make effective use of the words you already know, you need not have a remarkably large vocabulary. In fact, as shown by the example below, professional writers often choose short, familiar words.

> I saw her sitting at her desk, taking the rubber band off the roll-call cards, running it back upon the fingers of her right hand, and surveying us all separately with quick little henlike turns of her head.... She was forever climbing up the margins of books and crawling between their lines, hunting for the little gold of phrase, making marks with a pencil.
> —JAMES THURBER[1]

Of course, as you gain experience in writing and reading, you will become increasingly aware of the need to add new words, both short and long, to your vocabulary. When you discover a valuable new word, make it your own by mastering its spelling, its meaning, and its exact use.

20a

Consult a good dictionary for the exact word needed to express your idea.

(1) Make sure that the dictionary gives the exact meaning you have in mind.

WRONG WORD   I hope my mother will find the mountain air *enervating*. [*Enervating* means "weakening or destroying the vigor of."]

RIGHT WORD   I hope my mother will find the mountain air *invigorating*. [*Invigorating* means "animating or giving vigor to."]

INEXACT   A registration official *brainwashed* the freshmen for forty-five minutes. [*Brainwashing* is "the alteration of personal convictions, beliefs, habits, and attitudes by means of intensive, coercive indoctrination."]

EXACT   A registration official *briefed* the freshmen for forty-five minutes. [To *brief* is "to prepare in advance by instructing or advising."]

Be careful to use the right conjunction to express the exact relation between words, phrases, and clauses.

INEXACT   The halfback is clumsy *and* speedy. [*And* adds or continues.]

EXACT   The halfback is clumsy *but* speedy. [*But* contrasts.]

Caution: Do not confuse words that are similar in spelling or meaning. If necessary, review the list of similar words in Section 18, Exercise 2. See also **19i**.

WRONG WORD   Early Christians stressed the *immorality* of the soul.
RIGHT WORD   Early Christians stressed the *immortality* of the soul.

▶ **EXERCISE 1**   First, consult your dictionary in order to find the exact meaning of each word below. Then write a sentence using each word correctly.

[1] From "Here Lies Miss Groby" by James Thurber, reprinted from the *New Yorker*, March 21, 1942, by permission of the *New Yorker*.

1. eminent, imminent
2. persuade, dissuade
3. repentance, remorse
4. subconscious, unconscious
5. paradox, enigma
6. astronomy, astrology
7. opaque, translucent
8. imply, insinuate
9. jargon, dialect
10. sophomore, sophomoric

(2) Select the word with the connotation, as well as the denotation, proper to the idea you wish to express.

The denotation of a word is what the word actually points to. According to the dictionary, the word *birthday* denotes "the day of one's birth or its anniversary." The connotation of a word is what the word suggests or implies. For example, the word *birthday* may connote a cake with lighted candles, gifts, parties, a special date to remember —or forget.

Connotation includes the emotions or associations that surround a word. For instance, *taxi, tin lizzie, limousine, convertible, station wagon, dump truck, hot rod*—all denote much the same thing to a traffic officer. But to various readers, and in various contexts, each word may have a special connotation. *Taxi* may suggest a city rush hour; *tin lizzie*, an historical museum; *limousine*, an airport; *convertible*, a homecoming parade; *station wagon*, children and dogs; *dump truck*, highway construction; *hot rod*, noisy fun. Similarly, *jalopy, bus, sedan, bookmobile, moving van, ambulance, squad car*—all denote a means of transportation, but each word carries a variety of connotations.

A word may be right in one situation, wrong in another. *Female parent*, for instance, is a proper expression in a biology laboratory, but it would be very inappropriate to say "John wept because of the death of his female parent." *Female parent* used in this sense is literally correct, but the connotation is wrong. The more appropriate word, *mother*, not only conveys the meaning denoted by *female parent*; it also conveys the reason why John wept. The first expression simply implies a biological relationship; the second is full of imaginative and emotional suggestions.

▶ **EXERCISE 2**   Give one dictionary definition (denotation) and one connotation for each of the following words.

1. yellow
2. Christmas
3. tolerance
4. grandfather
5. New York City
6. dog
7. China
8. orchids
9. library
10. existentialism

▶ **EXERCISE 3**   Be prepared to explain why the italicized words in the following sentences, although literally correct, might be inappropriate because of their connotations.

1. At the sound of the organ, the professors in full regalia *scampered* down the aisle and *tramped* to their assigned seats.
2. We are building our new home on the rim of a most delightful little *gulch*.
3. The soloist *tucked* his *fiddle* under his chin.
4. For the *enlightenment* of the other ladies, Mrs. Bromley measured upon her *belly* the area of her recent operation.
5. Homer squeezed a quantity of *chlorophyllaceous extrusion* onto his toothbrush.

6. Small fry at the Saturday movies *consume* scads of popcorn and peanuts.
7. The conclusion of the Gettysburg Address indicates that President Lincoln *hankered* for a new *spurt* of freedom.

▶ **EXERCISE 4** Be prepared to discuss those words below which because of their connotative value intensify the author's meaning.

1. In all America, no one was so lucky as the Southerner who was a part of this social revolution, of this determination to reaffirm the principles of what we have called the American dream. —RALPH MC GILL
2. A man with courage knows how to die standing up; he's got more guts than you could hang on a fence, gravel in his gizzard, and is as salty as Lot's wife and as gritty as fish eggs rolled in sand. —GEORGE D. HENDRICKS

(3) Select the specific word and the concrete word rather than the general and abstract.

A *general* word is all-inclusive, indefinite, sweeping in scope. A *specific* word is precise, definite, limited in scope.

general	specific	more specific
food	dessert	apple pie
prose	fiction	short stories
people	Americans	Mr. and Mrs. Smith

An *abstract* word deals with concepts, with ideas, with what cannot be touched, heard, or seen. A *concrete* word has to do with particular objects, with the practical, with what can be touched, heard, or seen.

ABSTRACT WORDS   democracy, loyal, evil, hate, charity
CONCRETE WORDS   mosquito, spotted, crunch, wedding, car

All writers must sometimes use abstract words, like *wisdom* or *integrity*, and occasionally resort to generalizations, like "Men through the ages have sought freedom from tyranny." These abstractions and generalizations are vital to communication of ideas and theories. To be effective, however, the use of these words must be based upon clearly understood and well-thought-out ideas.

Professional writers usually have little difficulty handling general and abstract words. Inexperienced writers, however, tend to use too many general and abstract words. The writing becomes drab and lifeless, because of the scarcity of specific, concrete words. Be as specific as you can. For example, instead of writing "a *thin* speaker," consider the possibility of using *gaunt, slender, lanky,* or *frail.* When you are tempted to write *pretty,* ask yourself whether *graceful, delicate, stunning, shapely, becoming, ravishing,* or *picturesque* would not be more appropriate.

The test for the specific word is contained in one or more of these questions: Exactly who? Exactly what? Precisely when? Exactly where? Precisely how? As you study the examples below, notice what a difference specific, concrete words can make in the expression of an idea.

DULL   The Army team finally advanced the ball. [*How* did they do it?]
SPECIFIC Adams, the Army quarterback, received the ball from center Jim Hawkins, retreated to his ten-yard line,

and threw a pass to left-end Smith, who was tackled on the Army thirty-five-yard line. [Specific details expand the idea.]

DULL   After going up the famous mountain, we went on down and saw the sights of Pompeii.
SPECIFIC After exploring the crater of Mount Vesuvius, we wandered through the streets of Old Pompeii and saw the lava-covered bodies of four men and a dog that had been buried alive by the eruption of 79 A.D.

DULL   She worked in her flower bed, digging around in it and looking over the plants. She always saw to it that no bugs or other pests got into her flowers.
SPECIFIC She took off a glove and put her strong fingers down into the forest of new green chrysanthemum sprouts that were growing around the old roots. She spread the leaves and looked down among the close-growing stems. No aphids were there, no sowbugs or snails or cutworms. Her terrier fingers destroyed such pests before they could get started. —JOHN STEINBECK[2]

▶ **EXERCISE 5** Using a dictionary of synonyms if you wish, choose five specific words which might be appropriately substituted for each of the following: (1) *see,* (2) *walk,* (3) *great,* (4) *bad,* (5) *happy,* (6) *man,* (7) *get,* (8) *nice,* (9) *think,* (10) *love.*

EXAMPLE *eat:* munch, nibble, bolt, gulp, feast on

▶ **EXERCISE 6** Select from the words inside parentheses the specific word which best fits the context of the sentence.

1. Her moral indignation was always (high, evident, on the boil). —ALDOUS HUXLEY
2. A janitor collects garbage in a cart that (sounds, rumbles, squeaks) on the broken tile like a tumbril. —JOHN BARTLOW MARTIN
3. Her beauty was (outstanding, fabulous, paralyzing)— beyond all words, all experience, all dream. —CONRAD AIKEN
4. He had (flaxen, yellow, light) hair, weak blue eyes, and the general demeanor of a saintly but timid (person, animal, codfish). —P. G. WODEHOUSE
5. The plumber lifted his strong, (weathered, tough, dark) face and looked curiously at her. —KAY BOYLE
6. He (threw away, got rid of, flipped away) the dead match and blew (a puff of smoke, a stream of gray) into the evening. —FLANNERY O'CONNOR
7. Presently there came a spectacle of a man (getting, working, churning) himself into the deepest rage over the immobility of a house. —STEPHEN CRANE
8. From the main street outside came the echoes of holiday (celebration, hysteria, noises). —CARSON MC CULLERS
9. Two girls went (skittering, running, hurrying) by in short transparent raincoats, one green, one red, their heads (tucked, bent, held) against the drive of the rain. —KATHERINE ANNE PORTER
10. The women were disposed about a table of plate glass and their nine handbags lay in (polkadots, a pile, an archipelago) upon its great (lucid, opaque, serene) surface. —LIONEL TRILLING

[2] From *The Long Valley* by John Steinbeck. Copyright 1937, 1965 by John Steinbeck. Reprinted by the permission of The Viking Press, Inc.

▶ **EXERCISE 7** Using specific words, rewrite the following sentences.

1. My father looked at my grade in science and said what I least expected to hear.
2. At the store we priced a number of items.
3. The boy made a bad mistake the morning of his first day at school.
4. My relatives gave me two gifts which pleased me.
5. Only Fred was in the room; he sat slumped in a chair reading a magazine.
6. Marvin's car needs new parts before the family uses it for a trip.
7. Various aspects of the television show were criticized in the newspaper.
8. Many things in our back yard are unattractive.
9. The player moved forward quickly and caught the ball.
10. During that time the traffic officer arrested more than twenty people for the same violation.

(4) Use appropriate figurative language to create imaginative or emotional impressions.

A figure of speech is the use of a word in an imaginative rather than in a literal sense. The two chief figures of speech are the simile and the metaphor. A *simile* is an explicit comparison between two things of a different kind or quality, usually introduced by *like* or *as*. A *metaphor* is an implied comparison of dissimilar things; words of comparison, such as *like* and *as*, are not used.

SIMILES   This land is still there. The motorist on Highway 66 sees it swim toward him *like the blur of a microscope's field sharpening toward focus.*
— WALLACE STEGNER

As a parasol with many flounces, as a peacock with many feathers, shuts its flounces, folds its feathers, so she subsided and shut herself as she sank down in the leather armchair. — VIRGINIA WOOLF

METAPHORS   Thought is *the weariest of all the Titans.*
— J. FRANK DOBIE

There was some talk of expulsion, but his record showed *a neat picket fence of A's broken only twice by filigree B's.* — JOHN ANTHONY WEST

Metaphors and similes are especially valuable because they are concrete and tend to point up essential relationships that cannot otherwise be communicated. (For faulty metaphors see **23c.**)

Two other frequently used figures of speech are hyperbole and personification. *Hyperbole* is deliberate overstatement or fanciful exaggeration. *Personification* attributes to the nonhuman (inanimate objects, animals, ideas) those characteristics possessed only by the human.

HYPERBOLES
At our house, washing dishes is a *Sisyphean task.*

I, for one, don't expect till I die to be so good a man as I am at this minute, for just now I'm *fifty thousand feet high—a tower with all the trumpets shouting.* — G. K. CHESTERTON

PERSONIFICATIONS
The hurricane perversely changed her course, slashing her way through Louisiana swamps with malicious determination.

They sleep and the moon and the sun sleep and even the ocean sleeps sometimes on certain days when there is no current and a flat calm. — ERNEST HEMINGWAY

▶ **EXERCISE 8** Test the exactness and force of the metaphors, similes, hyperboles, and personifications in the following sentences by attempting to state the same ideas literally.

1. All these people zipped and caromed about the pristine world of the screen as jazzily as a convention of water bugs. — JAMES AGEE
2. Outside, evening had laid its blanket on the city. — ANDREW SINCLAIR
3. As the trout's back came up out of the water the minnows jumped wildly. They sprinkled the surface like a handful of shot thrown into the water. — ERNEST HEMINGWAY
4. When a headache and he went to bed together, they were a noisy pair. — CLARENCE DAY
5. Her eyes, lost in the fatty ridges of her face, looked like two small pieces of coal pressed into a lump of dough as they moved from one face to another while the visitors stated their errand. — WILLIAM FAULKNER
6. The odd thing about truth is that it keeps changing its clothes. — CURTIS BOK
7. She was ready half an hour before the time of departure and she paid some visits on the floor in her powder-blue gown and her hat that looked like one minute after an April shower. — F. SCOTT FITZGERALD
8. Every time a Cooper person is in peril, and absolute silence is worth four dollars a minute, he is sure to step on a dry twig. — MARK TWAIN
9. Ushers standing at fixed intervals wave their torches like regimented fireflies. — FRANCIS RUSSELL
10. To tell *all* about ourselves in one vast breath is really to press the whole round world in the lemon-squeezer of our minds . . . . — J. B. PRIESTLEY

▶ **EXERCISE 9** Complete each of the following by using a simile, metaphor, hyperbole, or personification. Use effective figures of speech. (For instance, instead of the familiar metaphor *Time is money!* you might use *Time is a physician.*)

1. My first in-class theme, as the professor read it to the class, sounded like . . . .
2. The father of the valedictorian was as proud as . . . .
3. The ragweed in Texas . . . .
4. Death is . . . .
5. Like a bewildered freshman during registration, the Pacific cold front . . . .
6. As it glistened in the sun, the jet was . . . .
7. Fans pushing into the stadium reminded me of . . . .
8. As George left art lab he resembled . . . .
9. Moaning in front of the full-length mirror, Gladys said, "I . . . ."
10. To Farmer Selby, that mangy, flea-ridden hound is . . . .
11. The steamer . . . .
12. Helen's hat looked like . . . .
13. As confident as . . . , I stepped forward.
14. Like . . . , the class sat speechless.
15. Driving on a crowded freeway, Uncle Robert is . . . .

20b
Use the exact idiom demanded by English usage.

At the very heart of the English language are idioms. These are everyday expressions which distinctly characterize a language and make it different from any other language. They are acceptable patterns of usage that do not conform to rules. One type of English idiom (such as *for many a year*) cannot be analyzed or justified grammatically; another type (such as *I completely lost my head!*) cannot be taken literally, cannot be sensibly translated word for word into another language. Dictionaries treat many idiomatic phrases. See, for instance, the idioms built around *go* and listed after *go* in your dictionary.

Ordinarily native speakers use idiomatic English naturally and effectively, but once in a while they may have difficulty choosing idiomatic prepositions. Be careful to use the exact phrasing for each idiom, not some unidiomatic approximation.

UNIDIOMATIC   comply to, superior than, buy off of
IDIOMATIC   comply with, superior to, buy from

When you are in doubt about what preposition to use after a given word, look up that word in the dictionary. Take, for instance, the word *angry*. The *Standard College Dictionary* lists these idiomatic phrases: "*angry with* (or *at*) his brother; *angry at* (or *about*) an insult."

Dictionaries also classify many idioms as *formal, informal, dialectal,* etc. For example, the *Standard College Dictionary* makes usage distinctions such as the following:

INFORMAL   Try and catch me.
FORMAL   Try to catch me.
DIALECTAL   I'll wait on you if it won't take long.
STANDARD   I'll wait for you if it won't take long.

Always choose the idiom that is both exact and appropriate.

▶ EXERCISE 10   Consult a good college dictionary to determine what prepositions are idiomatically used with (1) *agree*, (2) *compare*, (3) *differ*, (4) *consist*, and (5) *deal*. Use each of these verbs correctly in two sentences, each with a different preposition.

▶ EXERCISE 11   In a good college dictionary study the idiomatic phrases treated under *catch, put, set, tie,* and *win*. Select three different idioms formed with each verb, and illustrate each idiom in a sentence.

▶ EXERCISE 12   Choose the idiomatic preposition in each set of parentheses below. If you are not sure whether a given phrase is idiomatic, consult a good college dictionary.

1. Buy your car (from, off of) the man next door.
2. There was no sales tax prior (to, than) 1961.
3. That regiment is equal (for, to) the assignment.
4. Does Mr. Mason agree (with, on) the president's opinion?
5. Jo stays angry (with, at) himself.
6. We expect to be (at, to) home all day.
7. Barbara is utterly oblivious (about, of) noise when she studies chemistry.
8. In return for their labor, Americans expect to have the necessities (of, for) life.
9. Robert has gone in search (of, for) a secondhand car.
10. Drivers are expected to comply (with, to) traffic laws.

20c
Select fresh expressions instead of trite, worn-out ones.

Such trite expressions as *a word to the wise, as clear as mud, the almighty dollar,* and *the long arm of the law* were once striking and effective. What you may not know is that excessive use has made them trite. They are now stock phrases in the language, automatic clichés that have lost their effectiveness. Good writers do not use trite, well-known phrases when fresh, original expressions are more effective. Compare the effectiveness of the following sentences.

TRITE   *It goes without saying* that we often feel *as helpless as a baby* when we try to *hitch our wagon to a star.*
ORIGINAL   When we reach out for the stars, our limitations become grotesquely apparent.   —ARTHUR KOESTLER

To avoid trite phrases you must be aware of current usage. Catch phrases and slogans pass quickly from ephemeral popularity into the Old Words' Home. Glittering political shibboleths like *grass roots, pulse of public opinion,* and *the common man* are notoriously short-lived. Commercial advertising also bestows its *kiss of death* on an honorable phrase. When a mattress company bids you *sleep in peace* or promises a *midsummer night's dream* on their *airy fairy beds,* when blankets are publicized as *soft as down* or *gentle as a baby's breath,* mark the italicized words as trite expressions, for the time being at least.

Every writer uses a few clichés, such as *the weaker sex* or *beating about the bush.* And nearly every writer occasionally quotes familiar proverbs, Biblical verses, and lines from poetry—for example, "Who steals my purse steals trash . . . ." or "Three may keep a secret if two of them are dead." It is not unusual for a professional writer to give a new twist to an old saying—for instance, *easier done than said, to make a short story long,* or *There's madness in his method.* No good writer, however, relies heavily on the phraseology of others; he chooses his own words to communicate his own ideas.

▶ EXERCISE 13   Construct sentences which contain acceptable substitutes for ten of the hackneyed expressions listed below. In your sentences include within brackets the hackneyed expressions you replace. Be careful not to replace one hackneyed expression with another.

1. after all is said and done
2. agree to disagree
3. all work and no play
4. better late than never
5. cold as ice
6. easier said than done
7. green with envy
8. last but not least
9. white as a sheet
10. on the ball (on the beam)
11. bitter end
12. busy as a bee
13. by leaps and bounds
14. slow but sure
15. straight from the shoulder
16. sweat of his brow
17. this day and age
18. too funny for words
19. wee small hours
20. none the worse for wear
21. good personality
22. needless to say

▶ EXERCISE 14   First make a list of ten hackneyed expressions that you often use; then rewrite each by using exact, straightforward words of your own.

▶ EXERCISE 15   As you revise the following sentences, use original, specific diction in place of the italicized trite and general words.

TRITE (AND GENERAL)   I took the collie to chase rabbits in the upper fields, but its actions showed that it *did not have enough sense to come in out of the rain.*

ORIGINAL (AND SPECIFIC)   I took the one-eyed collie to chase rabbits in the upper fields, but it barked at ducks and brought me a tramp's shoe from a hedge, and lay down with its tail wagging in a rabbit hole.   —DYLAN THOMAS

1. *In this day and age* too much emphasis is placed on *filthy lucre.*
2. The telephone rang *at just the psychological moment.*
3. At the blast of the siren, the culprits *beat a hasty retreat.*
4. The professor spoke *straight from the shoulder.*
5. Fred was grateful to *the powers that be* for escaping the accident.
6. Father saw to it that my plans were *nipped in the bud.*
7. The *tall, dark, and handsome* actor was *on the ball.*
8. Examination week approached *slowly but surely.*
9. When the *blushing bride* entered the room, she was *the center of attraction.*
10. His *better half* was *busy as a bee* getting the house ready for company.
11. Though the score was forty to ten, the Eagles fought hard *to the bitter end.*
12. The ice cream was soup, and the hamburgers were *as cold as ice.*
13. *After all is said and done,* a student normally gets the grade he makes.
14. *Last but not least,* high taxes ought not discourage the small businessman.
15. *It stands to reason that* gravity is an important factor in space exploration.
16. On one side of the stage stood the American flag *in all its glory.*
17. Henry earns $52 a week by *the sweat of his brow.*
18. That highly ambitious secretary believes in *all work and no play.*
19. Knowing he was *doomed to disappointment,* he sank to *the depths of despair.*
20. After *working all day like a Trojan,* Mr. Gladwater *was tired but happy* as he *wended his way homeward.*

OTHER EXERCISES ON EXACTNESS

▶ EXERCISE 16   Look up the definitions of the following words in your dictionary; then use each word appropriately in an original sentence.

1. fabulous	6. cute	11. exotic	16. expedient
2. scandal	7. latent	12. dialect	17. equivocal
3. aspire	8. exploit	13. liberal	18. alleviate
4. judgment	9. amoral	14. simony	19. temperance
5. psychic	10. cynical	15. ironical	20. universality

▶ EXERCISE 17   The following passage from G. K. Chesterton is an excellent example of precise writing. Study the italicized expressions first with the aid of a dictionary and then in the context of the sentence and the paragraph. Substitute a synonym for each italicized word and compare its effectiveness with that of the original.

If a *prosperous* modern man, with a high hat and a frock-coat, were to solemnly *pledge* himself before all his clerks and friends to count the leaves on every third tree in Holland Walk, to hop up to the City on one leg every Thursday, to repeat the whole of Mill's "Liberty" seventy-six times, to collect three hundred dandelions in fields belonging to any one of the name of Brown, to remain for thirty-one hours holding his left ear in his right hand, to sing the names of all his aunts in order of age on the top of an omnibus, or make any such unusual undertaking, we should immediately *conclude* that the man was mad, or as it is sometimes expressed, was "an artist in life." Yet these *vows* are not more extraordinary than the vows which in the Middle Ages and in similar periods were made, not by *fanatics* merely, but by the greatest figures in civic and national civilization—by kings, judges, poets, and priests. One man swore to chain two mountains together, and the great chain hung there, it was said, for ages as a monument of that *mystical folly.* Another swore that he would find his way to Jerusalem with a patch over his eyes, and died looking for it. It is not easy to see that these two *exploits,* judged from a *strictly rational standpoint,* are any saner than the acts above suggested. A mountain is commonly a stationary and reliable object which it is not necessary to chain up at night like a dog. And it is not easy at first sight to see that a man pays a very high compliment to the Holy City by setting out for it under conditions which render it *to the last degree improbable* that he will ever get there.[3]

▶ EXERCISE 18   Carefully read the following paragraph, which sets forth in humorous fashion one of the home cures used by the English for the common cold. Be prepared for a class discussion of the author's appropriate diction, of his figurative language, of his choice of concrete, specific words.

[1] The Fresh-Air treatment is practiced only by those large red-faced men in check suits who look you in the eye, slap their chests, and declare they've never owned an overcoat or been to a doctor in their lives, as if claiming freedom from original sin. [2] They have a simple attitude to illness: it's all "psychological," from smallpox to fractured femurs. [3] But they are only human, and in time claimed by both death and colds. [4] The first sneeze affects them like a starter's pistol: they tear off their ties and waistcoats, stamp around the house throwing open the windows, jump into a cold bath, and upset their wives by doing breathing exercises all night in bed. [5] The discomfort in which they wallow for a fortnight makes no difference to the course of the disease, but by rendering their surroundings unfit for human habitation they rarely manage to infect anyone else.[4]

---

[3] From "A Defence of Rash Vows" by G. K. Chesterton, reprinted by permission of J. M. Dent & Sons, Ltd.

[4] From "The Common Cold" by Richard Gordon, reprinted from the *Atlantic Monthly,* January, 1955. By permission of the *Atlantic Monthly* and Curtis Brown, Ltd.

▶ EXERCISE 19   Analyze Paragraph 28 of Section **31**, page 901, for choice of words.

▶ EXERCISE 20   Choose the word inside parentheses which best suits the context of each item below.

1. To be an American and unable to play baseball is comparable to being a Polynesian unable to (swim, debate, drive).   —JOHN CHEEVER
2. Moonbeams (splash, twinkle, glow) and spill wildly in the rain.   —VIRGINIA WOOLF
3. Every evening at the rush hour the subway (releases, disgorges, gives out) its millions.   —JACQUES BARZUN
4. The scarecrow gave them an (unusual, eerie, elated) feeling when they saw it from the bedroom window at twilight.   —WILLIAM MAXWELL
5. Mr. Brook was a somewhat (pastel, ordinary, insipid) person.   —CARSON MC CULLERS
6. There was a roaring in my ears like the rushing of (music, rivers, breezes).   —STEPHEN VINCENT BENÉT
7. Superstitions, as Bacon said, like (birds, moths, bats) fly best in twilight, and the twilight of confused liberalism seems particularly favorable to them.   —BERGEN EVANS

Wordiness

21

Avoid wordiness. Repeat words only when needed for emphasis or clarity.

Today the best professional writers make each word count, avoiding the telegraphic as well as the verbose style. As you write and revise your composition, make sure that every word has a reason for being there, and eliminate all deadwood. When striking out unnecessary, meaningless, inappropriate words, keep in mind Allan Simpson's observation: "Every slaughtered syllable is a good deed."

21a

Omit words or phrases that add nothing to the meaning.[1]

Notice below that the words in brackets contribute nothing to meaning. Avoid such wordiness in your own writing.

1. all [of the] new styles [in this day and age]
2. yellow [in color], small [in size], eleven [in number]
3. circulated [around], cooperated [together], inside [of]
4. [true] facts, [erroneous] fallacies, a widow [woman]
5. [it was] in 1965 [that], at 9 A.M. [in the morning]

▶ EXERCISE 1   Without changing the meaning, strike out unnecessary words in the following sentences. Write *C* after each sentence that needs no revision.

[1] Bureaucratic jargon, called "gobbledygook," is often extremely wordy. See the example on page 858.

1. As a usual rule, all of the new cars of today have factory guarantees.
2. About midnight Halloween evening, Lucille dropped in for a short, unexpected visit.
3. It was in the year of 1964 that the joint partnership began to dissolve.
4. Architect James Hoban, the designer of the White House, was born in Dublin.
5. The venetian blind factory is close to the point of bankruptcy.
6. One reason why we honor Lincoln is because of the fact that he saved the Union.
7. The skillful English director made ruthless murder and flagrant blackmail the absurd hobbies of hilarious comedians.
8. The usual consensus of the majority is that Columbus discovered America.
9. Los Angeles is very different in various ways from the city of San Francisco.
10. In this day and time, it is difficult to find in the field of science a chemist who shows as much promise for the future as Joseph Blake shows.

21b

If necessary, revise the structure of the sentence to avoid wordiness.

Notice in the following examples how changes in sentence structure reduce two sentences of sixteen words to one sentence of eleven, ten, nine, and finally six words.

> There was a mist which hung like a veil. It obscured the top of the mountain.
> The mist *hung like a veil* and obscured the mountain top. [Part of a compound predicate]
> The mist, *hanging like a veil*, obscured the mountain top. [Participial phrase]
> The mist, *like a veil*, obscured the mountain top. [Prepositional phrase]
> The mist *veiled* the mountain top. [Word]

Any one of these sentences may, depending on the context, meet the special needs of the writer. By studying these examples, you can learn methods of revising the structure of your sentences to eliminate undesirable wordiness.

▶ EXERCISE 2   Revise the structure of the following sentences to eliminate wordiness.

1. There were six freshmen who volunteered.
2. When the Indians made tools, they used flint and bone as materials.
3. A new addition has been built at the side of the house, and this addition has been developed into a library.
4. Another thing is good health. It is one of our great blessings. It may be had through proper diet and exercise. Rest is also desirable.
5. My uncle was a tall man. He had a long nose. Over his right eye he had a deep scar.
6. If any workers were disgruntled, they made their complaints to the man who was in charge as manager.
7. Personally I believe it was the Spaniards rather than the Indians who first brought horses and ponies to America.

8. The grass was like a carpet. It covered the whole lawn. The color of the grass was a deep blue.
9. When anyone wants to start a garden, it is best to begin in the early part of the spring of the year.
10. Near the center of the campus of our university a new building has been erected, and it is constructed of red brick.

21c

Avoid careless or needless repetition of words or ideas.

Unless you are repeating intentionally for emphasis or for clarity in transitions, be careful not to write the same word twice or to write the same thing twice in slightly different words.

AWKWARD   Since the committee has already made three *reports*, only one *report* remains to be *reported* on.

BETTER   Since the committee has already made three reports, it has only one more to present.

REPETITIOUS   Julia delights in giving parties; entertaining guests is a real pleasure for her.

CONCISE   Julia delights in giving parties.

Use a pronoun instead of needlessly repeating a noun. Several pronouns in succession, even in successive sentences, may refer to the same antecedent noun, so long as the reference remains clear.

NEEDLESS REPETITION   The upper-middlebrow consumer takes his culture seriously, as seriously as his job allows, for *the consumer* is gainfully employed. In *the consumer's* leisure hours he reads Toynbee or Osbert Sitwell's serialized memoirs. *The upper-middlebrow consumer* goes to museum openings and to the theater, and *the consumer* keeps up on the foreign films.

BETTER   The upper-middlebrow consumer takes his culture seriously, as seriously as his job allows, for he is gainfully employed. In his leisure hours he reads Toynbee or Osbert Sitwell's serialized memoirs. He goes to museum openings and to the theater and he keeps up on the foreign films.

—RUSSELL LYNES

▶ EXERCISE 3   Revise the following sentences to eliminate wordiness and useless repetition.

1. In the last act of the play there is the explanation of the title of the play.
2. In the decade from 1950 to 1960, enrollments at universities doubled; in 1960 there were twice as many students as in 1950.
3. That morning we went to Jones Beach so that we could enjoy all the pleasures that that famous playground affords.
4. The National Gallery of Art, which is in Washington, D.C., and which contains the Mellon, Kress, and Widener collections of paintings and sculpture, is one of the largest marble structures in the entire world.
5. The radio announcer repeatedly kept saying, "Buy Peterson's Perfect Prawns," over and over and over again.
6. There were fifty people in the hospital ward who were among those who received great benefit from the new drug.

7. I had an advantage over the other contestants because of the fact that I had just looked up the word myself in a dictionary.
8. I got busy and got my assignment.
9. He found the problem of discovering the legal status of the migrant workers an almost insoluble problem.
10. In order that a man may apply to become a citizen of the United States he must make out an application stating his intention to become a citizen.

▶ EXERCISE 4   Rewrite the following passage to eliminate wordiness and useless repetition.

[1] Samuel Clemens (Mark Twain) was born in 1835 at Florida, County of Monroe, State of Missouri; but while he was still quite young, his family moved to Hannibal, a small Mississippi River town, where Samuel as a boy spent the days of his youth, and he grew up to young manhood there. [2] In 1853 Samuel Clemens left this small Mississippi River town of Hannibal to see something of the world. [3] In his itinerant wandering during the next four years which followed, Clemens worked at the printing trade in printing shops of various cities in the East and Middle West from the Mississippi to the Atlantic seaboard. [4] In Cincinnati, Ohio, in the year of 1857 Clemens took passage on a river steamboat bound down the river for New Orleans, Louisiana. [5] On this trip down the river Clemens met the pilot who steered the boat, named Mr. Horace Bixby, who agreed for the sum of five hundred dollars in money to teach young Clemens (Mark Twain) the art of piloting boats up and down the river. [6] One may read of Mark Twain's experience as a cub pilot apprentice in his book which he wrote about it and called *Life on the Mississippi*.

Omission of Necessary Words

22

Do not omit a word or phrase necessary to the meaning of the sentence.

Two reasons usually account for omissions of necessary words in student writing. The main reason is that the writer's mind is ahead of his pen; he thinks the word but does not write it. A second reason is that habits of informal speech reveal themselves in writing; an omission which may go unnoticed in spoken English may make a written sentence awkward or confusing.

The analyst talked about the tax dollar goes. [The writer thought "talked about where" but did not write *where*.]
I been considering changing my major. [Omission of *v* sound in saying *I've been* causes the omission of *have* in writing.]

To avoid omitting necessary words, you should not only carefully proofread your papers but also study the rules in this chapter.

22a

Do not omit an article, a pronoun, a conjunction, or a preposition that is necessary to make your meaning clear.

(1) Omitted article or pronoun

AWKWARD   Fog grounded all planes only week ago.
BETTER   Fog grounded all planes only *a* week ago.
CONFUSING   A man has a job there makes good money.
CLEAR   A man *who* has a job there makes good money.

Note: If it is necessary to indicate plural number, repeat a pronoun or an article before the second part of a compound.

> My mother and father were there. [Clearly two persons—repetition of *my* before *father* not necessary]
> A friend and *a* helper stood nearby. [Two persons clearly indicated by repetition of *a*]

(2) Omitted conjunction

CONFUSING   They noticed the young men who made up the crew were eager to start. [*Young men* can be momentarily mistaken for the object of *noticed*.]
BETTER   They noticed *that* the young men who made up the crew were eager to start.

Note: The conjunction *that* is frequently omitted as an introduction to clauses when the omission is not confusing.

> Sid thinks the National League will win.

(3) Omitted preposition

AWKWARD   Winter the Bakers ski at Chestnut Lodge.
BETTER   In winter the Bakers ski at Chestnut Lodge.

Note: Some idiomatic phrases indicating time or place regularly omit the preposition.

> The package was mailed Friday (*on Friday*).
> Mrs. Melton stayed home (*at home*).

22b

Do not omit a necessary verb or a necessary auxiliary.

AWKWARD   The play is good and the characters interesting. [Singular *is* may be used with singular *play* but not with plural *characters*.]
BETTER   The play is good and the characters *are* interesting. [The correct verb is supplied for *characters*.]
AWKWARD   He never has and never will be given proper recognition. [*Be* is the correct auxiliary for *will* but not for *has*.]
BETTER   He never has *been* given proper recognition, and he never will be. [The correct auxiliary is supplied for *has*.]

22c

Do not omit words necessary to complete comparisons (or other constructions).

INCOMPLETE   Ed's income is less than his wife.
COMPLETE   Ed's income is less than *that of* his wife.
INCOMPLETE   Snow here is as scarce as Miami.
COMPLETE   Snow here is as scarce as *it is in* Miami.

CONFUSING   Bruce likes me more than Ann.
CLEAR   Bruce likes me more than *he likes* Ann (OR more than Ann *does*).
INCOMPLETE   Harry is as old, if not older, than Paul.
COMPLETE   Harry is as old *as*, if not older than, Paul.
BETTER   Harry is as old *as* Paul, if not older.
INFORMAL   Mr. Perkins is as shrewd as any man in the office.
FORMAL   Mr. Perkins is as shrewd as any *other* man in the office.

Note: Incomplete comparisons often occur in advertising copy.

> Inferior detergents are far more expensive. [More expensive than what?]

Note: Once a frame of reference has been established, an intelligible comparison may be made without explicit mention of the second term of the comparison.

> From here, it is forty miles to the nearest ranch. The nearest town is even farther.

Formal writing avoids such intensives as *so, such,* and *too* without a completing phrase or clause.

INFORMAL   Peter was too ill.
FORMAL   Peter was too ill *to stay on the job.*
INFORMAL   Sue is so tone deaf.
FORMAL   Sue is so tone deaf *that she cannot tell "Three Blind Mice" from "The Star-Spangled Banner."*

▶ EXERCISE 1 Supply words that are omitted in the following sentences. Write *C* after every sentence that needs no revision.

1. The mystery of the stolen jewels reminds me of other mysteries like Sherlock Holmes.
2. The paint on sale is better than any paint on the market.
3. I found the performance too dull.
4. A girl has a face like that ought to win a beauty contest!
5. Our new car uses more gasoline.
6. In our state the winter is as mild as Louisiana.
7. Some people like cars with bucket seats much better.
8. Chifford cars are longer, faster, more economical to operate.
9. I always have and always will live in Kansas City.
10. The plains are mostly given over to cattle raising, not farming.
11. If Jack is in a profession he is not trained, he will not succeed.
12. The lawyer had to prove whatever the witness said was false.
13. You are as good, if not better, than anyone else.
14. Jim's wife and mother are standing beside him.
15. The merchandise is finest quality but the prices high.
16. Mr. Carter paid me more than Jim.
17. The pine trees here are as tall as Vermont.
18. Our city park is as attractive, if not more attractive, than yours.
19. The novels of Graham Greene are so controversial.
20. The work of the farmer requires longer hours than a plumber.

▶ EXERCISE 2 Supply words needed in the following paragraph.

¹ According to manual for drivers, every operator should know the state laws and traffic rules. ² For example, he should know legal speeds both in town and out of town, state highways and city streets. ³ He should also be aware of meaning of hand signals and blinking lights. ⁴ Every good driver knows that safety is so important. ⁵ He keeps at a safe distance from the ahead on the highway, he slows down before entering an intersection, and he is always in the proper lane for turning. ⁶ A safe driver understands policemen who give traffic orders take precedence over signs or lights that give conflicting directions. ⁷ Moreover, a driver who is safe is far more courteous, for he knows that at times discourtesy can actually break a law or even take a life. ⁸ Knowledge and courtesy have and always will be among the characteristics of an excellent driver.

EFFECTIVE SENTENCES

Unity and Logical Thinking

Unity, coherence, emphasis, variety—these are fundamental qualities of effective prose. Unity and coherence in sentences help to make ideas logical and clear. Emphasis makes them forceful. Variety lends interest. All these are usually found in good writing.

23

Write unified, logical sentences.

A sentence is unified when all its parts contribute to one clear idea or impression. The ideal sentence is, of course, one with parts that form a perfect whole so that a clause, a phrase, or even a word cannot be changed without disturbing the clarity of thought or the focus of the impression. A study of this section should help you to write logical, unified sentences, sentences which are not cluttered with obscurities, irrelevancies, or excessive details.

23a

Bring into the sentence only related thoughts; use two or more sentences for thoughts not closely related.

As you write a sentence, make sure that the ideas in it are related and that the relationship is immediately clear to the reader. Use two or more sentences to develop ideas which do not belong in one sentence because of the lack of close relationship.

UNRELATED   The ancient name for Paris, a city which today has about 2,800,000 inhabitants, was Lutetia.

IMPROVED   Paris today has about 2,800,000 inhabitants. The ancient name of the city was Lutetia. [The two unrelated ideas are put into separate sentences, possibly in different parts of the paper.]

UNRELATED   Yesterday Ted sprained his ankle, and he could not find his chemistry notes anywhere.

RELATED   Accident-prone all day yesterday, Ted not only sprained his ankle but also lost his chemistry notes. [The relationship of the two ideas is made clear by the addition of the opening phrase.]

▶ EXERCISE 1 All ten sentences below contain ideas which are apparently unrelated. Adding words when necessary, rewrite each of the sentences to indicate clearly a relationship between ideas. If you can establish no close relationship, put the ideas in separate sentences.

1. I hate strong windstorms, and pecans pelted my bedroom roof all night.
2. The fence and barn need repairs, and why are property taxes so high?
3. There are many types of bores at social gatherings, but personally I prefer a quiet evening at home.
4. A telephone lineman who works during heavy storms can prove a hero, and cowards can be found in any walk of life.
5. Although barbers are not often found in the unemployed ranks, haircuts contribute to the economy of the nation.
6. Jones was told to hire a tutor in French immediately, but the long hours of work at a service station kept his grades low.
7. Macbeth was not the only man to succumb to ambition, and Professor Stetson, for example, likes to draw parallels between modern men and literary characters.
8. Brad sent his sweetheart a dozen red roses, and she sang on a fifteen-minute program over KTUV.
9. The food in the cafeteria has been the subject of many jokes, and most college students do not look underfed.
10. Birds migrate to the warmer countries in the fall and in summer get food by eating worms and insects which are a pest to the farmer.

23b

Excessive detail and clumsy, excessive subordination should not be allowed to obscure the central thought of the sentence.

Bring into a sentence only pertinent details. Omit tedious minutiae and numerous side remarks. Avoid also clumsy, overlapping subordination, the house-that-Jack-built construction.

EXCESSIVE SUBORDINATION   Never before have I known a student who was so ready to help a friend who had gotten into trouble which involved money.

BETTER   Never before have I known a student so ready to help a friend in financial trouble.

EXCESSIVE DETAIL   In 1788, when Andrew Jackson, then a young man of twenty-one years who had been living in the Carolinas, still a virgin country, came into Tennessee, a turbulent place of unknown opportunities, to enforce the law as the new prosecuting attorney, he had the qualities in him which would make him equal to the task.

BETTER   In 1788, when Andrew Jackson came into Tennessee as the new prosecuting attorney, he had the necessary qualifications for the task.

As you strive to eliminate irrelevant details, remember that length alone does not make a sentence ineffective. Good writers can compose very long sentences, sometimes of paragraph length, without loss of unity. The use of parallel structure, balance, rhythm, careful punctuation, well-placed connectives can bind a sentence into perfect unity. Observe the effective repetition (indicated by italics) in Winston Churchill's famous sentence:

We shall go on to the end, *we shall fight* in France, *we shall fight* on the seas and oceans, *we shall fight* with growing confidence and growing strength in the air, *we shall defend* our Island, whatever the cost may be, *we shall fight* on the beaches, *we shall fight* on the landing grounds, *we shall fight* in the fields and in the streets, *we shall fight* in the hills; *we shall never surrender,* and even if, which I do not for a moment believe, this Island or a large part of it were subjugated and starving, then our Empire beyond the seas, armed and guarded by the British Fleet, *would carry on the struggle,* until, in God's good time, the New World, with all its power and might, steps forth to the rescue and the liberation of the old.   —WINSTON CHURCHILL[1]

In the following sentence Henry James maintains unity by balancing the "grand hotel" with the "small Swiss pension." (Italics have been added.)

The shore of the lake presents an unbroken array of establishments of this order, of every category, *from the "grand hotel" of the newest fashion,* with a chalk-white front, a hundred balconies, and a dozen flags flying from its roof, *to the small Swiss pension of an elder day,* with its name inscribed in German-looking lettering upon a pink or yellow wall and an awkward summer-house in the angle of the garden.
                                        —HENRY JAMES[2]

▶ EXERCISE 2   Recast the following sentences to eliminate excessive subordination or detail.

1. During the first period last Monday in Room 206 of the English building, we freshmen enjoyed discussing various dating codes.
2. The fan which Joan bought for her son who frets

[1] From *Their Finest Hour* by Winston Churchill. By permission of Houghton Mifflin Company.
[2] From *Daisy Miller.*

about any temperature that exceeds seventy arrived today.
3. When I was only four, living in a Colonial house, little of which remains today, I often walked alone the two miles from my house to the lake.
4. Four cars of various designs and makes jammed together on the freeway, which was completed in 1961 at a cost of over a half million dollars.
5. In a dark, pin-striped suit the senator advocated drastic reforms, occasionally taking time out for applause or a sip of water.
6. The dilapidated boat, though seaworthy ten years ago but badly in need of repairs now, moved out into the bay.
7. Flames from the gas heater given us by Aunt Tina before she died three years ago licked at the chintz curtains.
8. After finishing breakfast, which consisted of oatmeal, toast, and coffee, Martha called the tree surgeon, a man approximately fifty years old.
9. At last I returned the book that I had used for my report which I made Tuesday to the library.
10. A course in business methods helps the young man to get a job in order that he may prove whether he is fitted for business and thus avoid postponing the test, as so many do, until it is too late.

23c

Mixed, obscure, or illogical constructions should be avoided.

(1)   **Do not mix figures of speech by changing too rapidly from one to another.**

MIXED   Playing with fire can get a man into hot water.
BETTER   Playing with fire can result in burned fingers.

MIXED   Her plan to make it rain on Walter's parade was nipped in the bud.
BETTER   Walter thwarted her plan to make it rain on his parade.

(2)   **Do not mix constructions. Complete each construction logically.**

MIXED   When Mr. Green plays the hypochondriac taxes his wife's patience. [Adverb clause, part of a complex sentence, is here combined with the predicate of a simple sentence.]
CLEAR   Mr. Green's playing the hypochondriac taxes his wife's patience. [Simple sentence]
CLEAR   When Mr. Green plays the hypochondriac, he taxes his wife's patience. [Complex sentence]

Note: In defining, professional writers tell *what* the thing defined is, not when it is or where it is.

AWKWARD   A sonnet is when a poem has fourteen lines.
BETTER   A sonnet is a poem of fourteen lines.

AWKWARD   Banishing a person is where he is driven out of his country.
BETTER   Banishing a person is driving him out of his country.

(3)   **Make each part of the sentence agree logically with the other parts.**

Often a sentence is absurd because of failure in logical agreement resulting from a confusion of singular and plural words.

ILLOGICAL   Many of those attending the convention brought their wife with them.

BETTER   Many of those attending the convention brought their *wives* with them.

(4) Do not use the double negative.

NONSTANDARD   I don't want none.
STANDARD   I don't want any.

See **19i** under **but, hardly, scarcely.**

▶ EXERCISE 3   Revise the following sentences to eliminate mixed, obscure, or illogical constructions.

1. For Don, money does grow on trees, and he lets it go down the drain easily.
2. Because raindrops are not the same size explains the difference in the speed of their falling.
3. Friction is when one surface scrapes another.
4. These women we freshmen would not want for a mother.
5. I wouldn't take nothing for that experience!
6. Like a bat guided by radar, Hilda toes the mark.
7. To be discreet is where a person carefully avoids saying or doing something wrong.
8. Does anyone here know why Mr. James resigned or where did he find a better job?
9. Tourists are not permitted to bring their camera inside the area.
10. When a man needs glasses causes him to make mistakes.

23d

Do not make illogical statements.

One of the most important tests of good writing is the soundness of its reasoning. You should make sure that all your sentences are well thought out and contain no slips or weaknesses in your chain of reasoning. Be especially careful to avoid the common fallacies by observing the following principles of sound thinking.

(1) Be sure your generalizations are sufficiently supported.

FAULTY   None of the children in my family drink coffee; children do not like coffee. [The writer has jumped to a conclusion without finding a sufficient number of examples or instances to support his belief.]

FAULTY   When an automobile accident occurs in this city, the police are never on hand. [Unless the writer has himself seen or read an authoritative account of every automobile accident in the city, he cannot sensibly make this assertion. By avoiding such words as *never* and *always*, using instead such qualifiers as *sometimes* or *often*, the writer can generalize more safely.]

(2) Be sure your evidence is objective and relevant to your assertion.

FAULTY   Henry is an honest boy; he will make a success of anything he tries. [Obviously, Henry's honesty cannot guarantee his success at a task for which he may be intellectually unsuited. The writer's inference does not follow from the evidence.]

FAULTY   Donald is an atheist and a profligate; his arguments against a sales tax are worthless. [The writer here tries to discredit Donald's ideas by attacking him as a man. Donald might be a dissolute man, however, and still have excellent views on economic problems such as the sales tax.]

FAULTY   Joseph Jones, our distinguished candidate for mayor, has been endorsed by Miss Leila Lovely, Hollywood's brightest star. [This fallacy is the opposite of the previous one. The writer is using Miss Lovely's prestige as an actress to enhance the political reputation of Joseph Jones. But what are Miss Lovely's qualifications to be considered an expert on politics?]

▶ EXERCISE 4   Be prepared to contribute to a class discussion of the faulty reasoning in the sentences below.

1. Everybody goes to Florida in the winter.
2. Breaking a mirror will bring on seven years of bad luck.
3. Do not vote for my opponent as mayor; his parents were not born in America.
4. Young people nowadays do not obey their parents.
5. Joseph will be a good class president because all his classmates like him.
6. Of course the other car was at fault: the driver was a woman.
7. I am certain that all Germans like opera; I have never met one who did not like it.
8. I ate shrimp last night, and therefore I am sick today.
9. I always buy these razor blades because all the baseball players use them.
10. After the first atomic bomb was exploded, it rained for a week in my home town, and yet the scientists maintain that atomic explosions do not affect the weather!

▶ EXERCISE 5   Write approximately a hundred words either supporting or refuting one of the following statements. Make sure that you bring into each sentence only related ideas and pertinent details. Carefully avoid mixed or obscure constructions as you clearly present logical, convincing evidence in support of your point of view.

1. The learned think themselves superior to the common herd.   —W. T. STACE
2. Today Christmas is a major factor in our capitalist economy.   —ALDOUS HUXLEY
3. Few people see the long-range implications of juvenile delinquency.   —JUDGE ELIJAH ADLOW
4. Not one of us who has thought about it expects man as we know him to be on this planet a million years from now.   —HARLOW SHAPLEY
5. The notion that advertising can somehow "manipulate" people into buying products which they should not buy is both arrogant and naïve.   —MARTIN MAYER

Subordination

(An Aid to Unity)

24

Use subordination to relate ideas concisely and effectively; use coordination only to give ideas equal emphasis.

In grammar, subordination relates ideas by combining dependent elements with independent ones. (See Section 1, pages 804–06.) The principle of subordination is of great importance in composition since it is one of the best means of achieving sentence unity.

One of the marks of a mature style is effective use of subordination, particularly modifying phrases and clauses which give grammatical focus to main clauses. Inexperienced writers tend to use too many short simple sentences or stringy compound sentences. Compare the style of the groups of sentences below.

COORDINATION	Frank was listening to the radio. He heard the news then. His mother was killed in an automobile accident. The accident had occurred at ten o'clock.
SUBORDINATION	*Listening to the radio,* Frank heard *that his mother had been killed in an automobile accident at ten o'clock.* [A participial phrase, a noun clause, and a prepositional phrase replace three simple sentences.]
COORDINATION	Some students cheat, and they receive high grades, but they should be caught and penalized.
SUBORDINATION	Students *who cheat* should be caught and penalized *instead of receiving high grades.* [An adjective clause and a preposition with a gerund-phrase object replace two main clauses.]

As the subordinate clauses in the examples above indicate, grammatically subordinate structures may contain very important ideas.

24a

Use subordination to combine a related series of short, ineffective sentences into longer units.

When combining a series of related choppy sentences, first choose one complete idea for your sentence base; then use subordinate structures (such as modifying phrases or clauses, parenthetical elements, and appositives) to relate the ideas in the other simple sentences to the base.

CHOPPY	We must learn two things. We have to control ourselves. We must live in peace with our neighbors. If not, we shall not even be in a position to regret it.
BETTER	Unless we learn to control ourselves and to live in peace with our neighbors, we shall not even be in a position to regret it. —DANA L. FARNSWORTH

CHOPPY	He stood there in his buckskin clothes. One felt in him standards and loyalties. One also felt a code. This code is not easily put into words. But this code is instantly felt when two men who live by it come together by chance.
BETTER	As he stood there in his buckskin clothes, one felt in him standards, loyalties, a code which is not easily put into words, but which is instantly felt when two men who live by it come together by chance. —WILLA CATHER

Caution: Avoid excessive or clumsy, overlapping subordination. See 23b.

▶ EXERCISE 1   Combine the following short sentences into longer sentences in which ideas are properly subordinated.

¹ The miller was a large man.   ² He weighed well over two hundred pounds.   ³ He wore a red beard.   ⁴ It was thick and broad and was shaped like a spade.   ⁵ On his nose grew a wart.   ⁶ Red bristles sprouted out of the wart.   ⁷ This miller was a quarrelsome man.   ⁸ He was proud of his bull-like strength.   ⁹ He missed no chance to display it.   ¹⁰ He especially liked to show off by tearing down doors.   ¹¹ He would jerk them off their hinges.   ¹² He could also butt them to pieces with his head.   ¹³ Sometimes there was no door convenient.   ¹⁴ Then he would get attention in other ways.   ¹⁵ He was a loud-mouth.   ¹⁶ He always had a story ready to tell.   ¹⁷ His stories were ones he had picked up in barrooms.   ¹⁸ Usually they were filthy.   ¹⁹ It didn't matter that decent people were nearby.   ²⁰ He would tell his story anyhow.   ²¹ He had to make a noisy display of himself in one way or another.   ²² He never ran out of ways of doing it.   ²³ He might not be able to find a door to wreck.   ²⁴ People sometimes wouldn't listen to his stories.   ²⁵ He played a bagpipe.   ²⁶ His behavior had its reward.   ²⁷ It kept him from being a very well-liked man.

24b

Do not write a series of main clauses strung together with *and, so,* or *but* when ideas should be subordinated. Use coordination only to give ideas equal emphasis.

WEAK	There was a perfect full moon with theatrically silver light, and this should be a must for all future power failures, and so people peered into the faces of passersby, but they acted like children at a Halloween party, and they appeared to be trying to guess which friends were hiding behind which masks.
BETTER	In the theatrically silver light of a perfect full moon (a must for all future power failures) people peered into the faces of passersby like children at a Halloween party trying to guess which friends hide behind which masks.
	—LOUDON WAINWRIGHT
ACCEPTABLE	The offer was tempting, but I did not accept it. [Coordination used to stress equally the offer and the refusal]
USUALLY BETTER	Although the offer was tempting, I did not accept it. [Stress on one of the two—the refusal]

The conjunctive adverbs *however, therefore,* and *consequently* are often used in transitions when subordination would be preferable. Main clauses linked by these conjunctive adverbs can usually be combined and the proper relationship indicated by a subordinating conjunction. Subordinating conjunctions express such relationships as cause (*because, since*), concession (*although*), time (*after, before, since, whenever, while, until*), place (*where*), or condition (*if, unless*).

COORDINATION	I became increasingly uneasy; however, I kept my seat.
SUBORDINATION	Although I became increasingly uneasy, I kept my seat. [Subordination is usually better.]
COORDINATION	Fred knows almost nothing about farming; therefore I do not expect him to enjoy much success.
SUBORDINATION	Since Fred knows almost nothing about farming, I do not expect him to enjoy much success.

▶ EXERCISE 2   Revise the following sentences to achieve unity by way of effective subordination.

1. Jean Henri Dunant was a citizen of Switzerland, and he felt sorry for wounded Austrian soldiers in the Napoleonic Wars; therefore, he started an organization, and it was later named the Red Cross.
2. Yesterday I was daydreaming, so I did not hear the physics assignment, but anyway I passed the test today.
3. First he selected a lancet and sterilized it, and then he gave his patient a local anesthetic and lanced the infected part.
4. Father Latour was at a friend's house, and he saw two fine horses, and he induced the owner to part with them.
5. I graduated from high school, and then I worked in a bank, and so I earned enough to go to college.
6. The president of the bank walked into his office promptly at nine, and just then he saw the morning paper, and the headlines startled him.
7. We had just reached the bend in the road, for we were on our way home, and we saw a truckload of laborers crowded off the highway by an oncoming bus.
8. The Spanish started the custom in America of branding cattle, and the Mexicans kept it going, and Americans still brand cattle to show ownership.
9. Daniel Fahrenheit made a thermometer, and he used mercury in it; however, René Réaumur devised one too, but he used alcohol instead of mercury.
10. A wife wears a ring on the third finger of the left hand, for a vein runs from it to the heart, according to an old tale; therefore, the ring symbolizes the giving of the heart with the hand.

24c

Avoid illogical as well as awkward subordination.

When writing sentences such as the following, you are free to choose whatever you please for the subordinate structure. Your decision to subordinate one idea to another will depend upon what you wish to emphasize.

Although I know that the weather reports often err, I listen to them avidly.
Although I listen to the weather reports avidly, I know that they often err.

Placement of ideas in subordinate positions, however, is sometimes fixed. In the following sentence, for example, logic requires that one idea be subordinated rather than the other.

COORDINATION	I struck the match, and at that moment the oven exploded.
ABSURD SUBORDINATION	When the oven exploded, I struck the match.
LOGICAL SUBORDINATION	When I struck the match, the oven exploded. (OR The oven exploded when I struck the match.)

Many writers tend to avoid putting their most significant ideas in subordinate structures.

A cow that kicked a lantern over caused the great Chicago fire. (NOT A cow kicked a lantern over, causing the great Chicago fire.)

Note: Do not thwart subordination by inserting an inappropriate *and* or *but* before *which, who,* or *whom.*

AWKWARD	Law enforcement is a problem and which troubles the mayor.
IMPROVED	Law enforcement is a problem which troubles the mayor.

▶ EXERCISE 3   Revise the following sentences as necessary to eliminate awkward or illogical subordination.

1. Louise has had great success but which has not gone to her head.
2. Although David slept soundly, the deafening noise continued.
3. Mr. Dunbar is a good lawyer and who nearly always wins his cases.
4. As soon as we ate turkey, Thanksgiving arrived.
5. My father is an electrician and whom his customers depend on.
6. Even though I will not cut down the ragweed, I have hay fever.
7. Bruce found a lost hound and which needs a home.

▶ EXERCISE 4   Revise the following passage to achieve proper subordination.

[1] I was walking down the street when I found a purse containing fifty dollars. [2] It was just noon. [3] Thousands of people were on the streets. [4] I could not find the owner. [5] I went into the neighboring stores, and I inquired of the shopkeepers whether anyone had lost the money, and I approached the policeman with the same question. [6] No one could say who had lost the money, and so I thought I was the rightful owner, having found the purse myself. [7] But my father did not approve my keeping the purse. [8] He asked me to advertise it. [9] He said I might use the daily paper. [10] Next day I ran an advertisement in the paper, and now a week has passed and I have had no answers, and so I think the money is really mine.

▶ EXERCISE 5   Be prepared to contribute to a class discussion of the subordination of ideas in paragraphs 9 and 41, pages 896 and 903–04, of Section **31.**

Coherence:
Misplaced Parts;
Dangling Modifiers

25

Avoid needless separation of related parts of the sentence. Avoid dangling modifiers.

The meaning of an English sentence depends largely on the position of its parts. Usually these parts—especially the words, phrases, and subordinate clauses serving as modifiers—can be placed in various positions; and they should be placed to give just the emphasis or meaning desired. Note how the meaning in the following sentences changes according to the position of the modifier *only:*

She said that she loved *only* him.
  [She loved no one else.]
She said that *only* she loved him.
  [No one else loved him.]
She said *only* that she loved him.
  [She said nothing else.]
She *only* said that she loved him.
  [She didn't mean it.]
Only she said that she loved him.
  [No one else said it.]
She said that she *only* loved him.
  [Even love has its limitations.]

Normally the modifier should be placed as near the word modified as idiomatic English will permit.

Note: If you cannot distinguish readily the various modifiers and the parts of the sentence discussed in this chapter, review Section **1**, especially **1d**, and Section **4**.

Misplaced Parts

25a
Avoid needless separation of related parts of the sentence.

(1) **In standard written English, adverbs such as** *almost, only, just, even, hardly, nearly,* **or** *merely* **are regularly placed immediately before the words they modify.**

In spoken English, which tends to place these adverbs before the verb, ambiguity can be prevented by stressing the word to be modified.

AMBIGUOUS IN WRITING   He is *just* asking for a trifle.
CLEAR   He is asking for *just* a trifle.

INFORMAL   The house *only* costs $12,500.
FORMAL   The house costs *only* $12,500.

▶ EXERCISE 1   Place the adverbs in the following sentences immediately before the words they modify.

1. Some contemporary poets hardly show any interest in making their poems intelligible.
2. I only bet on the horse to take third place.
3. He took the penny home and polished it almost until it looked like new.

4. The man was only willing to sell a part of the farm.
5. He even works during his vacation.

(2) **The position of a modifying prepositional phrase should clearly indicate what the phrase modifies.**

A prepositional phrase used as an adjective nearly always immediately follows the word modified.

MISPLACED   Mother gave date muffins to my *friends with pecans in them.*
CLEAR   Mother gave my friends date *muffins with pecans in them.*

The position of a prepositional phrase used as an adverb is ordinarily not so fixed as that of an adjective phrase. Adverb phrases are usually placed near the word modified or at the beginning or end of a sentence. Sometimes, however, the usual placement can be awkward because the intended modification is not clear.

MISPLACED   One student said that such singing was not music but *a throat ailment in class.*
CLEAR   *In class* one student said that such singing was not music but a throat ailment. [OR One student said *in class* that such singing was not music but a throat ailment.]

▶ EXERCISE 2   Recast the following sentences to correct undesirable separation of related parts. Explain exactly what ambiguity each separation causes in each sentence.

1. Newspapers carried the story of the quarterback's fumbling all over the country.
2. At the age of two, my mother put me in a nursery school.
3. Students could not understand why Plato and Socrates were so wise in high school.
4. Gertrude served sundaes at the picnic to hungry guests in paper cups.
5. The professor made it clear why plagiarism is wrong on Monday.

(3) **Adjective clauses should be placed near the words they modify.**

AWKWARD   We bought gasoline in Arkansas at a small country store *which cost $3.12.* [*Which* does not refer to store.]
CLEAR   At a small country store in Arkansas, we bought gasoline *which cost $3.12.* [*Which* refers to *gasoline.*]
AWKWARD   I saw the horse stop at the edge of the precipice *that had raced ahead.*
CLEAR   I saw the horse *that had raced ahead* stop at the edge of the precipice.

(4) **Avoid "squinting" constructions—modifiers that may refer either to a preceding or to a following word.**

SQUINTING   I agreed *on the next day* to help him.
CLEAR   I agreed to help him *on the next day.*
CLEAR   *On the next day,* I agreed to help him.
SQUINTING   The tug which was whistling *noisily* chugged up the river.
CLEAR   The whistling tug chugged *noisily* up the river.
CLEAR   The tug whistled *noisily* as it chugged up the river.

(5) Avoid awkward separation of parts of verb phrases and awkward splitting of infinitives.

AWKWARD   There stood the old car which we *had* early last autumn *left* by our lake cottage.

IMPROVED   There stood the old car which we *had left* by our lake cottage early last autumn.

AWKWARD   You should now begin *to*, if you wish to succeed, *hunt* for a job.

IMPROVED   If you wish to succeed, you should now begin *to hunt* for a job. [In general avoid the "split" infinitive unless it is needed for smoothness or clarity.]

Note: Although all split infinitives were once considered questionable, those which are not awkward are now acceptable.

Americans seem to always be searching for something new.
—NEWSWEEK

Dangling Modifiers

25b

Avoid dangling modifiers.

Although any misplaced word, phrase, or clause dangles whenever it hangs loosely within a sentence, the term *dangling* is applied especially to incoherent verbal phrases and elliptical clauses. A dangling modifier is one that does not refer clearly and logically to some word in the sentence.

When verbal phrases or elliptical clauses come at the beginning of a sentence, the normal English word order requires that they immediately precede and clearly refer to the subject of the sentence.

PARTICIPLE   *Taking our seats,* we watched the game. [We took our seats.]

GERUND   After *watching the late show,* Nancy was tired. [Nancy watched the late show.]

INFINITIVE   *To avoid the rush-hour traffic,* Mr. Clark left the office early. [Mr. Clark avoided the rush-hour traffic.]

ELLIPTICAL CLAUSE   *When only a small boy,* I went with my father to Denver. [*I was* is implied in the elliptical clause.]

To correct a dangling modifier, (1) rearrange the words in the sentence to make the modifier sensibly refer to the right word, or (2) add words to make the meaning clear and logical.

(1) Avoid dangling participial phrases.

DANGLING   *Taking* our seats, the game started. [*Taking* does not refer to the subject *game*, nor to any other word in the sentence.]

IMPROVED   *Taking* (OR *Having taken*) our seats, *we* watched the opening of the game. [*Taking* refers to *we*, the subject of the sentence.]

IMPROVED   *After we had taken our seats,* the game started. [Participial phrase expanded into a clause]

DANGLING   The evening passed very pleasantly, *eating* candy and *playing* the radio. [*Eating* and *playing* refer to nothing in the sentence.]

IMPROVED   *We* passed the evening very pleasantly, *eating* candy and *playing* the radio. [*Eating* and *playing* refer to *we*, the subject of the main clause.]

Note: Participles do not dangle when they are used in an absolute phrase or used to introduce or refer to a general truth.

Weather permitting, we will have a cookout.
Generally speaking, a pessimist is an unhappy man.

(2) Avoid dangling phrases containing gerunds.

DANGLING   *By mowing the grass high and infrequently,* your lawn can be beautiful. [Who is to do the mowing?]

IMPROVED   *By mowing the grass high and infrequently, you* can have a beautiful lawn.

(3) Avoid dangling infinitive phrases.

DANGLING   *To write* well, good books must be read. [The understood subject of *to write* should be the same as the subject of the sentence.]

IMPROVED   *To write* well, a *student* must read good books. [*To write* refers to *student*, the subject of the sentence.]

DANGLING   *To run* efficiently, proper oiling is needed.

IMPROVED   *To run* efficiently, the *machine* must be properly oiled.

Note: Infinitives do not dangle when they introduce a general truth rather than designate the action of a specific person or thing.

To be brief, rats carry disease.
To judge from reports, all must be going well.

(4) Avoid dangling elliptical clauses (or phrases).

An elliptical clause—that is, a clause with an implied subject and verb—"dangles" unless the implied subject is the same as that of the main clause.

DANGLING   When only a small boy (OR At the age of nine), my father took me with him to Denver. [*I was* is implied in the elliptical clause.]

IMPROVED   When I was only a small boy (OR When I was nine years old), my father took me with him to Denver. [Elliptical clause expanded]

IMPROVED   When only a small boy (OR At the age of nine), *I* went with my father to Denver. [Subject of the main clause made the same as the implied subject of the subordinate clause]

DANGLING   Prepare to make an incision in the abdomen as soon as completely anesthetized.

IMPROVED   Prepare to make an incision in the abdomen as soon as the patient is completely anesthetized.

▶ EXERCISE 3   Revise the following sentences to eliminate dangling modifiers. Write *C* after each sentence that needs no revision.

1. While wondering about this phenomenon, the sun sank from view.
2. By standing and repeating the pledge, the meeting came to an end.
3. Once made, you must execute the decision promptly.
4. To speak effectively, eye contact is needed.
5. After sitting there awhile, it began to snow, and we went indoors.

6. Darkness having come, we stopped for the night.
7. Having taken his seat, we began to question the witness.
8. To grow good tomatoes, be sure to provide stakes for the vines.
9. Entering Chicago from the west, a whole network of stockyards is the first thing seen.
10. Before eating breakfast, the table had to be cleared.

▶ EXERCISE 4   Revise the following sentences to improve coherence. Write *C* after each sentence that needs no revision.

1. The car was advertised in last night's paper which is only two years old and is clean.
2. We have seed in a large can in our garage for sparrows.
3. Marvin wanted to, even during the 6:15 P.M. sports news, finish our game of checkers.
4. An official warned the hunter not to carry a rifle in a car that was loaded.
5. Selby said in the evening he would go.
6. To sum up, the candidate easily won the election.
7. Rusty ought to always be kept on a leash or in the yard.
8. Being in a hurry to leave Denver, the dented fender was not repaired then.
9. Mr. Waters promised again to visit the newcomers.
10. Having a broken arm and nose, I thought the statue was very ugly.
11. The slaves were unwilling to submit to his plans, thinking they could free themselves.
12. After taking only a few steps, I discovered that I had forgotten my keys.
13. You are, considering the whole affair, very fortunate.
14. The first thing a student must learn is to think for himself upon entering college.
15. Located on a mountain top, this made it an ideal place for a summer resort.
16. Henry promised when he was on his way home to stop at the library.
17. To irrigate successfully, water must flow through carefully planned ditches.
18. The Browns returned this morning from their vacation in the mountains on the bus.
19. Before taking a first trip by air, the thought of flying frightens one.
20. Keep stirring the water into the mixture until pale green.

Parallelism

26

Use parallel structure as an aid to coherence.

Words, phrases, clauses, or sentences are parallel when they have balanced grammatical structure. According to Simeon Potter, balanced sentences satisfy "a profound human desire for equipoise and symmetry." Use parallel form, especially with coordinating conjunctions, in order to express your ideas naturally and logically.

26a

For parallel structure, balance a word with a word, a phrase with a phrase, a clause with a clause, a sentence with a sentence.

As you study the following examples of parallelism, notice that a noun is balanced with nouns, an active verb with active verbs, an infinitive phrase with an infinitive phrase, a noun clause with a noun clause, a complex sentence with a complex sentence. Notice also that repetition of words can emphasize the parallel structure. One item in a series may be expanded without marring the total effect of the parallelism.

(1) Words

AWKWARD   The way we write reveals our bent, our inclinations, and what our inner drives are. [Nouns and subordinate clause not parallel]

PARALLEL   The way we write reveals || our *bent,*
our *inclinations,*
our inner *drives.*
—CHARLES W. FERGUSON

AWKWARD   As the forest lives, decays, and is devoured by itself, it spawns exotic creatures. [Active verbs not parallel to passive verb]

PARALLEL   As the forest || *lives,*
decays, and
devours itself,
it spawns exotic creatures. —NATIONAL GEOGRAPHIC

(2) Phrases

AWKWARD   It is easier to love humanity as a whole than loving one's neighbor. [Infinitive phrase and gerund phrase not parallel]

PARALLEL   It is easier || *to love humanity* as a whole than
to love one's *neighbor.*   —ERIC HOFFER

(3) Clauses

AWKWARD   What we say and the things that we do somehow seem out of joint. [Noun clause not parallel to noun modified by adjective clause]

PARALLEL || *What we say* and
what we do   somehow seem out of joint.
—NORMAN COUSINS

(4) Sentences

PARALLEL || *The danger of the past was that men became slaves.*
The danger of the future is that men may become robots.   —ERICH FROMM

Caution: Do not use parallel structure for sentence elements not parallel in thought. Never use an awkward or unidiomatic expression for the sake of a parallel. Lack of parallel structure is preferable.

MISLEADING   Our meetings were held on Friday afternoon, on Saturday morning, and on Saturday afternoon we started home.

CLEAR   Our meetings were held on Friday afternoon and on Saturday morning. On Saturday afternoon we started home.

AWKWARD   A teacher attempts to teach something, fails to inspire the pupil, kills the desire to learn, and hammers on cold iron. [Parallel structure used for ideas that could be related more clearly and effectively by way of subordination.]

BETTER   A teacher who is attempting to teach without inspiring the pupil with a desire to learn is hammering on cold iron.   —HORACE MANN

▶ EXERCISE 1   Underline the parallel structures in the following sentences, and be prepared to participate in a class discussion of the grammatical constructions. (If necessary, review Section 1, especially 1c and 1d.)

1. Not alone our physical acts but our ethics and our very emotions are to be channeled, standardized, massformulated.   —J. FRANK DOBIE
2. The birth of language is the dawn of humanity. The line between man and beast—between the highest ape and the lowest savage—is the language line.   —SUSANNE K. LANGER
3. Without criticism abuses will go unrebuked; without dissent our dynamic system will become static.   —HENRY STEELE COMMAGER
4. Not for a single moment did he ever compromise with what he believed, with what he dreamed.   —DEEMS TAYLOR
5. Broadly speaking, human beings may be divided into three classes: those who are toiled to death, those who are worried to death, and those who are bored to death.   —WINSTON CHURCHILL

▶ EXERCISE 2   Achieve parallelism in each of the following sentences (adapted from the *National Geographic Magazine*) by using the structure of the italicized words. When revising for parallel structure, do not copy the entire sentence; copy only the parallel items (properly punctuated), as in the example.

EXAMPLE   The trees are magnificent—*twisted by winds, hammered by storms,* and snows press them under.

REVISION   . . . twisted by winds, hammered by storms, pressed under snows.

1. The cameramen spent months *in primitive areas, in African heat, in Alaskan blizzards,* and where there are jungles in South America.
2. I missed the wild loneliness of the Cinqueterre, *its hard-won vineyards, its silent olive trees,* its villages that were isolated.
3. On the machinist's bench stood a variety of plastic birds, *opening and closing their beaks, turning their heads,* and their tails flipped.
4. During Divali festivals, the Indians like *to paint their houses, to buy new clothes,* exchanging visits, and offering prayers for prosperity.
5. They say in Arizona that men *tear down nature's mountains, run them through mills and smelters,* and of the waste new mountains are built.
6. We took advantage of exactly the right combination of *weather, temperature, equipment,* the surface of the mountain, and the moonlight which we were so grateful for.
7. We aimed to show the mothers the importance of a balanced diet—*that unpolished wheat has virtues, that vitamin B prevents beriberi,* and the value of protein foods.
8. Mainly *from the Central Highlands, from the Indian river section,* and the groves located near Tampa come a quarter of the world's oranges and tangerines.
9. Genoa is the *geographical, historical,* and logically the capital of the Ligurian coast.
10. *The lake was only a small sapphire glinting behind a tiny wall;* there were the canals which looked as if they were only silver threads as they wound across a plain.

26b

Whenever necessary to make the parallel clear, repeat a preposition, an article, an auxiliary verb, the sign of the infinitive, or the introductory word of a long phrase or clause. (See also **22c.**)

AWKWARD   I admire Tennyson *for the ideals* in his poems but not *his style.*

IMPROVED   I admire Tennyson || *for the ideals* in his peoms but not || *for his style.*

AWKWARD   In the wreck the circus lost *a camel* and *elephant.*

IMPROVED   In the wreck the circus lost || *a camel* and || *an elephant.*

OBSCURE   He explained *that* the advertising campaign had been successful, business had increased more than fifty per cent, and additional capital was sorely needed.

CLEARER   He explained || *that* the advertising campaign had been successful, *that* business had increased more than fifty per cent, and *that* additional capital was sorely needed.

▶ EXERCISE 3   Insert words that will bring out the parallel structure in the following sentences.

1. Take as much time as you need—a day, hour, year.
2. I intend to do two things: to try and succeed.
3. I told Katherine that I could not go and I had good reasons.
4. The professor assigned this poem and short story by Poe.
5. The sentences are difficult to understand, not because they are long but they are obscure.
6. The child learns in nursery school to take his turn, to respect the rights of others, and take care of his materials.
7. They would lie on the battlefield for hours and sometimes days.
8. Not only has he visited the patients, but also sung ballads for them.
9. One can learn much more by studying than worrying.
10. The hunter was outwitted by a tiny raccoon and buffalo herd.

26c

Correlatives (either . . . or, neither . . . nor, both . . . and, not only . . . but also, whether . . . or) should be followed by elements that are parallel in form.

FAULTY He was not only *kind* but also *knew* when to help people. [Adjective paralleled with verb]

BETTER He was ‖ *not only kind* ‖ *but also helpful.*

FAULTY I debated whether *I should give* the beggar money or *to offer* him food. [Subordinate clause paralleled with infinitive]

BETTER I debated ‖ *whether to give* the beggar money ‖ *or to offer* him food.

26d

Be sure that a who (or which) clause precedes and who (or and which).

FAULTY Inez Carter is a woman of great charm and who is popular. [A *who* clause does not precede the *and who;* the *of* phrase is not parallel to the *who* clause.]

BETTER Inez Carter is a woman ‖ *who has great charm* and ‖ *who is popular.*

▶ **EXERCISE 4** Revise the following sentences by using parallel structure to express parallel ideas. Write *C* after each sentence that needs no revision.

1. I like a detective story with exciting action and which keeps me guessing.
2. You will enjoy painting a favorite corner of the room, showing an armchair, drop-leaf table, and lamp.
3. Someone has said that Americans cannot enjoy life without a TV set, an automobile, and a summer cottage.
4. My friend told me that the trip would be delayed but to be ready to start on Friday.
5. William is a boy with a good mind and who has the highest principles.
6. A sea lion watches carefully the action of his fellows and how they obey their trainer.
7. He was quiet and in a serious mood after the talk.
8. I did not know whether I should go to some technical school or to enter a liberal arts college.
9. The secretary must attend all meetings, call the roll, and keep the minutes.
10. People fall naturally into two classes: the workers and those who like to lean on others.

▶ **EXERCISE 5** First carefully read the paragraphs below, observing all parallel constructions. Then write a similar composition of your own on a subject such as the importance of music, the value of travel, the beauty of friendship, or the impact of automation.

[1] Man's greatest source of enlightenment lies in the printed word. [2] No amount of persuasion can forever take away its imprint on the minds of a searching public. [3] Passing years cannot dilute its great truths nor still its gifts of laughter. [4] It alone passes from generation to generation the sum of mankind's knowledge and experience.

[5] Through the medium of printing you can live a thousand lives in one. [6] You can discover America with Columbus, pray with Washington at Valley Forge, stand with Lincoln at Gettysburg, work in the laboratory with Franklin, Edison, Pasteur or Salk and walk the fields with St. Francis. [7] Through printing you can encompass in your imagination the full sweep of world history. [8] You can watch the rise and fall of civilizations, the ebb and flow of mighty battles and the changing pattern of life through the ages. [9] Through printing you can live a mental life of adventure. [10] You can roam with Marco Polo, sail the seas with Magellan, be a swashbuckling Musketeer, a member of Robin Hood's band of merry men, a Knight of King Arthur's Round Table or a conqueror of space.

[11] Printing lets you enrich your spirit with the Psalms, the Sermon on the Mount, the Beatitudes and all the other noble writings that are touched with divine fire. [12] You can know the majesty of great poetry, the wisdom of great philosophers, the findings of the scientists.

[13] You can start today where the great thinkers of yesterday left off because printing has immortalized man's knowledge. [14] Thinkers dead a thousand years are as alive in their works today as when they walked the earth. [15] Through printing you can orient your life to the world you live in, for printing links the past, the present and the future. [16] It is ever-changing and immutably constant, as old as civilization and as new as this morning's newspaper.

[17] It is man's enduring achievement.[1]

▶ **EXERCISE 6** Indicate parallelism in Lincoln's Gettysburg Address. See Section 1, Exercise 14.

Point of View

27

Maintain a consistent point of view as an aid to coherence.

Sudden and illogical shifts in point of view tend to obscure the meaning and thus to cause needless difficulty in reading.

27a

Avoid needless shifts in tense. (See also 7d.)

SHIFT The boy *closed* his book and *hurries* away to the playground. [A shift from past tense to present tense]

BETTER The boy *closed* his book and *hurried* away to the playground. [Both verbs in the past tense]

Note: When the historical present is used, as in summarizing plots of narratives, care will be needed to avoid slipping from the present tense into the past tense.

Romeo *goes* in disguise to a Capulet feast, *falls* in love with Juliet, and *marries* (not *married*) her secretly.

[1] By permission of the Padgett Printing Corporation, Dallas.

27b

Avoid needless shifts in mood. (See also **7d**.)

SHIFT   First *rise* to your feet and then you *should address* the chairman. [A shift from imperative to indicative mood]

BETTER   First *rise* to your feet and then *address* the chairman. [Both verbs in the imperative mood]

27c

Avoid needless shifts in subject or voice.

A shift in subject often involves a shift in voice. A shift in voice nearly always involves a shift in subject.

SHIFT   James liked fishing, but hunting was also enjoyed by him. [The subject shifts from *James* to *hunting*. The voice shifts from active to passive.]

BETTER   James liked fishing, but he also enjoyed hunting. [The subject does not shift. Both verbs active]

SHIFT   Mary took summer courses and her leisure hours were devoted to tennis. [The subject shifts from *Mary* to *hours*. The voice shifts from active to passive.]

BETTER   Mary took summer courses and devoted her leisure hours to tennis. [One subject only. Both verbs active]

SHIFT   Paul hurried up the mountain path, and soon the laurel came into his sight. [The subject shifts from *Paul* to *laurel*.]

BETTER   Paul hurried up the mountain path and soon caught sight of the laurel. [One subject only]

27d

Avoid needless shifts in person.

SHIFT   *We* have reached a point where *one* ought to face the possibility of a great and sudden change. [A shift from first to third person]

BETTER   *We* have reached a point where *we* ought to face the possibility of a great and sudden change.

SHIFT   *Students* will find the University Book Shop a great convenience. *You* need not leave the campus to purchase any school supplies *you* may need. [A shift from third to second person]

BETTER   *The student* will find the University Book Shop a great convenience. *He* need not leave the campus to purchase any school supplies *he* may need.

27e

Avoid needless shifts in number. (See also agreement of pronoun and antecedent, **6b**.)

SHIFT   A *person* should be thoughtful of *their* neighbors. [A shift from singular *person* to plural *their*]

BETTER   A *person* should be thoughtful of *his* neighbors.

SHIFT   The United Nations *deserves* encouragement. Indeed *they deserve* much more than that. [If *United Nations* takes a singular verb (*deserves*), it should not be referred to by a plural pronoun (*they*).]

BETTER   The United Nations *deserves* encouragement. Indeed, *it deserves* much more than that.

27f

Avoid needless shifts from indirect to direct discourse.

SHIFT   My friend asked whether I knew the coach and will he be with the team. [Mixed indirect and direct discourse]

BETTER   My friend asked whether I knew the coach and whether he would be with the team. [Indirect discourse]

BETTER   My friend asked, "Do you know the coach? Will he be with the team?" [Direct discourse]

27g

Maintain the same tone or style throughout the sentence.

INAPPROPRIATE   Analysis of the principal obstacles to harmony in the United Nations reveals that Russia and her satellites refuse to *play ball* with the rest of the world. [A shift from formal to colloquial style. Substitute *cooperate*, or a similar word, for the italicized expression.]

INAPPROPRIATE   After distributing the grass seed evenly over the lawn, rake the ground at least twice and then *gently bedew it* with fine spray. [The italicized expression is too "poetic" in a sentence with a prosaic purpose. Substitute *water it lightly*.]

INAPPROPRIATE   It seemed to Juliet, as she gazed down from the balcony, that Romeo's face was as white as *the underside of a fish*. [The italicized expression clashes with the romantic beginning of the sentence.]

27h

Maintain a consistent perspective throughout the sentence (and also throughout the larger elements of discourse).

FAULTY PERSPECTIVE   From the top of the Washington Monument, the government offices seemed to be so many beehives, and the workers droned at their tasks behind long rows of desks. [The perspective shifts from the monument to the interior of government buildings.]

CONSISTENT PERSPECTIVE   From the top of the Washington Monument, the government buildings seemed to be so many beehives, and it was easy to imagine the workers droning at their tasks behind long rows of desks.

▶ EXERCISE 1   Correct in the following sentences all needless shifts in tense, mood, subject, voice, person, number, tone, or perspective. Explain each revision by writing the number of the appropriate rule in this chapter: **a, b, c, d, e, f, g,** or **h.** Write *C* after each sentence that needs no revision.

1. According to Helen Leath, Mr. Blake knows how to deal with annoying door-to-door salesmen; they are quickly frightened away by him.
2. Pretending to be a seller of knives, Mr. Blake waves a long butcher knife near the throat of the salesman. You can well imagine what they think.
3. When the policeman gave me a ticket for rolling past a stop sign, I ask him what the fine would be.
4. A woman stepped forward, grabs the culprit by the collar, and demands that he apologize to the child.
5. He said he had a convertible model in stock and would I like to try it out.
6. Jane likes to cook, but house cleaning is not a pleasant occupation.
7. Each person has some distinctive mannerism of their own.
8. When she saw him in the room, she thinks that she is dreaming.
9. If there is little enthusiasm among the students, we might ask, "Why they should be enthusiastic?"
10. No matter what her mother may say, Jane always took the opposite view.

11. It is a book everyone should read, for you can derive much good from it.
12. Gentlemen, we have finished our discussion about balancing the budget; bear with me awhile until I have said a few words about budgeting the balance.
13. The foreign ministers held their conference in Paris, and contrary to rumors, the peace pipe is passed around.
14. Pick the roses in the morning, and then they should be placed in water.
15. A vacation is enjoyed by all because it refreshes the mind and the body.
16. He told his aunt that there is someone in the room.
17. Every citizen should do his duty as they see it.
18. Aunt Jane spent her summers in Wisconsin, but Arizona is her favorite winter climate.
19. Jim wondered whether Jack had left and did he say when he would return?
20. Standing before the house, he thought of the many happy years he had spent there and how quickly they are passing.

▶ EXERCISE 2   Revise the following paragraph to avoid all needless shifts. If necessary, expand the paragraph.

¹ From behind the desk the shopkeeper emerged and comes toward me.   ² He is a heavy-set man, and his brown tweed coat was badly worn.   ³ An assistant gave me a chair and leaves the room, but not before he had welcomed us and even told me where one might find lodging.   ⁴ "First, look around in this vicinity and then you should find a comfortable place in a nearby hotel," he says.   ⁵ I hurried out of the shop and soon the hotel comes into view.   ⁶ Be thankful for suggestions when offered you.   ⁷ It usually helps one.

▶ EXERCISE 3   Follow the directions for Exercise 2.

¹ He was an artful old codger, it always had seemed to me.   ² He has a deceptively open face and his manner is that of a simple farmer.   ³ He tried to appear humble and said that "I am opposed to all pretense."   ⁴ Nevertheless he will let it be known that he has great influence with important people.   ⁵ Take these impressions for what they are worth; it may help one in your dealings with this reptile.

Reference of Pronouns

28

Make a pronoun refer unmistakably and definitely to its antecedent.[1]

A pronoun whose antecedent is not immediately obvious is at best an annoyance to the reader, who must pause to clarify the meaning, and at worst a cause of serious misunderstanding. You may find the faulty use of pronouns

[1] For agreement of pronoun and antecedent see **6b**.

one of the easiest errors to let slip by in your writing. Because you know just who or what you mean by *he, she, it; who, which, what; this, that; the same, such,* etc., you may not realize that you have not made your meaning obvious to the reader. Always check, therefore, to see that you have placed all pronouns as close as possible to their antecedents. If, having done this, you find that the reference of a pronoun is still not clear, repeat the antecedent or use a synonym for it. If repetition proves awkward, recast your sentence.

28a

Avoid ambiguous reference. Construct the sentence in such a way that the reader can easily distinguish between two possible antecedents.

AMBIGUOUS	John told William that he had made a mistake. [Who made the mistake?]
CLEAR	John said to William, "You have made a mistake."
CLEAR	John admitted to William that he had made a mistake.
AWKWARD	The books were standing on the shelf which needed sorting. (See also **25a[3]**.)
BETTER	The books which needed sorting were standing on the shelf. [Pronoun placed near its antecedent]

28b

Avoid remote reference—reference to an antecedent (1) too far removed from the pronoun or (2) so placed in a subordinate construction that it is not central in the mind of the reader.

Make your meaning immediately clear to the reader. Save him the annoyance of searching about for the antecedent.

REMOTE	The *lake* covers many acres. Near the shore water lilies grow in profusion, spreading out their green leaves and sending up white blossoms on slender stems. *It* is well stocked with fish. [The pronoun *it* is too far removed from the antecedent *lake*.]
IMPROVED	The *lake* covers many acres. Near the shore water lilies grow in profusion, spreading out their green leaves and sending up white blossoms on slender stems. The *lake* is well stocked with fish. [Repetition of the antecedent *lake*]
VAGUE	He sat by the little window all day and worked steadily at his translating. *It* was too small to give much light. [Temporarily confusing: antecedent of *it* not clear until reader finishes the sentence]
CLEAR	He sat by the little window all day and worked steadily at his translating. The *window* was too small to give much light. [Repetition of the noun]
OBSCURE	When *Johnson's* club was organized, *he* asked Goldsmith to become a member. [Reference to antecedent in the possessive case]
IMPROVED	When *Johnson* organized his club, *he* asked Goldsmith to become a member. (See also **27c**.)

Caution: As a rule avoid pronoun reference to the title of a theme, or to a word in the title.

Title: Is Work a Curse or a Blessing?

AWKWARD	To a man who is harassed by a nagging wife and undisciplined children, *it* can be a great blessing, a welcome escape.

BETTER   To a man who is harassed by a nagging wife and undisciplined children, *work* can be a great blessing, a welcome escape.

28c

Use broad reference only with discretion.

Informal English allows much latitude in the use of antecedents that must be inferred from the context. Even formal English accepts the general idea of a clause as an antecedent when the reference is unmistakable. But students who overuse *this, that, it,* or *which* to refer to the general idea of the preceding clause or sentence may be advised, as a means of insuring greater clarity, to make each of their pronouns refer to a specific noun (or noun substitute).

(1) Avoid reference to the general idea of a preceding clause or sentence unless the meaning is clear and unmistakable.

VAGUE   William was absent from the first performance, which caused much comment. [*Which* has no antecedent.]

CLEAR   William's absence from the first performance caused much comment. [Pronoun eliminated]

VAGUE   The story referred to James, but Henry misapplied it to himself. This is true in real life. [*This* has no antecedent.]

CLEAR   The story referred to James, but Henry misapplied it to himself. Similar mistakes occur in real life.

(2) As a rule do not refer to a noun not expressed but merely inferred from some word.

VAGUE   My mother is a music teacher. It is a profession I know nothing about.

CLEAR   My mother is a music teacher, but the teaching of music is a profession I know nothing about.

VAGUE   He wanted his teachers to think he was above average, as he could have been if he had used it to advantage.

CLEAR   He wanted his teachers to think he was above average, as he could have been if he had used his ability to advantage.

(3) Avoid the use of the indefinite *it, you,* or *they* in your formal writing.

INFORMAL (OR FORMAL)   If you break the law, you may be arrested. [Informal when *you* means "anyone," formal when *you* is addressed to a specific person or persons]

FORMAL   If a person breaks the law, he may be arrested.
OR Anyone breaking the law may be arrested.

INFORMAL   When *you* cannot swim, a leaking boat tossing in deep, stormy waters frightens *you.* I admit that I am afraid.

FORMAL   Since I cannot swim, I admit that a leaking boat tossing in deep, stormy waters frightens me.

INFORMAL   In France *they* could not understand William.
FORMAL   In France William could not be understood.

AWKWARD   In the book *it* says that many mushrooms are edible.
IMPROVED   The book says that many mushrooms are edible.

Note: The pronoun *it* is correctly used in such idiomatic expressions as *it seems, it is cold, it is raining, it is useless to go,* and *it is five miles to town.*

28d

Avoid the confusion arising from the repetition in the same sentence of a pronoun referring to different antecedents.

CONFUSING   Although *it* is very hot by the lake, *it* looks inviting. [The first *it* is an idiomatic pronoun; the second *it* refers to *lake.*]

CLEAR   Although it is very hot by the lake, the water looks inviting.

CONFUSING   We should have prepared for our examinations earlier. *It* is too late to do *it* now.

CLEAR   We should have prepared for our examinations earlier. It is too late now.

▶ EXERCISE   Reconstruct the following sentences as necessary to correct faults in reference. Write *C* after each sentence that needs no revision.

1. Howard was more intelligent than the average student, but he did not use it properly. His intelligence

2. I did not ever buy a season ticket, which was very disloyal to my school. My failure

3. Her ladylike qualities were reflected in the graciousness of her manner. This was apparent in her every act. ese qualities

4. Package wrapping has always been my job, because they say that I can do it better than anyone else.

5. When building roads the Romans tried to detour around valleys as much as possible for fear that flood waters might cover them and make them useless. the roads

6. If you are taken to the courthouse, they will fine you.

7. In the article it states that the inland sea is salt.

C 8. Our language is rich in connectives which express fine distinctions of meaning.

9. One summer while visiting my grandparents I was attracted by three pigeons that decided to settle in their barn loft. my grand

10. If all impurities are not removed from the iron, it will deprive steel of its ductility and prevent it from being rolled into bars or drawn into wire.

C 11. The speaker was eloquent, but he was annoyed by the intense heat in the auditorium.

12. My worst fault is the inability to express myself clearly in the presence of other people. But this is not true when I am with close friends. inability

13. I left home and hitchhiked to Chicago. This means of travel is not satisfactory, for it requires much waiting at the side of the road.

14. When the termite eggs are hatched, they grow wings and fly about the country in swarms. termites

15. Mary told Ann that she would be accepted as a member of the club. Ann

16. The story awakens your interest in radium, which continues to the end of the book. This inter

C 17. Visitors should heed the notice that is on the outside of the door.

18. Mary showed Jane that she had not made a mistake. Jane

19. It may freeze tonight and damage the pipe, and it should be protected. Pipe the

20. If a driver is guilty of violating a traffic law, the cost of your car insurance goes up. His

Emphasis

29

Select words and arrange the parts of the sentence to give emphasis to important ideas.

Since your ideas vary in importance, your expression of them should vary in stress. Short factual statements and routine description or narration cannot always be varied for emphasis without doing violence to the natural order of the English language. For example, it would be absurd for a sportswriter to describe a football play in this fashion: "Short was the pass that Randy caught, and across the goal line raced he." But in most types of writing, some sentences may be rearranged to achieve emphasis without sacrificing naturalness of expression.

You may gain emphasis through the use of concrete words, especially verbs and nouns (Section **20**), through economy of language (Section **21**), and through subordination (Section **24**). You may also emphasize ideas:

a. By placing important words in the important positions at the beginning and end of the sentence.
b. By changing loose sentences into periodic sentences.
c. By arranging ideas in the order of climax.
d. By using the active instead of the passive voice.
e. By repeating important words.
f. By putting words out of their usual order.
g. By using balanced construction.
h. By abruptly changing the sentence length.

29a

Gain emphasis by placing important words at the beginning or end of the sentence—especially at the end.

UNEMPHATIC   Science from the dawn of history has been intimately associated with war, and probably longer. [Parenthetical qualifier placed in an important position weakens the sentence.]

EMPHATIC   Science from the dawn of history, and probably longer, has been intimately associated with war.
—BERTRAND RUSSELL

UNEMPHATIC   In my opinion, the spirit of science is the spirit of progress, above all. By that I mean that science does not seek a utopia or heaven that is static. Generally speaking, there are ever newer horizons and higher peaks for men to climb, mentally, spiritually, materially. [The most important words are not placed at the beginning or end of the sentences. Word padding, such as *In my opinion* and *By that I mean that,* is unemphatic. In the last sentence, *materially* is the least important item in the series.]

EMPHATIC   Above all, the spirit of science is the spirit of progress. Science seeks no static utopia or heaven. It can afford men ever newer horizons and higher peaks to climb, materially, mentally, and spiritually.
—HERMANN J. MULLER

Note: Since semicolons are equivalent to weak periods, words placed before semicolons also have an important position.

▶ EXERCISE 1   Be prepared for a class discussion of emphasis in the following paragraph, giving special attention to the choice of words which begin and end sentences.

[1] By a strange perversity in the cosmic plan, the biologically good die young. [2] Species are not destroyed for their shortcomings but for their achievements. [3] The tribes that slumber in the graveyards of the past were not the most simple and undistinguished of their day, but the most complicated and conspicuous. [4] The magnificent sharks of the Devonian period passed with the period, but certain contemporaneous genera of primitive shellfish are still on earth. [5] Similarly, the lizards of the Mesozoic era have long outlived the dinosaurs who were immeasurably their biologic betters. [6] Illustrations such as these could be endlessly increased. [7] The price of distinction is death.
—JOHN HODGDON BRADLEY[1]

▶ EXERCISE 2   Revise each of the following sentences to gain emphasis for important ideas. (The sentences are adapted from the works of modern professional writers.)

1. In my opinion, rudeness luxuriates in the absence of self-respect more or less.
2. Frequently, dipping a paddle was like offering the torrent a toothpick, however.
3. Higher education has become a juvenile branch of the entertainment industry, if we may believe Mr. Daniels.
4. In any event, nothing in the fishing world makes as little sense as a short-sleeved fishing shirt, in the first place.
5. Shimmering buildings arrowed upward and glinted through the treetops, just ahead of us.
6. In the final analysis all he could see were the three double chins that her husband wore at the back of his neck conspicuously.
7. The search for truth is a subversive activity, and always has been.
8. In all probability not to engage in this pursuit of ideas is to live like ants instead of like men, however you look at it.
9. What they need is an awareness of their opportunities and potentialities, in fact; what they need is a philosophy, really.
10. One of the most exciting sports is whale watching, now in the prime of its season of course.

29b

Gain emphasis by changing loose sentences into periodic sentences. (Section **29b** is an extension of **29a**.)

A loose sentence is easily scanned, since the main idea comes toward the beginning and the reader can omit details, often parenthetical, placed later in the sentence. To

[1] From "Is Man an Absurdity?" by John H. Bradley, *Harper's Magazine,* October, 1936.

get the meaning of a periodic sentence, however, the reader cannot stop until he reaches the period.

LOOSE   Thousands of feet above the earth, the air is crowded with living creatures, drifting, flying, gliding, ballooning, or involuntarily swirling along on the high winds. [Notice how many effective details follow the main clause *the air is crowded with living creatures.*]
— RACHEL L. CARSON

PERIODIC   Once Columbus had shown the way to the West Indies and the Americas, once Balboa had seen the Pacific and Magellan had sailed around the globe, there arose, and long persisted, two new ideas. [The main idea comes at the end of the sentence.]
— RACHEL L. CARSON

Both types of sentences are effective. The loose sentence is, and should be, the more commonly used. But the periodic sentence, by holding the reader in suspense and reserving the main idea until the end, is more emphatic. Note the difference in tone in the following sentences.

LOOSE   There cannot be peace on earth as long as you see your fellow man as a being essentially to be feared, mistrusted, hated, and destroyed. [Main idea first—a good sentence]

PERIODIC   As long as you see your fellow man as a being essentially to be feared, mistrusted, hated, and destroyed, there cannot be peace on earth. [Main idea last—a more emphatic sentence]   — THOMAS MERTON

LOOSE   History has proved amply that mere numbers may be defeated by smaller forces who are superior in arms, organization, and morale.

PERIODIC   That mere numbers may be defeated by smaller forces who are superior in arms, organization, and morale history has amply proved.

Caution: Do not overuse the periodic sentence to the point of making your style unnatural. Variety is desirable. See Section 30.

▶ EXERCISE 3   Study the structure of the following sentences, and then label each as either *loose* or *periodic.*

1. On the moon, inside the air-filled domes that the future colonists will erect, a man could fly like a bird.
— ARTHUR C. CLARKE

2. So passionately do I love the usual, the commonplace, the everyday, that I turn off the television instantly if an adventure program comes on.   — PEARL BUCK

3. Polyphemus continued to melt round the room, staring malignly at nothing.   — ELIZABETH BOWEN

4. Out of this pain of loss, this bitter ecstasy of brief having, this fatal glory of the single moment, the tragic writer will therefore make a song for joy.
— THOMAS WOLFE

5. If great comedy must involve something beyond laughter, Lloyd was not a great comedian.
— JAMES AGEE

6. There are blustering signatures that swish across the page like cornstalks bowed before a tempest.
— F. L. LUCAS

7. Obscurity is the very opposite of culture as it is the opposite of good breeding.   — JACQUES BARZUN

8. Earline was a big, bouncy, uncomplicated girl who poked you in the ribs to make sure you got the point of her jokes.   — FRANCES GRAY PATTON

9. A small tree, rising between him and the light, stood there saturated with the evening, each gilt-edged leaf perfectly drunk with excellence and delicacy.
— E. B. WHITE

10. No one who has felt the fury of the fish charging like electric current through line and rod, who has heard the cacophonous screech of backing being ripped through guides, who has reeled with a madman's frenzy in the final seconds before boat and angler plunge into the Rogue's crashing, foaming white water, who has held on, bruised and shaken, until that sudden, inexplicable moment when the line goes slack and the contest is over as abruptly as it began—no one who has experienced such an encounter is ever the same again.   — VIRGINIA KRAFT[2]

▶ EXERCISE 4   Convert the loose sentences in Exercise 3 to periodic sentences, and then convert the periodic to loose; notice how your revisions make for varying emphasis.

29c

Gain emphasis by arranging ideas in the order of climax.

Notice in the examples below that words, phrases, clauses, and sentences are arranged in the order of importance, in stair-step fashion, with the strongest idea last.

Mr. Raleigh fears poverty, illness, and death. [Words placed in order of importance]

We could hear the roar of cannon, the crash of falling timbers, and the shrieks of the wounded. [Climax reached in *shrieks of the wounded*]

Sometimes their anguish was my anguish; sometimes their cussedness was my fury; occasionally their pleasure was my despair. [Clauses in order of importance]   — RUSSELL LYNES

In the language of screen comedians four of the main grades of laugh are the titter, the yowl, the belly laugh and the boffo. The titter is just a titter. The yowl is a runaway titter. Anyone who has ever had the pleasure knows all about a belly laugh. The boffo is the laugh that kills. [First words and then sentences are placed in climactic order.]   — JAMES AGEE

Note: A striking arrangement of ideas in reverse order of climax, called anticlimax, is sometimes used for comic effect.

To a distant cousin the rich old man willed his ranch, three oil wells, five apartment houses, and innumerable alley cats.

▶ EXERCISE 5   Arrange the ideas below in what you consider to be the order of climax.

1. Franklin used the ant as a symbol of industry, wisdom, and efficiency.

2. Everything on wheels—trains, bicycles, hot rods, roller skates—Archibald loved.

3. Images in the poem involve sun-drenched orchards, diamond-eyed children, and golden-flecked birds.

[2] From "Steelheads on a Rough River" by Virginia Kraft (*Sports Illustrated*, November 1, 1965) © 1965 Time Inc.

4. Like Patrick Henry, the young soldier wanted death or liberty.
5. He left the city because of his rapidly failing health, lack of success in business, and the loss of his club membership.
6. His confident manner, his knowledge of men, and his friendliness made him the logical man for the office.
7. Something must be done at once. The commission is faced with a deficit.
8. I gathered together the souvenirs of college days: my diploma, a textbook on mathematics, my fraternity pin, and a battered book bag.
9. His actions, his language, his clothes—these help reveal a man's character.
10. The would-be governor shook hands with the man on the street, autographed books for teenagers, promised prosperity to all, and wrote letters to senior citizens.

▶ EXERCISE 6   Be prepared for a class discussion of the arrangement of ideas in the following paragraphs.

I began to think about personal liability insurance the morning Mrs. Ehrlich, our cleaning woman, suddenly screamed down to me from her perch on the windowsill: "Mr. J., come help! I got another one of those dizzy spells!"

I had asked Mrs. Ehrlich time and again to stop climbing around on the windowsills. I had also asked her not to run so fast while carrying the big plate-glass top of the coffee table across the waxed floors, and to try not to pour quite so much water into the electrical outlets. These restrictions may seem harsh, but I don't think I am what you could call a tyrannical employer. I've left her plenty of room for fringe-benefit fun. I've said nothing about blowing out the pilot light, sticking her fingers into the vacuum cleaner's turbo-jet engine, or tossing all the naphthalene, paint cans, and oil-soaked rags she pleases into the incinerator.   —HAYES B. JACOBS[3]

29d

Gain emphasis by using the strong active voice instead of the weak passive voice.

UNEMPHATIC   Our picture window was punctured by hail, our frame garage was flattened by winds, and our basement was turned into a muddy swamp by the flash flood.

EMPHATIC   Hail punctured our picture window, winds flattened our frame garage, and the flash flood turned our basement into a muddy swamp.

Exception: If the receiver of the action is more important than the doer, the passive voice is more effective.

EMPHATIC   His only son was killed in Vietnam.
EMPHATIC   Any driver who exceeds the speed limit will be fined.

▶ EXERCISE 7   Substitute the active for the passive voice.

1. The speech on the state of domestic affairs was delivered by the President of the United States.
2. It is taken for granted by students in Dr. Boyer's class that a weekly quiz will be given to them.

[3] From Martin Levin's "The Phoenix Nest," *Saturday Review*, May 15, 1965, p. 6.

3. Victorian literature is being reevaluated by modern scholars.
4. As the station is reached, the train is seen coming around a curve.
5. A mink wrap was worn by the actress.
6. Paul was hesitant to enter the room, for he saw that a poster was being made by Jane.
7. Two maxims are often preached by Uncle Theodore: no moss will be gathered by a rolling stone; and, worms are always caught by early birds.
8. It was decided by the members that the meetings were to be held at their homes.
9. When the play was brought to an end, the actors were greeted with a loud burst of applause by the audience.
10. It is greatly feared by the citizens that adequate punishment will not be meted out by the judge.

29e

Gain emphasis by repeating important words.

Note the great difference between the careless repetition in **21c** and the effective repetition in the following passages. See also **31b(3)**.

EMPHATIC   The poet enters his world as an *as if:* he writes *as if* he were plowing a field, *as if* he were conducting a chemical experiment, *as if* he were analyzing a real man seated before him.   —JOHN CIARDI

EMPHATIC   In this whole matter of War and Peace especially, we have been at various times and in various ways *false* to ourselves, *false* to each other, *false* to the facts of history and *false* to the future.   —HENRY R. LUCE

See also the quotation from Winston Churchill in **23b**.

▶ EXERCISE 8   From your reading, copy three passages in which emphasis is gained by the repetition of an important word or phrase.

29f

Gain emphasis by putting a word or phrase out of its natural order.

EMPHATIC   *Trust her* I dare not.
EMPHATIC   *Never* will I vote for such a change!

Caution: This method of securing emphasis, if overused, will make the style distinctly artificial. And of course the order of the parts of the sentence should never be such as to make for ambiguity. (See **25a**.)

▶ EXERCISE 9   Copy from your reading and bring to class five passages in which emphasis is secured by putting a word or phrase out of natural order.

29g

Use balance to gain emphasis.

A sentence is balanced when identical or similar grammatical structure is used to express contrasted ideas. A balanced sentence uses parallel structure (see Section 26) and emphasizes the contrast between parts of similar length and movement.

UNBALANCED   Love is positive, but consider the negative aspects of tolerance. Passion is involved in love, and yet how humdrum and dull tolerance is.

BALANCED   Love is positive; tolerance negative. Love involves passion; tolerance is humdrum and dull.
—E. M. FORSTER

BALANCED   The slightest sense perception—a falling leaf, a twinkling star, a smiling child—awakens our minds as well as arouses our feelings, and forces us to ask: Why? What? Whence? Whither?
—MORTIMER ADLER

Caution: Do not overuse balance, which can make for artificiality rather than emphasis.

▶ EXERCISE 10   Copy from your reading and bring to class five examples of the balanced sentence.

▶ EXERCISE 11   Copy all examples of balanced structure from Lincoln's Gettysburg Address (at the end of Section 1, Exercise 20.)

▶ EXERCISE 12   Use balanced sentences to show the contrast between the following: Men and women, youth and age, success and failure.

29h
Abruptly change the sentence length to gain emphasis.

EXAMPLE   Across an expanse of new-turned earth stretches a new public housing project, with a playyard for the children, and at 32nd Street begins the new campus of the Illinois Institute of Technology, sleek brick-and-glass buildings surrounded by new trees and new grass. And just beyond the Institute rises a great gray hulk of brick, four stories high, topped by an ungainly smokestack, ancient and enormous, filling half the block north of 34th Street between State and Dearborn. It is the Mecca Building.   —JOHN BARTLOW MARTIN

[The last short sentence, which abruptly follows a group of longer sentences, is emphatic; the author stresses *Mecca Building* because the purpose of his essay is to describe this strange place.]

▶ EXERCISE 13   Revise the following sentences as necessary to give greater emphasis. Write *C* after each sentence that needs no revision.

1. The chairman will give his report after the meeting has been called to order.
2. The soldiers were outnumbered two to one, as you may have heard.
3. It was no fault of hers that the program was a failure.
4. Forceful prose was created by Hemingway because of his sensitivity to the real speech of Americans, however.
5. The zero hour had come. Already the armies were marching.
6. On the other hand, he had done the best he could, according to his story.

7. At any time I shall be ready, no matter how late the hour is.
8. He saw much to interest him: the Statue of Liberty, the art galleries, the tall buildings, and the crowds on the street.
9. A fast pass was thrown to Milburn, and a twenty-five yard gain was made by him before the whistle was blown by the referee.
10. Scouting develops a boy morally, mentally, and physically.
11. Convince her against her will I cannot.
12. The storm broke in all its fury at the close of a hot day.
13. Mr. Brown knew that he had made wrong decisions, that he should apologize, that he had made a mistake.
14. I asked her to marry me, many years ago, in a shop on Tremont Street, late in the fall.
15. Around her shoulders was draped a gorgeous Spanish shawl.
16. The art of the Indians was crude, but a great deal of originality was shown by some of them.
17. Her charm, her friendliness, her generosity, and her neat appearance made her a favorite with the girls.
18. As we approached the house, lights were turned on and faces appeared at the windows.
19. Make the most of it if this be treason.
20. The car overturned when we struck a rut in the road.

▶ EXERCISE 14   By pointing to specific sections of this chapter, indicate the methods of gaining emphasis used in the following sentences.

1. A rhythm, a musical motif, a brush stroke, a color can be malicious. But the melody in a work, sonata, picture or poem cannot be malicious.   —JACQUES MARITAIN
2. What money he could lay his hands on he spent like an Indian rajah.   —DEEMS TAYLOR
3. Beds he slept in are relics, stones he stepped on are sacred, battles he lost are victories.
—MARSHALL FISHWICK
4. The radio, except as it serves mariners, is a decivilizing achievement. It has destroyed the illusion of distance, invaded the privacy of walled enclosures, and coated the tongue of music.   —E. B. WHITE
5. When the loudspeaker announces "The Two-Fisted Killer from Ecuador," he rises on short, crooked legs, lowers his shaggy black head, aims himself and charges onto the court.   —MARSHALL SMITH
6. Why lands sink under the sea and rise again nobody knows.   —WOLFGANG LANGEWIESCHE
7. If a man can write a better book, preach a better sermon, or make a better mouse-trap than his neighbor, though he builds his house in the woods, the world will make a beaten path to his door.
—EMERSON
8. Gone are the people who owned these farms, their most lasting works faded like old ink, their names nothing but an echo in the land records.
—KENNETH ANDLER
9. Jet planes flashed a glance at us, after apparently ripping the old blue canvas of the sky. The monstrous voices roared out the half-time and three-quarter-time scores of other games. The cannon was fired at every

touchdown. The tumblers somersaulted. The cheer-leaders continued their idiot ballet.   —J. B. PRIESTLEY

10. The impression seems to be that the age we live in is the age of the masses. Half the times you open a book or start a discussion you find yourself dealing with mass production, mass consumption, mass media and mass culture. We blame the masses for all our ills: the vulgarization of culture and politics, the meaningless-ness of our way of life, the ferocity of our wars and, of course, the population explosion.   —ERIC HOFFER[4]

[4] From "Making a Mass Elite," *Holiday Magazine*, March, 1966.

Variety

30

Vary the structure and the length of your sentences to make your whole composition pleasing and effective.

The two following paragraphs have the same content, but the first is made up of eight short sentences, all simple or compound; the second has four sentences varied in length and structure: one simple, one complex, and two compound-complex. Note how variety in the second para-graph makes it more effective than the first.

UNVARIED   Even a climatic change can affect the rate of rotation. The earth's weather becomes warmer, for example, and some of the ice concentrated at the North and South poles melts. This releases water into the world's oceans. The mass of ice near the earth's axis of rotation is reduced, and the amount of water in the oceans is increased. The oceans are farther from the axis. As a result, the earth's movement of inertia becomes greater, and its speed of rotation decreases. This is like a twirling ice skater. He moves his arms out from his body; his speed of rotation decreases.

VARIED   Even a climatic change can affect the rate of rotation. When the earth's weather becomes warmer, for example, some of the ice concentrated at the North and South poles melts, releasing water into the world's oceans. The mass of ice near the earth's axis of rotation is reduced, and the amount of water in the oceans (which are farther from the axis) is increased. As a result, the earth's movement of inertia becomes greater and—like a twirling ice skater who moves his arms out from his body—its speed of rotation decreases.   —TIME[1]

Except for the loose, stringy sentences in **30c**, this sec-tion deals only with *good* sentences. Throughout Section **30** you are cautioned against monotonous repetition of any one type of sentence, not because these sentences are not good ones, but because they do not combine to form a pleasing and effective pattern. Even the best sentence can be boring if it follows a long series of sentences similar in design.

[1] From "Toward a Longer Day," *Time*, February 25, 1966. Courtesy *Time;* © Time Inc. 1966.

Note: Can you distinguish readily between main clauses and subordinate clauses, clauses and phrases, compound sen-tences and compound predicates? If necessary, review the fundamentals of the sentence treated in Section 1, Sen-tence Sense, especially 1d; then study Variety.

30a

Usually avoid a series of short, simple sentences. Vary the length. (See also 29h.)

UNVARIED   Consider what might happen on Venus. We could step off our rocket and meet a spider. Suppose he is ten feet tall. The spider might well be a creature of good will. He might be capable of right action. He might have an I.Q. incomparably higher than our own. But his terrible spider aspect would sur-prise us. We might not wait to test the creature's friendship. We might stomp on him with the largest boot available. [A series of choppy sentences]

VARIED   Consider what might happen should we step off our rocket on Venus to meet a 10-foot-tall spider. The spider might well be a creature of good will, capable of right action, and with an I.Q. incomparably higher than our own. But, surprised by his terrible spider aspect, we might not wait to test the creature's friendship. We might stomp on him with the largest boot available.   —RAY BRADBURY[2]

▶ EXERCISE 1   Revise the following paragraph to achieve variety in sentence length.

[1] A salesman's speech, recently recorded, has an inter-esting thesis. [2] A man should solve problems. [3] And a man should create problems to solve. [4] For instance, a woman's car will not start. [5] She has a problem. [6] An auto-parts man solves it by selling her a battery. [7] I think that by nature man is a solver of problems. [8] A teacher baffles his class with problems. Then he helps the students solve them. [9] A doctor solves the problems of his patients by recommending drugs or surgery. [10] In fact, even a garbage collector helps housewives clear their kitchens. [11] And a ditch digger eliminates the drainage problems of a city. [12] How to spend leisure hours in an age of computers is a problem for many Americans. [13] Singers, dancers, actors, and writers help solve this prob-lem. [14] Man can see problems everywhere. [15] And he does something about them.

30b

Avoid a long series of sentences beginning with the sub-ject. Vary the beginning.

The best writers begin about half their sentences with the subject—far more than in any other one way. But some students use this kind of beginning almost exclu-sively. To avoid overuse, they should vary the subject-first beginning.

Basic Sentence Patterns	*Variations*
SUBJECT—VERB.	VERB—SUBJECT.
The professor walked in.	In walked the professor.
A man lay beside the road.	Beside the road lay a man.

[2] From "Cry the Cosmos," *Life*, September 14, 1962.

SUBJECT—VERB—OBJECT.

Henry scorned honest men.
I will not do that again.

OBJECT—SUBJECT—VERB.

Honest men Henry scorned.
That I will not do again.

SUBJECT—LINKING VERB
—COMPLEMENT.

Bruce was a bungler then.
We shall never be completely
secure.

COMPLEMENT—SUBJECT
—LINKING VERB.

A bungler Bruce was then.
Completely secure we shall
never be!

In addition to shifting the word order of basic patterns, you can vary the beginnings of sentences in the following ways:

(1) **Begin with an adverb or an adverb clause.**

ADVERB   *Suddenly* the professor walked in.
ADVERB CLAUSE   *Although Bruce has good manners now,* he was a bungler then.

(2) **Begin with a prepositional phrase or a participial phrase.**

PREPOSITIONAL PHRASE   *At that moment* the professor walked in.
PARTICIPIAL PHRASE   *Waiting patiently for help,* a man lay beside the road.

(3) **Begin with a coordinating conjunction such as *but, and, or, nor,* or *yet.***

Effective sentences can often begin with a coordinating conjunction, but only when the conjunction shows the proper relation of the sentence to the preceding sentence. See 31b(4).

COORDINATING CONJUNCTION   The young woman wept and wrung her hands. *But* the injured man, lying beside the road, waited patiently for help. [*But* makes a contrast.]

▶ EXERCISE 2   Compose a good sentence that begins with the subject. Then revise the sentence to vary the beginning in as many ways as you can.

▶ EXERCISE 3   Classify the beginnings of the sentences in paragraph 32, page 901, into the types designated above.

30c

Avoid the loose, stringy compound sentence. (See also 24b.)

The ineffective compound sentence may be revised:

(1) **By converting it to a complex sentence.**

AIMLESSLY COMPOUND   The Mississippi River is one of the longest rivers in the world, and in the springtime it often overflows its banks, and many people are endangered.
COMPLEX   The Mississippi River, which is one of the longest rivers in the world, often endangers many people during the springtime by overflowing its banks.

(2) **By using a compound predicate in a simple sentence.**

COMPOUND   He put on his coat, and next he picked up his hat and cane, and then he hurried from the house.
SIMPLE   He put on his coat, picked up his hat and cane, and hurried from the house.

(3) **By using an appositive or a modifier in a simple sentence.**

COMPOUND   The town is north of the Red River, and a tornado struck it, and it was practically demolished.
SIMPLE   The town, located north of the Red River, was struck by a tornado and practically demolished.
COMPOUND   He was the mayor of the town, and he was a genial fellow, and he invited the four boys into his study.
SIMPLE   The mayor of the town, a genial fellow, invited the four boys into his study.

(4) **By using phrases in a simple sentence.**

COMPOUND   The streets were icy and we could not drive the car.
SIMPLE   Because of the icy streets we could not drive the car.
COMPOUND   You will reach your destination tomorrow, and then you can take a long rest.
SIMPLE   After reaching your destination tomorrow, you can take a long rest.

30d

Vary the conventional subject-verb sequence by occasionally separating subject and verb by words or phrases.

SUBJECT—VERB   The *auditorium is* across from the park and it is a gift of the alumni. [A compound sentence]
VARIED   The *auditorium,* across from the park, *is* a gift of the alumni. [A simple sentence]
SUBJECT—VERB   The *crowd sympathized* with the visitors and *applauded* every good play.
VARIED   The *crowd,* sympathizing with the visitors, *applauded* every good play.

Caution: Avoid awkward or needless separation of subject and verb.

30e

Vary a series of declarative statements by using an occasional exclamation, exhortation, command, or question.

STATEMENT   We will fight to the end.
EXCLAMATION   Imagine our nation not fighting to the very end!
EXHORTATION   Let us fight, then, to the very end.
COMMAND   Fight on. Fight to the end.
QUESTION   Who of us will not fight to the end? [A rhetorical question usually should not be answered.]

▶ EXERCISE 4   Be prepared for a class discussion of sentence variety in the following paragraphs.

1. ¹I will not dwell on the trials I endured from this horse. ²She was mean and never mean the same way twice. ³She would tolerate two automobiles and bolt from the third, the same with mailboxes or even a stone beside the road. ⁴At times she would stop and eye a telephone pole with such trembling, ears-cocked, ears-back panic that even I began to think the pole was doing something to scare her; if not at that moment, perhaps it had on some previous occasion. ⁵At that instant, after seeming to compose herself, she would bolt again. ⁶She very nearly threw me when the sleeve of my slicker, neatly tied on behind me, came adrift and touched her flank, to which her reaction was one of bucking and sun-fishing. ⁷If I left her at a hitching rack, she would lean back and pull

until she broke the reins.   ⁸ It was suicidal to light a cigarette while riding her in the dark.   ⁹ My worst moment with her came when we put up suddenly from the road just in front of us an eagle or a hawk which had been enjoying a dust bath.   ¹⁰ She went through her entire repertoire.   —CHARLES W. MORTON[3]

2. ¹ It was never a pilot that started the idea that night falls.   ² A pilot knows that it does not.   ³ It oozes up out of the ground, fills the hollows and low places with purple pools of shadow that spread and rise to the tops of the trees and the houses.   ⁴ Long before the sky has darkened, the world below is swimming in night.   ⁵ And then finally darkness begins washing up over the sky from the east, climbing over the zenith, closing down at last over the final gleams of the sunset.   ⁶ Here and there stars begin to prick through, larger and more liquid than ever seen from the ground, and the moon, big and white, outlines the earth.   ⁷ Below the plane, lights map the town, race along the roads, accenting but not relieving the blackness, for darkness clings to the ground.   ⁸ Whatever light there is clings to the sky to the last.   —ALMA HEFLIN[4]

3. ¹ Any Mediterranean knows what he wants, what it should be like, where it comes from.   ² In a restaurant he asks searching questions about each item of the food, how it is cooked, and he will complain on principle if there is the smallest doubt or disappointment, so that often the chef nervously comes up from the kitchen halfway through a meal to see how his customers are taking it.   ³ It is a point of honor to complain.   ⁴ In a shop he makes the same demands; patiently the assistant brings out all the cloth, all the shoes, and is not in the least upset if the customer refuses all.   ⁵ On the contrary, the assistant admires the discrimination.   ⁶ For life is not buying or selling; it is getting what you exactly wish for, what you can afford.   ⁷ The wish is everything, and for that, patience is indispensable and life is timeless.   —V. S. PRITCHETT[5]

³ From It Has Its Charms . . . by Charles W. Morton. Published by J. B. Lippincott Company. Copyright © 1966 by Charles W. Morton.
⁴ From Adventure Was the Compass by Alma Heflin McCormick. By permission of the author.
⁵ From "Europe's Mediterranean Coast" by V. S. Pritchett, Holiday, January, 1966.

4. ¹ All around the lakeshore the tormented water raced—not 80 feet high but, in places, clawing up to 800 feet above lake level.   ² It thundered at the dam—and the dam held.   ³ But the water went over the dam not five feet high but up to 300 feet high, and smashed to the bottom of the gorge 800 feet below.   ⁴ There it was constricted as in a deadly funnel, and its speed fearfully increased.   ⁵ It shot out of the short gorge as from a gun barrel and spurted across the wide Piave riverbed, scooping up millions of deadly stones.   ⁶ Ahead of it raced a strange icy wind and a storm of fragmented water, like rain, but flying upward.   ⁷ By now it was more than a wave, more than a flood.   ⁸ It was a tornado of water and mud and rocks, tumbling hundreds of feet high in the pale moonlight, leaping straight at Longarone.   —GORDON GASKILL[6]

5. ¹ Can you imagine any better example of divine creative accomplishment than the consummate flying machine that is a bird?   ² The skeleton, very flexible and strong, is also largely pneumatic—especially in the bigger birds.   ³ The beak, skull, feet, and all other bones of a 25-pound pelican have been found to weigh but 23 ounces.   ⁴ Yet the flesh too is pneumatic, and in some species there are air sacs around viscera, muscles, and, where balance and streamlining permit, immediately under the skin.   ⁵ The lungs are not just single cavities as with mammals but whole series of chambers around the main breathing tubes, connected also with all the air sacs of the body, including the hollow bones.   ⁶ Thus the air of the sky literally permeates the bird, flesh and bone alike, and aerates it entirely.   ⁷ And the circulation of sky through the whole bird acts as a radiator or cooling system of the flying machine, expelling excess humidity and heat as well as exchanging carbon dioxide for oxygen at a feverish rate.
—GUY MURCHIE[7]

⁶ From "The Night the Mountain Fell" by Gordon Gaskill. Reprinted from The Reader's Digest, May, 1965, by permission.
⁷ From Guy Murchie, Song of the Sky, 1954, reprinted by permission of and arrangement with Houghton Mifflin Company, the authorized publishers.

LARGER ELEMENTS

The Paragraph

31

Make paragraphs unified and coherent; develop them adequately.

A paragraph is a distinct unit of thought—usually a group of related sentences, though occasionally no more than one sentence—in a written or printed composition.

The form of a paragraph is easy to recognize: the first line is indented. The content of a unified paragraph deals with one central idea; every sentence contributes to this idea. Moreover, each sentence fits into a logical pattern of organization and is therefore carefully related to other sentences in the paragraph.

Below is an example of a unified, coherent, adequately developed paragraph. As you read it, observe (1) the clear statement of the controlling idea in the first sentence, (2) the development of that idea in the sentences which follow, (3) the orderly arrangement of the supporting facts, and (4) the close relationship of the sentences to the central idea and to one another. (For easy reference, each of the fifty-nine specimen paragraphs in this chapter is numbered.)

1 As a matter of fact, the educated man uses at least three languages. With his family and his close friends, on the ordinary, unimportant occasions of daily life, he speaks, much of the time, a monosyllabic sort of shorthand. On more important occasions and when dealing with strangers in his official or business relations, he has a more formal speech, more complete, less allusive, politely qualified, wisely reserved. In addition he has some acquaintance with the literary speech of his language. He understands this when he reads it, and often enjoys it, but he hesitates to use it. In times of emotional stress hot fragments of it may come out of him like lava, and in times of feigned emotion, as when giving a commencement address, cold, greasy gobbets of it will ooze forth.
—BERGEN EVANS[1]

The central idea of the above paragraph is "the educated man uses at least three languages." The sentences developing the central idea classify the languages and describe their uses; these points are well organized, progressing from informal speech in ordinary situations to formal speech on rare occasions. Repeated references to times and situations, the comparison of the languages, and transitional devices (such as the phrase "in addition") link the sentences within the paragraph and thus contribute to its coherence.

Since each paragraph in a composition is a distinct unit of thought, the beginning of a new paragraph is an important signal to the reader. It serves as a signpost of an approaching curve in the avenue of thought; or it warns him that he must take a new avenue of thought. It announces a new time, place, person, or thing in the course of a narrative, a different point of view in description, a new step in an exposition, or an advance in argument.

Length. Expository or argumentative paragraphs in current books and magazines are usually from 50 to 250 words in length, with the average perhaps 100 words. Paragraphs tend to run longer in books and shorter in the narrow columns of newspapers. Shorter paragraphs are more frequent in narrative writing, especially dialogue, in which each speech is paragraphed separately.

Indention. The first lines of paragraphs are indented uniformly, about one inch in longhand and five spaces in typewritten copy.

31a

Give unity to the paragraph by making each sentence contribute to the central thought.

A paragraph is said to have unity when each sentence contributes to the central thought. Any sentence that fails to contribute violates the unity of the paragraph and should be omitted. The central thought is usually expressed in a *topic sentence.* Although a topic sentence may come anywhere within a paragraph, the central idea of an expository paragraph is often stated in the first sentence.

In the illustrations of unified paragraphs below, the central idea, when expressed, is indicated by italics.

2 *We strolled across the campus after the last class one afternoon late in May, when the magnolia blossoms and the gentlemen were both out in force enjoying the balmy air.* A pair of men in running shorts and spiked shoes trotted by, not speeding, merely limbering up. Down by the rough stone wall that enclosed the campus another pair tossed a baseball languidly. Sheltered by low-swinging magnolia boughs, a group engaged in what looked suspiciously like a poker game. In the shade of a giant oak lay one man who actually had a book; but unfortunately the book, spread open, rested on his chest, and he slept blissfully.
—GERALD W. JOHNSON[2]

To achieve unity, you may find it helpful to make a plan for a paragraph, carefully listing points that clearly support your central topic. Paragraph 2, for example, reveals the following plan:

CENTRAL TOPIC	Observations during a campus stroll in May
DEVELOPMENT	1. two runners
	2. ball tossers
	3. card players
	4. sleeping scholar

When the topic sentence comes at or near the beginning, the conclusion of the paragraph may not only restate the central idea—and thus repeat key words or the main point of the topic sentence—but also emphasize its significance:

3 *Father got holes in his socks even oftener than we boys did in our stockings.* He had long athletic toes, and when he lay stretched out on his sofa reading and smoking, or absorbed in talking to anyone, these toes would begin stretching and wiggling in a curious way by themselves, as though they were seizing on this chance to live a life of their own. I often stared in fascination at their leisurely twistings and turnings, when I should have been listening to Father's instructions about far different matters. Soon one and then the other slipper would fall off, always to Father's surprise, but without interrupting his talk, and a little later *his busy great toe would peer out at me through a new hole in his sock.*
—CLARENCE DAY[3]

Occasionally the central idea of a paragraph may be stated in the last sentence only, especially when the writer progresses from particulars to a generalization:

4 When we watch a person walk away from us, his image shrinks in size. But since we know for a fact that he is not shrinking, we make an unconscious correcting and "see" him as retaining his full stature. Past experience tells us what his true stature is with respect to our own. Any sane and dependable expectation of the future requires that he have the same true stature when we next encounter him. *Our perception is thus a prediction; it embraces the past and the future as well as the present.*
—WARREN J. WITTREICH[4]

[1] From "Grammar for Today" by Bergen Evans, reprinted from the *Atlantic Monthly,* March, 1960. By permission of the author.

[2] From *Hod-Carrier: Notes of a Laborer on an Unfinished Cathedral* by Gerald W. Johnson. Reprinted by permission of William Morrow & Co., Inc. Copyright © 1963, 1964 by Gerald W. Johnson.

[3] From *Life with Father* by Clarence Day. Reprinted by permission of the publishers, Alfred A. Knopf, Inc.

[4] From "Visual Perception and Personality" by Warren J. Wittreich, reprinted from *Scientific American,* April, 1959. By permission of the publishers.

When not expressed in a topic sentence, the central idea of a unified paragraph is distinctly implied:

5   A man in cuffless shirt-sleeves with pink armgarters, wearing a linen collar but no tie, yawned his way from Dyer's Drug Store across to the hotel. He leaned against the wall, scratched a while, sighed, and in a bored way gossiped with a man tilted back in a chair. A lumber-wagon, its long green box filled with large spools of barbed-wire fencing, creaked down the block. A Ford, in reverse, sounded as though it were shaking to pieces, then recovered and rattled away. In the Greek candy-store was the whine of a peanut-roaster, and the oily smell of nuts.

—SINCLAIR LEWIS[5]

[Topic implied: *Such were the activities in Main Street.*]

▶ **EXERCISE 1**   Point out, or supply, the topic sentence for paragraph 16, page 898, and for any other paragraphs assigned by your instructor.

Caution: Do not make rambling statements that are vaguely related to your topic sentence. As you write a paragraph, hold to the main idea. For instance, if the controlling idea of a paragraph is "My roommate Bill Jones cannot keep a secret," irrelevant sentences about Bill Jones or about secrecy will disrupt the unity. Every statement should pertain to Bill Jones's inability to keep a secret.

CHECK LIST FOR REVISING A PARAGRAPH WHICH LACKS UNITY

1. Does the paragraph have a central idea clearly stated or implied? (If not, supply a topic sentence.)
2. Does the topic shift one or more times? (If so, either develop each topic in a separate paragraph, or supply a topic sentence to which each of the ideas can be made to contribute.)
3. Does every sentence contribute to the central idea? (If not, cross out each irrelevant sentence. If any sentence is related to the central idea, but not clearly so, revise it to make the relationship clear.)

REVISION OF A FAULTY PARAGRAPH

My friend Cliff is often late on   *Topic*
important occasions because of his   *sentence*
excessive courtesy.   *needed*

    On Christmas Eve, for example, Cliff was late to dinner. His unusually courteous habits had delayed him on a shopping trip. At the entrance of a large bargain basement, he had stood for a quarter of an hour holding doors open for last-minute shoppers. Once inside, he lost more time standing aside so that clerks could serve others first. ⟨Cliff bought a billfold for his brother.⟩ *Omit— irrelevant* When Cliff at last left the store, he took time out to carry heavy

packages for a woman whose car was parked two blocks away. *When he finally arrived* At home, his family was eating *make reference to central idea clear* dessert. The very next week, Cliff was late for an important business conference. He had stood outside a busy elevator letting everyone else on first; then he lost even more time insisting that he be the last person off. Who else besides Cliff would so courteously put others first? ⟨Cliff is the type of person who cannot sleep if a thank-you note remains unwritten.⟩ *Omit—topic shifts*

▶ **EXERCISE 2**   To achieve unity, revise the following faulty paragraph. Be prepared to give reasons for your revisions.

    At my place last night, a tornadic wind played several mischievous pranks. Whistling loudly through the weather stripping, it sprayed dirty water all over the freshly mopped kitchen floor. Next, as though chiding me for my earlier complaints about stuffy air, it created enormous drafts by breaking a half dozen window panes. The moment an announcer on television started reading a special bulletin from the weather bureau, the wind knocked down my television antenna and, just as I reached for the radio, blacked out the whole house. Later I learned that a pilot flying above the turbulent weather had reported that he had never seen such a violent thunderstorm. Traveling at ninety miles an hour, the wind leveled a two-car garage belonging to Mr. Fulton, my neighbor. The wind also turned on an outdoor water faucet, flooding my pansy bed, overturned the dog house, imprisoning my fox terrier, and dumped a stolen boat into the back yard, after ripping the motor off and breaking the oars. After that savage storm, my family and I are most grateful to be alive and uninjured.

31b

Give coherence to the paragraph by so interlinking the sentences that the thought may flow smoothly from one sentence to the next.

    A paragraph is said to have coherence when the relationship between sentences is clear, when the transition from one sentence to the next is easy and natural. The reader should be able to follow the thought without difficulty. In order to secure this coherence, this easy flow of the thought from sentence to sentence, the writer should rely first of all on (1) arrangement of the sentences in a clear order, and then on the use of (2) pronouns referring to the preceding sentence, (3) repeated words or ideas, (4) transitional expressions, and (5) parallel structure.

(1)   **Arrange the sentences of the paragraph in a clear, logical order.**

    There are several common, logical ways to order the sentences in a paragraph; the choice of an appropriate order depends upon the writer's purpose and the nature of his material. Perhaps the simplest and most common order is "time" order.

---

[5] From *Main Street* by Sinclair Lewis, copyright, 1920, by Harcourt, Brace & World, Inc.; renewed, 1948, by Sinclair Lewis. Reprinted by permission of the publishers.

POOR ARRANGEMENT OF SENTENCES

After the death of Saul, David ruled Israel for forty years. Once he incurred the king's anger and was driven ignominiously from court. As a shepherd lad he had lived in the hills of Judea. He had vanquished the mighty Philistine with his slingshot. The sad-faced Saul was charmed with his songs. He was the sweetest singer in all Israel.

[Confused time order]

ORDERLY SEQUENCE OF SENTENCES

6 David, the shepherd lad who lived in the hills of Judea, was the sweetest singer in all Israel. It was he who charmed the sad-faced Saul with his songs. It was he, too, who vanquished the mighty Philistine with his slingshot. Later he incurred the anger of Saul and was driven from court. But upon Saul's death David came back and ruled Israel for forty years.

[David's (1) *youth in Judea,* (2) *experiences with Saul,* and (3) *reign over Israel*]

This paragraph about David is made clearer by re-arrangement in time order. Narrative paragraphs lend themselves naturally to such arrangement, and other types of paragraphs often have a time element that makes possible and natural a chronological arrangement. For example, in explaining a process—how something is done or made—the writer can follow the process through, step by step, as in the following paragraph.

7 In *engraving,* the artist grooves out clean strips of metal from the plate with a steel instrument called a burin. The artist is actually drawing with the burin. After the picture is engraved, printing ink is rubbed over the entire plate. The surface is then wiped clean, leaving ink in the incised portions of the copper. A dampened sheet of paper is placed over the plate and together they are run through a roller press. The paper is dampened to retain the ink better and to avoid cracking or tearing, since a great deal of pressure must be exerted to force the paper into the incised areas. —MARVIN ELKOFF[6]

Sentences that have no evident time order can sometimes be arranged in "space" order, in which the paragraph moves from east to west, from west to east, from the near to the distant, from the distant to the near, from the left to the right, etc. This order is used especially for descriptive paragraphs. Note the movement from the warm, low coastal gardens to the cold, high areas in the following paragraph.

8 Late winter color heralds the approach of spring in all areas of the Southwest. In mild coastal gardens, this happens gradually as spring sneaks up without much fanfare. Farther inland, bulbs and flowering trees attract more attention. And in colder areas of the mountains and high desert, the appearance of the first buds on a deciduous shrub or tree is downright exciting after winter's snow.[7]

Another good arrangement of sentences is in order of "climax," according to which the least important idea is stated first and the others in order of increasing importance, as in the following paragraph. See also **29c.**

9 An ant cannot purposefully try anything new, and any ant that accidentally did so would be murdered by his colleagues. It is the ant colony as a whole that slowly learns over the ages. In contrast, even an earthworm has enough flexibility of brain to enable it to be taught to turn toward the left or right for food. Though rats are not able to reason to any considerable degree, they can solve such problems as separating round objects from triangular ones when these have to do with health or appetite. Cats, with better brains, can be taught somewhat more, and young dogs a great deal. The higher apes can learn by insight as well as by trial and error. —GEORGE R. HARRISON[8]

Sometimes the movement within the paragraph may be from the general to the particular, from the particular to the general, or from the familiar to the unfamiliar. A paragraph may begin with a general statement which is then supported by particular details, or, reversing the process, it may begin with a striking detail or series of details and conclude with a summarizing statement. Note the movement from the general to the particular in paragraph 10 and from particular to general in paragraph 11:

10 In the ten years we have been married, I have yet to see Maurine act deviously. Although caginess is presumed to be a prerequisite for politics, she has marched to the top of the ballot by blurting out exactly what is in her mind. When she was asked to back a bill allocating a portion of dog-racing revenues for 4-H clubs, Maurine scolded her constituents for tying a worthy cause to pari-mutuel gambling. The special interests which she has offended would terrify most politicians—utility companies, dairy farmers, the Bar-Tenders' Union, the fairs in all thirty-six Oregon counties, slot-machine operators, the Farm Bureau Federation, even the American Legion. —RICHARD L. NEUBERGER[9]

[The first sentence states the topic: *Maurine never acts deviously.* The second sentence begins the development with a general statement about her positive action. The third sentence shows specifically how she faced up to the 4-H clubs, and the fourth lists other special interests defied in the same way.]

11 Many years ago a graduate student inconvenienced himself greatly to come a long distance to see me to ask if I could help him secure some information about the term "poll tax." He was preparing a doctor's thesis, he told me, and needed to know how long this term had been in the language, what its basic meaning was, and what other meanings it may have had in the course of its use in English. He was most surprised when I opened the *OED* to the appropriate place and showed him that all he needed to know about this term had been available within a few feet of his desk in the school where he was studying. It is not at all likely that any but the exceptional student will ever need all the information about words that the larger dictionaries afford, but it is well worth the while of every student to become acquainted with the fact that such information is available for those who at any time need to make use of it. —MITFORD M. MATHEWS[10]

[This paragraph explains how one particular graduate student learned his lesson and then suggests the value of the lesson to all students.]

Paragraphs 6, 7, 8, 9, 10, and 11 above illustrate four of many possible types of clear sentence arrangement within the paragraph. Any order of sentences, or any combination

---

[6] From "Collecting Original Art Prints" by Marvin Elkoff, *Holiday,* February, 1966.
[7] From "The Earliest Color," reprinted from *Sunset,* January, 1959. By permission of the publishers.

[8] From "How the Brain Works" by G. R. Harrison, reprinted from the *Atlantic Monthly,* September, 1956. By permission of the author.
[9] From "My Wife Put Me in the Senate," *Harper's Magazine,* June, 1955.
[10] From "The Freshman and His Dictionary" by Mitford M. Mathews, reprinted from *College Composition and Communication,* December, 1955. By permission of the National Council of Teachers of English.

of orders, is satisfactory so long as it makes the sequence of thought clear. Proper arrangement of the sentences is the first, the basic, step to insure good transitions from sentence to sentence. All other steps presuppose that the sentences have first been arranged in the clearest possible order.

▶ EXERCISE 3 Analyze paragraph 4 above and paragraphs 32 and 39 below to determine the order used.

(2) **Link sentences by means of pronouns referring to antecedents in preceding sentences. (See also Section 28.)**

In the following paragraphs italics are used to indicate the pronouns serving as links between sentences. Such pronouns should usually come near the beginning of the sentence if they are to be of much use in paragraph coherence.

    12   I was becoming conditioned by what I saw each day on Pahlavi Avenue as I walked to the university. I would pass a squatting merchant on a blanket, his wares before him, chanting to attract business. *He* had for sale thirty empty Carter's ink bottles; *it* was puzzling to imagine where *he* had gotten them. Farther along a man specializing in art objects was selling a page from an old copy of the *Saturday Evening Post. It* was a four-color advertisement for Hotpoint showing a father, mother, and two crisply dressed daughters smugly regarding the legend in needlework on the wall behind them: "Bless Our Happy Hotpoint Home." Now *it* was handsomely encased behind glass with a gold baroque frame.   —CURTIS HARNACK[11]

    13   Amoebae are gray bits of jelly speckled with multitudes of grains and crystals. *They* have no particular form, although when *they*'re sleeping off a jag or just floating around passing the time of day, *they* assume a sort of star shape, like a splash of ink. Mostly *they* pour *themselves* along like a lava flow. Every once in a while *they* sit down on something and when *they* get up that something is inside *them.*   —ALFRED BESTER[12]

▶ EXERCISE 4 Underline the pronouns used to link sentences in paragraphs 24, 27, and 42, or in any others assigned by your instructor. Check the antecedent (in a preceding sentence) to which each pronoun refers. Underline the pronouns used to link sentences in your last paper or in your last two papers.

(3) **Link sentences by repeating words or ideas used in the preceding sentences.**

Notice in the next paragraph the repetition of the key words—*liberal, radical, leftist, left; conservative, rightist, right*—and of an idea—*labels, distinction, classifications,* "*ideological* positions," "This system of classifying political *philosophies.*" Notice also that the repetition of *world* and the use of *French* and *France's* link sentences within the paragraph.

    14   The *liberal-conservative labels* parallel the *left-right distinction* that grew out of the *French* Revolution. In *France's* National Assembly of 1789, the *conservatives* sat to the *right* of the

speaker, and became known as *rightists,* and the *radicals* sat at the *left* and became known as *leftists.* From then on, it was commonly assumed that you could place *ideological positions* somewhere on a list ranging from the *left* to the *right. This system of classifying political philosophies* is attractive because it seems so tidy. But it is woefully inadequate, since it is one-dimensional, whereas the *world* is three-dimensional. The *world* today is much too complex to hold still for the *left* versus *right* and the *liberal* versus *conservative* classifications.   —BOB SENSER[13]

▶ EXERCISE 5 In paragraphs 25 and 34, or in any others assigned by your instructor, underline each word or idea that is repeated in order to link the sentences within the paragraph. In your last paper underline words or ideas that are repeated as a means of linking sentences.

(4) **Link sentences by using such transitional expressions as the following:**

ADDITION   moreover, further, furthermore, besides, and, and then, likewise, also, nor, too, again, in addition, equally important, next, first, secondly, thirdly, finally, last, lastly
CONTRAST   but, yet, and yet, however, still, nevertheless, on the other hand, on the contrary, after all, notwithstanding, for all that, in contrast to this, at the same time, although this may be true, otherwise
COMPARISON   similarly, likewise, in like manner
PURPOSE   to this end, for this purpose, with this object
RESULT   hence, therefore, accordingly, consequently, thus, thereupon, as a result, then
TIME   meanwhile, at length, immediately, soon, after a few days, in the meantime, afterward, later
PLACE   here, beyond, nearby, opposite to, adjacent to, on the opposite side
SUMMARY, REPETITION, EXEMPLIFICATION, INTENSIFICATION   to sum up, in brief, on the whole, in sum, in short, as I have said, in other words, to be sure, as has been noted, for example, for instance, in fact, indeed, in any event

Note the transitional expressions in the following paragraph. See also paragraph 17.

    15   Since the major cost of advanced education, if the student is away from home, is board and lodging, one can argue that as far as possible the expansion of public education beyond high school should be arranged locally., *Otherwise* in order to offer equal opportunities we should have to envisage using public funds to provide years of free board and room for a considerable fraction of our high school graduates. *But* there are various types of professional and vocational education which can be given at only a few centers in even a very populous state. It is literally impossible, *for example,* to give adequate instruction in clinical medicine except in cities of sufficient size to support large hospitals. *Similarly,* advanced work in the arts, sciences, and letters can be done only where adequate libraries and laboratories are at hand. It is clearly in the national interest to find all the latent talent available for the lengthy training that research careers demand. *Yet* to establish research centers at every point in the United States where general education beyond the high school is desired would be not merely uneconomical, but impossible.   —JAMES BRYANT CONANT[14]

---

[11] From "The Wasteful Savers" by Curtis Harnack, first published in *The Reporter,* September 29, 1960. Reprinted by permission of the author.
[12] From "The Compleat Hobbyist" by Alfred Bester, *Holiday,* December, 1965.

[13] From "Don't Get Obsessed with Labels" by Bob Senser, reprinted from *Our Sunday Visitor,* May 7, 1961. By permission of the publishers.
[14] From "The University," reprinted from *Education in a Divided World* by James Bryant Conant. By permission of Harvard University Press.

▶ **EXERCISE 6** In paragraph 37, or in any others assigned by your instructor, underline all transitional expressions used to link sentences within the paragraph. In your last paper underline all transitional expressions used to link sentences.

(5) **Link sentences by means of parallel structure—that is, by repetition of the sentence pattern.**

Note how the following paragraph is made coherent by the parallel structure of the last four sentences.

16 In the minds and in the ideals of Americans we have untouched natural resources that need developing just as much as the material treasures still tucked away in unused patents, in undeveloped river valleys, and in the atomic nuclei. For the next war, if one is still required to iron out national vanities, we shall need not so much manpower as brain power and alertness. For the continuing fight against disease, we shall need trained technical skills and unlimited resources in laboratory equipment and service. For the advancement of knowledge generally, we need a deliberate plan to free contemplative men for quiet and respected contemplation. For the realization of "fuller and more fruitful employment and a fuller and more fruitful life," we need a National Science Foundation and a country-wide awareness that governmental support for knowledge-research is henceforth basic in the national policy.

                        —HARLOW SHAPLEY[15]

▶ **EXERCISE 7** In paragraph 27, or in any others assigned by your instructor, point out instances of parallel structure used to link sentences within the paragraph. Can you find instances in your own writing?

We have observed that easy transition from sentence to sentence within the paragraph depends on clear arrangement of the sentences and then on linking these sentences by means of pronouns, repeated words or ideas, transitional expressions, and parallel structure. Usually several of these aids to coherence are found in a single paragraph. In the following paragraph the linking devices are underlined and are explained in the margins.

17 It would seem that the great virtue of writing is its power to
[Repetition of word] arrest the swift process of thought for steady contemplation and analysis. Writing is the translation of
[Parallel structure] the audible into the visual. In _[Pronoun (referring to writing)]_ large measure it is the spatialization of thought. Yet writing on _[Repetition of word]_ papyrus and parchment fostered a
[Transitional word] very different set of mental habits _[Repetition of idea (process of thought)]_ from those we associate with print

[15] From "Status Quo or Pioneer," *Harper's Magazine*, October, 1945.

and books. In the first place, si- _[Transitional expression]_ lent reading was unknown until the macadamized, streamlined surfaces of the printed page arrived to per- _[Parallel structure]_ mit the swift traverse of the eye
[Repetition of idea (silent reading)] alone. In the second place, difficulty of access of manuscripts _[Transitional expression]_ impelled students to memorize so far as possible everything they
[Pronoun referring to necessary memorization] read. This led to encyclopedism, but also to having on tap in oral discourse one's entire erudition.[16]

▶ **EXERCISE 8** In paragraph 36 below, or in any other paragraphs assigned by your instructor, point out all devices used to insure easy transition from sentence to sentence.

(6) **Transitions between paragraphs.**

Transitions from one paragraph to the next are even more necessary than those between sentences within the paragraph. The reader takes it for granted that all sentences in one paragraph are on the same topic. But the paragraph break signals a new topic or a new phase of the preceding one, and the reader wants to know at once what the new one is to be. In the three connected paragraphs (18, 19, and 20) below, note how each opening sentence ties in with the preceding paragraph and also indicates the direction in which the new paragraph is to go.

18 In Philadelphia, the advantage of a small car was recently illustrated in a court of law. A baffled cop had dragged before a magistrate the owners of two MGs which had both been parked in the motor space designed for a single vehicle. It was the view of the cop that this arrangement resulted in an illicit mulcting of the city at the rate of a dime an hour. The magistrate disagreed; he commended the drivers for their ingenuity.

19 Another and no less precious asset arises not so much from size as from lighter and differently distributed weight. A small car is supremely handy in icy weather. It is almost never trapped by snow or mud, and it will almost never lose traction on a slippery grade. Its skids are rare and gentle. And its driver can enjoy the soul-satisfying experience of wending his way up a steep and snowy hill at an even speed among big cars which have skidded into the gutter or which lie helplessly athwart the highway.

20 For many of the more than a million Americans who own two or more cars, these and other advantages have dictated the choice of a small car as a supplement to the basic big car.

[16] From "Sight, Sound, and Fury" by Marshall McLuhan, reprinted from *Commonweal*, April 9, 1954, the weekly journal of opinion edited by Catholic laymen. By permission of *Commonweal*.

The combination of, say, a station wagon and an MG provides a nice balance between capacity and chic and provides an escape from the status of a two-car family with all the financial and social implications it involves. A small car doesn't seem to be *exactly* a car; its sheepish owner can treat it as a gadget and explain that it costs next to nothing to operate.

—LAURENCE LAFORE, R. W. LAFORE, AND R. W. LAFORE, JR.[17]

The topics of the three paragraphs may be stated thus: (18) *Ease of parking small cars was recently illustrated in Philadelphia.* (19) *The light weight of small cars is especially advantageous in icy weather.* (20) *The small car needs hardly to be considered a "second" car.* The opening sentence of paragraph 18 refers, by *advantage*, to the previously discussed ease of parking small cars and also leads up to the illustration to be used in the paragraph. The next paragraph begins with *another . . . asset*, showing at once that an additional advantage of small cars is to be pointed out (at the same time that *another* calls attention to the one just discussed). And *these and other advantages* in the opening sentence of paragraph 20 ties in with what has preceded while leading to what is to follow.

Sometimes a paragraph is used to make a transition. Paragraph 22 below is an example of a transitional paragraph.

21   I am overwhelmed by our material and materialistic culture—and its accomplishments. We have developed manufacturing and marketing techniques unsurpassed by any other country. The editors of *Fortune* magazine have observed, "The foreign visitor is drenched with sights and sounds and smells emanating from a man-made environment to which almost all Americans appear to give all their energies."

22   What are some of the factors that make us different from the rest of the world?

23   Our *standard of living* is considerably higher than that of any other nation. In fact, the American way of living is one in which an ever-increasing standard of living is considered our birthright. And with a high standard of living, we have not only great physical and material well-being but also an opportunity to expand our economy still further, especially in the last part of the twentieth century.   —STEUART HENDERSON BRITT[18]

[Note how paragraph 22 links paragraph 21 (which stresses our difference from the rest of the world) with paragraph 23 (which discusses one factor that makes us different). The paragraphs after 23 take up and develop separately the other factors.]

▶ EXERCISE 9   Analyze all of the transitions, not only those between sentences within a paragraph but also those between the paragraphs.

24   Language must convey all the complex organization of observations, ideas, and plain prejudices on which society and culture rest. It must reveal our individual moods, social status, origin, and appraisal of the situation in which we find ourselves. It must enable us to interact both with close friends and total strangers promptly and effectively. All this is complicated enough.

25   But language must do more than this. It must continually adjust itself to new needs. No language can be a fixed system of words and patterns. It must be open to receive new words

[17] From "The Small Cars: Fun on Wheels," *Harper's Magazine,* March, 1955.

[18] By permission from *The Spenders,* by Steuart Henderson Britt. Copyright 1960. McGraw-Hill Book Company, Inc.

and new structures, and to change the old. Change is inevitable, since language functions in a society in ceaseless flux. The continual change in language produces inevitable maladjustments in the system. The language must repeatedly repair itself, restoring and maintaining equilibrium by additional changes to counterbalance those forced upon it by changed environment. A language that could not adjust would deteriorate.   —H. A. GLEASON, JR.[19]

31c

Develop the paragraph adequately. Supply enough information to satisfy the reader but avoid excessively long paragraphs.

(1) Supply enough information to satisfy the reader.

Avoid inadequately developed paragraphs. A topic sentence is not in itself a paragraph. In ordinary writing a very short paragraph is sometimes used for emphasis or for transition between longer paragraphs. But a *series* of paragraphs each less than fifty words in length (except in dialogue and other special types of writing) suggests inadequate development of the thought. If such choppy paragraphs deal with the same topic, they should be combined into one or more longer paragraphs. If not, each paragraph should be expanded to the point where the thought is adequately developed.

PARAGRAPHS THAT SHOULD BE COMBINED

The line of demarcation between capitalism and socialism is sharp and clear.

Capitalism is that form of organization in which the means of production—and by that is meant the machine and the funds required to utilize the machine—are controlled by private individuals or by privately owned organizations.

Under a socialistic regime the control of the means of production, the control of capital—for even socialists concede the need for capital—is by the group. Under capitalism the profits accrue to the private individual; under socialism, to the group.

[These three short paragraphs, read together, actually make one unified paragraph of ninety words and should be so written. Taken separately, the paragraphs are short and choppy; together they form a paragraph of average length developing a clearly stated topic sentence: *The line of demarcation between capitalism and socialism is sharp and clear.*]

PARAGRAPHS THAT SHOULD BE EXPANDED

During his first term of office President Roosevelt introduced many laws to promote national recovery. These laws covered all phases of the national life.

[The reader wants to know specifically what some of these laws were.]

Forestry work is healthful, educational, and financially rewarding. A forester, for example, soon learns how to prevent and to fight forest fires.

[The reader expects to find out about three aspects of forestry work, and the writer comments briefly on only one. How is the work healthful? What else does a forester learn? What are the financial rewards?]

[19] From *Linguistics and English Grammar,* New York, 1965, p. 107.

The football game was much more like a movie than like real life. The most improbable things happened.
[Some of the improbable happenings should be mentioned, and the implied contrast between the movies and real life elaborated.]

Each of these short paragraphs begins with a promising topic sentence and then stops before supplying enough information to satisfy the reader. In other words, the paragraphs are not adequately developed. If the paragraphs in your compositions tend to be inadequately developed, study the seven methods of paragraph development described and illustrated in **31d**, pages 900–06.

(2) Avoid excessively long paragraphs.

In current writing, paragraphs seldom run to more than two or three hundred words, and the average is much shorter, perhaps not more than one hundred words. Whenever a writer finds that he needs more than 250 words to develop his central thought, he should, if possible, divide his material into two or more paragraphs. Let us notice, for example, how we may divide the following long paragraph, which Richard Steele wrote more than two hundred years ago when readers were less hurried than those of our generation.

[1] When a good artist would express any remarkable character in sculpture, he endeavors to work up his figure into all the perfections his imagination can form, and to imitate not so much what is, as what may or ought to be. [2] I shall follow their example, in the idea I am going to trace out of a fine gentleman, by assembling together such qualifications as seem requisite to make the character complete. [3] In order to do this I shall premise in general, that by a fine gentleman I mean a man completely qualified as well for the service and good as for the ornament and delight of society. [4] When I consider the frame of mind peculiar to a gentleman, I suppose it graced with all the dignity and elevation of spirit that human nature is capable of. [5] To this I would have joined a clear understanding, a reason free from prejudice, a steady judgment, and an extensive knowledge. [6] When I think of the heart of a gentleman, I imagine it firm and intrepid, void of all inordinate passions, and full of tenderness, compassion, and benevolence. [7] When I view the fine gentleman with regard to his manners, methinks I see him modest without bashfulness, frank and affable without impertinence, obliging and complaisant without servility, cheerful and in good humor without noise. [8] These amiable qualities are not easily obtained; neither are there many men that have a genius to excel this way. [9] A finished gentleman is perhaps the most uncommon of all the great characters in life. [10] Besides the natural endowments with which this distinguished man is to be born, he must run through a long series of education. [11] Before he makes his appearance and shines in the world, he must be principled in religion, instructed in all the moral virtues, and led through the whole course of the polite arts and sciences. [12] He should be no stranger to courts and to camps; he must travel to open his mind, to enlarge his views, to learn the policies and interests of foreign states, as well as to fashion and polish himself, and to get clear of national prejudices, of which every country has its share. [13] To all these more essential improvements he must not forget to add the fashionable ornaments of life, such as are the languages and the bodily exercises most in vogue; neither would I have him think even dress itself beneath his notice.

A careful reading shows that this whole paragraph of 404 words develops Steele's concept of the ideal gentleman. The paragraph has unity; except for the excessive

length, there would be no reason for dividing it. Fortunately it can (like most overlong paragraphs) be divided into shorter paragraphs, each developing a specific part of the general topic. Steele's long paragraph can be divided, without any rewriting, into three good paragraphs as follows:

FIRST PARAGRAPH (sentences 1–3) The method to be used in depicting the ideal gentleman and a general definition of him.
SECOND PARAGRAPH (sentences 4–7) The ideal gentleman's specific qualities of mind, heart, and manners.
THIRD PARAGRAPH (sentences 8–13) The education needed to develop these qualities.

If the long paragraph were thus divided into three, it would be much easier for the reader to comprehend. And each paragraph would be well unified, with good transitions from one to the other. Note especially the excellent transition to the third paragraph: "These amiable qualities are not easily obtained; neither are there many men that have a genius to excel this way."

31d

Master several different methods of paragraph development.

Analysis shows that good paragraphs may be developed by many methods and by innumerable combinations of methods. No one method, or combination of methods, is better than another except as it happens to fit the needs of a given paragraph. The experienced writer may be unaware of the method he is using. The inexperienced writer, however, can learn to develop his own paragraphs by studying the methods of professional writers.

(1) List specific details suggested by the topic sentence.

26 After the refrain she would give the night herding yodel of the cowboy, born of the vast melancholy of the plains; *a yodel to quiet a herd of restless cattle in the deep darkness of a rainy night,* when far-off flashes of lightning and the rumble of distant thunder meant danger. While the cattle milled around and refused to lie down, close to the fringe of the circle of moving animals rode the cowboys giving this wordless cry to the cattle, like the plea of a lonesome wolf calling for his mate, like the croon of a mother trying to quiet a restless babe in the long watches of the night, like the soft moo of a cow wooing her young offspring from its hiding place to come for its milk. "Quiet, cattle, quiet. Darkness is everywhere, but we, your friends, are near. Lie down, little dogies, lie down." The yodel was persuasive, far-reaching. Even in its high notes it was soothing and tender. —JOHN A. LOMAX[20]

[Notice that the carefully selected details bring into focus the nature and effect of the yodel at night. Effective writers choose details with care, and omit irrelevant details no matter how fascinating they may be in themselves.]

27 *My second great fortune was Lily Bess Campbell, professor of English literature at the University of California in Los Angeles.* She taught me to think exactly, to say the precise truth as nearly as I could perceive it. She taught me that there is vitality

[20] From "Songs of the Cowboy," *Atlantic Monthly,* March, 1947.

in logic, that there is logic in humor and in beauty, that in humor the greater the truth the funnier, that in lyricism the more consistent and clear the more moving. She made me brief a Shelley ode as though it were a legal argument. She taught me that a sentence was organic with bones and sinews and for this reason had life, that the power of logic was a passionate power and that Euclid and Grammar were one. And for the first time I recognized Pattern, which is Law as well as Magic.   —AGNES DE MILLE[21]

[The paragraph lists nine particulars in which Professor Campbell proved to be a "great fortune."]

28   When it was over and I escaped through the ropes, shaking, bleeding a little from the mouth, with rosin dust on my pants and a vicious throbbing in my head, *I knew all there was to know about being hit in the prize-ring.* It seems that I had gone to an expert for tuition. I knew the sensation of being stalked and pursued by a relentless, truculent professional destroyer whose trade and business it was to injure men. I saw the quick flash of the brown forearm that precedes the stunning shock as a bony, leather-bound fist lands on cheek or mouth. I learned more (partly from photographs of the lesson, viewed afterwards, one of which shows me ducked under a vicious left hook, an act of which I never had the slightest recollection) about instinctive ducking and blocking than I could have in ten years of looking at prizefights, and I learned, too, that as the soldier never hears the bullet that kills him, so does the fighter rarely, if ever, see the punch that tumbles blackness over him like a mantle, with a tearing rip as though the roof of his skull were exploding, and robs him of his senses.   —PAUL GALLICO[22]

[Details of this paragraph describe how the author learned what it is like to be a prizefighter. Note that in this paragraph and in paragraphs 26 and 27, the order of development is from the general to the particular.]

▶ EXERCISE 10   Develop one of the following topic sentences by using carefully selected specific details.

1. Americans know what two aspirins can do.
2. Television shows are influential babysitters.
3. Music shapes our moods.
4. My uncle was in almost perpetual emotion.
5. The comedian looked as distressed as a freshman on registration day.
6. One teacher influenced my thinking.
7. It was a perfect day for a trip to the lake.
8. At that moment, I knew how it felt to have stage fright.
9. I was the first one to arrive after the accident.
10. It is exciting to travel by jet.

(2) Illustrate the topic sentence by an example or examples.

29   *The belief in punishment at a distance was strikingly illustrated by a report from South Africa last April.* It seems that the caning of offenders was being carried out in a magistrates' court located near the center of Cape Town. Sentences of up to ten cuts were inflicted on malefactors, beginning with eight-year-old boys, in that particular jurisdiction. The matter became newsworthy when the public began to object to the practice. The objection, however, was not to the punishment itself but to the uncomfortable circumstance that it was administered in the business district of the city. One citizen complained, "We can clearly hear the swish and smack of the cane and the pleadings and screams of the people being beaten." It appears that this noise was upsetting women office workers. Not only the women were disturbed. One man said "that his conversations with important clients had been interrupted by the 'howling of somebody being thrashed.'" The problem was solved by police assurances that the beatings would thereafter be administered in the basement, where they would not disturb the public.   —JUDGE DAVID L. BAZELON[23]

[The topic sentence is developed by one striking example. Note that the example of the citizens' reactions to *nearby* punishment makes immediately clear what the author means by the rather abstract idea, "the belief in punishment at a distance." A good example is clearly related to the generalization it illustrates, and it makes that generalization easily understandable to the reader.]

30   *Tails serve animals as* fly-swatters, as signals, as instruments of communication, as extra hands and *tools of many uses.* A woolly monkey curls the tip of his tail into a circle, plants this loop on the ground, stiffens the rest of the tail into a supporting column, and has a portable chair. A honey bear, raiding a nest of bees, hangs head downward and then, when it wants to make its getaway, climbs its own tail. Pangolins, which are scaly anteaters living in West Africa, block their burrow entrances with their armored tails.   —ALAN DEVOE[24]

[Three sentences, each presenting a separate example, develop the topic sentence.]

31   The average cow hand is so conscious of brands that in season and out of season, appropriately and inappropriately, consciously and unconsciously, *he brands whatever he comes across.* He whittles brands on sticks; he burns them into the planks of branding chutes, on pasture gates, on the anchor posts of windmill towers. He smears them with axle grease across the doors of barns and garages. He paints them with charcoal on the rock walls of canyons in which he has made a campfire. He carves them into his spur traps, leggings, saddle—above all, into his boot tops. More pistols are etched with cattle brands than were ever notched for dead victims. Many a cook has stenciled the ranch coat of arms into the top crust of that gala-day treat—a wild-plum cobbler. Ranchboys are incorrigible when it comes to carving brands on their desks at school. They play ranch, and with bailing wire for running irons brand oak balls, the sawed-off tips of horns, spools, and other objects used to represent cattle and horses.   —J. FRANK DOBIE[25]

[The topic sentence is developed by numerous examples.]

32   *Perhaps the most extraordinary quality the Mohammedan religion developed in Jolo is its fanaticism.* For years, no Moro would attend school for fear of "invisible conversion" to Christianity. As recently as 1940 the students of one of the schools killed all their non-Moro teachers for no reason that the authorities were ever able to discern. And even today, some people of Jolo will not ride in a car, simply because Christians introduced automobiles to the island. It is also a problem for Moros to go to the hospital, because, according to their reasoning, if they died, a Christian would touch them, and this is not to be borne.   —FAUBION BOWERS[26]

[The topic sentence is developed by four instances or examples, each in a separate sentence.]

▶ EXERCISE 11   Analyze the development of paragraph 12, or any other paragraph selected by your instructor.

[21] From "The Valor of Teaching" by Agnes de Mille, *Atlantic Monthly*, June, 1955.
[22] From *Farewell to Sport* by Paul Gallico. Reprinted by permission of Alfred A. Knopf, Inc.
[23] From "The Imperative to Punish" by David L. Bazelon, reprinted from the *Atlantic Monthly*, June, 1960. By permission of the author.
[24] From *This Fascinating Animal World* by Alan Devoe. Copyright 1951 McGraw-Hill Book Company. Used by permission.
[25] From "The Heraldry of the Range," *Adventures in American Literature*, New York, 1958, p. 173.
[26] From "The Land-Locked Pirate of the Pacific," *Harper's Magazine*, June, 1955.

▶ EXERCISE 12   Develop one of the following topics by using a long example or several short ones.

1. The collie is a particularly loyal dog.
2. It is easy to coach at a distance.
3. A man uses his thumb in various ways.
4. There is a flower for every occasion.
5. My little brother is always fixing things.
6. Our science teacher encourages us really to see the things we look at.
7. In my collection are many greeting cards.
8. I have considered majoring in several subjects.
9. He makes everyone he meets feel important.
10. Almost anything can be bought on the installment plan.

(3) Develop the topic by definition.

33   *First, it is desirable to define the intellectuals.* They are all those who create, distribute and apply culture—the symbolic world of man, including art, science and religion. Within this group, three different levels can be set out. There is the hard core who are the creators of culture—authors, artists, philosophers, scholars, editors, some journalists. Second, there are those who distribute what others create—performers of various arts, most teachers, most reporters. Third, and the most peripheral group, are those who apply culture as part of their jobs—professionals such as physicians and lawyers.   —SEYMOUR MARTIN LIPSET[27]

[The topic sentence calls for a definition of *intellectuals;* the other sentences define and explain the word. A formal, or logical, definition such as Lipset uses has two parts: first, the thing being defined is put into a *class* of similar things; then it is differentiated from all other things in that class. Thus, *intellectuals* are defined as "those" men (*class*—i.e., mankind) "who create, distribute and apply culture" (*difference* from other kinds of men).]

34   *A guaranteed annual wage is money paid by an employer to people for all or some part of a year in which they are not making products.* The payments are part of the manufacturer's cost and hence part of the consumer's cost. If the manufacturer has ten employees but work for only eight, he must nevertheless reeover in the price he gets for his product the payments he makes to his employees for hours they did not work, or he must go out of business. This is true of any employer, whether he has ten or ten thousand employees.   —LELAND HAZARD[28]

[The topic sentence defines "guaranteed annual wage," and the remaining sentences serve to refine and clarify this definition.]

▶ EXERCISE 13   Select a suitable topic sentence and develop a paragraph by definition.

(4) Develop the topic by using classification.

35   There are three kinds of book owners. The first has all the standard sets and best-sellers—unread, untouched. (This deluded individual owns woodpulp and ink, not books.) The second has a great many books—a few of them read through, most of them dipped into, but all of them as clean and shiny as the day they were bought. (This person would probably like to make books his own, but is restrained by a false respect for their physical appearance.) The third has a few books or many—every one of them dog-eared

and dilapidated, shaken and loosened by continual use, marked and scribbled in from front to back. (This man owns books.)
    —MORTIMER J. ADLER[29]

[Classification is like definition in that it develops an idea by putting things into classes. But it does not differentiate one member of a class from another; instead, it simply gives a complete or representative listing of the members of the class. Thus, Adler in the paragraph above classifies book owners into three main classes and lists each class.]

▶ EXERCISE 14   Use classification to develop one of the following topics:

1. There are various kinds of newspapers (OR columnists, editors, comic strips).
2. I have known two (OR three, OR four) distinct types of hostesses (OR advisers, artists, lecturers).

(5) Develop the topic by using comparison or contrast.

36   To some of his contemporaries Socrates looked like a sophist. But *he distrusted and opposed the sophists wherever possible.* They toured the whole Greek world: Socrates stayed in Athens, talking to his fellow-citizens. They made carefully prepared continuous speeches; he only asked questions. They took rich fees for their teaching; he refused regular payment, living and dying poor. They were elegantly dressed, turned out like filmstars on a personal-appearance tour, with secretaries and personal servants and elaborate advertising. Socrates wore the workingman's clothes, bare feet and a smock; in fact, he had been a stonemason and carver by trade, and came from a working-class family. They spoke in specially prepared lecture-halls; he talked to people at street-corners and in the gymnasium (like public baths and bathing beaches nowadays), where every afternoon the young men exercised, and the old men talked, while they all sun bathed. He fitted in so well there that he sometimes compared himself to the athletic coach, who does not run or wrestle, but teaches others how to run and wrestle better: Socrates said he trained people to think. Lastly, the sophists said they knew everything and were ready to explain it. Socrates said he knew nothing and was trying to find out.
    —GILBERT HIGHET[30]

[The first sentence is transitional, linking this paragraph with the author's foregoing one; the second sentence states the topic, which is developed by contrasting the sophists with Socrates. In making a comparison or contrast, a writer will often choose the things he wants to compare or contrast from the same class. Socrates and the sophists both belong to the class "philosopher-teachers." This common class provides the *basis* of the contrast. Thus the two kinds of philosophers can be contrasted not only in their methods and their personal habits but, most important, in the ideas or theories of knowledge they taught.]

37   *In all the countries of Europe I have visited there is a patent difference between metropolises and smaller towns.* In the provinces of France, or Austria, or Germany you notice the difference in every shop window, in every coffee house, in the universities themselves. When, for instance, you go from Paris to Lille or to Orleans or to Bordeaux the dresses, the books, the furniture you see in the windows will lag some months if not years behind those you were used to seeing in Paris. The hotels and restaurants will be more modest, uncomfortable, and rather shabby. Universities will lack the stimulating élan of the Sorbonne. *Nothing of this kind distinguishes Madison from, let us say, New York or*

---

[27] From "The Egghead Looks at Himself" by Seymour M. Lipset, reprinted from the New York *Times Magazine,* November 17, 1957. By permission of the author.

[28] From "Can We Afford a Guaranteed Wage?" by Leland Hazard, *Atlantic Monthly,* March, 1955.

[29] From "How to Mark a Book" by Mortimer J. Adler, reprinted from the *Saturday Review,* July 6, 1940. By permission of the publishers.

[30] From *The Art of Teaching* by Gilbert Highet. Copyright 1950 by Gilbert Highet. Reprinted by permission of Alfred A. Knopf, Inc.

Chicago. Here you see just the same merchandise in the windows as in New York, the same neon lights, the same pictures in the same movie theaters, you read the same columns and comics in the local papers as in those of New York, and the university with its splendid installations, its rich library, its almost luxurious Students' Union certainly does not fall behind any university I saw in New York, though it is smaller. —PAUL SCHRECKER[31]

[The implied topic sentence, derived from the two italicized sentences, is: In Europe, but not in America, there is a patent difference between metropolises and smaller towns. European conditions (in four sentences following the first italicized sentence) are contrasted with American conditions (in one very long sentence following the second italicized sentence). Note that instances or examples are used to develop the separate parts of the contrast.]

▶ EXERCISE 15 Develop by contrast one of the following topics: (1) the service at a soda fountain and in a hotel dining room; (2) the dialogue of a motion picture and the dialogue of Shakespeare; (3) the architecture of the Washington Monument and of the Lincoln Memorial; (4) the relative effectiveness of radio and television.

38 *The living language is like a cowpath: it is the creation of the cows themselves, who, having created it, follow it or depart from it according to their whims or needs.* From daily use, the path undergoes change. A cow is under no obligation to stay in the narrow path she helped make, following the contour of the land, but she often profits by staying with it and she would be handicapped if she didn't know where it was and where it led to. Children obviously do not depend for communication on a knowledge of grammar; they rely on their ear, mostly, which is sharp and quick. But we have yet to see the child who hasn't profited from coming face to face with a relative pronoun at an early age, and from reading books, which follow the paths of centuries.
—E. B. WHITE[32]

[This paragraph compares the living language to a cowpath and the children who speak the language to the cows that use the path by pointing out similarities regarding creation, usage, change, and profitable knowledge and conformity. Note that, unlike the comparisons in paragraphs 35 and 36, the two things compared here are not members of the same class.]

Note that the last three paragraphs illustrate two different ways of making the contrast. In paragraphs 37 and 38 one side of the contrast is completely developed and then the other; in paragraph 36 both sides are contrasted in almost every sentence. Either way is good, and so is a combination of the two.

▶ EXERCISE 16 Develop a paragraph by analogy according to the organization used in paragraph 38.

(6) **Develop the topic by showing cause or effect.**

39 Tragedy was a Greek creation because in Greece thought was free. Men were thinking more and more deeply about human life, and beginning to perceive more and more clearly that it was bound up with evil and that injustice was of the nature of things. And then, one day, this knowledge of something irremediably wrong in the world came to a poet with his poet's power to see beauty in the truth of human life, and the first tragedy was

written. As the author of a most distinguished book on the subject says: "The spirit of inquiry meets the spirit of poetry and tragedy is born." Make it concrete: early Greece with her godlike heroes and hero-gods fighting far on the ringing plains of windy Troy; with her lyric world, where every common thing is touched with beauty —her twofold world of poetic creation. Then a new age dawns, not satisfied with beauty of song and story, an age that must try to know and to explain. And for the first time tragedy appears. A poet of surpassing magnitude, not content with the old sacred conventions, and of a soul great enough to bear new and intolerable truth—that is Aeschylus, the first writer of tragedy.
—EDITH HAMILTON[33]

[Miss Hamilton here states that tragedy began when the ancient Greeks discovered, through free inquiry, that evil is an inevitable part of human life. This discovery is, then, the *cause* of the writing of tragedy. But before this cause could have an effect in the creation of tragic plays, a great poet had to come along—that was Aeschylus. A paragraph developed by causal analysis must not only raise the question *why* but answer it to the satisfaction of the reader. The cause or causes must satisfactorily explain the result. Has Miss Hamilton done this?]

40 One might wonder why, after the Norman Conquest, French did not become the national language, replacing English entirely. The reason is that the Conquest was not a national migration, as the earlier Anglo-Saxon invasion had been. Great numbers of Normans came to England, but they came as rulers and landlords. French became the language of the court, the language of the nobility, the language of polite society, the language of literature. But it did not replace English as the language of the people. There must always have been hundreds of towns and villages in which French was never heard except when visitors of high station passed through. —PAUL ROBERTS[34]

[The topic sentence raises the question why the Norman Conquest did not, as might have been expected, make England a French-speaking country. The topic sentence thus states an *effect* or *result* of the Conquest. The sentences that follow develop the topic by showing *causes* to account for the result.]

▶ EXERCISE 17 Notice how paragraphs 39 and 40 are developed by explaining why the opening statement is true. In the same way develop a paragraph from one of the following topics:

1. Higher education has become more important than ever.
2. Our age is a dangerous one in which to live.

(7) **Develop the topic by a combination of methods.**

Many good paragraphs are developed not by any one specific method but by a combination of methods. Some good paragraphs almost defy analysis. The important consideration is not the specific method used but the adequacy of the development.

41 I wonder why American towns look so much alike that I sometimes mix them up in my memory. The reference to the standard influence of mass production whose agents are the traveling salesman, the mail-order houses, the five-and-ten cent stores, the chain stores, the movies, is not sufficient. If you stay two

[31] From "American Diary," *Harper's Magazine,* July, 1944.
[32] From the *New Yorker,* February 23, 1957. Reprinted by permission; Copr. © 1957, The New Yorker Magazine, Inc.

[33] Reprinted from *The Greek Way* by Edith Hamilton. By permission of W. W. Norton & Company, Inc. Copyright 1930, 1942 by W. W. Norton & Company, Inc.
[34] From "A Brief History of English," reprinted from *Understanding English* by Paul Roberts. By permission of Harper & Brothers.

days in Bologna and in Ferrara, or in Arles and in Avignon, you will never mix them up in all your life. But it may well happen that after you spend two days in St. Louis and in Kansas City the images of these towns soon merge into one. I think the real reason for this is that these towns have not yet had time enough to individualize and to crystallize visible local traditions of their own. Physiognomically speaking, children are much less differentiated from each other than grown people. —PAUL SCHRECKER[35]

[Note how this effective paragraph combines both cause or effect and comparison or contrast.]

42 I have heard rumors of visitors who were disappointed. The same people will be disappointed at the Day of Judgment. In fact, the Grand Canyon is a sort of landscape Day of Judgment. It is not a show place, a beauty spot, but a revelation. The Colorado River, which is powerful, turbulent, and so thick with silt that it is like a saw, made it with the help of the erosive forces of rain, frost, and wind, and some strange geological accidents; and all these together have been hard at work on it for the last seven or eight million years. It is the largest of the eighteen canyons of the Colorado River, is over two hundred miles long, has an average width of twelve miles, and is a good mile deep. It is the world's supreme example of erosion. But this is not what it really is. It is, I repeat, a revelation. The Colorado River made it, but you feel when you are there that God gave the Colorado River its instructions. It is all Beethoven's nine symphonies in stone and magic light. Even to remember that it is still there lifts up the heart. If I were an American, I should make my remembrance of it the final test of men, art, and policies. I should ask myself: Is this good enough to exist in the same country as the Canyon? How would I feel about this man, this kind of art, these political measures, if I were near that Rim? Every member or officer of the Federal Government ought to remind himself, with triumphant pride, that he is on the staff of the Grand Canyon. —J. B. PRIESTLEY[36]

▶ EXERCISE 18 Pick out the topic sentence in paragraph 42. Show how Priestley effectively develops his central idea. What specific methods or combination of methods of development are used?

▶ EXERCISE 19 Be prepared for a class discussion of the following paragraphs. Be able to point out topic sentences or central ideas and to designate methods of development.

43 Being a freethinking fisherman who will try anything, I borrowed the colonel's flimsy rod, only to find out that, while bread bait may not be immoral, it was in this case impractical. Mother Slonaker's loaf was so creamy good that it simply melted off the hook, and the trout would gobble it up as it drifted toward the bottom of the pool. At this point a conventional fisherman would have given up, but not an iconoclast with a fish crow to feed. Looking around for a bread substitute, I could hardly fail to see the piles of cigarette butts with which the colonel, while nervously dueling the trout, had littered the bank of the pool. Fortunately, he smoked Brand X, a filtered fag, suitably safe and masculine for a marine. Breaking off a firm, fibrous, buoyant filter, I put it on the hook and threw it in the water. A rainbow immediately rose, trout-lipped the butt, swallowed it, and was pulled out on the grass. —BIL GILBERT[37]

44 Except for the charred joke of a wall where the fire finally stopped, only our chimney guards the big hole now, and snow blankets most of the wreckage in it. The andirons, their burden of logs consumed along with the room they were supposed to warm, are squatting black in the fireplace. Six feet below, the fire screen is a twisted sculpture where it fell with the floor. Pipes poke at odd angles here and there. Scorched cables snake in and out of the snow piled in the cellar. On a cracked flagstone sits skull-like the metal top of a tape recorder. Near it, a scrap on a little drift, is a circular patch of blue. It is the center of a record, and the printing on it shows that it was Side 2 of Beethoven's Eroica. In the shell of the garage a pair of tires and a ping-pong table survive. —LOUDON WAINWRIGHT[38]

45 A pecking order has come into existence in science, in which the highest rank is assigned to the "purest" subjects, those whose connection with the directly observable elements of our physical environment is least obvious. Problems relating to the structure of the earth, the origin and history of the solar system, the conditions under which life developed on this planet—all the questions which directly concern the planet earth and man's physical existence on it—are considered impure and of lower intellectual content. Scientific investigations which have a direct bearing on human affairs are ranked at the bottom. The difficult and important problem of the weather is beneath the notice of most physicists. —ROBERT JASTROW[39]

46 Of the various factors that caused men to come to America, the economic was no doubt the most important. Throughout the period of the migrations, there was no free land in Europe; natural resources were limited; and the population was always in danger of increasing faster than the means of subsistence. Migration always occurred chiefly from areas of Europe where agriculture was still the chief occupation and where (owing to the growth of big estates or to genuine overcrowding) the demand for land was in excess of the supply. This was true of Spain in the sixteenth century, of England in the early seventeenth, and of Ireland, Germany, Scandinavia, Italy, and the Slavic countries of the east in the nineteenth. —HENRY BAMFORD PARKES[40]

47 Children are poetic. They love to feel of things. I suppose it is necessary to their preservation that they should be, for by random exercise of their organs of feeling they develop them and make them fit for their practical function. But that is not the chief reason why they are poetic; the chief reason is that they are not practical. They have not yet felt the necessity, or got addicted to the trick, of formulating a purpose and then achieving it. Therefore, this naive impulse of nature, the impulse toward realization, is free in them. Moreover, it is easy of satisfaction. It is easy for children to taste the qualities of experience, because experience is new, and its qualities are but loosely bound together into what we call "things." Each is concrete, particular, unique, and without an habitual use. —MAX EASTMAN[41]

48 There is Lou Martin, the class comedian, whose forte is facial expressions. No one can look more crestfallen over unprepared homework: hand clasped to brow, knees buckling, shoulders sagging with remorse, he is a penitent to end all penitents.

[35] From "American Diary," Harper's Magazine, July, 1944.
[36] From Midnight on the Desert by J. B. Priestley. By permission of the author.
[37] From "The Compleatest Angler" copyright © 1965 by Bil Gilbert. From the book Bears in the Ladies Room and Other Beastly Pursuits by Bil Gilbert. Reprinted by permission of the author and Doubleday & Company, Inc.

[38] From "After the Fire, a Sifting of Ashes," Life Magazine © 1966, Time Inc.
[39] From "Intuition in Science: Why Cover It Up?" Science and Humanity Supplement of Saturday Review, May 1, 1965.
[40] Reprinted from The American Experience by Henry Bamford Parkes, by permission of Alfred A. Knopf, Inc. Copyright 1947, 1955 by Henry Bamford Parkes.
[41] From The Enjoyment of Poetry by Max Eastman. Reprinted by permission of Charles Scribner's Sons.

No one can look more thirsty when asking for a pass: tongue hanging out, eyes rolling, a death-rattle in the throat, he can barely make it to the water fountain. No one can look more horrified at a wrong answer issuing from his own traitor lips; or more humble; or more bewildered; or more indignant. I know it's not in the syllabus, but I'm afraid I encourage him by laughing.   —BEL KAUFMAN[42]

49   We have always been a small people numerically and we shall remain a small people, unable to compete with our rivals in the size of population, extent of territory, richness of natural resources, and strength and equipment of the armed forces. But our place is in the history of humanity and the place of our country in the world cannot be measured in quantitative terms. Few people have had so profound an influence upon so large a part of the human race. And there are few countries which have played so central a role in world history as the Land of Israel. It must be our aim to achieve a future that can be worthy of our past.
—DAVID BEN GURION[43]

50   This, then, is how one might define jazz: it is a new music of a certain distinct rhythmic and melodic character, one that constantly involves improvisation—of a minor sort in adjusting accents and phrases of the tune at hand, of a major sort in creating music extemporaneously, on the spot. In the course of creating jazz, a melody or its underlying chords may be altered. The rhythmic valuations of notes may be lengthened or shortened according to a regular scheme, syncopated or not, or there may be no consistent pattern of rhythmic variations so long as a steady beat remains implicit or explicit. The beat is usually four quarternotes to the bar, serving as a solid rhythmic base for the improvisation of soloists or groups playing eight or twelve measures, or some multiple or dividend thereof.   —BARRY ULANOV[44]

51   The essential problem of man in a computerized age remains the same as it has always been. That problem is not solely how to be more productive, more comfortable, more content, but how to be more sensitive, more sensible, more proportionate, more alive. The computer makes possible a phenomenal leap in human proficiency; it demolishes the fences around the practical and even the theoretical intelligence. But the question persists and indeed grows whether the computer will make it easier or harder for human beings to know who they really are, to identify their real problems, to respond more fully to beauty, to place adequate value on life, and make their world safer than it now is.   —NORMAN COUSINS[45]

52   How does an amateur, or a professional, recognize a new comet when he finds one? Most new-found comets are as diffuse and formless as a squashed star, completely devoid of any tail. In this respect they resemble hundreds of faint nebulae that speckle the sky, with this difference: nebulae are fixed, but a comet will inevitably move. Consequently, a second observation made a few hours later will generally reveal a motion if the nebulous wisp is indeed a comet. However, most comet hunters compare the position of their suspected comet with a sky map that charts faint

nebulae and clusters. Then the discovery is quickly reported to a nearby observatory or directly to the Central Bureau.
—OWEN GINGERICH[46]

53   The herring gull is a creature of sufficient ingenuity that if he picks up a mussel with a shell too hard for his beak to break, he will carry it to a height and drop it on a hard road. He is a creature of sufficient loyalty and perception to guarantee that he will never attack his own mate, and will recognize her among dozens flying into the colony at a distance to defy human binoculars. He is a creature of sufficient social sophistication that, while many arrive in the spring already paired, definite areas in the colony which Tinbergen calls "clubs" will be set aside as meeting places for the unpaired. He is a creature also, as we have seen, of such sensitive social adjustment that the arriving flock will make "decisions" of mood and readiness as if it were one being. So dependent is the herring gull on the community of his citizenship that he would probably be unable to breed were he to return in the spring to the wrong gull town. So powerful and incomprehensible is his attachment for home that, like the albatross, a pair may return year after year to nest in precisely the same spot, although the North Sea's winter storms will have effaced all landmarks to guide his eye.
—ROBERT ARDREY[47]

54   This American devotion to music-making for pleasure is not an overnight development. During the Depression, millions of people attended the free WPA music classes. Thus the movement started. We dreamed of "good times," and when they finally came, amateur music-making on a mass scale followed. Since the end of World War II, the census of adult amateurs has risen considerably: from 16,500,000 in 1947 to 25,000,000 in 1964. In its continuing surveys, the American Music Conference, an organization that promotes amateur music, has found that music-making for the fun of it is now "second only to reading among the nation's leisure-time participative activities."   —JAMES T. MAHER[48]

55   Mathematics, the language of science, is not like other tongues. Its symbols are atoms of distilled logic, far more compact than words in some ways but uncolored by any of the associations, sights, and feelings that make words immediately meaningful. As a result, mathematics cannot be translated phrase for phrase or symbol by symbol like French or Sanskrit. Most of its content is no more interesting than a housewife's accounts—pure numbers and quantities. The rest, the part that gradually seeps into the core of a culture, is something that it does not really say at all but only implies. In this it is like poetry. And like a poem, a great formula is not so much translated as it is interpreted—rightly or wrongly according to the judgment and taste of each generation.
—DAVID BERGAMINI[49]

56   At the 1964 meeting of the American Association for the Advancement of Science a University of Colorado researcher named George A. Dulk predicted that a burst of radio signals from

[42] From *Up the Down Stair Case* by Bel Kaufman. Copyright 1964 by Bel Kaufman. Published by Prentice-Hall, Inc., Englewood Cliffs, New Jersey.

[43] From *Ben Gurion Looks Back*. Copyright © 1965 by Moshe Pearlman and David Ben Gurion. Reprinted by permission of Simon and Schuster and Weidenfeld & Nicolson, Ltd.

[44] From *A History of Jazz in America* by Barry Ulanov. Copyright 1952 by Barry Ulanov. Reprinted by permission of The Viking Press, Inc.

[45] From "The Computer and the Poet" by Norman Cousins, *Saturday Review*, July, 23, 1966. Reprinted by permission.

[46] From "The Great Comet of 1965" by Owen Gingerich. Copyright © 1966, by The Atlantic Monthly Company, Boston, Massachusetts 02116. Reprinted with permission.

[47] From *The Territorial Imperative* by Robert Ardrey. © 1966 by Robert Ardrey. Reprinted by permission of Atheneum Publishers.

[48] From "Holiday Handbook: Music-Making at Home" by James T. Maher. Copyright 1966 by Curtis Publishing Company. Reprinted by permission of Harold Matson Company, Inc.

[49] From "The Language of Science" by David Bergamini. Copyright 1960 by Reporter Magazine, Inc. Reprinted by permission of Harold Matson Company, Inc.

the planet Jupiter would be received in Colorado at midnight, December 31, 1964. On New Year's Eve, at 11:40 P.M.—just a few minutes ahead of schedule—a radio signal that sounded like the sizzle of a frying pan was picked up by the eighty-five-foot radio telescope at the National Center for Atmospheric Research. Since the signals did not come from intelligent creatures at the other end—there was never any question of that—the fulfillment of Dulk's prediction caused only a minor stir. For predictions—even startling predictions—of this kind are, of course, the bread and butter of science. They are entirely routine.   —ALVIN TOFFLER[50]

57   Bradley's play has just one somewhat unsound aspect, and it is the result of his mania for throwing the ball to his teammates. He can't seem to resist throwing a certain number of passes that are based on nothing but theory and hope; in fact, they are referred to by the Princeton coaching staff as Bradley's hope passes. They happen, usually, when something has gone just a bit wrong. Bradley is recovering a loose ball, say, with his back turned to the other Princeton players. Before he turned it, he happened to notice a screen, or pickoff, being set by two of his teammates, its purpose being to cause one defensive man to collide with another player and thus free an offensive man to receive a pass and score. Computations whir in Bradley's head. He hasn't time to look, but the screen, as he saw it developing, seemed to be working, so a Princeton man should now be in the clear, running toward the basket with one arm up. He whips the ball over his shoulder to the spot where the man ought to be. Sometimes a hope pass goes flying into the crowd, but most of the time they hit the receiver right in the hand, and a gasp comes from several thousand people. Bradley is sensitive about such dazzling passes, because they look flashy, and an edge comes into his voice as he defends them. "When I was halfway down the court, I saw a man out of the corner of my eye who had on the same color shirt I did," he said recently, explaining how he happened to fire a scoring pass while he was falling out of bounds. "A little later, when I threw the pass, I threw it to the spot where that man should have been if he had kept going and done his job. He was there. Two points."   —JOHN MCPHEE[51]

58   In many of the interviews and most of the essays and introductions there are three recurring themes. The first is the nature of poetry. Frost was no untutored swain, though the early interviewers liked to pretend he was, but a conscientious and brilliant student of both the practice and theory of poetry. He resented the suggestion that he was a simple sort of poet, especially when it was made by admirers who polemically contrasted his intelligibility with the obscurity of most of the poets who became influential in the Twenties. He could be impatient enough with what seemed to him a faked obscurity, put on to conceal failures of the imagination, but he never suggested that a poem was bad because it was difficult. He knew that his own poems were considerably less simple than most of his admirers believed. In whatever he wrote about the nature of poetry he was careful to avoid dogmatic definitions. He chose to be elusive, even coy, rather than to bind a poet in chains.   —GRANVILLE HICKS[52]

59   Mankind in the mass has often been compared, cynically or otherwise, to insects. To the historian proper the image

of an ant-heap is almost inevitable. When he looks back into the past, he sees no great men or famous names, but myriads of minute and nameless human insects, hurrying this way and that, making wars and laws, building and destroying cities and civilizations. The swarm ebbs and flows over the earth and through the centuries, the groups converging and coalescing or breaking up and scattering. The story of this ant-heap, of its impersonal groups and communities and of their ebb and flow upon the earth, is history. —LEONARD WOOLF[53]

▶ **EXERCISE 20** Indicate an appropriate method or combination of methods of developing each of the following topic sentences:

1. Like history, styles repeat themselves.
2. We are living in the Age of Computers.
3. Students have strange study habits.
4. *Irony* is harder to define than to illustrate.
5. I like Salinger better than Golding.
6. As Tennyson once said, a lie that is half a truth is the blackest lie of all.
7. A circus has many mouths to feed.
8. Before talking about democracy we should at least say what democracy is not.
9. I no longer believe in fortune tellers.
10. Some men think our great cities are monuments of progress; others say they are symptoms of social disease.
11. You can solve most problems by taking a walk.
12. Intelligence means the ability to discriminate.
13. At college I have discovered two kinds of friends.
14. A self-reliant person must know his predominant weakness as well as his predominant strength.
15. Automation may revolutionize education.
16. The ability to think and the ability to write are closely allied.
17. There is a great deal of difference between a state college and a state university.
18. When the storm was over we all set to work in earnest.
19. My jalopy reminds me of a frumpy old woman.
20. The itinerary of a typical American tourist will be fascinating in 1980.

[53] From *After the Deluge* by Leonard Woolf. Reprinted by permission of The Hogarth Press, Ltd.

Planning and Writing the Whole Composition

32

Arrange and express your ideas effectively.

The four units of composition, in an ascending order, are (1) the word—Sections **19-22**, (2) the sentence—Sections **23-30**, (3) the paragraph—Section **31**, and (4) the whole composition—Section **32**. Words make up the sentence, sentences make up the paragraph, and paragraphs make up the whole composition.

[50] From "The Future as a Way of Life" by Alvin Toffler. Reprinted from *Horizon*, Summer, 1965, by permission of the author.
[51] "A Sense of Where You Are" by John McPhee. © 1965, by John McPhee. Reprinted from *The New Yorker*, January 23, 1965, by permission of John McPhee and *The New Yorker*.
[52] From "Robert Frost Revisited" by Granville Hicks, *Saturday Review*, July 9, 1966. Reprinted by permission.

A paragraph is usually a series of sentences developing one topic. A composition is usually a series of paragraphs developing several topics which are closely related. Just as a unified paragraph has a stated or implied topic to which each sentence contributes, a unified composition has a central idea to which each paragraph contributes. Therefore, many of the techniques used to write paragraphs (e.g., developing a central idea, arranging supporting details logically and effectively, making appropriate transitions) are applicable to the composition as a whole. See Section **31**.

In fact, sometimes the major difference between a paragraph and a composition is merely a matter of scale. For example, the topic sentence of paragraph 1 on page 894 could easily be converted to the central idea of a composition. The three points made within paragraph 1 could then be topic sentences for separate paragraphs. Of course, more specific details would be necessary to develop each paragraph adequately; an introductory and a concluding paragraph might also be added.

32a

Choose an appropriate subject and limit it properly.

Be sure to select a topic that will enable you to say something interesting about what you know well. Limit the topic you choose so that you can develop it adequately, specifically.

A subject is appropriate:

1. If it appeals to you, or if you can develop an interest in it as you work on it.
2. If it is acceptable to the intended reader.

A subject is properly limited:

1. If you know enough about it or can learn enough in a reasonable period. (Subjects that require extensive reading should be reserved for the library paper. See Section **33**.)
2. If the topic is not too broad to treat in the time or space at your command. ("Amateur Photography" might be a satisfactory title for a paper of several thousand words; but if you must limit yourself to several hundred words, you will do better with "Developing a Film" or "The Growth of My Interest in Photography.")

Let us suppose that you have chosen (or have been assigned) "Sports" as a general subject for a paper of five hundred words. Obviously, you cannot cover everything to be said about sports in five hundred words. You must therefore find a more limited topic. You may be particularly interested in one sport, but "Football" or "Baseball" is still too broad for your short paper. Therefore you should concentrate on a narrow phase of the sport chosen, such as "The Importance of Fumbles in Saturday's Game" or "Characteristics of a Good Shortstop."

PURPOSE

Before making a final decision regarding the specific topic, you should consider your purpose in writing the composition. If your purpose is to inform the reader, either "The Importance of Fumbles in Saturday's Game" or "Characteristics of a Good Shortstop" would be appropriate. If, however, your primary aim is to describe your feelings as you watched a particularly heart-breaking defeat, you might want to title your theme "A Cold Day at Memorial Stadium." On the other hand, you might decide that you want to argue about the merits of watching football as compared with watching baseball. You might then write a theme on the topic "Football or Baseball as a Spectator Sport" or "I Would Rather Watch Football than Baseball." Finally, you might decide to write a narrative account of the most exciting five minutes of a football game. Then your topic might be "With Only Minutes to Go."

Each of the purposes you might select corresponds to one of the four main types of writing as they are conventionally classified in rhetoric—exposition or explanation (to inform), description, argument (or persuasion), and narration. *Exposition* is the most common kind of nonfiction writing and the kind most frequently written by college students. *Argument* is similar to exposition but written with the intention of convincing rather than simply explaining. In *narration*, events are presented in a time sequence, and in *description* a sensory impression of an object or feeling is conveyed. (See paragraph 5, Section **31**.) Very seldom is description written independently. Usually it is only part of a composition in which one of the other types dominates. In fact, few compositions are a single form of discourse. Most are mixtures in which one form predominates. Thus, a paper on "How to Drive a Car" would be primarily exposition but would also contain bits of description (perhaps of the steering mechanism) and narration (perhaps an anecdote about the author's first drive).

Whatever form of discourse a paper may take, it does not fall into order by chance. *Order is the result of careful planning.*

CENTRAL IDEA

After deciding upon your purpose, you will find it helpful to set down, in a single sentence, the central or controlling idea for your paper. If the purpose is to inform, the sentence may read, "A good shortstop thinks and acts quickly." This thesis statement helps to limit the subject and especially helps determine the items to be included in the outline. In fact, if in the beginning you can set down a central idea containing logically arranged main points (see Example 1 below), you will already have the main headings of your outline. If you do not give the main points in your central idea (see Examples 2 through 5 below), you may later wish to reword it in order to show its close relationship to the items in your outline. In dealing with some subjects, you may need to list your ideas and then find and consider more evidence before you can decide upon an appropriate central idea. If not determined in the process of limiting the subject, the central idea should be written out before the outline is completed and then used to test the contents of the outline.

1. *Purpose:* To inform by pointing out ways to appraise a used car [Exposition]
   Title: How to Buy a Good Used Car
   Central Idea: Before selecting a used car, a wise buyer will carefully inspect the car himself, talk to the former owner of it, and engage a good mechanic to examine its motor.

2. *Purpose:* To convince the reader of a need for change [Argument]
   Title: Why Have Final Examinations?
   Central Idea: Final examinations should be abolished.

3. *Purpose:* To describe Rushville and its surroundings [Description]
   Title: Rushville: A Beautiful City in the Mountains
   Central Idea: Rushville is a beautiful city in the mountains.

4. *Purpose:* To tell a story about a childhood experience [Narration]
   Title: I Will Never Play Post Office Again!
   Central Idea: Playing "postmaster," my brother once shocked my friends and me by wiring a group of old post office boxes.

5. *Purpose:* To describe Old Tony and show that he is a colorful individual [Exposition, Description, Narration]
   Title: Old Tony
   Central Idea: Old Tony is the most colorful individual that I know.

Each of the suggestions listed below is a suitable subject for a student paper. Some of the suggestions, as worded, may provide the exact title you need for your paper. In all likelihood, however, you will wish to limit the subject to the scope of your experience and to sharpen the wording to suit your purpose. (For the proper capitalization of titles, see 9c.)

Suggestions for Written Work

HOME AND THE INDIVIDUAL

1. Automation in the home
2. My home town in 1980
3. Our family's diets
4. Why I like my hobby
5. How children educate parents
6. If I could choose my relatives (OR parents)
7. Types of family friends
8. Our changing neighborhood
9. New styles in clothes
10. Being an only child (OR the youngest OR oldest)
11. My favorite author (book, actor, television show, etc.)

COLLEGE LIFE

1. Campus fads
2. Dating habits of college students
3. College slang
4. Earning one's way
5. My first field trip
6. The course I find most practical (OR difficult, interesting, etc.)
7. The student union
8. Campus politics
9. Why I should (OR should not) join a fraternity (OR sorority)
10. Boners of a freshman
11. The writing laboratory
12. Using a microscope
13. Are examinations fair?
14. The honor system
15. How to be a cheer leader
16. What makes school spirit?
17. Why I am going to college
18. Duties of the quarterback (OR halfback, fullback, etc.)
19. What is sportsmanship?
20. Life in a dormitory (OR fraternity house, sorority house, etc.)

ECONOMICS, HISTORY, SOCIOLOGY

1. Poverty in America
2. A nation of computers
3. Why the Spanish Armada was defeated
4. The Peace Corps
5. A four-hour work day
6. Conservation or Pollution
7. What our taxes buy
8. Our senior citizens
9. Our foreign aid
10. The Iron (or Bamboo) Curtain
11. Help for the retarded
12. Advertising schemes
13. The right to strike
14. The parole system
15. Status symbols
16. Socialized medicine
17. Social service as a career
18. Types of personalities
19. Tourists and the economy
20. Urban renewal
21. The guaranteed annual wage

SCIENCE AND MEDICINE

1. Discoveries in space
2. Underwater explorations
3. Extrasensory perception
4. Discoveries about the memory (OR heart, nerves, blood, etc.)
5. The common cold
6. Synthetic diamonds
7. New wonder drugs
8. Life expectancy
9. Uses of wild plants
10. The oxygen tent
11. Chemical warfare on insects
12. Uses of uranium
13. Plastic surgery
14. Predicting the weather
15. Beneficial bacteria
16. Experiments with animals

MISCELLANEOUS

1. Current English usage
2. Ghosts in literature
3. Poltergeists
4. Unidentified Flying Objects
5. Fads in music
6. Boom in water sports
7. City conveniences in the country
8. Political conventions
9. A choice involving conscience
10. Typical television characters (*such as* doctors, lawyers, etc.)
11. Pop (or Op) Art

▶ EXERCISE 1 After selecting five subjects from the preceding "Suggestions for Written Work," decide how it may be necessary to limit each one and what your purpose would be in writing a composition on each topic. Then write (1) your purpose, (2) an appropriate title, and (3) the central idea for each subject that you choose. (You may find it helpful to refer to the examples on pages 907–08.)

32b

Develop a working plan or an outline before writing a composition. See also 33c.

Although a formal outline may not be required for every paper, learning to make and use a good outline is important to inexperienced writers because it is a working plan that can make the actual writing of a composition easier.

The outline is the blueprint of the composition. Just as the carpenter or the engineer follows his blueprint implicitly in order to avoid costly structural blunders, so the writer—especially the student writer—follows his outline carefully so that he may arrange his ideas effectively.

But blueprints can be changed and improved, and so can outlines. The writer should make the outline his helpful tool; he should not become its slave. He should keep the outline a growing, developing plan which he will not hesitate to change at any stage of his composition whenever he hits upon a way to improve it. He will naturally try to perfect his outline before he starts to write the paper, but the actual writing will almost certainly suggest a few desirable changes in the arrangement of details.

The first step in the preparation of an outline is the jotting down of ideas on the topic. Keeping the purpose of the composition firmly in mind, the student should not hesitate to jot down a long list of ideas; and he should jot them down rapidly, without much concern for the proper order. When he begins to classify his ideas, he will find it easy to reject needless ones; he may find also that he needs to supplement his knowledge by further observation or reading.

Suppose, for example, a student has chosen to write on the subject "Books I Have Read." He first limits the subject to autobiographies. Then he limits it further by deciding upon his purpose: to inform his reader about the types of autobiographies he has read. Next, he selects a tentative title: "Types of Autobiographies." Finally, he writes out a tentative central idea and jots down a list of items closely related to the thesis statement.

LIST OF IDEAS FOR A COMPOSITION
ON AUTOBIOGRAPHIES

Tentative Central Idea: Autobiographies reveal significant facts about the authors' experiences.

Types of Autobiographies	*What They Reveal*
adventure stories	actions
success stories	achievements
journals like Pepys's *Diary*	contemporary life
travel books	explorations, sights
collections of letters	problems, attitudes
religious accounts	temptations
so-called war records	decisions, battles
disguised autobiographies	emotional conflicts
reports of events	personality

The next step in making an outline is the grouping of the listed items under a few main headings. After some thought, the writer will see that if he uses each of the nine types of autobiographies (listed in the first column above) as a main heading, the development of each would prove to be too unwieldy for a short paper. Therefore he may prefer to group these types further as subheadings under more general headings that will classify all autobiographies according to what they reveal about the authors' experiences; he could thus show that any autobiography could be appropriately entitled "What I Saw," "What I Felt," or "What I Did," and he could illustrate each type by representative examples. Then he would list these main headings in a logical order (see **31b** and **32e**):

    I. Autobiographies about "What I Did"
   II. Autobiographies about "What I Saw"
  III. Autobiographies about "What I Felt"

After more thought, the writer may limit his subject further by omitting some of the items listed in the first column—e.g., journals like Pepys's *Diary*, collections of letters, and disguised autobiographies. The logical arrangement of the remaining items as miscellaneous details (with further additions during the writing of the paper) under the three main headings gives the outline as it appears under **32c** below. The writer's purpose thus is to *inform* (exposition), and he decides to develop his central idea chiefly by the method of classification—see **31d(4)**—with exemplification as a subordinate method—see **31d(2)**. All the other methods of development described in Section 31 are equally adaptable to the development of the whole essay. (See also the examples under **32a**.)

Only one other decision in planning the composition remains: whether or not to include introductory and concluding paragraphs. See **32g(2)**. If these paragraphs are desirable or deemed necessary, the writer should add to his plan an explanation of each. In a topic or a sentence outline, these statements need not be numbered. See **32c**.

Once the writer has thought his subject through, he may wish to select a more appropriate or more interesting title. He may also change the wording of his tentative central idea.

32c

Use an outline of the type specified by your instructor.

The types of outlines most commonly used are (1) the topic outline, (2) the sentence outline, and (3) the paragraph outline. Topic outlines and sentence outlines have the same parts and the same groupings; they differ only in the fullness of expression. In the paragraph outline no effort is made to classify the material into major headings and subheadings: the topic of each paragraph is simply listed in the order in which it is to come. Paragraph outlines are especially helpful in writing short papers. Topic or sentence outlines may be adapted to papers of any length.

Topic Outline:

THE FACE IN THE MIRROR

CENTRAL IDEA Since the three types of autobiographies mirror their authors' experiences, any autobiography can be appropriately entitled "What I Did," "What I Saw," or "What I Felt."

INTRODUCTION An interesting autobiography—one of three possible kinds—inside of every person if he would tell the whole story of his life

  I. Autobiographies about "What I Did"
    A. Books by self-made men
    B. *The Second World War* by Churchill
 II. Autobiographies about "What I Saw"
    A. Books like *Kon-Tiki*
    B. *Travels in Arabia Deserta* by Doughty
    C. Some descriptions of wars
      1. *Recollections of Rifleman Harris*
      2. Documents concerning the Civil War
III. Autobiographies about "What I Felt"
    A. Books about failure, disaster, regeneration
    B. Descriptions of the process of growing up
      1. Edward Gibbon's autobiography
      2. Self-studies of Mill, Spencer, and Adams
    C. Records of religious struggles and spiritual victories
      1. *Confessions* of St. Augustine
      2. Journals of John Bunyan
      3. Writings of George Fox
    D. Many reports of contemporary events
      1. Reminiscences of Cellini, Rousseau, and Boswell
      2. Works of Yeats and Gide

CONCLUSION Difficulty in classifying autobiographies because the most interesting give something of all three kinds of experience

Sentence Outline:

THE FACE IN THE MIRROR

CENTRAL IDEA Since the three types of autobiographies mirror their authors' experiences, any autobiography can be appropriately entitled "What I Saw," "What I Did," or "What I Felt."

INTRODUCTION An interesting autobiography—one of three possible kinds—is inside of every person if he would tell the whole story of his life.

  I. The first group of autobiographies could be issued under the title "What I Did."
    A. Self-made men like Franklin and Cobbett have written books of this type.
    B. Churchill told about what he did in *The Second World War*.

II. The second group of autobiographies might be called "What I Saw."
  A. Books like *Kon-Tiki* place emphasis upon the authors' observations.
  B. *Travels in Arabia Deserta* by Doughty is probably the greatest autobiography of this type.
  C. Some documents about war describe what the authors saw.
    1. *Recollections of Rifleman Harris* gives scenes from the Napoleonic Wars.
    2. Other books describe scenes of the Civil War.

III. The third group of autobiographies could be entitled "What I Felt."
  A. Among these are books about failure, disaster, and regeneration.
  B. Other books of inner adventure describe the process of growing up.
    1. One example is Gibbon's autobiography.
    2. More famous examples are the self-studies of Mill, Spencer, and Adams.
  C. Some autobiographies mirror the inner struggles and spiritual victories of religious authors.
    1. One example is St. Augustine's *Confessions*.
    2. Another example is John Bunyan's journals.
    3. Still another example is George Fox's writings.
  D. Many autobiographies show how contemporary events affect the personalities of authors.
    1. Such are the reminiscences of Cellini, Rousseau, and Boswell.
    2. Such also are the works of Yeats and Gide.

CONCLUSION It is difficult to classify types of autobiographies because the most interesting give us something of all three kinds of experience.

Paragraph Outline:

THE FACE IN THE MIRROR

CENTRAL IDEA Since the three types of autobiographies mirror their authors' experiences, any autobiography can be appropriately entitled "What I Saw," "What I Did," or "What I Felt."

1. An interesting autobiography is inside of every person if he would tell the whole story of his life.
2. There are three different ways of telling the story of one's life.
3. The first group of autobiographies could be issued under the title "What I Did."
4. Churchill's *The Second World War* is an autobiographical record describing what the author did.
5. The second type of autobiography might be called "What I Saw."
6. The third kind of autobiography describes "What I Felt."
7. It is difficult to make divisions between types of autobiographies because the most interesting give us something of all three kinds of experience.

32d

Make sure that the outline covers the subject, that it treats of everything promised in the title.

An adequate outline is essential to a successful composition. The major headings (I, II, III, etc.) must be sufficient in number and in scope to satisfy the expectation aroused by the title. And each of these major headings must, in turn, be covered by its subheads just as the title

is covered by the major headings. These subheads, however, should not be unduly detailed.

TITLES NOT ADEQUATELY COVERED BY MAJOR HEADINGS

Characteristics of Ideal Parents	The Grading System
I. A father's sense of humor	I. What a *B* means
II. His generosity	II. What a *C* means
III. His understanding	

TITLES ADEQUATELY COVERED

Characteristics of Ideal Parents	The Grading System
I. Their sense of humor	I. Differences between an *A* and a *B*
II. Their generosity	II. Differences between a *C* and a *D*
III. Their understanding	III. The meaning of *F*

It would also be proper to leave the main headings unchanged and to alter the titles to agree, thus: "Characteristics of an Ideal Father" and "The Meaning of *B* and *C* in the Grading System."

In reality, making an outline is a kind of process of thinking through the paper. Ordinarily if your outline does not fit the rules for an outline, then there may be something awry with the paper itself—a missing element, a misstated title, or an inadequate purpose. Thus an outline can help you give focus to your paper and possibly show the need for further limitation.

32e

Make sure that the parts of the outline are logically arranged.

Logical arrangement is second in importance only to adequacy. If the outline is disorganized and ineffective, the paper that follows it will also be disorganized and ineffective. (See also **31b.**)

(1) Group related ideas.

Although you may begin your outline by hastily jotting down as many ideas on the topic as possible, without regard to order, you should later bring related ideas together, grouping them under major headings. Compare the first list of ideas on "The Face in the Mirror" (page 909) with the groupings in the finished outline (**32c**).

(2) Arrange the parts in a natural, logical order.

The problem of arrangement within the paper as a whole is much the same as that within each separate paragraph. (See pages 895–97.) The nature of the subject will suggest an appropriate arrangement, such as time order, space order, or order of climax.

Order of climax:
Subject: End of the drought

I. Rains soak the countryside.
II. Farmers rejoice.
III. Headlines all over the nation announce end of the drought.
IV. Rains steal attention from the most significant world affairs.

Time order:
Subject: Process of riveting

I. Preparation of rivets
II. Passing of red-hot rivets
III. Securing the rivets in place

▶ EXERCISE 2   First make a list of three, four, or five main points closely related to one of the following subjects; then arrange the items in a natural, logical order. (In parentheses are suggestions for appropriate arrangements.)

1. Ways to start an argument (order of climax)
2. An amusing practical joke (time order)
3. A walk across the campus (space order—see page 896)
4. A successful experiment (time order)
5. The joys of being a freshman in college (order of climax)

(3) **Do not allow headings to overlap.**

Overlapping often occurs when a writer attempts a division according to more than one principle.

TYPES OF ARRANGEMENT MIXED

Advertising on Television

I. Since the advent of color	Time
II. Its effect on sales	Result
III. Pain relievers	Group

TYPES OF ARRANGEMENT UNMIXED

Advertising on Television

Time	*Result*	*Group*
I. Before color	I. Creates demand	I. Detergents
II. After color	II. Influences sales	II. Household appliances
	III. Affects economy	III. Pain relievers

(4) **Do not coordinate any heading that should be subordinated. Do not subordinate any heading that should be coordinated.**

ILLOGICAL   Wonder Products in TV Advertisements

   I. Detergents
     A. Household appliances
  II. Washing machines
  III. Remedies for headaches
     A. Pain relievers
     B. Cures for upset stomachs

LOGICAL   Wonder Products in TV Advertisements

   I. Detergents
  II. Household appliances
     A. Washing machines
     B. Refrigerators
  III. Pain relievers
     A. For headaches
     B. For upset stomachs

(5) **Do not allow single headings or subheadings to stand anywhere in the outline.**

Headings and subheads stand for divisions, and a division denotes at least two parts. Therefore, each outline, to be logical, should have at least two main headings, I and II. If it has a subheading marked A, it should also have a B; if it has a 1, it should also have a 2.

INCOMPLETE   II. Household appliances
     A. Washing machines

Unless another subheading is added, the second main heading should be revised to read simply "Washing machines." The next heading in the outline would then name a different type of product.

32f

Check the outline for the formal details of (1) notation and indention and (2) parallel structure.

(1) In the outline use consistently one system of notation, and indent headings to indicate degrees of subordination.

Any intelligible system of notation is acceptable. The one used for the complete sentence outline and the topic outline in **32c** is in very common use and may well be adopted. This system, it will be noted, is as follows:

I.	[Used for major headings]
A.	[Used for subheadings of the first
B.	degree]
1.	[Used for subheadings of the second
2.	degree]

Seldom will a short outline (or even a longer one) need subordination beyond the first or second degree. If it does, it may use a, b, c, etc., for the third degree and (1), (2), (3), etc., for the fourth degree.

The indention, as well as the notation, should indicate the degree of subordination. Major headings (I, II, III, etc.) should be indented equally, subheadings of the first degree (A, B, C, etc.) should be indented more, and subheads of the second degree (1, 2, 3, etc.) should be indented still more. If a heading or subheading runs beyond the end of the line, it is given "hanging indention," as in the sentence outline above (**32c**).

(2) Give parallel structure to parallel parts of the outline to make clearer the coordination of the parts. (See the full discussion of parallel structure under Section **26**.)

PARALLEL STRUCTURE

   I. Autobiographies about "What I Did"
     [Noun—prepositional phrase]
     A. Books by self-made men
       [Noun—prepositional phrase]
     B. *The Second World War* by Churchill
       [Noun (a title)—prepositional phrase]
  II. Autobiographies about "What I Saw"
     [Noun—prepositional phrase]

The major headings (I, II, III, etc.) should be expressed in parallel structure, as should each group of subheads. But it is unnecessary to strive for parallel structure between different groups of subheads; for example, between A, B, C under I and A, B, C under II. (Parallel structure is no problem in the complete sentence outline, for parallelism is insured by the requirement of complete sentences.)

▶ EXERCISE 3   Make an outline (of the type specified by your instructor) on one of the subjects you used for Exercise 1. Then check your outline with the principles set forth in **32d–f.**

32g

Write the paper from the outline.

Once you have checked your outline to make sure that it covers the subject (see **32d**), is logically arranged (**32e**), and has proper notation, indention, and parallel structure

(32f), you are ready to write the paper. You simply write a series of effective paragraphs, with good transitions between them (see 31b[6]), to cover all items in the outline, taking up each item in the order in which it comes in the outline. The actual writing of the paper may very well suggest a better arrangement for some of the details.

(1) The paragraphs in relation to the outline. Although the paragraphs must develop the headings (including the subheadings) of the outline in the exact order in which they come in the outline, there is no rule regarding the number of these headings a paragraph may cover. In a general way, however, the writer is limited by the need to make each paragraph a unit and to keep it from being unduly long or short. Let us notice, for example, how the seven paragraphs of "The Face in the Mirror" (see Exercise 4 below) are related to the topic outline (see page 909):

Paragraphs	Relation to outline
1 and 2	Introduction
3	I and the subheading A
4	Subheading B (special treatment requires more words than for A)
5	II and all subheadings
6	III and all subheadings
7	Conclusion

Since each paragraph in the body of a composition (see paragraphs 3 through 6 above) should be easily identified with a main heading or subheading in the outline, the writer may wish to revise his outline to make it agree with his organization into paragraphs.

▶ EXERCISE 4 Carefully read the following essay so that you can intelligently participate in a class discussion of the (1) selection and limitation of the subject, (2) purpose of the writer, (3) choice of the title, (4) development of the central idea, (5) arrangement of main points, (6) transitions between ideas, and (7) relationship of the division into paragraphs to the topic outline on page 909.

THE FACE IN THE MIRROR[1]

(1) Every man and every woman has one book inside him or her. Some have more, but everybody has at least one—a volume of autobiography. We have all been talked almost to death by bores who attached themselves to us in a club car or a ship's smoking room and insisted on giving us a play-by-play account of their marital troubles or their complete medical history. I once met one who carried a set of his own x-rays. Yet even these people might be interesting if they could tell the whole truth. They are boring not because they talk about themselves but because they talk about only one aspect of themselves, that phase of their lives which fascinates and worries them personally. If they were really to tell us everything, we should listen with amazement.

(2) Apparently there are three kinds of autobiography: three different ways of telling the story of one's life. (We can leave out journals like Pepys's *Diary*, which was not meant to be published, and collections of letters and disguised autobiographies, which so many modern novels are.)

(3) The first group could all be issued under the same title. They could all be called "What I Did." They are essentially success stories. In them, a man who has achieved something of wide

[1] Abridged from *Talents and Geniuses*, copyright 1957 by Gibert Highet. Reprinted by permission of Oxford University Press, Inc.

importance explains how he did it, what were the obstacles in his way, how they were overcome, and what was the effect on the world. Self-made men often write such books—or have such books written for them. There is a splendid one by Ben Franklin and an equally good one by his English opposite number, William Cobbett: these are optimistic works, a good tonic for anyone who despairs of solving his own problems.

(4) Sir Winston Churchill's six-volume work *The Second World War* is really an autobiographical record. He himself says it is "the story as I knew and experienced it as Prime Minister and Minister of Defence of Great Britain." Therefore it cannot be called anything like a complete history of the war. For example, Churchill tells the story of one of the crucial events of the war, one of the crucial events of this century—the reduction of Japan to impotence and surrender by intensive bombardment culminating in what he calls the "casting" of two atomic bombs—in only eight pages, while a greater amount of wordage is devoted to a reprint of the broadcast which he made to British listeners on VE day.

(5) So much for the first type of autobiography: "What I Did." The second type might be called "What I Saw." Here the emphasis is not on the achievements of the narrator but rather on the strange sights he saw and the strange experiences through which he lived. Most good books of exploration are like this. Both the book *Kon-Tiki* and the film were absorbingly interesting, not because the author was an unusual man but because he could describe to us some unique adventures. We shall never cross New Guinea on foot or spend a whole year alone with two companions on the Arctic ice or climb Mount Everest; therefore we are delighted when a man who has done such a thing can tell us about it clearly—and modestly. The greatest of all such books in the English language is probably Doughty's *Travels in Arabia Deserta*. Some good adventure autobiographies have been written by ordinary soldiers and sailors. Many of our finest descriptions of the Napoleonic wars come from such books as the *Recollections of Rifleman Harris*, and there are similar documents from the American Civil War.

(6) Then there is a third kind of autobiography. It does not describe "What I Did" or "What I Saw" but "What I Felt," "What I Endured." These are the books of inner adventure. In them there is achievement, yes, but it is a struggle and a victory within the spirit. In them there are dangerous explorations and the discovery of unknown worlds, but the explorer is making his way through the jungles of the soul. Such are the books of failure, disaster, and regeneration which are now so popular: for example, Lillian Roth's *I'll Cry Tomorrow*, which tells how a woman wrecked her life with drink and then rebuilt it. Such also are the books which describe one of the most dangerous of all adventures: the process of growing up. My own favorite among them is Edward Gibbon's autobiography, partly because it is unconsciously funny. More famous perhaps are the self-studies of John Stuart Mill, Herbert Spencer, and Henry Adams—all of which seem to me excruciatingly pompous and dull. The famous records of religious suffering and conversion could all be subtitled "What I Felt": the *Confessions* of St. Augustine, the journals of John Bunyan and of the first Quaker, George Fox. And many of the most famous autobiographers have concentrated on reporting the events which happened during their lifetime, not as objective facts but simply as occurrences which impinged upon their own personalities: in books like the reminiscences of Benvenuto Cellini, of Rousseau, of Boswell, Yeats, and André Gide, we see the world as in an elaborate distorting mirror.

(7) "What I Did," "What I Saw," "What I Felt"—really, it is difficult to make a sharp division between these types of autobiographical writing. The emphasis in one book is more toward reporting of external happenings, in another toward self-analysis, but a man can scarcely describe what he did without also letting us know what he felt and saw. Even the most egoistic of men, like St. Augustine and James Boswell, do from time to time give us valuable information about their outer as well as their inner

worlds. The most interesting of these books give us something of all three kinds of experience. For a time, while we read them, it is possible to enjoy one of the rarest artistic pleasures—complete escape: escape into another sphere of action and perception. From that escape we return—with what relief!—to the real center of the universe, which is our own self.

▶ EXERCISE 5   After making an outline, write a paper on one of the following topics (or any other topic assigned by your instructor): (1) types of detective stories, (2) kinds of bores, (3) the heroes of TV Westerns, (4) what language habits reveal about a speaker, (5) what dogs (or any other pets) reveal about their owners, (6) the best reasons for going to college.

(2) Effective beginnings and endings.

Although formal introductions and conclusions are often not necessary for short papers, every composition should have an effective beginning and ending.

BEGINNINGS   There are two ways to begin a composition effectively. One way is to begin with a sentence which not only arouses the reader's interest but also starts the development of the topic by discussing the first main point in the outline. The second way is to begin with a formal introduction (often only one paragraph). This arouses the reader's interest and introduces the central idea of the paper but does not start the development of the topic. Sometimes the limitations of the subject are defined in a formal introduction. See the first two paragraphs of "The Face in the Mirror" in Exercise 4, page 912. The choice of the type of beginning depends upon the nature of the topic and the length of the composition.

Whichever method you use, remember that an effective beginning gains the reader's interest. One of the easiest and best ways to gain interest is to use specific facts and details instead of dull generalizations. See **20a(2)** and **31d**. Compare the effectiveness of the introductions on the next page.

Topic: A football game in the Rose Bowl

GENERAL

When football teams play an important bowl game, lots of fans are very enthusiastic supporters of the home-town team. I especially noticed this fact when I recently saw a game in the Rose Bowl.

SPECIFIC

There are two American cities that genuflect to no one in their uncontrollable—one could even say undying—affection for the home-town football team. When citizens of those two cities, Seattle and Minneapolis, assembled for a contest between their Washington Huskies and their Minnesota Gophers on the green grass of Pasadena, sensible natives took shelter. The less sensible—97,000 of them—were at the Arroyo Seco, where the Rose Bowl sits, and everyone but the ushers appeared to be related to a player on one or the other team. In its long history, the Rose Bowl had never been shaken by such passion from the stands.[2]

Another way to arouse interest is to refer to some common experience (such as shyness on a first date, an encounter with an eccentric door-to-door salesman, a clumsy slip of the tongue on an important occasion, the joy of winning a game or a special honor) which the reader will probably

---

[2] From "They Ran All the Way: The Wildest Rose," reprinted from *Sports Illustrated,* January 9, 1961. By permission of the publishers.

associate with himself; see the introduction to "Carousel—A New Experience" below. A third way to interest the reader is to start with a striking fact. Still another method is to begin with an interesting incident or anecdote that is closely related to the topic:

Title: The Elusive Dr. Szilard

At a party in a university community a few weeks ago the guests amused themselves by drawing up a list of men who have played unique roles in recent history. They finally agreed upon five who had done things which could not have been accomplished, in their times, by anybody else. The first four are familiar to everybody—Lincoln, Gandhi, Hitler, and Churchill. But the fifth might puzzle even many well-informed people. It was Leo Szilard.[3]

An effective beginning introduces a subject and is therefore directly related to it. As you read the following paragraph (written by a student), notice the repetition of the key words of the title: *Carousel, new, experience.* In the last sentence the controlling idea of the composition is given. Such an introduction is closely related to the topic and contributes to the unity of the whole composition.

Title: Carousel—A New Experience

All of us enjoy wearing a new pair of shoes, eating a dish we have not had before, seeing a movie with an unusual plot, or touring in a new section of the country; in other words, we like experiences which are novel, different. I happen to be one of those people who enjoy discovering an unfamiliar poem by a famous poet, reading a good book, or attending a choral or band concert. I like new and different cultural outlets, and a few weeks ago my English assignment brought me face to face with just such an experience: Carousel, theater-in-the-round. The play which I attended was an Irish drama by Paul Vincent Carroll, entitled *Shadow and Substance,* and I should like to use it as the vehicle in my description of Carousel itself—the interior of the theater, the actors, the techniques used.

Caution: Do not write aimless, dull introductions. If you have difficulty writing an interesting and pertinent introductory paragraph which contributes to the effectiveness of your whole composition, then begin with an immediate discussion of your first main point.

Title: Characteristics of a Nonconformist

One of the distinguishing characteristics of a nonconformist is his lack of respect for established authority. For example, ...

▶ EXERCISE 6   Evaluate the effectiveness of the following beginnings of student papers.

1. *Title:* A Description of My Home Town

It is early morning. A light drizzle falls upon the gray cobblestones, and you see two lace-shawled women hurrying to the Cathedral. The trolley-cars begin to clatter down the broad island of Canal Street, and the city begins to awake. This is a day in my city. This is New Orleans.

Soon the sun peeks through the misty heavens, and the city begins to erupt into a myriad of noises. . . .

2. *Title:* Justice in *The Unvanquished*

Justice is a word with many applications and definitions. This point is well illustrated in *The Unvanquished,* a novel

---

[3] From "The Elusive Dr. Szilard" by Alice Kimball, reprinted from *Harper's Magazine,* July, 1960. By permission of *Harper's Magazine.*

of Civil War times by William Faulkner. Justice, as practiced by Faulkner's characters, takes on many forms; indeed, the meaning of the word is warped to suit any occasion which may arise. Applications of justice may range all the way from mouth soaping to murder; many different situations call for different forms of justice.

Loosh, the old Negro slave, felt that he was justified in tearing down Bayard's and Ringo's model of the city of Vicksburg. . . .

ENDINGS   A composition should end; it should not merely stop. Two ways to end a composition effectively are (1) to stress the final point of the main discussion by using an emphatic last sentence and (2) to write a strong concluding paragraph. Often a concluding paragraph clinches, restates, or stresses the importance of the central idea or thesis of the composition. See the concluding paragraph of "The Face in the Mirror," pages 912–13. When the body of a composition describes an experiment or presents evidence, the conclusion often presents a discovery or a theory. A conclusion may also present a brief summary, a pertinent question, a suggestion or challenge, or a solution to a problem.

SUMMARY   (ending of an article giving reasons for the growing popularity of FM radio programs)

FM, in short, is prospering in direct ratio as it provides adults with a refuge from the blaring Children's Hour of the AM juke boxes and from the vacuity of most TV.

QUESTION   (ending of an essay describing the dangers of modern chemical, biological, and radiological warfare)

The question that cannot be avoided is whether any nation, even in its own defense, has the right to destroy half of the rest of the world.

SUGGESTION   (ending of an article discussing the interest of consumers in deceptive packaging which conceals rises in prices)

Efforts at industry self-government directed toward higher ethical standards are, of course, laudable and welcome. But consumers probably would do well to continue to hope, and to urge, that all existing Governmental agencies which exercise regulatory powers in this area—including the FTC, the FDA, certain divisions of the Department of Agriculture, and the Treasury's alcohol-control agency—will, in the future, act with more vigor and with a greater awareness of consumer needs.[4]

SOLUTION TO A PROBLEM   (ending of an essay explaining the problem of American doctors who are barred from hospitals)

What will help to solve the complicated and disturbing problem, he [John G. Steinle, management consultant to hospitals] says, is a greater public awareness of the role of the hospital as a community institution and a willingness on the part of the public to become involved in the management of its community affairs. Such a force of informed public opinion can right more wrongs than any laws devised.[5]

Caution: Do not devote too much space to introductions and conclusions. A short paper often has only one paragraph for a beginning or an ending; frequently one sentence for each is adequate. Remember that the bulk of your

[4] From *Consumer Reports,* January, 1961. By permission of Consumers Union, Mount Vernon, New York, a non-profit organization.
[5] From "Why Hospitals Lock Out Doctors," reprinted from *Look,* January 17, 1961. By permission of *Look.*

composition should be the development of the central idea, the discussion of the main headings and the subheadings in the outline.

▶ EXERCISE 7 In a magazine recommended by your instructor, find and copy a good conclusion to an article. Be prepared to explain why the conclusion is effective and how it is related to the central idea of the article.

▶ EXERCISE 8 Giving special attention to the beginning and ending, write a composition based on the outline you prepared for Exercise 3.

▶ EXERCISE 9 Revise the composition you wrote for Exercise 5, using the Check List for Revision (8d[1]).

▶ EXERCISE 10 Be prepared for a class discussion of the following outline and composition, which were written by a college freshman. Be prepared to support your comments by referring to parts of this section (32a–g).

MAYVILLE

CENTRAL IDEA   Visiting such familiar landmarks as Dr. Weaver's drugstore, the old fire hall, and Mel Tanner's service station proved to me that Mayville was still the same quiet, sleepy little town I had left.

INTRODUCTION   Mayville as seen from a train window
 I. Weaver's Drugs
    A. Characteristics sixteen years ago
    B. Characteristics at time of visit
 II. Mayville Fire Hall
 III. Tanner's Gulf Service
    A. Building and property
    B. Action going on at station

CONCLUSION   The small, quiet town, almost extinct

The trip from Lenox City had been a long and tiring one. As I peered through the blackened train window, Mayville came into view. From a distance it seemed even smaller than it actually is: it appeared only as a few boxes scattered beside the thin black line that is the railroad track. Then the conductor cried, "Mayville, all out for Mayville!" As the train huffed and lurched to a halt in front of the station, I took my single bag and stepped out onto the wooden platform in front of the train station; then, draping my coat over my arm, I walked toward town.

There were few cars on the Mayville streets and no noise or clamor to break the stillness of the air. (It was the same quiet, sleepy, little town I had left sixteen years before.) On the right stood Dr. Weaver's corner drugstore, its white plaster face cracked with wrinkles of age. The drugstore was always a place to go after school for a milkshake or a Coke. It would be so crowded with school children that Dr. Weaver could hardly get around to take orders and to speak to his young friends. When the children left, the drugstore fell into a deep silence broken only by the clinking of glasses as Dr. Weaver cleaned off the counter and the two small tables by the window. The drugstore was just as it had been then. The black tile floor was as spotless as ever, and the black counter-top shone like a mirror, reflecting the stacks of clean glasses on the shelf above. The wooden stools in front of the counter were worn from many pairs of blue jeans, and the brass rail was scuffed by countless shoes. The door hinges creaked as I left, just as I knew they would.

Across the street from the drugstore stood the Mayville Fire Hall. The old red brick building stood tall and erect as if indifferent to age, and the two doors facing the street were open. The antiquated fire engine had seen very little action and was covered with dust. On the pale green plaster wall hung buckets, axes, and hoses, all waiting in readiness. Everyone must have been out to lunch, for beside the fire engine stood a small table on which lay an unfinished checker game. The glass in the side window that Billy Joe Jacobs and I had broken when we were about twelve had not been replaced, and Chief Hansen's office door still lacked a doorknob. Brushing aside the cobwebs, I walked on out the back door.

Across the corner was Mel Tanner's Gulf Station, where I worked for three summers pumping gas and being an all-around junior grease monkey. High on the high building were orange metal letters spelling Tanner's Gulf Service. But the V in "service" had blown away during a storm one summer (before I ever worked there) and had never been replaced. Two stark gas pumps stood alone, projecting from the sea of concrete in front of the station. The often malfunctioning cold drink machine was creased and scarred from the kicks of disgruntled or persistent customers. Mel, unexpectedly aged, was leaning against the wall in a chair and smoking his pipe. A few cans of oil and one or two headlamps were stacked haphazardly on the metal shelves behind him, and a new set of tires for the old Ford service truck lay on the green concrete floor in front of his desk. Monte was in the back washing Mrs. Gillian's old Mercury and singing happily to himself. The grease-covered service rack was empty, and the tools from the open box were scattered on the wooden counter. Jumbled inside a rusted oil drum were discarded oil filter boxes, used paper towels, and a chamois, now beyond further use.

Saying good-by to Mel and Monte, I walked to the hotel and rented a room. The few restful days I spent in Mayville seemed more an escape than a vacation. With the world in a constant rush and everyone struggling to industrialize and urbanize all of the Mayville's in the world, it occurred to me that before many years the peace and quiet will vanish with the death of the small town. And there will no longer be any asylum for a homesick and tired assistant vice-president.   —BAYARD TARPLEY

Library Paper

33

Learn how to prepare a library paper.

A library paper (sometimes called a research or term paper) is usually a formal, well-documented composition based for the most part on outside readings. These readings may be from various books in the library or from a collection of essays on a specific subject, a collection commonly called a *sourcebook*. The usual steps in writing a library paper are as follows:

1. Select and limit a subject (**33a**).
2. Prepare a bibliography (**33b**).
3. Develop an outline (**33c**).
4. Take notes on readings (**33d**).
5. Write a properly documented paper (**33e**).

33a

Select and limit a subject.

If you do not know how to select an appropriate subject and to limit it properly, review **32a**, pages 907–08. How much you limit a subject for a library paper depends not only upon the assigned length but also upon the materials available in your library or sourcebook.

GENERAL   drama of the nineteenth century
LIMITED   the plays of Henrik Ibsen
MORE LIMITED   characterization in Ibsen's *A Doll's House*
EVEN MORE LIMITED   Ibsen's attitude toward women as seen in the character of Nora in *A Doll's House*

REPORT OR THESIS   The type of library paper you write will depend upon your purpose. Suppose, for example, that you have chosen the subject "The Meaning of Dreams." If you develop your subject by an organized presentation of the opinions of others, such as Jung and Adler, you will be writing a *report* paper. You may, however, wish to prove or disprove an opinion or theory. If you wish to convince your reader that dreams are significantly related to conscious behavior, that they are not merely mirrors of subconscious fears or wishes, you will be writing a *thesis* paper. Although either purpose should enable you to write an effective paper, the purpose you select will influence your collecting of facts and should therefore be determined as soon as possible.

▶ EXERCISE 1   List three general fields in which you have some interest. Then by process of limitation derive three topics (1) which are suitable for library papers of one to three thousand words each and (2) in which you have a special interest. The subject headings and the cross references in the card catalog or the *Readers' Guide* (see **33b** below) may suggest subjects and possible limitations of them. Determine, if possible, whether each topic lends itself to development as a *report* or a *thesis*.

33b

Prepare a bibliography in acceptable form.

The bibliography lists sources of information—such as books, pamphlets, and articles—from which you will draw the material for your paper. Use (1) the card catalog, (2) indexes to periodicals, and (3) reference books (as explained on the following pages) to make a preliminary bibliography by writing down the most promising titles you can find. Copy each title on a separate card (usually 3 × 5 inches) in the form shown on page 918. You should keep these cards in alphabetical order until you complete your paper, adding useful titles as you find them and discarding those that prove useless. The final bibliography to be copied at the end of your paper will most often include only those works that help in the writing—usually those cited in the footnotes.

(1) Use the card catalog.

The card catalog is the index to the whole library. It lists all books and all bound magazines, whether they are housed in the stacks, on the open shelves of the reference room, or in any other part of the building. In many libraries one general card catalog lists all books owned by the university and shows whether the book is in the general library or in a special collection in another building.

Usually the card catalog consists of cards arranged alphabetically in drawers. These may be "author" cards, "title" cards, or "subject" cards; for in most libraries each book is listed, alphabetically, once according to its author, again according to its title, and again according to its subject or subjects. These three cards (usually printed) are identical except that the title card has the title typewritten in black and the subject card has the subject typewritten in red.

SAMPLE CATALOG CARDS

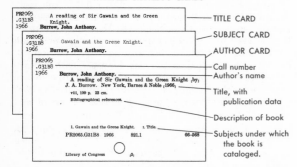

(2) Use indexes to periodicals.

When preparing your bibliography, remember that the periodical indexes do for articles what the card catalog does for books in the library. You will probably find the *Readers' Guide* (an index to over one hundred magazines) the most useful. You may have occasion, however, to use others of the following indexes to periodicals.

INDEXES TO PERIODICALS

GENERAL

Poole's Index. 1802–1906. (Subject index only)
Nineteenth Century Readers' Guide. 1890–99. (Author, subject)
Readers' Guide. 1900—. (Author, title, subject)
Book Review Digest. 1905—. (Author, title, subject)
International Index. 1907–65. Succeeded by *Social Sciences and Humanities.* 1965—. (Author, subject)
New York Times Index. 1913—. (A useful guide for finding the dates of important events which can then be looked up in all other newspapers)

SPECIAL

Agricultural Index. 1916–64. Succeeded by *Biological and Agricultural Index.* 1964—. (Subject)
Art Index. 1929—. (Author, subject)
Bibliographic Index. 1937—. (Subject)
Biography Index. 1946—. (Subject)
Book Review Index. 1965—.
Catholic Periodical Index. 1930—. (Subject)
Education Index. 1929—. (Author, subject)
Engineering Index. 1884—. (Subject)
Index Medicus. 1879–1926; *Quarterly Cumulative Index Medicus.* 1927—. (Author, subject)
Index to Book Reviews in the Humanities. 1960—.
Index to Legal Periodicals. 1908—. (Author, subject)
Industrial Arts Index. 1913–57. Succeeded by *Applied Science and Technology Index.* 1958—; *Business Periodicals Index.* 1958—. (Subject)
Music Index. 1949—. (Subject)

Public Affairs Information Service. 1915—. (Subject)
Technical Book Review Index. 1917–29; 1935—.

> [See also the various abstracts, such as *Biological Abstracts,* 1926—, *Chemical Abstracts,* 1907—, and *Psychological Abstracts,* 1927—.]

(3) Use reference books.

Dictionaries, encyclopedias, atlases, and other books especially helpful for reference are usually kept on the open shelves of the reference room, where students may use them directly without the trouble of having them brought from the stacks. Each of these books is listed in the card catalog, and the call number will often aid in finding the book. The student should learn the general location of the chief classes of reference books in order that he may turn to them without loss of time. For a detailed list of such books, with a short description of each, he should consult Constance M. Winchell's *Guide to Reference Books* (Seventh Edition, supplements 1950–52). Since many reference books, especially some of the encyclopedias, are kept up to date by frequent revisions, the student should cite the last copyright date of the edition he is using. A few of the more important reference books are listed below (with abbreviated entries).

GENERAL DICTIONARIES (UNABRIDGED)

Century Dictionary and Cyclopedia. 12 vols. 1911. 3 vols. 1927–33.
Dictionary of American English. 4 vols. 1936–44.
New Standard Dictionary. 1947, 1952.
Oxford English Dictionary. 12 vols. and supplement. 1933. Originally issued as *A New English Dictionary.* 10 vols. and supplement. 1888–1933.
Webster's New International Dictionary, Second ed., 1934.
Webster's Third New International Dictionary, 1961.

SPECIAL DICTIONARIES

Allen, F. S. *Allen's Synonyms and Antonyms.* 1938.
Evans, Bergen and Cornelia. *A Dictionary of Contemporary American Usage.* 1957.
Fowler, H. W. *Dictionary of Modern American Usage.* Second ed., revised by Sir Ernest Gowers. 1965.
Horwill, H. W. *Dictionary of Modern American Usage.* Second ed., 1944.
Lewis, Norman. *The New Roget's Thesaurus.* 1961.
Nicholson, Margaret. *A Dictionary of American-English Usage.* 1957. (Based on Fowler)
Partridge, Eric. *Dictionary of Slang and Unconventional English.* Fifth ed., 1961.
Roget's International Thesaurus. Third ed., 1962.
Webster's Dictionary of Synonyms. 1942.
Wright, Joseph. *English Dialect Dictionary.* 6 vols. 1961.

GENERAL ENCYCLOPEDIAS

Collier's Encyclopedia. 20 vols.
Columbia Encyclopedia. 1950, 1953.
Encyclopedia Americana. 30 vols.
Encyclopædia Britannica. 24 vols.

SPECIAL ENCYCLOPEDIAS

Adams, J. T. *Dictionary of American History.* 6 vols. 1942.
Bailey, L. H. *Cyclopedia of American Agriculture.* 4 vols. 1907–09.
Catholic Encyclopedia. 17 vols. 1907–22. New edition, 1936—.
Encyclopaedia of the Social Sciences. 15 vols. 1930–35.
Encyclopedia of World Art. 1959—.

Grove's Dictionary of Music and Musicians. 9 vols. 1954. Supplement, 1961.

Harris, Chester W. *Encyclopedia of Educational Research.* 1960.

Hastings, James. *Encyclopaedia of Religion and Ethics.* 13 vols. 1908–27.

———. *Interpreter's Dictionary of the Bible.* 4 vols. 1962.

Jewish Encyclopedia. 12 vols. 1925.

McGraw-Hill Encyclopedia of Science and Technology. 15 vols. 1966.

McLaughlin, A. C., and A. B. Hart. *Cyclopedia of American Government.* 3 vols. 1914. Reprint, 1949.

Monroe, Paul. *Cyclopedia of Education.* 5 vols. 1911–13.

Munn, Glenn G. *Encyclopedia of Banking and Finance.* Sixth ed., 1962.

New Schaff-Herzog Encyclopedia of Religious Knowledge. 13 vols. 1908–12.

New Standard Encyclopedia of Art. 2 vols. in 1. 1939.

Thompson, O. *International Cyclopedia of Music and Musicians.* Ninth ed., 1964.

Thorpe's Dictionary of Applied Chemistry. 12 vols. 1937–56.

Universal Jewish Encyclopedia. 10 vols. 1939–43.

Van Nostrand's Scientific Encyclopedia. 1958.

Worldmark Encyclopedia of the Nations. 5 vols. 1963.

ATLASES AND GAZETTEERS

Collier's New World Atlas and Gazetteer. 1953.

Columbia Lippincott Gazetteer of the World. 1952.

Encyclopædia Britannica World Atlas. 1962.

Hammond's Ambassador World Atlas. 1954.

Rand-McNally Commercial Atlas. 1962. Revised annually.

Times (London) *Atlas of the World.* 5 vols. 1955—.

Webster's Geographical Dictionary. Revised ed., 1962.

YEARBOOKS—CURRENT EVENTS

Americana Annual. 1923—.

Annual Register. 1758—.

Britannica Book of the Year. 1938—.

Economic Almanac. 1940—.

Facts on File. 1940—.

Information Please Almanac. 1947—.

New International Year Book. 1907—.

Statesman's Year-Book. 1864—.

Statistical Abstract of the United States. 1878—.

Whitaker's Almanack. 1869—.

World Almanac. 1868—.

BIOGRAPHY

Current Biography. 1940—.

Dictionary of American Biography. 20 vols. and index. 1928–43. Supplements to date.

Dictionary of National Biography. (British.) 22 vols. 1908–09. Indexes and supplements to date.

International Who's Who. 1935—.

Kunitz, S. J., and Howard Haycraft. *American Authors, 1600–1900.* 1938.

———. *British Authors of the Nineteenth Century.* 1936.

———. *Twentieth Century Authors.* 1942. Supplement, 1955.

———. *British Authors before 1800.* 1952.

Webster's Biographical Dictionary. 1943, 1956.

Who's Who. 1848—.

Who's Who in America. 1899—.

Who Was Who in America. 3 vols. 1897–1960.

LITERATURE—MYTHOLOGY

Barnhart, Clarence L. *The New Century Handbook of English Literature.* 1956.

Bartlett's Familiar Quotations. 1955.

Bateson, F. W. *Cambridge Bibliography of English Literature.* 5 vols. 1941–57.

Benét, William Rose. *The Reader's Encyclopedia.* Second ed., 1965.

Brewer's Dictionary of Phrase and Fable. 1953.

Cambridge History of American Literature. 4 vols. 1917–21.

Cambridge History of English Literature. 15 vols. 1907–27.

English Association. *Year's Work in English Studies.* 1920—.

Fiction Catalog. 1941. Seventh ed., 1960.

Frazer, Sir J. G. *The Golden Bough.* 12 vols. 1907–15.

Gayley, C. M. *Classic Myths in English Literature and in Art.* 1939.

Granger, Edith. *Index to Poetry and Recitations.* Fifth ed., 1962.

Harper's Dictionary of Classical Literature and Antiquities. 1897.

Hart, James D. *Oxford Companion to American Literature.* Fourth ed., 1965.

Harvey, Sir Paul. *Oxford Companion to Classical Literature.* 1937.

———. *Oxford Companion to English Literature.* 1946.

Modern Humanities Research Association. *Annual Bibliography of English Language and Literature.* 1920—.

Mythology of All Races, 13 vols. 1916–32.

Oxford Classical Dictionary. 1949.

Sears, Minnie Earl, and Marian Shaw. *Essay and General Literature Index.* 1900—.

Short Story Index. 1953. Supplements.

Spiller, Robert E., and others. *Literary History of the United States.* 3 vols. 1956. (Helpful bibliographies)

Stevenson, B. E. *Home Book of Quotations.* 1956.

Thrall, Hibbard, and Holman. *A Handbook to Literature.* 1960.

(4) Use a standard bibliographical form.

Put each item of your bibliography on a separate card (3 × 5 or 4 × 6 inches in size) so that you can readily drop or add a card and can arrange the list alphabetically without copying. Write in ink and follow exactly and consistently the bibliographical form you are directed to use. The form illustrated by the models below (and by the footnote forms on pages 920–21) is based in general on the revised *Style Sheet* of the Modern Language Association (MLA) but follows several other widely used style manuals in giving the name of the publisher.

MODEL BIBLIOGRAPHICAL ENTRIES

BOOKS

Burrow, John Anthony. *A Reading of Sir Gawain and the Green Knight.* New York: Barnes & Noble, 1966. [Capitalization of the title follows general usage (see **9c**) instead of the special library usage, which capitalizes only first words and proper names. Note that this bracketed comment and the others below are not a part of the bibliographical entries. These entries fall into three units: (1) the author's name; (2) the title; and (3) the place of publication, publisher, and date of publication taken from the latest copyright date as shown on the copyright page.]

Duverger, Maurice. *Political Parties.* Translated from the French by Barbara and Robert North. New York: John Wiley & Sons, Inc., 1954. [A translation]

Hervey, George F., and Jack Hems. *Freshwater Tropical Aquarium Fishes.* London: Batchworth Press, 1952. [Two authors]

Johnson, R. U., and C. C. Buel, editors. *Battles and Leaders of the Civil War.* 4 volumes. New York: The Century Company, 1887–88. [Edited work]

McConnell, F. J., and others. *The Creative Intelligence and Modern Life.* Boulder: The University of Colorado Press, 1928. (University of Colorado Semicentennial Series, 1877–1927. Vol. V.) [A book by more than two authors; also a book in a series]

Prescott, William Hickling. *History of the Reign of Philip the Second, King of Spain.* Edited by John Foster Kirk. 3 volumes. Philadelphia: J. B. Lippincott & Company, 1871. [Author and editor]

Ryan, Cornelius. *The Last Battle.* New York: Simon and Schuster, Inc., 1966.

MAGAZINES AND NEWSPAPERS

King, Larry L. "Requiem for a West Texas Town," *Harper's Magazine,* CCXXXII (January, 1966), 46–53.

"Latest on Getting into College," *U.S. News & World Report,* LX (January 3, 1966), 50–52.

Schonberg, Harold C. "Modern Literalism and Repeats," New York *Times,* March 20, 1966, Section 2, p. 11. [The *p.* or *pp.* (for *page* or *pages*) are not used when the volume number in Roman numerals precedes, as in the two items above.]

"Will the Credit Medicine Be Enough?" *Business Week* (August 13, 1955), pp. 26–28.

ENCYCLOPEDIAS

"Jackson, Andrew." *Encyclopædia Britannica,* 1954, XII, 851–53.

Lee, Edwin A. "Vocational Education." *Encyclopedia Americana,* 1950, XXVIII, 160–61. [A signed article]

BULLETINS AND PAMPHLETS

Standards of Practice for Radio Broadcasters of the United States of America. Washington: The National Association of Radio and Television Broadcasters, 1954.

Velvetbean Caterpillar, The. Dept. of Agriculture, Bureau of Entomology and Plant Quarantine Leaflet No. 348. Washington: Government Printing Office, 1953.

UNPUBLISHED DISSERTATION

Woodall, Guy Ramon. "Robert Walsh, Jr., as an Editor and Literary Critic: 1797–1836." Ph.D. dissertation, University of Tennessee, 1966.

The models given above, with hanging indention, show the proper form for the entries in the final bibliography, which is to be written out and submitted as a part of the library paper. On the separate bibliography cards, the same form may be used; or the author, title, and facts of publication may be written on separate lines.

These

> Watkins, Walter Barker Critz.
>
> <u>Johnson</u> *and* English Poetry
> before 1660.
> New York: Gordian Press, 1965.
>
> PR 3537
> .E6 W3 — card catalog number
>   your welcome

The form of the bibliographical models given above is commonly used by books and periodicals in languages and social sciences. Scientific periodicals tend to use boldface Arabic numerals for the volume number and to place the date at the end. Indexes to periodicals employ a compact form, but one not commonly used in books or periodicals and consequently not suitable as a model.

Whatever bibliographical form a writer adopts, he should give due heed to the three divisions of each entry: the author's name (if it is given), the title, and the facts of publication. He should take great pains to be consistent, each time using commas, periods, italics (underlining), and quotation marks exactly as they are called for by his model. This model will usually be suggested by the periodical, the organization, or the department for which the paper is being written. If the instructor does not specify a form, the student may adopt the commonly used form described in this handbook.

▶ EXERCISE 2   Prepare a preliminary bibliography on the topic selected for your library paper. Use at least ten of the most promising references (books, bulletins, articles in periodicals or reference books) you can find. (Often you will find helpful bibliographies in the books that you consult, especially at the end of articles in encyclopedias and other reference works.) Arrange your cards in alphabetical order.

33c

Prepare the outline.

After completing a preliminary bibliography and a minimum of general reading on your subject (an encyclopedia article and parts of one or two other works may suffice), make a preliminary outline that will give direction to your investigation. This tentative outline will enable you to discard irrelevant material from your bibliography and to begin spotting valuable passages on which you will want to take notes. There is nothing but frustration in store for anyone who attempts to take notes without first knowing what he is looking for.

Be careful, however, not to become a slave to your preliminary outline. For although the outline will direct your reading, your reading will almost certainly suggest ways in which the outline may be improved. No outline should be regarded as complete until the research paper has been finished. As you take notes, you will probably revise your original outline frequently, adding subheads to it, changing subheads to major headings, perhaps dropping some headings entirely.

Follow the general directions for outlining given in **32b–f**, pages 908–11. Make either a topic outline or a complete sentence outline. A paragraph outline would be less satisfactory for a paper as long as a library paper.

33d

Take notes (after evaluating the sources).

As you take notes on your readings, learn how to find and evaluate useful passages with a minimum of time and effort. Seldom will a whole book, or even a whole article, be of use as subject matter for any given research paper. To get what is needed for your paper, you will find that you must turn to many books and articles, rejecting most of them altogether and using from others only a section here and there. You cannot take the time to read each book carefully. Use the table of contents and the index of the book, and learn to scan the pages rapidly until you find the passages you need.

One important consideration always is the reliability of the source. Does the author seem to know his subject? Does he have an official position that implies competence? Do others speak of him as an authority? Is he prejudiced? Is the work recent enough to give the information needed? Is the edition being used the latest one available? Use your best judgment to determine the most dependable sources for your paper. You may find in the *Book Review Digest* convenient summaries of critical opinion on a book in your bibliography.

The common and best way to take notes is on cards or paper sheets of uniform size, usually 3×5 or 4×6 inches. (Often the smaller card is used for bibliography and the larger for notes.) Each card should contain a single note with a heading keyed to a significant word in the outline—not to the notation (IA, II, IIIC, etc.), which is especially subject to change. If the paper is to use the customary footnotes, each card must also show the source of the note, the exact page or pages.

A student preparing a library paper on Ibsen's drama might find the following passage and write from it the note given on the next page.

SOURCE

> And I know of no crime against virtue, good order and the revelation of God that he was not accused of. The product of all this pawing and bawling was the Ibsen legend, that fabulous picture of a fabulous monster, half Nietzsche and half Dr. Frank Crane, drenching the world with scandalous platitudes from a watch-tower in the chilblained North. The righteous heard of him with creepy shudders; there was bold talk of denying him the use of the mails; he was the Gog and the Magog, the Heliogabalus, nay, the downright Kaiser, of that distant and pious era.
>
> No such Ibsen, of course, ever really existed. The genuine Ibsen was anything but the Anti-Christ thus conjured up by imprudent partisans and terrified opponents.[1]

NOTE CARD

> Misunderstanding of Ibsen's purpose
> Ibsen loudly denounced as great sinner—criticisms gave rise to the "Ibsen legend," which made of him a "fabulous monster."
> "The righteous heard of him with creepy shudders ... he was the Gog and the Magog ... of that distant and pious era."
> Not true! The real Ibsen was not wicked.
>
> Mencken, p vii

The above note is an abbreviation or précis. Carefully observe that copied words are inside quotation marks.

[1] H. L. Mencken, Introduction to *Eleven Plays of Henrik Ibsen*, (New York, [1935]), p. vii. Permission by Random House copyright © 1935.

Notice that the words not enclosed in quotation marks are those of the student, not those in the source.

DIRECT QUOTATIONS

Very seldom should you write a note that is merely a quotation. Too many quotations in the library paper suggest a lack of mastery of the subject. And besides, the more you quote, the less practice you get in composition. A quotation must be a very telling and important one before you are justified in using it in your paper. Occasionally, however, you will discover such a passage. When you do, you should take down the passage verbatim—that is, write every word, every capital letter, every mark of punctuation exactly as in the original. Be sure to enclose the quoted passage in quotation marks. When you quote, quote accurately. When you are not quoting, use your own sentence structure and phraseology, getting entirely away from that of the original.

PLAGIARISM

If you fail to acknowledge borrowed material, then you are plagiarizing. Plagiarism is literary theft. When you copy the words of another, put those words inside quotation marks, and acknowledge the source with a footnote. When you paraphrase another's words, use your own words and your own sentence structure, and be sure to use a footnote giving the source of the idea. A plagiarist often merely changes a few words or simply rearranges the words in the source. As you take notes and as you write your paper, be especially careful to avoid plagiarism.

▶ EXERCISE 3   Read carefully the paragraph by Harlow Shapley reprinted on page 898. First write, in a single sentence, the central idea of the paragraph. Then write a note half as long as the paragraph. Finally write a note approximately as long as your source. [Avoid entirely the sentence patterns of the source. Choose your words carefully. Give variety to your sentences.]

33e

Using the outline, the bibliography, and the notes, write the library paper.

After you have made the outline as complete as possible and have taken a number of notes on every major section of the outline and every subsection, you are ready to begin writing. Arrange your notes in the order of the outline, and then use them as the basis of your paper, section by section. Naturally you will have to expand some parts, to cut others; and especially will you need to provide transitional sentences and even transitional paragraphs. Write the material in the best way you can—in your own style, in your own words. Follow the suggestions under **32g**.

(1) **Footnotes and Footnote Forms.** Since you will get your material for the library paper largely from others, you should, of course, give proper credit. To do so, use footnotes numbered consecutively throughout the paper and

placed at the bottoms of the pages (or in one list at the end of the paper, if so directed). The number needed will vary with the paper. Every quotation must have its footnote, and so must all the chief facts and opinions drawn from others. Usually from two to six footnotes per page will be needed for proper documentation of the average library paper.

In the model forms that follow, note that the first footnote reference to a source is similar to, but not identical with, the bibliographical entry.

Moorehead, Alan. *The White Nile*. New York: Harper & Brothers, 1960.

[Bibliographical entry]

[1] Alan Moorehead, *The White Nile* (New York, 1960), p. 351.

[First footnote reference]

The footnote has the normal paragraph indention (not the hanging indention used to make each entry stand out in a bibliography); the author's name comes in normal order with surname last (since the name is not to be alphabetized as in the bibliography); a comma replaces the period between author's name and title, and the facts of publication are put in parentheses without the publisher's name; and the exact page of the source is given.

MODEL FOOTNOTES—FIRST REFERENCES

BOOKS

[1] John Anthony Burrow, *A Reading of Sir Gawain and the Green Knight* (New York, 1966), p. 23.

[2] Maurice Duverger, *Political Parties,* trans. from the French by Barbara and Robert North (New York, 1954), p. 114. [A translation]

[3] George F. Hervey and Jack Hems, *Freshwater Tropical Aquarium Fishes* (London, 1952), p. 44. [Two authors]

[4] R. U. Johnson and C. C. Buel, eds, *Battles and Leaders of the Civil War* (New York, 1887–88), I, 9. [Edited work; also a work in several volumes]

[5] General James Longstreet, "Our March Against Pope," in *Battles and Leaders of the Civil War,* ed. R. U. Johnson and C. C. Buel (New York, 1887–88), II, 516. [Contributing author in an edited work]

[6] F. J. McConnell and others, *The Creative Intelligence and Modern Life,* University of Colorado Semicentennial Series, V (Boulder, Colo., 1928), pp. 29–30. [A book by more than two authors; also a book in a series]

[7] William Hickling Prescott, *History of the Reign of Philip the Second, King of Spain,* ed. John Foster Kirk (Philadelphia, 1871), III, 87.

[8] Cornelius Ryan, *The Last Battle* (New York, 1966), p. 31.

MAGAZINES AND NEWSPAPERS

[9] Larry L. King, "Requiem for a West Texas Town," *Harper's Magazine,* CCXXXII (January, 1966), 47.

[10] "Latest on Getting into College," *U.S. News & World Report, LX* (January 3, 1966), 50–51.

[11] Harold C. Schonberg, "Modern Literalism and Repeats," New York *Times,* March 20, 1966, Section 2, p. 11. [A signed article]

[12] Louisville *Times,* June 4, 1938, p. 16. [An unsigned news story]

[13] "Will the Credit Medicine Be Enough?" *Business Week* (August 13, 1955), pp. 26–27. [An unsigned magazine article]

ENCYCLOPEDIAS

[14] "Jackson, Andrew," *Encyclopædia Britannica,* 1954, XII, 853. [An unsigned encyclopedia article. The title here is given as "Jackson, Andrew" because it is found listed alphabetically under *J* and not under *A* in the encyclopedia.]

[15] Edwin A. Lee, "Vocational Education," *Encyclopedia Americana,* 1950, XXVIII, 160. [A signed encyclopedia article. Note the variant spellings: *Encyclopædia* for the *Britannica; Encyclopedia* for the *Americana.*]

BULLETINS AND PAMPHLETS

[16] *Standards of Practice for Radio Broadcasters of the United States of America* (Washington, 1954), p. 18.

[17] *The Velvetbean Caterpillar,* Department of Agriculture, Bureau of Entomology and Plant Quarantine Leaflet No. 348 (Washington, 1953), p. 3.

UNPUBLISHED DISSERTATION

[18] Guy Ramon Woodall, "Robert Walsh, Jr., as an Editor and Literary Critic: 1797–1836" (Ph.D. dissertation, University of Tennessee, 1966), p. 186.

MODEL FOOTNOTES—SECOND REFERENCES

The second (or later) footnote references below follow the order of the works cited in the Model Footnotes—First References.

BOOKS

[19] Burrow, p. 95. [20] Duverger, pp. 113–14. [It is permissible to place extremely short footnotes two, and even three, on a line, so long as there is no appearance of overcrowding.]

[21] Hervey and Hems, p. 41. [22] Johnson and Buel, I, 5.

[23] Longstreet, II, 515. [24] McConnell and others, p. 28.

[25] Prescott, III, 125.

[26] *Ibid.* [Same work, same volume, and same page as in footnote immediately preceding]

[27] *Ibid.,* II, 94–95. [Same work (Prescott's), but a different volume]

[28] *Ibid.,* p. 95. [Same work, same volume, but only one page this time]

[29] *Ibid.,* III, 125. [Same work, but back to a volume not cited in the *immediately* preceding footnote]

[30] Ryan, p. 133.

[31] Prescott, III, 127. [An *ibid.* here would refer to Ryan's work, not Prescott's.]

[32] Ryan, p. 133.

MAGAZINES AND NEWSPAPERS

[33] King, p. 279. [34] "Latest on Getting into College," p. 51.

[35] Schonberg, p. 1.

[36] Schonberg, "Modern Literalism and Repeats," p. 11. [This is the form that would have been needed if Schonberg had furnished more than one of the sources included in your bibliography.]

[37] Harold C. Schonberg, p. 11. [This is the form that would have to be used if another author also named Schonberg were included in your bibliography.]

[38] Louisville *Times,* p. 16. [Proper if only one article from this newspaper is used. If more than one are used, the secondary form is the same as the primary. See footnote 12.]

[39] "Will the Credit Medicine Be Enough?" p. 27.

ENCYCLOPEDIAS

[40] "Jackson, Andrew," pp. 851–52. [This is the proper form if only one article with this title has been used. It is possible that a research paper may use articles with identical titles from several different encyclopedias. In that case, the proper secondary footnote form would be as follows (footnote 41).]

[41] "Jackson, Andrew," *Encyclopædia Britannica*, pp. 851–52. [The year of publication and the volume number are cited in your primary footnote and need not be repeated here.]

[42] Lee, p. 160.

BULLETINS AND PAMPHLETS

[43] *Standards of Practice for Radio Broadcasters of the United States of America*, p. 17.

[44] *The Velvetbean Caterpillar*, p. 3.

UNPUBLISHED DISSERTATION

[45] Woodall, p. 135.

Abbreviations. Some abbreviations used in footnotes are as follows (those from Latin usually written in italics):

c. or *ca.* (*circa*)	about (*ca.* 1550)
cf. (*confer*)	compare [The English *see* is more common.]
ch., chs.	chapter, chapters
ed.	edited by, edition, editor
f., ff.	and the following page, pages
ibid. (*ibidem*)	in the same place
l., ll.	line, lines
loc. cit. (*loco citato*)	in the place cited
MS., ms., MSS., mss.	manuscript, manuscripts
n.d.	no date given
n.p.	no place (of publication)
op. cit. (*opere citato*)	in the work cited
p., pp.	page, pages
passim	here and there
rev.	revised
tr., trans.	translated by
vol., vols.	volume, volumes

(2) **Final Outline and Paper.** After writing the first draft of your paper, complete with footnotes, read it over carefully, correcting all errors in spelling, mechanics, and grammar, and making sure that the arrangement is logical and that the writing is as clear, concise, and pleasing in style as you can possibly make it. You will probably rewrite some sentences, strike out others, and add still others. Your outline, which has developed steadily throughout the note-taking and the first draft of the paper, should now be in its final form. It has served primarily, of course, as a guide to the writing of the paper; but it will also serve, if copied in its final stage, as a guide to the contents of the paper.

With your first draft corrected and revised, and with your outline put in its final form, write the final draft of your paper. Use a typewriter if possible; if not, use pen and ink, writing legibly and neatly.

(3) **Final Bibliography.** You assembled a preliminary bibliography early in your research. As you pursued your investigation, you eliminated some items and added others. Not until you have completed your paper can you know the items that should make up your final bibliography. Now, with your writing completed, look through your footnotes. Every book or article appearing even once in a footnote belongs in the bibliography. Your instructor may ask you to include everything that you have examined, whether you have actually used it in your writing or not. In that case your bibliography may have, instead of a dozen items, as many as fifty or a hundred. But, on the whole, the best practice is to include only items which have actually been used. Once you have determined the items that should be included, you can easily arrange the bibliography cards and copy them, either in one alphabetical list or in a list classified according to the instructor's directions.

The completed library paper will consist of three units (or four units if a separate page is used for title, author's name, instructor's name, course number, and date of writing):

1. Outline, serving as the table of contents (numbered with small Roman numerals if it occupies more than one page).
2. Text of the paper, with footnotes.
3. Bibliography, on a separate page or pages numbered with the text (with Arabic numerals).

Students are often asked to submit, along with the completed paper, the materials used in the preparation of the paper: (1) one of the preliminary outlines, (2) the notes, on cards, (3) the rough draft of the paper, with footnotes, and (4) the bibliography, on cards.

▶ EXERCISE 4   On the following pages is a library paper written by a college freshman. The pages facing those of the library paper contain passages from the sources used by the student in preparing the paper, so that you may compare the original material with the student's use of it. Be prepared for a class discussion of this paper—its strengths and weaknesses. Give special attention to both content and form, organization and documentation.

Ibsen's Nora

by Barbara J. Reid

OUTLINE

CENTRAL IDEA   The character of Nora reflects Ibsen's
       attitude toward women.

INTRODUCTION   The storm of controversy aroused by
       Ibsen's <u>A Doll's House</u>

  I. The early Nora

     A. Her doll-like qualities

     B. Her faulty sense of morality

 II. Nora's awakening

     A. Her latent instincts

     B. Her self-recognition

     C. Her reevaluation of her marriage

III. Nora as the Ibsen woman

     A. Foreshadows woman of the twentieth century

     B. Indicates needed reforms in the nineteenth
        century

CONCLUSION   Debated issues showing misunderstanding
       of Ibsen's purpose

Original Sources

The "problem play," a serious drama concentrated on a particular weakness or evil, presumably remediable if attacked from a new direction, brought the theatre into the arena of social reform. Because problem plays are pointed at existing problems which may in time be alleviated if the action they call for is taken, they sometimes seem dated by the problem, or limited to a sociological meaning only. The best of them, however, outlive the problem because it was only an external means for exhibiting universal human nature under tragic forces. Ibsen's plays, which served as powerful arguments both for realistic drama and realistic thought, have passed the "time test" and emerged as dateless serious dramas or tragedies. [From *Introduction to Literature: Plays*, eds. Lynn Altenbernd and Leslie L. Lewis. Reprinted by permission of The Macmillan Company.]

The theme of the play, with its insistence on the woman's right to individual self-development, provoked a storm of discussion, and, in many quarters, an outpouring of violent abuse. [From Introduction by R. Farquharson Sharp to *A Doll's House: And Two Other Plays*, by Henrik Ibsen (translated by R. Farquharson Sharp and Eleanor Marx-Aveling.) By permission of E. P. Dutton & Co. Inc. and J. M. Dent & Sons, Ltd.]

No work of Ibsen's, not even his beautiful Puritan opera of *Brand*, has excited so much controversy as *A Doll's House*. This was, no doubt, to a very great extent caused by its novel presentment of the mission of woman in modern society. In the dramas and romances of modern Scandinavia, and especially those of Ibsen and Björnson, the function of woman had been clearly defined. She was to be the helper, the comforter, the inspirer, the guerdon of man in his struggle towards loftier forms of existence. When man fell on the upward path, woman's hand was to be stretched to raise him; when man went wandering away on ill and savage courses, woman was to wait patiently over her spinning-wheel, ready to welcome and to pardon the returning prodigal; when the eyes of man grew weary in watching for the morning-star, its rays were to flash through the crystal tears of woman. [From *Northern Studies*, by Edmund Gosse.]

IBSEN'S NORA

Henrik Ibsen's A Doll's House is today regarded by many authorities as a timeless classic.[1] When it appeared in 1879, however, it aroused a heated controversy over the problem that Ibsen presented. A Doll's House has to do with woman's place in the home in the nineteenth century. The main theme, according to one critic, is the play's "insistence on the woman's right to individual self-development."[2] This was revolutionary doctrine in the nineteenth century, because woman's role at that time was to be "the helper, the comforter, the inspirer, the guerdon of man in his struggle towards loftier forms of existence."[3]

---

[1] See, for example, Lynn Altenbernd and Leslie L. Lewis, Introduction to Literature: Plays (New York, 1963), p. 164.

[2] R. Farquharson Sharp, Introduction to A Doll's House: And Two Other Plays, by Henrik Ibsen (New York, 1946), p. lx.

[3] Edmund Gosse, Northern Studies (London, 1890), p. 88.

The subject of *A Doll's House*—the awakening to the sense of individual responsibility on the part of a woman who has always been treated as a spoilt child— was of itself sufficient matter for any amount of discussion. Whether Nora acted rightly or wrongly, naturally or unnaturally, in leaving husband, home and children in order to develop her own "individuality"; whether her casting herself adrift was indispensable to her development—all this is hotly debated. [From Introduction by R. Farquharson Sharp to *A Doll's House: And Two Other Plays*, by Henrik Ibsen (translated by R. Farquharson Sharp and Eleanor Marx-Aveling.) By permission of E. P. Dutton & Co. Inc. and J. M. Dent & Sons, Ltd.]

. . . she [Nora] is now a mother, and the wife of a man who shields her carefully from all contact with the world. He refrains from sharing with her his work or his trouble; he fosters all her childish instincts; she is a source of enjoyment to him, a precious toy. [From *The New Spirit*, by Havelock Ellis.]

2

Therefore, Ibsen's implication that women ought to walk away from the shadows of men, to find their own place in the sun, caused quite a stir.

In the character of Nora in A Doll's House, Ibsen at first presents a nineteenth-century stereotype wife who is simple, flighty, childish, sweet, and irresponsible; then she gradually becomes aware of her individuality and breaks from the mold.[4] Her doll-like nature is caused by her upbringing. Both her husband, Helmer, and her father have babied her for many years; her opinions and ideas of morality are just echoes of these men in her life. As he refuses to tell her of his work and his difficulties, Helmer protects her from the outside world. Calling her his "little lark" and "little squirrel," he considers Nora as only "a source of enjoyment to him, a precious toy."[5]

---

[4]Sharp, p. ix.

[5]Havelock Ellis, The New Spirit (New York, 1892), p. 161.

. . . He is a man of aesthetic tastes, and his love for her has something of the delight that one takes in a work of art. Nora's conduct is the natural outcome of her training and experience. She tells lies with facility; she flirts almost recklessly to attain her own ends; when money is concerned, her conceptions of right are so elementary that she forges her father's name. But she acts from the impulses of a loving heart; her motives are always good; she is not conscious of guilt. Her education in life has not led her beyond the stage of the affectionate child with no sense of responsibility. But the higher instincts are latent within her; and they awake when the light of day at length penetrates her doll's house, and she learns the judgment of the world, of which her husband now stands forth as the stern interpreter. [From *The New Spirit*, by Havelock Ellis.]

3

According to Havelock Ellis, Nora's behavior can be traced to her experience and environment. It bothers her not at all to tell lies. For example, even when she is swallowing the last bite of the macaroons (which Helmer has forbidden her to buy), Nora answers Helmer's questions by saying that she has not bought macaroons nor is she eating them. To get what she wants, she also resorts to flirting with her own husband. When she wants to keep her husband from going to the mail box, she convinces him that without his constant help she could not learn the Tarantella dance before the party--though actually she knows the dance well. Although she has worthy motives, she does actually forge her father's signature. Her motives are always praiseworthy, and like a child who has no knowledge of wrong and right she has no guilty conscience.[6]

When Helmer explains to her the immorality involved in her forging the signature of her father,

---

[6]*Ibid.*

HELMER (*walking about the room*). What a horrible awakening! All these eight years —she who was my joy and pride—a hypocrite, a liar—worse, worse—a criminal! The unutterable ugliness of it all! For shame! For shame! [NORA *is silent and looks steadily at him. He stops in front of her.*] I ought to have suspected that something of the sort would happen. I ought to have foreseen it. All your father's want of principle—be silent!—all your father's want of principle has come out in you. No religion, no morality, no sense of duty—. How I am punished for having winked at what he did! I did it for your sake, and this is how you repay me.

NORA. Yes, that's just it.

HELMER. Now you have destroyed all my happiness. You have ruined all my future. It is horrible to think of! I am in the power of an unscrupulous man; he can do what he likes with me, ask anything he likes of me, give me any orders he pleases —I dare not refuse. And I must sink to such miserable depths because of a thoughtless woman!

NORA. When I am out of the way, you will be free.

.   .   .

HELMER. Nora—!

NORA. You mean that I would never have accepted such a sacrifice on your part? No, of course not. But what would my assurances have been worth against yours? That was the wonderful thing which I hoped for and feared; and it was to prevent that, that I wanted to kill myself.

HELMER. I would gladly work night and day for you, Nora—bear sorrow and want for your sake. But no man would sacrifice his honour for the one he loves.

NORA. It is a thing hundreds of thousands of women have done.

HELMER. Oh, you think and talk like a heedless child.

4

Nora begins to understand how naive she has been and how unkind and selfish her husband really is. Nora sees that he is selfishly concerned for his own reputation as she listens to him say these words:

> Now you have destroyed all my happiness. You have ruined all my future. It is horrible to think of! I am in the power of an unscrupulous man; he can do what he likes with me, ask anything he likes of me, give me any orders he pleases--I dare not refuse. And I must sink to such miserable depths because of a thoughtless woman.[7]

He is so concerned with himself that he does not stop to think what could have made her do such a thing.

The breach between Nora and Helmer widens. In the course of their quarrel, Helmer says,

> I would gladly work night and day for you, Nora--bear sorrow and want for your sake. But no man would sacrifice his honour for the one he loves.[8]

And Nora, with eyes newly opened, responds, "It is a

---

[7] Henrik Ibsen, A Doll's House, trans. by William Archer, in Interpreting Literature, eds. K. L. Knickerbocker and H. Willard Reninger (New York, 1960), pp. 638-39.

[8] Ibid., p. 643

. . . Wilder's play differs from Ibsen's in the conviction it creates in the minds of the audience that Nora's desertion is permanent rather than temporary, Ibsen's idea having been that the separation was to last only long enough for both husband and wife to make the adjustments necessary for a true marriage. [From *Milestones of the Drama,* ed. by Helen Louise Cohen. Reprinted by permission of Harcourt, Brace & World, Inc.]

I know no more important lessons for women than those contained in the *Doll's House* and *Ghosts.* They are full of the beautiful truth that Woman is a responsible being, as complete in herself, as capable of exercising self-government as Man. They sound a clarion call to women to throw off the yoke of the Past, to arise, to put aside their worn out ideal and to boldly assume the duties of the present age. In the *Doll's House,* there is shadowed forth the perfect marriage of the future. [From "Ibsen's Attitude Toward Woman," by Annie Nathan Meyer.]

6

play ends as Nora leaves.

What is this "most wonderful thing of all" or this "miracle of miracles" that Ibsen uses to hint that the separation of husband and wife will not be permanent? It is the development of perfect communion, which both Nora and Helmer may achieve by growing in individual responsibility, by making the adjustments needed for a happy marriage.[11] In this way, Ibsen does "sound a clarion call to women to throw off the yoke of the Past, to arise, to put aside their worn out ideal and to boldly assume the duties of the present age."[12] In a sense, Ibsen was foreseeing women in the twentieth century.

Because of the widespread misunderstanding of Ibsen's purposes, the dramatist was loudly denounced as a great sinner. A kind of "Ibsen legend" arose, which made the man a "fabulous monster." According to

---

[11]Helen Louise Cohen, *Milestones of the Drama* (New York, 1940), p. 271.

[12]Annie Nathan Meyer, "Ibsen's Attitude Toward Woman," *The Critic,* XVI (March 22, 1890), 148.

NORA. What do you consider my most sacred duties?

HELMER. Do I need to tell you that? Are they not your duties to your husband and your children?

NORA. I have other duties just as sacred.

HELMER. That you have not. What duties could those be?

NORA. Duties to myself.

HELMER. Before all else, you are a wife and a mother.

NORA. I don't believe that any longer. I believe that before all else I am a reasonable human being, just as you are—or, at all events, that I must try and become one. I know quite well, Torvald, that most people would think you right, and that views of that kind are to be found in books; but I can no longer content myself with what most people say, or with what is found in books. I must think over things for myself and get to understand them.

HELMER. Can you not understand your place in your own home? Have you not a reliable guide in such matters as that— have you no religion? [From *A Doll's House*, by Henrik Ibsen, trans. by William Archer.]

5

thing hundreds of thousands of women have done."[9] She now fully understands that her marriage has not been a true marriage, that she has really been living in a doll house. In fact, Nora has just courageously contradicted Helmer's statement that her function in life is to be a wife and mother. With new insight, she has clearly expressed her opposing view:

> I don't believe that any longer. I believe that
> before all else I am a reasonable human being,
> just as you are--or, at all events, that I must
> try and become one. I know quite well, Torvald,
> that most people would think you right, and that
> views of that kind are to be found in books; but
> I can no longer content myself with what most
> people say, or with what is found in books. I
> must think over things for myself and get to
> understand them.[10]

Nora knows that she must educate herself and must develop her own personality. She believes that the only way to do this is to leave her husband until he learns to understand her, an understanding which to her would be "the most wonderful thing of all." The

---

[9]Ibid.

[10]Ibid., p. 642.

9

BIBLIOGRAPHY

Altenbernd, Lynn, and Leslie L. Lewis, eds. Intro-
    duction to Literature: Plays. New York: The
    Macmillan Company, 1963.

Cohen, Helen Louise, ed. Milestones of the Drama.
    New York: Harcourt, Brace & World, Inc., 1940.

Ellis, Havelock. The New Spirit. 3rd ed. New York:
    The Walter Scott Publishing Company, Ltd., 1892.

Gosse, Edmund. Northern Studies. London: The Walter
    Scott Publishing Company, Ltd., 1890.

Huneker, James. Egoists: A Book of Supermen. New
    York: Charles Scribner's Sons, 1932.

Ibsen, Henrik. A Doll's House, trans. William Archer,
    in Interpreting Literature, eds. K. L. Knicker-
    bocker and H. Willard Reninger. Rev. ed. New
    York: Holt, Rinehart and Winston, Inc., 1960.

Mencken, H. L. Introduction to Eleven Plays of
    Henrik Ibsen. New York: Random House, [1935].

Meyer, Annie Nathan. "Ibsen's Attitude Toward Woman,"
    The Critic, XVI (March 22, 1890), 147-48.

Sharp, R. Farquharson. Introduction to A Doll's
    House: And Two Other Plays, by Henrik Ibsen.
    New York: E. P. Dutton & Company, Inc., 1946.

Watson, E. Bradlee, and Benfield Pressey, eds. Contem-
    porary Drama: Fifteen Plays. New York: Charles
    Scribner's Sons, 1959.

Letters

34

Letters should follow the forms prescribed by usage.

Many college graduates will find letter-writing a major part of their life's work. All the principles of good writing set forth in this handbook apply to letters and should be used by the student whenever he is called on to write letters.

Business letters are preferably typewritten on one side only of sheets 8½ × 11 inches in size. These sheets are folded either (1) once horizontally and twice in the other direction to fit an envelope about 3½ × 6½ inches in size or (2) twice horizontally to fit an envelope about 4 × 10 inches in size.

Personal letters and social notes are commonly written by hand on note paper—a four-page sheet to be folded once horizontally for insertion in a matching envelope; or on club paper—a sheet about 7¼ × 11 inches, to be folded twice horizontally to fit a matching envelope 3¾ × 7½ inches. Both sides of the sheets may be used.

34a

Business letters should follow prescribed usage with respect to the six essential parts:

(1) Heading.
(2) Inside address.
(3) Salutation (or greeting).
(4) Body of the letter.
(5) Complimentary close.
(6) Signature.

(1) The heading must give the full address of the writer and the date of the letter.

The heading is blocked as in the model.

860 Fremont Street [End punctuation is regularly
Bessemer, Alabama 35020 omitted with the blocked head-
February 3, 1967   ing.]

MODEL BUSINESS LETTER

(1) {
1288 Catawba Street
Columbia, Missouri 65201
May 3, 1966

(2) {
Mr. J. W. Rice
Editor, Rushville *News*
122 East Market Street
Rushville, Missouri 64484

(3) Dear Mr. Rice:

Mr. Erskine Freeman, of your City Room, has mentioned to me your regular practice of employing two student reporters every summer. I am now majoring in journalism at the University of Missouri, and I should like, therefore, to apply for one of those positions for this next summer.

By the end of this college year I shall have completed three quarters of the university program in journalism. Included in this work are two courses in reporting and one in copyreading. Before I began my college work, I had served four years as sports editor of my high school newspaper, where I learned some of the fundamentals of page make-up. Last year I was awarded the Missouri Press Association Scholarship for journalism.

I have permission to refer you to my employer of the last three summers:

(4) {
     Mr. George Armour
     Armour Drug Store
     Rushville, Missouri 64484

and to the professors under whom I have taken courses in journalism:

     Dr. James D. Turner
     Professor of Journalism
     University of Missouri
     Columbia, Missouri 65201

     Dr. John M. Cain
     Assistant Professor of Journalism
     University of Missouri
     Columbia, Missouri 65201

I shall be in Rushville after June 6 and should appreciate an opportunity to call at your office for an interview at your convenience.

(5)   Very truly yours,

(6) { *Donald Burke*
   Donald Burke

If there is a letterhead (which supplies the address), the date may be written either under the letterhead or flush with the right margin.

(2) **The inside address (identical with the address to appear on the envelope) must give the name and the full address of the person to whom the letter is written.**

The inside address must be consistent in form with the heading. The inside address is typed flush with the left margin about six spaces lower than the heading.

(3) **The salutation (or greeting) should be consistent with the tone of the letter, the first line of the inside address, and the complimentary close.**

The salutation is written flush with the left margin two spaces below the inside address and is followed by a colon. The following salutations are used:

FOR MEN	FOR WOMEN
Dear Sir:	Dear Madam:
Dear Mr. Smith:	Dear Mrs. Smith:
Gentlemen:	Ladies:

Note: The masculine salutation is used to address an organization (Gentlemen) or an individual (Dear Sir) whose name the writer does not know.

In some instances a business letter is addressed to a company or a department of a company but marked for the attention of a particular person. In such letters, the "attention line" is placed two lines above the salutation, thus:

<u>Attention</u>: Mr. L. W. Jones

Gentlemen:

For the proper form of salutation in letters to government officials, ecclesiastical dignitaries, etc., consult a good dictionary.

In salutations and addresses, abbreviations are generally disapproved except for *Mr.* (plural, *Messrs.*), *Mrs.* (plural, *Mmes.*), and *Dr.*

MODEL ADDRESSED ENVELOPE

Donald Burke
1288 Catawba Street
Columbia, Missouri 65201

Mr. J. W. Rice
Editor, Rushville <u>News</u>
122 East Market Street
Rushville, Missouri 64484

(4) **The body of the letter should follow the principles of good writing.**

Typewritten business letters are usually single-spaced, with double spacing between paragraphs. All paragraphs (1) should begin flush with the left-hand margin, as in the model business letter on page 932, or (2) should be indented equally (usually five spaces). The subject matter should be well organized and paragraphed, but the paragraphs will frequently be shorter than in ordinary writing. The style should be clear and direct. Indirect, abbreviated, or outdated phrasing should be avoided.

INDIRECT	I beg to inform you that we have . . . I beg to send . . . Permit us to report that we now supply . . .
BETTER	We have . . . I send . . . We now supply . . .
ABBREVIATED	Hope to have . . . Enclose check for six dollars.
BETTER	We hope to have . . . I enclose a check for six dollars.

Note: If the letter goes over to a second page, the sender's address (whether on letterhead or a typed heading) should not be repeated. The name (surname only) of the recipient, the page number, and the date should be given, arranged either across the top of the page or at the upper left margin.

(5) **The complimentary close should be consistent with the tone of the letter and with the salutation.**

Ordinary business letters addressed to strangers should close with *Yours truly, Yours very truly,* or *Very truly yours.* Professional letters, or business letters addressed to an individual with such an opening as *Dear Mr. White,* may well close with the more friendly *Yours sincerely, Sincerely yours, Sincerely, Faithfully yours,* or *Cordially yours.*

(6) **The signature should be written by hand directly below the complimentary close.**

If the writer's name does not appear in the letterhead, it may be typed just below the signature. Ordinarily, neither professional titles nor degrees should be used with the signature, but the writer's official capacity may be indicated:

INAPPROPRIATE	James M. Smith, LL.D.
PERMISSIBLE	James M. Smith President

A married woman should sign her own name (*Mary Hughes Black,* not *Mrs. John K. Black*). In business letters her status is indicated by the use of parentheses as follows:

CORRECT	Mary Hughes Black (Mrs. John K. Black)
CORRECT	(Mrs.) Mary Hughes Black

(7) **The letter should be folded to fit the envelope.**

Below are the steps for the proper folding of a business letter to fit the long standard envelope and for placing it inside the envelope.

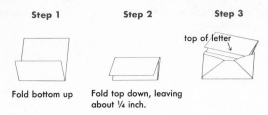

Step 1   Step 2   Step 3

top of letter

Fold bottom up   Fold top down, leaving about ¼ inch.

Fold the standard-sized paper to fit a small business envelope as follows:

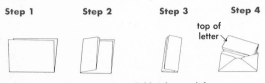

Step 1   Step 2   Step 3   Step 4

top of letter

Fold bottom up   Fold left side in   Fold right over left, leaving about ¼ inch.

34b
Personal letters and informal social notes follow in general the form of business letters.

Friendly letters usually omit the inside address. If it is included, it may be placed either at the beginning flush with the right margin or at the end of the letter flush with the left margin.

The salutation is usually followed by a comma instead of the more formal colon. As in the business letter, the salutation should be in keeping with the complimentary close and with the tone of the letter. A letter beginning with *Dear Mr. Brown* may close with *Sincerely yours, Yours sincerely*, or *Cordially yours*. A more familiar salutation and complimentary close may be justified by the intimacy of the correspondents.

The body of the letter will vary greatly with the occasion and with the personality of the writer. An easy, informal style is best.

34c
Formal social notes—announcements, invitations, answers to invitations—follow very definite conventions.

For the rare occasions when formal notes are required, engraving or handwriting (not typing) is the rule. Formal notes are always written in the third person. They have no inside address, no salutation, no complimentary close, and no signature. The writer's street address and the month and the date may be placed below at the left. Every word (except the street number and the abbreviations *Mr., Mrs.*, and *Dr.*) is spelled out in full. Acceptances and regrets follow the form of the invitation closely, repeating the hour and the date to insure understanding.

EXERCISES ON LETTERS

▶ EXERCISE 1   Write the following business letters:

1. Request the circulation manager of your newspaper to send your paper to a new address.

2. Ask the manager of a New York hotel to reserve a room for you.
3. Call the attention of your representative in the city government to some needed repairs in a street near your home.
4. Apply for a position that you are competent to fill. Be sure to include the following: (a) a brief description of the job desired—be specific; (b) your qualifications, including age, schooling, and experience; (c) at least three references—people who know you well and are able to evaluate your ability; (d) a request for an interview. See the model business letter on page 932.
5. Explain to your employer why you must resign your position at the end of the year.
6. Recommend to your employer (to fill the position you must resign) a young man or woman with whom you have worked.
7. Request permission of a former employer to use his name as a reference in applying for a new position.

▶ EXERCISE 2   Write the following personal letters:

1. Invite a friend to spend a weekend in your home.
2. Accept an invitation to spend a weekend with a friend.
3. Answer a friend's inquiry about the course in dramatics (or chemical engineering, astronomy, political science, etc.) in your college.
4. Congratulate a friend in another college on his election to some class office (or on any other honor).
5. Introduce a friend to one of your former classmates who lives in a distant city.

Grammatical Terms

35

Consult the following list as needed for explanations of grammatical terms.[1]

Absolute element. A parenthetical word or word group which qualifies a whole clause but which is not linked to it by a conjunction or a relative pronoun.

> *Rain or shine*, the class will have a cookout.
> *Oh*, that door, *I believe*, is locked.
> Fred has not read James Agee's novels, *has he?*

A NOMINATIVE ABSOLUTE is a phrase consisting of a noun or noun substitute followed by a participle (with any complements or modifiers).

> *Jobs being scarce*, competition was keen.

See also **12d(3)**.

Abstract noun. See **Noun.**

Active voice. See **Voice.**

---

[1] See the index for grammatical terms not in this list and for further treatment of those listed.

Adjective. A part of speech used to modify (qualify, describe, or limit) a noun or a noun substitute. The adjectives *a*, *an*, and *the* are often called "noun determiners." See **Articles**.

DESCRIPTIVE ADJECTIVES:

cloudy sky, *good* acting, *greatest* work, *reasonable* prices
They seem *happier* now. Were your neighbors very *friendly?*

LIMITING ADJECTIVES:

DEMONSTRATIVE	*this* one, *that* map, *these* rods, *those* keys
INDEFINITE	*some* milk, *more* effort, *many* others, *few* pets
INTERROGATIVE	*Whose* cap is it? *What* ticket? *Which* one?
NUMERICAL	*one* pear, *three* plums, *third* base, *tenth* year
POSSESSIVE	*my* opinion, *its* nest, *their* homes, *our* right
RELATIVE	The boy *whose* dog had died remained silent.

PROPER ADJECTIVES (capitalized) may be either descriptive or limiting, or both: *American* traditions, *Indian* territory, *English* classes.

Note: Nouns may function as adjectives: a *college* student.

See also Section **4, Adjectives and Adverbs**.

Adjective clause. A subordinate clause used as an adjective.

Velasquez, *whose work affected the French Impressionists,* was a famous Spanish realist. [The adjective clause modifies the noun *Velasquez.*]

Adverb. A part of speech used to modify a word (or word group) other than a noun or pronoun. An adverb may qualify or limit a verb, an adjective, another adverb, a verbal, or even a whole clause. An adverb often indicates time ("are *now* going"), place ("stayed *there*"), manner ("acting *quickly*"), or degree ("*very* eager").

Mildred owns an *extremely* old clock, which runs *very quietly*. [*Extremely* modifies the adjective *old; quietly* modifies the verb *runs; very* modifies the adverb *quietly*.]
Naturally, the villain succeeds at first by *completely* outwitting the hero. [*Naturally* modifies the rest of the sentence, and *completely* modifies the gerund *outwitting*.]

A noun functioning as an adverb is called an *adverbial noun:* "He left *home Monday.*" See also **Conjunctive adverb**.

See also Section **4, Adjectives and Adverbs**.

Adverb clause. A subordinate clause used adverbially. According to meaning, it may be classified as an adverb clause of time, place, manner, cause, purpose, condition, concession, comparison, or result.

The common mole is valuable *because it eats insects.*
Although George Mason is not famous, his ideas were used in our Bill of Rights.
Cartoonists make at least eighteen drawings *so that Woody Woodpecker can laugh victoriously.*

Agreement. The correspondence in form of one word with another (for example, a verb with its subject or a pronoun with its antecedent) to indicate person and number. See Section **6, Agreement**.

Antecedent. The name given to a word or group of words to which a pronoun refers.

This is the *man who* came to the house. [*Man* is the antecedent of the relative pronoun *who*.]
When *John* and *Mary* came, *they* told us the facts in the case. [*John* and *Mary* are the antecedents of the personal pronoun *they*.]

Appositive. A noun or noun substitute set beside another noun or noun substitute and indentifying or explaining it.

Dr. Smith, our *dentist,* is visiting England, his native *country.* [*Dentist* is in apposition with *Dr. Smith*, and *country* is in apposition with *England.*]

See also **12d(2)**.

Article. The definite article *the* and the indefinite articles *a* and *an* are adjectives. They are often called *determiners* because they indicate that a noun or a noun substitute is to follow.

Auxiliary. A verb helper in a verb phrase: *will* dine, *were* talking, *had* risen, *should be* studying, *ought to* pay. See also Sections **1a and 7**.

Case. The inflectional form of a noun (*man's*) or pronoun (*he, his, him*) to show such relations as subject (subjective or nominative case—*he*), possession (possessive case—*man's, his*), or object (objective case—*him*). See also **Inflection** and Section **5, Case**.

Clause. A group of words that contains a verb and its subject and is used as a part of a sentence. A clause may be main (independent, principal) or subordinate (dependent).

MAIN (INDEPENDENT, PRINCIPAL) CLAUSE A main clause can stand by itself as a simple sentence.

The moon rose, and the stars came out. [Two main clauses, either of which can stand by itself as a simple sentence]

SUBORDINATE (DEPENDENT) CLAUSE A subordinate clause cannot stand alone. It is used as a noun, an adjective, or an adverb.

That he will run for office is doubtful. [Noun clause: a subordinate clause used as subject of the sentence]

Collective noun. See **Noun**.

Colloquial. Appropriate for conversation and informal writing rather than for formal writing.

Common noun. See **Noun**.

Comparison. The change in the form of an adjective or adverb to indicate degrees in quality, quantity, or manner. There are three degrees: positive, comparative, and superlative.

Positive	Comparative	Superlative
good	better	best
high	higher	highest
quickly	more quickly	most quickly

See also **Inflection**.

Complement. A word or words used to complete the sense of the verb, the subject, or the object.

SUBJECT COMPLEMENTS
The boy is *obedient.* [The predicate adjective *obedient* modifies the subject *boy.*]
Samuel is a good *child.* [The predicate noun *child* refers to the subject *Samuel.*]

OBJECTS
William lent *Susan* his *book.* [*Book* is the direct object; *Susan* is the indirect object.]

OBJECT COMPLEMENTS
He called the man a *hero.* [*Hero* refers to *man*, which is the direct object.]
Jack painted his garage *blue.* [The adjective *blue* modifies the object *garage.*]

Complete predicate. See **Predicate**.

Complete subject. See **Subject.**

Complex (compound, compound-complex) sentence. See **Sentence.**

Concrete noun. See **Noun.**

Conjugation. A grouping of verb forms to indicate tense, voice, mood, as follows:

CONJUGATION OF THE VERB *TO SEE*
(Principal Parts: *see, saw, seen*)

Active Voice		Passive Voice	
Singular	*Plural*	*Singular*	*Plural*

INDICATIVE MOOD
PRESENT TENSE

1. I see	we see	I am seen	we are seen
2. you see	you see	you are seen	you are seen
3. he (she, it) sees	they see	he (she, it) is seen	they are seen

PAST TENSE

1. I saw	we saw	I was seen	we were seen
2. you saw	you saw	you were seen	you were seen
3. he saw	they saw	he was seen	they were seen

FUTURE TENSE

1. I shall see	we shall see	I shall be seen	we shall be seen
2. you will see	you will see	you will be seen	you will be seen
3. he will see	they will see	he will be seen	they will be seen

PRESENT PERFECT TENSE

1. I have seen	we have seen	I have been seen	we have been seen
2. you have seen	you have seen	you have been seen	you have been seen
3. he has seen	they have seen	he has been seen	they have been seen

PAST PERFECT TENSE

1. I had seen	we had seen	I had been seen	we had been seen
2. you had seen	you had seen	you had been seen	you had been seen
3. he had seen	they had seen	he had been seen	they had been seen

FUTURE PERFECT TENSE (seldom used)

1. I shall have seen	we shall have seen	I shall have been seen	we shall have been seen
2. you will have seen	you will have seen	you will have been seen	you will have been seen
3. he will have seen	they will have seen	he will have been seen	they will have been seen

---

SUBJUNCTIVE MOOD
PRESENT TENSE

Singular that I, you, he see   that I, you, he be seen
Plural that we, you, they see   that we, you, they be seen

PAST TENSE

Singular that I, you, he saw   that I, you, he were seen
Plural that we, you, they saw   that we, you, they were seen

PRESENT PERFECT TENSE

Singular that I, you, he have seen   that I, you, he have been seen
Plural that we, you, they have seen   that we, you, they have been seen

PAST PERFECT TENSE

(Same as the Indicative)

IMPERATIVE MOOD
PRESENT TENSE

see   be seen

Conjunction. A part of speech (often called a *function word*) used to connect words, phrases, or clauses. There are two kinds, coordinating conjunctions and subordinating conjunctions.

COORDINATING CONJUNCTIONS connect words, phrases, and clauses of equal rank: *and, but, or, nor, for,* and sometimes *so* and *yet.*

SUBORDINATING CONJUNCTIONS connect subordinate clauses with main clauses: *if, although, since, in order that, as, because, unless, after, before, until, when, whenever, where, while, wherever,* etc.

Conjunctive adverb. An adverb used to connect or relate main clauses: *however, therefore, nevertheless, hence, then, besides, moreover, thus, otherwise, consequently, accordingly,* etc.

Construction. See **Syntax.**

Coordinate. Of equal rank. For example, two nouns, two infinitives, or two main clauses.

Correlatives. Coordinating conjunctions used in pairs: *both . . . and, either . . . or, neither . . . nor, not only . . . but also.* See **26c.**

Declension. A grouping of pronoun forms. See **Inflection.**

Demonstrative. See **Adjective** and **Pronoun.**

Dependent clause. See **Clause.**

Descriptive adjective. See **Adjective.**

Determiner. A word such as *a, an,* or *the* which signals the approach of a noun.

Diagraming. An arrangement of words on lines to show relationships within the sentence. Various forms are used. Any form is serviceable if it helps the student to understand the sentence. A diagram is only a means to an end, not an end in itself. The following is a traditional form of diagraming.

THE SENTENCE BASE

SUBJECT—VERB.

The *students* always *cooperated.*

> Students | cooperated

SUBJECT—VERB—SUBJECT COMPLEMENT.

His *son seems* very *busy.*

> son | seems \ busy

Was he a skilled *mechanic?*

> he | Was \ mechanic

SUBJECT—VERB—OBJECT.

One of them *is buying* a *house.*

> One | is buying | house

SUBJECT—VERB—OBJECT—OBJECT COMPLEMENT.

Should we paint it green?

> we | Should paint | it \ green

INDIRECT OBJECT

He will not lend *her* a dollar.

> He | will lend | dollar
> \ her

EXPLETIVE

There were no complaints.

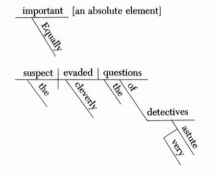

MODIFIERS

Equally important, the suspect *cleverly* evaded *the* questions of *very astute* detectives.

important   [an absolute element]

VERBALS

GERUND   *Taking* pictures is an art.

PARTICIPLE   *Seeing* a rat, she gasped.

she | gasped

INFINITIVES   The first thing *to do* is *to call* him.

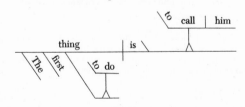

CLAUSES

MAIN   The moon rose, and the stars twinkled.

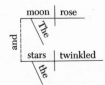

SUBORDINATE

adjective   The man *who is honest* should succeed.

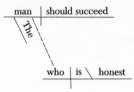

adverb   I shall leave the house *after she comes.*

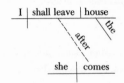

noun   *What the newspapers say* may be false.

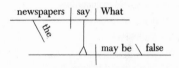

A COMPOUND-COMPLEX SENTENCE

Engines roared overhead, and a bomb fell where we had stood.

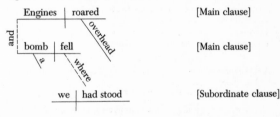

Engines | roared   [Main clause]

bomb | fell   [Main clause]

we | had stood   [Subordinate clause]

Direct address. A noun or pronoun used parenthetically to direct a speech to a definite person.

> I hope, *Mary*, that you will go. *Mary*, close the door.

Direct object. See **Object**.

Direct quotation. The exact oral or written words of others.

> DIRECT QUOTATION John asked, "Why didn't you join us, Martha?"
> INDIRECT QUOTATION John asked Martha why she had not joined the group.

See also **16a**.

Elliptical elements. Words which are omitted but are clearly understood.

> Mary is prettier than Helen (is pretty).
> Whenever (it is) possible, you should take exercise.

Expletive. *It* or *there* used merely as an introductory word or filler.

> *It* is true that he is not coming.
> *There* were few men present.

Finite verb. A verb or verb phrase that serves as a predicate. Infinitives, participles, and gerunds are **verbals**, not finite verbs.

Form change. See **Inflection.**

Function words. Words (such as prepositions, conjunctions, and articles) which indicate the grammatical relationship of the words connected or signaled.

Gerund. See **Verbals.**

Gerund phrase. See **Phrase.**

Idiom. An expression in good use that is peculiar to a language. (Idioms sometimes violate established rules of grammar but are nevertheless sanctioned by usage.)

> I have known him for *many a year.*
> He *gave himself away* by smiling.

Imperative. See **Mood.**

Indefinite pronoun. See **Pronoun.**

Independent clause (Main clause, principal clause). See **Clause.**

Independent element. See **Absolute element.**

Indicative. See **Mood.**

Indirect object. See **Object.**

Indirect quotation. See **Direct quotation.**

Infinitive. See **Verbals.**

Infinitive phrase. See **Phrase.**

Inflection. A change in the form of a word to show a change in meaning or in grammatical relationship to some other word or group of words. The inflection of nouns and pronouns is called **declension;** the inflection of verbs, **conjugation;** that of adjectives and adverbs, **comparison.**

> INFLECTIONS OF VERBS (indicating tense, person, mood)
> look, looking, looks, looked
> drink, drinking, drinks, drank, drunk
> know, knowing, knows, knew, known
> be, being, am, is, are, was, were, been

> INFLECTIONS OF NOUNS (indicating number, case)
> dog, dogs; dog's, dogs'
> child, children; child's, children's

> INFLECTIONS OF PRONOUNS (indicating case, person, number)
> I, me, my, mine   we, us, our, ours
> who, whom, whose   someone, someone's
> *This* is old. *These* are old. *That* is older than *those.*

> INFLECTIONS OF MODIFIERS (indicating comparison, number)
> fast, faster, fastest   bad, worse, worst
> attractive, more attractive, most attractive
> *this* letter, *these* letters, *that* letter, *those* letters

Intensive pronoun. See **Pronoun.**

Interjection. A part of speech used for simple exclamations: *Oh! Ouch! Whew!* When used in sentences, interjections are set off by commas. See **Absolute elements.**

Interrogative pronoun. See **Pronoun.**

Intransitive verb. See **Verb.**

Irregular verb (Strong verb). A verb that forms its principal parts in various ways *other than* by the addition of *-ed, -d,* or *-t.* See also **Inflection** and Section 7.

> *Vowel changes*   swim, swam, swum
> *Addition of -en*   beat, beat, beaten
> *No change*   set, set, set

Limiting adjective. See **Adjective.**

Linking verb. A verb which relates the subject to the subject complement. Words commonly used as linking verbs are *become, seem, appear, feel, taste, smell,* and parts of the verb *be.*

> The tires *look* good.   The surface *feels* rough.
> *Did* she *become* a nurse?   What *could* that *be?*

Main clause (Independent clause, principal clause). See **Clause.**

Mode. See **Mood.**

Modifier. Any word, phrase, or clause functioning as an adjective or an adverb.

Modify. To describe or qualify the meaning of a word or group of words.

> *A very old* man hobbled *slowly along the road.* [A and *old* modify *man; very* modifies *old; slowly* and *along the road* modify *hobbled; the* modifies *road.*]

Mood (Mode). The form of the verb that is used to indicate the manner in which the action or state is conceived. English has indicative, imperative, and subjunctive moods. See Section 7.

> The INDICATIVE MOOD states a fact or asks a question.
> You *have* a good mind.   *Have* you any ideas?
> Mother *is* here.   *Is* Mother here?

> The IMPERATIVE MOOD gives a command, makes a request, or gives directions.
> *Be* careful.   *Watch* your step, please.
> *Take* the next street on the right.

> The SUBJUNCTIVE MOOD is used in stating conditions contrary to fact and in certain idiomatic expressions. See **7c.**
> I wish Mother *were* here.
> If I *had* my way, you would not go.

Nominative. See **Case.**

Nominative absolute. See **Absolute element.**

Nominative of address. See **Direct address.**

Nonrestrictive modifier. A nonessential modifier. A parenthetical phrase or clause which does not identify the person or thing modified. See **12d.**

> The airplane, *now being manufactured in large numbers,* is of immense commercial value. [Phrase]
> The airplane, *which is now being manufactured in large numbers,* is of immense commercial value. [Clause]

See also **Restrictive modifier.**

Noun. A part of speech (the name of a person, place, thing, quality, or action: *Mary, America, apples, courage, departure*) that usually changes form to make the possessive case and the plural, as in *man, man's, men.* See also **Inflection.**

Types of nouns

COMMON   a *man,* the *cities,* some *trout* [General classes]
PROPER   *Mr. Ford,* in *Boston,* the *Forum* [Capitalized specifics]
COLLECTIVE a *flock,* the *jury,* my *family* [Groups—singular in form but singular or plural in meaning]
CONCRETE   an *apple,* the *radio,* his *face,* two *trees* [Tangibles]
ABSTRACT   *ambition, jealousy, pity, hatred* [Qualities, concepts]

Functions of nouns

SUBJECT OF VERB OR VERBAL *Dogs* barked. I want *Ed* to be here.
OBJECT OF VERB, VERBAL, OR PREPOSITION Someone opened the *door* to let the *dog* into the *house.*

SUBJECT COMPLEMENT (PREDICATE NOUN)   She is a *nurse*.
APPOSITIVE   Moses, a *prophet*, saw the promised land.
DIRECT ADDRESS   What do you think, *Angela?*
OBJECT COMPLEMENT   They named him *Jonathan*.

Noun clause. A subordinate clause used as a noun.

Whoever comes will be welcome. [Subject]
I hope *that he will recover.* [Direct object]
This is *what you need.* [Subject complement]
Spend it for *whatever seems best.* [Object of preposition]

Noun substitute. A pronoun or any group of words (especially a gerund phrase, an infinitive phrase, or a noun clause) functioning as a noun. See also **Substantive**.

Number. The change in the form of a word (e.g., noun, pronoun, etc.) to designate one (*singular*) or more than one (*plural*). See also **Inflection** and Section 6.

Object. A noun or noun substitute governed by a transitive active verb, by a verbal, or by a preposition.

DIRECT OBJECT   Any noun or noun substitute that answers the question *What?* or *Whom?* after a transitive active verb. A direct object frequently receives, or is in some way affected by, the action of the verb.

William raked *leaves.*   *What* did he say?
The Andersons do not know *where we live.*

A direct object may be converted to a subject with a passive verb. See **Voice**.

OBJECT OF A VERBAL   Any noun or its equivalent that follows and completes the meaning of a verbal.

Washing a *car* takes time. He likes to wear a *tie.*

INDIRECT OBJECT   Any noun or noun substitute that states *to whom* or *for whom* (or *to what* or *for what*) something is done. An indirect object ordinarily precedes a direct object.

He bought *her* a watch.
I gave the *painting* a second coat of varnish.

It is usually possible to substitute for the indirect object a prepositional phrase with *to* or *for.*

He bought a watch *for her.*

OBJECT OF PREPOSITION   Any noun or noun substitute which a preposition relates to another word or word group.

Cedars grow tall in these *hills.* [Object of *in*]
What am I responsible for? [Object of *for*]

Object complement. See **Complement**.

Objective. See **Case**.

Participial phrase. See **Phrase**.

Participle. See **Verbals**.

Parts of speech. The eight classes into which most grammarians group words according to their form changes, their positions, their meaning, and their uses in the sentence: *verb, noun, pronoun, adjective, adverb, conjunction, preposition,* and *interjection.* Each of these is discussed separately in this section. It is important to note that *part of speech* is determined by function. The same word is often used as several different parts of speech. See **1c**.

Passive voice. See **Voice**.

Person. Changes in the form of verbs and pronouns which indicate whether a person is speaking (first person), is spoken to (second person), or is spoken about (third person).

FIRST PERSON   *I* see the boy.
SECOND PERSON   Can *you* see the boy?
THIRD PERSON   *He* sees the boy.

Personal pronoun. See **Pronoun**.

Phrase. A group of related words not having a subject and a predicate and functioning as a single part of speech.

VERB   Don *will be calling* soon.
PREPOSITIONAL   A mower is *in the garage.* [Adverb]
     The man *at the door* smiled. [Adjective]
PARTICIPIAL   *Rearing its head,* the snake hissed.
GERUND   *Building a patio* can be fun.
INFINITIVE   Mrs. Raines went *to buy groceries.* [Adverb]

See also **1d**.

Predicate. The part of the sentence comprising what is said about the subject. The **Complete predicate** consists of the verb (the **Simple predicate**) along with its complements and modifiers.

He *runs* through the house. [*Runs* is the simple predicate; *runs through the house* is the complete predicate.]

Predicate adjective, predicate complement, predicate nominative, predicate noun, predicate objective. See **Complement**.

Preposition. A part of speech (often called a *function word*) that is used to show the relation of a noun or noun-equivalent (the *object of the preposition*) to some other word in the sentence.

The telephone is *in* the hall. [The preposition *in* shows the relationship of its object *hall* to the verb *is.*]
Across, after, at, before, between, by, for, from, in, of, on, over, to, under, with, up, and *near* are commonly used as prepositions.

See also **1c**.

Prepositional phrase. See **Phrase**.

Principal clause (Main clause, independent clause). See **Clause**.

Principal parts. The forms of any verb from which the various tenses are derived: (1) present stem (infinitive), (2) past tense, and (3) past participle.

see	saw	seen
take	took	taken
love	loved	loved

See also Section 7.

Progressive verb. A form of the verb (ending in *-ing* and accompanied by a part of the auxiliary *be*) used to express **continuous** action or state of being.

Sally *was singing* a cowboy ballad.
I *have been playing* tennis all afternoon.

See also Section. 7.

Pronoun. A part of speech (one of a special group of words) used as a noun substitute.

PERSONAL   *You* and *I* will see *him.*
INTERROGATIVE   *Who* is he? *Which* do you prefer? *What* is it?
RELATIVE   The boy *who* served us is the one *that* I tipped.
DEMONSTRATIVE   *This* is better than *that.*
INDEFINITE   *Each* of you should help *someone.*
RECIPROCAL   Help *each other.* They like *one another.*
REFLEXIVE   Carl blames *himself.* Did you hurt *yourself?*
INTENSIVE   We need a vacation *ourselves.* I *myself* saw it.

See also **Inflection** and Sections 5 and 7.

Proper adjective. An adjective formed from a proper noun, as *Spanish* from *Spain.*

Proper noun. See **Noun**.

Quotation. See **Direct quotation.**

Reciprocal pronoun. See **Pronoun.**

Reflexive pronoun. See **Pronoun.**

Regular verb (Weak verb). Any verb that forms its principal parts by adding *-ed*, *-d*, or *-t* to the infinitive: *love, loved, loved; weep, wept, wept.*

Relative pronoun. See **Pronoun.**

Restrictive modifier. An essential modifier. A phrase or clause which identifies the word modified and which therefore cannot be omitted without changing the essential meaning of the sentence.

> Any girl *who talks incessantly* is a bore.

See also **Nonrestrictive modifier.**

Sentence. An independent unit of expression. A grammatically complete sentence (with the exception of the imperative) has at least one subject and one predicate. (For the grammatically incomplete sentence, see page 807.) Sentences are classified structurally as (1) simple, (2) compound, (3) complex, or (4) compound-complex. See **1e.**

> SIMPLE   She may be a famous actress someday. [One main clause]
> COMPOUND   He lost the game, but he had done his best. [Two main clauses]
> COMPLEX   When the whistle blew, the parade began. [One subordinate clause and one main clause]
> COMPOUND-COMPLEX   The work stops when it rains, but the tools are kept in readiness. [Two main clauses and one subordinate clause]

See the ten patterns of simple sentences on pages 801–02.

See also **Diagraming.**

Simple predicate. See **Predicate.**

Simple sentence. See **Sentence.**

Simple subject. See **Subject.**

Strong verb. See **Irregular verb.**

Subject. A noun or a noun substitute about which something is asserted or asked. One of the two basic grammatical divisions of a sentence, the subject usually precedes the predicate and answers the question *Who?* or *What?* in front of the predicate. (Imperative sentences do not have stated subjects.) The subject and the words associated with it make up the **Complete subject.**

> The *dog* at the front of the house barked at the car. [*Dog* is the **Simple subject;** *the dog at the front of the house* is the complete subject.]

Subjective. See **Case.**

Subject complement. See **Complement.**

Subjunctive. See **Mood.**

Subordinate clause. A dependent clause. See **Clause.**

Substantive. Any word or group of words used as a noun. Substantives may be nouns, pronouns, phrases (especially gerund or infinitive phrases), or noun clauses. See **Noun substitute.**

Syntax (Construction). Sentence structure. The grammatical functions of words, phrases, clauses.

Tense. The time of occurrence indicated by the form of the verb. See **Inflection** and Section **7.**

Transitive. See **Verb.**

Verb. A predicator used to make a statement, ask a question, or to give a command or direction. Inflections indicate tense (and, in the present tense, a third-person singular subject) and mood. See **Inflection, Voice,** and Section **7.**

> TRANSITIVE VERB   A verb that requires an object to complete its meaning. Transitive verbs can usually be changed from active to passive voice. See **Object** and **Voice.**
>
> > The general *laid* a wreath on the tomb.
>
> INTRANSITIVE VERB   A verb, such as *go* or *sit*, that does not have an object to complete its meaning, is intransitive. Linking verbs, which take subject complements, are intransitive.
>
> > I *was* in New York last Christmas.
> > She *has been waiting* patiently for hours.
>
> The same verb may be transitive in one sentence and intransitive in another.
>
> > TRANSITIVE   Lydia *reads* novels. [Object: *novels*]
> > INTRANSITIVE   Lydia *reads* well. [No object]

Verb equivalent (Verb-adverb combination) A word group equal in meaning to a single-word verb.

> The parade *held up* [stopped] traffic.
> Please *turn on* [start] the motor.

Verb phrase. See **Phrase.**

Verbals. Verb forms used as nouns, adjectives, or adverbs. The three verbals are gerunds, participles, and infinitives. Like verbs, verbals may take objects, complements, and modifiers. Infinitives may have subjects.

> GERUND   Verb form used as a noun and always ending in *-ing.*
>
> > *Watching the new color television* kept our guests entertained. [Subject of *kept*]
> > By *swimming rapidly,* he escaped. [Object of preposition *by*]
>
> PARTICIPLE   Verb form used as an adjective. Endings of participles vary—for instance, *-ing, -ed, -t, -en.*
>
> > *Swimming rapidly,* he soon reached the dock. [*Swimming* modifies *he.*]
> > *Confused by improperly marked streets,* they lost their way. [*Confused* modifies *they; marked* modifies *streets.*]
>
> INFINITIVE   Verb form used chiefly as a noun, less frequently as an adjective or an adverb. The infinitive is usually made up of *to* plus a verb form but after such verbs as *let, make,* and *dare* the *to* may be omitted.
>
> > Hal wanted *to open the present.* [Object of *wanted*]
> > The noise made the baby *cry.* [*Baby* is subject of the infinitive *cry;* the infinitive phrase is object of *made.*]
> > I have work *to do.* [*To do* is adjective modifying *work.*]
> > *To tell the truth,* I never eat breakfast. [The infinitive phrase modifies the rest of the sentence and is therefore used as an adverb.]

Voice. Only verbs have voice. A verb having a direct object is in the active voice. When the direct object is converted to a subject, as is done in the sentences below, the verb is in the passive voice. A passive verb is always a verb phrase containing a part of the verb *be* as an auxiliary plus a past participle. The subject of an active verb acts. The subject of a passive verb does not act.

> | ACTIVE VOICE | PASSIVE VOICE |
> |---|---|
> | Priscilla *chose* John. | John *was chosen* by Priscilla. |
> | Ed *must learn* that. | That *must be learned.* |

Weak verb. See **Regular verb.**

Index to Part Eight, Harbrace College Handbook

[Numbers in **boldface** refer to rules; other numbers refer to pages. A colon is used after each boldface number to indicate that the following pages refer to the rule or the part of the rule concerned. An *ex* indicates that appropriate drill exercises are included. The **boldface** rule is given in detail—**9a(4)** or **20a(3)**, for example—in order to pinpoint a needed correction, but a less detailed reference (**9** or **9a**) will usually be sufficient for the student.]

a

A, an, **19i**: 860
A half a, for *a half* or *half a*, **19i**: 862
Abbreviations, **11**: 830–31 *ex*
  capitalization of, **9a(4)**: 826
  contractions, with apostrophe, **15c**: 842
  first names, spelled out, **11e**: 830
  from Latin, in italics, **33e(1)**: 921
  in footnotes, **11e**: 830, **33e(1)**: 920
  misused in letters, **34a**: 933
  names of organizations, permissible abbreviations of, **11**: 830
  names of states, months, days of week, **11b**: 830
  parts of proper names, **11c**: 830
  period after, **17a**: 845
  titles, **11a**: 830
  verified in dictionary, **11**: 830
  volume, chapter, page, **11d**: 830
  when permissible, **11**: 830
  with dates or numerals, when permissible, **11**: 830
Absolute element, defined, 934
Absolute phrase
  commas with, **12d(3)**: 836–37
  defined, 934
Abstract and general words, **20a(3)**: 867 *ex*
Abstract noun, defined, 838
Accent, shown in the dictionary, 855
Accept, except, **19i**: 860
Accidentally, incidentally, **19i**: 860
Accordingly, as a conjunctive adverb, **14a**: 839
Accusative case. *See* Objective case.
Acknowledgment of borrowed material, in footnotes, 918–19 *ex*
Active voice
  defined, 940
  for emphasis, **29d**: 889 *ex*
Ad, for *advertisement*, **19i**: 860
Address of a letter, **34a**: 932–33
  consistency, **34a(2)**: 933
  inside address, **34a(2)**: 933
  model addressed envelope, **34**: 933
  one of six essential parts, **34a**: 932
  shown in model letter, **34a**: 932
Adjective clause
  as modifier, 805 *ex*
  defined, 935
  position of, for coherence, **25a(3)**: 879
  restrictive or nonrestrictive, punctuation of, **12d(1)**: 835 *ex*
Adjectives, **4**: 811–13 *ex*
  adverbs identical with, **4**: 811 *ex*
  after linking verbs, **4b**: 812 *ex*
  among parts of speech, 803
  comparative form, **4c**: 812
  coordinate or in series, commas with, **12c**: 834 *ex*

defined and classified, 935
demonstrative, 935
descriptive, 935
distinguished from adverbs, **4**: 811–13 *ex*
forms of, **4**: 811
in sentence patterns, 812
indefinite and interrogative, 935
limiting, 935
need determined by use in sentence, **4**: 811 *ex*
nouns misused as, **4d**: 812 *ex*
position of, 803
possessive, 935
predicate, **4b**: 812
proper, capitalized, **9a**: 826, 935
relative, 935
superlative form, **4c**: 812
Adverb clause
  defined, 805, 935
  in sentence pattern, 805, 833–34
  misused as sentence, **2b**: 808 *ex*
  position of, 805, 833–34
  punctuation of, **12b**: 833–34
  to begin sentence, for variety, **30b**: 891–92 *ex*
Adverb phrase
  defined, 804
  used as modifier, 804
Adverbs, **4**: 811–13 *ex*
  adjectives identical with, **4**: 811 *ex*
  among parts of speech, 803
  comparative form, **4c**: 812
  conjunctive, 812, 839
  defined, 935
  distinguished from adjectives, **4**: 811–13 *ex*
  forms of, **4**: 811
  modifiers of verbs, adjectives, adverbs, **4a**: 811 *ex*
  modifiers of whole clauses, 803, 935
  not used after linking verbs or verbs of senses, **4b**: 812
  position of, for coherence, **25a**: 879 *ex*
  superlative form, **4c**: 812
  to begin sentence, for variety, **30b**: 891–92 *ex*
  verb-adverb combinations, 803
Advice, advise, **19i**: 860
Affect, effect, **19i**: 860
Aggravate, for *annoy*, **19i**: 860
Agreement, **6**: 815–18 *ex*, 935
Agreement of pronoun and antecedent, **6b**: 817–18 *ex*
  antecedents joined by *and* or *or*, **6b(2)**: 817
  collective nouns, **6b(3)**: 817–18 *ex*
  man, person, each, etc., **6b(1)**: 817
Agreement of subject and verb, **6a**: 815–17 *ex*
  after *there is, there are*, **6a(4)**: 816
  collective nouns, **6a(7)**: 816
  don't, doesn't, **19i**: 862
  each, either, etc., **6a(6)**: 816
  expletive *it*, followed by singular verb, **6a(4)**: 816
  intervening nouns or pronouns, **6a(1)**: 815

none, **6a(6)**: 816
nouns in *-st*, **6b(1)**: 817
plural form, singular meaning, **6a(9)**: 816
predicate noun, mistaken agreement with, **6a(8)**: 816
relative pronoun, agreement with antecedent, **6a(5)**: 816
singular subjects joined by *or* or *nor*, **6a(3)**: 815
subjects joined by *and*, **6a(2)**: 815
titles of books, etc., **6a(10)**: 816 *ex*
Ain't, **19i**: 860
Alibi, for *excuse*, **19i**: 860
All, agreement with, **6a(6)**: 816
All-, hyphen with, **18f(4)**: 852
All ready, already, **19i**: 860
All the farther, all the faster, **19i**: 860
Alliteration, overuse of, **19h(3)**: 859
Allusion, illusion, **19i**: 860
Almost, most, **19i**: 860
Almost, position of, **25a(1)**: 879 *ex*
A lot, lots, **19i**: 860
Already, all ready, **19i**: 860
Alright, for *all right*, **19i**: 860
Also, as a conjunctive adverb, **14a**: 839
Altogether, all together, **19i**: 860
Alumnus, alumna, **19i**: 860
A.M., P.M., **19i**: 860
Ambiguous reference, **28a**: 885
Among, between, **19i**: 860
Amount, number, **19i**: 860
An, a, **19i**: 860
And, thwarting subordination, **24c**: 878 *ex*
And, used to excess, **24b**: 877 *ex*
And etc., **19i**: 860
And which, but which, etc., thwarting subordination, **24c**: 878 *ex*
And who, and which, in parallel structure, **26d**: 883 *ex*
Another, agreement with, **6a(6)**: 816
Antecedent
  agreement with pronoun, **6b**: 817–18 *ex*
  ambiguous reference to, **28a**: 885
  defined, 935
  far from pronoun, **28b**: 885
  not expressed, **28c**: 886
Any, anybody, anyone, anything, agreement with, **6a(6)**: 816
Anyhow, as a conjunctive adverb, **14a**: 839
Anyone, any one, **19i**: 860–61
Anyways, for *anyway*, **19i**: 861
Anywheres, for *anywhere*, **19i**: 861
Apostrophe, **15**: 841–42 *ex*
  misuse of, with pronouns and nouns in plural, **15b**: 842
  to form plurals of letters, figures, etc., **15d**: 842
  to form possessives, **15a**: 841–42 *ex*
  compounds, **15a(4)**: 842 *ex*
  joint possession, **15a(4)**: 842 *ex*

See page 406 for the original passage in Mencken and the student's note card on it.

Ibsen himself refused to admit that he had purposed writing a play on the subject of a woman's rights. He did not wish to distinguish in his mind between the rights of men and the rights of women, but liked to think that the liberty of all human beings was uppermost in his mind when he wrote the play. "In our times," said Ibsen in 1882, "every literary work has the mission of extending boundary lines." [From *Milestones of the Drama*, edited by Helen Louise Cohen. Reprinted by permission of Harcourt, Brace & World, Inc.]

. . . search Ibsen throughout and it will be found that his subject matter is fundamentally the same as that of all great masters of tragedy. It is his novel manner of presentation, his transposition of themes hitherto treated epically, to the narrow, unheroic scale of middle-class family life that blinded critics to his true significance. This tuning down of the heroic, this reversal of the old aesthetic order extorted bitter remonstrances. [From *Egoists: A Book of Supermen*, by James Huneker. Reprinted by permission of Charles Scribner's Sons, Inc.]

H. L. Mencken, Ibsen was "the Gog and the Magog . . . of that distant and pious era."[13] Many angry critics accused Ibsen of being an advocate of "the emancipated woman." All of these were false accusations. Ibsen himself said that he had no patience with women who abandoned their own world for the man's world. Ibsen firmly insisted that a woman should not only develop her own individuality but also use her feminine gifts as a mother. Actually, Ibsen did not set out to write a play on the rights of emancipated women; instead he was insisting upon the rights of all human beings, both women and men.[14]

Perhaps it was Ibsen's use of the "unheroic scale of middle-class family life that blinded critics [of Ibsen's time] to his true significance."[15] They debated the morality of Nora's leaving her husband and

---

[13]Introduction to *Eleven Plays of Henrik Ibsen* (New York, [1935]), p. vii.

[14]Cohen, p. 270.

[15]James Huneker, *Egoists: A Book of Supermen* (New York, 1932), p. 323.

. . . yet Nora Helmer, when she slammed the door of her doll's home, caused an echo in the heart of every intelligent woman in Christendom. It is not necessary now to ask whether a woman would, or should, desert her children; Nora's departure was only the symbol of her liberty, the gesture of a newly awakened individuality. [From *Egoists: A Book of Supermen*, by James Huneker. Reprinted by permission of Charles Scribner's Sons, Inc.]

His reply to those who accused him of a merely destructive philosophy was that his task, as he conceived it, was to point out the weaknesses of the social fabric, and to leave constructive philosophy to those who were not dramatists. He diagnosed, and left the cure to others. [From Introduction by R. Farquharson Sharp to *A Doll's House: And Two Other Plays*, by Henrik Ibsen (translated by R. Farquharson Sharp and Eleanor Marx-Aveling). By permission of E. P. Dutton & Co. Inc. and J. M. Dent & Sons, Ltd.]

. . . unity lies not in the said but in the saying.
In this saying is Ibsenism. Modern drama, as a historical development, is surely partly created by Ibsenism. And Ibsenism is not so much a system as an attitude: thoughtfulness, seriousness, and especially searching characterization. [From *Contemporary Drama: Fifteen Plays*, eds. E. Bradlee Watson and Benfield Pressey. Reprinted by permission of Charles Scribner's Sons.]

8

children in order to develop herself. They completely missed Ibsen's message; to him, Nora's leaving was a symbol, a kind of declaration of independence.[16] Ibsen did present, as Sharp has pointed out, "the weaknesses of the social fabric,"[17] but he did this as an artist. He was content to leave the solutions of the problems he presented to the philosophers. Certainly Ibsenism is not a philosophy. As one modern critic has written: "Ibsenism is not so much a system as an attitude: thoughtfulness, seriousness, and especially searching characterization."[18] And the characterization of Nora striving to develop her own personality shows one of Ibsen's most important attitudes: his belief that every woman has a right to be a person.

---

[16]*Ibid.*, p. 331.

[17]Sharp, p. x.

[18]E. Bradlee Watson and Benfield Pressey, *Contemporary Drama: Fifteen Plays* (New York, 1959), p. 4.

GRAMMAR

1 ss — Sentence Sense
a Verbs
b Subjects and objects
c All parts of speech
d Phrases and subordinate clauses
e Main clauses and sentence types

2 frag — Fragment
a Phrase
b Subordinate clause
c Other fragments

3 cs — Comma Splice and Fused Sentence
a Methods of correction
b Caution: Conjunctive adverb, etc.

4 ad — Adjectives and Adverbs
a Adverb form
b Adjective as subject complement
c Comparative and superlative
d Awkward noun form as adjective

5 ca — Case
a Appositives; compounds
b Use in own clause
c Whom in formal use
d Possessive with gerund
e Objective with infinitive
f Subjective for complement of be

6 agr — Agreement
a Subject and verb
 (1) Intervening word; pronunciation
 (2) Subjects joined by and
 (3) Subjects joined by or, etc.
 (4) Subject following verb
 (5) Relative pronoun
 (6) Each, either, etc.
 (7) Collective nouns
 (8) Predicate noun
 (9) Plural form, singular meaning
 (10) Title of book, etc.
b Pronoun and antecedent
 (1) Antecedents such as man, one, etc.
 (2) Antecedents joined by and; by or
 (3) Collective nouns as antecedents

7 t — Tense and Mood
a Confused verbs; principal parts
b Sequence of tenses
c Subjunctive mood
d Needless shifts in tense or mood
e Should, would, shall, and will

MECHANICS

8 ms — Manuscript
a Proper materials
b Arrangement on page; syllabication
c Legibility
d Revision
e Record of errors

9 cap — Capitals
a Proper names
b Titles preceding name, etc.
c Titles of books, etc.
d I and O
e First word of sentence, etc.
f Unnecessary capitals

10 ital — Italics
a Titles of publications
b Foreign words and phrases
c Names of ships, etc.
d Words, etc., used as such
e Overuse for emphasis

11 ab — Abbreviations and Numbers
a Titles
b Names of states, etc.
c Street, road, etc.
d References to volume, page, etc.
e First names
f Usage regarding numbers

PUNCTUATION

12 , — The Comma
a Main clauses
b Introductory elements
c Series; coordinate adjectives
d Nonrestrictive elements
e Misreading

13 ◦ — Superfluous Commas
a Subject and verb, etc.
b Words, phrases joined by and
c Slight parenthesis
d Restrictive elements
e First item of series, etc.

14 ; — The Semicolon
a Main clauses
b Elements containing commas
c Caution: Misuse with parts of unequal rank

15 ap — The Apostrophe
a Indicating possession
b Misused with personal pronouns
c Marking omissions
d Forming plurals of letters, etc.

16 " " — Quotation Marks
a Direct quotations
b Minor titles
c Special sense
d Overuse
e Position with other marks

17 — The Period and Other Marks
a . / Period
b ? / Question mark
c ! / Exclamation point
d : / Colon
e — / Dash
f ( ) / Parentheses
g [ ] / Brackets

18 sp — Spelling
a Mispronunciation
b Similar words
c Prefix and root
d Suffixes
e Confusion of ei and ie
f Hyphenated words

SPELLING

DICTION

19 g — Good Use
a Use of dictionary
b Colloquialisms
c Slang and jargon
d Dialectal words
e Illiteracies
f Obsolete and archaic words
g Technical words
h Fine writing, etc.
i Glossary

20 e — Exactness
a Exact words
b Exact idioms
c Fresh expressions

21 w — Wordiness and Useless Repetition
a Needed omission
b Needed revision
c Useless repetition

22 ∧ — Omission of Necessary Words
a Article, pronoun, etc.
b Verb
c Completion of comparisons, etc.

EFFECTIVE SENTENCES

23 u — Unity and Logical Thinking
a Unrelated ideas
b Excessive detail
c Mixed, obscure, or illogical constructions
d Caution: Illogical statements

24 sub — Subordination
a Short, choppy sentences
b And sentences
c Illogical subordination

25 coh — Coherence
a Misplaced parts
 (1) Adverbs (2) Phrases (3) Clauses
 (4) "Squinting" constructions
 (5) Split infinitives, etc.
b Dangling modifiers

26 ‖ — Parallelism
a Balanced parts
b Repetition of preposition, etc.
c Correlatives
d And who, and which

27 pv — Point of View
a Tense
b Mood
c Subject or voice
d Person
f Indirect and direct discourse
g Tone or style
h Perspective

28 ref — Reference of Pronouns
a Ambiguous
b Remote antecedent
c Broad
d Repeated pronoun with different antecedents

29 emp — Emphasis
a Position
b Periodic sentence
c Order of climax
d Active voice
e Repetition
f Unusual order
g Balance
h Short sentence

30 var — Variety
a Length
b Beginning
c Avoiding compound sentences
d Subject-verb sequence
e Statement